Honoring America

For Americans, the flag has always had a special meaning. It is a symbol of our nation's freedom and democracy.

Flag Etiquette

Over the years, Americans have developed rules and customs concerning the use and display of the flag. One of the most important things every American should remember is to treat the flag with respect.

- The flag should be raised and lowered by hand and displayed only from sunrise to sunset. On special occasions, the flag may be displayed at night, but it should be illuminated.

- The flag may be displayed on all days, weather permitting, particularly on national and state holidays and on historic and special occasions.

- No flag may be flown above the American flag or to the right of it at the same height.

- The flag should never touch the ground or floor beneath it.

- The flag may be flown at half-staff by order of the president, usually to mourn the death of a public official.

- The flag may be flown upside down only to signal distress.

- The flag should never be carried flat or horizontally, but always carried aloft and free.

- When the flag becomes old and tattered, it should be destroyed by burning. According to an approved custom, the Union (stars on blue field) is first cut from the flag; then the two pieces, which no longer form a flag, are burned.

★ ★ ★ ★ ★ ★ ★ ★

The American's Creed

I believe in the United States of America as a Government of the people, by the people, for the people, whose just powers are derived from the consent of the governed; a democracy in a republic; a sovereign Nation of many sovereign States; a perfect union, one and inseparable; established upon those principles of freedom, equality, justice, and humanity for which American patriots sacrificed their lives and fortunes.

I therefore believe it is my duty to my Country to love it; to support its Constitution; to obey its laws; to respect its flag, and to defend it against all enemies.

The Pledge of Allegiance

I pledge allegiance to the Flag of the United States of America and to the Republic for which it stands, one Nation under God, indivisible, with liberty and justice for all.

The Star-Spangled Banner

O! say, can you see, by the dawn's early light,
What so proudly we hail'd at the twilight's last gleaming?
Whose broad stripes and bright stars, thro' the perilous fight,
O'er the ramparts we watched were so gallantly streaming?
And the rockets' red glare, the bombs bursting in air,
Gave proof thro' the night, that our flag was still there.
O! say, does that Star-Spangled Banner yet wave
O'er the land of the free and the home of the brave?

On the shore, dimly seen thro' the mist of the deep,
Where the foe's haughty host in dread silence reposes,
What is that which the breeze, o'er the towering steep,
As it fitfully blows, half conceals, half discloses?
Now it catches the gleam of the morning's first beam,
In full glory reflected now shines on the stream.
'Tis the Star-Spangled Banner. O long may it wave
O'er the land of the free and the home of the brave.

And where is that band who so vauntingly swore,
That the havoc of war and the battle's confusion
A home and a country should leave us no more?
Their blood has wash'd out their foul footstep's pollution.
No refuge could save the hireling and slave
From the terror of flight or the gloom of the grave,
And the Star-Spangled Banner in triumph doth wave
O'er the land of the free and the home of the brave.

O thus be it e'er when free men shall stand
Between their lov'd home and war's desolation,
Blest with vict'ry and peace, may the Heav'n-rescued land
Praise the pow'r that hath made and preserv'd us a nation.
Then conquer we must, when our cause it is just,
And this be our motto, "In God is our Trust."
And the Star-Spangled Banner in triumph shall wave
O'er the land of the free and the home of the brave.

Teacher Wraparound Edition

Economics
Principles & Practices

WITH FEATURES FROM
BusinessWeek
STANDARD
&POOR'S

WITH FEATURES FROM
BusinessWeek

STANDARD
&POOR'S

Teacher Wraparound Edition

GLENCOE

Economics
Principles & Practices

Gary E. Clayton, Ph.D.

New York, New York   Columbus, Ohio   Chicago, Illinois   Peoria, Illinois   Woodland Hills, California

About the Author

Gary E. Clayton teaches economics at Northern Kentucky University in Highland Heights, Kentucky. Dr. Clayton received his Ph.D. in economics from the University of Utah, has taught economics and finance at several universities, and has authored textbooks, including several at the college level, as well as a number of articles in various educational, professional, and technical journals.

Dr. Clayton has also appeared on a number of radio and television programs, and was a guest commentator specializing in economic statistics for *Marketplace*, which is broadcast on American Public Radio.

Dr. Clayton has a long-standing interest in economic education. He has participated in and directed numerous economic education workshops. He received the Outstanding Citizen Certificate of Recognition from the state of Arkansas for his work in economic education. He has served as vice president for the Kentucky Council on Economic Education and received the state's highest honor when he received a commission as an honorary Kentucky colonel. More recently, Dr. Clayton was the year 2000 Leavey Awards Winner for Excellence in Private Enterprise Education, which is presented annually by the Freedoms Foundation, in Valley Forge, Pennsylvania. During the summer months he participates in various study-abroad programs that take college students to Europe.

STANDARD &POOR'S

Standard & Poor's is a leading source for information on regional, national, and global economic developments. Standard & Poor's data, information, news and analysis on the United States, regional, and world economies is used by industrial firms, financial institutions, and government agencies for setting policy, managing financial positions, planning production, formulating marketing strategies, and a range of similar activities. Standard & Poor's information services represent the single most sophisticated source of information for organizations that need to understand the impact of the path of economic growth and of government fiscal and monetary policy on their activities.

BusinessWeek

Business Week is the most widely read business publication in the world and is the only weekly business news publication in existence. *Business Week* provides incisive and comprehensive interpretations of events by evaluating the news and its implications for the United States, regional, and world economies. *Business Week* offers writing that is informative and often inspiring to uncover what is crucial to understanding the economy —today's as well as tomorrow's. *Business Week* features in *Economics: Principles and Practices* are a tool that enables students to see real-world economics in action.

About the Cover: The Golden Dollar, first minted in 2000, depicts Sacagawea and her infant son Jean Baptiste.

A Division of The **McGraw·Hill** *Companies*

Send all inquiries to:
Glencoe/McGraw-Hill
8787 Orion Place
Columbus, OH 43240

ISBN 0-07-825977-0 (Student Edition)   ISBN 0-07-825978-9 (Teacher Wraparound Edition)

1 2 3 4 5 6 7 8 9 10 027/043 10 09 08 07 06 05 04 03 02

Table of Contents

UNIT ①

Fundamental Economic Concepts — 2

UNIT ②

Microeconomics — 86

UNIT ③

Macroeconomics: Institutions — 190

Table of Contents

Features

ECONOMICS IN ACTION
WORKSHOP

Features

Profiles in Economics

THE GLOBAL ECONOMY

ISSUES IN FREE ENTERPRISE

Features

Skill Activities

Careers

Did you know?

Charts, Graphs, and Maps

Charts, Graphs, and Maps

Charts, Graphs, and Maps

Charts, Graphs, and Maps

NATIONAL GEOGRAPHIC **Reference Atlas**

STANDARD &POOR'S **Databank**

Photo Credits
T4-5 Horizons [Companies]; **T16** Walter Hodges/Stone; **T17** (l)Geoff Butler, (r)Security Industries Foundation for Economic Education; **T18 T18-T19** Martucci Studio

National Council on Economic Education

THE **Economics**America AND **Economics**International PROGRAMS

National Council on Economic Education

THE **Economics**America AND **Economics**International PROGRAMS

January 21, 2000
*In Our 51st Year of Leadership and Service as the
Nation's Premier Economic Education Organization*

Dear Educator,

We commend this textbook to teachers. The Principles and Practices of sound, standards-based Economics are needed for our students and our society, now, more than ever. These lessons are correlated with the Voluntary National Content Standards in Economics written and published by the National Council on Economic Education.

Economics is no longer (if it ever was) the "dismal science." It is an essential set of reasoning and decision-making skills for surviving, let alone thriving, in a changing, competitive global economy.

As we confront the issues of the increasing number of personal bankruptcies, uncontrolled credit card debt, ignorance of the value of saving and investing, and the inability of many of our students and their families to grasp the repercussions of international trade, these public concerns magnify the need for increasing economic literacy in our young adults and for enhancing economic education in our nation's schools.

The challenge was expressed over fifty years ago in the founding of the National Council on Economic Education (NCEE): "There is no aspect of education more important than that which makes all our citizens intelligent and truly informed about the economic system in which they live and work."

In principle and in practice, teaching standards-based economics is an excellent thing to be doing.

Respectfully,

Robert F. Duvall
President & Chief Executive Officer

The Campaign for Economic Literacy

1140 Avenue of the Americas, New York, NY 10036   212.730.7007   fax 212.730.1793   ncee@eaglobal.org

T14

Text Correlation to NCEE Standards

Voluntary National Content Standards in Economics

In 1994 the United States Congress designated economics as one of the nine core subjects to be taught in American schools. As a result, the National Council on Economic Education (NCEE) developed the Voluntary National Content Standards in Economics for use in economics curricula. **Economics: Principles and Practices** provides extensive coverage for each of the 20 voluntary content standards. For a complete discussion of the standards, you can reach the National Council on Economic Education through the Internet at **www.nationalcouncil.org** or by telephoning 1-800-338-1192.

For each standard, students will understand that:	Economics: Principles and Practices Chapter and Section coverage
1 **Productive resources are limited. Therefore, people cannot have all the goods and services they want; as a result, they must choose some things and give up others.**	**Chapter 1** Section 1: Scarcity and the Science of Economics Section 3: Economic Choices and Decision Making **Chapter 20** Section 3: Applying the Economic Way of Thinking
2 **Effective decision making requires comparing the additional costs of alternatives with the additional benefits. Most choices involve doing a little more or a little less of something; few choices are all or nothing decisions.**	**Chapter 1** Section 3: Economic Choices and Decision Making **Chapter 5** Section 3: Cost, Revenue, and Profit Maximization
3 **Different methods can be used to allocate goods and services. People, acting individually or collectively through government, must choose which methods to use to allocate different kinds of goods and services.**	**Chapter 2** Section 1: Economic Systems **Chapter 18** Section 1: The Spectrum of Economic Systems
4 **People respond predictably to positive and negative incentives.**	**Chapter 6** Section 1: Prices as Signals **Chapter 20** Section 2: Economic Incentives and Resources

For each standard, students will understand that:	Economics: Principles and Practices Chapter and Section coverage
5 Voluntary exchange occurs only when all participating parties expect to gain. This is true for trade among individuals or organizations within a nation, and among individuals or organizations in different nations.	**Chapter 17** Section 1: Absolute and Comparative Advantage Section 2: Barriers to International Trade Section 3: Financing and Trade Deficits
6 When individuals, regions, and nations specialize in what they can produce at the lowest cost and then trade with others, both production and consumption increase.	**Chapter 17** Section 1: Absolute and Comparative Advantage
7 Markets exist when buyers and sellers interact. This interaction determines market prices and thereby allocates scarce goods and services.	**Chapter 6** Section 1: Prices as Signals Section 2: The Price System at Work **Chapter 17** Section 3: Financing and Trade Deficits
8 Prices send signals and provide incentives to buyers and sellers. When supply or demand changes, market prices adjust, affecting incentives.	**Chapter 4** Section 1: What Is Demand? **Chapter 5** Section 1: What Is Supply? **Chapter 6** Section 1: Prices as Signals Section 2: The Price System at Work **Chapter 20** Section 2: Economic Incentives and Resources
9 Competition among sellers lowers costs and prices, and encourages producers to produce more of what consumers are willing and able to buy. Competition among buyers increases prices and allocates goods and services to those people who are willing and able to pay the most for them.	**Chapter 7** Section 1: Competition and Market Structures Section 2: Market Failures

For each standard, students will understand that:	Economics: Principles and Practices Chapter and Section coverage
10 Institutions evolve in market economies to help individuals and groups accomplish their goals. Banks, labor unions, corporations, legal systems, and not-for-profit organizations are examples of important institutions. A different kind of institution, clearly defined and well enforced property rights, is essential to a market economy.	**Chapter 3** Section 1: Forms of Business Organization Section 3: Other Organizations **Chapter 8** Section 1: The Labor Movement **Chapter 12** Section 1: Savings and the Financial System
11 Money makes it easier to trade, borrow, save, invest, and compare the value of goods and services.	**Chapter 11** Section 1: The Evolution of Money Section 2: Early Banking and Monetary Standards
12 Interest rates, adjusted for inflation, rise and fall to balance the amount saved with the amount borrowed, thus affecting the allocation of scarce resources between present and future uses.	**Chapter 15** Section 3: Monetary Policy, Banking, and the Economy **Chapter 16** Section 3: Stabilization Policies
13 Income for most people is determined by the market value of the productive resources they sell. What workers earn depends, primarily, on the market value of what they produce and how productive they are.	**Chapter 8** Section 3: Labor and Wages Section 4: Employment Trends and Issues **Chapter 14** Section 4: Poverty and the Distribution of Income
14 Entrepreneurs are people who take the risks of organizing productive resources to make goods and services. Profit is an important incentive that leads entrepreneurs to accept the risks of business failure.	**Chapter 1** Section 1: Scarcity and the Science of Economics **Chapter 3** Section 2: Business Growth and Expansion

For each standard, students will understand that:	Economics: Principles and Practices Chapter and Section coverage
15 Investment in factories, machinery, new technology, and the health, education, and training of people can raise future standards of living.	**Chapter 13** Section 4: Economic Growth **Chapter 19** Section 1: Economic Development Section 3: Financing Economic Development
16 There is an economic role for government to play in a market economy whenever the benefits of a government policy outweigh its costs. Governments often provide for national defense, address environmental concerns, define and protect property rights, and attempt to make markets more competitive. Most government policies also redistribute income.	**Chapter 2** Section 3: Capitalism and Economic Freedom **Chapter 3** Section 3: Other Organizations **Chapter 7** Section 2: Market Failures Section 3: The Role of Government **Chapter 9** Section 1: The Economics of Taxation Section 2: The Federal Tax System Section 3: State and Local Tax Systems Section 4: Current Tax Issues **Chapter 10** Section 1: The Economics of Government Spending **Chapter 18** Section 1: The Spectrum of Economic Systems Section 3: The Transition to Capitalism Section 4: The Various Faces of Capitalism **Chapter 20** Section 2: Economic Incentives and Resources
17 Costs of government policies sometimes exceed benefits. This may occur because of incentives facing voters, government officials, and government employees, because of actions by special interest groups that can impose costs on the general public, or because social goals other than economic efficiency are being pursued.	**Chapter 6** Section 2: The Price System at Work **Chapter 17** Section 2: Barriers to International Trade

For each standard, students will understand that:	Economics: Principles and Practices Chapter and Section coverage
18 A nation's overall levels of income, employment, and prices are determined by the interaction of spending and production decisions made by all households, firms, government agencies, and others in the economy.	**Chapter 13** Section 1: Measuring the Nation's Output Section 2: GDP and Changes in the Price Level Section 4: Economic Growth **Chapter 14** Section 1: Business Cycles and Fluctuations Section 2: Unemployment Section 3: Inflation **Chapter 16** Section 2: Macroeconomic Equilibrium **Chapter 19** Section 1: Economic Development
19 Unemployment imposes costs on individuals and nations. Unexpected inflation imposes costs on many people and benefits some others because it arbitrarily redistributes purchasing power. Inflation can reduce the rate of growth of national living standards, because individuals and organizations use resources to protect themselves against the uncertainty of future prices.	**Chapter 14** Section 1: Business Cycles and Fluctuations Section 2: Unemployment Section 3: Inflation Section 4: Poverty and the Distribution of Income
20 Federal government budgetary policy and the Federal Reserve System's monetary policy influence the overall levels of employment, output, and prices.	**Chapter 10** Section 1: The Economics of Government Spending Section 4: Deficits, Surpluses, and the National Debt **Chapter 15** Section 1: The Federal Reserve System Section 2: Monetary Policy Section 3: Monetary Policy, Banking, and the Economy **Chapter 16** Section 2: Macroeconomic Equilibrium Section 3: Stabilization Policies

Alternate Course Outlines

Economics: Priciples and Practices is organized so that it can be adjusted easily for alternative lengths or varied course emphases. The models on the following pages are based on the basic concepts listed below, which are provided in "A Framework for Teaching Basic Economic Concepts," written by the National Council on Economic Education (NCEE).

NCEE Basic Concepts

Fundamental Economic Concepts

- Scarcity and Choice
- Opportunity Cost and Trade-Offs
- Productivity
- Economic Systems
- Economic Institutions and Incentives
- Exchange, Money, and Interdependence

Macroeconomic Concepts

- Gross Domestic Product
- Aggregate Supply and Aggregate Demand
- Unemployment
- Inflation and Deflation
- Monetary Policy
- Fiscal Policy

Microeconomic Concepts

- Markets and Prices
- Supply and Demand
- Competition and Market Structures
- Income Distribution
- Market Failures
- The Role of Government

International Economic Concepts

- Absolute and Comparative Advantage and Barriers to Trade
- Exchange Rates and the Balance of Payments
- International Aspects of Growth and Stability

Measurement Concepts and Methods

- ✓ Tables
- ✓ Charts and Graphs
- ✓ Ratios and Percentages
- ✓ Index Numbers
- ✓ Real vs. Nominal Values
- ✓ Averages and Distributions Around the Average

Broad Social Goals

- ✓ Economic Freedom
- ✓ Economic Efficiency
- ✓ Economic Equity
- ✓ Economic Security
- ✓ Full Employment
- ✓ Price Stability
- ✓ Economic Growth
- ✓ Other Goals

Emphasis on Microeconomic Concepts

Chapter or Section	Basic Concepts	Length of Study in Days
Economic Handbook	• Measurement Concepts and Methods	3
Chapter 1 What Is Economics?	• Fundamental Economic Concepts	4
Chapter 2 Economic Systems and Decision Making	• Fundamental Economic Concepts	4
Chapter 3 Business Organizations	• Fundamental Economic Concepts	4
Chapter 4 Demand	• Microeconomic Concepts	6
Chapter 5 Supply	• Microeconomic Concepts	6
Chapter 6 Prices and Decision Making	• Microeconomic Concepts	6
Chapter 7 Market Structures	• Microeconomic Concepts	6
Chapter 8, Section 3 Labor and Wages	• Microeconomic Concepts	2
Chapter 8, Section 4 Employment Trends and Issues	• Microeconomic Concepts	2
Chapter 14, Section 4 Poverty and the Distribution of Income	• Microeconomic Concepts	2
	Total Days:	45

Course Length: 12 Weeks

Emphasis on Macroeconomic Concepts

Chapter or Section	Basic Concepts	Length of Study in Days
Economic Handbook	• Measurement Concepts and Methods	4
Chapter 1 What Is Economics?	• Fundamental Economic Concepts	4
Chapter 2 Economic Systems and Decision Making	• Fundamental Economic Concepts	4
Chapter 3, Section 1 Forms of Business Organization	• Macroeconomic Concepts	2
Chapter 8 Employment, Labor, and Wages	• Macroeconomic Concepts	5
Chapter 9 Sources of Government Revenue	• Macroeconomic Concepts	5
Chapter 10 Government Spending	• Macroeconomic Concepts	5
Chapter 11 Money and Banking	• Macroeconomic Concepts	5
Chapter 13 Economic Performance	• Macroeconomic Concepts	6
Chapter 14 Economic Instability	• Macroeconomic Concepts	6
Chapter 15 The Fed and Monetary Policy	• Macroeconomic Concepts	6
Chapter 16 Achieving Economic Stability	• Macroeconomic Concepts	6
	Total Days:	58

Course Length: 18 Weeks (Semester)

Emphasis on Fundamental, Macroeconomic, and International Economic Concepts

Chapter or Section	Basic Concepts	Length of Study in Days
Economic Handbook	• Measurement Concepts and Methods	5
Chapter 1 What Is Economics?	• Fundamental Economic Concepts	6
Chapter 2 Economic Systems and Decision Making	• Fundamental Economic Concepts & Broad Social Goals	6
Chapter 3 Business Organizations	• Fundamental Economic Concepts	6
Chapter 4, Section 1 What Is Demand?	• Microeconomic Concepts	2
Chapter 5, Section 1 What Is Supply?	• Microeconomic Concepts	2
Chapter 6, Section 1 Prices as Signals	• Microeconomic Concepts	2
Chapter 13 Economic Performance	• Macroeconomic Concepts & Broad Social Goals	7
Chapter 14 Economic Instability	• Macroeconomic Concepts	7
Chapter 15 The Fed and Monetary Policy	• Macroeconomic Concepts	7
Chapter 16 Achieving Economic Stability	• Macroeconomic Concepts & Broad Social Goals	7
Chapter 17 International Trade	• International Economic Concepts	7
Chapter 18 Comparative Economic Systems	• International Economic Concepts	7
Chapter 19 Developing Countries	• International Economic Concepts	6
Chapter 20 Global Economic Challenges	• International Economic Concepts	5
	Total Days:	82

Course Length: 18 Weeks (Semester)

Emphasis on Fundamental and Microeconomic Concepts

Chapter or Section	Basic Concepts	Length of Study in Days
Economic Handbook	• Measurement Concepts and Methods	5
Chapter 1 What Is Economics?	• Fundamental Economic Concepts	7
Chapter 2 Economic Systems and Decision Making	• Fundamental Economic Concepts & Broad Social Goals	6
Chapter 3 Business Organizations	• Fundamental Economic Concepts	6
Chapter 4 Demand	• Microeconomic Concepts	6
Chapter 5 Supply	• Microeconomic Concepts	7
Chapter 6 Prices and Decision Making	• Microeconomic Concepts & Broad Social Goals	6
Chapter 7 Market Structures	• Microeconomic Concepts	7
Chapter 11 Money and Banking	• Fundamental Economic Concepts	6
Chapter 14 Economic Instability	• Macroeconomic Concepts	6
Chapter 17 International Trade	• International Economic Concepts	6
Chapter 18 Comparative Economic Systems	• International Economic Concepts	6
Chapter 20 Global Economic Challenges	• International Economic Concepts & Broad Social Goals	5
pp. A30–A39 Life Skills	• Microeconomics: Fundamental Economic Concepts	3
	Total Days:	82

Emphasis on Microeconomic Concepts

Chapter or Section	Basic Concepts	Length of Study in Days
Economic Handbook	• Measurement Concepts and Methods	6
Chapter 1 What Is Economics?	• Fundamental Economic Concepts	8
Chapter 2 Economic Systems and Decision Making	• Fundamental Economic Concepts & Broad Social Goals	8
Chapter 3 Business Organizations	• Fundamental Economic Concepts	8
Chapter 4 Demand	• Microeconomic Concepts	9
Chapter 5 Supply	• Microeconomic Concepts	9
Chapter 6 Prices and Decision Making	• Microeconomic Concepts & Broad Social Goals	9
Chapter 7 Market Structures	• Microeconomic Concepts	9
Chapter 8 Employment, Labor, and Wages	• Macroeconomic Concepts	9
Chapter 9 Sources of Government Revenue	• Macroeconomic Concepts	8
Chapter 10 Government Spending	• Macroeconomic Concepts	8
Chapter 11 Money and Banking	• Fundamental Economic Concepts	9
Chapter 12 Financial Markets	• Macroeconomic Concepts	8
Chapter 13 Economic Performance	• Macroeconomic Concepts & Broad Social Goals	9
Chapter 14 Economic Instability	• Macroeconomic Concepts	8
Chapter 15 The Fed and Monetary Policy	• Macroeconomic Concepts	8
Chapter 16 Achieving Economic Stability	• Macroeconomic Concepts & Broad Social Goals	9
Chapter 17 International Trade	• International Economic Concepts	8
Chapter 18 Comparative Economic Systems	• International Economic Concepts	9
Chapter 19 Developing Countries	• International Economic Concepts	8
Chapter 20 Global Economic Challenges	• International Economic Concepts	8
pp. A30–A39 Life Skills	• Microeconomics: Fundamental Economic Concepts	5
	Total Days:	180

Reading Strategies

How Can I Help My Students Read and Understand the Textbook?

Social studies teachers do not have to be reading teachers to help students read and understand their textbooks. Often poor readers lack interest in the topic, have trouble concentrating, cannot understand a word or sentence, or are confused as to how the information fits together. These problems can frustrate the student and the teacher, but there are strategies that can be used to improve comprehension and retention of information. Using these reading strategies not only helps poor readers, but also strengthens the reading skills of strong readers.

Activate Prior Knowledge

Activating prior knowledge provides opportunities for students to discover and articulate what they already know about key concepts and ideas. It stimulates student interest and prepares students to incorporate new information into a larger picture. In addition, it helps the teacher to determine a starting place for instruction.

✔ Write the topic on the board and have students brainstorm what they know about it. Record their responses on the board.

✔ Ask general or specific questions about the topic and see how students respond to them.

✔ Present an anticipation guide. An anticipation guide provides a series of statements about an idea or topic. Students read each statement and tell whether they agree or disagree, based on their prior understandings and experiences.

✔ Use a K-W-L-H or K-W-L chart to activate prior knowledge and set reading purposes. Students identify what they already **know** (or think they know) and what they **want** to find out about the topic. After reading, students complete the chart.

K	W	L	H
What I **Know**	What I **Want** to Find Out	What I **Learned**	**How** I Can Learn More

Set Reading Purposes

Reading is a purposeful activity. We read to find answers to specific questions, to satisfy curiosity, and to be entertained.

✔ Have students preview the reading selection. Tell students to read the title, headings, and subheadings. Draw students' attention to diagrams, tables, and other visuals and their captions. Discuss how these will help comprehension.

✔ Prompt students to predict what they might learn in the selection, based on their preview. Invite them to list additional questions they hope to answer through the reading.

Have them identify possible problems, such as unfamiliar words or ideas, to watch for as they read.

✔ Discuss the need to "shift gears" in reading speed and attention when reading. Support students as they plan how best to read a selection—slowly to watch for new vocabulary and ideas or quickly to review previously learned ideas. They can also discuss new information with a buddy as they read.

Vocabulary Development

Vocabulary knowledge and reading comprehension are closely related.

✔ Before students read, preteach vocabulary that is crucial for understanding key topics and concepts.

✔ Relate new vocabulary to known words and ideas. After introducing a word and its definition, have students name synonyms or related words they know.

✔ If a student encounters an unfamiliar word while reading, have him or her try to pronounce it aloud. Sometimes saying the word will trigger one's memory of its meaning.

✔ As students read, help them use prefixes (word parts added to the beginning of base words), suffixes (word parts added to the end of base words), and roots (word elements from which other words are formed) as clues to decipher the meaning of words.

✔ Encourage students to use the context of surrounding words and sentences to determine a word's meaning.

✔ If context clues and structural analysis fail to help a student understand an important word as

Tom & DeeAnn McCarthy/CORBIS STOCK MARKET

Common Prefixes	Meanings	Examples
un-, dis-, non-, im- and il-	"not" or "the opposite of"	unwrapped, dishonest, nonprofit, immortal, illogical
re-	"again" or "back"	reheat
post-	"after"	postwar
uni-	"one"	unicycle

Common Suffixes	Meanings	Examples
-ship, -hood	"state of" or "condition of"	friendship, neighborhood
-ment	"act of" or "state of"	management
-ish	"like"	childish
-ous	"full of" or "like"	joyous

they read, have students find the definition in a glossary or dictionary. If the word is not critical for understanding, have students note the word and read on. Later, have students reread the word in context. If the meaning is still unclear, have students consult the dictionary.

Taking Notes

Taking notes challenges readers to determine what is most important and to organize information in a way that makes sense. Note-taking can also help students stay focused as they read. Reviewing notes can build students' retention of important information.

✔ Have students take notes after they have read long paragraphs in the section rather than the entire chapter. This helps them focus on important ideas and details and prevents them from losing track of the flow of information.

✔ Remind students that as they take notes on the section, they should not take a long time to do it. Students should read, think, write, and move on.

✔ Have students take notes using note cards. Notes should be recorded in the students' own words and labeled with the page number where the entire text appears.

✔ To use notes to review a passage, have students read through the notes, highlighting the most impor-

tant information. As they review, encourage students to annotate their notes, making connections between related ideas and clarifying difficult concepts.

Summarizing

Summarizing demands that students identify the most important ideas and

details to create a streamlined version of the text.

✔ After reading the section, have students recall as much of the information as possible. If the main idea and its supporting details are presented in a certain order, make sure students can recall that organization.

✔ As they summarize, students should try to answer as many of the following questions as possible: *who, what, where, when, why,* and *how.*

✔ If the section does not have a main idea that is clearly stated, have students create one that is concise but comprehensive. Have students state the main idea in a topic sentence at the beginning of their summaries.

✔ Sometimes summaries seem disconnected when details are left out. Students should use connector words such as "and" or "because," along with introductory or closing statements, to make ideas more connected.✦

Reading Comprehension: Be Aware, Reread, and Connect (BARC)

Advice from Dr. Elizabeth Pryor, Ph.D.
Research Center for Educational Technology
Kent State University, Kent, Ohio

Many students think silent reading means just looking at words and saying them in their heads. They do not make the connection that reading is supposed to make sense! Have you ever read a paragraph or a page and then said to yourself, "What was that?" As a good reader, you were aware of your lack of understanding. Poor readers, on the other hand, just keep on reading the words, unaware that they do not understand them.

What strategies do good readers use when this happens? Most reread the text they did not understand. Before rereading I study key words I might have missed. When I reread, sometimes I "whisper read" so I can hear the text as well as read it. As I reread, I try to connect what I am reading with something I already know. If I reread and still don't understand, I read it a third (or fourth) time. Each rereading increases comprehension.

In summary, **Be aware** of understanding as you read, **reread,** and **connect** the reading to what you already know. **BARC!**

Test-Taking Strategies
How Can I Help My Students Succeed on Tests?

It's not enough for students to learn social studies facts and concepts—they must be able to show what they know in a variety of test-taking situations.

How Can I Help My Students Do Well On Objective Tests?

Objective tests may include multiple choice, true/false, and matching questions. Applying the following strategies can help students do their best on objective tests.

Multiple Choice Questions

✔ Students should read the directions carefully to learn what answer the test requires—the best answer or the right answer. This is especially important when answer choices include "all of the above" or "none of the above."

✔ Advise students to watch for negative words in the questions, such as *not, except, unless, never,* and so forth. If the question contains a negative, the correct answer choice is the one that does not fit.

✔ Students should try to mentally answer the question before reading the answer choices.

✔ Students should read all the answer choices and cross out those that are obviously wrong. Then they should choose an answer from those that remain.

True/False Questions

✔ It is important that students read the entire question before answering. For an answer to be true, the entire statement must be true. If one part of a statement is false, the answer should be marked *False.*

✔ Remind students to watch for words like *all, never, every,* and *always.* Statements containing these words are often false.

Matching Questions

✔ Students should read through both lists before they mark any answers.

✔ Unless an answer can be used more than once, students should cross out each choice as they use it.

✔ Using what they know about grammar can help students find the right answer. For instance, when matching a word with its definition, the definition is often the same part of speech (noun, verb, adjective, and so forth) as the word.

How Can I Help My Students Do Well On Essay Tests?

Essay tests require students to provide thorough and well-organized written responses, in addition to telling what they know. Help students use the following strategies on essay tests.

Analyze:	To **analyze** means to systematically and critically examine all parts of an issue or event.
Classify or Categorize:	To **classify** or **categorize** means to put people, things, or ideas into groups, based on a common set of characteristics.
Compare and Contrast:	To **compare** is to show how things are similar, or alike. To **contrast** is to show how things are different.
Describe:	To **describe** means to present a sketch or impression. Rich details, especially details that appeal to the senses, flesh out a description.
Discuss:	To **discuss** means to systematically write about all sides of an issue or event.
Evaluate:	To **evaluate** means to make a judgment and support it with evidence.
Explain:	To **explain** means to clarify or make plain.
Illustrate:	To **illustrate** means to provide examples or to show with a picture or other graphic.
Infer:	To **infer** means to read between the lines or to use knowledge and experience to draw conclusions, make a generalization, or form a prediction.
Justify:	To **justify** means to prove or to support a position with specific facts and reasons.
Predict:	To **predict** means to tell what will happen in the future, based on an understanding of prior events and behaviors.
State:	To **state** means to briefly and concisely present information.
Summarize:	To **summarize** means to give a brief overview of the main points of an issue or event.
Trace:	To **trace** means to present the steps or stages in a process or event in sequential or chronological order.

Read the Question

The key to writing successful essay responses lies in reading and interpreting questions correctly. Teach students to identify and underline key words in the questions, and to use these words to guide them in understanding what the question asks. Help students understand the meaning of some of the most common key words, listed in the chart on page T28.

Plan and Write the Essay

After students understand the question, they should follow the writing process to develop their answer. Encourage students to follow the steps below to plan and write their essays.

---

1. Map out an answer. Make lists, webs, or an outline to plan the response.

2. Decide on an order in which to present the main points.

3. Write an opening statement that directly responds to the essay question.

4. Write the essay. Expand on the opening statement. Support key points with specific facts, details, and reasons.

5. Write a closing statement that brings the main points together.

6. Proofread to check for spelling, grammar, and punctuation.

How Can I Help My Students Prepare for Standardized Tests?

Students can follow the steps below to prepare for a test.

✔ **Read About the Test** Students can familiarize themselves with the format of the test, the types of questions that will be asked, and the amount of time they will have to complete the test.

✔ **Review the Content** Consistent study throughout the school year will help students build social studies knowledge and understanding. If there are specific objectives or standards that are tested on the exam, help students review these facts or skills to be sure they are proficient.

✔ **Practice** Provide practice, ideally with real released tests, to build students' familiarity with the content, format, and timing of the real exam. Students should practice all the types of questions they will encounter on the test—multiple choice, short answer, and extended response.

✔ **Analyze Practice Results** Help students improve test-taking performance by analyzing their test-taking strengths and weaknesses. Spend time discussing students' completed practice tests, explaining why particular answers are right or wrong. Help students identify what kinds of questions they had the most difficulty with. Look for patterns in errors and then tailor instruction to review the appropriate test-taking skills or social studies content. ✦

Jose L. Pelaez/CORBIS STOCK MARKET

Help Students Learn by Reviewing Graded Tests

Advice from Tara Musslewhite
Humble Independent School District
Humble, Texas

Frequently reviewing graded tests is a great way for students to assess their test-taking skills. It also gives teachers the opportunity to teach test-taking strategies and review content. As the class re-reads each test question, guide students to think logically about their answer choices. Show students how to:

1. Read each question carefully to determine its meaning.
2. Look for key words in the question to support their answers.
3. Recognize synonyms in the answer choices that may match phrases in the question.
4. Narrow down answer choices by eliminating ones that don't make sense.
5. Anticipate the answer before looking at the answer choices.
6. Circle questions of which they are unsure and go back to them later. Sometimes a clue will be found in another question on the test.

Alternative Assessment Strategies

How Can I Go Beyond Tests to Assess Students' Understanding of Social Studies Facts and Concepts?

In response to the growing demand for accountability in the classroom, educators must use multiple assessment measures to accurately gauge student performance. In addition to quizzes, tests, essay exams, and standardized tests, assessment today incorporates a variety of performance-based measures and portfolio opportunities.

What Are Some Typical Performance-Based Assessments?

There are many kinds of performance-based assessments. They all share one common characteristic—they challenge students to create products that demonstrate what they know. One good way to present a performance assessment is in the form of an open-ended question.

Writing

Performance-based writing assessments challenge students to apply their knowledge of social studies concepts and information in a variety of written ways. Writing activities are most often completed by one student, rather than by a group.

✔ **Journals** Students write from the perspective of a historical character or a citizen of a particular historical era.

✔ **Letters** Students write a letter from one historical figure to another or from a historical figure to a family member or other audience.

✔ **Position Paper or Editorial** Students explain a controversial issue and present their own opinion and recommendations, supported with strong evidence and convincing reasons.

✔ **Newspaper** Students write a variety of stories from the perspective of a reporter living in a particular historical time period.

✔ **Biographies and Autobiographies** Students write about historical figures either from the third person point of view (biography) or from the first person (autobiography).

✔ **Creative Stories** Students integrate historical events into a piece of fiction, incorporating the customs, language, and geography of the period.

✔ **Poems and Songs** Students follow the conventions of a particular type of song or poem as they tell about a historical event or person.

✔ **Research Reports** Students synthesize information from a variety of sources into a well-developed research report.

Oral Presentations

Oral presentations allow students to demonstrate their social studies literacy before an audience. Oral presentations are often group efforts, although this need not be the case.

✔ **Simulations** Students hold simulations, or reenactments, of actual events, such as trials, acts of civil disobedience, battles, speeches, and so forth.

✔ **Debates** Students debate two or more sides to a historical policy or issue. Students can debate from a contemporary perspective or in a role play in which they assume a viewpoint held by a historical character.

✔ **Interview** Students conduct a mock interview of an historical character or bystander.

✔ **Oral Reports** Students present the results of research efforts in a lively oral report.

✔ **Skits and Plays** Students use historical events as the basis for a play or skit. Details should accurately reflect customs, language, and the setting of the period.

Visual Presentations

Visual presentations allow students to demonstrate their social studies understandings in a variety of visual formats. Visual presentations can be either group or individual projects.

✔ **Model** Students make a model to demonstrate or represent a process, place, event, battle, artifact, or custom.

✔ **Museum Exhibit** Students create a rich display of materials around a topic. Typical displays might include models, illustrations, photographs, videos, writings, and audiotaped explanations.

✔ **Graph or Chart** Students analyze and represent historical data in a line graph, bar graph, table, or other chart format.

✔ **Drawing** Students represent or interpret a historical event or period through illustration, including political cartoons.

✔ **Posters and Murals** Posters and murals may include maps, time lines, diagrams, illustrations, photographs, and written explanations that reflect students' understandings of historical information.

- ✔ **Quilt** Students sew or draw a design for a patchwork quilt that shows a variety of perspectives, events, or issues related to a key topic.
- ✔ **Videotapes** Students film a video to show historical fiction or to preserve a simulation of a historical event.
- ✔ **Multimedia Presentation or Slide Show** Students create a computer-generated multimedia presentation containing historical information and analysis.

How Are Performance Assessments Scored?

There are a variety of means used to evaluate performance tasks. Some or all of the following methods may be used.

- ✔ **Scoring Rubrics** A scoring rubric is a set of guidelines for assessing the quality of a process and/or product. It sets out criteria used to distinguish acceptable responses from unacceptable ones, generally along a scale from excellent to poor.
- ✔ **Models of Excellent Work** Teacher-selected models of excellent work concretely illustrate expectations and help students set goals for their own projects.
- ✔ **Student Self-Assessment** Common methods of self-assessment include ranking work in relation to the model, using a scoring rubric, and writing their own goals and then evaluating how well they have met the goals they set for themselves. Regardless of which method or methods students use, they should be encouraged to evaluate their behaviors and processes, as well as the finished product.
- ✔ **Peer or Audience Assessment** Many of the performance tasks target an audience other than the classroom teacher. If possible, the audience of peers should give the student feedback. Have the class create rubrics for specific projects together.

- ✔ **Observation** As students carry out their performance tasks, you may want to formally observe students at work. Start by developing a checklist, identifying all the specific behaviors and understandings you expect students to demonstrate. Then observe students as they carry out performance tasks and check off the behaviors as you observe them.
- ✔ **Interviews** As a form of ongoing assessment, you may want to conduct interviews with students, asking them to analyze, explain, and assess their participation in performance tasks. When projects take place over an extended period of time, you can hold periodic interviews as well as exit interviews. In this way the interview process allows you to gauge the status of the project and to guide students' efforts along the way. ✦

Targeting Multiple Intelligences

Advice from John Cartaina
Consultant, New Jersey Council of Social Studies

Authentic performance assessment provides students with different learning styles opportunities to demonstrate their successful learning. The table below list types of learning styles.

Learning Style	Characteristics of Students
Linguistic	Read regularly, write clearly, and easily understand the written word
Logical-Mathematical	Use numbers, logic, and critical thinking skills
Visual-Spatial	Think in terms of pictures and images
Auditory-Musical	Remember spoken words and produce rhythms and melodies
Kinesthetic	Learn from touch, movement, and manipulating objects
Interpersonal	Understand and work well with other people
Intrapersonal	Have a realistic understanding of their strengths and weaknesses
Naturalist	Can distinguish among, classify, and use features of the environment

You may want to assign activities to students that accommodate their strongest learning styles, but frequently ask them to use their weakest learning styles.

Cooperative Group Strategies
How Can I Use Cooperative Learning to Teach Social Studies?

Today's social and economic climate requires flexibility. Workers must be able to function independently, work well with groups, and engage in fair-minded competition. For this reason, most educators recommend a healthy balance of instructional strategies to foster cooperative, competitive, and individualistic styles of problem solving and learning. Cooperative learning requires students to work together—each with a specific task—to pursue a common goal. Because part of each student's evaluation is determined by the overall quality of the group's work, students help one another accomplish the group goal.

How Do I Form Cooperative Groups?

✔ **Composition** Most experts recommend that cooperative groups be heterogeneous, reflecting a range of student abilities, backgrounds, and learning styles. However, this does not necessarily mean that students should be assigned to groups on a random basis.

✔ **Group Size** The size of cooperative groups can change, depending upon the task. Some cooperative tasks are best accomplished in pairs. For most projects, groups of three to five students are ideal.

✔ **Abilities** Consider the tasks and projects the groups will undertake as you make group assignments. You may want to make sure each group has a strong manager, a strong writer, a strong artist, a good listener, and so forth.

✔ **Balance** Some teachers use a "family-of-five" approach to grouping. A strong leader heads each group. Two pairs of students with opposing styles or strengths complete the "family." Paired students might exhibit traits such as outgoing and shy, creative and conventional, spontaneous and methodical, and so on. Each group continues to work together throughout the semester or year, with the goal that students develop greater flexibility in their own problem-solving abilities and greater respect for the contributions of others.

✔ **Roles** In most instances, you will want to assign a specific role for each student to play in a group, such as designer, moderator, recorder, researcher, presenter, graphic artist, actor, and so forth. Roles should be interdependent, requiring students to rely upon one another in order to successfully carry out their individual responsibilities. As students gain experience in working in cooperative groups, turn over more of the responsibility for establishing individual roles and responsibilities to the group.

How Do I Help Groups Run Smoothly?

✔ **Seating Arrangements** Explain how and where groups should sit. Pairs can sit with desks or chairs face-to-face. Larger groups do well with desks or chairs gathered in a circle or with students seated around a table.

✔ **Warm-Ups** Provide an introductory activity for new groups. Even when students know one another, they can benefit by making formal introductions and sharing their thoughts on a sentence starter, such as "If I could go anywhere in the world, I would go to . . ." or "If I could have lived at any period in history, I would choose. . ."

✔ **Rules** Set clear expectations and rules for groups. Typical rules include addressing group members by name, making eye contact, listening politely, expressing disagreement with respect, welcoming others' questions, valuing others' contributions, providing positive feedback, and assisting others when asked.

How Do I Use Cooperative Groups in My Classroom?

✔ **Share and Tell** Have students form groups of four. Assign each group member a number between one and four. Ask a factual recall question. Have group members discuss the question and come up with an answer. Call out a number between one and four. The student with that number who is first to raise his or her hand answers the question. The group earns a point for a correct answer.

✔ **Circle Partners** Have the class separate into two equal groups and form two circles, with one circle inside the other. Each student faces a partner in the

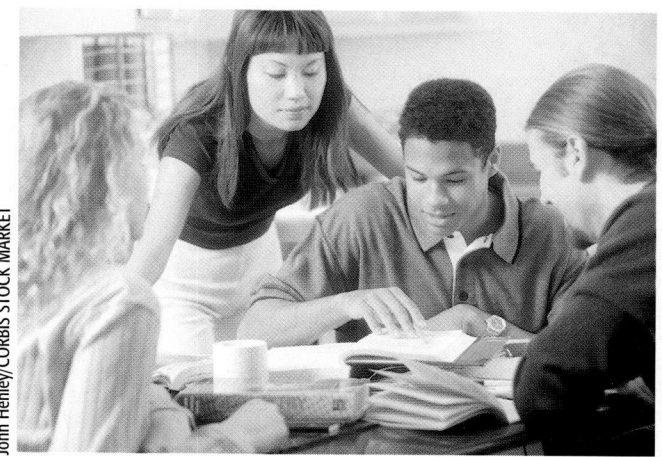

John Henley/CORBIS STOCK MARKET

opposing circle. Ask a question and have partners discuss the answer. If partners do not know the answer they can ask another pair for help. Then, call on students in the inside circle, the outside circle, or all students to say the answer aloud together.

✔ **In the Know** Provide students with a set of end-of-chapter questions or other questions covering content you want students to master. Tell students to circulate around the room to find someone who can answer a question on the worksheet. After listening to the answer, the student paraphrases it, writes the answer on the worksheet, and asks the "expert" to read and sign off on the answer if it is correct. Students move on to find a student to answer the next question. The process continues until students have completed their worksheets.

✔ **Open-Ended Projects** The best long-term projects for cooperative groups are those that are open-ended and multidimensional. That is, the task or question should have many possible answers and should lend itself to many different presentation possibilities.

Multiple intelligences Appropriate projects should challenge students and allow students of various abilities and backgrounds to contribute significantly to solving the problem and executing the project. One way to assess the validity of a potential project is to see whether it requires the use of many different strengths or "intelligences."

Assigning roles
Because of the complexity of long-term projects, it is essential that students have clearly assigned roles and responsibilities. Once cooperative groups are established and successful in your classroom, be sure to vary the assignments given to each student from project to project.

Deadlines Define interim and final deadlines to encourage students to pace their efforts appropriately.

How Do I Assess Group and Individual Efforts?

✔ **Expectations** As with any assignment, set clear guidelines and high expectations for projects. Show models of excellent past projects, if possible, and define what criteria projects must meet to earn the highest grade.

✔ **Group and Individual Grades** Before students begin, define what percentage of the grade will be based on group work and how much will be based on individual effort. Many teachers give two equally weighted grades: a group grade—the same for each team member—and an individual grade.

✔ **Self-Assessment** Provide a checklist or rating scale for each group member. Have students evaluate their own contribution to the group, as well as the contributions of other group members. In addition to assessing the quality of the finished product, have students evaluate the processes they used within the group, such as showing respect for others' ideas. Provide space on the evaluation sheet for students to explain why they rated themselves and group members as they did.✦

Troubleshooting

Advice from Carey Boswell, M.Ed.
Humble Independent School District
Humble, Texas

Modern research overwhelmingly suggests that student learning is enhanced when cooperative groups are used in the classroom. Like many other teachers, I was uncertain of how much learning was taking place when I set up cooperative groups. I struggled with noise and control issues and off-task behavior by some students. I found a solution, though.

A cooperative group activity occurs whenever a student works with another student. Cooperative groups do not have to be large groups. Smaller groups ensure that all students are engaged and contribute to the group effort. Smaller groups also guarantee that members perform multiple tasks so that real learning occurs. I often combine two or more small groups into a larger group for short comparative tasks. After making this small adjustment, I am able to assign cooperative group tasks to students at least once a week and student performance, comprehension, and learning has increased in my classroom.

Web Strategies
How Can I Use the Internet to Teach Social Studies?

From the Internet to round-the-clock live newscasts, teachers and students have never before had so much information at their fingertips. Yet never before has it been so confusing to determine where to turn for reliable content and what to do with it once you have found it. In today's world, social studies teachers must not only use the Internet as a source of up-to-the-minute information for students; they must teach students how to find and evaluate sources on their own.

What's Available On the Internet?

✔ **Teacher-Focused Web Sites** These Web sites provide teaching tips, detailed lesson plans, and links to other sites of interest to teachers and students.

✔ **Historical Documents** Thousands of primary source documents have now been cataloged and placed on the Web. Some sites provide text-only versions. Others provide photographs of actual documents and artifacts as well as insightful commentary and analysis.

✔ **Geographical Information** The Web holds a variety of geographical resources, from historical, physical, and political maps; to interactive mapping programs; to information about people and places around the world.

✔ **Statistics** Government Web sites are rich depositories for statistics of all kinds, including census data and information about climate, education, the economy, and political processes and patterns.

✔ **Reference Sources** Students can access full-text versions of encyclopedias, dictionaries, atlases, and other reference books, as well as databases containing millions of journal and newspaper articles.

✔ **News** Traditional media sources, including television, radio, newspapers, and newsmagazines, sponsor Internet sites that provide almost instantaneous news updates, as well as in-depth news coverage and analysis. Extensive archives facilitate research on past news stories.

✔ **Topical Information** Among the most numerous Web sites are those organized around a particular topic or issue, such as the Civil War or the stock market. These Internet pages may contain essays, analyses, and other commentaries, as well as primary source documents, maps, photographs, video and audio clips, bibliographies, and links to related online resources.

✔ **Organizations** Many organizations such as museums post Web pages that provide online exhibits, archives, and other information.

Glencoe Online

Glencoe provides an integrated Web curriculum for your textbook. The **Chapter Overview** Web link provides previews and reviews to help students better understand each chapter's organization and content. Engaging **Student Web Activities** challenge students to apply what they've learned. **Self-Check Quizzes** at the end of each chapter let you and your students assess their knowledge. You can also access additional resources, including links relevant to your state.

Finding Things on the Internet

The greatest asset of the Internet—its vast array of materials—is also its greatest deterrent. Many excellent social studies-specific sites provide links to relevant content. Using Internet search engines can also help you find what you need.

✔ A search engine is an Internet search tool. You type in a keyword, name, or phrase, and the search engine lists the URLs for Web sites that match your search. However, a search engine may find things that are not at all related or may miss sites that you would consider of interest. The key is to find ways to define your search.

✔ Not all search engines are the same. Each seeks out information a little bit differently. Different search engines use different criteria to determine what constitutes a "match" for your search topic. The Internet holds numerous articles

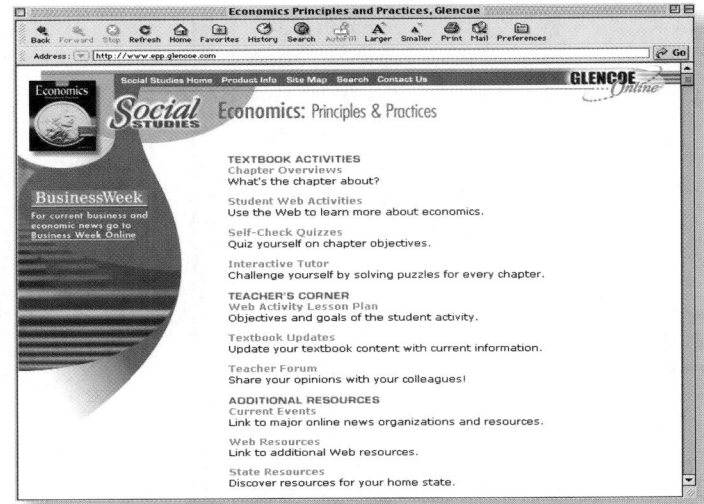

that compare search engines and offer guidelines for choosing those that best meet your needs.

✔ An advanced search allows you to refine the search by using a phrase or a combination of words. The way to conduct an advanced search varies from search engine to engine; check the search engine's Help feature for information. Encourage students to review this information regularly for each of the search engines they use.

How Do I Teach Students to Evaluate Web Sites?

Anyone can put up a Web site. Web content is easy to change, too, so Webmasters constantly update their Web sites by adding, modifying, and removing content. These characteristics make evaluating Web sites both more challenging and more important than traditional print resources. Teach students to critically evaluate Web resources, using the questions and criteria below.

1 Purpose: What is the purpose of the Web site or Web page? Is it an informational Web page, a news site, a business site, an advocacy site, or a personal Web page? Many sites serve more than one purpose. For instance, a news site may provide current events accompanied by banner ads that market the products advertisers think readers might want.

2 URL: What is the URL, or Web address? Where does the site originate? That can sometimes tell you about the group or business behind the Web page. For example, URLs with .edu and .gov domain names indicate that the site is connected to an educational institution or a government agency, respectively. A .com suffix usually means that a commercial or business interest hosts the Web site, but may also indicate a personal Web page. A nonprofit organization's Web address may end with .org.

3 Authority: Who wrote the material or created the Web site? What qualifications does this person or group have? Who has ultimate responsibility for the site? If the site is sponsored by an organization, are the organization's goals clearly stated?

4 Accuracy: How reliable is the information? Are sources listed so that they can be verified? Is the Web page free from surface errors in spelling and grammar? How does it compare with other sources you've found on the Web and in print?

5 Objectivity: If the site presents itself as an informational site, is the material free from bias? If there is advertising, is it easy to tell the difference between the ads and other features? If the site mixes factual information with opinion, can you spot the difference between the two? If the site advocates an opinion or viewpoint, is the opinion clearly stated and logically defended?

6 Currency: When was the information first placed on the Web? Is the site updated on a regular basis? When was the last revision? If the information is time-sensitive, are the updates frequent enough?

7 Coverage: What topics are covered on the Web site? What is the depth of coverage? Are all sides of an issue presented? How does the coverage compare with other Web and print sources? ✦

See the *Glencoe Social Studies Guide to Using the Internet* for additional information and teaching strategies.

Avoiding Online Pitfalls

Advice from Jim Matiya
Carl Sandburg High School
Orland Park, Illinois

Integrating technology into your social studies curriculum can have its pitfalls. Because something often goes wrong when you least expect it, here is some advice about technology, computers, and students.

1. Make sure the hyperlinks work—check them yourself.
2. Design assignments that go from easy to complex. Students have varying degrees of success with computers so start with simple, concrete assignments and move to complex, abstract assignments.
3. Vary the selection of sites for students. You can use a search engine and a museum site for one assignment and then use a historical document page and a statistical site for another assignment. Varying the sites negates predictability and breaks the routine.
4. Make sure you have given students enough information to find what you want. Do not give them a question that can lead to thousands of different answers on different sites.
5. Design Web assignments so that students with less Internet experience can achieve some degree of success. Have computer-literate students become mentors for their classmates.
6. Have alternative assignments in case the Internet is temporarily down, the computers are locked inside a closet, or lightning has wiped out a bank of computers.

Primary Source Strategies

How Do I Use Primary Sources in My Classroom?

A primary source is direct evidence of an event, idea, period, or development. It is an oral or written account obtained from actual participants in an event. Examples of primary sources include the following:

✔ official documents (records, statistics)
✔ political declarations, laws, and rules for governance
✔ speeches and interviews
✔ diaries, memoirs, and oral histories
✔ autobiographies
✔ recipes and cookbooks
✔ advertisements and posters
✔ letters

Physical objects, such as tools and dishes, can be primary sources; so can visual evidence in the form of fine art, photographs, maps, films, and videotapes. Primary sources can also include songs and audio recordings.

Why Use Primary Sources in Your Classroom?

Using primary sources to teach transforms the study of social studies from a passive process to an active one. Students become investigators—finding clues, formulating hypotheses and drawing inferences, making judgments, and reaching conclusions. Bringing primary sources into the classroom stimulates students to think critically about events, issues, and concepts rather than just memorizing dates, names, and generalizations reached by others.

Choosing Primary Sources

✔ Provide exposure to a variety of source types, including historic photographs, folk or popular music, financial records or household accounts, as well as letters, journals, and historic documents.
✔ When choosing print sources, consider the interests and reading levels of your students. Many texts contain challenging vocabulary and unfamiliar sentence structure. You may need to create a reader's guide that defines key vocabulary and paraphrases the main points of the reading.
✔ Some documents may be too long. Decide whether using an excerpt will provide enough information for students to draw conclusions.
✔ Depending upon the topic and your instructional objectives, you may need to provide several different primary sources to expose students to a variety of perspectives.
✔ Decide how students will access the primary sources: through the Internet, the library, a museum, or other print resources. Consider the possibility of an Internet virtual field trip for students. Moving from URL to URL, students can visit museum sites and other Web pages to view artifacts; interpret economic or census data; and read journals, letters, and official documents.

How Do I Introduce Students to Primary Sources?

Carefully explain the nature of primary sources when you introduce them to students. Although primary sources contain valuable clues, be sure to alert students that primary sources contain biases and prejudices, and must be approached with caution. Every primary source reflects the creator's point of view to some degree.

Using Primary Sources in the Classroom

Primary sources provide a rich source of inspiration for a variety of instructional strategies. They can be used to spark interest in a new topic, foster deeper exploration into a historical era, or assess students' understanding of social studies concepts and facts.

✔ **Pre-Reading Activities** Present a primary source for students to study at the beginning of a new chapter or topic. Have students analyze the source, using the questions and guidelines presented on the next page. Then have students make

Anthony Redpath/CORBIS STOCK MARKET

PhotoDisc

Aaron Haupt

Interpreting a Primary Source

Before students interpret a primary source, they need to know the context into which the source fits. Then they can use questions and guidelines, such as those below, to help them analyze and interpret the primary source.

Print Sources

- Who created the source, and what was the purpose for doing so?
- Did the writer personally experience or witness the event(s)?
- At what point did the writer record the information—as it happened or afterward? How long after?
- Who was the intended audience?
- Was the writer trying to record facts, express an opinion, or persuade others to take action?
- What is the author's main message?
- What values does the document convey?
- What bias does it reflect?
- What information about the topic can you gather from this document?
- Compare this document with what you know about the topic. Does it confirm those ideas or introduce a new perspective?
- How might other accounts about this topic support or modify the message this source delivers?

Visual Sources

- Who created the source, and what was the purpose for doing so?
- What does the image show?
- What mood does the image convey?
- Who or what dominates the image or catches your eye?
- How does the view impact the message?
- What details can you learn from the image?
- What is excluded from view?
- What bias does the visual reflect?
- What information about the topic can you gather from this visual?
- How might other visuals about this topic support or modify the message this one delivers?

Audio Sources

- Who created the source? What was the purpose for creating this source?
- What is the main idea of the audio?
- What mood does the recorder's voice convey?
- What bias does the audio text reflect?
- What information about the topic can you gather from this audio source?
- Compare the information in this source with what you already know about the topic. Does it confirm those ideas or introduce a new perspective?
- How might other sources about this topic support or modify the message that this one delivers?

predictions about what they might learn in the upcoming lessons.

✔ **Exploring Information** Provide a variety of primary sources related to a topic or time period. Have students compare and contrast the items, analyzing the information, making inferences, and drawing conclusions about the period.

✔ **Evaluation Activities** Have students evaluate a primary source and tell how it supports or refutes what they learned in the textbook or have students read a primary source document that provides one perspective on a topic, and have students write their own account, presenting another perspective or opinion.◆

How to Use the Declaration of Independence in Your Classroom

Advice from Susan Hirsch
East Wake High School
Wendell, North Carolina

Divide students into groups of three or four. Tell students that it is 1777, and one member of their group has been arrested for joining the revolutionary struggle against Great Britain. This person will be sent to London to be tried on charges of treason. Hanging is the punishment for those found guilty of treason. Each group must prepare a defense using only one source—the Declaration of Independence. One person from each group will speak to the class, acting as either the defendant or the defendant's attorney. After all the presentations, the class will vote to determine which person did the best job of defending himself or herself or the client.

Using Maps, Graphs, and Charts

How Can I Use Visuals to Improve Students' Reading Comprehension?

Maps, graphs, and charts are visual tools. By using images rather than words, these tools present complex information in an easy-to-understand format. Teach students the following generalized viewing strategies, and encourage them to apply these strategies as they study each chapter.

✔ **Asking Questions** Students should start by looking over the graphic and asking themselves questions, such as "What is my purpose for looking at this image?" Then students can identify questions they hope to answer, such as "What is being compared?" or "What are the most important features?"

✔ **Finding Answers** Next, students should use the graphic's structural features, such as the title, labels, colors, and symbols, to help them find the answers to their questions. If the source of the graphic is available, students should also determine its reliability.

✔ **Drawing Conclusions** After studying the visual, students should summarize its main points and draw conclusions.

✔ **Connecting** Before moving on, students should relate what they learned from the visual with what they gained from reading the text selection. Students can examine how the visual supports or extends the meaning of the text.

Maps

Maps show the relative size and location of specific geographic areas. There are as many different kinds of maps as there are uses for them. Two of the most common general purpose maps are political maps and physical maps. Political maps show human-made boundaries, such as state and country borders. Physical maps show physical features, such as mountains and lakes. Special purpose maps might show historical change, cultural features, population, land use, or climate.

Parts of Maps

All maps contain parts that assist in interpreting the information. Help students learn to identify the following map parts.

✔ **Title** The map title identifies the area shown on the visual. The title can also identify a map's special focus.

✔ **Map Key** The map key, or legend, explains the symbols presented on the map, thus unlocking the map's information.

✔ **Compass Rose** A compass rose is a direction marker. It is a symbol that points out where the cardinal directions—north, south, east, and west—are positioned.

✔ **Scale** A measuring line, often called a scale bar, indicates the relationship between the distances on the map and the actual distances on Earth. Distance on a map can be determined by measuring the distance between points, then multiplying that measure by the number of miles or kilometers specified in the map scale ratio.

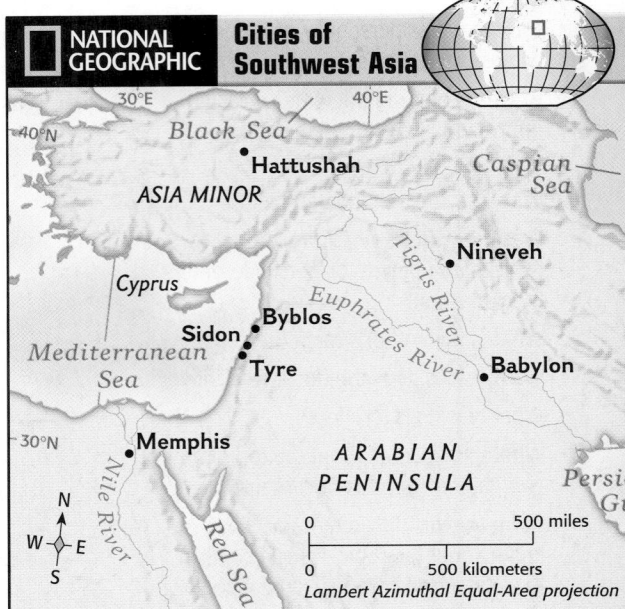

NATIONAL GEOGRAPHIC

Cities of Southwest Asia

✔ **Latitude and Longitude** Mapmakers use lines of latitude and longitude to pinpoint exact locations on maps and globes. The imaginary horizontal lines that circle the globe from east to west are lines of latitude, also called parallels. The imaginary vertical lines are lines of longitude, also called meridians. Both parallels and meridians are measured in degrees.

Graphs

Graphs are a way of showing numbers or statistics in a clear, easy-to-read way. Because graphs summarize and present information visually, readers have an easier time understanding the data and drawing conclusions. The most common types of graphs are bar graphs, line graphs, circle graphs, and pictographs.

Populations: Selected Countries

Morocco

Libya

Algeria

Tunisia

Egypt

= 5,000,000

Source: National Geographic Atlas of the World, 7th edition

Charts

While all charts present information or data in a visual way, the type of chart is often dictated by the nature of the information and by the chart-maker's purposes.

✔ **Tables** Tables show information, including numerical data, in columns and rows. This organized arrangement facilitates comparisons between categories of information. Labels are usually located at the top of each column and on the left-hand side of the table.

✔ **Diagrams** Diagrams are specialized drawings. They can show steps in a process; point out parts of an object, organization, or idea; or explain how something works. Arrows or lines may join parts of a figure and can show relationships between parts or the flow of steps.✦

✔ **Bar Graphs** A bar graph shows how two or more subjects or statistics compare. It provides information along two sides or axes. The horizontal axis is the line across the bottom of the graph. The vertical axis is the line along the side. The bars may be either vertical or horizontal. In most cases the labels on one axis show quantity, while the labels on the opposite axis show the categories of data being compared.

✔ **Line Graphs** A line graph shows change over time. Like a bar graph, it organizes information along the horizontal and vertical axes. The horizontal axis usually shows passing time, such as months, years, or decades. The vertical axis usually shows quantity or amount. Sometimes more than one set of data is shown in a line graph. A double-line graph, for instance, plots data for two related quantities, which may be represented in different colors or patterns.

✔ **Circle Graphs** A circle graph, also called a pie graph, shows how each part or percentage relates to the whole. A circle graph enables a viewer to make comparisons between parts and to analyze the relationship of each part to the whole.

✔ **Pictograph** A pictograph uses rows of small symbols or pictures, each representing a particular amount. Like a bar graph, a pictograph is useful for making comparisons.

Classroom Activity: Create a Graph

Advice from Faith Vautour
Camden Hills Regional High School
Rockport, Maine

Graphs can be difficult to interpret and understand. Help students by having them create their own graph. To help students begin thinking about graphs, separate students into small groups. Then explain that each group should take a quick survey of classmates and make a graph to show their survey results. Suggest that students make either a bar graph, line graph, circle graph, or pictograph to show their data. To prompt students' thinking, ask the following questions.

• *Do you play on a sports team? Which sport(s)?*
• *What do you plan to do after high school?*
• *About how much time do you spend watching TV each day? About how much time did you spend on TV when you were 10 years old? When you were five years old?*

After students are done graphing their data, invite each group to share its work. Discuss the types of graphs students made and their reasons for choosing them. Each group should then take the graph that another group has prepared and transfer the information into another type of graph.

Addressing the Needs of Special Students

How Can I Help ALL my Students Learn Social Studies?

Today's classroom contains students from a variety of backgrounds and with a variety of learning styles, strengths, and challenges. With careful planning, you can address the needs of all students in the social studies classroom. The following tips for instruction can assist your efforts to help all students reach their maximum potential.

✔ Survey students to discover their individual differences. Use interest inventories of their unique talents so you can encourage contributions in the classroom.

✔ Model respect of others. Adolescents crave social acceptance. The student with learning differences is especially sensitive to correction and criticism—particularly when it comes from a teacher. Your behavior will set the tone for how students treat one another.

✔ Expand opportunities for success. Provide a variety of instructional activities that reinforce skills and concepts.

✔ Establish measurable objectives and decide how you can best help students meet them.

✔ Celebrate successes and praise "work in progress."

✔ Keep it simple. Point out problem areas—if doing so can help a student affect change. Avoid overwhelming students with too many goals at one time.

✔ Assign cooperative group projects that challenge all students to contribute to solving a problem or creating a product.

How Do I Reach Students with Learning Disabilities?

✔ Provide support and structure. Clearly specify rules, assignments, and responsibilities.

✔ Practice skills frequently. Use games and drills to help maintain student interest.

✔ Incorporate many modalities into the learning process. Provide opportunities to say, hear, write, read, and act out important concepts and information.

✔ Link new skills and concepts to those already mastered.

✔ Allow students to record answers on audiotape.

✔ Allow extra time to complete tests and assignments.

✔ Let students demonstrate proficiency with alternative presentations, including oral reports, role plays, art projects, and with music.

✔ Provide outlines, notes, or tape recordings of lecture material.

✔ Pair students with peer helpers, and provide class time for pair interaction.

How Do I Reach Students with Behavioral Disorders?

✔ Provide a structured environment with clear-cut schedules, rules, seat assignments, and safety procedures.

✔ Reinforce appropriate behavior and model it for students.

✔ Cue distracted students back to the task through verbal signals and teacher proximity.

✔ Set very small goals that can be achieved in the short term. Work for long-term improvement in the big areas.

How Do I Reach Students with Physical Challenges?

✔ Openly discuss with the student any uncertainties you have about when to offer aid.

✔ Ask parents or therapists and students what special devices or procedures are needed, and whether any special safety precautions need to be taken.

✔ Welcome students with physical challenges into all activities, including field trips, special events, and projects.

Michael Newman/PhotoEdit

Jose L. Pelaez/CORBIS STOCK MARKET

✔ Provide information to help able-bodied students and adults understand other students' physical challenges.

How Do I Reach Students with Visual Impairments?

✔ Facilitate independence. Modify assignments as needed.
✔ Teach classmates how and when to serve as guides.
✔ Limit unnecessary noise in the classroom, if it distracts the student with visual impairments.
✔ Provide tactile models whenever possible.
✔ Foster a spirit of inclusion. Describe people and events as they occur in the classroom. Remind classmates that the student with visual impairments cannot interpret gestures and other forms of nonverbal communication.
✔ Provide taped lectures and reading assignments.
✔ Team the student with a sighted peer for written work.

How Do I Reach Students with Hearing Impairments?

✔ Seat students where they can see your lip movements easily and where they can avoid visual distractions.

✔ Avoid standing with your back to the window or light source.
✔ Use an overhead projector to maintain eye contact while writing.
✔ Seat students where they can see speakers.
✔ Write all assignments on the board, or hand out written instructions.
✔ If the student has a manual interpreter, allow both student and interpreter to select the most favorable seating arrangements.
✔ Teach students to look directly at each other when they speak.

How Do I Reach English Language Learners?

✔ Remember, students' ability to speak English does not reflect their academic abilities.

✔ Try to incorporate the students' cultural experience into your instruction. The help of a bilingual aide may be effective.
✔ Avoid cultural stereotypes.
✔ Pre-teach important vocabulary and concepts.
✔ Encourage students to preview text before they begin reading, noting headings, graphic organizers, photographs, and maps.

How Do I Reach Gifted Students?

✔ Make arrangements for students to take selected subjects early and to work on independent projects.
✔ Ask "what if" questions to develop high-level thinking skills. Establish an environment safe for risk taking.
✔ Emphasize concepts, theories, ideas, relationships, and generalizations.
✔ Promote interest in the past by inviting students to make connections to the present.
✔ Let students express themselves in alternate ways, such as creative writing, acting, debate, simulations, drawing, or music.
✔ Provide students with a catalog of helpful resources, listing such things as agencies that provide free and inexpensive materials, appropriate community services and programs, and community experts.
✔ Assign extension projects that allow students to solve real-life problems related to their communities.◆

Customize Your Classroom!

Advice from Marilyn Gerken
Pickerington Local Schools
Pickerington, Ohio

Provide individualized activities and assignments for a variety of student ability levels. Develop learning packets for chapters and units of study with varying formats, levels, and types of assignments. Assign points and contract students based on their selection of activities to be completed. The activities in the Student Edition can be used for many of the learning activities and assignments.

More THAN A GAME. AN *education* FOR LIFE.

What is the Stock Market Game?

The Stock Market Game (SMG) is an educational simulation that teaches about the stock markets, the American economic system, and the global economy.

Participants develop skills in math, language arts, research and critical thinking, while building and maintaining a stock portfolio.

SMG is used in grades 4–12, college courses, and by those who seek to learn more about investing.

Since 1977, over 8 million students have participated in this national program.

How does it work?

Teams of three to five students invest a hypothetical $100,000 in a portfolio of common stocks listed on the New York and American stock exchanges and the NASDAQ stock market.

Most teams use the Internet to follow their portfolios, research stocks, enter trades at end-of-day prices, and see their weekly division ranking.

Those without Internet access use a paper-based version of SMG. These team portfolios are updated and mailed back once a week.

In each state, the program is administered by an SMG Coordinator who provides introductory workshops, training and on-going support.

How do I get more information?

Contact your local SMG Coordinator by visiting our Web site *www.smgww.org* or by calling the **Securities Industry Foundation for Economic Education** at (212) 618-0519.

Are curriculum materials provided?

Lesson plans, curriculum guides, teacher resources and videos for all grade and ability levels are available through the SMG Coordinator. Additional materials are available on the Web site to participants.

What's the cost?

The small registration fee varies from state to state. Internet access costs are determined by local Internet providers.

Who sponsors The SMG Program?

The Stock Market Game is a trademarked program of the Securities Industry Foundation for Economic Education (SIFEE), an affiliate of the Securities Industry Association (SIA). SMG is supported nationally and locally by securities industry firms, SIA Districts, the National Council on Economic Education, Newspapers in Education, and other organizations involved in economic and financial literacy education.

Securities Industry Foundation for Economic Education

120 Broadway, 35th Floor,
New York, NY 10271-0080

212-618-0519   212-791-5020 fax

sifee@sia.com

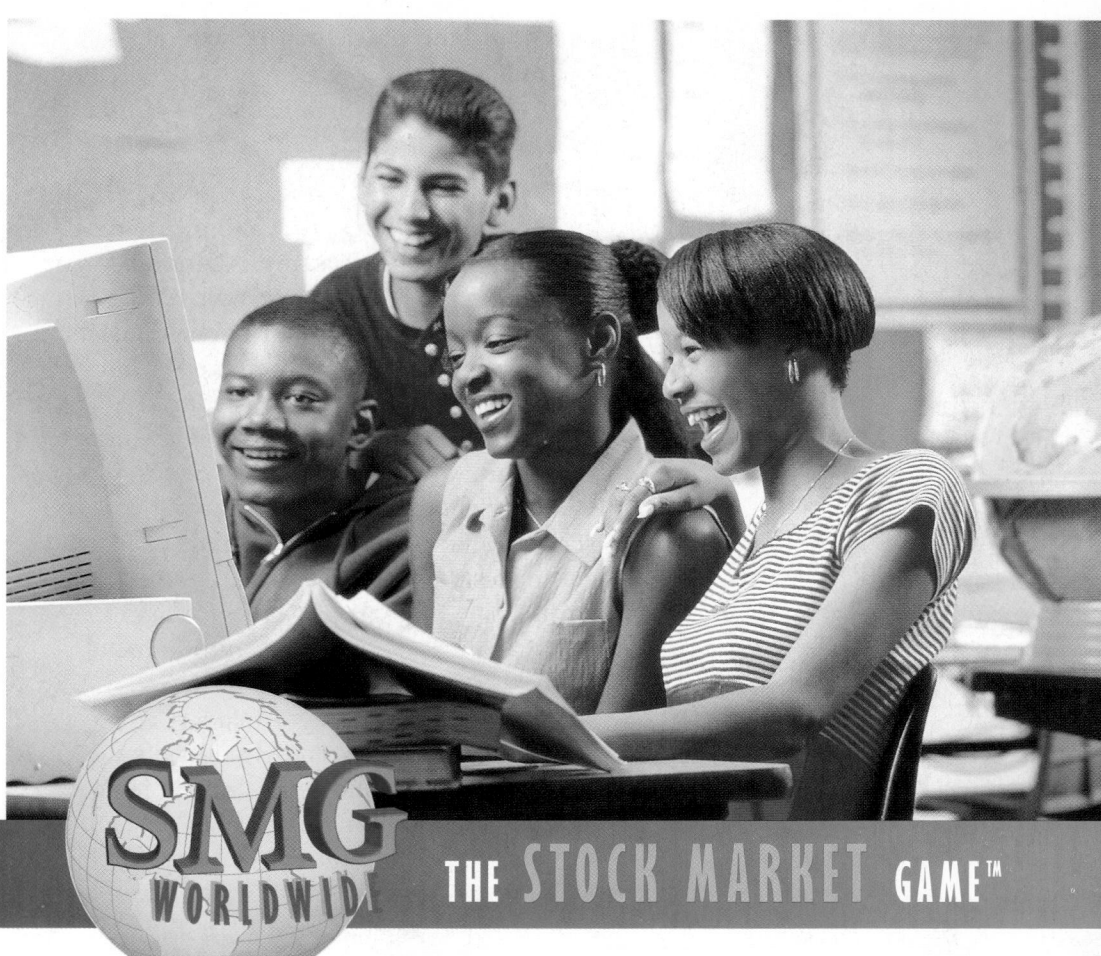

SMG WORLDWIDE THE STOCK MARKET GAME™

Fed Challenge

The Challenge

The Federal Reserve Banks invite high school teams to enter the Fed Challenge. This multi-level national competition is designed to bring real-world economics into the classroom.

Goals

- To increase understanding of the Federal Reserve's role in setting U.S. Monetary Policy
- To develop students' research, cooperation, presentation, and critical-thinking skills
- To promote interest in economics, not only as a subject for undergraduate and postgraduate study, but as the basis for a career
- To foster a closer relationship between schools and participating Federal Reserve Banks

How It Works: Presentations and Judges' Q&A

The Fed Challenge is a **25-minute performance-based assessment** conducted at participating Federal Reserve Banks and Branches. Each performance consists of two parts: a **15-minute presentation**—inspired by the work of the Federal Open Market Committee (FOMC)—and a **10-minute question-and-answer session**.

High School teams (only one per school), made up of five students each, gather research to make a presentation including:

- An analysis of economic and financial conditions (as of the day of the presentation)
- A forecast of economic, financial, and international conditions, for the near-term, of critical importance in developing monetary policy (e.g., unemployment, inflation, output, etc.)
- Identification of pressing economic, financial, and international issues that should be of special concern for monetary policy-makers
- A recommendation to increase, decrease, or leave unchanged the level of short-term interest rates

Following the presentation, a panel of judges, typically made up of Federal Reserve staff members, financial professionals, and educators, question the team about its analysis, forecast, recommendation, and the Federal Reserve's role in developing and implementing monetary policy.

Scoring

Judges will score teams based on five criteria:

1. Knowledge of the Federal Reserve's role in developing and implementing monetary policy
2. Responses to judge's questions
3. Quality of the presentation
4. Quality of the research and analysis
5. Evidence of teamwork and cooperation

All rounds of the Fed Challenge—from district competitions to NATIONAL championship—use the same scoring rubric and adhere to the following rules: Students may refer to, but not read from, notes or scripts. Each team member must play a substantial role in making the presentation. More than one team member may answer a judge's question. While huddling to formulate a response to a judge's question is permitted, teams are cautioned that lengthy and excessive huddling will result in points being deducted, to the extent that it significantly limits the number of questions posed.

Awards, Prizes and Endorsements

Citibank has established the **Citibank Scholarships and Grants for the Fed Challenge**. As a result, the team that wins the National Championship will be awarded $100,000, comprised of $50,000 in scholarships ($10,000 per team member), a $10,000 achievement award (for the teacher), and a $40,000 grant to set up an in-school economics laboratory.

Each of the other national finalist teams will take home a total of $35,000, comprised of $20,000 in scholarship money ($4,000 per student), a $4,000 achievement award (for the teacher), and an $11,000 grant to set up an in-school economics laboratory.

The **McGraw-Hill Companies** will sponsor a reception in Washington, D.C., for all students and teachers of Federal Reserve District champions.

Registration and More Information

- Outside the 212 area code, call toll free: 1-877-FED-CHLG (1-877-333-2454)
- In area codes 212, 718, 516 and 914, call: 212-720-1836

Sample Fed Challenge Questions

Questions from Fed Challenge judges generally are from the following categories:
- Questions based upon the presentation
- Interpretive questions
- Hypothetical questions
- Program learning or evaluative questions

The following questions from previous competitions provide examples of these types of questions.

1. On the fiscal policy side, how would the passage of a federal balanced budget measure affect the Fed's monetary policy decisions? Do you think balancing the federal budget is an important goal?

2. What is the impact of the nation's trade deficit on U.S. growth prospects?

3. What did you learn from participating in the Fed Challenge?

4. What is the primary goal of monetary policy? What do you think the goal(s) should be?

5. In your own words, explain the Phillips Curve. What is it and what does it show? Why do some economists question the validity of the Phillips Curve? Is there any justification to question its validity?

6. The CPI (consumer price index) and PPI (producer price index) are recognized measures of inflation. Why in your presentation did you include capacity utilization as a measure of inflation?

7. How would movement in the unemployment rate, wages, salaries, benefits, and total compensation figure into your analysis of an inflationary trend? Are you worried about recent gas and food price movements? Explain the concept of Core CPI and why it is important.

8. Should all FOMC (Federal Open Market Committee) members be appointed by the U.S. President and confirmed by the U.S. Senate?

9. Talk about the issues involved in trying to balance inflation and unemployment in the short-run and in the long-run.

10. The most recent rate hike resulted in letters of protest from several members of Congress. How would you respond to criticism that the Fed is not considering the consequences of unemployment, which may arise from rate hikes?

Teach

Discuss with students any difficulties they have in understanding economic statistics and graphic information. Point out that the steps described in this Handbook will help them simplify the task of learning economics. The Handbook will also give them tools they need to analyze and understand other forces shaping their lives—figuring sales tax, averaging their semester grade, and figuring how much interest their savings account will earn, for example.

Each skill in this Handbook is accompanied by a reproducible master in the **Reinforcing Economic Skills** booklet in the Teacher's Classroom Resource package.

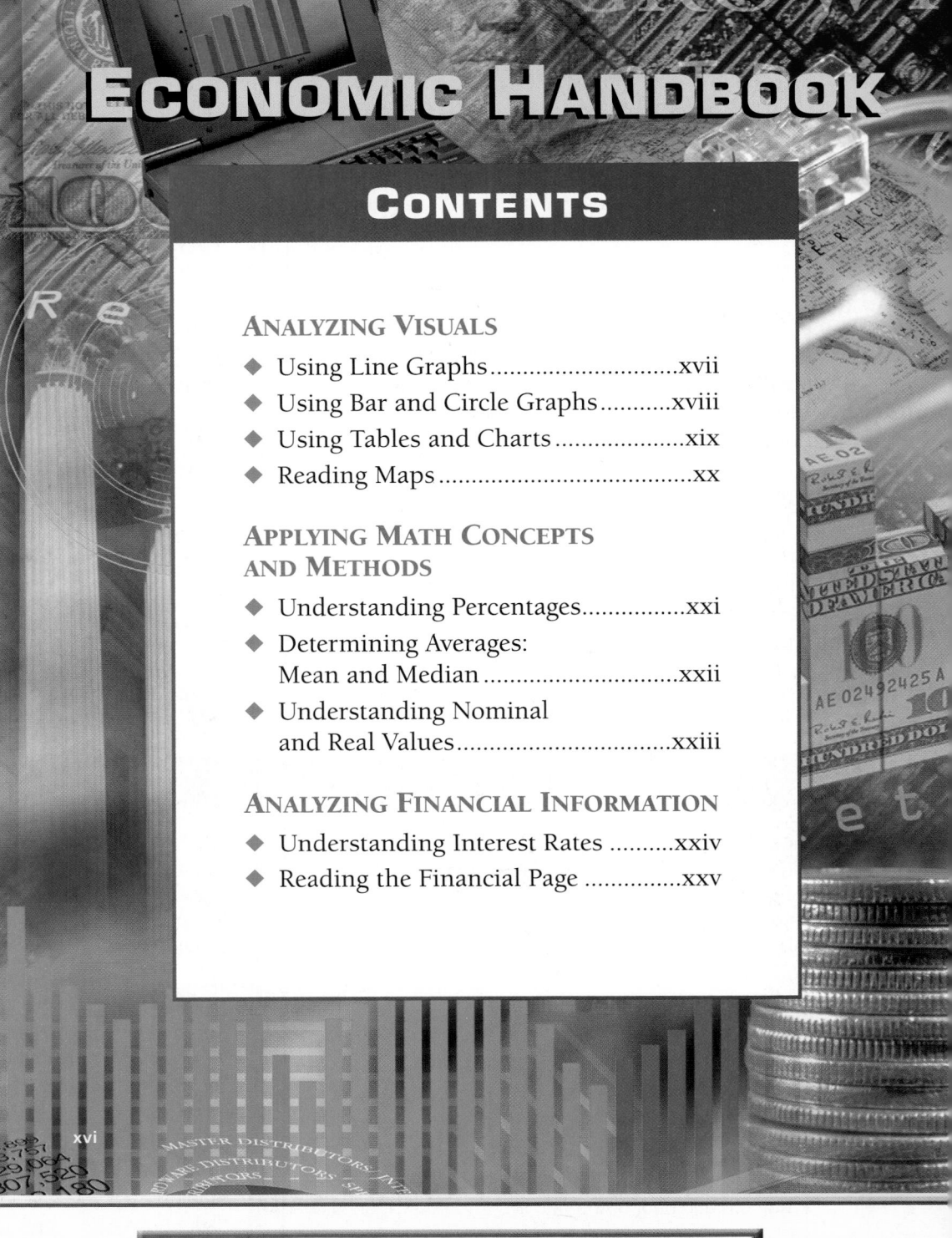

ECONOMIC HANDBOOK

CONTENTS

ANALYZING VISUALS

APPLYING MATH CONCEPTS AND METHODS

ANALYZING FINANCIAL INFORMATION

xvi

Teacher's Notes / Internet Bookmarks

Using Line Graphs

A graph, like a picture, may present information in a more concise way than words.
Line graphs are drawings that compare numerical values. They often are used to compare
changes over time or differences between places, groups of items, or other related events.

LEARNING THE SKILL

Follow these steps to learn how to understand and use line graphs. Then answer the questions below.

1. Read the title of the graph. This should tell you what to expect or look for.

2. Note the information on the left side of the graph—the vertical axis. The information being compared usually appears on this axis.

3. Note the information along the bottom of the graph—the horizontal axis. Time often appears along this axis.

4. Determine what the line(s) or curve(s) symbolizes.

5. Select a point on the line, then note the date below this point on the horizontal axis and the quantity measured on the vertical axis.

6. Analyze the movement of the line (whether increasing or decreasing over time) or compare lines (if more than one are on the graph) to determine the point being made.

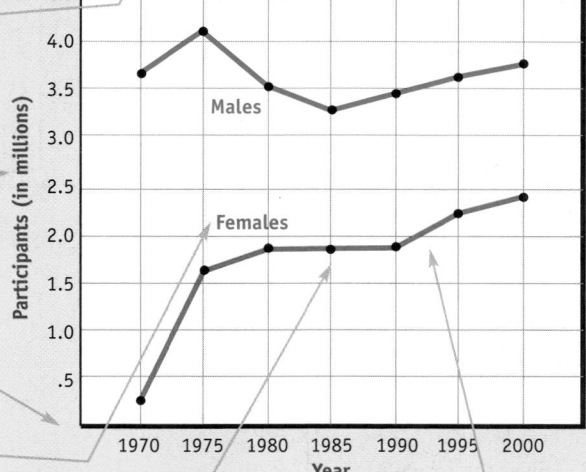

Participation in High School Athletic Programs

Participants (in millions)

Males

Females

1970 1975 1980 1985 1990 1995 2000
Year

PRACTICING THE SKILL

1. About how many males participated in high school athletic programs in 1970? In 1997?

2. About how many females participated in high school athletic programs in 1970? In 1997?

Applying the Skill to Economics

1. What trends are shown on the graph?

2. How do you think these trends affected the manufacture and sale of sports-related products from the early to late 1990s?

Teach

Using Line Graphs

Tell students that graphs present data in a way that readers can grasp easily and quickly. Inform them that graphs come in many forms—line graphs, bar graphs, and circle graphs are the most common. (How to use bar graphs and circle graphs is explained on page xviii.)

Each type of graph has a different way of displaying information. Line graphs show data and how they have changed over time, which is good for showing trends and predictions. Remind students to familiarize themselves with the label on the vertical axis. This label tells what is being compared—often quantities or percentages. The label along the horizontal axis is usually time-related—years, months, and so on.

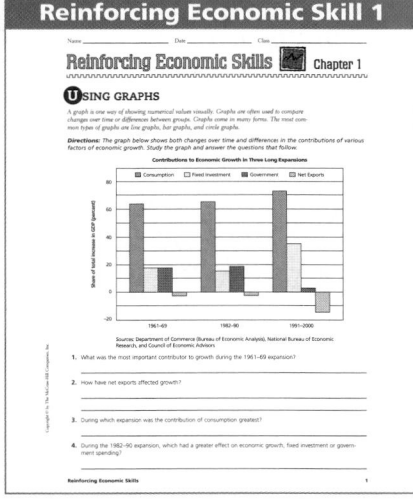

Reinforcing Economic Skill 1

ANSWERS

PRACTICING THE SKILL

1. about 3.6 million; about the same number
2. about 250,000; about 2.3 million

Applying the Skill to Economics

1. Answers may note that the number of males participating in high school athletic programs peaked around 1975, then decreased and is slowly increasing again. The number of females in high school athletic programs increased dramatically from 1970 to 1975, and has been increasing slowly since then.

2. Answers may note that manufacturers of sports-related products for both males and females experienced increased sales from the early to late 1990s.

Teach

Using Bar and Circle Graphs

Unlike line graphs, which usually show how data change over time, bar graphs show data in relation to a fixed scale, which is good for comparing items to each other. Have students sit in five rows. Direct each row of students to total the amount of money they have in their pockets. Note the totals on the board. Then have students present the information on the board in the form of a bar graph.

Explain to students that a circle graph is like a sliced pie; often, it is even called a pie chart. Circle graphs show proportions rather than absolute amounts. They often are used when the information being compared totals 100 percent.

Reinforcing Economic Skill 1

Using Bar Graphs

LEARNING THE SKILL
Follow these steps to learn how to understand and use bar graphs.

1. Read the title and labels. They tell you the topic, what is being compared, and how it is counted or measured.

3. Analyze the change over time or compare bars to determine the point being made.

2. Examine a bar on the graph. Note the date below the bar on the horizontal axis and the quantity measured on the vertical axis.

New Vehicle Sales, 1994–2000

Vehicles (in millions)

Model Year

☐ Cars   ☐ Trucks

Source: U.S. Bureau of Economic Analysis

PRACTICING THE SKILL
1. What year had the lowest new car sales?
2. About how many trucks sold in 2000?

Using Circle Graphs

LEARNING THE SKILL
Follow these steps to learn how to understand and use circle graphs.

1. Examine the title to determine the subject.

3. Compare the relative sizes of the circle segments, thus analyzing the relationship of the parts to the whole.

2. Read the legend to see what each segment represents.

High School Student Foreign Language Enrollment

23%   67%
7%
3%

☐ Spanish
☐ French
☐ German
☐ Other

Source: *Statistical Abstract of the United States, 2000*

PRACTICING THE SKILL
1. What percent of foreign language students are studying German?
2. What foreign language has the greatest student enrollment?

Applying the Skill to Economics
1. Using the bar graph, what projection could you make about the future of new car sales?
2. Based on the circle graph, which foreign language textbooks probably have the greatest sales volume?

ANSWERS

PRACTICING THE SKILL
Using Bar Graphs
1. 1998
2. about 8.4 million
Using Circle Graphs
1. 7 percent
2. Spanish

Applying the Skill to Economics
1. Answers will vary, but students should infer that new car sales are beginning to rise slightly each year.
2. Spanish

Using Tables and Charts

Tables and charts are often used to show comparisons between similar categories of information. Tables usually compare statistical or numerical data. Tabular data is presented in columns and rows. Charts often show a wider variety of information than tables.

LEARNING THE SKILL

Follow these steps to learn how to understand and use tables. Then answer the questions below.

1. Read the title of the table to learn what content is being presented.

2. Read the headings in the top row. They define the groups or categories of information to be compared.

3. Examine the labels in the left-hand column. They describe ranges or subgroups, and are often organized chronologically or alphabetically.

Average Earnings of Full-Time Workers by Age and Education, 1999				
Age and Sex	All Workers	Some High School	High School Graduate	Four-Year College Degree
Male	**$47,573**	**$25,558**	**$35,121**	**$62,543**
18–24	20,913	17,563	20,416	28,380
25–34	38,978	22,881	31,945	51,097
35–44	49,833	27,175	37,155	65,469
45–54	57,252	29,723	39,493	73,820
55–64	56,125	31,471	40,124	67,686
Female	**$31,129**	**$19,419**	**$23,498**	**$40,263**
18–24	18,825	17,973	16,665	26,217
25–34	29,766	17,750	21,633	37,562
35–44	32,711	17,432	24,258	43,471
45–54	34,099	18,398	25,756	43,337
55–64	32,887	28,492	25,935	42,649

Source: CPS Annual Demographic Survey (Bureau of Labor Statistics and Bureau of the Census)

4. Note the source of the data. It may tell you about the reliability of the table.

5. Compare the data presented in the other columns. This is the body of the table.

PRACTICING THE SKILL

1. What are the average earnings for 25- to 34-year-old women with college degrees?

2. What are the average earnings for 18- to 24-year-old males without high school diplomas?

Applying the Skill to Economics

1. What age-related trends do you notice?

2. What conclusions could you draw from this data about the economic effect of education on earnings?

Teach

Using Tables and Charts

Ask students how many of them have after-school jobs. How many play on a sports team? Then tell them that statistics like these could be explained in text form, but a table or a chart would present the information in a more concise and easily interpreted format.

Have students analyze the information in the table on this page. **Ask:** What information is being compared? *(average full-time worker earnings for sex and age groups, based on education level)* How is the information grouped into categories? *(by sex and age and by education level)*

Reinforcing Economic Skill 2

Name _____ Date _____ Class _____

Reinforcing Economic Skills Chapter 2

USING CHARTS AND TABLES

Tables and charts are often used to compare information. Tables present data in columns and rows. By looking at a table, you can see trends and relationships more easily than if the information were written in text form.

Directions: *Study the table below and answer the questions that follow.*

Population and Gross National Product of Selected Countries, 1999		
Country	Population (in millions)	Gross National Product (in billions of dollars)
Australia	19	380.6
Botswana	2	5.6
Canada	31	612.2
China	1,239	928.9
Honduras	6	4.5
Nepal	23	4.8
United States	270	7,921.3

Source: World Development Report 1999/2000; The World Bank

1. How does the population of Nepal compare with the population of Australia?

2. Which country listed in the table has the largest population?

3. Which country listed in the table has the highest gross national product?

4. If you divide the GNP by the population, which country has the highest per capita GNP: Honduras or Botswana?

5. How does the per capita GNP of China compare with that of Canada?

2   *Reinforcing Economic Skills*

ANSWERS

PRACTICING THE SKILL

1. $37,562
2. $17,563

Applying the Skill to Economics

1. Answers will vary, but students should infer that for men and women of all education levels, average earnings rise through the 40s or 50s and then decline.
2. Answers will vary, but students should infer that the higher the education level, the greater the earnings.

Teach

Reading Maps

Discuss with students their use of maps. Most have probably used a map to locate a particular geographic region or land feature. In addition, most have probably used a map to help them navigate from one place to another. Have students study the map on this page. **Ask:** In which regions of the United States is ranching an important economic activity? *(the Far West, Midwest, and Southwest)* What does the color green on the map represent? *(commercial farming)*

Have students draw their own maps showing the route they use to come to school. They should incorporate symbols representing buildings, vegetation, and unusual landmarks. Ask them to include a compass rose, a map scale, and a key on their maps. If possible, also have them indicate at what latitude and longitude their location is.

Reinforcing Economic Skill 3

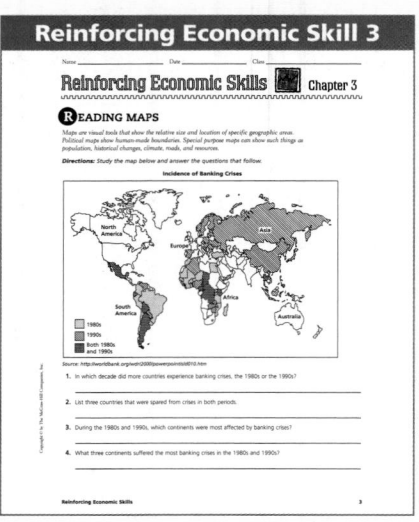

Reading Maps

Maps are visual tools that show to scale the relative size and location of specific geographic areas. There are political maps, which show human-made boundaries. There are physical maps, which show physical features of an area. There are also special purpose maps that can show historical change, cultural features, population, climate, land use, or resources. Regardless of type, all maps use symbols to convey information.

LEARNING THE SKILL

Follow these steps to learn how to understand and use maps. Then answer the questions below.

THE UNITED STATES: Land Use and Resources

1. Read the title to determine the map's content.

2. Examine the map's scale, which indicates the ratio between the map's size and the actual area being represented.

3. Look for a compass rose or directional arrow to find the map's directions.

4. Examine the lines of latitude and longitude to find the absolute location of specific places.

5. Read the legend, or key, to interpret any shapes, colors, boundary lines, or symbols.

PRACTICING THE SKILL

1. What is the primary content shown on this map?

2. Which region of the United States has the heaviest concentration of manufacturing areas?

Applying the Skill to Economics

1. How could this map be a helpful reference if you were planning to buy ranch land to raise cattle?

2. What generalizations could you draw from this map about energy resources in the United States?

xx ECONOMIC HANDBOOK

ANSWERS

PRACTICING THE SKILL

1. land use and resources in the United States
2. the Northeast

Applying the Skill to Economics

1. Answers will vary, but students should infer that the map shows where ranch land is located.
2. Answers will vary, but students should infer that the map shows abundant petroleum and coal resources, as well as some natural gas and forest resources.

Understanding Percentages

If you shop, you probably like seeing the word *percent.* Stores often advertise sale prices as a percent of regular price. *Percent* means "parts per hundred." So, 30 percent means the same thing as 30/100 or 0.30. Expressing change as a percentage allows you to analyze the relative size of the change.

LEARNING THE SKILL

Follow these steps to learn how to calculate and use percentages. Then answer the questions below.

2. Find the sale price by subtracting the discount from the regular price.

1. Suppose a pair of shoes is on sale for 30 percent off the regular price. Calculate the discount by multiplying the original price by the sale percentage. Change percent to a decimal before you multiply.

Calculating Percent

Regular price of shoes	$57.00	Regular price	$57.00			$57.00
30%	× .30	Discount	−17.10	OR		× .70
Discount	$17.10	Sale price	$39.90			$39.90

3. Or, figure the sale price by multiplying the regular price by the percent you *will* pay. (Subtract the sale percentage from 100 to get the percent you will pay.) Change percent to a decimal before you multiply.

Arithmetic Change vs. Percentage Change

4. Calculate an increase in sales by subtracting the quantity sold last year from the quantity sold this year.

Arithmetic change

1.6 billion pounds of butter sold this year
−1.5 billion pounds of butter sold last year

.1 billion pounds

Percentage change $\frac{0.1}{1.5} = .067 \times 100 = 6.7$ percent

5. Determine the percentage change by dividing the arithmetic difference by the original quantity. Multiply by 100 to change the decimal to percent.

PRACTICING THE SKILL

1. A store advertises a shirt at 25 percent off the original price of $44. What is the sale price?

2. What is the percentage increase in high school enrollment from 1,165 students to 1,320?

Applying the Skill to Economics

In 1997 about 32 percent of all music recordings sold were classified as rock music. That year about $12 billion was spent on all recordings. How much was spent on rock music?

Teach

Understanding Percentages

Empty two rolls of pennies (100 coins) into a container. Remove five pennies and ask students what percentage of the total number of pennies the five represent. Write the decimal .05 on the board. Tell students that *percent* means parts per hundred, just as cents are a portion or percentage of a dollar.

Call on a student to determine the sales tax on an item that sells for $10.00 if the tax rate is 4 percent. Have the student write the calculation on the board. *(.04 × $10.00 = $.40)*

Reinforcing Economic Skill 4

Name _____ Date _____ Class _____

Reinforcing Economic Skills ◼ Chapter 4

UNDERSTANDING PRECENTAGES

Understanding percentages is very important in business and economics. Discounts, taxes, price changes, and inflation rates are all given in percentages. A percentage is a figure expressed in hundredths. The figure 2 percent is equal to the fraction 2/100 or the decimal 0.02. For example, to figure out how much 2 percent of 250 is, state the percentage as a decimal and multiply the decimal times 250 (.02 × 250 = 5).

Directions: Read the following paragraph, and then answer the questions that follow.

You order 12 cartons of notebooks at $50 a carton. Because you ordered a dozen cartons, you receive a quantity discount of 10 percent. You also purchase 50 pens that are on sale for 20 percent of the regular price of $.69 apiece. Finally, you purchase a package of copier paper priced at $6.99 instead of the regular price of $9.99. The tax in your state is 5 percent.

1. How much did you pay for the 12 cartons of notebooks? How did you figure it out?
_____
_____

2. How much would you have paid for the 50 pens you purchased if they had not been on sale?
_____
_____

3. How much did you pay for the pens? How did you figure it out?
_____
_____

4. By what percentage was the price of the copier paper you purchased reduced? How did you figure it out?
_____
_____

5. How much tax did you pay on your purchase? How did you figure it out?
_____
_____

Reinforcing Economic Skills

ANSWERS

PRACTICING THE SKILL
1. $33.00
2. 13.3 percent

Applying the Skill to Economics
$3.84 billion

ECONOMIC HANDBOOK

Teach

Determining Averages: Mean and Median

Mean and *median* are used often in economics to summarize information. They are particularly useful for comparing data over time or among different categories, such as showing an increase or a decrease in average wages in manufacturing over five years.

Make sure students understand the difference between mean and median. Have them go through the steps and calculations several times to be certain they know how to determine both measures.

Have students read steps 1–3. **Ask:** What is the primary reason for the difference between the mean ($60) and the median ($41) in this example? *Students should infer that one student earns more than twice as much ($175) as any other student. This high salary skews the mean, which makes the median the more useful statistic in this case.*

Reinforcing Economic Skill 5

Determining Averages: Mean and Median

The most commonly used summary statistic is the average. There are two ways to compute the average: by using the mean or the median. The *mean* is the average of a series of items. When your teacher computes the class average, he or she is really computing the mean. Sometimes using the mean to interpret statistics is misleading, however. This is especially true if one or two numbers in the series are much higher or lower than the others. The median can be more accurate. The *median* is the midpoint in any series of numbers arranged in order.

LEARNING THE SKILL

Follow these steps to learn how to determine and use averages. Then answer the questions below.

1. Suppose you want to find the mean weekly salary for a group of teenagers. First, add all the earnings together.

3. Locate the median by finding the midpoint in the series ($41). Compare the mean with the median. Determine which is the more useful statistic.

Students' Weekly Earnings From After-School Jobs

| $ 20 |
| 32 |
| 34 |
| 41 |
| 53 |
| 65 |
| 175 |
| $420 |

$420 ÷ 7 = $60

2. Divide the sum by the number of students to find the mean.

Median Weekly Income of the Four Highest-Paid Students

$ 41	$ 53
53	+ 65
65	$118
175	

$118 ÷ 2 = $59

5. When an even number of figures is in the series, the median is the mean of the two middle numbers. Follow steps 1 and 2 to find the mean.

4. Suppose you want to calculate the median for the four highest-paid students. First, arrange the numbers in order.

PRACTICING THE SKILL

1. What is the median salary for all seven students?

2. What is the median salary for the four lowest-paid students?

Applying the Skill to Economics

Average Monthly Rent: 2-Bedroom Apartment

| Atlanta, GA | $1,059 | Dallas, TX | $ 933 |
| Boston, MA | $2,287 | San Jose, CA | $1,930 |

1. What is the mean monthly rent for these four cities?

2. What is the median monthly rent?

ANSWERS

PRACTICING THE SKILL
1. $41
2. $33

Applying the Skill to Economics
1. $1,552.25
2. $1,494.50

Understanding Nominal and Real Values

The rise in the economy's average price level is called inflation. To make comparisons between the prices of things in the past and those of today, you have to make the distinction between *nominal*, or current, and *real*, or adjusted for inflation, values. You can use the consumer price index (CPI), an index of average prices for consumer goods, to calculate real values. Then you can *accurately* compare changes in income and prices over time.

LEARNING THE SKILL

Follow these steps to learn how to understand and calculate nominal and real values. Then answer the questions below.

1. Suppose a family sells a house after living there for 10 years. To calculate whether they made any profit from the sale, they need to know the real sale price of their house. First, find the nominal price increase.

4. Determine the percentage increase in real price. Subtract the percentage increase in CPI from the percentage increase in nominal price. Evaluate the sale in real values.

Purchase price of house in 1990: $50,000
Sale price of house in 2000: $100,000

CPI in 1990: 100
CPI in 2000: 200

$100,000
− 50,000
$ 50,000

$\frac{\$50,000}{\$50,000} = 1 \times 100 = 100\%$

200
−100
100

$\frac{100}{100} = 1 \times 100 = 100\%$

100%
−100%
0%

2. Calculate the nominal percentage increase in price. Divide the amount of increase by the original price and multiply by 100 to express the answer as a percent.

3. Determine the percentage increase in the consumer price index. First find the actual change in CPI. Then divide the amount of increase by the original CPI and multiply by 100.

5. Suppose that last year you earned $10 per hour. You receive a 5 percent raise. The CPI is 3 percent higher than last year's CPI, which means there is a 3 percent inflation rate.

Earnings: $10 per hour
Raise: 5%
Inflation Rate: 3%
  5%
−3%
  2%

6. Calculate the real salary increase by subtracting the inflation rate from the nominal raise.

PRACTICING THE SKILL

1. What was the nominal price increase on the sale of the house?

2. How much money, in real dollars, was made on the house?

3. How much was the real value of the raise?

Applying the Skill to Economics

Between 1980 and 1997, the amount spent on advertising in the United States increased by 240 percent. How could you adjust this figure for inflation?

ECONOMIC HANDBOOK

Teach

Understanding Nominal and Real Values

Ask students if they have ever heard their parents, grandparents, or other older friend or relative talk about how much things cost when they were teenagers. Throughout the history of the United States, prices have tended to increase over time. This phenomenon is called inflation, and students must take current, inflated prices into account when comparing them against prices of the past.

Remind students that to calculate nominal versus real prices, they must know four figures: the price in the original year, the price today, the consumer price index in the original year, and the consumer price index today. **Ask:** To receive a real 5 percent raise in a year with 3 percent inflation, what would the nominal raise need to be?

8 percent

Reinforcing Economic Skill 6

Reinforcing Economic Skills Chapter 6

UNDERSTANDING REAL AND NOMINAL VALUES

ANSWERS

PRACTICING THE SKILL

1. $50,000
2. none
3. 2 percent

Applying the Skill to Economics

You must subtract the inflation rate for the same time period from the increase in advertising expenditures.

Teach

Understanding Interest Rates

Use the following activity to guide students through the mathematics for calculating simple and compound interest. Have students imagine that they have $100 to deposit in a savings account. They can place the money in an account that pays 5 percent compound interest or an account that pays 6 percent simple interest.

Lead them through the steps of calculating the total savings per year at 5 percent interest on $100 compounded annually for eight years: $105, $110.25, $115.76, $121.55, $127.63, $134.01, $140.71, $147.75.

Then guide students to calculate that 6 percent simple interest over eight years would amount to $48, for a total savings of $148. Help students conclude that the first account would be more profitable for long-term savings, and the second would be more profitable for short-term savings.

Reinforcing Economic Skill 7

Understanding Interest Rates

When you deposit money in a savings account, the bank pays you interest for the use of your money. The amount of interest is expressed as a percent, such as 6 percent, for a time period, such as per year. Two types of interest exist: simple and compound. *Simple interest* is figured only on the principal, or original deposit, not on any interest earned. *Compound interest* is paid on the principal plus any interest that has been earned. Over time, there is a significant difference in earnings between simple and compound interest.

LEARNING THE SKILL

Follow these steps to learn how to understand and calculate interest rates. Then answer the questions below.

1. Suppose you deposit $100 in a savings account that earns 6 percent simple interest per year. Get ready to figure your earnings by converting 6 percent to a decimal.

2. To calculate the simple interest earned, multiply the principal by the interest rate.

3. Calculate the account balance for the first two years, assuming the bank pays the same interest rate each year. Add the principal, the first year's interest, and the second year's interest.

Simple Interest		
6% = .06	$ 100	$100
	× .06	+ 6
	$6.00	6
		$112

4. Suppose you deposit $100 in a savings account that earns 6 percent compound interest per year. Calculate the interest earned the first year.

6. Determine the interest earned in the second year. Multiply the new balance by the interest rate.

7. Figure the total bank balance after two years. Add the second year's interest to the first year's balance.

Compound Interest			
$ 100	$100	$ 106	$106.00
× .06	+ 6	× .06	+ 6.36
$6.00	$106	$6.36	$112.36

5. Find the bank balance for the end of the first year. Add the principal and first year's interest.

PRACTICING THE SKILL

1. What would be the difference in earnings between simple and compound interest if your initial balance was $1,000 rather than $100?

2. What would be the difference in earnings between simple and compound interest on your $100 savings after five years?

Applying the Skill to Economics

1. What would be the impact of compounding interest on a daily basis rather than an annual basis?

2. Banks often pay higher rates of interest on money you agree to keep in the bank for longer periods of time. Explain why this might be.

ANSWERS

PRACTICING THE SKILL
1. $3.60
2. $3.82

Applying the Skill to Economics
1. You would earn more interest.
2. Answers will vary, but students should infer that the bank benefits by having longer use of the money, so the bank is willing to pay more for that benefit.

Reading the Financial Page

A stock market report alphabetically lists stocks and provides information about stock prices and trades. Every business day, shares of stock are bought and sold. At the beginning of each trading day, stocks open at the same prices they closed at the day before. Prices generally go up and down throughout the day as the conditions of supply and demand change. At the end of the day, each stock's closing price is recorded.

LEARNING THE SKILL

Follow these steps to learn how to understand and use the financial page. Then answer the questions below.

1. Locate the stock in the alphabetical list. Names are abbreviated.

2. Examine the stock's history over the last 52 weeks. The high and low prices for one share of stock appear.

3. Note the ticker symbol, or computer code, for the stock.

4. Evaluate the annual dividend. Stockholders receive this dividend, or payment, for each share of stock they own.

5. Review the yield. The yield is the return on investment per share of stock. It is calculated by dividing the dividend by the closing price.

6. Read the price/earnings ratio. Lower price/earnings ratios generally mean more earnings per share.

7. Note the volume, or number of shares of stock, traded that day. The number given represents hundreds of shares.

8. Examine the day's high, low, and closing stock price.

9. Examine how the day's closing stock price compares with the prior business day's closing price. Positive numbers indicate a price increase. Negative numbers mean a price drop.

Stock Quotations

| 52 Weeks | | Stock | Sym | Div | Yld % | PE | Vol 100s | Hi | Lo | Close | Net Chg |
Hi	Lo										
94.15	29.25	TxInstr	TXN	.17	.2	57	39008	80.80	77.55	79.60	+1.5
59.50	41	TexPacTr	TPL	.40	.9	28	23	44.25	43.85	44.25	+ .15
48	35.50	TX Util	TXU	2.30	6.2	13	17307	37.20	36.45	36.80	− .15

PRACTICING THE SKILL

1. How many shares of Texas Instruments stock were traded on the day shown?

2. What was the day's highest price for a share of Texas Utilities stock?

3. Which stock had the greatest increase in closing price from the previous day?

Applying the Skill to Economics

If you had purchased 100 shares of Texas Instruments stock at its lowest 52-week price and sold it at this day's closing price, how much money would you earn?

ECONOMIC HANDBOOK **xxv**

Teach

Reading the Financial Page

Because so much information is provided on page xxv, it might be useful to have students read aloud the explanations for each entry. To show students how this format is used in the everyday financial world, display the New York Stock Exchange (NYSE) list from a current newspaper. A stock market report from *The Wall Street Journal*, like the one shown here, provides a complete listing of information. Your local newspaper, however, may delete some of the information to save space.

Tell students that the NYSE has approved a plan to use decimals rather than the centuries-old tradition of quoting price changes in fractions of a dollar. Most non-U.S. equities markets trade in decimals. According to the NYSE, the change will take effect as soon as the securities industry's computer systems are reprogrammed.

ANSWERS

PRACTICING THE SKILL

1. 3,900,800
2. $37.20
3. Texas Instruments

Applying the Skill to Economics

$5,035.00

Reading for Information

Think about your textbook as a tool that helps you learn more about the world around you. It is an example of nonfiction writing—it describes real-life events, people, ideas, and places. Here is a menu of reading strategies that will help you become a better textbook reader. As you come to passages in your textbook that you don't understand, refer to these reading strategies for help.

✓ BEFORE YOU READ

Set a Purpose
- Why are you reading the textbook?
- How does the subject relate to your life?
- How might you be able to use what you learn in your own life?

Preview
- Read the chapter title to find what the topic will be.
- Read the subtitles to see what you will learn about the topic.
- Skim the photos, charts, graphs, or maps. How do they support the topic?
- Look for vocabulary words that are boldfaced. How are they defined?

Draw From Your Own Background
- What have you read or heard about concerning new information on the topic?
- How is the new information different from what you already know?
- How will the information that you already know help you understand the new information?

✓ AS YOU READ

Question
- What is the main idea?
- How do the photos, charts, graphs, and maps support the main idea?

Connect
- Think about people, places, and events in your own life. Are there any similarities with those in your textbook?
- Can you relate the textbook information to other areas of your life?

Predict
- Predict events or outcomes by using clues and information that you already know.
- Change your predictions as you read and gather new information.

Visualize
- Pay careful attention to details and descriptions.
- Create graphic organizers to show relationships that you find in the information.

LOOK FOR CLUES AS YOU READ

- **Comparison-and-Contrast Sentences:**

  Look for clue words and phrases that signal comparison, such as *similarly, just as, both, in common, also,* and *too.*

  Look for clue words and phrases that signal contrast, such as *on the other hand, in contrast to, however, different, instead of, rather than, but,* and *unlike.*

- **Cause-and-Effect Sentences:**

  Look for clue words and phrases such as *because, as a result, therefore, that is why, since, so, for this reason,* and *consequently.*

- **Chronological Sentences:**

  Look for clue words and phrases such as *after, before, first, next, last, during, finally, earlier, later, since,* and *then.*

✓ AFTER YOU READ

Summarize
- Describe the main idea and how the details support it.
- Use your own words to explain what you have read.

Assess
- What was the main idea?
- Did the text clearly support the main idea?
- Did you learn anything new from the material?
- Can you use this new information in other school subjects or at home?
- What other sources could you use to find more information about the topic?

Basic Concepts in Economics

Economics: Principles and Practices incorporates the 21 basic concepts established in *A Framework for Teaching Basic Economic Concepts*, published by the National Council on Economic Education.

FUNDAMENTAL ECONOMIC CONCEPTS

1. **Scarcity and Choice** *Scarcity* is the universal problem that faces all societies because there are not enough resources to produce everything people want. Scarcity requires people to make *choices* about the goods and services they use.

2. **Opportunity Cost and Trade-Offs** *Opportunity cost* is the foregone benefit of the next best alternative when scarce resources are used for one purpose rather than another. *Trade-offs* involve choosing less of one thing to get more of something else.

3. **Productivity** *Productivity* is a measure of the amount of output (goods and services) produced per unit of input (productive resources) used.

4. **Economic Systems** *Economic systems* are the ways in which people organize economic life to deal with the basic economic problem of scarcity.

5. **Economic Institutions and Incentives** *Economic institutions* include households and families and formal organizations such as corporations, government agencies, banks, labor unions, and cooperatives. *Incentives* are factors that motivate and influence human behavior.

6. **Exchange, Money, and Interdependence** *Exchange* is a voluntary transaction between buyers and sellers. It is the trading of a good or service for another good or service, or for money. *Money* is anything that is generally accepted as final payment for goods and services, and thus serves as a medium of exchange. *Interdependence* means that decisions or events in one part of the world or in one sector of the economy affect decisions and events in other parts of the world or sectors of the economy.

MICROECONOMIC CONCEPTS

7. **Markets and Prices** *Markets* are arrangements that enable buyers and sellers to exchange goods and services. *Prices* are the amounts of money that people pay for a unit of a particular good or service.

8. **Supply and Demand** *Supply* is defined as the different quantities of a resource, good, or service that will be offered for sale at various possible prices during a specific time period. *Demand* is defined as the different quantities of a resource, good, or service that will be purchased at various possible prices during a specific time period.

9. **Competition and Market Structure** *Competition* is the struggle between businesses that strive for the same customer or market. Competition depends on *market structure*—the number of buyers and sellers, the extent to which firms can control price, the nature of the product, the accuracy and timeliness of information, and the ease with which firms can enter and exit the market.

10. **Income Distribution** *Income distribution* refers to the way the nation's income is distributed by function—to those who provide productive resources—and by recipient, primarily individuals and families.

11. **Market Failures** *Market failures* occur when there is inadequate competition, lack of access to reliable information, resource immobility, externalities, and the need for public goods.

12. **The Role of Government** *The role of government* includes establishing a framework of law and order in which a market economy functions. The government plays a direct and an indirect role in the economy as both a producer and a consumer of goods and services.

MACROECONOMIC CONCEPTS

13. **Gross Domestic Product** *Gross Domestic Product (GDP)* is defined as the market value of the total output of all final goods and services produced within a country's boundaries during one year.

14. **Aggregate Supply and Aggregate Demand** *Aggregate supply* is the total amount of goods and services produced by the economy during a period of time. *Aggregate demand* is the total amount of spending on goods and services in the economy during a period of time.

15. **Unemployment** *Unemployment* is defined as the number of people without jobs who are actively seeking work. This is also expressed as a rate when the number of unemployed is divided by the number of people in the labor force.

16. **Inflation and Deflation** *Inflation* is a sustained increase in the average price level of the entire economy. *Deflation* is a sustained decrease in the average price level of an entire economy.

17. **Monetary Policy** *Monetary policy* consists of actions initiated by a nation's central bank that affect the amount of money available in the economy and its cost (interest rates).

18. **Fiscal Policy** *Fiscal policy* consists of changes in taxes, in government expenditures on goods and services, and in transfer payments that are designed to affect the level of aggregate demand in the economy.

INTERNATIONAL ECONOMIC CONCEPTS

19. **Absolute and Comparative Advantage and Barriers to Trade** *Absolute advantage* and *comparative advantage* are concepts that are used to explain why trade takes place. *Barriers to trade* include tariffs, quotas, import licenses, and cartels.

20. **Exchange Rates and the Balance of Payments** An *exchange rate* is the price of one nation's currency in terms of another nation's currency. The *balance of payments* of a country is a statistical accounting that records, for a given period, all payments that the residents, businesses, and governments of one country make to the rest of the world as well as the receipts that they receive from the rest of the world.

21. **International Aspects of Growth and Stability** *International aspects of growth and stability* are more important today than in the past because all nations are much more interdependent.

Unit 1 Resource Manager

Materials listed may be used at any time during the study of the unit.

Economics Forms and Financial Pages Transparencies

Transparency 5
Map of the United States

Transparency 6
Circle Graph

Transparency 7
Bar Graph

Economic Concepts Transparencies

Transparency 1
Scarcity

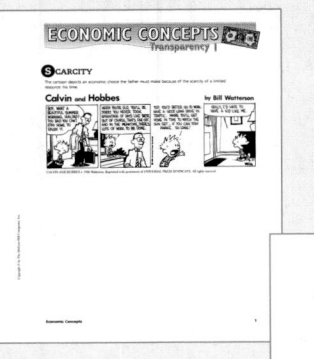

Transparency 2
Opportunity Costs and Trade-Offs

Transparency 3
Productivity

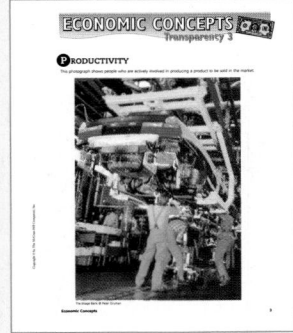

Transparency 4
Economic Systems

REAL-WORLD ECONOMICS

*Have your students learn about investing and managing their financial future by participating in the exciting simulation **The Stock Market Game**™. See Teacher pages in front of book for more information.*

*Strengthen students' research, cooperation, presentation and critical-thinking skills by having them compete in the **Fed Challenge**. See Teacher pages in front of book for more information.*

Additional Glencoe Resources for This Unit:

- **Interactive Economics!**
- **Glencoe Skillbuilder Interactive Workbook, Level 2**
- **Nightly Business Report Economics & You Video Program**
- **Economic Survival: A Financial Simulation**

Unit 1 Resource Manager

ASSESSMENT

Unit 1 Test

APPLICATION AND ENRICHMENT

Economics Laboratory 1

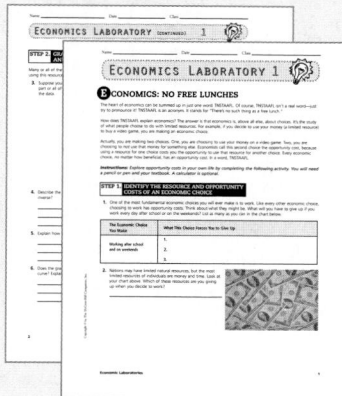

Unit 1 Business Week Focus on the New Economy

Use the following tools to easily assess student learning in a variety of ways:

- Performance Assessment Strategies and Activities
- Section Quizzes
- Chapter and Unit Tests
- Interactive Tutor Self-Assessment Software
- ExamView® Pro Testmaker
- MindJogger Videoquiz
- SAT I/II Test Practice
- epp.glencoe.com

*inter*NET CONNECTION

Economics: Principles and Practices
Visit the *Economics: Principles and Practices* Web site for economics overviews, activities, assessments, and updated charts and graphs.
epp.glencoe.com

Glencoe Social Studies
Visit the Glencoe Web site for social studies activities updates, and links to other sites.
socialstudies.glencoe.com

 Glencoe's Guide to Using the Internet
Provides an introduction to many of the current technologies on the Internet. Professional resources and teaching strategies included.

***Business Week* Online**
Visit the *Business Week* Web site for up-to-date news and special reports.
www.businessweek.com

Our Web sites provide additional resources. All essential content is covered in the Student Edition.

BIBLIOGRAPHY

Readings for the Student

Friedman, David D., *Hidden Order: The Economics of Everyday Life.* Harper-Collins Publishing, Inc., 1996.

"A Partnered World," by Debra Sparks, *Business Week*, October 25, 1999.

Readings for the Teacher

Friedman, Thomas L., *The Lexus and the Olive Tree.* Farrar, Straus & Giroux, Inc., 1999.

"Europe Ten Years Later . . ." by John

Rossant, *Business Week*, November 8, 1999.

Multimedia Resources

Videocassette. *Fundamental Economic Concepts.* United Learning, 1997. Available from Social Studies School Service, 10200 Jefferson Boulevard, P.O. Box 802, Culver City, CA 90232-0802. VHS videocassette, photocopy masters, guide. History of economic systems, scarcity, opportunity costs, market economies, world marketplace.

`0:00` OUT OF TIME?

If time does not permit teaching each chapter in this unit, you may use the Audio Program that includes a one-page activity and a one-page test for each chapter.

Unit Objectives

After studying this unit, students will be able to:

1. Define economics and its fundamental principles.
2. Differentiate between traditional, command, and market economies.
3. Discuss the major characteristics of the American free enterprise economy.
4. Identify the major types of economic organizations in the United States.

Unit Overview

Unit 1 provides a basic introduction to and an overview of economics. **Chapter 1** focuses on the fundamental economic problem of scarcity and introduces terms necessary to the study and understanding of economics. **Chapter 2** continues the discussion of decision making and focuses on the different economic systems. **Chapter 3** covers the various kinds of economic institutions that operate in our economy.

UNIT 1
Fundamental Economic Concepts

CHAPTER 1
What Is Economics?

CHAPTER 2
Economic Systems and Decision Making

CHAPTER 3
Business Organizations

Why It's Important

As you read this unit, learn how the study of economics helps answer the following questions:

- How do you make the decision between buying gas for your car or taking your friend out for pizza?

- Why is your friend from Russia stunned by all the shoes available at your local shoe store?

- Why is an item at a department store less expensive than that same item at a specialty shop?

The factors of production—land, labor, capital, and entrepreneurship—make production possible.

2 UNIT 1 FUNDAMENTAL ECONOMIC CONCEPTS

MAKING IT RELEVANT

Future Entrepreneurs In a phone survey, the Gallup organization questioned a random sample of approximately 1,000 teenagers across the country on their thoughts about entrepreneurship. The sample ranged in age from 14 to 19 years, and was evenly divided between males and females. Almost 7 out of every 10 respondents said that they wanted to be entrepreneurs. Asked if they would rather be a manager of a large company or the owner of a small company, most chose the latter. **Ask:** What is your opinion of the subject?

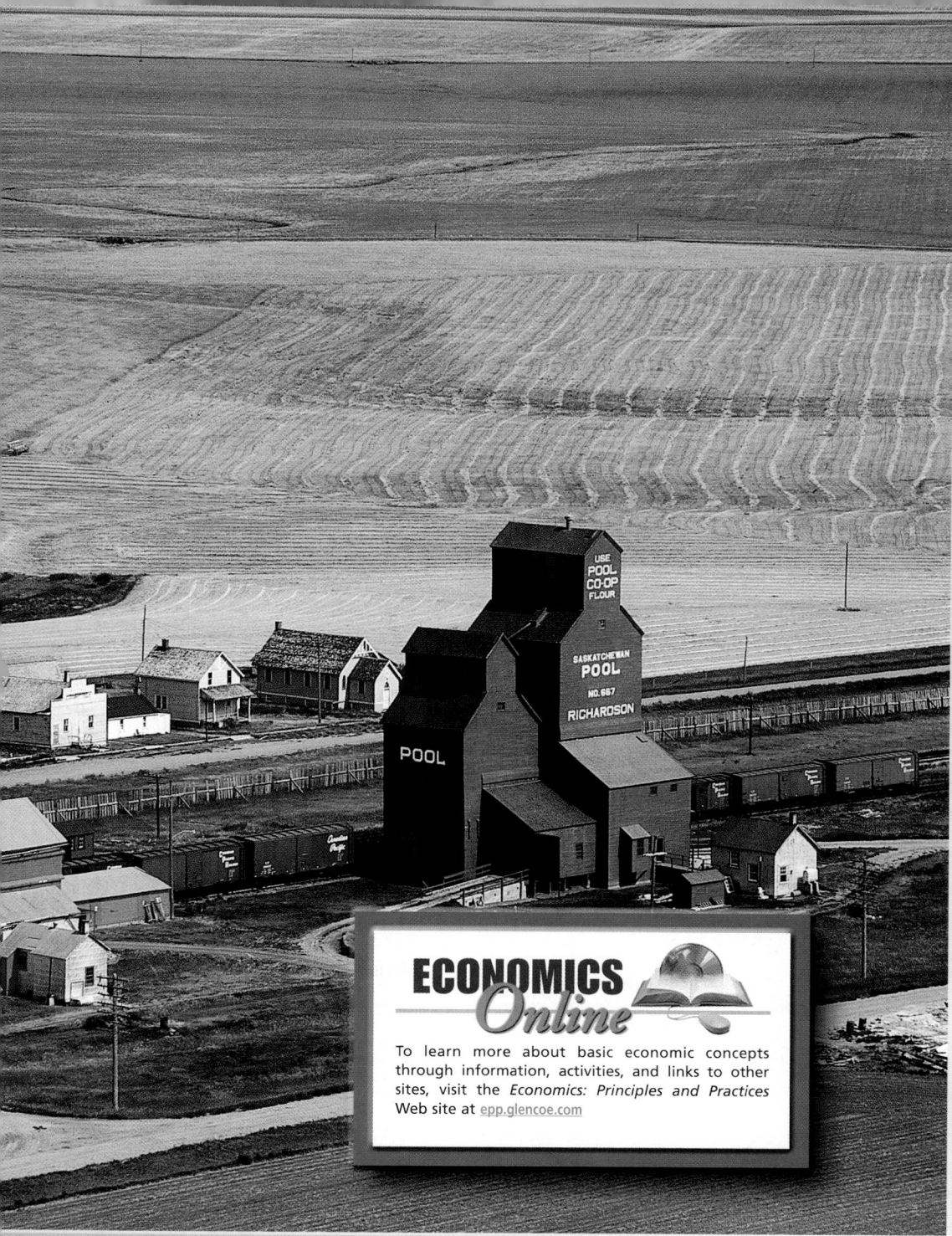

ECONOMICS
Online

To learn more about basic economic concepts through information, activities, and links to other sites, visit the *Economics: Principles and Practices* Web site at epp.glencoe.com

Introducing the Unit

Organize students in pairs and ask pair members to interview their partners to obtain the following information:

1. Give an example of a want.
2. What inputs are necessary to produce the want? *(factors of production—land, labor, capital, and entrepreneurship)*
3. Do you have any part in the process necessary to get your want? *(Does the student work?)*
4. What can you do to get your want?

After each person has been interviewed, ask the class what is necessary in our society to obtain their wants. Point out that wants are purchased in the marketplace and cost money that most people must earn by selling their labor, or working. In other words, we trade our productive efforts to satisfy our wants.

Visual Instruction

Economic development is linked to the factors of production. Ask students to identify what factors of production are represented in the photograph. *(farmland, grain elevator, and so on)*

ECONOMIC SURVIVAL
A FINANCIAL SIMULATION

To help students learn to manage their own finances, have them participate in the game **Economic Survival: A Financial Simulation** in which each student enters the workforce, rents an apartment, and deals with everyday events.

ECONOMICS
Online

Have students use the data from the Children's Advertising Review Unit (CARU) from the Better Business Bureau.

To access the data, follow these steps:

1. Log on to the **Economics: Principles and Practices** Web site at epp.glencoe.com
2. From the options on the opening screen, select Web Resources, then select the Better Business Bureau.
3. Select Programs & Services. Scroll and click on (CARU).

What to Do When You Are There

Have students choose three businesses from the list of CARU supporters and access each company's Web site. Have students evaluate each site for appropriate advertising and analyze any propoganda or bias directed at children. Students should create a chart to document results. If students have limited access to the Internet, have them use other resources to access the information.

Chapter 1 Resource Manager

SECTION RESOURCES

Daily Objectives	Reproducible Resources	Technology/Multimedia Resources
Section 1 **Scarcity and the Science of Economics** 1. Explain the fundamental economic problem. 2. Examine the three basic economic questions every society must decide.	Reproducible Lesson Plan 1-1 Daily Lecture Notes 1-1 Guided Reading Activity 1-1 Reading Essentials and Study Guide 1-1 Section Quiz 1-1*	Daily Focus Transparency 1 Interactive Tutor Self-Assessment Software ExamView® Pro Testmaker Presentation Plus!
Section 2 **Basic Economic Concepts** 1. Explain the relationship among scarcity, value, utility, and wealth. 2. Understand the circular flow of economic activity.	Reproducible Lesson Plan 1-2 Daily Lecture Notes 1-2 Guided Reading Activity 1-2 Reading Essentials and Study Guide 1-2 Section Quiz 1-2*	Daily Focus Transparency 5 Interactive Economics! Interactive Tutor Self-Assessment Software ExamView® Pro Testmaker Presentation Plus!
Section 3 **Economic Choices and Decision Making** 1. Analyze trade-offs and opportunity costs. 2. Explain decision-making strategies.	Reproducible Lesson Plan 1-3 Daily Lecture Notes 1-3 Guided Reading Activity 1-3 Reading Essentials and Study Guide 1-3 Section Quiz 1-3*	Daily Focus Transparency 2 Vocabulary PuzzleMaker CD-ROM Interactive Economics! NBR Economics & You Video Program Interactive Tutor Self-Assessment Software ExamView® Pro Testmaker Presentation Plus!

Also available in Spanish

Transparency   CD-ROM   Software   Blackline Master

Videodisc   Audio Program   Videocassette

0:00 OUT OF TIME?
Assign the Chapter 1 Audio Program activity and test.

Block Schedule

Activities that are particularly suited to use within the block scheduling framework are identified throughout this chapter by the following designation: **BLOCK SCHEDULING**

KEY TO ABILITY LEVELS

Teaching strategies have been coded for varying learning styles and abilities.

L1 BASIC activities for all students
L2 AVERAGE activities for average to above-average students
L3 CHALLENGING activities for above-average students
ELL ENGLISH LANGUAGE LEARNER activities

Chapter 1 Resource Manager

TeacherWorks™ All-In-One Planner and Resource Center

- **Interactive Teacher Edition** Access your Teacher Wraparound Edition and your classroom resources with a few easy clicks.
- **Interactive Lesson Planner** Planning has never been easier! Organize your week, month, semester, or year with all the lesson helps you need to make teaching creative, timely, and relevant.

Use Glencoe's **Presentation Plus!** multimedia teacher tool to easily present dynamic lessons that visually excite your students. Using Microsoft PowerPoint® you can customize the presentations to create your own personalized lessons.

ACTIVITY

From the Classroom of...

Sarah T. Makepeace
McCallie School
Chattanooga, TN

Production Possibilities Frontiers

This is a good way to illustrate the curved nature of the production possibilities frontier.

Choose two teams of two students each. Each team should have students of different talents. For instance, I choose one student who seems to have good gross motor skills and one who seems to have good fine motor skills. Give the teams a limited amount of time, usually 15 seconds, to "produce" as many push-ups as they can. A quality control person counts the push-ups, and another serves as a timer. On the board, draw a graph, and label the x-axis "push-ups" and the y-axis "chain." Plot each team's number of push-ups on the horizontal axis. Next, challenge each team to make paper clip chains in the same amount of time. Plot the data.

Now, question the teams about how many push-ups they could produce if one person produced push-ups and the other produced paperclip chains. **Ask:** Which team member would you choose to produce which good? Why? Students should recognize that some resources are better suited to the production of one good than another.

National Council on Economic Education

THE **Economics**America AND **Economics**International PROGRAMS

Voluntary National Content Standards in Economics
Emphasized in Chapter 1

Content Standard 1

Content Standard 2

Content Standard 14

For a complete listing of NCEE Standards and entire text correlation, see Teacher pages in front of book.

Resources Available from NCEE
- Capstone: The Nation's High School Economics Course
- Focus: High School Economics
- Entrepreneurship in the U.S. Economy
- Personal Decision Making: Focus on Economics

To order these materials or to contact your state Council on Economic Education about workshops and programs, call 1-800-338-1192 or visit www.nationalcouncil.org

Chapter 1 Resource Manager

TEACHING TRANSPARENCY

Economic Concept Transparency 1: Scarcity

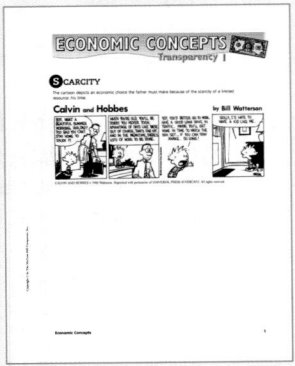

APPLICATION AND ENRICHMENT

Consumer Application Activity 1

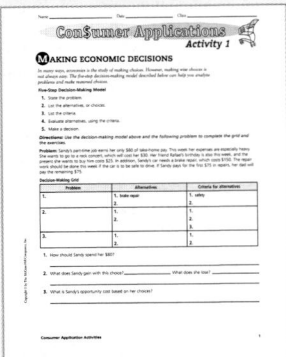

Free Enterprise Activity 1

APPLICATION AND ENRICHMENT

Enrichment Activity 1

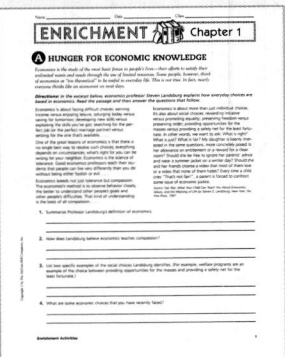

Cooperative Learning Activity 1

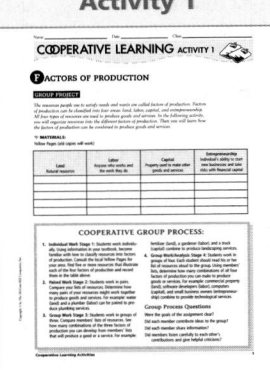

Math Practice Activity 1

Economic Cartoon 1

Primary and Secondary Source Reading 1

REVIEW AND REINFORCEMENT

Economic Vocabulary Activity 1

Reteaching Activity 1

Critical Thinking Activity 1

Reinforcing Economic Skill 9

Chapter 1 Resource Manager

ASSESSMENT AND EVALUATION

Chapter 1 Test Form A

Chapter 1 Test Form B

Performance Assessment Activity 1

ExamView® Pro Testmaker

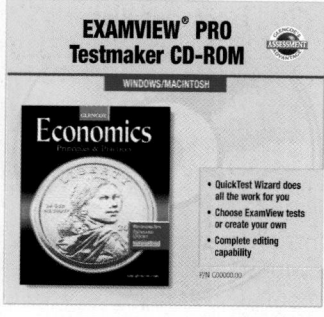

SPANISH RESOURCES

The following Spanish language materials are available in the Spanish Resources binder:

 Spanish Economic Vocabulary Activities

 Spanish Reteaching Activities

 Spanish Section Quizzes

 Spanish Economic Concepts Transparencies

Also available:

  Spanish Chapter 1 Audio Program Activity and Test

TECHNOLOGY/MULTIMEDIA

- Vocabulary PuzzleMaker CD-ROM
- Interactive Tutor Self-Assessment Software
- ExamView® Pro Testmaker
- Audio Program (English or Spanish)
- NBR Economics & You Video Program (English or Spanish)
- MindJogger Videoquiz
- Interactive Economics! CD-ROM
- Presentation Plus!
- TeacherWorks CD-ROM
- Glencoe Skillbuilder Interactive Workbook CD-ROM, Level 2

ECONOMICS Online

Use our Web site for additional resources. All essential content is covered in the Student Edition.

You and your students can visit epp.glencoe.com, the Web site companion to **Economics: Principles and Practices.** This innovative integration of electronic and print media offers your students a wealth of opportunities. The student text directs students to the Web site for the following options:

- **Chapter Overviews**
- **Student Web Activities**
- **Self-Check Quizzes**
- **Textbook Updates**

Answers are provided for you in the Web Activity Lesson Plan. Additional Web resources and interactive puzzles are also available.

CHAPTER 1

What Is Economics?

Economics & You

The study of economics will help you become a better decision maker—it helps you develop a way of thinking about how to make the best choices for you. To learn more about the scope of economics, view the Chapter 2 video lesson:

What Is Economics?

ECONOMICS *Online*

Chapter Overview Visit the *Economics: Principles and Practices* Web site at epp.glencoe.com and click on *Chapter 1—Chapter Overviews* to preview chapter information.

Consumers must make choices from many alternatives.

✚ EXTRA CREDIT PROJECT

Have students create a television-viewing log chronicling the number and types of economics-related items presented on the nightly news. Suggest that some students watch national newscasts on the networks, that others watch CNN national newscasts, and that still others watch local newscasts. They should record the date, the subject of the item, and the length of time devoted to the item. When study of the chapter is completed, have students compare and discuss their logs, noting how much news related to economics is presented.

Scarcity and the Science of Economics

Study Guide

Main Idea
Scarcity forces us to make choices. We can't have everything we want, so we are forced to choose what we want most.

Reading Strategy
Graphic Organizer As you read the section, complete a graphic organizer like the one below by listing and describing the three economic choices every society must make.

Key Terms
scarcity, economics, need, want, factors of production, land, capital, financial capital, labor, entrepreneur, production, Gross Domestic Product (GDP)

Objectives
After studying this section, you will be able to:
1. **Explain** the fundamental economic problem.
2. **Examine** the three basic economic questions every society must decide.

Applying Economic Concepts
Scarcity Read to find out why scarcity is the basic economic problem that faces everyone.

Cover Story

Harris Poll Shows High Interest in Economics

American adults have an exceptionally keen interest in economics. More than seven in ten say they share the same high level of interest in economics as they do politics, business and finance. A full 96% believe basic economics should be taught in high school. Yet, half of these same adults and two out of three high school students flunked an elementary quiz on basic economic concepts. Clearly the time has come [to] place economic literacy higher on the national education agenda.

The focus on economics education is growing.

—April 27, 1999 press release, The National Council on Economic Education

Do you think the study of economics is worth your time and effort? According to the Harris poll in the cover story, a huge percentage of Americans think it is. They must know what economists know—that a basic understanding of economics can help make sense of the world around us.

The Fundamental Economic Problem

Have you ever noticed that very few people are satisfied with the things they have? Someone without a home may want a small one; someone else with a small home may want a larger one; someone with a large home may want a mansion. Others want things like expensive sports cars, lavish jewelry, and exotic trips. Whether they are rich or poor, most people seem to want more than they already have. In fact, if each of us were to make a list of all the things we want, it would include more things than we could ever hope to obtain.

The fundamental economic problem facing all societies is that of scarcity. **Scarcity** is the condition that results from society not having enough resources to produce all the things people would like to have.

CHAPTER 1: WHAT IS ECONOMICS? **5**

CHAPTER 1
Section 1, pages 5–10

1 FOCUS

Section Overview
This section examines the three basic economic questions.

BELLRINGER
Motivational Activity

 Project **transparency** and have students answer questions.

 Available as blackline master.

Daily Focus Transparency 1

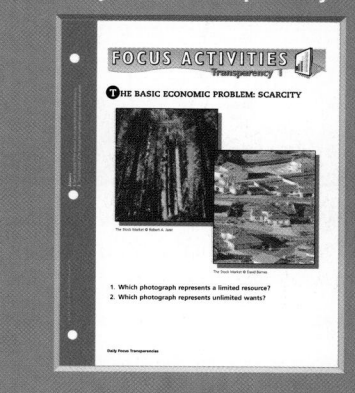

Study Guide

Reading Strategy
Have students create the graphic organizer.
Answers to Graphic: *what to produce, how to produce, for whom to produce*

Preteaching Vocabulary
Have students provide examples of scarce resources in their daily lives.

RESOURCE MANAGER

📁 Reproducible Masters
- Reproducible Lesson Plan 1-1
- Daily Lecture Notes 1-1
- Guided Reading Activity 1-1
- Reading Essentials and Study Guide 1-1
- Section Quiz 1-1

Multimedia
- 💾 Interactive Tutor Self-Assessment Software
- ⊗ ExamView® Pro Testmaker
- ⊗ Presentation Plus!

🎮 Transparencies
- Daily Focus Transparency 1

TEACH

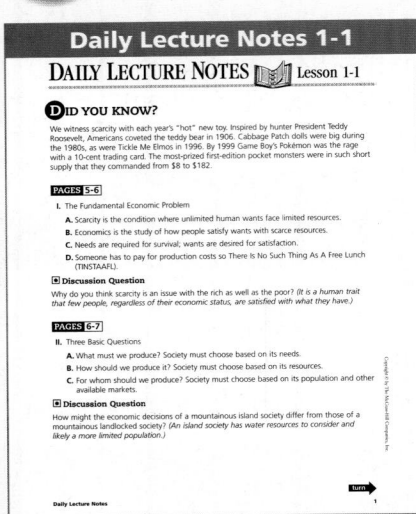

ECONOMICS
AT A GLANCE

Answer: *because people all over the world need goods and services produced with limited resources*

L1 Bulletin Board

Have students bring to class photographs or magazine clippings that illustrate scarce economic resources. Then have volunteers create an annotated bulletin-board display titled *Scarcity*. **ELL**

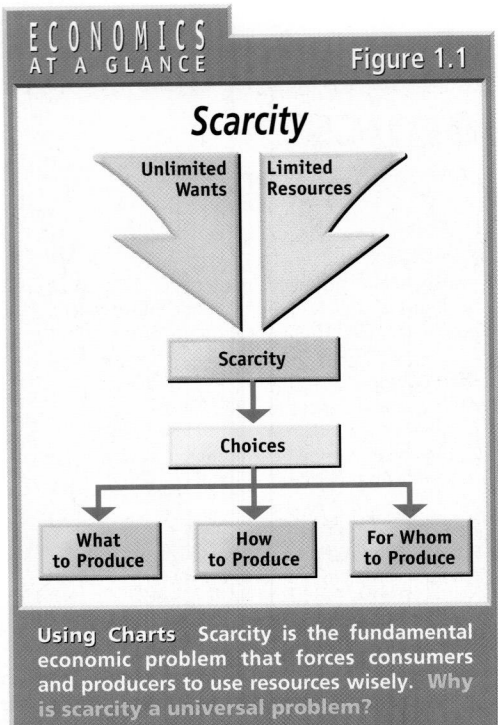

ECONOMICS
AT A GLANCE
         Figure 1.1

Scarcity

Unlimited Wants → ← Limited Resources

Scarcity

Choices

| What to Produce | How to Produce | For Whom to Produce |

Using Charts Scarcity is the fundamental economic problem that forces consumers and producers to use resources wisely. **Why is scarcity a universal problem?**

As shown in **Figure 1.1**, scarcity affects almost every decision we make. This is where the study of economics comes in. **Economics** is the study of how people try to satisfy what appears to be seemingly unlimited and competing wants through the careful use of relatively scarce resources.

Needs and Wants

Economists often talk about people's needs and wants. A **need** is a basic requirement for survival and includes food, clothing, and shelter. A **want** is a way of expressing a need. Food, for example, is a basic need related to survival. To satisfy the need for food, a person may "want" a pizza or other favorite meal. Because any number of foods will satisfy the need for nourishment, the range of things represented by the term *want* is much broader than that represented by the term *need*.

"There Is No Such Thing as a Free Lunch"

Because resources are limited, virtually everything we do has a cost—even when it seems as if we are getting something "for free."

For example, you may think you are getting a free lunch when you use a "buy one, get one free" coupon. However, while you may not pay for the extra lunch then and there, someone had to pay the farmer for raising the food, the truck driver for delivering the food, the chef for preparing the food, and the server for serving the food.

How does business recover these costs? Chances are that the price of the giveaway is usually hidden somewhere in the prices the firm charges for its products. As a result, the more a business gives away "free," the more it has to raise the prices for the items it sells. In the end, someone always pays for the supposedly "free" lunch—and that someone may be you!

Unfortunately, most things in life are not free because someone has to pay for the production in the first place. Economic educators use the term *TINSTAAFL* to describe this concept. In short, this term means that *There Is No Such Thing As A Free Lunch.*

Three Basic Questions

Because we live in a world of relatively scarce resources, we have to make wise economic choices. **Figure 1.1** presents three of the basic questions we have to answer. In so doing, we make decisions about the ways our limited resources will be used.

WHAT to Produce

The first question is that of WHAT to produce. Should a society direct most of its resources to the production of military equipment or to other items such as food, clothing, or housing? Suppose the decision is to produce housing. Should its limited resources be used for low-income, middle-income, or upper-income housing? How many of each will be needed? A society cannot have everything its people want, so it must decide WHAT to produce.

MEETING SPECIAL NEEDS ACTIVITY

Learning Disabled For students who have problems with reading, you might wish to help them organize their study of the section by examining the section objectives given in the Study Guide at the beginning of each section. Point out that the tasks required by the objectives are signaled in the first word of the objective. Some emphasize collection ("List," "Identify"), while others call for description ("Describe," "Explain"). Still others ask students to compare, analyze, and so on. Ask students to look through the objectives for this section and to note the first word of each. Have students explain what they believe they will have to do to meet each objective. Tell students to keep their answers in mind as they read the section.

📁 Refer to *Inclusion for the Social Studies Classroom Strategies and Activities* in the TCR.

HOW to Produce

A second question is that of HOW to produce. Should factory owners use mass production methods that require a lot of equipment and few workers, or should they use less equipment and more workers? If an area has many unemployed people, the second method might be better. On the other hand, mass production methods in countries where machinery and equipment are widely available can often lower production costs. Lower costs make manufactured items less expensive and, therefore, available to more people.

FOR WHOM to Produce

The third question deals with FOR WHOM to produce. After a society decides WHAT and HOW to produce, the things produced must be allocated to someone. If the society decides to produce housing, should it be distributed to workers, professional people, or government employees? If there are not enough houses for everyone, a choice must be made as to who will receive the existing supply.

These questions concerning WHAT, HOW, and FOR WHOM to produce are not easy for any society to answer. Nevertheless, they must be answered as long as there are not enough resources to satisfy people's seemingly unlimited wants.

The Factors of Production

The reason people cannot satisfy all their wants and needs is the scarcity of productive resources. The **factors of production,** or resources required to produce the things we would like to have, are land, capital, labor, and entrepreneurs. As shown in **Figure 1.2,** all four are required if goods and services are to be produced.

Land

In economics, **land** refers to the "gifts of nature," or natural resources

not created by humans. "Land" includes deserts, fertile fields, forests, mineral deposits, livestock, sunshine, and the climate necessary to grow crops. Because only so many natural resources are available at any given time, economists tend to think of land as being fixed, or in limited supply.

For example, there is not enough good farmland to adequately feed all of the earth's population, nor enough sandy beaches for everyone to enjoy, nor enough oil and minerals to meet our expanding energy needs indefinitely. Because the supply of a productive factor like land is relatively fixed, the problem of scarcity is likely to become worse as population grows in the future.

Capital

Another factor of production is **capital**—the tools, equipment, machinery, and factories used in the production of goods and services. Such items are also called capital goods to distinguish them from **financial capital,** the money used to buy the tools and equipment used in production.

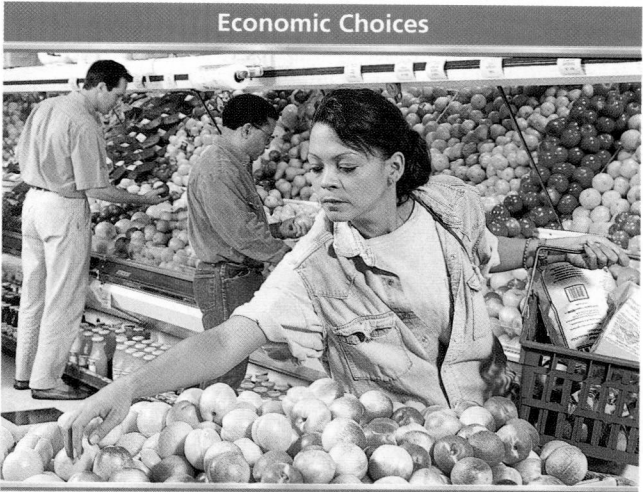

Economic Choices

Making Decisions If we cannot have everything we want, then we have to choose what we want the most. *Why must a society face the choices about what, how, and for whom to produce?*

Guided Reading Activity 1-1

GUIDED READING Activity 1-1

For use with textbook pages 5–10

SCARCITY AND THE SCIENCE OF ECONOMICS

RECALLING THE FACTS

Directions: Use the information in your textbook to answer the questions. Use another sheet of paper if necessary.

1. What is the basic economic problem facing all societies? _____
2. How is need different from want? _____
3. What do the letters TINSTAAFL stand for and what does it mean to consumers? _____
4. What are the three basic questions societies have to answer about the way their resources are used?
   a. _____
   b. _____
   c. _____
5. List the factors of production and define each one.
   a. _____
   b. _____
   c. _____
   d. _____
6. What is production? _____
7. What are the four key elements of economics? Explain briefly why each one is important.
   a. _____

CYBERNOMICS

Stock Trading One area of economic activity that computers and the Internet have revolutionized is stock trading. For certain stocks, traders no longer have to use a stockbroker to buy or sell stock. Instead, using computers, they can trade directly with one another. They also use certain software programs to help them analyze stocks. Using a number of sites on the Internet, traders can keep track of stocks as they are being bought and sold, and keep track of the buyers and sellers as well. Have students discuss how this new technology may affect the rules and regulations of stock trading.

Visual Instruction

Answer to Caption:
because people's wants are greater than available resources

FREE ENTERPRISE ACTIVITY

Just as consumers are faced with scarcity of goods and services, entrepreneurs must deal with scarcity of the other three factors of production—land, capital, and labor. Have students imagine that they are entrepreneurs in the business of producing and selling CDs. Inform them that the price of the raw material used for making CDs has doubled. Encourage students to make economic predictions about what will happen in the CD business. *(Fewer CDs will be produced; the price of CDs will go up; consumers will purchase fewer CDs.)*

L2 Designing a Poster

Have students work individually or in small groups to design posters that illustrate the three basic economic questions. **ELL**

L3 Writing Commercials

Have students write storyboards for a television commercial "selling" economics as a subject that should be studied. The commercial should describe the nature of economics, discuss the relevance of the subject to class members, and point out how they may benefit from an understanding of the subject.

③ ASSESS

Assign Section 1 Assessment as homework or as an in-class activity.

📖 Have students use **Interactive Tutor Self-Assessment Software** to review Section 1.

Section Quiz 1-1

ECONOMICS
AT A GLANCE

Figure 1.2

The Factors of Production

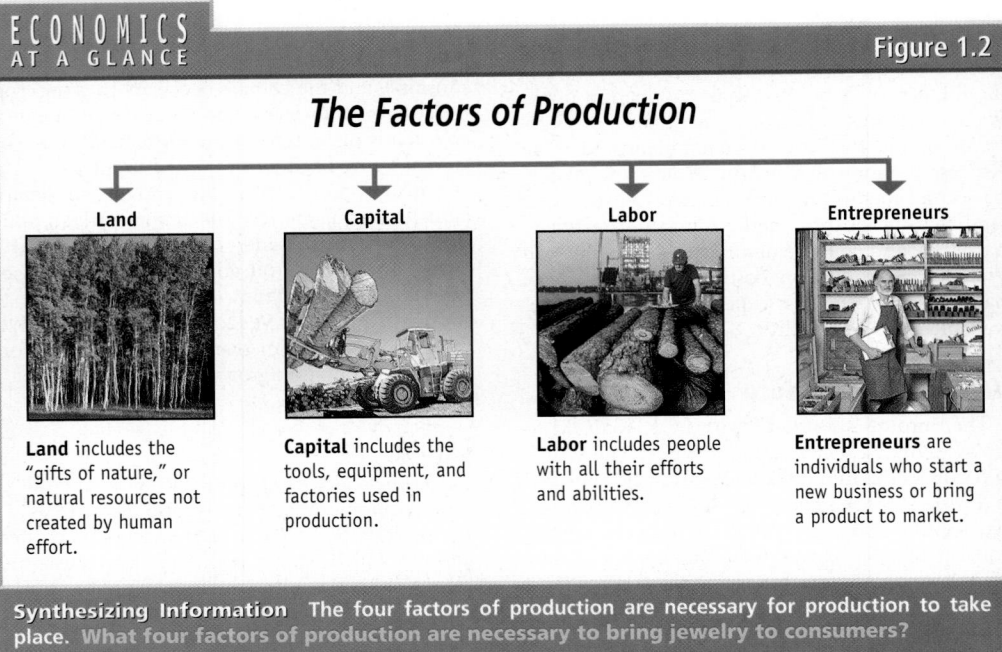

Land	Capital	Labor	Entrepreneurs

Land includes the "gifts of nature," or natural resources not created by human effort.

Capital includes the tools, equipment, and factories used in production.

Labor includes people with all their efforts and abilities.

Entrepreneurs are individuals who start a new business or bring a product to market.

Synthesizing Information The four factors of production are necessary for production to take place. **What four factors of production are necessary to bring jewelry to consumers?**

Capital is unique in that it is the result of production. A bulldozer, for example, is a capital good used in construction. It also was built in a factory, which makes it the result of earlier production. Like the bulldozer, the cash register in a neighborhood store is a capital good, as are the computers in your school that are used to produce the service of education.

Labor

A third factor of production is **labor**—people with all their efforts, abilities, and skills. This category includes all people except for a unique group of individuals called entrepreneurs, which we single out because of their special role in the economy.

Unlike land, labor is a resource that may vary in size over time. Historically, factors such as population growth, immigration, famine, war, and disease have had a dramatic impact on both the quantity and quality of labor.

Entrepreneurs

Some people are special because they are the innovators responsible for much of the change in our economy. Such an individual is an **entrepreneur,** a risk-taker in search of profits who does something new with existing resources. Entrepreneurs often are thought of as being the driving force in an economy because they exhibit the ability to start new businesses or bring new products to market. They provide the initiative that combines the resources of land, labor, and capital into new products.

Production

When all factors of production—land, capital, labor, and entrepreneurs—are present, **production,** or the process of creating goods and services, can take place. In fact, everything we produce requires these factors. For example, the chalkboards, desks, and audiovisual equipment used in schools are capital goods. The labor is in the form of services supplied

8 UNIT 1 FUNDAMENTAL ECONOMIC CONCEPTS

CRITICAL THINKING

Analyzing Information On the board, list a number of economic activities from both the service and manufacturing sectors. For example, you might list manufacturing computer hardware (the processor, keyboard, screen), creating a new computer word processing program, teaching a high school course on computers, running a computer store, and growing wheat. Ask students to make and complete a chart using the listed economic activities for the rows and the factors of production for the columns. When students have finished, discuss as a class how the factors of production are involved in each economic activity.

by teachers, administrators, and other employees. Land, such as the iron ore, granite, and timber used to make the building and desks, as well as the land where the school is located, is also needed. Finally, entrepreneurs are needed to organize the other three factors and make sure that everything gets done.

The Scope of Economics

 Economics is the study of human efforts to satisfy what appear to be unlimited and competing wants through the careful use of relatively scarce resources. As such, it is a *social science* because it deals with the behavior of people as they deal with this basic issue. There are four key elements to this study: description, analysis, explanation, and prediction.

Description

Economics deals with the description of economic activity. For example, you will often hear about the **Gross Domestic Product (GDP)**—the dollar value of all final goods and services, and structures produced within a country's borders in a 12-month period. GDP is the most comprehensive measure of a country's total output and is a key measure of the nation's economic health. Economics is also concerned with what is produced and who gets how much, as well as with topics such as unemployment, inflation, international trade, the interaction of business and labor, and the effects of government spending and taxes.

Description is important because we need to know what the world around us looks like. However, description is only part of the picture because it leaves many important "why" and "how" questions unanswered.

Analysis

In order to answer such questions, economics must focus on the analysis of economic activity as well. Why, for example, are prices of some items high while others are low? Why do some people earn higher incomes than others? How do taxes affect people's desire to work and save?

THE GLOBAL ECONOMY

United States Leads in Entrepreneurs Just as students in the United States participate in programs on entrepreneurship, students in other countries study the same principles. In Ireland, students aged 12 to 18 can be part of the Young Entrepreneurs Programme. The purpose of the program is to encourage students to learn about starting their own businesses. Students sometimes sell their products or services to other students and sometimes to the general public. During the 1996–1997 school year, more than 7,000 students in 250 schools took part in the program, starting about 2,300 businesses.

Answers:
1. *United States; Finland*
2. *North America's entrepreneurial activity is, per capita, twice that of Europe.*
3. *Answers will vary, but students should consider the opportunities strong economic growth offers.*

THE GLOBAL ECONOMY

UNITED STATES LEADS IN ENTREPRENEURS

A vast majority of the owners of the nearly 20 million businesses in the United States are entrepreneurs. Most either work for themselves or have a few employees.

A 10-nation study found that the United States leads when it comes to entrepreneurs. According to the survey, nearly 1 in 12 Americans is trying to start a new business. In second place is Canada. The study also shows a strong link between business start-up rates and overall economic growth. The graph shows the percentage of the adult population starting new businesses.

Country	Percentage
Italy	3.4%
Britain	3.3%
Germany	2.2%
Denmark	2.0%
France	1.8%
Finland	1.4%
U.S.	8.5%
Canada	6.8%

Source: *1999 Global Entrepreneurship Monitor*

Critical Thinking

1. **Analyzing Information** In which nation is entrepreneurial activity strongest? Weakest?
2. **Making Comparisons** How does the level of North America's entrepreneurial activity compare with Europe's?
3. **Drawing Conclusions** Do you think there is a link between business start-up rates and overall economic growth? Why or why not?

CHAPTER 1: WHAT IS ECONOMICS? **9**

EXTENDING THE CONTENT

Importance of Economics Economics is becoming increasingly important in people's lives, and interest in the subject is growing among the general public. To accommodate this interest, the media have enlarged their coverage of economics. Newspapers, for example, are devoting more space to economic matters. Economic commentators are a part of evening newscasts, and television newsbreaks often feature the economic events of the day. Education is also focusing more on economics, with many states now mandating economics instruction. These mandates take different forms, such as consumer economics, free enterprise, and economic principles and institutions.

Reteach

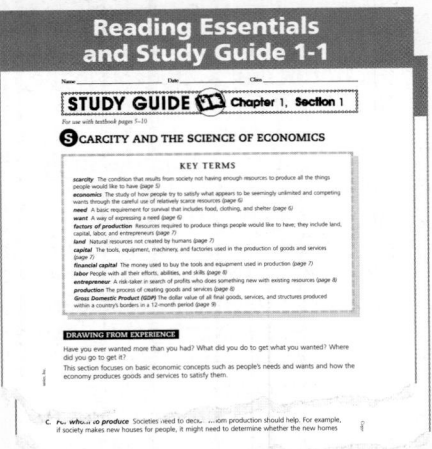

Reading Essentials and Study Guide 1-1

Enrich

Provide students with copies of business and financial newspapers and magazines, such as *The Wall Street Journal, Forbes,* and *Business Week.* Have students search through the publications to locate and discuss articles that address the concepts they have examined so far in this chapter.

 CLOSE

Ask students to consider how the element of prediction in economics might be important in their own lives. For example, have they ever examined reports on the expected growth or decline in certain jobs? Is the demand for auto mechanics or computer programmers going to grow over the next 10 years? Or, is the trend in their region toward a growth or a decline in the overall number of jobs? How might such economic predictions be important for their futures?

CYBERNOMICS SPOTLIGHT

Capital

"Capital" comprises the tools, equipment, and factories used to produce goods and services. As the economy changes, some economists are adjusting the definition to include "tools" such as knowledge and intellectual property. An example of such knowledge and intellectual property are databases and software.

The importance of analysis is that it helps us to discover why things work and how things happen. This, in turn, will help us deal with problems that we would like to solve.

Explanation

Economics is also concerned with the explanation of economic activity. After economists understand why and how things work, it is useful and even necessary to communicate this knowledge to others. If we all have a common understanding of the way our economy works, some economic problems will be much easier to address or even fix in the future. When it comes to the GDP, you will soon discover that economists spend much of their time explaining why the measure is, or is not, performing in the manner expected.

Prediction

Finally, economics is concerned with prediction. For example, we may want to know if people's incomes are going to rise or fall in the future, affecting their spending habits in the marketplace. Or, perhaps a community trying to choose between higher taxes on homeowners or higher taxes on businesses needs to know the consequences of each alternative before it makes its choice.

The study of economics can help to make the best decision in both situations. Because economics deals with the study of what is, or what tends to be, it can help predict what may happen in the future, as well as the likely consequences of different courses of action.

Finally, it is also important to realize that the actual decisions about the economic choices to be made are the responsibility of all citizens in a free and democratic society. Therefore, the study of economics helps all of us to become more informed citizens and better decision makers.

Section 1 Assessment

Checking for Understanding

1. **Main Idea** Using your notes from the graphic organizer activity on page 5, explain why a society must face the choices about WHAT, HOW, and FOR WHOM to produce.

2. **Key Terms** Define scarcity, economics, need, want, factors of production, land, capital, financial capital, labor, entrepreneur, production, Gross Domestic Product (GDP).

3. **Describe** the fundamental economic problem.

4. **List** the three basic economic questions every society must answer.

5. **Describe** the factors of production.

6. **List** the four key elements of economics.

Applying Economic Concepts

7. **Scarcity** How does scarcity affect your life? Provide several examples of items you had to do without because of limited resources. Explain how you adjusted to this situation. For example, were you able to substitute other items for those you could not have?

Critical Thinking

8. **Synthesizing Information** Give an example of a supposedly "free" item that you see every day. Explain why the item is not really free by stating who or what actually pays for it.

   Practice and **assess** key social studies skills with the *Glencoe Skillbuilder Interactive Workbook, Level 2.*

Section 1 Assessment Answers

1. Choices must be made as long as wants are greater than the resources available.

2. All vocabulary terms are defined in the text.

3. Answers should describe scarcity.

4. what to produce, how to produce, for whom to produce

5. The factors of production are land, capital, labor, and entrepreneurs. Students should provide descriptions of each factor.

6. description, analysis, explanation, prediction

7. Students should recognize items that are scarce because of limited resources.

8. Students should give appropriate examples.

Newsclip

Alexis de Tocqueville, a French traveler, wrote about his travels in the United States during the 1830s. His book, Democracy in America, a two-volume study of the American people and their institutions, is still relevant today.

The Role of the Entrepreneur

> What astonishes me in the United States is not so much the marvelous grandeur of such undertakings as the innumerable multitude of small ones.
>
> –Alexis de Tocqueville, 1835

What [de Tocqueville noticed nearly 160 years ago]—before the advent of Apple Computer, Genentech, Microsoft, or Nucor—is just as true today. The only difference is that the spirit of enterprise is more than ever a global phenomenon with few bounds.

From the row of kiosks selling goods on nearly every block in Moscow to the cramped factories in Taiwan, Russian *biznez-men* and Chinese *chang-shang* are reshaping their nations' economies in much the same way as those ingenious old Yankees created the basis for America's business cultures just after independence was won.

Any [de Tocqueville of modern times] would notice something else about this global shift:

Changes in the rules of the business game are putting a premium on the entrepreneurial qualities of [the smaller] companies. Today's successful enterprises are nimble, innovative, close to the customer, and quick to the market. They're not bureaucratic, centrally controlled institutions that are slow to change. It adds us to a new management catechism with many of the hallmarks of small business. . . .

Sure, some industries, such as auto making and petrochemicals, still require size and scale. But the swift pace of technological change and the fragmentation of markets are eroding the traditional economies of scale. Indeed, some management thinkers now speak of the "diseconomies of scale," the unresponsiveness, sluggishness, and high costs that come with bureaucracy. While the behemoths try to adjust to new competitive realities, younger and smaller companies have emerged as the agents of change in economies around the world. . . .

–Reprinted from *Small Business Trends and Entrepreneurship*, by the editors of *Business Week*, copyright © 1995 by The McGraw-Hill Companies, Inc.

Examining the Newsclip

1. **Summarizing Information** What are the entrepreneurial qualities of small companies?

2. **Finding the Main Idea** What does the writer mean by "diseconomies of scale"?

11

BusinessWeek ONLINE

Visit the Business Week Web site at www.businessweek.com for up-to-date news, analysis on the economy, editorials, special reports, market updates, book reviews, personal finance information, and an archive of past articles.

TEACH

After students have read the article, have them to think of any small entrepreneurial ventures in their own neighborhoods. **Ask:** What sorts of small, privately owned businesses have opened in your area—pizza shops, bakeries, comic book shops, hair salons, convenience stores? What advantages do these smaller businesses offer to the consumer? *(Students should recognize that a smaller company can often provide specialized products and more individualized service.)*

Refer to **Business Week Focus on the New Economy** in the TCR for additional unit-based articles.

Answers to Examining the Newsclip

1. They are nimble, innovative, close to the customer, and quick to the market.

2. The writer is referring to the slowness to change and the high costs that can result when companies become too large.

① FOCUS

Section Overview
This section discusses the relationship among scarcity, value, utility, and wealth.

BELLRINGER
Motivational Activity

Project **transparency** and have students answer questions.

Available as blackline master.

Daily Focus Transparency 5

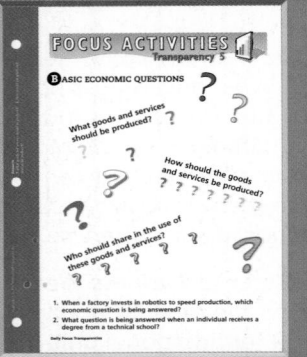

Study Guide

Reading Strategy
Have students create the graphic organizer.
Answers to Graphic: *producers sell goods and services, money returns to businesses, businesses produce more goods and services*

Preteaching Vocabulary
Have students name recent purchases and identify the purchase as either a service or a good.

SECTION 2

Basic Economic Concepts

Study Guide

Main Idea
An economic product is a good or service that is useful, relatively scarce, and exchangeable.

Reading Strategy
Graphic Organizer As you read the section, describe three different transactions that could take place in the factor market. Use a web like the one below to help you organize your answer.

Key Terms
economic product, good, consumer good, capital good, service, value, paradox of value, utility, wealth, market, factor market, product market, economic growth, productivity, division of labor, specialization, human capital, economic interdependence

Objectives
After studying this section, you will be able to:
1. **Explain** the relationship among scarcity, value, utility, and wealth.
2. **Understand** the circular flow of economic activity.

Applying Economic Concepts
Specialization Read to discover how specialization increases production.

Cover Story

On Specialization

To take an example, . . . One man draws out the wire, another straightens it, a third cuts it, a fourth points it, a fifth grinds it at the top for receiving the head; to make the head requires two or three distinct operations; to put it on, is a peculiar business, to whiten the pins is another; it is even a trade by itself to put them into the paper; and [the making of] a pin is, in this manner, divided into about eighteen distinct operations.

—Adam Smith, *The Wealth of Nations*, 1776

Adam Smith

Economics, like any other social science, has its own vocabulary. To understand economics, a review of some key terms is necessary. Fortunately, most economic terms are widely used, and many will already be familiar to you.

Goods, Services, and Consumers

Economics is concerned with **economic products**—goods and services that are useful, relatively scarce, and transferable to others. Economic products are scarce in an economic sense. That is, one cannot get enough to satisfy individual wants and needs. Because of these characteristics, economic products command a price.

Goods

The first type of economic product is a **good**—an item that is economically useful or satisfies an economic want, such as a book, car, or compact disc player. A **consumer good** is intended for final use by individuals. When manufactured goods are used to produce other goods and services, they are called **capital goods.** An example

12

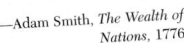

RESOURCE MANAGER

📂 Reproducible Masters
- Reproducible Lesson Plan 1-2
- Daily Lecture Notes 1-2
- Guided Reading Activity 1-2
- Reading Essentials and Study Guide 1-2
- Section Quiz 1-2

📖 Transparencies
- Daily Focus Transparency 5

Multimedia
- 🌐 Interactive Economics!
- 💾 Interactive Tutor Self-Assessment Software
- 🌐 ExamView® Pro Testmaker
- 🌐 Presentation Plus!

of a capital good would be a robot welder in a factory, an oven in a bakery, or a computer in a high school.

Any good that lasts three years or more when used on a regular basis is called a durable good. Durable goods include both capital goods, such as robot welders, and consumer goods such as automobiles. A nondurable good is an item that lasts for less than three years when used on a regular basis. Examples of nondurable goods include food, writing paper, and most clothing items.

Services

The other type of economic product is a **service,** or work that is performed for someone. Services include haircuts, home repairs, and forms of entertainment such as concerts. They also include the work that doctors, lawyers, and teachers perform. The difference between a good and a service is that a service is intangible, or something that cannot be touched.

Consumers

The consumer is a person who uses goods and services to satisfy wants and needs. As consumers, people indulge in consumption, the process of using up goods and services in order to satisfy wants and needs.

Value, Utility, and Wealth

In economics, **value** refers to a worth that can be expressed in dollars and cents. Why, however, does something have value, and why are some things worth more than others? To answer these questions, it helps to review an early problem faced by economists.

Paradox of Value

At first, early economists were puzzled by a contradiction between necessities and value called the **paradox of value.** The paradox of value is the situation where some necessities, such as water, have little monetary value, whereas some non-necessities, such as diamonds, have a much higher value.

Economists knew that scarcity is required for value. For example, water was so plentiful in many areas that it had little or no value. On the other hand, diamonds were so scarce that they had great value. The problem was that scarcity by itself is not enough to create value.

Utility

It turned out that for something to have value, it must also have **utility,** or the capacity to be useful and provide satisfaction. Utility is not something that is fixed or measurable, like weight or height. Instead, the utility of a good or service may vary from one person to the next. One person may get a great deal of satisfaction from a home computer; another may get very little. One person may enjoy a rock concert; another may not. A good or service does not have to have utility for everyone, only utility for some.

For something to have value, economists decided, it must be scarce *and* have utility. This is the solution to the paradox of value. Diamonds are scarce and have utility—and therefore they possess a value that can be stated in monetary terms. Water has utility, but is not scarce enough in most places to give it much value. Therefore, water is less expensive, or has less value, than diamonds.

STANDARD &POOR'S INFOBYTE

Durable Goods Orders The Department of Commerce's report on durable goods orders highlights the number of new orders placed with domestic manufacturers for goods intended to last over three years. The report is divided into broad categories; these include defense, nondefense, and capital and noncapital goods. Noncapital goods are generally of the consumer spending variety and include automobiles and large appliances. Capital goods tend to be of the investment spending nature, while defense goods indicate government spending.

CHAPTER 1: WHAT IS ECONOMICS? **13**

 TEACH

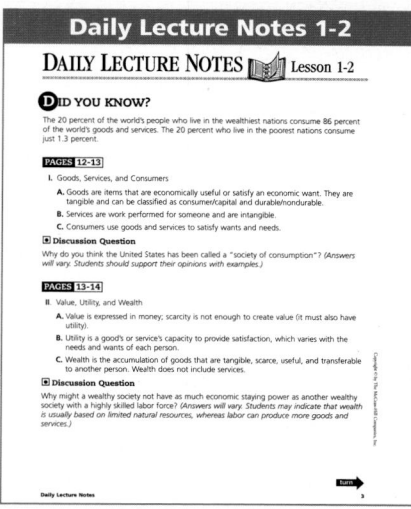

Daily Lecture Notes 1-2

DAILY LECTURE NOTES Lesson 1-2

DID YOU KNOW?
The 20 percent of the world's people who live in the wealthiest nations consume 86 percent of the world's goods and services. The 20 percent who live in the poorest nations consume just 1.3 percent.

PAGES 12-13
I. Goods, Services, and Consumers
  A. Goods are items that are economically useful or satisfy an economic want. They are tangible and can be classified as consumer/capital and durable/nondurable.
  B. Services are work performed for someone and are intangible.
  C. Consumers use goods and services to satisfy wants and needs.

Discussion Question
Why do you think the United States has been called a "society of consumption"? (Answers will vary. Students should support their opinions with examples.)

PAGES 13-14
II. Value, Utility, and Wealth
  A. Value is expressed in money; scarcity is not enough to create value (it must also have utility).
  B. Utility is a good's or service's capacity to provide satisfaction, which varies with the needs and wants of each person.
  C. Wealth is the accumulation of goods that are tangible, scarce, useful, and transferable to another person. Wealth does not include services.

Discussion Question
Why might a wealthy society not have as much economic staying power as another wealthy society with a highly skilled labor force? (Answers will vary. Students may indicate that wealth is usually based on limited natural resources, whereas labor can produce more goods and services.)

Daily Lecture Notes

L1 Collage

Have students collect pictures representing both durable and nondurable goods from advertisements. Students should use the pictures to make a collage with a section for each type of good. Students should be prepared to explain why they chose to put the pictures in the sections that they did. **ELL**

The term *conspicuous consumption*—which means the use of a good or service to impress others—was coined by economist and social critic Thorstein Veblen in his study *The Theory of the Leisure Class* (1899).

MEETING SPECIAL NEEDS ACTIVITY

Learning Disabled For students who have trouble with reading, the organization, modified sentence construction, and special features of the text should facilitate their comprehension of the material. Because poor decoding (work attack) skills impede the reading process, it will be important for you to know the level at which each student has mastered these skills. Present each student with a list of 20 words from Section 2 to read aloud. Judge responses by both fluency (time) and power (correctness) criteria.

Refer to *Inclusion for the Social Studies Classroom Strategies and Activities* in the TCR.

Visual Instruction

Answer to Caption:
because they are tangible, scarce, useful, and transferable from one person to another

L1 Analyzing Information

Tell students to imagine that they are managers of the Straight and True Paper Airplane Company. Ask volunteers to describe airplane-construction procedures that might be followed if the company were a one-person operation. Ask others how airplanes might be made if the company's staff consisted of 12 people who specialized in various tasks. **Ask:** Which company would be more efficient? Why?

L2 Economic Interdependence

Have students list the various ways they are dependent on others and how others are dependent on them. **Ask:** Which ways illustrate economic interdependence?

Wealth

Another concept is **wealth.** Wealth, in an economic sense, is the accumulation of those products that are tangible, scarce, useful, and transferable from one person to another. Consequently, a nation's wealth is comprised of all items, including natural resources, factories, stores, houses, motels, theaters, furniture, clothing, books, highways, video games, and even footballs.

While goods are counted as wealth, services are not because they are intangible. However, this does not mean that services are not useful. Indeed, when Adam Smith wrote *The Wealth of Nations* in 1776, he was referring specifically to the ability and skills of a nation's people as the source of its wealth. To illustrate, if a country's material possessions were taken away, its people, through their skilled efforts, could restore these possessions. On the other hand, if a country's people were taken away, its wealth would deteriorate.

Wealth

Natural Resources Fertile land is a natural resource and an item of wealth. *Why are natural resources considered part of the nation's wealth?*

The Circular Flow of Economic Activity

The wealth that an economy generates is made possible by the circular flow of economic activity. The key feature of this circular flow is the **market,** a location or other mechanism that allows buyers and sellers to exchange a certain economic product. Markets may be local, regional, national, or global. More recently, markets have evolved in cyberspace, with buyers and sellers interacting through computer networks without leaving the comfort of their homes.

Factor Markets

How does this circular flow operate? As shown in **Figure 1.3,** individuals earn their incomes in **factor markets,** the markets where productive resources are bought and sold. This is where entrepreneurs hire labor for wages and salaries, acquire land in return for rent, and borrow money for interest. The concept of a factor market is a simplified version of the real world, of course, but it is nevertheless realistic. To illustrate, you participate in the factor market whenever you go to work and sell your labor to an employer.

Product Markets

After individuals receive their income from the resources they sell, they spend it in **product markets,** markets where producers sell their goods and services to consumers. Thus, the money that individuals receive from businesses in the factor markets returns to businesses in the product markets. Businesses then use this money to produce more goods and services—and the cycle, through economic activity, repeats itself.

As you can see from **Figure 1.3,** markets serve as the main links between individuals and businesses. Note that money circulates on the outside, illustrating payments for goods, services, and the factors of production. The actual factors of production, and the products made with these productive inputs, flow in the opposite direction on the inside.

FREE ENTERPRISE ACTIVITY

Have students apply their understanding of several of the economic terms found in Section 2. They can do this by giving an illustration—not used in the text—for each of the following fundamental economic concepts: consumer durable goods *(refrigerators, dishwashers, CD players)*; consumer nondurable goods *(soap, gasoline)*; wealth *(oil reserves, airplanes, computers, bicycles)*; human capital *(education, ideas)*.

Productivity and Economic Growth

Economic growth occurs when a nation's total output of goods and services increases over time. This means that the circular flow in **Figure 1.3** becomes larger, with more factors of production, goods, and services flowing in one direction, and more payments flowing in the opposite direction. A number of factors are responsible for economic growth, but productivity is the most important.

Productivity

Everyone benefits when scarce resources are used efficiently. This is described by the term **productivity,** which is a measure of the amount of output produced by a given amount of inputs in a specific period of time. Productivity goes up whenever more output can be produced with the same amount of inputs in the same amount of time. For example, if a company produced 500 units of a product in one period, and if it produced 510 in

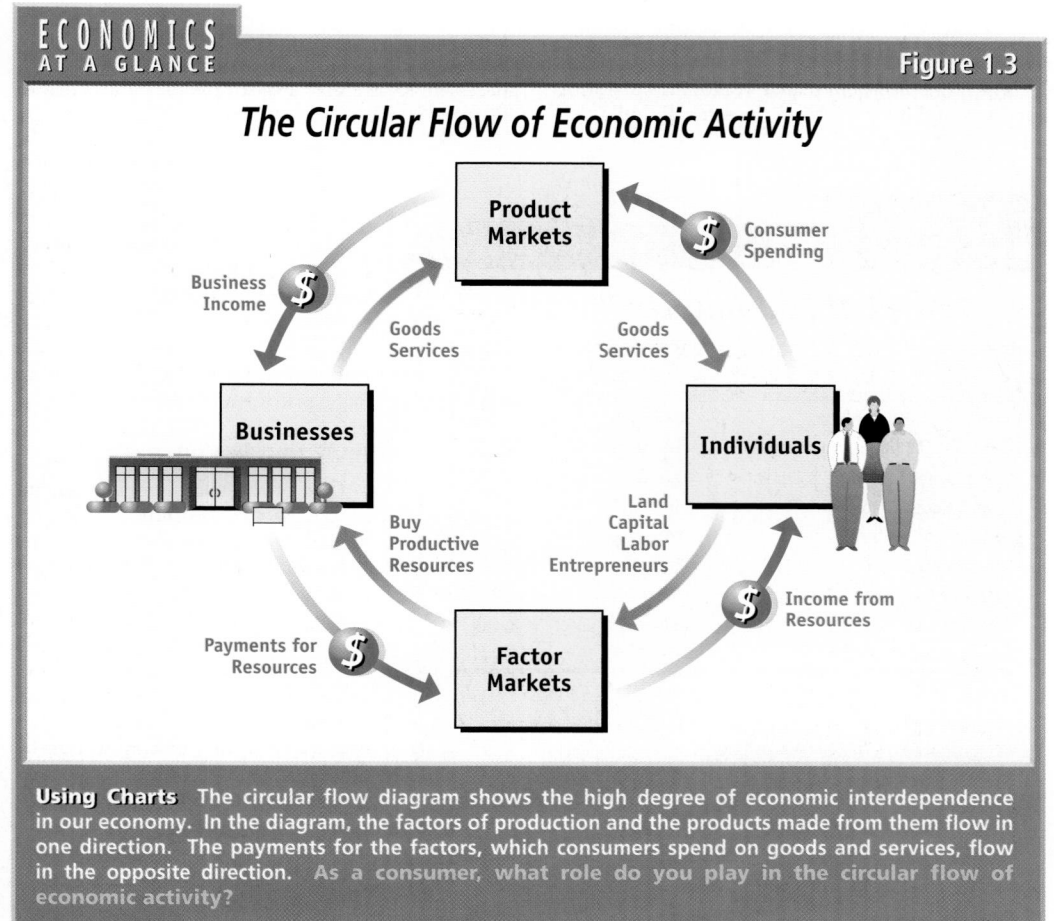

ECONOMICS AT A GLANCE

Figure 1.3

The Circular Flow of Economic Activity

- Product Markets
- $ Consumer Spending
- Business Income $
- Goods Services
- Goods Services
- Businesses
- Individuals
- Buy Productive Resources
- Land Capital Labor Entrepreneurs
- $ Income from Resources
- Payments for Resources $
- Factor Markets

Using Charts The circular flow diagram shows the high degree of economic interdependence in our economy. In the diagram, the factors of production and the products made from them flow in one direction. The payments for the factors, which consumers spend on goods and services, flow in the opposite direction. As a consumer, what role do you play in the circular flow of economic activity?

CHAPTER 1: WHAT IS ECONOMICS? **15**

CRITICAL THINKING

Identifying Alternatives Organize the class into small groups. Explain to students that they are going to do an activity related to specialization and the division of labor. Tell each group to choose a product to produce in a factory; for example, frozen pizza. Ask students in each group to divide the job of making their product into a number of tasks. Have them assign one or two of the tasks to a single worker. Ask students to discuss the advantages of having workers do the same few tasks every day. **Ask:** What might be some disadvantages? Ask students to devise ways to balance the advantages and disadvantages. Finish the activity by holding a class discussion about how and why students changed or did not change their division of labor. **BLOCK SCHEDULING**

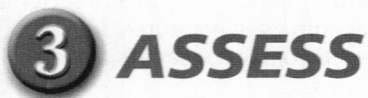

Answer: *Studies show that as education levels increase, so does income expectancy.*

③ ASSESS

Assign Section 2 Assessment as homework or as an in-class activity.

■ Have students use **Interactive Tutor Self-Assessment Software** to review Section 2.

Section Quiz 1-2

L2 Drawing Conclusions

Have students develop a chart comparing different factors of production found in the United States and in a developing nation. What conclusions can be drawn about the unequal distribution of the factors of production?

---

the next period with the same number of inputs, then productivity went up.

Productivity is often discussed in terms of labor, but it applies to all factors of production. For this reason, business owners try to buy the most efficient capital goods, and farmers try to use the most fertile land for their crops.

Division of Labor and Specialization

Division of labor and specialization can improve productivity. **Division of labor** takes place when work is arranged so that individual workers do fewer tasks than before. In most cases, a worker who performs a few tasks many times every day is likely to become more proficient than a worker who performs hundreds of different tasks in the same period.

Specialization takes place when factors of production perform tasks that they can do relatively more efficiently than others. Note that specialization is not limited to a single factor of production such as labor. For example, complex industrial robots are often built to perform just one or two simple assembly line tasks. In regional specialization, different regions of the country often specialize in the things they can produce best—as when Idaho specializes in potatoes, Iowa in corn, and Texas in oil, cotton, and cattle.

One of the best examples of the advantages offered by the division of labor and specialization is Henry Ford's introduction of the assembly line into automobile manufacturing. This process cut the time necessary to assemble a car from a day and a half to just over 90 minutes. It also cut the price of a new car by more than 50 percent. The result was an improvement in productivity.

Another example of the changes that can result from specialized tools can be seen in American agriculture. In 1910 it took more than 13 million farmers to feed the U.S. population, at that time about 90 million. Today, 2 million farmers can feed a population that is more than three times as large as it was in 1910.

Investing in Human Capital

One of the main contributions to productivity comes from investments in **human capital,** the sum of the skills, abilities, health, and motivation of people. Government can invest in human capital by helping to provide education and health care. Businesses can invest in training and other programs that improve the skill and motivation of its workers. Individuals can invest in their own education by completing high school, going to technical school, or going to college.

Figure 1.4 shows that investments in education can have substantial payoffs. According to the data in the table, high school graduates have substantially higher incomes than

ECONOMICS AT A GLANCE

Figure 1.4

Effect of Education on Income

Education	Average Income For Males	Average Income For Females
Less Than 9th Grade	$23,139	$16,636
9th to 12th Grade (no diploma)	$27,067	$19,620
High School Graduate & Equivalency	$36,805	$24,228
Some College, no degree	$44,558	$30,157
Associate Degree	$45,876	$31,855
Bachelor's Degree	$63,491	$41,106
Master's Degree	$75,527	$49,844
Professional Degree	$130,711	$72,188
Doctorate Degree	$108,334	$69,085

Source: U.S. Department of Commerce, Bureau of the Census, 2001

Using Tables Education is one way to invest in human capital. How does this type of investment pay off for both employers and their employees?

ECONOMICS *Online*

Visit epp.glencoe.com and click on **Textbook Updates—Chapter 1** for an update of the data.

16 UNIT 1 FUNDAMENTAL ECONOMIC CONCEPTS

EXTENDING THE CONTENT

Capital Goods To produce most goods and services, it takes all four factors of production—land, labor, capital, and entrepreneurs. Although a nation may have abundant natural resources, human labor, and entrepreneurship, it may not have enough capital goods to produce needed consumer goods and services. Thus, its people may still be denied a high standard of living. For example, although some developing nations have large supplies of labor and natural resources, they are barely able to provide enough food for their people because they lack machinery, equipment, and factories.

nongraduates, and college graduates make even more than high school graduates. Educational investments require that we make a sacrifice today so we can have a better life in the future—and few investments generate higher returns.

Investing in the Future

Businesses, government, and other organizations face many of the same choices that individuals do. Investments in human capital and physical capital can eventually increase production and promote economic growth. Faster economic growth, in turn, increases the amount of goods and services available to us.

Economic Interdependence

The American economy has a remarkable degree of **economic interdependence.** This means that we rely on others, and others rely on us, to provide the goods and services that we consume.

Events in one part of the country or the world often have a dramatic impact elsewhere. To illustrate, a labor dispute between several hundred professional basketball players and a handful of owners can affect

---

---

the lives of tens of thousands of people who park cars, sell tickets, serve food at the games, and sell NBA apparel and memorabilia all across the country. Or, bad weather in countries where sugar cane is grown can affect sugar prices in the United States, which in turn can affect the price of snack foods and the demand for sugar substitutes elsewhere.

This does not mean that economic interdependence is necessarily bad. The gain in productivity and income as a result of increased specialization almost always offsets the costs associated with the loss in self-sufficiency. However, we need to understand how all the parts fit together, which is one reason why we study economics.

Section 2 Assessment

Checking for Understanding

1. **Main Idea** Using your notes from the graphic organizer activity on page 12, explain the different transactions that take place in the product market.

2. **Key Terms** Define economic product, good, consumer good, capital good, service, value, paradox of value, utility, wealth, market, factor market, product market, economic growth, productivity, division of labor, specialization, human capital, economic interdependence.

3. **Discuss** the relationship among scarcity, value, utility, and wealth.

4. **Describe** the circular flow of economic activity.

5. **Explain** why productivity is important to economic growth.

Applying Economic Concepts

6. **Specialization** Provide at least three examples each of specialized workers and capital that are used in your school to provide the service of education. Would productivity go up or down if these specialized capital goods and workers were not available to your school? Explain why or why not.

Critical Thinking

7. **Making Comparisons** What is the difference between a durable good and a nondurable good?

8. **Drawing Conclusions** In what way do businesses and households both supply and demand in the circular flow model?

 Practice and **assess** key social studies skills with the *Glencoe Skillbuilder Interactive Workbook, Level 2.*

Reteach

Reading Essentials and Study Guide 1-2

Name _____ Date _____ Class _____

STUDY GUIDE Chapter 1, Section 2

For use with textbook pages 12–17

BASIC ECONOMIC CONCEPTS

KEY TERMS

economic product A good or service that is useful, relatively scarce, and transferable to others (page 12)
good An item that is economically useful or satisfies an economic want (page 12)
consumer good A good intended for final use by individuals (page 12)
capital good A manufactured item used to produce other goods and services (page 12)
service Work that is performed for someone (page 13)
value A worth that can be expressed in dollars and cents (page 13)
paradox of value The situation in which some non-necessities have a much higher value than some necessities (page 13)
utility The capacity to be useful and provide satisfaction (page 13)
wealth The accumulation of those economic products that are tangible, scarce, useful, and transferable from one person to another (page 14)
market A location or other mechanism that allows buyers and sellers to exchange a certain economic product (page 14)
factor market A market where productive resources are bought and sold (page 14)
product market A market where producers sell their goods and services to consumers (page 14)
economic growth The increase in a nation's total output of goods and services over time (page 15)
productivity A measure of the amount of output produced by a given amount of inputs in a specific period of time (page 15)
division of labor Work arranged so that individual workers do fewer tasks than before (page 16)
specialization Situation in which a factor of production performs tasks that it can do relatively more efficiently than others (page 16)
human capital The sum of the skills, abilities, health, and motivation of people (page 16)
economic interdependence Reliance on one another to provide the goods and services that people

...of using goo... ...onsumption.

1. Do durable goods include consumer goods and capital goods? Explain your answer.

Enrich

Refer students to the circular flow diagram on page 15. Have students construct a similar diagram that represents their own economic activity if they have a job, or the economic activity of a family member if they do not.

④ CLOSE

Discuss ways in which your community, state, or region specializes in the goods or services it provides. Analyze and evaluate the areas these resources come from. What makes them unique?

Section 2 Assessment Answers

1. buying/selling goods and services, and using money from sales to produce more goods

2. All vocabulary terms are defined in the text.

3. Answers should reflect an understanding of the interrelationships.

4. Answers should reflect material in diagram on page 15.

5. When productivity goes up, more output is produced with the same amount of inputs in the same amount of time.

6. Students should recognize that without specialized workers and goods, productivity would be reduced.

7. durable: lasts three or more years when used on a regular basis; nondurable: lasts for less than three years

8. Businesses supply goods while demanding resources; households supply labor and income while demanding goods.

BACKGROUND

Adam Smith's famous metaphor—the "invisible hand" of the market—did not mean that in *all* cases government should refrain from interfering in the economy. In fact, Smith was devoted to moral philosophy. He wrote of the need for both individual and societal responsibility, and thought that government intervention was at times required to prevent injustices. He wrote, "People of the same trade seldom meet together, even for merriment and diversion, but the conversation ends in a conspiracy against the public, or in some contrivance to raise prices." Smith, then, was not the apologist for a free-for-all market that some today have made him out to be. He was a broad thinker who devoted his mind to improving society as a whole.

TEACH

Share with students this assessment of Smith, made by a historian: "[Smith] is a major figure in the history of human thought." Emphasize the weight of the claim. Challenge students to create detailed graphic organizers that link Smith's ideas to various areas (economic thought, government policies, modern economies), to show a visual representation of Smith's influence. Have students use their graphic organizers to evaluate the historian's claim.

Profiles IN Economics

The Father of Modern Economics:
Adam Smith
(1723–1790)

Take a look at a Scottish penny and you'll be surprised by what you see. The person pictured was not a political or military figure, but an economist: Adam Smith. It is a fitting tribute to a man who contributed so much to economics.

HIS LIFE

Smith was born in Kirkcaldy, Scotland. After graduating from Glasgow University, he traveled to England and enrolled at Oxford University. Six years later, Smith returned to Scotland to lecture at Edinburgh University and at his alma mater, where he was immensely popular with his students. Smith became a tutor to a young duke, and traveled throughout Europe.

HIS IDEAS

Smith met and exchanged ideas with French writer Voltaire, Benjamin Franklin, and the French economist Quesnay. His travels helped him formulate the ideas put forth in *The Wealth of Nations* (1776). In *The Wealth of Nations*, Smith observed that labor becomes more productive as each worker becomes more skilled at a single job. He said that new machinery and the division of labor and specialization would lead to an increase in production and greater "wealth of nations." Smith also put forth what was then a radical new idea: that the wealth of a nation should be defined as the sum of its labor-produced goods, not by who owned those goods.

Smith's most influential contribution, however, concerned competition in the marketplace. Every individual, Smith wrote, "intends only his own gain, and he is in this . . . led by an invisible hand. . . . By pursuing his own interest he frequently promotes that of the society. . . ." Smith argued that a free market isn't chaotic, but that competition acts as an "invisible hand" that guides resources to their most productive uses. A truly free, competitive market—operating with a minimum of government intervention—would bring about the greatest good for society as a whole.

The English aristocracy ridiculed *The Wealth of Nations*. Business people, however, were delighted to have a moral justification for their growing wealth and power. Soon, Smith's doctrine of *laissez-faire* (French, "let it be"), meaning minimal government intervention in economic affairs, became the economic watchword in Europe, and is today the economic watchword of much of the world.

Examining the Profile

1. **Summarizing Ideas** Summarize Smith's contribution to economic thought.

2. **Synthesizing Information** Explain how Smith's ideas are evident in the workings of the American economy.

Answers to Examining the Profile

1. Answers will vary, but should allude to Smith's description of fundamental economic principles; his idea that labor productivity increases with skill, new machinery, division of labor and specialization; his vision of the "invisible hand" that refers to the self-regulating nature of a free market; and his lasting influence on economic thought.

2. Answers will vary, but students should note that the United States has a market economy, composed of a myriad of small markets, each of which operates essentially in the way Smith described: buyers and sellers operate in their own best interests.

Economic Choices and Decision Making

Study Guide

Main Idea
Trade-offs are present whenever choices are made.

Reading Strategy
Graphic Organizer As you read this section, complete a graphic organizer similar to the one below by explaining what you need to know to become a good decision maker.

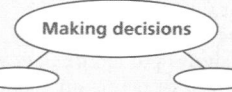

Making decisions

Key Terms
trade-off, opportunity cost, production possibilities frontier, cost-benefit analysis, free enterprise economy, standard of living

Objectives
After studying this section, you will be able to:
1. **Analyze** trade-offs and opportunity costs.
2. **Explain** decision-making strategies.

Applying Economic Concepts
Opportunity Costs Read to find out how your decisions are measured in terms of opportunity costs.

FOCUS

Section Overview
This section analyzes trade-offs and opportunity costs.

BELLRINGER
Motivational Activity

 Project **transparency** and have students answer questions.

 Available as blackline master.

Daily Focus Transparency 2

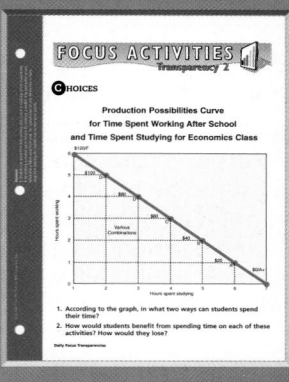

Cover Story

Cost Benefit Analysis

Research has long demonstrated the educational value of early intervention for America's at-risk children, but a new study also shows the federal programs are a wise public investment.

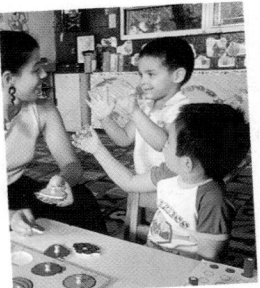

Social programs involve trade-offs and opportunity costs.

[A] cost-benefit analysis of the federally funded Chicago Child-Parent Center program, which serves children from low-income families in Chicago's inner city [shows that] an average annual cost of $6,730 per child. . . . generated a total return to society at large of $47,759 per participant.

- AScribe Newswire, June 26, 2001

The process of making a choice is not always easy. Still, individuals, businesses, and government agencies, like the Chicago Child-Parent Center program, who try to satisfy people's wants and needs, must make decisions. Because resources are scarce, consumers need to make wise choices. To become a good decision maker, you need to know how to identify the problem and then analyze your alternatives. Finally, you have to make your choice in a way that carefully considers the costs and benefits of each possibility.

Trade-Offs and Opportunity Cost

There are alternatives and costs to everything we do. In a world where "there is no such thing as a free lunch," it pays to examine these concepts closely.

Trade-Offs

The first thing we must recognize is that people face **trade-offs,** or alternative choices, whenever they make an economic decision. To help make the decision, constructing a grid such as that in **Figure 1.5** shows one way to approach the

CHAPTER 1: WHAT IS ECONOMICS? **19**

Study Guide

Reading Strategy
Have students create the graphic organizer.
Answers to Graphic: *trade-offs, opportunity costs*

Preteaching Vocabulary
Use the Vocabulary Puzzle-Maker to create crossword and word-search puzzles.

RESOURCE MANAGER

Reproducible Masters
- Reproducible Lesson Plan 1-3
- Daily Lecture Notes 1-3
- Guided Reading Activity 1-3
- Reading Essentials and Study Guide 1-3
- Section Quiz 1-3

Transparencies
- Daily Focus Transparency 2

Multimedia
- Vocabulary PuzzleMaker CD-ROM
- NBR Economics & You
- Interactive Economics!
- Interactive Tutor Self-Assessment Software
- ExamView® Pro Testmaker
- Presentation Plus!

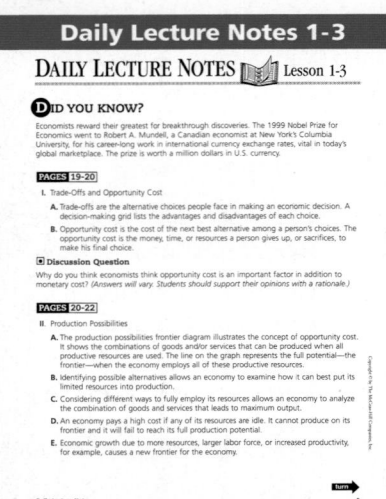

L1 Analyzing Information

Ask students to imagine that they are officers of a school social club who must decide how to spend a $500 grant. Call on volunteers to explain the decision-making process they would follow. (Refer students to Figure 1.5.)

ECONOMICS
AT A GLANCE

Answer: *Economists think in terms of opportunity costs, the cost of the next best alternative use of time, money, or resources when one choice is made rather than another.*

---

problem. This grid summarizes a decision to be made by Jesse, a newspaper carrier, whose dilemma is how to spend a gift of $50 in the best way possible.

Jesse realizes that several alternatives are appealing—a soccer ball, jeans, a portable CD player, several CDs, or concert tickets. At the same time, he realizes that each item has advantages and disadvantages. Some of these items are more durable than others, and some might require his parents' consent. Some even have additional costs while others do not—the CD player would require batteries and the concert tickets would require the use of his parents' car.

To help with his decision, Jesse draws a grid that lists his alternatives and several criteria by which to judge them. Then he evaluates each alternative with a "yes" or "no." In the end, Jesse chooses the jeans because they satisfy more of his criteria than any other alternative.

Using a decision-making grid is one way to analyze an economic problem. Among other things, it forces you to consider a number of relevant alternatives. For another, it requires you to identify the criteria used to evaluate the alternatives. Finally, it forces you to evaluate each alternative based on the criteria you selected.

Opportunity Cost

People often think of cost in terms of dollars and cents. To an economist, however, cost often means more than the price tag placed on a good or service. Instead, economists think broadly in terms of **opportunity cost**—the cost of the next best alternative use of money, time, or resources when one choice is made rather than another. When Jesse made his choice and decided to purchase the jeans, his opportunity cost was the next best choice—the soccer ball or the CD player—that he gave up.

Suppose you spend $5,000 on a used car. The opportunity cost of the purchase is the value of the stereo, apartment, vacation, or other items and activities that you could have purchased with the money spent on the car.

Even time has an opportunity cost, although you cannot always put a monetary value on it. The opportunity cost of taking an economics class, for example, is the history or math class that you could not take at the same time. Thus, part of making economic decisions involves recognizing and evaluating the cost of the alternatives as well as making choices from among the alternatives.

ECONOMICS
AT A GLANCE

Figure 1.5

Jesse's Decision-Making Grid

Alternatives	Criteria				
	Costs $50 or less?	Durable?	Will parents approve?	Future expense unnecessary?	Can use anytime?
Several CDs	yes	yes	yes	yes	no
Concert tickets	yes	no	no	no	no
CD player	yes	yes	yes	no	yes
Soccer ball	yes	yes	yes	yes	no
Jeans	yes	yes	yes	yes	yes

Adapted from *A Framework for Teaching Basic Economics,*
Economics America National Council on Economic Education, 1996

Using Tables A decision-making grid is a good way to list and then evaluate alternatives when a decision must be made. **What do economists mean when they talk about costs?**

MEETING SPECIAL NEEDS ACTIVITY

Learning Style: Visual/Spatial Locate several examples of editorial cartoons that deal with economic issues and share them with students. Then ask students to draw an editorial-type cartoon related to a concept from this section; for example, opportunity costs, the classic guns vs. butter model, the free enterprise economy, or our standard of living. Have students attach a short, two- or three-sentence explanation, with proper sentence structure, to the back of their artwork. Display the cartoons in the classroom.

 Refer to *Inclusion for the Social Studies Classroom Strategies and Activities* in the TCR.

Economic Choices

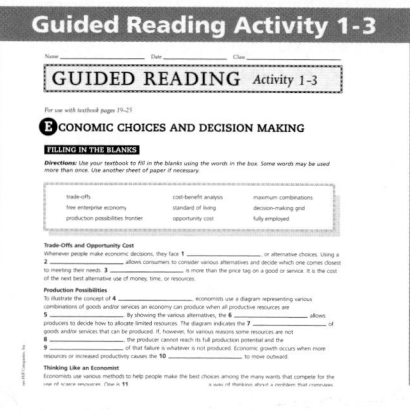

Trade-Offs In this cartoon, the king faces a trade-off between crops and catapults. *What is the opportunity cost of obtaining two more catapults?*

Production Possibilities

A popular model economists use to illustrate the concept of opportunity cost is the **production possibilities frontier,** a diagram representing various combinations of goods and/or services an economy can produce when all productive resources are fully employed. In the classic example shown in **Figure 1.6,** a mythical country called Alpha produces two goods—guns and butter.

Identifying Possible Alternatives

Even though Alpha only produces two goods, the country has a number of alternatives available to it. For example, it could choose to use all of its resources to produce 70 units of guns and 300 units of butter, which is shown as point **a** in **Panel A.** Or, it could shift some of its resources out of gun production and into butter, thereby moving to point **b.** Alpha could even choose to produce at point **c,** which represents all butter and no guns, or at point **e,** which is inside the frontier.

Alpha has many alternatives available to it, which is why the figure is called a production "possibilities" frontier. Eventually though, Alpha will have to settle on a single combination such as point **a, b,** or any other point on or inside the curve, because its resources are limited.

Fully Employed Resources

All points *on* the curve such as **a, b,** and **c** represent *maximum* combinations of output possible if all resources are fully employed. To illustrate, suppose that Alpha is producing at point **a** and the people would like to move to point **d,** which represents the same amount of guns, but more butter.

As long as all resources are fully employed at point **a,** however, there are no extra resources available to produce the extra butter. Therefore, point **d** cannot be reached, nor can any other point outside the curve. This is why the figure is called a production possibilities "frontier"—to indicate the maximum combinations of goods and/or services that can be produced.

CHAPTER 1: WHAT IS ECONOMICS? **21**

Guided Reading Activity 1-3

Visual Instruction

Answer to Caption:
the peasants' crops

Math Practice

Opportunity Cost Gerard has two choices for a summer job. The first opportunity is at a computer manufacturer, where he would earn $10.25 per hour. The second opportunity is with a landscaping company, where he could work and have lunch with three of his closest friends every day. The landscaping job would pay $8.65 per hour. For one 40-hour workweek, what would be the opportunity cost, in dollars, of accepting the landscaping job? *($64.00)* What would be the opportunity cost of accepting the job with the computer manufacturer? *(not working or eating lunch with his friends every day)*

FREE ENTERPRISE ACTIVITY

Point out that in a free enterprise system, the emphasis is on the individual and their economic rights and responsibilities. Identify some roles the individual may play in a free enterprise system, including consumer, producer, owner of factors of production, voting citizen, investor, and saver. Next, have students assume each role, explaining why their assigned role is important in a free enterprise economy and illustrating how their role is interdependent with others. Direct the rest of the class to discuss how the economic rights and responsibilities of individuals overlap with those of businesses.

CURRICULUM CONNECTION

History During World War II, the American economy temporarily produced beyond its production possibilities frontier. Individuals not normally part of the workforce—housewives, retirees, and teenagers—were called on to work, both to replace men serving in the armed forces and to drastically increase production. For a short time, the country actually produced beyond its normal capacity.

Objectives, goals, and answers to the student activity can be found in the **Web Activity Lesson Plan** feature at epp.glencoe.com

L2 Compare and Contrast

Some economists refer to the production possibilities frontier as a curve. Ask students which term they believe is most accurate.

Opportunity Cost

Making Choices The nation incurs opportunity costs when it makes choices. The money spent on defense cannot at the same time be spent on health services; money spent on health services cannot be spent on education, and so on. *Why does every choice involve an opportunity cost?*

Opportunity Cost

Suppose that Alpha was producing at point **a** and that it wanted to move to point **b.** This is clearly possible so long as point **b** is not outside the frontier. As shown in **Panel B,** the opportunity cost of producing the 100 additional units of butter is the 30 units of guns given up.

As you can see, opportunity cost is a general concept that is expressed in terms of trade-offs, or in terms of things given up to get something else. Opportunity cost is not always measured in terms of dollars and cents. For example, you need to balance the time you spend studying and doing homework and spending time with your friends. If you decide to spend extra hours on your homework, the opportunity cost of this action is less time with your friends.

The Cost of Idle Resources

If some resources were not fully employed, then it would be impossible for Alpha to reach its potential. To illustrate, suppose that Alpha was producing at point **b** in **Panel A** when workers in the butter industry decided to go on strike. Butter production would fall, causing total output to change to point **e.** The opportunity cost of the unemployed resources would be the 100 units of lost butter production.

Production at **e** could also be the result of other idle resources, such as factories or land that are available but are not being used. As long as some resources are idle, the country cannot produce on its frontier—which is another way of saying that it cannot reach its full production potential, although it can produce at some point inside it.

Economic Growth

The production possibilities frontier represents potential output at a given point in time. Eventually, however, population may grow, the capital stock may grow, and productivity may increase. If this happens, then Alpha will be able to produce more in the future than it can today.

The effect of economic growth is shown in **Panel C** of **Figure 1.6.** Economic growth made possible by having more resources or increased productivity causes the production possibilities frontier to move outward. Economic growth will eventually allow Alpha to produce at point **d,** which it could not do earlier.

Student Web Activity Visit the *Economics: Principles and Practices* Web site at epp.glencoe.com and click on *Chapter 1—Student Web Activities* to learn more about what economists do.

CRITICAL THINKING

Identifying Central Issues Ask students to find an article on a recent labor dispute. The dispute can be an ongoing strike or lockout, or one that has been recently settled. It can even be a holdout by a star athlete at the beginning of the season. Have students identify and summarize each side's position. Ask them to include in their summary at least one cost and one benefit for each side's argument. Have students present their analyses to the class. Discuss as a class how using a cost-benefit analysis could help an individual or a group decide whether or not to go on strike.

Thinking Like an Economist

Because economists study how people satisfy seemingly unlimited and competing wants with the careful use of scarce resources, they are also concerned with strategies that will help us make the best choices. Some of these strategies are discussed here; others will be discussed in later chapters.

Build Simple Models

One of the most important strategies of economists is the economic model. A model is a simplified theory or a simplified picture of what something is like or how something works. Simple models can often be constructed that reduce complex situations to their most basic elements. To illustrate, the circular flow diagram in **Figure 1.3** is an example of how complex economic activity can be reduced to a simple model.

Another basic model is the production possibilities frontier illustrated in **Figure 1.6.** Realistically, of course, economies are able to produce more than two goods or services, but the concepts of trade-offs and opportunity costs are easier to illustrate if only two products are examined. As a result, simple models such as these are sometimes all that economists need to analyze or describe an actual situation.

It is important to remember that models are based on assumptions, or things that we take for granted as true. We use them as facts even though we can't be sure that they are. For example, you might assume that a restaurant is out of your price range. You might not even try it because you assume you cannot afford it. However, you might be wrong—the prices at the restaurant might be quite reasonable. The quality of a model is no better than the assumptions that it is based on.

It is also important to keep in mind that models can be revised. Economists use models to better understand the past or present and to predict the future. If an economic model results in a prediction that turns out to be right, the model can be used again. If the prediction is wrong, the model might be changed to make better predictions the next time.

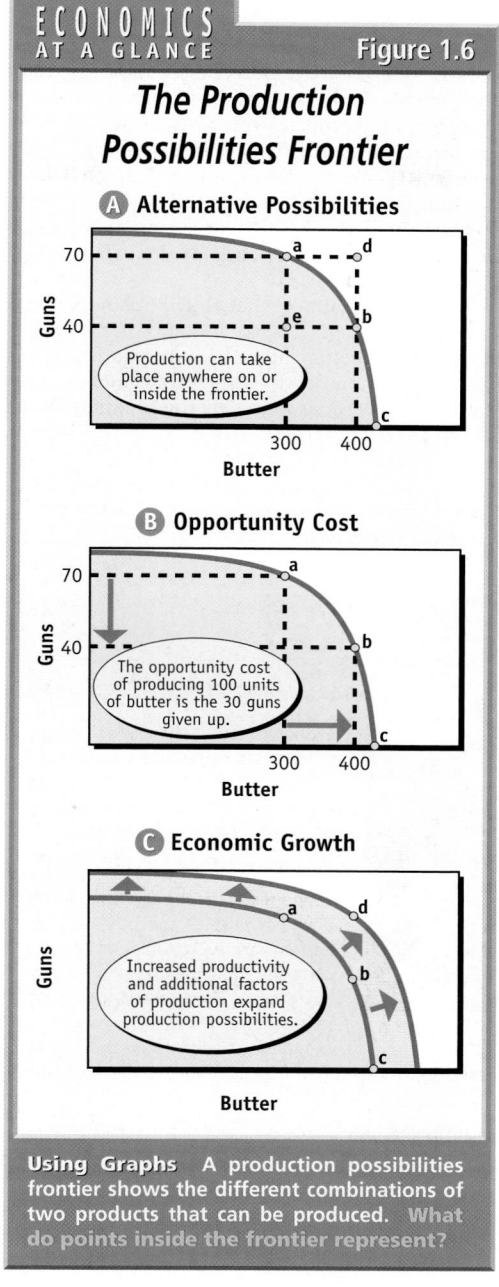

ECONOMICS AT A GLANCE   Figure 1.6

The Production Possibilities Frontier

A Alternative Possibilities

Production can take place anywhere on or inside the frontier.

B Opportunity Cost

The opportunity cost of producing 100 units of butter is the 30 guns given up.

C Economic Growth

Increased productivity and additional factors of production expand production possibilities.

Using Graphs A production possibilities frontier shows the different combinations of two products that can be produced. **What do points inside the frontier represent?**

L2 Cooperative Learning

Organize students into groups. Instruct students to use a decision-making process in order to select an appropriate gift for a high school graduate. Groups should list and consider the advantages and disadvantages of their options. Information should be organized into a grid like that in Figure 1.5. Then have groups discuss their criteria, filling in the grid and finally choosing the best gift to buy. Allow groups to present and justify their decisions to the class.

NIGHTLY BUSINESS REPORT

⊙ **ECONOMICS & YOU**

|||||| Chapter 9
Disc 1, Side 1

Your Role As A Consumer
After students have viewed the segment:
Ask: What is the difference between disposable income and discretionary income?
(disposable: the money left after taxes that is spent on basics; discretionary: the money left over for nonessentials.)

▭▭ Also available in VHS.

ECONOMICS AT A GLANCE

Answer: *different production levels*

EXTENDING THE CONTENT

Economists and Economic Models When economists are asked to help develop economic policy, their suggestions often lead to a great amount of debate. Two of the main reasons economists disagree over policy matters is that the economists themselves may have different assumptions, and/or differing views of the correct economic model to employ. Such disagreements might focus on whether the consumers and businesses have an accurate view of the market, or whether the market is competitive or noncompetitive. Even if economists agree on a model to use, they may disagree about the relevancy of the data to be used within the model. Data collected just 10 years ago may be irrelevant to today's changing economy.

INTERACTIVE ECONOMICS!

CD-ROM

OPPORTUNITY COSTS Have students complete the "Economics Lab" and "Math Practice" sections of Lesson 1 on opportunity costs. Students will determine whether firms have an absolute or a comparative advantage of certain goods. Based on this information, students will decide which goods the firms should produce.

💾 Also supplied in disk format.

③ ASSESS

Assign Section 3 Assessment as homework or as an in-class activity.

💾 Have students use **Interactive Tutor Self-Assessment Software** to review Section 3.

Section Quiz 1-3

Employ Cost-Benefit Analysis

Most economic decisions can be made by using **cost-benefit analysis,** a way of thinking about a problem that compares the costs of an action to the benefits received. This is what Jesse did in the decision-making matrix shown in **Figure 1.5.** This decision can be made subjectively, as when Jesse selected the jeans. Or, the decision can be more formal, especially if the costs of the various alternatives are different.

To illustrate, suppose that you like choices A and B equally well. If B costs less, however, then it would be the better choice because you would get more satisfaction per dollar spent. Businesses make investment decisions in exactly this manner, choosing to invest in projects which give the highest return per dollar spent. Cost-benefit studies, like the one described in the cover story, can also be used to evaluate the effectiveness of many public assistance programs.

Careers

Economist

Economists study the way society distributes scarce resources to produce goods and services. They carry on inquiries, collect and analyze data, and observe economic trends.

The Work

Economists in the private sector advise businesses and other organizations on such topics as energy costs, inflation, imports, and employment levels. Those who work for various government agencies may study economic conditions in the United States or in other countries to estimate the economic effects of new legislation or public policies.

Qualifications

Graduate training is required for most economists in the private sector. Individuals who wish to secure an entry-level job in the federal government must have a bachelor's degree, with a focus on economics and on statistics, accounting, or calculus.

24 UNIT 1 FUNDAMENTAL ECONOMIC CONCEPTS

Take Small, Incremental Steps

Finally, and whenever possible, it also helps to make decisions by taking small, incremental steps toward the final goal. This is especially valuable whenever we are unsure of the exact, or total, cost involved. If the cost turns out to be larger than we anticipated, then the resulting decision can be reversed, without too much being lost.

For example, if someone offers you a hot beverage, it might be best to take a small sip first. This will allow you to find out if the beverage is cool enough to drink, without paying too high a price if it is not. Few decisions are all-or-nothing decisions—sometimes it helps to do a little bit at a time.

The Road Ahead

The study of economics does more than explain how people deal with scarcity. Economics also includes the study of how things are made, bought, sold, and used. It helps answer such questions as, Where do these products come from? Who makes them? How are they made? How do they get to the stores? Who buys them? It provides insight as to how incomes are earned and spent, how jobs are created, and how the economy works on a daily basis. It also provides a more detailed understanding of a **free enterprise economy**—one in which consumers and privately owned businesses, rather than the government, make the majority of the WHAT, HOW, and FOR WHOM decisions.

Topics and Issues

The study of economics will provide a working knowledge of property rights, competition, supply and demand, the price system, and the economic incentives that make the American economy function. Along the way, topics such as unemployment, the business cycle, inflation, productivity, and economic growth will be covered. The role of business, labor, and government in the American economy also will be examined, along with the relationship of the United States economy to the international community. All of these have a bearing on our

INTERDISCIPLINARY CONNECTIONS ACTIVITY

The Environment Determining value can be very difficult when economic decisions are related to environmental concerns. When the Northern Spotted Owl was declared a threatened species, the owls' nesting sites and surrounding locations became protected by the government. This helped the chances for the owls' survival, but it greatly impacted the logging industry in parts of the northwest. Because fewer trees could be cut down, logging decreased dramatically. Many workers lost their jobs in an area with few other economic opportunities. Have students report on another case in which environmental government policy impacted the economy. Discuss how the value of the environment might be weighed against other economic concerns. **BLOCK SCHEDULING**

standard of living—the quality of life based on the possession of the necessities and luxuries that make life easier. You will learn how we measure the value of our production and how productivity helps determine our standard of living. You will find, however, that the way the American people make economic decisions is not the only way to make these decisions. Economists have identified three basic kinds of economic systems. You will analyze these systems in Chapter 2.

Economics for Citizenship

The study of economics helps us to become better decision makers—both in our personal lives and in the voting booths. Economic issues often are debated during political campaigns, and we need to understand the issues before deciding which candidate to support. Most of today's political problems have important economic aspects: How important is it that we balance the federal budget? How can we best keep inflation in check? What methods can we use to strengthen our economy? The study of economics will not provide you with clear-cut answers to all questions, of course, but it will give you a better understanding of the issues involved.

Making the Rational Choice

You have already learned in this chapter that economists study how decisions are made. Every time a choice is made something is given up. Rational choice is taking the things with greater value and giving up those with lesser value. That's the rational thing to do.

But which things have greater value? If everyone felt the same about what they did and did not want, deciding how to use our resources would be simple; the problem is we don't all agree. When you make a decision for yourself alone, it doesn't make much difference how others feel. But many of your decisions will affect other people who may not share your ideas. Making the best choices for groups of people is hard to do.

Textbook economics can be divided into neat sections for study, but the real world is not so orderly. Society is dynamic and things are always changing. In addition, people have different degrees of ambition, strength, and luck. Opinions also differ, and some issues never seem to be settled.

In practice, the world of economics is complex and the road ahead is bumpy. Studying and understanding economics, however, is vital to our understanding of how the world around us works.

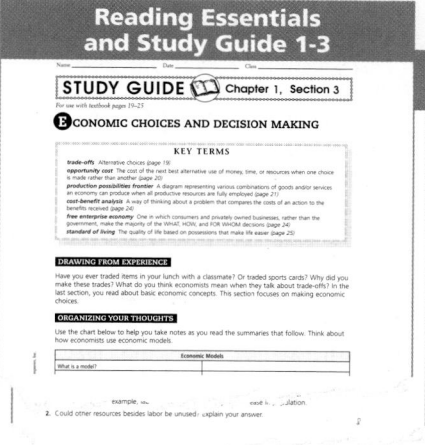

Reading Essentials and Study Guide 1-3

Enrich

The dropout rate among high school students generally declines during a recession. Have students use the concept of opportunity cost to explain why this might happen.

CLOSE

Have students discuss how the production possibilities frontier might change if new technology were applied to the production of guns but not to the production of butter. *(More guns could be produced than before; a new graph would show the frontier increasing along the axis showing guns, but not along the axis showing butter.)*

Section 3 Assessment

Checking for Understanding

1. **Main Idea** Using your notes from the graphic organizer activity on page 19, explain what people try to achieve when they make decisions or trade-offs.

2. **Key Terms** Define trade-offs, opportunity cost, production possibilities frontier, cost-benefit analysis, free enterprise economy, standard of living.

3. **Describe** the relationship between trade-offs and opportunity costs.

4. **List** the decision-making strategies that economists use.

5. **Explain** why the study of economics is important to the American free enterprise system.

Applying Economic Concepts

6. **Opportunity Costs** Identify several possible uses of your time that will be available to you after school today. What will you actually do, and what will be the opportunity cost of your decision? Explain how your decision will or will not affect your friends and members of your family.

Critical Thinking

7. **Making Generalizations** Study the decision-making grid on page 20. Explain the advantages of using such a grid to evaluate alternatives.

    Practice and **assess** key social studies skills with the *Glencoe Skillbuilder Interactive Workbook, Level 2.*

CHAPTER 1: WHAT IS ECONOMICS? **25**

Section 3 Assessment Answers

1. When making economic decisions, people try to get the most value for their investment, whether it be time, money, or something else.

2. All vocabulary terms are defined in the text.

3. All economic decisions involve trade-offs. The opportunity cost of a choice is the cost of the next best use of money, time, or resources.

4. circular flow diagram, production possibilities frontier, cost-benefit analysis

5. Economic issues are an important part of many political campaigns. An understanding of the issues will help a citizen decide how to vote in an election.

6. Answers should reflect an understanding of the concept of opportunity costs.

7. Students should recognize that such a grid helps organize and explain the various choices when decision making.

CRITICAL THINKING
Skill

Sequencing and Categorizing Information

Sequencing involves placing facts in the order in which they occur. *Categorizing* entails organizing information into groups of related facts and ideas. Both actions help you deal with large quantities of information in an understandable way.

Learning the Skill

Follow these steps to learn sequencing and categorizing skills:

- Look for dates or clue words that provide you with a chronological order: *in 2004, the late 1990s, first, then, finally,* and so on.

Steelworker tends blast furnace

- If the information does not happen in sequence, you may categorize it instead. To do so, look for information with similar characteristics.
- List these characteristics, or categories, as the headings on a chart.
- As you read, fill in details under the proper category on the chart.

Practicing the Skill

Read the excerpts that follow, compare the information they contain, then answer the questions.

Excerpt A

In the 1950s and early 1960s, the United States dominated the world steel market. However, construction of new facilities in other countries hurt the domestic steel industry in the 1980s. During the next ten years, U.S. steel firms improved production methods and reduced hourly wages. By 1990 the number of work-hours required to produce a ton of steel fell from 10.5 in 1980 to just 5.3 in 1990. Trade protection, beginning with the 1947 General Agreement on Tariffs and Trades, and later agreements protected many American jobs.

Excerpt B

Competition is the rivalry among producers or sellers of similar goods to win more business by offering the lowest prices or best quality. In many industries effective competition requires a large number of independent buyers and sellers. This large number of competitors means that no one company can noticeably affect the price of a particular product. Competition also requires that companies can enter or exit any industry they choose. Those who feel they could make more profit in another industry are free to get out of the industry they are in.

1. Which passage's information can be organized sequentially? List the main ideas in chronological order.
2. What categories can you use to organize the information in the other excerpt?

Answers to Practicing the Skill

1. Excerpt A; the U.S. dominated the world steel market (1950s, 1960s), foreign competition cut into U.S. dominance (1980s), U.S. steel production improved (1990), work-hours required to produce a ton of steel dropped in the U.S. (1990), beginning in 1947 trade agreements protected U.S. jobs.
2. Answers will vary, but should reflect a logical organization and placement of facts.

Section 1

Scarcity and the Science of Economics (pages 5–10)

- The basic economic problem of **scarcity** is due to the combination of people's seemingly unlimited wants and relatively scarce resources.

- In a world of scarce resources, There Is No Such Thing As A Free Lunch (TINSTAAFL).

- Because of scarcity, society has to decide WHAT, HOW, and FOR WHOM to produce.

- **Land, capital, labor,** and **entrepreneurs** are the four **factors of production** required to produce the things that people use.

- Entrepreneurs are risk-taking individuals who go into business in order to make a profit; they organize the other factors of production.

- The scope of economics deals with description, analysis, explanation, and prediction.

Section 2

Basic Economic Concepts (pages 12–17)

- **Consumers** use **goods** and **services** to satisfy their **wants** and **needs.**

- Something has **value** when it has **utility** and is relatively scarce.

- Wealth consists of products that are scarce, useful, and transferable to others, but wealth does not include services, which are intangible.

- **Markets** link individuals and businesses in the circular flow of economic activity; the factors of production are traded in **factor markets;** goods and services are traded in the **product markets.**

- **Productivity** and investments in **human capital** help economic growth; investments in human capital are among the most profitable of all investments.

- Increases in **specialization** and **division of labor** cause more **economic interdependence.**

Section 3

Economic Choices and Decision Making (pages 19–25)

- The **opportunity cost** of doing something is the next best alternative, or **trade-off,** that you give up.

- A decision-making grid can be used to help evaluate alternatives.

- A **production possibilities frontier** shows the various possible combinations of output that can be produced when all resources are fully employed; production inside the frontier occurs when some resources are idle or are not being used to their maximum capability.

- When economic growth takes place, the production possibilities frontier shifts outward, showing that more products are produced than before.

- The economic way of thinking involves simplification with model building, **cost-benefit analysis** to evaluate alternatives, and incremental decision making.

- The study of economics will make you a better decision maker and will help you to understand the world around you; however, the study of economics will not tell you which decisions to make.

- The study of economics helps people understand how a **free enterprise economy** makes the WHAT, HOW, and FOR WHOM decisions.

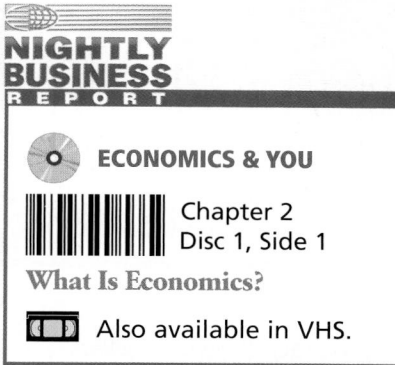

Using the Chapter 1 Summary

Use the Chapter 1 Summary to preview, review, condense, or reteach the chapter.

Preview/Review

🔵 Vocabulary PuzzleMaker CD-ROM reinforces Key Terms.

💾 Interactive Tutor Self-Assessment Software provides a review of Chapter 1 content.

Condense

🎧 🗂 Have students listen to the Chapter 1 Audio Program. Spanish also available.

🗂 🗂 Assign the Chapter 1 Audio Program Activity and give students the Chapter 1 Audio Program Test.

🗂 🗂 Have students complete the Guided Reading Activities and Reading Essentials and Study Guides for Chapter 1.

Reteach

🗂 🗂 Have students complete Reteaching Activity 1 in the TCR. Spanish also available.

Teacher's Notes / Internet Bookmarks

_____

_____

_____

_____

_____

_____

_____

_____

GLENCOE
TECHNOLOGY

Use **MindJogger Videoquiz** to review the Chapter 1 content.

Have students visit the Web site at epp.glencoe.com to review Chapter 1 and take the **Self-Check Quiz.**

Identifying Key Terms

1. consumer goods
2. value
3. services
4. scarcity
5. opportunity cost
6. human capital
7. utility
8. capital goods
9. factors of production
10. consumers

Reviewing the Facts

Section 1

1. having only limited resources to meet seemingly unlimited wants
2. WHAT to produce? HOW to produce? FOR WHOM to produce?
3. land: land itself and natural resources; capital: school building, computers, financial capital; labor: teachers, other workers, publishers; entrepreneurs: people who devise new products and methods of delivery of educational material.
4. It deals with people's behavior as they cope with scarcity.

Section 2

5. Consumers use goods and services to satisfy their wants and needs.
6. because they are intangible and it is difficult to measure their value accurately
7. Product markets are producers offering goods and services for sale.

Self-Check Quiz Visit the *Economics: Principles and Practices* Web site at epp.glencoe.com and click on *Chapter 1—Self-Check Quizzes* to prepare for the chapter test.

Identifying Key Terms

Write the key term that best completes the following sentences.

capital goods	opportunity cost
consumer goods	scarcity
consumers	services
factors of production	utility
human capital	value

1. Economic products designed to satisfy people's wants and needs are called _____ .
2. The _____ of a CD player can be expressed in dollars and cents.
3. Haircuts, repairs to home appliances, and entertainment are examples of _____ .
4. _____ arises because society does not have enough resources to produce all the things people would like to have.
5. The _____ of going to a football game instead of working would include the money not earned at your job.
6. _____ is the sum of the skills, abilities, health, and motivation of people.
7. _____ is another name for the capacity of a product to be useful.
8. The only factors of production that are themselves the result of earlier production are _____ .
9. Land, capital, labor, and entrepreneurs are _____ .
10. People who use goods and services to satisfy their wants and needs are called _____ .

Reviewing the Facts

Section 1 (pages 5–10)

1. **Identify** the cause of scarcity.
2. **List** the three basic economic questions that every society must face.
3. **Describe** the factors of production required to deliver a service like education.
4. **Explain** why economics is considered a social science.

Section 2 (pages 12–17)

5. **Describe** the relationship between goods, services, and consumers.
6. **Explain** why services are excluded from the measure of wealth.
7. **Distinguish** between product markets and factor markets.
8. **Explain** why economists argue that productivity is important.

Section 3 (pages 19–25)

9. **Describe** the nature of an opportunity cost.
10. **Identify** the economic concept illustrated by the production possibilities frontier.
11. **Describe** incremental decision making.
12. **Explain** why economic education is important.

Thinking Critically

1. **Understanding Cause and Effect** Suppose that Alpha, shown in Figure 1.6 on page 23, decided to produce more guns and less butter. What would Alpha have to do to make the change? What would be the opportunity cost of producing more guns? What conditions would have to be met for the new mix of guns and butter to be on the production possibilities frontier?

Factor markets are productive resources being bought and sold.
8. Productivity is the efficient use of productive resources. The more efficiently productive resources are used, the greater the number of goods and services that are produced.

Section 3

9. the cost of the next best alternative use of money, time, or resources when one choice is made rather than another
10. opportunity cost

11. making a decision in small stages or steps so that the decision can be reversed without too much being lost
12. It helps people become better decision makers.

Thinking Critically

1. Resources have to be shifted from guns to butter. The opportunity cost of producing more guns is the production of less butter. All of Alpha's resources would have to be employed.

28

2. Understanding Cause and Effect Copy the two diagrams of the production possibilities frontiers shown below. Then, write captions that explain what each diagram is showing.

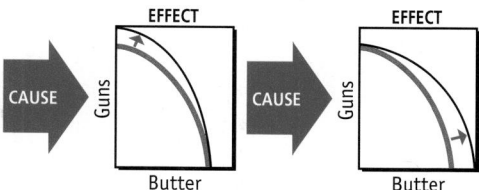

Applying Economic Concepts

1. **Scarcity** What three choices must a society make because of scarcity?

2. **Utility** How is a product's utility related to its value?

3. **Cost-Benefit Analysis** How would you apply the concept of cost-benefit analysis to the decision to finish high school? To further your education?

Math Practice

A city administrator with a $100,000 annual budget is trying to decide between fixing potholes or directing traffic at several busy intersections after school. Studies have shown that 15 cars hit potholes every week, causing average damages of $200. Collisions at the intersections are less frequent, averaging one per month at an average cost of $6,000, although none have ever caused injuries or deaths. Use this information to answer the following questions.

1. What are the annual costs from the pothole damage?

2. What are the annual costs due to damage from collisions?

3. Given the size of the annual budget, make your recommendation as to which project should be undertaken. Explain you answer in terms of dollar benefits per dollar spent.

Thinking Like an Economist

Use a problem-solving process to gather information about the alternatives, trade-offs, and opportunity costs facing the city administrator. List and consider possible options the administrator may choose to implement. Consider the advantages and disadvantages of implementing the possible solutions.

Technology Skill

Using a Spreadsheet Keep track of your economic decisions for one week. Use your data to create a spreadsheet, highlighting your weekly spending habits.

1. In cells B1 through E1, type *Food, Clothing, Entertainment,* and *Other.* In cell F1, type *Total.*

2. In cells A2 through A8, type the days of the week, starting with *Monday* in cell A2. In cell A9, type *Total.*

3. In cells B2 through E2, enter the amount spent in each category on Monday.

4. In cell F2, use a formula such as =SUM(B2:E2) to calculate total expenditures on Monday. Click and drag this formula to cells F3 through F8 to find the other weekday sums.

5. Compute total expenditures for cells B9–F9.

Building Skills

Sequencing and Categorizing Information
Identify a reasonably large purchase you recently made or are about to make. What are the trade-offs involved, and what are the criteria you use to evaluate the alternatives? On a separate sheet of paper, illustrate your decision in the form of a decision-making grid like the one below.

	Decision-Making Grid			
Alternatives	Criteria 1	Criteria 2	Criteria 3	Criteria 4

 Practice and **assess** key social studies skills with the *Glencoe Skillbuilder Interactive Workbook, Level 2.*

Thinking Like an Economist

Answers may include a solution that will split the budget between the two problems. Students may look at the problems from the standpoint of which is more likely to threaten people's lives.

Technology Skill

Check students' answers for accuracy.

Building Skills

Answers should reflect an understanding of opportunity costs and trade-offs. Grids should contain elements to aid in the decision-making process.

? Bonus Test Question

Suppose that scientists invented a car that ran efficiently on water. Explain, in terms of scarcity, how this might affect the price of water. Explain, in terms of utility, how this might affect the price of gasoline. *(The more water that is needed, the scarcer it becomes, and so the price of water might go up. The less gasoline that is needed, the less utility it has, and so the price of gasoline might go down.)*

---

2. The diagram on the left shows increase in productivity/resources in gun industry; the diagram on right shows increase on resources/productivity in butter industry.

Applying Economic Concepts

1. WHAT to produce? HOW to produce? FOR WHOM to produce?

2. For a product to have value, it must have utility.

3. Make a matrix listing choices and the costs and benefits (including time, money, and satisfaction) of each educational choice.

Math Practice

1. $156,000

2. $72,000

3. Fixing the potholes is a better economic choice since for every dollar spent, the city would get $1.56 back in benefits. For every dollar spent in directing traffic at intersections, the city would get $0.72 in benefits.

① FOCUS

The purpose of this activity is to provide students with a concrete example of the problem of scarcity and hands-on experience in answering the three fundamental questions of economics.

② TEACH

- Prepare by filling several lunch bags each with three chocolate bars, five marshmallows, and two graham crackers, or some other uneven combination of ingredients. Label each bag "Resources."
- Begin the workshop organizing students into groups of three or four. Distribute a "Resources" bag to each group. Then direct students to follow the steps.
- After students examine the contents of their bags, make sure they understand what "s'mores" are and how they are made.
- As students conduct the workshop activity, offer mini-lectures at the appropriate points on the problem of scarcity (Step 1) and on the three fundamental questions of economics: what to produce (Step 5), how to produce it (Step 6), and how to distribute what is produced (Step 6).

ECONOMICS WORKSHOP IN ACTION

Working with Resource Scarcity

From the classroom of . . .
Douglas Ide
Mt. Ararat High School
Topsham, Maine

Our resources are limited while our wants are relatively unlimited. In this workshop, you will experiment with methods to overcome the problem of scarcity. You will also answer the three fundamental questions of economics: what to produce, how to produce it, and how to distribute what you produce. Finally, you will analyze why it is important to determine the answers to these questions.

Setting Up the Workshop

For this activity you will need:
- small paper "lunch" bags
- miniature chocolate bars
- marshmallows
- graham crackers

Procedures

STEP 1

Review the concept of scarcity with your group. Remember that scarcity is the economic term that describes a situation where there are not enough products available to satisfy people's needs or wants. Discuss why scarcity *always* exists.

STEP 2

Review the concept of production. Note that production—the creation of goods and services—requires four factors.

The Four Factors of Production:
- Natural Resources
- Labor
- Capital
- Entrepreneurship

STEP 3

Your teacher will provide you with your group's "resources." Do not open the bag.

Participating in Economics

Scarcity in the Classroom Organize the class into groups, or keep the same groupings from the workshop activity. Have each group choose a single element in the classroom—a chair, for example, a piece of chalk, a brick in the wall—and focus on it as an economic good. Allow groups 15 minutes to develop brief narratives of their chosen good's production history, explaining how its manufacturer had to confront scarcity and answer the three fundamental questions of economics. Students should record their narratives in note form, which a group representative can consult while relating his or her group's analysis to the class.

STEP 4

Read and discuss these instructions:

This bag contains your resources. You must use these resources and no other, but you may use them in any way you choose. The resources are exactly what they appear to be: chocolate, marshmallows, and graham crackers; they may not be used to represent anything other than that.

STEP 5

Open your bag and study the contents. Discuss what item or items your group can produce with these "resources." Due to **scarcity,** your group may have difficulty in producing one complete unit of "product" for each group member.

STEP 6

Compare the available resources in your bag to the "demand" for the finished product. How many units can be produced? How will you produce them? How will you distribute them? (e.g. Will each member of the group receive a completed unit, or will only some of the members receive the product? If not everyone receives one, how will you determine who receives one?)

Summary Activity

Once you've produced the product, answer the following questions. Take notes as you determine the answers.

1. What was your first thought when you opened the bag and examined the amount of resources?

2. What did you then have to decide?

3. Why did you have to think about how to produce them, and how they would be distributed?

4. Were each of the four factors of production used in making your product?

5. What resources were used?

6. What type of skills and tools did the workers need?

7. Create a chart showing the factors of production that are combined into different consumer products that the members of your group buy.

The world's oldest "industry" is flint knapping (chipping) to make tools, which originated some 2.5 million years ago in what is now Ethiopia. These ancient crafts-people had to deal with scarcity (limits of stone, time, and so on) and "answer" the same fundamental economic questions that people do today.

③ ASSESS

Have students write paragraphs that explain how the problem of scarcity impacts a local manufacturing business of their own choosing.

④ CLOSE

Invite student comments on this thought: "The basic ideas of economics are really quite simple."

ECONOMIC SURVIVAL
A FINANCIAL SIMULATION

To help students learn to manage their own finances, have the class play the game **Economic Survival: A Financial Simulation** in which each student enters the workforce, rents an apartment, and deals with everyday events.

Summary Activity Answers

Answers will vary. For question 1, reward thoughtful answers and indicate for students how their responses relate to the problem of scarcity and/or the three fundamental questions of economics. For question 2, reward responses that indicate an understanding of the three fundamental questions of economics. For question 3, students should demonstrate an awareness of how scarcity forces producers to address the three fundamental questions of economics.

Chapter 2 Resource Manager

SECTION RESOURCES

Daily Objectives	Reproducible Resources	Technology/Multimedia Resources
Section 1 **Economic Systems** 1. Describe the characteristics of the traditional, command, and market economies. 2. Explain the advantages and disadvantages of the traditional, command, and market economies.	Reproducible Lesson Plan 2-1 Daily Lecture Notes 2-1 Guided Reading Activity 2-1 Reading Essentials and Study Guide 2-1 Section Quiz 2-1*	Daily Focus Transparency 6 Interactive Tutor Self-Assessment Software ExamView® Pro Testmaker Presentation Plus!
Section 2 **Evaluating Economic Performance** 1. Describe the basic economic and social goals used to evaluate economic performance. 2. Evaluate the tradeoffs among economic and social goals.	Reproducible Lesson Plan 2-2 Daily Lecture Notes 2-2 Guided Reading Activity 2-2 Reading Essentials and Study Guide 2-2 Section Quiz 2-2*	Daily Focus Transparency 8 Interactive Tutor Self-Assessment Software ExamView® Pro Testmaker Presentation Plus!
Section 3 **Capitalism and Economic Freedom** 1. Explore the characteristics of a free enterprise system. 2. Describe the role of the entrepreneur, the consumer, and government in a free enterprise economy.	Reproducible Lesson Plan 2-3 Daily Lecture Notes 2-3 Guided Reading Activity 2-3 Reading Essentials and Study Guide 2-3 Section Quiz 2-3*	Daily Focus Transparency 7 Vocabulary PuzzleMaker CD-ROM Interactive Tutor Self-Assessment Software ExamView® Pro Testmaker Presentation Plus!

*Also available in Spanish

 Transparency   CD-ROM   Software   Blackline Master

 Videodisc   Audio Program   Videocassette

0:00 OUT OF TIME?
Assign the Chapter 2 Audio Program activity and test.

 Block Schedule

Activities that are particularly suited to use within the block scheduling framework are identified throughout this chapter by the following designation: **BLOCK SCHEDULING**

KEY TO ABILITY LEVELS

Teaching strategies have been coded for varying learning styles and abilities.

L1 BASIC activities for all students
L2 AVERAGE activities for average to above-average students
L3 CHALLENGING activities for above-average students
ELL ENGLISH LANGUAGE LEARNER activities

Chapter 2 Resource Manager

ACTIVITY

From the Classroom of...

**Suzanne Johnston
Jeff Tech
Reynoldsville, PA**

Characteristics of Economic Systems

To help my students review the differences between traditional, command, and market economies, I have them play a game. I take two different colored sets of index cards and prepare two identical lists of characteristics for the systems—the advantages and disadvantages of each of the systems. I place one characteristic on each card. The characteristics I choose come from the chart on page 38 of their textbook. Students are then organized into two teams. They decide as a group which characteristic belongs to which economic system and then individually place their cards into one of three manila folders I have taped to the board, which are marked "traditional," "command," or "market."

I then take the cards out and read them. Because the teams used different colored cards, it is easy to identify which team you are dealing with. A scorekeeper keeps track of the number of correct answers and gives each team a point for each correct answer. The team with the most points gets a bonus point added to their grade.

National Council on Economic Education

THE **Economics**America AND **Economics**International PROGRAMS

Voluntary National Content Standards in Economics
Emphasized in Chapter 2

Content Standard 3

Content Standard 16

For a complete listing of NCEE Standards and entire text correlation, see Teacher pages in front of book.

Resources Available from NCEE
- Capstone: The Nation's High School Economics Course
- United States History: Eyes on the Economy
- Economics and Entrepreneurship, Teaching Strategies
- Entrepreneurship in the U.S. Economy
- Civics and Government: Focus on Economics
- Economics in Transition: Command to Market

To order these materials or to contact your state Council on Economic Education about workshops and programs, call 1-800-338-1192 or visit www.nationalcouncil.org

Chapter 2 Resource Manager

TEACHING TRANSPARENCY

Economic Concept Transparency 4: Economic Systems

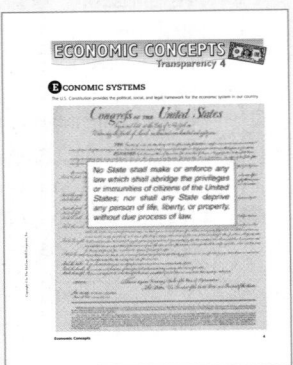

APPLICATION AND ENRICHMENT

Consumer Application Activity 2

Free Enterprise Activity 2

APPLICATION AND ENRICHMENT

Enrichment Activity 2

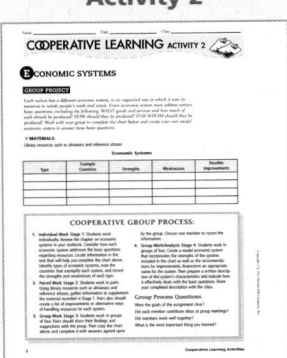

Cooperative Learning Activity 2

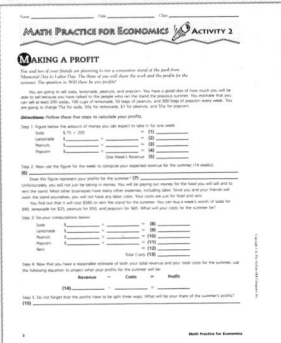

Math Practice Activity 2

Economic Cartoon 2

Primary and Secondary Source Reading 2

REVIEW AND REINFORCEMENT

Economic Vocabulary Activity 2

Reteaching Activity 2

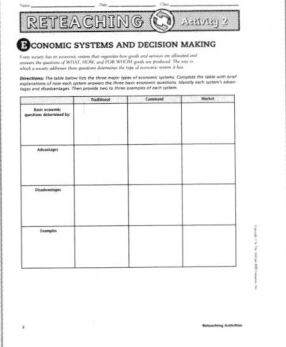

Critical Thinking Activity 2

Reinforcing Economic Skill 11

Chapter 2 Resource Manager

ASSESSMENT AND EVALUATION

Chapter 2 Test Form A

Chapter 2 Test Form B

Performance Assessment Activity 2

ExamView® Pro Testmaker

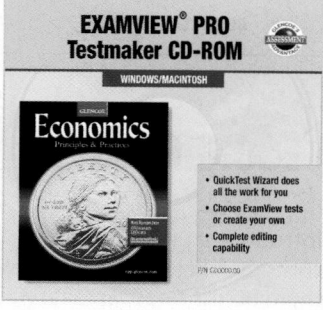

SPANISH RESOURCES

The following Spanish language materials are available in the Spanish Resources binder:

 Spanish Economic Vocabulary Activities

 Spanish Reteaching Activities

 Spanish Section Quizzes

 Spanish Economic Concepts Transparencies

Also available:

  Spanish Chapter 2 Audio Program Activity and Test

TECHNOLOGY/MULTIMEDIA

- Vocabulary PuzzleMaker CD-ROM
- Interactive Tutor Self-Assessment Software
- ExamView® Pro Testmaker
- Audio Program (English or Spanish)
- NBR Economics & You Video Program (English or Spanish)
- MindJogger Videoquiz
- Interactive Economics! CD-ROM
- Presentation Plus!
- TeacherWorks CD-ROM
- Glencoe Skillbuilder Interactive Workbook CD-ROM, Level 2

ECONOMICS Online

Use our Web site for additional resources. All essential content is covered in the Student Edition.

You and your students can visit epp.glencoe.com, the Web site companion to **Economics: Principles and Practices.** This innovative integration of electronic and print media offers your students a wealth of opportunities. The student text directs students to the Web site for the following options:

- **Chapter Overviews**
- **Student Web Activities**
- **Self-Check Quizzes**
- **Textbook Updates**

Answers are provided for you in the Web Activity Lesson Plan. Additional Web resources and interactive puzzles are also available.

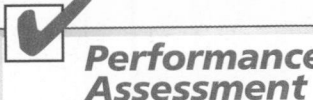
ECONOMICS
Online

Introduce students to chapter content and key terms by having them access **Chapter Overview 2** at epp.glencoe.com

NIGHTLY BUSINESS
R E P O R T

 ECONOMICS & YOU

 Chapter 3
Disc 1, Side 1

Economic Systems and the American Economy

After viewing this segment, students should be able to:
- Explain how a free enterprise system works.

 Also available in VHS.

GLENCOE
TECHNOLOGY

 Use **MindJogger Videoquiz** to preview the Chapter 2 content.

Economic Systems and Decision Making

Economics & You

In **Chapter 2**, you will learn how economic systems differ and what makes up the major characteristics of the United States market system. To learn more about how economic systems operate, view the Chapter 3 video lesson:

Economic Systems and the American Economy

A wide range of choices is characteristic of a market economy.

ECONOMICS
Online

Chapter Overview Visit the *Economics: Principles and Practices* Web site at epp.glencoe.com and click on **Chapter 2—Chapter Overviews** to preview chapter information.

✚ EXTRA CREDIT PROJECT

Organize students into groups of three or four. Direct groups to develop a lesson plan and teaching materials for a 30-minute class, suitable for junior high students, titled "Free Enterprise—The American Economic System." (See Section 3 CLOSE activity.)

Economic Systems

Study Guide

Main Idea
An economic system is a set of rules that governs what goods and services to produce, how to produce them, and for whom they are produced.

Reading Strategy
Graphic Organizer As you read the section, complete a graphic organizer like the one below to identify ways in which a market economy differs from, and is similar to, a command economy.

Market economy
Similarities
Command economy

Key Terms
economy, economic system, traditional economy, command economy, market economy

Objectives
After studying this section, you will be able to:
1. **Describe** the characteristics of the traditional, command, and market economies.
2. **Explain** the advantages and disadvantages of the traditional, command, and market economies.

Applying Economic Concepts
Tradition Tradition plays a stabilizing role in our lives. Even the U.S. economy, characterized by freedom and competition, has some elements of tradition.

Cover Story

Bombay, India

McDonald's in India

The Golden Arches finally have arrived in India, but if you get a Big Mac Attack, you're still out of luck. . . . In coming to this predominately Hindu nation, where cows are sacred and most people don't eat beef, McDonald's Corp. ditched the Big Mac for an Indian stand-in, the Maharaja Mac. That's two all-mutton patties, special sauce, lettuce, cheese, pickles and onions, all on a sesame-seed bun.

—*The Wall Street Journal,* October 14, 1996

The survival of any society depends on its ability to provide food, clothing, and shelter for its people. Because these societies face scarcity, decisions concerning WHAT, HOW, and FOR WHOM to produce must be made.

All societies have something else in common. They have an **economy,** or **economic system**—an organized way of providing for the wants and needs of their people. The way in which these provisions are made determines the type of economic system they have. Three major kinds of economic systems exist—traditional, command, and market. Most countries in the world can be identified with one of these systems.

Traditional Economies

Many of our actions spring from habit and custom. Why, for example, do so many Americans eat turkey on Thanksgiving? Why does the bride toss the bouquet at a wedding? Why do most people shake hands when they meet, or leave tips in restaurants? These practices have generally been handed down from one generation to the next and have become tradition—they are a part of American culture.

CHAPTER 2: ECONOMIC SYSTEMS AND DECISION MAKING **33**

RESOURCE MANAGER

Reproducible Masters
- Reproducible Lesson Plan 2-1
- Daily Lecture Notes 2-1
- Guided Reading Activity 2-1
- Reading Essentials and Study Guide 2-1
- Section Quiz 2-1

Transparencies
- Daily Focus Transparency 6

Multimedia
- Interactive Tutor Self-Assessment Software
- Examview® Pro Testmaker
- Presentation Plus!

2 TEACH

Objectives, goals, and answers to the student activity can be found in the **Web Activity Lesson Plan** feature at epp.glencoe.com

L1 Illustrating Ideas

Have students use library resources to find visual images that illustrate each of the three economic systems. Call on volunteers to present and justify their selections in an oral report. **ELL**

Visual Instruction

Answer to Caption:
ritual, habit, custom

In a society with a **traditional economy,** the allocation of scarce resources, and nearly all other economic activity, stems from ritual, habit, or custom. Habit and custom also dictate most social behavior. Individuals are not free to make decisions based on what they want or would like to have. Instead, their roles are defined by the customs of their elders and ancestors.

Examples

Many societies—such as the central African Mbuti, the Australian Aborigines, and other indigenous peoples around the world—are examples of traditional economies. The Inuits of northern Canada in the 1800s provide an especially interesting case of a traditional economy.

For generations, Inuit parents taught their children how to survive in a harsh climate, make tools, fish, and hunt. Their children, in turn,

Traditional Economy

Way of Life This woman uses the methods for weaving passed on by her ancestors. *What drives economic activity in a traditional economy?*

Student Web Activity Visit the *Economics: Principles and Practices* Web site at epp.glencoe.com and click on *Chapter 2—Student Web Activities* for an activity on the role of tradition in Inuit society.

taught these skills to the next generation. The Inuit hunted, and it was traditional to share the spoils of the hunt with other families. If a walrus or bear was taken, hunters divided the kill evenly into as many portions as there were heads of families in the hunting party. The hunter most responsible for the kill had first choice, the second hunter to help with the kill chose next, and so on.

Later, members of the hunting party shared their portions with other families, because the Inuit shared freely and generously with one another. The hunter had the honor of the kill and the respect of the village, rather than a physical claim to the entire kill. Because of this tradition of sharing, and as long as skilled hunters lived in the community, a village could survive the long harsh winters. This custom was partially responsible for the Inuit's survival for thousands of years.

Advantages

The main strength of a traditional economy is that everyone knows which role to play. Little uncertainty exists over WHAT to produce. If you are born into a family of hunters, you hunt. If you are born into a family of farmers, you farm. Likewise, little uncertainty exists over HOW to produce, because you do everything the same way your parents did.

Finally, the FOR WHOM question is determined by the customs and traditions of the society. Life is generally stable, predictable, and continuous.

Disadvantages

The main drawback of the traditional economy is that it tends to discourage new ideas and new ways of doing things. The strict roles in a traditional society have the effect of punishing people

---

MEETING SPECIAL NEEDS ACTIVITY

Learning Disability For students who have trouble with reading, consider that visual processing problems often impair a student's ability to recall words by sight, affecting reading and comprehension. Confusion between similar words is common because of weaknesses in visual attention to detail or visual memory problems. In private sessions, have students read aloud two paragraphs from this section. Note if they confuse "from" and "form" or "saw" and "was." Encourage students to reread and self-correct their mistakes.

📁 Refer to *Inclusion for the Social Studies Classroom Strategies and Activities* in the TCR.

TEACHING CAPITALISM IN RUSSIA

In Nadeshda Shilyayeva's first-grade class, the words of the day are "profit" and "inventory." As the kindly teacher bounces her pointer along the curly blackboard script, her 26 students at School 139 sing the syllables in unison.

"Now what do we call the money left over in Misha's wallet after all his expenses are paid?" asked Miss Shilyayeva. "Profit!" shouted a pig-tailed 7-year-old girl named Dasha. The teacher continued, "And why does Misha need this profit?"

Silence. Then a small voice ventured, "So he can"—a pause—"expand his store?"

"Excellent, Andrushka!" boomed the teacher's voice.

Ten years ago, this kind of aggressive attempt to plant a seed of capitalism in her young students would have landed Miss Shilyayeva in the *gulag* [Soviet labor camp]. Today she is among a growing number of elementary school teachers in Russia who have seen the future and know that in order to survive, her students will need to be able to compute interest rates.

"If we don't teach children about the market economy from an early age," said Miss Shilyayeva, 57, "they will end up like us. The older generation knew nothing about economics. We never gave it a thought. As a result, we are like blind kittens, bumping into walls, looking for a way out."

—*The New York Times,* Feb. 9, 1997

Critical Thinking

1. **Analyzing Information** What topics are the first graders studying?

2. **Finding the Main Idea** Why does the teacher believe it is important for her students to learn about the market economy?

---

who act differently or break rules. The lack of progress leads to a lower standard of living than in other types of economic societies.

Command Economies

Other societies have a **command economy,** one in which a central authority makes most of the WHAT, HOW, and FOR WHOM decisions. Economic decisions are made by the government: the people have little, if any, influence over how the basic economic questions are answered.

Examples

There are few command economies in the world today, but they still can be found in North Korea and Cuba. Until recently, the People's Republic of China, the communist bloc countries of Eastern Europe, and the former Soviet Union also had command economies.

In the former Soviet Union, for example, the government made the major economic decisions. The State Planning Commission directed nearly every aspect of the Soviet economy. It determined needs, decided goals, and set production quotas for major industries. If the State Planning Commission wanted growth in heavy manufacturing, it shifted resources from consumer goods to that sector. If it wanted to strengthen national defense, it directed resources to the production of military equipment and supplies.

Advantages

The main strength of a command system is that it can change direction drastically in a relatively short time. The former Soviet Union went from a rural (or primitive) agricultural society to a leading industrial nation in just a few decades. It did so by emphasizing heavy industry and industrial growth rather than the production of consumer goods.

During this period, the central planning agency shifted resources around on a massive scale. Consumer goods were virtually ignored, and when the country faced a shortage of male workers on construction projects, the government put women to work with picks and shovels.

CHAPTER 2: ECONOMIC SYSTEMS AND DECISION MAKING **35**

Guided Reading Activity 2-1

> **GUIDED READING** Activity 2-1
>
> *For use with textbook pages 33–39*
>
> **ECONOMIC SYSTEMS**
>
> **RECALLING THE FACTS**
>
> *Directions: Use the information in your textbook to answer the questions. Use another sheet of paper if necessary.*
>
> 1. Define the term economic system.
>
> 2. Describe each type of economic system. Then briefly state its major advantages and disadvantages.
>   a. Traditional economy
>   Advantages:
>
>   Disadvantages:
>
>   b. Command economy
>   Advantages:
>
>   Disadvantages:
>
>   c. Market economy
>   Advantages:
>
>   Disadvantages:
>
> Guided Reading Activities

THE GLOBAL ECONOMY

Teaching Capitalism in Russia Switching to a market economy has not been easy for Russia and other Eastern European nations. In Russia, for example, real money plays a small role in the current economy. The Russian currency, the ruble, is used to buy basic necessities such as food. IOUs, barter, and alternate currencies are used in most dealings involving companies. Some companies, such as the Magnitogorsk Metal Works, issue their employees cards, rather than currency, that can be used in company-owned shops and the city department stores.

Answers:

1. *profit, inventory*
2. *In order to survive in a market economy, students will need to understand what makes the economy work, and be able to compute interest rates.*

FREE ENTERPRISE ACTIVITY

Prepare a one-page handout listing the six strengths of a market economy, leaving space under each strength. Distribute copies of the handout to the class and instruct students to find at least two current examples of each strength from newspapers, magazines, radio, or television. Have them enter brief descriptions of examples under the appropriate strength. Allow students one week to complete the assignment. Upon completion, have students compare and discuss their examples.

L2 Journalism

Write the following statement on the board: Dollar "votes" tell producers what consumers want. Tell students that this is the headline of a brief newspaper article on the role of the consumer in a market economy and ask them to write the article.

L2 Applying Ideas

Have students write a paragraph analyzing how each of the three types of economic systems might respond to the introduction of new technology. How might the technology affect the manufacturing, marketing, and distribution of goods and services. Select students to present and discuss their paragraphs.

CURRICULUM CONNECTION

Government Fascist governments also employ command economies to meet their state goals. In Nazi Germany in the 1930s and 1940s, the fascist government under Adolf Hitler left the ownership of factories and resources in private hands, but strictly controlled industrial output. Much of this output was directed toward military goods. While no true fascist governments exist today, some military dictatorships in Africa and South America, and in Iraq under Saddam Hussein, are similar to fascist states.

Another advantage is that there is little uncertainty in this type of economy. People do not have to worry about what they will study, or where they will work, or if they might lose their job because these decisions are made for them. Most command economies tend to provide minimum levels of education, health, and other public services at little or no cost to its people.

Disadvantages

One disadvantage of a command system is that it is not designed to meet the wants of consumers, even though many basic needs are provided. In the case of Soviet industrial development, generations were forced to do without such consumer goods as cars, home appliances, and adequate housing. People often were told to sacrifice for the good of the state and the benefit of future generations.

A second disadvantage is that the system does not give people the incentive to work hard. In most command economies, workers with different skills and responsibilities receive similar wages. In addition, people seldom lose their jobs, regardless of the quality of their work. As a result, many people work just hard enough to fill the production quotas set by planners.

This can have unexpected results. At one time in the former Soviet Union, central planners set production quotas for electrical motors to be measured in tons of output per year. Workers soon discovered that the easiest way to fill the quota was to add weight to the motors. As a result, Soviet workers made some of the heaviest electrical motors in the world. They also produced some of the heaviest chandeliers in the world for the same reason. Some were so heavy that they fell from ceilings.

A third weakness is that the command economy requires a large decision-making bureaucracy. Many clerks, planners, and other administrators are needed to operate the system. Most decisions cannot be made until after consulting a number of people and processing a large amount of paperwork. These procedures slow decision making and raise the costs of production.

Yet a fourth weakness of a command economy is that it does not have the flexibility to deal with minor, day-to-day problems. Even when some change is needed, the sheer size of the bureaucracy

discourages even the smallest adjustments. As a result, command economies tend to lurch from one crisis to the next—or collapse completely as in the case of the former Soviet Union.

Finally, people with new or unique ideas find it difficult to get ahead in a command economy. Rewards for individual initiative are rare. Each person is expected to perform a job in a factory, in the bureaucracy, or on a farm, according to the economic decisions made by central planners.

Market Economies

In a **market economy,** people and firms act in their own best interests to answer the WHAT, HOW, and FOR WHOM questions. In economic terms, a market is an arrangement that allows buyers and sellers to come together in order to exchange goods and services. A market might be in a specific location, such as a farmers' market or a flea market. A list of phone numbers for lawn-mowing services posted on a local bulletin board also acts as a market. As long as a mechanism exists for buyers and sellers to get together, a market can exist.

In a market economy, people's decisions act as votes. When consumers buy a particular product, they are casting their dollar "votes" for that product. After the "votes" are counted, producers know what people want. Because producers are always looking for goods and services that consumers will buy, the consumer plays a key role in determining WHAT to produce.

Examples

Many of the largest and most prosperous economies in the world, such as the United States, Canada, Japan, South Korea, Singapore, Germany, France, Great Britain, and other parts of Western Europe, are based on the concept of a market economy. While there are also many significant differences among these countries, the common thread of the market binds them together.

Advantages

One advantage of a market economy is that, over time, it can adjust to change. During the gasoline shortage of the 1970s, for example, consumers

---

CRITICAL THINKING

Making Comparisons Ask students to find an article about a nation that has undergone a major economic change. Have students summarize the article, citing specific changes to the economy and to the lives of citizens and workers. Ask students to compare the old economic system with the new economic system and form an opinion about whether the change has yielded positive benefits for the citizens based on the culture's societal values. How have societal values affected the level of economic development and vice versa? Have students present their analyses to the class. Discuss as a class how a major economic change can affect a country and its people. **BLOCK SCHEDULING**

reduced their demand for large, gas-guzzling automobiles and increased their demand for smaller, fuel-efficient ones. Because auto makers still wanted to sell cars, they moved resources from the production of large cars to small ones.

When gas prices finally declined in the mid-1980s, the trend slowly began to reverse. Consumers wanted to buy large cars again, so auto makers began making large, although more fuel-efficient, vehicles again. Changes in a market economy, then, tend to be gradual. Unlike the traditional economy, change is neither prohibited nor discouraged. Unlike the command economy, change is neither delayed because of bureaucracy, nor suddenly forced on people by others.

A second major strength of the market economy is its high degree of individual freedom. Producers may make whatever they think will sell. They also decide the HOW question by producing their products in the most efficient manner. Consumers, on the other hand, spend their money on the goods and services they prefer. Meanwhile, individuals are free to choose where and when they want to work, and if they should invest further in their own education and training.

A third strength is the relatively small degree of government interference. Except for certain important concerns, such as national defense and environmental protection, the government tries to stay out of the way so that buyers and sellers can go about their business. As long as competition exists, the market economy tends to take care of itself.

A fourth advantage is that decision making is decentralized, or not concentrated in the hands of a few. Literally billions—if not trillions—of individual economic decisions are made daily. Collectively, these decisions direct scarce resources into uses that consumers favor. Because individuals make these decisions, everyone has a voice in the way the economy runs.

THE GLOBAL ECONOMY

Gang of Four South Korea, Taiwan, Singapore, and Hong Kong are collectively known as the "gang of four" because they have successfully instituted market economies. The economy of South Korea has been bolstered by the production of automobiles and computers. Taiwan's economy depends heavily on the manufacturing of textiles, cement, plastics, and electronic appliances. Singapore's economy encompasses international banking, finance, communications, high-technology manufacturing, and tourism. Hong Kong's economy relies heavily on the exportation of the textiles, electronic equipment, plastic products, and watches and clocks that it produces. Discuss with students how societal values affect the level of economic development.

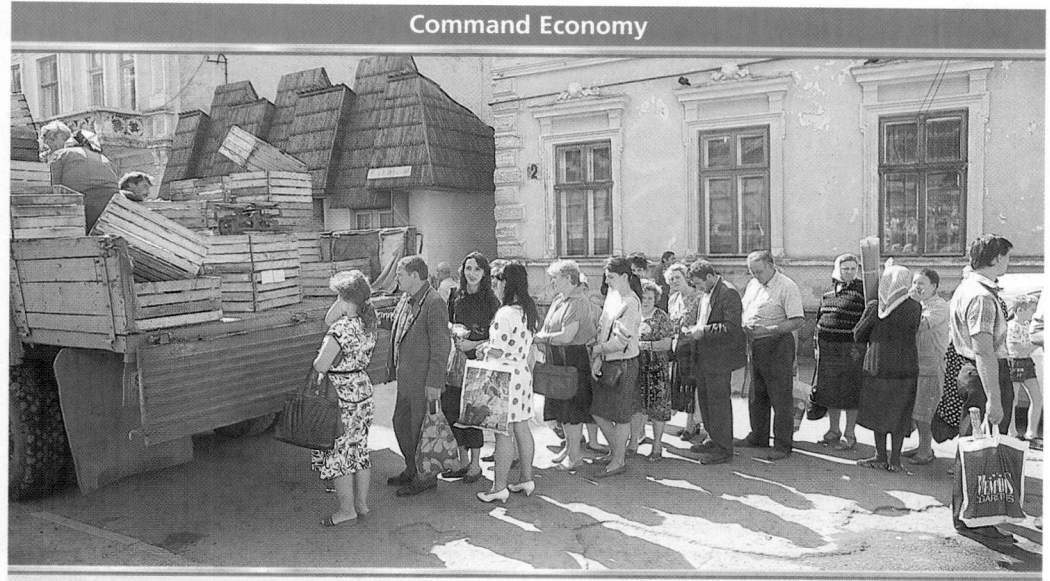

Command Economy

Economic Choices Consumers line up to buy scarce goods at a marketplace in the western Ukraine. In a command economy, like the former Soviet Union, many products are unavailable or in short supply, while other overproduced goods sit in warehouses. *Who is responsible for making the basic economic decisions in a command economy?*

CHAPTER 2: ECONOMIC SYSTEMS AND DECISION MAKING **37**

The word *market* derives from the Latin word *mercari,* which means "to trade." Its first use in its present meaning—the place where trading goes on—probably appeared in the twelfth century.

Visual Instruction

Answer to Caption:
the government

EXTENDING THE CONTENT

Ideal Types Social scientists refer to the three kinds of economic systems as *ideal types.* An ideal type is a simplified description of a particular phenomenon, focusing on the phenomenon's most common features. In other words, an ideal type provides a picture of the essential nature of the phenomenon and thus makes the task of analysis much easier. Ideal types rarely, if ever, exist in reality, and most economic systems have elements of one or more types. A socialist economic system, for example, may have elements of the command and market ideal types. The government owns and controls important means of production. At the same time, however, consumer decisions on what to purchase may influence what is produced with the means of production.

ECONOMICS
AT A GLANCE

Answer: *must be reasonably competitive; resources must be reasonably free to move from one activity to another; adequate information available to everyone*

3 ASSESS

Assign Section 1 Assessment as homework or as an in-class activity.

💾 Have students use **Interactive Tutor Self-Assessment Software**.

Section Quiz 2-1

A fifth strength of the market economy is the incredible variety of goods and services available to consumers. Almost any product can and will be produced if a buyer for it exists. Recent products include everything from Internet bookstores to 24-hour cable television cartoon and comedy networks to ultrasound devices that keep the neighbor's dog out of your yard. In short, if a product can be imagined, it can be produced in hopes that people are willing to buy it.

A sixth strength is the high degree of consumer satisfaction. In a market economy, almost everyone can satisfy his or her wants because the choice one group makes does not mean that another group cannot have what it wants. To illustrate, if 51 percent of the people want blue shirts, and 49 percent want white ones, people in both groups can still get what they want. Unlike an election, the minority does not have to live with choices the majority makes.

ECONOMICS
AT A GLANCE

Figure 2.1

Comparing Economic Systems

	Traditional	Command	Market
Advantages	• Sets forth certain economic roles for all members of the community • Stable, predictable, and continuous life	• Capable of dramatic change in a short time • Little uncertainty over choice of career, where to work, or losing job • Many basic education, public health, and other public services available at little or no cost	• Able to adjust to change gradually • Individual freedom for everyone • Lack of government interference • Decentralized decision making • Incredible variety of goods and services • High degree of consumer satisfaction
Disadvantages	• Discourages new ideas and new ways of doing things • Stagnation and lack of progress • Lower standard of living	• Does not meet wants and needs of consumers • Lacks effective incentives to get people to work • Requires large bureaucracy, which consumes resources • Has little flexibility to deal with small, day-to-day changes • New and different ideas discouraged, no room for individuality	• Rewards only productive resources; does not provide for people too young, too old, or too sick to work • Workers and businesses face uncertainty as a result of competition and change • Does not produce enough public goods such as defense, universal education, or health care • Must guard against market failures

Using Charts Every society has an economic system. The type of system that is best for a society depends on the ability of that system to satisfy people's wants and needs, and to fulfill its economic goals. What conditions must be met for a market economy to be effective?

38 UNIT 1 FUNDAMENTAL ECONOMIC CONCEPTS

INTERDISCIPLINARY CONNECTIONS ACTIVITY

Geography List on the board the names of several nations—Great Britain, Mexico, Japan, South Korea, North Korea, China, Hungary, Poland, Indonesia, and Saudi Arabia, for example—and have each student choose a nation to research. Instruct students to gather either current or historical information about the economic system of their selected nation. Suggest that they focus on the extent to which the system has characteristics of traditional, command, or market economies. Ask students to gather the information in a report, showing direct relationships between the country's societal values and characteristics of its economic system. Call on students to present their reports to the class. 📦 **BLOCK SCHEDULING**

Disadvantages

One of the disadvantages of the market economy is that it does not provide for the basic needs of everyone in the society—some members of the society may be too young, too old, or too sick to care for themselves. These people would have difficulty surviving in a pure market economy without assistance from government or private groups.

Another disadvantage of a market economy is that it does not provide enough of the services that people value highly. For example, private markets cannot adequately supply a system of justice, national defense, universal education, or comprehensive health care. This is because private producers concentrate on providing products they can sell. Therefore, government must provide these services, paid for with tax dollars.

A third disadvantage of a market economy is the relatively high degree of uncertainty that workers and businesses face as the result of change. Workers, for example, worry that their company will move to another city or country in order to lower the cost of production. Employers worry that another company will produce a better and less expensive product, thereby taking their customers.

Finally, market economies can fail if three conditions are not met. First, markets must be reasonably competitive, allowing producers to compete with one another to offer the best value for the price. Second, resources must be reasonably free to move from one activity to another. Workers, for example, need the freedom to change jobs if they have a better opportunity elsewhere. Producers need the freedom to produce goods and services in the best way they know how. Third, consumers need access to adequate information so that they can weigh the alternatives and make wise choices.

When markets fail, some businesses become too powerful and some individuals receive incomes much larger than that justified by their productivity. Because of this, we often have to rely on government to ensure that sufficient competition, freedom of resource movement, and adequate information exist.

 Did you know?

Worth Its Weight Many currencies get their names from words meaning "weight" because merchants in ancient times would weigh coins made from precious metals to assess their value. Among these currencies are the Spanish *peseta*, the Mexican *peso*, and the Italian *lira*.

Section 1 Assessment

Checking for Understanding

1. **Main Idea** Using your notes from the graphic organizer activity on page 33, explain how a market economy determines who will receive the benefits from what is produced and sold.

2. **Key Terms** Define economy, economic system, traditional economy, command economy, market economy.

3. **Describe** the characteristics of a traditional economy.

4. **Identify** the advantages and disadvantages of a command economy.

5. **Identify** the advantages and disadvantages of a market economy.

Applying Economic Concepts

6. **Tradition** Give an example of an economic activity from a traditional economy that is seen in today's market economy. Describe how important this activity is for the economy.

Critical Thinking

7. **Analyzing Information** How are roles defined in a traditional economy?

8. **Making Comparisons** How are the WHAT, HOW, and FOR WHOM questions answered in the command and market economies?

Practice and **assess** key social studies skills with the *Glencoe Skillbuilder Interactive Workbook, Level 2.*

Reteach

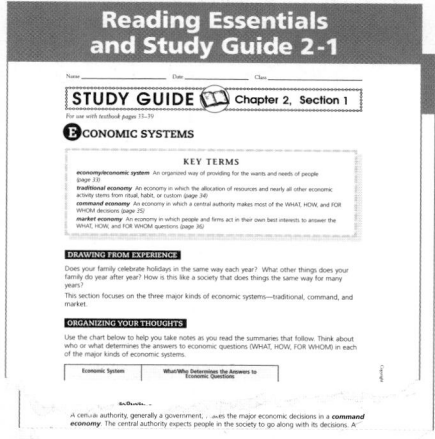

Reading Essentials and Study Guide 2-1

Enrich

Have students consider their part in the economy. What are some of their rights? Responsibilities? What goods and services do they consume? What labor do they provide.

 CLOSE

Ask: Which of the three economic systems you would prefer to live under? Why?

Section 2 Assessment Answers

1. Those who act in their own best interests will receive the benefits.

2. All vocabulary terms are defined in the text.

3. sets economic roles; life is stable, predictable, continuous; discourages ideas

4. advantages: great change in short time; disadvantages: does not meet needs and wants of consumers; lacks incentives to work hard; large bureaucracy; little flexibility; ideas discouraged

5. advantages: adjusts to change gradually; individual freedom; lack of government interference; produces great variety of goods and services; high consumer satisfaction; disadvantages: does not provide basic needs of everyone; lacks services people want and need; workers and businesses face high uncertainty as a result of change.

6. Answers will vary. Based on students' answers, the importance of this activity will vary.

7. Roles are set by long-standing customs.

8. command: central authority answers questions; market: people and firms acting in own best interests provide answers.

Teaching Skills

Write *New York* and *California* on the board. Ask students what factors they would consider in making a comparison of these two states and note responses on the board. (*area, geography, population, economy, government, major cities, and so on*)

Point out that comparing such factors will help establish the similarities and differences between the states.

Conclude by pointing out that this is a major step in making comparisons.

Additional Practice

GLENCOE
TECHNOLOGY

Glencoe Skillbuilder Interactive Workbook, Level 2

This interactive CD-ROM reinforces student mastery of essential social studies skills.

CRITICAL THINKING
Skill

Making Comparisons

When you make comparisons, you determine similarities and differences among ideas, objects, or events. Making comparisons is an important skill because it helps you choose among alternatives.

Learning the Skill

Follow these steps to make comparisons:

- Identify or decide what will be compared.
- Determine the common area or areas in which comparisons can be drawn.
- Look for similarities and differences within these areas.

Practicing the Skill

Read the passages below, then answer the questions that follow.

Viewpoint A

Russians are readily embracing the middle-class lifestyle of Western democracies. Nothing better symbolizes the changes sweeping this nation than the flea market that has taken over Moscow's Exhibition of Economic Achievements park. Built as a shrine to the Soviet system, it is now the center of free enterprise in the city. Muscovites swarm here to get deals on all sorts of goods. A park pavilion once housed an exhibit celebrating the Soviet space program. It has now become an auto showroom. A few space capsules remain, scattered among the used cars. But the crowds are here to see the new Fords and Jeeps.

Viewpoint B

Besides the inefficiency of many Russian factories, capitalism there is not yet the same as it is in the United States. Private capital apparently is steered into projects controlled by small groups in power. There is a strong criminal organization in Russia that imposes serious costs on anybody wishing to do business.

"The West supports Russia, despite the corruption there, because of the former Soviet state's economic and military stature on the world stage," said a World Bank spokesperson. "The reason we need to help is that the whole of the former Soviet Union represents not only an economic threat or economic opportunity, but politically it does have a somewhat different weight than some other countries because of its defense and offensive capabilities."

The spokesperson also noted, "I don't doubt that there has been corrupt practice . . . but the overall question of global stability is also an issue."

1. What is the topic of these passages?

2. How are the passages similar? Different?

3. What conclusions can you draw about the opinions of the writers?

Statue of farm workers at the Exhibition of Economic Achievement

Application Activity

Survey your classmates about an issue in the news. Summarize the opinions and write a paragraph comparing the different opinions.

 Practice and **assess** key social studies skills with the *Glencoe Skillbuilder Interactive Workbook, Level 2.*

Answers to Practicing the Skill

1. the Russian economy
2. While both passages examine the Russian economy, Viewpoint A discusses the products now available to the Russian people, and Viewpoint B examines the economy in a global context.
3. The writer of the first passage holds a more optimistic view of the new Russian economy and what it offers the Russian people. The writer of the second passage voices concerns about Russia's progress toward capitalism.

Evaluating Economic Performance

Study Guide

Main Idea
The social and economic goals of the United States include economic freedom, economic security, and economic equity.

Reading Strategy
Graphic Organizer As you read the section, indentify seven major economic and social goals by completing a graphic organizer like the one below.

Economic and social goals

Key Terms
Social Security, inflation, fixed income

Objectives
After studying this section, you will be able to:
1. **Describe** the basic economic and social goals used to evaluate economic performance.
2. **Evaluate** the trade-offs among economic and social goals.

Applying Economic Concepts
Freedom and Equity Read to find out how freedom and equity are related to the level of satisfaction people have with their economic system.

1 FOCUS

Section Overview
This section describes basic economic and social goals and the trade-offs among them.

BELLRINGER
Motivational Activity

Project **transparency** and have students answer questions.

Daily Focus Transparency 8

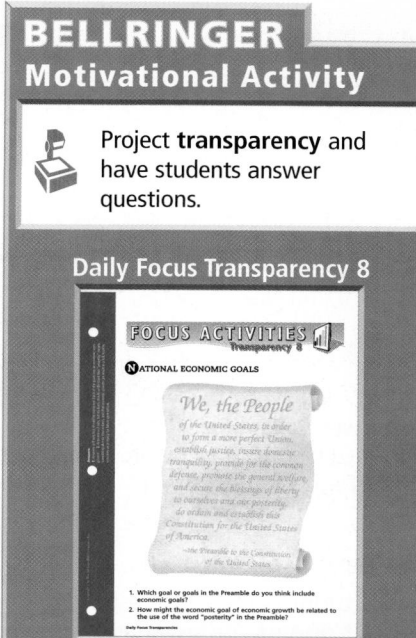

Cover Story

Minimum Wage Revisited on the Hill

It happens every seven years or so, the last time in 1997. So look for a hike in the minimum wage before too long. Sen. Tom Daschle, D-S.D., the Senate's new majority leader, has already said it's a Democratic priority. He wants to raise the rate $1.50 over a year and a half, to $6.65 an hour. He's likely to get it, too, even if now may not be the best time....

Minimum-wage workers might get a raise.

Critics say hiking the minimum wage cuts down on the number of new jobs employers can add. It may also force employers to cut back on the hours workers work.

- Investor's Business Daily, June 6, 2001

Every economic system has goals such as financial security and freedom to carry out economic choices. Goals are important because they serve as benchmarks that help us determine if the system meets most—if not all—of our needs. If the system falls short, then we may demand laws to change the system until the needs are met.

Economic and Social Goals

In the United States, people share many broad social and economic goals. While it might be difficult to find them listed in any one place, they are repeated many times in the statements that friends, relatives, community leaders, and elected officials make. We can categorize those statements into seven major economic and social goals.

Economic Freedom

In the United States, people place a high value on the freedom to make their own economic decisions. People like to choose their

CHAPTER 2: ECONOMIC SYSTEMS AND DECISION MAKING **41**

Study Guide

Reading Strategy
Have students create the graphic organizer.
Answers to Graphic: *economic freedom, economic efficiency, economic equity, economic security, full employment, price stability, economic growth*

Preteaching Vocabulary
Have students explain how inflation affects people on fixed incomes.

RESOURCE MANAGER

📁 Reproducible Masters
- Reproducible Lesson Plan 2-2
- Daily Lecture Notes 2-2
- Guided Reading Activity 2-2
- Reading Essentials and Study Guide 2-2
- Section Quiz 2-2

🖨 Transparencies
- Daily Focus Transparency 8

Multimedia
- 💾 Interactive Tutor Self-Assessment Software
- 🔊 ExamView® Pro Testmaker
- 🔊 Presentation Plus!

② TEACH

Daily Lecture Notes 2-2

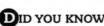

DAILY LECTURE NOTES 📖 Lesson 2-2

❶ DID YOU KNOW?
A minimum wage was mandated by the federal government with passage of the Fair Labor Standards Act in 1938. That federal law set the nation's minimum wage at 25 cents per hour. About 40 states also have set minimum wages, but those usually are lower than the nationally set minimum wage.

PAGES 41-43
I. Economic and Social Goals
   A. Economic freedom, the freedom for people to make their own economic decisions, is a goal highly valued in the Unites States.
   B. Economic efficiency means that resources are used wisely and that the benefits gained are greater than the costs incurred.
   C. Economic equity is the social goal that explains why so many people support laws against wage and job discrimination.
   D. Economic security is a social goal that results in programs to help support the ill, the elderly, and workers who have lost their jobs.
   E. Most economic systems strive for full employment, the providing of as many jobs as possible.
   F. Price stability, or freedom from inflation, is important to anyone trying to provide basic necessities on a limited income and for anyone planning their economic future.
   G. Economic growth is an important goal because populations tend to increase and existing populations tend to want more goods and services.

❶ Discussion Question
In your opinion, which of these economic goals is most important? Why? *(Answers will vary. Students may support their choices by explaining what would happen if the goal was not met.)*

Visual Instruction

Answer to Caption:
legislation that bans discrimination for any reason

L1 Economic and Social Goals

Ask students to create a poster about one of the seven major economic and social goals. Students can use magazine and newspaper photos to illustrate their chosen goal. Have students write a short sentence explaining how each photo represents their goal. **ELL**

Guided Reading Activity 2-2

Name _____ Date _____ Class _____

GUIDED READING Activity 2-2

For use with textbook pages 41–44

❶ EVALUATING ECONOMIC PERFORMANCE

OUTLINING

Directions: *Locate the heading in your textbook. Then use the information under the heading to help you write each answer. Use another sheet of paper if necessary.*

I. Economic and Social Goals
   A. Introduction
      1. What are two kinds of goals people may share? _____
      2. How many major kinds of goals are there? _____
   B. Economic Freedom
      1. What are three examples of economic freedom for individuals? _____
      2. What kind of economic freedom do business owners want? _____
   C. Economic Efficiency
      1. What happens if resources are wasted? _____
      2. Why must economic decision making be efficient? _____
   D. Economic Equity
      1. What are two examples of economic equity? _____
      2. What is a "lemon law"? _____
   E. Economic Security
      1. What do American workers want protection from? _____
      2. What kind of protection does Social Security offer? _____
   F. Full Employment
      1. What happens when people work? _____
      2. What happens when people do not have jobs? _____
   G. Price Stability
      1. What is inflation? _____

Economic and Social Goals

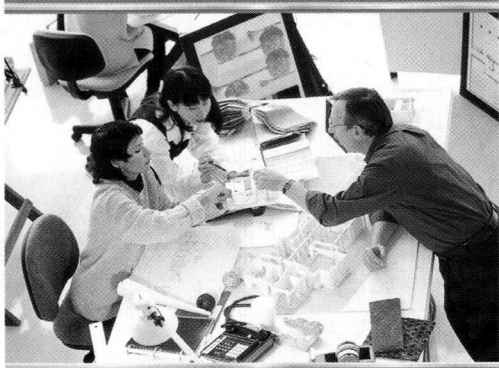

Economic Equity Our nation values the ideal of equal pay for equal work. *What legislation safeguards economic equity?*

own occupations, employers, and uses for their money. Business owners like the freedom to choose where and how they produce. The belief in economic freedom, like political freedom, is one of the cornerstones of American society.

Economic Efficiency

Most people recognize that resources are scarce and that factors of production must be used wisely. If resources are wasted, fewer goods and services can be produced and fewer wants and needs can be satisfied. Economic decision making must be efficient so that benefits gained are greater than costs incurred.

Economic Equity

Americans have a strong sense of justice, impartiality, and fairness. Many people, for example, believe in equal pay for equal work. As a result, it is illegal to discriminate on the basis of age, sex, race, religion, or disability in employment. When it comes to selling products, most people feel that advertisers should not be allowed to make false claims about their products. Many states even have "lemon laws" that allow new car buyers to return their cars if they have too many repairs.

42 UNIT 1 FUNDAMENTAL ECONOMIC CONCEPTS

Economic Security

Americans desire protection from such adverse economic events as layoffs and illnesses. States have set up funds to help workers who lose their jobs. Many employers have insurance plans to cover the injuries and illnesses of their workers. On the national level, Congress has set up **Social Security**—a federal program of disability and retirement benefits that covers most working people.

More than 90 percent of American workers participate in the Social Security system. Retirees, survivors, disabled persons, and medicare recipients are eligible for benefits. Survivors are spouses and children of deceased persons covered by Social Security. Medicare provides health insurance for persons 65 or older.

Full Employment

When people work, they earn income for themselves while they produce goods and services for others. If people do not have jobs, however, they cannot support themselves or their families, nor can they produce output for others. As a result, people want their economic system to provide as many jobs as possible.

STANDARD & POOR'S INFOBYTE

Economic Indicators Economic indicators are economic statistics reflecting the general direction of the economy. Some indicators are termed *leading* indicators because they tend to lead or forecast the direction of the economy or business cycle; the stock market is known as a leading indicator. Another important indicator is the U.S. Department of Labor's quarterly Employment Cost Index, which measures the rate of change in employee compensation. Like the average hourly earnings data, it allows economists to keep a beat on wage inflation, which is often seen as a catalyst to overall inflation.

MEETING SPECIAL NEEDS ACTIVITY

Reading Disability Even students with adequate decoding and visual-word-skill development have reading comprehension problems. To assess students' abilities to comprehend this text, do the following: Copy the four paragraphs from the Trade-Offs Among Goals section on page 43, deleting every sixth or seventh word. Provide students with copies of these adjusted paragraphs, asking them to fill in the deleted words. Those who enter the correct words or synonyms show good comprehension.

📂 Refer to *Inclusion for the Social Studies Classroom Strategies and Activities* in the TCR.

Price Stability

Another goal is to have stable prices. If **inflation**—a rise in the general level of prices—occurs, workers need more money to pay for food, clothing, and shelter. People who live on a **fixed income**—an income that does not increase even though prices go up—find that bills are harder to pay and that planning for the future is more difficult. High rates of inflation can discourage business activity. When there is inflation, interest rates tend to increase. High interest rates discourage businesses both from borrowing and spending. Price stability makes budgeting easier and adds a degree of certainty to the future.

Economic Growth

The last major goal of most Americans is economic growth. Most people hope to have a better job, a newer car, better clothes, their own home, and a number of other things in the future. Growth is needed so that people can have more goods and services. Because the nation's population is likely to grow, economic growth is necessary to meet everyone's needs.

Future Goals

These goals are ones on which most people seem to agree. As our society evolves, however, it is entirely possible that new goals will be added. Do people feel that a cleaner environment is important enough to be added to the list of goals? Should we add the preservation of an endangered species, such as the timber wolf and the wild tiger, to the list? In the end, Americans must decide on the goals important to them.

Other countries and their leaders and citizens must also make important choices regarding their goals. For example, an economic goal for many developing nations from the 1950s through the mid-1970s was to increase the goods and services they produced. The idea was that big gains in production would "trickle down" to the poorest people.

By the mid-1990s, many developing nations had achieved regular increases in their production. Living conditions for the poor in most countries, however, did not improve much. Today, basic human needs have become a focus of development policies. These needs include food, shelter, health, protection, and the freedom to make choices about one's life.

Math Practice

Fixed Income Ruth, a retiree, lives on a fixed income of $625 a month. Each month she spends $315 for rent, and she budgets $85 for food, $25 for clothing, and $50 for various items. She deposits the money that is left over into her savings account. How much money does she put into savings each month? *($150)* If her rent is increased by 15 percent, how much money does she have left to put into savings? *($102.75)*

Visual Instruction

Answer to Caption: *Social Security*

③ ASSESS

Assign Section 2 Assessment as homework or as an in-class activity.

💾 Have students use **Interactive Tutor Self-Assessment Software**.

Section Quiz 2-2

Economic and Social Goals

Economic Security One aspect of economic security is protecting people against the economic loss of natural disasters. *What federal program protects economic security for working people?*

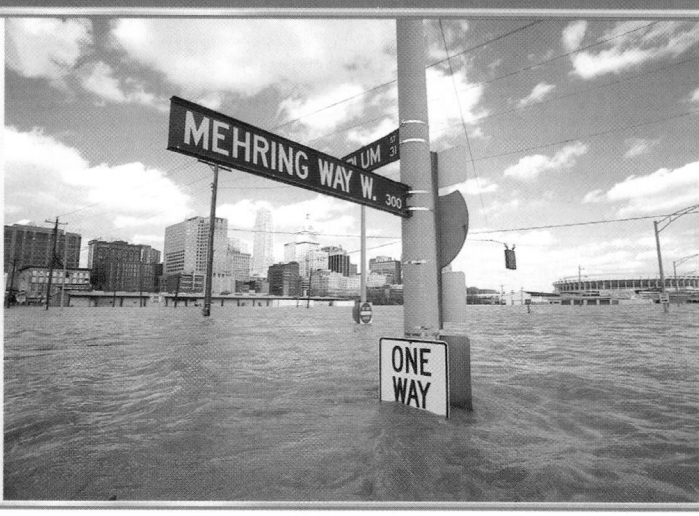

CHAPTER 2: ECONOMIC SYSTEMS AND DECISION MAKING **43**

FREE ENTERPRISE ACTIVITY

Write the following incomplete sentence on the board: *The economic and social goal of _____ is illustrated in the economy by _____ .* Organize students into pairs and have each pair complete seven sentences, one for each of the social and economic goals of the United States market economy. (Suggest the following as an example: *The economic and social goal of economic freedom is illustrated in the economy by the choices people have on how to spend their money.*) After the activity is completed, ask pairs to share their sentences with the class.

Reteach

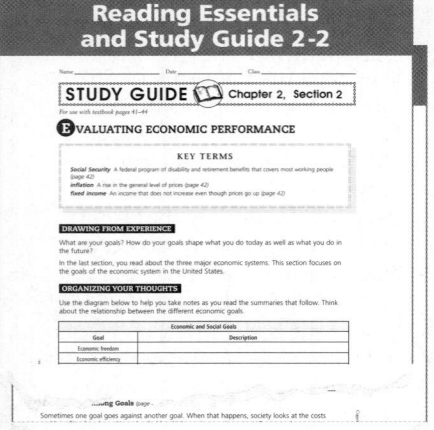

Reading Essentials and Study Guide 2-2

Enrich

Write on the board the terms *economic freedom* and *economic security*. Ask students to write a short paragraph, using proper grammar, spelling, sentence structure, and punctuation, to explain how these two goals might conflict.

4 CLOSE

Have students rank and justify the economic and social goals in order of importance as they see them.

Job Outlook

The freedom to make our own economic decisions—including choosing our occupations and where to work—is a cherished right for many people. Information available on the World Wide Web can provide help with making those decisions. One useful online source is the Occupational Outlook Handbook from the U.S. Bureau of Labor Statistics. It provides job descriptions, earnings, job outlooks, and educational requirements about hundreds of occupations—from "able seamen" to "zoologists."

Trade-Offs Among Goals

People sometimes have different ideas about how to reach a goal. At other times, the goals themselves might conflict with one another because even economic policies have opportunity costs. For example, a policy that keeps foreign-made shoes out of the United States could help the goal of full employment in the local shoe industry. This policy might work against individual freedom, however, if people ended up with fewer choices of shoes to buy. Or, a new shopping center built near a highway may stimulate economic growth in one area of a community. At the same time, it could threaten the stability and security of merchants who run stores in the downtown area.

Even an increase in the minimum wage involves a conflict of goals. On one hand, supporters of the increase might argue that an increase is the equitable, or "right," thing to do. Opponents might argue that increasing the minimum wage would do more harm than good. A higher minimum wage increases costs of production for firms that pay this wage. In addition, it restricts the freedom of employers to pay wages that they think are fair.

So, how are trade-offs among goals resolved? In the case of the minimum wage, people compare their estimates of the costs against their estimates of benefits—and then exercise their right to vote for political candidates that support their position. If the majority of people feel that it is too low, then it will be raised. The minimum wage then tends to stay at a higher level for a while until the majority of people feel that it again needs changed.

For the most part, people, businesses, and government usually are able to resolve conflicts among goals. Fortunately, the economic system of the United States is flexible enough to allow choices, accommodate compromises, and still satisfy the majority of Americans most of the time.

Section 2 Assessment

Checking for Understanding

1. **Main Idea** Using your notes from the graphic organizer activity on page 41, explain why it is important to set economic goals.
2. **Key Terms** Define Social Security, inflation, fixed income.
3. **Describe** the seven major goals of the United States economy.
4. **Explain** how an increase in the minimum wage might involve a conflict of goals.
5. **Describe** some of the economic choices people and producers in the United States are free to make.

Applying Economic Concepts

6. **Freedom and Equity** How do laws against false advertising promote the goal of economic equity?

Critical Thinking

7. **Analyzing Information** Why is economic growth an important goal?
8. **Making Generalizations** What characteristics does the United States economy have that allow it to resolve conflicts among goals?

 Practice and **assess** key social studies skills with the Glencoe *Skillbuilder Interactive Workbook, Level 2.*

Section 2 Assessment Answers

1. They help us determine if the system meets our needs.
2. Vocabulary terms defined in text.
3. economic freedom, economic efficiency, economic equity, economic security, full employment, price stability, economic growth
4. Some believe that an increase furthers the goal of economic equity because it is fair. Others might argue that it conflicts with the goal of full employment by raising unemployment, and with the goal of economic freedom by preventing employers from paying what they feel are fair wages.
5. People choose their own occupations, employers, and uses for their money; producers choose where/how they produce.
6. prevent unscrupulous business owners from telling falsehoods; promote economic equity by ensuring justice in market
7. so people have more goods/services
8. It allows choices, accommodates compromises, and satisfies most people most of the time.

BusinessWeek

APRIL 5, 1999

Newsclip

The Internet provides millions with quick access to information. There are trade-offs, however. One is privacy. Powerful database technologies have made it possible to quickly gather personal information on millions of Americans who cruise the Web.

The Internet and the Right of Privacy

Like all new technologies, the Internet is creating undreamed-of conflicts. Case in point: The very nature of the Web makes it easy to collect and collate information about people who shop at or even simply visit a Web site, without their knowledge. Indeed, using such information is an important part of the business model of many Net companies.

But Net companies are discovering that consumers also care about their privacy. Examples of a growing concern are [evident] everywhere. GeoCities had to settle with the Federal Trade Commission when it sold personal data collected from children without parents' consent. Microsoft Corp. was red-faced and apologetic when it was discovered that the Windows 98 operating system could be used to create a giant database of information about Microsoft customers. Perhaps most notable was the response to Intel Corp.'s plans to ship its new Pentium III microprocessor with a component that could transmit a serial number whenever the user visits a Web site. The idea of consumers unknowingly leaving behind an ID number when on-line set off howls of protest, and Intel promised to ship the Pentium III with the identifier in the "off" position.

What's happening is that people are worried that their essential democratic right to privacy is being surreptitiously eroded. The idea of the Net building "dossiers" without customers' knowledge conjures up images of secret files, police states, and the loss of freedom. That will create a backlash that can only injure Internet commerce. . . .

Equally germane is a truism of the Information Age: Information is a hugely valuable good in its own right. From that perspective, Net companies have been appropriating information that rightfully does not belong to them. It is akin to stealing for Net companies to gather, use, and resell information on consumers without asking permission.

Net companies have to realize that individuals have the right of first refusal on the information of their lives. For companies to use it, they have to say "please" and exchange something for the information. The Net marketplace has made progress in posting privacy policies on Web sites and curbing intrusions. But time is running out for companies to agree on rules of the game to protect privacy before the backlash does permanent damage to the future of E-commerce.

Examining the Newsclip

1. **Analyzing Information** What issue is the article addressing?
2. **Drawing Conclusions** What solution to protecting the right of privacy does the article present? In your opinion is this a good solution, or should others be suggested?

BusinessWeek *ONLINE*

Visit the Business Week Web site at www.businessweek.com for up-to-date news, analysis on the economy, editorials, special reports, market updates, book reviews, personal finance information, and an archive of past articles.

TEACH

A "cookie" is a message sent to your Internet browser that contains personal information to be stored for future use. For example, if you visit a Web site such as an online bookstore that displays your name each time you access the site, your name is stored in a cookie. As a user, you have the option of disabling cookies if you do not want your personal information to be stored. If you allow cookies to be stored, you are allowing each Web site that you visit to access your information and potentially pass it on to other Web sites and advertisers. Discuss the potential need for rules and regulations to protect possible economic information stored in cookies.

📁 Refer to ***Business Week Focus on the New Economy*** in the TCR for additional unit-based articles.

Answers to Examining the Newsclip

1. a person's right to privacy on the Internet and how that right is being exploited
2. The article suggests that companies should be required to request permission to use personal information and that they offer something in exchange for that information. Students' opinions will vary based on how they feel about the right-to-privacy issue.

① FOCUS

Section Overview
This section discusses characteristics of capitalism and economic freedom.

BELLRINGER
Motivational Activity

- Project **transparency** and have students answer questions.
- Available as blackline master.

Daily Focus Transparency 7

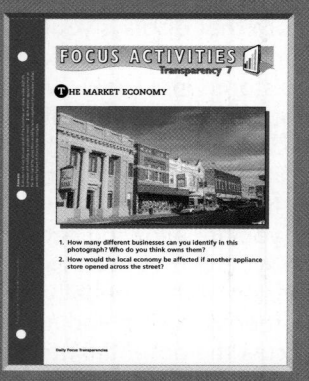

Study Guide

Reading Strategy
Have students create the graphic organizer.
Answers to Graphic: *Examples for the characteristics (economic freedom, voluntary exchange, private property rights, the profit motive, competition) will vary.*

Preteaching Vocabulary
Use the Vocabulary Puzzle-Maker to create crossword and word-search puzzles.

SECTION 3

Capitalism and Economic Freedom

Study Guide

Main Idea
Under capitalism, the basic economic decisions are made through the free interaction of individuals looking out for their own best interests.

Reading Strategy
Graphic Organizer As you read the section, complete a graphic organizer like the one below to identify the five characteristics of a free enterprise economy. Then provide an example of each.

Characteristic	Example

Key Terms
capitalism, free enterprise, voluntary exchange, private property rights, profit, profit motive, competition, consumer sovereignty, mixed economy, modified private enterprise economy

Objectives
After studying this section, you will be able to:
1. **Explore** the characteristics of a free enterprise system.
2. **Describe** the role of the entrepreneur, the consumer, and government in a free enterprise economy.

Applying Economic Concepts
Voluntary Exchange Read to find out why voluntary exchange is one of the most popular features of a market economy.

Cover Story

Madame C.J. Walker

Madame C.J. Walker—Sarah Breedlove—was a highly successful entrepreneur, widely considered to be the first African-American millionairess. Walker was known and respected not only for her business acumen but for her inspirational political and social advocacy and her philanthropy.

Madame C.J. Walker

The daughter of former slaves, Walker worked initially as a washerwoman until she devised a hair care and grooming system to meet the needs of African-American women in 1905. Supervising the manufacture of a variety of products, she also developed an enormous marketing network, headquartered in Indianapolis, that employed thousands of African-American women and was the largest African-American owned business in the nation. Walker encouraged women's independence by training others and by serving as a powerful role model.

—National Women's Hall of Fame, ©1998

46

A market economy is normally based on a system of **capitalism,** where private citizens, many of whom are entrepreneurs, own the factors of production. **Free enterprise** is another term used to describe the American economy. In a free enterprise economy, competition is allowed to flourish with a minimum of government interference.

Competition and Free Enterprise
A free enterprise economy has five important characteristics—economic freedom, voluntary exchange, private property rights, the profit motive, and competition.

Economic Freedom
Individuals as well as businesses enjoy economic freedom, the first characteristic of capitalism. People, for example, have the freedom to choose their occupation and their employer. To a lesser extent, they can choose to work where and when they want. They may work on the west coast, east coast, or in Alaska. They may work days, nights, indoors, outdoors, in offices, or in their homes.

RESOURCE MANAGER

Reproducible Masters
- Reproducible Lesson Plan 2-3
- Daily Lecture Notes 2-3
- Guided Reading Activity 2-3
- Reading Essentials and Study Guide 2-3
- Section Quiz 2-3

Transparencies
- Daily Focus Transparency 7

Multimedia
- Vocabulary PuzzleMaker CD-ROM
- Interactive Tutor Self-Assessment Software
- ExamView® Pro Testmaker
- Presentation Plus!

With economic freedom, people can choose to have their own business or to work for someone else. They can apply for jobs, and they have the right to accept or reject employment if offered. Economic freedom also means that people can leave jobs and move on to others that offer greater opportunity.

Businesses also enjoy economic freedom. They are free to hire the best workers, and they have the freedom to produce the goods and services they feel will be the most profitable. Businesses can make as many or as few goods and services as they want, and they can sell them wherever they please. They have the right to charge whatever price they feel is profitable, and they are free to risk success or failure.

Voluntary Exchange

A second characteristic of capitalism is **voluntary exchange**—the act of buyers and sellers freely and willingly engaging in market transactions. Moreover, transactions are made in such a way that both the buyer and the seller are better off after the exchange than before it occurred. Buyers, for example, can do many things with their money. They can deposit it in the bank, hide it under a mattress, or exchange it for goods or services. If they spend their money on a product, they must believe that the item being purchased is of greater value to them than the money they gave up.

With voluntary exchange, sellers also have many opportunities to sell their products. If they exchange their goods and services for cash, they must feel that the money received is more valuable than the product being sold, or they would not sell in the first place. In the end, the transaction benefits both buyer and seller or it would not have taken place. Both the buyer and the seller obtained something they believed had more value than the money or products they gave up.

Private Property Rights

Another major feature of capitalism is the concept of **private property rights,** the privilege that entitles people to own and control their possessions as they wish. Private property includes both tangible items such as houses and cars, and intangible items such as skills and talents. People are free to make decisions about their property and their own abilities.

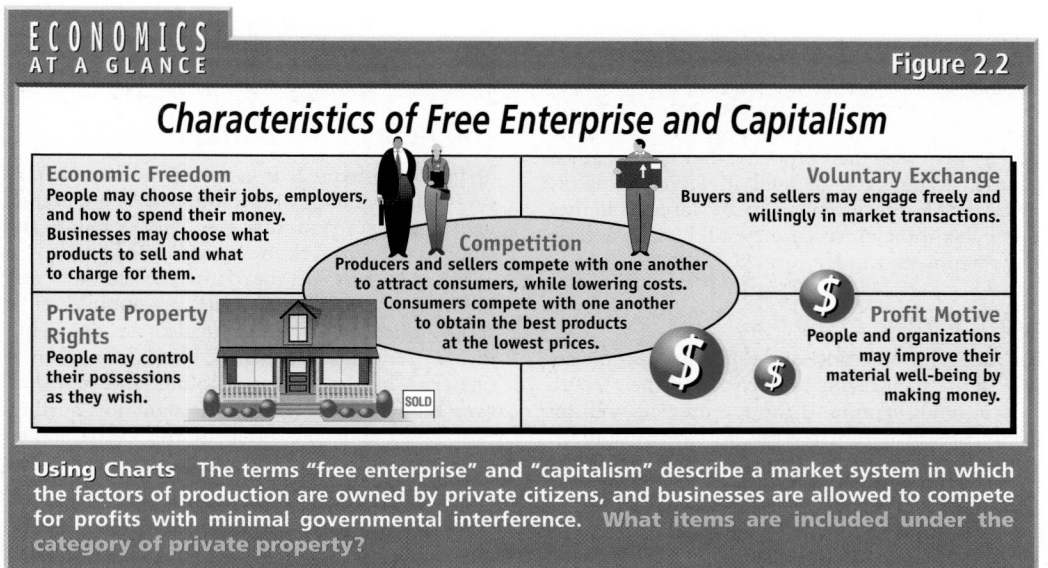

ECONOMICS
AT A GLANCE

Figure 2.2

Characteristics of Free Enterprise and Capitalism

Economic Freedom
People may choose their jobs, employers, and how to spend their money. Businesses may choose what products to sell and what to charge for them.

Voluntary Exchange
Buyers and sellers may engage freely and willingly in market transactions.

Competition
Producers and sellers compete with one another to attract consumers, while lowering costs. Consumers compete with one another to obtain the best products at the lowest prices.

Private Property Rights
People may control their possessions as they wish.

Profit Motive
People and organizations may improve their material well-being by making money.

SOLD

Using Charts The terms "free enterprise" and "capitalism" describe a market system in which the factors of production are owned by private citizens, and businesses are allowed to compete for profits with minimal governmental interference. What items are included under the category of private property?

MEETING SPECIAL NEEDS ACTIVITY

English Language Learners Students often benefit by using a form of rapid reading called "scanning" to locate specific information. Demonstrate the scanning procedure by sliding your finger rapidly down the middle of both columns on this page. Tell students to use scanning to find the word "capitalism" on page 47. Time students as they search the rest of the section for the word "capitalism." Discuss the results, then have pairs of students practice the exercise. Partners should take turns identifying a word for which to search. **ELL**

⬚ Refer to *Inclusion for the Social Studies Classroom Strategies and Activities* in the TCR.

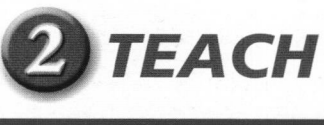 **TEACH**

Daily Lecture Notes 2-3

DAILY LECTURE NOTES 📖 Lesson 2-3

DID YOU KNOW?
Bill Gates is perhaps the nation's most successful entrepreneur. In 1975 he cofounded Microsoft Corporation and 20 years later, that company made him the world's richest man. But in 1998, the federal government took Microsoft to court. The government charged that the software giant used unfair practices to try to put its competition out of business. In 1999 the court agreed with the government and found Microsoft guilty of antitrust practices.

PAGES 46-48
I. Competition and Free Enterprise
   A. Capitalism is a market economy in which private citizens own the factors of production. In a free enterprise system there is limited government interference and businesses are free to compete.
   B. With economic freedom, both people and businesses make their own economic choices.
   C. The result of voluntary exchange, in which buyers and sellers are free to decide whether or not to complete a transaction, results in both buyers and sellers believing that the good or service obtained is of more value than the money or product given up.
   D. Private property rights give people the motivation to succeed. They keep any rewards they earn.
   E. The profit motive encourages entrepreneurship and is largely responsible for the growth of a free enterprise economy.
   F. Competition helps lower prices.

☐ Discussion Question

L1 Classifying

Some economists classify consumer decisions in three major categories —habitual, impulsive, or rational. Habitual decisions are those made routinely, such as purchasing gasoline. Impulsive decisions are those made on the spur of the moment. Rational decisions are given great thought and usually involve the purchase of an expensive item. Have students give three examples for each classification and decide which purchase is the most responsible. **ELL**

ECONOMICS
AT A GLANCE

Answer: *both tangible items, such as houses and cars, and intangible items, such as skills and talents*

Guided Reading Activity 2-3

Visual Instruction

Answer to Caption:

voluntary exchange, private property rights, the profit motive, competition

CURRICULUM CONNECTION

Language Arts Free enterprise with private property ownership, is essentially, an American invention. The ideas on which it is based, however, derive from many cultures. Some of the terms used to describe aspects of the system originated elsewhere. "Entrepreneur," for example, derives from the French word *entreprendre*, which means "to undertake," "to try," or "to adventure."

L2 Analyzing Ideas

On the board draw a concept web to explain the basic principles of the free enterprise system. Place *Economic Freedom* at the center and *Voluntary Exchange*, *Private Property*, and *Profit Motive* around it. Call on volunteers to explain the relationship of each satellite idea to the central idea of economic freedom.

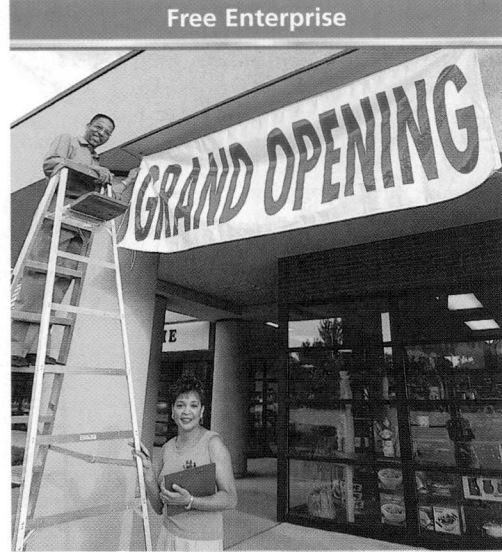

Economic Freedom The freedom to own a business is a hallmark of free enterprise. *What other characteristics does a free enterprise economy have?*

They have the right to use or abuse their property as long as they do not interfere with the rights of others.

Private property gives people the incentive to work, save, and invest. When people are free to do as they wish with their property, they are not afraid to use, accumulate, or lend it. Private property gives people the incentive to be successful; they know that if they succeed they will be able to keep any rewards they might earn.

Profit Motive

Under free enterprise and capitalism, people are free to risk their savings or any part of their wealth in a business venture. If the venture goes well for them, they will earn rewards for their efforts. If things go poorly, they could lose part or all of their investment. The very possibility of financial gain, however, encourages many people to become *entrepreneurs*, or those who risk entering business in hopes of earning a profit.

What, however, is profit? Consider the earlier case of voluntary exchange. Remember that the buyer gives up money to obtain a product, and the seller gives up the product to obtain money. Unless both parties believe they will be better off afterward than before, neither will make the exchange. When exchange takes place, it does so only because both parties feel they will make a profit.

Profit, then, is the extent to which persons or organizations are better off at the end of a period than they were at the beginning. The **profit motive**—the driving force that encourages people and organizations to improve their material well-being—is largely responsible for the growth of a free enterprise system based on capitalism.

Competition

Finally, capitalism thrives on **competition**—the struggle among sellers to attract consumers while lowering costs. Competition is possible because private individuals, acting as entrepreneurs, own the factors of production and have the freedom to produce the products they think will be the most profitable.

Because capitalism is based on freedom and voluntary exchange, buyers compete to find the best products at the lowest prices. The result is that goods and services are produced at the lowest cost and are allocated to those who are willing and able to pay for them.

The Role of the Entrepreneur

The entrepreneur is one of the most important people in the economy. The entrepreneur organizes and manages land, capital, and labor in order to seek the reward called profit.

Entrepreneurs are the ones who start up new businesses such as restaurants, automobile repair shops, Internet stores, and video arcades. They include people who may have worked for others at one time, but have decided to quit and start their own businesses. Entrepreneurs want to "be their own boss" and are willing to risk everything to make their dreams come true.

Many entrepreneurs fail. Of course, others survive and manage to stay in business with varying degrees of success. A few, and only a very few, manage to become fantastically wealthy and famous.

48 UNIT 1 FUNDAMENTAL ECONOMIC CONCEPTS

FREE ENTERPRISE ACTIVITY

Organize students into three groups to conduct interviews. The goal of the interviews is to establish how various groups of people view the term *free enterprise*. Work with groups to develop a list of questions dealing with voluntary exchange, private property rights, profit motive, and competition. Then have members of one group interview local business owners or managers, members of the second group interview employees at local businesses, and members of the third group interview shoppers at a mall or shopping area. Ask groups to collate their findings and present them to the class in the form of an oral report. Have students discuss the reasons for any differences in views among the interview subjects.

Well-known entrepreneurs include Bill Gates, who founded Microsoft, John Johnson of Johnson Publishing Co., and Mary Kay Ash, who founded Mary Kay Cosmetics.

Despite the high rate of failure among entrepreneurs, the dream of success is often too great to resist. The entrepreneur is both the sparkplug and the catalyst of the free enterprise economy. When an entrepreneur is successful, everybody benefits. The entrepreneur is rewarded with profits, a growing business, and the satisfaction of a job well done. Workers are rewarded with more and better-paying jobs. Consumers are rewarded with new and better products. The government is rewarded with a higher level of economic activity and larger tax receipts. These receipts can be used to build roads, schools, and libraries for people not even connected with the original entrepreneur.

Nor does it stop there. Successful entrepreneurs attract other firms to the industry who rush in to "grab a share" of the profits. To remain competitive

and stay in business, the original entrepreneur may have to improve the quality or cut prices, which means that customers can buy more for less. In the end, the entrepreneur's search for profits can lead to a chain of events that involves new products, greater competition, more production, higher quality, and lower prices for consumers.

The Role of the Consumer

 In the United States, consumers often are thought of as having power in the economy because they determine which products are ultimately produced. For example, a company may try to sell a certain item to the public. If consumers like the product, it will sell and the producer will be rewarded for his or her efforts. If consumers reject the product and refuse to purchase it, the firm may

The Role of the Entrepreneur

Building a Business John Johnson started his publishing business in 1942 with a $500 loan on his mother's furniture. Today, Johnson Publishing is the world's largest African American–owned publishing company. *What aspects of the economy benefit when an entrepreneur succeeds?*

Careers

Law Enforcement Officer

Law enforcement work can range from keeping order in public places and investigating crimes to controlling traffic and lecturing the public on safety.

The Work

Every level of government needs law enforcement officers. In small communities, officers may be called on to do many tasks. In larger cities, work may be highly specialized, including chemical and firearms analysis, fingerprint identification, and harbor and border patrol. The challenges of the work are numerous. Working long hours, risking injury, and taking the chances involved in pursuing and apprehending lawbreakers demands dedication to the job.

Qualifications

Most law enforcement jobs are covered by civil service regulations. Usually candidates must be at least 21 years old and must be U.S. citizens. Most jobs require a high school education or more. The more specialized jobs require college training.

49

CYBERNOMICS

Toys Online At the start of the 1999 Christmas shopping season, online toy stores such as KBkids.com, Toysrus.com, and eToys.com logged nearly twice the number of visitors compared with a year earlier. Traffic to the toy sites rose 99 percent overall as consumers became more comfortable using the Internet and making online purchases. Have students discuss how scientific discoveries and technological advances cause the need for rules and regulations to protect businesses and consumers.

Visual Instruction

Answer to Caption:
workers, consumers, government

L2 Designing a Poster

Have students design a poster about the life and career of a famous entrepreneur. Some possible examples might include Andrew Carnegie, John D. Rockefeller, Mary Kay Ash, or Bill Gates.

CRITICAL THINKING

Synthesizing Information Ask each student to select one of the economic roles of government—protector, provider, consumer, regulator, or promoter of national goals. Have students research historical and current materials to determine if the government role they chose has changed over time. Students should present their findings in a report containing visuals, if appropriate. Call on volunteers to present and discuss their reports.

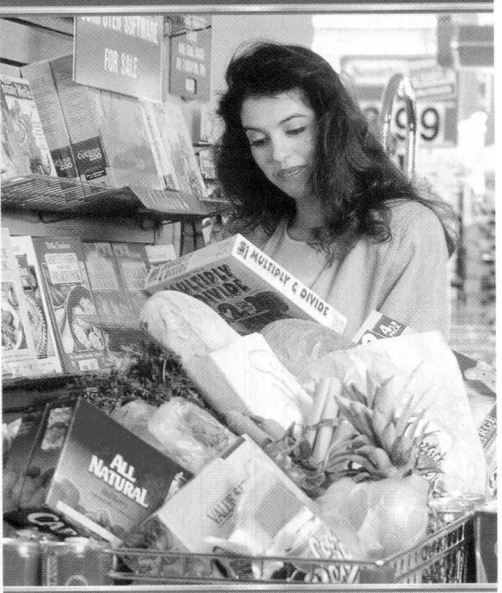

The Role of the Consumer

Consumer Sovereignty The principle of consumer sovereignty says that in a competitive economy, customers determine what is produced by choosing what they will buy. *Why do firms have to sell products customers want in order to earn a profit?*

go out of business. **Consumer sovereignty** describes the role of the consumer as sovereign, or ruler, of the market. More commonly, this is expressed in a different way by saying that "the customer is always right."

In recent years, producers have had outstanding successes with various products, including home video games, sport utility vehicles, and personal computers. Many other products—including "New" Coke, celery flavored Jell-O, chewable toothpaste in tablet form, and bacon you cook in your toaster—were promptly rejected by consumers.

Consumers' wants change constantly as modern communications and travel expose people to new ideas and products. Today, Americans purchase more home computers every year than TV sets,

even though computers were barely known just 20 years ago. Consumers buy products from all over the world, and more and more often they use the Internet to find product reviews and other information about the goods before they purchase.

Consumers, then, play an important role in the American free enterprise economy. They have a say in what is—and what is not—produced when they express their wants in the form of purchases in the marketplace. The dollars they spend are the "votes" used to select the most popular products.

The Role of Government

Government—whether national, state, or local—has an economic role to play that reflects the desires, goals, and aspirations of its citizens. Government has become involved in the economy because Americans want its involvement. Consequently, it has become a protector, provider of goods and services, consumer, regulator, and promoter of national goals. The role of government is normally justified whenever its benefits outweigh its costs.

Protector

As protector, the United States government enforces laws such as those against false and misleading advertising, unsafe food and drugs, environmental hazards, and unsafe automobiles. It also enforces laws against abuses of individual freedoms. Employers, for example, cannot discriminate against workers because of their age, gender, race, or religion. In short, the government protects property rights, enforces contracts, and generally tries to make sure that everyone follows the "rules of the game" to ensure an efficient and fair economy.

Provider and Consumer

All levels of government provide goods and services for citizens. The national government, for example, supplies defense services. State governments provide education and public welfare. Local governments provide, among other things, parks, libraries, and bus services.

EXTENDING THE CONTENT

Role of Government Government-owned businesses provide public services that private companies often cannot. For instance, the amount of money needed to start a project such as the Tennessee Valley Authority is usually more than a private business can afford to spend. Since its inception in 1933, this federal corporation has worked to develop the natural resources of the Tennessee Valley. The TVA pays no federal income taxes, but it does pay more than $100 million a year in interest and repayments to the U.S. treasury.

In the process of providing, government consumes factors of production just like any other form of business. In recent years the government has grown so large that it is now the second largest consuming unit in the economy, trailing only the consumer sector.

Regulator

In its role as a regulator, the national government is charged with preserving competition in the marketplace. It also oversees interstate commerce, communications, and even entire industries such as banking and nuclear power. Many state governments regulate insurance rates and automobile registrations. Local governments even regulate business activity with building and zoning permits.

The regulatory role of government is often controversial. Most businesses do not like to be told how to run their affairs, and they argue that consumers can always sue in court if there are problems. On the other hand, many consumers feel that they do not always know when they are at risk—as in the case of potential food poisoning from unsafe food preparation practices. As a result,

consumers usually think that the government is in a better position to monitor and regulate such activities.

Promoter of National Goals

Government reflects the will of a majority of its people. As a result, many government functions reflect people's desire to modify the economic system to achieve the economic goals of freedom, efficiency, equity, security, full employment, price stability, and economic growth. A government program such as Social Security, as well as laws dealing with child labor and the minimum wage, reveal how Americans have modified their free enterprise economy.

Because of these modifications, and because there are some elements of tradition in our economy, the United States is said to have a **mixed economy,** or a **modified private enterprise economy.** In a mixed economy people carry on their economic affairs freely, but are subject to some government intervention and regulation. This system most likely will undergo further change as the goals and objectives of the American people change.

Reteach

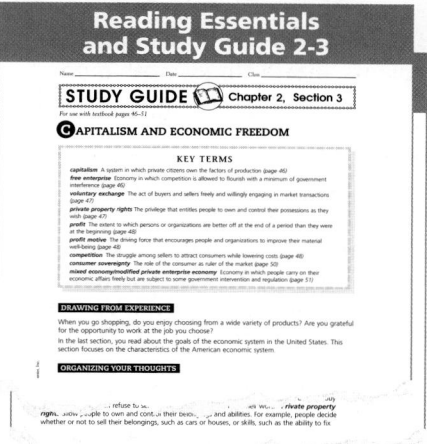

Reading Essentials and Study Guide 2-3

Enrich

Have students research and report on the various ways in which the federal government regulates or restricts businesses and promotes national goals.

 CLOSE

Call on groups to make brief presentations on the lesson plans they developed for the Extra Credit Project on page 32. Then have students discuss the following: What makes the free enterprise system unique?

Section 3 Assessment

Checking for Understanding

1. **Main Idea** Using your notes from the graphic organizer on page 46, explain how basic economic decisions are made under capitalism.

2. **Key Terms** Define capitalism, free enterprise, voluntary exchange, private property rights, profit, profit motive, competition, consumer sovereignty, mixed economy, modified private enterprise economy.

3. **List** the five major characteristics of a free enterprise system.

4. **Describe** the role of the entrepreneur.

5. **Analyze** the consequences of consumer economic decisions in a free enterprise economy.

6. **Identify** the role of the government in a free enterprise economy.

Applying Economic Concepts

7. **Voluntary Exchange** Cite at least three examples of voluntary exchanges you made this week. How are you better off by having made the exchanges? Did the person with whom you exchanged gain too? How?

Critical Thinking

8. **Understanding Cause and Effect** Americans have varying economic goals. How have these often-competing goals modified our free enterprise economy?

Practice and assess key social studies skills with the *Glencoe Skillbuilder Interactive Workbook, Level 2.*

CHAPTER 2: ECONOMIC SYSTEMS AND DECISION MAKING **51**

Section 3 Assessment Answers

1. They are made through free interaction of individuals looking out for own best interests.

2. All vocabulary terms are defined in the text.

3. economic freedom, voluntary exchange, private property, profit motive, competition

4. the entrepreneur organizes and manages land, capital, and labor; starts up businesses

5. The consequences involve what is, and what is not, produced when consumers express their

wants in the form of purchases in the marketplace.

6. protector, provider and consumer, regulator, promoter of national goals

7. Answers should recognize that all parties gained something they considered of value.

8. increased government intervention in the economy in the form of programs like Social Security and laws dealing with minimum wage and child labor

BACKGROUND

Both George Lucas and Walt Disney became entertainment industry giants. Interestingly, both men faced and overcame failures early in their careers. Their triumphs were a result of personal qualities, but also of technology. Disney embraced animation, which was the cutting edge at the time. Lucas embraced computer-generated special effects, the cutting edge for his generation.

The histories of economics and technology are tightly interwoven. In boom times the funds exist to research and develop new technology; in bust times necessity often leads to invention. New technologies create new economic opportunities, as Lucas and Disney demonstrated.

TEACH

Review with students the powerful influence that the Walt Disney Company has had, and continues to have, on the cultures of the United States and other countries. Then organize students into teams to debate this resolution: "Resolved: That private companies should not be allowed to shape the culture of a nation."

Walt Disney won more Oscars than anyone ever has—twenty "Oscar" statuettes and a dozen more special plaques and certificates.

Profiles IN Economics

More Than Star Wars:
George Lucas
(1944–)

"The crossroad in my career," filmmaker giant George Lucas recalls, "happened very early on. I was in an automobile accident. Before that I wasn't really a very good student. I wasn't really focused in my life. I came through an automobile accident that I should never have survived. And, in the process of that, I realized that there must be some purpose for me to be here and I'd better figure out what it is. . . . That really motivated me in a very direct way which sent me off, ultimately, searching for the things I loved and winding up in the film business."

George Lucas did more than just "wind up" in the film business: he conquered it. Lucas, as a writer, director, producer, and film business owner, has had a hand in more than half of the top 20 box office hits of all time. His credits include many of the world's best-known films, including the *Indiana Jones* series, and, his most famous work, the *Star Wars* series.

Lucas has won many awards, the most prestigious of which is the Irving G. Thalberg Award, given by the Academy of Motion Pictures. Lucas seems, indeed, to have found his purpose.

A Household Name:
Walt Disney
(1901–1966)

The name Disney is known around the world. Yet as a young man, Walt Disney was a failed filmmaker operating out of a makeshift studio in a garage in Los Angeles. Disney had moved there from Kansas City, where he had helped create cartoon advertisements for showings in movie theaters. Dreaming of making full-scale movies, he headed to Los Angeles—then, as now, the film industry capital—to pursue his dream. For five years, he struggled to make ends meet. Then he released an animated film featuring a character that would soon become a household name: Mickey Mouse.

The year was 1928, and the film industry was about to explode: the ability to add sound to movies had just been developed; color movies would emerge in just a few years.

Disney and his workers made full use of . . . new technologies.

Today, Walt Disney Company is a business giant. With income from four motion-picture units (Walt Disney Pictures, Touchstone Pictures, Hollywood Pictures, and Miramax Films), television (Disney owns ABC), videocassettes, recordings, theme parks, resorts, publications, and merchandise based on Disney characters, "Disney" is practically an industry unto itself. This huge media presence has brought Disney characters to millions of people around the world. Walt Disney combined economic success with a cultural impact that few, if any, others have achieved.

Examining the Profiles

1. **Making Comparisons** What similarities are there in the early lives of Lucas and Disney?

2. **Evaluating Information** Both Lucas and Disney have influenced millions of people through their films. Do you view this as something positive or something negative? Explain your answer.

Answers to Examining the Profile

1. Answers will vary, but should note that neither Lucas nor Disney achieved early success in their careers.

2. Answers will vary, but should be explained. Students who view their influence as positive might refer to the importance of free speech and free markets. Students who view it as negative might refer to the commercialization of culture.

Section 1

Economic Systems (pages 33–39)

- Every society has an **economy** or **economic system,** a way of allocating goods and services to satisfy the WHAT, HOW, and FOR WHOM questions.

- In a **traditional economy,** the major economic decisions are made according to custom and habit. Life in these economies tends to be stable, predictable, and continuous.

- In a **command economy,** government makes the major economic decisions. Command economies can change direction drastically in a short time, focusing on whatever the government chooses to promote.

- Command economies tend to have little economic freedom, few consumer goods, and little uncertainty.

- A **market economy** features decentralized decision making with people and firms operating in their own self-interests.

- A market economy adjusts gradually to change, has a high degree of individual freedom and little government interference, is highly decentralized, and offers a wide variety of goods and services that help to satisfy consumers' wants and needs.

Section 2

Evaluating Economic Performance
(pages 41–44)

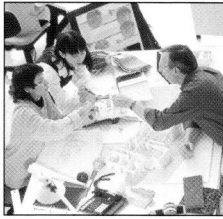

- The social and economic goals of U.S. society include economic freedom, economic efficiency, economic equity, economic security, full employment, price stability, and economic growth.

- When goals conflict, society evaluates the costs and benefits of each in order to promote one goal over another; many election issues reflect these conflicts and choices.

- People's goals are likely to change in the future, as our economy evolves.

Section 3

Capitalism and Economic Freedom (pages 46–51)

- **Capitalism** is a competitive economic system in which private citizens own the factors of production.

- The five characteristics of capitalism are **economic freedom, voluntary exchange, private property rights, profit motive,** and **competition.**

- The entrepreneur is the individual who organizes land, capital, and labor for production in hopes of earning a **profit:** the profit motive is the driving force in capitalism.

- In capitalism, firms are in business to make a profit. To do this they must offer products consumers want at competitive prices.

- **Consumer sovereignty** states that the consumer is the one who decides WHAT goods and services to produce.

- The national government plays the role of protector, provider and consumer, regulator, and promoter of economic goals.

- The United States has a **mixed economy,** or a **modified private enterprise economy,** in which its citizens carry on their economic affairs freely but are subject to some government intervention and regulation.

Teacher's Notes / Internet Bookmarks

NIGHTLY BUSINESS REPORT

 ECONOMICS & YOU

Chapter 3
Disc 1, Side 1

Economic Systems and the American Economy

📼 Also available in VHS.

Using the Chapter 2 Summary

Use the Chapter 2 Summary to preview, review, condense, or reteach the chapter.

Preview/Review

Vocabulary PuzzleMaker CD-ROM reinforces Key Terms.

Interactive Tutor Self-Assessment Software provides a review of Chapter 2 content.

Condense

Have students listen to the Chapter 2 Audio Program. Spanish also available.

Assign the Chapter 2 Audio Program Activity and give students the Chapter 2 Audio Program Test.

Have students complete the Guided Reading Activities and Reading Essentials and Study Guides for Chapter 2.

Reteach

Have students complete Reteaching Activity 2 in the TCR. Spanish also available.

GLENCOE
TECHNOLOGY

Use **MindJogger Videoquiz** to review the Chapter 2 content.

Have students visit the Web site at epp.glencoe.com to review Chapter 2 and take the **Self-Check Quiz.**

Identifying Key Terms

1. c	6. g
2. d	7. i
3. h	8. b
4. f	9. e
5. a	10. j

Reviewing the Facts

Section 1

1. strength: everyone knows which role to play; weakness: discourages new ideas and new ways
2. does not meet needs and wants of consumers; lacks effective incentives for people to work hard; requires large bureaucracy that consumes resources; has little flexibility; new ideas and individuality discouraged
3. Traditional: often punishes those who attempt to change the way things are done. Command: problems adjusting to changes because of inflexibility. Market: flexible and can adjust to change.

Section 2

4. economic freedom—freedom to make one's own economic decisions; economic efficiency—recognition that resources are scarce and need to be used wisely; economic equity—belief that the economy should be managed justly, impartially, and fairly; economic security—protection from

ECONOMICS
Online

Self-Check Quiz Visit the *Economics: Principles and Practices* Web site at epp.glencoe.com and click on *Chapter 2—Self-Check Quizzes* to prepare for the chapter test.

Identifying Key Terms

On a separate sheet of paper, write the letter of the key term that best matches each statement below.

a. capitalism	**f. inflation**
b. command economy	**g. private property rights**
c. consumer sovereignty	**h. profit motive**
d. economic system	**i. traditional economy**
e. fixed income	**j. voluntary exchange**

1. the idea that people rule the market
2. a society's organized way of providing for its people's wants and needs
3. the driving force that encourages people and organizations to try to improve their material well-being
4. a rise in the general level of prices
5. a system in which the factors of production are owned by private citizens
6. the right and privilege to control one's own possessions
7. an economic system in which ritual, habit, and custom dictate most economic and social behavior
8. an economic system in which a central authority makes economic decisions
9. the situation in which the money an individual receives does not increase even though prices go up
10. the act of buyers and sellers freely conducting business in a market

Reviewing the Facts

Section 1 (pages 33–39)

1. **Describe** the main strength and weakness of a traditional economy.
2. **List** the five major weaknesses of the command economy.
3. **Describe** how a market economy, a traditional economy, and a command economy adapt to change.

Section 2 (pages 41–44)

4. **Describe** the seven major economic goals which most Americans agree on.
5. **Explain** how society resolves the conflict among goals which conflict.

Section 3 (pages 46–51)

6. **State** how people and businesses benefit from economic freedom.
7. **Explain** the importance of the entrepreneur in a free enterprise economy.
8. **Provide** examples of how the government acts as protector, provider and consumer of goods and services, regulator, and promoter of national goals.

Thinking Critically

1. **Drawing Conclusions** Some people believe the profit motive conflicts with the goals of economic security and equity. Do you agree or disagree? Why or why not?
2. **Understanding Cause and Effect** How has the development of transportation and communication systems affected the type of economy that exists in the United States?
3. **Making Inferences** What incentive does owning private property give people?

---

effects of adverse economic events; full employment—desire for the economic system to provide as many jobs as possible; price stability—desire for stable prices; economic growth—production of more and better goods and services

5. economic system is flexible, allows choices, and accommodates compromises

Section 3

6. People can choose their employer, where and when they work, and how they spend their money. Businesses hire the best workers,

decide what and how to produce, and what prices to charge.

7. When entrepreneurs succeed, they benefit by gaining profits; workers benefit through jobs and higher wages; consumers benefit by having more and better products to buy; and government benefits through greater tax revenues.

8. protector—enforces laws against false advertising; provider and consumer—provides highways, uses productive resources; regulator—oversees interstate commerce; promoter of goals—minimum wage promotes equity

4. **Making Comparisons** Reproduce the following diagram on a separate sheet of paper. Then, in the spaces indicated, identify several elements of command and tradition in the U.S. economy that make it a mixed, or modified private enterprise, economy.

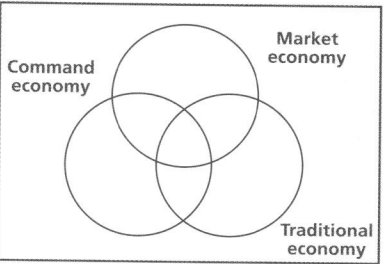

Applying Economic Concepts

1. **Tradition** Most people tip for service in restaurants, but not for service at clothing stores or gas stations. Explain how this illustrates economic behavior by tradition rather than by market or command.

2. **Freedom and Equity** Explain the role you as a consumer must play in obtaining economic equity for yourself.

3. **Voluntary Exchange** How does the principle of voluntary exchange operate in a market economy?

Math Practice

If the typical minimum-wage employee works 40 hours a week and takes two weeks off for vacation, how much will that person earn annually if the minimum wage is $5.15/hour? How much extra will that person earn for every $0.25 increase per hour in the wage?

Thinking Like an Economist

Not all societies have market economies. Some have command or traditional economies. Use the discussion of incremental reasoning and cost-benefit analysis in Chapter 1 on pages 22 and 23 to explain why you would or would not like to live in a society with a different economic system.

Technology Skill

Using the Internet Search for information on the Internet about the Russian economy. Use a search engine. Type in the word *Russia*. After typing in *Russia*, enter words like the following to focus your search: *goods and services, government controls, competition, economic freedom,* and *transition economy.*

As you analyze the information that you find, answer these questions: What progress has Russia achieved in its transition to a market economy? What problems remain? Write a one-page paper that describes your findings.

Building Skills

Making Comparisons Compare the figures below and then answer the questions that follow.

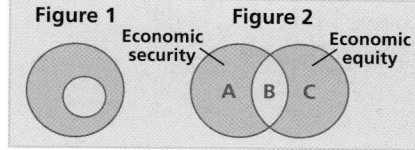

1. If the diagram in Figure 1 represents "needs" and "wants," how would you label the two diagrams in the figure? Explain your choice.

2. If the two circles in Figure 2 represent the goals of economic security and economic equity, where would you place a federal policy such as the minimum wage law—in area A, B, or C? Explain your choice.

3. If you were to change economic security to economic efficiency in Figure 2, how would this change your placement of the minimum wage policy? Or, would it?

 Practice and **assess** key social studies skills with the *Glencoe Skillbuilder Interactive Workbook, Level 2.*

3. Both buyers and sellers must believe that something they want has more value than the money or products they want to give up.

Math Practice

$10,300; $500

Thinking Like an Economist

Students should provide a logical explanation for their response.

Technology Skill

Students' papers should reflect accurate research.

Building Skills

Answers will vary.

 Bonus Test Question

Ask students to identify the type of economy in the following situations.

1. After hearing complaints about postal service, Jack starts a delivery service. *(market)*

2. Production has remained the same for generations. *(traditional)*

3. A proposal to introduce new production methods is held up for months while paperwork is prepared. *(command).*

Thinking Critically

1. Some might argue that the profit motive does conflict with those goals, pointing out that business owners, in their drive for profits, may be less than fair. Others may argue that there is no conflict, because the drive for profits eventually leads to economic success for all.

2. The freedom of movement of people and ideas has allowed the United States to develop a strong market economy.

3. Private property gives people the incentive to work harder, to save, to invest, and to succeed.

4. Answers should reflect an understanding of both traditional and command economies.

Applying Economic Concepts

1. Tipping for service in a restaurant is a long-established tradition; tipping at clothing stores and gas stations is not.

2. Suggestions may include reporting unfair pricing or false advertising.

Chapter 3 Resource Manager

SECTION RESOURCES

Daily Objectives

Section 1
Forms of Business Organization
1. Describe the characteristics of the sole proprietorship.
2. Understand the advantages and disadvantages of the partnership.
3. Describe the structure and features of the corporation.

Section 2
Business Growth and Expansion
1. Explain how businesses can reinvest their profits to grow and expand.
2. Recognize the reasons that cause firms to merge.
3. Identify two different types of mergers.

Section 3
Other Organizations
1. Describe nonprofit organizations.
2. Explain the direct and indirect role of government in our economy.

Reproducible Resources

Section 1
- Reproducible Lesson Plan 3-1
- Daily Lecture Notes 3-1
- Guided Reading Activity 3-1
- Reading Essentials and Study Guide 3-1
- Section Quiz 3-1*

Section 2
- Reproducible Lesson Plan 3-2
- Daily Lecture Notes 3-2
- Guided Reading Activity 3-2
- Reading Essentials and Study Guide 3-2
- Section Quiz 3-2*

Section 3
- Reproducible Lesson Plan 3-3
- Daily Lecture Notes 3-3
- Guided Reading Activity 3-3
- Reading Essentials and Study Guide 3-3
- Section Quiz 3-3*

Technology/Multimedia Resources

Section 1
- Daily Focus Transparency 15
- Interactive Economics!
- Interactive Tutor Self-Assessment Software
- ExamView® Pro Testmaker
- Presentation Plus!

Section 2
- Daily Focus Transparency 17
- Interactive Tutor Self-Assessment Software
- ExamView® Pro Testmaker
- Presentation Plus!

Section 3
- Daily Focus Transparency 18
- Vocabulary PuzzleMaker CD-ROM
- Interactive Tutor Self-Assessment Software
- ExamView® Pro Testmaker
- Presentation Plus!

Also available in Spanish

Key:
- Transparency
- Videodisc
- CD-ROM
- Audio Program
- Software
- Videocassette
- Blackline Master

0:00 OUT OF TIME?
Assign the Chapter 3 Audio Program activity and test.

Block Schedule
Activities that are particularly suited to use within the block scheduling framework are identified throughout this chapter by the following designation: **BLOCK SCHEDULING**

KEY TO ABILITY LEVELS

Teaching strategies have been coded for varying learning styles and abilities.

L1 BASIC activities for all students
L2 AVERAGE activities for average to above-average students
L3 CHALLENGING activities for above-average students
ELL ENGLISH LANGUAGE LEARNER activities

Chapter 3 Resource Manager

TeacherWorks™ All-In-One Planner and Resource Center

- **Interactive Teacher Edition** Access your Teacher Wraparound Edition and your classroom resources with a few easy clicks.

- **Interactive Lesson Planner** Planning has never been easier! Organize your week, month, semester, or year with all the lesson helps you need to make teaching creative, timely, and relevant.

Use Glencoe's **Presentation Plus!** multimedia teacher tool to easily present dynamic lessons that visually excite your students. Using Microsoft PowerPoint® you can customize the presentations to create your own personalized lessons.

ACTIVITY

From the Classroom of...

**Theresa Jacobson
Culver Community
  Jr./Sr. High School
Culver, IN**

Business Organizations

This activity allows the students to learn more about the variety of business organizations in their community. Each student contacts a different business in the community and interviews the business owner. The student's job is to determine whether the business is a sole proprietorship, partnership, or corporation, and to gather information about the business. Students are also to obtain a business card from the business. The students then share their information with the rest of the class.

We then take poster board and construct a map of the area. Once the map is completed, the students paste the business cards at the appropriate locations on the map. A variation is to ring the map with 3" × 5" cards that contain a summary of each business, connecting each index card to the corresponding business card with a piece of colored yarn or string. As a class, discuss the kinds of businesses in the community and the relationship between location and competition.

National Council on Economic Education

THE **Economics**America AND **Economics**International PROGRAMS

Voluntary National Content Standards in Economics
Emphasized in Chapter 3

Content Standard 10

Content Standard 14

Content Standard 16

For a complete listing of NCEE Standards and entire text correlation, see Teacher pages in front of book.

Resources Available from NCEE
- Capstone: The Nation's High School Economics Course
- Civics and Government: Focus on Economics
- Entrepreneurship in the U.S. Economy
- Geography: Focus on Economics
- Economics at Work
- Learning from the Market: Integrating the Stock Market Game™ Across the Curriculum

To order these materials or to contact your state Council on Economic Education about workshops and programs, call 1-800-338-1192 or visit www.nationalcouncil.org

Chapter 3 Resource Manager

Economic Concept Transparency 2: Opportunity Cost and Trade-Offs

Consumer Application Activity 3

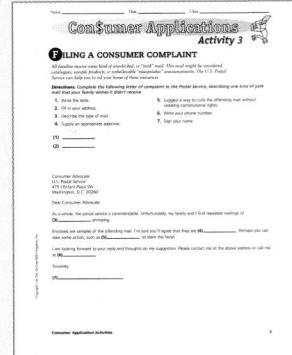

Free Enterprise Activity 3

Enrichment Activity 3

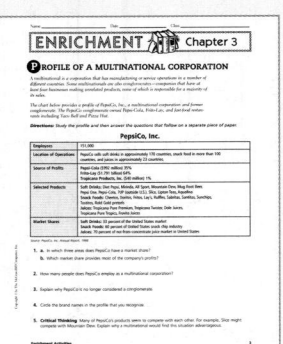

Cooperative Learning Activity 3

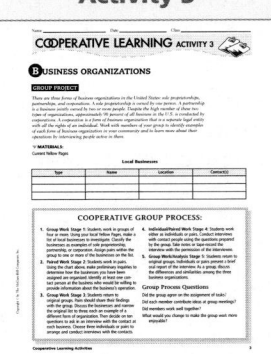

Math Practice Activity 3

Economic Cartoon 3

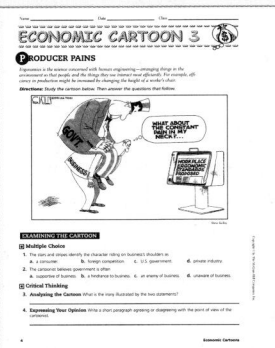

Primary and Secondary Source Reading 3

Economic Vocabulary Activity 3

Reteaching Activity 3

Critical Thinking Activity 3

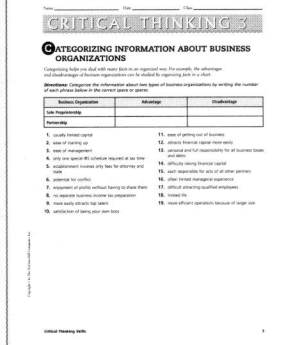

Reinforcing Economic Skill 26

Chapter 3 Resource Manager

Chapter 3 Test Form A

Chapter 3 Test Form B

Performance Assessment Activity 3

ExamView® Pro Testmaker
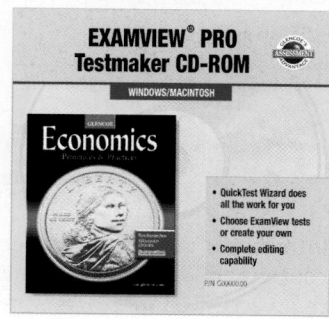

SPANISH RESOURCES

The following Spanish language materials are available in the Spanish Resources binder:

 Spanish Economic Vocabulary Activities

 Spanish Reteaching Activities

Spanish Section Quizzes

Spanish Economic Concepts Transparencies

Also available:

Spanish Chapter 3 Audio Program Activity and Test

TECHNOLOGY/MULTIMEDIA

 Vocabulary PuzzleMaker CD-ROM

Interactive Tutor Self-Assessment Software

ExamView® Pro Testmaker

Audio Program (English or Spanish)

 NBR Economics & You Video Program (English or Spanish)

MindJogger Videoquiz

Interactive Economics! CD-ROM

Presentation Plus!

TeacherWorks CD-ROM

Glencoe Skillbuilder Interactive Workbook CD-ROM, Level 2

ECONOMICS Online

Use our Web site for additional resources. All essential content is covered in the Student Edition.

You and your students can visit epp.glencoe.com, the Web site companion to **Economics: Principles and Practices.** This innovative integration of electronic and print media offers your students a wealth of opportunities. The student text directs students to the Web site for the following options:

• **Chapter Overviews**

• **Student Web Activities**

• **Self-Check Quizzes**

• **Textbook Updates**

Answers are provided for you in the Web Activity Lesson Plan. Additional Web resources and interactive puzzles are also available.

Performance Assessment

Refer to Activity 3 in the *Performance Assessment Strategies and Activities* booklet.

 BLOCK SCHEDULING

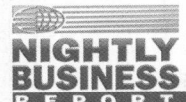
ECONOMICS Online

Introduce students to chapter content and key terms by having them access **Chapter Overview 3** at epp.glencoe.com

NIGHTLY BUSINESS REPORT

 ECONOMICS & YOU

Chapter 4
Disc 1, Side 1

Business Organizations
After viewing this segment, students should be able to:
• Name common types of business organizations.

 Also available in VHS.

GLENCOE
TECHNOLOGY

 Use **MindJogger Videoquiz** to preview the Chapter 3 content.

CHAPTER

3

Business Organizations

Economics & You

Do you work at a business? Belong to a church? Participate in a club? Chances are these institutions play a significant role in your life. To learn more about how business organizations and economic institutions operate, view the Chapter 4 video lesson:

Business Organizations

ECONOMICS Online

Chapter Overview Visit the *Economics: Principles and Practices* Web site at epp.glencoe.com and click on **Chapter 3—Chapter Overviews** to preview chapter information.

Running a business involves risks as well as expectations.

✚ EXTRA CREDIT PROJECT

Have students visit their local chamber of commerce. They should investigate the procedures for establishing various forms of businesses. For example, what local regulations and ordinances apply when forming a partnership? Allow students to share their findings with the class.

Forms of Business Organization

Study Guide

Main Idea
Businesses may be organized as individual proprietorships, partnerships, or corporations.

Reading Strategy
Graphic Organizer As you read about business organizations, complete a graphic organizer similar to the one below to explain how the three types of business organizations differ from one another.

Proprietorships	
Partnerships	
Corporations	

Key Terms
sole proprietorship, proprietorship, unlimited liability, inventory, limited life, partnership, limited partnership, bankruptcy, corporation, charter, stock, stockholder, shareholder, dividend, bond, principal, interest, double taxation

Objectives
After studying this section, you will be able to:
1. **Describe** the characteristics of the sole proprietorship.
2. **Understand** the advantages and disadvantages of the partnership.
3. **Describe** the structure and features of the corporation.

Applying Economic Concepts
Unlimited Liability Some forms of business organization can leave you holding the bag—including all the bills—for the entire business. Read to see how personal liability is affected by the type of business owned.

Cover Story

Raw Feelings

Scott Melton thinks he got a raw deal. Melton, who recently opened Sushi Nights on Main Street in Deep Ellum [Texas], filed for Chapter 11 bankruptcy in April for Sushi Deep Ellum Inc., the general partnership he formed to operate Deep Sushi. . . . Last June, Deep Sushi's limited partners, a group

Mounting bills are one of the risks of business.

of 10 or so anesthesiologists and other human meat menders, gave Melton the boot. Not only that, they stiffed him, he says. "They left me holding the bag for $57,000 worth of unpaid taxes . . . including utilities and vendor bills. . . .

—*Dallas Observer Online*, May 20–26, 1999

There are three main forms of business organizations in the economy today—the sole proprietorship, the partnership, like the one Scott Melton describes in the cover story, and the corporation. Each offers its owners significant advantages and disadvantages.

Sole Proprietorships

The most common form of business organization in the United States is the **sole proprietorship** or **proprietorship**—a business owned and run by one person. Although relatively the most numerous and profitable of all business organizations, proprietorships are the smallest in size. As **Figure 3.1** on page 58 shows, proprietorships earn almost one-fifth of the net income earned by all businesses, even though they make only a fraction of total sales.

Forming a Proprietorship

The sole proprietorship is the easiest form of business to start because it involves almost no requirements except for occasional business

Section Overview
This section describes the characteristics of the sole proprietorship, the partnership, and the corporation.

BELLRINGER
Motivational Activity

Project **transparency** and have students answer questions.

Available as blackline master.

Daily Focus Transparency 15

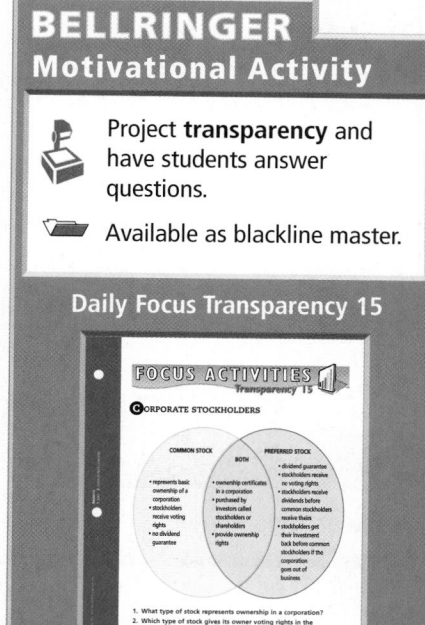

Study Guide

Reading Strategy
Have students create the graphic organizer.
Answers to Graphic: owned and run by one person; jointly owned by two or more persons; formal legal entities, owned by shareholders

Preteaching Vocabulary
Ask students to define *proprietorship, partnership,* and *corporation.*

RESOURCE MANAGER

Reproducible Masters
- Reproducible Lesson Plan 3-1
- Daily Lecture Notes 3-1
- Guided Reading Activity 3-1
- Reading Essentials and Study Guide 3-1
- Section Quiz 3-1

Transparencies
- Daily Focus Transparency 15

Multimedia
- Interactive Economics!
- Interactive Tutor Self-Assessment Software
- ExamView® Pro Testmaker
- Presentation Plus!

②TEACH

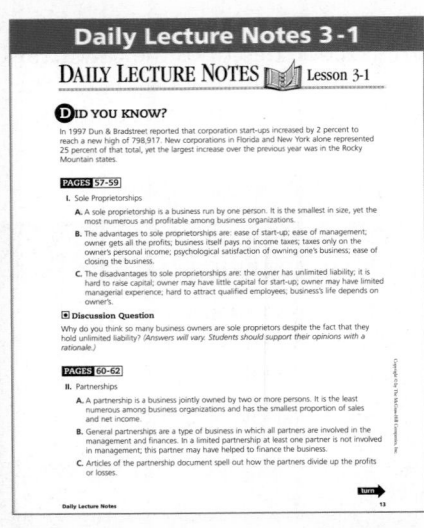

Daily Lecture Notes 3-1

Answer: *corporations*

L1 Generalizing

On the board draw a table with *Sole Proprietorship, Partnership,* and Corporation as vertical headings and *Features, Advantages,* and *Disadvantages* as horizontal headings. Ask students to complete the table. **ELL**

ECONOMICS
AT A GLANCE   Figure 3.1

Corporations, Partnerships, and Sole Proprietorships

- Corporations
- Partnerships
- Sole Proprietorships

Type of Organization
19.9%   73.0%
7.1%

Sales
6.2%
5.0%   88.8%

Net Income (profit)
71.4%   12.9%
15.7%

Source: *2000 Statistical Abstract of the United States*

Using Graphs Businesses can be organized in the United States in a number of ways. Which business organization accounts for the largest amount of sales?

ECONOMICS
Online
Visit epp.glencoe.com and click on *Textbook Updates—Chapter 3* for an update of the data.

---

licenses and fees. Most proprietorships are ready for business as soon as they set up operations. You could start a proprietorship simply by putting up a lemonade stand in your front yard. Someone else might decide to mow lawns, do gardening, or open a restaurant. A proprietorship can be run on the Internet, out of a garage, or from an office in a professional building.

Advantages

The first advantage of a sole proprietorship is the ease of starting up. If someone has an idea or an opportunity to make a profit, he or she has only to decide to go into business and then do it.

The second advantage is the relative ease of management. Decisions may be made quickly, without having to consult a co-owner, boss, or "higher-up." This flexibility means that the owner can make an immediate decision if a problem comes up.

A third advantage is that the owner enjoys the profits of successful management without having to share them with other owners. The possibility of suffering a loss exists, but the lure of profits makes people willing to take risks.

Fourth, the proprietorship does not have to pay separate business income taxes because the business is not recognized as a separate legal entity. The owner still must pay individual income taxes on profits taken from the sole proprietorship, but the business itself is exempt from any tax on income.

Suppose, for example, Mr. Winters owns and operates a small hardware store in a local shopping center and a small auto repair business in his garage next to his home. Because neither business depends on the other, and because the only thing they have in common is ownership, the two businesses appear as separate and distinct economic activities. For tax purposes, however, everything is lumped together at the end of the year. When Mr. Winters files his personal income taxes, the profits from each business, along with wages and salaries earned from other sources, are combined. He does not pay taxes on each of the businesses separately.

A fifth advantage of the proprietorship is the psychological satisfaction. Some people want the personal satisfaction of being their own boss. Other people have a strong desire to see their name in print, have dreams of great wealth or community status, or want to make their mark in history.

A sixth advantage is the ease of getting out of business. In this case, all the proprietor has to do is pay any outstanding bills and then stop offering goods or services for sale.

Disadvantages

One main disadvantage of a proprietorship is that the owner has **unlimited liability.** This means that the owner is personally and fully responsible for all losses and debts of the business. If the business fails, the owner's personal possessions may be taken away to satisfy business debts.

MEETING SPECIAL NEEDS ACTIVITY

Learning Disabled Students who have trouble reading may have problems decoding unfamiliar words and will often skip over them. Many times, however, students can successfully comprehend the words based on the context of the sentence. Ask students to scan Section 1 for words with which they are unfamiliar. Ask them to write these words in their notebooks and to guess at the meanings based on the context. Some words that may need definition or review are: *relatively, liability, capital, minimum, entity, shares, proxy, revenue, chartered.*

📁 Refer to *Inclusion for the Social Studies Classroom Strategies and Activities* in the TCR.

Business Organizations

Sole Proprietorships The sole proprietorship is the most common form of business organization. *What are some of the reasons for setting up a sole proprietorship?*

To illustrate, consider the earlier case of Mr. Winters who owns and operates two businesses. If the hardware business should fail, Mr. Winters' personal wealth, which includes the automobile repair shop, may be legally taken away to pay off debts arising from the hardware store.

A second disadvantage of a proprietorship is the difficulty in raising financial capital. Generally, a great deal of money is needed to set up a business, and even more is required to support its expansion. A problem may arise because the personal financial resources available to most sole proprietors are limited. Banks and other lenders usually do not want to lend money to new or very small businesses. As a result, the proprietor often has to raise financial capital by tapping savings, using credit cards, or borrowing from family members.

A third disadvantage of a proprietorship is that of size and efficiency. A retail store, for example, may need to hire a minimum number of employees just to stay open during normal business hours. It may also need to carry a minimum **inventory**—a stock of finished goods and parts in reserve—to satisfy customers or to keep production flowing smoothly. Because of limited capital, the proprietor may not be able to hire enough personnel or stock enough inventory to operate the business efficiently.

A fourth disadvantage is that the proprietor often has limited managerial experience. The owner-manager of a small company may be an inventor who is highly qualified as an engineer, but lacks the "business sense" or time to oversee the orderly growth of the company. This owner may have to hire others to do the types of work—sales, marketing, and accounting—that he or she cannot do.

A fifth disadvantage is the difficulty of attracting qualified employees. Because proprietorships tend to be small, employees often have to be skilled in several areas. In addition, many top high school and college graduates are more likely to be attracted to positions with larger, well-established firms than small ones. This is especially true when larger firms offer *fringe benefits*—employee benefits such as paid vacations, sick leave, retirement, and health or medical insurance—in addition to wages and salaries.

A sixth disadvantage of the sole proprietorship is **limited life.** This means that the firm legally ceases to exist when the owner dies, quits, or sells the business.

STANDARD & POOR'S INFOBYTE

Business Inventories The Business Inventories report measures the monthly percentage changes in inventories from manufacturers, retailers, and wholesalers. The report is useful in predicting inventories within the gross domestic product (GDP), which can be volatile from quarter to quarter. Business inventories are reported monthly by the Commerce Department. Business inventories data, released in the third week of each month, show the monthly percentage change in inventories from manufacturers, retailers, and wholesalers. Because the majority of the data is old by the time it is released, it is usually not a key report to the markets. One portion of the report that does draw a bit of attention, though, is the inventory-to-sales ratio. This particular component is useful in forecasting, since increasing inventory-to-sales ratios signals a cutback in production.

CHAPTER 3: BUSINESS ORGANIZATIONS **59**

Visual Instruction

Answer to Caption:
easy to establish or discontinue; do not have to share profits; no separate income taxes; personal satisfaction

F.Y.I.

Each year, *Fortune* magazine provides a list of the top 500 U.S. companies, called the "Fortune 500." The companies are ranked by sales revenue. In 2001, the top ten companies were:

1. Exxon Mobil
2. Wal-Mart Stores
3. General Motors
4. Ford Motor
5. General Electric
6. Citigroup
7. Enron
8. International Business Machines
9. AT&T
10. Verizon Communications

Source: *Fortune* Magazine

FREE ENTERPRISE ACTIVITY

Ask students to imagine that they are entrepreneurs who have developed a product that is bound to succeed—a frisbee that, when heated, can be eaten like a pizza. Ask students to consider how they would organize to manufacture and sell their new product. Have them write an essay stating which form of business organization they would choose, defending their choice in terms of the advantages and disadvantages of the form of business organization.

L2 Applying Ideas

Write the following on the board: **1.** General partnership of five accountants. **2.** Limited partnership in the retail business; five general partners, five limited partners.

Ask students to suggest what the partners in these two businesses might have to consider in their articles of partnership, such as local ordinances and regulations. Then have students work in small groups to write business agreements.

Math Practice

Types of Firms/Total Sales
Write the data below on the board. Have students use the data to answer the questions that follow.

Number of firms (1992)

Sole Proprietorships	14,599,000
Partnerships	1,090,000
Corporations	3,597,000
Total	19,286,000

Total sales by different types of firms (1992)

Sole Proprietorships	$722,000,000
Partnerships	$665,000,000
Corporations	$12,685,000,000
Total	$14,072,000,000

Source: U.S. Census Bureau

What percentage of the total number of firms do corporations comprise? *(19%)* What percentage of the total sales by different types of firms are made by corporations? *(90%)*

Partnerships

A **partnership** is a business jointly owned by two or more persons. It shares many of the same strengths and weaknesses of a sole proprietorship. As shown in **Figure 3.1**, partnerships are the least numerous form of business organization, accounting for the smallest proportion of sales and net income.

Types of Partnerships

The most common form of partnership is a *general* partnership, one in which all partners are responsible for the management and financial obligations of the business. In a *limited* partnership, at least one partner is not active in the daily running of the business, although he or she may have contributed funds to finance the operation.

Forming a Partnership

Like a proprietorship, a partnership is relatively easy to start. Because more than one owner is involved, formal legal papers called articles of partnership are usually drawn up to specify arrangements between partners. Although not always required, these papers state ahead of time how profits (or losses) will be divided.

The articles of partnership may specify that the profits be divided equally or by any other arrangement suitable to the partners. They also may state the way future partners can be taken into the business and the way the property of the business will be distributed if the partnership ends. Individuals who join as partners must be very careful because they are financially responsible for personal as well as business debts of their partners (except for those debts specifically exempted in the partnership contract).

CYBERNOMICS SPOTLIGHT

Entrepreneurs of the New Economy

During the 1700s and 1800s, a series of innovations in agriculture and industry led to profound economic and social change throughout many regions of the world. Urban industrial economies emerged in these areas and eventually spread around the world. This transformation, which became known as the Industrial Revolution, began when power-driven machinery in factories replaced work done in homes, altering the way people had lived and worked for hundreds of years.

In the late twentieth century, the world underwent a technological revolution as significant as the Industrial Revolution. Computers and the Internet are at the heart of this transformation.

Dell Computer Few have done more to take advantage of the promise of the Internet than Michael Dell. Under his leadership Dell Computer is in the forefront of making the Web the foundation of an existing business. Many producers, like Dell, are bypassing regular channels of trade and reaching out to their customers directly. Dell Computer grew twice as fast as other personal computer manufacturers by allowing buyers to configure their own PCs online.

Michael Dell

Another reason for Dell's success is velocity. According to Dell, business velocity is shrinking time and distance between a company and its suppliers as well as its customers. "The reduction of time, the reduction of inventory, and the reduction of physical materials and assets can drive a tremendous improvement in business efficiency," notes Dell. "Customers' purchasing decisions become faster and they have direct access to information they need immediately. Customers can compare products around the world over the Internet. This has dramatic implications for companies that previously had based their strategies on having a physical location, and having customers go and buy their products."

60 UNIT 1 FUNDAMENTAL ECONOMIC CONCEPTS

CYBERNOMICS SPOTLIGHT

More About . . . Dell Computers and Online Auctions Michael Dell started Dell Computers from his dorm room at the University of Texas at Austin with a few computers and $1,000. His biggest innovation was eliminating the middleman by selling computers directly to customers. That enabled Dell not only to keep prices down, but also to offer more reliable service and support to customers. Dell's superior service was very well received by consumers and eventually prodded other computer manufacturers to offer better service.

There are now many online auction sites, but eBay has a distinct advantage over all of them—it's the largest. Sellers are drawn to eBay since it gives them access to the greatest number of potential

Advantages

Like the sole proprietorship, the first advantage of the partnership is its ease of establishment. Even the costs of the partnership articles, which normally involve attorney fees and a filing fee for the state, are minimal if they are spread over several partners.

Ease of management is the second advantage. Generally, each partner brings different areas of expertise to the business: one might have a talent for marketing, another for production, another for bookkeeping and finance, and yet another for shipping and distribution. While partners usually agree ahead of time to consult with each other before making major decisions, partners generally have a great deal of freedom to make lesser ones.

A third advantage is the lack of special taxes on a partnership. As in a proprietorship, the partners withdraw profits from the firm and then pay individual income taxes on them at the end of the year. Each partner has to submit a special schedule to the Internal Revenue Service detailing the profits from the partnership, but this is for informational purposes only and does not give a partnership any special legal status.

Fourth, partnerships can usually attract financial capital more easily than proprietorships. They are generally a little bigger and, if established, have a better chance at getting a bank loan. If money cannot be borrowed, the existing partners can always take in new partners who bring financial capital with them as part of their price for joining the business.

A fifth advantage of a partnership is the slightly larger size, which often makes for more efficient operations. In some areas, such as medicine and law, a

Did You Know?

Internet Commerce As use of the Internet spreads throughout the world, the U.S. share of Internet commerce will fall. In 2003, the United States will account for about 50% of Internet-based commerce, compared with 75% in 1998.

Online Auctions The auction, a centuries-old tradition that links communities of buyers and sellers, is taking a new form on the Internet. One of the first to sell used goods online was the Gibson Guitar Company. The company offered older-model, used guitars for sale on the Web in 1996. Gibson's site was a huge success, in large part due to the celebrated reputation of its products.

The pioneer of person-to-person online trading is eBay. Launching its site in 1995, eBay at first offered only small collectibles such as Beanie Babies and Pez dispensers. Today, the company connects millions of buyers and sellers worldwide. It helps people buy and sell products in more than 1,000 categories, including antiques, books, collectibles, electronics, sports memorabilia, and toys.

Under the leadership of CEO Margaret Whitman, eBay helped establish negotiated pricing, a concept that influenced Web selling on items such as airplane tickets. The success of eBay has proven that customers will buy used merchandise online—a significant step for many businesses in accepting the idea of the online auction.

An abundance of collectibles and other goods are available through online auctions.

CHAPTER 3: BUSINESS ORGANIZATIONS **61**

L3 Writing

To emphasize the importance of corporations in the U.S. economy, provide students with recent issues of *Fortune, Forbes, Business Week, The Wall Street Journal,* or the business sections of various newspapers. Direct students to review the periodicals to locate articles about corporations. Suggest that they take notes on the various items they find. Then ask students to write a few paragraphs on their findings, using the key terms introduced in the discussion on corporations on pages 62–65. Call on volunteers to read their paragraphs to the class.

CURRICULUM CONNECTION

History The first recorded use of the word "corporation" appeared in the works of Tertullian, one of the founders of the Christian church, in A.D. 190. Tertullian employed the term, which he derived from the Latin word *corporare,* "to make into a body," in his writings on church law. The word first appeared in English in the fifteenth century, and referred to the trade guilds of merchants. By the seventeenth century, the word had begun to be used in its modern-day sense.

buyers. Buyers flock there because it offers the largest selection. One rival, Rbid.com, promoted its new auction site in May 1999 by offering $60,000 in prize money. It didn't work. On August 13, 1999 for example, the auction site had only 16 items listed, and no bidders for any of them. A new site called AuctionRover.com also sprang up in an attempt to diminish eBay's advantage. This site enabled buyers to check out several auction sites at once by doing the searching for them. By 2001, both Rbid.com and AuctionRover.com were out of business, leaving eBay as the reigning auction site. Have students research and report on other innovative companies that have benefitted from advances in communication.

C Y B E R N O M I C S

Internet Business Forms

What kind of business organization is best suited to selling books on the Internet? The largest online bookstores, such as Amazon and Barnes & Noble, are corporations. This allows them to acquire large amounts of financial capital so that they can maintain a huge inventory of books, provide reliable service to their customers, and advertise heavily. But some sole proprietorships and partnerships are also succeeding at selling books on the Internet. While it's difficult for them to offer the selection, low prices, and service of the larger online bookstores, some of them have found a niche selling used, rare, or out-of-print books. Since these bookstores are usually too small to attract many users to their own sites, many of them list their books on Web sites like Bibliofind.com, which puts potential buyers in contact with sellers.

relatively small firm with three or four partners may be just the right size for the market. Other partnerships, such as accounting firms, may have hundreds of partners offering services throughout the United States.

A sixth advantage is that many partnerships find it easier to attract top talent into their organizations. Because most partnerships offer specialized services, top graduates seek out stable, well-paying firms to apply their recently acquired skills in law, accounting, and other fields.

Disadvantages

The main disadvantage of a general partnership is that each partner is fully responsible for the acts of all other partners. If one partner causes the firm to suffer a huge loss, each partner is fully and personally responsible for the loss. This is the same as

Business Organizations

Partnerships Finding the right partner or partners is essential in a partnership. *What is the difference between a general partnership and a limited partnership?*

the unlimited liability feature of a sole proprietorship. It is more complicated, however, because more owners are involved. As a result, most people are extremely careful when they choose a business partner.

In the case of a **limited partnership,** the limited partners have limited liability. This means that the investor's responsibility for the debts of the business is limited by the size of his or her investment in the firm. If the business fails and large debts remain, the limited partner loses only his or her original investment, leaving the general partners to make up the rest.

Like the proprietorship, a partnership has limited life. When a partner dies or leaves, the partnership must be dissolved and reorganized. However, the new partnership may try to reach an agreement with the older partnership to keep its old name for public image purposes.

Another weakness is the potential for conflict between partners. Sometimes partners discover that they do not get along, and they either have to learn to work together or leave the business. If the partnership is large, it is fairly easy for these types of problems to develop, even though everyone thought they would get along well in the first place.

Partnerships offer entrepreneurs increased access to financial capital, but—as Scott Melton the former general partner of Deep Sushi found out—things do not always work out as planned. First, his business filed for **bankruptcy,** a court-granted permission to an individual or business to cease or delay debt payments. Then, because the limited partners had no liability beyond their initial investments, Scott was left with the rest of the bills. As a result, he also filed for bankruptcy.

Corporations

As shown in **Figure 3.1,** corporations account for approximately one-fifth of the firms in the United States and about 90 percent of all sales. A **corporation** is a form of business organization recognized by law as a separate legal entity having all the rights of an individual. This status gives the corporation the right to buy and sell property, enter into legal contracts, and to sue and be sued.

CRITICAL THINKING

Identifying Central Issues To help illustrate the difficulties partnerships sometimes encounter, ask students to answer the following questions in a two- or three-paragraph essay. What problems would you expect to have if you were assigned to do a graded team project with one other student? Would there be more or fewer problems if more students were assigned to each team? Explain.

Forming a Corporation

Unlike a sole proprietorship or partnership, a corporation is a very formal and legal arrangement. People who would like to *incorporate,* or form a corporation, must file for permission from the national government or the state where the business will have its headquarters. If approved, a **charter**–a government document that gives permission to create a corporation–is granted. The charter states the name of the company, address, purpose of business, and other features of the business.

The charter also specifies the number of shares of **stock,** or ownership certificates in the firm. These shares are sold to investors, called **stockholders** or **shareholders.** The money is then used to set up the corporation. If the corporation is profitable, it may eventually issue a **dividend**–a check representing a portion of the corporate earnings–to each stockholder.

Corporate Structure

When an investor purchases stock, he or she becomes an owner with certain ownership rights. The extent of these rights depends on the type of stock purchased, common or preferred.

Common stock represents basic ownership of a corporation. The owner of common stock usually receives one vote for each share of stock. This vote is used to elect a board of directors whose duty is to direct the corporation's business by setting broad policies and goals. The board also hires a professional management team to run the business on a daily basis.

Preferred stock represents nonvoting ownership shares of the corporation. These stockholders receive dividends before common stockholders receive theirs. If the corporation goes out of business, and if some property and funds remain after other debts have been paid, preferred stockholders get their investment back before common stockholders. Because the stock is nonvoting, preferred stockholders do not have the right to elect members to the board of directors.

In theory, a stockholder who owns a majority of a corporation's common stock can elect board members and control the company. In some cases,

the common stockholder might even elect himself or herself, and other family members, to the board of directors.

In practice, this is not done very often because most corporations are so large and the number of shares held by the typical stockholder is so small. Most small stockholders either do not vote, or they turn their votes over to someone else. This is done with the use of a proxy, a ballot that gives a stockholder's representative the right to vote on corporate matters.

Finally, **Figure 3.3** presents an organizational chart which shows how the different parts of the organization relate to one another. The chart shows the basic components of the business—sales, production, finance, payroll, etc.—as well as the lines of authority so that everybody knows who they report to.

CHAPTER 3: BUSINESS ORGANIZATIONS **63**

ECONOMICS
AT A GLANCE

Answer: *Common stock represents basic ownership of a corporation. Owners of common stock can vote for the corporation's board of directors. Preferred stock owners own shares in the company but cannot vote. They also receive dividends before common stockholders.*

THE GLOBAL ECONOMY

Corporations in Japan
Annual shareholder meetings in Japan are much different than in the United States. Every corporation in that country holds its annual meeting on the same day. The meetings are usually packed with loyal employees, and some meetings last less than an hour.

INTERACTIVE ECONOMICS!

  CD-ROM

PERSONAL FINANCE Have students study the Lesson 10 "Tutorial," which focuses on stocks, stock markets, and mutual funds. After students read the "Tutorial," have them attempt to complete the "Economics Lab" dealing with terms related to personal finance.

 Also supplied in disk format.

EXTENDING THE CONTENT

Bankruptcy If a firm files for bankruptcy under *Chapter 7,* it simply liquidates and goes out of business. If it files bankruptcy under *Chapter 11,* it is given one year to reorganize and is allowed to stay in business. Individuals with regular incomes may file bankruptcy under *Chapter 13,* which is less complicated and less expensive than filing under *Chapter 11. Chapter 13* is not available to corporations or partnerships. Have students investigate the schedule of priorities in a bankruptcy case, for both individuals and businesses. How is personal and business property disposed of in order to pay off creditors? Students should share their findings with the class.

CURRICULUM CONNECTION

History State charters issued during the 1800s, for the most part, greatly restricted the powers of corporations. By the end of the century, however, courts and legislatures, yielding to pressure from business interests, began to ease controls on corporate activities. Exposés of business corruption by muckraking journalists at the turn of the century stirred demands for renewed restrictions. As a result, federal and state governments passed laws regulating practically every aspect of corporate operations.

L2 Writing an Article

Have students write a newspaper article describing the three forms of business organizations and the economic advantages and disadvantages of each.

ECONOMICS AT A GLANCE

Figure 3.3

Ownership, Control, and Organization of a Typical Corporation

The Owners *Shareholders elect the*

Board of Directors *who selects*

The President *who hires*

Vice President Sales

Vice President Production

Vice President Finance

Domestic | **International** | **Quality Control** | **Research & Development** | **Payroll**

Using Charts This organizational chart shows the chain of command of a typical organization. Who reports directly to the vice president of production?

Advantages

The main advantage of a corporation is the ease of raising financial capital. If the corporation needs more capital, it can sell additional stock to investors. The revenue can then be used to finance or expand operations. A corporation may also borrow money by issuing bonds. A **bond** is a written promise to repay the amount borrowed at a later date. The amount borrowed is known as the **principal.** While the money is borrowed, the corporation pays **interest,** the price paid for the use of another's money.

A second advantage of a corporation is that the directors of the corporation can hire professional managers to run the firm. This means that the owners, or stockholders, can still own a portion of the corporation without having to know a great deal about the business itself.

A third advantage is that the corporation provides limited liability for its owners. This means that the corporation itself, not its owners, is fully responsible for its debts and obligations. To illustrate, suppose a corporation cannot pay all of its obligations and goes out of business. Because of limited liability, stockholder losses are limited to the money they invested in stock. Even if other debts remain, the stockholders are not responsible for them.

Because limited liability is so attractive, many firms incorporate just to take advantage of it. Suppose Mr. Winters, who owns the hardware store and the auto repair business, now decides to set up each business as a corporation. If the hardware business should fail, his personal wealth, which includes the automobile repair business, is safe. Mr. Winters may lose all the money invested in the hardware business, but that would be the extent of his loss.

Another advantage is unlimited life, meaning that the corporation continues to exist even when ownership changes. Because the corporation is recognized as a separate legal entity, the name of the company stays the same, and the corporation continues to do business.

The ease of transferring ownership is also a strength of the corporation. If a shareholder no

INTERDISCIPLINARY CONNECTIONS ACTIVITY

Daily Life Have students keep a record of the businesses they visit for one week. Ask them to classify each business according to its formal structure—sole proprietorship, partnership, or corporation. In some cases, the firm's name may reveal the form of organization. In other cases, students may have to ask the manager. Students should also note the kinds of goods and services offered at each business. At the end of the week, have students identify in a class discussion any patterns in the types of goods and services provided by particular forms of business organizations. Also discuss whether a particular form of organization is the best provider for their everyday needs.

longer wants to be an owner, he or she simply sells the stock to someone else, who then becomes the new owner. As a result, it is much easier for the owner of a corporation to find a new buyer than it is for a sole proprietor or a partnership.

Disadvantages

One disadvantage of the corporate structure is the difficulty and expense of getting a charter. Depending on the state, attorney's fees and filing expenses can cost several thousand dollars. Because of this expense, many people prefer to set up proprietorships or partnerships.

A second disadvantage of the corporation is that the owners, or shareholders, have little say in how the business is run after they have voted for the board of directors. This is because the directors turn day-to-day operations over to a professional management team, resulting in the separation of ownership and management. This is different from

the proprietorship and partnership, where ownership and management are one and the same.

A third disadvantage is the **double taxation** of corporate profits. Stockholders' dividends are taxed twice—once as corporate profit and again as personal income. This tax status is a consequence of the corporation's special status as a separate legal entity. This also means that the corporation is required to keep detailed records of sales and expenses so that it can compute and pay taxes on its profits.

Finally, corporations are subject to more government regulation than other forms of business. Corporations must register with the state in which they are chartered. If a corporation wants to sell its stock to the public, it must register with the federal Securities and Exchange Commission (SEC). It will also have to provide financial information concerning sales and profits on a regular basis to the general public. Even an attempt to take over another business may require federal government approval.

Business Organizations

Corporations A corporation is an organization owned by many people but treated by law as though it were a person. As a corporation the company can raise money by selling shares of ownership in the business to hundreds or thousands of people. Owners of common stock elect a board of directors. The board of directors, in turn, hires managers to run the business. *How do the holders of common stock differ from the holders of preferred stock?*

CHAPTER 3: BUSINESS ORGANIZATIONS **65**

EXTENDING THE CONTENT

Sole Proprietorships and Partnerships Although sole proprietorships and partnerships account for only a small part of total business sales, they still play a very important role in the overall economy. These relatively small operations usually have close personal ties with their customers and often are the first to notice—and respond to—changes in consumer demand. In addition, small businesses are able to produce certain specialty items—fine jewelry, for example—more economically than larger companies.

L3 Illustrating Ideas

Have students use library resources to locate an annual report of a major American corporation. Have them use information in the report on the corporation's organizational structure to construct an organizational chart like that on page 64.

Visual Instruction

Answer to Caption:
Common stockholders have the right to elect the corporation's directors. Preferred stockholders have no voting rights but receive dividends before common shareholders and have higher claims on assets if the corporation fails.

3 ASSESS

Assign Section 1 Assessment as homework or as an in-class activity.

Have students use **Interactive Tutor Self-Assessment Software.**

Section Quiz 3-1

Reteach

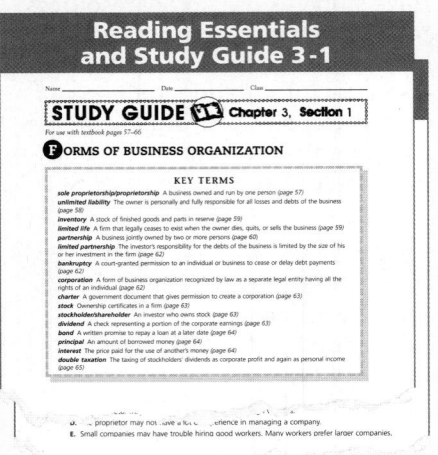

Reading Essentials and Study Guide 3-1

Enrich

Invite representatives from each of the three types of business organizations to participate in a panel discussion. Have students ask the panel members questions on the advantages and disadvantages of the various business forms.

 CLOSE

Ask students to discuss which business form they think is the most important for the American economy.

Government and Business Regulation

 The concept of competitive markets, free from government intervention, has always been a strong part of the U.S. economy. However, in the mid-nineteenth century, states tried to restrict the powers of corporations. By the 1890s, however, courts and legislatures, influenced by business interests and aware that giant corporations were becoming indispensable, had relaxed control over business. States that continued to restrict corporations found their major businesses moving to other states where the laws were more lenient.

Business Regulation

In the twentieth century, various consumer groups demanded regulation of giant corporations. In response, federal and state governments passed stronger regulations. States helped set insurance companies' rates, administered licensing exams, and generally protected consumer interests. Legislation regulated all kinds of corporations, but laws regulating banks, insurance companies, and companies providing such necessities as electricity, gas, telephone service, or transportation service, were especially rigorous. Recently, states have reduced regulations in order to encourage competition. In the next section, you will read about the ways businesses can grow and expand.

Business Development

State governments are very active in trying to attract new industry. Governors often travel throughout the country or even to foreign countries to draw new business to their states. Television advertising, billboards, brochures, and newspaper advertisements promote travel or business opportunities.

Beginning in the 1930s, state governments sold industrial development bonds to people or institutions and used the money to help finance industries that relocated or expanded within the state. The state paid off the bond within a specified time period from money that the industry paid back to the state in the form of taxes. Today a state may offer an incentive such as a tax credit, or a reduction in taxes, in return for the creation of new jobs or new business investment.

Section 1 Assessment

Checking for Understanding

1. **Main Idea** Using your notes from the graphic organizer activity on page 57, explain why partnerships are able to attract more capital than sole proprietorships.

2. **Key Terms** Define sole proprietorship, proprietorship, unlimited liability, inventory, limited life, partnership, limited liability, bankruptcy, corporation, charter, stock, stockholder, shareholder, dividend, bond, principal, interest, double taxation.

3. **Identify** the characteristics and organization of the sole proprietorship.

4. **Discuss** the advantages and disadvantages of the partnership.

5. **Discuss** the structure and features of the corporation.

Applying Economic Concepts

6. **Unlimited Liability** Interview one or two business owners in your community and ask them about the formal structure of their business. Ask them how they feel about the issue of unlimited liability. Inquire whether the issue had any influence on the legal form of business they selected.

Critical Thinking

7. **Drawing Conclusions** When a corporation wants to introduce a potentially profitable but risky product, it frequently sets up a separate company that has its own corporate structure. Why do you think the corporation does this?

Practice and assess key social studies skills with the *Glencoe Skillbuilder Interactive Workbook, Level 2.*

Section 1 Assessment Answers

1. partnerships are bigger, better established, have a better chance of getting a bank loan; new partners bring financial capital.

2. All vocabulary terms are defined in the text.

3. owned by one individual; all decisions made by owner; owner receives all profits, responsible for all debts, losses; limited life

4. adv: ease of establishment and management, no special taxes, can attract financing and top talent, more efficient; disadv: all partners equally responsible for business losses (except in limited partnerships), limited life, potential conflict among partners

5. It is a separate legal entity with all the rights of the individual. It possesses a charter and shares of stock that are sold to investors. Investors purchase common stock or preferred stock.

6. Answers should demonstrate an understanding of the concepts.

7. limited liability—the first corporation limits its exposure by setting up a separate corporation

Profiles IN Economics

A Pioneer in Corporate America:
Kenneth I. Chenault
(1952–)

What does it take to succeed at one of America's largest and most prestigious corporations? Kenneth Chenault knows the answer. At the young age of 45, Chenault became president and chief operating officer (COO) of American Express, the sixty-fifth largest company in the country.

Chenault is the first African American to serve as president of a top-100 company. Some people have compared him to Jackie Robinson, who broke the color barrier in baseball in 1947. Coincidentally—and perhaps fittingly—Chenault became COO in 1997, the 50th anniversary year of Robinson's breakthrough.

STEPPING STONES

Remarkably, Kenneth Chenault did not start his career in business. Instead, he obtained an undergraduate degree in history, and then earned a law degree at Harvard. He had keen instincts for business, however, and worked for

a management consulting firm before joining American Express in 1981.

CHALLENGES AND OPPORTUNITIES

At first Chenault was responsible for strategic planning. His intelligence and hard work led him up the corporate ranks. Promotions brought Chenault new challenges—and opportunities.

His greatest opportunity now is as president and chief executive officer (CEO). Chenault is responsible for integrating strategies across all of American Express's many business units. He has been in the forefront of company efforts to increase market share by expanding product offerings, globalizing the business, and opening American Express's card network to bank partners around the world. Chenault is also responsible for global advertising and brand management.

How does Chenault view his tremendous responsibilities as the highest-ranking African American in corporate America?

"With American Express being a large, publicly held company, I would be scrutinized under any circumstances," Chenault said "If you don't enhance shareholder value, it doesn't matter who you are, you will have a problem. . . . [I]f I do well, I would be very hopeful that it would encourage other companies to give people the opportunity to succeed."

Kenneth Chenault himself had the opportunity to succeed. And he has proven he knew how to take advantage of it.

Examining the Profile

1. **Drawing Conclusions** What personal ethics and qualities do you think help make Chenault a success?

2. **For Further Research** Learn about and report on Chenault's philanthropic contributions in New York City.

BACKGROUND

Kenneth Chenault sets an example of someone who uses his economic success to benefit others. His community service has earned him numerous awards, among them the Arthur Ashe Institute for Urban Health's Leadership Award, given "to men and women who have used their personal success to help others" in the areas of corporate social responsibility, urban medical education, and humanitarian service.

TEACH

Share this quotation from Chenault with students and have them explain, in writing or orally, how they develop each trait in school.

Question: What is the most important trait for someone to develop to be successful in today's global business environment?
Chenault: I would say that there are several important traits. One would be an openness to ideas and different perspectives, which requires excellent listening skills. Another would be the ability to synthesize ideas to create unifying themes and make specific recommendations that solve business problems. A final one would be to become adept at taking good ideas that are global in scope and making them locally relevant. . . .

Answers to Examining the Profile

1. Answers will vary, but students should at least imply that Chenault is intelligent, hard working and wants others to succeed.

2. Answers will vary. Chenault is very active and is a recipient of the Arthur Ashe Institute for Urban Health's Leadership Award, the Torch of Liberty from the Anti-Defamation League of B'Nai Brith, the Candle in the Dark Award from Morehouse College, the Friend of the Children Award from Rheedlan Centers for Children and Families, an American Black Achievement Award, and is recognized as Corporate Patron of the Arts by the Studio Museum of Harlem.

FOCUS

Section Overview
This section describes how businesses can grow.

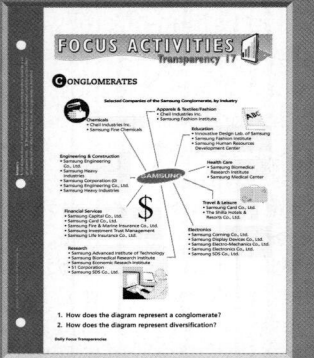
Study Guide

Reading Strategy
Have students create the graphic organizer.
Answers to Graphic: *Similarities include: to grow faster, to become more efficient, to acquire or deliver a better product*

Preteaching Vocabulary
Ask students to speculate on the meanings of the Key Terms. Have them check their accuracy by finding the correct definitions in the text.

SECTION 2

Business Growth and Expansion

Study Guide

Main Idea
Businesses grow through merging with other companies and by investing in the machinery, tools, and equipment used to produce goods and services.

Reading Strategy
Graphic Organizer As you read the section, complete a graphic organizer similar to the one below by comparing a vertical merger to a horizontal merger.

- Vertical merger
- Similarities
- Horizontal merger

Key Terms
merger, income statement, net income, depreciation, cash flow, horizontal merger, vertical merger, conglomerate, multinational

Objectives
After studying this section, you will be able to:
1. **Explain** how businesses can reinvest their profits to grow and expand.
2. **Recognize** the reasons that cause firms to merge.
3. **Identify** two different types of mergers.

Applying Economic Concepts
Business Growth Businesses can grow by reinvesting their profits in themselves, or they can combine with another business. Read to find out what influences growth.

Cover Story

Kroger Bags Fred Meyer

Grocery store giant Kroger Co. agreed Monday to purchase rival Fred Meyer Co. in a $12.8 billion deal that will enable Kroger to reclaim its status as the nation's largest supermarket company. . . . [Analysts say] the merger is a good deal

Supermarket companies are growing through mergers.

for both companies, one that should create the economies of scale necessary to remain competitive in the tough supermarket industry.

The merger also will enable Kroger to [stay] ahead of rival Albertson's, which otherwise would have eclipsed Kroger through its $11.7 billion buyout of American Stores Co. in August. . . . Combined with Meyer, currently the fifth-largest grocery chain, Kroger will operate 2,200 supermarkets in 31 states, boasting $43 billion in annual sales.

—*CNNfn*, October 19, 1998

68

A business can grow in one of two ways. First, it can grow by reinvesting some of its profits. A business can also expand by engaging, much like Kroger did, in a **merger**—a combination of two or more businesses to form a single firm.

Growth Through Reinvestment

Most businesses use some of the revenue they receive from sales to invest in factories, machinery, and new technologies. We can use the **income statement**—a report showing a business's sales, expenses, and profits for a certain period—to illustrate the process. An income statement can reflect various periods of financial activity, such as three months or a year.

Estimating Cash Flows

As illustrated in **Figure 3.4**, the business first records its total sales for the period. Next, it finds its **net income** by subtracting all of its expenses, including taxes, from its revenues. These expenses include the cost of any goods such as inventory,

---

RESOURCE MANAGER

Reproducible Masters
- Reproducible Lesson Plan 3-2
- Daily Lecture Notes 3-2
- Guided Reading Activity 3-2
- Reading Essentials and Study Guide 3-2
- Section Quiz 3-2

Transparencies
- Daily Focus Transparency 17

Multimedia
- Interactive Tutor Self-Assessment Software
- ExamView® Pro Testmaker
- Presentation Plus!

wages and salaries, interest payments, and **depreciation,** a non-cash charge the firm takes for the general wear and tear on its capital goods.

Depreciation is called a *non-cash charge* because, unlike other expenses shown in the figure, the money is never paid to anyone else. For example, interest may be paid to a bank, wages may be paid to employees, but the money allocated to depreciation never goes anywhere–it simply stays in the business.

The concept of **cash flow,** the sum of net income and non-cash charges such as depreciation, is the *bottom line,* or real measure of profits for the business. This is because the cash flow represents the total amount of new funds the business generates from operations.

Reinvesting Cash Flows

The business owners, either directly in the case of the proprietorship or partnership, or indirectly through the board of directors in the case of the corporation, decide how the cash flow will be allocated. Some of it can be paid back to owners as their reward for risk taking, or the funds can be reinvested in the form of new plant, equipment, and technologies.

When cash flows are reinvested in the business, the firm can produce additional products. This generates additional sales and a larger cash flow during the next sales period. As long as the firm remains profitable, and as long as the reinvested cash flow is larger than the wear and tear on the equipment, the firm will grow.

Growth Through Mergers

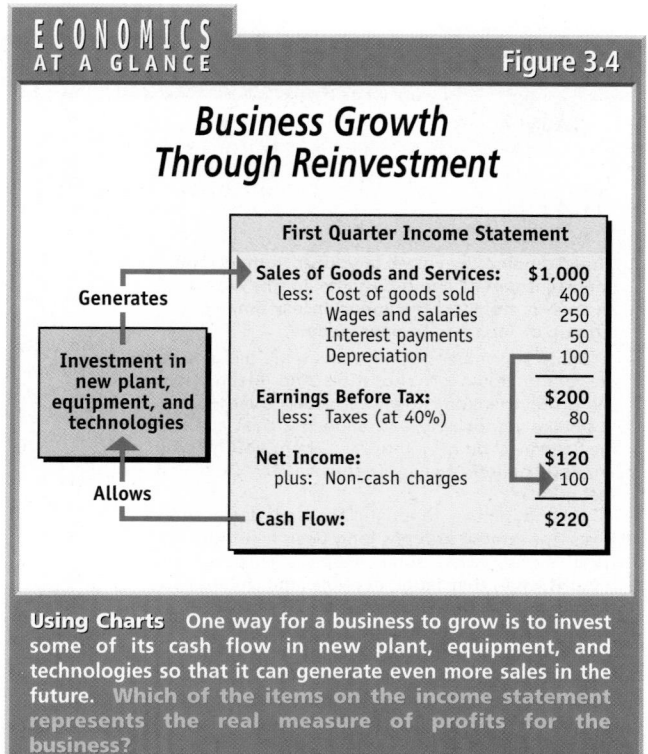

When firms merge, one gives up its separate legal identity. For public recognition purposes, however, the name of the new company may reflect the identities of the merged companies. When Chase National Bank and Bank of Manhattan merged, the new organization was called the Chase Manhattan Bank of New York–a name later changed to Chase Manhattan Corporation to reflect its geographically expanding business.

Mergers take place for a variety of reasons. A firm may seek a merger to grow faster, to become more efficient, to acquire or deliver a better product, to eliminate a rival, or to change its image.

Reasons for Merging

Some managers find that they cannot grow as fast as they would like using the funds they generate internally. As a result, the firm may look for another firm with which to merge. Sometimes a merger makes sense, and other times it may not, but the desire to be bigger–if not the biggest–is one reason that mergers take place.

CHAPTER 3: BUSINESS ORGANIZATIONS **69**

ECONOMICS AT A GLANCE | Figure 3.4

Business Growth Through Reinvestment

First Quarter Income Statement

Generates →

Investment in new plant, equipment, and technologies

Allows →

Sales of Goods and Services:		$1,000
less: Cost of goods sold	400	
Wages and salaries	250	
Interest payments	50	
Depreciation	100	
Earnings Before Tax:		**$200**
less: Taxes (at 40%)	80	
Net Income:		**$120**
plus: Non-cash charges	100	
Cash Flow:		**$220**

Using Charts One way for a business to grow is to invest some of its cash flow in new plant, equipment, and technologies so that it can generate even more sales in the future. Which of the items on the income statement represents the real measure of profits for the business?

---

② TEACH

ECONOMICS AT A GLANCE

Answer: *the cash flow*

Chart Skills Practice

Have students quickly sketch this chart on a sheet of paper. Ask them to draw another arrow and box showing where the cash flow would go if it was not reinvested into the business. *(arrows should point to box labeled "owners")*

L1 Diversification

To illustrate the benefits of diversification, **ask:** What may be the consequenses of a store that sells snowboards merging with a store that sells surfboards? Would this be a responsible use of both businesses?

MEETING SPECIAL NEEDS ACTIVITY

Learning Disabled For students who have trouble with reading, skimming may help them organize information and improve their reading comprehension. Explain to students that skimming a section will help them formulate ideas about what will be covered in the section. Demonstrate skimming by saying: "First, I look at the chapter title, then I read the section and subsection headings. Next, I look at the photographs and other illustrations and, finally, I read the words in bold type, the section Study Guide, and the first and last paragraphs of the section." Have students practice each step after you announce it.

📂 Refer to *Inclusion for the Social Studies Classroom Strategies and Activities* in the TCR.

Guided Reading Activity 3-2

Name _____ Date _____ Class _____

GUIDED READING Activity 3-2

For use with textbook pages 68–73

B USINESS GROWTH AND EXPANSION

OUTLINING

Directions: Locate the heading in your textbook. Then use the information under the heading to help you write each answer. Use another sheet of paper if necessary.

I. Growth Through Reinvestment
   A. Estimating Cash Flows—What does cash flow represent?
   B. Reinvesting Cash Flows
      1. What can business owners do with cash flow to further help their businesses?
      2. What can happen when cash flows are reinvested in the business?
II. Growth Through Mergers
   A. Introduction
      1. What happens when two firms merge?
      2. What are five possible reasons for mergers?
   B. Types of Mergers—What is the difference between a horizontal merger and a vertical merger?
   C. Conglomerates—What is the main reason for a conglomerate to want diversification?
   D. Multinationals—What are the advantages and disadvantages of multinationals?

Guided Reading Activities

THE GLOBAL ECONOMY

When You Say Profits, Smile

Just as foreigners are striving to learn more about American culture, Americans traveling abroad are wise to learn more about foreign cultures. The following are examples of taboos in other countries:

- In many parts of the world, it's deeply offensive to offer something or to eat with the left hand.
- In parts of Latin America, it's considered rude to yawn in public.
- It's insulting to tip in China.

Answers:
1. *Friendliness toward clients is likely to increase sales.*
2. *If business people know their clients' values, they can avoid accidentally offending their clients and, in the process, improve relations and sales.*

THE GLOBAL ECONOMY

WHEN YOU SAY PROFITS, SMILE

Understanding the values of your customers is an important part of doing business. In this excerpt, an analyst promotes the importance of smiling to a group of Japanese businesspeople.

Some 30 somber businessmen in plain blue suits are biting down on chopsticks and feeling silly. "Now pull them out slowly," instructs their teacher, Yoshihiko Kadokawa, and suddenly the Japanese men seem to be grinning. . . . "There you go, you are now smiling," beams Kadokawa, 47. "Doesn't it feel great?"

Second nature to politicians and game show hosts, the toothy grin has long been a cultural no-no in Japan, where some people still cover their mouths when they laugh in public and children are taught to limit their expressiveness, lest they upset the *wa*, or sense of group harmony. But Kadokawa, a former department store executive who noticed that his friendliest clerks racked up the biggest sales, wants to turn Japan into the land of happy lips. He charges up to $1,000 to host his two-to-three-hour "Let's Smile Operation" seminars, in which students exercise recalcitrant facial muscles and try to grasp the notion that smiles equal sales. "If you do not smile, you cannot make a profit," says Kadokawa, mindful that his country is mired in its worst economic crisis in decades. "If Japan smiled more, perhaps this nasty recession would end."

Look what it has done for Kadokawa, who has also written a popular book, *The Power of a Laughing Face*. His clients, however, mostly men, are having a harder time of it. "Won't I look stupid if I smile?" asks one. "Is it good for your health?" inquires another. Kadokawa assures them that showing their pearly whites is the key to prosperity. Perhaps his most helpful tip: Study Bill Clinton. "Look at the way he smiles," says Kadokawa. "That is real power."

—*People Weekly*, May 10, 1999

Critical Thinking

1. **Analyzing Information** What is Kadokawa trying to teach the group?
2. **Synthesizing Information** How important is it for business people who work with people from other countries to understand their values?

Efficiency is another reason for mergers. When two firms merge, they no longer need two presidents, two treasurers, and two personnel directors. The firm can have more retail outlets or manufacturing capabilities without significantly increasing management costs. In addition, the new firm may be able to get better discounts by making volume purchases, and make more effective use of its advertising. Sometimes the merging firms can achieve two objectives at once—such as dominant size and improved efficiency—as in the case of the Kroger-Meyer merger.

Some mergers are driven by the need to acquire new product lines. Recent telecommunications industry mergers, for example, were driven by the desire for some firms to provide better communications services. As a result, former telephone companies like AT&T bought cable TV firms so that they could offer faster internet access and telephone service in a single package.

Sometimes firms merge to catch up with, or even eliminate, their rivals. Royal Caribbean Cruises acquired Celebrity Cruise Lines in 1997 and nearly doubled in size, becoming the second largest cruise line behind Carnival. When the office supply store Staples tried to acquire Office Depot in the same year, however, the government blocked the merger on the grounds that it would reduce competition in the industry.

Finally, a company may use a merger to *lose* its corporate identity. In 1997 ValuJet merged with AirWays to form AirTran Holdings Corporation. The new company flew the same planes and routes as the original company, but AirTran hoped the name change would help the public forget ValuJet's tragic 1996 Everglades crash that claimed 110 lives.

70 UNIT 1 FUNDAMENTAL ECONOMIC CONCEPTS

FREE ENTERPRISE ACTIVITY

To emphasize the role of large business corporations in the American free enterprise system, select a number of large corporations that produce and sell a variety of consumer goods and services. You might designate Proctor & Gamble, Ford, PepsiCo, Phillip Morris, Inc., and Microsoft, for example. Organize the class into groups and assign each group one of the large corporations. Have groups research the goods and services their corporation produces and sells. Then have groups illustrate those products in a bulletin-board display.

 BLOCK SCHEDULING

Types of Mergers

Economists generally recognize two types of mergers. The first is a **horizontal merger,** which takes place when two or more firms that produce the same kind of product join forces. The merger of the two banks, Chase National and the Bank of Manhattan, is one such example.

When firms involved in different steps of manufacturing or marketing join together, we have a **vertical merger.** An automaker merging with a tire company is one example of a vertical merger. Another is the U.S. Steel Corporation. At one time, it mined its own ore, shipped it across the Great Lakes, smelted it, and made steel into many different products. Vertical mergers take place when companies believe that it is important to protect themselves against the loss of suppliers.

Conglomerates

A corporation may become so large through mergers and acquisitions that it becomes a conglomerate. A **conglomerate** is a firm that has at least four businesses, each making unrelated products, none of which is responsible for a majority of its sales.

Diversification is one of the main reasons for conglomerate mergers. Some firms believe that if they do not "put all their eggs in one basket," their overall sales and profits will be protected. Isolated economic happenings, such as bad weather or the sudden change of consumer tastes, may affect some product lines at some point, but not all at one time.

During the 1970s and early 1980s, conglomerate mergers were popular in the United States. The cigarette and tobacco firm of R.J.

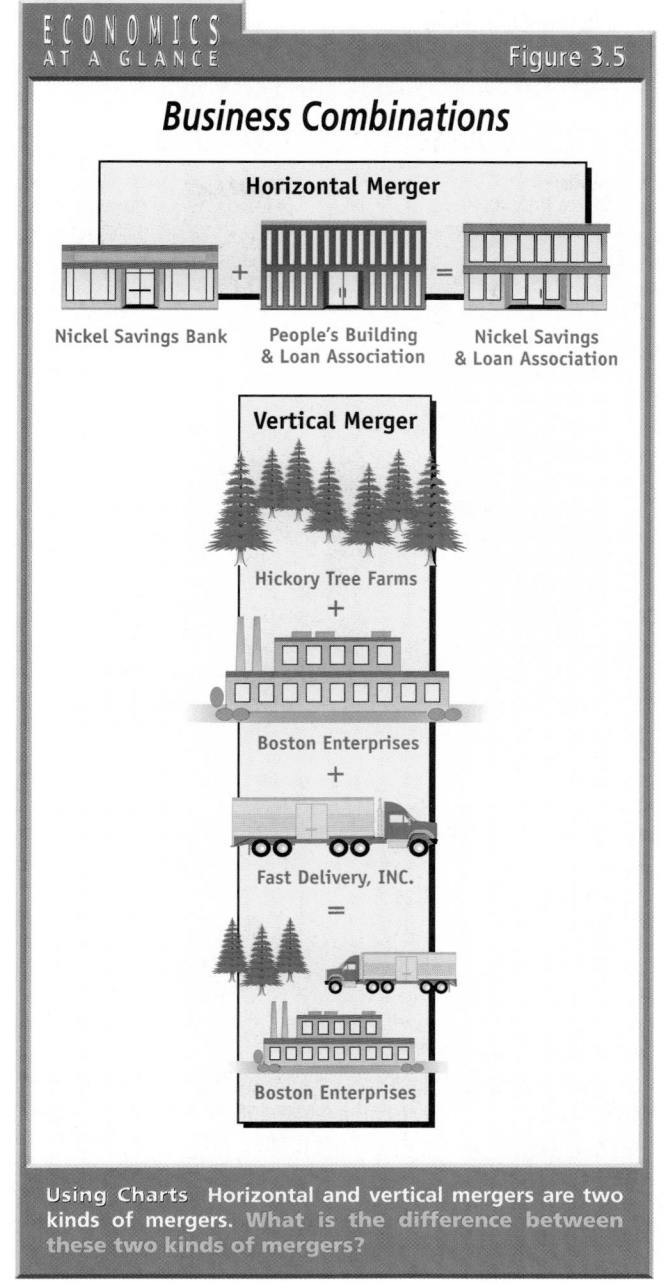

ECONOMICS AT A GLANCE Figure 3.5

Business Combinations

Horizontal Merger

Nickel Savings Bank + People's Building & Loan Association = Nickel Savings & Loan Association

Vertical Merger

Hickory Tree Farms
+
Boston Enterprises
+
Fast Delivery, INC.
=
Boston Enterprises

Using Charts Horizontal and vertical mergers are two kinds of mergers. What is the difference between these two kinds of mergers?

CHAPTER 3: BUSINESS ORGANIZATIONS **71**

CHAPTER 3
Section 2, pages 68–73

L2 Journalism

Have students choose two corporations in the community and imagine that they have merged. Ask students to write a fictitious newspaper article about the merger and its results.

ECONOMICS AT A GLANCE

Answer: *In a horizontal merger, two or more firms that produce the same kind of product join forces. In a vertical merger, firms involved in different steps of manufacturing and marketing join together.*

THE GLOBAL ECONOMY

World Markets In the 1990s, Avon Products found its sales lagging in the United States and Europe. With more women in the labor force, fewer people are at home when the Avon sales representative calls, or are willing to work for Avon as part-time salespeople. In Asia, Eastern Europe, Africa, and Latin America, however, people (typically women) are eager to supplement their incomes as Avon representatives, and their customers are happy to buy what they consider to be chic American products. Since Avon relies on door-to-door sales, it fits in well in developing countries that don't have good retailing infrastructures.

CRITICAL THINKING

Making Comparisons Have students discuss the reasons behind mergers, noting especially the desire for efficiency and for new product lines. Then discuss in general whether bigger is always better when it comes to businesses. Have each student choose a large business and a small business in the neighborhood to compare in a report. Students might compare, for example, a large grocery chain versus a small neighborhood market, or a local bicycle shop versus a major retail store that sell bikes. Encourage students to create a chart with headings such as *Price, Selection, Knowledgeable Staff, Speed of Service*, and so on, as a part of their report. Discuss students' findings as a class. **BLOCK SCHEDULING**

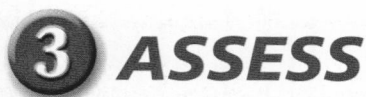

ECONOMICS
AT A GLANCE

Answer: *conglomerate: a firm that has at least four businesses; multinational: a corporation that has manufacturing or service organizations in a number of different countries*

L3 Writing

Have students research corporate mission statements. Then have them write a paper on how businesses view rights and responsibilities.

3 ASSESS

Assign Section 2 Assessment as homework or as an in-class activity.

■ Have students use **Interactive Tutor Self-Assessment Software** to review Section 2.

Section Quiz 3-2

ECONOMICS
AT A GLANCE

Figure 3.6

Conglomerate Structure

Office Products
ACCO office supplies
Swingline staplers
Day-Timers personal organizers

Golf Products
Titleist golf balls
Foot-Joy golf shoes
Cobra golf clubs

Home Products
Moen faucets
Master Lock
Waterloo toolboxes

Spirits and Wines

Sales by Category

Home Products	38%
Office Products	25%
Spirits and Wines	21%
Golf Products	16%

Pie chart: 25%, 21%, 16%, 38%

Source: http://www.fortunebrands.com, 2001

Using Charts A conglomerate is a firm that has at least four businesses, each of which makes unrelated products and none of which is responsible for a majority of its sales. Fortune Brands is an American conglomerate with a wide range of products. About 25 percent of Fortune Brand's sales come from international sales. **How does a conglomerate differ from a multinational?**

Reynolds became a leading conglomerate, at one time owning the largest containerized shipping firm in the country (Sea-Land), the nation's second largest fast-food chain (Kentucky Fried Chicken), the nation's largest fruit and vegetable processor (Del Monte), and the second largest producer of wine and distilled spirits (Heublein).

Since the late 1980s, the number of conglomerates in the United States has declined. In Asia, however, conglomerates remain strong. Samsung, Gold Star, and Daewoo are still very dominant in Korea, as are Mitsubishi, Panasonic, and Sony in Japan.

Multinationals

Other large corporations have become international in scope. A **multinational** is a corporation that has manufacturing or service operations in a number of different countries. It is, in effect, a citizen of several countries at one time. As such, a multinational is subject to the laws of, and is likely to pay taxes in, each country where it has operations. General Motors, Nabisco, British Petroleum, Royal Dutch Shell, Mitsubishi, and Sony are examples of global corporations that have attained worldwide economic importance.

Multinationals are important because they have the ability to move resources, goods, services, and financial capital across national borders. A multinational with its headquarters in Canada, for example, is likely to sell bonds in France. The proceeds may then be used to expand a plant in Mexico that makes products for sale in the United States. Multinationals may

EXTENDING THE CONTENT

Alliances Instead of merging, firms often form alliances with others. McDonald's, for example, is allied with Coca-Cola, Disney, Wal-Mart, and Chevron. McDonald's helps Coca-Cola by being its biggest customer. Coca-Cola, which has operations in many different countries, returns the favor by helping McDonald's enter new foreign markets. McDonald's helps Disney by promoting its films with tie-in products like Happy Meal toys, while Disney has allowed McDonald's to open restaurants at the Walt Disney World Resort and Disneyland Paris. McDonald's restaurants also are cropping up in Wal-Marts and Chevron stations. Alliances like these are becoming increasingly common. It's estimated that there are more than 30,000 such arrangements throughout the world.

also be conglomerates if they make a number of unrelated products, but when they conduct their operations in several different countries they are more likely to be called a multinational.

Multinationals are usually welcome because they transfer new technology and generate new jobs in areas where jobs are needed. Multinationals also produce tax revenues for the host country, which helps that nation's economy.

At times, multinationals have been known to abuse their power by paying low wages to workers, exporting scarce natural resources, or by adversely interfering with the development of local businesses. Some analysts point out that multinational corporations will be increasingly able to demand tax, regulatory, and wage concessions by threatening to move their operations to another country. Only highly educated people or those with skills will benefit as wages remain low. Other analysts predict uneven development. One region of the world will grow at the expense of another.

Most economists, however, welcome the low-cost production and quality that competition in the global economy brings. They also believe a greater use of research and new technology will raise the standard of living for all people. On balance, the advantages of multinationals far outweigh the disadvantages.

Careers

Buyer

Buyers purchase merchandise for resale to the public. They choose the suppliers, negotiate the price, and award contracts.

The Work

Duties include anticipating consumer demand, staying informed about new products, attending trade shows, and checking shipments. Buyers assist in sales promotions and advertising campaigns, as well as checking on displays. Buyers must have the ability to plan, make decisions quickly, work under pressure, and identify products that will sell. Most buyers work in wholesale and retail trade companies, such as grocery or department stores, or in manufacturing. Many others work in government or in service industries.

Qualifications

Most buyers have completed a college degree with a business emphasis. Familiarity with the merchandise as well as with wholesaling and retailing practices is important.

Reteach

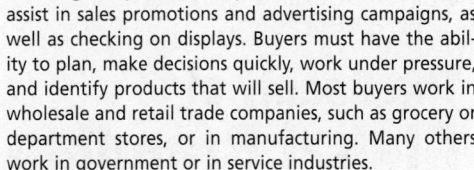

Reading Essentials and Study Guide 3-2

STUDY GUIDE — Chapter 3, Section 2

For use with textbook pages 68–73

B USINESS GROWTH AND EXPANSION

KEY TERMS

merger A combination of two or more businesses to form a single firm (page 68)
income statement A report showing a business's sales, expenses, and profits for a certain period (page 68)
net income Revenues minus expenses and taxes (page 68)
depreciation A non-cash charge the firm takes for the general wear and tear on its capital goods (page 69)
cash flow The sum of net income and non-cash charges such as depreciation (page 69)
horizontal merger The kind of merger in which two or more firms that produce the same kind of product join forces (page 71)
vertical merger The kind of merger in which firms involved in different steps of manufacturing or marketing join together (page 71)
conglomerate A firm that has at least four businesses, each making unrelated products, none of which is responsible for the majority of the firm's sales (page 71)
multinational A corporation that has manufacturing or service operations in a number of different countries (page 72)

DRAWING FROM EXPERIENCE

Do you read the information on products' labels? Have you ever noticed the name of the same company on the labels of unrelated products, such as books and household appliances? How would you describe a company like that? In the last section, you read about the different ways businesses are organized. This section focuses on how businesses grow.

2. List expenses that would appear on a business's income statement.

Enrich

Have students research and construct a time line showing how a major American corporation has grown over the years.

4 CLOSE

Ask students to discuss the statement "The world is shrinking," in relation to the role that multinationals play in the global economy.

Section 2 Assessment

Checking for Understanding

1. **Main Idea** Using your notes from the graphic organizer activity on page 68, explain how mergers improve efficiency.

2. **Key Terms** Define merger, income statement, net income, depreciation, cash flow, horizontal merger, vertical merger, conglomerate, multinational.

3. **Describe** how a firm can generate funds internally to grow and expand.

4. **Identify** five reasons why firms merge.

5. **Describe** the different ways a business can merge.

Applying Economic Concepts

6. **Business Growth** In a newspaper or magazine, find an article about a merger. What companies merged? What reasons, if any, were given for the merger? What statistics were provided? Write a one-page paper in which you answer these questions.

Critical Thinking

7. **Making Comparisons** What are the possible ethical benefits and drawbacks of multinationals to their host countries?

 Practice and **assess** key social studies skills with the *Glencoe Skillbuilder Interactive Workbook, Level 2.*

CHAPTER 3: BUSINESS ORGANIZATIONS **73**

Section 3 Assessment Answers

1. Mergers can diminish costs and increase buying power.

2. All vocabulary terms are defined in the text.

3. A firm can reinvest revenue from sales into the company in the form of new plants, equipment, and technologies.

4. grow faster, increase efficiency, acquire new product lines, eliminate rivals, or change corporate image

5. horizontal: two or more firms that produce same product merge; vertical: firms in different steps of manufacturing or marketing merge.

6. Answers should accurately discuss the concepts related to mergers.

7. benefits: help spread new technology, generate new jobs, produce tax revenues for host countries; drawbacks: may exploit workers, export scarce natural resources, or adversely interfere with local businesses

TEACH

Have students discuss clothes that are currently considered trendy. **Ask:** Where do you think these clothes originate? Point out that any garment sold in the United States (except for hats and shoes) must have a label telling where it was made. Have students research some of the major brands to find out where the items are made and where the company headquarters is located. Discuss their findings as a group.

Refer to *Business Week Focus on the New Economy* in the TCR for additional unit-based articles.

BusinessWeek

JUNE 28, 1999 ————————— Newsclip

Cosmetic companies like L'Oréal have found a profitable strategy: acquire smaller cosmetic companies and promote the culture from which they came. With this formula, and with the help of chief executive Lindsay Owen-Jones, L'Oréal's profits have dramatically increased.

The Beauty of
Global Branding

It's a sunny afternoon outside Parkson's department store in Shanghai, and a marketing battle is raging for the attention of Chinese women. Tall, pouty models in beige skirts and sheer tops pass out flyers promoting Revlon's new spring colors. But their efforts [are being] drowned out by L'Oréal's eye-catching show for its Maybelline brand.

To a pulsating rhythm, two gangly models in shimmering lycra tops dance on a podium before a large backdrop depicting the New York City skyline. The music stops, and a makeup artist transforms a model's face while a Chinese saleswoman delivers the punch line. "This brand comes from America. It's very trendy," she shouts into the microphone. "If you want to be fashionable, just choose Maybelline."

Few of the women in the admiring crowd realize that the trendy "New York" Maybelline brand belongs to French cosmetics giant L'Oréal. In the battle for global beauty markets, $12.4 billion L'Oréal has developed a winning formula: a growing portfolio of international brands that have transformed the French company into the U.N. of beauty. . . .

Its secret: conveying the allure of different cultures through its many products. Whether it's selling Italian elegance, New York street smarts, or French beauty through its brands, L'Oréal is reaching out to a vast range of people across incomes and cultures. . . .

L'Oréal's work with Maybelline is a prime example. In 1996, L'Oréal acquired Maybelline for $758 million and began a makeover of the brand. The key: figuratively stamping "urban American chic" all over Maybelline products to promote their American origins. . . .

"That's a big challenge for this company to add brands, yet keep the differentiation," says Marlene Eskin, publisher of *Market View* research reports on the cosmetics industry.

Department store in Shanghai, China

Examining the Newsclip

1. **Analyzing Information** How has L'Oréal become more competitive in the global market?

2. **Summarizing Information** In your own words, explain why it is a challenge for a company to "add brands, yet keep differentiation"?

74 UNIT 1 FUNDAMENTAL ECONOMIC CONCEPTS

Answers to Examining the Newsclip

1. by acquiring smaller companies and promoting the cultures from which they came

2. It is usually easier and more efficient to make all company products look the same; in L'Oréal's case, however, differentiation gives the company a competitive edge.

Other Organizations

Study Guide

Main Idea
Producer and worker cooperatives are associations in which the members join in production and marketing to lower costs for their members' benefit.

Reading Strategy
Graphic Organizer As you read the section, complete a graphic organizer similar to the one below by describing the different kinds of cooperatives.

Key Terms
nonprofit organization, cooperative, co-op, credit union, labor union, collective bargaining, professional association, chamber of commerce, Better Business Bureau, public utility

Objectives
After studying this section, you will be able to:
1. **Describe** nonprofit organizations.
2. **Explain** the direct and indirect role of government in our economy.

Applying Economic Concepts
Nonprofit Organizations Do you belong to a church, club, or civic organization? Read to find out how these organizations fit into our economic system.

① FOCUS

Section Overview
This section discusses nonprofit organizations, and the role of government in our economy.

BELLRINGER
Motivational Activity

- Project **transparency** and have students answer questions.
- Available as blackline master.

Daily Focus Transparency 18

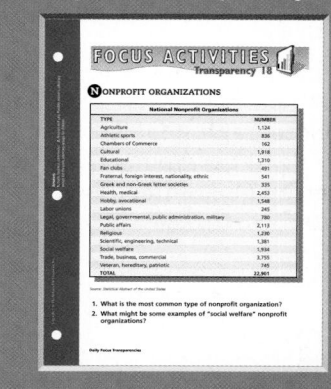

Cover Story

Baby-Sitting Co-Ops a Growing Trend

Baby-sitting duties

When Candace and Roger Kuebel of Larchmont, N.Y., flew to Grenada for a week's vacation, they did something most parents of young children do only in their dreams. The Kuebels left their two-year-old daughter, Heather, in the care of two responsible adults—parents themselves . . . they also didn't pay a child care service any costly fees.

The couple's secret: They belong to a baby-sitting cooperative.

The idea behind the baby-sitting co-op is simple: Families swap baby-sitting duties without ever exchanging money. Co-ops usually rely on a coupon system: members with coupons have an incentive to use them, while those low on coupons need to sit.

—*The New York Times On the Web*, February 1, 1998

 Most businesses use scarce resources to produce goods and services in hopes of earning a profit for their owners. Other organizations, like the baby-sitting co-op described in the cover story, operate on a "not-for-profit" basis. A **nonprofit organization** operates in a businesslike way to promote the collective interests of its members rather than to seek financial gain for its owners.

Community and Civic Organizations

 Examples of nonprofit institutions include organizations such as schools, churches, hospitals, welfare groups, and adoption agencies. Most of these organizations are legally incorporated to take advantage of unlimited life and limited liability. They are similar to profit-seeking businesses, but do not issue stock, pay dividends, or pay income taxes.

These organizations often provide goods and services to their members while they pursue other rewards such as improving educational standards, seeing the sick become well, and helping those in need. Their activities often produce revenues in excess of expenses, but they use the surplus to further the work of their institutions.

CHAPTER 3: BUSINESS ORGANIZATIONS **75**

Study Guide

Reading Strategy
Have students create the graphic organizer.
Answers to Graphic: *consumer, service, and producer cooperatives*

Preteaching Vocabulary
Use the Vocabulary Puzzle-Maker.

RESOURCE MANAGER

Reproducible Masters
- Reproducible Lesson Plan 3-3
- Daily Lecture Notes 3-3
- Guided Reading Activity 3-3
- Reading Essentials and Study Guide 3-3
- Section Quiz 3-3

Transparencies
- Daily Focus Transparency 18

Multimedia
- Vocabulary PuzzleMaker CD-ROM
- Interactive Tutor Self-Assessment Software
- ExamView® Pro Testmaker
- Presentation Plus!

② TEACH

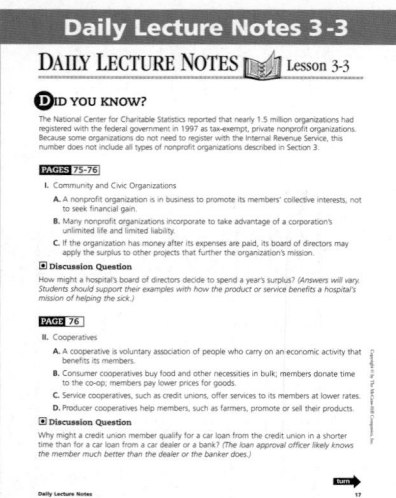

Daily Lecture Notes 3-3

DAILY LECTURE NOTES 📖 Lesson 3-3

① DID YOU KNOW?

The National Center for Charitable Statistics reported that nearly 1.5 million organizations had registered with the federal government in 1997 as tax-exempt, private nonprofit organizations. Because some organizations do not need to register with the Internal Revenue Service, this number does not include all types of nonprofit organizations described in Section 3.

PAGES 75-76

I. Community and Civic Organizations

A. A nonprofit organization is in business to promote its members' collective interests, not to seek financial gain.

B. Many nonprofit organizations incorporate to take advantage of a corporation's unlimited life and limited liability.

C. If the organization has money after its expenses are paid, its board of directors may apply the surplus to other projects that further the organization's mission.

⊡ Discussion Question

How might a hospital's board of directors decide to spend a year's surplus? (Answers will vary. Students should support their examples with how the product or service benefits a hospital's mission of helping the sick.)

PAGE 76

II. Cooperatives

A. A cooperative is a voluntary association of people who carry on an economic activity that benefits its members.

B. Consumer cooperatives buy food and other necessities in bulk; members donate time to the co-op; members pay lower prices for goods.

C. Service cooperatives, such as credit unions, offer services to its members at lower rates.

D. Producer cooperatives help members, such as farmers, promote or sell their products.

⊡ Discussion Question

Why might a credit union member qualify for a car loan from the credit union in a shorter time than for a car loan from a car dealer or a bank? (The loan approval officer likely knows the member much better than the dealer or the banker does.)

Daily Lecture Notes 17

L1 Using Photographs

Have students search newspapers for photographs that illustrate the dual role of government. Ask volunteers to discuss their selections with the class. **ELL**

ECONOMICS
AT A GLANCE

Answer: *consumer cooperative buys bulk goods on behalf of members; service cooperative offers members various services; producer cooperative helps members promote or sell their products*

Nonprofit community and civic organizations use scarce factors of production to serve many needs. Their efforts are difficult to analyze economically, however, because the value of their products is not easy to measure. Even so, the large number of these organizations shows that they are an important part of our economic system.

Cooperatives

Another example of a nonprofit organization is the **cooperative,** or **co-op.** A cooperative is a voluntary association of people formed to carry on some kind of economic activity that will benefit its members. Cooperatives fall into three major classes: consumer, service, and producer.

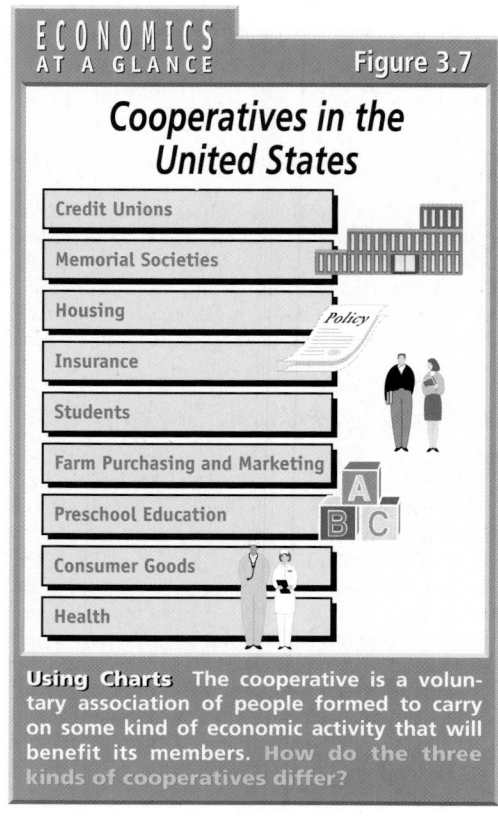

ECONOMICS
AT A GLANCE

Figure 3.7

Cooperatives in the United States

- Credit Unions
- Memorial Societies
- Housing
- Insurance
- Students
- Farm Purchasing and Marketing
- Preschool Education
- Consumer Goods
- Health

Using Charts The cooperative is a voluntary association of people formed to carry on some kind of economic activity that will benefit its members. **How do the three kinds of cooperatives differ?**

Consumer Cooperatives

The consumer cooperative is a voluntary association that buys bulk amounts of goods such as food and clothing on behalf of its members. Members usually help keep the cost of the operation down by devoting several hours a week or month to the operation. If successful, the co-op is able to offer its members products at prices lower than those charged by regular businesses.

Service Cooperatives

A service cooperative provides services such as insurance, credit, and baby-sitting to its members, rather than goods. One example is a **credit union,** a financial organization that accepts deposits from, and makes loans to, employees of a particular company or government agency. In most cases, credit union members can borrow at better rates and more quickly than they could from for-profit banks or commercial loan companies.

Producer Cooperatives

Producers, like consumers, can also have co-ops. A producer cooperative helps members promote or sell their products. In the United States, most cooperatives of this kind are made up of farmers. The co-op helps the farmers sell their crops directly to central markets or to companies that use the members' products. Some co-ops, such as the Ocean Spray cranberry co-op, market their products directly to consumers.

Labor, Professional, and Business Organizations

Non-profit organizations are not just limited to co-ops and civic groups. Many other groups also organize this way to promote the interests of their members.

Labor Unions

Another important economic institution is the **labor union,** an organization of workers formed to represent its members' interests in various

---

MEETING SPECIAL NEEDS ACTIVITY

Learning Disabled For students who have problems with reading, consider the following strategy to help them differentiate main ideas from details. Teach them to skim for a main idea in the subsection above titled "Labor Unions." Have students tell in their own words what the subsection is about. Next, have students read the first sentence of each paragraph in the subsection. Point out that main ideas are often, but not always, stated in the first sentence of paragraphs. Students should then state the main idea of this subsection.

📁 Refer to *Inclusion for the Social Studies Classroom Strategies and Activities* in the TCR.

Cooperatives

Benefits A cooperative is an organization that is owned by and operated for the benefit of those using its services. Consumer cooperatives, service cooperatives, and producer cooperatives perform different functions. *What are the benefits of a consumer cooperative?*

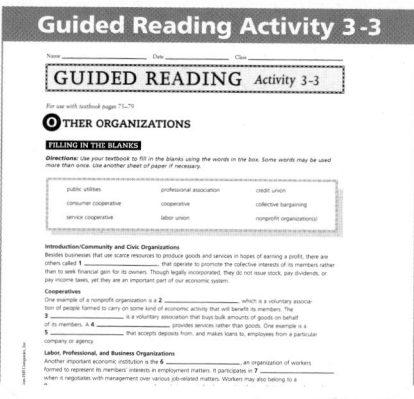

employment matters. The union participates in **collective bargaining** when it negotiates with management over issues such as pay, working hours, health care coverage, life insurance, vacations, and other job-related matters.

Unions pressure the government to pass laws that will benefit and protect their workers. The largest labor organization in the United States is the American Federation of Labor-Congress of Industrial Organizations (AFL-CIO), an association of unions whose members do all kinds of work. The American Postal Workers Union and the American Federation of Teachers, for example, are both AFL-CIO unions. Many other unions, such as the National Education Association for Teachers, are independent and represent workers in specific industries.

Professional Associations

Many workers belong to professional societies, trade associations, or academies. While these groups are similar to unions, they do not work in quite the same way. One such organization is a **professional association**—a group of people in a specialized occupation that works to improve the

working conditions, skill levels, and public perceptions of the profession.

The American Medical Association (AMA) and the American Bar Association (ABA) are two examples of interest groups that include members of specific professions. Basically, these two groups influence the licensing and training of doctors and lawyers, and both groups are actively involved in political issues. Professional associations also represent bankers, teachers, college professors, police officers, and hundreds of other professions. While these associations are concerned primarily with the standards of their professions, they also seek to influence government policy on issues that are important to them.

Student Web Activity Visit the *Economics: Principles and Practices* Web site at epp.glencoe.com and click on *Chapter 3—Student Web Activities* for an activity on the Better Business Bureau.

Visual Instruction

Answer to Caption:
Because a co-op buys goods in bulk, it can offer its members reduced prices.

L2 Conducting an Interview

Have students interview officers of local nonprofit organizations to discover what services the organization offers and who uses those services.

Objectives, goals, and answers to the student activity can be found in the **Web Activity Lesson Plan** feature at epp.glencoe.com

FREE ENTERPRISE ACTIVITY

Point out that the first successful cooperative in the United States—the Philadelphia Contributionship for the Insurance of Houses from Loss of Fire—was organized by Benjamin Franklin in 1752. It is still operating today, making it the oldest continuously operating cooperative in the country. Have students research the development of cooperatives in the United States, from their beginnings in the mid-1700s to the present day. Suggest that students present their findings in a written report using proper grammar, spelling, sentence structure, and punctuation, that discusses how the focus of cooperatives has expanded over the years.

L3 Journalism

Quiz students on the dual role that government plays in linking consumers and resources. Ask students to prepare a news release titled either "Government Plays a Direct Role" or "Government Plays an Indirect Role."

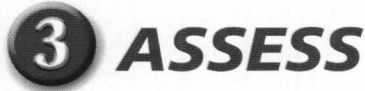 **ASSESS**

Assign Section 3 Assessment as homework or as an in-class activity.

Have students use **Interactive Tutor Self-Assessment Software** to review Section 3.

Section Quiz 3-3

L2 Using a Diagram

Tell students to refer to their circular flow diagram from the Enrich activity on page 17. Have them develop a list of government actions that might affect their diagram.

Business Associations

Businesses also organize to promote their collective interests. Most cities and towns have a **chamber of commerce** that promotes the welfare of its members and of the community. The typical chamber sponsors activities ranging from educational programs to neighborhood clean-up campaigns to lobbying for favorable business legislation.

Many business organizations represent specific kinds of businesses. These are called industry or trade associations. Trade associations are interested in shaping the government's policy on such economic issues as free enterprise, imports and tariffs, the minimum wage, new construction, and government contracts for construction and manufacturing. The Telecommunications Industry Association, for instance, represents manufacturers and suppliers of communications and information technology products on issues affecting its members.

Some business associations help protect the consumer. The **Better Business Bureau,** a nonprofit organization sponsored by local businesses

CYBERNOMICS SPOTLIGHT

The Changing Workplace

In studying the workplace, some analysts feel that certain trends will continue. People will change jobs several times during their lifetimes. The compressed work schedule—working a shorter workweek with more hours per day—will continue to make inroads. Analysts also believe that lifelong learning is a key to career success. New jobs require advanced skills, education, and training. Therefore, the need for continuing to learn and develop new skills is more important than ever before.

—Source: *Computer Industry Almanac*

to provide general information on companies, is one of these. It maintains records on consumer inquiries and complaints and sometimes offers various consumer education programs.

Government

Government is another nonprofit economic organization. Sometimes government plays a direct role in the economy, while at other times the role is indirect.

Direct Role of Government

Many government agencies produce and distribute goods and services to consumers, giving government a direct role in the economy. The role is "direct" because the government supplies a good or service that competes with private businesses.

One example is the Tennessee Valley Authority (TVA). The TVA supplies electric power for almost all of Tennessee and parts of Alabama, Georgia, Kentucky, Mississippi, North Carolina, and Virginia. This power competes directly with the power supplied by other, privately owned, power companies.

Another example is the Federal Deposit Insurance Corporation (FDIC), which insures deposits in our nation's banks. Because the insurance the FDIC supplies could be provided by privately owned insurance companies, the FDIC is also an example of the direct role of government.

Perhaps the best known of the government corporations is the U.S. Postal Service (USPS). Originally an executive department called the Post Office Department, the USPS became a government corporation in 1970.

Many of these federal agencies are organized as government-owned corporations. Like those of privately owned businesses, these corporations have a board of directors that hires a professional management team to oversee daily operations. These corporations charge for the products they produce, and the revenue goes back into the "business." If the corporation has losses, however, they are covered by funds supplied by Congress.

State and local governments provide police and fire protection, rescue services, schools, and court systems. At the same time, all levels of government

CRITICAL THINKING

Drawing Conclusions The government often provides goods and services that people value highly but that private firms find unprofitable to sell. For example, city governments often provide free fireworks exhibitions for the Fourth of July. Ask your students to imagine that they are setting up a private firm that wishes to sell tickets to a fireworks show. Ask them how the company would make money doing that. Students should recognize that it would be difficult to make money on a fireworks show because they wouldn't be able to exclude non-payers.

help develop and maintain roads, libraries, and parks. In these ways, government plays a direct part in the productive process.

Indirect Role of Government

The government plays an indirect role when it acts as an umpire to make sure the market economy operates smoothly and efficiently. One such case is the regulation of **public utilities,** investor- or municipal-owned companies that offer important products to the public, such as water or electric service.

Because many public utilities have few competitors, people often want government supervision. For example, government established regulatory control over the cable television industry in 1993 because it felt that some operators were charging too much. Without competition, utilities and other companies having exclusive rights in certain areas may not offer services at reasonable rates.

The government also plays an indirect role when it grants money to people in the form of Social Security, veterans' benefits, financial aid to college students, and unemployment compensation. Such payments give the recipients of these funds a power

Promoting Interests

Methods Labor unions, professional and business organizations, and interest groups draw from the financial resources and expertise of their members. *Who makes up the membership of a professional association?*

they otherwise might not have—the power to "vote" and to make their demands known in the market. This power influences the production of goods and services that, in turn, affects the allocation of scarce resources.

Section 3 Assessment

Checking for Understanding
1. **Main Idea** Using your notes from the graphic organizer activity on page 75, describe the different types of cooperatives.

2. **Key Terms** Define nonprofit organization, cooperative, co-op, credit union, labor union, collective bargaining, professional association, chamber of commerce, Better Business Bureau, public utility.

3. **Identify** the purpose of the different types of nonprofit organizations.

4. **Provide** examples that illustrate the government's direct and indirect roles as an economic institution.

Applying Economic Concepts
5. **Nonprofit Organizations** Name a nonprofit organization that you or one of your friends

have joined. Research the history of the organization to find out how it began and its stated goals. State the purpose of the organization, and then compare its activities to profit-making organizations. If your organization collects more than it spends, what does it do with the extra money?

Critical Thinking
6. **Classifying Information** Make a list of 10 activities performed by your local government. Classify each as to its direct or indirect influences on the local economy.

7. **Making Comparisons** Why do many people prefer to deal with credit unions rather than banks?

> **Practice** and **assess** key social studies skills with the *Glencoe Skillbuilder Interactive Workbook, Level 2.*

Visual Instruction

Answer to Caption:
people in a specialized occupation

Reteach

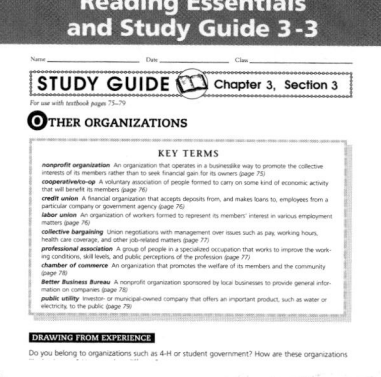

Reading Essentials and Study Guide 3-3

Enrich

Ask students to write an editorial discussing the importance of nonprofit organizations to the American economy.

4 CLOSE

Ask students to discuss which of the institutions examined in Section 3 has the most impact on their lives and why.

Section 3 Assessment Answers

1. consumer: buy goods in bulk/offer members reduced prices; service: provide services instead of goods; producer: help members promote/sell products.

2. All vocabulary terms are defined in the text.

3. community/civic organizations: provide goods and services and promote a common good; cooperatives: carry on activities that benefit members; labor, professional, and business organizations: promote interests of members; government: regulate economy

4. direct: police and fire protection, schools, court systems; indirect: regulation of public utilities and quasi-monopolies, subsidies

5. Answers should demonstrate an understanding of nonprofit organizations.

6. Lists should demonstrate an understanding of the economic roles of government.

7. They can borrow at better rates.

79

Study and Writing Skill

Teaching Skills

Have students read through each section, noting the longer, commonly used terms. Ask them to devise abbreviations for those terms and to list the abbreviations by section. Discuss as a class students' ideas, as well as any accepted abbreviations for the chapter's terms. Also discuss how the use of abbreviations makes note-taking easier.

Additional Practice

Reinforcing Economic Skill 26

Reinforcing Economic Skills **Chapter 26**

TAKING NOTES

Effective note taking involves separating what you read or hear into meaningful parts so that you can understand and remember it. To take good notes, write down the key points and important facts. When taking notes in class, copy words, statements, or diagrams the teacher draws on the board. When taking notes on textbook material include a heading that contains the main idea of the section and then write a few phrases to recall the facts. When taking notes for a research report, use note cards. Be sure to include the title, author, and page number of the sources you use.

Directions: *Read the excerpt below and take notes on a separate sheet of paper that summarize its main ideas.*

U.S. Trade in Information Technology (IT) Goods and Services

[body text]

Goods Trade

[body text]

Services Trade

[body text]

Source: The Emerging Digital Economy II, U.S. Department of Commerce, June 1999

GLENCOE
TECHNOLOGY

Glencoe Skillbuilder Interactive Workbook, Level 2

This interactive CD-ROM reinforces student mastery of essential social studies skills.

Taking Notes

Effective note taking involves more than just writing facts in short phrases. It involves breaking up the information into meaningful parts so that it can be understood and remembered.

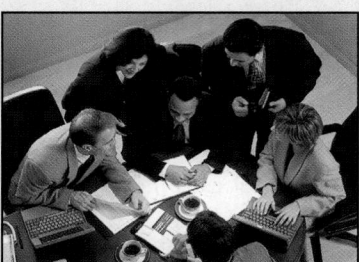

Business in the United States can be organized in a number of ways.

Learning the Skill

To take good notes, follow these steps.

- When taking notes on material presented in class, write the key points, along with the important facts and figures, in a notebook.

- Write quickly and neatly, using abbreviations and phrases.

- Copy words, statements, or diagrams drawn on the chalkboard.

- Ask the teacher to repeat important points you have missed or do not understand.

- When studying textbook material, organize your notes into an outline. When outlining written material, first read the material to identify the main ideas. Next, identify the subheads. Place details supporting or explaining subheads under the appropriate head.

- For a research report, take notes on cards. Note-cards should include the title, author, and the page number of sources.

Practicing the Skill

Suppose you are writing a research report on the topic, Business Organizations. First, identify main idea questions about this topic, such as "What are the different kinds of business organizations?" "How are they formed?" and "What are their advantages and disadvantages?" Then find material about each main-idea question.

Using this textbook as a source, read the material on "Forms of Business Organization," beginning on page 57. Then, review the material and prepare notes like those below.

Topic: Business Organizations
Main Idea: Different kinds
1. The sole proprietorship is one kind of bus. org.
2.
3.
Main Idea: Formation differs by kind of org.
1.
2.
3.

Application Activity

Scan a local newspaper for a short editorial or an article about an event pertaining to business or the economy. Take notes by writing the main idea and supporting facts. Summarize the article using only your notes.

 Practice and **assess** key social studies skills with the *Glencoe Skillbuilder Interactive Workbook, Level 2.*

Answers to Practicing the Skill

Answers will vary. Students should note main ideas of each section.

Section 1

Forms of Business Organization
(pages 57–66)

- **Sole proprietorships** are small, easy-to-manage enterprises owned by one person. They are relatively numerous and profitable. Disadvantages include raising financial capital and attracting qualified employees.

- **Partnerships** are owned by two or more persons. Their slightly larger size makes it easier to attract financial capital and qualified workers. Disadvantages include the **unlimited liability** of each general partner for the acts of the other partners, the **limited life** of the partnership, and the potential for conflict among partners.

- **Corporations** are owned by **shareholders** who vote to elect the board of directors. Shareholders have **limited liability** and are not liable for the actions or debts of the corporation. The relatively large size of the corporation allows for specialized functions and large-scale manufacturing within the firm.

- Disadvantages of corporations include the cost of obtaining charters, limited shareholder influence over corporate policies, and having to deal with some government regulations.

- The corporation is recognized as a separate legal entity and so must pay a separate corporate income tax not paid by proprietorships and partnerships.

Section 2

Business Growth and Expansion (pages 68–73)

- Businesses can grow by reinvesting their **cash flows** in plant, equipment, and new technology.

- Businesses can also expand through **mergers.** Most mergers take place because firms want to become bigger, more efficient, acquire a new product, catch up to or eliminate a competitor, or change its corporate identity.

- A **horizontal merger** takes place when two firms that produce similiar products come together. A **vertical merger** is one that involves two or more firms at different stages of manufacturing or marketing.

- A **conglomerate** is a large firm that has at least four different businesses, none of which is responsible for a majority of sales.

- A **multinational** can be an ordinary corporation or a conglomerate, but it has manufacturing or service operations in several different countries. Multinationals introduce new technology, generate jobs, and produce tax revenues for the host countries.

Section 3

Other Organizations (pages 75–79)

- **Nonprofit organizations** function like a business, but on a not-for-profit basis to further a cause or for the welfare of their members.

- The **cooperative, or co-op,** is one of the major nonprofit organizations. The co-op can be organized to provide goods and services, or to help producers.

- **Professional associations** work to improve the working conditions, skill levels, and public perceptions of their profession.

- Businesses often form a **chamber of commerce** or a **Better Business Bureau** to promote their collective interests.

- Government plays a direct role in the economy when it provides goods and services directly to consumers; it plays an indirect role when it provides Social Security, veterans' benefits, unemployment compensation, and financial aid to college students, or when it regulates businesses.

Teacher's Notes / Internet Bookmarks

_____
_____
_____
_____
_____
_____
_____
_____
_____

NIGHTLY BUSINESS REPORT

💿 **ECONOMICS & YOU**

Chapter 4
Disc 1, Side 1

Business Organizations

📼 Also available in VHS.

Using the Chapter 3 Summary

Use the Chapter 3 Summary to preview, review, condense, or reteach the chapter.

Preview/Review

💿 Vocabulary PuzzleMaker CD-ROM reinforces Key Terms.

💾 Interactive Tutor Self-Assessment Software provides a review of Chapter 3 content.

Condense

🎧 📁 Have students listen to the Chapter 3 Audio Program. Spanish also available.

📁 📁 Assign the Chapter 3 Audio Program Activity and give students the Chapter 3 Audio Program Test.

📁 📁 Have students complete the Guided Reading Activities and Reading Essentials and Study Guides for Chapter 3.

Reteach

📁 📁 Have students complete Reteaching Activity 3 in the TCR. Spanish also available.

GLENCOE
TECHNOLOGY

Use **MindJogger Videoquiz** to review the Chapter 3 content.

ECONOMICS
Online

Have students visit the Web site at epp.glencoe.com to review Chapter 3 and take the **Self-Check Quiz.**

Identifying Key Terms

1. **corporations**
2. **corporations**
3. **nonprofit organizations**
4. **corporations**
5. **sole proprietorships; partnerships**
6. **corporations; nonprofit organizations**
7. **nonprofit organizations**
8. **nonprofit organizations**
9. **partnerships**
10. **nonprofit organizations**

Reviewing the Facts

Section 1

1. ease of establishment, ease of management, owner keeps all profits, no separate taxes, psychological benefits, ease of getting out of business
2. all partners equally responsible for business losses (except limited partnerships), limited life, potential conflict among partners
3. structure: A board of directors, elected by owners of common stock, sets broad policies and goals. The board hires a professional management team to run the business on a daily basis. Strengths: ease of raising financial capital, ability to hire best managers, limited liability for owners, unlimited life, and ease of transfer of ownership

Self-Check Quiz Visit the *Economics: Principles and Practices* Web site at epp.glencoe.com and click on *Chapter 3—Self-Check Quizzes* to prepare for the chapter test.

Identifying Key Terms

On a separate sheet of paper, classify each of the numbered terms below into the following categories (some terms may apply to more than one category):

- • **Sole Proprietorships**
- • **Partnerships**
- • **Corporations**
- • **Nonprofit Organizations**

1. bond
2. stock
3. cooperative
4. dividend
5. unlimited liability
6. charter
7. labor union
8. professional association
9. limited partner
10. credit union

Reviewing the Facts

Section 1 (pages 57–66)

1. **Explain** the strengths of a sole proprietorship.
2. **Identify** the weaknesses of a partnership.
3. **Explain** the structure and strengths of a corporation.

Section 2 (pages 68–73)

4. **Explain** how the firm obtains, and then disposes of, its cash flow.
5. **Describe** the difference between a horizontal and a vertical merger.

6. **Explain** why a corporation might choose to become a conglomerate.

Section 3 (pages 75–79)

7. **Describe** the difference between a nonprofit institution and other forms of business organizations.
8. **List** three examples of cooperative associations.
9. **Describe** the purpose of a labor union.
10. **Identify** three types of business or professional organizations.
11. **Compare** the direct and the indirect roles of government.

Thinking Critically

1. **Making Comparisons** If you were planning to open your own business, such as a sportswear store or a lawn service, which form of business organization would you prefer—sole proprietorship, partnership, or corporation? Give reasons for your answer. To help you organize your response, begin by setting up a diagram like the one below.

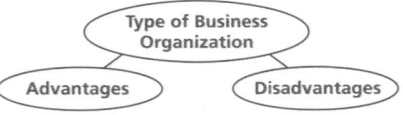

2. **Drawing Conclusions** Do you think mergers are beneficial for the U.S. economy? Defend your response.
3. **Synthesizing Information** List the strengths and weaknesses of each type of business organization. Then share the list with the owner of a business in your community. Ask the owner which items on the list were the most influential in deciding how to organize his or her business. Write a report summarizing your findings.

Section 2

4. Cash flow is obtained by adding net income to non-cash charges. A firm may pay this sum back to the owners or reinvest in itself.
5. horizontal merger: two or more firms that produce the same product join forces; vertical merger: firms in different steps of manufacturing or marketing come together
6. Its overall sales and profits will be protected from isolated economic happenings.

Section 3

7. Nonprofits do not seek financial gain.
8. consumer: a food co-op; service: a credit union; producer: a farmers' co-op
9. to work for its members' interests
10. professional: (American Bar Association); business to promote members' interests: (chamber of commerce); business to help consumers (Better Business Bureau)
11. direct role: producer and consumer of goods and services; indirect role: regulates, makes payments to individuals

Applying Economic Concepts

1. **Economic Institutions** Cite a case in your community where a cooperative would fulfill a definite economic need. Explain why you think so, and then tell what kind of cooperative you would set up.

2. **The Role of Government** Which do you think is more appropriate–the direct or indirect role of government? Defend your position.

3. **Unlimited Liability** What is the difference between the unlimited liability of proprietorships and partnerships, and the limited liability of corporations?

4. **Business Growth** What advantages might a multinational bring to a host nation?

5. **Nonprofit Organizations** In what ways does a consumer cooperative differ from a service cooperative?

Math Practice

Study the table that follows. Then answer the questions.

Sole Proprietorships, 1987–1997			
	1987	**1992**	**1997**
Business Receipts	610,823	737,082	870,392
Business Deductions	505,362	725,666	858,453
Net Income			

In millions of dollars
Source: *Statistical Abstract of the United States, 2000*

1. What is the net income for each of the three years listed? How did you find the answer?

2. In what year did sole proprietorships have the largest net income?

3. In what year did sole proprietorships have the largest net income as a percentage of business receipts? How did you find your answer?

Thinking Like an Economist

Identify two ways a firm's cash flow can be used. Explain why these uses are a trade-off and explain the opportunity costs of these choices in terms of the firm's future growth.

Technology Skill

Using the Internet With the increase in multinational corporations, many American citizens are interacting more and more with different cultures in other countries. Imagine that you and a partner have set up a multinational corporation that operates in the global economy. Select a country and use the Internet to research its culture in relation to business protocol. Use the information to create a report that lists procedures and key words your employees will need to know in order to properly conduct business in the country. Share your findings with the members of your class.

Building Skills

Taking Notes Research to find out more about an American entrepreneur and his or her role in shaping the U.S. economy. Before you do any research, compile a list of questions to serve as a guide and to narrow your topic. Consider such questions as:

1. Whom shall I research?
2. What did he or she invent or promote?
3. How did he or she become a successful entrepreneur?
4. What effect did this entrepreneur have on the U.S. economy?

Use your notes to help you write a two-page typewritten sketch of the entrepreneur.

 Practice and **assess** key social studies skills with the *Glencoe Skillbuilder Interactive Workbook, Level 2.*

CHAPTER 3: BUSINESS ORGANIZATIONS **83**

Math Practice

1. 1987, $105,461; 1992, $11,416; 1997, $11,939; by subtracting deductions from receipts.
2. 1987
3. 1987–17.27%; by dividing net income by business receipts

Thinking Like an Economist

A firm's cash flow can either be paid back to the owners or reinvested in the business. If the money is paid back, it is taken out of the business. If it is put back into the business, the firm can produce more products, generate more sales, and eventually have larger cash flow. The firm will grow as long as it remains profitable and reinvested cash flow is greater than wear and tear on equipment.

Technology Skill

Answers should reflect accurate research.

Building Skills

Check that students have thoroughly investigated their entrepreneur.

 Bonus Test Question

List one similarity and one difference between someone who owns common stock and a citizen of our country. *(Both have the right to vote for people who direct the entity's business by setting policies and goals. Differences include how many votes a citizen or stockholder has. A citizen has only one vote while a stockholder may have many votes.)*

Thinking Critically

1. Answers should demonstrate understanding of advantages offered by the form chosen.
2. Answers should include reasons for response.
3. Answers should identify strengths and weaknesses of each organization.

Applying Economic Concepts

1. Answers will vary, but should indicate an understanding of the concept.
2. Answers should indicate an understanding of the concept.

3. unlimited: the owner(s) is/are personally and fully responsible for all losses and debts of the business. limited: the corporation itself, not the owners, is fully responsible for its debts and losses.
4. Multinationals transfer new technology, generate new jobs, and produce tax revenues for the host nation.
5. A consumer co-op offers goods to its members, whereas a service co-op offers services.

Issues in Free Enterprise are case studies that allow students to investigate opposing views of economic issues. The case study contains background information about a current topic related to economics. Two differing opinions are presented that debate the issue and how it should be resolved. Students answer questions that evaluate their understanding of the arguments. They are then asked to identify which opinion they agree with, and explain the reason for their decision.

FOCUS

Challenge students to estimate the size, in dollars, of the largest business deal in history. Record their estimates on the board and guide the class toward a consensus. Reveal that the largest business deal was the Exxon/Mobil merger, valued at a mind-boggling $80 billion. The largest pending merger, in January 2000, was AOL/Time Warner, valued at around $162 billion. Have students compare this figure to the GDP figures of several countries listed in the *Statistical Abstract* or in a world atlas. Explain the term *megamerger*. As they read the selections, tell students to think about how megamergers might affect them and the country as a whole.

TEACH

L2 Recognizing Bias
Challenge students to find instances of bias in each selection. Have students look for words and figures of speech that are not neutral and discuss how they might help sway readers to the author's point of view.

A Case Study:

ARE MEGAMERGERS HARMFUL?

Financial analysts called the 1990s "the decade of the megamerger," and it's easy to see why. The decade saw an unprecedented number of "megamergers"—multi-*billion* dollar deals that combine already huge firms into even larger business giants.

In the oil industry, two giants—Exxon and Mobil—agreed to merge. The value of the deal? A stunning $80 billion—Wall Street's biggest deal ever. In the telecommunications industry, AT&T acquired cable giant Tele-Communications, Inc. for $48 billion. Daimler-Benz AG, an auto industry giant, acquired Chrysler Corporation in a $38 billion deal. In the financial industry, German bank Deutshe Bank took over Bankers Trust Corporation (a $10 billion-plus deal), creating the world's largest bank.

These megamergers are only a few highlights of the trend toward megamergers in many industries—a trend that shows no signs of stopping. But what are the consequences of megamergers?

> As you read the selections, ask yourself:
> Are megamergers beneficial or harmful?

 PRO Megamergers Are a Threat

The fierce competitive pressures forcing megamergers, such as cost-cutting and the need to achieve scale in the global economy, are understandable. But the mergers raise a broad issue that goes beyond traditional concerns. . . .

The big problem with these gigantic mergers is the growing imbalance between public and private power in our society. . . . [N]owadays an era of Big Government is being superseded by the age of global goliaths.

Superlarge companies with interests and commitments stretching from Boston to Brisbane are unlikely to focus as intensely as smaller ones do on support for the local neighborhoods—the schools, the arts, the development of research activities, the training of potential workers. . . .

Big companies have disproportionate clout on national legislation. Our scandalously porous laws for campaign contributions leave little doubt that megacompanies will exercise huge power over politicians when it comes to such issues as environmental standards, tax policy, Social Security, and health care. . . .

Megacompanies are almost beyond the law, too, because their deep pockets allow them to stymie prosecutors in ways smaller defendants cannot. Or, if they lose in court, they can pay large fines without much damage to their operations.

Corporate giants will also exert massive pressure on America's international behavior. Defense contractors such as Lockheed Martin, the result of a 1995 merger, have successfully pushed for NATO expansion and for related military sales to Poland, the Czech Republic, and others. Combined entities such as Boeing-McDonnell Douglas will tighten their already formidable grip on U.S. trade policy. Companies like Exxon-Mobil Corp. will deal with oil-producing countries

Behind the Viewpoints

 PRO **Jeffrey E. Garten** is the Dean of the Yale School of Management.

 CON **Robert J. Samuelson** is a writer for *The Washington Post*.

ENTERPRISE

almost as equals, conducting the most powerful private diplomacy since the British East India Company wielded near-sovereign clout throughout Asia. . . .

The American economic system is at its best when public and private needs are balanced. The sheer magnitude of mergers is skewing the equilibrium.

—Jeffrey E. Garten, Dean of the Yale School of Management

Megamergers Are Harmless

We are witnessing an interesting collision between history and headlines. The headlines herald a new era of menacing corporate power. . . .

Big business seems to be getting ever bigger and more powerful.

Well, not exactly. The correct lesson from history is just the opposite: corporate power is on the wane.

If this seems counterintuitive, it's also common sense. Big business has been brought to heel politically. Everything from child labor to the environment has been regulated. Government is the final arbiter of business behavior, even if government is often arbitrary. This is an old story. Less recognized—or perhaps forgotten—is the fact that companies have also lost much market power to set prices and determine what customers buy. . . .

We can all identify the major forces that have corroded corporate market power: new technology (personal computers and cable TV); foreign competition (automobiles); the end of legal monopoly (telephones). But there is a less visible force that subverts overall corporate power, and that is economic growth itself. As society becomes richer, people buy a greater array of goods and

services. When the typical market basket grows, producers of traditional goods become less important. . . .

Megamergers do not contradict this picture. One reason is that today's merger is often tomorrow's bust-up. Some mergers fail because they're driven more by personal ambition than true efficiency. . . .

Some mergers may also be blatantly collusive. Corporate executives regularly complain about lost "pricing power" (this may be a reason inflation has stayed tame). What better way to restore it than by buying a competitor? This is a genuine antitrust worry, but it's wrong to see bigness as automatically anti-competitive. Sometimes it's the other way around. One reason manufacturers have held down prices is that their superstore customers—the Wal-Marts and Home Depots—have the purchasing power to insist on low prices.

In truth, the inefficient firm—however big—is its own worst enemy. Its inefficiency curbs its power. Its products become vulnerable to competition; its managers become vulnerable to takeover. . . .

—Robert J. Samuelson, Washington Post Writers Group

Analyzing the Issue

1. What is Garten's basic objection to megamergers? How does he support his position?

2. What fundamental forces, in Samuelson's view, curb the power of giant corporations?

3. Explain whose position you agree with, and why, or explain your reasons for a third position.

L3 Diagramming an Argument

Direct students to summarize each argument in the form of a series of premises and conclusions. Have them next assign each premise and conclusion a number, and link the numbers with arrows to show relationships. Conclude by having students write a paragraph about each argument that evaluates it in terms of weak and strong points in its construction.

③ ASSESS

Have students answer the **Analyzing the Issue** questions.

④ CLOSE

Have students analyze the societal value of megamergers in terms of the seven economic and social goals of the United States discussed in Chapter 2: economic freedom, economic efficiency, economic equity, economic security, price stability, economic growth, and full employment. Do megamergers promote or detract from each goal? In what way(s)? Have students present their answers orally or in writing.

Answers to Analyzing the Issue

1. Garten's basic objection to megamergers is that they create an "imbalance between public and private power in our society." He cites a lack of business support for communities, business influence on legislation, avoidance of legal repercussions, and influence on foreign policy to support his position.

2. According to Samuelson, the power of giant corporations is curbed by government regulation by a loss of market power (from technology and economic growth), the failure of many giant corporations, and inefficiency.

3. Answers will vary. Students should provide cogent explanations for their positions.

Unit 2 Resource Manager

Materials listed may be used at any time during the study of the unit.

TEACHING TRANSPARENCIES

Economics Forms and Financial Pages Transparencies

Transparency 8
Grid Line Graph

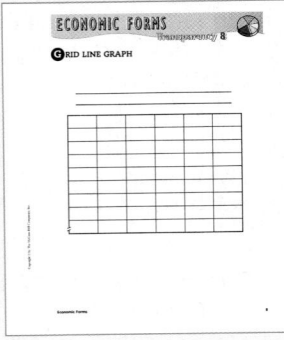

Transparency 9
X-Y Axis Line Graph

Transparency 12
Commodities Indexes

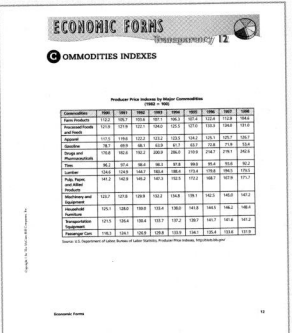

Economic Concepts Transparencies

Transparency 7
Markets and Prices

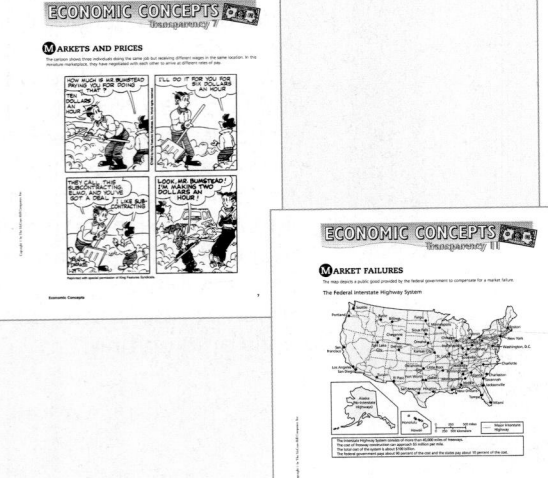

Transparency 8
Supply and Demand

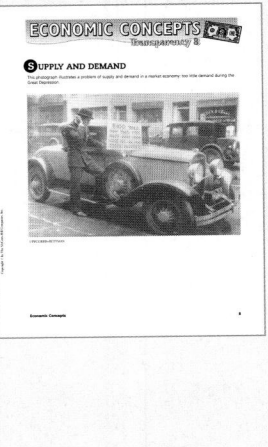

Transparency 9
Competition and Market Structure

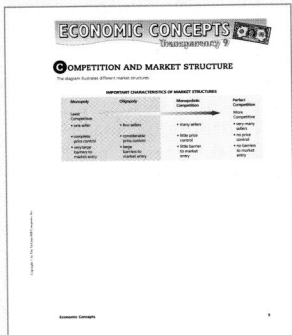

Transparency 11
Market Failures

REAL-WORLD ECONOMICS

*Have your students learn about investing and managing their financial future by participating in the exciting simulation **The Stock Market Game**TM. See Teacher pages in front of book for more information.*

*Strengthen students' research, cooperation, presentation and critical-thinking skills by having them compete in the **Fed Challenge**. See Teacher pages in front of book for more information.*

Additional Glencoe Resources for This Unit:
- Interactive Economics!
- Glencoe Skillbuilder Interactive Workbook, Level 2
- Nightly Business Report Economics & You Video Program
- Economic Survival: A Financial Simulation

Unit 2 Resource Manager

APPLICATION AND ENRICHMENT

Unit 2 Test

Economics Laboratory 2

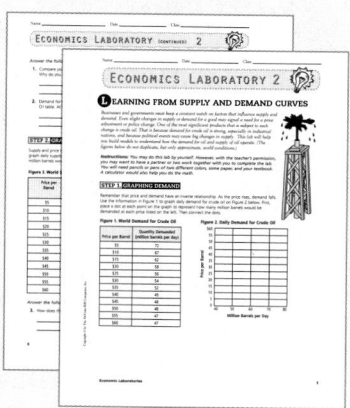

Unit 2 Business Week Focus on the New Economy

Use the following tools to easily assess student learning in a variety of ways:

- Performance Assessment Strategies and Activities
- Section Quizzes
- Chapter and Unit Tests
- Interactive Tutor Self-Assessment Software

- ExamView® Pro Testmaker
- MindJogger Videoquiz
- SAT I/II Test Practice
- epp.glencoe.com

*inter*NET CONNECTION

Economics: Principles and Practices
Visit the *Economics: Principles and Practices* Web site for economics overviews, activities, assessments, and updated charts and graphs.
epp.glencoe.com

Glencoe Social Studies
Visit the Glencoe Web site for social studies activities updates, and links to other sites.
socialstudies.glencoe.com

 Glencoe's Guide to Using the Internet
Provides an introduction to many of the current technologies on the Internet. Professional resources and teaching strategies included.

***Business Week* Online**
Visit the *Business Week* Web site for up-to-date news and special reports.
www.businessweek.com

Our Web sites provide additional resources. All essential content is covered in the Student Edition.

BIBLIOGRAPHY

Readings for the Student
Ambry, Margaret K., and Cheryl Russell, *The Official Guide to the American Marketplace.* Ithaca, NY: New Strategies Publications, 1995.

"I'd Like to Teach the World to Sell," ed. by Ellen Neuborne, *Business Week*, June 7, 1999.

Readings for the Teacher
Supply and Demand. Gainesville, FL: Center for Economic Education, University of Florida, 1996. Resource guide providing ideas on how to teach this basic principle of the free market system.

"amazon.com vs. e-bay," by Robert D. Hof and Linda Himelstein, *Business Week,* May 31, 1999.

Multimedia Resources
Videocassette. *The Illustrious Yet Elusive World of Microeconomics.* Cerebellum, 1995. Video, 113 minutes. The Standard Deviants mix comedy and concepts to help students master supply and demand.

Unit Objectives
After studying this unit, students will be able to:
1. Explain how supply and demand interact to determine price.
2. Describe the major types of economic markets in the United States.
3. Discuss how competition and monopolies affect prices.

Unit Overview
Unit 2 examines major markets with respect to the degree of competition within each type and how this affects buyers and sellers. **Chapter 4** explains the concept of demand, while **Chapter 5** discusses supply, the theory of production, and profit maximization. **Chapter 6** brings demand and supply together in a relationship focusing on price and explains how the price system operates. **Chapter 7** introduces competition and market structures. It also discusses market failures and the government's role in the economy.

UNIT 2
Microeconomics

Why It's Important

As you read this unit, learn how the study of economics helps answer the following questions:

- Why are tickets for some sporting events sold out?

- Why does the price of local farm products such as corn and tomatoes decrease during the summer?

Buyers and sellers in the stock market exemplify the forces of supply and demand.

MAKING IT RELEVANT

Demand In 1996, a much-publicized study by the Cleveland Clinic reported that people who took zinc lozenges appeared to beat colds faster. Although other studies were not as conclusive, demand for zinc tablets skyrocketed. Cold-Eeze, the brand that was used in the Cleveland Clinic study, saw an increase in sales from about $500,000 in 1995 to more than $16 million in 1997. **Ask:** What factors might have led to such an increase in sales?

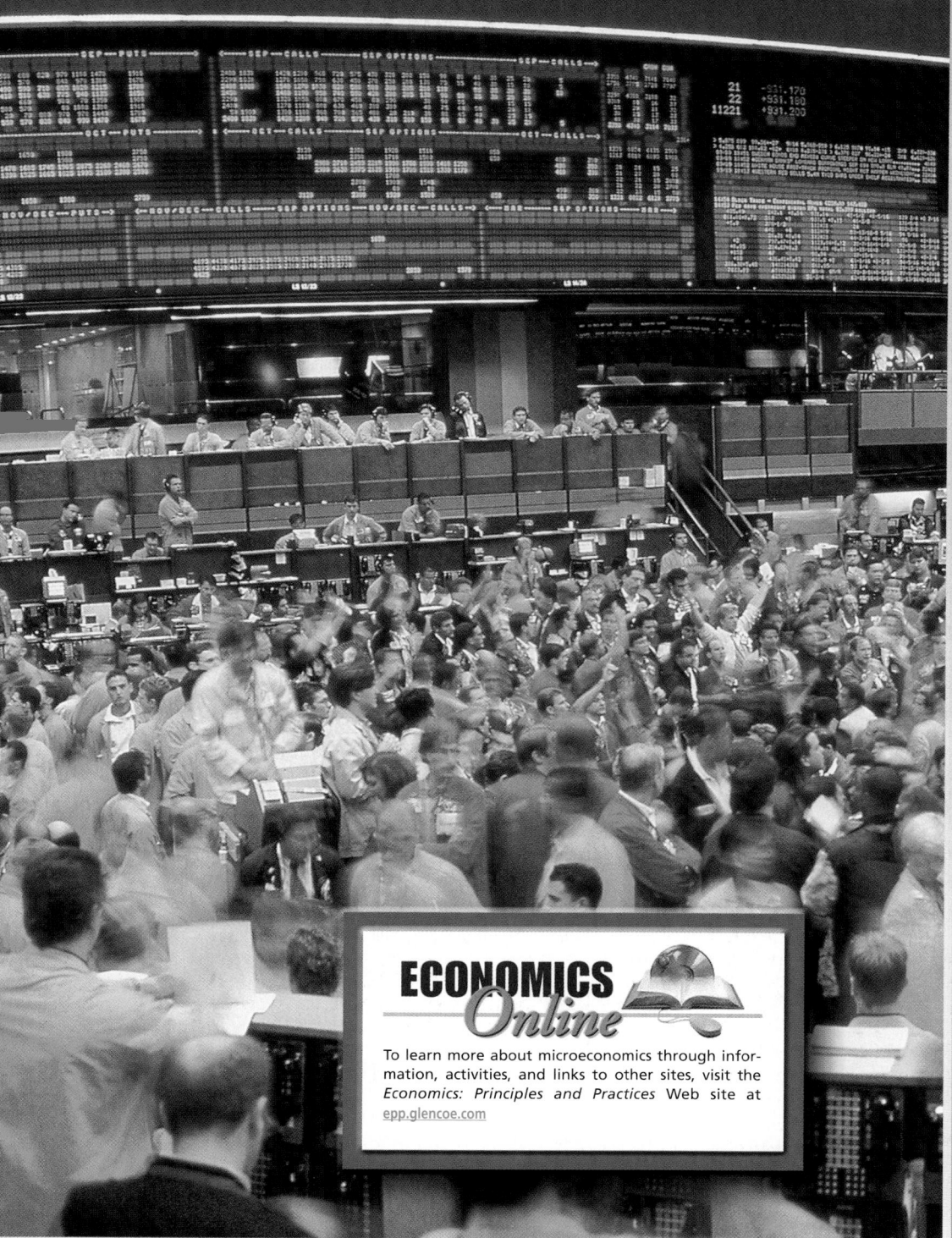

Introducing the Unit
Ask students to select a business in their community that they patronize. Have them write a short analysis of the business by responding to the following:
1. What is the name and location of the business?
2. Why do you purchase from this business? *(convenience, price, service, quality of product)*
3. What is the competition for the business that you selected? *(stores nearby, malls, mail order)*
4. How does the selected business compete? *(price competition, sales, advertising, special service)*

Have students share their analyses. Point out that in this unit, students will study how prices are determined, how businesses compete, and the roles that consumers and businesses play in our economy.

Visual Instruction

The stock market is where stocks are bought and sold. The oldest stock market, founded in 1817, is the New York Stock Exchange (NYSE) in New York City.

ECONOMIC SURVIVAL
A FINANCIAL SIMULATION

To help students learn to manage their own finances, have them participate in the game **Economic Survival: A Financial Simulation** in which each student enters the workforce, rents an apartment, and deals with everyday events.

ECONOMICS
Online

To learn more about microeconomics through information, activities, and links to other sites, visit the *Economics: Principles and Practices* Web site at epp.glencoe.com

ECONOMICS
Online

To access the data, follow these steps:
1. Log on to the **Economics: Principles and Practices** Web site at epp.glencoe.com
2. From the options on the opening screen, select Web Resources.
3. Select the Bureau of Labor Statistics.
4. Then select Surveys & Programs.
5. From there, click on Consumer Price Indexes.

What to Do When You Are There
From the list of items in the Consumer Price Index, have students identify four expenditures that are purchased regularly. Then have them track the changes over the last five years for these items and create a line graph that shows how the price changes. **Ask:** How have prices changed over the last five years? Why? If students have limited access to the Internet, have them use other resources.

Chapter 4 Resource Manager

SECTION RESOURCES

Daily Objectives	Reproducible Resources	Technology/Multimedia Resources
Section 1 **What Is Demand?** 1. Describe and illustrate the concept of demand. 2. Explain how demand and utility are related.	Reproducible Lesson Plan 4-1 Daily Lecture Notes 4-1 Guided Reading Activity 4-1 Reading Essentials and Study Guide 4-1 Section Quiz 4-1*	Daily Focus Transparency 9 Interactive Tutor Self-Assessment Software ExamView® Pro Testmaker Presentation Plus!
Section 2 **Factors Affecting Demand** 1. Explain what causes a change in quantity demanded. 2. Describe the factors that could cause a change in demand.	Reproducible Lesson Plan 4-2 Daily Lecture Notes 4-2 Guided Reading Activity 4-2 Reading Essentials and Study Guide 4-2 Section Quiz 4-2*	Daily Focus Transparency 10 Interactive Economics! Interactive Tutor Self-Assessment Software ExamView® Pro Testmaker Presentation Plus!
Section 3 **Elasticity of Demand** 1. Explain why elasticity is a measure of responsiveness. 2. Analyze the elasticity of demand for a product. 3. Understand the factors that determine demand.	Reproducible Lesson Plan 4-3 Daily Lecture Notes 4-3 Guided Reading Activity 4-3 Reading Essentials and Study Guide 4-3 Section Quiz 4-3*	Daily Focus Transparency 12 Vocabulary PuzzleMaker CD-ROM NBR Economics & You Video Program Interactive Tutor Self-Assessment Software ExamView® Pro Testmaker Presentation Plus!

*Also available in Spanish

Transparency   CD-ROM   Software   Blackline Master

Videodisc   Audio Program   Videocassette

0:00 OUT OF TIME?
Assign the Chapter 4 Audio Program activity and test.

Block Schedule

Activities that are particularly suited to use within the block scheduling framework are identified throughout this chapter by the following designation: **BLOCK SCHEDULING**

KEY TO ABILITY LEVELS

Teaching strategies have been coded for varying learning styles and abilities.

L1 BASIC activities for all students
L2 AVERAGE activities for average to above-average students
L3 CHALLENGING activities for above-average students
ELL ENGLISH LANGUAGE LEARNER activities

Chapter 4 Resource Manager

Timesaving Tools

TeacherWorks™ All-In-One Planner and Resource Center

- **Interactive Teacher Edition** Access your Teacher Wraparound Edition and your classroom resources with a few easy clicks.

- **Interactive Lesson Planner** Planning has never been easier! Organize your week, month, semester, or year with all the lesson helps you need to make teaching creative, timely, and relevant.

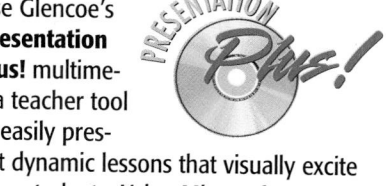

Use Glencoe's **Presentation Plus!** multimedia teacher tool to easily present dynamic lessons that visually excite your students. Using Microsoft PowerPoint® you can customize the presentations to create your own personalized lessons.

ACTIVITY

From the Classroom of...

Sandy Hayes
Logan County
High School
Russellville, KY

Elastic and Inelastic Demand

I call this activity "Let's Stretch." Have the class watch several television commercials that you have prerecorded. Then discuss elastic and inelastic demand using three questions that help determine elasticity:
1. Can the purchase be delayed?
2. Are adequate substitutes available?
3. Does the purchase use a large portion of income?

Organize the class into groups of three or four students, and ask each group to find eight to ten (or any number) newspaper or magazine advertisements for goods or services of their choice. They should mount these on poster board and draw a chart below the ads that asks and answers, for each product, the three questions previously discussed. Have students write under each good or service whether it has elastic or inelastic demand based on their answers to the questions. Allow each group to discuss its findings with the class.

National Council on Economic Education

THE **Economics**America AND **Economics**International PROGRAMS

Voluntary National Content Standards in Economics
Emphasized in Chapter 4

Content Standard 8

For a complete listing of NCEE Standards and entire text correlation, see Teacher pages in front of book.

Resources Available from NCEE
- Capstone: The Nation's High School Economics Course
- Economics and Entrepreneurship, Teaching Strategies
- Entrepreneurship in the U.S. Economy
- Focus: High School Economics
- United States History: Focus on Economics

To order these materials or to contact your state Council on Economic Education about workshops and programs, call 1-800-338-1192 or visit www.nationalcouncil.org

Chapter 4 Resource Manager

Economic Concept Transparency 8: Supply and Demand

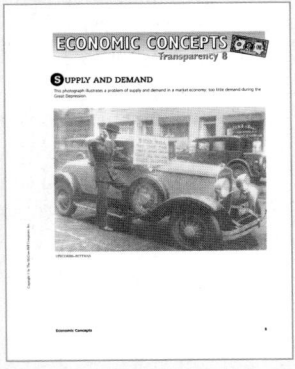

Consumer Application Activity 4

Free Enterprise Activity 4

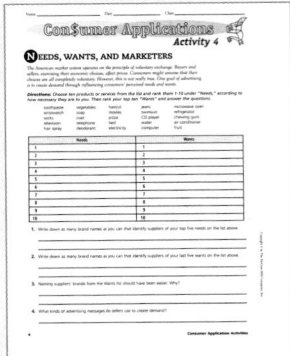

Enrichment Activity 4

Cooperative Learning Activity 4

Math Practice Activity 4

Economic Cartoon 4

Primary and Secondary Source Reading 4

Economic Vocabulary Activity 4

Reteaching Activity 4

Critical Thinking Activity 4

Reinforcing Economic Skill 10

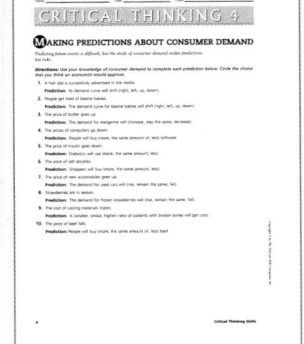

Chapter 4 Resource Manager

ASSESSMENT AND EVALUATION

Chapter 4 Test Form A

Chapter 4 Test Form B

Performance Assessment Activity 4

ExamView® Pro Testmaker

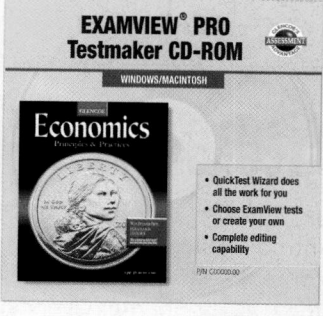

SPANISH RESOURCES

The following Spanish language materials are available in the Spanish Resources binder:

 Spanish Economic Vocabulary Activities

 Spanish Reteaching Activities

 Spanish Section Quizzes

 Spanish Economic Concepts Transparencies

Also available:

  Spanish Chapter 4 Audio Program Activity and Test

TECHNOLOGY/MULTIMEDIA

- Vocabulary PuzzleMaker CD-ROM
- Interactive Tutor Self-Assessment Software
- ExamView® Pro Testmaker
- Audio Program (English or Spanish)
- NBR Economics & You Video Program (English or Spanish)
- MindJogger Videoquiz
- Interactive Economics! CD-ROM
- Presentation Plus!
- TeacherWorks CD-ROM
- Glencoe Skillbuilder Interactive Workbook CD-ROM, Level 2

ECONOMICS Online

Use our Web site for additional resources. All essential content is covered in the Student Edition.

You and your students can visit epp.glencoe.com, the Web site companion to **Economics: Principles and Practices.** This innovative integration of electronic and print media offers your students a wealth of opportunities. The student text directs students to the Web site for the following options:

- **Chapter Overviews**
- **Student Web Activities**
- **Self-Check Quizzes**
- **Textbook Updates**

Answers are provided for you in the Web Activity Lesson Plan. Additional Web resources and interactive puzzles are also available.

Performance Assessment

Refer to Activity 4 in the *Performance Assessment Strategies and Activities* booklet.

 BLOCK SCHEDULING

ECONOMICS
Online

Introduce students to chapter content and key terms by having them access **Chapter Overview 4** at epp.glencoe.com

NIGHTLY BUSINESS REPORT

 ECONOMICS & YOU

Chapter 5
Disc 1, Side 1

What is Demand?
After viewing this segment, students should be able to:
• Explain the law of demand.
• Differentiate between elastic and inelastic demand.

 Also available in VHS.

GLENCOE
TECHNOLOGY

 Use **MindJogger Videoquiz** to preview the Chapter 4 content.

CHAPTER

4

Demand

Economics & You

In **Chapter 4,** you will learn that demand is more than a desire to buy something: it is the ability and willingness to actually buy it. To learn more about how demand operates in the marketplace, view the Chapter 5 video lesson:

What is Demand?

Chapter Overview Visit the *Economics: Principles and Practices* Web site at epp.glencoe.com and click on **Chapter 4—Chapter Overviews** to preview chapter information.

People demonstrate demand by their desire, ability, and willingness to pay.

✚ EXTRA CREDIT PROJECT

Have students research and write about a product or service for which they believe there will be a high demand in the twenty-first century. Students should explain why they think such a high demand will exist and use the Internet and financial magazines to make predictions about the product or service's potential growth. Have students create charts and graphs to support their positions.

What Is Demand?

Study Guide

Main Idea
Demand is a willingness to buy a product at a particular price.

Reading Strategy
Graphic Organizer As you read this section, use a web diagram similar to the one below to note characteristics of demand.

Characteristics of demand

Key Terms
demand, microeconomics, demand schedule, demand curve, Law of Demand, market demand curve, marginal utility, diminishing marginal utility

Objectives
After studying this section, you will be able to:
1. **Describe** and illustrate the concept of demand.
2. **Explain** how demand and utility are related.

Applying Economic Concepts
Demand You express your *demand* for a product when you are willing and able to purchase it. Read to find out how demand is measured.

1 FOCUS

Section Overview
This section defines demand and the conditions necessary for it to exist.

BELLRINGER
Motivational Activity

 Project **transparency** and have students answer questions.

 Available as blackline master.

Daily Focus Transparency 9

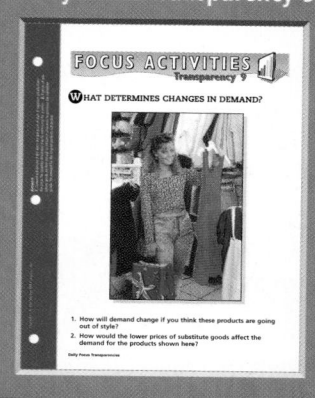

Cover Story

Forecasting Demand

Keith Clinkscales realizes that he must pinpoint what his readers want if his new magazine, *Blaze*, is to succeed. *Blaze* is a magazine for the hip hop movement—focusing on rap music and fashion. As reported in *USA Today*, Clinkscales watches the comings and goings of teenagers at [nearby] Norman Thomas High School. He studies

Successful magazines gauge demand.

their clothes, hairstyles, and, of course, their music. . . . Clinkscales, 34, notes, "It's amazing to watch them and observe the passion they have about their music and fashion and overall lifestyle. . . ."

The magazine targets readers ages 12 to 24. "Hip-hop is the octane of the urban culture. We decided to create a publication that will focus on that culture," says Clinkscales.

—*USA Today*, December 30, 1998

P eople sometimes think of demand as the desire to have or to own a certain product. In this sense, anyone who would like to own a swimming pool could be said to "demand" one. In order for demand to be counted in the marketplace, however, desire is not enough; it must coincide with the ability and willingness to pay for it. Only those people with **demand**–the desire, ability, and willingness to buy a product–can compete with others who have similar demands.

Demand, like many other topics in Unit 2, is a microeconomic concept. **Microeconomics** is the area of economics that deals with behavior and decision making by small units, such as individuals and firms. Collectively, these concepts of microeconomics help explain how prices are determined and how individual economic decisions are made.

An Introduction to Demand

A knowledge of demand is essential to understand how a market economy works. As you read in Chapter 2, in a market economy people and firms act in their own best interests to

CHAPTER 4: DEMAND **89**

Study Guide

Reading Strategy
Have students create the graphic organizer.
Answers to Graphic: *the desire, ability, and willingness to buy a product*

Preteaching Vocabulary
Have students write questions for which each Key Term is an answer.

RESOURCE MANAGER

Reproducible Masters
- Reproducible Lesson Plan 4-1
- Daily Lecture Notes 4-1
- Guided Reading Activity 4-1
- Reading Essentials and Study Guide 4-1
- Section Quiz 4-1

Transparencies
- Daily Focus Transparency 9

Multimedia
- Interactive Tutor Self-Assessment Software
- ExamView® Pro Testmaker
- Presentation Plus!

2 TEACH

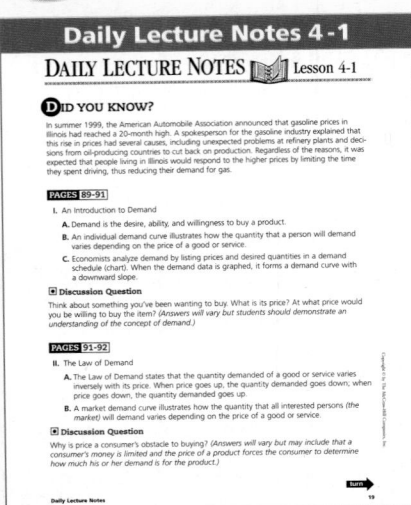

Daily Lecture Notes 4-1

DAILY LECTURE NOTES Lesson 4-1

DID YOU KNOW?

In summer 1999, the American Automobile Association announced that gasoline prices in Illinois had reached a 20-month high. A spokesperson for the gasoline industry explained that this rise in prices had several causes, including unexpected problems at refinery plants and decisions from oil-producing countries to cut back on production. Regardless of the reasons, it was expected that people living in Illinois would respond to the higher prices by limiting the time they spent driving, thus reducing their demand for gas.

PAGES 89-91

I. An Introduction to Demand

A. Demand is the desire, ability, and willingness to buy a product.

B. An individual demand curve illustrates how the quantity that a person will demand varies depending on the price of a good or service.

C. Economists analyze demand by listing prices and desired quantities in a demand schedule (chart). When the demand data is graphed, it forms a demand curve with a downward slope.

Discussion Question

Think about something you've been wanting to buy. What is its price? At what price would you be willing to buy the item? (Answers will vary but students should demonstrate an understanding of the concept of demand.)

PAGES 91-92

II. The Law of Demand

A. The Law of Demand states that the quantity demanded of a good or service varies inversely with its price. When price goes up, the quantity demanded goes down; when price goes down, the quantity demanded goes up.

B. A market demand curve illustrates how the quantity that all interested persons (the market) will demand varies depending on the price of a good or service.

Discussion Question

Why is price a consumer's obstacle to buying? (Answers will vary but may include that a consumer's money is limited and the price of a product forces the consumer to determine how much his or her demand is for the product.)

Daily Lecture Notes 19

L1 Relating Concepts

Have students draw a cartoon that illustrates the relationship between price and demand. **ELL**

ECONOMICS
AT A GLANCE

Answer: *The Law of Demand describes the inverse relationship between demand and price as shown in the curve.*

ECONOMICS
AT A GLANCE
Figure 4.1

The Demand for Compact Digital Discs

Ⓐ Demand Schedule

Price	Quantity Demanded
$30	0
25	0
20	1
15	3
10	5
5	8

Ⓑ Demand Curve

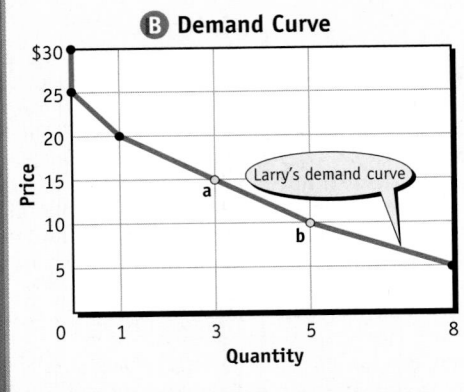

Larry's demand curve

Using Graphs The demand schedule on the top lists the quantity demanded at each and every possible price. The demand curve (below) shows the same information in the form of a graph. The demand curve is downward sloping, which means that more will be demanded at lower prices, and fewer at higher prices. **How does the demand curve illustrate the Law of Demand?**

---

answer the WHAT, HOW, and FOR WHOM questions. Knowledge of demand is also important for sound business planning. This is what an entrepreneur like Keith Clinkscales must do: Find out what type of magazine the hip-hop set is willing and able to buy in order for his project to become a success.

Demand Illustrated

To illustrate more fully how demand affects business planning, imagine you are opening a bicycle repair shop. Before you begin, you need to know where the demand is. You will want to set up your shop in a neighborhood with many bicycle riders and few repair shops.

After you identify an area in which to locate the shop, how do you measure the demand for your services? You may visit other shops and gauge the reactions of consumers to different prices. You may poll consumers about prices and determine demand from this data. You could study data compiled over past years, which would show consumer reactions to higher and lower prices.

All of these methods would give you a general idea as to the desire, willingness, and ability of people to pay. Gathering precise data on how consumers actually behave, however, is not easy. Even so, it is possible to treat the concept of demand in a more formal manner.

The Individual Demand Schedule

To see how an economist would analyze demand, look at **Panel A** of **Figure 4.1.** It shows the amount of a product that a consumer, whom we'll call Larry, would be willing and able to purchase over a range of *possible* prices that go from $5 to $30. The information in Panel A is known as a **demand schedule.** The demand schedule is a listing that shows the various quantities demanded of a particular product at all prices that might prevail in the market at a given time.

As you can see, Larry would not buy any CDs at a price of $25 or $30, but he would buy one if the price fell to $20, and he would buy three if the price were $15, and so on. Just like the rest of us, he is generally willing to buy more units of a product as the price gets lower.

MEETING SPECIAL NEEDS ACTIVITY

Learning Disabled For students who have trouble with reading, note that transition words and key words in the text can help focus the reader's attention. Students who read superficially often need help to notice these "markers." Have students skim the first two paragraphs on page 89 with you as you point to these words: *in this sense, in order, however, like, such as,* and *collectively.* Discuss the use of these words and the kind of information students might expect to follow such words. Have students skim another subsection to find other transitions or key words.

➤ Refer to *Inclusion for the Social Studies Classroom Strategies and Activities* in the TCR.

The Individual Demand Curve

The demand schedule information in **Panel A** of **Figure 4.1** can also be shown graphically as the downward-sloping line in **Panel B**. All we have to do to is to transfer each of the price-quantity observations in the demand schedule to the graph, and then connect the points to form the curve. Economists call this the **demand curve,** a graph showing the quantity demanded at each and every price that might prevail in the market.

For example, point **a** in **Panel B** shows that three CDs are purchased at a price of $15 each, while point **b** shows that five will be bought at a price of $10. The demand schedule and the demand curve are similar in that they both show the same information—one just shows the data in the form of a table while the other is presented in the form of a graph.

The Law of Demand

The prices and quantities illustrated in **Figure 4.1** point out an important feature of demand: For practically every product or service, higher prices are associated with a smaller amount demanded. Conversely, lower prices are associated with larger amounts demanded. This is known as the **Law of Demand,** which states that the quantity demanded of a good or service varies inversely with its price. In other words, when the price goes up, quantity demanded goes down. Likewise, when the price goes down, quantity demanded goes up.

Foundations for the Law of Demand

Stating something in the form of a "law" may seem like a strong statement for a social science like economics to make, but there are at least two reasons why economists prefer to do so. First, the inverse relationship between price and quantity demanded is something that we find in study after study, with people almost always stating that they would buy more of an item if its price goes down, and less if the price goes up. Price is an obstacle, which discourages consumers from buying. The higher this obstacle, the less of a product they will buy; the lower the obstacle, the more they will buy. Second, common sense

and simple observation are consistent with the Law of Demand. This is the way people behave in normal everyday life. People ordinarily do buy more of a product at a low price than at a high price. All we have to do is to observe the increased traffic and purchases at the mall whenever there is a sale.

The Market Demand Curve

Figure 4.1 shows a particular *individual's* demand for a product. Sometimes, however, we are more concerned with the **market demand curve,** the demand curve that shows the quantities demanded by everyone who is interested in purchasing the product. **Figure 4.2** shows the market demand curve **DD** for Larry and his friend Curly, the only two people whom (for simplicity) we assume to be willing and able to purchase CDs.

The Law of Demand

Demand and Prices If the prices of televisions drop, consumers will be better able and more willing to buy. *How does this situation reflect the Law of Demand?*

CHAPTER 4: DEMAND **91**

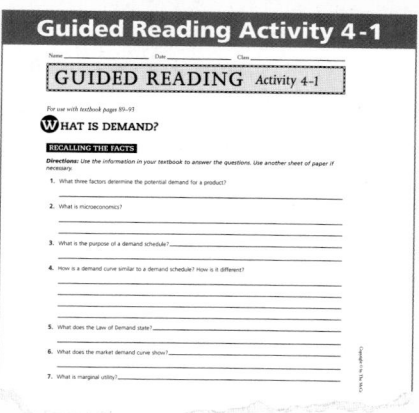

Guided Reading Activity 4-1

GUIDED READING Activity 4-1

For use with textbook pages 89–93

WHAT IS DEMAND?

RECALLING THE FACTS

Directions: Use the information in your textbook to answer the questions. Use another sheet of paper if necessary.

1. What three factors determine the potential demand for a product?
2. What is microeconomics?
3. What is the purpose of a demand schedule?
4. How is a demand curve similar to a demand schedule? How is it different?
5. What does the Law of Demand state?
6. What does the market demand curve show?
7. What is marginal utility?

CURRICULUM CONNECTION

Family and Consumer Science Lifestyle changes can create new market demands. As people spend more time working and less time on housework, soap and detergent companies are creating cleansers for those who want timesaving, easy-to-use products for their homes. Sales boomed for products like Clean Shower, a cleaning spray for shower walls that requires no scrubbing. Net sales for Clean Shower climbed to $11 million from 1995 to 1998.

Visual Instruction

Answer to Caption:
The Law of Demand states that the quantity demanded of a good varies inversely with its price; therefore, if the prices of televisions drop, the quantity demanded will increase.

FREE ENTERPRISE ACTIVITY

As a class, discuss how store sales affect students' demand for a variety of products. **Ask:** Do you tend to make more purchases during sales? Then organize the class into groups. Assign each group a different type of store, for example a grocery store, a department store, a convenience store, or a specialty store. Have each group develop a list of general questions to ask the stores' managers about the effect that sale prices have on consumer demand. A volunteer from each group can then interview a store manager using the group's questions. (Caution students that managers may be unwilling to discuss specific sales figures; general answers to their questions will be sufficient.) Discuss students' findings as a class. **BLOCK SCHEDULING**

Answer: *The curve will begin to level off as the extra satisfaction from using additional CDs begins to diminish.*

③ ASSESS

Assign Section 1 Assessment as homework or as an in-class activity.

💾 Have students use **Interactive Tutor Self-Assessment Software** to review Section 1.

ECONOMICS
AT A GLANCE

Figure 4.2

Individual and Market Demand Curves

Quantity of CDs Demanded by:

Price	Larry	+	Curly	=	Market
$30	0		0		0
25	0		1		1
20	1		2		3
15	3	+	3	=	6
10	5		5		10
5	8		7		15

Using Graphs The market demand curve, DD, is the sum of all individual demand curves in the market. The market demand curve, like the individual demand curve, is also downward sloping. **How does diminishing marginal utility help explain the shape of the demand curve?**

To get the market demand curve is a simple matter. All we need to do is add together the number of CDs that Larry and Curly would purchase at every possible price, and then plot them on a separate graph. To illustrate, point **a** in **Figure 4.2** represents the three CDs that Larry would purchase at $15, plus the three that Curly would buy at the same price. Likewise, point **b** represents the quantity of CDs that both would purchase at a price of $10.

The market demand curve in **Figure 4.2** is very similar to the individual demand curve in **Figure 4.1.** Both show a range of possible prices that might prevail in the market at a given time. Both are downward sloping, showing that more will be bought at lower prices, and fewer at higher prices. The only real difference between the two is that the market demand curve shows the demand for *everyone* that is interested in buying the product. Thus, the market demand curve shows the demand for everyone in the market.

92 UNIT 2 MICROECONOMICS

CRITICAL THINKING

Formulating Questions Ask students to imagine that they are going to open a restaurant. While the location for the restaurant has been determined—a prime business location with adequate parking along a busy street—no other details have been finalized. Have students develop a questionnaire to be circulated throughout the neighborhood that, when answered by a majority of local residents, will help them determine local demands. Students should consider the restaurant's menu, pricing, and type of service (fast food, drive-through, sit-down), to help in their decision. Tell students to think about the types of questions that will provide them with the most information, but to also consider ease-of-answering for those participating in the survey.

Demand and Marginal Utility

 As you may recall from Chapter 1, economists use the term *utility* to describe the amount of usefulness or satisfaction that someone gets from the use of a product. **Marginal utility**—the extra usefulness or satisfaction a person gets from acquiring or using one more unit of a product—is an important extension of this concept because it explains so much about demand.

The reason we buy something in the first place is because we feel the product is useful and that it will give us satisfaction. However, as we use more and more of a product, we encounter the principle of **diminishing marginal utility,** which states that the extra satisfaction we get from using additional quantities of the product begins to diminish.

Because of our diminishing satisfaction, we are not willing to pay as much for the second, third, fourth, and so on, as we did the first. This is why our demand curve is downward-sloping, and this is why Larry and Curly won't pay as much for the second CD as they did for the first. This is something that happens to all of us all the time. For example, when

you buy a cola, why not buy two, or three, or even more? The answer is that you get the most satisfaction from the first purchase, and so you buy one. You get less satisfaction from the second purchase and even less from the next—so you simply are not willing to pay as much. When you reach the point where the marginal utility is less than the price, you stop buying.

STANDARD &POOR'S INFOBYTE

Housing Starts The number of housing starts shows the demand for new homes. Economists forecast housing starts by using the current month's permits as a predictor. Building permits tend to move in tandem with starts on a month-to-month basis. They are also considered to be a leading indicator of the economy in general. Increases in building permits and starts are common during periods following a drop in mortgage rates.

Section 1 Assessment

Checking for Understanding

1. **Main Idea** Using your notes from the graphic organizer activity on page 89, write a definition of demand in your own words.

2. **Key Terms** Define demand, microeconomics, demand schedule, demand curve, Law of Demand, market demand curve, marginal utility, diminishing marginal utility.

3. **Describe** the relationship between the demand schedule and demand curve.

4. **Describe** how the slope of the demand curve can be explained by the principle of diminishing marginal utility.

Applying Economic Concepts

5. **Demand** Record the names and approximate prices of the last two items you purchased. In general, would you have spent your money

differently if the price of each item was twice as high? Would you have spent your money differently if each of the items cost half as much as it did? Explain your responses.

Critical Thinking

6. **Using Graphs** Create your own demand schedule for an item you currently purchase. Next, plot your demand schedule on a demand curve. Be sure to include correct labels.

7. **Analyzing Information** Analyze several magazine or newspaper ads to determine how the ads reflect or use the law of diminishing marginal utility.

> **Practice** and **assess** key social studies skills with the *Glencoe Skillbuilder Interactive Workbook, Level 2.*

Section 1 Assessment Answers

1. Answers should include the desire, ability, and willingness to buy a product.

2. All vocabulary terms are defined in the text.

3. Both provide information about demand—the schedule in the form of a table and the curve in the form of a graph.

4. Diminishing marginal utility says that as we use more of a product, we are not willing to pay as much for it. Therefore, the demand

curve is downward sloping. People will not pay as much for the second and third product as they will for the first.

5. Answers should reflect an understanding of the economic concepts studied in the section.

6. Answers should reflect an understanding of demand schedules and curves.

7. Answers should show an understanding of the law of diminishing marginal utility.

Reteach

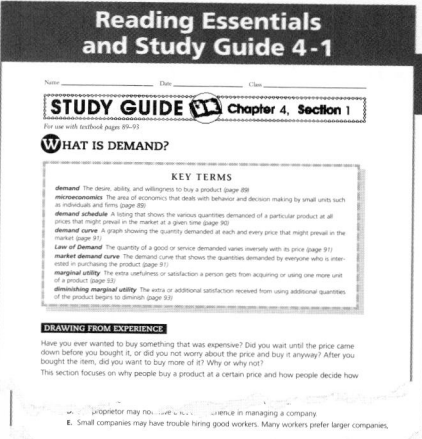

Reading Essentials and Study Guide 4-1

Enrich

Encourage students to interview store managers to discover how they measure demand for their products.

 CLOSE

Have each student choose an item that he or she buys regularly, for example a food item or jeans, and create a simple demand schedule and curve for that item.

BACKGROUND

Students are probably familiar with Oprah Winfrey, and may even recognize the influence she holds. What they might not know is that Winfrey comes from a background of poverty, and had to overcome many obstacles in her personal life. Instead of allowing such disadvantages to limit her, Winfrey embraces and promotes an ethic of self-reliance and responsibility in all that she does. Winfrey maintains that responsibility should extend to others, as she has demonstrated through her key roles in the enactment of the National Childhood Protection Act, philanthropy, and funding of programs that help women and children. "My mission," Winfrey said, "is to use [my] position, power, and money to create opportunities for other people."

TEACH

Share this fact with students: a recent survey indicated that, on average, whenever *The Oprah Winfrey Show* airs, some 7 percent of households with televisions are tuned into it. Then focus students on the viewership information in the Profile (10 million people, 190 cities, 13 countries). Direct students to put these figures into larger demographic and geographic contexts (e.g., percent of total population), and write paragraphs that evaluate Winfrey's influence in such quantitative terms. **Ask:** Which is a better measure of her influence, these figures, or her charity work? Why?

Profiles IN Economics

Wealth and Influence:
Oprah Winfrey
(1954–)

Oprah Winfrey–known to millions simply as "Oprah"–is one of the richest and most powerful women in America. Most people know her as a talk show host, but she has other talents. As an actress, she received an Oscar nomination for Best Supporting Actress in *The Color Purple*. As a businessperson, she is the third woman in history (after Mary Pickford and Lucille Ball) to own a major television and film studio. With an annual income of about $100 million, she is poised to become the country's first African American billionaire.

AGAINST ALL ODDS

Winfrey's beginnings were humble. She was born to unwed teenage parents in rural Mississippi and grew up in poverty. A troubled childhood followed. Eventually, the teenager went to live with her father, whose insistence on discipline and education soon turned her life around.

At the age of 17, Winfrey became a part-time radio newscaster at Nashville's WVOL. Two years later, while attending Tennessee State University, she was hired as a reporter and anchor at WTVF-TV.

In 1976 Winfrey moved to Baltimore, where she found her niche in television as co-host of a Baltimore morning show, *People Are Talking*. Winfrey's successful experience in Baltimore paved the way for her to become the undisputed "Queen of Talk" in Chicago.

In 1984 Winfrey took over the ailing *AM Chicago* talk show on WLS-TV. She turned it into a smash hit, driving the successful *Phil Donahue Show* to another city and another time slot. In 1986 *The Oprah Winfrey Show* became nationally syndicated. Within months, it was the third-highest-rated show in syndication. It became the number-one talk show, reaching up to ten million people daily in more than 190 cities in 13 countries.

Winfrey became the first African American woman to own her own television and film production complex, Harpo Productions, Inc. (Harpo is Oprah spelled backwards.)

MAKING A DIFFERENCE

Winfrey uses her wealth and influence to make a difference in the lives of others. Under her guidance, *The Oprah Winfrey Show* avoids sensationalism, focusing instead on issues of empowerment and self-improvement.

Winfrey is also a staunch children's rights activist. She proposed a bill to create a national database of convicted child abusers, which President Clinton signed into law in 1994.

> ### Examining the Profile
> 1. **Drawing Conclusions** Why is Oprah Winfrey considered one of the most powerful women in America?
> 2. **For Further Research** Make an annotated time line of Winfrey's career, highlighting her major achievements.

Answers to Examining the Profile

1. Answers will vary, but students might equate power with influence, and note that Winfrey's influence stems from the popularity of her television show, her wealth (and what she has done with it), and the programs in which she has participated.

2. Time lines will vary. Possible entries include: 1971—became newscaster at WVOL; 1973—became reporter/anchor at WTVF; 1976—became co-host of *People are Talking*; 1984—became host of *AM Chicago*; 1986—*The Oprah Winfrey Show* went into national syndication.

Factors Affecting Demand

Study Guide

Main Idea
There are a number of factors that will cause demand to either increase or decrease.

Reading Strategy
Graphic Organizer As you read about the determinants of demand, list each on a table similar to the one below and provide an example of each.

Determinants of Demand

Determinant	Example

Key Terms
change in quantity demanded, income effect, substitution effect, change in demand, substitutes, complements

Objectives
After studying this section, you will be able to:
1. **Explain** what causes a change in quantity demanded.
2. **Describe** the factors that could cause a change in demand.

Applying Economic Concepts
Change in Demand Would you buy more clothes if your employer doubled your salary? Read to find out what causes a *change in demand*.

Cover Story

America's Pastime?

Myles Monaghan could almost be the next Alex Rodriguez. He's got a cannon for an arm. He almost never drops the ball. And on a good day, he can knock a pitch clear out of the park. So how come he spent his last few springs playing lacrosse?

Consumer preferences cause a change in demand.

"BASEBALL IS BORING," says the 12-year-old Larchmont, N.Y., jock.

Nationwide, the average number of children playing America's once-favorite pastime has tumbled nearly 20% according to the Sporting Goods Manufacturers Association. Sales of everything from balls to baseball cards are falling.

—*MSNBC News* (online), June 15,2001

The demand curve is a graphical representation of the quantities that people are willing to purchase at all possible prices that might prevail in the market. Occasionally, however, something happens to change people's willingness and ability to buy, as exemplified in the cover story. These changes are usually of two types: a change in the quantity demanded, and a change in demand.

Change in the Quantity Demanded

 Point **a** on the demand curve in **Figure 4.3** shows that six CDs are demanded when the price is $15. When the price falls to $10, however, 10 CDs are demanded. This movement from point **a** to point **b** shows a **change in quantity demanded**—a movement along the demand curve that shows a change in the quantity of the product purchased in response to a change in price.

We already know that the principle of diminishing marginal utility provides an intuitive explanation of why the demand curve is downward sloping. As we will see below, the income and substitution effects can also add to our understanding of demand.

CHAPTER 4: DEMAND **95**

① FOCUS

Section Overview
This section distinguishes between a change in quantity demanded and a change in demand.

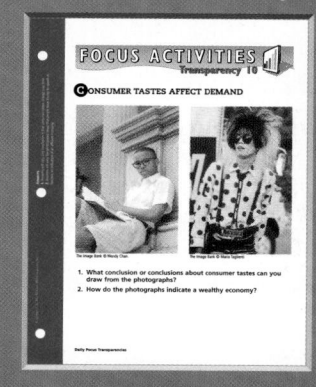
Study Guide

Reading Strategy
Have students create the graphic organizer.
Answers to Graphic: *Answers should reflect real-life economic changes.*

Preteaching Vocabulary
Ask students to suggest how a change in demand and in the quantity demanded might differ.

RESOURCE MANAGER

📂 Reproducible Masters
- Reproducible Lesson Plan 4-2
- Daily Lecture Notes 4-2
- Guided Reading Activity 4-2
- Reading Essentials and Study Guide 4-2
- Section Quiz 4-2

🎙 Transparencies
- Daily Focus Transparency 10

Multimedia
- 🔘 Interactive Economics!
- 💾 Interactive Tutor Self-Assessment Software
- 🔘 ExamView® Pro Testmaker
- 🔘 Presentation Plus!

② TEACH

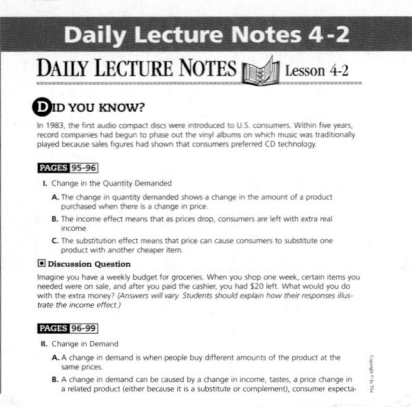

Daily Lecture Notes 4-2

DAILY LECTURE NOTES 📖 Lesson 4-2

DID YOU KNOW?
In 1983, the first audio compact discs were introduced to U.S. consumers. Within five years, record companies had begun to phase out the vinyl albums on which music was traditionally played because sales figures had shown that consumers preferred CD technology.

PAGES 95-96

I. Change in the Quantity Demanded

A. The change in the quantity demanded shows a change in the amount of a product purchased when there is a change in price.

B. The income effect means that as prices drop, consumers are left with extra real income.

C. The substitution effect means that price can cause consumers to substitute one product with another cheaper item.

☐ Discussion Question

Imagine you have a weekly budget for groceries. When you shop one week, certain items you needed were on sale, and after you paid the cashier, you had $20 left. What would you do with the extra money? (Answers will vary. Students should explain how their responses illustrate the income effect.)

PAGES 96-99

II. Change in Demand

A. A change in demand is when people buy different amounts of the product at the same prices.

B. A change in demand can be caused by a change in income, tastes, a price change in a related product (either because it is a substitute or complement), consumer expecta-

ECONOMICS
AT A GLANCE

Answer: *As a change in price alters consumers' real income and consumers tend to substitute, the quantity demanded moves in an opposite direction.*

L1 Demonstrating Concepts

Write: **(1)** Minimum wage raised to $6.00 per hour; **(2)** Prices of CD players fall; **(3)** Powerful advertisements make CDs much more appealing. **Ask:** What would happen to the demand for CDs? Why? *(Demand would increase in all situations. Reasons: 1. rise in income enables consumers to buy more at all prices; 2. CD players and CDs are complementary goods; 3. consumer tastes change, stimulated by advertising.)* **ELL**

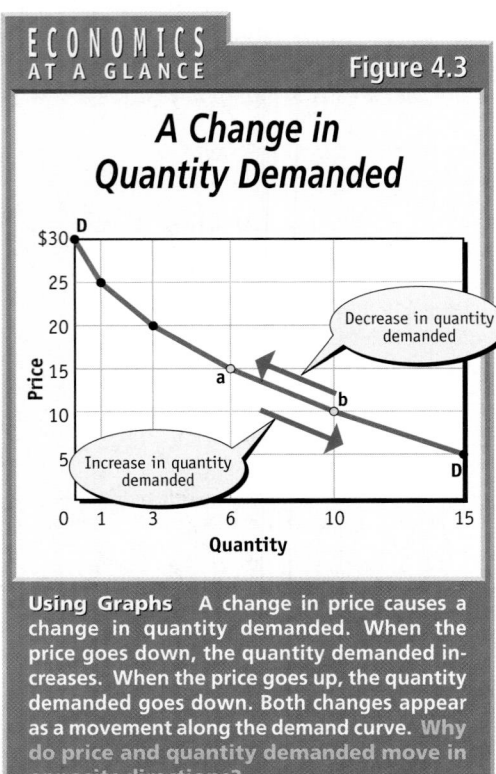

ECONOMICS
AT A GLANCE   Figure 4.3

A Change in Quantity Demanded

Using Graphs A change in price causes a change in quantity demanded. When the price goes down, the quantity demanded increases. When the price goes up, the quantity demanded goes down. Both changes appear as a movement along the demand curve. Why do price and quantity demanded move in opposite directions?

The Income Effect

When prices drop, consumers pay less for the product and, as a result, have some extra real income to spend. At a price of $15 per CD, Larry and Curly spent $90 to buy six CDs. If the price drops to $10, they would spend only $60 on the same quantity—leaving them $30 "richer" because of the drop in price. They may even spend some of their savings on more CDs. As a result, part of the increase from 6 to 10 units purchased is due to consumers feeling richer.

Of course, the opposite would have happened if the price had gone up. Larry and Curly would have felt a bit poorer and would have bought fewer. This illustrates the **income effect**, the change in quantity demanded because of a change in price that alters consumers' real income.

The Substitution Effect

A lower price also means that CDs will be relatively less expensive than other goods and services such as concerts and movies. As a result, consumers will have a tendency to replace a more costly item—say, going to a concert—with a less costly one—CDs. The **substitution effect** is the change in quantity demanded because of the change in the *relative* price of the product. Together, the income and substitution effects explain why consumers increase consumption of CDs from 6 to 10 when the price drops from $15 to $10.

Note that whenever a change in price causes a change in quantity demanded, the change appears graphically as a movement *along* the demand curve. The change in quantity demanded, as illustrated in **Figure 4.3,** can be either an increase or a decrease—but in either case the demand curve itself does not shift.

Change in Demand

Sometimes something happens to cause the demand curve itself to shift. This is known as a **change in demand** because people are now willing to buy *different* amounts of the product at the same prices. As a result, the entire demand curve shifts—to the right to show an increase in demand or to the left to show a decrease in demand for the product. Therefore, a change in demand results in an entirely new curve.

A change in demand is illustrated in the schedule and graph in **Figure 4.4.** Note that there is a new column in the demand schedule showing that people are willing to buy more at each and every price. At a price of $15, for example, consumers are now willing to buy 10 CDs instead of 6, moving from point **a** to point **a'**. At $10, they are willing to buy 15 CDs instead of 10, and so on. When this information is transferred to the graph, the demand curve appears to have shifted to the right to show an increase in demand.

The demand curve can change for several reasons. When this happens, a new schedule or curve must be constructed to reflect the new demand at all possible prices. Demand can change because of changes in income, tastes, the price of related goods, expectations, and the number of consumers.

MEETING SPECIAL NEEDS ACTIVITY

English Language Learners Students less familiar with English often have difficulty seeing differences between similar words. Common objectives used throughout this text require students to identify, discuss, and explain. Point out that *identifying* usually involves listing by category, *discussing* requires giving pros and cons, and *explaining* requires giving reasons in a complete form. Provide opportunities for identification, discussion, and explanation in the context of normal lesson-time conversations. **ELL**

📂 Refer to *Inclusion for the Social Studies Classroom Strategies and Activities* in the TCR.

Economics *Online*

Student Web Activity Visit the *Economics: Principles and Practices* Web site at epp.glencoe.com and click on *Chapter 4—Student Web Activities* for an activity on change in demand.

Consumer Income

Changes in consumer income can cause a change in demand. When your income goes up, you can afford to buy more goods and services. As incomes rise, consumers are able to buy more products at each and every price. When this happens, the demand curve shifts to the right. Suppose, for example, that Larry and Curly get a raise, which allows them to buy more CDs. Instead of Larry and Curly each buying 3 for a total of 6, they can now each buy 5—for a total of 10. If we find out how many CDs would be purchased at every possible price in the market, and if we plot the information as a demand curve as in **Figure 4.4,** then it appears as if the curve has shifted to the right.

Exactly the opposite could happen if there was a decrease in income. If Larry and Curly's raise turned out to be temporary, then the loss in income would cause them to buy less of the good at each and every price. The demand curve then shifts to the left, showing a decrease in demand.

Consumer Tastes

Consumers do not always want the same things. Advertising, news reports, fashion trends, the introduction of new products, and even changes in the season can affect consumer tastes. For example, when a product is successfully advertised in the media or on the Internet, its popularity increases and people tend to buy more of it. If consumers want more of an item, they would buy more of it at each and every price. As a result, the demand curve shifts to the right.

On the other hand, if people get tired of a product, they will buy less at each and every price, causing the demand curve to shift to the left. This is exactly what happened to the demand for baseball products described in the cover story. When fewer people play baseball, the demand for related products declines, with fewer items demanded at each and every price.

In addition, the development of new products can have an effect on consumer tastes. Years ago, many students carried slide rules to school to work out math and science problems. Now they use pocket calculators instead of slide rules. The demand for calculators has increased while the demand for slide rules has decreased.

Sometimes tastes and preferences change by themselves over time. In recent years, consumer concerns about health have greatly increased the demand for healthier, less-fattening foods. Demand for smaller, more fuel-efficient cars has grown, driven by a change in tastes.

Careers

Statistician

Who will win the next election? How many consumers will buy a certain new product? People who try to answer such questions are statisticians.

The Work

Statisticians work for the government and in industry gathering and interpreting data about the economy, health trends, and so on. They also work for industries and public opinion research organizations. One way statisticians gather information is by taking samples. They cannot question all the adults in this country about their activities, but they can get a fairly accurate picture by asking a sample of a few hundred people.

Qualifications

To become a statistician, you should have an aptitude for and an interest in mathematics and computers. Although some jobs are available for people with a bachelor's degree, many jobs require a graduate degree in mathematics or statistics. If you think you want a career in statistics, you should take business, math, and science courses.

CHAPTER 4: DEMAND **97**

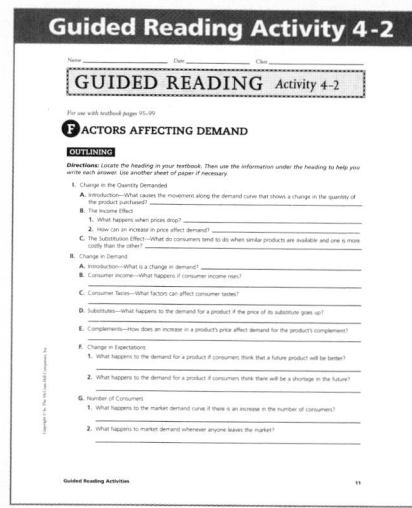

Guided Reading Activity 4-2

GUIDED READING Activity 4-2

For use with textbook pages 95–99

FACTORS AFFECTING DEMAND

OUTLINING

Directions: Locate the heading in your textbook. Then use the information under the heading to help you write each answer. Use another sheet of paper if necessary.

I. Change in the Quantity Demanded
   A. Introduction—What causes the movement along the demand curve that shows a change in the quantity of the product purchased?
   B. The Income Effect
      1. What happens when prices drop?
      2. How can an increase in price affect demand?
   C. The Substitution Effect—What do consumers tend to do when similar products are available and one is more costly than the other?
II. Change in Demand
   A. Introduction—What is a change in demand?
   B. Consumer Income—What happens if consumer income rises?
   C. Consumer Tastes—What factors can affect consumer tastes?
   D. Substitutes—What happens to the demand for a product if the price of its substitute goes up?
   E. Complements—How does an increase in a product's price affect demand for the product's complement?
   F. Change in Expectations
      1. What happens to the demand for a product if consumers think that a future product will be better?
      2. What happens to the demand for a product if consumers think there will be a shortage in the future?
   G. Number of Consumers
      1. What happens to the market demand curve if there is an increase in the number of consumers?
      2. What happens to market demand whenever anyone leaves the market?

Guided Reading Activities   11

ECONOMICS *Online*

Objectives, goals, and answers to the student activity can be found in the **Web Activity Lesson Plan** feature at epp.glencoe.com

INTERACTIVE ECONOMICS!

  CD-ROM

DEMAND Have students review "A Change in Demand" and "A Change in the Quantity Demanded" in **Lesson 3.** Then have them draw two graphs—one showing a change in quantity demanded, the other showing a change in demand.

💾 Also supplied in disk format.

FREE ENTERPRISE ACTIVITY

To increase students' understanding of the effects of a change in quantity demanded and a change in demand in a free enterprise economy, present the following scenario: A disease destroys much of the coffee crop in South America. **Ask:** How might this affect the price of coffee? The demand for substitute products? The demand for complementary products? *(price increases; demand for substitute drinks, such as soft drinks and juices, might increase; demand for complementary products, such as sugar, might fall)* Have students present these changes in the form of graphs.

THE GLOBAL ECONOMY

Demand Finland is becoming the leader of cell-phone technology. Some 58 percent of all Finns own a cell phone; by the year 2004, the devices will outnumber Finland's population of five million people.

③ ASSESS

Assign Section 2 Assessment as homework or as an in-class activity.

💾 Have students use **Interactive Tutor Self-Assessment Software** to review Section 2.

ECONOMICS AT A GLANCE

Figure 4.4

A Change in Demand

Quantity Demanded

Price	Old (DD)	New (D'D')
$30	0	1
25	1	3
20	3	6
15	6	10
10	10	15
5	15	20

Using Graphs A change in demand means that a different quantity is demanded at each and every possible price in the market. An increase in demand appears as a shift of the demand curve to the right. A decrease appears as a shift to the left. *What might cause a change in demand for CDs?*

Substitutes

A change in the price of related products can cause a change in demand. Some products are known as **substitutes** because they can be used in place of other products. For example, butter and margarine are substitutes. A rise in the price of butter causes an increase in the demand for margarine. Likewise, a rise in the price of margarine would cause the demand for butter to increase. In general, the demand for a product tends to increase if the price of its substitute goes up. The demand for a product tends to decrease if the price of its substitute goes down.

Complements

Other related goods are known as **complements,** because the use of one increases the use of the other. Personal computers and software are two complementary goods. When the price of computers decreases, consumers buy more computers *and* more software. In the same way, if the price of computers spirals upward, consumers would buy

fewer computers and less software. Thus, an increase in the price of one good usually leads to a decrease in the demand for its complement.

Companies have made use of this relationship for a number of years. For example, the Gillette Corporation makes razor handles and razor blades. To generate a high demand for their products, the price of razor handles is kept low. The profit earned on each razor handle is small, but the razor blades are sold at very profitable prices. As a result, the company is able to use the profits on the blades to more than offset the losses on the handles. Given the complementary nature of the two products, it is unlikely that demand for Gillette blades would have been as high if the handles had been more expensive.

Change in Expectations

"Expectations" refers to the way people think about the future. For example, suppose that a leading maker of audio products announces a technological

CRITICAL THINKING

Making Generalizations Ask students to name a number of popular, "trendy" items from recent years. Attempt to list a wide range of products, from food items to popular clothing to laptop computers and minivans. Have students try to determine which of the factors related to a change in demand apply to each of the items listed. If students are unsure which of the factors apply, have volunteers research the answer and report back to the class.

breakthrough that would allow more music to be recorded on a smaller disk at a lower cost than before. Even if the new product might not be available for another year, some consumers might decide to buy fewer musical CDs today simply because they want to wait for a better product. Purchasing less at each and every price would cause demand to decline, which is illustrated by a shift of the demand curve to the left.

Of course, expectations can also have a very different effect on market demand. For example, if the weather service forecasts a bad year for crops, people might stock up on some foods before they actually become scarce. The willingness to buy more at each and every price because of expected future shortages would cause demand to increase, which is demonstrated by a shift of the demand curve to the right.

Number of Consumers

A change in income, tastes, and prices of related products affects *individual* demand schedules and curves—and hence the *market* demand curve, which is the sum of all individual demand curves. It follows, therefore, that an increase in the number of consumers can cause the market demand curve to shift.

To illustrate, suppose Moe, one of Larry's and Curly's old friends, now decides to purchase compact discs. If we add the number of CDs that Moe would demand at each and every possible price to the others shown in **Figure 4.2**, the market demand curve **DD** would shift to the right. This would not affect the other individual demand curves, of course, but, as we shall see later in Chapter 6, it will affect the prices that everyone will pay for CDs. If Larry or Moe should leave the market the total number of CDs purchased at each and every price would decrease. This shifts the market demand curve to the left. The result is a decline in market demand whenever anyone leaves the market.

Reteach

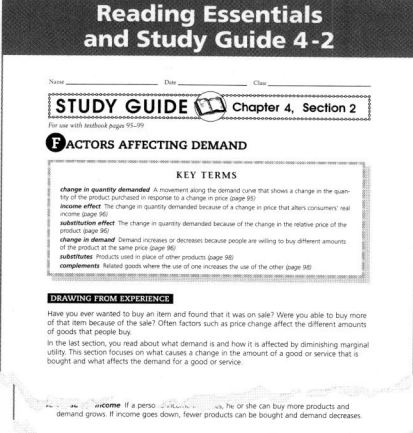

Reading Essentials and Study Guide 4-2

Name _____ Date _____ Class _____

STUDY GUIDE 📖 Chapter 4, Section 2

For use with textbook pages 95–99

❻ FACTORS AFFECTING DEMAND

KEY TERMS

change in quantity demanded A movement along the demand curve that shows a change in the quantity of the product purchased in response to a change in price (page 95)
income effect The change in quantity demanded because of a change in price that alters consumers' real income (page 96)
substitution effect The change in quantity demanded because of the change in the relative price of the product (page 96)
change in demand Demand increases or decreases because people are willing to buy different amounts of the product at the same price (page 96)
substitutes Products used in place of other products (page 98)
complements Related goods where the use of one increases the use of the other (page 98)

DRAWING FROM EXPERIENCE

Have you ever wanted to buy an item and found that it was on sale? Were you able to buy more of that item because of the sale? Often factors such as price change affect the different amounts of goods that people buy.
In the last section, you read about what demand is and how it is affected by diminishing marginal utility. This section focuses on what causes a change in the amount of a good or service that is bought and what affects the demand for a good or service.

... the **income** If a person ... ..., he or she can buy more products and demand grows. If income goes down, fewer products can be bought and demand decreases.

Enrich

Have students develop a marketing strategy, excluding lowering prices, to increase demand for a particular product.

 CLOSE

Have students write a paragraph explaining all of the determinants that can lead to a change in individual demand.

CHAPTER 4: DEMAND **99**

BusinessWeek

TEACH

As students read the article, have them think about the concepts that it addresses. Discuss how the lack of a product in high demand forces suppliers to find alternatives. Relate this conversation to the discussion on substitutes in this chapter.

☞ Refer to *Business Week Focus on the New Economy* in the TCR for additional unit-based articles.

CURRICULUM CONNECTION

History In 1998, a severe financial crisis hit Indonesia. Government mishandling of the economy sparked strikes and riots. These protests forced Suharto, Indonesia's long-standing president, to resign. A new government promised reform and fair elections.

DECEMBER 14, 1998

Newsclip

McDonald's opened its first restaurant in Des Plaines, Illinois, in 1955. In 1967 McDonald's opened its first restaurants in cities in other countries. Today, the company operates nearly 25,000 McDonald's restaurants in 115 countries on six continents. Multinational companies, like McDonald's, are huge companies that carry out their activities on a global scale, selling their products worldwide. Read to find out how McDonald's must adapt its menu to local tastes.

Holding the Fries "At the Border"

Your stomach starts growling and you want a quick fix, so you head to the nearest Gold Arches for a Big Mac and . . . rice?

Rice is what you'll probably end up with these days if your local McDonald's is in Indonesia. With the collapse of the Indonesian currency, the rupiah, in 1998, potatoes, the only ingredient McDonald's imports to the island nation, have quintupled in price. That means rice is turning with an increasing frequency as an alternative to the french fry. In September 1998 McDonald's introduced a rice and eggs dish, and its value meals now consist of just chicken and a drink—but no potatoes. It's not hard to fathom why fries are an

endangered menu item says Jack Greenberg, CEO of McDonald's: "No one can afford them."

The company has long tailored menus at its 24,000 worldwide restaurants to local tastes, though not out of economic distress. In other Asian markets weakened currencies have made it cheaper to build new outlets: 2,000 are anticipated [by the year 2002]. But Indonesia's situation is so disastrous, says Greenberg, that McDonald's will close 30 of its 100 stores there.

Examining the Newsclip

1. **Understanding Cause and Effect** Why did McDonald's change its menu in Indonesia?
2. **Synthesizing Information** Did McDonald's introduce rice to its Indonesian menu in response to a change in consumer tastes? Explain your reasoning.
3. **Making Predictions** What will happen if the change in the menu increases demand? Explain your answer.

麦当劳

Answers to Examining the Newsclip

1. The collapse of the rupiah made the cost of imports such as potatoes quintuple in price. Since people could not afford to pay for potatoes, McDonald's was forced to find a substitute product, rice, which could be used instead.

2. Answers will vary, but should reflect knowledge of consumer tastes and substitutes.

3. More rice will be produced, stimulating the Indonesian economy; prices may increase.

Elasticity of Demand

Study Guide

Main Idea
Consumers react differently to price changes depending on whether the good is a necessity or a luxury.

Reading Strategy
Graphic Organizer As you read about price elasticity, complete a web like the one below to illustrate what effect a change in price has on products that are elastic, inelastic, or unit elastic.

Change in price

Effects

Key Terms
elasticity, demand elasticity, elastic, inelastic, unit elastic

Objectives
After studying this section, you will be able to:
1. **Explain** why elasticity is a measure of responsiveness.
2. **Analyze** the elasticity of demand for a product.
3. **Understand** the factors that determine demand elasticity.

Applying Economic Concepts
Elasticity of Demand What are you willing to pay to see a popular movie? Read to find out about the *elasticity of demand* for a product and what factors influence your willingness and ability to pay for a product.

1 FOCUS

Section Overview
This section analyzes demand elasticity.

BELLRINGER
Motivational Activity

 Project **transparency** and have students answer questions.

 Available as blackline master.

Daily Focus Transparency 12

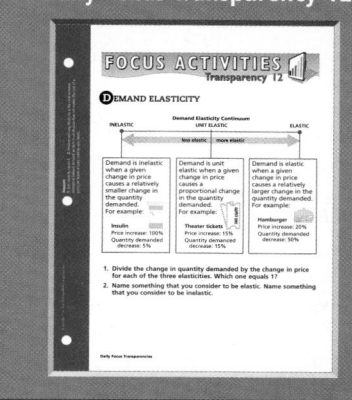

Cover Story

Setting Prices

It is always a difficult problem knowing how best to price a product. . . . When the product is one in a new and rapidly evolving industry,

Demand helps determine price.

like the microcomputer industry in the 1980s, the decision is doubly difficult. Was it best to charge a high price and sell a smaller number of disks or charge a lower price and aim for volume? One software producer decided to [test] the market for its new accounting program at different prices. The firm, Noumenon Corporation, raised prices in increments of $20 all the way up to $210. They found that total revenue was maximized at a price of $90. As a result of this experiment, they decided to advertise and market the Intuit Accounting program at $89.95, much lower than the prices of competing software programs.

—Adapted from *The Study of Economics,* by Turley Mings, Dushkin Publishing

ause-and-effect relationships are important in the study of economics. For example, we often ask, "if one thing happens, how will it affect something else?" The software manufacturer in the cover story used a cause-and-effect relationship to set the price for its product.

An important cause-and-effect relationship in economics is **elasticity,** a measure of responsiveness that tells us how a dependent variable such as quantity responds to a change in an independent variable such as price. Elasticity is also a very general concept. It can be applied to income, the quantity of a product supplied by a firm, or to demand.

Demand Elasticity

 In the case of demand, you will consider whether a given change in price will cause a relatively *larger,* a relatively *smaller,* or a *proportional* change in quantity demanded. Consumers are sensitive to prices and that is why the Noumenon Corporation conducted so many experiments to find the best price for its accounting software. An understanding of **demand elasticity**—the extent to which a change in price causes a change in the

CHAPTER 4: DEMAND **101**

Study Guide

Reading Strategy
Have students create the graphic organizer.
Answers to Graphic: *greater change in demand; lesser change in demand; a proportional change in demand*

Preteaching Vocabulary
Use the Vocabulary PuzzleMaker.

RESOURCE MANAGER

Reproducible Masters
- Reproducible Lesson Plan 4-3
- Daily Lecture Notes 4-3
- Guided Reading Activity 4-3
- Reading Essentials and Study Guide 4-3
- Section Quiz 4-3

Transparencies
- Daily Focus Transparency 12

Multimedia
- Vocabulary PuzzleMaker CD-ROM
- NBR Economics & You Video Program
- Interactive Tutor Self-Assessment Software
- ExamView® Pro Testmaker
- Presentation Plus!

② TEACH

Daily Lecture Notes 4-3

DAILY LECTURE NOTES 📖 Lesson 4-3

ⒹID YOU KNOW?
The drugs needed to get or stay well can take a large portion of a consumer's income, especially if that income is fixed. However, the use of generic drugs has offered consumers a cheaper alternative to drugs with brand names. After the founding drug company's patent on a brand-name drug has expired, another drug company can create a generic drug.

PAGES 101–103
I. Demand Elasticity
  A. Elasticity measures how sensitive consumers are to price changes.
  B. Demand is elastic when a change in price causes a large change in demand.
  C. Demand is inelastic when a change in price causes a small change in demand.
  D. Demand is unit elastic when a change in price causes a proportional change in demand.

▣ Discussion Question
What are examples of items for which an increase in price would cause you or your family to reconsider buying them? (Answers will vary but should illustrate an understanding of elastic demand.)

PAGES 103–105
II. The Total Expenditures Test
  A. Price times quantity demanded equals total expenditures.
  B. Changes in expenditures depend on the elasticity of a demand curve—if the change in price and expenditures move in opposite directions on the curve, the demand is elastic; if they move in the same direction, the demand is inelastic; if there is no change in expenditures, demand is unit elastic.

THE GLOBAL ECONOMY

Trading Gold for Salt Just as gold and salt were necessary trading commodities in some parts of Africa, so are oil and iron ore in some regions of the world today. The Japanese, for example, produce automobiles. They must trade with other countries, however, to obtain the raw materials needed to produce those automobiles.

Answers:
1. *The Akan traded gold for salt with the people of North Africa.*
2. *Answers should point out that the Akan could use the salt to trade for other commodities.*

Guided Reading Activity 4-3

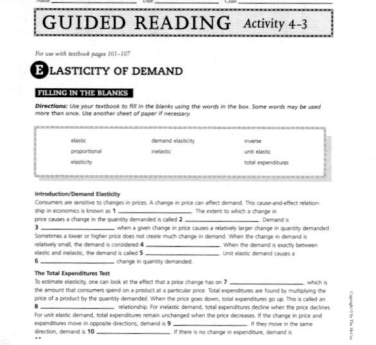

GUIDED READING Activity 4-3

Name____ Date____ Class____

For use with textbook pages 101–107

Ⓔ ELASTICITY OF DEMAND

FILLING IN THE BLANKS

Directions: Use your textbook to fill in the blanks using the words in the box. Some words may be used more than once. Use another sheet of paper if necessary.

elastic	demand elasticity	inverse
proportional	inelastic	unit elastic
elasticity		total expenditures

Introduction/Demand Elasticity
Consumers are sensitive to changes in prices. A change in price can affect demand. This cause-and-effect relationship in economics is known as **1** ____. The extent to which a change in price is proportional to the change in the quantity demanded is called **2** ____. Demand is **3** ____ when a given change in price causes a relatively larger change in quantity demanded. Sometimes a lower or higher price does not create much change in demand. When the change in demand is relatively small, the demand is considered **4** ____. When the change in demand is exactly between elastic and inelastic, the demand is called **5** ____. Unit elastic demand causes a **6** ____ change in quantity demanded.

The Total Expenditures Test
To estimate elasticity, one can look at the effect that a price change has on **7** ____, which is the amount that consumers spend on a product at a particular price. Total expenditures are found by multiplying the price of a product by the quantity demanded. When the price goes down, total expenditures go up. This is called an **8** ____ relationship. For inelastic demand, total expenditures decline when the price declines. For unit elastic demand, total expenditures remain unchanged when the price decreases. If the change in price and expenditures move in opposite directions, demand is **9** ____. If they move in the same direction, demand is **10** ____. If there is no change in expenditure, demand is ____.

THE GLOBAL ECONOMY

TRADING GOLD FOR SALT

What determines how much demand there will be for a good or service? The scarcity of the good or service plays an important role.

If you could choose between a pile of salt and a pile of gold, you would probably choose the gold. After all, you know that you can always buy a container of salt for about forty-five cents at the local supermarket. But what if you could not easily get salt?

Throughout history, salt has been very difficult to obtain in many parts of the world. Salt was used in food as a preservative and for flavor. People feared a lack of salt as we fear a shortage of fuel oil today.

Long ago, the Akan people of West Africa could not mine salt and always needed to trade for it. Gold, however, was much easier to come by. The people who lived in the desert of North Africa could easily mine salt, but not gold. These mutual differences led to the establishment of long-distance trade routes that connected very different cultures. Trade centers, such as Djenne and Timbuktu on the Niger River, flourished, as a demand for goods was satisfied.

—Adapted from *Smithsonian In Your Classroom*

Critical Thinking

1. **Analyzing Information** How did the Akan people meet their demand for salt?

2. **Drawing Conclusions** Suppose the Akan found a method to produce all the salt they needed. What changes in trade do you think might occur? Explain your reasoning.

---

quantity demanded—will help analyze these issues. The demand for most products is such that consumers do care about changes in prices—and the concept of elasticity tells us just how sensitive consumers are to these changes.

Elastic Demand

Economists say that demand is **elastic** when a given change in price causes a relatively larger change in quantity demanded. To illustrate, look at how price and quantity demanded change between points **a** and **b** on the demand curve in **Panel A** of **Figure 4.5.**

As we move from point **a** to point **b,** we see that price declines by one-third, or from $3 to $2. At the same time, the quantity demanded doubles from two to four units. Because the percentage change in quantity demanded was relatively larger than the percentage change in price, demand between those two points is elastic.

This type of elasticity is typical of the demand for products like green beans, corn, tomatoes, or other fresh garden vegetables. Because prices are lower in the summer, consumers increase the

amount they purchase. When prices are considerably higher in the winter, however, consumers normally buy fewer fresh vegetables and use canned products instead.

Inelastic Demand

For other products, demand may be largely **inelastic,** which means that a given change in price causes a relatively smaller change in the quantity demanded. We can see the case of inelastic demand in **Panel B** of **Figure 4.5.** In this case, the one-third drop in price from point **a'** to **b'** only causes quantity demanded to increase by 25 percent, or from two to two and one-half units.

This is typical of the demand elasticity for a product like table salt. A lower or higher price for table salt does not bring about much change in the quantity purchased. If the price was cut in half, the quantity demanded would not increase by much because people can consume only so much salt. Or, if the price doubled, we would expect consumers to demand about the same amount because the portion of a person's budget that is spent on salt is so small.

102 UNIT 2 MICROECONOMICS

MEETING SPECIAL NEEDS ACTIVITY

Learning Style: Visual/Spatial Draw the graphic organizer on the chalkboard and have students complete it to understand how price change affects quantity demanded. Students should list how the quantity demanded for elastic, unit elastic, and inelastic products changes as price changes.

Elastic Demand
(A change in price causes a relatively larger change in the quantity demanded.)

Demand Elasticity

Inelastic Demand
(A change in price causes a relatively smaller change in the quantity demanded.)

Unit Elastic Demand
(A change in price causes proportional change in the quantity demanded.)

 Refer to *Inclusion for the Social Studies Classroom Strategies and Activities* in the TCR.

Unit Elastic Demand

Sometimes demand for a product or service falls midway between elastic and inelastic. When this happens, demand is **unit elastic,** meaning that a given change in price causes a proportional change in quantity demanded. In other words, when demand is unit elastic, the percent change in quantity roughly equals the percent change in price. For example, a five percent drop in price would cause a five percent increase in quantity demanded. Unit elastic demand is illustrated in **Panel C of Figure 4.5.**

The Total Expenditures Test

To estimate elasticity, it is useful to look at the impact of a price change on total expenditures, or the amount that consumers spend on a product at a particular price. This is sometimes called the total expenditures test.

Determining Total Expenditures

Total expenditures are found by multiplying the price of a product by the quantity demanded for any point along the demand curve. To illustrate, the total

L1 Categorizing

Ask students to plan for a camping trip. In their preparation for the trip, they should list the goods that they'll need and the quantity of each good. Have students indicate if demand for the items is elastic, inelastic, or unit elastic. **ELL**

CYBERNOMICS

Textbooks Companies now sell college textbooks over the Internet. Universities enroll online and provide the required reading lists for their classes. Students can buy new and used textbooks from these lists, saving up to 40 percent. There is an economic incentive for colleges to use these Internet companies: the colleges receive a share in the revenue.

ECONOMICS AT A GLANCE

Answer: *The concept of elasticity helps businesses analyze the sensitivity of consumers to price changes.*

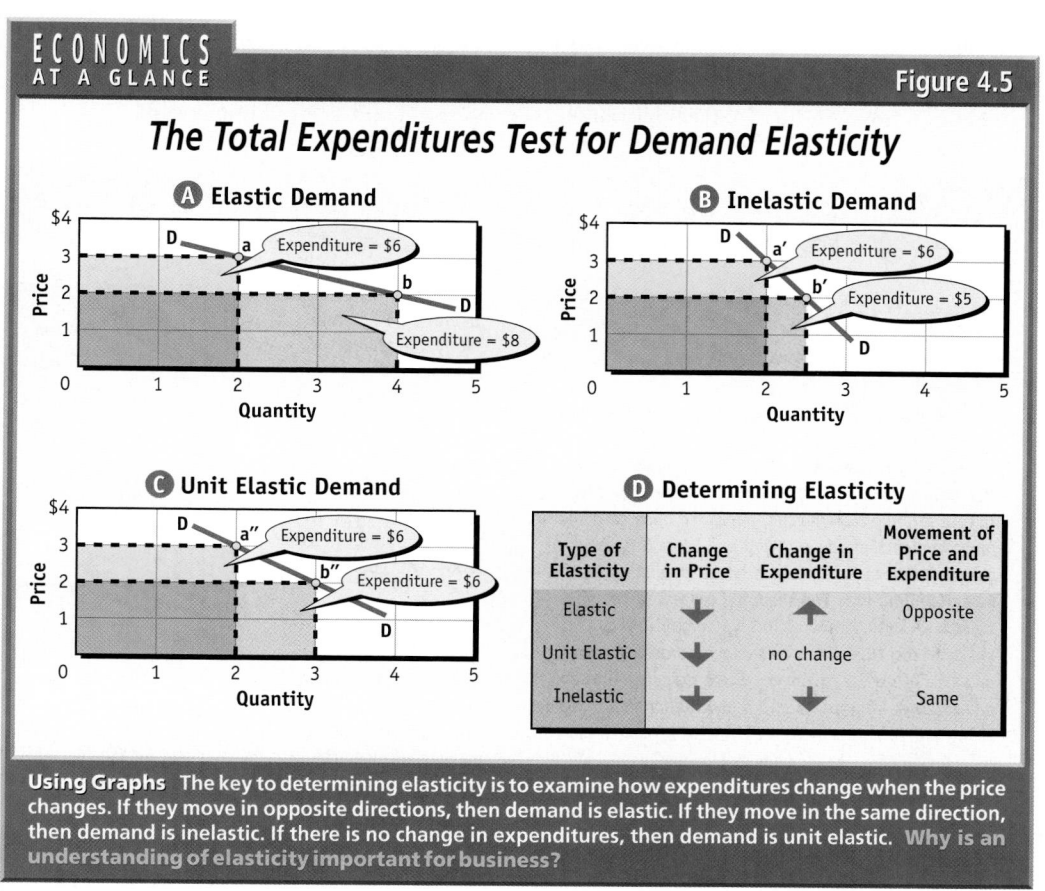

ECONOMICS AT A GLANCE

Figure 4.5

The Total Expenditures Test for Demand Elasticity

A Elastic Demand
- Expenditure = $6
- Expenditure = $8

B Inelastic Demand
- Expenditure = $6
- Expenditure = $5

C Unit Elastic Demand
- Expenditure = $6
- Expenditure = $6

D Determining Elasticity

Type of Elasticity	Change in Price	Change in Expenditure	Movement of Price and Expenditure
Elastic	↓	↑	Opposite
Unit Elastic	↓	no change	
Inelastic	↓	↓	Same

Using Graphs The key to determining elasticity is to examine how expenditures change when the price changes. If they move in opposite directions, then demand is elastic. If they move in the same direction, then demand is inelastic. If there is no change in expenditures, then demand is unit elastic. **Why is an understanding of elasticity important for business?**

CHAPTER 4: DEMAND **103**

FREE ENTERPRISE ACTIVITY

Present students with the following scenario: You own a restaurant that is fully booked during the weekends. In mid-week, however, you rarely have enough bookings to stay open. To make more money during this slow period, you decide to cut dinner prices by one-third—from $15 to $10—on Wednesdays and Thursdays. **Ask:** Do you think this action will increase your revenues? Suggest that students draw graphs similar to those in Figure 4.5 to illustrate their answers. Call on volunteers to present and discuss their graphs.

L2 Analyzing Demand

Review as a class the three types of demand elasticity discussed in the section. Then, on the board, list several consumer products that have not been used in the text as illustrations of demand elasticity. Organize the class into small groups and assign two or three consumer products to each group. Have groups apply what they have learned about demand elasticity to the assigned products to decide whether the demand for each product is elastic, inelastic, or unit elastic. Have group representatives explain their decisions. **ELL**

Math Practice

Elasticity Present students with the following problem: The managers of a rock band plan to give a concert in an auditorium that seats 800 people. They believe they can sell 600 tickets at $20 each or 800 tickets at $15 each. Have students use the total expenditures test to discover what kind of elasticity exists between the price and demand for the tickets. (*Unit elasticity, because total expenditures are the same at either price.*) Then tell students that the managers decide to charge $15. Have them suggest why the managers may have made this decision. (*The 800 people who are willing to attend for $15 may spend the $5 they saved on tickets on concert complements such as food, T-shirts, and other souvenirs.*)

---

expenditure under point **a** in **Panel A** of **Figure 4.5** is $6, which is determined by multiplying two units times the price of $3. Likewise, the total expenditure under point **b** in **Panel A** is $8, or $2 times four units. By observing the change in total expenditures when the price changes, we can test for elasticity.

Three Results

The relationship between changing prices and total expenditures is summarized in **Figure 4.5**. For each of the demand curves, the impact on total expenditures for a decrease in price from $3 to $2 is shown. In each case, the change in expenditures depends on the elasticity of the demand curve.

The demand curve in **Panel A** is elastic. When the price drops by $1 per unit, the increase in the quantity demanded is large enough to raise total expenditures from $6 to $8. The relationship between the change in price and total expenditures for the elastic demand curve is described as "inverse." In other words, when the price goes down, total expenditures go up.

The demand curve in **Panel B** is inelastic. In this case, when the price drops by $1, the increase in the quantity demanded is so small that total expenditures fall below $6. For inelastic demand, total expenditures decline when the price declines. Finally, the demand curve in **Panel C** is unit elastic. This time, total expenditures remain unchanged when the price decreases from $3 to $2.

The relationship between the change in price and the change in total expenditures is shown in **Panel D** of **Figure 4.5**. As you can see, if the change in price and expenditures move in opposite directions, demand is elastic. If they move in the same direction, demand is inelastic. If there is no change in expenditure, demand is unit elastic.

CYBERNOMICS SPOTLIGHT

Revolution in E-Commerce

Innovations in shopping are nothing new. The growth of the department store at the turn of the century answered the needs of the growing number of urban consumers. Meanwhile, generations of Americans, especially those in remote farming communities, depended upon catalog shopping through Montgomery Ward and Sears & Roebuck to get the latest in fashion, housewares, appliances, and even home-building kits. The shopping centers of the mid-twentieth century were replaced by gigantic shopping malls. In the 1990s, new technologies provided convenience and ease of use for customers. Home shopping—catalog, TV, and Internet—has grown into a multibillion dollar business. Today, entrepreneurs such as Jeff Bezos of Amazon.com Inc. are transforming our shopping habits.

Birth of an Internet Company Just as Sears and Montgomery Ward reached customers through their catalogs, today's entrepreneurs do the same online. Few, however, have been as successful as Jeff Bezos with

Amazon. In 1994, Bezos decided to stake a claim on the unknown frontier of Internet retail. He quit his job on Wall Street and moved to Seattle. He rented a garage and borrowed money to start a business where people could make their book purchases over the Internet. Amazon debuted on the World Wide Web in July 1995.

Jeff Bezos, founder of Amazon.com

Unique Appeal to Customers What are the reasons for Amazon's success? An important factor is that Amazon provides services that regular stores don't. People who search for a book at the Amazon site often find a description accompanied by excerpts from reviews—not only from print sources but from customers. Authors, too, are invited to comment on their own works. And Amazon asks customers which kinds of books they like. When books in the same category or by

CYBERNOMICS SPOTLIGHT

More About . . . Online Shopping E-commerce is finally becoming a popular method of shopping. Although there has been no significant change in the technology, sales over the Internet are increasing due to the confidence level of the user. In 1998, more than half of Web users had been online for over a year. More people are comfortable with navigating the Internet and using it for information. Other factors have led to increased usage of the Web for shopping. Safety features have improved, so there is diminishing fear of hackers stealing credit card numbers. Web sites are better, too, and are often interactive, colorful, and informative. Many people find that the Internet allows them to save money because it is convenient for quick price comparisons.

Finally, and even though all the price changes discussed above were decreases, the results would be the same if prices had gone up instead of down. If the price rises from $2 to $3 in **Panel A,** spending falls from $8 to $6. Prices and expenditures still move in opposite directions, as shown in the table.

Elasticity and Profits

All of this discussion about elasticity may seem technical and somewhat unnecessary, but knowledge of demand elasticity is extremely important to businesses. Suppose, for example, that you are in business and that you want to do something that will raise your profits. Of course you could try to cut costs, or you could even try to advertise in order to increase the number of units sold. You might, however, be tempted to raise the price of your product in order to increase total revenue from sales.

This might actually work in the case of table salt, or even medical services, because the demand for both products is generally inelastic. But, what if you sell a product that has an elastic demand? If you raise the price of your product, your total revenues—which is the same thing as consumer expenditures—will go *down* instead of up. This outcome is exactly the opposite of what you intend!

This is exactly why the Noumenon Corporation in the cover story experimented with so many different prices when they introduced their accounting software program. By discovering the elastic nature of demand for their new product, they were able to increase their total revenues by charging a relatively low price rather than a much higher one. This example illustrates that demand elasticity is more important than most people realize.

F.Y.I.

The demand for some products has become more elastic because of technological innovations. VCRs, for example, have allowed consumers to substitute home viewing of movies for going to a movie theater. As a result, demand for tickets to movie theaters has become more elastic.

L3 Determining Elasticity

Point out to students that, while the demand for some products may seem inelastic, over time demand may grow somewhat more elastic. For example, the major rise in gasoline prices in the 1970s did not at first adversely affect demand. Over time, however, as people purchased more fuel-efficient cars and used more public transportation, the demand for gasoline grew more elastic. Have students find other examples of such products.

the same author appear, the company sends E-mail inviting people to buy them.

Growth and Development Bezos has even bigger plans for the future. He wants Amazon to serve as the gateway for more products. Among its innovations, Amazon added auctions in March 1999. The company retooled its warehouses to offer more varied selection and faster service. Bezos believes Amazon is successful because it values its customers. "The Internet is this big, huge hurricane," Bezos notes. "The only constant in that storm is the customers." Today Amazon serves more than 29 million customers in 160 countries. Although buying books over the Internet accounts for 3 percent of books sold, Amazon claims 76 percent of online book sales. In June 1998, the company began selling music selections. Today, Amazon is one of the leading online music retailers, with sales of $33.1 million. As use of the Web grows, so too does the future of Amazon.

Amazon's Strategy

- Make it easy for visitors to find what they want.
- Encourage visitor participation.
- Win repeat customers.

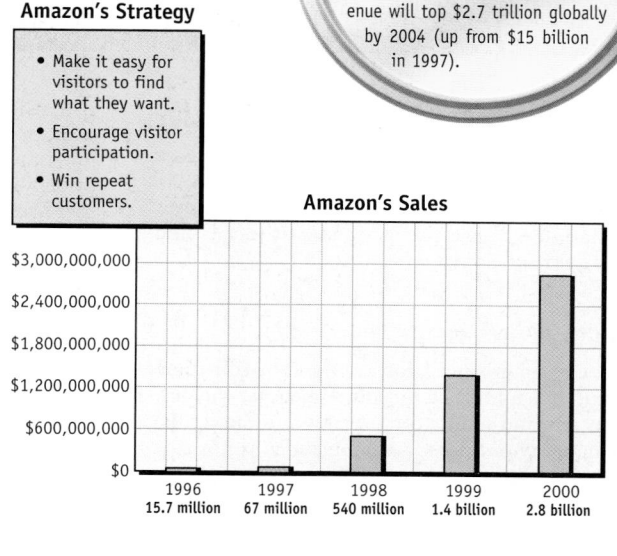

Amazon's Sales

$3,000,000,000				
$2,400,000,000				
$1,800,000,000				
$1,200,000,000				
$600,000,000				
$0				
1996	1997	1998	1999	2000
15.7 million	67 million	540 million	1.4 billion	2.8 billion

Did You Know?

Internet Shopping According to research analysts, two billion orders were placed over the Internet in 1999, generating $95 billion in revenue. Researchers estimate e-commerce revenue will top $2.7 trillion globally by 2004 (up from $15 billion in 1997).

CHAPTER 4: DEMAND **105**

ECONOMICS & YOU

 Chapter 5
Disc 1, Side 1

What is Demand?
After the segment: **Ask:** How does inelastic demand differ from elastic demand? *(When the demand for a product or service does not change in reaction to price changes, the demand is inelastic.)*

There are drawbacks to shopping on the Internet, however. If you know what you want to buy, electronic shopping is almost always faster than traditional shopping. If you don't know, it can become tedious waiting for images to download. If a site doesn't take credit cards, you must print out an order sheet and order the item offline. If the computer crashes, orders are lost, and you must shop for the same items again. For many people, though, the benefits of being able to shop in your pajamas at any time of the day outweigh the drawbacks of online shopping. Have students discuss if they believe online shopping will make traditional shopping obsolete.

Answer: *If the luxury product uses a large portion of income, demand would generally be elastic.*

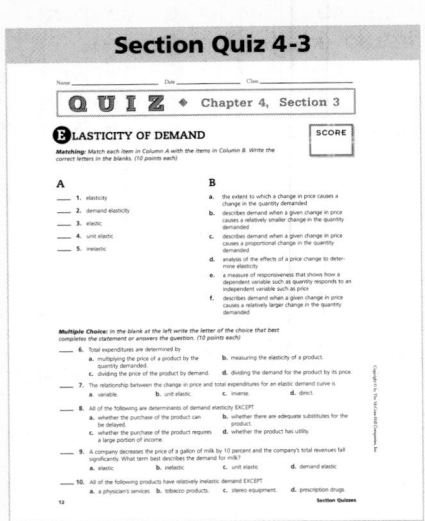

③ ASSESS

Assign Section 3 Assessment as homework or as an in-class activity.

💾 Have students use **Interactive Tutor Self-Assessment Software** to review Section 3.

Section Quiz 4-3

ECONOMICS AT A GLANCE

Figure 4.6

Estimating the Elasticity of Demand

Products

Determinants of elasticity Yes (elastic) No (inelastic)	Fresh tomatoes, corn, or green beans	Table salt	Gasoline from a particular station	Gasoline in general	Services of medical doctors	Insulin	Butter
Can purchase be delayed?	yes	no	yes	no	no	no	yes
Are adequate substitutes available?	yes	no	yes	no	no	no	yes
Does purchase use a large portion of income?	no	no	yes	yes	yes	no	no
Type of elasticity	Elastic	Inelastic	Elastic	Inelastic	Inelastic	Inelastic	Elastic

Using Tables The elasticity of demand can usually be estimated by examining the answers to three key questions. All three answers do not have to be the same in order to determine elasticity, and in some cases the answer to a single question is so important that it alone might dominate the answers to the other two. **If you applied the three questions to a luxury product, what would be the elasticity of demand for that product?**

Determinants of Demand Elasticity

 What makes the demand for a specific good elastic or inelastic? To find out, we can ask three questions about the product. The answers will give us a reasonably good idea as to the product's demand elasticity.

Can the Purchase Be Delayed?

A consumer's need for a product is sometimes urgent and cannot be put off. Whenever this happens, demand tends to be inelastic, meaning that the quantity of the product demanded is not especially sensitive to changes in price.

For example, persons with diabetes need insulin to control the disorder. An increase in its price is not likely to make diabetes sufferers delay buying and using the product. Likewise, the demand for tobacco

also tends to be inelastic because the product is addictive. As a result, a sharp increase in price will lower the quantity purchased by consumers, but not by very much. The change in quantity demanded is also likely to be relatively small for these products when their prices go down instead of up.

If the product were corn, tomatoes, or gasoline from a particular station, however, people might react differently to price changes. If the prices of these products increase, consumers could delay buying any of these items without suffering any great inconvenience. Being able to delay or postpone the purchase of a product, then, is a characteristic of elastic demand.

Figure 4.6 summarizes some of these observations. Note that if the answer is yes to the question "Can the purchase be delayed?" then the demand for the product is likely to be elastic. If the answer is no, then demand is likely to be inelastic.

106 UNIT 2 MICROECONOMICS

CRITICAL THINKING

Drawing Conclusions Have students research consumer demand for a high-tech product over a recent five-year period. Items may include laptop computers, digital cameras, fax machines, or cordless telephones. Ask students to graph annual sales volume against average price. Have them explain in the graph's caption the reason for the price-volume relationship. Ask volunteers to present their findings in a class discussion.

📦 **BLOCK SCHEDULING**

Are Adequate Substitutes Available?

If adequate substitutes are available, consumers can switch back and forth between a product and its substitute to take advantage of the best price. If the price of beef and butter goes up, buyers can switch to chicken and margarine. With enough substitutes, even small changes in the price of a product will cause people to switch, making the demand for the product elastic. The fewer substitutes available for a product, the more inelastic the demand.

Sometimes the consumer only needs to have a single adequate substitute in order to make the demand for the product elastic. Historically, for example, there were few adequate substitutes for a letter sent through the post office. As technology has progressed, fax machines allow messages to be transmitted over phone lines, and, perhaps most significantly, the personal computer has helped make electronic mail (E-mail) popular. As a result, it is extremely difficult for the U.S. Postal Service to increase its total revenues by significantly raising the price of a first-class letter.

Also, note that the availability of substitutes also depends on the extent of the market. For example, the demand for gasoline from a particular station tends to be elastic because the consumer can buy gas at another station. If we ask about the demand for gasoline in general, however, demand is much more inelastic because there are few adequate substitutes for gasoline.

Does the Purchase Use a Large Portion of Income?

The third determinant is the amount of income required to make the purchase. Whenever the answer to the question "Does the purchase use a large portion of income?" is yes, then demand tends to be elastic. Demand tends to be inelastic whenever the answer to this question is no.

Finally, you may have noticed that for any given product, the answer is not necessarily yes or no. For example, some products such as salt or insulin may be easy to classify, but we have to use our judgment on others. For example, the demand for medical services tends to be inelastic even though these services require a large portion of income. As far as most people are concerned, the lack of adequate substitutes and the reluctance to put off seeing a doctor when they are sick are more important than the relatively large portion of income that medical services consume.

Section 3 Assessment

Checking for Understanding

1. **Main Idea** What luxuries do you think would have a higher price elasticity than others? Give three examples and explain why you think they would have an exceptionally high elasticity.

2. **Key Terms** Define elasticity, demand elasticity, elastic, inelastic, unit elastic.

3. **Describe** the three determinants of demand elasticity.

4. **Explain** why the demand for insulin is inelastic.

5. **Explain** why an item that has many close substitutes tends to have an elastic demand.

Applying Economic Concepts

6. **Elasticity of Demand** Why are airlines reluctant to offer reduced round-trip airfares during holidays such as Christmas, Easter, and Thanksgiving? Refer to the three determinants of demand elasticity in your answer.

Critical Thinking

7. **Understanding Cause and Effect** A hamburger stand raised the price of its hamburgers from $2.00 to $2.50. As a result, its sales of hamburgers fell from 200 per day to 180 per day. Was the demand for its hamburgers elastic or inelastic? How can you tell?

 Practice and **assess** key social studies skills with the *Glencoe Skillbuilder Interactive Workbook, Level 2*.

Reteach

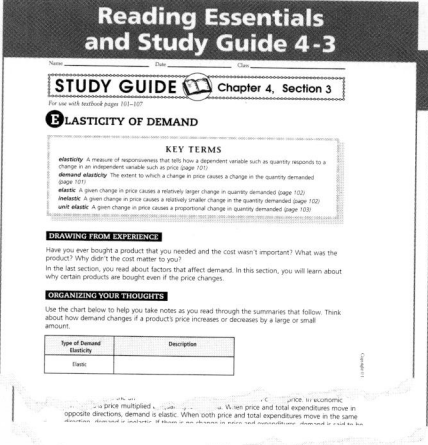

Reading Essentials and Study Guide 4-3

Enrich

Have students use library resources to locate a photograph that illustrates the concept of demand elasticity.

 CLOSE

On the board, draw graphs and write definitions and examples of the various types of elasticity. Call on students to identify the elasticity illustrated or described.

Section 3 Assessment Answers

1. Answers will vary but should reflect an understanding of price elasticity.

2. All vocabulary terms are defined in the text.

3. Can the purchase be delayed? Are adequate substitutes available? Does the purchase use a large portion of income?

4. lack of adequate substitutes for insulin

5. because consumers can switch among the various substitutes

6. Demand tends to be inelastic because the purchase of tickets cannot be delayed since holiday travel is time specific; there are few adequate substitutes for air travel; the ticket price would not represent a large portion of income for many people.

7. Students should argue that the demand is inelastic because a 25 percent increase in price resulted in a 10 percent decrease in units for sale.

Teaching Skills

Call on volunteers to summarize the guidelines for recognizing cause-and-effect relationships. Then read through Section 3 with students, asking them to identify any cause-and-effect relationships they notice.

Conclude by working through the practice examples, asking students to identify any cause-and-effect clue words for each example.

Additional Practice

Reinforcing Economic Skill 10

Reinforcing Economic Skills — Chapter 10

UNDERSTANDING CAUSE AND EFFECT

Understanding cause and effect involves considering why an event occurred. A cause is the action or situation that produces an event or outcome. What happens as a result of a cause is an effect.

Directions: *Read the following passage, look for logical relationships between events, and answer the questions that follow.*

Following the stock market crash of 1929, consumer spending fell dramatically in the United States. Products sat unsold on store shelves. Demand diminished and factories found themselves without orders. In response, manufacturers cut back production, and were forced to layoff many workers in the process. As more and more workers lost their jobs, consumer spending fell significantly. Economic conditions all over the country worsened as millions of men and women lost their jobs.

Decisive action was needed, but President Herbert Hoover's actions were insufficient so fix the situation. In 1932, an election year, voters decided they wanted to give another person a chance and elected Hoover's opponent, Franklin D. Roosevelt.

Roosevelt immediately took drastic action. He created the Civil Works Administration (CWA), which put four million Americans back to work in public works projects. During his administration, Congress also passed the Social Security Act and increased taxes on the rich.

List five effects mentioned in this excerpt. Then list the cause of each.

Cause	Effects
1.	
2.	
3.	
4.	
5.	

10 — Reinforcing Economic Skills

CRITICAL THINKING
Skill

Understanding Cause and Effect

Understanding cause and effect involves considering *why* an event occurred. A *cause* is the action or situation that produces an event. What happens as a result of a cause is an *effect*.

One of the key factors that determines demand is people's tastes.

Learning the Skill

To identify cause-and-effect relationships, follow these steps:

• Identify two or more events or developments.

• Decide whether one event caused the other. Look for clue words such as *because, led to, brought about, produced, as a result of, so that, since,* and *therefore.*

• Look for logical relationships between events, such as "She overslept, and then she missed her bus."

• Identify the outcomes of events. Remember that some effects have more than one cause, and some causes lead to more than one effect. Also, an effect can become the cause of yet another effect.

Practicing the Skill

Analyze the statements below. Then, on a separate piece of paper, list the causes and effects found in each statement.

1. Historically, prices have shown their greatest fluctuations in times of war.

2. The government also is confronted with scarcity, and must make choices.

3. Because of scarcity, people, businesses, and the government must all make trade-offs in choosing the products they want the most.

4. When a choice is made, an opportunity cost is paid.

5. It is impossible for us to produce all the products we would like to have because the factors of production exist in limited quantities.

6. Because consumers don't always want the same things, items that are popular now may not sell in the future.

7. If income increases, people can afford to buy more products.

8. If the price of butter goes up, more people would buy margarine instead.

Application Activity

In your local newspaper, read an article describing a current event. Determine at least one cause and one effect of that event. Show the cause-and-effect relationship in a diagram like the one here.

Cause → Effect

Practice and **assess** key social studies skills with the *Glencoe Skillbuilder Interactive Workbook, Level 2.*

Answers to Practicing the Skill

1. cause: war; effect: greater price fluctuation
2. cause: scarcity; effect: government must make choices
3. cause: scarcity; effect: trade-offs
4. cause: making a choice; effect: paying an opportunity cost
5. cause: limited factors of production; effect: impossible to produce all wanted products
6. cause: consumers' changing wants; effect: popular items may not sell in future
7. cause: income increase; effect: people can buy more products
8. cause: price of butter goes up; effect: demand for margarine goes up

Section 1

What Is Demand? (pages 89–93)

- **Microeconomics** is the area of economic study that deals with individual units in an economy, such as households, business firms, labor unions, and workers.

- You express **demand** for a product when you are both willing and able to purchase it.

- Demand can be summarized in a **demand schedule,** which shows the various quantities that would be purchased at all possible prices that might prevail in the market.

- Demand can also be shown graphically as a downward sloping **demand curve.**

- The **Law of Demand** refers to the inverse relationship between price and quantity demanded.

- Individual demand curves for a particular product can be added up to get the **market demand curve.**

- **Marginal utility** is the amount of satisfaction an individual receives from consuming one additional unit of a particular good or service.

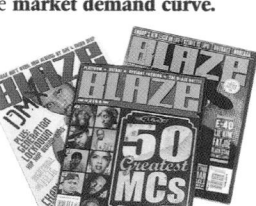

- **Diminishing marginal utility** means that with each succeeding unit, satisfaction decreases.

Section 2

Factors Affecting Demand (pages 95–99)

- Demand can change in two ways—a change in quantity demanded or a change in demand.

- A **change in quantity demanded** means people buy a different quantity of a product if that product's price changes, appearing as a movement *along* the demand curve.

- A **change in demand** means that people have changed their minds about the amount they would buy at each and every price. It is represented as a *shift* of the demand curve to the right or left.

- A change in consumer incomes, tastes and expectations, and the price of related goods causes a change in demand.

- Related goods include substitutes and complements. A **substitute** is a product that is interchangeable in use with another product. A **complement** is a product that is used in conjunction with another product.

- The market demand curve changes whenever consumers enter or leave the market, or whenever an individual's demand curve changes.

Section 3

Elasticity of Demand (pages 101–107)

- **Elasticity** is a general measure of responsiveness that relates changes of a dependent variable such as quantity to changes in an independent variable such as price.

- **Demand elasticity** relates changes in the quantity demanded to changes in price.

- If a change in price causes a relatively *larger* change in the quantity demanded, demand is **elastic.**

- If a change in price causes a relatively *smaller* change in the quantity demanded, demand is **inelastic.**

- When demand is elastic, it stretches as price changes. Inelastic demand means that price changes have little impact on quantity demanded.

- Demand is **unit elastic** if a change in price causes a *proportional* change in quantity demanded.

- The total expenditures test can be used to estimate demand elasticity.

- Demand elasticity is influenced by the ability to postpone a purchase, by the substitutes available, and by the proportion of income required for the purchase.

CHAPTER 4: DEMAND 109

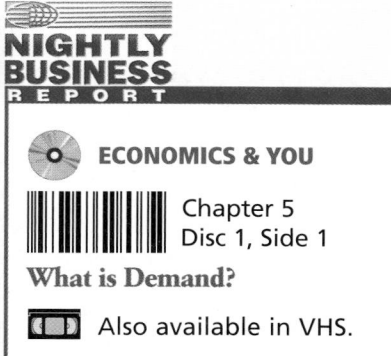

NIGHTLY BUSINESS REPORT

ECONOMICS & YOU

Chapter 5
Disc 1, Side 1

What is Demand?

Also available in VHS.

Using the Chapter 4 Summary

Use the Chapter 4 Summary to preview, review, condense, or reteach the chapter.

Preview/Review

Vocabulary PuzzleMaker CD-ROM reinforces Key Terms.

Interactive Tutor Self-Assessment Software provides a review of Chapter 4 content.

Condense

Have students listen to the Chapter 4 Audio Program. Spanish also available.

Assign the Chapter 4 Audio Program Activity and give students the Chapter 4 Audio Program Test.

Have students complete the Guided Reading Activities and Reading Essentials and Study Guides for Chapter 4.

Reteach

Have students complete Reteaching Activity 4 in the TCR. Spanish also available.

Teacher's Notes / Internet Bookmarks

GLENCOE
TECHNOLOGY

Use **MindJogger Videoquiz** to review the Chapter 4 content.

ECONOMICS *Online*

Have students visit the Web site at epp.glencoe.com to review Chapter 4 and take the **Self-Check Quiz.**

Identifying Key Terms

1. b	2. f	3. g	4. a
5. d	6. c	7. h	8. e

Reviewing the Facts

Section 1

1. A demand schedule is a list that shows the quantities demanded for a product at all prices that prevail in the market. A demand curve shows the same data in graphic form.

2. Diminishing marginal utility states that as we use more of a product, we are not willing to pay as much for it. People will not pay as much for the second and third product as they did for the first, therefore the demand is downward sloping.

Section 2

3. The income effect is the change in quantity demanded because of a change in price that alters consumers' real income. The substitution effect is the change in quantity demanded because of the change in the relative price of the product.

4. consumer income, consumer tastes, substitutes and complements, change in expectations, number of consumers

Section 3

5. When demand is elastic, there is a relatively large change in quantity

---

ECONOMICS
Online

Self-Check Quiz Visit the *Economics: Principles and Practices* Web site at epp.glencoe.com and click on *Chapter 4—Self-Check Quizzes* to prepare for the chapter test.

Identifying Key Terms

On a separate sheet of paper, match the letter of the term best described by each statement below.

a. demand schedule
b. demand
c. microeconomics
d. change in demand
e. demand curve
f. change in quantity demanded
g. Law of Demand
h. elastic demand

1. the desire, ability, and willingness to buy a product

2. a movement along the demand curve showing that a different quantity is purchased in response to a change in price

3. a statement that more will be demanded at lower prices and less at higher prices

4. a listing in a table that shows the quantity demanded at all possible prices in the market at a given time

5. a principle illustrating that consumers demand different amounts at every price, causing the demand curve to shift to the left or the right

6. the field of economics that deals with behavior and decision making by individuals and firms

7. a principle illustrating that a relatively small change in price causes a relatively large change in the quantity demanded

8. a graph that shows the quantity demanded at all possible prices in the market at a given time

---

Reviewing the Facts

Section 1 (pages 89–93)

1. **Describe** a demand schedule and a demand curve. How are they alike?

2. **Explain** how the principle of diminishing marginal utility is related to the downward-sloping demand curve.

Section 2 (pages 95–99)

3. **Describe** the difference between the income effect and the substitution effect.

4. **Identify** the five factors that can cause a change in market demand.

Section 3 (pages 101–107)

5. **Describe** the difference between elastic demand and inelastic demand.

6. **Explain** how the total expenditures test can be used to determine demand elasticity.

Thinking Critically

1. **Making Generalizations** Do you think the Law of Demand accurately reflects most people's behavior regarding certain purchases? Explain.

2. **Drawing Conclusions** What would normally happen to a product's market demand curve in a growing and prosperous community if consumer tastes, expectations, and the prices of related products remained unchanged? Create a web like the one below to explain your answer.

No change in consumer tastes → No change in price of related products → Effect on Product A

---

demanded when price changes, giving the demand curve a flat slope. The change in quantity demanded is much smaller for inelastic demand, making the slope of the demand curve steeper.

6. By observing the change in total expenditures when the price changes, you can determine demand elasticity. If expenditures and price move in opposite directions, demand is elastic. If they move in the same direction, demand is inelastic. If expenditures don't change, demand is unit elastic.

Thinking Critically

1. Answers will vary, but most students will note that when prices fall, consumers tend to demand more of a product.

2. An increase in the number of consumers would shift the market demand curve to the right. Students' webs should reflect an increase in quantity demanded for the product.

Applying Economic Concepts

1. **Demand** Why do you think a knowledge of demand would be useful to an individual like yourself? To a businessperson like Keith Clinkscales (cover story, page 89)?

2. **Demand** How do you think the market demand curve for pizza would be affected by **(1)** an increase in everyone's pay, **(2)** a successful pizza advertising campaign, **(3)** a decrease in the price of hamburgers, and **(4)** new people moving into the community? Explain your answers.

3. **Demand Elasticity** How would you, as a business owner, use your knowledge of demand elasticity to determine the price of your product?

Math Practice

Mindy is trying to estimate the elasticity of demand for a product she wants to sell at a craft fair. She has been told that she can expect to sell 10 items if she charges a price of $10, six items if she charges a price of $20, and 18 items at a price of $5.

1. Make a demand schedule to show the quantities demanded at each price.

2. Use the information in the demand schedule to create a demand curve and to graph the results.

3. At which price would the total expenditures by consumers be greatest for the product? At what price would expenditures be the smallest?

Thinking Like an Economist

Write a paragraph describing a business that you might like to own and the major product that the business would produce. Next, use the three determinants of demand elasticity to predict the elasticity of demand for that product. Describe the pricing policy you would use to get consumers to maximize their expenditures on that product.

Technology Skill

Using the Internet Use a search engine to find the Web site for the U.S. Department of Commerce. Select the option "Economics and Statistics Administration." Next select "STAT-USA." Then click on "State of the Nation." From the options on the screen, select "Manufacturing and Trade, Inventories and Sales." Locate the information on "Apparel and accessory stores," and answer the questions that follow.

1. How many months does the data cover?

2. Compare the monthly data on inventory. Is the inventory increasing, decreasing, or about the same? Then, compare the data on sales.

3. Are there any sharp fluctuations in inventory or sales from one month to the next? If so, what might have caused these changes?

4. Do you think demand for apparel increases or decreases according to the season or time of year? How do you think this change in demand relates to inventory and sales?

Building Skills

Understanding Cause and Effect Draw the two demand curves below on separate sheets of paper. Then, show how the rise in the cost of razor blade handles affects the demand curve for its complementary and its substitute products.

Demand for double-edged razor blades

Demand for electric razors

Sharp increase in the price of double-edged razor blade handles

Practice and *assess* key social studies skills with the Glencoe *Skillbuilder Interactive Workbook, Level 2*.

Applying Economic Concepts

1. Answers will vary but should note that a knowledge of demand will help an individual make more informed decisions as a consumer. Students should note that businesspeople need such knowledge in order to run their businesses effectively.

2. (1) Demand would increase since more people could afford to buy more pizza.
(2) Demand would increase as more people became aware of pizza. (3) Demand would decrease since people would buy more hamburgers. (4) Demand would increase as more consumers would buy pizza.

3. If demand is elastic, lower the price to increase total business revenues. If demand is inelastic, raise the price to increase business revenues.

Math Practice

1. Price Quantity Demanded
$20   6
$10   10
$ 5   18

2. Students' demand curves should accurately reflect the figures in the demand schedule.

3. $20; $5

Thinking Like an Economist

Answers will vary but should reflect an understanding of how to determine elasticity of demand and the use of the total expenditures test.

Technology Skill

Check students' answers for accuracy.

Building Skills

Students' graphs should reflect a decrease in demand for double-edged razor blades and an increase in demand for electric razors.

? Bonus Test Question

How would a successful advertising campaign affect the elasticity of demand for the advertised product? Explain. *(It would make demand more inelastic. Some people would be influenced by the advertising and would demand the advertised product rather than buy a substitute.)*

Chapter 5 Resource Manager

SECTION RESOURCES

Daily Objectives	Reproducible Resources	Technology/Multimedia Resources
Section 1 **What is Supply?** 1. Understand the difference between the supply schedule and the supply curve. 2. Explain how market supply curves are derived. 3. Specify the reasons for a change in supply.	Reproducible Lesson Plan 5-1 Daily Lecture Notes 5-1 Guided Reading Activity 5-1 Reading Essentials and Study Guide 5-1 Section Quiz 5-1*	Daily Focus Transparency 13 Interactive Economics! Interactive Tutor Self-Assessment Software ExamView® Pro Testmaker Presentation Plus!
Section 2 **The Theory of Production** 1. Explain the theory of production. 2. Describe the three stages of production.	Reproducible Lesson Plan 5-2 Daily Lecture Notes 5-2 Guided Reading Activity 5-2 Reading Essentials and Study Guide 5-2 Section Quiz 5-2*	Daily Focus Transparency 23 Interactive Tutor Self-Assessment Software ExamView® Pro Testmaker Presentation Plus!
Section 3 **Cost, Revenue, and Profit Maximization** 1. Define four key measures of cost. 2. Identify two key measures of revenue. 3. Apply incremental analysis to business decisions.	Reproducible Lesson Plan 5-3 Daily Lecture Notes 5-3 Guided Reading Activity 5-3 Reading Essentials and Study Guide 5-3 Section Quiz 5-3*	Daily Focus Transparency 24 Vocabulary PuzzleMaker CD-ROM Interactive Tutor Self-Assessment Software ExamView® Pro Testmaker Presentation Plus!

Also available in Spanish

Transparency   CD-ROM   Software   Blackline Master

Videodisc   Audio Program   Videocassette

0:00 OUT OF TIME?
Assign the Chapter 5 Audio Program activity and test.

Block Schedule

 Activities that are particularly suited to use within the block scheduling framework are identified throughout this chapter by the following designation: **BLOCK SCHEDULING**

KEY TO ABILITY LEVELS

Teaching strategies have been coded for varying learning styles and abilities.
L1 BASIC activities for all students
L2 AVERAGE activities for average to above-average students
L3 CHALLENGING activities for above-average students
ELL ENGLISH LANGUAGE LEARNER activities

Chapter 5 Resource Manager

TeacherWorks™ **All-In-One Planner and Resource Center**

- **Interactive Teacher Edition** Access your Teacher Wraparound Edition and your classroom resources with a few easy clicks.
- **Interactive Lesson Planner** Planning has never been easier! Organize your week, month, semester, or year with all the lesson helps you need to make teaching creative, timely, and relevant.

Use Glencoe's **Presentation Plus!** multimedia teacher tool to easily present dynamic lessons that visually excite your students. Using Microsoft PowerPoint® you can customize the presentations to create your own personalized lessons.

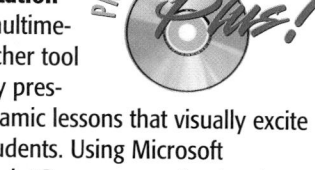

ACTIVITY

From the Classroom of...

**Laura Wagner
Bryan High School
Bryan, TX**

Understanding Supply

Give each student about 1 foot of plastic lanyard rope and about 30 beads of various colors in a plastic bag. Ask students to string the beads together to make a bracelet. They may use as many beads as they like and may trade with others.

Then give students a table with the prices for the different colored beads (rounded to the nearest dollar). Ask them to count their beads and calculate the cost of producing the bracelet. Ask how many students would be willing to sell their bracelet at $30, $40, and so on. The class can use this information to construct a supply schedule and graph the information to construct a corresponding supply curve. Ask students to explain the Law of Supply based on what happened in the game. Give each student a revised list of increased bead prices and ask them to recalculate the cost of their bracelet. As the class reconstructs the supply schedule and graph, students will understand that increased costs of production lead to a lower supply.

Number	Color	×	Price	=	Cost
	Red	×	$1.00	=	
	Green	×	$2.00	=	

National Council on Economic Education

THE **Economics**America AND **Economics**International PROGRAMS

Voluntary National Content Standards in Economics
Emphasized in Chapter 5

Content Standard 2

Content Standard 8

For a complete listing of NCEE Standards and entire text correlation, see Teacher pages in front of book.

Resources Available from NCEE
- Capstone: The Nation's High School Economics Course
- United States History: Focus on Economics
- Focus: High School Economics
- Entrepreneurship in the U.S. Economy
- Civics and Government: Focus on Economics
- Economics at Work
- The Great Economic Mysteries Book

To order these materials or to contact your state Council on Economic Education about workshops and programs, call 1-800-338-1192 or visit www.nationalcouncil.org

Chapter 5 Resource Manager

TEACHING TRANSPARENCY

Economic Concept Transparency 8: Supply and Demand

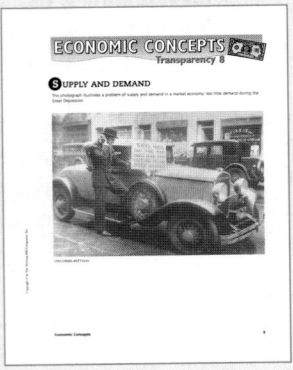

APPLICATION AND ENRICHMENT

Consumer Application Activity 5

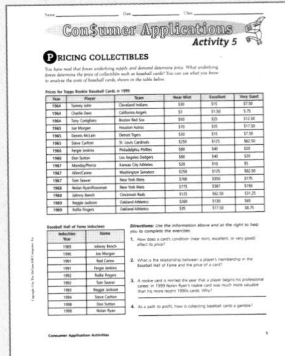

Free Enterprise Activity 5

APPLICATION AND ENRICHMENT

Enrichment Activity 5

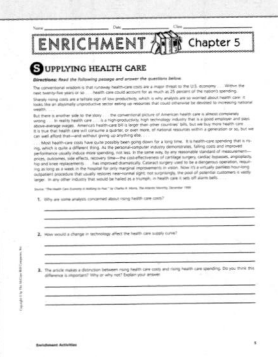

Cooperative Learning Activity 5

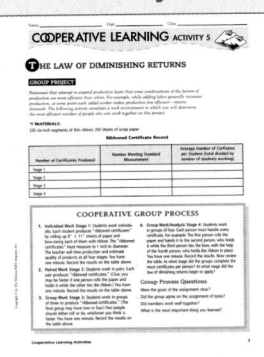

Math Practice Activity 5

Economic Cartoon 5

Primary and Secondary Source Reading 5

REVIEW AND REINFORCEMENT

Economic Vocabulary Activity 5

Reteaching Activity 5

Critical Thinking Activity 5

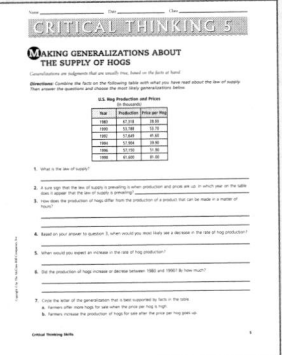

Reinforcing Economic Skill 28

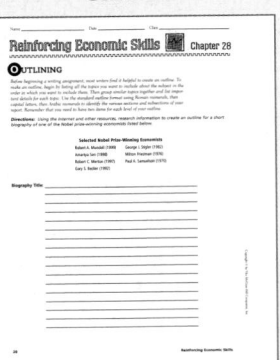

Chapter 5 Resource Manager

ASSESSMENT AND EVALUATION

Chapter 5 Test Form A

Chapter 5 Test Form B

Performance Assessment Activity 5

ExamView® Pro Testmaker

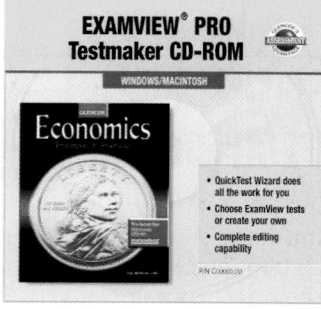

SPANISH RESOURCES

The following Spanish language materials are available in the Spanish Resources binder:

 Spanish Economic Vocabulary Activities

 Spanish Reteaching Activities

 Spanish Section Quizzes

 Spanish Economic Concepts Transparencies

Also available:

 Spanish Chapter 5 Audio Program Activity and Test

TECHNOLOGY/MULTIMEDIA

- Vocabulary PuzzleMaker CD-ROM
- Interactive Tutor Self-Assessment Software
- ExamView® Pro Testmaker
- Audio Program (English or Spanish)
- NBR Economics & You Video Program (English or Spanish)
- MindJogger Videoquiz
- Interactive Economics! CD-ROM
- Presentation Plus!
- TeacherWorks CD-ROM
- Glencoe Skillbuilder Interactive Workbook CD-ROM, Level 2

ECONOMICS Online

Use our Web site for additional resources. All essential content is covered in the Student Edition.

You and your students can visit epp.glencoe.com , the Web site companion to **Economics: Principles and Practices.** This innovative integration of electronic and print media offers your students a wealth of opportunities. The student text directs students to the Web site for the following options:

- **Chapter Overviews**
- **Student Web Activities**
- **Self-Check Quizzes**
- **Textbook Updates**

Answers are provided for you in the Web Activity Lesson Plan. Additional Web resources and interactive puzzles are also available.

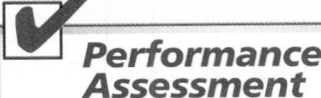

Performance Assessment

Refer to Activity 5 in the *Performance Assessment Strategies and Activities* booklet.

 BLOCK SCHEDULING

Introduce students to chapter content and key terms by having them access **Chapter Overview 5** at epp.glencoe.com

 ECONOMICS & YOU

 Chapter 6
Disc 1, Side 1

What Is Supply?
After viewing this segment, students should be able to:
- Identify some factors that can cause a change in the supply of a product.

 Also available in VHS.

GLENCOE
TECHNOLOGY

Use **MindJogger Videoquiz** to preview the Chapter 5 content.

CHAPTER 5

Supply

Economics & You

About how many hours do you spend studying every night? How many hours would you study if you were paid $1 an hour? $10 an hour? If you will study more for a higher price, you are following the Law of Supply. To learn more about supply, view the Chapter 6 video lesson:

What Is Supply?

ECONOMICS
Online

Chapter Overview Visit the *Economics: Principles and Practices* Web site at epp.glencoe.com and click on *Chapter 5—Chapter Overviews* to preview chapter information.

A firm's willingness to supply products depends on the price it can charge and on its cost of production.

✚ EXTRA CREDIT PROJECT

Have students monitor television newscasts and newspapers to find three stories that discuss supply. Have students write a brief explanation of how the situation in each story might affect price and supply.

What Is Supply?

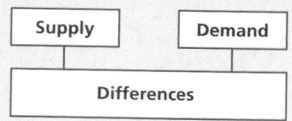

Study Guide

Main Idea
For almost any good or service, the higher the price, the larger the quantity that will be offered for sale.

Reading Strategy
Graphic Organizer As you read the section, complete a graphic organizer similar to the one below by describing how supply differs from demand.

```
  Supply        Demand

        Differences
```

Key Terms
supply, Law of Supply, supply schedule, supply curve, market supply curve, quantity supplied, change in quantity supplied, change in supply, subsidy, supply elasticity

Objectives
After studying this section, you will be able to:
1. **Understand** the difference between the supply schedule and the supply curve.
2. **Explain** how market supply curves are derived.
3. **Specify** the reasons for a change in supply.

Applying Economic Concepts
Supply The Law of Supply tells us that firms will produce and offer for sale more of their product at a high price than at a low price. On another level, think about your own labor. You are the supplier, and the higher the pay, the more work you are willing to supply.

Cover Story

Sell It on the Web

By now, just about everyone has heard the breathless prediction about the coming explosion in e-commerce. From the corner store to the corporate boardroom, entrepreneurs recognize that there's

Online business grows.

money to be made online. The debate is no longer about whether you should put your business online but about what is the best way to do it. . . .

A new group of e-commerce solutions lets small businesses take a dip into e-commerce without getting in over their heads. These turnkey solutions offer several advantages. . . . No knowledge of HTML is required, because all the site design is done using ready-made templates (and) authoring tools. . . .

—*PC Magazine*, September 17, 1998

The concept of supply is based on voluntary decisions made by producers, whether they are proprietorships working out of home offices or large corporations operating out of downtown corporate headquarters. For example, a producer might decide to offer one amount for sale at one price and a different quantity at another price. **Supply,** then, is defined as the amount of a product that would be offered for sale at all possible prices that could prevail in the market.

Because the producer is *receiving* payment for his or her products, it should come as no surprise that more will be offered at higher prices. This forms the basis for the **Law of Supply,** the principle that suppliers will normally offer more for sale at high prices and less at lower prices.

An Introduction to Supply

 All suppliers of economic products must decide how much to offer for sale at various prices—a decision made according to what is best for the individual seller. What is best depends, in

1 FOCUS

Section Overview
This section focuses on the nature of supply.

BELLRINGER
Motivational Activity

Project **transparency** and have students answer questions.

Available as blackline master.

Daily Focus Transparency 13

Study Guide

Reading Strategy
Have students create the graphic organizer.
Answers to Graphic: *supply: prices and quantities move in the same direction; demand: they vary inversely.*

Preteaching Vocabulary
Call on volunteers to tell what they think each Key Term means.

RESOURCE MANAGER

Reproducible Masters
- Reproducible Lesson Plan 5-1
- Daily Lecture Notes 5-1
- Guided Reading Activity 5-1
- Reading Essentials and Study Guide 5-1
- Section Quiz 5-1

Transparencies
- Daily Focus Transparency 13

Multimedia
- Interactive Economics!
- Interactive Tutor Self-Assessment Software
- ExamView® Pro Testmaker
- Presentation Plus!

2 TEACH

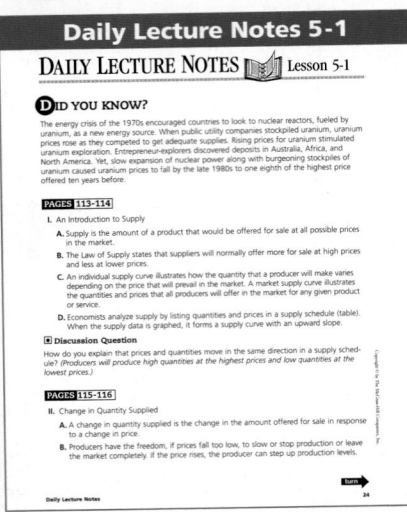

Daily Lecture Notes 5-1

DAILY LECTURE NOTES 📖 Lesson 5-1

DID YOU KNOW?
The energy crisis of the 1970s encouraged countries to look to nuclear reactors, fueled by uranium, as a new energy source. When public utility companies stockpiled uranium, uranium prices rose as they competed to get adequate supplies. Rising prices for uranium stimulated uranium exploration. Entrepreneur-explorers discovered deposits in Australia, Africa, and North America. Yet, slow expansion of nuclear power along with burgeoning stockpiles of uranium caused uranium prices to fall by the late 1980s to one eighth of the highest price offered ten years before.

PAGES 113-114
I. An Introduction to Supply
   A. Supply is the amount of a product that would be offered for sale at all possible prices in the market.
   B. The Law of Supply states that suppliers will normally offer more for sale at high prices and less at lower prices.
   C. An individual supply curve illustrates how the quantity that a producer will make varies depending on the price that will prevail in the market. A market supply curve illustrates the quantities and prices that all producers will offer in the market for any given product or service.
   D. Economists analyze supply by listing quantities and prices in a supply schedule (table). When the supply data is graphed, it forms a supply curve with an upward slope.

□ Discussion Question
How do you explain that prices and quantities move in the same direction in a supply schedule? (Producers will produce high quantities at the highest prices and low quantities at the lowest prices.)

PAGES 115-116
II. Change in Quantity Supplied
   A. A change in quantity supplied is the change in the amount offered for sale in response to a change in price.
   B. Producers have the freedom, if prices fall too low, to slow or stop production or leave the market completely. If the price rises, the producer can step up production levels.

Daily Lecture Notes

ECONOMICS
AT A GLANCE

Answer: *For the Law of Supply, quantity varies directly with the price, rather than inversely as with the Law of Demand.*

L1 Applying Economics

Ask: What role do you play as producers in the market? As guidance, remind students that producers provide services as well as goods. Then ask if any students have part-time jobs or do baby-sitting or household chores for an allowance. Point out that by taking part in these activities, they are acting as producers supplying an economic product—their labor—to buyers in the marketplace.

ECONOMICS
AT A GLANCE
Figure 5.1

Supply of Compact Discs

Ⓐ Supply Schedule

Price	Quantity Supplied
$30	8
25	7
20	6
15	4
10	2
5	0

Ⓑ Supply Curve

[Graph showing supply curve with Price on y-axis ($5 to $30) and Quantity on x-axis (0 to 8). Labels: "Decrease in quantity supplied", "Increase in quantity supplied", points a and b.]

Using Tables and Graphs The supply curve is drawn from the values on the schedule. How does the Law of Supply differ from the Law of Demand?

---

turn, upon the cost of producing the goods or services. The concept of supply, like demand, can be illustrated in the form of a table or a graph.

The Supply Schedule

The **supply schedule** is a listing of the various quantities of a particular product supplied at all possible prices in the market. **Panel A** of **Figure 5.1** is a hypothetical supply schedule for compact digital discs. It shows the quantities of CDs that will

---

be supplied at various prices, other things being equal. If you compare it to the demand schedule in **Panel A** of **Figure 4.1** on page 90 you will see that the two are remarkably similar. The only real difference between the two is that prices and quantities now move in the same direction for supply—rather than in opposite directions as in the case of demand.

The Individual Supply Curve

The data presented in the supply schedule can also be illustrated graphically as the upward-sloping line in **Panel B** of **Figure 5.1**. To draw it, we transfer each of the price-quantity observations in the schedule over to the graph, and then connect the points to form the curve. The result is a **supply curve,** a graph showing the various quantities supplied at each and every price that might prevail in the market.

All normal supply curves slope from the lower left-hand corner of the graph to the upper right-hand corner. This is a positive slope and shows that if one of the values goes up, the other will go up too.

While the supply schedule and curve in the figure represent a single, hypothetical producer of compact digital discs, we should realize that supply is a very general concept. In fact, you are a supplier when you look for a job and offer your services for sale. Your economic product is your labor, and you would probably be willing to supply more labor for a high wage than for a low one.

The Market Supply Curve

The supply schedule and curve in **Figure 5.1** show the information for a single firm. Frequently, however, we are more interested in the **market supply curve,** the supply curve that shows the quantities offered at various prices by all firms that offer the product for sale in a given market.

To obtain the data for the market supply curve, add the number of CDs that individual firms would produce at each and every price, and then plot them on a separate graph. In **Figure 5.2**, point **a** on the market supply curve represents six CDs—four from the first firm and two from the second—that are offered for sale at a price of $15. Correspondingly, point **b** on the curve represents a total of nine CDs offered for sale at a price of $20.

MEETING SPECIAL NEEDS ACTIVITY

English Language Learners One of the most common problems of students with language difficulties is an inability to ask questions of their teachers. Form small groups to practice developing questions about information in Section 1. Reward groups for the following achievements: producing the most questions and producing the most varied questions. **ELL**

📂 Refer to *Inclusion for the Social Studies Classroom Strategies and Activities* in the TCR.

ECONOMICS AT A GLANCE

Figure 5.2

Individual and Market Supply Curves

Firm A

Firm B

Market

. . . to get the Market Supply Curve.

Quantity of CDs Supplied by:

Price	Firm A	+	Firm B	=	Market
$30	8		5		13
25	7		4		11
20	6		3		9
15	4	+	2	=	6
10	2		1		3
5	0		0		0

Using Graphs The market supply curve, SS, is the sum of all individual supply curves in the market. **Why are the supply curves upward sloping?**

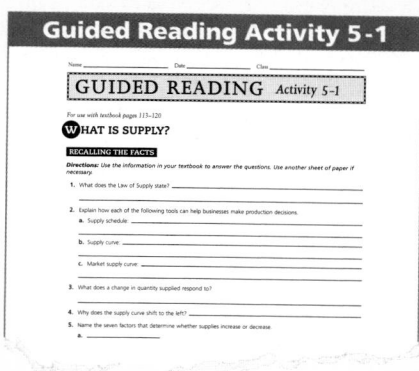

Change in Quantity Supplied

The **quantity supplied** is the amount that producers bring to market at any given price. A **change in quantity supplied** is the change in amount offered for sale in response to a change in price. In **Figure 5.1,** for example, four CDs are supplied when the price is $15. If the price increases to $20, six CDs are supplied. If the price then changes to $25, seven units are supplied.

These changes illustrate a change in the quantity supplied which—like the case of demand—shows as a movement along the supply curve. Note that the change in quantity supplied can be an *increase* or a *decrease*, depending on whether more or less of a product is offered. For example, the movement from **a** to **b** in **Figure 5.1** shows an increase because the number of products offered for sale goes from four to six when the price goes up.

L2 Illustrating Ideas

Draw a two-column table on the board with *Pay Per Hour* and *Students Willing to Work* as column headings. In the *Pay* column, list the figures $1 through $10. State that you need help to clean the classroom. Ask who would be interested in the job at a wage of $1 an hour. Record the number and repeat the process for all other hourly rates. Tell students they have provided an example of the Law of Supply. Have students use the data in the chart to construct a graph similar to Figure 5.1. **ELL**

FREE ENTERPRISE ACTIVITY

The productivity of the factors of production can have a major impact on the costs of doing business and, therefore, on the supply of goods and services available to consumers. Invite a local businessperson to talk to the class about the importance of productivity in his or her business. In a follow-up discussion, ask students to speculate about the effects of changes in productivity on supply. **BLOCK SCHEDULING**

Math Practice

Labor Costs The Jolly Music Company has three employees. Two work 40-hour weeks, and one works a 25-hour week. Each worker just received a raise from $8.40 an hour to $9.92 an hour. Ask students to figure out the company's old and new weekly labor costs and the amount of the increase. *(old weekly labor costs: $882; new weekly labor costs: $1041.60; increase in weekly labor costs: $159.60)* **Ask:** How might this increase affect supply? *(Fewer products might be offered for sale.)*

THE GLOBAL ECONOMY

Oil Supply OPEC, the Organization of Petroleum Exporting Countries, uses adjustments in oil production to counter changes in prices. In the late 1990s, just after OPEC agreed to increase production, the Asian economy unexpectedly collapsed. With demand down, an oil glut resulted, and oil prices fell sharply. In time, the members of OPEC agreed to cut production, leading to a rise in oil prices.

Supply

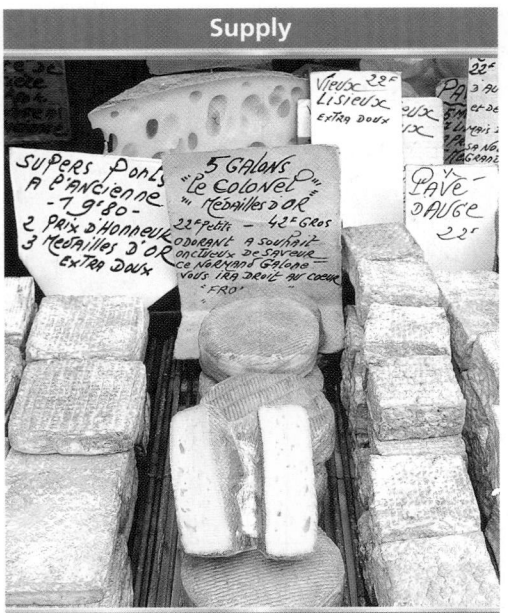

The Effect of Price A delicatessen offers different kinds of cheeses at various prices. *How does the price of a product affect the quantity offered for sale?*

In a competitive economy, producers usually react to changing prices in just this way. While the interaction of supply and demand usually determines the final price for the product, the producer has the freedom to adjust production. Take oil as an example. If the price of oil falls, the producer may offer less for sale, or even leave the market altogether if the price goes too low. If the price rises, the oil producer may offer more units for sale to take advantage of the better prices.

Change in Supply

Sometimes something happens to cause a **change in supply,** a situation where suppliers offer different amounts of products for sale at all possible prices in the market. For example, the supply schedule in **Figure 5.3** shows that producers are now willing to offer more CDs for sale at every

price than before. Where 6 units were offered at a price of $15, now there are 13. Where 11 were offered at a price of $25, 18 are now offered, and so on for every price shown in the schedule.

When both old and new quantities supplied are plotted in the form of a graph, it appears as if the supply curve has shifted to the right, showing an *increase in supply.* For a *decrease in supply* to occur, less would be offered for sale at each and every price, and the supply curve would shift to the left.

Changes in supply, whether increases or decreases, can occur for several reasons. As you read, keep in mind that all but the last reason—the number of sellers—affects both the individual and the market supply curves.

Cost of Inputs

A change in the cost of inputs can cause a change in supply. Supply might increase because of a decrease in the cost of inputs, such as labor or packaging. If the price of the inputs drops, producers are willing to produce more of a product at each and every price, thereby shifting the supply curve to the right.

An increase in the cost of inputs has the opposite effect. If labor or other costs rise, producers would not be willing to produce as many units at each and every price. Instead, they would offer fewer products for sale, and the supply curve would shift to the left.

Productivity

When management motivates its workers, or if workers decide to work more efficiently, productivity should increase. The result is that more CDs are produced at every price, which shifts the supply

Did you know?

Economic Efficiency In 1814 Francis Lowell combined all the stages of textile production—spinning, weaving, bleaching, dyeing, and printing—under one roof. His efficient mill launched the nation's Industrial Revolution, changing the system of manufacturing from the home to the factory.

CRITICAL THINKING

Determining Cause and Effect Ask students to find a news story about a change in supply—an increase or a decrease—of a basic product, such as oil or wheat. Have them explain the cause or causes for the change in supply and analyze how the change will affect prices. Then ask students to try to identify businesses whose costs may be affected by the change.

curve to the right. On the other hand, if workers are unmotivated, untrained, or unhappy, productivity could decrease. The supply curve shifts to the left because fewer goods are brought to the market at every possible price.

Technology

New technology tends to shift the supply curve to the right. The introduction of a new machine, chemical, or industrial process can affect supply by lowering the cost of production or by increasing productivity. For example, improvements in the fuel efficiency of aircraft engines have lowered the cost of providing passenger air service. When production costs go down, the producer is usually able to produce more goods and services at each and every price in the market.

New technologies do not always work as expected, of course. Equipment can break down, or the technology—or even replacement parts—might be difficult to obtain. This would shift the supply curve to the left. These examples are exceptions, however. New technology far more often increases supply.

Taxes and Subsidies

Firms view taxes as costs. If the producer's inventory is taxed or if fees are paid to receive a license to produce, the cost of production goes up. This causes the supply curve to shift to the left. Or, if taxes go down production costs go down, supply then increases and the supply curve shifts to the right.

A **subsidy** is a government payment to an individual, business, or other group to encourage or protect a certain type of economic activity. Subsidies lower the cost of production, encouraging current producers to remain in the market and new

producers to enter. When subsidies are repealed, costs go up, producers leave the market, and the supply curve shifts to the left.

Historically, many farmers in the milk, corn, wheat, and soybean industries received substantial subsidies to support their income. While many farmers would have gone out of business without these subsidies, the fact that they were paid ensured their ability to remain operational, and the market supply curve shifted to the right.

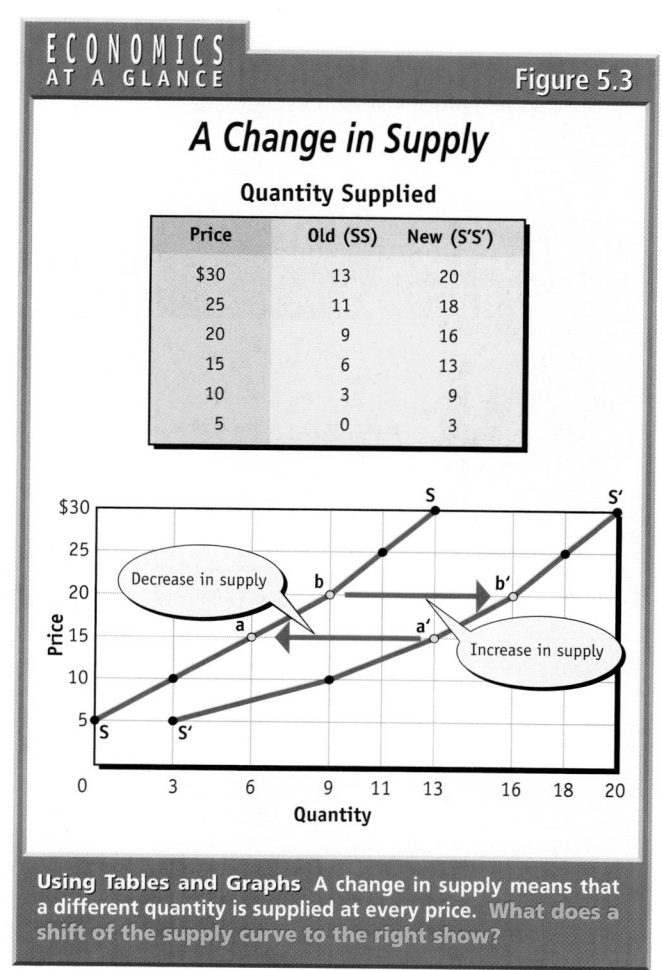

ECONOMICS AT A GLANCE   Figure 5.3

A Change in Supply

Quantity Supplied

Price	Old (SS)	New (S'S')
$30	13	20
25	11	18
20	9	16
15	6	13
10	3	9
5	0	3

Using Tables and Graphs A change in supply means that a different quantity is supplied at every price. What does a shift of the supply curve to the right show?

CYBERNOMICS

Technology and Farming
Many U.S. farmers now use computers, the Internet, and e-mail to get information about the supply of crops that will come to market, prices offered, yield per acre, and other data. This information helps farmers decide how much to plant and where to sell their products. State agricultural departments and universities have Web sites to help farmers use electronic information effectively.

ECONOMICS AT A GLANCE

Answer: *an increase in supply at each price*

L2 Journal Writing

Suggest that students consider their attitudes toward working for pay and working without pay. Have them describe any difference in attitude they may have toward unpaid work. Then have them write a paragraph explaining why students should get paid for the hours they spend studying and going to school.

EXTENDING THE CONTENT

Changing Supply of Farmland The supply of arable farmland would seem to be fairly constant. Over a relatively long period of time, however, the location and supply of arable land can change because alternative uses for the land are developed. For example, suburban developments, new highways, and shopping centers may encroach upon farmland, thereby decreasing the available amount of arable land.

L1 Applying Ideas

Have students construct supply schedules and supply curves of the amount of time per week they would be willing to work as a store clerk, a server at a fast-food restaurant, or some other part-time position at various possible wages. **ELL**

L2 Journalism

Ask students to write a newspaper story describing one of the possible determinants of a change in supply. Suggest that they illustrate the story with graphs showing how supply changed.

INTERACTIVE ECONOMICS!

CD-ROM

SUPPLY Have students click on "Supply Schedules and Curves" in Lesson 4. Then have students write a paragraph explaining why the concept of supply involves a direct relationship rather than an inverse relationship between prices and quantity.

💾 Also supplied in disk format.

Expectations

Expectations about the future price of a product can also affect the supply curve. If producers think the price of their product will go up, they may withhold some of the supply. This causes supply to decrease and the supply curve to shift to the left. On the other hand, producers may expect lower prices for their output in the future. In this situation, they may try to produce and sell as much as possible right away, causing the supply curve to shift to the right.

Government Regulations

When the government establishes new regulations, the cost of production can be affected, causing a change in supply. For example, when the

Careers

Real Estate Agent

Real estate agents assist in renting, selling, and buying property for clients. In return, they receive a percentage of the rent or sale prices of the property.

The Work

Responsibilities include obtaining listings—owner agreements to place properties for rent or sale—advertising the property, and showing the property to prospective renters and buyers. Agents need to be familiar with fair-market values, zoning laws, local land-use laws, housing and building codes, insurance coverage, mortgage and interest rates, and credit and loan policies. They may also need to know about leasing practices, business trends, location needs, transportation, utilities, and labor supply. Agents often work evenings and weekends because they must accommodate their schedule to that of the client.

Qualifications

Agents should have a high school education at the minimum and possess a real estate license.

government mandates new auto safety features such as air bags or emission controls, cars cost more to produce. Producers adjust to the higher production costs by producing fewer cars at each and every price in the market.

In general, increased—or tighter—government regulations restrict supply, causing the supply curve to shift to the left. Relaxed regulations allow producers to lower the cost of production, which results in a shift of the supply curve to the right.

Number of Sellers

All of the factors you just read about can cause a change in an individual firm's supply curve and, consequently, the market supply curve. It follows, therefore, that a change in the number of suppliers causes the market supply curve to shift to the right or left.

As more firms enter an industry, the supply curve shifts to the right. In other words, the larger the number of suppliers, the greater the market supply. If some suppliers leave the market, fewer products are offered for sale at all possible prices. This causes supply to decrease, shifting the curve to the left.

In the real world, sellers are entering the market and leaving the market all the time. Some economic analysts believe that, at least initially, the development of the Internet will result in larger numbers entering the market than in leaving. They point out that almost anyone with Internet experience and a few thousand dollars can open up his or her own Internet store. Because of the ease of entry into these new markets, being a seller is no longer just for the big firms.

Elasticity of Supply

Just as demand has elasticity, there is elasticity of supply. **Supply elasticity** is a measure of the way in which quantity supplied responds to a change in price. If a small increase in price leads to a relatively larger increase in output, supply is elastic. If the quantity supplied changes very little, supply is inelastic.

What is the difference between supply elasticity and demand elasticity? Actually, there is very little difference. If quantities are being purchased, the

---

INTERDISCIPLINARY CONNECTIONS ACTIVITY

Geography Tell students that geography helps determine the supply of products and affects the unequal distribution of the factors of production. Students should recognize obvious geographical influences on supply, such as climate, growing season, and proximity to transportation routes. For example, the supply of pineapples is relatively limited in the continental United States because of geographical influences. Pineapples are tropical plants and cannot be widely grown in the 48 continental states. Have students identify geographical influences on the supply of products in their region. Have them choose one particular product, analyze the geographical influences that affect its supply, and present their findings to the class. 📦 **BLOCK SCHEDULING**

ECONOMICS AT A GLANCE

Figure 5.4

Supply Elasticity

A Elastic Supply

B Inelastic Supply

C Unit Elastic Supply

D Change in Supply Due to Change in Price

Type of Elasticity	Change in Quantity Supplied Due to a Change in Price
Elastic	More than proportional
Unit Elastic	Proportional
Inelastic	Less than proportional

Using Graphs The elasticity of supply, like the elasticity of demand, is a measure of responsiveness. The key to elasticity is the way the dependent variable (quantity supplied) changes in response to a change in the independent variable (price). **What determines whether a business's supply curve is elastic or inelastic?**

ECONOMICS AT A GLANCE

Answer: *how fast a business can adjust to new prices*

③ ASSESS

Assign Section 1 Assessment as homework or as an in-class activity.

💾 Have students use **Interactive Tutor Self-Assessment Software** to review Section 1.

Section Quiz 5-1

---

concept is demand elasticity. If quantities are being brought to market for sale, the concept is supply elasticity. Keep in mind that elasticity is simply a measure of the way quantity adjusts to a change in price.

Three Elasticities

Examples of supply elasticity are illustrated in **Figure 5.4.** The supply curve in **Panel A** is elastic because the change in price causes a relatively larger change in quantity supplied. Doubling the price from $1 to $2 causes the quantity brought to market to triple.

Panel B shows an inelastic supply curve. A change in price causes a relatively smaller change in quantity supplied. When the price is doubled

from $1 to $2, the quantity brought to market goes up only 50 percent, or from two units to three units.

Panel C shows a unit elastic supply curve. A change in price causes a proportional change in the quantity supplied. The price doubles from $1 to $2, which causes the quantity brought to market also to double.

Determinants of Supply Elasticity

The elasticity of a business's supply curve depends on the nature of its production. If a firm can adjust to new prices quickly, then supply is likely to be elastic. If the nature of production is such that adjustments take longer, then supply is likely to be inelastic.

CHAPTER 5: SUPPLY **119**

EXTENDING THE CONTENT

Elasticity of Supply Toy manufacturers may face a temporary inelasticity of supply if a toy turns out to be more popular than expected during the holiday buying season and it cannot be manufactured quickly enough to satisfy the seasonal demand. That was the situation in December 1996, when the Tickle Me Elmo doll turned out to be the hottest toy of the season. The toy, regularly priced at $23.99, was advertised in newspapers for as much as $500. Some customers said they would pay any price to buy the toy in time for Christmas.

119

Visual Instruction

Answer to Caption:
The number of substitutes and ability to delay the purchase are important for demand elasticity, but not supply elasticity.

Reteach

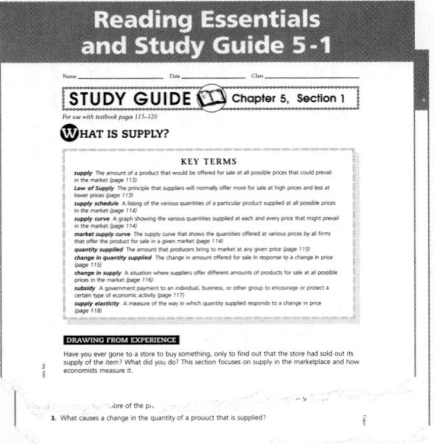

Reading Essentials and Study Guide 5-1

Enrich

Have students write a report on how a technological innovation like the microchip affected the communications industry.

4 CLOSE

Ask students to write a poem, a proverb, or a riddle that illustrates the relationship between price and supply.

Supply and Demand

Elasticity Business owners need to be aware of the relationship between supply and demand. *What is the difference between supply elasticity and demand elasticity?*

The supply curve for shale oil, for example, is likely to be inelastic in the short run. No matter what price is being offered, companies will find it difficult to increase output because of the huge amount of capital and technology needed before production can be increased very much.

However, the supply curve is likely to be elastic for kites, candy, and other products that can be made quickly without huge amounts of capital and skilled labor. If consumers are willing to pay twice the price for any of these products, most producers will be able to gear up quickly to significantly increase production.

The elasticity of supply is different from the elasticity of demand in several important respects. First, the number of substitutes has no bearing on the elasticity of supply. In addition, considerations such as the ability to delay the purchase or the portion of income consumed have no relevance to supply elasticity even though they are essential for demand elasticity. Instead, only production considerations determine supply elasticity. If a firm can react quickly to higher or lower prices, then supply is likely to be elastic. If the firm takes longer to react to a change in prices, then supply is likely to be inelastic. For these reasons, there is no supply elasticity table equivalent to **Figure 4.6** on page 106.

Section 1 Assessment

Checking for Understanding

1. **Main Idea** Using your notes from the graphic organizer activity on page 113, describe how supply is different from demand.

2. **Key Terms** Define supply, Law of Supply, supply schedule, supply curve, market supply curve, quantity supplied, change in quantity supplied, change in supply, subsidy, supply elasticity.

3. **Describe** the difference between the supply schedule and the supply curve.

4. **Describe** how market supply curves are obtained.

5. **List** the factors that can cause a change in supply.

Applying Economic Concepts

6. **Supply** Provide an example of an economic good whose producer would increase the quantity supplied if the price were to go up.

Critical Thinking

7. **Understanding Cause and Effect** According to the Law of Supply, how does price affect the quantity offered for sale?

> **Practice** and **assess** key social studies skills with the *Glencoe Skillbuilder Interactive Workbook, Level 2.*

Section 1 Assessment Answers

1. Demand is the desire, ability, and willingness to buy, and deals with how prices affect consumer spending. Supply is the amount of a product for sale and deals with how prices affect quantity supplied.

2. All vocabulary terms are defined in the text.

3. schedule: information on supply in table form; curve: same information in graphic form

4. Determine amount produced by individual firms. Add numbers and plot on a graph.

5. costs of inputs, productivity, technology, number of sellers, taxes and subsidies, expectations, government regulations

6. Examples should represent products for which supply is directly related to price.

7. Sellers will offer more at higher prices and less at lower prices.

Profiles in Economics

Enterprising Entrepreneurs

There have been literally millions of American entrepreneurs. A few, however, are noteworthy for taking modest business dreams to stunning heights. Three of the most impressive are Richard Sears, Milton Hershey, and John Johnson.

RICHARD SEARS

In 1886, 23-year-old Richard Sears was a railway station agent in North Redwood, Minnesota. Sears had free time on his hands, so he decided to make a little money on the side. He bought a surplus shipment of watches and started selling them to other station agents.

Encouraged by his profits, Sears moved to Chicago, where he partnered with Alvah C. Roebuck, who could repair watches. They founded Sears, Roebuck and Company in 1893, and published their first catalog a year later. Rural residents, who could "Shop at Sears and Save" by avoiding middlemen, loved the catalog, and the company prospered. Within a decade, Sears was the largest mail-order firm in the world. In 1935, Sears opened its first retail store. Today, Sears, Roebuck and Company is one of the largest retail businesses in the world, employing more than 300,000 people.

MILTON HERSHEY

Milton Hershey started as a poor farm boy, and received little education. He failed as a candy seller in Philadelphia, Denver, New York, Chicago, and New Orleans. At 30, he was flat broke and shunned by his family. But one more try at the candy business— this time making a caramel candy of his own recipe—made him a success. In fact, his "Hershey's Crystal A" made him a millionaire. In 1895, Hershey sold his caramel company and went into the chocolate business. In just a few years, the name Hershey became synonymous with chocolate. It still is, due to the dogged persistence of a man who failed for decades before he succeeded.

JOHN JOHNSON

In 1942, John Johnson set off to publish a magazine called *Negro Digest*. Most white magazine sellers, doubting that there was a sufficient African American readership, refused to carry it. So Johnson convinced hundreds of acquaintances to ask for the magazine at newsstands, and then to buy all the copies once they came in. Circulation soared. Johnson then persuaded the first lady, Eleanor Roosevelt, to write a piece called "If I Were a Negro" for the magazine. The publicity tripled circulation.

Johnson followed this success in 1945 by founding *Ebony*, a magazine aimed at African American veterans of World War II. The magazine proved even more popular than his first. A third magazine, *Jet*, was produced, and whereas there had been no national magazines for African Americans before, there were now three. And they were all a result of the hard work of just one enterprising entrepreneur.

Examining the Profile

1. **Making Generalizations** Explain how persistence played a role in the success of each of these men.

2. **For Further Research** Find out the etymology of *entrepreneur* and explain why the word is used as it is today.

Profiles in Economics

BACKGROUND

Every entrepreneur takes risks. In economic terms, the risk is solely financial, but in a larger sense entrepreneurs also risk their reputations and self-esteem. Thus, entrepreneurs are economic heroes, the most successful of whom inspire others.

TEACH

Challenge students to create tables that identify the risks each of the three entrepreneurs in the Profile took. Students should use the column headings *Financial Risks, Personal Risks, Social Risks,* and *Other Risks,* and identify as many of each as possible.

Entrepreneur Invite a local entrepreneur to class to discuss the risks and rewards of entrepreneurship with students.

Answers to Examining the Profile

1. Answers will vary. Sears persisted for 24 years before he opened his first retail store; Hershey was poor, uneducated, a multiple-business failure, and broke before he achieved success; Johnson persisted in the face of racism.

2. The word *entrepreneur* comes from the French, and it means "one who undertakes some task." Its deeper root is Latin, originating in words that mean "to grasp" or "to seize." It shares these roots with the word "enterprise." Entrepreneurship thus means something akin to seizing an opportunity. Today, it denotes one who seizes a business opportunity.

1 FOCUS

Section Overview
This section introduces the theory of production.

The Theory of Production

Study Guide

Main Idea
A change in the variable input called labor results in a change in production.

Reading Strategy
Graphic Organizer As you read about production, complete a graphic organizer similar to the one below by listing what occurs during the three stages of production.

Stage I	Stage II	Stage III

Key Terms
theory of production, short run, long run, Law of Variable Proportions, production function, raw materials, total product, marginal product, stages of production, diminishing returns

Objectives
After studying this section, you will be able to:
1. **Explain** the theory of production.
2. **Describe** the three stages of production.

Applying Economic Concepts
Diminishing Returns Has the quality of your work ever declined because you worked too hard at something? Sometimes you reach a stage where you still make progress but at a diminished rate.

BELLRINGER
Motivational Activity

 Project **transparency** and have students answer questions.

 Available as blackline master.

Daily Focus Transparency 23

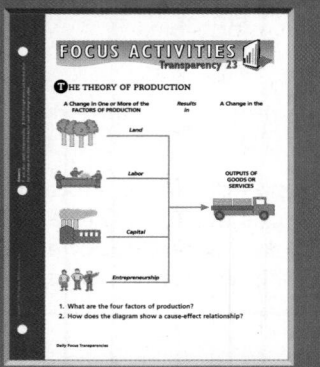

Study Guide

Reading Strategy
Have students create the graphic organizer.
Answers to Graphic: *I—increasing returns: each new worker increases output; II—diminishing returns: each new worker increases output by a smaller amount; III—negative returns: each new worker decreases output*

Preteaching Vocabulary
Refer students to the list of Key Terms. Have volunteers locate the terms and read them in context.

Cover Story

The Effects Are Getting Less Special All the Time

When George Lucas declares that digital effects are a technological advance as profound as the advent of sound and color, he is exactly right. . . .

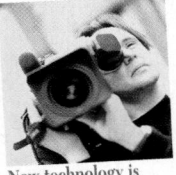

New technology is altering moviemaking.

But is the revolution already over?

Mixed reaction to his new movie, *Star Wars Episode I: The Phantom Menace,* suggest that it may be, in the same way that revolutions ushered in by color and sound were profound but brief affairs. . . . after all, none of us is amazed when we go to the movies and hear an actor speak. Nor are we amazed when we go to the movies and see color images.

What this creates, for effects-driven movies, is a scale of diminishing returns. The more Lucas achieves in the digital arena, the smarter we become, the harder we are to impress. . . .

—*Philadelphia Daily News,* May 21, 1999

122

W hether they are film producers of multi-million-dollar epics or small firms that market a single product, suppliers face a difficult task. Producing an economic good or service requires a combination of land, labor, capital, and entrepreneurs. The **theory of production** deals with the relationship between the factors of production and the output of goods and services.

The theory of production generally is based on the **short run,** a period of production that allows producers to change only the amount of the variable input called labor. This contrasts with the **long run,** a period of production long enough for producers to adjust the quantities of all their resources, including capital. For example, Ford Motors hiring 300 extra workers for one of its plants is a short-run adjustment. If Ford builds a new factory, this is a long-run adjustment.

Law of Variable Proportions

The **Law of Variable Proportions** states that, in the short run, output will change as one input is varied while the others are held constant. Although the name of the law is probably new to you, the concept is not.

RESOURCE MANAGER

Reproducible Masters
- Reproducible Lesson Plan 5-2
- Daily Lecture Notes 5-2
- Guided Reading Activity 5-2
- Reading Essentials and Study Guide 5-2
- Section Quiz 5-2

Transparencies
- Daily Focus Transparency 23

Multimedia
- Interactive Tutor Self-Assessment Software
- ExamView® Pro Testmaker
- Presentation Plus!

For example, if you are preparing a meal, you know that a little bit of salt will make the food taste better. A bit more may make it tastier still. Yet, at some point, too much salt will ruin the meal. As the amount of the input—salt—varies, so does the output—the quality of the meal.

The Law of Variable Proportions deals with the relationship between the input of productive resources and the output of final products. The law helps answer the question: How is the output of the final product affected as more units of one variable input or resource are added to a fixed amount of other resources?

A farmer, for example, may have all the land, machines, workers, and other items needed to produce a crop. However, the farmer, may have some questions about the use of fertilizer. How will the crop yield be affected if different amounts of fertilizer are added to fixed amounts of the other inputs? In this case, the variable input is the fertilizer added per acre.

Of course, it is possible to vary all the inputs at the same time. The farmer may want to know what will happen to output if the fertilizer and other factors of production are varied. Economists do not like to do this, however, because when more than one factor of production is varied, it becomes harder to gauge the impact of a single variable on total output.

The Production Function

The Law of Variable Proportions can be illustrated by using a **production function**—a concept that describes the relationship between changes in output to different amounts of a single input while other inputs are held constant. The production function can be illustrated with a schedule, such as the one in **Panel A** of **Figure 5.5**, or with a graph like the one in **Panel B.**

The production schedule in the figure lists hypothetical output as the number of workers is varied from zero to 12. With no workers, for example, there is no output. If the number of workers increases by one, output rises to seven. Add yet another worker and total output rises to 20. This information is used to construct the production function that appears as the graph in **Panel B,** where the variable input is shown on the horizontal axis with total production on the vertical axis.

In this example, only the number of workers changes. No changes occur in the amount of machinery used, the level of technology, or the quantities of **raw materials**—unprocessed natural products used in production. Under these conditions, any change in output must be the result of the variation in the number of workers.

Total Product

The second column in the production schedule in **Figure 5.5** shows **total product,** or total output produced by the firm. The numbers indicate that the plant barely operates when it has only one or two workers. As a result, some resources stand idle much of the time.

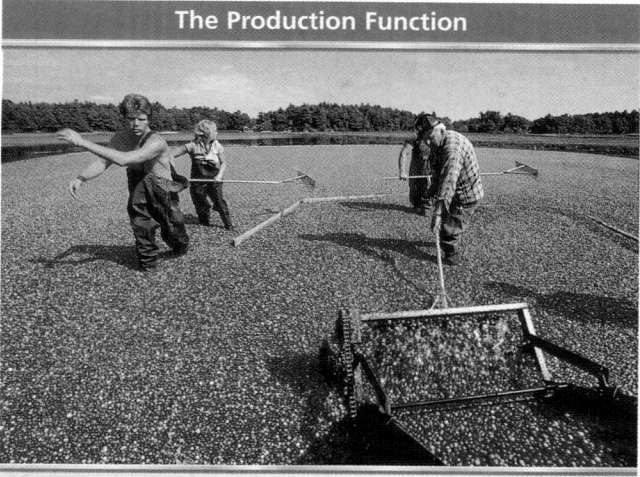

The Production Function

Inputs and Outputs All businesses must deal with the questions that surround the production relationship. *Why is the use of the production function important in business?*

CHAPTER 5: SUPPLY **123**

CHAPTER 5
Section 2, pages 122–125

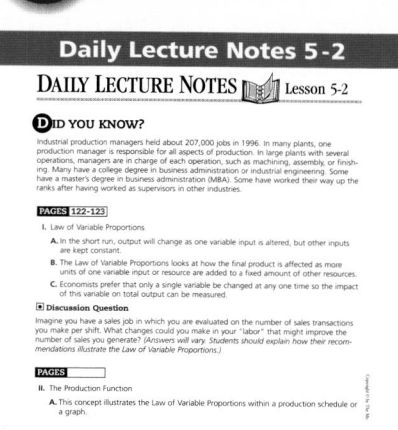

TEACH

Daily Lecture Notes 5-2

DAILY LECTURE NOTES 📖 Lesson 5-2

ⅅID YOU KNOW?
Industrial production managers held about 207,000 jobs in 1996. In many plants, one production manager is responsible for all aspects of production. In large plants with several operations, managers are in charge of each operation, such as machining, assembly, or finishing. Many have a college degree in business administration or industrial engineering. Some have a master's degree in business administration (MBA). Some have worked their way up the ranks after having worked as supervisors in other industries.

PAGES 122-123
I. Law of Variable Proportions
  A. In the short run, output will change as one variable input is altered, but other inputs are kept constant.
  B. The Law of Variable Proportions looks at how the final product is affected as more units of one variable input or resource are added to a fixed amount of other resources.
  C. Economists prefer that only a single variable be changed at any one time so the impact of this variable on total output can be measured.

⯐ Discussion Question
Imagine you have a sales job in which you are evaluated on the number of sales transactions you make per shift. What changes could you make in your "labor" that might improve the number of sales you generate? (Answers will vary. Students should explain how their recommendations illustrate the Law of Variable Proportions.)

PAGES
II. The Production Function
  A. This concept illustrates the Law of Variable Proportions within a production schedule or a graph.

Visual Instruction

Answer to Caption:
It allows businesses to gauge whether additional input will result in extra output.

L1 Draw a Diagram
To reinforce the concept of changing just one variable, have students draw a before-and-after diagram. Ask them to create the "before" diagram by showing 3 units of labor, 5 units of land, and 6 units of capital. Then ask them to draw an "after" diagram in which they change the number of units of just one of the categories—land, labor, or capital. Ask students to explain how entrepreneurs can use a change in one variable to evaluate effects.

MEETING SPECIAL NEEDS ACTIVITY

Learning Style: Kinesthetic Organize students into groups of four and secretly assign each group a concept developed in Chapter 5. Have the groups brainstorm ideas for a skit, scenario, or charade that illustrates their assigned concept. Then have groups use these ideas to develop a script. Call on groups to perform their skits, scenarios, or charades for the class. Have class members attempt to identify the concept being portrayed.

🗁 Refer to *Inclusion for the Social Studies Classroom Strategies and Activities* in the TCR.

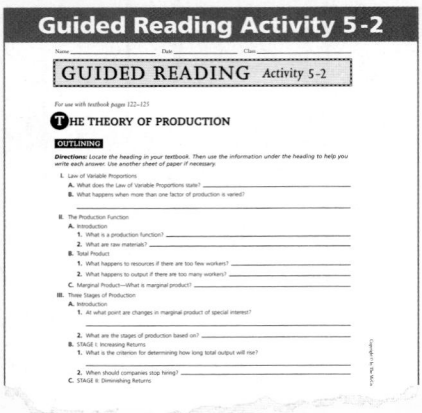
ECONOMICS
AT A GLANCE

Answer: *as increasing returns, diminishing returns, and negative returns as determined by marginal product*

③ ASSESS

Assign Section 2 Assessment as homework or as an in-class activity.

■ Have students use **Interactive Tutor Self-Assessment Software.**

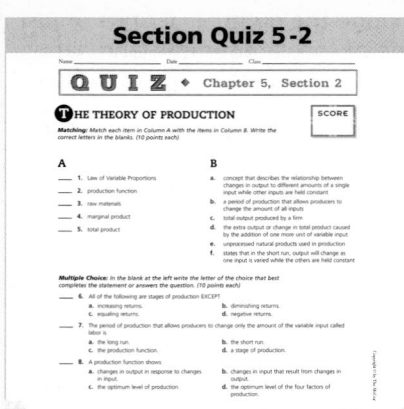
ECONOMICS
AT A GLANCE
Figure 5.5

The Law of Variable Proportions

Ⓐ The Production Schedule

Number of Workers	Total Product	Marginal Product*	Regions of Production
0	0	0	Stage I
1	7	7	
2	20	13	
3	38	18	
4	62	24	
5	90	28	
6	110	20	Stage II
7	129	19	
8	138	9	
9	144	6	
10	148	4	
11	145	–3	Stage III
12	135	–10	

*All figures in terms of output per day

Ⓑ The Production Function

Synthesizing Information The law can be shown as the production schedule in A, or as the production function shown in B. **How are the three stages of production defined?**

Total Product Rises

As more workers are added, however, total product rises. More workers can operate more machinery, and plant output rises. Additional workers also means that the workers can specialize. For example, one group runs the machines, another handles maintenance, and a third group assembles the products. By working in this way—as a coordinated whole—the firm can be more productive.

Total Product Slows

As even more workers are added output continues to rise, but it does so at a slower rate until it can grow no further. Finally, the addition of the eleventh and twelfth workers causes total output to go down because these workers just get in the way of the others. Although the ideal number of workers cannot be determined until costs are considered, it is clear that the eleventh and twelfth workers will not be hired.

Marginal Product

The measure of output shown in the third column of the production schedule in **Figure 5.5** is an important concept in economics. The measure is known as **marginal product,** the extra output or change in total product caused by the addition of one more unit of variable input.

As we can see in the figure, the marginal product, or extra output of the first worker, is seven. Likewise, the marginal product of the second worker—which is equal to the change in total product—is 13. Together, both workers account for 20 units of total product.

FREE ENTERPRISE ACTIVITY

Productivity is measured in different ways. The productivity of labor is gauged by output per hour worked. Because a higher rate of output per hour worked will lead to increased profits, businesses are constantly seeking ways to boost labor productivity. The methods businesses use to achieve this goal include providing attractive working environments, offering pay incentives and bonuses, subsidizing further education so that workers gain new skills, investing in modern capital equipment, and building or purchasing larger, more efficient plants. Have students research the ways local businesses have tried to increase labor productivity. Have them present the consequences of the business' economic decisions in a brief oral report. 📦 **BLOCK SCHEDULING**

Three Stages of Production

When it comes to determining the optimal number of variable units to be used in production, changes in marginal product are of special interest. **Figure 5.5** shows the three **stages of production**–increasing returns, diminishing returns, and negative returns–that are based on the way marginal product changes as the variable input of labor is changed.

In Stage I, the first workers hired cannot work efficiently because there are too many resources per worker. As the number of workers increases, they make better use of their machinery and resources. This results in increasing returns (or increasing marginal products) for the first five workers hired.

As long as each new worker hired contributes more to total output than the worker before, total output rises at an increasingly faster rate. Because marginal output increases by a larger amount every time a new worker is added, Stage I is known as the stage of increasing returns. Companies, however, do not knowingly produce in Stage I for very long. As soon as a firm discovers that each new worker adds more output than the last, the firm is tempted to hire another worker.

In Stage II, the total production keeps growing, but by smaller and smaller amounts. Any additional workers hired may stock shelves, package parts, and do other jobs that leave the machine operators free to do their jobs. The rate of increase in total production, however, is now starting to slow down. Each additional worker, then, is making a diminishing, but still positive, contribution to total output.

Stage II illustrates the principle of **diminishing returns,** the stage where output increases at a diminishing rate as more units of a variable input are added. In **Figure 5.5,** Stage II begins when the sixth worker is hired, because the 20-unit marginal product of that worker is less than the 28-unit marginal product of the fifth worker.

The third stage of production begins when the eleventh worker is added. By this time, the firm has hired too many workers, and they are starting to get in each other's way. Marginal product becomes negative and total plant output decreases.

Most companies do not hire workers whose addition would cause total production to decrease. Therefore, the number of workers hired would be found only in Stage II. The exact number of workers hired depends on the cost of each worker. If the cost is low, the firm should hire at least six, but no more than 10, workers.

Reteach

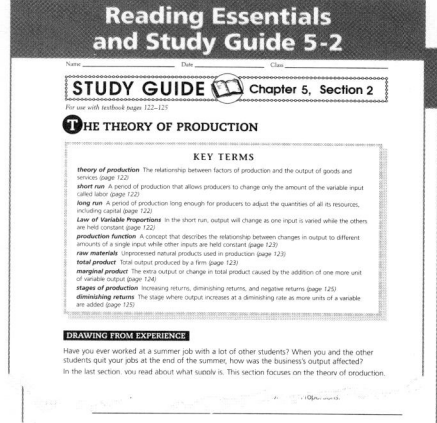

Reading Essentials and Study Guide 5-2

STUDY GUIDE — Chapter 5, Section 2

For use with textbook pages 122–125

THE THEORY OF PRODUCTION

KEY TERMS

theory of production The relationship between factors of production and the output of goods and services (page 122)

short run A period of production that allows producers to change only the amount of the variable input called labor (page 122)

long run A period of production long enough for producers to adjust the quantities of all its resources, including capital (page 122)

Law of Variable Proportions In the short run, output will change as one input is varied while the others are held constant (page 122)

production function A concept that describes the relationship between change in output to different amounts of a single input while other inputs are held constant (page 123)

raw materials Unprocessed natural products used in production (page 123)

total product Total output produced by a firm (page 123)

marginal product The extra output or change in total product caused by the addition of one more unit of variable output (page 124)

stages of production Increasing returns, diminishing returns, and negative returns (page 125)

diminishing returns The stage where output increases at a diminishing rate as more units of a variable are added (page 125)

DRAWING FROM EXPERIENCE

Have you ever worked at a summer job with a lot of other students? When you and the other students quit your jobs at the end of the summer, how was the business's output affected? In the last section, you read about what supply is. This section focuses on the theory of production.

Enrich

Ask students to investigate different types of job specialization used by businesses. Have them present their findings in a report that shows the role specialization plays in production.

4 CLOSE

Discuss: The most important economic concept for business managers to understand is that of marginal product.

Section 2 Assessment

Checking for Understanding

1. **Main Idea** Using your notes from the graphic organizer activity on page 122, explain how production is affected by a change in inputs.

2. **Key Terms** Define theory of production, short run, long run, Law of Variable Proportions, production function, raw materials, total product, marginal product, stages of production, diminishing returns.

3. **Describe** the relationship on which the theory of production is based.

4. **Explain** how marginal product changes in each of the three stages of production.

5. **Identify** what point will eventually be reached if companies continue adding workers.

Applying Economic Concepts

6. **Diminishing Returns** Provide an example of a time when you entered a period of diminishing returns or even negative returns. Explain why this might have occurred.

Critical Thinking

7. **Sequencing Information** You need to hire workers for a project you are directing. You may add one worker at a time in a manner that will allow you to measure the added contribution of each worker. At what point will you stop hiring workers? Relate this process to the three stages of the production function.

 Practice and assess key social studies skills with the *Glencoe Skillbuilder Interactive Workbook, Level 2.*

Section 2 Assessment Answers

1. As input changes, production of outputs also changes. First, each input will cause an increase. Then, each input will cause an increase, but in increasingly smaller increments. Finally, each input will cause a decrease.

2. All vocabulary terms are defined in the text.

3. The theory of production states that changing factors of production (inputs) will change the output of goods and services.

4. In Stage I, marginal product increases. In Stage II, marginal product continues to increase, but at a slower rate. In Stage III, marginal product becomes negative.

5. Workers will be in each other's way and output will decrease.

6. Examples should reflect an understanding of the concept of diminishing or negative returns.

7. just before Stage II begins; In Stage I, as each worker is added, total product and marginal product increase. In Stage II, as each worker is added, marginal product is positive but decreasing. Therefore, the marginal product is greatest just before Stage II.

BusinessWeek

TEACH

As students read the article, ask if they can identify any other products that are given away free in order to sell a service. For instance, some companies that provide cellular telephone service offer the telephone free with the purchase of service. Others offer a certain number of free minutes when you buy their service. **Ask:** Why are companies giving away products with the purchase of a different product or service? How does this benefit the company and the consumer?

Refer to **Business Week Focus on the New Economy** in the TCR for additional unit-based articles.

APRIL 19, 1999

Newsclip

The price of the average desktop computer shrank by 17.3% in just one year. As prices continue to fall, computer makers are scrambling to find other ways to make a profit.

New Directions for
PC Makers

Hardly a week goes by that some wild-eyed startup doesn't announce a scheme to give away personal computers—as if the PC were some throwaway rather than the machine that ushered in the Information Age. On March 31, following in the footsteps of Free-PC, NuAction, and DirectWeb, New York-based Gobi said it would hand out free PCs to consumers who sign up for three years of Internet service. Meanwhile, emachines Inc. keeps cranking out PCs priced as low as $399, and startup Microworkz Computer Corp. says it will soon sell them for $299. . . .

. . . Two years of free-falling prices are squeezing the life out of margins, threatening to leave PC makers gasping for profits. . . . Analysts expect prices to plummet nearly 15% [in one year], capping industrywide sales growth at less than 5%. . . .

Suddenly, PC makers are heading off in surprising new directions. Dell and Compaq are developing E-commerce businesses—whether it's collecting monthly Internet service fees or becoming online sellers of everything from printers to carrying cases. . . .

Other PC makers think new gizmos are the answer. Compaq and Packard Bell NEC Inc. are preparing non-PC products such as cell phones and newfangled devices that act as Web-access machines. . . .

Ultimately, these launches into cyberspace could morph into sweeping new business models in which PC companies make money not on their hardware but on the services they can bundle with their boxes. Already, Gateway and Compaq get a share of monthly revenues from Internet service providers featured on their machines. And the more subscribers they sign up, the more advertisers will pay to get their ads to these potential shoppers.

–Reprinted from April 19, 1999 issue of *Business Week,* by special permission, copyright © 1999 by The McGraw-Hill Companies, Inc.

Examining the Newsclip

1. **Understanding Cause and Effect** Why are companies moving away from producing PCs?

2. **Making Generalizations** What are some companies doing in order to stay competitive in the computer industry?

Answers to Examining the Newsclip

1. The price of PCs has been plummeting for the past two years. Companies are not producing as many PCs because they are not making much profit from them.

2. Some companies are developing e-commerce business and producing non-PC products like cell phones and Web access machines.

Cost, Revenue, and Profit Maximization

Study Guide

Main Idea
Profit is maximized when the marginal costs of production equal the marginal revenue from sales.

Reading Strategy
Graphic Organizer As you read the section, complete a graphic organizer similar to the one below by explaining how total revenue differs from marginal revenue. Then provide an example of each.

Total revenue is: → Example:

Marginal revenue is: → Example:

Key Terms
fixed cost, overhead, variable cost, total cost, marginal cost, e-commerce, total revenue, marginal revenue, marginal analysis, break-even point, profit-maximizing quantity of output

Objectives
After studying this section, you will be able to:
1. **Define** four key measures of cost.
2. **Identify** two key measures of revenue.
3. **Apply** incremental analysis to business decisions.

Applying Economic Concepts
Overhead Overhead is one type of fixed cost that we try to avoid whenever we can. Read to see how overhead can even change the way people do business.

Cover Story

More Retailers Discover Net Auctions

Johnelle Lentner rarely made more than $250 a month peddling benches, chests, pie safes and other collectibles from the space she rented in an Isanti, Minnesota-based antiques shop.

Collectible available online

But last August, Lentner gave up brick-and-mortar retailing and took her business entirely online. Since ending the $60-a-month lease with Isanti Antiques to sell over Internet auction site eBay, Lentner's monthly income has shot up 700%.

"You get the highest dollar amount for what you're trying to sell online, and there is no overhead. . . ."

—USA Today, May 17, 1999

J ohnelle Lentner talked about eliminating overhead for her business. Overhead is one of many different measures of costs.

Measures of Cost

Because the cost of inputs influences efficient production decisions, a business must analyze costs before making its decisions. To simplify decision making, cost is divided into several different categories.

The first category is **fixed cost**—the cost that a business incurs even if the plant is idle and output is zero. It makes no difference whether the business produces nothing, very little, or a large amount. Total fixed cost, or **overhead,** remains the same.

Fixed costs include salaries paid to executives, interest charges on bonds, rent payments on leased properties, and local and state property taxes. Fixed costs also include depreciation, the

TEACH

ECONOMICS
AT A GLANCE

Answer: *Total cost is the sum of fixed and variable costs. Marginal cost is the extra cost incurred by producing one additional unit of product.*

L1 Classifying Costs

Review with students the different kinds of costs examined in this section. Then invite the principal to the class to discuss the cost of running the school. After the principal's talk, ask students to draw charts using *Fixed Costs* and *Variable Costs* as headings. Have students place in the proper category the various costs noted by the principal. Call on volunteers to present and explain their classifications. **ELL**

ECONOMICS
AT A GLANCE
Figure 5.6

Production, Costs, and Revenues

Regions of Production	Production Schedule			Costs				Revenues		Profit
	Number of Workers	Total Product	Marginal Product	Total Fixed Costs	Total Variable Costs	Total Costs	Marginal Costs	Total Revenue	Marginal Revenue	Total Profit
Stage I	0	0	0	$50	$0	$50	--	$0	--	–$50
	1	7	7	50	90	140	$13	105	$15	–35
	2	20	13	50	180	230	6.92	300	15	70
	3	38	18	50	270	320	5.00	570	15	250
	4	62	24	50	360	410	3.75	930	15	520
	5	90	28	50	450	500	3.21	1,350	15	850
Stage II	6	110	20	50	540	590	4.50	1,650	15	1,060
	7	129	19	50	630	680	4.74	1,935	15	1,210
	8	138	9	50	720	770	10.00	2,070	15	1,300
	9	144	6	50	810	860	15.00	2,160	15	1,300
	10	148	4	50	900	950	22.50	2,220	15	1,270
Stage III	11	145	–3	50	990	1,040	--	2,175	15	1,135
	12	135	–10	50	1,080	1,130	--	2,025	15	895

Using Tables The concepts of marginal product, marginal cost, and marginal revenue are central to economic analysis. Marginal product is used to define the three stages of production. Marginal cost and marginal revenue are used to determine the profit-maximizing quantity of output. **How do total costs differ from marginal costs?**

gradual wear and tear on capital goods over time and through use. A machine, for example, will not last forever because its parts will wear out slowly and eventually break.

The nature of fixed costs is illustrated in the fourth column of the table in **Figure 5.6,** which is an extension of the production schedule in **Figure 5.5.** Note that, regardless of the level of total output, fixed costs amount to $50.

Another kind of cost is **variable cost,** a cost that changes when the business rate of operation or output changes. While fixed costs generally are associated with machines and other capital goods, variable costs generally are associated with labor and raw materials. For example, wage-earning workers may be laid off or worked overtime as

output changes. Other examples of variable costs include electric power to run the machines and freight charges to ship the final product.

In **Figure 5.6** the only variable cost is labor. If one worker costs $90 per day, the total variable cost for one worker is $90. Two workers, or two units of variable input, cost $180, and so on.

The **total cost** of production is the sum of the fixed and variable costs. Total cost takes into account all the costs a business faces in the course of its operations. The business represented in **Figure 5.6,** for example, might employ six workers—costing $90 each for a total of $540—to produce 110 units of total output. If no other variable costs existed, and if fixed costs amounted to $50, the total cost of production would be $590.

MEETING SPECIAL NEEDS ACTIVITY

Learning Disabled For students who have problems with reading, model the use of the "Questions" component of the study routine. Explain that this exercise should be practiced whenever reading for information in a text. Read aloud the first sentence of each paragraph under the subheading "Marginal Analysis" on page 131. For the first paragraph, **ask:** What is marginal analysis? For the second paragraph, **ask:** What is meant by breaking even? Have students form other questions for the remaining paragraphs.

CYBERNOMICS SPOTLIGHT

Costs and Information Goods

Information goods, rather than industrial goods, are the key forces in many world markets. What are information goods? Essentially, they are anything that can be digitized—baseball scores, music, and stock quotes are all information goods. The cost structure of information goods is unusual. Production of information goods requires high fixed costs but low marginal costs. In other words, producing the first copy of an information good is costly, but the cost of reproducing additional copies is much less.

Another category of cost is **marginal cost**—the extra cost incurred when a business produces one additional unit of a product. Because fixed costs do not change from one level of production to another, marginal cost is the per-unit increase in variable costs that stems from using additional factors of production.

Figure 5.6 shows that the addition of the first worker increased the total product by seven units. Because total variable costs increased by $90, each of the additional seven units cost $12.86, or $90 divided by seven. If another worker is added, 13 more units of output will be produced for an additional cost of $90. The marginal, or extra, cost of each unit of output is $90 divided by 13, or $6.92.

Applying Cost Principles

The cost and combination, or mix, of inputs affects the way businesses produce. The following examples illustrate the importance of costs to business firms.

Self-Service Gas Station

Consider the case of a self-serve gas station with many pumps and a single attendant who works in an enclosed booth. This operation is likely to have large fixed costs, such as the cost of the lot, the pumps and tanks, and the taxes and licensing fees paid to state and local governments.

The variable costs, on the other hand, are relatively small. The station's variable costs include the hourly wage paid to the employee, the cost of electricity for lights and pumps, and the cost of the gas sold. When all costs are included, however, the ratio of variable to fixed costs is low.

As a result, the owner may operate the station 24 hours a day, seven days a week for a relatively low cost. Even the extra cost of keeping the station open between the hours of midnight and 6:00 A.M. is minimal. As a result, the extra wages, the electricity, and other variable costs are minor and may be covered by the profits of the extra sales.

Internet Stores

Stores are flocking to the Internet, making it one of the fastest-growing areas of business today, and for reasons largely related to cost. Specifically, many stores are using the Internet because the overhead, or the fixed cost of operation, is so low.

An individual engaged in **e-commerce**—electronic business or exchange conducted over the Internet—does not need to spend large sums of money to rent a building and stock it with inventory. Instead, for just a fraction of the cost of a store, the e-commerce business owner can purchase Web access along with an e-commerce software package

STANDARD & POOR'S INFOBYTE

Measures of Cost Variable costs represent expenses a corporation incurs that change with that company's level of business activity. Fixed costs represent expenses a corporation incurs that remain relatively stable despite a change in the level of that company's business activity. Expense items which generally remain fixed for any given reporting period include rent, depreciation, property tax, and executive salaries.

CHAPTER 5: SUPPLY **129**

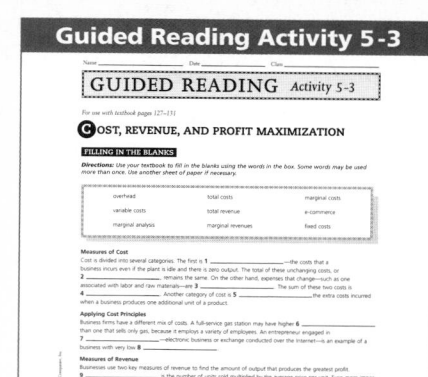

Guided Reading Activity 5-3

GUIDED READING Activity 5-3

For use with textbook pages 127–131

COST, REVENUE, AND PROFIT MAXIMIZATION

FILLING IN THE BLANKS

Directions: Use your textbook to fill in the blanks using the words in the box. Some words may be used more than once. Use another sheet of paper if necessary.

overhead	total costs	marginal costs
variable costs	total revenue	e-commerce
marginal analysis	marginal revenue	fixed costs

Measures of Cost

Cost is divided into several categories. The first is 1 _____—the costs that a business incurs even if the plant is idle and there is zero output. The total of these unchanging costs, or 2 _____, remains the same. On the other hand, expenses that change—such as one associated with labor and raw materials—are 3 _____. The sum of these two costs is 4 _____. Another category of cost is 5 _____, the extra costs incurred when a business produces one additional unit of a product.

Applying Cost Principles

Business firms have a different mix of costs. A full-service gas station may have large 6 _____ than one that sells only gas, because it employs a variety of employees. An entrepreneur engaged in 7 _____—electronic business or exchange conducted over the Internet—is an example of a business with very low 8 _____.

Measures of Revenue

Businesses use two key measures of revenue to find the amount of output that produces the greatest profit. 9 _____ is the number of units sold multiplied by the average price per unit. Even more important are 10 _____, which are the extra revenues associated with the production and sale of one additional unit of output.

CURRICULUM CONNECTION

Language Arts In everyday usage, the words "cost" and "price" often are used interchangeably. For example, when someone says, "The cost of living is going up," he or she is comparing the prices of goods and services today with prices during an earlier time. For economists, however, the terms "price" and "cost" are distinct. Economists define price as the amount consumers are willing and able to pay for goods and services. Cost is expressed in terms of opportunity cost, or that which is given up to do something else. To accountants, cost entails all the expenses directly related to doing business, while business managers define it as anything that reduces profits.

FREE ENTERPRISE ACTIVITY

More than 200 years ago, the U.S. Constitution established a climate for profit maximizing. First, there were no barriers to trade among the states, which allowed businesses to expand markets for their products and services. Second, the federal government assumed control over monetary matters, creating relative confidence about monetary stability. Third, the Constitution supported property rights and the enforcement of contracts. Today, the American economy is still driven by the opportunity to make profits. Ask students to investigate the Constitution, as well as federal and state laws that affect business's drive to maximize profits. Have students share their findings with the class. **BLOCK SCHEDULING**

F.Y.I.

All costs are variable in the long run.

3 ASSESS

Assign Section 3 Assessment as homework or as an in-class activity.

◾ Have students use **Interactive Tutor Self-Assessment Software.**

Section Quiz 5-3

QUIZ ◆ Chapter 5, Section 3

COST, REVENUE, AND PROFIT MAXIMIZATION [SCORE]

Matching: Match each item in Column A with the items in Column B. Write the correct letters in the blanks. (10 points each)

A
1. fixed cost
2. variable cost
3. marginal cost
4. total revenue
5. e-commerce

B
a. cost that a business incurs even if the plant is idle and output is zero
b. extra cost incurred when a business produces one additional unit of a product
c. sum of the fixed and variable costs
d. cost that changes when the business rate of operation or output changes
e. electronic business or exchange conducted over the Internet
f. the number of units sold multiplied by the average price per unit

Multiple Choice: In the blank at the left write the letter of the choice that best completes the statement or answers the question. (10 points each)

6. Cost-benefit decision making that compares the extra benefits to the extra costs of an action is called
   a. marginal revenue   b. marginal costs.
   c. marginal analysis.   d. marginal output.
7. The total cost of production is determined by
   a. adding fixed and variable costs.   b. adding marginal and fixed costs.
   c. multiplying fixed and variable costs. d. multiplying marginal and fixed costs.
8. All of the following are examples of variable costs EXCEPT
   a. labor.   b. height.
   c. interest payments on bonds.   d. electricity.
9. If a business's fixed costs are large relative to its variable costs, it is likely to

MASTER MARKETER

Kathryn Leary helps entrepreneurs enter new markets. Among the services Leary offers are establishing contacts and coordinating trade missions.

After viewing the proverbial glass ceiling first-hand at a majority of firms, Leary, 47, felt it was time to venture off on her own.

"Once I realized the large companies had overseas offices, it became my goal to go abroad," Leary says. "But this was denied me. I started my company to help Americans market in other countries."

To prepare for doing business in Japan, Leary took language classes to master basic greetings and common phrases, studied the culture at the Asia Society in New York, subscribed to the international edition of the Japan *Times* and other magazines and newsletters and read books on Japanese business customs. . . .

—*Black Enterprise,* August 1999

Critical Thinking

1. **Finding the Main Idea** Why did Leary start her own company?

2. **Analyzing Information** What services does Leary's company provide? Why do you think her service is useful?

that provides everything from Web catalog pages to ordering, billing, and accounting software. The e-commerce business owner inserts pictures and descriptions of the products for sale into the software and loads the program.

When customers visit the "store" on the Web, they see what appears to be a full range of merchandise for sale. In some cases, the owner has the goods in stock, as with Johnelle Lentner's antique auction site. In other cases, the store takes the orders and forwards them to the manufacturer or to specialty warehouses that handle the shipping.

Measures of Revenue

Businesses use two key measures of revenue to find the amount of output that will produce the greatest profits. The first is total revenue, and the second is marginal revenue.

The **total revenue** is the number of units sold multiplied by the average price per unit. If 7 units are sold at $15 each, the total revenue is $105, as shown in the total revenue column in **Figure 5.6.** The second, and more important, measure of revenue is **marginal revenue,** the extra revenue associated with the production and sale of one additional unit of output.

The marginal revenues in **Figure 5.6** are determined by dividing the change in total revenue by the marginal product. When a business has no workers, it produces no output, and it receives no revenue. When it adds the first worker, total output jumps to 7 units, and $105 of total revenue is generated. Because the $105 is earned from the sale of 7 units of output, each unit must have added $15. Therefore, the marginal, or extra, revenue each unit of output brings in is $15.

Keep in mind that whenever an additional worker is added, the marginal revenue computation remains the same. If the business employs five workers, it produces 90 units of output and generates $1,350 of total revenue. If a sixth worker is added, output increases by 20 units, and total revenues increase to $1,650. To have increased total revenue by $300, each of the 20 additional units of output must have added $15.

If each unit of output sells for $15, the marginal or extra revenue earned by the sale of one more unit is $15. For this reason, the marginal revenue appears to be constant at $15 for every level of output. While marginal revenue is constant in **Figure 5.6,** this will not always be the case. Businesses often find that marginal revenues start high and then decrease as more and more units are produced and sold.

130 UNIT 2 MICROECONOMICS

CRITICAL THINKING

Identifying Alternatives Have students discuss their assumptions about a product that a business advertises and sells through a store, a catalog, or over the Internet. Students should recognize that buyers assume that an advertised product is available. At times, the seller's supply is too small because the demand was underestimated. Have students use newspapers, periodicals, and the Internet to research situations when the supply of a product ran short. Have them discuss the situations and how the businesses handled them. Next, have students predict how companies can prevent and react to future product shortages. Discuss students' ideas as a class.

Marginal Analysis

 Economists use **marginal analysis,** a type of cost-benefit decision making that compares the extra benefits to the extra costs of an action. Marginal analysis is helpful in a number of situations, including break-even analysis and profit maximization. In each case the process involves comparing the costs and benefits of decisions that are made in small, incremental steps.

The **break-even point** is the total output or total product the business needs to sell in order to cover its total costs. In **Figure 5.6,** the break-even point is between 7 and 20 units of total product, so at least two workers would have to be hired to break even.

A business wants to do more than break even, however. It wants to make as much profit as it can. We know that the business represented in **Figure 5.6** will break even when it hires the second worker. But, how many workers and what level of output are needed to generate the maximum profits?

The owners of the business can decide by comparing marginal costs and marginal revenues. The business would probably hire the sixth worker, for example, because the extra output would only cost $4.50 to produce, and would generate $15 in revenues. In general, as long as the marginal cost is less than the marginal revenue, the business will keep hiring workers.

Having made a profit with the sixth worker, the business probably would hire the seventh and eighth workers. If it hired the ninth worker, however, the cost of the additional output would equal the additional revenue earned when the product was sold. The addition of the ninth worker neither adds to nor takes away from total profits—so the firm would have little incentive to hire the tenth worker. If it did, it would quickly discover that profits would go down, and it would go back to using nine workers.

When marginal cost is less than marginal revenue, more variable inputs should be hired to expand output. The **profit-maximizing quantity of output** is reached when marginal cost and marginal revenue are equal. In **Figure 5.6,** profits are maximized when the ninth worker is hired. Other combinations may generate equal profits, but no other combination will be more profitable.

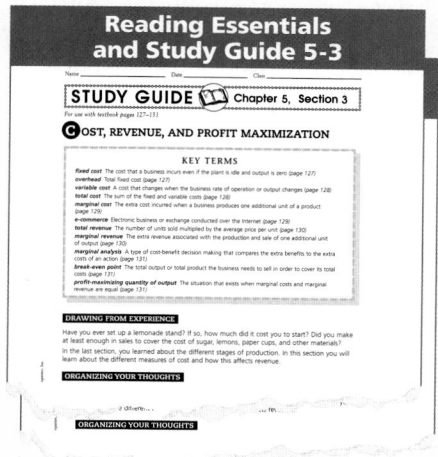

Student Web Activity Visit the *Economics: Principles and Practices* Web site at epp.glencoe.com and click on *Chapter 5—Student Web Activities* for an activity on the operation of a company.

Section 3 Assessment

Checking for Understanding

1. **Main Idea** Using your notes from the graphic organizer activity on page 127, describe how cost affects total revenue.

2. **Key Terms** Define fixed cost, overhead, variable cost, total cost, marginal cost, e-commerce, total revenue, marginal revenue, marginal analysis, break-even point, profit-maximizing quantity of output.

3. **List** the four measures of cost.

4. **Describe** the two measures of revenue.

5. **Explain** the use of marginal analysis for break-even and profit-maximizing decisions.

Applying Economic Concepts

6. **Overhead** How might overhead affect the price of a new car?

Critical Thinking

7. **Understanding Cause and Effect** Many oil-processing plants operate 24 hours a day, using several shifts of workers to maintain operations. How do you think a plant's fixed and variable costs affect its decision to operate around the clock?

Practice and *assess* key social studies skills with the *Glencoe Skillbuilder Interactive Workbook, Level 2.*

CHAPTER 5: SUPPLY **131**

Section 3 Assessment Answers

1. The cost of inputs influences supply. The supply influences the number sold. The number sold multiplied by the average price per unit is the total revenue.

2. All vocabulary terms are defined in the text.

3. fixed cost, variable cost, total cost, marginal cost

4. See page 130 for descriptions of total revenue and marginal revenue.

5. By comparing the marginal revenue and the marginal cost of adding units of variable input, break-even and profit-maximizing points can be established.

6. A car manufacturer or dealer with high overhead may need to charge more.

7. When variable costs are small relative to fixed costs, the additional cost of operating around the clock is low.

Reteach

Reading Essentials and Study Guide 5-3

Name_____ Date_____ Class_____

STUDY GUIDE 📀 Chapter 5, Section 3

For use with textbook pages 127–131

COST, REVENUE, AND PROFIT MAXIMIZATION

KEY TERMS

fixed cost The cost that a business incurs even if the plant is idle and output is zero (page 127)
overhead Total fixed cost (page 127)
variable cost A cost that changes when the business rate of operation or output changes (page 128)
total cost The sum of the fixed and variable costs (page 128)
marginal cost The extra cost incurred when a business produces one additional unit of a product (page 129)
e-commerce Electronic business or exchange conducted over the Internet (page 129)
total revenue The number of units sold multiplied by the average price per unit (page 130)
marginal revenue The extra revenue associated with the production and sale of one additional unit of output (page 130)
marginal analysis A type of cost-benefit decision making that compares the extra benefits to the extra costs of an action (page 131)
break-even point The total output or total product the business needs to sell in order to cover its total costs (page 131)
profit-maximizing quantity of output The situation that exists when marginal costs and marginal revenue are equal (page 131)

DRAWING FROM EXPERIENCE

Have you ever set up a lemonade stand? If so, how much did it cost you to start? Did you make at least enough in sales to cover the cost of sugar, lemons, paper cups, and other materials? In the last section, you learned about the different stages of production. In this section you will learn about the different measures of cost and how this affects revenue.

ORGANIZING YOUR THOUGHTS

ORGANIZING YOUR THOUGHTS

Enrich

Have students interview local business owners and managers, asking them to explain why profit maximization is important to them.

Objectives, goals, and answers to the student activity can be found in the **Web Activity Lesson Plan** feature at epp.glencoe.com

4 **CLOSE**

Ask students to consider which, if any, of society's economic goals are furthered by profit maximization. *(economic freedom, economic efficiency)*

Teaching Skills

Ask a student to identify the main ideas in Section 2. Review the system of outlining with Roman numerals, capital letters, Arabic numerals, and lowercase letters. Work through a portion of an outline for Section 2 with the students, writing their ideas on the board. Have students explain their choices for each of the outline points.

Additional Practice

Reinforcing Economic Skill 28

Name _____ Date _____ Class _____

Reinforcing Economic Skills   **Chapter 28**

⊙ OUTLINING

Before beginning a writing assignment, most writers find it helpful to create an outline. To make an outline, begin by listing all the topics you want to include about the subject in the order in which you want to include them. Then group similar topics together and list important details for each topic. Use the standard outline format using Roman numerals, then capital letters, then Arabic numerals to identify the various sections and subsections of your report. Remember that you need to have two items for each level of your outline.

Directions: Using the Internet and other resources, research information to create an outline for a short biography of one of the Nobel prize-winning economists listed below.

Selected Nobel Prize-Winning Economists

Robert A. Mundell (1999)   George J. Stigler (1982)
Amartya Sen (1998)   Milton Friedman (1976)
Robert C. Merton (1997)   Paul A. Samuelson (1970)
Gary S. Becker (1992)

Biography Title: _____

_____
_____
_____
_____
_____

GLENCOE TECHNOLOGY

Glencoe Skillbuilder Interactive Workbook, Level 2

This interactive CD-ROM reinforces student mastery of essential social studies skills.

Outlining

Outlining may be used as a starting point for a writer. The writer begins with the rough shape of the material and gradually fills in the details in a logical manner. You may also use outlining as a method of note taking and organizing information as you read.

Learning the Skill

There are two types of outlines—formal and informal. Making an informal outline is similar to taking notes—you write words and phrases needed to remember main ideas. A formal outline has a standard format. Follow these steps to formally outline material.

- Read the text to identify the main ideas. Label these with Roman numerals.

- Write subtopics under each main idea. Label these ideas with capital letters.

- Write supporting details for each subtopic. Label these with Arabic numerals.

- Each level should have at least two entries and should be indented from the level above.

Production on the assembly line

- All entries use the same grammatical form, whether phrases or complete sentences.

I. An Introduction to Supply
  A. The Supply Schedule
    1.
    2. Prices and quantities move in same direction.
  B. The Individual Supply Curve
    1.
    2.
  C. The Market Supply Curve
    1.
    2.
  D.
    1.
    2.
II. Change in Supply
  A.
  B. Productivity
  C.
  D.
  E. Expectations
  F.
  G.

Practicing the Skill

On a separate sheet of paper, copy the following outline of the main ideas in the first part of Section 1 of Chapter 5. Then use your textbook to fill in the missing subtopics and details.

Application Activity

Following the guidelines above, prepare an outline for Section 3 of Chapter 5.

 Practice and **assess** key social studies skills with the *Glencoe Skillbuilder Interactive Workbook, Level 2.*

Answers to Practicing the Skill

Answers should include the appropriate subtopics and details from Section 1.

Section 1

What Is Supply? (pages 113–120)

- **Supply** is the quantities of output that producers will bring to market at each and every price. Supply can be represented in a **supply schedule,** or graphically as a **supply curve.**

- The **Law of Supply** states that the quantities of an economic product offered for sale vary directly with its price. If prices are high, suppliers will offer greater quantities for sale. If prices are low, they will offer smaller quantities for sale.

- The **market supply curve** is the sum of the individual supply curves.

- A **change in quantity supplied** is represented by a movement along the supply curve.

- A **change in supply** is a change in the quantity that will be supplied at each and every price. An increase in supply is presented graphically as a shift of the supply curve to the right, and a decrease in supply appears as a shift of the supply curve to the left.

- Changes in supply can be caused by a change in the cost of inputs, productivity, new technology, taxes, **subsidies,** expectations, government regulations, and number of sellers.

- **Supply elasticity** describes how a change in quantity supplied responds to a change in price.

- If supply is elastic, a given change in price will cause a more than proportional change in quantity supplied. If supply is inelastic, a given change in price will cause a less than proportional change in quantity supplied. If supply is unit elastic, a given change in price will cause a proportional change in quantity supplied.

Section 2

The Theory of Production (pages 122–125)

- The **theory of production** deals with the relationship between the factors of production and the output of goods and services.

- The theory of production deals with the **short run,** a production period so short that only the variable input (usually labor) can be changed. This contrasts to the **long run,** a production period long enough for all inputs—including capital—to vary.

- The **Law of Variable Proportions** states that the quantity of output will vary as increasing units of a single input are added. This law is presented graphically in the form of a **production function.**

- The two most important measures of output are **total product** and **marginal product,** the extra output gained from adding one additional unit of input.

- Three **stages of production**—increasing returns, **diminishing returns,** and negative returns—show how marginal product changes when additional variable inputs are added. Production takes place in Stage II under conditions of diminishing returns.

Section 3

Cost, Revenue, and Profit Maximization (pages 127–131)

- Four important measures of cost exist: **total cost,** which is the sum of **fixed cost** and **variable cost,** and **marginal cost,** which is the increase in total cost that stems from producing one additional unit of output.

- The mix of variable and fixed costs that a business faces affects the way the business operates.

- The key measure of revenue is **marginal revenue,** which is the change in total revenue when one more unit of output is sold.

- The **profit-maximizing quantity of output** occurs when marginal cost is exactly equal to **marginal revenue.** Other quantities of output may yield the same profit, but none yield more.

ECONOMICS & YOU

Chapter 6
Disc 1, Side 1

What Is Supply?

Also available in VHS.

Using the Chapter 5 Summary

Use the Chapter 5 Summary to preview, review, condense, or reteach the chapter.

Preview/Review

Vocabulary PuzzleMaker CD-ROM reinforces Key Terms.

Interactive Tutor Self-Assessment Software provides a review of Chapter 5 content.

Condense

Have students listen to the Chapter 5 Audio Program. Spanish also available.

Assign the Chapter 5 Audio Program Activity and give students the Chapter 5 Audio Program Test.

Have students complete the Guided Reading Activities and Reading Essentials and Study Guides for Chapter 5.

Reteach

Have students complete Reteaching Activity 5 in the TCR. Spanish also available.

Teacher's Notes / Internet Bookmarks

GLENCOE TECHNOLOGY

Use **MindJogger Videoquiz** to review the Chapter 5 content.

Have students visit the Web site at epp.glencoe.com to review Chapter 5 and take the **Self-Check Quiz.**

Identifying Key Terms

1. c	7. f
2. d	8. a
3. b	9. i
4. j	10. h
5. g	11. l
6. e	12. k

Reviewing the Facts

Section 1

1. quantities of a product offered for sale at all possible prices that could prevail in the market
2. Individual supply curves show quantities of a product supplied at each and every market price; market supply curves show quantities of a product at various prices by all firms that market the product.
3. the change in the amount of a product offered for sale in response to a price change
4. cost of inputs, productivity, technology, number of sellers, taxes and subsidies, expectations, government regulations

Section 2

5. In the short run, output will change as one input is varied while others remain constant.
6. Total product is total output produced by a firm; marginal product is extra output generated by adding one more unit of variable input.

Self-Check Quiz Visit the *Economics: Principles and Practices* Web site at epp.glencoe.com and click on *Chapter 5—Self-Check Quizzes* to prepare for the chapter test.

Identifying Key Terms

On a separate sheet of paper, write the letter of the key term that best matches each definition below.

a. depreciation	g. production function
b. diminishing returns	h. profit-maximizing
c. fixed cost	i. total cost
d. marginal analysis	j. variable cost
e. marginal product	k. overhead
f. marginal revenue	l. total product

1. a production cost that does not change as total business output changes
2. decision making that compares the additional costs with the additional benefits of an action
3. associated with Stage II of production
4. a production cost that changes when output changes
5. a graphical representation of the theory of production
6. the additional output produced when one additional unit of input is added
7. change in total revenue from the sale of one additional unit of output
8. the gradual wearing out of capital goods
9. the sum of variable and fixed costs
10. when marginal revenue equals marginal cost
11. total output produced by a firm
12. total fixed costs

Reviewing the Facts

Section 1 (pages 113–120)

1. **Describe** what is meant by supply.
2. **Distinguish** between the individual supply curve and the market supply curve.
3. **Explain** what is meant by a change in quantity supplied.
4. **Identify** the factors that cause a change in supply.

Section 2 (pages 122–125)

5. **Describe** the Law of Variable Proportions.
6. **Explain** the difference between total product and marginal product.
7. **Identify** the three stages of production.

Section 3 (pages 127–131)

8. **Describe** the relationship between marginal cost and total cost.
9. **Identify** four measures of cost.
10. **Describe** one practical application of cost principles.

Thinking Critically

1. **Making Comparisons** Create a chart like the one below to help you explain how supply differs from demand.

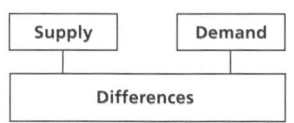

2. **Making Generalizations** Why might production functions tend to differ from one firm to another?
3. **Understanding Cause and Effect** Explain why e-commerce reduces fixed costs.

---

7. increasing returns, diminishing returns, and negative returns

Section 3

8. Marginal cost is the change in total cost incurred by producing one additional unit of a product. Total cost is the sum of fixed and variable costs.
9. total cost, fixed cost, variable cost, marginal cost
10. Answers should reflect an understanding of the importance of cost to business firms.

Thinking Critically

1. Charts should reflect an understanding of supply and demand.
2. Because different firms have different technologies and use different amounts of variable inputs, the production function for each firm will vary.
3. Fixed costs, like interest charges on bonds, rent payments, and property taxes do not apply to e-commerce. Web access and software are the only fixed costs for e-commerce businesses.

Applying Economic Concepts

1. **Supply** According to the Law of Supply, what will happen to the number of products a firm offers for sale when prices go down? What will happen to the cost of additional units of production when a firm starts having diminishing returns? What will happen to the number of products a firm will offer for sale if its cost of production increases while prices remain the same?

2. **Marginal Analysis** Give an example of a recent decision you made in which you used the tools of marginal analysis.

Math Practice

Create a supply schedule and a supply graph that shows the following information: American automakers are willing to sell 200,000 cars per year when the price of a car is $6,000. They are willing to sell 400,000 when the price is $12,000, and 600,000 at a price of $18,000.

Thinking Like an Economist

Label the following actions according to their placement in the stages of production: (a) After many hours of studying, you are forgetting some of the material you learned earlier. (b) You are studying for a test and learning rapidly. (c) After a few hours, you are still learning but not as fast as before.

Technology Skill

Using a Database For one week, record every service or job you perform for anyone else. Organize the services and the amount of time spent on each into two columns: Paid Work and Unpaid Work. Use this information to help you build an "employment" database.

1. Define and name the fields in your database. The following can be used as examples:

Field Name	Field Type
Job/Service	Text
Employer's Name	Text
Employer's Phone	Number
Hourly Wage/Fee	Number
Hours Worked	Number

2. Save the database.

3. Change field size as needed so that all information in each field is visible.

4. Use the speller, proofread, and preview the database. Save the database again.

5. Print your database while in list view.

Building Skills

Outlining On a separate sheet of paper, add supporting details to the outline of Section 2 below.

```
I.   Law of Variable Proportions
     A.
          1.
          2.
     B.
          1.
          2.
II.  The Production Function
     A.
          1.
          2.
     B.
          1.
          2.
III. Three Stages of Production
     A.
     B.
     C.
```

 Practice and **assess** key social studies skills with the *Glencoe Skillbuilder Interactive Workbook, Level 2.*

Technology Skill

Check students' databases for correct form.

Building Skills

Outlines should demonstrate knowledge of the outlining process.

? Bonus Test Question

Suppose economists predict that the price of oil will rise by 25 percent in the next two years. How might this affect the number of wildcatters—people who drill for oil in hopes of finding new supplies? Explain. *(The number of wildcatters would likely go up, as more people would seek oil to sell at the higher prices.)*

Applying Economic Concepts

1. When prices go down, the amount offered for sale will also go down. Each unit of production will cost more. There will be a decrease in supply.

2. Examples should reflect an understanding of marginal analysis.

Math Practice

The supply schedule should show prices and quantities moving in the same direction (increasing). The supply graph should be upward sloping to the right for price and quantity.

Thinking Like an Economist

(a) Stage III—negative returns
(b) Stage I—increasing returns
(c) Stage II—diminishing returns

Chapter 6 Resource Manager

SECTION RESOURCES

Daily Objectives	Reproducible Resources	Technology/Multimedia Resources
Section 1 **Prices as Signals** 1. Explain how prices act as signals. 2. Describe the advantages of using prices as a way to allocate economic products. 3. Understand the difficulty of allocating scarce goods and services without using prices.	Reproducible Lesson Plan 6-1 Daily Lecture Notes 6-1 Guided Reading Activity 6-1 Reading Essentials and Study Guide 6-1 Section Quiz 6-1*	Daily Focus Transparency 25 Interactive Tutor Self-Assessment Software ExamView® Pro Testmaker Presentation Plus!
Section 2 **The Price System at Work** 1. Understand how prices are determined in competitive markets. 2. Explain how economic models can be used to predict and explain price changes. 3. Apply the concepts of elasticity to changes in prices.	Reproducible Lesson Plan 6-2 Daily Lecture Notes 6-2 Guided Reading Activity 6-2 Reading Essentials and Study Guide 6-2 Section Quiz 6-2*	Daily Focus Transparency 14 Interactive Economics! Interactive Tutor Self-Assessment Software ExamView® Pro Testmaker Presentation Plus!
Section 3 **Social Goals vs. Market Efficiency** 1. Describe the consequence of having a fixed price in a market. 2. Explain how loan supports and deficiency payments work. 3. Understand what is meant when "markets talk."	Reproducible Lesson Plan 6-3 Daily Lecture Notes 6-3 Guided Reading Activity 6-3 Reading Essentials and Study Guide 6-3 Section Quiz 6-3*	Daily Focus Transparency 26 Vocabulary PuzzleMaker CD-ROM Interactive Economics! NBR Economics & You Video Program Interactive Tutor Self-Assessment Software ExamView® Pro Testmaker Presentation Plus!

Also available in Spanish

 Transparency   ● CD-ROM   💾 Software   Blackline Master

◎ Videodisc   ∩ Audio Program   ▦ Videocassette

0:00 **OUT OF TIME?**
Assign the Chapter 6 Audio Program activity and test. ∩

Block Schedule

Activities that are particularly suited to use within the block scheduling framework are identified throughout this chapter by the following designation: 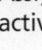 **BLOCK SCHEDULING**

KEY TO ABILITY LEVELS

Teaching strategies have been coded for varying learning styles and abilities.
L1 **BASIC** activities for all students
L2 **AVERAGE** activities for average to above-average students
L3 **CHALLENGING** activities for above-average students
ELL **ENGLISH LANGUAGE LEARNER** activities

Chapter 6 Resource Manager

Timesaving Tools

TeacherWorks™ All-In-One Planner and Resource Center

- **Interactive Teacher Edition** Access your Teacher Wraparound Edition and your classroom resources with a few easy clicks.

- **Interactive Lesson Planner** Planning has never been easier! Organize your week, month, semester, or year with all the lesson helps you need to make teaching creative, timely, and relevant.

Use Glencoe's **Presentation Plus!** multimedia teacher tool to easily present dynamic lessons that visually excite your students. Using Microsoft PowerPoint® you can customize the presentations to create your own personalized lessons.

PRESENTATION *Plus!*

ACTIVITY

From the Classroom of...

Cari Gray
New Braunfels
High School
New Braunfels, TX

Price Ceilings and Floors

My students need a great deal of practice to understand and graph supply and demand curves. I use the concepts of price ceilings and floors as an opportunity to practice these skills in conjunction with the new knowledge from the chapter.

1. **Price ceilings:** Using an example of rent control and some brochures for area apartment complexes, ask students to graph the supply and demand curves for 2-bedroom, 1-bath apartments. Note the equilibrium price and discuss the results of their graphs. Then set a price ceiling, which students mark and label on their graphs. Discuss how and why price ceilings might help or hurt renters or discourage suppliers.

2. **Price floors:** Have students graph the supply and demand curves for grocery clerk jobs at area grocery stores. After noting the equilibrium wage, have students graph the current minimum wage and label it as a price floor. Discuss how price floors affect the availability of jobs (such as waiting tables) that allow employers to pay below the price floor. You might also want to discuss whether there should be a "lower" price floor for teenagers.

National Council on Economic Education

THE **Economics**America AND **Economics**International PROGRAMS

Voluntary National Content Standards in Economics
Emphasized in Chapter 6

Content Standard 4

Content Standard 7

Content Standard 8

Content Standard 17

For a complete listing of NCEE Standards and entire text correlation, see Teacher pages in front of book.

Resources Available from NCEE
- Capstone: The Nation's High School Economics Course
- Focus: High School Economics
- Personal Decision Making: Focus on Economics

To order these materials or to contact your state Council on Economic Education about workshops and programs, call 1-800-338-1192 or visit www.nationalcouncil.org

Chapter 6 Resource Manager

Economic Concept Transparency 7: Markets and Prices

APPLICATION AND ENRICHMENT

Consumer Application Activity 6

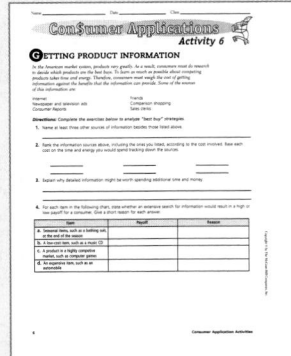

Free Enterprise Activity 6

APPLICATION AND ENRICHMENT

Enrichment Activity 6

Cooperative Learning Activity 6

Math Practice Activity 6

Economic Cartoon 6

Primary and Secondary Source Reading 6

REVIEW AND REINFORCEMENT

Economic Vocabulary Activity 6

Reteaching Activity 6

Critical Thinking Activity 6

Reinforcing Economic Skill 20

Chapter 6 Resource Manager

ASSESSMENT AND EVALUATION

Chapter 6 Test Form A

Chapter 6 Test Form B

Performance Assessment Activity 6

ExamView® Pro Testmaker

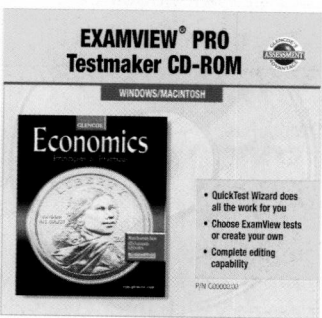

SPANISH RESOURCES

The following Spanish language materials are available in the Spanish Resources binder:

 Spanish Economic Vocabulary Activities

 Spanish Reteaching Activities

 Spanish Section Quizzes

 Spanish Economic Concepts Transparencies

Also available:

  Spanish Chapter 6 Audio Program Activity and Test

TECHNOLOGY/MULTIMEDIA

- Vocabulary PuzzleMaker CD-ROM
- Interactive Tutor Self-Assessment Software
- ExamView® Pro Testmaker
- Audio Program (English or Spanish)
- NBR Economics & You Video Program (English or Spanish)
- MindJogger Videoquiz
- Interactive Economics! CD-ROM
- Presentation Plus!
- TeacherWorks CD-ROM
- Glencoe Skillbuilder Interactive Workbook CD-ROM, Level 2

ECONOMICS Online

Use our Web site for additional resources. All essential content is covered in the Student Edition.

You and your students can visit epp.glencoe.com, the Web site companion to **Economics: Principles and Practices.** This innovative integration of electronic and print media offers your students a wealth of opportunities. The student text directs students to the Web site for the following options:

- **Chapter Overviews**
- **Student Web Activities**
- **Self-Check Quizzes**
- **Textbook Updates**

Answers are provided for you in the Web Activity Lesson Plan. Additional Web resources and interactive puzzles are also available.

CHAPTER 6

Prices and Decision Making

Economics & You

What factors do you consider when you need to make a decision to buy something? Price may be one of the most important factors of all. In this chapter, you will learn how price serves as a signal to both buyers and sellers. To learn more about the effect of supply and demand on prices, view the Chapter 12 video lesson:

The Price System at Work

ECONOMICS Online

Chapter Overview Visit the *Economics: Principles and Practices* Web site at epp.glencoe.com and click on **Chapter 6—Chapter Overviews** to preview chapter information.

Dakota Whole Wheat $4.75

Spinach Feta $5.25

Prices for products in a market economy are determined by the interaction of supply and demand.

Prices as Signals

Study Guide

Main Idea
Competitive markets and prices are important to capitalism.

Reading Strategy
Graphic Organizer As you read the section, complete a graphic organizer similar to the one below by providing examples from your own experience that show how the price system provides for freedom of choice.

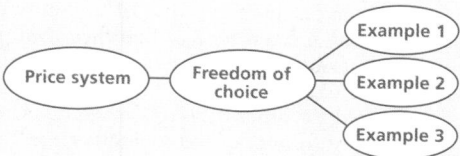

Price system → Freedom of choice → Example 1 / Example 2 / Example 3

Key Terms
price, rationing, ration coupon, rebate

Objectives
After studying this section, you will be able to:
1. **Explain** how prices act as signals.
2. **Describe** the advantages of using prices as a way to allocate economic products.
3. **Understand** the difficulty of allocating scarce goods and services without using prices.

Applying Economic Concepts
Rationing Have you and your friends ever tried to share something—a candy bar, cake, or pizza—when there really wasn't enough to go around? Read to find out about different ways to deal with making allocations.

① FOCUS

Section Overview
This section discusses prices as signals to producers and consumers.

BELLRINGER
Motivational Activity

- Project **transparency** and have students answer questions.

- Available as blackline master.

Daily Focus Transparency 25

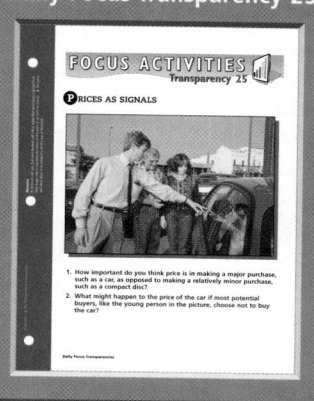

FOCUS ACTIVITIES
Transparency 25
PRICES AS SIGNALS

1. How important do you think price is in making a major purchase, such as a car, as opposed to making a relatively minor purchase, such as a compact disc?
2. What might happen to the price of the car if most potential buyers, like the young person in the picture, choose not to buy the car?

Daily Focus Transparency

Cover Story

Cuban Fans Left Out of O's Game

HAVANA—Cuban baseball fans expressed dismay Thursday that attendance at Sunday's highly anticipated exhibition game with the Baltimore Orioles would be by invitation only.

Only Cubans invited by the Communist Party or trade unions will be allowed to attend the game with the Orioles,

Off-the-field controversy over-shadowed the game.

the first Major League team to play here since Fidel Castro came to power in 1959. . . .

Baseball fans here have made no secret of their distress. At Havana's *Esquino Caliente* (Hot Corner), . . . (fans) complained that "90% of the people who got the invitations don't know baseball. The real fans are the people who deserve the seats."

—*USA Today*, March 26, 1999

Life is full of signals that help us make decisions. For example, when we pull up to an intersection, we look to see if the traffic light is green, yellow, or red. We look at the other cars to see if any have their blinkers on, and in this way receive signals from other drivers regarding their intentions to turn. Doctors even tell us that pain is a signal that something is wrong with our body and may need attention. But have you ever thought about the signals that help us make our everyday economic decisions?

It turns out that something as simple as a **price**—the monetary value of a product as established by supply and demand—is a signal that helps us make our economic decisions. Prices communicate information and provide incentives to buyers and sellers. High prices are signals for producers to produce more and for buyers to buy less. Low prices are signals for producers to produce less and for buyers to buy more.

Advantages of Prices

Prices serve as a link between producers and consumers. In doing so, they help decide the three basic WHAT, HOW, and FOR WHOM questions all societies face. Without

CHAPTER 6: PRICES AND DECISION MAKING **137**

Study Guide

Reading Strategy
Have students create the graphic organizer.
Answers to Graphic: *Answers should reflect understanding of price and its importance to buyers/sellers.*

Preteaching Vocabulary
Have students define "rationing" and provide real-life examples.

RESOURCE MANAGER

📁 Reproducible Masters
- Reproducible Lesson Plan 6-1
- Daily Lecture Notes 6-1
- Guided Reading Activity 6-1
- Reading Essentials and Study Guide 6-1
- Section Quiz 6-1

📽 Transparencies
- Daily Focus Transparency 25

Multimedia
- 💾 Interactive Tutor Self-Assessment Software
- ⓘ ExamView® Pro Testmaker
- ⓘ Presentation Plus!

TEACH

Daily Lecture Notes 6-1

DAILY LECTURE NOTES Lesson 6-1

DID YOU KNOW?
During the oil crisis in the early 1970s, the proposed gas rationing program raised serious differences of opinion among Americans. Some people argued that every adult American should get the same number of gas rationing coupons. Others argued that owners of newer, more fuel-efficient cars would not need as many coupons as owners of older, gas-guzzling models. Those who lived in western states believed they should receive more coupons than Easterners because they traveled longer distances. Some people called for every car owner to receive a certain number of coupons; others said this plan discriminated against families with several drivers who shared one car.

PAGES 137-139
I. Advantages of Prices
   A. Prices are neutral because they do not favor the buyer or the consumer. They are the result of competition.
   B. Prices are flexible, allowing for the "shocks" of unforeseen events and changes in the market.
   C. Prices have no administration costs.
   D. Prices are familiar and easily understood.

☐ **Discussion Question**
In your opinion, why does the neutrality of prices stimulate competition? (Student answers will vary but should indicate an understanding that buyers pay the price because they choose to accept it; otherwise, they would go to another producer with a lower price and buy there.)

PAGE 139

L1 Organizing Information
Have students draw a chart using *Price Allocation* and *Nonprice Allocation* as horizontal headings, and *Neutral, Flexible, No Administrative Costs,* and *Familiar* as vertical headings. Ask them to complete the chart by writing brief explanations of how the two allocation systems do or do not exhibit the listed characteristics. **ELL**

THE GLOBAL ECONOMY

Comparing Food Prices The top ten countries in terms of cost of living are, in order from highest to lowest: Japan, Hong Kong, Russia, Norway, Switzerland, France, Gabon, United Kingdom, Singapore, and Taiwan. The United States is ranked 17th in cost of living.

Answers:
1. *Tokyo, Japan*
2. *Answers should reflect knowledge of price allocation.*

---

prices, the economy would not run as smoothly, and decisions about allocating goods and services would have to be made some other way. Prices perform the allocation function very well for the following reasons.

First, prices in a competitive market economy are neutral because they favor neither the producer nor the consumer. This is because prices are the result of competition between buyers and sellers and, in this way, represent compromises that both sides can live with. The more competitive the market, the more efficient the price adjustment process.

Second, prices in a market economy are flexible. Unforeseen events such as natural disasters and war affect the prices of many items. Buyers and sellers react to the new level of prices and adjust their consumption and production accordingly. Before long, the system functions as smoothly again as it had before. The ability of the price system to absorb unexpected "shocks" is one of the strengths of a market economy.

Price flexibility also allows the market economy to accommodate change. The development of the personal computer provides an example. The early personal computers were relatively scarce and expensive, which attracted new producers. The resulting competition, along with advances in technology and production methods, soon drove prices lower, which attracted more consumers. More computers were needed to meet the demand, which brought more producers into the market. This new round of competition lowered prices even more, which attracted even more buyers. Consequently, a major innovation—the computer—entered the economy with the help of the price system and without the involvement of government or one of its bureaucracies.

Third, prices have no cost of administration. Competitive markets tend to find their own prices without outside help or interference. No bureaucrats need to be hired, no committees formed, no laws passed, or other decisions made. Even when prices adjust from one level to another, the change is usually so gradual that people hardly notice.

THE GLOBAL ECONOMY
COMPARING FOOD PRICES

The cost for a market basket of staple items varies widely around the world. The prices shown are for capital cities.

$18.79 United States	$28.14 Madrid, Spain
$23.19 London, England	$30.10 Paris, France
$27.38 Rome, Italy	$74.23 Tokyo, Japan

Source: USDA, 1999

One way to compare prices is to study a representative sample, called the market basket. The figures in the chart are based on a market basket that includes these staples:
• 1 gallon of milk
• 1 dozen eggs
• 1 pound of cheddar cheese
• 2 pounds of sirloin steak
• 2 pounds of apples
• 5 pounds of sugar

Critical Thinking
1. **Analyzing Information** In which location are these items the costliest?
2. **Drawing Conclusions** What factors do you think account for the wide range of prices?

MEETING SPECIAL NEEDS ACTIVITY

Learning Style: Logical/Mathematical Discuss as a class the advantages that using prices offers to both buyers and sellers. Then ask each student to choose a simple service he or she could perform after school to earn income, for example, baby-sitting, pet care, lawn mowing, or computer repair. **Ask:** How would you go about setting an hourly price for your service in order to be competitive? Have students set a reasonable price. Then, to simulate the flexibility of prices, ask students to think of some changing conditions that might affect that price, for example, another child to baby-sit. Have students set what they consider reasonable prices to accommodate these changes.

▷ Refer to *Inclusion for the Social Studies Classroom Strategies and Activities* in the TCR.

Finally, prices are something that we have known about all our lives, from the time we were old enough to ask our parents to buy us something to the age where we were old enough to buy it ourselves. As a result, prices are familiar and easily understood. There is no ambiguity over a price—if something costs $1.99, then we know exactly what we have to pay for it. This allows people to make decisions quickly and efficiently, with a minimum of time and effort.

Allocations Without Prices

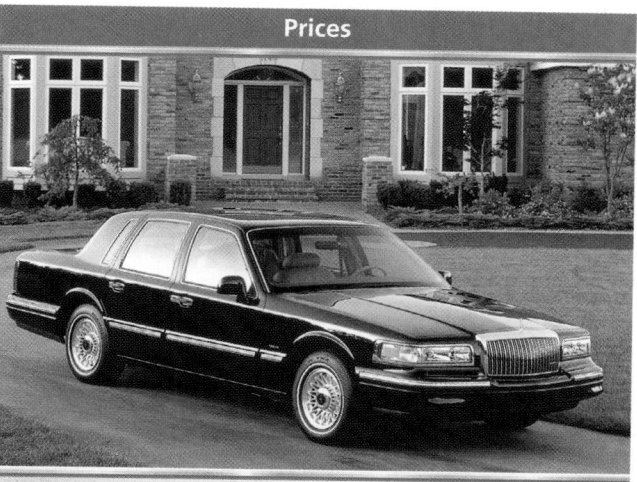

Prices
Prices are important because they help us make the everyday economic decisions that allocate scarce resources and the products made from them. But what would life be like without a price system? How would a car dealer allocate a limited supply of sports cars? Would intelligence, or perhaps good looks, or even political connections, determine who could get a car?

These criteria may seem far-fetched, but they are used in many parts of the world today, especially in countries with command economies, such as Cuba. After all, the local baseball fans did not get to see the exhibition game with the Baltimore Orioles in Havana. Instead, the seats were reserved for Communist Party and trade union members.

Without prices, another system must be used to decide who gets what. One method is **rationing**—a system under which an agency such as government decides everyone's "fair" share. Under such a system, people receive a **ration coupon,** a ticket or a receipt that entitles the holder to obtain a certain amount of a product. Rationing is used in many societies today, and it has been widely used during wartime, but it can lead to problems.

The Problem of Fairness

The first problem with rationing is that almost everyone feels his or her share is too small. During the oil crisis of the early 1970s, for example, the government made plans for, but never implemented, a gas rationing program. One of the major problems with the program was determining how to allocate the gas rationing coupons. Any number of ways to allocate the gas coupons were formulated, but the issue of fairness was never resolved.

High Administrative Cost

A second problem is the cost. Someone has to pay for printing the coupons and the salaries of the people who distribute them. In addition, no matter how much care is taken, some coupons will be stolen, sold, or counterfeited and used to acquire a product intended for someone else.

Diminishing Incentive

A third problem is that rationing has a negative impact on people's incentive to work and produce. Suppose that authorities went ahead with a rationing system and that you were given a certain number of coupons. How would this affect your incentive to work? If you could not get more

Advantages When energy prices rose, demand for luxury cars fell, while demand for smaller, more fuel-efficient autos jumped. *Why are prices considered neutral?*

CHAPTER 6: PRICES AND DECISION MAKING **139**

Guided Reading Activity 6-1

GUIDED READING Activity 6-1

For use with textbook pages 137–140

PRICES AS SIGNALS

RECALLING THE FACTS

Directions: Use the information in your textbook to answer the questions. Use another sheet of paper if necessary.

1. What are the four reasons that prices in a market economy perform the allocation function so well?
   a.
   b.
   c.
   d.
2. What is rationing and when is it most likely to be used?

3. Describe the problems that rationing can lead to
   a.

   b.

   c.

Visual Instruction

Answer to Caption:
because they favor neither the producer nor the consumer

3 ASSESS

Assign Section 1 Assessment as homework or as an in-class activity.

■ Have students use **Interactive Tutor Self-Assessment Software.**

Section Quiz 6-1

QUIZ ◆ Chapter 6, Section 1

PRICES AS SIGNALS   SCORE

Matching: Match each item in Column A with the items in Column B. Write the correct letters in the blanks. (10 points each)

A		B
1. price	a.	system under which an agency allocates products
2. price flexibility	b.	allows the market economy to accommodate change
3. rationing	c.	signals that convey information to buyers and sellers
4. rebate	d.	a ticket or receipt that entitles the holder to obtain a certain amount of a product
5. ration coupon	e.	the monetary value of a product as established by supply and demand
	f.	a partial refund of the original price of the product

Multiple Choice: In the blank at the left write the letter of the choice that best completes the statement or answers the question. (10 points each)

6. Prices perform the allocation function well because they do all of the following EXCEPT
   a. provide neutrality favoring neither the producer or consumer.
   b. provide flexibility absorbing unexpected "shocks."
   c. enable the government to use rationing.
   d. provide ways for consumers to make decisions
7. All of the following are characteristics of rationing EXCEPT
   a. rationing is often viewed as unfair.
   b. rationing creates high administrative costs.
   c. rationing decreases the incentive to work.
   d. rationing provides an efficient link between producers and consumers.
8. In a market economy, a high price is a signal for
   a. producers to produce more and buyers to buy less.
   b. producers to produce more and buyers to buy more.
   c. producers to produce less and buyers to buy less.
   d. producers to produce less and buyers to buy more.
9. In a market economy, a low price is a signal for

FREE ENTERPRISE ACTIVITY

Organize students into groups and assign each group one of the advantages of prices— neutrality, flexibility, lack of administrative cost, and familiarity. Direct groups to identify a real-life example of their assigned advantage in operation. Have groups develop a brief presentation on their example. Presentations could take the form of an illustrated lecture, a skit, a television or radio news story, or a small museum exhibit. Call on groups to make their presentations to the class. 🖿 **BLOCK SCHEDULING**

Reteach

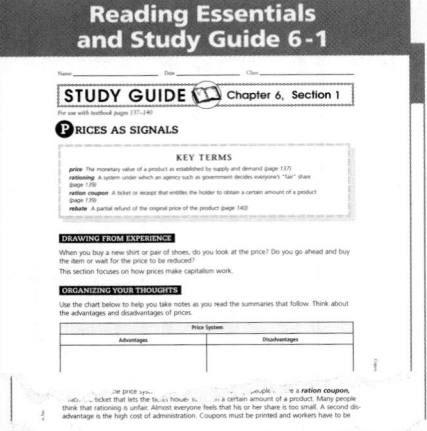

Reading Essentials and Study Guide 6-1

Enrich

Encourage students to write a research paper on a situation where rationing has been used to allocate economic products.

④ CLOSE

Have students debate the following: In every respect, price is the best system of allocating goods and services.

coupons by working harder, and if you got the same amount of coupons if you worked less, you certainly would lose some of your incentive to work.

Nonprice allocation mechanisms, such as rationing, raise issues that do not occur under a price allocation system. As long as we have prices, goods can be allocated through a system that is neutral, flexible, efficient, and easily understood by all.

Prices as a System

 Because of the many difficulties with nonprice allocation systems, economists overwhelmingly favor the price system. In fact, prices do more than help individuals in specific markets make decisions: they also serve as signals that help allocate resources between markets.

Consider the way in which higher oil prices affected producer and consumer decisions when the price of oil went from $5 to over $40 a barrel in the 1970s. Because the demand for oil is basically inelastic, people spent a greater part of their income on energy. Higher energy costs left them with less to spend elsewhere.

The market for full-size automobiles was one of the first to feel the effects. Because most large cars got poor gas mileage, people bought fewer large cars and more smaller ones, leaving dealerships with huge inventories of gas guzzlers.

At first, automakers thought the increase in gas prices would be temporary, so they were reluctant to switch over to smaller, more fuel-efficient models. As time went on, however, the surplus of unsold cars remained. To move their inventories, some manufacturers began to offer a **rebate**–a partial refund of the original price of the product. The rebate was the same as a temporary price reduction, because consumers were offered $500, $600, and even $1,000 back on each new car they bought.

Finally, automakers began reducing their production of large cars. They closed plants, laid off workers, and started to change to small car production. Many of the automobile workers who lost their jobs eventually found new ones in other industries. The result of higher prices in the international oil market, then, was a shift of productive resources out of the large car market into other markets. Although the process was a painful one for many in the industry, it was natural and necessary for a market economy.

In the end, prices do more than convey information to buyers and sellers in a market–they also help buyers and sellers allocate resources between markets. This is why economists think of prices as a "system"–part of an informational network–that links all markets in the economy.

Section 1 Assessment

Checking for Understanding

1. **Main Idea** Using your notes from the graphic organizer activity on page 137, describe how price affects decisions that consumers make.

2. **Key Terms** Define price, rationing, ration coupon, rebate.

3. **Describe** how producers and consumers react to prices.

4. **List** the advantages of using prices to distribute economic products.

5. **Explain** the difficulties of allocating goods and services without a price system.

Applying Economic Concepts

6. **Rationing** From your own experience, describe a situation that required some form of rationing. What criteria were used to allocate the good or service, and what were some of the problems with each of the criteria?

Critical Thinking

7. **Understanding Cause and Effect** List five items you would like to buy. How does the price of each item affect your decision to allocate your scarce resources—your money and your time? Explain.

> **Practice** and **assess** key social studies skills with the *Glencoe Skillbuilder Interactive Workbook, Level 2.*

Section 1 Assessment Answers

1. Consumers will purchase less at a high price and more at a low price. Consumers also weigh the price against their need.

2. All vocabulary terms are defined in the text.

3. high prices: producers produce more, consumers buy less; low prices: producers produce less, consumers demand more.

4. neutrality, flexibility, lack of administrative costs, familiarity

5. unfair system of allocation; high cost of administering system; negative impact of system on incentive to work and produce

6. Answers should reflect an understanding of the concept of rationing.

7. Answers will vary.

Profiles IN Economics

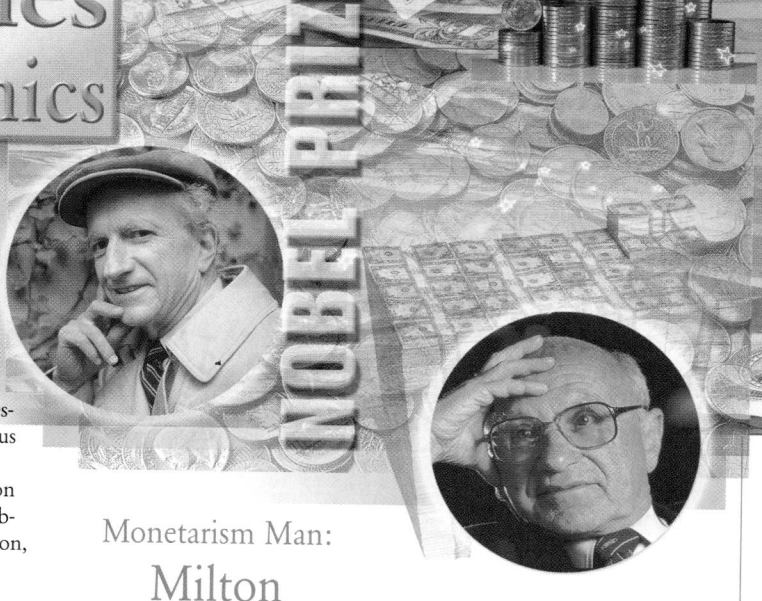

Society and Economics:
Gary Becker
(1930–)

Gary Stanley Becker is a professor of economics at the prestigious University of Chicago. Becker's work? The pioneering application of *economic* analysis to *social* problems such as crime, discrimination, and drug abuse. For his unique insight, Becker was awarded the Nobel Prize in economics in 1992.

Professor Becker views individuals as rational decision makers. People, he says, make life decisions largely in the economic terms of self-interest and the incentives of the market. He argues that viewing individual decisions in this way—as choices based on costs and benefits—helps explain individual human behaviors and their societal results. Becker offered an example of a life choice based on economic thinking: "The number of children a couple has depends on the costs and benefits of child rearing. . . . [C]ouples tend to have fewer children when the wife works and has a better-paying job, when subsidies and tax deductions for dependents are smaller, when the cost of educating and training children rises, and so forth."

Monetarism Man:
Milton Friedman
(1912–)

Milton Friedman is one of the best-known economists working today. His popular column in *Newsweek* helped make his a household name.

Friedman's writings have covered an extraordinary variety of topics, many of which were put forth in his book, *Capitalism and Freedom* (1962), which has become a standard. Friedman voiced opposition to such popular policies as agricultural subsidies, price controls, and a minimum wage.

Friedman has been most influential as an unwavering supporter of monetarism—the theory that the quantity of money in an economy is a critical factor in the overall state of the economy. The key to his argument is that changes in the rate of growth of the money supply have varying and unpredictable lags, which makes fine-tuning the economy virtually impossible. Friedman claims that the Federal Reserve System should let the money supply grow at a constant rate to avoid destabilizing the economy. For his theories on economic stabilization, Friedman was awarded the Nobel Prize in economics in 1976.

Examining the Profiles

1. **Making Comparisons** How are Becker's and Friedman's ideas similar and different?
2. **For Further Research** Read an article or book by Becker or Friedman. Present a summary of the work to the class.

BACKGROUND

Gary Becker and Milton Friedman—relatively well-known to the general public—stand out in a profession whose practitioners are generally not famous. Yet lesser-known economists are often among the most influential people in the country. Their ideas, first put forth in obscure journals, are given serious consideration by politicians and policy analysts who can apply or enact them. Thus, many public policy decisions are based on the work of economists. Economists, therefore, famous and otherwise, have a profound influence on the lives and fortunes of millions of Americans.

TEACH

Draw students' attention to Friedman's argument that "competitive capitalism [is] a necessary condition for political freedom." Organize students into teams to debate this statement as a resolution.

L3 Oral Report

Have students research and report on the contributions of other economic philosophers that have impacted the United States. Students might report on Adam Smith, John Stuart Mill, John Maynard Keynes, or Karl Marx.

Answers to Examining the Profile

1. Becker's and Friedman's ideas are similar in that they view economic conditions and decisions as fundamental to other aspects of life; they differ in that Becker focuses on the micro, specifically the decision-making of individuals, while Friedman focuses on the macro, specifically the importance of the supply of money or monetary policy.
2. Answers will vary. Reward summaries that are cogent, and that demonstrate a complete reading and an understanding of the main ideas.

FOCUS

Section Overview
This section explains how equilibrium prices are determined, and describes shortages and surpluses.

BELLRINGER
Motivational Activity

Project **transparency** and have students answer questions.

Available as blackline master.

Daily Focus Transparency 14

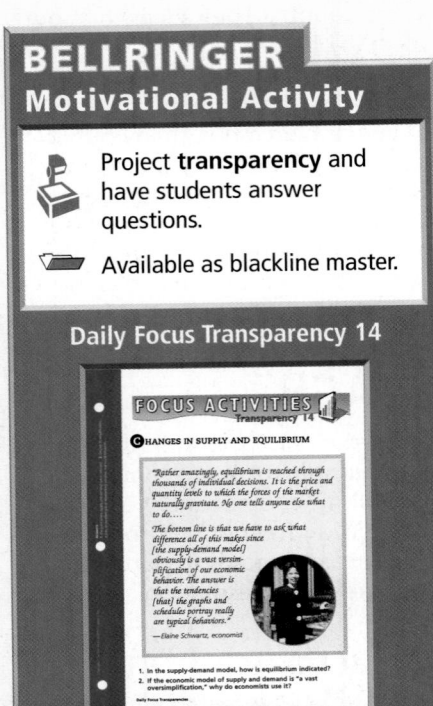

Study Guide

Reading Strategy
Have students create the graphic organizer.
Answers to Graphic: *surplus: prices fall, low demand, producers lower production; shortage: prices rise, high demand, producers raise production*

Preteaching Vocabulary
Ask students to define the terms *surplus* and *shortage* in their own words.

The Price System at Work

Study Guide

Main Idea
Changes in demand and supply cause prices to change.

Reading Strategy
Graphic Organizer As you read the section, complete a graphic organizer similar to this, showing how a surplus and shortage affect prices, demand, and supply.

The effects of a SURPLUS
on prices
on demand
on supply

The effects of a SHORTAGE
on prices
on demand
on supply

Key Terms
economic model, market equilibrium, surplus, shortage, equilibrium price

Objectives
After studying this section, you will be able to:
1. **Understand** how prices are determined in competitive markets.
2. **Explain** how economic models can be used to predict and explain price changes.
3. **Apply** the concepts of elasticity to changes in prices.

Applying Economic Concepts
Equilibrium Price When something is at equilibrium, it tends to remain at rest. Read to find out what causes prices to reach, and then stay at, equilibrium.

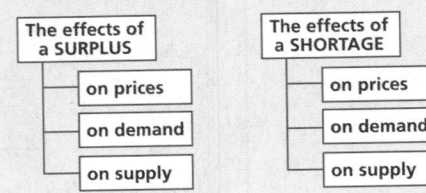

Cover Story

Engineering Extra Tickets

If Massachusetts Institute of Technology students don't know the law of supply and demand coming into school, they sure have it down by graduation. Just ask Steve Shapiro.

Like all graduating seniors, he was allotted four free tickets to his June 4 commencement. But 11 relatives are planning to attend. . . .

UN Secretary-General Kofi Annan addresses MIT graduates.

Enter the Graduation Ticket Trading Center, a Web site set up by MIT's class of 1999 for seniors who want to buy or sell tickets to the ceremony. . . .

It's clearly a seller's market. Most suppliers were looking for about $100 a ticket, though one fellow had four tickets for anyone who would take a final exam for him. . . .

—*USA Today*, May 27, 1999

142

One of the most appealing features of a competitive market economy is that everyone who participates has a hand in determining prices. This is why economists consider prices to be neutral and impartial.

The process of establishing prices, as illustrated by the example of the Graduation Ticket Trading Center, is remarkable because buyers and sellers have exactly the opposite hopes and desires. Buyers want to find good buys at low prices. Sellers hope for high prices and large profits. Neither can get exactly what they want, so some adjustment is necessary to reach a compromise.

The Price Adjustment Process
Because transactions in a market economy are voluntary, the compromise that eventually takes place must be to the benefit of both parties, or the compromise would not occur in the first place.

An Economic Model
To show how the adjustment process takes place, we use the supply and demand illustration shown in **Figure 6.1**—one of the more popular

---

RESOURCE MANAGER

Reproducible Masters
- Reproducible Lesson Plan 6-2
- Daily Lecture Notes 6-2
- Guided Reading Activity 6-2
- Reading Essentials and Study Guide 6-2
- Section Quiz 6-2

Transparencies
- Daily Focus Transparency 14

Multimedia
- Interactive Economics!
- Interactive Tutor Self-Assessment Software
- ExamView® Pro Testmaker
- Presentation Plus!

"tools" used by economists. The figure illustrates an **economic model**—a set of assumptions that can be listed in a table, illustrated with a graph, or even stated algebraically—to help analyze behavior and predict outcomes.

The data in the figure is already familiar to you. The numbers in the first two columns in the schedule and the market demand curve **DD** are from **Figure 4.2** on page 92. The information in the schedule and curve reflects the Law of Demand, showing that consumers will buy more at lower prices and less at higher prices.

The numbers in the first and third column of the schedule and the market supply curve **SS** come from **Figure 5.2** on page 117. This information reflects the Law of Supply, showing that suppliers will offer more for sale at higher prices and less at lower ones.

Separately, each of these graphs represents the demand and the supply sides of the market. When they are combined, as in **Panel B** of **Figure 6.1**, we have a complete model of the market, which will allow us to analyze how the interaction of buyers and sellers results in a price that is agreeable to all.

Market Equilibrium

In a competitive market, the adjustment process moves toward **market equilibrium**—a situation in which prices are relatively stable, and the quantity of goods or services supplied is equal to the quantity demanded. In **Figure 6.1,** equilibrium is reached when the price is $15 and the quantity supplied is six units.

How does the market find this equilibrium on its own? Why did the market settle at $15, rather than $20, or $10, or at some other price? To answer these questions, we have to examine the reactions of buyers and sellers to market prices. In addition, we assume that neither knows the final price, so we'll have to find it using trial and error—like the MIT seniors did when they introduced their Graduation Ticket Trading Center Web site described in the cover story.

Surplus

We start on Day 1 with sellers thinking that the price for musical CDs will be $25. If you examine the supply schedule and curve in **Figure 6.1,** you see that suppliers will produce 11 units for sale at that price. However, the suppliers soon discover that buyers will purchase only one CD at a price of $25, leaving a surplus of 10.

CHAPTER 6: PRICES AND DECISION MAKING **143**

ECONOMICS
AT A GLANCE   Figure 6.1

A Model of the CD Market

A Market Demand and Supply Schedules

Price	Quantity Demanded	Quantity Supplied	Surplus/ Shortage
$30	0	13	13
25	1	11	10
20	3	9	6
15	6	6	0
10	10	3	−7
5	15	0	−15

B Market Demand and Supply Curves

Using Tables and Graphs An economic model of the CD market includes both supply and demand. At what price does quantity demanded equal quantity supplied?

Daily Lecture Notes 6-2

DAILY LECTURE NOTES 📖 Lesson 6-2

🅓ID YOU KNOW?

In spring and summer 1988, drought hit the United States, drying out a broad band of the country from the eastern Appalachian Mountains all the way to the Pacific coast. Parts of Iowa, Illinois, and other North Central farm states went for months with little or no rain. By the end of June, more than 1,300 counties in 30 states had been declared drought-disaster areas. The drought resulted in a grain shortage (typical harvest dropped by almost one-third, but stored grain eased the blow), as well as a meat shortage (farmers had to slaughter live-stock early because they had no grain for the animals). By year's end, food prices were up 5.2 percent.

PAGES 142-145

I. The Price Adjustment Process
   A. Together, demand and supply make a complete picture of the market.
   B. Price adjustments help a competitive market reach market equilibrium, with fairly equal supply and demand.
   C. Surpluses occur when supply exceeds demand.
   D. Shortages occur when demand exceeds supply.
   E. The equilibrium price is the price at which supply meets demand.

☑ Discussion Question

Imagine that you want to go to a concert but you find it is sold out at ticket outlets. What effect will this shortage of tickets have on the price of any remaining concert tickets? *(Their price will increase.)*

PAGES 146-148

ECONOMICS
AT A GLANCE

Answer: *$15*

➕ Math Practice

Graphing Equations Supply and demand curves can be written as equations. Have your students graph the following equations on graph paper (with P on the vertical axis and Q on the horizontal axis).
Supply: $P = 14 − 2Q$
Demand: $P = 2 + Q$
Find the equilibrium price P and quantity Q. Next have them find the equilibrium price and quantity algebraically by solving the two equations for P and Q.
(P = 6, Q = 4)

MEETING SPECIAL NEEDS ACTIVITY

English Language Learners Students with language concept problems will need practice in categorizing information. Direct students' attention to the headings in Section 2: The Price Adjustment Process, An Economic Model, Market Equilibrium, Surplus, Shortage, Equilibrium Price, Explaining and Predicting Prices, Changes in Supply, Importance of Elasticity, Changes in Demand, and The Competitive Price Theory. After reading each subsection, have students think of alternative titles such as "Sellers and Buyers Compromise," and so on. **ELL**

🖿 Refer to *Inclusion for the Social Studies Classroom Strategies and Activities* in the TCR.

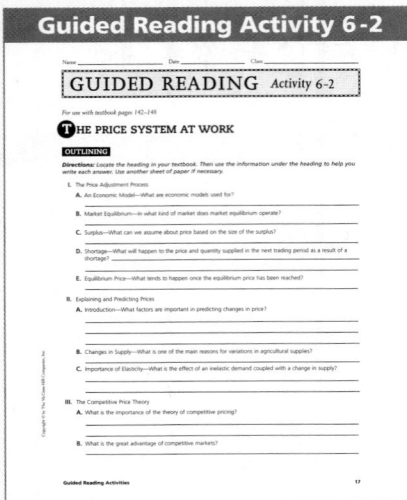

Guided Reading Activity 6-2

Visual Instruction

Answer to Caption:
Demand will be so great that there will be a shortage.

L2 Market Model

Have students construct demand and supply schedules and a market model for a brand of blue jeans, using the information below. Then ask at what prices surpluses and shortages appear.

Price	Demand	Supply
$22	60,000	20,000
24	50,000	28,000
26	44,000	32,000
28	36,000	36,000
30	30,000	40,000
32	24,000	46,000

Price Determination

Price Adjustment Bicycle shops and other businesses often price certain goods below cost to attract customers. *What can occur if the price for a given product is too low?*

A **surplus** is a situation in which the quantity supplied is greater than the quantity demanded at a given price. The 10 unit surplus at the end of Day 1 is shown in column four of **Panel A** in **Figure 6.1** as the difference between the quantity supplied and the quantity demanded at the $25 price. It is also shown graphically in **Panel A** of **Figure 6.2** as the horizontal distance between the supply and demand curves.

This surplus shows up as unsold products on suppliers' shelves, and it begins to take up space in the suppliers' warehouses. Sellers now know that $25 is too high, and they know that they have to lower their price if they want to attract more buyers and dispose of the surplus.

Therefore, the price tends to go down as a result of the surplus. The model cannot tell us how far the price will go down, but we can reasonably assume that the price will go down only a little if the surplus is small, and much more if the surplus is larger.

Shortage

Suppliers are more cautious on Day 2, and so they anticipate a much lower price of $10. At that price, the quantity they are willing to supply changes

144 UNIT 2 MICROECONOMICS

to three compact discs. However, as **Panel B** in **Figure 6.2** shows, this price turns out to be too low. At a market price of $10, only three CDs are supplied and 10 are demanded—leaving a shortage of seven CDs.

A **shortage** is a situation in which the quantity demanded is greater than the quantity supplied at a given price. When a shortage happens, producers have no more CDs to sell, and they end the day wishing that they had charged higher prices for their products.

As a result, both the price and the quantity supplied will go up in the next trading period. While our model does not show exactly how much the price will go up, we can assume that the next price will be less than $25, which we already know is too high.

Equilibrium Price

If the new price is $20 on Day 3, the result will be the surplus of six CDs shown in **Panel C** of **Figure 6.2.** This surplus will cause the price to drop, but probably not below $10, which already proved to be too low. If the price drops to $15, as shown in **Panel D** in **Figure 6.2**, the market will have found its equilibrium price. The **equilibrium price** is the price that "clears the market" by leaving neither a surplus nor a shortage at the end of the trading period.

While our economic model of the market cannot show exactly how long it will take to reach equilibrium, equilibrium will be reached because of the pressure that temporary surpluses and shortages put on prices. Whenever the price is set too high, the surplus will tend to force it down. Whenever the price is set too low, the shortage

CYBERNOMICS SPOTLIGHT

The Internet and Prices
When you buy a $100 sweater at a stylish boutique, most of the money you pay goes to the distribution channels. The Internet lessens the need for most go-betweens, thus it eliminates most distribution costs and increases the possible savings for both the consumer and the manufacturer.

FREE ENTERPRISE ACTIVITY

To help students understand the role of price in dealing with a surplus, and to give them some math practice, provide them with the following problem. At the end of spring, the manager of a clothing store notices that his stockroom is stacked with designer sweaters priced at $80 each. To clear his stock, the manager decides to mark down the sweater price by 45 percent. What will be the markdown price of the sweaters?

For students who need guidance, explain that the markdown price is determined by: **1.** multiplying the regular price by the percentage of markdown, and **2.** subtracting the result from the regular price. *(**1.** $80 × 45% = $36; **2.** $80 − $36 = $44. The markdown price is $44.)*

ECONOMICS AT A GLANCE

Figure 6.2

Dynamics of the Price Adjustment Process

Ⓐ At a price of $25, a surplus of ten causes the price to drop.

Surplus = 10

Ⓑ At a price of $10, a shortage of seven causes the price to rise.

Shortage = 7

Ⓒ At a price of $20, a surplus of six causes the price to drop again.

Surplus = 6

Ⓓ Alternating surpluses and shortages cause equilibrium to be reached.

Equilibrium price

Equilibrium quantity

Using Graphs In a competitive market, prices are drawn toward equilibrium as a result of the constant pressures from temporary surpluses and shortages. Panel A shows that a price of $25 will create a surplus. A surplus is also created on Day 3, as shown in Panel C. Why did a surplus occur on Day 1?

CHAPTER 6: PRICES AND DECISION MAKING **145**

ECONOMICS AT A GLANCE

Answer: *No one is sure what the equilibrium price for a new product will be, so they estimate on the first day, then adjust the price.*

Economists may refer to a surplus as *excess supply* and a shortage as *excess demand.*

CURRICULUM CONNECTION

Family and Consumer Science A practical lesson of market equilibrium theory is that "if it sounds too good to be true, it probably is." For example, legitimate TV stores would never sell new TVs for only $10, no strings attached. They would know that they could sell their TVs for a much higher price. Ask students to find examples of prices (or wages) that seem too good to be true, then have them do research on the deals being offered to see if there's a "catch."

CRITICAL THINKING

Identifying Central Issues Have students visit an area shopping mall and look for examples of surpluses and shortages, listing 5 to 10 items for each concept. Note that almost any sale or clearance item can be an example of a surplus, while rain checks or sold-out items signal a shortage. **Ask:** Did the stores visited have more surpluses or more shortages? Ask students to write short essays in which they examine the prices and other determinants related to the items they found and hypothesize as to why the surplus or shortage occurred.

will tend to force it up. As a result, the market tends to seek its own equilibrium.

When the equilibrium price of $15 is reached, it will tend to remain there because the quantity supplied is exactly equal to the quantity demanded. Something could come along to disturb the equilibrium, but then new shortages or new surpluses, or both, would appear to push the price to its new equilibrium level.

Explaining and Predicting Prices

Economists use their market models to explain how the world around us works and to predict how certain events such as changes in prices might occur. A change in price is normally the result of a change in supply, a change in demand, or changes in both. Elasticity of demand is also important when predicting prices.

Changes in Supply

Consider the case of agriculture, which often experiences wide swings in prices from one year to the next. A farmer may keep up with all the latest developments and have the best advice experts can offer, but the farmer never can be sure what price to expect for the crop. A soybean farmer may put in 500 acres of beans, expecting a price of $9 a bushel. The farmer knows, however, that the actual price may end up being anywhere from $5 to $20.

Weather is one of the main reasons for the variation in agricultural prices. If it rains too much after

ECONOMICS
AT A GLANCE

Figure 6.3

Factors Affecting Price Changes in Agriculture

A Inelastic Supply and Demand

B Same Supply with Elastic Demand

Using Graphs Diagram A shows that larger price changes occur when both the supply and demand curves are highly inelastic. When the demand curve is more elastic, as in Diagram B, price fluctuations are smaller. *What happens to the slope of a supply curve when it becomes more elastic?*

146 UNIT 2 MICROECONOMICS

the farmer plants the seeds, the seeds may rot or be washed away and the farmer must replant. If it rains too little, the seeds may not sprout. Even if the weather is perfect during the growing season, rain can still prevent the harvest from being gathered. The weather, then, often causes a change in supply.

The result, shown in **Panel A** of **Figure 6.3**, is that the supply curve is likely to shift, causing the price to go up or down. At the beginning of the season, the farmer may expect supply to look like curve **SS.** If a bumper, or record, crop is harvested, however, supply may look like **S¹S¹.** If bad weather strikes, supply may look like **S²S².** Because both demand and supply for food is inelastic, a small change in supply is enough to cause a large change in the price.

Importance of Elasticity

What would happen to prices if the demand for soybeans were highly elastic, as in **Panel B** of **Figure 6.3**? The results would be quite different. Because this demand curve is much more elastic, the prices would only range from $8 to $10 a bushel instead of from $5 to $20 a bushel.

Economists consider elasticity of demand whenever a change in supply occurs. When a given change in supply is coupled with an inelastic demand curve, as in **Panel A** of **Figure 6.3**, price changes dramatically. When the same change in supply is coupled with a very elastic demand curve, such as that in **Panel B** of **Figure 6.3**, the change in price is much smaller.

In general, price changes in any given market are likely to be wider if both supply and demand are inelastic. The same price changes are likely to be less volatile if both curves are elastic.

Changes in Demand

A change in demand, like a change in supply, can also affect the price of a good or service. All of the factors we examined in Chapter 4—changes in income, tastes, prices of related products, expectations, and the number of consumers—affect the market demand for goods and services. One example is the demand for gold.

Figure 6.4 shows why gold prices have changed so dramatically over a 20-year period. In 1980, rising prices, uncertain economic conditions, and other factors created a high demand for gold. When

ECONOMICS AT A GLANCE   Figure 6.4

The Price of Gold When Supply and Demand Change

Using Graphs A change in supply, a change in demand, or a change in both can influence prices. What could cause the price of gold to go back up?

this demand, shown as **DD** in the figure, was combined with a relatively tight supply, **SS,** the price of gold reached $850 per ounce.

By the mid-1990s, economic fears declined and people lost some of their desire for gold. This had the effect of shifting the demand curve to **D¹D¹.**

Meanwhile, gold producers reacted to the sky-high price in a predictable manner—they reopened mines that had been closed because of low gold prices and resumed production. This had the effect of increasing the supply of gold to **S¹S¹.** The combination of increased supply and reduced demand drove the price of gold down to the $400 level.

In early 1999, more bad news hit the gold market. The Bank of England announced plans to sell about 400 tons of gold, or slightly more than half of its official gold stock, causing the supply curve to shift to **S²S²** and the price of gold to reach a new low of $280 an ounce.

However the price of gold fluctuates, one thing is certain—everything depends on the demand and

CHAPTER 6: PRICES AND DECISION MAKING **147**

ECONOMICS AT A GLANCE

Answer: *bad news, such as war, disaster, or possible recession*

③ ASSESS

Assign Section 2 Assessment as homework or as an in-class activity.

💾 Have students use **Interactive Tutor Self-Assessment Software** to review Section 2.

Section Quiz 6-2

INTERDISCIPLINARY CONNECTIONS ACTIVITY

Science In science, as in economics, equilibrium refers to a situation in which there is no longer a tendency for change to occur unless something happens to upset the balance. To demonstrate this, perform the following two simple experiments with students. First, fill a large clear container with water and add a few drops of food coloring. It will take a few minutes for the coloring to disperse evenly throughout the container. When the liquid stops changing color, it will have achieved a state of equilibrium. Next, mix some oil with water in a clear plastic bottle. The contents of the bottle will reach a state of equilibrium when the water has completely separated from the oil.

Objectives, goals, and answers to the student activity can be found in the **Web Activity Lesson Plan** feature at epp.glencoe.com

Reteach

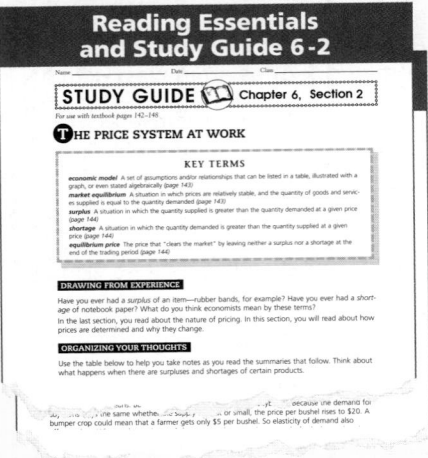

Reading Essentials and Study Guide 6-2

STUDY GUIDE 📖 Chapter 6, Section 2

For use with textbook pages 142–148

❶ THE PRICE SYSTEM AT WORK

KEY TERMS

economic model A set of assumptions and/or relationships that can be listed in a table, illustrated with a graph, or even stated algebraically (page 143)

market equilibrium A situation in which prices are relatively stable, and the quantity of goods and services supplied is equal to the quantity demanded (page 143)

surplus A situation in which the quantity supplied is greater than the quantity demanded at a given price (page 144)

shortage A situation in which the quantity demanded is greater than the quantity supplied at a given price (page 144)

equilibrium price The price that "clears the market" by leaving neither a surplus nor a shortage at the end of the trading period (page 144)

DRAWING FROM EXPERIENCE

Have you ever had a surplus of an item—rubber bands, for example? Have you ever had a shortage of notebook paper? What do you think economists mean by these terms?

In the last section, you read about the nature of pricing. In this section, you will read about how prices are determined and why they change.

ORGANIZING YOUR THOUGHTS

Use the table below to help you take notes as you read the summaries that follow. Think about what happens when there are surpluses and shortages of certain products.

... the same whether the supply ... or small, the price per bushel rises to $20. A bumper crop could mean that a farmer gets only $5 per bushel. So elasticity of demand also

Enrich

Have students scan the business sections of newspapers to locate stories about price changes. Have students share stories and explain what signals the price changes send.

❹ CLOSE

Discuss the following: Price represents the balancing of the forces of demand and supply.

---

the supply. Whenever economic conditions or political instability threatens, people tend to increase their demand for gold and drive the price up. Whenever the supply of gold increases dramatically—as when a major holder of gold like the Bank of England sells half of its gold holdings—the supply of gold increases, driving the price down.

The Competitive Price Theory

The theory of competitive pricing represents a set of ideal conditions and outcomes. The theory is important because it serves as a model by which to measure the performance of other, less competitive market structures. Even so, many markets come reasonably close to the ideal.

The prices of some foods such as milk, flour, bread, and many other items in your community will be relatively similar from one store to the next. When the prices of these items vary, it may be because advertisers have convinced some people that its brand is slightly better than others. Another reason may be that buyers are not well informed. The price of gasoline, for example, is usually higher at stations near an expressway because gas station owners know that travelers do not know the location of lower cost stations in an unfamiliar area.

Student Web Activity Visit the *Economics: Principles and Practices* Web site at epp.glencoe.com and click on *Chapter 6—Student Web Activities* for a price comparison activity.

Fortunately, markets only have to be reasonably competitive—rather than perfect—to be useful. The great advantage of competitive markets is that they allocate resources efficiently. As sellers compete to meet consumer demands, they are forced to lower the price of their goods, which in turn encourages them to keep their costs down. At the same time, competition among buyers helps prevent prices from falling too far.

In the final analysis, the market economy is one that "runs itself." There is no need for a bureaucracy, planning commission, or other agency to set prices because the market tends to find its own equilibrium. In addition, the three basic economic questions of WHAT, HOW, and FOR WHOM to produce are decided by the participants—the buyers and sellers—in the market.

Section 2 Assessment

Checking for Understanding
1. **Main Idea** Explain how a change in demand can affect prices.
2. **Key Terms** Define economic model, market equilibrium, surplus, shortage, equilibrium price.
3. **Describe** how prices are determined in a competitive market.
4. **Explain** why economic models are useful.
5. **Explain** how different cases of demand and supply elasticity are related to price changes.

Applying Economic Concepts
6. **Equilibrium Price** Choose one good or service—for example, unleaded gasoline, a gallon of milk, a local newspaper, or a haircut. Visit at least five stores that sell the product, and note its price at each location. What do the individual prices tell you about the equilibrium price for the good or service?

Critical Thinking
7. **Understanding Cause and Effect** What signal does a high price send to buyers and sellers?
8. **Making Inferences** What do merchants usually do to sell items that are overstocked? What does this tell you about the equilibrium price for the product?

💿 **Practice** and **assess** key social studies skills with the *Glencoe Skillbuilder Interactive Workbook, Level 2.*

Section 2 Assessment Answers

1. Changes in income, tastes, and so on affect demand and, therefore, price.
2. All vocabulary terms are defined in the text.
3. Prices are adjusted through competition between buyers and sellers.
4. They show how markets work by helping analyze behavior and predict outcomes.
5. The more elastic, the smaller the price change; the less elastic, the larger the price change.
6. If there is little difference in prices, the equilibrium price has been reached.
7. tells buyers that they should buy less and tells sellers they should offer more
8. They lower the price of the items. The equilibrium price is lower than the present price.

Synthesizing Information

Synthesizing information involves integrating information from two or more sources. The ability to synthesize, or combine, information is important because information gained from one source often sheds new light upon other information.

Learning the Skill

To synthesize information, follow these steps:

- Analyze each source separately to understand its meaning.
- Determine what information each source adds to the subject.
- Identify points of agreement and disagreement between the sources. Ask: Can Source A give me new information or new ways of thinking about Source B?
- Find relationships between the information in the sources.

Practicing the Skill

Study the sources below, then answer the questions that follow.

Source A

A common decision consumers make is whether to borrow money for a new car, or to pay cash for a less expensive used one. Studies show that more than 80 percent of all new cars sold in any given year in the United States are financed. There are advantages to owning a new car, but there are also significant costs consumers should keep in mind when they make this decision.

The interest a consumer pays on a new car loan is a significant part of its cost. Insuring a new car costs more than insuring a used car because new cars are more likely to be stolen or vandalized. In addition, there is a higher sales tax to pay for a more costly new car.

Source B

Most Americans are accustomed to borrowing and buying on credit. At times, especially when buying such expensive consumer durables as automobiles and fine furniture, they consider borrowing to be necessary.

In a sense, people feel forced to buy items on credit because they believe they need them immediately. They do not want to wait. Of course, consumers are not really "forced" to buy most goods and services on credit. They could decide instead to save the money needed to make their purchases.

Because people have limited resources, most people have to borrow to buy a car.

1. What is the main subject of each excerpt?
2. What kind of information does Source A add to this subject?
3. What kind of information does Source B add to this subject?
4. Does Source B support or contradict Source A? Explain.
5. Summarize what you have learned from both sources.

Application Activity

Find two sources of information on a topic dealing with the price of goods. Write a short report answering these questions: What are the main ideas in the sources? How does each source add to your understanding of the topic? Do the sources support or contradict each other?

 Practice and **assess** key social studies skills with the *Glencoe Skillbuilder Interactive Workbook, Level 2.*

Teaching Skills

Locate a number of pairs of related articles on economic subjects. Copy and distribute articles to students. Have students read the articles. As a class, examine the related stories. Make a chart on the board for each pair of stories, noting the main subjects of each, agreements and disagreements within the pair, and the relationship between the information in the articles. Ask volunteers to explain how the related articles led to a better understanding of the common subject.

Additional Practice

Reinforcing Economic Skill 20

Reinforcing Economic Skills — Chapter 20

SYNTHESIZING INFORMATION

Synthesizing information involves integrating information from two or more sources. To synthesize information, analyze each source separately to understand its meaning. Determine what each source of information adds to the subject. Then identify points of agreement and disagreement.

Directions: Read both of the excerpts below and answer the questions that follow.

What Is the "Debt Crisis"?
Fergus Nicoll, BBC News Online

Campaigners for urgent debt relief say that huge sums of money are going back to wealthy countries instead of feeding and educating children in the world's poorest nations.

In its 1997 report, the United Nations Development Programme (UNDP) said that governments in Africa alone, if relieved of their debt obligations, could use the funds "to save the lives of millions of children . . ."

Why Debt Relief Will Not Benefit Poor
Karl Ziegler, Director of the Centre for Accountability and Debt Relief

The main reason why unconditional debt relief to the world's over-borrowed nations will not help their poorest citizens, is that those citizens will never experience the benefits of such relief.

Most over-borrowed nations are dominated by ruling elites, familial, tribal or military, whose first priority is to feed their offshore bank accounts and provide sustenance and support to the military or police forces that maintain them in power.

Indeed, some of the world's "poorest" over-borrowed countries include Nigeria, Democratic Republic of Congo (formerly Zaire), Zimbabwe, Tanzania and Zambia, inherently wealthy countries.

In most cases, the total debt owed by the nation's [sic] could be repaid immediately if monies, stolen by rulers and their cronies and nested into offshore tax havens, were returned to the nations from which they had been exported illegally. The highly visible . . . campaign by poor countries has attracted well-meaning supporters based on intellectually dishonest arguments. Debt, per se, does not starve children in Africa or elsewhere, but corruption does have that effect.

1. What is the main subject of each excerpt?

GLENCOE
TECHNOLOGY

Glencoe Skillbuilder Interactive Workbook, Level 2

This interactive CD-ROM reinforces student mastery of essential social studies skills.

Answers to Practicing the Skill

1. Source A is about the consumer's decision to either borrow money for a new car, or to pay cash for a less expensive used car. Source B is about borrowing and buying on credit.
2. Source A adds research results, and advantages and disadvantages.
3. Source B considers consumers' feelings and opinions.
4. Both Sources A and B provide information about the economic decision of whether to make purchases using credit.
5. Answers should provide an accurate summary of the articles' information.

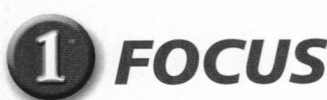

1 FOCUS

Section Overview
This section describes how prices operate in the economy as a whole.

BELLRINGER
Motivational Activity

- Project **transparency** and have students answer questions.
- Available as blackline master.

Daily Focus Transparency 26

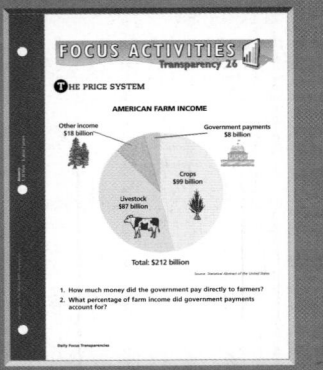

Study Guide

Reading Strategy
Have students create the graphic organizer.
Answers to Graphic: *Price ceilings cut into profits, causing suppliers to supply less, leading to a shortage.*

Preteaching Vocabulary
Use the Vocabulary Puzzle-Maker to create crossword and word-search puzzles.

Social Goals vs. Market Efficiency

Study Guide

Main Idea
To achieve one or more of its social goals, government sometimes sets prices.

Reading Strategy
Graphic Organizer As you read the section, complete a cause-and-effect chart similar to the one below by explaining how price ceilings affect quantity supplied.

Price ceilings → Effect on quantity supplied

Key Terms
price ceiling, minimum wage, price floor, target price, nonrecourse loan, deficiency payment

Objectives
After studying this section, you will be able to:
1. **Describe** the consequence of having a fixed price in a market.
2. **Explain** how loan supports and deficiency payments work.
3. **Understand** what is meant when "markets talk."

Applying Economic Concepts
Price Floor Chances are that you have worked for the minimum wage at some time in your life. Read to see why this is an example of a price floor.

Cover Story

Congress Sews a Safety Net for Farmers

Various farmer aid proposals considered

Three years after a major farm bill ended the nation's decades-old program of agricultural price supports, Congress is considering beefing up safety nets to aid farmers around the country hit by dramatically low crop prices, shrinking exports, and falling incomes.

But the proposed solutions—ranging from an expanded crop-insurance program to a return to commodity price supports—are both costly and tend to divide market-oriented Republicans and Democrats who favor subsidies.

Moreover, such remedies take time. So, as financially strapped farmers begin a new planting season, Congress could end up passing another emergency aid package this year like the more than $5 billion approved for farmers last October. . . .

—*The Christian Science Monitor*, March 12, 1999

150

In Chapter 2 we examined seven broad economic and social goals that most people seem to share. We also observed that these goals, while commendable, were sometimes in conflict with one another. These goals were also partially responsible for the increased role that government plays in our economy.

The goals most compatible with a market economy are freedom, efficiency, full employment, price stability, and economic growth. Attempts to achieve the other two goals—equity and security—usually require policies like the "safety net for farmers" in the cover story that distort market outcomes. In other words, we may have to give up a little efficiency and freedom in order to achieve equity and security.

Whether this is good or bad often depends on a person's perspective. After all, the person who receives a subsidy is more likely to support it than is the taxpayer who pays for it. In general, however, it is usually wise to evaluate each situation on its own merits, as the benefits of a program may well exceed the costs. What is common to all of these situations, however, is that the outcomes can be achieved only at the cost of interfering with the market.

RESOURCE MANAGER

📁 Reproducible Masters
- Reproducible Lesson Plan 6-3
- Daily Lecture Notes 6-3
- Guided Reading Activity 6-3
- Reading Essentials and Study Guide 6-3
- Section Quiz 6-3

🖳 Transparencies
- Daily Focus Transparency 26

Multimedia
- 🔘 Vocabulary PuzzleMaker CD-ROM
- 📼 🔘 NBR Economics & You Video
- 🔘 Interactive Economics!
- 💾 Interactive Tutor Self-Assessment Software
- 🔘 ExamView® Pro Testmaker
- 🔘 Presentation Plus!

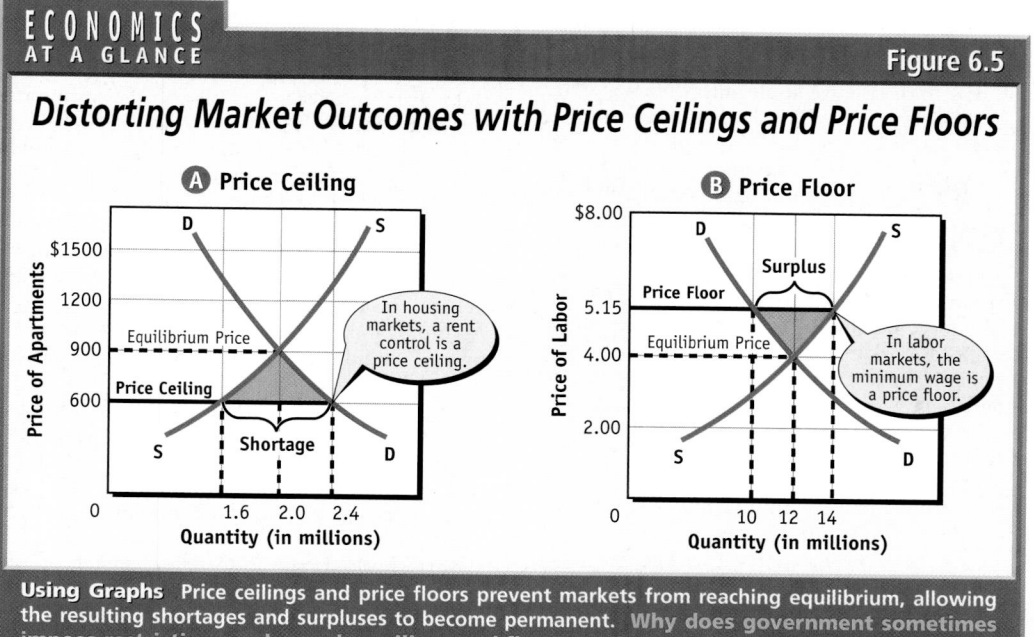

ECONOMICS AT A GLANCE

Figure 6.5

Distorting Market Outcomes with Price Ceilings and Price Floors

A Price Ceiling

In housing markets, a rent control is a price ceiling.

B Price Floor

In labor markets, the minimum wage is a price floor.

Using Graphs Price ceilings and price floors prevent markets from reaching equilibrium, allowing the resulting shortages and surpluses to become permanent. **Why does government sometimes impose restrictions such as price ceilings and floors on the market?**

② TEACH

Daily Lecture Notes 6-3

DAILY LECTURE NOTES 📖 Lesson 6-3

ⅅID YOU KNOW?

During the nation's Great Depression, prices for farm products tumbled. Farmers lost much money, and many even lost their farms. At the same time, the farms produced surplus crops. To combat this, in 1933, the government passed the Agricultural Adjustment Act. In part, this act authorized payments to farmers who agreed to reduce the acreage they farmed. This effectively reduced the crop surplus and boosted farmer income.

PAGES 151-152

I. Distorting Market Outcomes
  A. Achieving equity and security (two of the seven broad economic and social goals) usually requires policies that distort market outcomes.
  B. One way to achieve these goals is to set "socially desirable" prices, which interferes with the pricing system.
  C. Setting price ceilings affects the allocation of resources.
  D. The minimum wage is an example of a price floor.

☒ Discussion Question
Do you agree with economists who argue that the minimum wage actually contributes to unemployment rates? Why or why not? (Answers will vary but should reflect an understanding of the purpose of price floors.)

PAGES 153-155

II. Agricultural Price Supports
  A. Government loan support was offered in the 1930s through the Commodity Credit Corporation to help stabilize agricultural prices. The CCC loan program led to food surpluses.

Distorting Market Outcomes

One of the common ways of achieving social goals involves setting prices at "socially desirable" levels. When this happens, prices are not allowed to adjust to their equilibrium levels, and the price system cannot transmit accurate information to other buyers and sellers in the market.

Price Ceilings

Some cities, especially New York City, have a long history of using rent controls to make housing more affordable. This is an example of a **price ceiling,** a maximum legal price that can be charged for a product.

The case of a price ceiling is shown in **Panel A** of **Figure 6.5.** Without the ceiling, the market establishes monthly rents at $900, which is an equilibrium price because 2 million apartments

would be supplied and rented at that rate. If authorities think $900 is too high, and if they want to achieve the social goals of equity and security for people who cannot afford these rents, they can establish, arbitrarily, a price ceiling at $600 a month.

No doubt consumers would love the lower price and might demand 2.4 million apartments. Landlords, on the other hand, would try to convert some apartments to other uses, such as condos and office buildings that offer higher returns. Therefore, the supply might only reach 1.6 million apartments at $600 per month, leaving a *permanent* shortage of 800,000 apartments.

Are consumers better off? Perhaps not. More than likely, the better apartments will be converted to condos or offices—leaving the poorer ones to be rented. In addition, 800,000 people are now unhappy because they cannot get an apartment, although they are willing and able to pay for one. Prices no longer allocate apartments.

CHAPTER 6: PRICES AND DECISION MAKING **151**

ECONOMICS AT A GLANCE

Answer: *They feel a market price is too high or too low.*

INTERACTIVE ECONOMICS!

💿 **CD-ROM**

PRICE DETERMINATION Have students click on "Price Ceilings and Floors" in Lesson 5. Then have them write a paragraph describing the advantages and disadvantages of a price ceiling on rents. *(advantage: to control prices of rents; disadvantage: shortage of rental units).*

💾 Also supplied in disk format.

MEETING SPECIAL NEEDS ACTIVITY

Learning Style: Verbal/Linguistic Organize students into groups and assign each group a government price control policy, like the minimum wage, rent control, or agricultural price supports. Have students in each group identify people or firms who might benefit or suffer economically because of the policy. Then have each student individually assume the role of one of the people or firms discussed in the group, and explain to the class in a brief speech how the policy affects that character in particular.

📂 Refer to *Inclusion for the Social Studies Classroom Strategies and Activities* in the TCR.

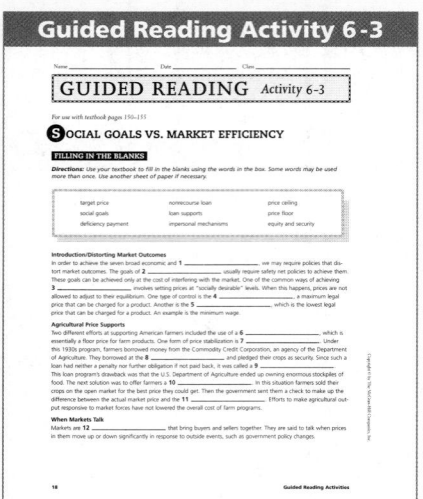

L1 Price Ceilings

Have students draw political cartoons depicting a concern related to a price ceiling, such as rent controls. The cartoon can show the frustrations of the consumers or producers involved, or the benefits of the policy. **ELL**

CYBERNOMICS

Outside the Law In the case of body organs, the government has imposed a price control of zero. While people are allowed to donate organs upon their death, anyone caught selling human organs can get up to five years in prison or a $50,000 fine. Price controls like this, however, often engender black markets. In 1999, for example, someone offered to sell a kidney on eBay, an online auction site. The bidding rose to $5.7 million before eBay cancelled the illegal auction.

Instead, landlords resort to long waiting lists or other nonprice criteria such as excluding children and pets to discourage applicants.

Rent controls freeze a landlord's total revenue and threaten his or her profits. As a result, the landlord tries to lower costs by providing the absolute minimum upkeep, thereby protecting profits. Landlords may have no incentive at all to add additional units if they feel rents are too low. Some apartment buildings may even be torn down to make way for shopping centers, factories, or high-rise office buildings.

The price ceiling, like any other price, affects the allocation of resources—but not in the way intended. The attempt to limit rents makes some people happy, until their buildings begin to deteriorate. Others, including landlords and potential renters on waiting lists, are unhappy from the beginning. Finally, some scarce resources—those used to build and maintain apartments—are slowly shifted out of the rental market.

Careers

Sales Clerk

The primary purpose of a sales clerk is to interest customers in the merchandise. How successful a business is depends in large part on how efficient and courteous its sales force is.

The Work

Sales clerks' duties include stocking shelves, taking inventory, and dealing directly with customers. Clerks must be able to demonstrate the product, record the sales transaction, and, if necessary, arrange for the product's safe delivery. For those selling complex items such as computers or automobiles, knowing special features and what they can do is essential.

Qualifications

Ability to work under pressure is helpful. Other required skills include a strong working knowledge of business math for calculating prices and taxes, and the ability to communicate clearly and tactfully.

152 UNIT 2 MICROECONOMICS

Price Floors

Other prices often are considered too low and so steps are taken to keep them higher. The **minimum wage,** the lowest legal wage that can be paid to most workers, is a case in point. The minimum wage is actually a **price floor,** or lowest legal price that can be paid for a good or service.

Panel B in **Figure 6.5** uses a minimum wage of $5.15 per hour as an illustration of a price floor. At this wage, the supply curve shows that 14 million people would want to offer their services. According to the demand curve for labor, however, only 10 million would be hired—leaving a surplus of 4 million workers.

The figure also shows that without the minimum wage, the actual demand and supply of labor would establish an equilibrium price of $4.00 per hour. At this wage, 12 million workers would offer their services and the same number would be hired—which means that there would be neither a shortage nor a surplus in the labor market.

Some economists argue that the minimum wage actually increases the number of people who do not have jobs because employers hire fewer workers. In the case of **Figure 6.5,** the number of people who lose jobs amounts to 2 million—the difference between the 12 million who would have worked at the equilibrium price and the 10 million who actually work at the higher wage of $5.15 per hour.

Is the minimum wage good or bad for the economy? Certainly the minimum wage is not as efficient as a wage set by supply and demand, but not all decisions in our economy are made on the basis of efficiency. The basic argument in favor of the minimum wage is that it raises poor people's incomes. A federal minimum wage is evidence that the small measure of equity provided by the minimum wage—with equity being one of our seven major economic and social goals—is preferred to the loss of efficiency.

Finally, some people argue that the minimum wage is irrelevant anyway because it is actually lower than the lowest wages paid in many areas. Consider the wages in your area. Do you think that your employer would pay you less if he or she were allowed to do so? Your response will provide a partial answer to the question.

FREE ENTERPRISE ACTIVITY

Invite a farmer from the area, or a representative of a farmers' association, to visit the class. Encourage the visitor to talk about farm operations in the area, why farmers have difficulty predicting prices for their crops from year to year, and the removal of agricultural price supports. Ask the speaker to evaluate government's role in agriculture. In a follow-up discussion, have students review the meaning of target prices, nonrecourse loans, and deficiency payments. **BLOCK SCHEDULING**

Price Stabilization

Loan Supports The government plays a role in helping farmers market their products and stabilizing agricultural prices. *What problems did the program of loan supports create?*

Agricultural Price Supports

In the 1930s, the federal government established the Commodity Credit Corporation (CCC), an agency in the Department of Agriculture, to help stabilize agricultural prices. The stabilization took two basic forms—the first involved loan supports, and the second involved deficiency payments. Both made use of a **target price,** which is essentially a price floor for farm products.

Loan Supports

Under the loan support program, a farmer borrowed money from the CCC at the target price and pledged his or her crops as security in return. The farmer used the loan to plant, maintain, and harvest the crop. The farmer sold the crop in the

market and used the proceeds to repay the CCC loan, or the farmer kept the proceeds of the loan and let the CCC take possession of the crop. Because the loan was a **nonrecourse loan**—a loan that carries neither a penalty nor further obligation to repay if not paid back—the farmer could get at least the target price for his or her crops.

Panel A in **Figure 6.6** illustrates the CCC loan program using a $4-per-bushel target price for wheat. In the end, the farmer received $4 a bushel for each of the 10,000 bushels produced—with 8,000 sold in the market and the remaining 2,000 picked up by the CCC—for a total of $40,000. Without the loan program, the farmer would have produced 9,000 bushels and then sold them at $3 each for a total revenue of $27,000.

Deficiency Payments

The CCC loan program created problems because the U.S. Department of Agriculture soon owned enormous stockpiles of food. Surplus wheat was stored in rented warehouses or on open ground. Surplus milk was made into cheese and stored in underground caves. Some food was given to the military, and other food was donated to public schools for use in "free lunch" programs. Still the surpluses persisted, leaving CCC officials to consider how they could support farm prices and still avoid holding large surpluses.

The solution was to have farmers sell their crops on the open market for the best price they could get and then have the CCC make up the difference with a deficiency payment. A **deficiency payment** is a

Did you know?

Gender Pricing Women often pay higher prices for haircuts, dry cleaning, and clothes than do men. Massachusetts found that women were charged up to $2.50 more per dry cleaned item than men. Dry cleaners claimed that women's clothing was harder to press because the equipment was designed for men's shirts. Although some states have laws against gender-biased pricing, these laws are hard to enforce across the many industries.

CHAPTER 6: PRICES AND DECISION MAKING **153**

CRITICAL THINKING

Analyzing Information Some people are outraged that the government subsidizes tobacco farmers and at the same time funds programs to discourage people from consuming tobacco. Explain to your students that these subsidies are in the form of price supports. Have your students draw supply and demand diagrams for tobacco with a price floor above the equilibrium price, then ask them if the price support encourages or discourages tobacco consumption. They should discover that, paradoxically, subsidies to tobacco farmers discourage tobacco use.

③ ASSESS

Assign Section 3 Assessment as homework or as an in-class activity.

📕 Have students use **Interactive Tutor Self-Assessment Software** to review Section 3.

Section Quiz 6-3

QUIZ ◆ Chapter 6, Section 3

SOCIAL GOALS VS. MARKET EFFICIENCY SCORE

Matching: Match each item in Column A with the items in Column B. Write the correct letters in the blanks. (10 points each)

A	B
___ 1. price ceiling	a. a check sent to producers that makes up the difference between the actual market price and the target price
___ 2. price floor	b. the lowest legal price that can be paid to most workers
___ 3. target price	c. floor price for farm products
___ 4. nonrecourse loan	d. carries neither a penalty nor further obligation to repay if not paid back
___ 5. deficiency payment	e. a maximum legal price that can be charged for a product
	f. partial refund of the original price of a product

Multiple Choice: In the blank at the left write the letter of the choice that best completes the statement or answers the question. (10 points each)

___ 6. Which of the following is an example of a price ceiling?
   a. minimum wage   b. "free lunch" program
   c. rent control   d. government subsidies

___ 7. Price ceilings that are artificially low are likely to create
   a. a price floor   b. a surplus.
   c. an equilibrium.   d. a shortage.

___ 8. Price floors that are artificially high are likely to create
   a. a price ceiling.   b. a surplus.
   c. an equilibrium.   d. a shortage.

___ 9. Why might a government interfere in a market economy by setting prices?
   a. to achieve the goals of equity and security   b. to insure an entrepreneur's profit
   c. to distort market outcomes   d. to allow the price system to transmit accurate information

___ 10. What is meant by the phrase "markets talk"?
   a. Market changes are written about in newspapers and magazines.   b. Government officials base decisions on the stock market.
   c. Businesspeople rely on good communication to conduct business.   d. Markets reflect the thoughts and feelings of buyers and sellers.

16   Section Quizzes

ECONOMICS
AT A GLANCE

Figure 6.6

Agricultural Price Support Programs

A CCC Loan Program

Price of Wheat — Target Price $4.00; $3.00; $2.00; $5.00

CCC acquires unsold portion of crop in exchange for loan default.

Quantity in Thousands of Bushels — 0 4 8 9 10 12 16

B CCC Deficiency Payments

Price of Wheat — Target Price $5.00; $4.00; $3.00; $2.50

The farmer is paid the difference between the target and the market price.

Quantity in Thousands of Bushels — 0 4 8 9 10 12 16

Using Graphs The farmer sells surplus crops to the government under the plan shown in Panel A. The farmer receives a payment equal to the difference between the target price and the prices the farmer received for the crops. What was the total payment the farmer received under the loan program? Under the deficiency payment program?

check sent to producers that makes up the difference between the actual market price and the target price.

Panel B in **Figure 6.6** illustrates the deficiency payment approach. Under this program, the farmer made $25,000 by selling 10,000 bushels at $2.50 each on the open market. Because this was $1.50 below the target price of $4.00 a bushel, the farmer received a deficiency payment of $1.50, times 10,000 bushels, or the $15,000 represented by the shaded area.

When the $15,000 deficiency payment was added to the $25,000 market sale, the farmer made $40,000—the same as under the loan program. Under this program, however, the CCC does not have the political and economic problem of disposing of the surplus. Farmers liked this program and would have produced even more crops if they could. Instead, they had to promise the CCC that they would limit production. In many cases, aerial photographs were taken to verify that the acreage planted was within the limits of the agreement with the CCC.

154 UNIT 2 MICROECONOMICS

Reforming Price Supports

In an effort to make agricultural output responsive to market forces, Congress passed the Federal Agricultural Improvement and Reform (FAIR) Act of 1996. Under this law, eligible producers of grains, cotton, and rice can enter into a seven-year program that allows them almost complete flexibility to plant any crop on any land. Other products, such as milk, sugar, fruits, and vegetables, are not affected.

Under FAIR, cash payments take the place of price supports and deficiency payments. Because these new payments have turned out to be as large as the ones they replaced, however, the overall cost of farm programs has not gone down. Instead, in 1998 a drop in worldwide food prices made things even worse for farmers. This, as we saw in the cover story, prompted Congress to pass a $5 billion aid bill for farmers—with possibly more in the works.

EXTENDING THE CONTENT

Price Changes The Civil War almost halted American exports of cotton to England. As a result, the price of cotton in Liverpool rose from 8 pence (English pennies) per pound in 1860 to 31 1/2 pence per pound in 1864. There was a subsequent decrease in the demand for people working in the cotton industry. Another result of the price increase was the great increase in production of substitute fabrics. In Ireland, flax production quadrupled from 1861 to 1864. During this relatively short period, then, the increase in the price of cotton caused changes in the demand for workers and in the production and demand for substitute fabrics. Ask students to draw diagrams showing the shift in the demand and supply curves for cotton and various substitutes in the first half of the 1860s.

When the program expires in the year 2002, farmers will cease to receive all payments. By then, farmers should have had enough experience with the laws of supply and demand to no longer need government help. If farm income is still down when the bill expires, Congress may decide to bring farm support back–thereby choosing the goal of economic security over efficiency.

When Markets Talk

 Markets are impersonal mechanisms that bring buyers and sellers together. Although markets do not talk in the usual sense of the word, they do communicate in that they speak collectively for all of the buyers and sellers who trade in the markets. Markets are said to talk when prices in them move up or down significantly.

Suppose the federal government announced that it would raise personal income taxes and corporate taxes to pay off some of the federal debt. If investors thought this policy would not work or that other policies might be better, they might decide to sell some of their stocks and other investments for cash and gold. As the selling takes place, stock prices fall, and gold prices rise. In effect, the market would "talk"–voicing its disapproval of the new tax policy.

In this example, individual investors made decisions on the likely outcome of the new policy and sold stocks for cash or gold. Together, their actions were enough to influence stock prices and to send a signal to the government that investors did not favor the policy. If investors' feelings were divided about the new policy, some would sell while others bought stocks. As a result, prices might not change, and the message would be that, as yet, the market has not made up its mind.

STANDARD &POOR'S INFOBYTE

Consumer Confidence A statistic called the Consumer Confidence Index attempts to gauge consumers' feelings about the current condition of the economy and their expectations about the economy's future direction. The index is weighted 60% in favor of expectations and 40% in favor of current conditions. Large movements in this index indicate or signal changes in consumer spending patterns.

Section 3 Assessment

Checking for Understanding

1. **Main Idea** Using your notes from the graphic organizer activity on page 150, describe why price ceilings are often set.

2. **Key Terms** Define price ceiling, minimum wage, price floor, target price, nonrecourse loan, deficiency payment.

3. **Describe** two effects of having a fixed price other than the equilibrium price forced on a market.

4. **Explain** how loan supports and deficiency payments work.

5. **Describe** how markets speak collectively for buyers and sellers.

Applying Economic Concepts

6. **Price Floor** Would small businesses be more affected by a change in the minimum wage than large businesses? Explain your answer.

Critical Thinking

7. **Understanding Cause and Effect** The price of fresh fruit over the course of a year may go up or down by as much as 100 percent. Explain the causes for these changes in terms of changes in demand, changes in supply, and the elasticity of demand for fresh fruit.

  Practice and **assess** key social studies skills with the *Glencoe Skillbuilder Interactive Workbook, Level 2.*

CHAPTER 6: PRICES AND DECISION MAKING **155**

Reteach

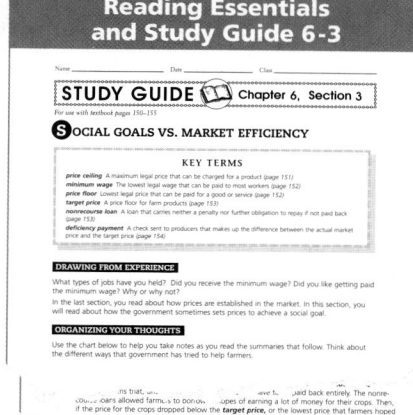

Reading Essentials and Study Guide 6-3

Name _____ Date _____ Class _____

STUDY GUIDE Chapter 6, Section 3

For use with textbook pages 150–155

SOCIAL GOALS VS. MARKET EFFICIENCY

KEY TERMS

price ceiling A maximum legal price that can be charged for a product (page 151)
minimum wage The lowest legal wage that can be paid to most workers (page 152)
price floor Lowest legal price that can be paid for a good or service (page 152)
target price A price floor for farm products (page 153)
nonrecourse loan A loan that carries neither a penalty nor further obligation to repay if not paid back (page 153)
deficiency payment A check sent to producers that makes up the difference between the actual market price and the target price (page 154)

DRAWING FROM EXPERIENCE

What types of jobs have you held? Did you receive the minimum wage? Did you like getting paid the minimum wage? Why or why not?
In the last section, you read about how prices are established in the market. In this section, you will read about how the government sometimes sets prices to achieve a social goal.

ORGANIZING YOUR THOUGHTS

Use the chart below to help you take notes as you read the summaries that follow. Think about the different ways that government has tried to help farmers.

Enrich

Have students collect examples of "when markets talk" by reading newspapers and periodicals, watching television news, and listening to the radio. Ask students to share their examples with the class and discuss how the market reacted to certain events.

 CLOSE

Remind students that prices can be viewed as signals. Ask them to create a logo or symbol that illustrates this idea.

Section 3 Assessment Answers

1. to achieve equity and security

2. All vocabulary terms are defined in the text.

3. Shortages result if prices are set below equilibrium; surpluses result if prices are set above it.

4. Loan supports allow farmers to borrow against crops. Deficiency payments supply farmers with checks for the difference between the target price and the actual price.

5. The significant movement of prices, either up or down, signals the collective decisions.

6. Salaries represent a larger percentage of costs for small businesses.

7. Supply is affected by seasons and by weather. Because demand tends to be stable and slightly inelastic, a change in supply can cause a large change in price.

TEACH

Use a supply and demand diagram to illustrate how the quantity of physicians is changing in different areas. Draw two supply and demand diagrams for physicians: one for metro areas with a strong HMO presence and one for metro areas with a weak HMO presence. Show on the diagram how the supply of physicians decreased between 1990 and 1994 in metro areas with a strong HMO presence and how it increased during that period in metro areas with a weak HMO presence.

📁 Refer to *Business Week Focus on the New Economy* in the TCR for additional unit-based articles.

BusinessWeek

DECEMBER 21, 1998

Newsclip

Many considerations are involved in an individual's choice of jobs. These include not only whether and how much to work, but where to work. As you read this article, think about what influences affect labor demand. What influences affect labor mobility?

Doctors: Charting New Territory

Health officials have long bemoaned the fact that new doctors tend to choose to practice in large, relatively affluent communities, with the result that many smaller towns and rural areas are often undersupplied. Now, changes in the health-care market itself may be starting to cure the "maldistribution" of doctors.

According to a new RAND study, the growth of health-maintenance organizations is shifting the locales where new docs decide to practice. At the start of the 1990s, reports Jose J. Escarce of RAND, newly graduated general practitioners tended to locate in large metro areas where HMOs were well established, while new specialists chose metro areas regardless of HMO presence. By 1994, however, new generalists and especially specialists tended to locate in metro areas with low HMO penetration.

Why is this happening? Noting that general practitioners are in high demand throughout the U.S., Escarce and his fellow researchers theorize that many are seeking to avoid HMOs and the cost-control pressures they impose on primary physicians. And new specialists may be relocating because HMOs have been particularly successful in curbing demand for their services.

The RAND study looked only at larger metro areas. But the results offer the hopeful prospect that continued HMO growth in such areas could result in more new docs hanging their shingles up in smaller cities and rural locations.

Many physicians are relocating to rural areas. A major reason is avoiding cost-control pressures that health-maintenance organizations place on them.

Examining the Newsclip

1. **Sequencing Information** What trend does the RAND research show regarding doctors' choices of location?

2. **Finding the Main Idea** What theory do the researchers offer to support this relocation trend?

3. **Understanding Cause and Effect** Do you think the theory is the best explanation for the trend? What other factors affect where doctors locate their practices?

Answers to Examining the Newsclip

1. RAND research shows that generalists and specialists are settling in metro areas with low HMO penetration.

2. Doctors are trying to avoid HMOs because these organizations often curb the demand for their services.

3. Answers should recognize that various other factors may influence where doctors locate.

Section 1

Prices as Signals (pages 137–140)

- **Prices** serve as signals to both producers and consumers. In doing so, they help decide the three basic WHAT, HOW, and FOR WHOM questions that all societies face.

- High prices are signals for businesses to produce more and for consumers to buy less. Low prices are signals for businesses to produce less and for consumers to buy more.

- Prices have the advantages of neutrality, flexibility, efficiency, and clarity.

- Other nonprice allocation methods such as **rationing** can be used. Under such a system, people receive **ration coupons,** which are similar to tickets or receipts that entitle the holder to purchase a certain amount of a product.

- Nonprice allocation systems suffer from problems regarding fairness, high administrative costs, and diminished incentives to work and produce.

- A market economy is made up of many different markets, and different prices prevail in each. A change in price in one market affects more than the allocation of resources in that market. It also affects the allocation of resources between markets.

Section 2

The Price System at Work

(pages 142–148)

- Economists often use an **economic model** to help analyze behavior and predict outcomes. Models of economic markets are often represented with supply and demand curves in order to examine the concept of **market equilibrium,** a situation in which prices are relatively stable, and the quantity of output supplied is equal to the quantity demanded.

- In a competitive market, prices are established by the forces of supply and demand. If the price is too high, a temporary **surplus** appears until the price goes down. If the price is too low, a temporary shortage appears until the price rises. Eventually the market reaches the equilibrium price where there is neither a shortage nor a surplus.

- A change in price can be caused by a change in supply or a change in demand. The size of the price change is affected by the elasticity of both curves. The more elastic the curves, the smaller the price change; the less elastic the curves, the larger the price change.

- The theory of competitive pricing represents a set of ideal conditions and outcomes. The theory serves as a model by which to measure the performance of other, less competitive markets. Because of this, absolutely pure competition is not needed for the theory of competitive pricing to be practical.

Section 3

Social Goals vs. Market Efficiency (pages 150–155)

- Governments sometimes fix prices at levels above or below the equilibrium price to achieve the social goals of equity and security.

- If the fixed price is a **price ceiling,** as in the case of rent controls, a shortage usually appears for as long as the price remains fixed below the equilibrium price.

- Agricultural price supports were introduced during the 1930s to support farm incomes. **Nonrecourse loan** support programs allowed farmers to borrow against crops, and then keep the loan and forfeit the crop if market prices were low.

- Later, **deficiency payments** were used, supplying the farmer with a check that made up the difference between the **target price** and the actual price received for the product.

NIGHTLY BUSINESS REPORT

ECONOMICS & YOU

Chapter 12
Disc 1, Side 1

The Price System at Work

Also available in VHS.

Using the Chapter 6 Summary

Use the Chapter 6 Summary to preview, review, condense, or reteach the chapter.

Preview/Review

Vocabulary PuzzleMaker CD-ROM reinforces Key Terms.

Interactive Tutor Self-Assessment Software provides a review of Chapter 6 content.

Condense

Have students listen to the Chapter 6 Audio Program. Spanish also available.

Assign the Chapter 6 Audio Program Activity and give students the Chapter 6 Audio Program Test.

Have students complete the Guided Reading Activities and Reading Essentials and Study Guides for Chapter 6.

Reteach

Have students complete Reteaching Activity 6 in the TCR. Spanish also available.

Teacher's Notes / Internet Bookmarks

157

GLENCOE
TECHNOLOGY

Use **MindJogger Videoquiz** to review the Chapter 6 content.

Have students visit the Web site at epp.glencoe.com to review Chapter 6 and take the **Self-Check Quiz.**

Identifying Key Terms

1. **d**
2. **a**
3. **e**
4. **c**
5. **c**

Reviewing the Facts

Section 1

1. Prices are neutral, favoring neither producer nor consumer, and flexible, allowing the market economy to accommodate change. Prices have no administrative costs and are efficient because they are understood by all.

2. establishing fair system of allocation; cost of administering system; negative impact system has on incentive to work and produce

Section 2

3. Examples may include graphs of supply and demand curves.
4. shortage: the quantity demanded is greater than the quantity supplied at a given price, and prices will go up; surplus: the quantity supplied is greater than the quantity demanded, and prices will go down.
5. a change in supply, a change in demand, or a change in both

---

Self-Check Quiz Visit the *Economics: Principles and Practices* Web site at epp.glencoe.com and click on *Chapter 6—Self-Check Quizzes* to prepare for the chapter test.

Identifying Key Terms

Write the key term that is an effect of the five causes stated below. Some causes may have more than one effect.

a. rationing
b. economic model
c. surplus
d. shortage
e. equilibrium price
f. loss leader
g. price ceiling
h. price floor

1. **Cause:** The government tries to keep prices down by legislating price ceilings. **Effect:** _____
2. **Cause:** The government wants to allocate scarce goods and services without the help of a price system. **Effect:** _____
3. **Cause:** A reasonably competitive market is experiencing alternating, yet consecutively smaller, surpluses and shortages. **Effect:** _____
4. **Cause:** People decide that farmers should receive a higher price for milk and cheese, so a price floor for these products is established. **Effect:** _____
5. **Cause:** A market is at equilibrium, but the product falls out of style before producers can reduce production. **Effect:** _____

Reviewing the Facts

Section 1 (pages 137–140)

1. **Describe** four advantages of using price as an allocating mechanism.
2. **List** three problems of allocating goods and services using nonprice-related methods.

Section 3

6. At lower prices there is no incentive for producers to produce more, so shortages continue. At higher prices there is no incentive to buy, so surpluses remain.
7. loan supports, deficiency payments
8. The significant movement of prices up or down reflects the judgments of all buyers and sellers in the market. Enough buyers or sellers cause significant price movements that communicate to all buyers and sellers.

Section 2 (pages 142–148)

3. **Cite** an example of an economic model used in this chapter.
4. **Explain** the role of shortages and surpluses in competitive markets.
5. **Describe** three causes of a price change in a market.

Section 3 (pages 150–155)

6. **Explain** why shortages and surpluses are not temporary when price controls are used.
7. **Identify** two programs that have historically been used to stabilize farm incomes.
8. **Explain** what is meant by the statement that markets "talk."

Thinking Critically

1. **Making Generalizations** Some people argue that the minimum wage is not a fair price. Use a web like the one below to help you identify reasons for this argument. Explain why you agree or disagree.

Minimum wage		Reason #1
		Reason #2

2. **Making Predictions** Suppose that your state wanted to make health care more affordable for everyone. To do this, state legislators put a series of price controls–price ceilings–in place that cut the cost of medical services in half. What would happen to the demand for medical services at the new, lower price? What would happen to the supply of medical services that doctors would be willing to provide at the new, lower price? Where do you think new doctors would prefer to set up practice? Explain the reasons for your answers.

Thinking Critically

1. Answers will vary.
2. Because demand for medical services tends to be inelastic, the quantity demanded will increase only moderately. Because prices for services would be set below market level, there would be less incentive for doctors to offer services. Quantity supplied would probably decrease. New doctors might want to set up practice in states where there were no price ceilings.

Applying Economic Concepts

1. **Rationing** Suppose that a guest speaker visited your class and left 20 ballpoint pens as samples—not knowing that there were 30 students in the class. Devise a nonprice rationing system that would fairly allocate the scarce item to everyone in the class.

2. **Equilibrium Price** Many people feel that the minimum wage is too low. If it increased by $1 per hour, what would happen to the number of students who would want to work after school? What would happen to the number of workers that stores in your community would want to hire? Would the combination of these factors cause a shortage or a surplus of workers in your community? Provide an explanation for each of your answers.

Math Practice

A shoe store is having a sale. The first pair of shoes sells for $40. The second pair sells for half price, or $20. The next pair sells for half of that, and so on. Make a table, like the one below, that tracks the total cost of the shoes as each pair is added.

Number of Pairs	Total Cost

Thinking Like an Economist

Economists like to use cost-benefit analysis to analyze the merits of any program. Use this decision-making strategy to evaluate the desirability of continuing to support and stabilize farm income.

Technology Skill

Using a Spreadsheet Use your personal buying decisions to create a spreadsheet and graph showing how a market equilibrium price is reached.

1. Select a product that costs about $5.00.

2. In cells A1 through C1, enter the words *Price, Demand,* and *Supply.*

3. In cells A2 through A11, enter prices that range from $1.00 to $10.00.

4. In the next two columns, enter quantities that might be demanded and supplied at those prices.

5. Highlight the three columns on the spreadsheet, then click on "Chart Wizard" or a similar icon, or click on "Insert" and then "Chart."

6. Click on "line graph," then highlight a 2-line chart sub-type.

7. Follow the spreadsheet directions to title your graph.

Building Skills

Synthesizing Information Examine the figure, then answer the questions that follow.

1. What is the quantity demanded at a price of $20? At $15?

2. What is the quantity supplied at a price of $10? At a price of $20?

3. How large is the shortage or surplus at $5? Explain your answer.

4. If the price started out at $5 today, what would likely happen to the price tomorrow? Why?

 Practice and **assess** key social studies skills with the *Glencoe Skillbuilder Interactive Workbook, Level 2.*

Thinking Like an Economist

Answers will vary. Some may note that the government does not receive in return what it pays into programs for farmers, so farm supports should be stopped.

Technology Skill

Check spreadsheets for accuracy.

Building Skills

1. 3; 6
2. 3; 9
3. a shortage of 14; supply is 1, but demand is 15, leaving shortage of 14.
4. It would go up until an equilibrium between supply and demand is reached.

Bonus Test Question

Have students identify what will happen to prices in the following situations:

1. Supply decreases and demand is elastic. *(prices rise slightly)*
2. Supply increases and demand is inelastic. *(prices fall markedly)*
3. A surplus exists. *(prices fall)*
4. Supply remains constant but demand increases. *(prices rise)*
5. A shortage exists. *(prices rise)*

Applying Economic Concepts

1. Rationing systems will vary.
2. At a higher minimum wage, there would be more incentive for workers to sell their labor. The number of students wanting to work after school would increase. The higher cost of labor would result in store managers hiring fewer workers, so there might be a surplus of workers.

Math Practice

Number of Pairs	Total Cost
1	$40
2	$60
3	$70
4	$75
5	$77.50

Economics in Action Workshop

① FOCUS

The purpose of this activity is to provide students with a hands-on opportunity to analyze an economic process and describe it clearly in the form of a training manual.

② TEACH

- Introduce the workshop activity by displaying and discussing training manuals for a variety of products and processes. Challenge students to identify what all of the descriptions have in common and why these elements are critical. **Ask:** Why are analyzing and describing processes vital economic skills?

- After students have read the introduction, invite volunteers to suggest appropriate topics for manuals. Record salient responses on the board and invite student pairs to choose their topics from the list.

- Encourage students to create comprehensive, detailed flow-charts as a way to take notes during their research, as an outline for their manuals, and for use as illustrations in their manuals.

- Arrange to meet with student pairs after they have conducted their research in order to guide them in the preparation of their manuals. Emphasize that they are participating in a process, and not an act, and so should plan and craft their manuals carefully, and make necessary revisions.

ECONOMICS WORKSHOP IN ACTION

Developing a Training Manual

From the classroom of . . .
Juan C. Ledesma
Flanagan High School
Pembroke Pines, Florida

*The forces of supply and demand determine what is produced and made available to the consumer. Many products in the marketplace would have little value if you—the consumer—did not know how to use the product. Thus, as new products and technology are developed, a **demand** is created for manuals that illustrate the correct way to use the product. In this workshop, you will write a "how-to" manual or report. The manual will illustrate how to accomplish a process or function that you've chosen to describe.*

160 UNIT 2 MICROECONOMICS

Setting Up the Workshop

For this workshop you should work with one other person. Your task is to write a technical manual or report that explains how to construct, instruct, build, rebuild, or just plain create a product or process. Your audience must be real—fellow students, your teachers, your family members, etc. Keep this goal in mind as you do your work: The reader will learn something important, functional, and worthwhile after using your manual.

Criteria for Manuals

Your finished manual should include all of the following:

- Numbered pages
- Title page
- Statement of purpose
- Table of contents that includes at least five sections
- At least five sections that explain "how to"
- Scaled pictures or drawings of important parts, plans, and procedures, placed appropriately in the manual
- Chart, or graphic organizer, that reveals some important, usable data (e.g. a survey)
- Reference list of at least five other resource materials that could be utilized
- Information gained from an interview with an expert on the topic
- Alphabetized index of the important topics in the manual
- Checklist for procedures
- Troubleshooting guide with at least ten "what if" problems
- Review/rating/recommendation by someone who has tried the manual

Participating in Economics

How-To Manuals From the Real World Assign one or more working pairs of students the following task: contact a local business and ask to borrow (or copy representative pages from) a manual the business uses to train or guide workers. Try to have students collect manuals from a variety of businesses (manufacturing, retail, and so on). Have students interview managers about the importance of the manuals to the proper operation of their businesses. Have students share what they learn with the class.

Procedures

STEP 1

Determine what process you will describe.

STEP 2

Do research in your school library or on the Internet for information about your process. Interview a person locally who is familiar with the process.

STEP 3

Make an outline of the process you hope to describe. A flowchart, like the example shown below, is often a good way to get started "mapping" the steps in a process.

Process to get ready for school

Start
1 → 2 → 3 → 4 → 5a End

| Wake up | Shower | Dress | Eat breakfast | Catch the bus |

→ 5b

| Drive to school |

STEP 4

Put your manual together following the criteria listed at left.

Summary Activity

Present your training manual to your class, using the following guidelines:

1. Explain the rationale for your manual's subject.

2. Describe the aspirations you hold for your product and its user.

3. Describe any technology you used to create your manual.

4. Describe the trials and errors you encountered in developing your manual.

5. Describe the problems that you might foresee that could still be addressed (and even solved) if you had the time.

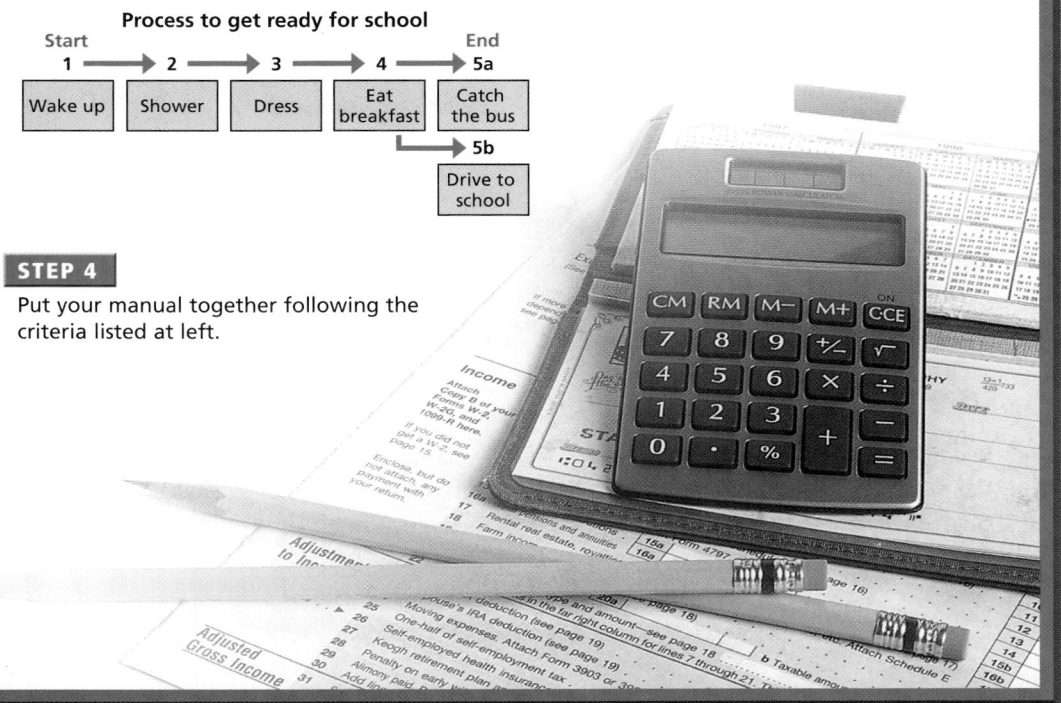

③ ASSESS

Have students write paragraphs that explain in general terms *what* manuals are, *how* they are developed, *who* uses them, *when* they are used, *where* they are used, and *why* they are important.

④ CLOSE

Invite students to present their manuals in a hallway display with appropriate explanatory cards.

Summary Activity Answers

Student summaries will vary. Reward students who address each of the five summary points thoroughly, in turn. Interrupt student summaries to ask questions that elicit details or make general points. Invite the class to ask appropriate questions after students have finished their presentations.

Chapter 7 Resource Manager

SECTION RESOURCES

Daily Objectives	Reproducible Resources	Technology/Multimedia Resources
Section 1 **Competition and Market Structures** 1. Explain the characteristics of perfect competition. 2. Understand the nature of monopolistic competition. 3. Describe the behavior and characteristics of the oligopolist. 4. Identify several types of monopolies.	Reproducible Lesson Plan 7-1 Daily Lecture Notes 7-1 Guided Reading Activity 7-1 Reading Essentials and Study Guide 7-1 Section Quiz 7-1*	Daily Focus Transparency 20 NBR Economics & You Video Program Interactive Tutor Self-Assessment Software ExamView® Pro Testmaker Presentation Plus!
Section 2 **Market Failures** 1. Discuss the problems caused by inadequate competition. 2. Understand the importance of having adequate information. 3. Describe the nature of resource immobility. 4. Explain the nature of positive and negative externalities.	Reproducible Lesson Plan 7-2 Daily Lecture Notes 7-2 Guided Reading Activity 7-2 Reading Essentials and Study Guide 7-2 Section Quiz 7-2*	Daily Focus Transparency 21 Interactive Tutor Self-Assessment Software ExamView® Pro Testmaker Presentation Plus!
Section 3 **The Role of Government** 1. Discuss major antitrust legislation in the United States. 2. Understand the need for limited government regulation. 3. Explain the value of public disclosure. 4. Discuss the modifications to our free enterprise economy.	Reproducible Lesson Plan 7-3 Daily Lecture Notes 7-3 Guided Reading Activity 7-3 Reading Essentials and Study Guide 7-3 Section Quiz 7-3*	Daily Focus Transparency 22 Vocabulary PuzzleMaker CD-ROM Interactive Tutor Self-Assessment Software ExamView® Pro Testmaker Presentation Plus!

 Transparency   CD-ROM   Software   Blackline Master

*Also available in Spanish

 Videodisc   Audio Program   Videocassette

KEY TO ABILITY LEVELS

Teaching strategies have been coded for varying learning styles and abilities.

L1 BASIC activities for all students

L2 AVERAGE activities for average to above-average students

L3 CHALLENGING activities for above-average students

ELL ENGLISH LANGUAGE LEARNER activities

Block Schedule

Activities that are particularly suited to use within the block scheduling framework are identified throughout this chapter by the following designation: **BLOCK SCHEDULING**

Chapter 7 Resource Manager

Timesaving Tools

TeacherWorks™ All-In-One Planner and Resource Center

- **Interactive Teacher Edition** Access your Teacher Wraparound Edition and your classroom resources with a few easy clicks.
- **Interactive Lesson Planner** Planning has never been easier! Organize your week, month, semester, or year with all the lesson helps you need to make teaching creative, timely, and relevant.

Use Glencoe's **Presentation Plus!** multimedia teacher tool to easily present dynamic lessons that visually excite your students. Using Microsoft PowerPoint® you can customize the presentations to create your own personalized lessons.

ACTIVITY

From the Classroom of...

**Joanne Benjamin
Los Gatos High School
Los Gatos, CA**

Oligopolies

One fun activity that I have my students do when we study oligopolies is to have them go to the grocery store with a list of products (cereal, detergents, frozen foods, and so on). They are to find which companies produce each of the products.

These questions can be used in a class discussion and can be repeated for a variety of products:

1. How many different manufacturers did you find in the ___ (example: *cereal section*)?
2. How many brands of ___ (*cereal*) does each manufacturer produce?
3. What type of market structure does this industry represent? (*oligopoly*)
4. What do you think the concentration ratio is of this industry? (*Let students guess. For cereals, the four largest firms produce about 85 percent of the industry output. For an AP class, you can also discuss the Herfindahl index.*)
5. How do firms in this industry build sales for their products? (*advertising, coupons, and so on*)

This activity can lead to a variety of other discussions—for example, on different types of nonprice competition, the positive and negative effects of advertising, price leadership, and price wars.

National Council on Economic Education

THE **Economics**America AND **Economics**International PROGRAMS

Voluntary National Content Standards in Economics
Emphasized in Chapter 7

Content Standard 9

Content Standard 16

For a complete listing of NCEE Standards and entire text correlation, see Teacher pages in front of book.

Resources Available from NCEE
- Capstone: The Nation's High School Economics Course
- Focus: High School Economics
- Civics and Government: Focus on Economics
- Economics in Transition: Command to Market
- From Plan to Market
- Entrepreneurship in the U.S. Economy

To order these materials or to contact your state Council on Economic Education about workshops and programs, call 1-800-338-1192 or visit www.nationalcouncil.org

Chapter 7 Resource Manager

TEACHING TRANSPARENCY

Economic Concept Transparency 9: Competition and Market Structure

APPLICATION AND ENRICHMENT

Consumer Application Activity 8

Free Enterprise Activity 8

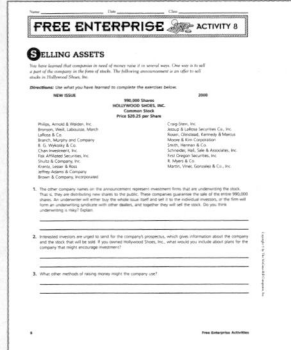

APPLICATION AND ENRICHMENT

Enrichment Activity 7

Cooperative Learning Activity 8

Math Practice Activity 8

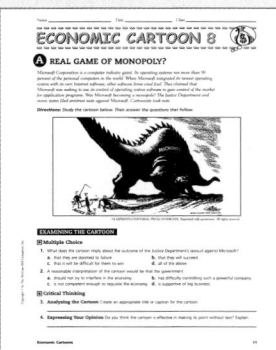

Economic Cartoon 8

Primary and Secondary Source Reading 8

REVIEW AND REINFORCEMENT

Economic Vocabulary Activity 7

Reteaching Activity 7

Critical Thinking Activity 8

Reinforcing Economic Skill 12

Chapter 7 Resource Manager

ASSESSMENT AND EVALUATION

Chapter 7 Test Form A

Chapter 7 Test Form B

Performance Assessment Activity 8

ExamView® Pro Testmaker

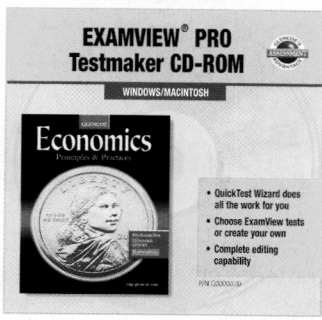

SPANISH RESOURCES

The following Spanish language materials are available in the Spanish Resources binder:

 Spanish Economic Vocabulary Activities

 Spanish Reteaching Activities

 Spanish Section Quizzes

 Spanish Economic Concepts Transparencies

Also available:

  Spanish Chapter 7 Audio Program Activity and Test

TECHNOLOGY/MULTIMEDIA

- Vocabulary PuzzleMaker CD-ROM
- Interactive Tutor Self-Assessment Software
- ExamView® Pro Testmaker
- Audio Program (English or Spanish)
- NBR Economics & You Video Program (English or Spanish)
- MindJogger Videoquiz
- Interactive Economics! CD-ROM
- Presentation Plus!
- TeacherWorks CD-ROM
- Glencoe Skillbuilder Interactive Workbook CD-ROM, Level 2

ECONOMICS Online

Use our Web site for additional resources. All essential content is covered in the Student Edition.

You and your students can visit epp.glencoe.com, the Web site companion to **Economics: Principles and Practices.** This innovative integration of electronic and print media offers your students a wealth of opportunities. The student text directs students to the Web site for the following options:

- **Chapter Overviews**
- **Student Web Activities**
- **Self-Check Quizzes**
- **Textbook Updates**

Answers are provided for you in the Web Activity Lesson Plan. Additional Web resources and interactive puzzles are also available.

CHAPTER 7

Market Structures

Advertisers try to persuade consumers to purchase their products.

Economics & You

Why are some products available at competitive prices? Why are other products priced higher? In **Chapter 7,** you will learn about the various effects competition and market structures have on the prices you pay. To learn more about competition in a free enterprise system, view the Chapter 8 video lesson:

Competition and Monopolies

ECONOMICS *Online*

Chapter Overview Visit the *Economics: Principles and Practices* Web site at epp.glencoe.com and click on **Chapter 7—Chapter Overviews** to preview chapter information.

Competition and Market Structures

Study Guide

Main Idea
Market structures include perfect competition, monopolistic competition, oligopoly, and monopoly.

Reading Strategy
Graphic Organizer As you read the section, complete a graphic organizer similar to the one below by identifying five conditions that characterize perfectly competitive markets.

Perfect competition

Key Terms
laissez-faire, market structure, perfect competition, imperfect competition, monopolistic competition, product differentiation, nonprice competition, oligopoly, collusion, price-fixing, monopoly, natural monopoly, economies of scale, geographic monopoly, technological monopoly, government monoply

Objectives
After studying this section, you will be able to:
1. **Explain** the characteristics of perfect competition.
2. **Understand** the nature of monopolistic competition.
3. **Describe** the behavior and characteristics of the oligopolist.
4. **Identify** several types of monopolies.

Applying Economic Concepts
Product Differentiation Think of a popular brand of shoes or clothing. Read to find out why sellers go to such lengths to differentiate their products.

Cover Story

Air fares cut for business travel

NEW YORK (AP)—In a nod to the importance of corporate travel to their bottom lines, three of the nation's biggest airlines introduced discounts on business fares at a time when planes are flying half-empty nationwide. . . .

Airlines lower fares

The discounts, available for travel through Dec. 31, were adopted Tuesday by Houston-based Continental and Fort-Worth, Texas-based American after Chicago-based United announced its fare change late Monday. Other carriers are expected to follow.

—*The Columbus Dispatch*, October 3, 2001

When Adam Smith published *An Inquiry into the Nature and Causes of the Wealth of Nations* in 1776, the average factory was small, and business was competitive. **Laissez-faire,** the philosophy that government should not interfere with commerce or trade, dominated Smith's writing. "Laissez-faire" is a French term that means "allow them to do." Under laissez-faire, the role of government is confined to protecting private property, enforcing contracts, settling disputes, and protecting businesses against increased competition from foreign goods.

By the late 1800s, however, competition was weakening. In some markets mergers and acquisitions had combined many small firms into a few very large businesses. As industries developed, the nature of competitive markets changed. *Industry* refers to the supply side of the market, or all producers collectively. Many modern markets, such as the one discussed in the cover story, are now dominated by a few very large firms.

CHAPTER 7: MARKET STRUCTURES **163**

Section Overview
This section explains the four market structures.

BELLRINGER
Motivational Activity

 Project **transparency** and have students answer questions.

 Available as blackline master.

Daily Focus Transparency 20

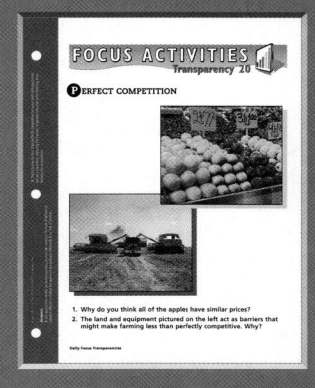

Study Guide

Reading Strategy
Have students create the graphic organizer.
Answers to Graphic: *large number of buyers/sellers, buyers/sellers deal in identical products, buyers/sellers act independently, buyers/sellers well informed, ease of entry into market*

Preteaching Vocabulary
Have students write sentences that use each Key Term in context.

RESOURCE MANAGER

Reproducible Masters
- Reproducible Lesson Plan 7-1
- Daily Lecture Notes 7-1
- Guided Reading Activity 7-1
- Reading Essentials and Study Guide 7-1
- Section Quiz 7-1

Transparencies
- Daily Focus Transparency 20

Multimedia
- Interactive Tutor Self-Assessment Software
- NBR Economics & You Video Program
- ExamView® Pro Testmaker
- Presentation Plus!

② TEACH

Daily Lecture Notes 7-1

DAILY LECTURE NOTES 📖 Lesson 7-1

❶ DID YOU KNOW?

Advertising Age reported that Microsoft Corporation responded to the federal court's 1999 ruling of its monopolistic power in the software industry by launching its largest advertising campaign, designed to portray the company's humility, humaneness, and humor. Microsoft wants its customers to know that the company "empathizes with the situations customers find themselves in," especially in facing "the practical realities of the Internet."

PAGES 164-166

I. Perfect Competition
  A. Perfect competition is when a large number of buyers and sellers exchange identical products under five conditions.
    1. There should be a large number of buyers and sellers.
    2. The products should be identical.
    3. Buyers and sellers should act independently.
    4. Buyers and sellers should be well-informed.
    5. Buyers and sellers should be free to enter, conduct, or get out of business.
  B. Under perfect competition, supply and demand set the equilibrium price, and each firm sets a level of output that will maximize its profits at that price.
  C. Imperfect competition refers to market structures that lack one or more of the five conditions of perfect competition.

▣ Discussion Question

Imagine that your town had an open farmers' market during the spring and summer. How would it meet each condition for a perfectly competitive market? *(Students should indicate that it would draw many buyers and sellers; the products would be farm-grown vegetables and fruits; prices would be set based on the week's harvest (supply) and buyers' demand; buyers examine and select products firsthand; and buyers may choose not to purchase and sellers may choose not to participate or not to offer all farm products.)*

Daily Lecture Notes   36

Visual Instruction

Answer to Caption:
according to conditions that prevail in them

F.Y.I.

The term *laissez-faire* originated with a group of eighteenth-century French economists who supported free trade. Their slogan, *laissez faire, laissez passer* ("let us alone, let us have free circulation of goods") was adopted by Adam Smith to describe the idea of no government interference in the economy.

Market Structures

Conditions A market is a place where buyers and sellers can exchange products. *How do economists classify markets?*

Today, economists classify markets according to conditions that prevail in them. They ask questions such as: How many buyers and suppliers are there? How large are they? Does either have any influence over price? How much competition exists between firms? What kind of product is involved—is everyone trading the exact same product, or are they simply similar? Is it easy or difficult for new firms to enter the market?

The answers to these questions help determine **market structure,** or the nature and degree of competition among firms operating in the same industry. Economists group industries into four different market structures—perfect competition, monopolistic competition, oligopoly, and monopoly.

Perfect Competition

Perfect competition is characterized by a large number of well-informed independent buyers and sellers who exchange identical products. It represents a theoretically ideal situation that is used to evaluate other market structures. Five major conditions characterize perfectly competitive markets.

Necessary Conditions

The first condition is that there are a large number of buyers and sellers. No single buyer or seller is large enough or powerful enough to affect the price.

The second condition is that buyers and sellers deal in identical products. With no difference in quality, there is no need for brand names and no need to advertise. One seller's merchandise is just as good as another's. The market for table salt shares some of these features. Because salt is always the same chemical—sodium chloride—there is no logical reason to prefer one brand of salt over another.

The third condition is that each buyer and seller acts independently. This ensures that sellers compete against one another for the consumer's dollar, and that consumers compete against one another to obtain the best price. This competition is one of the forces that keeps prices low.

The fourth condition is that buyers and sellers are reasonably well-informed about products and prices. Well-informed buyers shop at the stores that have the lowest prices. Well-informed sellers match the lowest prices of their competitors to avoid losing customers.

The fifth condition is that buyers and sellers are free to enter into, conduct, or get out of business. This freedom makes it difficult for producers in any industry to keep the market to themselves. Producers have to keep prices competitive or new firms can take away some of their business.

Perfect Competition and Profit Maximization

Under perfect or pure competition, each individual firm is too small to influence price. The firm views demand differently than the market does. In a perfectly competitive market, supply and demand set

---

MEETING SPECIAL NEEDS ACTIVITY

Learning Style: Interpersonal Have students work in small groups and research the early economic life of your state, including information about early industry, government regulation, and specialization. Within each group, have students who prefer visual or hands-on learning experiences draw detailed pictures showing the early economy of your state. Ask volunteers from each group to present their research project to the class and display the drawings they created on the bulletin board.

 Refer to *Inclusion for the Social Studies Classroom Strategies and Activities* in the TCR.

the equilibrium price. Then, each firm selects a level of output that will maximize its profits at that price.

The relationship between an individual firm and the entire industry under perfect competition is shown graphically in **Figure 7.1**. In **Panel A,** the market forces of supply and demand set the equilibrium price at $15. This price, as shown in **Panel B,** now becomes a horizontal demand curve facing each perfectly competitive firm. Because the firm receives $15 for every additional unit it makes, the demand curve is the same as the marginal revenue (MR) curve.

Panel B also shows the cost and revenue information for the firm presented earlier, in **Figure 5.6** on page 128. This firm, as you may recall, also received $15 for every unit of output sold—which is why the price is the same as the marginal revenue shown in the second-to-last column. When the firm wanted to maximize its profits, it did so by finding the level of output that equated its marginal cost with its marginal revenue.

Panel B in **Figure 7.1** shows this same information graphically. For example, the firm's marginal cost (MC) for producing the 110th unit of output was $4.50. Because this unit could be sold in the market for $15, the firm made a profit of $10.50. When the firm added the seventh worker, total output rose to 129 units, and marginal costs rose to $4.74—thereby earning additional profits for the firm.

The eighth worker helped increase total output to 138 units. This was also profitable since the marginal cost of producing 138 units was less than the marginal revenue from the sale of those products. When the firm hired the ninth worker, however, marginal cost was exactly equal to marginal revenue, so at this point the firm would stop hiring labor and maintain production at 144 units. Had the firm hired the tenth variable input, increasing total output to 148 units, total profits would have gone down because the $22.50 marginal cost of production was larger than the $15 marginal revenue.

Guided Reading Activity 7-1

GUIDED READING Activity 7-1

For use with textbook pages 163–171

COMPETITION AND MARKET STRUCTURES

RECALLING THE FACTS

Directions: Use the information in your textbook to answer the questions. Use another sheet of paper if necessary.

1. What is the role of government under Adam Smith's laissez-faire philosophy?

2. Define market structure.

3. What are the four different types of market structure?
   a.
   b.
   c.
   d.

4. What are the five major conditions that characterize perfectly competitive markets? Explain each condition briefly.
   a.
   b.
   c.
   d.
   e.

5. Name and describe the four different types of monopolies.
   a.
   b.
   c.
   d.

Guided Reading Activities   19

ECONOMICS
AT A GLANCE

Figure 7.1

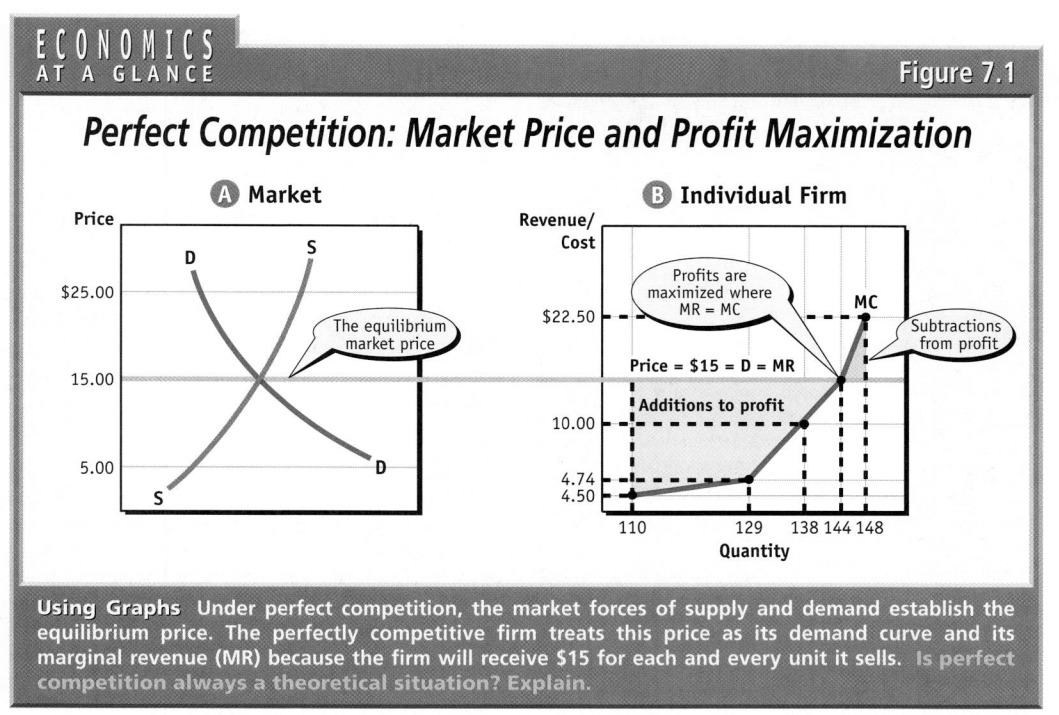

Perfect Competition: Market Price and Profit Maximization

A Market

B Individual Firm

Using Graphs Under perfect competition, the market forces of supply and demand establish the equilibrium price. The perfectly competitive firm treats this price as its demand curve and its marginal revenue (MR) because the firm will receive $15 for each and every unit it sells. **Is perfect competition always a theoretical situation? Explain.**

CHAPTER 7: MARKET STRUCTURES **165**

Math Practice

Profit A business sells an average of 300 units a day at a unit price of $1.50. Fixed costs are $.50 per unit; variable costs average $.65 per unit. Ask students to figure out the profit per unit and the profit for an average day's sale. *(profit per unit = $.35; profit per day at 300 units = $105)*

ECONOMICS
AT A GLANCE

Answer: *Perfect competition rarely exists; local vegetable farming is the closest example.*

FREE ENTERPRISE ACTIVITY

To demonstrate the concept of product differentiation, have students take part in a blind taste test of a variety of colas. First, ask students to note the name of their favorite brand of cola and to list reasons they like it. Suggest that they limit their reasons to physical attributes—taste, color, aroma, effervescence, and so on. Then conduct the taste test and determine how many students picked the brand they named as their favorite. Conclude by leading a class discussion on why product differentiation may be as much a matter of perception as of reality.

L1 Advertising

List the following products on the board: jeans, shampoo, perfume, gasoline, aspirin. Ask students to name their favorite brands of these items, explaining why they made particular choices. Point out that this is an illustration of product differentiation, because student preferences were based on slight differences among several similar brands.

L2 Design a Package

Have students design a package to differentiate a product from its competition. Students should select a product such as salt, butter, tomatoes, or another item involved in nearly perfect competition. The package design should suggest that the product is somewhat different from the competition.

ECONOMICS & YOU

Chapter 8
Disc 1, Side 1

Competition and Monopolies

Ask: How is a monopoly different than an oligopoly?
(A monopoly exists when only one product or service exists; an oligopoly when only a few producers compete in a market.)

 Also available in VHS.

The profit maximizing quantity of output is found where the marginal cost of production is equal to the marginal revenue from sales, or where MC = MR. This occurs at 144 units of output, shown in both **Figure 5.6** and **Panel B** of **Figure 7.1**. Other levels of output may generate the same amount of profits, but none will generate more.

A Theoretical Situation

Few, if any, perfectly competitive markets exist, although local vegetable farming ("truck" farming) comes close to satisfying all five conditions. In these markets many sellers offer nearly identical products. Individual sellers are unable to control prices, and both buyers and sellers have reasonable knowledge of products and prices. Finally, anyone who wants to enter the business by growing tomatoes, corn, or other products can easily do so.

Careers

Market Researcher

Can you organize and evaluate data? Can you be impartial when you compile your findings?

The Work

Market researchers gather, record, and analyze facts about products and sales. Information may be gathered from company or government records, published materials, statistical files, and other sources. Researchers often print and circulate questionnaires, or survey people over the phone or door-to-door. The information is used to prepare forecasts of future sales trends, offer recommendations on product design, and define the market toward which advertising should be directed.

Qualifications

Strong analytical and writing skills and experience with computerized data are essential. Courses in marketing, statistics, English composition, speech, psychology, and economics are required.

166 UNIT 2 MICROECONOMICS

Although perfect competition is rare, it is important because economists use it to evaluate other market structures. **Imperfect competition** is the name given to a market structure that lacks one or more of the conditions of perfect competition. Most firms and industries in the United States today fall into this classification, which has three categories—monopolistic competition, oligopoly, and monopoly.

Monopolistic Competition

Monopolistic competition is the market structure that has all the conditions of perfect competition except for identical products. By making its product a little different, the monopolistic competitor tries to attract more customers and monopolize a small portion of the market.

Product Differentiation

In contrast to perfect competition, monopolistic competition utilizes **product differentiation**—real or imagined differences between competing products in the same industry. Most items produced today—from the many brands of athletic footwear to personal computers—are differentiated. The differentiation may even be extended to store location, store design, manner of payment, delivery, packaging, service, and other factors.

Sometimes differences between products are real. For example, some brands of athletic footwear have special shock-absorbing soles. Others have certain construction materials to reduce weight. Some are just designed to look more appealing, or are linked to star athletes.

Nonprice Competition

Monopolistic competitors want to make consumers aware of product differences. **Nonprice competition**—the use of advertising, giveaways, or other promotional campaigns to convince buyers that the product is somehow better than another brand—often takes the place of price competition. Therefore, monopolistic competitors usually advertise or promote heavily to make their products seem different from everyone else's.

CRITICAL THINKING

Synthesizing Information Organize the class into four groups and assign each group one of the four market structures. Instruct groups to identify and visit local businesses that exhibit characteristics of their market structure. Have groups prepare a list of common questions to ask managers regarding product differentiation, ease of entry into the market, the number of firms in the industry, and the ability of firms to influence price.

After the visits and interviews, have groups summarize the information obtained and present their findings to the class. Emphasize that these presentations should compare the businesses visited with the market structures discussed in the chapter. **BLOCK SCHEDULING**

THE GLOBAL ECONOMY

MARKETING IN CHINA

An important part of any product is its name. It must convey what the producers intend.

Potential exporters must understand cultural characteristics when considering brand management. Because the Chinese continue to favor names that convey goodness, luck, happiness, long life, prosperity or historical significance, it is sometimes difficult to translate a Western brand name into Chinese.

The Coca-Cola Company took 11 years to make a profit, in part due to an ill-advised brand name, after it came back to China in 1979. Today, Coke dominates the vast soft drink market across the Chinese continent after creating an improved name meaning "delicious, enjoyable and makes you happy."

PepsiCo, Inc., came up with "everything makes you happy" to capture market share for Pepsi. . . .

—Alcinda Hatfield, Foreign Agricultural Service, July 1999

Critical Thinking

1. **Making Generalizations** Why is it sometimes difficult to translate a brand name into a name acceptable to people in another country?

2. **Categorizing Information** What part does the brand name and labeling of a product play in product differentiation?

This explains why producers of designer jeans spend so much on advertising and promotion. If the seller can *differentiate* a product in the mind of the buyer, the firm may be able to raise the price above its competitors' prices.

Monopolistic Competition and Profit Maximization

Under monopolistic competition, similar products generally sell within a narrow price range. The monopolistic aspect is the seller's ability to raise the price within this narrow range. The competitive aspect is that if sellers raise or lower the price enough, customers will forget minor differences and change brands.

The profit maximization behavior of the monopolistic competitor is no different from that of other firms. The firm produces the quantity of output where its marginal cost is equal to its marginal revenue. If the firm convinces consumers that its product is better, it can charge a higher price. If it cannot convince them, the firm cannot charge as much.

The monopolistic competitor can enter the market easily. The possibility of profits draws new firms, each of which produces a product only a little different from the ones already on the market.

In time, both the number of firms in an industry and the supply of the product becomes fairly stable with no great profits or losses.

Oligopoly

Oligopoly is a market structure in which a few very large sellers dominate the industry. The product of an oligopolist may be differentiated—as in the auto industry, or standardized—as in the steel industry. The exact number of firms in the industry is less important than the ability of any single firm to cause a change in output, sales, and

Did you know?

Competing in the Market On an average shopping trip, a consumer's eye lingers on a product for only about 2.5 seconds. In order to stay competitive, companies experiment with new formulas, along with the color and size of the product's packaging. These research and development costs can range from $100,000 for adding a new color to an existing product line to millions of dollars for the creation of a new product.

THE GLOBAL ECONOMY

Marketing in China In addition to brand names, brand logos are significant in selling American products abroad. For example, the Coca-Cola logo is recognizable even when written in other alphabets, such as Arabic or Hebrew. The McDonald's golden arches and Nike swoosh are other internationally known logos.

Answers:

1. *Cultural characteristics influence how people perceive names, and sometimes translations result in different meanings from what was expected.*

2. *Brand names and labeling are a vital part of product differentiation, as they influence people's perceptions of a product.*

L2 Recognizing Ideas

Ask students to identify three businesses in the community that are in monopolistic competition. Direct students to write a brief description of the competitive strategies employed by these businesses. Call on volunteers to read their descriptions to the class.

EXTENDING THE CONTENT

Agriculture and Perfect Competition Few markets today meet the conditions of the perfectly competitive market model. However, the grain market for number two yellow corn—a standard product that does not vary—closely fits this description. There are many farmers who grow and sell number two yellow corn, as well as a large number of buyers. The farmers do not advertise or band together to control price. There is open communication between buyers and sellers about the market price. The grain market for number two yellow corn, however, falls short of satisfying the fifth condition for perfect competition—ease of access to the market. Entry is limited because it takes a sizeable investment to start a farm focused on the growing of grain.

L3 Do Market Research

Have students research cereals in a supermarket. Ask them to focus on one kind of cereal and list the brands available, the price per ounce for a specified size (15 ounce or another size), and the ways companies differentiate their cereals. Ask student researchers to compare the nutritional values of store (generic) brands and national brands and make a chart comparing all factors they find.

Visual Instruction

Answer to Caption:
to make each product seem different, and therefore better, so that people will buy it

---

prices in the industry as a whole. Because of these characteristics, oligopoly is further from perfect competition than is monopolistic competition.

In the United States, many markets are already oligopolistic, and many more are becoming so. Pepsi and Coke dominate the soft drink market. McDonald's, Burger King, and Wendy's dominate the fast-food industry. A few large corporations dominate other industries, such as the domestic airline, automobile, and long-distance telephone service industries.

Interdependent Behavior

Because oligopolists are so large, whenever one firm acts the other firms usually follow. As demonstrated in the cover story on airline pricing, if one airline announces discount fares, the other airlines generally match the lower prices in a matter of days, if not hours. Each oligopolist knows that the

Competition

Advertising Advertisers often use celebrities, such as star athletes, to increase the popularity of their products. *What is the purpose of product differentiation?*

other firms in the industry have considerable power and influence over consumer choices. Therefore, firms tend to act together.

Sometimes the interdependent behavior takes the form of **collusion,** a formal agreement to set prices or to otherwise behave in a cooperative manner. One form of collusion is **price-fixing**–agreeing to charge the same or similar prices for a product. In almost every case these prices are higher than those determined under competition. The firms also might agree to divide the market so that each is guaranteed to sell a certain amount. Because collusion usually restrains trade, it is against the law.

Pricing Behavior

The tendency of oligopolists to act together usually shows up in their pricing behavior. For example, one firm may try to implement a price increase in hopes that other firms in the industry will follow. If the other firms do not follow, then the oligopolist that initiated the price change will usually be forced to take it back–or lose customers to its competitors.

An oligopolist may also try to lower the price of its product, knowing that other oligopolists are likely to follow suit. When one firm lowers prices, it can lead to a price war, or a series of price cuts that result in unusually low prices. Oligopolistic price wars are usually short but intense—and almost always provide welcome relief for consumers in the form of lower prices.

Because oligopolists usually act together when it comes to changing prices, most firms tend to compete on a nonprice basis by advertising, or by enhancing their products with new or different features. Nonprice competition has the advantage of making it more difficult for rivals to respond quickly. If an oligopolist finds a new advertising gimmick or a way to enhance a product, the other firms are at a disadvantage for a period of time. After all, it takes longer to develop a better advertising campaign or a new physical attribute for a product than it does to match a price cut.

Oligopoly and Profit Maximization

The oligopolist, like any other firm, maximizes its profits when it finds the quantity of output

---

INTERDISCIPLINARY CONNECTIONS ACTIVITY

Technology Tell students that U.S. biological scientists use a process called genetic engineering to make plants more resistant to diseases and destructive pests. The companies that produce genetically engineered seeds have patents that give them a virtual monopoly on them. Some individuals and some nations are concerned about both the costs and possible side effects of genetic engineering. Ask students to research arguments for and against this new scientific discovery. Have volunteers share their findings with the class.

ECONOMICS AT A GLANCE

Figure 7.2

Characteristics of Market Structures

	Number of Firms in Industry	Influence Over Price	Product Differentiation	Advertising	Entry Into Market	Examples
Perfect Competition	Many	None	None	None	Easy	Perfect: None Near: Truck Farming
Monopolistic Competition	Many	Limited	Fair Amount	Fair Amount	Easy	Gas Stations Women's Clothing
Oligopoly	Few	Some	Fair Amount	Some	Difficult	Automobiles Aluminum
Pure Monopoly	One	Extensive	None	None	Almost Impossible	Perfect: None Near: Water

Using Tables The term market structure refers to the nature and degree of competition among firms operating in the same industry. Individual market structures—perfect competition, monopolistic competition, oligopoly, and monopoly—are determined by the five characteristics listed in the columns above. **In which market structure does nonprice competition play a major role?**

where its marginal cost is equal to its marginal revenue. Having found this level of production, the oligopolist will charge the price consistent with this level of sales.

The product's final price is likely to be higher than it would be under monopolistic competition, and much higher than it would be under perfect competition. Even when oligopolists do not collude formally, they still tend to act conservatively and seldom protest price hikes by their rivals.

Monopoly

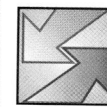 At the opposite end of the spectrum from perfect competition is the monopoly. A **monopoly** is a market structure with only one seller of a particular product. This situation—like that of perfect competition—is an extreme case. In fact, the American economy has very few, if any, cases of

pure monopoly—although the local telephone company or cable TV operator may come close.

Even the telephone company, however, faces competition from other communication companies, from the United States Postal Service, and from Internet providers that supply E-mail and voice-mail services. Local cable providers face competition from video rental stores, satellite cable systems, and the Internet. Consequently, when people talk about monopolies, they usually mean near monopolies.

One reason we have so few monopolies is that Americans traditionally have disliked and tried to outlaw them. Another reason is that new technologies often introduce products that compete with existing monopolies. The development of the fax machine allowed businesses to send electronic letters that compete with the United States Postal Service. Later, E-mail became even more popular than the fax.

CHAPTER 7: MARKET STRUCTURES **169**

ECONOMICS AT A GLANCE

Answer: *monopolistic competition*

L3 Research

Encourage students to research one of the following: fast-food industry, soft drink industry, domestic airlines, automobile industry, long-distance telephone service. Have students write a report showing how the subject of their research matches the characteristics and behavior of an oligopoly. Ask volunteers to share their reports with the class.

CURRICULUM CONNECTION

History The U.S. Patent Office issued its first patent in 1790. It was for a new method of making potash. A little more than 200 years later, in 1991, it issued the 5,000,000th patent—for a genetically engineered microbe.

EXTENDING THE CONTENT

The Kinked Demand Curve As noted in the text, oligopolists are willing to lower prices because they feel that their rivals will follow suit. They are reluctant to raise prices, however, because they cannot be certain that competitors will do the same. Economists sometimes use a "kinked" demand curve to explain this situation. On this curve, demand for products at prices above the present price is highly elastic. At prices below the present price, however, demand is less elastic and may become inelastic.

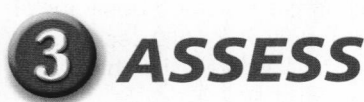

Visual Instruction

Answer to Caption:
Answers will vary depending on special product characteristics individuals prefer.

❸ ASSESS

Assign Section 1 Assessment as homework or as an in-class activity.

💾 Have students use **Interactive Tutor Self-Assessment Software** to review Section 1.

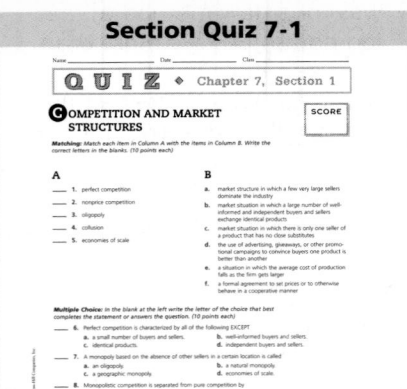

Section Quiz 7-1

Types of Monopolies

Sometimes the nature of a good or service dictates that society would be served best by a monopoly. One such case is a **natural monopoly**–a market situation where the costs of production are minimized by having a single firm produce the product.

Natural monopolies can provide services more cheaply as monopolies than could several competing firms. For example, two or more competing telephone companies serving the same area would be inefficient if they each needed their own telephone poles and lines. Public utility companies fall into this category because it would be wasteful to duplicate the networks of pipes and wires that distribute water, gas, and electricity throughout a city. To avoid these problems, the government often gives a public utility company a *franchise*, the exclusive right to do business in a certain area without competition. By accepting such franchises, the companies also accept a certain amount of government regulation.

The justification for the natural monopoly is that a larger firm can often use its personnel, equipment, and plant more efficiently. This results in **economies of scale,** a situation in which the average cost of production falls as the firm gets larger. When this happens, it makes sense for the firm to be as large as is necessary to lower its production costs.

Sometimes a business has a monopoly because of its location. A drugstore operating in a town that is too small to support two or more such businesses becomes a **geographic monopoly,** a monopoly based on the absence of other sellers in a certain geographic area. Similarly, the owner of the only gas station on a lonely interstate highway exit also has a type of geographic monopoly.

A **technological monopoly** is a monopoly that is based on ownership or control of a manufacturing method, process, or other scientific advance. The government may grant a *patent*–an exclusive right to manufacture, use, or sell any new and useful invention for a specific period. Inventions are covered for 20 years; however, the product's designs can be patented for shorter periods, after which they become public property available for the benefit of all. Art and literary works are protected through a *copyright,* the exclusive right of authors or artists to publish, sell, or reproduce their work for their lifetime plus 50 years.

Still another kind of monopoly is the **government monopoly**–a monopoly the government owns and operates. Government monopolies are found at the national, state, and local levels. In most cases they involve products or services that private industry cannot adequately provide.

Competition

Nonprice Competition If advertisers can make you believe their product is better than others, you might pay more for it. *How has nonprice competition affected your buying habits?*

170 UNIT 2 MICROECONOMICS

FREE ENTERPRISE ACTIVITY

Have students select one of the four types of markets described in Section 1—perfect competition, monopolistic competition, oligopoly, and monopoly. Ask students to imagine that they are entrepreneurs in the selected market. Tell them to choose a specific, appropriate business to be involved in and to write an essay describing their entrepreneurial activities. They should apply their understanding of the characteristics of the selected market in their essays.

Many towns and cities have monopolies that oversee water use. Some states control alcoholic beverages by requiring that they be sold only through state stores. The federal government controls the processing of weapons-grade uranium for military and natural security purposes.

Monopoly and Profit Maximization

Monopolies maximize profits the same way other firms do: they equate marginal cost with marginal revenue to find the profit-maximizing quantity of output. Even so, there are differences between the monopolist and other profit-maximizing firms—especially the perfect competitor.

First, the monopolist is very much larger than the perfect competitor. This is because there is only one firm—the monopolist—supplying the product, rather than thousands of smaller ones. Second, this large size, along with the lack of meaningful competition, allows the monopolist to behave as a *price maker*—as opposed to the perfect competitor who is a *price taker*.

Because there are no competing firms in the industry, there is no equilibrium price facing the

Monopoly

Geographic Monopoly A lone general store in an isolated area enjoys a geographic monopoly. *How does a geographic monopoly differ from a natural monopoly?*

monopolist. Instead, the monopolist determines the price that will equate its marginal revenue with its marginal cost, and then produces the quantity of output consistent with that price. In every case, the monopolist will charge more for its product—hence the term *price maker*—and then limit the quantity for sale in the market.

Section 1 Assessment

Checking for Understanding

1. **Main Idea** Describe the four basic market structures. Explain how they differ from one another.

2. **Key Terms** Define laissez-faire, market structure, perfect competition, imperfect competition, monopolistic competition, product differentiation, nonprice competition, oligopoly, collusion, price-fixing, monopoly, natural monopoly, economies of scale, geographic monopoly, technological monopoly, government monopoly.

3. **List** the five characteristics of perfect competition.

4. **Describe** monopolistic competition.

5. **Explain** why the actions of one oligopolist affect others in the same industry.

6. **Identify** the types of monopolies.

Applying Economic Concepts

7. **Product Differentiation** Make a list of as many clothing stores in your community as possible. Describe how each store tries to differentiate itself from the others.

Critical Thinking

8. **Synthesizing Information** Provide at least two examples of oligopolies in the United States today.

Practice and assess key social studies skills with the *Glencoe Skillbuilder Interactive Workbook, Level 2.*

CHAPTER 7: MARKET STRUCTURES **171**

Section 1 Assessment Answers

1. Student descriptions should include basic information from pages 164–169.

2. All vocabulary terms are defined in the text.

3. large number of buyers and sellers, deal in identical products, act independently, are well informed, ease of entry into market

4. many competitors, similar item or service, and entry into the market is easy

5. Others must follow to maintain market share.

6. natural, geographic, technological, government

7. advertising and other forms of promotion, differing brands, and so on

8. Answers may include the fast-food industry, soft drink industry, domestic airlines.

CHAPTER 7
Section 1, pages 163–171

Visual Instruction

Answer to Caption:
Natural monopoly is a market situation where costs are minimized by having one producer; geographic monopoly exists because of its location.

Reteach

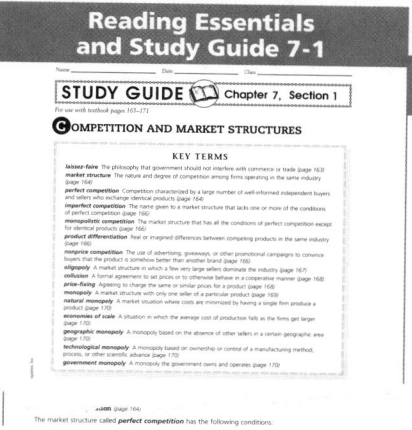

Reading Essentials and Study Guide 7-1

STUDY GUIDE 📖 Chapter 7, Section 1

For use with textbook pages 163–171

COMPETITION AND MARKET STRUCTURES

KEY TERMS

laissez-faire The philosophy that government should not interfere with commerce or trade (page 163)
market structure The nature and degree of competition among firms operating in the same industry (page 164)
perfect competition Competition characterized by a large number of well-informed independent buyers and sellers who exchange identical products (page 164)
imperfect competition The name given to a market structure that lacks one or more of the conditions of perfect competition (page 166)
monopolistic competition The market structure that has all the conditions of perfect competition except for identical products (page 166)
product differentiation Real or imagined differences between competing products in the same industry (page 166)
nonprice competition The use of advertising, giveaways, or other promotional campaigns to convince buyers that the product is somehow better than another brand (page 168)
oligopoly A market structure in which a few very large sellers dominate the industry (page 167)
collusion A formal agreement to set prices or to otherwise behave in a cooperative manner (page 168)
price-fixing Agreeing to charge the same or similar prices for a product (page 168)
monopoly A market structure with only one seller of a particular product (page 169)
natural monopoly A market situation where costs are minimized by having a single firm produce a product (page 170)
economies of scale A situation in which the average cost of production falls as the firms get larger (page 170)
geographic monopoly A monopoly based on the absence of other sellers in a certain geographic area (page 170)
technological monopoly A monopoly based on ownership or control of a manufacturing method, process, or other scientific advance (page 170)
government monopoly A monopoly the government owns and operates (page 170)

...ion (page 164)
The market structure called *perfect competition* has the following conditions.

Enrich

Invite a farmer or member of a farm association to speak about how market conditions affect farming. Have students use this information to write an essay titled "The Economics of Farming."

4 CLOSE

Have students write a brief report on the role of competition in the American free enterprise economy.

BACKGROUND

Charles Wang's success as an entrepreneur coincided with, and not just by chance, the beginnings of a considerable change in the American economy. Computer Associates' growth during the 1980s paralleled the growth of the computer hardware and software industries; Wang and his company rode an economic wave. The fortunes at the microeconomic level, of individuals and of companies, are highly correlated with developments at the macroeconomic level. This holds true across industries, countries, and time. Wang, then, is emblematic of the type of entrepreneur who sensed macroeconomic developments and exploited them at a microeconomic level.

TEACH

Challenge students to reflect on this question in a journal: How much of an individual's economic success can be contributed to macroeconomic forces beyond that individual's control?

Profiles IN Economics

"I Love the Challenge":
Charles Wang
(1944–)

"There are CEOs who brag about never having touched a PC," says Charles Wang, chairman of Computer Associates International. "I say to them, 'Get your head out of the sand, kid.'" Wang's aggressive approach has helped him grow his company from a four-person operation to one that earns more than $5 billion in computer software sales a year. Today, Computer Associates is the largest independent supplier of software for business computing.

A DIFFICULT START

Born in Shanghai, China, in 1944, Charles Wang and his family fled the communist regime in 1952 to settle in the United States. Wang attended Queens College in New York and then opened an American subsidiary of Swiss-owned Computer Associates in New York City in 1976. Wang began his operations with just one product.

STRATEGY FOR GROWTH

Wang believed that the best growth strategy for the fledgling company was to purchase existing software firms and market their products. This would spare his company the risk of developing its own products and enable it to get products to market sooner. The strategy paid off. Computer Associates purchased a number of firms throughout the 1980s, and increased its sales more than tenfold, from $85 million in 1984 to $1 billion in 1989.

The recession of 1990–1991 put a damper on business, but Wang remained optimistic about the future of his company and launched a campaign to purchase even more companies. His efforts were amply rewarded, and Computer Associates soon found itself back on the fast track.

PROGRESSIVE MANAGEMENT

Despite its enormous growth, the company still remains focused on its people. Wang supplies on-site fitness facilities and child development centers for employees. He brought together 2,000 members of Computer Associates' development staff for "Nerd Weekend"—a celebration for the people who fueled Computer Associates' growth. Wang also sponsors "Technology Boot Camps" to help chief executives get over their fear and ignorance of computers. In 1994, he wrote a book urging business people to start thinking like technology people, and vice versa.

How has Wang accomplished so much? "I love it when people say it can't be done," he says. "I love the challenge."

Examining the Profile

1. **Identifying Cause and Effect** What business strategy helped Wang's fledgling company become successful?
2. **Evaluating Information** How important do you think Wang's "Nerd Weekend" and similar activities are to his company's success?

Answers to Examining the Profile

1. Wang, in order to avoid certain risks and speed products to market, purchased existing software firms and marketed their products.
2. Answers will vary. Some students might maintain that such activities are morale boosters and thus promote the success of the company as a whole. Other students might argue that the success of Computer Associates relies more on Wang's business strategy and the growth of the computer industry.

Market Failures

Study Guide

Main Idea
Inadequate competition, inadequate information, and immobile resources can result in market failures.

Reading Strategy
Graphic Organizer As you read the section, think about why maintaining adequate competition is a worthwhile goal. Use a graphic organizer like the one below to list effects of competition.

If markets are competitive . . . → Effects

Key Terms
market failure, externality, negative externality, positive externality, public goods

Objectives
After studying this section, you will be able to:
1. **Discuss** the problems caused by inadequate competition.
2. **Understand** the importance of having adequate information.
3. **Describe** the nature of resource immobility.
4. **Explain** the nature of positive and negative externalities.

Applying Economic Concepts
Market Failure Have you ever felt that the perfect part-time job is waiting for you—but you just can't seem to find it? If so, you are experiencing market failure. A market failure usually occurs when we don't have adequate information about the market. The result is that productive resources—including you—do not reach their maximum potential.

Cover Story

Mum's the Word

We live in increasingly intolerant times. . . . Mobile telephones are the latest target: some trains, airline lounges, restaurants and even golf courses are being designated "no phone" areas.

Woman on cell phone

The Economist would like to suggest restrictions on another source of noise pollution: children. . . . Smoking, driving and mobile phones all cause what economists call "negative externalities" . . . [the] costs of these activities to other people tend to exceed the costs to the individuals [who are doing it].

For children, just like cigarettes or mobile phones, clearly impose a negative externality on people who are near them. Anybody who has suffered a 12-hour flight with a bawling baby in the row immediately ahead or a bored youngster viciously kicking their seat from behind, will grasp this quickly. . . .

—*The Economist*, December 5, 1998

The writer of the article cited in the cover story went on to suggest that airlines should create "child-free zones" by seating children in the back of the aircraft—and by charging parents more. This "rare outbreak of humor at *The Economist*," according to London's *Daily Telegraph*, was a hit with readers, resulting in bulging mailbags and publicity.

The cover story, however, reminds us of another, more serious, fact of economic life—that markets sometimes fail. How they fail, and how the failures can be remedied, is a concern for economists. We now want to take a look at how markets fail. Ways to deal with these failures will be discussed in the next section of this chapter.

A competitive free enterprise economy works best when four conditions are met. Adequate competition must exist in all markets. Buyers and sellers must be reasonably well-informed about conditions and opportunities in these markets. Resources must be free to move from one industry to another. Finally, prices must reasonably

CHAPTER 7: MARKET STRUCTURES **173**

① FOCUS

Section Overview
This section describes how market failures can occur when there is inadequate competition.

BELLRINGER
Motivational Activity

 Project **transparency** and have students answer questions.

 Available as blackline master.

Daily Focus Transparency 21

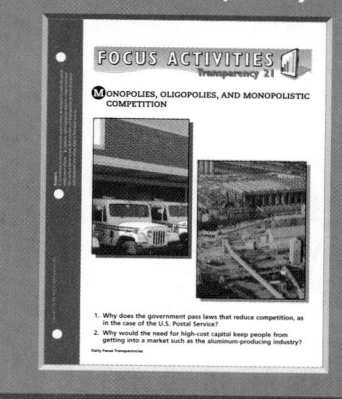

Study Guide

Reading Strategy
Have students create the graphic organizer.
Answers to Graphic: *Adequate competition prevents inefficient resource allocation; higher prices will cause reduced output.*

Preteaching Vocabulary
Have students write questions for which each Key Term is an answer.

RESOURCE MANAGER

📁 Reproducible Masters
- Reproducible Lesson Plan 7-2
- Daily Lecture Notes 7-2
- Guided Reading Activity 7-2
- Reading Essentials and Study Guide 7-2
- Section Quiz 7-2

🖐 Transparencies
- Daily Focus Transparency 21

Multimedia
- 💾 Interactive Tutor Self-Assessment Software
- 💿 ExamView® Pro Testmaker
- 💿 Presentation Plus!

2 TEACH

CURRICULUM CONNECTION

Geography For many years, electricity was generated locally and sold to people and businesses in the same region. Now, local electric companies in the United States may buy electricity from more distant companies—sometimes from Canada or Mexico—and base their choices on price and availability.

L2 Informative Writing

Have students find newspaper articles about federal, state, or local public goods. Ask them to write short essays summarizing what the article is about and analyzing why the public good discussed is not provided by markets.

---

reflect the costs of production, including the rewards to entrepreneurs. Accordingly, a **market failure** can occur when any of these four conditions are significantly altered.

The most common market failures involve cases of inadequate competition, inadequate information, resource immobility, external economies, and public goods. These failures occur on both the demand and supply sides of the market.

Inadequate Competition

Over time, mergers and acquisitions have resulted in larger and fewer firms dominating various industries. The decrease in competition has several consequences.

Inefficient Resource Allocation

Inadequate competition tends to curb efficient use of scarce resources—resources that could be put to other, more productive uses if they were available. For example, why would a firm with few or no competitors have the incentive to use resources carefully? If a firm is free to do as it pleases, it likely will spend its profits on bonuses and extras like executive jets, lucrative salaries, and generous retirement benefits. This is one of the reasons that public utilities such as electricity are regulated by the government—to make sure that they do not use their monopoly status to waste or abuse resources.

Higher Prices and Reduced Output

An imperfect competitor such as a monopoly can use its position to prevent competition and restrict production. This situation brings about artificial shortages that cause higher prices than under other market structures.

Economic and Political Power

Inadequate competition may enable a business to influence politics by wielding its economic might. In the past, many firms have used their huge capital resources to further the political careers of owners and their relatives and friends.

A large corporation does not even have to be a monopoly for its economic power to translate to political power. A large corporation, for example, may demand tax breaks from the state or local government. If the government refuses, the corporation may threaten to move elsewhere, causing economic loss to the community. Because the community does not want to risk the loss, the corporation may get its way.

Both Sides of the Market

If we consider the supply side of the market, it is clear that perfectly competitive or monopolistically competitive markets usually have enough firms to ensure competition. When it comes to oligopoly, however, we know that the temptation to collude is strong. No competition exists if a monopolist dominates the supply side of the market.

Inadequate competition may occur on the demand side of the market as well. In most cases, such as in the consumer goods and services markets, many buyers can be found. How many buyers are there, though, for space shuttles, hydroelectric dams, super computers, M-1 tanks, and high technology fighter jets? While failures on the demand side of the market do occur, they are more difficult to correct than failures on the supply side.

Inadequate Information

If resources are to be allocated efficiently, everyone—consumers, businesspeople, and government officials—must have adequate information about market conditions. A secretary or an accountant may receive a competitive wage in the automobile industry, but are wages for the same skills higher in the insurance industry, or in the banking industry? Even the treasurer of a small community needs to know if the town's surplus funds can earn a higher return if invested in Dallas, New York, Indianapolis, or Seattle. Information about conditions in many markets is needed before these questions can be answered.

Some information is easy to find, such as want-ads or sale prices found in the local newspaper. Other information is more difficult to obtain. If this

---

MEETING SPECIAL NEEDS ACTIVITY

Learning Disabled For students who have problems with reading, practice a focused reading exercise. Have students read the subsection, "Inadequate Information." When students have finished reading, have them write in their notebooks what they remember of the subsection. Then have them reread the subsection to look for answers to the following questions: What is needed to allocate resources efficiently? How can information be obtained? Ask students to check whether they wrote this information in their notebooks. If not, discuss why they might have left it out.

📑 Refer to *Inclusion for the Social Studies Classroom Strategies and Activities* in the TCR.

knowledge is important to buyers, and is difficult to obtain, then it is an example of a market failure.

Resource Immobility

One of the more difficult problems in any economy is that of resource immobility. This means that land, capital, labor, and entrepreneurs do not move to markets where returns are the highest. Instead they tend to stay put and sometimes remain unemployed.

What happens, for example, when a large auto assembly plant, steel mill, or mine closes, leaving hundreds of workers without employment? Certainly some workers can find jobs in other industries, but not all can. Some of the newly unemployed may not be able to sell their homes. Others may not want to move away from friends and relatives to find new jobs in other cities.

Consider the problems caused when the federal government closed military bases to save taxpayers' dollars. Thousands of workers were laid off in communities that had no immediate means of employing them. Resource mobility, an ideal in the competitive free enterprise economy, is much more difficult to accomplish in the real world. When resources are immobile or refuse to move, markets do not always function efficiently.

Externalities

Many activities generate some kind of **externality,** or unintended side effect that either benefits or harms a third party not involved in the activity that caused it.

A **negative externality** is the harm, cost, or inconvenience suffered by a third party because of actions by others. The classic case of a negative externality is

Externalities

Positive and Negative   Most economic activities generate externalities. *Do you think the nearby airport expansion was a positive or a negative externality for the people living in this neighborhood? Why?*

FREE ENTERPRISE ACTIVITY

List several public goods or services on the board—flood control, national defense, county roads, fire protection, and police protection, for example. Organize students into several small groups and assign each group one of the listed public goods. Have groups develop a brief oral presentation giving reasons their assigned item should remain a public good or why it should be provided as a private good by competitive markets. Have groups make presentations and discuss them as a class.   **BLOCK SCHEDULING**

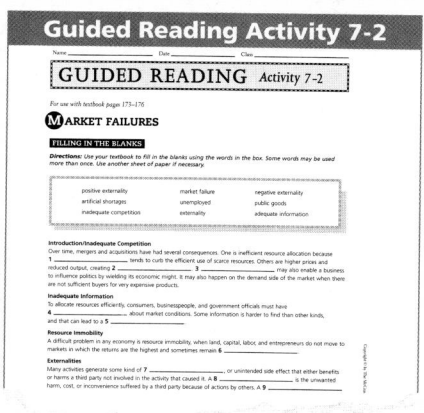

Guided Reading Activity 7-2

Visual Instruction

Answer to Caption:
negative; people living near the airport may experience inconvenience from construction, airplane noise, drop in property value

❸ ASSESS

Assign Section 2 Assessment.

 Have students use **Interactive Tutor Self-Assessment Software.**

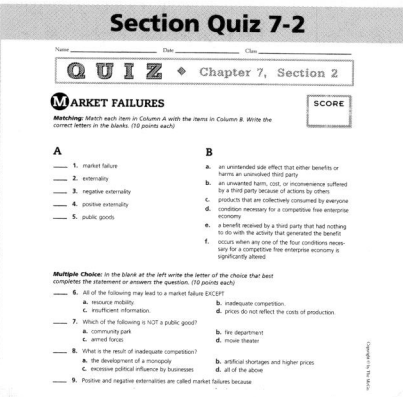

Section Quiz 7-2

Reteach

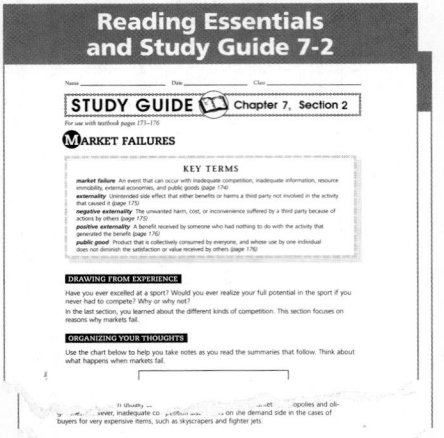

Reading Essentials and Study Guide 7-2

Enrich

Invite the mayor or a police officer to visit the class and discuss negative and positive externalities in your community.

④ CLOSE

Ask students to choose the one factor they believe is the most serious obstacle to efficient market competition and to justify their choices in writing.

---

the noise and inconvenience some people suffer when an airport expands.

A **positive externality** is a benefit received by someone who had nothing to do with the activity that generated the benefit. For example, people living on the other side of town may benefit from the additional jobs generated by the airport expansion, or a nearby restaurant may sell more meals, make a greater profit, and hire more workers. Both the owners of the restaurant and the new workers gain from the airport expansion even though they had nothing to do with the expansion in the first place.

Externalities are classified as market failures because their costs and benefits are not reflected in the market prices that buyers and sellers pay for the original product. For example, does the airline or the air traveler compensate the homeowner for the diminished value of the property located near the new runway extension? Does the restaurant owner share the additional good fortune derived from the new business with the airport or the air traveler? In both cases the answer is no. As a result, the prices that travelers pay for air travel will not reflect the external costs and benefits that the airport expansion generates.

Public Goods

 Another form of market failure shows up in the need for public goods. **Public goods** are products that are collectively consumed by everyone, and whose use by one individual does not diminish the satisfaction or value available to others. Examples of public goods are uncrowded highways, flood control measures, national defense, and police and fire protection.

The market, however, when left to itself, does not supply these items—or only supplies them inadequately. This is because a market economy produces only those items that can be withheld if people refuse to pay for them. It would be difficult, for example, to deny one person the benefits of national defense while supplying it to others. Because it is so difficult to get everyone to pay for their fair share of a public good, private markets cannot efficiently produce them and will therefore produce other things.

The case of public goods illustrates that while the market is very successful in satisfying *individual* wants and needs, it may fail to satisfy them on a *collective* basis. If public goods are to be supplied, the government usually has to provide them.

Section 2 Assessment

Checking for Understanding

1. **Main Idea** Using your notes from the graphic organizer activity on page 173, explain why maintaining adequate competition is a worthwhile goal.

2. **Key Terms** Define market failure, externality, negative externality, positive externality, public goods.

3. **Define** "adequate competition" in your own words and explain why markets need adequate competition.

4. **Explain** the importance of having adequate information.

5. **Explain** why resources are not always mobile and willing to move.

6. **Describe** the similarities and differences between positive and negative externalities.

Applying Economic Concepts

7. **Market Failures** Cite at least two examples of situations in your community in which resources did not move from one market or industry to another because they were either unable or unwilling to move.

Critical Thinking

8. **Understanding Cause and Effect** Identify one possible positive externality and one possible negative externality from the closing of a military base.

   Practice and assess key social studies skills with the *Glencoe Skillbuilder Interactive Workbook, Level 2.*

Section 2 Assessment Answers

1. Without it, productive resources will not be allocated efficiently.

2. All vocabulary terms are defined in the text.

3. Students should note that it keeps any one competitor from becoming too powerful.

4. Without it, producers and consumers are unaware of products or services that would benefit them.

5. unable to sell homes; not willing to leave

6. Both affect a third party. positive: benefits; negative: harms, costs, inconveniences

7. Answers should reflect an understanding of the concept of resource immobility.

8. Possible answers: positive—the base may have disrupted traffic; negative—businesses near base might lose customers

BusinessWeek

AUGUST 3, 1998

——— Newsclip

Coca-Cola and Pepsi are competing for control of the U.S. beverage market. The cola giants are experimenting with new marketing strategies in New York City, where the consumer market is considered one of the toughest in the country.

Cola Wars

With $30 billion in beverage sales between them, Coca-Cola Co. and Pepsico Inc. have long battled each other with multimillion dollar ad campaigns and country-by-country marketing coups. . . .

But to make sure all that marketing money translates into bottles sold, both Coke and Pepsi are intensifying their efforts at the local level. . . . And nowhere is the fighting more heated than in the intensely competitive, intensely difficult New York market. "Many soft-drink executives think New York is the toughest market in the country," says John Sicher, editor of industry newsletter *Beverage Digest.* "The traffic is huge, the population is dense, and the neighborhoods are complicated."

But it's also a huge price—and one PepsiCo, headquartered in Purchase, N.Y., would be loath to lose. Pepsi has always spent big to stay ahead on its home turf. New York is one of only four U.S. markets where Pepsi-Cola outsells Coca-Cola Classic. . . .

The showdown over the Big Apple began . . . when Coke's largest bottler, Coca-Cola Enterprises Inc. (CCE), moved into the New York market. CCE has since added 600 more marketing people and 60 new trucks to its delivery fleet. . . .

. . . Each marketing representative visits up to 120 small stores a week, [where they are] pushing for snazzier displays, better placement, and more promotions. . . .

. . . Pepsi is pushing its own New York campaign to the hilt. But rather than send out fresh new troops, Pepsi is relying heavily on its bottler's local distribution force to boost its presence in stores, with new racks, coolers, and giveaways. It is also making a big push to get the most from its sponsorships of Lincoln Center, Radio City Music Hall, and the Bronx Zoo with ticket giveaways and advertising tie-ins. . . .

. . . In this hard-fought battle, Coke and Pepsi are doing everything they can to come out on top.

—Reprinted from August 3, 1998 issue of Business Week, *by special permission, copyright © 1998 by The McGraw-Hill Companies, Inc.*

Examining the Newsclip

1. **Finding the Main Idea** Explain how the cola companies are trying to dominate the New York consumer markets.

2. **Making Predictions** What might you expect to happen to Pepsi and Coke prices as the companies try to dominate the New York City market?

CHAPTER 7: MARKET STRUCTURES **177**

TEACH

After students read the article, have them examine the competition between Coke and Pepsi in their own community. Ask students to work in small groups to research the availability of each soft drink in local restaurants and other places of entertainment (stadiums, movie theaters, and so on). Have them do market research to find out which fast-food restaurants, diners, and other businesses carry only one of the two products, and whether any carry competing cola drinks. Have students make a chart to show the availability of Coke, Pepsi, and other cola brands at businesses in their community. **Ask:** Do you feel that one of the major cola brands has a more intensive marketing strategy in your community? Why?

▱ Refer to *Business Week Focus on the New Economy* in the TCR for additional unit-based articles.

Answers to Examining the Newsclip

1. nonprice competition, such as better store displays, better store placement, promotions, giveaways, and sponsorships

2. Answers may speculate that the price of both Pepsi and Coke could drop as the companies try to sway consumers.

FOCUS

Section Overview

This section discusses antitrust legislation and the need for limited government regulation.

BELLRINGER
Motivational Activity

 Project **transparency** and have students answer questions.

 Available as blackline master.

Daily Focus Transparency 22

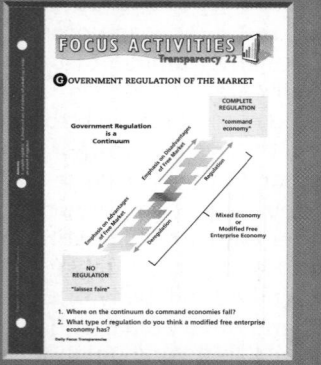

Study Guide

Reading Strategy

Have students create the graphic organizer.
Answers to Graphic: *to encourage competition, to regulate monopolies, to reinforce public disclosure*

Preteaching Vocabulary

⚙ Use the Vocabulary Puzzle-Maker to create crossword and word-search puzzles.

The Role of Government

Study Guide

Main Idea
One of the economic functions of government in a market economy is to maintain competition.

Reading Strategy
Graphic Organizer As you read the section, give three reasons government takes part in economic affairs. Complete an organizer similar to the one below to help you organize your answer.

Government in economic affairs ◯ ◯ ◯

Key Terms
trust, price discrimination, cease and desist order, public disclosure

Objectives
After studying this section, you will be able to:
1. **Discuss** major antitrust legislation in the United States.
2. **Understand** the need for limited government regulation.
3. **Explain** the value of public disclosure.
4. **Discuss** the modifications to our free enterprise economy.

Applying Economic Concepts
Public Disclosure Do you have a credit card or a car loan? Do you know the size of the monthly payments, the computation of the interest, and other important terms of the agreement? Did someone take the time to explain all these details? Disclosing this information is not merely an act of kindness on the part of the business: it is required by a federal public disclosure law to assure that you are a well-informed consumer.

Cover Story

New Parents Face Steep Costs

Parents of Y2K babies may gasp when they check out he final tab.

The average cost of rearing a child born last year will be about $165,630—or $233,530 factoring in inflation—for food, shelter, and other necessities over the next 17 years, according to an annual report by the Agriculture Department released Monday.

Cost of raising children is rising

The USDA report "Expenditures on Children by Families," is used by state agencies and courts in determining child support guidelines and foster care payments.

—*Associated Press*, June 12, 2001

178

Today, government has the power to encourage competition and to regulate monopolies that exist for the public welfare. In some cases, government has taken over certain economic activities and runs them as government-owned monopolies. In other cases, the United States government even makes estimates—such as those described in the cover story—in order to carry out its legal and social obligations.

Antitrust Legislation

In the late 1800s, the United States passed laws to restrict monopolies, combinations, and **trusts**—legally formed combinations of corporations or companies. Since then, a number of key laws have been passed that allow the government to either prevent or break up monopolies. Collectively, this legislation is designed to prevent market failures due to *inadequate competition*.

RESOURCE MANAGER

📁 Reproducible Masters
- Reproducible Lesson Plan 7-3
- Daily Lecture Notes 7-3
- Guided Reading Activity 7-3
- Reading Essentials and Study Guide 7-3
- Section Quiz 7-3

🔲 Transparencies
- Daily Focus Transparency 22

Multimedia
- ⚙ Vocabulary PuzzleMaker CD-ROM
- 🔲 Interactive Tutor Self-Assessment Software
- ⚙ ExamView® Pro Testmaker
- ⚙ Presentation Plus!

In 1890 Congress passed the Sherman Antitrust Act "to protect trade and commerce against unlawful restraint and monopoly." The Sherman Act, described in **Figure 7.3,** was the country's first significant law against monopolies. It sought to do away with monopolies and restraints that hindered competition. By the early 1900s, a number of business organizations had been convicted under the Sherman Act.

The Sherman Act laid down broad foundations for maintaining competition. The act was not specific enough, however, to stop many practices that restrained trade and competition. In 1914 Congress passed the Clayton Antitrust Act to give the government greater power against monopolies. Among other provisions, this act outlawed **price discrimination**—the practice of charging customers different prices for the same product.

The Federal Trade Commission Act was passed in the same year to enforce the Clayton Antitrust Act. The act set up the Federal Trade Commission (FTC) and gave it the authority to issue cease and desist orders. A **cease and desist order** is an FTC ruling requiring a company to stop an unfair business practice, such as price-fixing, that reduces or limits competition among firms.

In 1936 Congress passed the Robinson-Patman Act in an effort to strengthen the Clayton Act, particularly the provisions that dealt with price

discrimination. Under this act, companies could no longer offer special discounts to some customers while denying them to others. This law primarily affected national organizations and chain stores that were offering goods and services at lower prices than those paid by small independent businesses.

Government Regulation

Not all monopolies are bad, and for that reason not all should be broken up. In the case of a natural monopoly, it makes sense to let the firm expand to take advantage of lower production costs—then regulate its activities so that it cannot take advantage of the consumer. Ideally, the regulator's goal is to set the same level of price and service that would exist under competition.

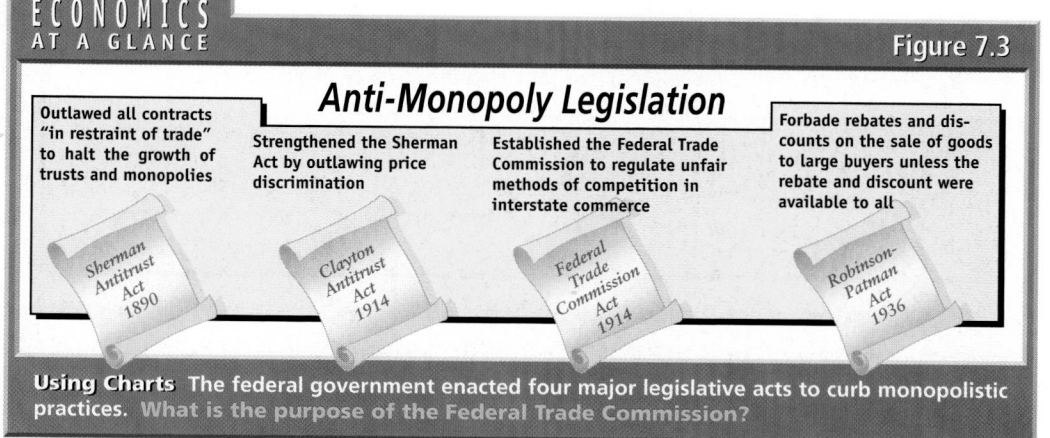

ECONOMICS AT A GLANCE

Figure 7.3

Anti-Monopoly Legislation

Outlawed all contracts "in restraint of trade" to halt the growth of trusts and monopolies

Strengthened the Sherman Act by outlawing price discrimination

Established the Federal Trade Commission to regulate unfair methods of competition in interstate commerce

Forbade rebates and discounts on the sale of goods to large buyers unless the rebate and discount were available to all

Sherman Antitrust Act 1890

Clayton Antitrust Act 1914

Federal Trade Commission Act 1914

Robinson-Patman Act 1936

Using Charts The federal government enacted four major legislative acts to curb monopolistic practices. What is the purpose of the Federal Trade Commission?

CHAPTER 7: MARKET STRUCTURES **179**

② TEACH

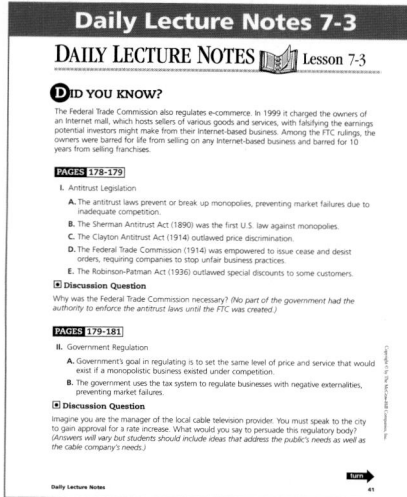

Daily Lecture Notes 7-3

DAILY LECTURE NOTES 📖 Lesson 7-3

ⓓ DID YOU KNOW?
The Federal Trade Commission also regulates e-commerce. In 1999 it charged the owners of an Internet mall, which hosts sellers of various goods and services, with falsifying the earnings potential investors might make from their Internet-based business. Among the FTC rulings, the owners were barred for life from selling on any Internet-based business and barred for 10 years from selling franchises.

PAGES 178-179
I. Antitrust Legislation
  A. The antitrust laws prevent or break up monopolies, preventing market failures due to inadequate competition.
  B. The Sherman Antitrust Act (1890) was the first U.S. law against monopolies.
  C. The Clayton Antitrust Act (1914) outlawed price discrimination.
  D. The Federal Trade Commission (1914) was empowered to issue cease and desist orders, requiring companies to stop unfair business practices.
  E. The Robinson-Patman Act (1936) outlawed special discounts to some customers.

▣ Discussion Question
Why was the Federal Trade Commission necessary? (No part of the government had the authority to enforce the antitrust laws until the FTC was created.)

PAGES 179-181
II. Government Regulation
  A. Government's goal in regulating is to set the same level of price and service that would exist if a monopolistic business existed under competition.
  B. The government uses the tax system to regulate businesses with negative externalities, preventing market failures.

▣ Discussion Question
Imagine you are the manager of the local cable television provider. You must speak to the city to gain approval for a rate increase. What would you say to persuade this regulatory body? (Answers will vary but students should include ideas that address the public's needs as well as the cable company's needs.)

Daily Lecture Notes   41

L1 Conducting a Survey

Have students conduct an informal survey of family members, friends, students, and teachers on government's role in the economy. Suggest that they ask such questions as: Is there too much or not enough government regulation? Which regulatory agencies, if any, should be abolished? Have students share their survey results with the class.

ECONOMICS AT A GLANCE

Answer: *to ensure fair methods of competition in interstate commerce*

MEETING SPECIAL NEEDS ACTIVITY

Learning Style: Visual/Spatial Have students choose one of the subsections in Section 3—Antitrust Legislation, Government Regulation, or Public Disclosure. Have each student create an illustrated poster explaining that particular role of government using pictures from magazines or other sources that are related to the concept. For example, to illustrate Government Regulation, students might collect pictures related to monopolies regulated by the government, such as telephone companies. Posters should also use captions or short paragraphs to make clear government's role in maintaining competition.

Refer to *Inclusion for the Social Studies Classroom Strategies and Activities* in the TCR.

THE GLOBAL ECONOMY

International Price-Fixing
OPEC, the Organization of Petroleum Exporting Countries, is an international oligopoly that tries to set world oil prices and to determine the amount of petroleum produced by its 11 member nations.

ECONOMICS
AT A GLANCE

Answer: *Answers will vary.*

L2 Government Restrictions
Students should research various regulatory agencies. Have them identify and evaluate restrictions placed on individuals and businesses.

Federal Regulatory Agencies

Food and Drug Administration (FDA), 1906	Enforces laws to ensure purity, effectiveness, and truthful labeling of food, drugs, and cosmetics; inspects production and shipment of these products
Federal Trade Commission (FTC), 1914	Administers antitrust laws forbidding unfair competition, price fixing, and other deceptive practices
Federal Communications Commission (FCC), 1934	Licenses and regulates radio and television stations and regulates interstate telephone, telegraph rates and services
Securities and Exchange Commission (SEC), 1934	Regulates and supervises the sale of listed and unlisted securities and the brokers, dealers, and bankers who sell them
National Labor Relations Board (NLRB), 1935	Administers federal labor-management relations laws; settles labor disputes; prevents unfair labor practices
Federal Aviation Administration (FAA), 1958	Oversees the airline industry
Equal Employment Opportunity Commission (EEOC), 1964	Investigates and rules on charges of discrimination by employers and labor unions
Environmental Protection Agency (EPA), 1970	Protects and enhances the environment
Occupational Safety and Health Administration (OSHA), 1970	Investigates accidents at the workplace; enforces regulations to protect employees at work
Consumer Product Safety Commission (CPSC), 1972	Develops standards of safety for consumer goods
Nuclear Regulatory Commission (NRC), 1974	Regulates civilian use of nuclear materials and facilities
Federal Energy Regulatory Commission (FERC), 1977	Supervises transmission of the various forms of energy

Using Charts The government has created a number of federal regulatory agencies to oversee the economy. Because of government's involvement in the economy, we have a modified free enterprise system. With which of the agencies listed in the table are you familiar? Which affect you directly? Why?

180 UNIT 2 MICROECONOMICS

FREE ENTERPRISE ACTIVITY

Select teams of students to debate the following proposition: "Resolved: That the government is too involved in regulating our economy." Before the debate, review Section 3 with the students. Then have them conduct research in the library to obtain additional information on the subject. During the debate, have students not directly involved serve as judges, recording a mark when each side makes a point that supports its position. Have judges tally scores and announce the winner of the debate. **BLOCK SCHEDULING**

Examples of Regulation

Local and state governments regulate many monopolies, such as cable television companies, water and electric utilities, and even telephone companies. A public commission or other government agency usually approves prices for their services. If a company wants to raise rates, it must argue and prove its case before the commission.

Agencies of the national government, such as those listed in **Figure 7.4,** regulate many businesses. Privately owned agencies, such as the Federal Reserve System, have certain regulatory powers, including the power to regulate the money supply, some daily bank operations, and even bank mergers.

Internalizing Externalities

The government can also use the tax system to lessen some of the negative externalities in the economy. Suppose, for example, that firms in a certain industry are causing pollution, which is flowing into a nearby river or even affecting the atmosphere. Because they are using the environment as a giant waste-disposal system, their costs of production are lower than they should be.

If government taxes these producers, several things happen. First, every firm's cost of production goes up, causing each to produce a little less at every possible price. This causes the market supply curve to shift and the price of the product to rise. Consumers of the product react predictably by buying less of the product. Meanwhile, the government uses the tax proceeds to clean up the pollution.

Figure 7.5 shows how this works. First, a $1 tax is placed on every unit of output that a firm produces. This shifts the supply curve up by exactly $1. The new intersection of supply and demand takes place at $15.60—indicating that the firm paid 40¢ of the tax and passed 60¢ on to the consumer.

Economists call this "internalizing an externality" because it forces the polluting firm and its customers, rather than innocent third parties, to pay for the cost of pollution. Consequently, the government uses policies like this to prevent market failures due to *negative externalities.*

Public Disclosure

The purpose of public disclosure is to provide the market with enough data to prevent market failures due to *inadequate information.* While there is some cost involved, and while some businesses might prefer to not disclose anything, the benefits to society far outweigh the costs.

One of the more potent weapons available to the government is **public disclosure,** or the requirement that businesses reveal information to the public. The degree of disclosure is more extensive than most people realize, going beyond the content labels that the Food and Drug Administration requires on foods and medicines.

For example, the government requires that all corporations selling stock to the public must disclose financial and operating information on a regular basis to both its shareholders and to the Securities and Exchange Commission (SEC). The

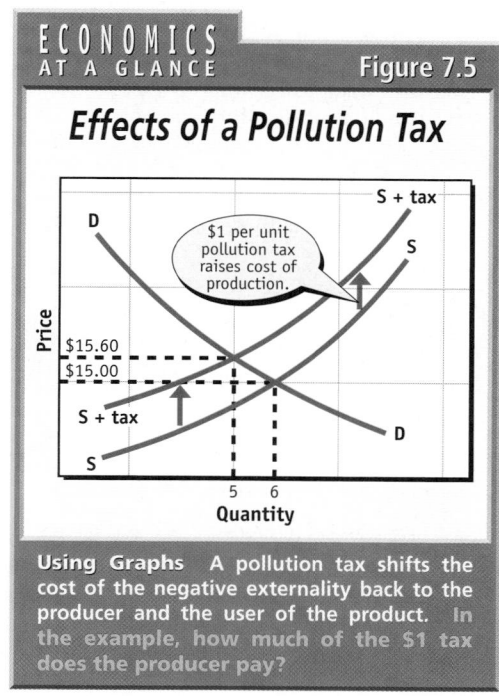

ECONOMICS AT A GLANCE
Figure 7.5

Effects of a Pollution Tax

$1 per unit pollution tax raises cost of production.

Using Graphs A pollution tax shifts the cost of the negative externality back to the producer and the user of the product. **In the example, how much of the $1 tax does the producer pay?**

CHAPTER 7: MARKET STRUCTURES **181**

L2 Journalism

Write the section's main headings on the board and tell students that the headings are headlines for news stories. Then have students write two news stories.

L3 Government

Ask students to find articles in current news stories about government attempts to regulate a monopoly. Have students write a one-sentence summary of the nature of the regulation attempt.

ECONOMICS AT A GLANCE

Answer: *40¢*

CYBERNOMICS

Business Info on the Internet
The SEC (Securities and Exchange Commission) home page on the Internet offers a variety of information for investors as well as a place to list complaints. The SEC's Web site provides information for small businesses and individual investors, and lists current SEC rulings and information about enforcement of its rules.
www.sec.gov

CRITICAL THINKING

Evaluating Information Discuss as a class whether students commonly refer to the nutritional content labels found on food products. **Ask:** Do you find these labels useful? Why or why not? Then have each student choose a type of food product and examine the nutritional content labels on several different brands and/or sizes of that product. What information is available on the label? Have students write short reports describing what they found, noting especially any differences, such as serving sizes, that made comparing the information on the labels difficult.

Visual Instruction

Answer to Caption:
promote competition and enable consumers to make better decisions

L3 Analyzing Ideas

Have students review the section. Then **ask:** Which government activity plays the greatest role in maintaining competition in the marketplace? Why? After the discussion, have students write a few paragraphs outlining their own ideas.

③ ASSESS

Assign Section 3 Assessment as homework or as an in-class activity.

💾 Have students use **Interactive Tutor Self-Assessment Software** to review Section 3.

Section Quiz 7-3

The Role of Government Truth-in-advertising laws are one way the federal government tries to improve the quality of information in the economy. *How do these laws protect consumers?*

SEC retains this data electronically in its Electronic Data Gathering Analysis and Retrieval (EDGAR) system, which can be accessed by anyone over the Internet. Access is free, and you need not be an owner to see the extremely detailed financial and operating information for any firm.

Banks are required to file periodic reports to the Federal Reserve System and other federal agencies such as the Federal Deposit Insurance Corporation (FDIC) that insures the nation's banks. Most of this information is available to the bank's competitors as well as to its shareholders, and it is highly sought after by almost all firms in the industry.

There are also disclosure regulations for businesses that lend to consumers. If you obtain a credit card or borrow money to buy a car, the lender will take considerable time to explain how the monthly interest is computed, the length of the loan, the size of the payments, and other important terms of the agreement. This is not an act of kindness on the lender's part—federal law requires that lenders make these disclosures so that consumers know what they are getting into. Finally, there are "truth-in-advertising" laws that prevent sellers from making false claims about their products.

Indirect Disclosure

The government has also worked indirectly to improve the quality of information available to consumers. One example is the government's support for the Internet, and its attempt to provide low-cost access to all public schools. Government has also agreed to not collect some fees, such as taxes on e-commerce sales, in order to help the Internet grow.

STANDARD & POOR'S INFOBYTE

The SEC The Securities and Exchange Commission (SEC) is a regulatory agency that is responsible for administering federal securities laws. The purpose of these laws is to protect investors from improper practices in securities markets and to ensure that they have access to disclosure of all material information concerning publicly traded securities. The commission also regulates firms engaged in the purchase or sale of securities, people who provide investment advice, and investment companies.

182 UNIT 2 MICROECONOMICS

EXTENDING THE CONTENT

Disclosure Rules Have on hand a sampling of disclosure forms from banks and lending institutions. Distribute them to students and discuss information on these forms. Have students compare interest rates on various credit cards based on a bill of $1,000. Ask students to use the disclosure information to identify the rate that is best for the borrower as well as the rate that gains the greatest profit for the lender.

ECONOMICS Online

Student Web Activity Visit the *Economics: Principles and Practices* Web site at epp.glencoe.com and click on **Chapter 7—Student Web Activities** for an activity on the government's role in promoting fair business practices.

Businesses have joined the rush to the Web by posting extensive information about their activities. The Internet provides other information to consumers as well. The savvy user can talk to others in chat rooms, participate in user forums, or read product reviews to find out more about a good or service before making a purchase. Other services allow consumers to search for the best prices.

Finally, virtually every government document, study, and report is available in some fashion on the Internet. This includes the annual budget of the U.S. government, and reports by the President's Council of Economic Advisors. Also available online are information from the *Statistical Abstract of the United States,* bulletins by the Bureau of Labor Statistics, reports by the Census Bureau, and almost every other publication that you can find in the government documents section of a major research library.

Modified Free Enterprise

Concern over the costs of imperfect competition is one reason the government intervenes in the economy. Historically, the freedom to pursue self-interests led some people and businesses to seek economic gain at the expense of others. Under the label of competition, some larger firms used their power to take advantage of smaller ones. In some markets, monopoly replaced competition.

Because of such conditions, Congress passed laws to prevent "evil monopolies" and to protect the rights of workers. Its support of labor unions gave workers more bargaining power. New food and drug laws protected people from false claims and harmful products. Government strictly regulated some industries, such as public utilities. All these actions led to a modification of free enterprise.

In summary, government takes part in economic affairs for several reasons. One is to promote and to encourage competition for the benefit of society. Another is to prevent monopolies and reduce the costs of imperfect competition wherever possible. A third is to regulate industries in which a monopoly is clearly in the best interest of the public. A fourth is to fulfill the need for public goods. As a result, today's modified private enterprise economy is a mixture of different market structures, different kinds of business organizations, and varying degrees of government regulation.

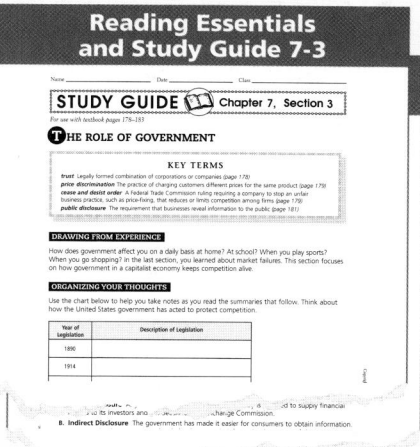

ECONOMICS Online

Objectives, goals, and answers to the student activity can be found in the **Web Activity Lesson Plan** feature at epp.glencoe.com

Reteach

Reading Essentials and Study Guide 7-3

STUDY GUIDE — Chapter 7, Section 3

For use with textbook pages 178–183

THE ROLE OF GOVERNMENT

Enrich

Have students research one of the federal agencies listed in Figure 7.4 on page 180.

④ CLOSE

Have students explain whether they think "modified free enterprise" is an appropriate description of the American economic system.

Section 3 Assessment

Checking for Understanding

1. **Main Idea** Using your notes from the graphic organizer activity on page 178, explain why the government is involved in economic affairs.

2. **Key Terms** Define trust, price discrimination, cease and desist order, public disclosure.

3. **Describe** four important antitrust laws.

4. **Explain** why there is a need for limited government regulation within the economy.

5. **Describe** the value of public disclosure.

6. **Explain** why the United States has a modified free enterprise economy.

Applying Economic Concepts

7. **Public Disclosure** Visit a bank in your community and ask for literature describing the computation of interest and conditions for withdrawal on various savings accounts. Why do you think the bank is so forthcoming on these issues?

Critical Thinking

8. **Synthesizing Information** Identify five examples of how government has intervened in your community.

> **Practice** and **assess** key social studies skills with the *Glencoe Skillbuilder Interactive Workbook, Level 2.*

CHAPTER 7: MARKET STRUCTURES **183**

Section 3 Assessment Answers

1. to encourage competition, regulate monopolies, and punish companies when they act in a manner that restrains competition

2. All vocabulary terms are defined in the text.

3. Answers should offer descriptions of the Sherman Antitrust Act (1890); Clayton Antitrust Act (1914); Federal Trade Commission Act (1914); Robinson-Patman Act (1936).

4. to prevent market failures due to negative externalities, and to regulate natural and government monopolies

5. it promotes competition and enables consumers to make informed decisions

6. People carry on economic affairs freely but are subject to some government regulation

7. Government requires public disclosure.

8. Examples should reflect government's role in maintaining competition.

Teaching Skills

Find and copy several newspaper or magazine articles dealing with the government's role in maintaining competition. Give each student an article and several different colored pens or highlighters. Have students skim articles and mark the headings and subheadings with one color. Have them use another color to highlight details that support a larger idea or issue. If a sentence or paragraph summarizes the article's main idea, have students mark that passage in a third color.

Reinforcing Economic Skill 12

Reinforcing Economic Skills Chapter 12

FINDING THE MAIN IDEA

Finding the main idea will help you see the "big picture" by assessing the most important concepts in what you read. To find the main idea, skim the material to identify its general subject. Then ask yourself what the purpose of the article is. Finally, identify details that support the main idea.

Directions: Read the letter below and answer the questions that follow.

Letter to Shareholders

Improving consumers' lives by doing things that have never been done before is what Procter & Gamble is all about. In more than 140 countries around the world, we work to understand what consumers want and need. Then we develop innovative brands to serve those needs—creating new products, new categories and new growth opportunities for our Company.

More than 110,000 P & G employees around the world, committed to breakthrough innovation and superior execution, drive our growth. Again this year, we delivered record performance: net earnings of $3.78 billion, up 11%; basic net earnings per common share of $2.74, up 13 percent; and worldwide net sales of $37.2 billion, up 4% on 6% unit volume growth.

These results fueled solid performance in the areas that matter most to you, our shareholders. Over the past three years, we've delivered an average annual Total Shareholder Return (TSR) of 37 percent, compared to a TSR of 30% for the S&P 500. And we concluded the 1997/1998 fiscal year by increasing common share dividends 13% to $1.14—marking the 43rd consecutive year of increased dividend payments.

1. What is the purpose of this letter?

2. What is its main idea?

3. What details support the main idea?

GLENCOE
TECHNOLOGY

Glencoe Skillbuilder Interactive Workbook, Level 2

This interactive CD-ROM reinforces student mastery of essential social studies skills.

CRITICAL THINKING
Skill

Finding the Main Idea

Finding the main idea will help you see the "big picture." Organizing information will help you understand and assess the most important concepts.

Learning the Skill

To find the main idea, follow these steps:

• Find out the setting of the article.

• As you read the material, ask "What is the purpose of this article?"

• Skim the material to identify its general subject. Look at headings and subheadings.

• Identify any details that support a larger idea or issue.

• Identify the central issue. Ask "What part of the selection conveys the main idea?"

Chimneys obscured by smoke at coal-fired power plant

Practicing the Skill

Read the excerpt below, then answer the questions that follow.

Does [economic] growth threaten the environment? The connection between growth and environment is tenuous, say growth proponents.

Increases in economic growth need not mean increases in pollution. Pollution is not so much a by-product of growth as it is a "problem of the commons." Much of the environment—streams, lakes, oceans, and the air—is treated as "common property," with no restrictions on its use. The commons have become our dumping grounds; we have overused and debased them. Environmental pollution is a case of spillover or external costs, and correcting this problem involves regulatory legislation or specific taxes to remedy misuse of the environment.

There are serious pollution problems. But limiting growth is the wrong solution. Growth has allowed economies to reduce pollution, be more sensitive to environmental considerations, set aside wilderness, and clean up hazardous waste, while still enabling rising household incomes.

—Alice M. Rivlin, *Reviving the American Dream*
Washington Brookings Institutions, 1992

1. Who wrote this passage?

2. When was it written?

3. What was the purpose of this article?

4. What is the main idea that the author of the article is expressing?

5. What additional details in the excerpt support the main idea?

6. Do you find the article persuasive? Explain your response.

Application Activity

Bring to class a news article that deals with competition in the marketplace. Identify the main idea and explain why it is important.

 Practice and **assess** key social studies skills with the *Glencoe Skillbuilder Interactive Workbook, Level 2.*

Answers to Practicing the Skill

1. Alice M. Rivlin
2. 1992
3. to persuade readers that growth is not a problem
4. Economic growth does not result in pollution.
5. Answers may mention the "problem of the commons" and the benefits of economic growth.
6. Answers should specify what details made the article more or less persuasive.

Section 1

Competition and Market Structures (pages 163–171)

- **Perfect competition** is a **market structure** with a large numbers of buyers and sellers, identical economic products, independent action by buyers and sellers, reasonably well-informed participants, and freedom for firms to enter or leave the market.

- Perfect competition is a largely theoretical situation used as a benchmark to evaluate other market structures. Market situations lacking one or more of these conditions are called **imperfect competition.**

- **Monopolistic competition** has all the characteristics of **perfect competition** except for identical products.

- **Oligopoly** is a market structure dominated by a few very large firms, and the actions by one affects the welfare of others.

- The **monopolist** is a single producer with the most control over supply and price. Various forms of monopoly include the **natural monopoly,** the **geographic monopoly,** the **technological monopoly,** and the **government monopoly.**

- All private firms, regardless of market structure, maximize profits by producing at the level of output where marginal cost is equal to marginal revenue.

Section 2

Market Failures (pages 173–176)

- **Market failures** occur when sizable deviations from one or more of the conditions required for perfect competition take place.

- Three of the five common market failures include *inadequate competition, inadquate information,* and *resource immobility.*

- **Externalities,** or economic side effects to third parties, are a fourth market failure. A **negative externality** is a harmful side effect and a **positive externality** is a beneficial side effect.

- Externalities are regarded as market failures because they are not reflected in the market prices of the activities that caused the side effects.

- Finally, a market economy often fails to provide **public goods** such as national defense and public education because it cannot withhold supply from those who refuse to pay.

Section 3

The Role of Government (pages 178–183)

- The Sherman Antitrust Act of 1890 was enacted to prohibit **trusts,** monopolies, and other arrangements that restrain competition. The Clayton Antitrust Act was passed in 1914 to outlaw **price discrimination.** The Robinson-Patman Act of 1936 was passed to strengthen the price discrimination provisions of the Clayton Antitrust Act.

- **Public disclosure** is used as a tool to promote competition. Any corporation that sells its stock publicly is required to supply periodic financial reports to both its investors and to the SEC.

- Banks are covered by additional disclosure laws and report to various federal agencies.

- Today, government takes part in economic affairs to promote and encourage competition. As a result, the modern economy is a mixture of different market structures, different forms of business organizations, and some degree of government regulation.

NIGHTLY BUSINESS REPORT

○ **ECONOMICS & YOU**

Chapter 8
Disc 1, Side 1

Competition and Monopolies

▭ Also available in VHS.

Using the Chapter 7 Summary

Use the Chapter 7 Summary to preview, review, condense, or reteach the chapter.

Preview/Review

⊙ Vocabulary PuzzleMaker CD-ROM reinforces Key Terms.

▯ Interactive Tutor Self-Assessment Software provides a review of Chapter 7 content.

Condense

⌒ ▭ Have students listen to the Chapter 7 Audio Program. Spanish also available.

▭ ▭ Assign the Chapter 7 Audio Program Activity and give students the Chapter 7 Audio Program Test.

▭ ▭ Have students complete the Guided Reading Activities and Reading Essentials and Study Guides for Chapter 7.

Reteach

▭ ▭ Have students complete Reteaching Activity 7 in the TCR. Spanish also available.

Teacher's Notes / Internet Bookmarks

CHAPTER 7
Assessment and Activities

Use **MindJogger Videoquiz** to review the Chapter 7 content.

ECONOMICS Online

Have students visit the Web site at epp.glencoe.com to review Chapter 7 and take the **Self-Check Quiz.**

Self-Check Quiz Visit the *Economics: Principles and Practices* Web site at epp.glencoe.com and click on **Chapter 7—Self-Check Quizzes** to prepare for the chapter test.

Identifying Key Terms

Use all the terms below in four paragraphs, with each paragraph describing one of the major types of market structures.

collusion
geographic monopoly
imperfect competition
monopolistic competition
natural monopoly
oligopoly
product differentiation
technological monopoly
price-fixing
monopoly
nonprice competition
perfect competition

Reviewing the Facts

Section 1 (pages 163–171)

1. **Describe** the five characteristics of perfect competition.
2. **Explain** the main characteristics of the monopolistic competitor.
3. **Contrast** the oligopolist and the perfect competitor.
4. **Describe** the four types of monopolies.

Section 2 (pages 173–176)

5. **Explain** what happens when markets do not have enough competition.
6. **Provide** two examples of inadequate information in a market.

7. **Explain** what is meant by resource immobility.
8. **Explain** what is meant by positive and negative externalities.
9. **Account** for the reluctance of the private sector to produce public goods.

Section 3 (pages 178–183)

10. **Identify** four major antitrust laws.
11. **List** 10 major federal government regulatory agencies.
12. **Explain** how public disclosure is used as a tool to prevent market failures.
13. **Describe** a modified free enterprise economy.

Thinking Critically

1. **Drawing Inferences** Do you think there would be any advantages to making monopolies or near monopolies break up into smaller, competing firms? If so, what are they? If not, why would there not be? Use a chart like the one below to help you organize the answers to these questions.

| Monopolies should be broken up | → | Reasons |
| Monopolies should not be broken up | → | Reasons |

2. **Understanding Cause and Effect** How are natural monopolies prevented from practicing monopolistic practices?
3. **Making Generalizations** To what extent do you think government should be involved in the free enterprise economy? Defend your answer.
4. **Finding the Main Idea** What problems do the Federal Trade Commission, the Securities and Exchange Commission, and the Consumer Product Safety Commission address?
5. **Summarizing Information** Why do private producers fail to provide public goods?

Identifying Key Terms
Paragraphs will vary but should include relevant chapter content.

Reviewing the Facts

Section 1

1. large number of buyers/sellers; buyers/sellers deal in identical products; buyers/sellers act independently; buyers/sellers are well informed; ease of entry into market
2. Competitor uses product differentiation, nonprice competition, price competition
3. oligopolist: few large competitors dealing in differentiated products may take actions that can change output, sales, and prices in the industry as a whole; perfect competitor: one of many producers dealing in identical products, and the actions he or she may take have no effect on prices
4. natural: costs are minimized by having single producer; geographic: business has monopoly because of its geographic location; technological: firm or individual has discovered new manufacturing technique or has created something new; government: government owns and operates the business

Section 2

5. Productive resources will not be allocated efficiently; prices may rise and output decrease.
6. a lack of information about wages for the same job in different industries, or lack of information about returns on investments
7. Resources are unable or unwilling to move to markets where returns are highest.
8. positive: economic action benefits uninvolved third party; negative: harms an uninvolved third party

9. private sector only willing to produce items that can be withheld if people unwilling to pay

Section 3

10. Sherman Antitrust Act (1890); Clayton Antitrust Act (1914); Federal Trade Commission Act (1914); Robinson-Patman Act (1936)
11. See Figure 7.4 on p. 180 for possible entries.
12. It requires businesses to provide information that helps prevent failures.
13. economy in which people carry on their economic affairs freely, but are subject to government regulation in certain cases

186

Applying Economic Concepts

1. **Market Failures** Explain how your newspaper, with its help-wanted ads and weekly sale prices, helps prevent market failures.

2. **Market Structures** Identify a fast-food product that you consume regularly. Count the number of firms in your community that supply a similar product, and then identify the market structure for that product in your community.

3. **Free Enterprise** How does the federal government attempt to preserve competition among business enterprises?

Math Practice

The table below shows the price, market demand, market supply, and the surplus and shortage for a firm providing a product under perfect competition. Study the information in the table, then answer the questions.

Price	Market Demand	Market Supply	Surplus/ Shortage
10	600	1550	950
9	-----	1500	780
8	850	1450	-----
7	990	1400	-----
6	-----	1350	210
5	1300	-----	0
4	1470	-----	−220
3	1650	1200	-----
2	1840	1150	−690

1. Some of the information is missing from the table. Calculate the correct information.

2. What is the equilibrium price? How can you tell?

3. What price(s) will produce a surplus?

4. What price(s) will produce a shortage?

Thinking Like an Economist

Profit Maximization Economists like to analyze decisions incrementally—taking small steps and analyzing the costs and benefits of the steps as they are made. How is this way of thinking similar to the profit maximization logic illustrated in **Figure 7.1** on page 165?

Technology Skill

Developing Multimedia Presentations Choose a product offered by several producers that is advertised in newspapers or magazines. For one week, clip and save at least three different advertisements about your product. Keep a journal in which you evaluate each advertisement and summarize why you would or would not buy a particular brand. Use your evaluations and a video camera to develop a commercial advertising a product of your choice. Have other students evaluate your commercial for its effectiveness.

Building Skills

Finding the Main Idea Read the excerpt below, then answer the questions that follow.

> *Monopolistic competition occurs when there are many producers of products that are almost the same. Firms in such a market try to make customers believe that the similar products are actually different. Each producer uses advertising to persuade the customer that his or her brand is superior. Firms that are successful have a monopoly on their name and reputation more than on their product. Customers are willing to pay more for the product because they associate its name with quality or value. Many beauty products, soaps, household cleaners, and over-the-counter medicines fall into this group.*

1. What is monopolistic competition?

2. What main idea is expressed?

3. What details support the main idea?

 Practice and **assess** key social studies skills with the *Glencoe Skillbuilder Interactive Workbook, Level 2.*

Thinking Critically

1. Dividing monopolies would increase competition and prevent monopolies from taking advantage of consumers. Some monopolies are beneficial because they can operate more efficiently. Students may mention the possible inability to divide geographic or technological monopolies.

2. Government regulations ensure that the natural monopoly sets the same level of price and service that would exist under competition.

3. Answers will vary but students should support their answers.

4. Students should provide specific examples.

5. It is difficult to get everyone to pay for their share of a public good.

Applying Economic Concepts

1. by providing people with additional information on markets

2. Answers may note that the fast-food market is an oligopoly.

3. federal regulation agencies, antitrust regulations, public disclosure, and individualized regulations

Math Practice

1. demand at price 9 is 720, at price 6 is 1140, supply at price 5 is 1300, at price 4 is 1250; surplus at price 8 is 600, at price 7 is 410; shortage at price 3 is −450

2. The equilibrium price is 5; neither a surplus nor a shortage.

3. price 6 and above

4. price 4 and below

Thinking Like an Economist

Students might note that profit maximization also entails the analysis of increments of change.

Technology Skill

Evaluate students' presentations for insight and effectiveness.

Building Skills

1. a situation in which there are many producers of similar products

2. Firms in a monopolistic competition market try to make customers believe their product is different.

3. types of nonprice competition such as advertising; the effect of nonprice competition on consumers; examples of products

Bonus Test Question

Provide examples, other than those mentioned in the chapter, of industries that match, or closely match, each of the four forms of market structure. *(Examples will vary.)*

1 FOCUS

Have several students bring in paycheck stubs from their part-time jobs. Respect students' privacy while pointing out how money is taken out for federal, state, county, and city taxes. Show students how 6.2 percent of the money from each paycheck is deducted to pay the Social Security tax. Ask students to define what "social security" is, based on what they have read or heard about in the media. As students read in the selections about the problems that the system faces, have them try to think of possible solutions of their own.

2 TEACH

L1 Applying Basic Concepts

Write "PRO" and "CON" on the board and ask students to identify the major points of the two arguments about Social Security. Note responses under the appropriate heading. Then have students write a summary paragraph for each of the arguments using information on the board. Make sure they include terms such as "tax" and "insurance" when writing their paragraphs.

L2 Analyzing Cartoons

Have students find political cartoons that satirize how people view the Social Security issue. Students may also draw their own cartoons that reflect their opinions of the debate.

A Case Study:

THE FUTURE OF SOCIAL SECURITY

The Social Security Act of 1935 and its later amendments created a social insurance system to help America's most needy: elderly, ill, and unemployed citizens. The core of the program was retirement benefits, funded by taxes on workers and employers, that people could collect when they stopped working at age 65. For decades the system, though criticized, was largely recognized as fundamentally sound.

But in the 1980s the system faced a severe cash shortage: outgoing payments rose faster than incoming taxes. The federal government responded with some changes (such as raising the retirement age from 65 to 67 by the year 2027) that forestalled the problem. But as the baby boomer generation ages, Social Security may be facing another crisis.

Many experts fear that the system will be drained of funds in the twenty-first century, leaving whole generations bereft of benefits. The solution, they say, is the privatization of the system. Others maintain that the problems facing Social Security are overstated and that, while some fine-tuning may be necessary, a fundamental change like privatization is uncalled for, and dangerous.

> Who is right? As you read the selections, ask yourself: Is Social Security working, or does the United States need a new system?

PRO Social Security Is Secure

During the 21st century, when all the Boomers have put work behind them, 20 percent of all Americans will be elderly—a larger percentage than ever before in our history. And these retirees will get Social Security benefits from taxes collected from a much smaller pool of working people. . . .

While it's true that in 2030 there will be fewer workers per retiree than there are today, a more reliable measure is to look at workers per

dependent—which means not just the elderly but also those too young to work. Why is this important? Because it allows us to point out, reassuringly, that in 1965, the last year of the Baby Boom, there were 95 dependents for every 100 workers, compared to 71 today and 79 in 2030. If society could handle the massive needs (education, health care, for example) of our generation in our pre-productive years, it can manage to see us through our post-productive years as well. . . .

Social Security works because it offers universal coverage. . . . Certainly some people would rake in more money under privatization than they would under the current

188 UNIT 2 MICROECONOMICS

Behind the Viewpoints

PRO **John Shure** writes for the Twentieth Century Fund, a nonpartisan foundation that researches and writes about progressive approaches to public policies.

CON **Carrie Lips** writes for the Cato Institute, a nonpartisan research foundation that supports the beliefs of limited government, individual liberty, and peace.

system. But others would get less and some would lose everything. . . . If that doesn't make you uneasy, try this: these privatization schemes would increase taxes and add considerably to the administrative costs of Social Security (which today stand at an almost unbelievable 1 percent compared to 12–14 percent for private sector insurance). Social Security isn't without problems. Quite simply, people are living longer and so there will have to be adjustments like a higher retirement and maybe somewhat lower benefits phased in gradually over decades so no one gets a surprise they can't plan for. But Social Security ain't broke–in the fiscal or structural sense. . . .

–John Shure, Vice President of the Twentieth Century Fund

CON A New System Is Needed

Back in 1940, when the Social Security program was just getting under way, average life expectancy was less than 64 years. The program's designers expected that many people would contribute to the program most of their lives and die before collecting a dime in retirement benefits. . . . Today, average life expectancy in the United States is more than 75 years. More important, the population that reaches age 65 is also living longer. An average person that lives to 65 will live for approximately another 17 years. . . .

As life expectancy has soared, birthrates have declined, leaving fewer and fewer workers to support the ballooning number of retirees. In 1950, this pyramid scheme was solidly supported with 16 workers paying for each retiree; today, there are just over three workers per beneficiary. The [Social Security Administration's] own estimates indicate that the ratio of workers to beneficiaries will continue to decrease, reaching just two workers per beneficiary by 2030.

Moreover, those projections ignore one of the most promising facts of our time: Not only does life expectancy continue to grow; the rate of growth is accelerating. From 1940 to 1965, life expectancy for men over age 65 increased by one year; during the next quarter century it grew by 2.1 years. . . .

Social Security needs fundamental reform if it is to cope with our increasing longevity. . . . [A]ll workers should be given the option of redirecting their payroll taxes to personal retirement accounts.

Those accounts, which will be invested in productive enterprises, will grow and all workers will accrue a substantial asset of far greater value than the benefits promised–but not yet paid for–by the current Social Security system. . . . As the savings rate increases, young innovative companies . . . will have easier access to investment capital and will flourish.

–Carrie Lips, Cato Institute's Project on Social Security Privatization

Analyzing the Issue

1. How does Shure's discussion of the "workers-per-dependent" ratio suggest that the Social Security system is not in crisis? Why does he oppose privatization of the system?

2. What evidence does Lips use to support her argument that "Social Security needs fundamental reform"? Why does she support privatization?

3. With which opinion do you agree? Explain your reasoning.

Have students answer the **Analyzing the Issue** questions.

4 CLOSE

Have students evaluate the pro and con positions using the seven economic and social goals discussed in Chapter 1: economic freedom, economic efficiency, economic equity, economic security, price stability, and economic growth.

LINKING PAST & PRESENT

Spending for Social Programs Since the end of World War II, the United States has greatly increased its funding for social insurance and public assistance. In 1950, for instance, the federal government spent $2.1 billion on social insurance. About 40 years later the amount was nearly $400 billion. Public aid expenditures went from $1.1 billion to $80 billion in about the same time period.

Answers to Analyzing the Issue

1. Benefits are paid for by taxes on workers and employers that people can collect when they retire; because it would increase taxes and administration cost.

2. decreasing ratio of workers to beneficiaries and increased average life span; Lips believes that workers should be given the option of redirecting their payroll taxes to personal retirement accounts.

3. Answers will vary. Students should support their opinions.

Unit 3 Resource Manager

Materials listed may be used at any time during the study of the unit.

Economics Forms and Financial Pages Transparencies

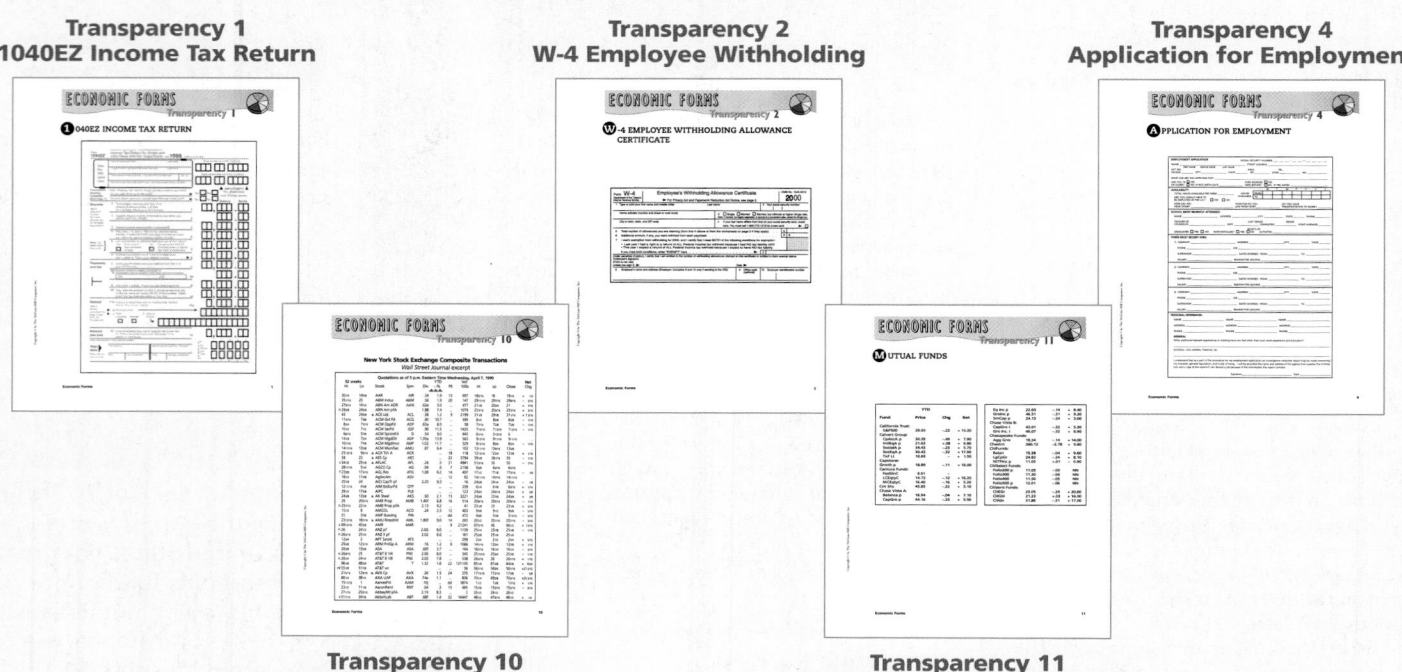

Transparency 1
1040EZ Income Tax Return

Transparency 2
W-4 Employee Withholding

Transparency 4
Application for Employment

Transparency 10
Stock Quotations

Transparency 11
Mutual Fund Quotations

Economic Concepts Transparencies

Transparency 5
Economic Institutions and Incentives.

Transparency 6
Exchange, Money, Interdependence

Transparency 12
The Role of the Government

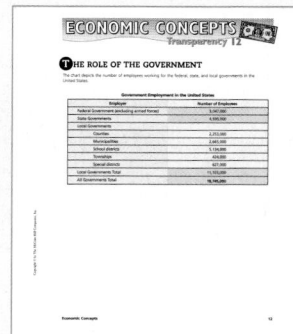

REAL-WORLD ECONOMICS

*Have your students learn about investing and managing their financial future by participating in the exciting simulation **The Stock Market Game**™. See Teacher pages in front of book for more information.*

*Strengthen students' research, cooperation, presentation and critical-thinking skills by having them compete in the **Fed Challenge**. See Teacher pages in front of book for more information.*

Additional Glencoe Resources for This Unit:
- **Interactive Economics!**
- **Glencoe Skillbuilder Interactive Workbook, Level 2**
- **Nightly Business Report Economics & You Video Program**
- **Economic Survival: A Financial Simulation**

Unit 3 Resource Manager

ASSESSMENT

Unit 3 Test

APPLICATION AND ENRICHMENT

Economics Laboratory 3

Unit 3 Business Week Focus on the New Economy

Use the following tools to easily assess student learning in a variety of ways:

- Performance Assessment Strategies and Activities
- Section Quizzes
- Chapter and Unit Tests
- Interactive Tutor Self-Assessment Software
- ExamView® Pro Testmaker
- MindJogger Videoquiz
- SAT I/II Test Practice
- epp.glencoe.com

inter NET CONNECTION

Economics: Principles and Practices
Visit the *Economics: Principles and Practices* Web site for economics overviews, activities, assessments, and updated charts and graphs.

epp.glencoe.com

Glencoe Social Studies
Visit the Glencoe Web site for social studies activities updates, and links to other sites.

socialstudies.glencoe.com

 Glencoe's Guide to Using the Internet
Provides an introduction to many of the current technologies on the Internet. Professional resources and teaching strategies included.

Business Week **Online**
Visit the *Business Week* Web site for up-to-date news and special reports.

www.businessweek.com

Our Web sites provide additional resources. All essential content is covered in the Student Edition.

BIBLIOGRAPHY

Readings for the Student

Geisst, Charles R. and Richard A. Grasso, *100 Years of Wall Street*. New York: McGraw-Hill Companies, 1999.

"The Wild New Workforce," by Michelle Conlin, Peter Coy, Ann Therese Palmer, and Gabrielle Saveri, *Business Week*, Dec. 6, 1999.

Readings for the Teacher

Snowdon, Brian and Howard R. Vane, *Conversations With Leading Economists: Interpreting Modern Macroeconomics.*

Cheltenham, UK: Edward Elgar Publishing, 1999.

"Brain Drain," by Jennifer Reingold and Diane Brady, *Business Week*, Sept. 20, 1999.

Multimedia Resources

Software. *Oikonomos: The Economist.* Brighter Paths, 1997. Available from Social Studies School Service, 10200 Jefferson Boulevard, P.O. Box 802, Culver City, California 90232-0802. Macroeconomics simulation, students role-play foreign minister.

0:00 OUT OF TIME?

If time does not permit teaching each chapter in this unit, you may use the Audio Program that includes a one-page activity and a one-page test for each chapter.

Unit Objectives

After studying this unit, students will be able to:
1. Trace the development and influence of labor unions.
2. Explain how government raises revenues and allocates expenditures.
3. Describe the evolution of money and the banking system.
4. Explain the organization and role of financial markets.

Unit Overview

Unit 3 discusses the role of labor, government, and financial institutions in the American economy. **Chapter 8** describes organized labor in the United States and examines its influence on employment and wages. **Chapter 9** focuses on how government raises revenue and discusses the nature of taxation, while **Chapter 10** details how government spends revenues. **Chapter 11** discusses the development of the banking system. **Chapter 12** explains the importance of savings to the economy and describes investments in financial assets, equities, and markets.

UNIT 3

Macroeconomics: Institutions

CHAPTER 8
Employment, Labor, and Wages

CHAPTER 9
Sources of Government Revenue

CHAPTER 10
Government Spending

CHAPTER 11
Money and Banking

CHAPTER 12
Financial Markets

Why It's Important

As you read this unit, learn how the study of economics helps answer the following questions:

- Why are deductions taken out of your paycheck?
- How do taxes pay for your education?
- Why does your savings account probably earn less than other investments?

190 UNIT 3 MACROECONOMICS: INSTITUTIONS

MAKING IT *activity* RELEVANT

Public Goods and Services Tell students that local, state, and federal taxes pay for items that are public goods and services. Ask students to make a list of public goods and services that they use, such as road maintenance and police protection. Ask students to look at deductions from their paychecks or a generic paycheck to see how much money is deducted by each level of government. **Ask:** What are some positive uses of tax money? How much might you have to pay out of pocket to buy such goods or services if the government did not provide them? What goods and services would be difficult for individuals to provide?

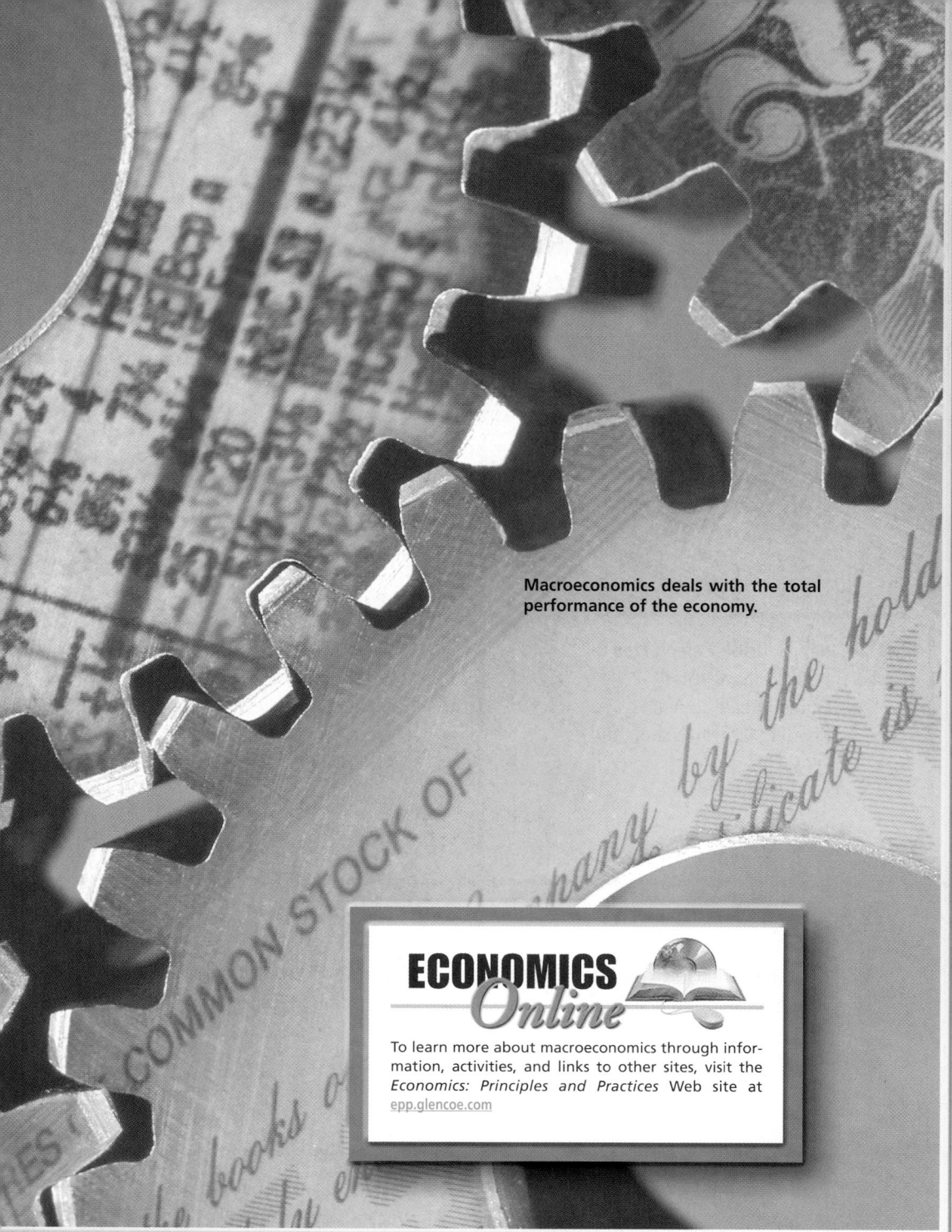

Macroeconomics deals with the total performance of the economy.

Introducing the Unit

Have each student list what he or she thinks are the three most controversial topics in economics today. Call on volunteers to share their lists with the class, noting new issues on the board as they are offered. Circle topics such as labor unions, taxes, government spending, deficit, national debt, social security, and so on. Then point out that the circled issues will be discussed at some length in Unit 3.

Visual Instruction

Macroeconomics operates on the level of huge aggregates like national production, employment, and the money supply.

ECONOMIC SURVIVAL
A FINANCIAL SIMULATION

To help students learn to manage their own finances, have them participate in the game **Economic Survival: A Financial Simulation** in which each student enters the workforce, rents an apartment, and deals with everyday events.

ECONOMICS
Online

To learn more about macroeconomics through information, activities, and links to other sites, visit the *Economics: Principles and Practices* Web site at epp.glencoe.com

ECONOMICS
Online

To access the data, follow these steps:

1. Log on to the **U.S. Bureau of Labor Statistics** at stats.bls.gov. Use the search tool to locate **"How the Government Measures Unemployment."**

What To Do When You Are There
Instruct students to read this information carefully. Discuss the major points of this summary. Students should then develop a pamphlet outlining how the government measures unemployment and provide reasons as to why this information is so important to our overall economy. If students have limited or no access to the Internet, have them use the library's computerized or traditional card catalog to find this information.

Chapter 8 Resource Manager

SECTION RESOURCES

Daily Objectives	Reproducible Resources	Technology/Multimedia Resources
Section 1 **The Labor Movement** 1. Explain why unions are still important today. 2. Discuss the development of the labor movement from the late 1700s to the 1930s. 3. Relate labor's successes during the Great Depression. 4. Describe the major labor developments since World War II.	Reproducible Lesson Plan 8-1 Daily Lecture Notes 8-1 Guided Reading Activity 8-1 Reading Essentials and Study Guide 8-1 Section Quiz 8-1*	Daily Focus Transparency 39 Interactive Tutor Self-Assessment Software ExamView® Pro Testmaker Presentation Plus!
Section 2 **Resolving Union and Management Differences** 1. Explain the differences among kinds of union arrangements. 2. Describe several ways to resolve labor and management differences when collective bargaining fails.	Reproducible Lesson Plan 8-2 Daily Lecture Notes 8-2 Guided Reading Activity 8-2 Reading Essentials and Study Guide 8-2 Section Quiz 8-2*	Daily Focus Transparency 40 Interactive Tutor Self-Assessment Software ExamView® Pro Testmaker Presentation Plus!
Section 3 **Labor and Wages** 1. Identify four main categories of labor. 2. Explain the importance of noncompeting labor grades. 3. Describe three different approaches to wage determination.	Reproducible Lesson Plan 8-3 Daily Lecture Notes 8-3 Guided Reading Activity 8-3 Reading Essentials and Study Guide 8-3 Section Quiz 8-3*	Daily Focus Transparency 38 Interactive Tutor Self-Assessment Software ExamView® Pro Testmaker Presentation Plus!
Section 4 **Employment Trends and Issues** 1. Explain why union membership has declined. 2. Describe reasons for the discrepancy in pay between men and women.	Reproducible Lesson Plan 8-4 Daily Lecture Notes 8-4 Guided Reading Activity 8-4 Reading Essentials and Study Guide 8-4 Section Quiz 8-4*	Daily Focus Transparency 41 Vocabulary PuzzleMaker CD-ROM Interactive Tutor Self-Assessment Software ExamView® Pro Testmaker Presentation Plus!

Also available in Spanish

 Transparency   CD-ROM   Software   Blackline Master

 Videodisc   Audio Program   Videocassette

0:00 OUT OF TIME?
Assign the Chapter 8 Audio Program activity and test.

Activities that are particularly suited to use within the block scheduling framework are identified throughout this chapter by the following designation: **BLOCK SCHEDULING**

Chapter 8 Resource Manager

TeacherWorks™
All-In-One Planner and Resource Center

- **Interactive Teacher Edition** Access your Teacher Wraparound Edition and your classroom resources with a few easy clicks.

- **Interactive Lesson Planner** Planning has never been easier! Organize your week, month, semester, or year with all the lesson helps you need to make teaching creative, timely, and relevant.

Use Glencoe's **Presentation Plus!** multimedia teacher tool to easily present dynamic lessons that visually excite your students. Using Microsoft PowerPoint® you can customize the presentations to create your own personalized lessons.

ACTIVITY

From the Classroom of...

Tim Brewton
Fairhill High School
Dallas, TX

Starting a Company

Tell students that they are going to start a new company. Have them work in groups of two or three. Ask students to:

- Choose a name for their company and decide on the product or service they want to provide.
- Determine how much money to allocate to overhead, such as rent, utilities, equipment, and advertising.
- Determine the number and kinds of employees they will need. Have them categorize employees according to the four major categories of labor presented in the chapter.
- Determine the salaries and wages of employees.
- Prepare a plan for hires and layoffs.
- Discuss how they might handle union issues.
- Specify whether the Civil Rights Act of 1964 will apply to their business and explain why or why not.

Ask students to prepare a presentation for the class. After all the groups have finished hold a class discussion about running a business from the point of view of an employer and an employee.

National Council on Economic Education

THE **Economics**America AND **Economics**International PROGRAMS

Voluntary National Content Standards in Economics
Emphasized in Chapter 8

Content Standard 10

Content Standard 13

For a complete listing of NCEE Standards and entire text correlation, see Teacher pages in front of book.

Resources Available from NCEE

- Capstone: The Nation's High School Economics Course
- Focus: High School Economics
- Civics and Government: Focus on Economics
- Personal Finance Economics: Wallet Wisdom
- United States History: Eyes on the Economy, Vols. I and II
- Geography: Focus on Economics
- Economics and the Environment

To order these materials or to contact your state Council on Economic Education about workshops and programs, call 1-800-338-1192 or visit www.nationalcouncil.org

Chapter 8 Resource Manager

TEACHING TRANSPARENCY

Economic Concept Transparency 12: The Role of the Government

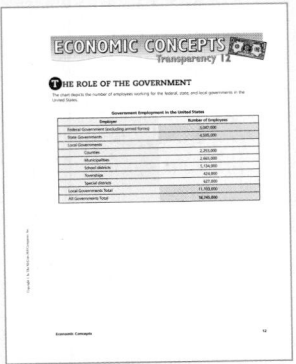

APPLICATION AND ENRICHMENT

Consumer Application Activity 13

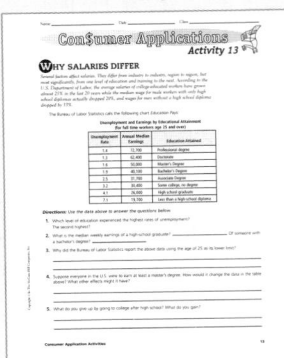

Free Enterprise Activity 13

APPLICATION AND ENRICHMENT

Enrichment Activity 8

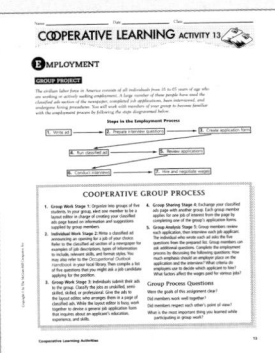

Cooperative Learning Activity 13

Math Practice Activity 13

Economic Cartoon 13

Primary and Secondary Source Reading 13

REVIEW AND REINFORCEMENT

Economic Vocabulary Activity 8

Reteaching Activity 8

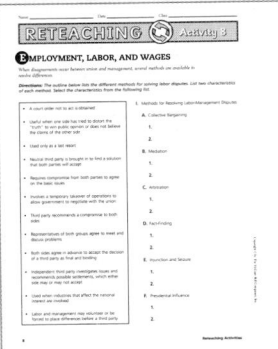

Critical Thinking Activity 13

Reinforcing Economic Skill 17

Chapter 8 Resource Manager

ASSESSMENT AND EVALUATION

Chapter 8 Test Form A

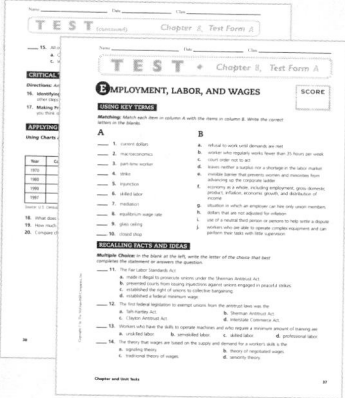

Chapter 8 Test Form B

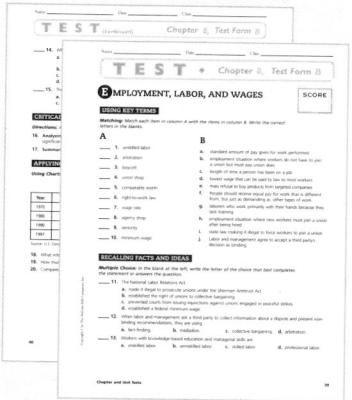

Performance Assessment Activity 13

ExamView® Pro Testmaker

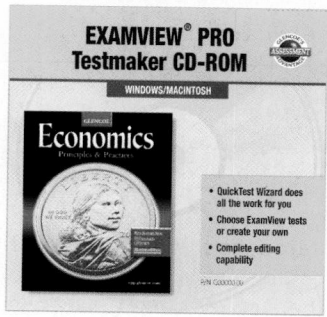

SPANISH RESOURCES

The following Spanish language materials are available in the Spanish Resources binder:

 Spanish Economic Vocabulary Activities

 Spanish Reteaching Activities

 Spanish Section Quizzes

 Spanish Economic Concepts Transparencies

Also available:

 Spanish Chapter 8 Audio Program Activity and Test

TECHNOLOGY/MULTIMEDIA

- Vocabulary PuzzleMaker CD-ROM
- Interactive Tutor Self-Assessment Software
- ExamView® Pro Testmaker
- Audio Program (English or Spanish)
- NBR Economics & You Video Program (English or Spanish)
- MindJogger Videoquiz
- Interactive Economics! CD-ROM
- Presentation Plus!
- TeacherWorks CD-ROM
- Glencoe Skillbuilder Interactive Workbook CD-ROM, Level 2

ECONOMICS Online

Use our Web site for additional resources. All essential content is covered in the Student Edition.

You and your students can visit epp.glencoe.com, the Web site companion to **Economics: Principles and Practices.** This innovative integration of electronic and print media offers your students a wealth of opportunities. The student text directs students to the Web site for the following options:

- **Chapter Overviews**
- **Student Web Activities**
- **Self-Check Quizzes**
- **Textbook Updates**

Answers are provided for you in the Web Activity Lesson Plan. Additional Web resources and interactive puzzles are also available.

Performance Assessment

Refer to Activity 13 in the *Performance Assessment Strategies and Activities* booklet.

BLOCK SCHEDULING

ECONOMICS *Online*

Introduce students to chapter content and key terms by having them access **Chapter Overview 8** at epp.glencoe.com

NIGHTLY BUSINESS REPORT

 ECONOMICS & YOU

Chapter 14
Disc 1, Side 2

The American Labor Force
After viewing this segment, students should be able to:
• Differentiate among the major categories of workers.

 Also available in VHS.

GLENCOE TECHNOLOGY

 Use **MindJogger Videoquiz** to preview the Chapter 8 content.

Employment, Labor, and Wages

Economics & You

What level of income do you want to earn after you graduate? Will your current training and skills allow you to reach your income goal? In **Chapter 8**, you will learn about the labor force and employment issues. To learn more about important labor issues, view the Chapter 14 video lesson:

The American Labor Force

ECONOMICS *Online*

Chapter Overview Visit the *Economics: Principles and Practices* Web site at epp.glencoe.com and click on **Chapter 8—Chapter Overviews** to preview chapter information.

Labor is human resources—people who produce goods and services.

EXTRA CREDIT PROJECT

Have students use library resources to develop a statistical report on labor in the United States. Suggest that they use charts and graphs to illustrate topics such as changes in the labor force, average wages over the years, union membership, and so on.

The Labor Movement

Study Guide

Main Idea
Labor unions are organizations that attempt to improve the working conditions of their members through joint action.

Reading Strategy
Graphic Organizer As you read the section, compare how an industrial union differs from a trade union. Complete a graphic organizer similar to the one below by listing the differences.

Industrial Union	Trade Union

Key Terms
macroeconomics, civilian labor force, craft union, trade union, industrial union, strike, picket, boycott, lockout, company union, Great Depression, right-to-work law, independent union

Objectives
After studying this section, you will be able to:
1. **Explain** why unions are still important today.
2. **Discuss** the development of the labor movement from the late 1700s to the 1930s.
3. **Relate** labor's successes during the Great Depression.
4. **Describe** the major labor developments since World War II.

Applying Economic Concepts
Civilian Labor Force Do you have a part-time job? If so, read to find out more about your role in the civilian labor force.

① FOCUS

Section Overview
This section covers the history of the organized labor movement in the United States.

BELLRINGER
Motivational Activity

Project **transparency** and have students answer questions.

Daily Focus Transparency 39

Cover Story

N.F.L. Officials Approve Pact ...

Replacement official signals an extra point.

N.F.L. game officials voted yesterday to accept a new contract that the league had recently offered, ending a lockout during which replacements officiated N.F.L. games for the first time....

A majority of the 119 officials ratified the contract, which league and union officials had agreed to on Monday. ... The contract, which is good for four years with an option for six, gives the officials a 50 percent raise this season and a 100 percent raise by the fourth year....

Many coaches, fans and players had scoffed at the idea of a lockout, but the league ended up using 15 replacement officiating crews, with many of them pulled from below the Division I-A college level.

—*The New York Times, September 20, 2001*

L Labor issues, like the one discussed in the cover story, appear in the news all the time. After all, working for a living is one of the single most important things we do. How well we do, as measured by the satisfaction we get and the income we receive, affects virtually every other aspect of our lives. Accordingly, any study of economics that ignores the way the "labor" factor of production earns its income would be incomplete.

The study of labor is part of **macroeconomics.** Macroeconomics is the branch of economics that deals with the economy as a whole, including employment, gross domestic product, inflation, economic growth, and the distribution of income. For example, the population of the United States by mid-2001 was approximately 284 million people. Slightly less than half, or about 140 million, belonged to the **civilian labor force**—men and women 16 years old and over who are either working or actively looking for a job. The civilian classification excludes members of the armed forces, the prison population, and other institutionalized persons.

CHAPTER 8: EMPLOYMENT, LABOR, AND WAGES **193**

Study Guide

Reading Strategy
Have students create the graphic organizer.
Answers to Graphic: *An industrial union is an association of all workers in a given industry, regardless of the job each person performs. A trade union is an association of skilled workers who perform the same kind of work.*

Preteaching Vocabulary
Have students write sentences using each Key Term in context.

RESOURCE MANAGER

📁 Reproducible Masters
- Reproducible Lesson Plan 8-1
- Daily Lecture Notes 8-1
- Guided Reading Activity 8-1
- Reading Essentials and Study Guide 8-1
- Section Quiz 8-1

📠 Transparencies
- Daily Focus Transparency 39

Multimedia
- 💾 Interactive Tutor Self-Assessment Software
- 🎧 ExamView® Pro Testmaker
- 🎧 Presentation Plus!

TEACH

Daily Lecture Notes 8-1

DAILY LECTURE NOTES 📖 Lesson 8-1

DID YOU KNOW?
The stock market crash on October 29, 1929, signaled the start of the Great Depression. In that year, national income was more than $87 billion. By 1933, just four years later, national income had plummeted by more than 50 percent, to just over $40 billion. More than 80,000 businesses had failed, and nine million savings accounts had been cleaned out.

PAGES 194-196
I. Early Union Development
  A. The nation's first unions were comprised of skilled workers.
  B. After the Civil War, as industry expanded, the labor force became more unified.
  C. Two types of unions developed—the trade union and the industrial union.
  D. Unions used strikes, pickets, and boycotts to help members get better pay, better hours, and job security.
  E. Employers resisted unions through lockouts, firings, and even setting up company unions.
  F. Historically, the courts have viewed unions with hostility.

Discussion Question
Webster's Dictionary says that to conspire is "to join in a secret agreement to do an unlawful or wrongful act or an act which becomes unlawful as a result of the secret agreement." Do you agree with those who viewed unions as conspiracies against business? Why or why not? *(Answers will vary but should focus on the conflict between unions and business.)*

PAGE 196
II. Labor During the Great Depression

STANDARD & POOR'S

Answer: *about six to one*

L1 Constructing a Time Line
Ask students to construct an annotated time line of the American labor movement from its beginnings to the present day. Have students limit their time lines to 12 entries. Discuss completed time lines. **ELL**

Guided Reading Activity 8-1

GUIDED READING Activity 8-1

For use with textbook pages 193-198

THE LABOR MOVEMENT

RECALLING THE FACTS

Directions: Use the information in your textbook to answer the questions. Use another sheet of paper if necessary.

1. What is macroeconomics? _____
2. Which workers are not counted as being part of the civilian labor force? _____
3. How do a trade union and an industrial union differ? _____
4. What actions could unions take if negotiations with industry employers failed? Explain each one.
  a. _____
  b. _____
5. What actions could employers take in their fight against unions? Explain each one.
  a. _____
  b. _____
6. How did the Clayton Antitrust Act help labor unions? _____
7. What did the National Labor Relations Act (NLRA) of 1935 do for unions? _____

As you examine **Figure 8.1,** note that nearly 85 percent of those employed had no connection with unions, 13.5 percent were members of unions, and 1.4 percent were nonunion members being represented by unions. Although the percentage of union workers is small, unions are important for two reasons. First, they played a major role in promoting legislation that affects pay levels and working conditions today. Second, unions are a force in the economy, with membership of nearly 16.3 million people.

Historically, unions tended to be concentrated in heavy manufacturing industries. More recently, unions have made inroads in the service sector, especially among government workers. As **Figure 8.2** shows, 42 percent of all government workers in 2001 were either unionized or represented by a union.

Early Union Development

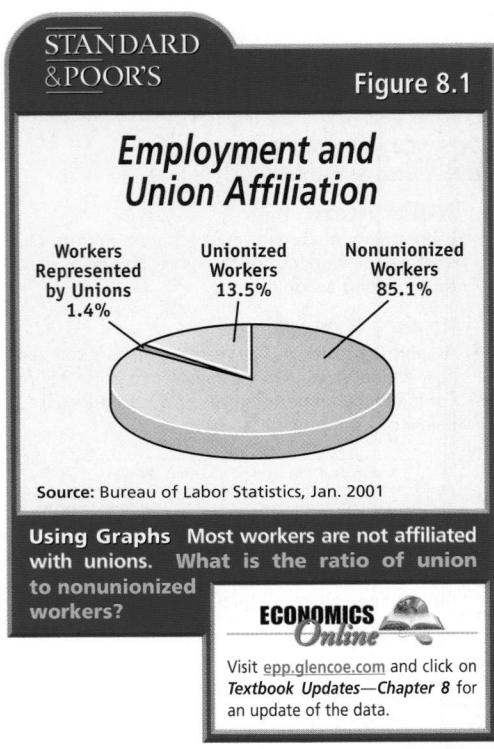

The development of unions in the United States started in the colonial period. From there, unions waged a long uphill struggle that peaked in the 1930s.

Colonial Times to the Civil War

In 1778, printers in New York City joined together to demand higher pay. This protest was the first attempt to organize labor in America. Before long, unions of shoemakers, carpenters, and tailors developed, each hoping to negotiate agreements covering hours, pay, and working conditions. While only a very small percentage of workers belonged to unions, most unions were comprised of skilled workers and possessed strong bargaining power.

Until about 1820, most of America's workforce was made up of farmers, small business owners, and the self-employed. Shortly after, however, immigrants began to arrive in great numbers. Because they provided a supply of cheap, unskilled labor, they posed a threat to existing wage and labor standards.

Even so, public opinion was against union activity and some parts of the country even banned labor unions. Labor organizers often were viewed as troublemakers, and many workers believed they

194 UNIT 3 MACROECONOMICS: INSTITUTIONS

could better negotiate with their employers on a one-to-one basis.

Civil War to the 1930s

During and after the Civil War, attitudes toward unions began to change. The Civil War led to higher prices, a greater demand for goods and services, and a shortage of workers. Industry expanded, and the farm population declined. Hourly workers in industrial jobs made up about one-fourth of the country's working population. Many of the cultural and linguistic differences between immigrants and American-born workers began to fade, and the labor force became more unified.

Types of Unions

By the end of the Civil War, two main types of labor unions had come into existence. One was

---

STANDARD & POOR'S
Figure 8.1

Employment and Union Affiliation

Workers Represented by Unions 1.4%

Unionized Workers 13.5%

Nonunionized Workers 85.1%

Source: Bureau of Labor Statistics, Jan. 2001

Using Graphs Most workers are not affiliated with unions. **What is the ratio of union to nonunionized workers?**

ECONOMICS *Online*
Visit epp.glencoe.com and click on **Textbook Updates—Chapter 8** for an update of the data.

MEETING SPECIAL NEEDS ACTIVITY

Learning Disabled For students who have problems with reading, restating information can be difficult. They often have trouble finding synonyms for words in the text. Explain that the point of this procedure is for them to use common language and not to make it sound like the textbook. In the subsection "Civil War to the 1930s," have students look for words that might be somewhat complex and replace them with synonyms.

📁 Refer to *Inclusion for the Social Studies Classroom Strategies and Activities* in the TCR.

the **craft union,** or **trade union,** an association of skilled workers who perform the same kind of work. The Cigar Makers' Union, begun by union leader Samuel Gompers, is an example of this type of union. Other, more recent examples are shown in **Figure 8.3** on page 197.

The second type of union was the **industrial union**—an association of all workers in the same industry, regardless of the job each worker performs. The development of basic mass-production industries such as steel and textiles provided the opportunity to organize this kind of union. Because many of the workers in these industries were unskilled and could not join trade unions, they organized as industrial unions instead.

Union Activities

Unions tried to help workers by negotiating for higher pay, better hours and working conditions, and job security. If an agreement could not be reached, workers could **strike,** or refuse to work until certain demands were met. Unions also pressured employers by having the striking workers **picket,** or parade in front of the employer's business carrying signs about the dispute. The signs might ask other workers not to seek jobs with the company, or they might ask customers and suppliers to take their business elsewhere.

If striking and picketing did not settle the dispute, a union could organize a **boycott**—a mass refusal to buy products from targeted employers or companies. If a boycott was effective, it hurt the company's business.

Employer Resistance

Employers fought unions in a number of ways. Sometimes the owners called for a **lockout,** a refusal to let the employees work until management demands were met. Often violence erupted during lockouts, and troops were sometimes brought in to keep peace. At other times, management responded to a strike, or the threat of a strike, by hiring all new workers. Some owners even set up a **company union**—a union organized, supported, or run by employers—to head off efforts by others to organize workers.

Attitude of the Courts

Historically, the courts had an unfavorable attitude toward unions. Under English common law, unions were considered to be conspiracies against business and were prosecuted as such in the United States. Even the Sherman Antitrust Act of 1890, aimed mainly at curbing monopolies, was used to keep labor in line.

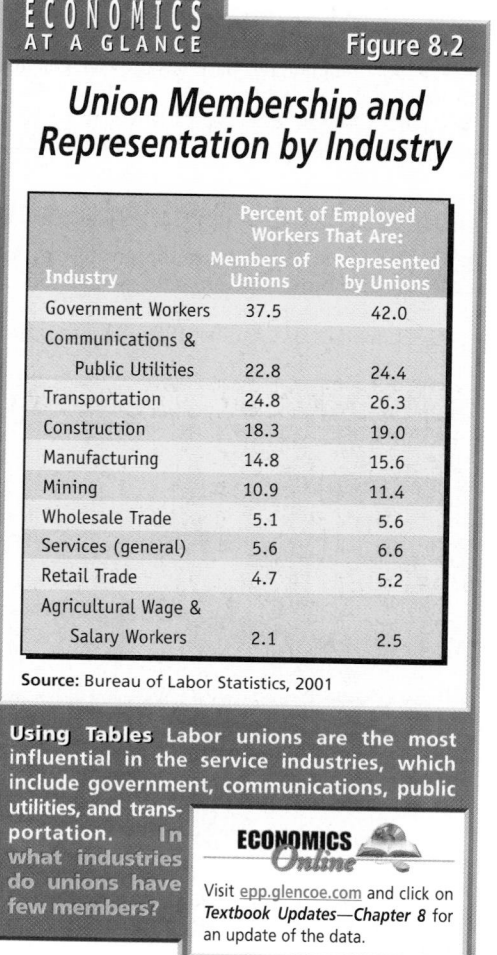

ECONOMICS AT A GLANCE — Figure 8.2

Union Membership and Representation by Industry

Industry	Percent of Employed Workers That Are: Members of Unions	Percent of Employed Workers That Are: Represented by Unions
Government Workers	37.5	42.0
Communications & Public Utilities	22.8	24.4
Transportation	24.8	26.3
Construction	18.3	19.0
Manufacturing	14.8	15.6
Mining	10.9	11.4
Wholesale Trade	5.1	5.6
Services (general)	5.6	6.6
Retail Trade	4.7	5.2
Agricultural Wage & Salary Workers	2.1	2.5

Source: Bureau of Labor Statistics, 2001

Using Tables Labor unions are the most influential in the service industries, which include government, communications, public utilities, and transportation. **In what industries do unions have few members?**

ECONOMICS Online
Visit epp.glencoe.com and click on *Textbook Updates—Chapter 8* for an update of the data.

CHAPTER 8: EMPLOYMENT, LABOR, AND WAGES **195**

L2 Journalism

Have students select one of the events discussed in the section. Then have them write a newspaper story, with headlines and illustrations, describing the event and noting its significance for the organized labor movement in the U.S.

THE GLOBAL ECONOMY

International Unions Many trade unions have regional organizations on various continents. In addition, the International Labor Organization (ILO), a branch of the United Nations, has a mission to promote and realize standards, fundamental principles, and rights at work. It also has training centers for employers and potential employees.

ECONOMICS AT A GLANCE

Answer: *Agricultural wage and salary workers*

FREE ENTERPRISE ACTIVITY

Inform students that, if they have not done so already, at some time they will have to complete a job application. Tell them a completed job application should contain clear and accurate information; should be filled out carefully; and should be typed, or printed in blue or black ink. Point out that, along with an application form, they will have to provide several pieces of information, including their Social Security number, references, and a list of former employers with dates of employment. Have students prepare to fill out a job application by bringing the above information to class. Distribute sample job applications to students, asking each to fill them in as completely and accurately as possible.

L3 Defending a Position

Write the following question on the board: Were better working conditions and wages for the American labor force the result of labor unions or the result of increased demand for skilled labor? Call on volunteers to offer information supporting either side of the question. Have students write a paragraph arguing their position.

CURRICULUM CONNECTION

History The Noble Order of the Knights of Labor, founded in 1869, sought to bring "men and women of every craft, creed, and color" into one big union. The Knights not only welcomed women members but also gave them leadership opportunities. For example, Elizabeth Rodgers led a Chicago division of the Knights that represented some 50,000 male and female workers. Married with a family, Rodgers registered her occupation as "housewife." To underscore their feelings about race, leaders of the Knights decided to hold the 1886 General Assembly in Richmond, Virginia—which had served as the capital of the Confederacy—and gave African Americans a prominent role in the proceedings.

In 1902, the United Hatters Union called a strike against a Danbury, Connecticut, hat manufacturer that had rejected a union demand. The union applied pressure on stores to not stock hats made by the Danbury firm. The hat manufacturer, charging a conspiracy in restraint of trade under the Sherman Act, filed a damage suit in the state court but lost. Later, the Supreme Court ruled that the union had organized an illegal boycott that was in restraint of trade. This ruling dealt a severe blow to organized labor.

The Danbury Hatters case and several subsequent antiunion decisions pushed organized labor to call for relief. The passage of the Clayton Antitrust Act (1914) helped to remedy the situation. The Clayton Act expressly exempts labor unions from prosecution under the Sherman Act.

Labor During the Great Depression

The **Great Depression**—the greatest period of economic decline and stagnation in United States history—began with the collapse of the stock market in October 1929. The economy

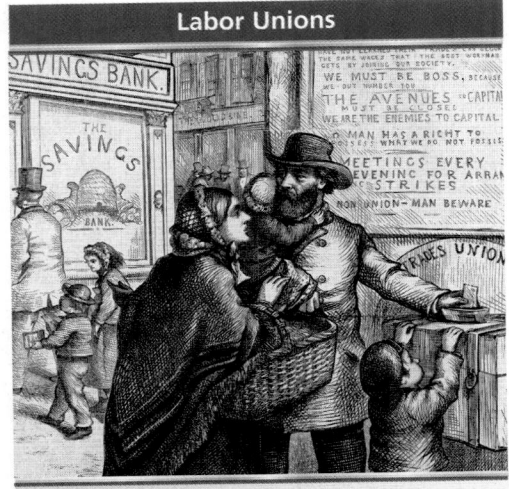

Labor Unions

Union Activities Early American labor unions had few rights to organize. *What tactics did the early unions take to improve their working conditions?*

reached bottom in 1933, and did not recover to its 1929 level until 1939.

Unemployment and Wages

During the depths of the Depression as many as one in four workers were without a job. Many who kept their jobs had their pay cut. In 1929, the average manufacturing wage was 55 cents per hour. By 1933, however, wages had plummeted to 5 cents per hour.

The Great Depression brought misery to millions, but it also changed attitudes toward the labor movement. Common problems united factory workers, and union promoters renewed their efforts to organize workers.

Pro-Union Legislation

New legislation aided labor. The Norris-LaGuardia Act of 1932 prevented federal courts from issuing rulings against unions engaged in peaceful strikes, picketing, or boycotts. This forced companies to negotiate directly with their unions, rather than take them to court.

The National Labor Relations Act (NLRA), or Wagner Act, of 1935 established the right of unions to collective bargaining. The act also created the National Labor Relations Board (NLRB), giving it the power to police unfair labor practices. The NLRB also had the power to oversee and certify union election results. If a fair election resulted in a union becoming the employees' bargaining agent, employers were required to recognize and negotiate with it.

The Fair Labor Standards Act (1938) applies to businesses that engage in interstate commerce. The act fixes a federal minimum wage for many workers and establishes time-and-a-half pay for overtime, which is defined as more than 40 hours per week. It also prohibits oppressive child labor, which includes any labor for a child under 16 and work that is hazardous to the health of a child under 18.

Labor Since World War II

Many Americans viewed organized labor favorably in the 1930s, but public opinion shifted again by the end of World War II. Some people believed that Communists had secretly

Visual Instruction

Answer to Caption:
strikes, pickets, boycotts

CRITICAL THINKING

Formulating Questions Ask students to use this section's headings to formulate questions to guide their reading. For example, "Attitude of the Courts" can become the question, "What was the attitude of the courts toward labor unions?" Then have students read the passage carefully to determine the answers to the questions. Finally, ask students to examine how answers to the questions changed over time.

ECONOMICS AT A GLANCE

Figure 8.3

Trade (Craft) and Industrial Unions

Trade (Craft) Unions

Printers' Union · Electricians' Union · Machinists' Union · Carpenters' Union · Plumbers' Union

Industrial Unions

Using Charts Labor unions can be categorized as either trade or industrial unions. How do trade unions differ from industrial unions?

ECONOMICS AT A GLANCE

Answer: *trade: an association of skilled workers who perform the same kind of work; industrial: an association of all workers in a given industry, regardless of the job each person performs*

③ ASSESS

Assign Section 1 Assessment as homework or as an in-class activity.

💾 Have students use **Interactive Tutor Self-Assessment Software** to review Section 1.

Section Quiz 8-1

entered the unions. Others were upset by the loss of production resulting from strikes. In 1946 alone, more than 116 million workdays were lost due to work stoppages. People began to feel that management, not labor, was the victim.

Antiunion Legislation

Growing antiunion feelings led to the Labor-Management Relations Act, or Taft-Hartley Act, of 1947. The act puts limits on what unions can do in labor-management disputes. Among its provisions, Taft-Hartley gives employers the right to sue unions for breaking contracts, and prohibits unions from making union membership a condition for hiring.

The Taft-Hartley Act had two other provisions that worked against organized labor. The first was an 80-day cooling-off period that federal courts could use to delay a strike in the case of a national emergency.

The second (Section 14(b)) was a tough anti-union provision, which allowed individual states to pass right-to-work laws. A **right-to-work law** is a state law making it illegal to force workers to join a union as a condition of employment, even though a union may already exist at the company. If a state does not have a right-to-work law, new workers may

have to join the existing union as a condition for employment shortly after being hired.

If a state has a right-to-work law, then new hires have the option to join or not to join a union—even if the overwhelming majority of workers at the company support the union. Lawmakers have supported a national right-to-work law, requiring all states to give workers this option, whether the states want to or not.

In the mid-1900s, other legislation was passed to stop the criminal influences that had begun to emerge in the labor movement. The Labor-Management Reporting and Disclosure Act, or Landrum-Griffin Act, of 1959 tried to protect individual union members from unfair actions of unions and union officials. The act requires unions to file regular financial reports with the government, and it limits the amount of money officials can borrow from the union.

The AFL-CIO

The American Federation of Labor (AFL) began in 1886 as an organization of craft unions. Later, it added several industrial unions. The trade and industrial unions, however, did not always agree over the future of the union movement. As a result, eight of the AFL industrial unions formed the

CHAPTER 8: EMPLOYMENT, LABOR, AND WAGES **197**

EXTENDING THE CONTENT

The AFL-CIO The merger of the AFL with the CIO in 1955 brought together some 16 million workers—more than 85 percent of all union members. Some major unions, however, refused to affiliate with the AFL-CIO. The United Mine Workers of America (UMW) was one of the most prominent of those unions that chose to remain independent. This decision, in large part, was due to disagreements UMW president John L. Lewis had with the leadership of the AFL. Even so, the UMW remained unaffiliated long after Lewis resigned his post. The UMW did not join the AFL-CIO until 1989.

Objectives, goals, and answers to the student activity can be found in the **Web Activity Lesson Plan** feature at epp.glencoe.com

Visual Instruction

Answer to Caption:
The National Labor Relations Act, or Wagner Act

Reteach

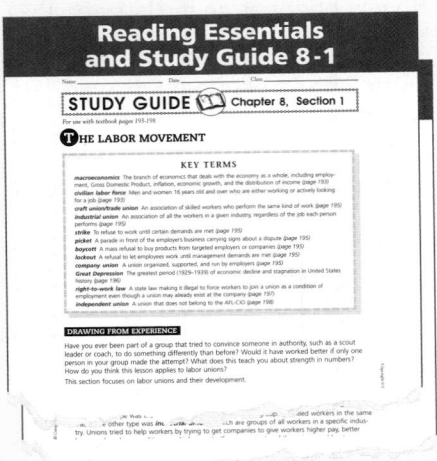

Reading Essentials and Study Guide 8-1

Enrich

Have students research to learn how one of the pieces of legislation mentioned in the section affected the development of organized labor.

CLOSE

Have students compare the role of the labor movement in the late 1800s to its present-day role.

Labor Unions

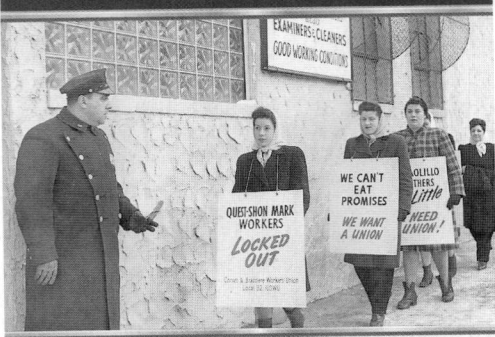

Legislation Three sisters lead the picket line in a demonstration calling for organization of a union. *What legislation gave unions the right to engage in collective bargaining?*

Committee for Industrial Organization in 1935. Headed by John L. Lewis, president of the United Mine Workers of America, its goal was to bring about greater unionization in industry.

The AFL and Lewis, however, did not get along, so the AFL expelled the Committee for Industrial Organization unions in 1937. Those unions then formed the Congress of Industrial Organizations

(CIO). The CIO quickly set up unions in industries that had not been unionized before, such as the steel and automobile industries. By the 1940s, the CIO had nearly 7 million members.

As the CIO grew stronger, it began to challenge the dominance of the AFL. In 1955 the AFL and the CIO joined to form the American Federation of Labor and Congress of Industrial Organizations (AFL-CIO).

Independent Unions

Although the AFL-CIO is a major force, other unions are also important in the labor movement. Many are **independent unions**—unions that do not belong to the AFL-CIO, such as the Brotherhood of Locomotive Engineers.

Student Web Activity Visit the *Economics: Principles and Practices* Web site at epp.glencoe.com and click on *Chapter 8—Student Web Activities* for an activity on labor unions.

Section 1 Assessment

Checking for Understanding

1. **Main Idea** Using your notes from the graphic organizer activity on page 193, describe the purpose of labor unions.

2. **Key Terms** Define macroeconomics, civilian labor force, craft or trade union, industrial union, strike, picket, boycott, lockout, company union, Great Depression, right-to-work law, independent union.

3. **Explain** why unions are important today.

4. **Describe** several reasons for the rise of unions prior to 1930.

5. **State** why unions became successful during the Great Depression.

6. **Describe** the major labor developments since World War II.

Applying Economic Concepts

7. **Civilian Labor Force** How would your participation in the civilian labor force be affected if you joined the armed services?

Critical Thinking

8. **Making Generalizations** How did the major legislative acts discussed in the section reflect the rise and decline of the labor movement?

 Practice and **assess** key social studies skills with the *Glencoe Skillbuilder Interactive Workbook, Level 2.*

Section 1 Assessment Answers

1. to promote legislation and decisions that allow higher pay, better hours and working conditions, job security

2. All vocabulary terms are defined in the text.

3. They continue to influence legislation affecting pay levels and working conditions.

4. Descriptions should include information from pages 194–196.

5. Common problems united workers; union

organizers renewed efforts; federal legislation increased the power of unions.

6. Descriptions should be based on information from pages 196–198.

7. You would not be in the civilian labor force.

8. Legislation prior to World War II tended to be pro-union, giving labor more power. Legislation passed after the war was generally antiunion and limited labor's power.

CRITICAL THINKING
Skill

Evaluating Primary and Secondary Sources

Primary sources are original records of events made by people who witnessed them. They include letters, journals, legal documents, drawings, photographs, and artifacts. *Secondary sources* are documents created after an event occurred. They pull together information from many sources and provide an overview of events.

Learning the Skill

To interpret primary and secondary sources, follow these steps:

- Identify the author of the document.
- Identify when and where the document was written.
- Read the document for its content.
- Identify the author's opinions and biases.
- Determine what kind of information the document provides and what is missing.

Practicing the Skill

Read the excerpt below, then answer the questions that follow.

For the past two decades, economists and social observers have bemoaned the rapid growth in income inequality in the U.S. Pointing to the widening gap between the wages of high school graduates and those with college degrees, some critics have claimed that the nation is in danger of developing a rigid class system out of sync with traditional American democratic values.

Lately, such concerns have abated. For one thing, there has been a general upgrading of the labor force as more and more Americans have graduated from high school and gone on to college. For another, low unemployment has finally begun to lift the wages of those at the bottom of the income ladder. Still, as a recent study by economist Maria E. Enchautegui of the University of Puerto Rico suggests, there is one group whose economic status may

Bookstore for Russian immigrants

actually deteriorate in the years ahead despite their adherence to the work ethic: low-skilled immigrants.

Between 1980 and 1994, notes Enchautegui, the number of working-age immigrants in the U.S. without a high school degree jumped from 2.8 million to 5.1 million—as the number of U.S.-born high school dropouts fell sharply from 20 million to 13 million. . . .

. . . The problem is that their very numbers, combined with declining demand for low-skilled workers, are driving their wages down. . . .

—*Business Week*, June 7, 1999

1. When was this document published?

2. What was the general feeling of the person who wrote this document?

3. What economic trend is the writer describing? Is information missing from this passage?

Application Activity

Look through the letters to the editor in your local newspaper. Prepare a report analyzing one of the letters. Summarize the article, the writer's point of view and frame of reference, and any primary sources cited.

 Practice and **assess** key social studies skills with the *Glencoe Skillbuilder Interactive Workbook, Level 2.*

Answers to Practicing the Skill

1. June 7, 1999
2. concern for the dropping wages of low-skilled immigrants
3. The writer is describing how a surplus of workers is driving their wages down. Yes, it is an excerpt from an article, not the entire article.

1 FOCUS

Section Overview
This section explains ways of resolving disputes between unions and management.

BELLRINGER
Motivational Activity

Project **transparency** and have students answer questions.

Available as blackline master.

Daily Focus Transparency 40

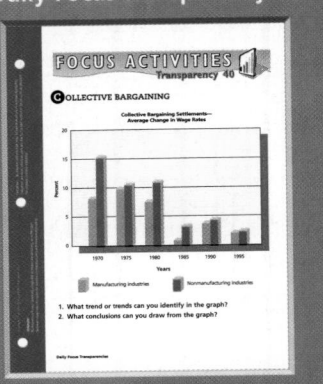

Study Guide

Reading Strategy
Have students create the graphic organizer.
Answers to Graphic: *mediation, arbitration, fact-finding, injunction and seizure, presidential intervention*

Preteaching Vocabulary
Have students write each Key Term and its definition on large sheets of paper to display in the classroom.

Resolving Union and Management Differences

Study Guide

Main Idea
Unions and management negotiate contracts through a process that is known as collective bargaining.

Reading Strategy
Graphic Organizer As you read the section, complete a graphic organizer similar to the one below that describes the different ways labor disputes are resolved.

Resolution

Key Terms
closed shop, union shop, modified union shop, agency shop, grievance procedure, mediation, arbitration, fact-finding, injunction, seizure

Objectives
After studying this section, you will be able to:
1. **Explain** the differences among kinds of union arrangements.
2. **Describe** several ways to resolve labor and management differences when collective bargaining fails.

Applying Economic Concepts
Union Arrangements Does the company that you or your parents work for have a union? Read to learn more about the different kinds of unions that exist today.

Cover Story

American Airlines Flight Attendants Reject Arbitration

The union representing flight attendants at American Airlines rejected an offer of arbitration from federal mediators yesterday, assuring the start of a 30-day cooling-off period after which its members will be legally free to strike.

American Airlines Strike

The major issue dividing the two sides is pay. The flight attendants now earn $15,000 to $35,000 a year, the union said. American said that the union's last proposal would cost the airline $570 million more over six years than its final offer. The union said that the gap was closer to $200 million.

—The New York Times, May 31, 2001

200

O ver the years, many disputes have occurred between labor and management. Sometimes employees take action against their employer, as during the 1981 air traffic controllers' strike. Sometimes the employer takes action against its employees, as in the case of the 1998–1999 NBA lockout. While the NBA was finally able to settle its difficulties, there are still other ways to resolve the deadlock had they needed them.

Kinds of Union Arrangements

The labor movement has organized workers in various ways to deal more effectively with management. Four kinds of union arrangements are discussed below.

Closed Shops
The most restrictive arrangement is the **closed shop,** a situation in which the employer agrees to hire only union members. In effect, this allows the union to determine who is hired by giving or denying a person union membership.

RESOURCE MANAGER

Reproducible Masters
- Reproducible Lesson Plan 8-2
- Daily Lecture Notes 8-2
- Guided Reading Activity 8-2
- Reading Essentials and Study Guide 8-2
- Section Quiz 8-2

Transparencies
- Daily Focus Transparency 40

Multimedia
- Interactive Tutor Self-Assessment Software
- ExamView® Pro Testmaker
- Presentation Plus!

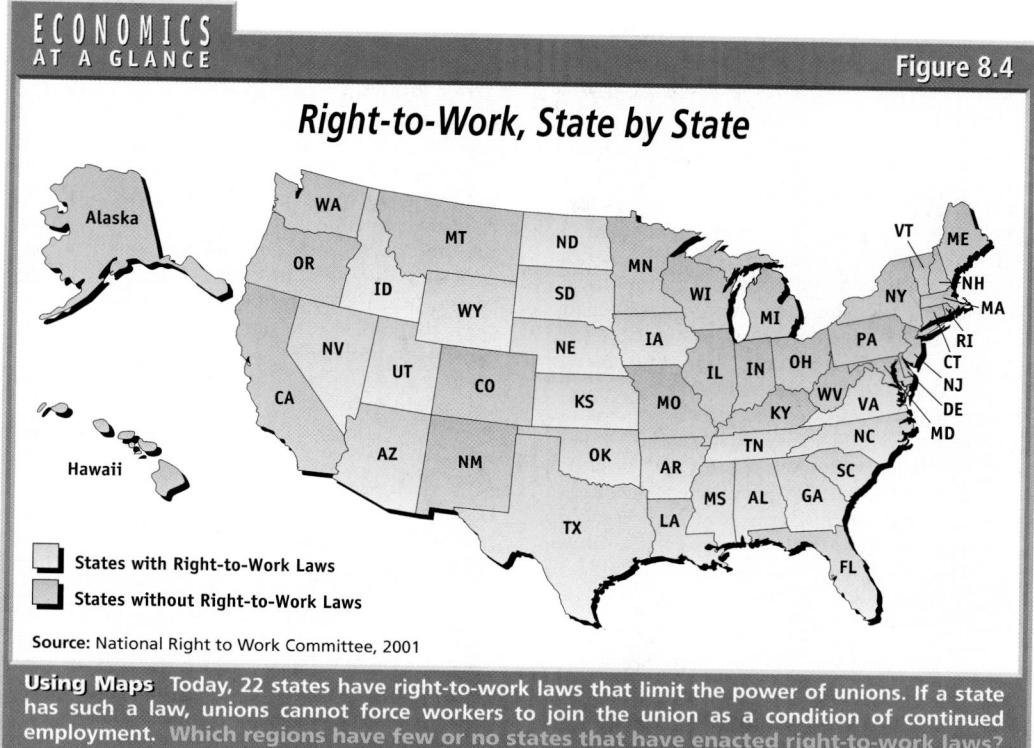

ECONOMICS AT A GLANCE

Figure 8.4

Right-to-Work, State by State

☐ States with Right-to-Work Laws

☐ States without Right-to-Work Laws

Source: National Right to Work Committee, 2001

Using Maps Today, 22 states have right-to-work laws that limit the power of unions. If a state has such a law, unions cannot force workers to join the union as a condition of continued employment. Which regions have few or no states that have enacted right-to-work laws?

Although this kind of union arrangement was common in the 1930s and early 1940s, the Taft-Hartley Act of 1947 made the closed shop illegal for companies involved in interstate commerce. Because most firms in the United States today are directly or indirectly engaged in interstate commerce, few, if any, closed shops exist.

Union Shops

The second arrangement is the **union shop,** an employment situation where workers do not have to belong to the union to be hired, but must join soon after and remain a member for as long as they keep their jobs. Today, the 22 states shown in **Figure 8.4** have taken advantage of Section 14(b) to pass right-to-work laws that prohibit mandatory union membership.

Modified Union Shops

The third kind of arrangement is a **modified union shop.** Under this arrangement, workers do not have to belong to a union to be hired and cannot be made to join one to keep their jobs. If workers voluntarily join the union, however, they must remain members for as long as they hold their jobs.

Agency Shops

Another arrangement is the **agency shop**—an agreement that does *not* require a worker to join a union as a condition to get or keep a job, but *does* require the worker to pay union dues to help pay collective bargaining costs. Nonunion workers are also subject to the contract negotiated by the union, whether or not they agree with it. Agency

CHAPTER 8: EMPLOYMENT, LABOR, AND WAGES **201**

CHAPTER 8
Section 2, pages 200–203

 TEACH

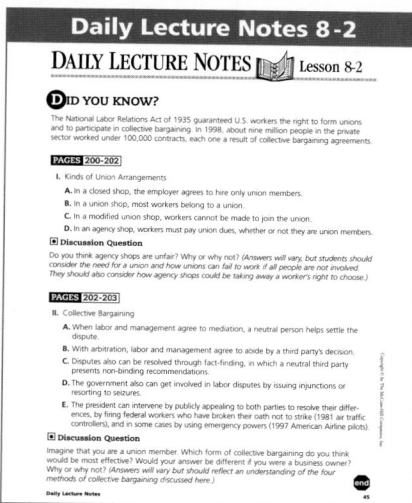

Daily Lecture Notes 8-2

DAILY LECTURE NOTES 📖 Lesson 8-2

DID YOU KNOW?
The National Labor Relations Act of 1935 guaranteed U.S. workers the right to form unions and to participate in collective bargaining. In 1998, about nine million people in the private sector worked under 100,000 contracts, each one a result of collective bargaining agreements.

PAGES 200-202
I. Kinds of Union Arrangements
  A. In a closed shop, the employer agrees to hire only union members.
  B. In a union shop, most workers belong to a union.
  C. In a modified union shop, workers cannot be made to join the union.
  D. In an agency shop, workers must pay union dues, whether or not they are union members.

☐ Discussion Question
Do you think agency shops are unfair? Why or why not? (Answers will vary, but students should consider the need for a union and how unions can fail to work if all people are not involved. They should also consider how agency shops could be taking away a worker's right to choose.)

PAGES 202-203
II. Collective Bargaining
  A. When labor and management agree to mediation, a neutral person helps settle the dispute.
  B. With arbitration, labor and management agree to abide by a third party's decision.
  C. Disputes also can be resolved through fact-finding, in which a neutral third party presents non-binding recommendations.
  D. The government also can get involved in labor disputes by issuing injunctions or resorting to seizures.
  E. The president can intervene by publicly appealing to both parties to resolve their differences, by firing federal workers who have broken their oath not to strike (1981 air traffic controllers), and in some cases by using emergency powers (1997 American Airline pilots).

☐ Discussion Question
Imagine that you are a union member. Which form of collective bargaining do you think would be most effective? Would your answer be different if you were a business owner? Why or why not? (Answers will vary but should reflect an understanding of the four methods of collective bargaining discussed here.)

Daily Lecture Notes   45

ECONOMICS AT A GLANCE

Answer: *Northeast and Midwest*

L2 Cooperative Learning
Provide students with the following situation: They are workers who have issued a demand for a 25¢-an-hour wage increase, but management has rejected the demand. Then organize students into groups of five and have groups review the grievance procedures discussed in the section. Ask groups to prepare a brief report on which procedure they would prefer to use and why. Have groups present and discuss their reports.

MEETING SPECIAL NEEDS ACTIVITY

English Language Learners Discuss with English language learners the differences between closed shops, union shops, modified union shops, and agency shops. Help students understand these differences by illustrating each with a drawing to show membership rules. Carry out the same process for the various forms of collective bargaining, using photos from news items related to the subject. Encourage such learners to use illustrations whenever possible to help them understand or recall economic concepts. **ELL**

📁 Refer to *Inclusion for the Social Studies Classroom Strategies and Activities* in the TCR.

201

Guided Reading Activity 8-2

③ ASSESS

Assign Section 2 Assessment as homework or as an in-class activity.

💾 Have students use **Interactive Tutor Self-Assessment Software** to review Section 2.

Section Quiz 8-2

---

shops are primarily responsible for the 1.4 percent of employed wage and salary workers represented by unions, as shown in **Figure 8.1.**

Collective Bargaining

 When labor and management take part in collective bargaining, representatives from both sides meet. A group of elected union officials represents workers, and company officials in charge of labor relations represent management. Collective bargaining requires compromise from both parties, and the discussions may go on for months.

If the negotiations are successful, both parties agree on basic issues such as pay, working conditions, and benefits. Because it is difficult to anticipate future problems, a **grievance procedure**—a provision for resolving issues that may come up later—may also be included in the final contract. Normally, union and management are able to reach an agreement. If not, other methods are available to resolve the differences.

Careers

Labor Relations Specialist

Are you a people person? Are you patient, fair-minded, and persuasive? Can you function under pressure?

The Work

Labor relations specialists formulate labor policy, oversee industrial labor relations, negotiate collective bargaining agreements, and coordinate grievance procedures to handle complaints resulting from contract disputes. Knowledge about wages and salaries, benefits, pensions, and union and management practices is necessary.

Qualifications

Courses in labor law, collective bargaining, labor economics, labor history, and industrial psychology are essential. Most often, labor relations specialists hold a degree in labor relations.

202 UNIT 3 MACROECONOMICS: INSTITUTIONS

Mediation

One way to resolve differences is through **mediation,** the process of bringing in a neutral third person or persons to help settle a dispute. The mediator's primary goal is to find a solution that both parties will accept. A mediator must be unbiased so that neither party benefits at the expense of the other. If the mediator has the confidence and trust of both parties, he or she will be able to learn what concessions each side is willing to make.

In the end, the mediator recommends a compromise to both sides. Neither side has to accept a mediator's decision, although it often helps break the deadlock.

Arbitration

Another way to resolve differences is through **arbitration,** a process in which both sides agree to place their differences before a third party whose decision will be accepted as final.

Arbitration is finding its way into areas beyond labor-management relations as well. American Express revised the agreement it had with its credit card holders and now requires disputes to be solved by an arbitrator rather than in the courts. This means that a credit card holder can no longer sue American Express in the event of a dispute—the matter goes to arbitration instead.

Fact-Finding

A third way to resolve a dispute is through **fact-finding,** an agreement between union and management to have a neutral third party collect facts about a dispute and present nonbinding recommendations. This process can be especially useful in situations where each side has deliberately distorted the issues to win public support, or when one side simply does not believe the claims made by the other side. Neither labor nor management has to accept the recommendations the fact-finding committee makes.

Injunction and Seizure

A fourth way to settle labor-management disputes is through injunction or seizure. During a

---

FREE ENTERPRISE ACTIVITY

Select a recent labor-management dispute covered in the local newspaper to present to the class. After students have reviewed all the information on both sides of the dispute, ask for volunteers to represent labor and management at a collective bargaining session to resolve the differences and negotiate a new contract. Have the remaining members of the class act as government mediators who help resolve the conflict. After the session, ask students to identify the type of union arrangement that was part of this conflict. 📦 **BLOCK SCHEDULING** dispute, one of the parties may resort to an **injunction**—a court order not to act. If issued against a union, the injunction may direct the union not to strike. If issued against a company, it may direct the company not to lock out its workers. In 1995, after professional baseball players ended their strike and went back to work, the owners promptly called a lockout. The players then got an injunction against the owners, and the 1995 baseball season began—without a labor agreement.

Under extreme circumstances, the government may resort to **seizure**—a temporary takeover of operations—to allow the government to negotiate with the union. This occurred in 1946 when the government seized the bituminous coal industry. While operating the mines, government officials worked out a settlement with the miners' union.

Presidential Intervention

The president of the United States may enter a labor-management dispute by publicly appealing to both parties to resolve their differences. This can be effective if the appeal has public support. The president also can fire federal workers. In 1981 President Ronald Reagan fired striking air traffic controllers because they were federal employees

who had gone on strike despite having taken an oath not to do so.

The president also has emergency powers that can be used to end some strikes. When pilots from American Airlines went on strike in 1997 during a peak travel weekend, President Clinton used a 1926 federal law, the Railway Labor Relations Act, to order an end to the strike less than 30 minutes after it began.

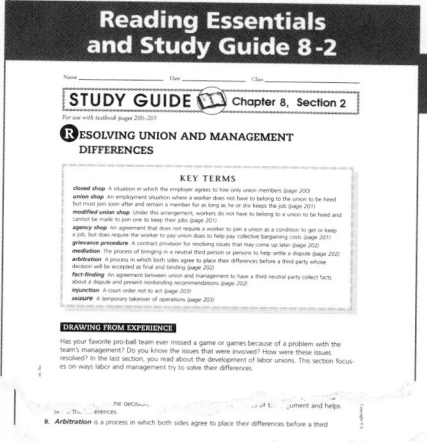

Negotiating Washington, D.C., was the scene of a major labor rally in the early 1990s. *What is the process through which unions and management negotiate contracts called?*

Section 2 Assessment

Checking for Understanding

1. **Main Idea** Using your notes from the graphic organizer activity on page 200, explain the purpose of collective bargaining.

2. **Key Terms** Define closed shop, union shop, modified union shop, agency shop, grievance procedure, mediation, arbitration, fact-finding, injunction, seizure.

3. **List** four kinds of union arrangements.

4. **Explain** six ways to resolve union and management differences when collective bargaining fails.

Applying Economic Concepts

5. **Union Arrangements** Contact a firm in your community that has a union. Ask if all

workers in the company are required to join, or if only some are. Based on your information, determine if the union arrangement is a closed shop, a union shop, a modified union shop, or an agency shop.

Critical Thinking

6. **Sequencing Information** If you represented a company during a collective bargaining session, and if negotiations were deadlocked, what course of action would you recommend? Why?

7. **Making Comparisons** How does voluntary arbitration differ from mediation?

 Practice and **assess** key social studies skills with the *Glencoe Skillbuilder Interactive Workbook, Level 2.*

Visual Instruction

Answer to Caption:
collective bargaining

Reteach

Reading Essentials and Study Guide 8-2

Name _____ Date _____ Class _____

STUDY GUIDE Chapter 8, Section 2

For use with textbook pages 200–203

RESOLVING UNION AND MANAGEMENT DIFFERENCES

KEY TERMS

closed shop A situation in which the employer agrees to hire only union members (page 200)
union shop An employment situation where a worker does not have to belong to the union to be hired but must join soon after and remain a member for as long as he or she keeps the job (page 201)
modified union shop Under this arrangement, workers do not have to belong to a union to be hired and cannot be made to join one to keep their jobs (page 201)
agency shop An agreement that does not require a worker to join a union as a condition to get or keep a job, but does require the worker to pay union dues to help pay collective bargaining costs (page 201)
grievance procedure A contract provision for resolving issues that may come up later (page 202)
mediation The process of bringing in a neutral third person or persons to help settle a dispute (page 202)
arbitration A process in which both sides agree to place their differences before a third party whose decision will be accepted as final and binding (page 202)
fact-finding An agreement between union and management to have a third neutral party collect facts about a dispute and present nonbinding recommendations (page 202)
injunction A court order not to act (page 203)
seizure A temporary takeover of operations (page 203)

DRAWING FROM EXPERIENCE

Has your favorite pro-ball team ever missed a game or games because of a problem with the team's management? Do you know the issues that were involved? How were these issues resolved? In the last section, you read about the development of labor unions. This section focuses on ways labor and management try to solve their differences.

the decision _____
_____ the _____ erences. _____ of the _____ ument and helps

8. **Arbitration** is a process in which both sides agree to place their differences before a third

Enrich

Ask students to write a research paper on a recent strike, noting the reasons for the work stoppage, the procedures used to end the dispute, and the final resolution.

4 CLOSE

Have students speculate how arrangements between employees and employers might be handled other than through collective bargaining.

Section 2 Assessment Answers

1. to discuss the demands of labor and management and reach a compromise

2. All vocabulary terms are defined in the text.

3. closed shop, union shop, modified union shop, agency shop

4. mediation, arbitration, fact-finding, injunction, seizure, presidential intervention; descriptive information on pages 202–203.

5. Answers should correctly determine the union arrangement of the company contacted.

6. Answers should reflect an understanding of the various forms of collective bargaining.

7. voluntary: both sides agree that decision of third party will be accepted as final; mediation: decision of third party does not have to be accepted by either party

BACKGROUND

American labor leaders are among the most colorful characters in American economic history. It's no wonder: becoming a successful union leader requires combinations of traits that seem paradoxical. Successful labor leaders like John Lewis and Cesar Chavez have had to be tough enough to stand up to hard-fighting companies, yet compassionate enough to devote their lives to common workers. They have had to believe passionately in their causes, yet be willing to seek and make compromises to achieve their goals. Finally, although many have lacked much formal education, they have had to be intelligent enough to understand all aspects of business, economic conditions, and the interplay between the economic and the social.

TEACH

Focus students' attention on the quotation from Chavez in the first line of his profile. Have them write journal entries or paragraphs in which they explain why they agree or disagree with Chavez's statement. Have them further address the idea of "economic courage." Is there such a thing? What does it entail?

Profiles IN Economics

Labor Giant:
John L. Lewis
(1880–1969)

For more than four decades, John L. Lewis stood as a giant in the American labor movement. As president of the United Mine Workers of America (UMW), his powerful leadership and dynamic style made him an influential—and controversial—figure.

Lewis, the son of Welsh immigrants, had little education. As a young man, Lewis worked in mines, earning a living by his physical strength and ingenuity. He later told a convention of miners, "I have always found that if I could not make a living in one place, I could in another. . . ."

As a leading figure in both the UMW and CIO, Lewis was instrumental in using strikes and negotiation to benefit union workers. He succeeded in raising wages and improving working conditions. His concern for the safety and well-being of miners was a hallmark of his leadership.

Lewis was often criticized for ruling his union with an iron hand. Yet no one can deny his many contributions to poor workers—or the giant role he played in U.S. labor history.

Acts of Courage:
Cesar Chavez
(1927–1993)

"The truest act of courage," Cesar Chavez said, "is to sacrifice ourselves for others in a totally non-violent struggle for justice." Chavez lived by these words. He founded the nation's first successful union for agricultural workers, the National Farm Workers of America (NFWA), in 1962. Its goal was justice for poor, migrant farm workers, largely Hispanic, who were among the most exploited workers in the country.

Chavez learned about the hard life of the migrant worker from bitter, early experience. He first worked in California's farm fields when he was just ten years old. Like other migrant workers, Chavez's family had to move to where work could be found.

In 1965, Chavez organized a strike of migrant grape pickers in California. Later, Chavez called for a nationwide boycott of California grapes. Under his slogan "Long live the strike!" the union kept the pressure on until, in 1970, the grape growers agreed to recognize the union. The results? Better working conditions and better pay, and a long sought-after voice for migrant workers.

Today, Chavez is revered. His life stands as a symbol for the battle for economic justice.

Examining the Profiles

1. **Making Comparisons** What similarities are there between Lewis and Chavez?

2. **For Further Research** Find out how a clash between Lewis and President Harry Truman led to a government seizure of mines in 1946. Write a newspaper article about the event.

Answers to Examining the Profile

1. Answers will vary. Students might note the obvious fact that both were successful labor leaders, that both founded or helped to found a union, that both devoted themselves to the betterment of the common worker, that both grew up in poor working families, and that both men had little education.

2. Newspaper articles will vary. Articles should answer the basic questions of *who, what, when, where, why,* and *how* in relation to Lewis's leading 400,000 United Mine Workers coal miners on strike, and Truman's response.

Labor and Wages

Study Guide

Main Idea
Wages differ for a variety of reasons, including skills, type of job, and location.

Reading Strategy
Graphic Organizer As you read the section, complete a graphic organizer similar to the one below by listing the reasons wages differ from one region to another.

Wage differences

Key Terms
unskilled labor, semiskilled labor, skilled labor, professional labor, noncompeting labor grades, wage rate, traditional theory of wage determination, equilibrium wage rate, theory of negotiated wages, seniority, signaling theory, labor mobility

Objectives
After studying this section, you will be able to:
1. **Identify** four main categories of labor.
2. **Explain** the importance of noncompeting labor grades.
3. **Describe** three different approaches to wage determination.

Applying Economic Concepts
Signaling Theory Believe it or not, diplomas have something in common with prices. Read to find out more about the signals they send.

FOCUS

Section Overview
This section identifies categories of labor and explains theories of wage determination.

BELLRINGER
Motivational Activity

- Project **transparency** and have students answer questions.
- Available as blackline master.

Daily Focus Transparency 38

Cover Story

People Are What's Most Important

Rhetoric aside, today we live in a capitalist economy.

Now while the word "capitalist" often conjures up images of those icons to capitalism—large buildings or factories and other symbols of worth—it is said that today's capitalist economy is built on people.

Computer education class

Nobel economics prize winner Gary Becker . . . asserted that human capital is the backbone of the capitalist economy and he noted that in the United States, between 17 and 25 percent of the GDP was being spent on the field of education and career training. . . .

He also observed that around the world, advances in technology now favored people with a greater command of knowledge and skills. . . .

—*The Bangkok Post,* January 27, 1999

The cover story stresses that investment in human capital is one of the more important investments we can make. The extent to which we invest in our own level of skills, experience, and knowledge even affects the way we describe and classify labor.

Categories of Labor

The four major categories of labor are based on the general level of knowledge and skills needed to do a particular kind of job. These categories are unskilled, semiskilled, skilled, and professional.

Unskilled Labor

Those who work primarily with their hands because they lack the training and skills required for other tasks make up the category of **unskilled labor.** These people work at jobs such as digging ditches, picking fruit, and mopping floors. Unskilled workers are likely to have the least amount of human capital invested in them—and therefore they often earn the lowest wages.

CHAPTER 8: EMPLOYMENT, LABOR, AND WAGES **205**

Study Guide

Reading Strategy
Have students create the graphic organizer.
Answers to Graphic: *labor mobility, cost of living differences, attractiveness of location*

Preteaching Vocabulary
Have students explain the differences between the four major categories of labor.

RESOURCE MANAGER

Reproducible Masters
- Reproducible Lesson Plan 8-3
- Daily Lecture Notes 8-3
- Guided Reading Activity 8-3
- Reading Essentials and Study Guide 8-3
- Section Quiz 8-3

Transparencies
- Daily Focus Transparency 38

Multimedia
- Interactive Tutor Self-Assessment Software
- ExamView® Pro Testmaker
- Presentation Plus!

② TEACH

Daily Lecture Notes 8-3

DAILY LECTURE NOTES 📖 Lesson 8-3

DID YOU KNOW?

In the first quarter of 1997, full-time U.S. workers in the bottom 10 percent of the wage range actually made an average of $6.48 an hour, despite the fact that the federal minimum wage was set at $4.75 an hour. In fact, during that time of low unemployment rates, wages for those lowest-paid workers actually increased at a faster rate than the wages of workers in the middle wage range.

PAGES 205-206

I. Categories of Labor
  A. Unskilled laborers make some of the lowest wages.
  B. Semiskilled workers do jobs that require a minimum amount of training.
  C. Skilled workers hold jobs that require experience and training.
  D. Professional workers do jobs that require a high level of knowledge-based education and managerial skills.

Discussion Question

In your opinion, should a higher investment in human capital be rewarded with higher wages? Why or why not? (Answers will vary but should reflect an understanding of the relationship between human capital and levels of knowledge and skills.)

PAGES 206-207

II. Noncompeting Labor Grades
  A. People must have the ability, the initiative, and the money to obtain additional education and training.
  B. Sometimes people are faced with a lack of opportunity for additional training and

---

THE GLOBAL ECONOMY

Percent of Income Spent on Food Some farmers raise cash crops—products they grow in large quantities to be sold. Cash crops include sugar, bananas, and soybeans. Farmers receive money for these crops, but must buy much of their own food. Other farmers are subsistence farmers, who grow food for themselves and sometimes sell a small amount to buy other things. There is no good way to figure out the costs of food to subsistence farmers or to people who grow food in their own garden plots.

Answers:

1. *The United States spends about 5 percent less than France.*
2. *Answers should reflect information from the graph.*

THE GLOBAL ECONOMY

United States	10.9		New Zealand	15.7		Spain	21.0
United Kingdom	11.5		Italy	17.6		South Africa	27.0
Sweden	14.5		Germany	17.7		Mexico	33.2
Australia	14.6		Japan	17.8			
France	15.2		Israel	21.0			

Source: USDA, United Nations System of National Accounts

PERCENT OF INCOME SPENT ON FOOD

How much does food cost you and your family? Depicted here is the percentage of income that the average citizen of the country spends on food.

Critical Thinking

1. **Making Comparisons** How do the expenditures in the United States compare with those in France?
2. **Making Generalizations** Is the statement "Most nations' citizens spend about 20 percent of their income on food" a valid statement? Why or why not?

Semiskilled Labor

A higher category is **semiskilled labor**—workers with enough mechanical abilities and skills to operate machines that require a minimum amount of training. These workers may operate basic equipment such as electric floor polishers, dishwashers, lawnmowers, and other machines that call for a minimal amount of training.

Skilled Labor

Skilled labor includes workers who are able to operate complex equipment and can perform their tasks with little supervision. These workers represent a higher investment of human capital, especially in the areas of experience and training. Examples include carpenters, typists, tool and die makers, computer technicians, chefs, and computer programmers.

Professional Labor

The final category is **professional labor,** or those individuals with the highest level of knowledge-based education and managerial skills. Examples include doctors, scientists, lawyers, and corporate

executives. These people usually have invested the most in their own human capital, and normally earn some of the highest incomes.

Noncompeting Labor Grades

Workers in one labor category generally do not compete with those in another category. For example, unskilled workers do not compete directly with semiskilled and skilled laborers. Because of this, it is useful to think of labor as being grouped into **noncompeting labor grades,** broad categories of labor that do not directly compete with one another because of experience, training, education, and other human capital investments.

This does not mean that some people in one category can never make it to a higher category—workers often do when they acquire additional skills and training. Others, however, often find it difficult to make the transition for reasons of cost, opportunity, and initiative.

Cost is one of the more difficult barriers to advancement. Some individuals have the ability and initiative to obtain additional technical skills, but they may not have the money to pay for the training. Many students have the aptitude to become college

---

MEETING SPECIAL NEEDS ACTIVITY

Learning Style: Logical/Mathematical Have students discuss a number of high-paying and low-paying jobs. Discuss the supply and demand related to those jobs and have students create graphs similar to those in Figure 8.5 on page 207 for four or five selected jobs, using their best estimates for average wages. Finally, have students create similar graphs for two or three careers that they are considering for the future.

Refer to *Inclusion for the Social Studies Classroom Strategies and Activities* in the TCR.

professors, but they lack the resources needed for up to six years of post-college study.

A lack of opportunity poses another barrier. Some people may live in areas where additional training and education are not available. Others may have the resources and grades to enter a specialized program such as law or medical school, but still may not be able to enter because schools have limited openings.

Although they know that more skills are needed to get a better job, other individuals simply lack the initiative to get ahead. These people may never acquire additional training or education because they are not willing to put forth the extra effort.

Wage Determination

Most occupations have a **wage rate,** a standard amount of pay given for work performed. Wage rates usually differ from one occupation to the next, and wages are sometimes different even within the same occupation.

Differences in wage rates can be explained in three ways. The first relies on the traditional tools of supply and demand. The second recognizes the influence of unions in the bargaining process. The third is known as "signaling theory."

Traditional Theory of Wages

Some of the highest paid people are the professional athletes, performers, and managers with skills so exceptional that they are above and beyond the norm in their professions. Their pay can be explained by the **traditional theory of wage determination.** The theory states that the supply and demand for a worker's skills and services determine the wage or salary.

Note that **Panel A** in **Figure 8.5** shows what happens to wages when a relatively large supply of ditch diggers is coupled with a relatively low level of demand. **Panel B** shows what happens when a relatively small supply of professional athletes is paired with a relatively high level of demand. The intersection of supply and demand determines the **equilibrium wage rate**—the wage rate that leaves neither a surplus nor a shortage in the labor market.

In most cases, the higher the level of human capital, the higher the skill of labor required, and the

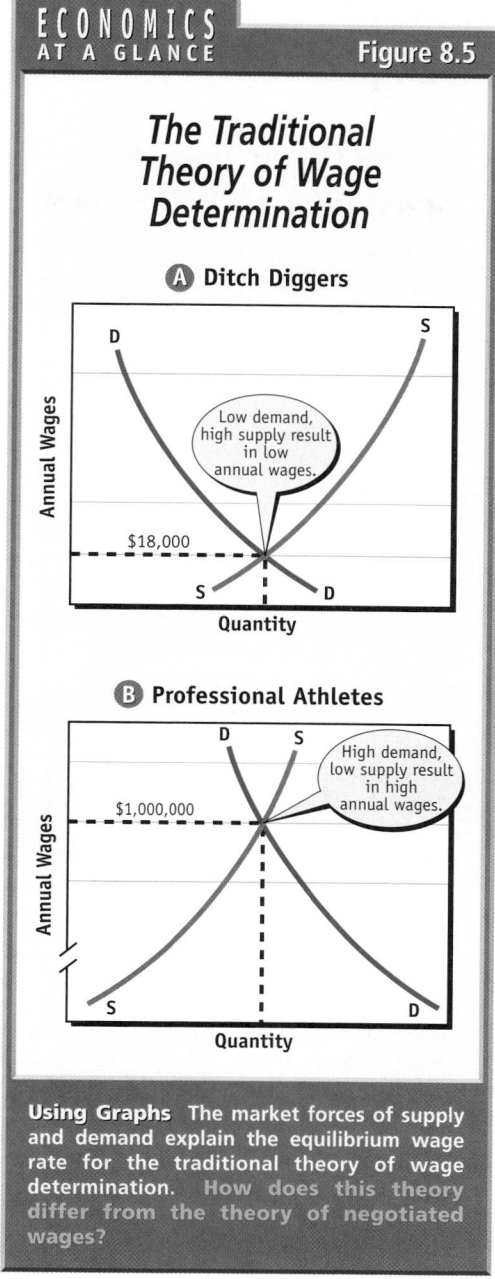

The Traditional Theory of Wage Determination

Ⓐ Ditch Diggers

Low demand, high supply result in low annual wages.

$18,000

Annual Wages / Quantity

Ⓑ Professional Athletes

High demand, low supply result in high annual wages.

$1,000,000

Annual Wages / Quantity

Using Graphs The market forces of supply and demand explain the equilibrium wage rate for the traditional theory of wage determination. **How does this theory differ from the theory of negotiated wages?**

CHAPTER 8: EMPLOYMENT, LABOR, AND WAGES **207**

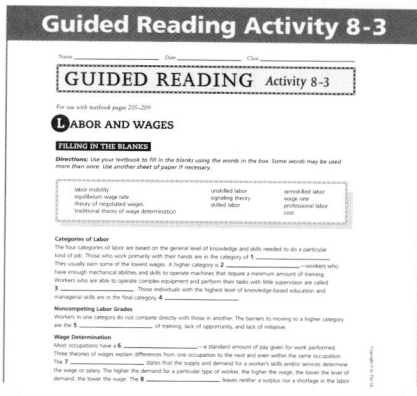

Guided Reading Activity 8-3

GUIDED READING Activity 8-3

For use with textbook pages 205–209

LABOR AND WAGES

FILLING IN THE BLANKS

Directions: Use your textbook to fill in the blanks using the words in the box. Some words may be used more than once. Use another sheet of paper if necessary.

labor mobility	unskilled labor	semiskilled labor
equilibrium wage rate	signaling theory	wage rate
theory of negotiated wages	skilled labor	professional labor
traditional theory of wage determination		cost

Categories of Labor

The four categories of labor are based on the general level of knowledge and skills needed to do a particular kind of job. Those who work primarily with their hands are in the category of **1** _____. They usually earn some of the lowest wages. A higher category is **2** _____—workers who have enough mechanical abilities and skills to operate machines that require a minimum amount of training. Workers who are able to operate complex equipment and perform their tasks with little supervision are called **3** _____. Those individuals with the highest level of knowledge-based education and managerial skills are in the final category, **4** _____.

Noncompeting Labor Grades

Workers in one category do not compete directly with those in another. The barriers to moving to a higher category are the **5** _____ of training, lack of opportunity, and lack of initiative.

Wage Determination

Most occupations have a **6** _____—a standard amount of pay given for work performed. Three theories of wages explain differences from one occupation to the next and even within the same occupation. The **7** _____ states that the supply and demand for a worker's skills and/or services determine the wage or salary. The higher the demand for a particular type of worker, the higher the wage. The lower the level of demand, the lower the wage. The **8** _____ leaves neither a surplus nor a shortage in the labor

Answer: *traditional theory of wage determination: the supply and demand for a worker's skills and services determine the wage or salary; theory of negotiated wages: organized labor's bargaining strength is a factor that helps determine wages*

L1 Advertising

List the four categories of labor on the board. Ask students to write brief classified advertisements for a job in each category. Have students compare and discuss their advertisements. **ELL**

L2 Debate

Ask students to debate the following: Professional athletes should command a high salary for their labors.

FREE ENTERPRISE ACTIVITY

Have students work in small groups to investigate job opportunities in the United States. Encourage groups to note the education and training required for each position, starting wage or salary, chances for advancement, and so on, for each position they list. Have groups present their findings to the class. Use these presentations as the starting point for a discussion on the kinds of positions students might seek in the future. **BLOCK SCHEDULING**

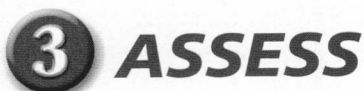

Answer: *that unionization does help determine wages and can help make wages higher*

③ ASSESS

Assign Section 3 Assessment as homework or as an in-class activity.

💾 Have students use **Interactive Tutor Self-Assessment Software** to review Section 3.

Section Quiz 8-3

(Section Quiz 8-3 reproduction)

ECONOMICS AT A GLANCE

Figure 8.6

Median Weekly Earnings by Occupation and Union Affiliation

Occupation	Represented by Unions	Nonunion Workers
Managerial and Professional Specialty	$834	$836
Precision Production, Craft and Repair	778	570
Government Workers	726	609
Operators, Fabricators, and Laborers	602	411
Technical, Sales, and Administrative Support	590	497
Farming, Forestry, and Fishing	506	325

Source: Bureau of Labor Statistics, 2001

Using Tables Weekly earnings are significantly higher for highly skilled occupations. Workers represented by unions also make substantially more than their nonunion counterparts. What can you infer about the theory of negotiated wages from Figure 8.6?

---

higher the average wage rate. Semiskilled workers generally receive more than unskilled workers, and skilled workers receive more than semiskilled or unskilled workers. Professional workers generally earn more than any of the other grades. This relationship is evident in **Figure 8.6,** which ranks occupations in descending order according to the level of skills and training required.

At times, exceptions to the traditional theory may appear to exist. Some unproductive workers may receive high wages because of family ties or political influence. Other highly skilled workers may receive low wages because of discrimination

based on their race or gender. In addition, workers and employers do not always know what the market wage rate is or should be.

Theory of Negotiated Wages

Sometimes other theories are useful when explaining wage differentials. The **theory of negotiated wages** states that organized labor's bargaining strength is a factor that helps determines wages. A strong union, for example, may have the power to force higher wages on some firms.

Figure 8.6 helps validate the theory of negotiated wages. The table shows that when workers are either unionized or represented by unions, weekly salaries are significantly higher than for nonunion workers. This situation applies to all occupations except for the "managerial and professional specialty" category, whose members are seldom unionized.

A final factor important to unions and collective bargaining is **seniority**—the length of time a person has been on the job. Because of their seniority, some workers receive higher wages than others who perform similar tasks.

Signaling Theory

The last explanation is known as **signaling theory.** This theory states that employers are willing to pay more for people with certificates, diplomas, degrees, and other indicators or "signals" of superior ability. For example, a sales firm might prefer to hire—or be willing to pay more for—a college graduate with a major in modern dance and a minor in theatre, than a high school graduate who excelled in business courses.

While this may seem odd at first, some firms view the college degree as a signal that the individual possesses the intelligence, perseverance, and maturity to succeed in his or her endeavors.

You might hear from friends and acquaintances that they did not need their high school or college degree to do the job they currently have—as if their education was unimportant. What these people overlook is signaling theory—the theory that helps explain *why* they got the job in the first place. The theory says nothing about what they needed to know to actually perform the job once they got it.

CRITICAL THINKING

Making Generalizations Direct students to draw a chart with three columns headed *Jobs, Category of Labor,* and *Wage Determination.* In the first column, have them list the jobs or occupations of 10 people they know. In the second column, have them note the category of labor (unskilled, semiskilled, skilled, or professional) into which the corresponding position falls. In the third column, have them hypothesize as to how the wage or salary for the position is determined. Encourage students to compare and discuss their results with other class members.

Regional Wage Differences

 Regardless of how wage rates are determined, they can still be different for the same job from one part of the country to another. Labor mobility, cost of living differences, and attractiveness of location can all make a difference.

Skilled workers often are scarce in some parts of the country and abundant in others, causing differences in wage rates. These differences, however, can be minimized by **labor mobility**—the ability and willingness of workers to relocate in markets where wages are higher.

Not all workers are equally mobile. Some are reluctant to move away from relatives. Some may want to move, but find that the cost is too high. Others do not want the inconvenience of buying a new house or renting a new apartment. As a result, the demand for certain skills remains high in some areas and low in others, and so wages tend to vary.

Another factor that affects wages is the cost of living. In many southern states, fresh fruits and vegetables are readily available. In addition, little money is spent on heavy clothing or on heating a home. In Alaska, however, food must be shipped in from thousands of miles away, people must have warm clothing, and every home must be well heated. Because the cost of living is higher in Alaska than in southern states, employers tend to offer higher wages in Alaska.

Finally, location can also make a difference because some places are thought to be so attractive that lower wages can be offered there. A person who likes to hunt and fish may be willing to work for less pay in Colorado or Montana than in New York City. Others may want to flee the busy—and expensive—city life for life in the country.

STANDARD & POOR'S INFOBYTE

Personal Income Personal income is a measure of income that is published by the Department of Commerce. It represents the total income that consumers receive, including most of the national income earned in the production of gross domestic product. It measures wages, salaries and other income sources, including rental income, government subsidy payments, interest income, and dividend income.

Section 3 Assessment

Checking for Understanding

1. **Main Idea** Using your notes from the graphic organizer activity on page 205, explain why wage rates differ among regions.

2. **Key Terms** Define unskilled labor, semiskilled labor, skilled labor, professional labor, noncompeting labor grades, wage rate, traditional theory of wage determination, equilibrium wage rate, theory of negotiated wages, seniority, signaling theory, labor mobility.

3. **List** the four categories of labor.

4. **Explain** the importance of noncompeting labor grades.

5. **Describe** three different approaches to wage determination.

Applying Economic Concepts

6. **Signaling Theory** Look at some help-wanted ads in your local paper. What criteria do they often specify, and how do these criteria relate to signaling theory?

Critical Thinking

7. **Making Comparisons** How does the category of semiskilled labor differ from unskilled labor?

8. **Making Generalizations** If you were a semiskilled worker, what could you do to move into a higher category of noncompeting labor?

Practice and assess key social studies skills with the *Glencoe Skillbuilder Interactive Workbook, Level 2.*

CHAPTER 8: EMPLOYMENT, LABOR, AND WAGES **209**

Reteach

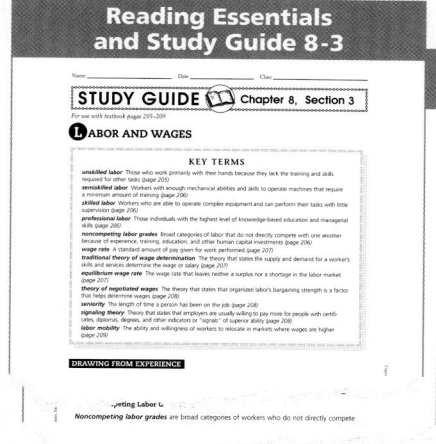

Reading Essentials and Study Guide 8-3

STUDY GUIDE — Chapter 8, Section 3

LABOR AND WAGES

Enrich

Point out that wages often include fringe benefits such as paid vacation and health insurance. Have students interview personnel officers at local firms to see what fringe benefits those firms offer. Have students share their findings with the class.

 CLOSE

Have students discuss the following: The forces of supply and demand should be the only factors that determine wages.

Section 3 Assessment Answers

1. Wage rates differ among regions due to lack of labor mobility, cost of living, and attractiveness of location.

2. All vocabulary terms are defined in the text.

3. unskilled labor, semiskilled labor, skilled labor, professional labor

4. Individuals with different levels of experience, training, and education do not compete against one another for jobs.

5. Descriptions found on pages 207–208.

6. Answers should demonstrate an understanding of the signaling theory.

7. semiskilled: individuals with enough mechanical abilities and skills to operate machines requiring minimum training; unskilled: those working primarily with their hands due to lack of skills required for other tasks.

8. obtain additional skills, education, or training

TEACH

As students read the article, have them think about how they define "disability." Ask them to identify disabilities that would clearly disqualify people—for example, a blind person cannot drive a bus. Also have students identify "impairments that can be corrected." Select students to conduct a debate about Vaughn Murphy's case. Ask one side in the debate to argue in favor of Murphy and the other side to argue against him. Ask the rest of the class to determine which side has the stronger argument.

📁 Refer to *Business Week Focus on the New Economy* in the TCR for additional unit-based articles.

BusinessWeek

Newsclip

APRIL 26, 1999

The passage of the Americans with Disabilities Act in 1990 was the first national civil rights bill for people with disabilities. The law requires all public places to be accessible. It also prohibits job discrimination against persons with physical or mental disabilities. Disputes over the meaning of the act's language have led to challenges in court.

The Disabled and the Marketplace

[I]n recent years, many courts have refused to assist people without serious disabilities. The reason is the language of the ADA, which only covers disabilities that "substantially limit" important activities such as work. Often, judges have interpreted it to exclude anybody whose impairments can be corrected.

That narrow legal reasoning has put many people with treatable disabilities in a Catch-22. Just because someone can lead a relatively normal life doesn't mean they don't face workplace discrimination as a result of their disability. "A person is judged too disabled to qualify for work but not disabled enough to be covered by the

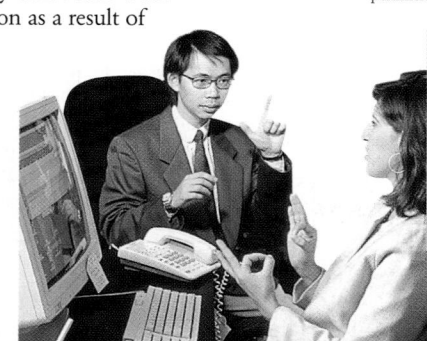

act," says Catherine A. Hanssens, director of the Lambda Legal Defense & Education Fund. Taken to its extreme, the employers' position would have the law cover only persons with disabilities so severe they can barely work, thereby rendering the law almost meaningless. . . .

By narrowly construing the ADA, the courts are preventing many able-bodied people from pursuing productive careers. Consider the case of Vaughn Murphy, who sued

Atlanta-based United Parcel Service Inc. after the company fired him as a truck mechanic in 1994. . . . His job included road tests of the trucks he fixed, and UPS said Murphy's blood pressure exceeded federal standards for driving. Murphy counters that the driving took up only 1% of his time, so it would not have been expensive to hire another driver.

"Truck work has been my life. When you've dedicated 23 years, it's hard to up and change your occupation," says Murphy. . . . UPS attorney William Kilberg says that Murphy understates the amount of driving that his old job required and that if the Supreme Court rules against the company, it "would be a blow to a company's ability to set quality standards."

Examining the Newsclip

1. **Analyzing Information** How has the government attempted to reduce the effect of discrimination against disabled workers?

2. **Drawing Conclusions** Have these efforts changed societal values towards the disabled? Why or why not?

210

Answers to Examining the Newsclip

1. through passage of the Americans with Disabilities Act in 1990, which prohibits job discrimination against persons with physical or mental disabilities

2. Answers should reflect an understanding of how attitudes have changed about the disabled.

Employment Trends and Issues

Study Guide

Main Idea
Important employment issues include union decline, unequal pay, and the minimum wage.

Reading Strategy
Graphic Organizer As you read the section, complete a graphic organizer similar to the one below to explain why *comparable worth* is difficult to apply.

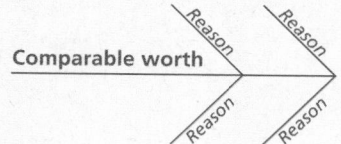

Key Terms
giveback, two-tier wage system, glass ceiling, comparable worth, set-aside contract, part-time worker, minimum wage, current dollars, real or constant dollars, base year

Objectives
After studying this section, you will be able to:
1. **Explain** why union membership has declined.
2. **Describe** reasons for the discrepancy in pay between men and women.

Applying Economic Concepts
Minimum Wage Have you ever worked at a job and earned exactly $5.15 an hour? Read to find out more about the minimum wage.

① FOCUS

Section Overview
This section discusses the decline of union membership and pay discrepancy.

BELLRINGER
Motivational Activity

 Project **transparency** and have students answer questions.

 Available as blackline master.

Daily Focus Transparency 41

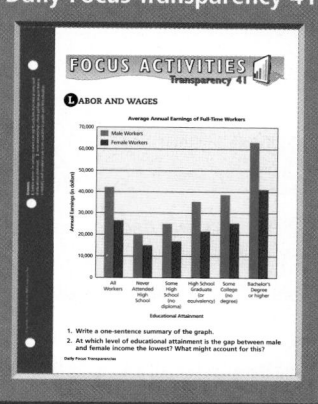

Cover Story

Two-Tier Pay More Common

Between corporate takeovers and energetic cost-cutting, more workers than ever are finding themselves on the same runway as the pilots of American Airlines and its subsidiary, Reno Air: They're working the same jobs for the same employer but taking home vastly different paychecks.

Pilots' pay may show striking differences.

Whether a "two-tier" wage system is the result of a formal union contract, a merger of two companies with different pay practices, or an increasing use of temporary workers . . . such wage differentials create a veritable caste system in the workplace, critics contend. . . .

Employers consider such wages a valuable tool for keeping payrolls under control . . . (but) the concept of tiered wages, which became something of a fad in the 1980s, has become decidedly unpopular among employees.

—The Los Angeles Times, February 28, 1999

Important issues abound in today's labor market. The two-tier wage structure discussed in the cover story, along with other issues, have an enormous impact on morale—and consequently, productivity—in the economy.

Decline of Union Influence

A significant trend in today's economy is the decline in both union membership and influence. As **Figure 8.7** shows, 35.5 percent of nonagricultural workers were members of unions in 1945. This number fell to 21.9 percent by 1980, and then dropped to about 13.5 percent by 2001.

Reasons for Decline

Several reasons account for the decline in union membership and influence. The first is that many employers made a determined effort to keep unions out of their businesses. Some activists even hired consultants to map out legal strategies to fight unions. Other employers made workers part of the management team, adding employees to the board of directors or setting up profit-sharing plans to reward employees.

CHAPTER 8: EMPLOYMENT, LABOR, AND WAGES **211**

Study Guide

Reading Strategy
Have students create the graphic organizer.
Answers to Graphic: *lack of legislation, occupational hazards, educational requirements, and degree of physical difficulty*

Preteaching Vocabulary
Use the Vocabulary Puzzle-Maker.

RESOURCE MANAGER

📁 Reproducible Masters
- Reproducible Lesson Plan 8-4
- Daily Lecture Notes 8-4
- Guided Reading Activity 8-4
- Reading Essentials and Study Guide 8-4
- Section Quiz 8-4

🗞 Transparencies
- Daily Focus Transparency 41

Multimedia
- Vocabulary PuzzleMaker CD-ROM
- Interactive Tutor Self-Assessment Software
- ExamView® Pro Testmaker
- Presentation Plus!

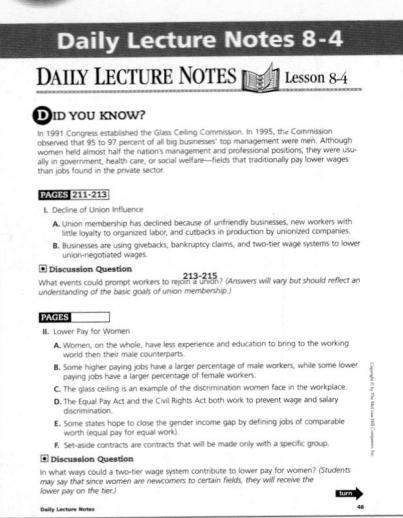

② TEACH

Daily Lecture Notes 8-4

ECONOMICS
AT A GLANCE

Answer: *steadily decreasing; also steadily decreasing*

L2 Television News Report

Have students work in groups of five to prepare a two- or three-minute television newscast on one of the issues discussed in the section. Some students might act as reporters, others might play experts or "people on the street," and still others might take the roles of news anchors. Have groups "broadcast" the news programs to the rest of the class.

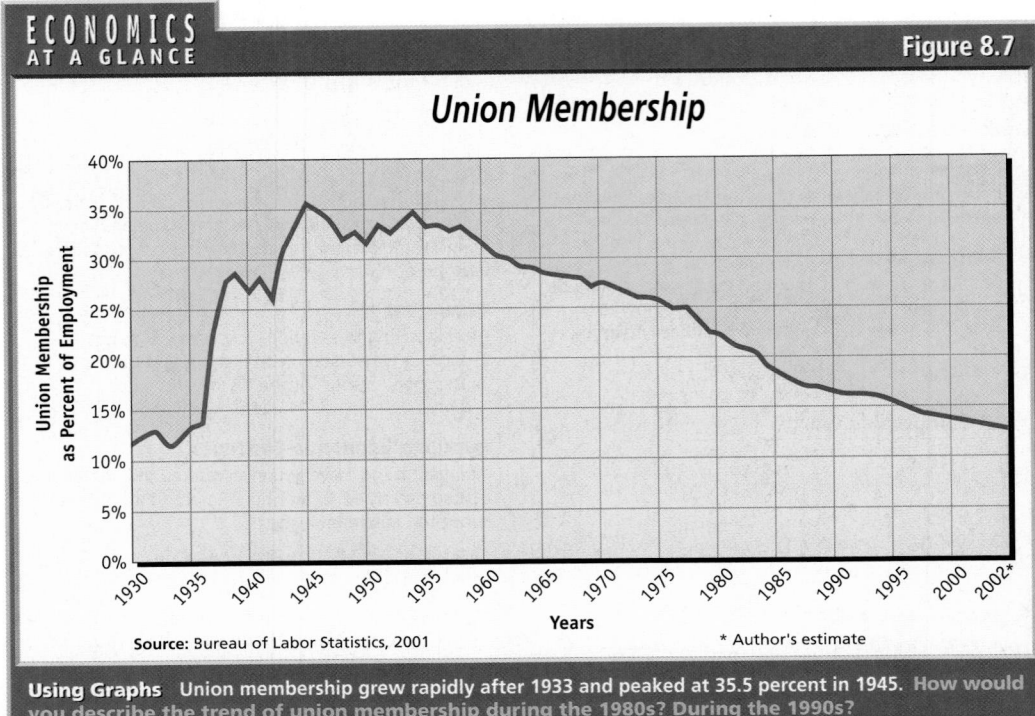

ECONOMICS
AT A GLANCE
Figure 8.7

Union Membership

Source: Bureau of Labor Statistics, 2001   * Author's estimate

Using Graphs Union membership grew rapidly after 1933 and peaked at 35.5 percent in 1945. **How would you describe the trend of union membership during the 1980s? During the 1990s?**

A second reason for union decline is that new additions to the labor force—especially women and teenagers—traditionally had little loyalty to organized labor. Because many of these workers represent second incomes to families, they have a tendency to accept lower wages.

The third and perhaps most important reason for the decline is that unions are the victims of their own success. When unions raise their wages substantially above the wages paid to nonunion workers, some union-made products become more expensive and sales are lost to lower-cost foreign and nonunion producers. This forces unionized companies to cut back on production, which causes layoffs and unions to lose some of their members.

Renegotiating Union Wages

Because unions have generally kept their wages above those of their nonunion counterparts, union wages have been under pressure.

One way employers have been able to reduce union wages is by asking for givebacks from union workers. A **giveback** is a wage, fringe benefit, or work rule given up when a labor contract is renegotiated.

Some companies have been able to get rid of labor contracts by claiming bankruptcy. If a company can show that wages and fringe benefits contributed significantly to its problems, federal bankruptcy courts usually allow a company to terminate its union contract and establish lower wage scales.

Another way to reduce union salary scales is with a **two-tier wage system**—a system that keeps

212 UNIT 3 MACROECONOMICS: INSTITUTIONS

MEETING SPECIAL NEEDS ACTIVITY

Learning Disabled For students who have problems with reasoning, illustrate the importance of headings and subheads for understanding the framework for each section. Model student use by asking a question such as: "What would I do if I wanted to know what each section was about?" For Section 4, read: Decline of Union Influence, Reasons for Decline, Renegotiating Union Wages, Lower Pay for Women, Human Capital Differences, Gender and Occupation, Discrimination, Legal Remedies, Comparable Worth, Set-Aside Contracts, and so on. Ask students to rephrase the headings using complete sentences.

▱ Refer to *Inclusion for the Social Studies Classroom Strategies and Activities* in the TCR.

high wages for current workers, but has a much lower wage for newly hired workers. As noted in the cover story, this practice is becoming widespread in industry, and often has union approval. In Ohio, for example, locals of the International Union of Electronic Workers have multitiered contracts with General Motors, Ford, and Chrysler. One contract even pays starting workers 55 percent of standard pay, and requires 17 years before a worker can reach the top scale.

Lower Pay for Women

Overall, women face a considerable gap between their income and the income received by men. As **Figure 8.8** shows, female income has been only a fraction of male income over a 40-year period—with a 28-percentage-point gap for the most recent year.

This gap has been the subject of much study. In 1998, the President's Council of Economic Advisors released an extensive report called *Explaining Trends in the Gender Wage Gap* that sheds light on the situation.

Human Capital Differences

According to the report, about one-third of the gap was due to differences in the skills and experience that women bring to the labor market. For example, women tend to drop out of the labor force to raise families, whereas men often do not. The report found that working women had lower levels of education than their male counterparts. If these two factors—experience and education—were the same for both men and women, one-third of the wage gap would disappear.

Gender and Occupation

The study also concluded that slightly less than one-third of the wage gap was due to the uneven distribution of men and women among various occupations. To illustrate, **Figure 8.9** shows that

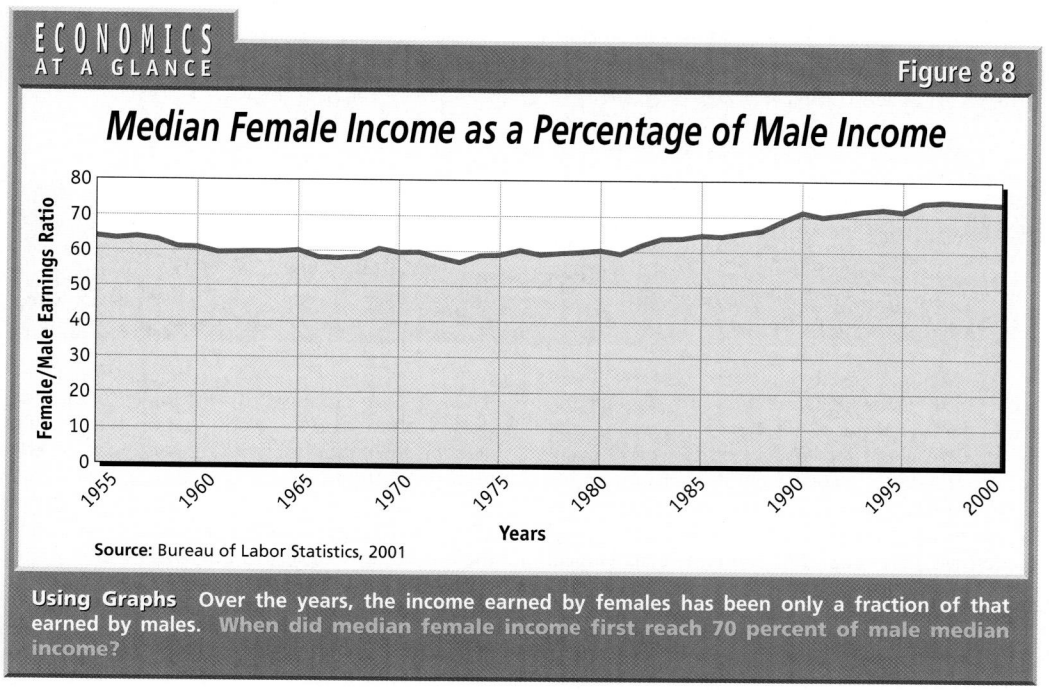

ECONOMICS AT A GLANCE

Figure 8.8

Median Female Income as a Percentage of Male Income

Female/Male Earnings Ratio (y-axis: 0–80)
Years (x-axis: 1955–2000)

Source: Bureau of Labor Statistics, 2001

Using Graphs Over the years, the income earned by females has been only a fraction of that earned by males. When did median female income first reach 70 percent of male median income?

ECONOMICS AT A GLANCE

Answer: *the late 1980s or 1990*

CHAPTER 8: EMPLOYMENT, LABOR, AND WAGES **213**

FREE ENTERPRISE ACTIVITY

Have students write a one-page summary of what they have learned in the chapter that will be helpful to a person thinking about entering the labor force in a full-time job. As guidance, write the following issues on the board and ask students to focus their summaries on any three: Pay, Education or Training, the Role of Unions, Two-Tier Wage System, Discrimination, Comparable Worth. Call on volunteers to present and discuss their summaries.

ECONOMICS
AT A GLANCE

Answer: *sales, retail and personal services; teachers, except college and university; health service workers; private household service workers; secretaries, stenographers, and typists*

F.Y.I.

In 1998, the median income for women was $26,855 compared to $36,252 for men, or about 74 cents for each dollar a man earned. Women with a bachelor's degree or more had a median income of $39,786, higher than the median income for all men, but considerably lower than the $56,524 for men with at least a bachelor's degree. Women with at least a bachelor's degree earned about 70 cents for each dollar a man in this category earned.

L2 Interviews

To learn more about the difficulties in making comparable worth decisions, have each student interview two people in different jobs that the student believes require the same level of skill, effort, and responsibility. After the interviews are completed, ask students to make oral presentations noting whether they think the jobs are comparable, giving reasons for their decisions. Use the presentations as a starting point for a class discussion on whether comparable worth is a viable method of setting wages.

ECONOMICS
AT A GLANCE

Figure 8.9

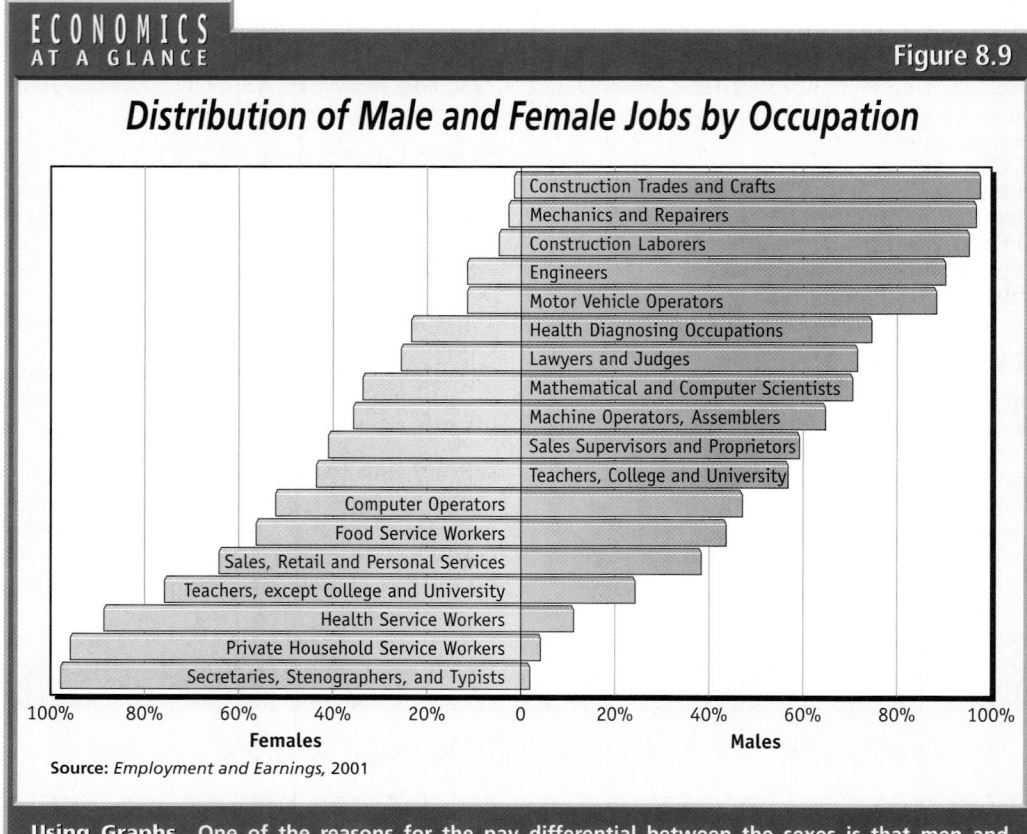

Distribution of Male and Female Jobs by Occupation

Source: Employment and Earnings, 2001

Using Graphs One of the reasons for the pay differential between the sexes is that men and women are not evenly distributed among occupations. If men tend to cluster in higher-paid occupations, and if women tend to cluster in lower-paid occupations, the average pay for men and women will differ. **In what occupations do women make up between 60 and 80 percent of the workforce?**

more men enter construction and engineering trades than do women. Likewise, women enter the private household service and office-worker occupations in relatively greater numbers than men.

As long as construction and engineering wages are higher than private household and office worker wages, men, on average, will earn more than women.

Discrimination

The study also found that more than one-third—or about 11 percentage points—of the gap

could not be explained. Accordingly, many analysts attribute this to discrimination that women face in the labor market. In fact, women and minorities often feel that their difficulties in getting raises and promotions are like encountering a **glass ceiling,** an invisible barrier that obstructs their advancement up the corporate ladder.

Legal Remedies

Two federal laws are designed to fight wage and salary discrimination. The first is the Equal Pay

214 UNIT 3 MACROECONOMICS: INSTITUTIONS

CRITICAL THINKING

Identifying Alternatives Have students work in small groups to brainstorm alternatives for creating greater equality in wages between people who do comparable work. Ask students to try to find solutions that do not require government interference in the marketplace. Have each group present its alternative solutions to the class, then have the entire class rank the ideas beginning with the one they consider most workable.

Act of 1963 which prohibits wage and salary discrimination for jobs that require equivalent skills and responsibilities. This act applies only to men and women who work at the same job in the same business establishment.

The second law is the Civil Rights Act of 1964. Title VII of this act prohibits discrimination in all areas of employment on the basis of gender, race, color, religion, and national origin. The law applies to employers with 15 or more workers, although it specifically excludes religious associations and their educational institutions.

The Civil Rights Act of 1964 also set up the Equal Employment Opportunity Commission (EEOC). The EEOC investigates charges of discrimination, issues guidelines and regulations, conducts hearings, and collects statistics. If a pattern of discrimination is discovered, the government can bring suit against a company.

Comparable Worth

One measure used to close the income gap between men and women is **comparable worth**, the principle stating that people should receive equal pay for work that is different from, but just as demanding as, other types of work.

In the state of Washington, for example, a federal judge ruled that work performed by social service workers—most of whom were female—was just as demanding as some traditionally male occupations. The judge ordered the state to raise wages and give workers several years' back pay. In Illinois, job evaluators determined that the work done by highway workers was roughly equivalent to that done by nurses.

Comparable-worth decisions are not easy to make because so many factors, such as occupational hazards, educational requirements, and degree of physical difficulty must be taken into consideration.

Some people—including most economists—believe that fair and unbiased comparisons of occupations are almost impossible to make. This group also argues that comparable worth is not needed as long as people are free to obtain training and to enter the profession of their choice. Others argue that comparable worth is necessary to remove gender discrimination in the marketplace.

These issues, along with a lack of federal legislation and the reluctance of the courts to interfere with the market, have limited the popularity of comparable worth in the United States. Comparable worth is widely used in Europe and Canada, however.

Set-Aside Contracts

Another corrective measure is the government **set-aside contract,** a guaranteed contract reserved exclusively for a targeted group. The federal government, for example, requires that a certain percentage of defense contracts be reserved exclusively for minority-owned businesses.

Another example is a 1988 California law requiring that 5 percent of the state's bond contracts be set aside exclusively for women lawyers, bankers, and other females who help place the bonds with investors. Such laws ensure that states do not give all of their business to males in a male-dominated profession.

Most set-aside programs are beginning to add "graduation" clauses that "promote" minority-owned businesses out of the program once they reach a certain size or have received set-aside contracts for a certain number of years. After all, the intent of the program is to give these firms a boost, not a permanent subsidy.

CYBERNOMICS SPOTLIGHT

The End of Work?
Some analysts in the past contended that the computer age would result in less work for humans. What's happening, however, is that more people are working *more* hours. The average number of hours worked per week has increased from 40 hours in 1973 to 50 hours today. Why is this happening? One explanation is that computers don't replace human thought and endeavor, they extend it. By allowing people to communicate easily at any time from any place, computers increase the amount of time people work.

CHAPTER 8: EMPLOYMENT, LABOR, AND WAGES **215**

THE GLOBAL ECONOMY

Reverse Brain Drain For decades, highly skilled workers in India, Caribbean nations, and other countries have not found work in their own lands. They have migrated to the United States and other countries that need individuals trained in science, technology, and computers. This has resulted in "brain drain," the loss of skilled workers. Some countries are making efforts to stop the loss of educated workers. Thailand, for example, has started project Reverse Brain Drain (RBD) to create and attract more high-tech industry in order to keep their skilled workers.

 Math Practice

Weekly Wages Ask students to figure out the before-tax wages for a 40-hour week at hourly rates of $5.15, $9.50, $15.10, and $25.00. *($206.00, $380.00, $604.00, $1,000.00)*

EXTENDING THE CONTENT

Minimum Wage and Productivity Some economists suggest that raising the minimum wage may have a positive impact on productivity. First, employers of low-wage workers often are inefficient in the way they use labor. Having to pay higher wages through an increased minimum wage rate might force the employers to use labor more efficiently and thus improve productivity. In addition, higher wages increase the real income of workers, which in turn might increase worker motivation, also translating into increased productivity.

CYBERNOMICS

The Electronic Office Job listings on the Internet sometimes involve work for people with home offices. Often a person can work for a company in another city and receive assignments and send completed work by e-mail. The availability of such jobs has created a national—and sometimes international—workplace.

CURRICULUM CONNECTION

History In its proposed form, Title VII of the Civil Rights Act of 1964 prohibited job discrimination on the basis of race, color, religion, or national origin. During the House debate on this provision, a dissenting representative introduced an amendment forbidding discrimination based on gender. The aim of this action was to ridicule the whole idea of discrimination in the workplace and thus defeat the provision. The result, however, was very different. Women representatives rallied support for the amendment, and it—and the act as a whole—passed.

Did you know?

Big Macroeconomics The magazine *The Economist* uses the price of a McDonald's Big Mac sandwich, converted to U.S. dollars, as an indicator of the comparative value of major world currencies. It operates on the notion that a dollar should buy the same amount in all countries. In July 1999, the average American price (including tax) of the Big Mac was $2.42. A Big Mac in Switzerland costs the most—$4.02. The price of the sandwich in the People's Republic of China costs the least—$1.16. In other words, the Swiss *franc* is the most overvalued currency and the Chinese *yuan* is the most undervalued.

Part-Time Workers

One of the more remarkable trends in the labor market has been the rise in part-time employment. **Part-time workers**—or those workers who regularly work fewer than 35 hours per week—account for one out of five jobs in the U.S. economy. In some states, like North Carolina, part-time labor accounts for nearly 25 percent of the workforce.

Reasons for Growth

Part of the reason for the part-time job growth is the evolving nature of the economy. When retail stores stay open for more hours, they often need workers to fill in at odd times—and the checks received by part-time workers are often welcome additions to the family income. Also, the odd hours give some workers the opportunity to do other things, such as take college classes, that would normally interfere with the standard 40-hour workweek.

The use of part-time workers also gives employers more flexibility to schedule workers for peak periods, such as during lunch or supper at fast-food restaurants. Businesses also like the lower cost of part-time workers because they receive few of the health, retirement, and other benefits received by full-time workers. When the savings from these fringe benefits are combined with lower part-time hourly salaries, the sums can be substantial. Today, figures from the Bureau of Labor Statistics show that part-time employee wages and fringe benefits averaged slightly over $10 per hour, as compared to more than $20 for full-time workers.

Critics of Part-Time Employment

The arguments against part-time jobs are that wages are too low, and the hours too few, for workers to earn a decent living. In addition, no benefits are offered. Some part-time workers feel that they are being abused by the system and forced to work at inconvenient times. Others feel that the system denies full-time employment to a large number of capable workers.

Unions are especially opposed to part-time workers. The 1997 strike at United Parcel Service (UPS) was partially over this issue. According to the union, lower paid, part-time workers were routinely scheduled into four-hour shifts even though they wanted full-time employment.

The Minimum Wage

The **minimum wage**—the lowest wage that can be paid by law to most workers—was first set in 1939 at $.25 per hour. As **Panel A** in **Figure 8.10** shows, the minimum wage increased over time until it reached $5.15 in 1997.

Debate Over the Minimum Wage

The minimum wage has always been controversial. Its original intent was to prevent the outright exploitation of workers and to provide some degree of equity and security to those who lacked the skills needed to earn a decent income.

Supporters of the minimum wage argue that these objectives—equity and security—are consistent with the economic goals of the United States. Besides, they say, the wage is not very high in the first place. Opponents of the minimum wage object to it on the grounds of economic freedom—also a U.S. economic goal. This group also believes that the wage discriminates against young people and is one of the reasons that many teenagers cannot find jobs.

Some parts of the country have even instituted their own equivalent of a minimum wage. The city of Los Angeles, for example, has a "living wage" that is substantially higher than the federal minimum wage. Any company doing business with the city is required to pay its workers at least that amount.

INTERDISCIPLINARY CONNECTIONS ACTIVITY

Literature Many biographies of successful people recount how they overcame poverty or other difficulties. Have students read biographies (brief or book-length) of individuals fitting this description and prepare a time line of events in that person's life that demonstrates how the individual achieved success. Have students share their time lines and brief reports on their subjects with the class.

ECONOMICS AT A GLANCE

The Minimum Wage

A The Minimum Wage in Current Dollars

Current Dollars per Hour — axis from 0 to $7.00

1939, 1949, 1959, 1969, 1979, 1989, 1999, 2001

B The Minimum Wage Adjusted for Inflation

Constant 1996 Dollars per Hour — axis from 0 to $6.00

1939, 1949, 1959, 1969, 1979, 1989, 1999, 2001

C The Minimum Wage as a Percent of the Average Manufacturing Wage

% of Average Wage — axis from 0 to 60

1939, 1949, 1959, 1969, 1979, 1989, 1999, 2001

Sources: *Statistical Abstract of the United States, Economic Report of the President,* various issues

Using Graphs The minimum wage is expressed in current dollars in Panel A, adjusted for inflation in Panel B, and as a percent of the average wage for workers in manufacturing in Panel C. Even though the minimum wage was $3.35 an hour during most of the 1980s, the minimum wage adjusted for inflation decreased. Explain why this occurred.

Figure 8.10

CHAPTER 8: EMPLOYMENT, LABOR, AND WAGES **217**

ECONOMICS AT A GLANCE

Answer: *Because prices increased during that period, the purchasing power of the minimum wage declined.*

Graph Skills Practice

In what year was the minimum wage as a percent of the average manufacturing wage the highest? *(1950)* Approximately what was the minimum wage adjusted for inflation that year? *(about $4.00)*

ASSESS

Assign Section 4 Assessment as homework or as an in-class activity.

💾 Have students use **Interactive Tutor Self-Assessment Software** to review Section 4.

Section Quiz 8-4

EXTENDING THE CONTENT

Finding Workers Point out that workers have more difficulty finding jobs or getting raises in difficult economic times, but in good times companies have a difficult time getting and keeping workers. At the end of the 1990s, many companies found new pools of workers among women in the workforce. Many women who had been working part-time upgraded to full-time work, according to the Bureau of Labor Statistics. In addition, unions were able to get higher hourly wages for their members.

Reteach

Enrich

Have students choose a state with comparable worth laws and research and write a report describing that law's provisions.

4 CLOSE

In a class discussion, have students speculate on what the major employment trends and issues in the next century might be.

Measured in Current Dollars

Panel A in **Figure 8.10** shows the minimum wage in **current dollars,** or in dollars that are not adjusted for inflation. The minimum wage is recorded exactly as it was from 1939 to 2001.

When viewed in this manner, it seems as if the minimum wage increased dramatically over time. The figure, however, does not take into account inflation, which erodes the purchasing power of the minimum wage.

Adjusted for Inflation

To compensate for inflation, economists like to use **real or constant dollars**–dollars that are adjusted in a way that removes the distortion of inflation. This involves the use of a **base year**–a year that serves as a comparison for all other years.

Although the computations are complex, the results are not. **Panel B,** using constant base-year prices, shows that the minimum wage had relatively more purchasing power in 1968 than in any other year. As long as the base year serves as a common denominator for comparison purposes, the results would be the same regardless of the base year used.

Panel B also shows that the purchasing power of the minimum wage goes up whenever it increases faster than inflation, as it did in 1997 when the wage

went to $5.15. However, the minimum wage remained the same through 2001 while prices went up, so the wage actually purchased a little less as time went by. As long as the minimum wage remains unchanged, and as long as inflation continues, its purchasing power will continue to decline.

Compared to Manufacturing Wages

In **Panel C,** the minimum wage is shown as a percent of the average manufacturing wage. In 1968, for example, the minimum wage was $1.60 and the average manufacturing wage was $3.01. If we divide the two, the minimum wage works out to be 53.2 percent of the manufacturing wage for that year.

When measured in this manner, 1968 was the peak year. After 1968, the ratio slowly declined to approximately 35 percent by 2001. As long as the minimum wage stays fixed, and as long as manufacturing wages continue to go up, this ratio will continue to decline.

The minimum wage will certainly be raised again. What is not certain is when this will happen. When the minimum wage becomes unacceptably low to voters and their elected officials, Congress will increase it. Some people even want to link the minimum wage to inflation, so that the wage will automatically rise when prices rise.

Section 4 Assessment

Checking for Understanding

1. **Main Idea** Using your notes from the graphic organizer activity on page 211, write a definition of comparable worth in your own words.

2. **Key Terms** Define giveback, two-tier wage system, glass ceiling, comparable worth, set-aside contract, part-time worker, minimum wage, current dollars, real or constant dollars, base year.

3. **List** three reasons for the decline of unions.

4. **Describe** three reasons for the income gap between men and women.

5. **Describe** the current trends in part-time employment.

6. **Explain** why it is necessary to consider inflation when examining the minimum wage.

Applying Economic Concepts

7. **Minimum Wage** A number of arguments exist both in favor of and against having a minimum wage. With which side do you agree? Why?

Critical Thinking

8. **Drawing Conclusions** In your opinion, do cultural stereotypes influence the income gap between men and women?

 Practice and **assess** key social studies skills with the *Glencoe Skillbuilder Interactive Workbook, Level 2.*

---

218 UNIT 3 MACROECONOMICS: INSTITUTIONS

Section 4 Assessment Answers

1. Definitions should reflect material on page 215.

2. All vocabulary terms are defined in the text.

3. many employers have kept unions out; additions to labor force have little loyalty to organized labor; unions are victims of own success

4. Women tend to fill lower-paying positions; discrimination prevents them from getting promotions; career interruptions for child-bearing affect women's seniority.

5. It has been growing due to increasing hours in retail and the need to fill extra positions during peak periods.

6. As prices tend to increase over time, purchasing power of fixed minimum wage decreases.

7. Answers should reflect understanding of the advantages/disadvantages of minimum wage.

8. Answers should show grasp of reasons behind income gap between men and women.

Section 1

The Labor Movement (pages 193–198)

- **Craft or trade unions,** and **industrial unions** were established by the end of the Civil War.

- Unfavorable public attitudes existed toward labor: The Sherman Antitrust Act was used against labor and even the Clayton Act was ignored by the courts.

- Attitudes shifted in favor of labor during the **Great Depression** with the passage of the Norris-LaGuardia Act, the Wagner Act, and the Fair Labor Standards Act.

- Public opinion shifted against labor again after World War II. The Taft-Hartley Act in 1947 limited union activity and allowed states to pass **right-to-work laws.**

- The union movement was dominated by the AFL and the CIO, which merged in 1955 to form the AFL-CIO.

Section 2

Resolving Union and Management Differences (pages 200–203)

- The **closed shop** (now illegal), requires that employers hire only union members selected by the union. The **union shop** requires that an employee join the union shortly after being hired. The **modified union shop** gives the employee the option to join the union after being hired. The **agency shop** requires that workers pay dues to the union, but does not require the workers to join, even though the union represents all workers.

- When collective bargaining fails, several other methods are available to settle labor disputes, including mediation, arbitration, fact-finding, the use of injunctions, and seizure.

Section 3

Labor and Wages (pages 205–209)

- Four noncompeting labor grades are **unskilled labor, semiskilled labor, skilled labor,** and **professional labor.**

- Workers usually find it difficult to move to a higher income group because of the cost of education and training, the lack of opportunities for education and training, and lack of individual initiative.

- The **traditional theory of wage determination** uses the market forces of supply and demand to explain wage rates; the **theory of negotiated wages** argues that the relative strength of a union is a factor; **signaling theory** argues that certificates and diplomas are signals of ability.

- Wages also differ because of **labor mobility,** the cost of living, and attractiveness of work locations.

Section 4

Employment Trends and Issues (pages 211–218)

- Union membership is declining because of anti-union activities by firms, labor force additions that have little loyalty to labor, and unions that have priced themselves out of some markets.

- Corrective measures include anti-discrimination laws, the principle of **comparable worth,** and **set-aside contracts.**

- Part-time jobs are increasing, providing flexible, low cost options to employers.

- The **minimum wage** has lost much of its purchasing power because of inflation. It is also falling behind when measured as a percent of the average manufacturing wage.

 ECONOMICS & YOU

 Chapter 14
Disc 1, Side 2
The American Labor Force

 Also available in VHS.

Using the Chapter 8 Summary

Use the Chapter 8 Summary to preview, review, condense, or reteach the chapter.

Preview/Review

Vocabulary PuzzleMaker CD-ROM reinforces Key Terms.

Interactive Tutor Self-Assessment Software provides a review of Chapter 8 content.

Condense

Have students listen to the Chapter 8 Audio Program. Spanish also available.

Assign the Chapter 8 Audio Program Activity and give students the Chapter 8 Audio Program Test.

Have students complete the Guided Reading Activities and Reading Essentials and Study Guides for Chapter 8.

Reteach

Have students complete Reteaching Activity 8 in the TCR. Spanish also available.

Teacher's Notes / Internet Bookmarks

219

GLENCOE
TECHNOLOGY

Use **MindJogger Videoquiz** to review the Chapter 8 content.

Have students visit the Web site at epp.glencoe.com to review Chapter 8 and take the **Self-Check Quiz**.

Identifying Key Terms

1. **pro-union**
2. **pro-union**
3. **antiunion**
4. **neither**
5. **neither**
6. **antiunion**
7. **neither**
8. **antiunion**
9. **neither**
10. **neither**
11. **neither**
12. **pro-union**
13. **antiunion**
14. **neither**
15. **pro-union**
16. **antiunion**
17. **neither**
18. **neither**

Reviewing the Facts

Section 1

1. Less then 14.5 percent of employed wage and salary workers belong to unions; a further 1.7 percent of nonunion members are represented in collective bargaining; total of nearly 18.1 million workers.
2. industrial: represented all workers in an industry; trade or craft: represented skilled workers who performed same kind of job
3. workers united; leaders renewed efforts; federal legislation increased power of unions
4. Unions have made limited progress, membership has dwindled, and some legislation has limited the power of unions.

Section 2

5. closed shop, union shop, modified union shop, agency shop; descriptions found pages 200–202

ECONOMICS
Online

Self-Check Quiz Visit the *Economics: Principles and Practices* Web site at epp.glencoe.com and click on *Chapter 8—Self-Check Quizzes* to prepare for the chapter test.

Reviewing Key Terms

Classify each of the terms below as pro-union, antiunion, or neither.

1. boycott
2. closed shop
3. company union
4. compulsory arbitration
5. fact-finding
6. giveback
7. grievance procedure
8. lockout
9. modified union shop
10. seizure
11. injunction
12. picket
13. right-to-work law
14. agency shop
15. strike
16. two-tier wage system
17. arbitration
18. mediation

Reviewing the Facts

Section 1 (pages 193–198)

1. **Describe** current union influence in terms of membership and workers represented by unions.
2. **Compare** the two types of unions in the post-Civil War period.
3. **Describe** the advances made by unions during the Great Depression.

---

4. **Outline** the progress of unions since the end of World War II.

Section 2 (pages 200–203)

5. **Describe** the four types of union arrangements.
6. **Explain** five approaches to resolving a deadlock that may occur between a union and a company's management.

Section 3 (pages 205–209)

7. **Explain** the differences between the four major categories of noncompeting labor.
8. **Explain** why it is so difficult for workers to move from one category of labor to another.
9. **Compare** the three theories of wage determination.
10. **Discuss** the reasons for regional wage differences.

Section 4 (pages 211–218)

11. **Explain** why unions have lost members, as well as influence, in recent years.
12. **Describe** two corrective measures being taken to close the income gap between men and women workers.
13. **Explain** the popularity of part-time employment.
14. **Identify** three ways to evaluate the minimum wage.

Thinking Critically

1. **Making Generalizations** Unions generally argue that the best interests of workers can be served when employees are members of a union. Do you agree or disagree with this statement? Defend your answer.
2. **Analyzing Information** Some people believe that in today's economy, the theory of negotiated wages is more useful than the traditional theory of wage determination. Explain why you agree or disagree.

---

6. mediation, arbitration, fact-finding, injunction, seizure; descriptions found pages 202–203

Section 3

7. Differences between unskilled, semiskilled, skilled, professional found pages 205–206.
8. cost of training and education, lack of opportunity, and lack of initiative

9. traditional: supply/demand for a worker's skills and services determine the wage or salary; negotiated wages: organized labor's bargaining strength helps determine wages; signaling theory: employers willing to pay more for people with certificates, diplomas, degrees
10. labor mobility, cost of living differences, attractiveness of location

Section 4

11. Many employers have kept unions out; additions to labor force have little loyalty

Create webs like the ones below to help you organize your answer.

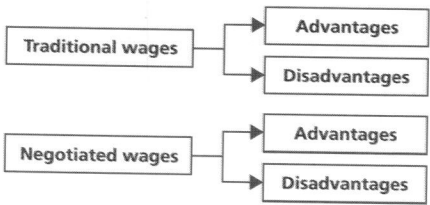

Applying Economic Concepts

1. **Civilian Labor Force** As you go to and from school, take note of the various occupations around you. List at least 10 occupations, then classify them according to the four major categories of labor.

2. **Minimum Wage** Poll at least 10 people of various ages, asking for their opinions on the following statement: There should be no minimum wage. Compile the responses and present your findings to the class.

Math Practice

The Bureau of Labor Statistics issued these statistics on workers between the ages of 16 and 24, who were employed in July 1998: "About 7 in 8 employed youth were wage and salary workers in the private sector this summer, with retail trade (7.4 million) and services (5.8 million) the largest employers. There also were sizable numbers of youth employed in manufacturing (2.2 million) and construction (1.2 million). Government employed a total of 1.5 million young people in July. Nearly 3 in 5 of the young people with government jobs were employed in local governments."

1. Total the number of individuals employed in retail, services, manufacturing, construction, and government.

2. Use the data to create a circle graph that illustrates the percentages of individuals ages 16–24 in the different economic sectors.

Thinking Like an Economist

Economists think of transactions in a market economy as being voluntary, with participants evaluating their decisions *incrementally,* meaning that they evaluate the costs and benefits of every action as they go along. Use this way of thinking to explain the rise of part-time employment.

Technology Skill

Using the Internet Visit the Bureau of Labor Statistics Web site. Search and find the summary of current employment. Then rewrite the paragraph that follows. Employment (rose/fell/remained unchanged). The unemployment rate stands at (?) percent in the latest month. Average weekly hours (declined/increased/remained unchanged), and average hourly earnings (fell/rose/were unchanged) at the end of the month.

Building Skills

Evaluating Primary and Secondary Sources Economists define wages and wage rates as the price paid for labor. Variations in wages are influenced by differences in workers' skills and nonmonetary differences in jobs. Examine the cartoon below. Explain what economists mean by a "competitive" salary.

 Practice and **assess** key social studies skills with the *Glencoe Skillbuilder Interactive Workbook, Level 2.*

CHAPTER 8: EMPLOYMENT, LABOR, AND WAGES **221**

2. Findings should demonstrate an understanding of both sides.

Math Practice

1. 18.1 million
2. Graphs should show correct percentages.

Thinking Like an Economist

Each time a company hired more part-time employees, it saw more work completed and less money spent; it was better able to fill shifts at odd hours, and it saved money because the new part-time employees had few benefits and worked less than 35 hours a week.

Technology Skill

Check students' answers for accuracy.

Building Skills

Salary is comparable to what others are paying.

Bonus Test Question

Opponents of the minimum wage believe that if the minimum wage were abolished: *(b)*

a. wages for unskilled workers would rise and employment would fall.

b. wages for unskilled workers would fall and employment would rise.

c. wages for unskilled workers rise and employment would rise.

d. wages for unskilled workers would fall and employment would fall.

to organized labor; unions are victims of their own success.

12. comparable worth: people should receive equal pay for work that is different from, but just as demanding as, other work; set-aside contracts: guaranteed contracts reserved for targeted groups

13. It enables employers to pay part-time employees less and offer them few or no benefits; flexibility of part-time workers' hours enables employers to fill shifts at odd hours.

14. in current dollars, in constant dollars, and as a percentage of average manufacturing wage

Thinking Critically

1. Answers should demonstrate an understanding of the benefits and drawbacks of union membership.

2. Answers should show understanding of theories.

Applying Economic Concepts

1. Answers should show understanding of labor categories.

Chapter 9 Resource Manager

SECTION RESOURCES

Daily Objectives

Section 1
The Economics of Taxation
1. Explain the economic impact of taxes.
2. List three criteria for effective taxes.
3. Understand the two primary principles of taxation.
4. Understand how taxes are classified.

Section 2
The Federal Tax System
1. Explain the progressive nature of the individual income tax.
2. Describe the importance of the corporate tax structure.
3. Identify other major sources of federal revenue.

Section 3
State and Local Tax Systems
1. Explain how state governments collect taxes and other revenues.
2. Differentiate between state and local revenue systems.
3. Interpret paycheck deductions.

Section 4
Current Tax Issues
1. Describe the major tax reforms since 1980.
2. Debate the advantages and disadvantages of the value-added tax.
3. Explain the features of a flat tax.
4. Discuss why future tax reforms will occur.

Reproducible Resources

Section 1
- Reproducible Lesson Plan 9-1
- Daily Lecture Notes 9-1
- Guided Reading Activity 9-1
- Reading Essentials and Study Guide 9-1
- Section Quiz 9-1*

Section 2
- Reproducible Lesson Plan 9-2
- Daily Lecture Notes 9-2
- Guided Reading Activity 9-2
- Reading Essentials and Study Guide 9-2
- Section Quiz 9-2*

Section 3
- Reproducible Lesson Plan 9-3
- Daily Lecture Notes 9-3
- Guided Reading Activity 9-3
- Reading Essentials and Study Guide 9-3
- Section Quiz 9-3*

Section 4
- Reproducible Lesson Plan 9-4
- Daily Lecture Notes 9-4
- Guided Reading Activity 9-4
- Reading Essentials and Study Guide 9-4
- Section Quiz 9-4*

Technology/Multimedia Resources

Section 1
- Daily Focus Transparency 65
- Interactive Tutor Self-Assessment Software
- ExamView® Pro Testmaker
- Presentation Plus!

Section 2
- Daily Focus Transparency 66
- Interactive Tutor Self-Assessment Software
- ExamView® Pro Testmaker
- Presentation Plus!

Section 3
- Daily Focus Transparency 67
- Interactive Tutor Self-Assessment Software
- ExamView® Pro Testmaker
- Presentation Plus!

Section 4
- Daily Focus Transparency 69
- Vocabulary PuzzleMaker CD-ROM
- Interactive Tutor Self-Assessment Software
- ExamView® Pro Testmaker
- Presentation Plus!

 Transparency   CD-ROM   Software Blackline Master

 Videodisc   Audio Program Videocassette

Also available in Spanish

Chapter 9 Resource Manager

TeacherWorks™ All-In-One Planner and Resource Center

- **Interactive Teacher Edition** Access your Teacher Wraparound Edition and your classroom resources with a few easy clicks.
- **Interactive Lesson Planner** Planning has never been easier! Organize your week, month, semester, or year with all the lesson helps you need to make teaching creative, timely, and relevant.

Use Glencoe's **Presentation Plus!** multimedia teacher tool to easily present dynamic lessons that visually excite your students. Using Microsoft PowerPoint® you can customize the presentations to create your own personalized lessons.

ACTIVITY

From the Classroom of...

Mark Rothman
Paul D. Schreiber
High School
Port Washington, NY

Taxation: Goals and Side Effects

Explain to students that, theoretically, any tax action is undertaken to advance an accepted social goal, for example, to promote freedom through a strong military, or to decrease unemployment through public projects. Whether these social goals have actually been advanced is a source of debate. Even the most effective use of taxation sometimes produces totally unforeseen side effects.

Write the list below on the board or on a handout. For each tax action, ask the students to tell **(1)** what they think the goal is, and **(2)** what, if any, unexpected side effects (positive or negative) might result.

1. Property taxes are used to fund public education.
2. Business taxes are decreased.
3. High taxes are levied on cigarettes and alcohol.
4. Sales tax is no longer allowed as a deduction on federal income tax returns.
5. Income tax rates are lowered for most people.
6. High import taxes are imposed on foreign-made cars.
7. Corporate tax rates are lowered.

National Council on Economic Education

THE **Economics**America AND **Economics**International PROGRAMS

Voluntary National Content Standards in Economics
Emphasized in Chapter 9

Content Standard 16

For a complete listing of NCEE Standards and entire text correlation, see Teacher pages in front of book.

Resources Available from NCEE
- Capstone: The Nation's High School Economics Course
- Civics and Government: Focus on Economics
- Personal Decision Making: Focus on Economics

To order these materials or to contact your state Council on Economic Education about workshops and programs, call 1-800-338-1192 or visit www.nationalcouncil.org

Chapter 9 Resource Manager

Economic Concept Transparency 12:
The Role of the Government

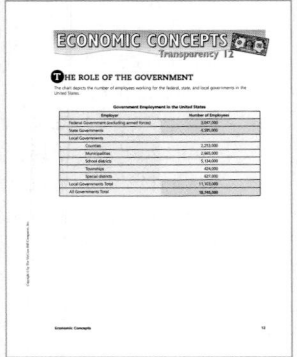

Consumer Application
Activity 14

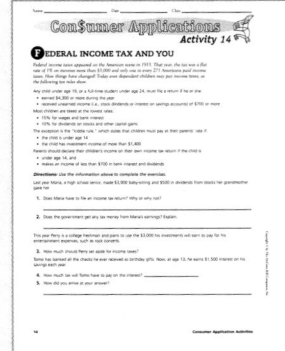

Free Enterprise
Activity 14

Enrichment Activity 9

Cooperative Learning
Activity 14

Math Practice
Activity 14

Economic Cartoon 14

Primary and Secondary
Source Reading 14

Economic Vocabulary
Activity 9

Reteaching Activity 9

Critical Thinking
Activity 14

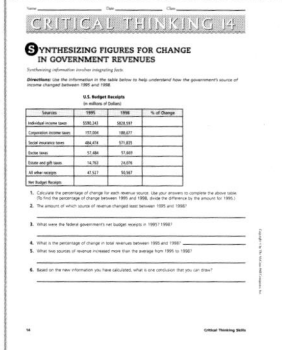

Reinforcing Economic
Skill 27

Chapter 9 Resource Manager

ASSESSMENT AND EVALUATION

Chapter 9 Test Form A

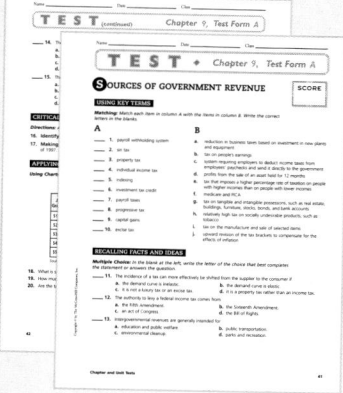

Chapter 9 Test Form B

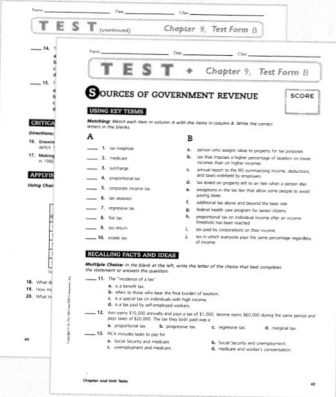

Performance Assessment Activity 14

ExamView® Pro Testmaker

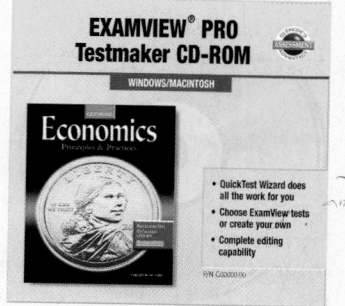

- QuickTest Wizard does all the work for you
- Choose ExamView tests or create your own
- Complete editing capability

SPANISH RESOURCES

The following Spanish language materials are available in the Spanish Resources binder:

 Spanish Economic Vocabulary Activities

 Spanish Reteaching Activities

 Spanish Section Quizzes

 Spanish Economic Concepts Transparencies

Also available:

  Spanish Chapter 9 Audio Program Activity and Test

TECHNOLOGY/MULTIMEDIA

- Vocabulary PuzzleMaker CD-ROM
- Interactive Tutor Self-Assessment Software
- ExamView® Pro Testmaker
- Audio Program (English or Spanish)
- NBR Economics & You Video Program (English or Spanish)
- MindJogger Videoquiz
- Interactive Economics! CD-ROM
- Presentation Plus!
- TeacherWorks CD-ROM
- Glencoe Skillbuilder Interactive Workbook CD-ROM, Level 2

ECONOMICS Online

Use our Web site for additional resources. All essential content is covered in the Student Edition.

You and your students can visit epp.glencoe.com, the Web site companion to **Economics: Principles and Practices.** This innovative integration of electronic and print media offers your students a wealth of opportunities. The student text directs students to the Web site for the following options:

- Chapter Overviews
- Student Web Activities
- Self-Check Quizzes
- Textbook Updates

Answers are provided for you in the Web Activity Lesson Plan. Additional Web resources and interactive puzzles are also available.

Performance Assessment

Refer to Activity 14 in the *Performance Assessment Strategies and Activities* booklet.

 BLOCK SCHEDULING

ECONOMICS Online

Introduce students to chapter content and key terms by having them access **Chapter Overview 9** at epp.glencoe.com

NIGHTLY BUSINESS REPORT

 ECONOMICS & YOU

Chapter 15
Disc 1, Side 2

How the Government Spends, Collects, and Owes

After viewing this segment, students should be able to:

• Describe how the government finances budget deficits.

Also available in VHS.

GLENCOE TECHNOLOGY

Use **MindJogger Videoquiz** to preview the Chapter 9 content.

Sources of Government Revenue

Economics & You

Have you wondered or questioned why the paychecks you've seen have so many deductions? In **Chapter 9,** you will learn more about taxes and revenues raised by all levels of government. To learn about the different types of taxes collected by state and federal governments, view the Chapter 15 video lesson:

How Government Collects

ECONOMICS Online

Chapter Overview Visit the *Economics: Principles and Practices* Web site at epp.glencoe.com and click on **Chapter 9—Chapter Overviews** to preview chapter information.

While governments receive revenue from a variety of sources, the most important source is taxes.

➕ EXTRA CREDIT PROJECT

Have students create a television-viewing log for news items concerning government and the economy—with specific reference to taxation. Students should record the date, the subject of the item, and the length of time given to the item. When study of the chapter is completed, have students compare and discuss their logs.

The Economics of Taxation

Study Guide

Main Idea
Taxes are the single most important way of raising revenue for the government.

Reading Strategy
Graphic Organizer As you read the section, complete a graphic organizer similar to the one below by listing the criteria for taxes to be effective. Then, define each of the criteria in your own words.

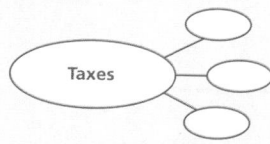

Taxes

Key Terms
sin tax, incidence of a tax, tax loophole, individual income tax, sales tax, benefit principle of taxation, ability-to-pay principle of taxation, proportional tax, average tax rate, progressive tax, marginal tax rate, regressive tax

Objectives
After studying this section, you will be able to:
1. **Explain** the economic impact of taxes.
2. **List** three criteria for effective taxes.
3. **Understand** the two primary principles of taxation.
4. **Understand** how taxes are classified.

Applying Economic Concepts
Equity Read to find out what role equity, or fairness, plays in administering taxes.

Cover Story

America to Celebrate Tax Freedom Day

WASHINGTON, D.C.—America can celebrate Tax Freedom Day® on May 3, 2001, according to the Tax Foundation's annual calculation. That means that the nation's taxpayers have to work from January 1, 2001,

Taxpayer fills out tax form

to the 123rd day of the year before earning enough money to pay for government—federal, state and local—and start spending money on themselves. . . . Individual income taxes represent the largest component of Americans' tax bills. . . .

—Tax Foundation, April 23, 2001

An enormous amount of money is required to run the federal, state, and local governments of the United States. In 2001, all three levels of government collected approximately $3.3 trillion–or about $11,800 for every man, woman, and child in the United States. Whether we count the dollars, or the days needed to earn the dollars as illustrated in the cover story, it all adds up to a staggering sum.

Total revenue collections by all levels of government have grown dramatically over the years. **Figure 9.1** shows that these revenues, even when adjusted for inflation and population growth, increased by approximately 800 percent since 1940.

Economic Impact of Taxes

 Taxes and other governmental revenues influence the economy by affecting resource allocation, consumer behavior, and the nation's productivity and growth. In addition, the burden of a tax does not always fall on the party being taxed, because some of the tax can be transferred to others.

CHAPTER 9: SOURCES OF GOVERNMENT REVENUE **223**

2 TEACH

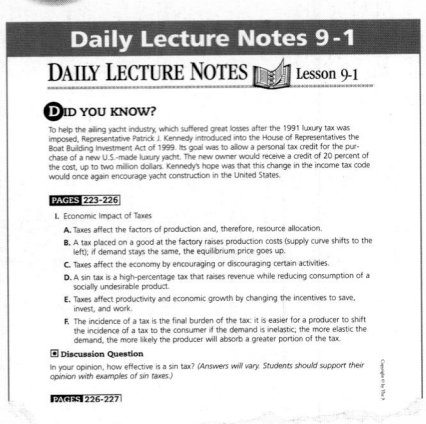

Daily Lecture Notes 9-1

ECONOMICS
AT A GLANCE

Answer: *Total government receipts grew from 500% of the 1940 level to over 700%.*

L1 Developing Graphs

Direct students' attention to the discussion of the economic importance of taxes on pages 223–226. Ask students to draw demand and supply curves to graphically illustrate the situations considered in the discussion. **ELL**

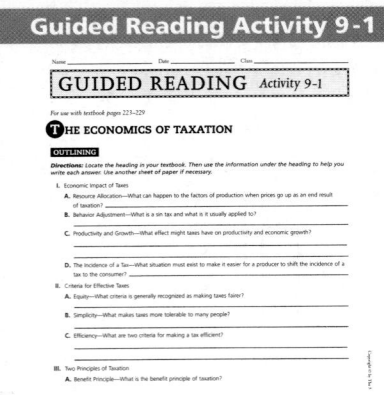

Guided Reading Activity 9-1

STANDARD & POOR'S

Figure 9.1

Total Government Receipts Per Capita, Adjusted for Inflation

As a percentage of 1940

- 800%
- 700%
- 600%
- 500%
- 400%
- 300%
- 200%
- 100%
- 0%

1940 1950 1960 1970 1980 1990 2000 2001

1950–1999 - Spending by all levels of government increases 2.72% annually

1990s - Economic growth and higher marginal tax rates contribute to increased revenues.

Source: Bureau of Economic Analysis and the Department of the Census, various forms

Using Graphs Total receipts by all levels of government have increased significantly over time. **What information does the graph show for the period 1980 to 2000?**

ECONOMICS Online
Visit epp.glencoe.com and click on *Textbook Updates—Chapter 9* for an update of the data.

Resource Allocation

The factors of production are affected whenever a tax is levied. A tax placed on a good or service at the factory raises the cost of production, which shifts the supply curve to the left. If demand remains unchanged, the equilibrium price of the product goes up.

People react to the higher price in a predictable manner—they buy less. When sales fall, some firms cut back on production and some productive resources—land, capital, labor, and entrepreneurs—will have to go to other industries to be employed.

In 1991, for example, Congress enacted a luxury tax on expensive cars, private aircraft, yachts, and other costly items in order to raise additional tax revenue from the wealthy. Because the demand for luxury goods was elastic, however, higher prices drove customers away, and unemployment soared in some of these industries.

Behavior Adjustment

Often taxes are used to encourage or discourage certain types of activities. For example, homeowners are allowed to use interest payments on mortgages as tax deductions—a practice that encourages home ownership. Interest payments on other consumer debt, such as credit cards, is not deductible—a practice that makes credit card use less attractive.

The so-called **sin tax**—a relatively high tax designed to raise revenue and reduce consumption of a socially undesirable product such as liquor or tobacco—is another example of how a tax can be used to change behavior. Canada used a sin tax in the 1980s when it quadrupled the tobacco tax, pushing the price of a pack of cigarettes to more than $4, and reducing cigarette consumption by one-third.

Efforts to tax tobacco in the United States, however, show that tobacco, because of its addictive nature, is still an inelastic product. For example, it is

224 UNIT 3 MACROECONOMICS: INSTITUTIONS

MEETING SPECIAL NEEDS ACTIVITY

Learning Style: Intrapersonal Have students who outline the information on pages 223–226. Tell them to write the title "Economic Impact of Taxes" and the pages' bold-type headings on a sheet of paper, leaving space for supporting ideas. Copy the outline sample below on the board for students to use as a model.

Economic Impact of Taxes

I. Resource Allocation
   A. Taxes raise the cost of production.
   B. Prices go up.
   C. People buy less.

▸ Refer to *Inclusion for the Social Studies Classroom Strategies and Activities* in the TCR.

estimated that a $1 tax per pack is not enough to significantly affect consumption–and thus the government could raise billions of dollars in tax revenues.

Productivity and Growth

Finally, taxes can affect productivity and economic growth by changing the incentives to save, invest, and work. Some people think that taxes are already so high that it affects their incentive to work. Why, they argue, should a person earn additional income if much of it will be paid out in taxes?

While these arguments have validity, it is difficult to tell if we have reached the point where taxes are too high. For example, even the wealthiest individuals pay less than half of their taxable income to state and local governments in the form of income taxes. Are these taxes so high that they do not have the incentive to earn an additional $10 million because they can only keep half? Would they work any harder if income taxes only took thirty percent of their income? Or, would they work just as hard if they paid seventy percent of the extra income in taxes?

While we do not have exact answers to these questions, we do know that there must be some level of taxes at which productivity and growth would suffer. This is just one of many reasons why people favor lower taxes.

The Incidence of a Tax

The party being taxed is not always the one that bears the burden of a tax. For example, suppose a city wants to tax a local utility company to raise revenue. If the utility is able to raise its rates, consumers will likely bear most of the burden in the form of higher utility bills. If a company's rates are regulated, and if the company's profits are not large enough to absorb the tax increase, shareholders may receive smaller dividends–placing the burden of the tax on the owners. Another alternative is that the company may postpone a pay raise–shifting the burden of the tax to its employees.

The **incidence of a tax**–or the final burden of the tax–can be predicted with the help of supply and demand analysis. Examine the demand curve in **Panel A** of **Figure 9.2**. You see that it is relatively more elastic than the one shown in **Panel B,** although the supply curves are exactly the same in both. A $1 tax

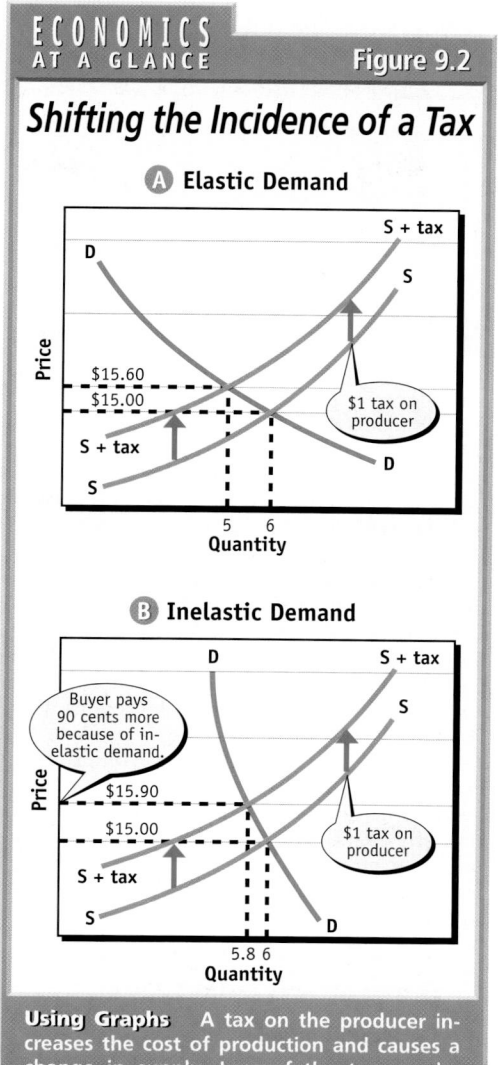

ECONOMICS AT A GLANCE
Figure 9.2

Shifting the Incidence of a Tax

A Elastic Demand

Price

$15.60
$15.00

S + tax

S

D

D

S + tax

S

$1 tax on producer

5 6
Quantity

B Inelastic Demand

Price

D

S + tax

S

Buyer pays 90 cents more because of inelastic demand.

$15.90

$15.00

S + tax

S

D

$1 tax on producer

5.8 6
Quantity

Using Graphs A tax on the producer increases the cost of production and causes a change in supply. Less of the tax can be shifted back to the taxpayer if demand is elastic, as in A. More of the tax can be shifted to the taxpayer if demand is inelastic, as in B. Who is likely to bear the greater burden—the producer or the consumer—if a tax is placed on medicine?

CHAPTER 9: SOURCES OF GOVERNMENT REVENUE 225

ECONOMICS AT A GLANCE

Answer: *The demand for medicine is generally inelastic, and the consumer will bear the greater burden of a tax on medicine.*

L1 Creating Posters

Have students work in small groups to create posters that illustrate one or all three of the criteria for taxes. Have groups display and explain their posters. **ELL**

CYBERNOMICS

Electronic Tax Forms Income-tax payers who once picked up tax forms at the library or the local accountant's office can now stay home and order a Federal Tax Products CD-ROM on the Internet. The CD contains current year tax forms, including forms that may be filled in and filed electronically.

FREE ENTERPRISE ACTIVITY

Ask students to raise their hands if they pay taxes. Ask a student whose hand was not raised if he or she buys clothing, gasoline, food, or magazines, and point out that in almost all states such articles are taxed when they are purchased. Ask another student whose hand was not raised if he or she attends music concerts or sporting events, and point out that the cost of the ticket probably includes a special entertainment tax. Then have students make a list of goods or services they may have purchased in the last week on which they paid a tax. Have students compare and discuss their lists.

ECONOMICS Online

Objectives, goals, and answers to the student activity can be found in the **Web Activity Lesson Plan** feature at epp.glencoe.com

F.Y.I.

The effect of a tax depends on the elasticities of the demand and supply curves.

L2 Journalism

Encourage students to imagine that they are writers for a current affairs magazine whose readers are mostly junior high students. Ask them to write a 250- to 300-word article titled "The Economics of Taxation" suitable for their readership.

CURRICULUM CONNECTION

History In the United States the idea of taxing income goes back to the 1640s when the colony of New Plymouth taxed the "faculties" (earning power) of individuals and the "returns and gains" of tradespeople and craftspersons.

STANDARD & POOR'S INFOBYTE

Taxable Income Taxable income is the amount of income that is subject to taxation by the state and federal government. It is the adjusted gross income of wages, salaries, dividends, interest, capital gains, etc., less allowable adjustments deductions, which include but are not limited to contributions to retirement accounts, business expenses, and capital losses.

on the producer in **Panel A** increases the price of the product by 60 cents—which means that the producer must have absorbed the other 40 cents. On the other hand, the demand curve in **Panel B** is relatively inelastic. Here we can see that the exact same tax on the producer results in a 90-cent increase in price, which means that the producer must have absorbed the other 10 cents. The figure clearly shows that it is much easier for a producer to shift the incidence of a tax to the consumer if the consumer's demand curve is relatively inelastic. The more elastic the demand curve, the greater the portion of the tax that will be absorbed by the producer.

In the case of the 1991 luxury tax on private aircraft, the burden of the tax fell on the producer because the demand for small private aircraft was relatively elastic. The unemployment that resulted in the aircraft industry, along with the costs of coping with the unemployment, convinced Congress to remove the tax.

Criteria for Effective Taxes

Some taxes will always be needed, so we want to make them as effective as possible. To do so, taxes must meet criteria: they must be equitable, simple, and efficient.

Equity

The first criterion is equity or fairness. Most people feel that taxes should be impartial and just. Problems arise, however, when we ask, *what is fair?*

226 UNIT 3 MACROECONOMICS: INSTITUTIONS

You might believe that a tax is fair only if everyone pays the same amount. Your friend concludes, on the other hand, that a tax is fair only if wealthier people pay more than those with lower incomes.

There is no overriding guide that we can use to make taxes completely equitable. However, it does make sense to avoid **tax loopholes**—exceptions or oversights in the tax law that allow some people and businesses to avoid paying taxes. Loopholes are a fairness issue, and most people oppose them on the grounds of equity. Taxes generally are viewed as being fairer if they have fewer exceptions, deductions, and exemptions.

Simplicity

A second criterion is simplicity. Tax laws should be written so that both the taxpayer and the tax collector can understand them. This task is not easy, but people seem more willing to tolerate taxes when they understand them.

The **individual income tax**—the tax on people's earnings—is a prime example of a complex tax. The entire code is thousands of pages long, and even the simplified instructions the Internal Revenue Service (IRS) sends out to taxpayers are lengthy and often difficult to understand. As a result, many people dislike the individual income tax code, in part because they do not fully understand it.

A **sales tax**—a general tax levied on most consumer purchases—is much simpler. The sales tax is paid at the time of purchase, and the amount of the tax is computed and collected by the merchant. Some goods such as food, child care, and medicine may be exempt, but if a product is taxed then everyone who buys the product pays it.

ECONOMICS Online

Student Web Activity Visit the *Economics: Principles and Practices* Web site at epp.glencoe.com and click on **Chapter 9—Student Web Activities** for an activity on the individual income tax.

CRITICAL THINKING

Distinguishing Fact from Opinion Tell students that failure to distinguish fact from opinion can muddy the debate over fairness and taxes. Remind students that facts can be proven but opinions are based on people's differing values and beliefs. Read aloud the statements below and ask students to identify which is a fact and which is an opinion:

a. The fairest tax is the one that everybody pays. *(opinion)*
b. The luxury tax on private aircraft led to higher unemployment among workers in that industry. *(fact)*

Have students search for editorials dealing with taxes in newspapers or magazines and identify other examples of facts and opinions in the writing.

Efficiency

A third criterion for an effective tax is efficiency. A tax should be relatively easy to administer and reasonably successful at generating revenue.

The individual income tax satisfies this requirement fairly well. Whenever someone is paid, the employer withholds a portion of the employee's pay and sends it to the IRS. At the end of the year, the employer notifies each employee of the amount of tax withheld. Because most payroll records are now computerized, neither the employer nor the employee is unduly burdened by this withholding system.

Other taxes, especially those collected in toll booths on state highways, are considerably less efficient. The state invests millions of dollars in heavily reinforced booths that span the highway. The cost to commuters, besides the toll, is the wear and tear on their automobiles. After giving a few quarters and dimes to the attendant, drivers take off again to repeat the process a few miles down the road.

Efficiency also means that the tax should raise enough revenue to be worthwhile. If it does not, or if it harms the economy in other ways, the tax has little value. One example is the luxury tax on small private aircraft in 1991. According to the IRS, only $53,000 in luxury tax revenues were collected that year because so few planes were sold. This turned out to be less than the unemployment benefits paid to workers who lost jobs in that industry. This is the reason Congress quickly repealed the luxury tax on small aircraft.

Two Principles of Taxation

Taxes in the United States are based on two principles that have evolved over the years. These principles are the benefit principle and the ability-to-pay principle.

Benefit Principle

Many taxes are based on the **benefit principle of taxation:** Those who benefit from government goods and services should pay in proportion to the amount of benefits they receive.

Think about the taxes you pay for gasoline. Because the gas tax is built into the price of gasoline at the pump, people who drive more than others pay more gas taxes—and therefore pay for

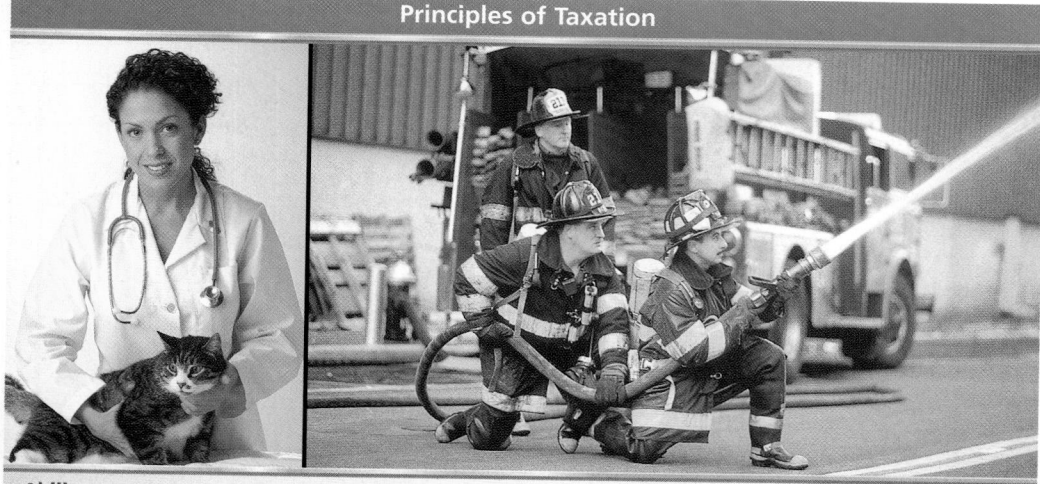

Principles of Taxation

Ability-to-Pay The veterinarian (left) and the firefighters (right) both have to pay taxes. **According to the ability-to-pay principle, how is the amount each person has to pay determined?**

CHAPTER 9: SOURCES OF GOVERNMENT REVENUE **227**

CHAPTER 9
Section 1, pages 223–229

L2 Applying Ideas

Have students review the discussion of the three criteria for effective taxes on pages 226–227, and the two principles of taxation on pages 227–229. Then organize the class into five groups, assigning each group one criterion or principle. Have groups analyze the property, state sales, and income taxes to see which tax best fits their assigned principle or criterion. Have group representatives present their findings, and then have students vote on which taxes they prefer.

THE GLOBAL ECONOMY

Taxes Around the World If each student were to ask 10 people the question, "Do you pay too much in taxes?" the vast majority of responses would be in the affirmative. A recent study suggests, however, that Americans are among the least taxed people in the industrialized world. In the United States all taxes account for about 30 percent of gross domestic product (GDP). Of the world's 24 wealthiest nations, only Turkey and Australia collect a smaller percentage of GDP in taxes. Most leading industrialized nations pay close to 40 percent. The study concluded that taxes in the U.S. could be raised substantially and the country would still remain among the least taxed nations.

Visual Instruction

Answer to Caption:
The amount each pays depends on how much income each earns.

EXTENDING THE CONTENT

Tax Equity Although the tax system has been modified to make it more equitable, it is impossible to have a system that is fair for everyone and that is seen by everyone as fair. An analysis of the benefit and ability-to-pay principles of taxation illustrates this point. As is noted in the text on pages 228–229, it is often hard to measure exactly who benefits from a particular government service and even harder to assess how much benefit each person receives. In addition, although two families may have equal incomes, because of different circumstances they may not have the same ability to pay. This difficulty in determining equity is one reason why there are several different kinds of taxes at the federal, state, and local levels.

③ ASSESS

Assign Section 1 Assessment as homework or as an in-class activity.

💾 Have students use **Interactive Tutor Self-Assessment Software** to review Section 1.

ECONOMICS
AT A GLANCE

Answer: *progressive tax*

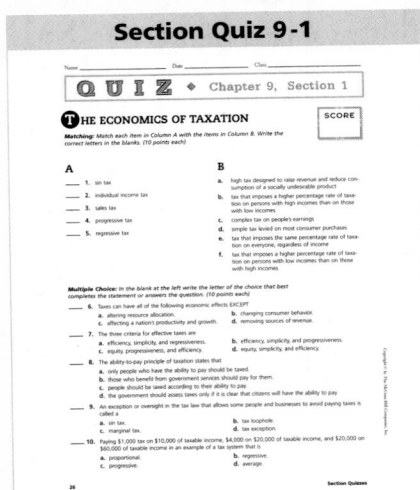

more of the upkeep of our nation's highways. Taxes on truck tires operate on the same principle. Because heavy vehicles like trucks are likely to put the most wear and tear on roads, the tire tax is another way to tie the cost of repair and upkeep to the user.

The benefit principle has two limitations. The first is that many government services provide the greatest benefit to those who can least afford to pay for them. People who receive welfare payments or live in subsidized housing, for example, usually have the lowest incomes. Even if they could pay something, they would not be able to pay in proportion to the benefits they receive.

The second limitation is that the benefits often are hard to measure. Are people who pay for gas the only ones who benefit from the roads built with gas taxes? What about property owners whose property increases in value because of the improved access? What about hotel and restaurant owners who profit from tourists arriving by car or bus? These people may buy very little gasoline, but they still benefit from the facilities that the gas tax helps provide.

Ability-to-Pay Principle

The second principle is the **ability-to-pay principle of taxation**—the belief that people should be taxed according to their ability to pay, regardless of the benefits they receive. An example is the individual income tax, which requires individuals with higher incomes to pay more than those with lower incomes.

The ability-to-pay principle is based on two factors. First, it recognizes that societies cannot always measure the benefits derived from government spending. Second, it assumes that people with higher incomes suffer less discomfort paying taxes than people with lower incomes.

ECONOMICS
AT A GLANCE

Figure 9.3

Three Types of Taxes

Type of Tax	Income of $10,000	Income of $100,000	Summary
Proportional	*City Occupational Tax* $97.50 or .975% of income	*City Occupational Tax* $975.00 or .975% of income	As income goes up, the percent of income paid in taxes *stays the same*.
Progressive	*Federal Income Tax* $1,000 paid in taxes, or 10% of total income	*Federal Income Tax* $25,000 paid in taxes, or 25% of total income	As income goes up, the percent of income paid in taxes *goes up*.
Regressive	*State Sales Tax* $5,000 in food and clothing purchases, taxed at 4% for a total tax of $200 or 2% of income.	*State Sales Tax* $20,000 in food and clothing purchases, taxed at 4% for a total tax of: $800 or .8% of income	As income goes, up the percent of income paid in taxes *goes down*.

Using Tables Proportional, progressive, and regressive are the three main types of taxes. Under which type of tax do individuals with lower incomes pay a smaller percentage than do those with higher incomes?

INTERDISCIPLINARY CONNECTIONS ACTIVITY

The Environment To curtail pollution, governments are levying more taxes based on the benefit principle. France was the first nation to levy a direct pollution tax, which requires manufacturers to pay tax on every unit of pollution they discharge. Ask students to imagine that they are environmental consultants whom world leaders ask for tax suggestions. **Ask:** Whom would you recommend the leaders of Mexico City tax to raise money for cleaning up air pollution from cars? *(tax car dealers who sell cars without antipollution devices)* **Ask:** Whom would you recommend Canadian leaders tax to combat the acid rain caused by U.S. factories? *(a tax on goods coming into Canada from the United States, the factors that caused acid rain)*

For example, a family of four with an annual taxable income of $20,000 needs every cent to pay for necessities. At a tax rate of 14 percent, this family pays $2,800—a huge amount for them. On the other hand, a comparable family with a $100,000 taxable income could afford to pay a higher tax rate and suffer much less discomfort.

Types of Taxes

 Three general types of taxes exist in the United States today—proportional, progressive, and regressive. Each type of tax is classified according to the way in which the tax burden changes as income changes.

A **proportional tax** imposes the same percentage rate of taxation on everyone, regardless of income. If the income tax rate is 20 percent, an individual with $10,000 in taxable income pays $2,000 in taxes. A person with $100,000 in taxable income pays $20,000.

If the percentage tax rate is constant, the **average tax rate**—total taxable income divided by the total income—is constant, regardless of income. If a person's income goes up, the *percentage* of total income paid in taxes does not change.

A **progressive tax** is a tax that imposes a higher percentage rate of taxation on persons with higher incomes. A progressive tax claims not only a larger absolute (dollar) amount but also a larger percentage of income as income increases. Progressive taxes usually use a **marginal tax rate,** the tax rate that applies to the next dollar of taxable income, that increases as the amount of taxable income increases. Therefore, the *percentage* of income paid in taxes increases as income goes up.

Suppose the tax system requires a person to pay $1,000 on $10,000 of taxable income, $4,000 on $20,000 of taxable income, or $30,000 on $100,000 of taxable income. The tax is progressive over this range because the percent of income paid in taxes—10, 20, and 30 percent respectively—rises as income rises.

A **regressive tax** is a tax that imposes a *higher* percentage rate of taxation on low incomes than on high incomes. For example, a person with an annual income of $10,000 may spend $5,000 on food and clothing, while another person with an annual income of $100,000 may spend $20,000 on the same essentials. If the state sales tax is 4 percent, the person with the lower income is paying a higher percentage of total income in taxes.

Section 1 Assessment

Checking for Understanding

1. **Main Idea** Using your notes from the graphic organizer activity on page 223, list the ways that taxes influence the economy.

2. **Key Terms** Define sin tax, incidence of a tax, tax loophole, individual income tax, sales tax, benefit principle of taxation, ability-to-pay principle of taxation, proportional tax, average tax rate, progressive tax, marginal tax rate, regressive tax.

3. **Describe** the economic impact of taxes.

4. **List** three criteria used to evaluate taxes.

5. **Summarize** the two main principles of taxation.

6. **Explain** the characteristics of proportional, progressive, and regressive taxes.

Applying Economic Concepts

7. **Equity** Which of the two principles of taxation—the benefit principle or the ability-to-pay principle—do you feel is the most equitable? Explain your answer. Be sure to include in your answer how the two principles differ from one another.

Critical Thinking

8. **Drawing Inferences** Think about the last tax you paid. Using the criteria for progressive, proportional, and regressive taxes, determine which type of tax you think it is and explain why.

Practice and assess key social studies skills with the Glencoe Skillbuilder Interactive Workbook, Level 2.

CHAPTER 9: SOURCES OF GOVERNMENT REVENUE **229**

Section 1 Assessment Answers

1. resource allocation, behavior adjustment, productivity and growth, incidence of a tax

2. All vocabulary terms are defined in the text.

3. They affect resource allocation, consumer behavior, and the nation's productivity and growth.

4. equity, simplicity, efficiency

5. Answers should reflect content on pages 227–229.

6. proportional: impose same percentage rate of taxation on everyone; progressive: impose higher percentage rate on persons with higher incomes; regressive: impose a higher percentage rate on lower incomes as compared to high incomes

7. Answers should show application of content from pages 227–229.

8. Answers should demonstrate an understanding of the various forms of taxes.

Reteach

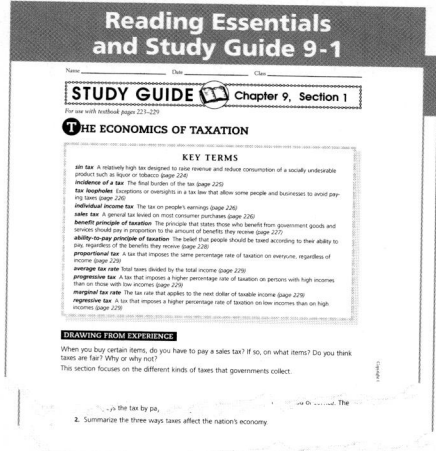

Reading Essentials and Study Guide 9-1

Enrich

Have students prepare handouts with brief explanations of the three criteria for effective taxes and the three types of taxes. Have students distribute the handouts to family members, neighbors, and friends, asking them which kind of tax would be best in terms of the criteria. Have students collate their findings to see which type of tax is most favored.

4 CLOSE

Write the following on the board: *The only fair tax is a tax on someone else.* Then have students discuss how equity can be achieved in the tax system.

Teaching Skills

On the board, list the following topics and ask students to identify the library resource or resources that would contain information about each topic.

- Information about the president in office when the first major federal income tax was levied *(an encyclopedia, a biographical dictionary, or a computer database)*
- Distribution of income by country *(an atlas or an almanac)*
- Recent debates over tax reform in Congress *(an almanac or periodical guide)*
- Titles of books on income tax preparation *(card catalog)*
- A brief history of taxes *(encyclopedia)*

Additional Practice

Reinforcing Economic Skill 27

Name _____ Date _____ Class _____

Reinforcing Economic Skills **Chapter 27**

USING LIBRARY RESOURCES

Libraries contain many resources. These resources include traditional resources, such as encyclopedias, atlases, almanacs, and periodicals, as well as online resources, such as computer databases and access to the World Wide Web. Knowing which resources to use will improve the quality and efficiency of your research.

Directions: *You are writing a term paper on trade between the United States and Japan. To make the report interesting, you want to include many real-world examples. You also want to make sure that your report covers very recent developments. Choose sources from among the following:*

Business Week, Fortune, Forbes—business magazines published weekly
Statistical Abstract of the United States—published yearly
World Almanac, Information Please Almanac—published yearly
World Development Report—published yearly
The World Wide Web

1. What source would you use to find out the value of Japan's exports to the United States between 1985 and 1995?

2. What source would you use to find out how economic conditions in Japan differ from economic conditions in the United States?

3. Where would you find examples of U.S. businesses that have been successful in Japan?

GLENCOE TECHNOLOGY

Glencoe Skillbuilder Interactive Workbook, Level 2

This interactive CD-ROM reinforces student mastery of essential social studies skills.

Using Library Resources

Your teacher has assigned a major research report, so you go to the library. As you wander the aisles surrounded by books, you wonder: Where do I start my research? Which reference works should I use?

Deciding where to start your research and which reference works to use are important in doing a research report.

Learning the Skill

Libraries contain many resources. Here are brief descriptions of important ones:

Reference Books Reference books include encyclopedias, biographical dictionaries, atlases, and almanacs.

- An encyclopedia is a set of books containing short articles on many subjects arranged alphabetically.

- A biographical dictionary includes brief biographies listed alphabetically by last names.

- An atlas is a collection of maps and charts for locating geographic features and places. An atlas can be general or thematic.

- An almanac is an annually updated reference that provides current statistics and historical information on a wide range of subjects.

Card Catalogs Every library has a card catalog, either on cards or computer or both, which lists every book in the library. Search for books by author, subject, or title. Computerized card catalogs will also advise you on the book's availability.

Periodical Guides A periodical guide is a set of books listing topics covered in magazines and newspaper articles.

Computer Databases Computer databases provide collections of information organized for rapid search and retrieval. For example, many libraries carry reference materials on CD-ROM.

Internet Libraries can often suggest clearinghouse sites, online databases, and other reputable sites.

Practicing the Skill

Suppose you are assigned a research report dealing with the introduction of the U.S. income tax. Read the questions below, then decide which of the sources described above you would use to answer each question and why.

1. During which year was the federal income tax established?

2. What was the purpose of the income tax when it was introduced in 1913?

3. How did the public react to the tax?

Application Activity

Using library resources, research the origins of Social Security taxes. Present the information you find to the class.

 Practice and assess key social studies skills with the Glencoe Skillbuilder Interactive Workbook, Level 2.

Answers to Practicing the Skill

Answers should include an appropriate resource and explanation as to why student chose that resource.

1. almanac
2. encyclopedia
3. encyclopedia or card catalog

The Federal Tax System

Study Guide

Main Idea
The federal government raises revenue from a variety of taxes.

Reading Strategy
Graphic Organizer As you read the section, complete a graphic organizer like the one below to identify the federal government's most important revenue sources.

Revenue sources

Key Terms
payroll withholding system, Internal Revenue Service (IRS), tax return, indexing, FICA, medicare, payroll

tax, corporate income tax, excise tax, luxury good, estate tax, gift tax, customs duty, user fee

Objectives
After studying this section, you will be able to:
1. **Explain** the progressive nature of the individual income tax.
2. **Describe** the importance of the corporate tax structure.
3. **Identify** other major sources of federal revenue.

Applying Economic Concepts
Federal Taxes You, the American taxpayer, are the source of most of the money the government spends. Almost all federal government revenue comes from taxation.

① FOCUS

Section Overview
This section describes sources of federal revenue.

BELLRINGER
Motivational Activity

 Project **transparency** and have students answer questions.

 Available as blackline master.

Daily Focus Transparency 66

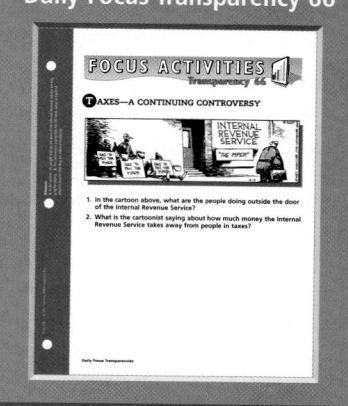

Cover Story

The Costs of Taxation

Taxes are often a source of heated political debate. In 1776 the anger of the American Colonies over British taxes sparked the American Revolution. More than two centuries later Ronald Reagan was elected president on a platform of large cuts in personal income taxes, and during his eight years in the White House the top tax rate on income fell from 70 percent to 28 percent. In 1992 Bill Clinton was elected in part because incumbent George Bush had broken his 1988 campaign promise, "Read my lips: no new taxes."

American colonists protested against British taxes and collectors.

—N. Gregory Mankiw, *Microeconomics*, 1998

The federal government collects taxes from a number of sources. The most important sources of government revenue are individual income taxes, Social Security taxes, and corporate income taxes.

Individual Income Taxes

In 1913 the Sixteenth Amendment to the United States Constitution was ratified, allowing Congress to levy an income tax. The amendment states that:

> The Congress shall have power to lay and collect taxes on incomes, from whatever source derived, without apportionment among the several States, and without regard to any census or enumeration.

Since the amendment was ratified, the federal government has relied heavily on the individual income tax—the tax on people's earnings—to finance its operations. As **Figure 9.4** shows, the federal government collected nearly 50 percent of its total revenue from taxes on people's earnings.

CHAPTER 9: SOURCES OF GOVERNMENT REVENUE **231**

Study Guide

Reading Strategy
Have students create the graphic organizer.
Answers to Graphic: *individual income taxes, FICA taxes, corporate income taxes*

Preteaching Vocabulary
Ask students to use any Key Terms they know in written sentences.

RESOURCE MANAGER

Reproducible Masters
- Reproducible Lesson Plan 9-2
- Daily Lecture Notes 9-2
- Guided Reading Activity 9-2
- Reading Essentials and Study Guide 9-2
- Section Quiz 9-2

Transparencies
- Daily Focus Transparency 66

Multimedia
- Interactive Tutor Self-Assessment Software
- ExamView® Pro Testmaker
- Presentation Plus!

2 TEACH

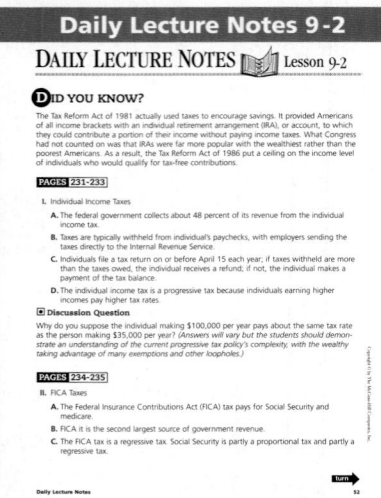

Daily Lecture Notes 9-2

L1 Constructing a Chart

Draw a two-column chart on the board using *Federal Taxes* and *Type of Tax* as headings. Ask students to copy the chart in their notebooks. Have students complete the chart by listing the federal taxes described in the section in the first column, and classifying each as proportional, progressive, or regressive in the second column. Call on students to present their charts and explain why they chose the various classifications. **ELL**

STANDARD &POOR'S

Answer: *It ended completely.*

Payroll Deductions

In most cases, the individual income tax is paid over time through a **payroll withholding system,** a system that requires an employer to automatically deduct income taxes from an employee's paycheck and send it directly to the government. The agency that receives the tax payment is the **Internal Revenue Service (IRS),** the branch of the U.S. Treasury Department in charge of collecting taxes.

After the close of the tax year on December 31, and before April 15 of the following year, the employee files a **tax return**—an annual report to the IRS summarizing total income, deductions, and the taxes withheld by employers. Any difference between the amount already paid and the amount actually owed, as determined by official tax tables like those shown in **Figure 9.5,** is settled when the return is filed. Most differences are caused by deductions and expenses that lower the amount of taxes owed, as well as by additional income received that was not subject to tax withholding.

People who are self-employed do not have money withheld from their paychecks. Instead, they are required to send quarterly estimates of their taxes to the Internal Revenue Service. These individuals must also make a final settlement for the previous year sometime before April 15.

A Progressive Income Tax

The individual income tax is a progressive tax. According to the individual tax tables in **Figure 9.5,** single individuals paid a flat 10 percent on all income up to $6000. After that, the marginal tax rate jumps to 14 percent, 27 percent, 30 percent, 35 percent, and 38.6 percent depending on the amount of taxable income. The tax schedule is

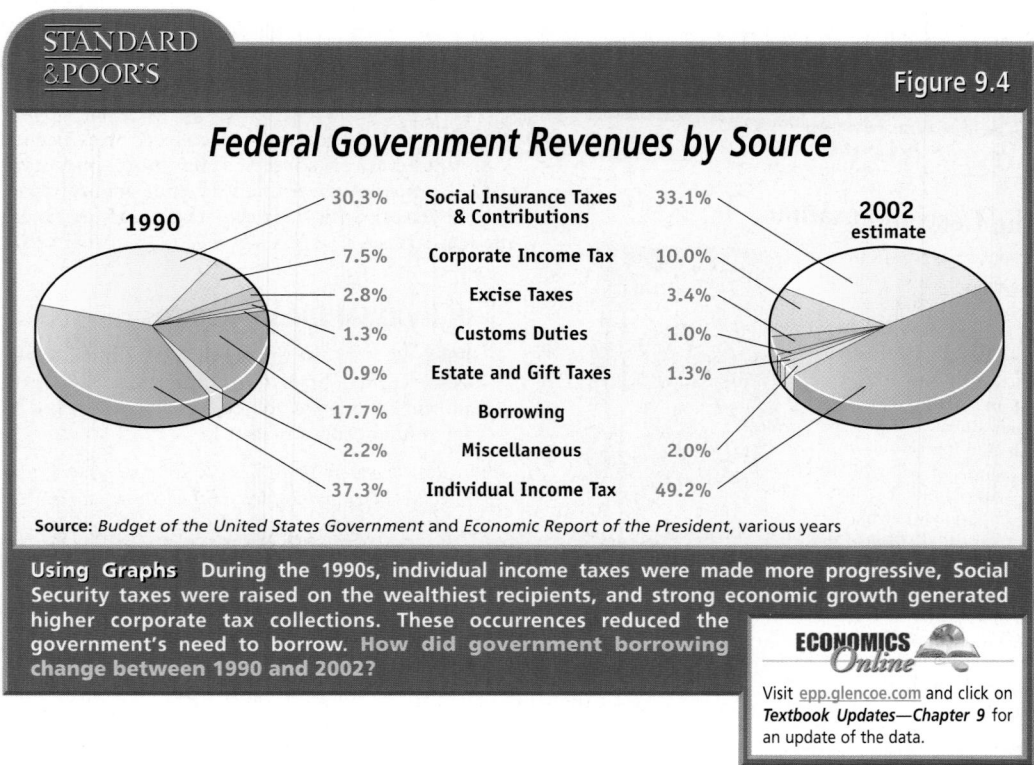

STANDARD &POOR'S

Figure 9.4

Federal Government Revenues by Source

1990

		2002 estimate
30.3%	Social Insurance Taxes & Contributions	33.1%
7.5%	Corporate Income Tax	10.0%
2.8%	Excise Taxes	3.4%
1.3%	Customs Duties	1.0%
0.9%	Estate and Gift Taxes	1.3%
17.7%	Borrowing	
2.2%	Miscellaneous	2.0%
37.3%	Individual Income Tax	49.2%

Source: *Budget of the United States Government* and *Economic Report of the President,* various years

Using Graphs During the 1990s, individual income taxes were made more progressive, Social Security taxes were raised on the wealthiest recipients, and strong economic growth generated higher corporate tax collections. These occurrences reduced the government's need to borrow. **How did government borrowing change between 1990 and 2002?**

ECONOMICS Online

Visit epp.glencoe.com and click on **Textbook Updates—Chapter 9** for an update of the data.

---

232 UNIT 3 MACROECONOMICS: INSTITUTIONS

MEETING SPECIAL NEEDS ACTIVITY

Learning Disabled For students who have problems with reading, consider helping them locate specific information in the text. Without direction, these students often cannot distinguish between important facts and elaboration. The notes they take may be filled with nonessential information. Have students read the subsection titled "Payroll Deductions." Tell them to find one sentence in each paragraph that best states the main idea. Have students discuss and defend their choices.

Refer to *Inclusion for the Social Studies Classroom Strategies and Activities* in the TCR.

ECONOMICS AT A GLANCE

Figure 9.5

Tax Table for Single Individuals—2002

If the amount on Form 1040, line 39, is over . . .	but not over . . .	enter on Form 1040, line 40		of the amount over . . .
$0	$6,000	------------	10.0%	$0
$6,000	$27,050	$600 +	14.0%	$6,000
$27,050	$65,550	$3,652 +	27.0%	$27,050
$65,550	$136,750	$14,240 +	30.0%	$65,550
$136,750	$297,300	$35,956 +	35.0%	$136,750
$297,300	------------	$92,951 +	38.6%	$297,300

Source: Schedule X, IRS Individual Tax Table

Using Tables   According to the individual income tax table, a single individual with $6,000 of taxable income would pay $6,000 × .10, or $600 in taxes. How much in taxes would an individual with $40,000 of taxable income pay?

Guided Reading Activity 9-2

GUIDED READING   Activity 9-2

For use with textbook pages 231–236

❶ THE FEDERAL TAX SYSTEM

FILLING IN THE BLANKS

Directions: Use your textbook to fill in the blanks using the words in the box. Some words may be used more than once. Use another sheet of paper if necessary.

similar for married individuals, with rates scaled so that couples earning higher incomes pay a larger percentage of their income in taxes.

When a tax is progressive, the average tax rate goes up when income goes up. **Figure 9.6** illustrates this point. The single individual with $6,000 of taxable income pays an average of 10 cents for every dollar earned. If the person has $35,000 of taxable income, the marginal tax rate is higher (at 27 percent), which raises the average tax on every dollar to 16.7 cents. Likewise, the individual with $145,000 of taxable income pays an average of 26.8 cents on every dollar.

Indexing

Suppose a worker receives a small raise, just enough to offset the rate of inflation. Although that worker is no better off, the raise may still push the worker into a higher tax bracket. Because of this possibility, the individual income tax has a provision for **indexing,** an upward revision of the tax brackets to keep workers from paying more in taxes just because of inflation.

To illustrate, suppose that a single individual with no dependents had exactly $27,050 of taxable income in 2002. If the person receives a 5 percent raise the following year to offset expected inflation, the $1,352.50 raise would be taxed at the next marginal tax bracket of 27 percent. The result is that the individual gets pushed into a higher tax bracket simply because of inflation. If the bracket is indexed, or

adjusted upward by 5 percent, the 27 percent marginal rate for the next 6 years would not apply until $28,402.50 is earned.

FICA Taxes

The second most important federal tax is FICA. **FICA** is the Federal Insurance Contributions Act tax levied on both employers and employees to pay for Social Security and medicare. **Medicare** is a federal health-care program available to all senior citizens, regardless of income. Employees and employers share equally in paying the tax for Social Security and medicare. These two taxes are also called **payroll taxes** because they are deducted from your paycheck.

Social Security Taxes

In 2002 the Social Security component of FICA was 6.2 percent of wages and salaries up to $80,400. After that amount, Social Security taxes are not collected, regardless of income. This means that a person with taxable income of $80,400 pays a Social Security tax of $4,985, the same as someone who earns $1,000,000.

Because the Social Security tax is capped, it is proportional up to $80,400, and regressive thereafter. For example, a single individual with $80,400 of taxable income would pay an average of 6.2 cents of Social Security taxes on every dollar earned (.062 times $80,400). If that same individual

CHAPTER 9: SOURCES OF GOVERNMENT REVENUE **233**

ECONOMICS AT A GLANCE

Answer: *$7,148.50*

L2 Debate

Lead the class in a debate of the following proposition: The only equitable type of tax is the individual income tax. Encourage students to take notes during the debate. Have them use these notes to write a paragraph supporting or challenging the proposition.

L3 Research

Have students undertake research on the Social Security tax. Topics they might cover include its history, original purpose, connection to the U.S. Constitution, changes in collections and payments, or problems with the system. Suggest that students present their findings in a written report.

FREE ENTERPRISE ACTIVITY

To learn more about how taxes affect the behavior of taxpayers, ask pairs of students to interview a variety of taxpayers in your community, including small-business owners, high school students with part-time jobs, large-business managers, and retired persons. Instruct students to ask their subjects to name the taxes they pay and then to describe how paying taxes affects their economic behavior—hiring new workers, expanding the business, buying products, saving, and so on. Have pairs of students summarize their findings, making special note of any differences among the four groups of taxpayers interviewed.

Taxpayers send their income tax returns to one of the IRS's 10 tax-processing centers. These centers receive and process around 200 million returns and other related documents each year. Using computers, IRS staff members quickly check each return. A small percentage of each year's returns are selected for audit—a more thorough examination. The IRS also investigates suspected violations of the tax laws.

Math Practice

Paycheck Withholding Have students determine what would be withheld for Social Security and medicare from the paycheck of an individual who worked 40 hours at $6.50/hour. *(40 × $6.50 = $260 total pay; 6.2 % of $260 = $16.12 for Social Security tax; 1.45 % of $260 = $3.77 for medicare)*

ECONOMICS
AT A GLANCE

Answer: *a regressive tax; because the Social Security portion of FICA is capped at a certain income level—the higher the income, the lower the FICA tax*

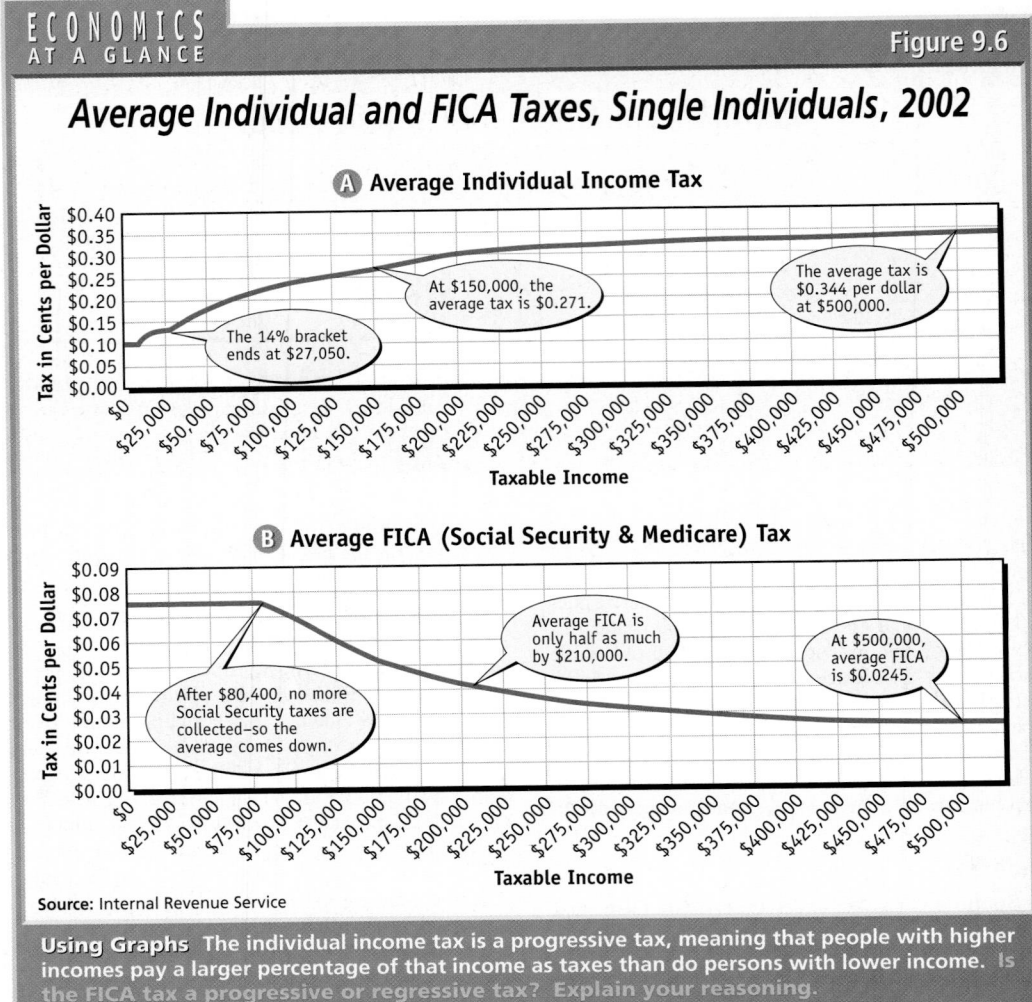

ECONOMICS AT A GLANCE

Figure 9.6

Average Individual and FICA Taxes, Single Individuals, 2002

Ⓐ Average Individual Income Tax

At $150,000, the average tax is $0.271.

The average tax is $0.344 per dollar at $500,000.

The 14% bracket ends at $27,050.

Ⓑ Average FICA (Social Security & Medicare) Tax

Average FICA is only half as much by $210,000.

At $500,000, average FICA is $0.0245.

After $80,400, no more Social Security taxes are collected–so the average comes down.

Source: Internal Revenue Service

Using Graphs The individual income tax is a progressive tax, meaning that people with higher incomes pay a larger percentage of that income as taxes than do persons with lower income. Is the FICA tax a progressive or regressive tax? Explain your reasoning.

made $300,000, the average tax per dollar would drop to 1.7 cents (.062 times $80,400 divided by $300,000).

Medicare

In 1965 Congress added medicare to the Social Security program. More than 30 million senior citizens participate in medicare. The basic plan pays a major share of an eligible person's total hospital bills. The medicare component of FICA is taxed at a flat rate of 1.45 percent. Unlike Social Security, there is no cap on the amount of income taxed, which means that wealthy individuals pay the same percent of income to medicare taxes as do the poor.

When medicare and Social Security are considered together, as in **Panel B** of **Figure 9.6,** we can see the overall regressive nature of the FICA tax.

234 UNIT 3 MACROECONOMICS: INSTITUTIONS

CRITICAL THINKING

Making Comparisons Ask students to compare the Social Security tax and the medicare tax. They may wish to make a chart stating the purpose of each tax, and the similarities and differences between the two taxes. They may also wish to provide several examples of incomes and the taxes levied on those amounts. Finally, ask students to hypothesize why the government handles the two taxes differently. *(The taxes are both payroll deductions. However, Social Security is a proportional tax up to a $72,600 income and regressive thereafter. Medicare tax is proportional because the individual pays the same percentage regardless of the amount of income.)*

For single individuals in 2002, the tax was level at 7.65 percent up to $80,400, and then declined. A single individual earning $35,000 in 2002 paid an average FICA tax of 7.65 cents per dollar. If that same individual made $150,000, the average FICA tax paid dropped to 4.77 cents per dollar.

Corporate Income Taxes

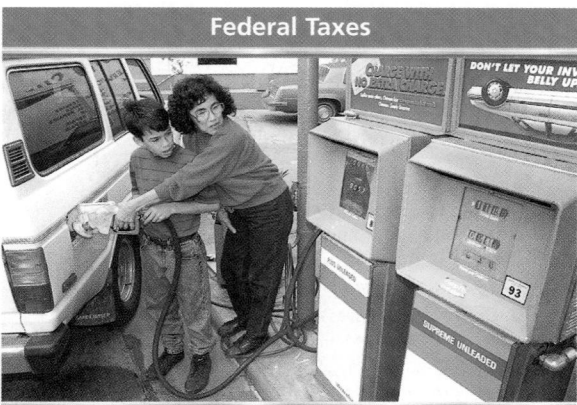 Corporations as well as individuals must pay income taxes. The third largest category of taxes the federal government collects is the **corporate income tax**—the tax a corporation pays on its profits. The corporation is taxed separately from individuals because the corporation is recognized as a separate legal entity.

Several marginal tax brackets, which are slightly progressive, are placed on corporations. The first is at 15 percent on all income under $50,000. The second is at 25 percent on income from $50,000 to $75,000. The third tax bracket is at 34 percent on income starting at $75,000. Eventually, a 35 percent marginal tax applies to all profits in excess of $18.3 million.

Other Federal Taxes

In addition to income, FICA, and corporate taxes, the federal government receives revenue in the form of excise taxes, estate and gift taxes, and customs duties.

Excise Taxes

The **excise tax**—a tax on the manufacture or sale of selected items, such as gasoline and liquor—is the fourth largest source of federal government revenue. The Constitution permits levying excise taxes, and since 1789 Congress has placed taxes on a variety of goods. Some early targets for excise taxes were carriages, snuff, and liquor. Today, federal excise taxes also are found on telephone services, tires, legal betting, and coal. Because low-income families spend larger portions of their incomes on these goods than do high-income families, excise taxes tend to be regressive.

In 1991 Congress expanded the excise tax to include certain luxury goods. An economic product is called a **luxury good** (or service) if the demand for the good rises faster than income when income grows. At first, the 19 percent luxury tax was indexed to keep up with inflation and was applied to many goods, including passenger vehicles in excess of $30,000. The tax was unpopular, however, so boats, aircraft, jewelry, and furs were dropped in 1993. Later, Congress decided to phase out the luxury tax by the year 2002.

Estate and Gift Taxes

An **estate tax** is the tax the government levies on the transfer of property when a person dies. Estate taxes can range from 18 to 50 percent of the value of the estate. Estates worth less than $675,000 were exempt in 2002, although this limit will soon be raised to $1,000,000.

The **gift tax** is a tax on donations of money or wealth and is paid by the person who makes the gift. The gift tax is used to make sure that wealthy people do not try to avoid taxes by giving away their estates before their deaths. As shown in **Figure 9.4**, these two taxes account for only a small fraction of total federal government revenues.

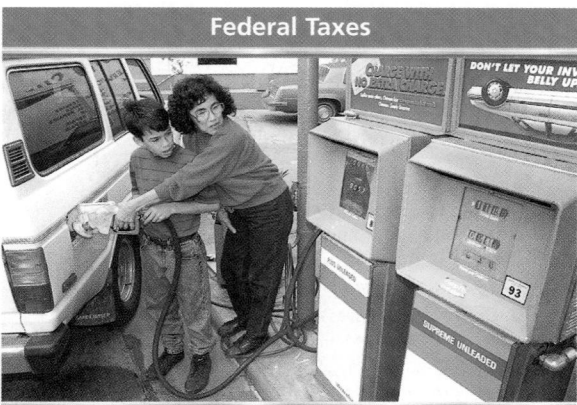

Federal Taxes

Excise Taxes The Constitution permits levying excise taxes. Since 1789 Congress has placed taxes on a variety of goods, including gasoline, coal, and luxury goods. *What are luxury goods?*

CHAPTER 9: SOURCES OF GOVERNMENT REVENUE **235**

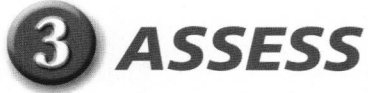

③ ASSESS

Assign Section 2 Assessment as homework or as an in-class activity.

💾 Have students use **Interactive Tutor Self-Assessment Software** to review Section 2.

Section Quiz 9-2

Visual Instruction

Answer to Caption:
goods or services for which the demand rises faster than income when income grows

---

EXTENDING THE CONTENT

Government Revenue in the 1800s Before the Civil War, the federal government collected most of its revenues from tariffs, or taxes on imports, and from the sale of public lands. During the war, a variety of taxes, including a 5 percent income tax, were imposed to pay the costs of fighting. After the war, many of these taxes were dropped, but others, including increased property taxes, were added. However, the typical homeowner paid only about $90 in annual property taxes and only about 1 percent of the population ever paid income tax. By 1872 no one was paying income tax because the tax had been repealed. Have students identify which parts of the U.S. Constitution deal with taxation.

Reteach

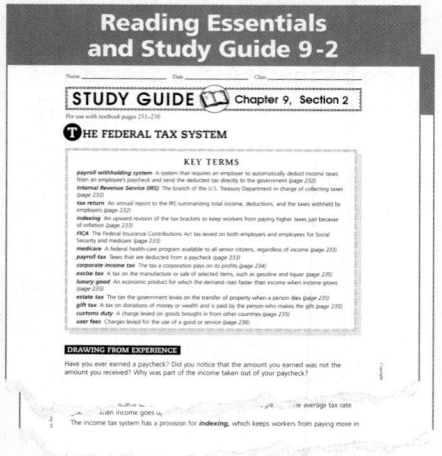

Enrich

Invite a tax accountant to visit the class and discuss federal taxes, tax filing, and other information that young people with part-time jobs need to know.

 CLOSE

Ask students to discuss what they think the three most important sources of federal revenue should be.

The estate tax and the gift tax are progressive taxes—the larger the estate or gift, the higher the tax rate. These two taxes accounted for about 1.3 percent of federal government revenue.

Customs Duties

A **customs duty** is a charge levied on goods brought in from other countries. The Constitution gives Congress the authority to levy customs duties. Congress can decide which foreign imports will be taxed and at what rate. Congress, in turn, has given the president authority by executive order to raise or lower the existing tariff rates by as much as 50 percent. Many types of goods are covered, ranging from automobiles to silver ore. The duties are relatively low, and they produce little federal revenue today, although they were the largest source of federal government income prior to 1913.

Miscellaneous Fees

Finally, about 2 percent of federal revenue is collected through various miscellaneous fees. Since the 1980s, when taxes were politically unpopular,

user fees—charges levied for the use of a good or service—have been suggested with increasing frequency. President Ronald Reagan was one of the first presidents to aggressively push for user fees instead of taxes.

These fees include entrance charges you pay to visit national parks, as well as the fees ranchers pay when their animals graze on federal land. These fees are essentially taxes based on the benefit principle; politicians just seem to think that we won't recognize them as taxes if they call them "user fees" instead.

CYBERNOMICS SPOTLIGHT

E-Filing

There are benefits to filing taxes online. E-filing speeds up tax-processing time so that computer users can get their refunds twice as fast as those who mail in paper. E-filing also prevents errors, since no IRS keypunchers are needed to type in the information from paper returns. In 1998, 20 percent of taxpayers filed their tax returns online. By the year 2007, the IRS hopes to have 80 percent of returns filed electronically.

Section 2 Assessment

Checking for Understanding

1. **Main Idea** Using your notes from the graphic organizer activity on page 231, list the federal government's most important revenue sources.

2. **Key Terms** Define payroll withholding system, Internal Revenue Service, tax return, indexing, FICA, medicare, payroll tax, corporate income tax, excise tax, luxury good, estate tax, gift tax, customs duty, user fee.

3. **Describe** the progressive nature of the individual income tax.

4. **Identify** the main marginal tax brackets in the corporate income tax structure.

5. **Describe** the other sources of government revenue.

Applying Economic Concepts

6. **Federal Taxes** User fees have been compared to taxes based on the benefit principle of taxation. Define user fees in your own words. What are the pros and cons of having user fees as a way to charge admission to national parks?

Critical Thinking

7. **Categorizing Information** Explain and use an example to explain the regressive nature of the current FICA tax.

8. **Finding the Main Idea** What is indexing? What is its purpose?

Practice and *assess* key social studies skills with the *Glencoe Skillbuilder Interactive Workbook, Level 2.*

Section 2 Assessment Answers

1. individual income taxes, FICA taxes, corporate income taxes

2. All vocabulary terms are defined in the text.

3. It imposes a higher percentage rate of taxation on persons with higher incomes.

4. 15 percent, 25 percent, 34 percent, 35 percent

5. excise taxes, estate taxes, gift taxes, customs duties, user fees levied for use of a good or service

6. User fees would place burden of payment on those who benefit most from the parks—visitors, but lower-income individuals may no longer be able to use the parks.

7. It is regressive because persons with large incomes pay no Social Security tax on income greater than $80,400.

8. an upward revision of the tax brackets; to keep workers from paying more in taxes due to inflation

Profiles IN Economics

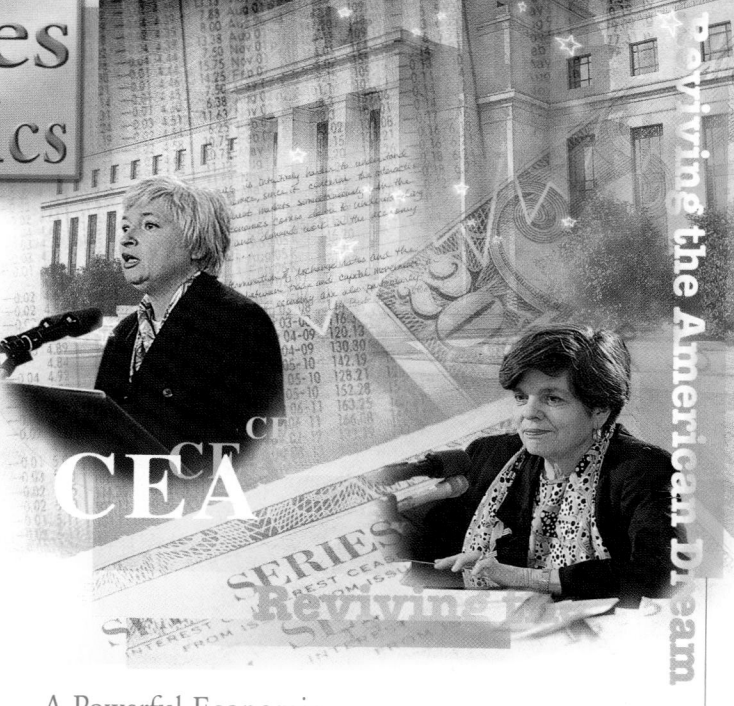

Adviser to a President:
Janet Yellen
(1946–)

Janet Yellen, former Chair of the President's Council of Economic Advisers (CEA), has a knack for explaining things. When she was a student pursuing her Ph.D. in economics in the early 1970s, the lecture notes she took became a legend in their own time. The "Yellen Notes," as they were known, were passed around and became the unofficial textbook for several generations of graduate students.

As a member of the Board of Governors of the Federal Reserve, she frequently briefed the White House on labor markets and welfare reform. As a result of these encounters, President Clinton knew just where to look when he needed a new Chair for the CEA in early 1997.

As Chair of the CEA, Yellen's top priorities were a balanced federal budget and welfare reform, including measures that would punish fathers who do not support their children. The distribution of income was another priority. "I'm concerned about rising inequality of earnings and its long-term social implications," Dr. Yellen said. "Education is the answer."

A Powerful Economic Voice:
Alice Rivlin
(1931–)

Alice Rivlin, founding director of the Congressional Budget Office (CBO), former Director of the Office of Management and Budget (OMB) in the Clinton administration, and former Vice Chair of the Fed's Board of Governors, is one of the most respected economists in Washington. As a seasoned professional with a wealth of experience, her knowledge of government finance is virtually unparalleled.

She has written extensively and is known for the straightforward—sometimes searing—views put forth in her many writings. Rivlin is a blunt and outspoken critic of budget deficits, and argues that spending cannot be brought under control until Congress is willing to reform the politically sensitive spending measures, such as pension systems, subsidies, and other types of transfer payments. Rivlin is now a senior fellow for the Brookings Institute, a Washington-based research group.

Examining the Profiles

1. **Making Comparisons** Compare and contrast the work and views of Yellen and Rivlin.

2. **Synthesizing Information** What significance is there in the fact that both Yellen and Rivlin are women?

BACKGROUND

In 1931, an official of the New York state government, echoing the feelings of many others at the time, called employed married women "undeserving parasites" and called for "our federal, state, and local governments" to cooperate to keep married women from working. Little could he know that Alice Rivlin, born that very year, would eventually belie his ideology. Rivlin, Janet Yellen, and other women have contributed greatly to economic thought and the government. Rivlin and Yellen stand as testament to both the progress women made during the twentieth century, and how that progress has benefited the country as a whole.

TEACH

Challenge the class to brainstorm a list of obstacles Rivlin and Yellen may have faced because of their gender. For each item on the list, have students identify qualities and actions these women could have employed to overcome it.

Answers to Examining the Profile

1. Answers will vary. Similarities students might note are that both economists lead important federal economic agencies, both are critical of federal deficit spending, and both focus on macroeconomic issues. A difference is that Yellen's top priority is balancing the federal budget, and Rivlin is a strong critic of the budget.

2. Answers will vary. Students might note that their success belies discriminatory attitudes.

① FOCUS

Section Overview
This section discusses taxes for state and local governments.

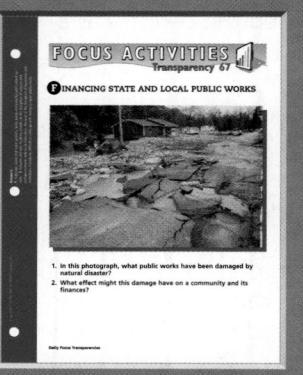
Study Guide

Reading Strategy
Have students create the graphic organizer.
Answers to Graphic: *Sales taxes are levied on nearly all products; they are added to the final price the consumer pays; merchants collect the tax at the time of sale.*

Preteaching Vocabulary
Have students read the Glossary definition of each Key Term.

State and Local Tax Systems

Study Guide

Main Idea
State and local governments each rely on different revenue sources.

Reading Strategy
Graphic Organizer As you read the section, complete a graphic organizer like the one below by describing why sales taxes are effective ways to raise revenue.

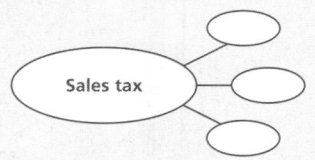

Sales tax

Key Terms
intergovernmental revenue, property tax, tax assessor, payroll withholding statement

Objectives
After studying this section, you will be able to:
1. **Explain** how state governments collect taxes and other revenues.
2. **Differentiate** between state and local revenue systems.
3. **Interpret** paycheck deductions.

Applying Economic Concepts
Sales Tax Read to find out why, when you purchase an item in most states, you pay a fee in the form of a sales tax.

Cover Story

Federal Tax Cut Could Bolster State Revenues

Iowa residents can take solace in knowing that they'll likely help the state with its budget crunch if President Bush cuts federal taxes.

Iowa's softening economy has left state government revenue stagnant, a problem caused by a lack of spending by Iowans. Sales-tax receipts have barely bumped up from last year, and it's coming back to hit the state budget.

President Bush calls for tax relief

In Iowa, residents get to deduct their federal income taxes from their state income taxes. So if the federal government saves Iowans $1 billion in income taxes, that's $1 billion that the state will get to tax.

–The Omaha World-Herald, February 9, 2001

238

State and local governments, like the federal government, raise revenue in many ways. They receive funds from sales taxes, property taxes, utility revenues, and through other methods. Sometimes state and local governments even tax us when we die.

State Government Revenue Sources

State governments collect their revenues from several sources. **Figure 9.7** shows the relative proportions of each source, the largest of which are examined below.

Intergovernmental Revenues

The largest source of state revenue is the category called **intergovernmental revenue**—funds collected by one level of government that are distributed to another level of government for expenditures. States receive these funds from the federal government to help with expenditures on welfare, education, highways, health, and hospitals. As **Figure 9.7** shows, they represent over 20 percent of all state revenues.

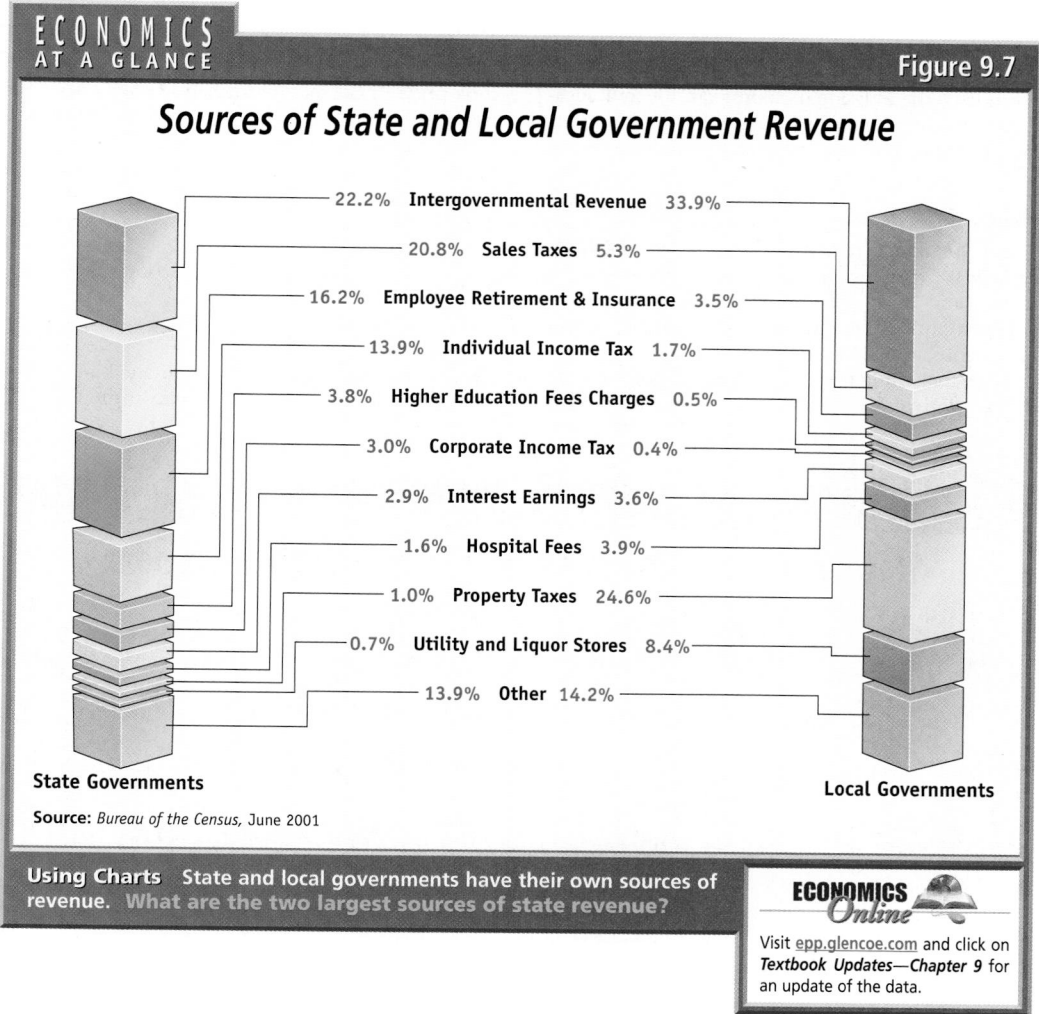

Sources of State and Local Government Revenue

State		Source		Local
22.2%		Intergovernmental Revenue		33.9%
20.8%		Sales Taxes		5.3%
16.2%		Employee Retirement & Insurance		3.5%
13.9%		Individual Income Tax		1.7%
3.8%		Higher Education Fees Charges		0.5%
3.0%		Corporate Income Tax		0.4%
2.9%		Interest Earnings		3.6%
1.6%		Hospital Fees		3.9%
1.0%		Property Taxes		24.6%
0.7%		Utility and Liquor Stores		8.4%
13.9%		Other		14.2%

State Governments

Local Governments

Source: *Bureau of the Census,* June 2001

Using Charts State and local governments have their own sources of revenue. **What are the two largest sources of state revenue?**

ECONOMICS *Online*

Visit epp.glencoe.com and click on **Textbook Updates—Chapter 9** for an update of the data.

Taxes and Fees

The sales tax is a general tax levied on consumer purchases of nearly all products. The tax is a percentage of the purchase price which is added to the final price the consumer pays. Merchants collect the tax at the time of sale. The taxes are then turned over to the proper state government agency on a weekly or monthly basis. Most states allow merchants to keep a small portion of what they collect to compensate for their time and bookkeeping costs.

The sales tax is the second largest source of revenue for states, accounting for 20.8 percent of total revenues collected. Only five states—Alaska, Delaware, Montana, New Hampshire, and Oregon—do not have a general sales tax.

Many states levy taxes, fees, or other assessments on their employees to cover the cost of state retirement funds and pension plans. **Figure 9.7** shows that employee retirement contributions were the third largest source of state revenue.

CHAPTER 9: SOURCES OF GOVERNMENT REVENUE **239**

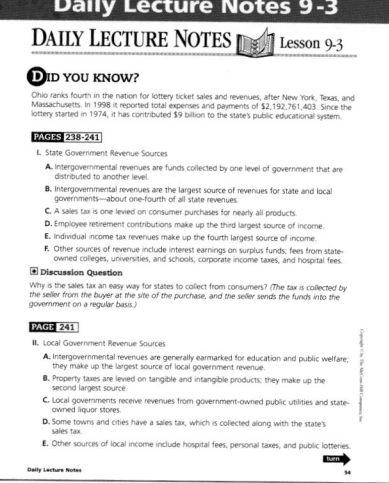

Daily Lecture Notes 9-3

DAILY LECTURE NOTES 📖 Lesson 9-3

DID YOU KNOW?
Ohio ranks fourth in the nation for lottery ticket sales and revenues, after New York, Texas, and Massachusetts. In 1998 it reported total expenses and payments of $2,192,761,403. Since the lottery started in 1974, it has contributed $9 billion to the state's public educational system.

PAGES 238–241
I. State Government Revenue Sources
  A. Intergovernmental revenues are funds collected by one level of government that are distributed to another level.
  B. Intergovernmental revenues are the largest source of revenues for state and local governments—about one-fourth of all state revenues.
  C. A sales tax is one levied on consumer purchases for nearly all products.
  D. Employee retirement contributions make up the third largest source of income.
  E. Individual income tax revenues make up the fourth largest source of income.
  F. Other sources of revenue include interest earnings on surplus funds; fees from state-owned colleges, universities, and schools; corporate income taxes, and hospital fees.

Discussion Question
Why is the sales tax an easy way for states to collect from consumers? *(The tax is collected by the seller from the buyer at the site of the purchase, and the seller sends the funds into the government on a regular basis.)*

PAGE 241
II. Local Government Revenue Sources
  A. Intergovernmental revenues are generally earmarked for education and public welfare; they make up the largest source of local government revenue.
  B. Property taxes are levied on tangible and intangible products; they make up the second largest source.
  C. Local governments receive revenues from government-owned public utilities and state-owned liquor stores.
  D. Some towns and cities have a sales tax, which is collected along with the state's sales tax.
  E. Other sources of local income include hospital fees, personal taxes, and public lotteries.

Daily Lecture Notes

ECONOMICS AT A GLANCE

Answer: *intergovernmental revenue and sales taxes*

L1 Constructing a Chart

On the board draw a chart similar to that used for the activity on page 232 in Section 2, but label the columns *State/Local Taxes* and *Type of Tax.* Have students copy and complete the chart by listing the various kinds of state and local taxes in the first column and classifying each tax as proportional, progressive, or regressive in the second column. **ELL**

MEETING SPECIAL NEEDS ACTIVITY

Learning Disabled For students who have problems speaking, asking their teacher questions can pose a challenge. Organize students into small groups and instruct group members to develop questions about the sources of state and local revenues using the chart and text on page 239. Have group members take turns reading the questions to the class. Students from other groups can volunteer answers.

📁 Refer to *Inclusion for the Social Studies Classroom Strategies and Activities* in the TCR.

Guided Reading Activity 9-3

GUIDED READING Activity 9-3

Name _____ *Date* _____ *Class* _____

For use with textbook pages 238–242

STATE AND LOCAL TAX SYSTEMS

RECALLING THE FACTS

Directions: Use the information in your textbook to answer the questions. Use another sheet of paper if necessary.

1. What is intergovernmental revenue?
   _____

2. What are the two largest sources of revenue for states? How are they collected?
   a. _____
   b. _____

3. What are the third and fourth largest sources of revenue for states?
   a. _____
   b. _____

4. Name four other sources of revenue for state governments.
   a. _____
   b. _____
   c. _____
   d. _____

5. What are the three largest local government revenue sources?
   a. _____
   b. _____

L1 Applying Ideas

Ask students to keep a record of the total amount of sales taxes they pay during a week. Then **ask:** Did sales taxes play a role in your purchasing decisions? How would your spending behavior have differed if there were no sales tax?

L2 Writing a Report

Have students research and write a report on the economic importance of major types of revenue for their state, county, and municipal governments.

ECONOMICS
AT A GLANCE

Answer: *highest: Maine and New York; lowest: Alaska, New Hampshire, and Tennessee*

On average, the fourth largest source of state revenues is the individual income tax. Overall, individual income tax revenues are about five times as large as the income tax collected from corporations.

Other Revenues

The remaining revenues that state governments collect are interest earnings on surplus funds; tuition and other fees collected from state-owned colleges, universities, and technical schools; corporate income taxes; and hospital fees.

Note that while the percentages in **Figure 9.7** are representative for most states, wide variations among states still exist. For years, New Hampshire took pride in the fact that it had neither a sales tax nor an income tax. Even so, as **Figure 9.8** shows, the state made up the difference with other types of taxes. The same is true for Alaska, Delaware, Montana, and Oregon—the other four states without a general sales tax.

The Choice of Tax

The choice of tax is something that most states feel strongly about. Sooner or later, however, they all discover that if they do not use one kind of tax, then they have to rely on another. In the end, the

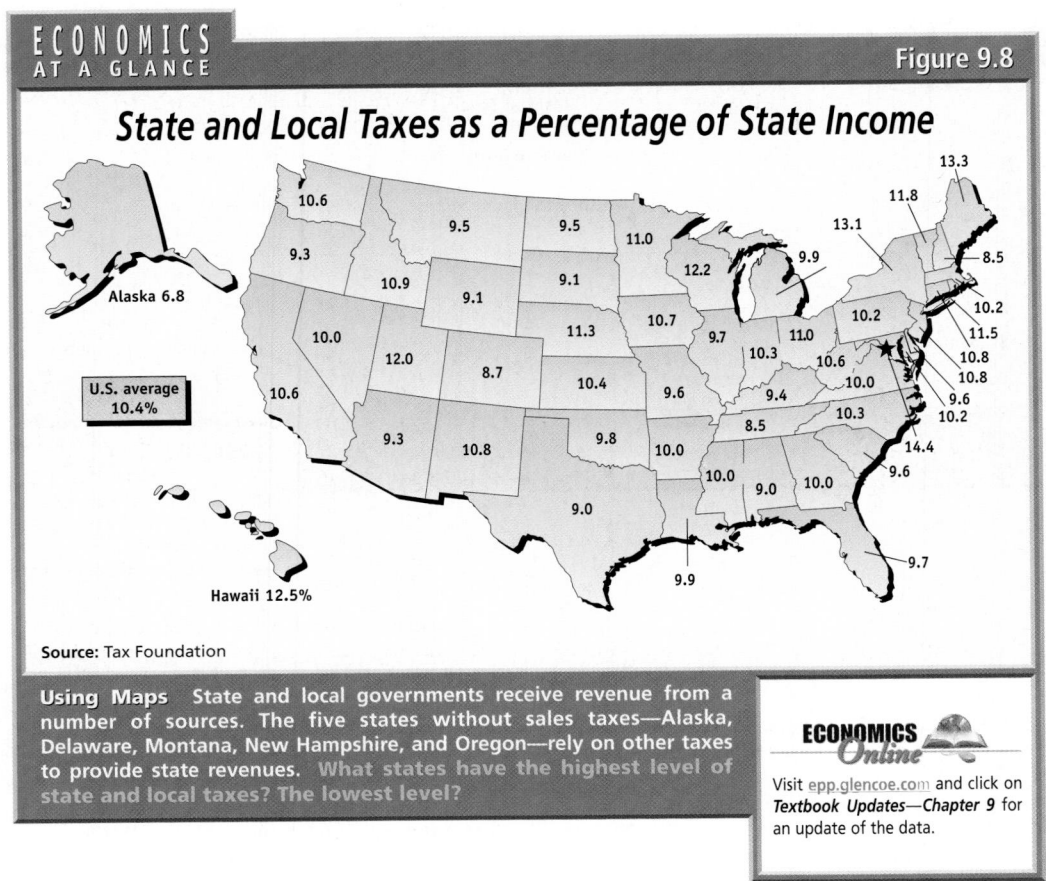

ECONOMICS
AT A GLANCE

Figure 9.8

State and Local Taxes as a Percentage of State Income

Alaska 6.8

U.S. average 10.4%

Hawaii 12.5%

Source: Tax Foundation

Using Maps State and local governments receive revenue from a number of sources. The five states without sales taxes—Alaska, Delaware, Montana, New Hampshire, and Oregon—rely on other taxes to provide state revenues. What states have the highest level of state and local taxes? The lowest level?

ECONOMICS
Online

Visit epp.glencoe.com and click on **Textbook Updates—Chapter 9** for an update of the data.

FREE ENTERPRISE ACTIVITY

Ask students who work to bring paycheck stubs to class. Then have students turn to page 241 and study the paycheck and withholding statement in Figure 9.9. Review the categories on the statement, pointing out that while paycheck stubs may differ in appearance, most contain similar information, such as pay period, hours worked, gross and net pay, and tax figures. Have students locate where the federal, state, city, and Social Security tax amounts are noted on the paycheck stub, and ask which of these taxes are federal taxes. *(federal income, FICA)* Conclude the activity by having students who brought paycheck stubs locate the various categories on their withholding statements.

choices that states face are like the choices individuals face–and we already know that there is no such thing as a free lunch.

Nearly three-fourths of the states run public lotteries to raise revenue. Lotteries became the fastest-growing source of state revenues in the 1980s. The states spend about half the lottery income on prizes and 6 percent on administration.

Local Government Revenue Sources

The major sources of local government revenue are also shown in **Figure 9.7**. These include taxes and funds from state and federal governments. The main categories are discussed below.

Intergovernmental Revenues

Local governments receive the largest part–slightly more than one-third–of their revenues in the form of intergovernmental transfers from state governments. These funds are generally intended for education and public welfare. A much smaller amount comes directly from the federal government, mostly for urban renewal.

Property Taxes

The second largest source of revenue for local governments is the **property tax**–a tax on tangible and intangible possessions such as real estate, buildings, furniture, automobiles, farm animals, stocks, bonds, and bank accounts.

The property tax that raises the most revenue is the tax on real estate. Taxes on other personal property, with the exception of automobiles, is seldom collected because of the problem of valuation. For example, how would the **tax assessor**–the person who assigns value to property for tax

purposes–know the reasonable value of everyone's wedding silver, furniture, coin collections, clothing, and other tangible property items? Instead, most communities find it more efficient to hire one or more individuals to assess the value of a few big-ticket items like buildings, real estate, and motor vehicles.

Other Sources

The third largest source of local revenue is derived from the earnings of public utilities and

---

ECONOMICS AT A GLANCE Figure 9.9

Biweekly Paycheck and Withholding Statement

Weaver & Higginson
Attorneys at Law

21-2/000 Number 2,195,903
Date June 25 20 02

Pay to the order of   Sara Peña $ 586.89

Five Hundred Eighty-Six Dollars and 89/100 Dollars

THE CENTRAL BANK
Memo _____
5:5555555: 555:55555   Ton (on)
                                Treasurer

PLEASE DETACH AND RETAIN THIS PORTION
AS YOUR RECORD OF EARNINGS AND DEDUCTIONS

Date	Pay End	Vo. No.	Emp. No.	Hrs.	Misc.	Cr. Un.	Ins.	Gross
6/10/02	6/21/02		1376	80	3.20			800 00

104 70	40 01	4 00	61 20					586 89
Federal	State	City	FICA	Ret.	Bonds	Other		Net

Understanding Percentages The withholding statement attached to your paycheck summarizes many of the federal, state, and local taxes. Federal and state income tax withholdings are always shown, as is the FICA (Social Security and medicare) tax. Other withholdings may include city income taxes and voluntary deductions, such as health insurance payments and savings plans. **What percentage of this individual's pay has been deducted from her paycheck?**

L2 Identifying Ideas

Have students identify the state and local taxes they pay. *(Responses might include sales tax, individual income tax, and various license and user fees.)* Then have them consider the state and local taxes they might pay if they were business owners. *(Responses might include corporate income tax, property tax, and various license and user fees.)*

ECONOMICS AT A GLANCE

Answer: *about 27 percent ($800 − $586.89) ÷ $800*

③ ASSESS

Assign Section 3 Assessment as homework or as an in-class activity.

📖 Have students use **Interactive Tutor Self-Assessment Software.**

Section Quiz 9-3

QUIZ ◆ Chapter 9, Section 3

STATE AND LOCAL TAX SYSTEMS SCORE

Matching: Match each item in Column A with the items in Column B. Write the correct letters in the blanks. (10 points each)

A
___ 1. intergovernmental revenue
___ 2. property tax
___ 3. tax assessor
___ 4. sales tax
___ 5. public lotteries

B
a. fastest-growing source of state revenues in the 1980s
b. second largest source of revenue for state governments
c. person who assigns value to property for tax purposes
d. funds collected by one level of government that are distributed to another level of government for expenditures
e. a tax on tangible and intangible possessions
f. real estate, buildings, and anything permanently attached to them

Multiple Choice: In the blank at the left write the letter of the choice that best completes the statement or answers the question. (10 points each)

___ 6. The largest source of revenue for states is
a. property taxes.   b. sales taxes.
c. income taxes.   d. intergovernmental revenues.
___ 7. The property tax that raises the most revenue for local governments is the tax on
a. automobiles.   b. intangible personal property.
c. real estate.   d. tangible personal property.
___ 8. The three largest sources of revenue for local governments are
a. utility and liquor store income, property tax, and intergovernmental revenue.
b. utility and liquor store income, property tax, and sales taxes.
c. sales taxes, intergovernmental revenue, and property tax.

CHAPTER 9: SOURCES OF GOVERNMENT REVENUE **241**

CRITICAL THINKING

Analyzing Information Ask a volunteer to write the general categories of local taxes, found in Figure 9.7 (page 239), on the board *(property taxes, public utilities and state liquor store income, sales taxes, other sources)*. Then read aloud the following taxes and ask students to categorize each one under the correct heading: a bank account *(property tax)*, the purchase of a pair of jeans *(sales tax)*, a herd of cattle *(property tax)*, interest on savings *(other sources: income tax)*, the use of an emergency room *(other sources: hospital fees)*, last month's electricity bill *(utility and liquor store income)*, an automobile *(property tax)*, a house and a lot *(property tax)*.

Reteach

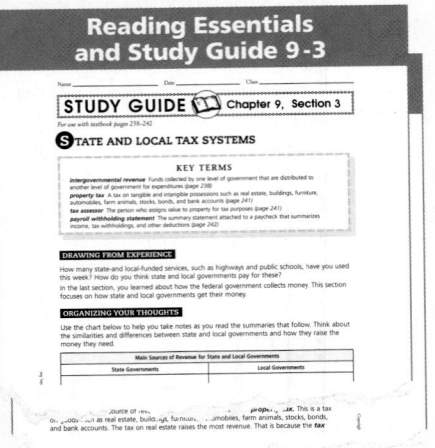

Reading Essentials and Study Guide 9-3

Enrich

Invite the tax assessor in your school district to explain the procedures for evaluating real property, focusing on the inherent problems in collecting the property tax. Students should prepare questions to ask the speaker.

4 CLOSE

Have students select what they think is the most equitable way of raising revenue for state and local governments. Call on volunteers to explain their selections.

---

state-owned liquor stores. **Figure 9.7** shows that local governments acquired 8.4 percent of their revenues from these sources.

Many towns and cities have their own sales taxes. Merchants collect these taxes right along with the state sales tax, at the point of sale. As indicated in **Figure 9.7**, sales taxes are the fourth most important source of local government revenues.

Local governments also collect a portion of funds in the form of hospital fees and personal income taxes. In general, the revenue sources available to local governments are much more limited than those available to the state and federal levels of government.

Examining Your Paycheck

 Many of the taxes you pay to federal, state, and local governments are deducted directly from your paycheck. By examining the **payroll withholding statement**—the summary statement attached to a paycheck that summarizes income, tax withholdings, and other deductions—shown in **Figure 9.9**, we can identify many of the revenue sources described in this chapter.

The worker to whom the check belongs makes $10 an hour and receives a check every two weeks. If the length of the workweek is 40 hours, the worker's gross pay amounts to $800. The worker is single, has no deductions, and lives and works in Kentucky.

According to withholding tables the federal government supplied for that year, biweekly workers making at least $800, but less than $820, have $104.70 withheld from their paychecks. Similar tables for the state of Kentucky specify that $40.01 is withheld for state income taxes. Because these are both estimates, and because even minor differences between the amounts withheld and the amount actually owed can grow, the worker will file state and federal tax returns between January 1 and April 15 of 2003 to settle the differences.

Another deduction is the half-percent city income tax that amounts to $4. Because the amount is relatively small, cities seldom require workers to file separate year-end tax forms.

The federal FICA tax amounts to 7.65 percent (6.20 percent for Social Security and 1.45 percent for medicare) of $800, or $61.20. The FICA is deducted from the gross pay, along with $3.20 in miscellaneous deductions, which leaves the worker with a net pay of $586.89.

If the worker has insurance payments or retirement contributions, purchases savings bonds, or puts money into a credit union, even more deductions will appear on the paycheck.

Section 3 Assessment

Checking for Understanding

1. **Main Idea** Using your notes from the graphic organizer activity on page 238, write a definition in your own words of what intergovernmental revenues are.

2. **Key Terms** Define intergovernmental revenue, property tax, tax assessor, payroll withholding statement.

3. **Explain** the four major sources of state tax revenues.

4. **Explain** the difference between state and local revenue systems.

5. **List** the major types of state, local, and federal taxes reflected on a paycheck.

Applying Economic Concepts

6. **Sales Taxes** Why do you think sales taxes are applied to food and beverages purchased at restaurants, but not to food and beverages purchased at grocery stores?

Critical Thinking

7. **Drawing Conclusions** State and local governments receive revenue from various sources. Which source do you think best satisfies the tax criteria listed in the chapter? Defend your answer.

Practice and assess key social studies skills with the *Glencoe Skillbuilder Interactive Workbook, Level 2.*

242 UNIT 3 MACROECONOMICS: INSTITUTIONS

Section 3 Assessment Answers

1. funds collected by one level of government distributed to another for expenditures

2. All vocabulary terms are defined in the text.

3. sales tax, intergovernmental revenues, individual income taxes, employee retirement contributions, assessments levied on state employees

4. state: collect from intergovernmental revenues, sales taxes, employee retirement contributions, individual income taxes; local: collect from intergovernmental revenues, property taxes, public utilities and state liquor store sales, sales taxes

5. federal income tax, state income tax, city income tax, FICA tax

6. Groceries represent necessities, meals out do not.

7. Answers should show an understanding of tax criteria and sources for revenue.

JANUARY 18, 1999

Newsclip

The Sixteenth Amendment, which gives Congress the power to tax people's incomes to generate revenue for the federal government, was added to the Constitution in 1913. Today, taxes are placed on income, sales, and property to raise money for services such as transportation and education.

Do Taxes Spell Good News?

Taxes, as the saying goes, may be as unavoidable as death, but do they have to be so high?

. . . In recent years, federal individual income and payroll taxes have been claiming an ever larger share of personal income. . . .

As some critics see it, this growing tax bite is squeezing consumers. With more income being siphoned off by taxes, they say, struggling households have had to dip into savings simply to maintain consumption patterns. And the fact that the monthly savings rate recently turned negative for the first time in 60 years underscores the problem.

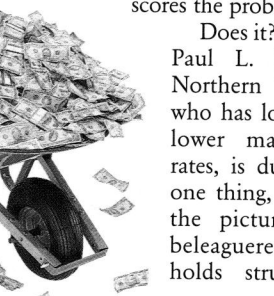

Does it? Economist Paul L. Kasriel of Northern Trust Co., who has long favored lower marginal tax rates, is dubious. For one thing, he regards the picture of tax-beleaguered households struggling to

maintain consumption as highly exaggerated. In actuality, he notes, people have been spending with exuberance. . . .

As for the rising tax take, Kasriel claims that the main cause has been increases in inflation-adjusted income, which have been pushing tax filers into higher marginal brackets. . . .

Similarly, more income has become subject to taxation as more households have moved off welfare rolls and onto payrolls in response to welfare reform and a tight labor market. . . .

Finally, Kasriel points to a development others have cited in explaining the falling savings rate and rising tax bite: the huge increase in household net worth generated by the stock market boom. With the value of their past savings and investments rising so rapidly, consumers have felt free to curtail current savings so they can enjoy the fruits of their past thrift now. . . .

–Reprinted from January 18, 1999 issue of *Business Week*, by special permission, copyright © 1999 by The McGraw-Hill Companies, Inc.

Examining the Newsclip

1. **Making Inferences** How would having negative monthly savings rates imply that taxes are too high?

2. **Drawing Conclusions** Do you agree with Paul Kasriel's opinion about taxes and lower savings rates? Why or why not?

CHAPTER 9: SOURCES OF GOVERNMENT REVENUE **243**

TEACH

Ask students if they think the generalizations that Kasriel makes apply to the worker whose paycheck is shown in Figure 9.9 on page 241. Then have students figure out a monthly budget for the worker including $600 per month for rent or mortgage, at least $200 per month for food, at least $100 per month for utilities, and allowances for clothing, entertainment, car maintenance, car insurance, and an emergency fund. Compare how much the worker has left over for savings and investment with Kasriel's ideas. *(The students probably will discover that the worker has little left to save or invest and conclude that Kasriel's generalizations apply to people making substantially more than $1,600 a month.)*

Refer to *Business Week Focus on the New Economy* in the TCR for additional unit-based articles.

Answers to Examining the Newsclip

1. Negative monthly savings rates imply that too much income was taken in taxes, forcing households to use savings to pay monthly bills.

2. Answers should reflect an understanding of the effect of taxes on personal economics.

FOCUS

Section Overview
This section deals with tax reforms and issues.

BELLRINGER
Motivational Activity

 Project **transparency** and have students answer questions.

 Available as blackline master.

Daily Focus Transparency 69

Study Guide

Reading Strategy
Have students create the graphic organizer.
Answers to Graphic: *adv: simplicity for taxpayers, minimized or closed loopholes, reduced need for tax accountants, tax preparers, and portions of the IRS; disadv: few behavior incentives, benefit for high-income individuals at the expense of low-income individuals*

Preteaching Vocabulary
Use the Vocabulary Puzzle-Maker to create crossword and word-search puzzles.

SECTION 4

Current Tax Issues

Study Guide

Main Idea
The consequence of tax reform was to make the individual tax code more complex than ever.

Reading Strategy
Graphic Organizer As you read the section, complete a graphic organizer like the one below by listing the advantages and the disadvantages of the flat tax. Include a definition of flat tax in your own words.

```
        Flat tax
       /        \
  Advantages   Disadvantages
```

Key Terms
accelerated depreciation, investment tax credit, surcharge, alternative minimum tax, capital gains, value-added tax (VAT), flat tax

Objectives
After studying this section, you will be able to:
1. **Describe** the major tax reforms since 1980.
2. **Debate** the advantages and disadvantages of the value-added tax.
3. **Explain** the features of a flat tax.
4. **Discuss** why future tax reforms will occur.

Applying Economic Concepts
Flat Tax Have you ever noticed how much time your parents spend filling out their income tax returns? Read to find out what a flat tax would mean to them.

Cover Story

How the Tax Code Got This Way

Every year at this time, Congress discovers, with a great public show of dismay and indignation, the existence of the American tax code and the agency that administers it, the Internal Revenue Service.

There are high-minded calls for abolishing the current tax system and replacing it. . . .

Around April 15, Congress likes to pretend that the tax code just sort of appeared or [just] happened. But the Constitution puts the burden of taxes solely, exclusively and entirely on Congress' shoulders.

The tax code is the way it is because a majority of Congress wants it that way. Hope you enjoyed this year's tax day.

IRS employee sorts tax returns

—*Denver Rocky Mountain News,* April 16, 1999

244

The editorial in the cover story sums it up quite well. The complexity of our tax code is not accidental: it is the result of adjustments and amendments by Congress to both influence and reward behavior.

Tax Reform

Tax reform has received considerable attention in recent years, due to more changes in the tax code, and more changes in direction, than at any time in our nation's history.

Tax Reform in 1981

When Ronald Reagan was elected president in 1980, he believed that high taxes were the main stumbling block to economic growth. Accordingly, he proposed the Economic Recovery Tax Act of 1981, which substantially reduced taxes for individuals and businesses.

Before the Recovery Act, the individual tax code had 16 marginal tax brackets ranging from 14 percent to 70 percent. In comparison, today's

---

RESOURCE MANAGER

Reproducible Masters
- Reproducible Lesson Plan 9-4
- Daily Lecture Notes 9-4
- Guided Reading Activity 9-4
- Reading Essentials and Study Guide 9-4
- Section Quiz 9-4

Transparencies
- Daily Focus Transparency 69

Multimedia
- Vocabulary PuzzleMaker CD-ROM
- Interactive Tutor Self-Assessment Software
- ExamView® Pro Testmaker
- Presentation Plus!

tax code, shown in **Figure 9.5**, has six marginal brackets ranging from 10 to 38.6 percent. The 1981 act lowered the marginal rates in all brackets, but, more importantly, it capped the highest marginal tax wealthy individuals paid at 50 percent.

Businesses also got tax relief in the form of **accelerated depreciation**—larger than normal depreciation charges—which allowed firms to reduce federal income tax payments. Another section of the act introduced the **investment tax credit**—a reduction in business taxes that are tied to investment in new plants and equipment. For example, a company might purchase a $50,000 machine that qualified for a 10 percent, or $5,000, tax credit. If the firm owed $12,000 in taxes, the credit reduced the tax owed to $7,000.

These provisions produced a dramatic impact on the federal budget. In 1980, the proportion of total federal government revenues from the corporate income tax was 12.5 percent. This dropped to 10.2 percent in 1981, and then to 8.0 percent in 1982, and finally to 6.2 percent in 1983.

Tax Reform: 1986, 1993

By the mid-1980s, the idea that the tax code favored the rich and powerful was gaining momentum. In 1983 more than 3,000 millionaires paid no income taxes. Additionally, many corporations were able to legally avoid paying taxes. Boeing, ITT, General Dynamics, Transamerica, and Greyhound were profitable from 1981 to 1984. Instead of paying corporate income taxes, however, these companies applied tax losses in earlier years to current profits—and then collected tax *refunds* during each of those four years.

In 1986 Congress passed sweeping tax reform. First, it ended the traditionally progressive individual income tax structure by reducing the 16 marginal tax brackets to two brackets (15 percent and 28 percent). Then, a 5 percent **surcharge**—or additional tax above and beyond the base rate—was added to bring the top bracket to 31 percent.

The law made it difficult for the very rich to avoid taxes altogether. The **alternative minimum tax**—the personal income rate that applies whenever the amount of taxes paid falls below some designated level—was strengthened. Under this provision, people had to pay a minimum tax of 20 percent, regardless of other circumstances or loopholes in the tax code.

The reform act shifted about $120 billion of taxes from individuals to corporations over a five-year period by removing a number of tax breaks for business. The proportion of total federal government revenues from the corporate income tax increased to 10.3 percent in 1988—a percentage much closer to the 10.0 percent shown in **Figure 9.4.**

Taxation

Reform   Some people think any tax is too high, but this viewpoint is not very realistic. *What tax credits were part of the Taxpayer Relief Act of 1997?*

CHAPTER 9: SOURCES OF GOVERNMENT REVENUE   **245**

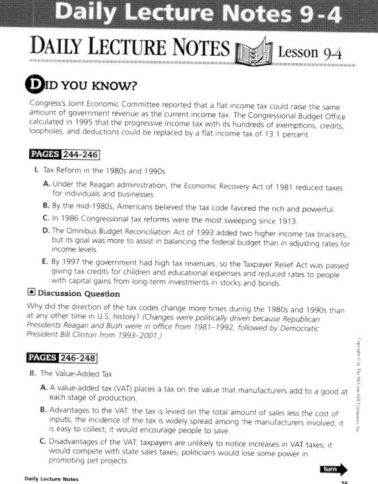

Daily Lecture Notes 9-4

L1 Constructing a Chart

Draw on the board a three-column chart with the headings *Element of Act, Criterion,* and *Principle*. Direct students to review the discussion of the Omnibus Budget Reconciliation Act of 1993 and the Taxpayer Relief Act of 1997 on pages 245–246. Then have them copy and complete the chart by noting the various parts of the acts in the first column, and the criterion and principle of taxation that apply to each part in the second and third columns.

Visual Instruction

Answer to Caption:
tax credits for children

MEETING SPECIAL NEEDS ACTIVITY

English Language Learners Make copies of the following terms and their definitions: *accelerated depreciation*—larger than normal depreciation charges; *investment tax credit*—a reduction in business taxes that are tied to investment in new plants and equipment; *surcharge*—additional tax above and beyond the base rate; *alternative minimum tax*—the personal income tax rate that applies whenever the amount of taxes paid falls below some designated level. Give a copy to each student who is an English language learner. Ask the student to look up unfamiliar terms from the definitions in a translation dictionary. If they cannot find equivalents for certain English words, suggest synonyms that might be in their dictionaries. **ELL**

Refer to *Inclusion for the Social Studies Classroom Strategies and Activities* in the TCR.

Guided Reading Activity 9-4

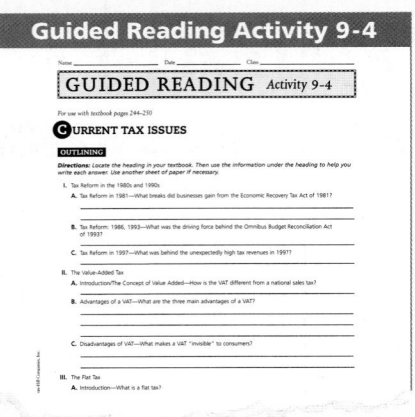

Visual Instruction

Answer to Caption:
10 years

L2 Writing a Letter

Have students assume the role of a worker or the head of a business. Direct them to write a letter to a newspaper editor or to one of their congressional representatives explaining why they support or oppose tax reform. Suggest that they focus on one of the tax reform acts discussed in the section. Encourage students to refer to the criteria and principles of taxation to support their positions.

L3 Research

Have students conduct research to find instances in American history of tax reform. Direct students to present their findings in written reports that note why tax reform was proposed, how the tax laws were changed, and whether or not the legislation achieved its aims.

Tax Cut

Tax Relief The possibility of a budget surplus and a slowing economy prompted President Bush to call for a tax cut. *How long will his tax reduction plan take to implement?*

As the United States entered the 1990s, the impact of 10 years of tax cuts was beginning to show. Government spending was growing faster than revenues, and the government had to borrow more.

The Omnibus Budget Reconciliation Act of 1993 was driven more by the need for the government to balance its budget than to overhaul the tax brackets. As a result, the law added two top marginal tax brackets of 36 and 39.6 percent.

Tax Reform in 1997

The next significant reform was the Taxpayer Relief Act of 1997. The forces that created it were both economic and political.

On the economic side, the government found itself with unexpectedly high tax revenues in 1997. The higher marginal tax brackets introduced in 1993, along with the closure of some tax loopholes, meant that individuals and corporations paid more taxes than before. In addition, unexpectedly strong

economic growth resulted in an increased number of people and businesses paying taxes.

On the political side, the balance of power had dramatically shifted in the 1996 elections. Both political parties felt they had commitments to fulfill to the people who had voted them into office. For many Republicans, this meant a tax break for people with long-term investments in stocks, bonds, and other assets. The tax on **capital gains**—profits from the sale of an asset held for 12 months—was reduced from 28 to 20 percent. Inheritance taxes—the so-called "death taxes"—were also lowered, which tended to favor the well-to-do.

The tax reductions reflected the "family-friendly" theme of the 1996 elections. Tax credits of $500 per child and other deductions for educational expenses were included in the legislation. The marginal tax brackets remained virtually unchanged, however, which resulted in an unbalanced distribution of tax cuts. People who had neither children nor capital gains from the sale of houses, stocks, or bonds received virtually no benefit.

At the time, an analysis by the United States Treasury Department determined that nearly half of the benefits went to the top 20 percent of wage and income earners. The lowest 20 percent received less than 1 percent of the tax reductions. With all its categories, the 1997 federal tax law became the most complicated ever.

Did you know?

Tax Freedom Day It takes 40 days, on average, for most Americans to earn enough money to pay for their food supply for the entire year. It takes the average American 123 days—until the first week of May—to earn enough money to pay federal, state, and local taxes for the year.

FREE ENTERPRISE ACTIVITY

Tell students that they are going to determine the economic importance of a tax in their community. Have students choose a product and determine its demand elasticity. Next, have them draw, on a single graph, hypothetical supply and demand curves for their chosen product. Tell students to assume a 10 percent tax has been placed on their product. Have students use their supply and demand curves to determine where the incidence of tax will fall. *(If demand is inelastic, burden of tax will fall on consumers; if demand is elastic, burden will be shared by producers and consumers.)* Point out that when a community decides to place a tax on a product, it must consider the elasticity of the product and who will ultimately pay the tax.

Tax Reform in 2001

By 2001, politicians faced a new issue—that of growing government surpluses rather than deficits. The surpluses, projected to continue to the year 2010, could be used to pay down the federal debt, fund additional federal spending, or, pay for a federal tax cut. President Bush backed tax reduction in 2001, and the result was a $1.35 billion, ten-year tax cut.

One component of the tax cut was to add the 10 percent bracket shown in **Figure 9.5**. The top four tax brackets would then be gradually reduced to 25, 28, 33, and 35 percent by 2006. A third component of the tax cut was to make the tax reductions retroactive to the beginning of the year so that individual taxpayers could receive immediate refund checks of up to $300 (or $600 for married couples)—the announcement of which cost approximately $21 million.

Other components of the tax bill included higher child tax credits and increased deductions for college educational expenses. Even other pro-visions of the law were scheduled to take effect much later, such as the elimination of the estate tax in 2010.

Because the law is being phased in slowly, the majority of the reductions will not take place until after 2006, so the exact cost of the tax bill is not known. Also, because of Congressional rules regarding new legislation, the entire tax bill is scheduled to expire (or be renewed) in 2011.

The Value-Added Tax

Some people want to change the personal income tax; others want to scrap it altogether. One controversial proposal is to shift the tax from income to consumption. This shift would be accomplished with the use of a **value-added tax** (VAT)—a tax placed on the value that manufacturers add at each stage of production.

The VAT has the potential to raise enormous amounts of revenues for the federal government. The United States currently does not have a VAT, although it is widely used in Europe.

CURRICULUM CONNECTION

History Until 1989 local governments in Great Britain had only one source of revenue—the ability-to-pay-based property tax on residential and business property. The Conservative Party government under the leadership of Prime Minister Margaret Thatcher objected to the property tax and replaced it with a flat rate community charge—or poll tax—which was levied on all adults, regardless of income or wealth.

THE GLOBAL ECONOMY

HIGH TAXES? ARE YOU SURE?

The ratio of tax revenues to the GDP is one measure of a country's tax burden.

Have you ever thought about living in another country to avoid high taxes in the United States? If you did move, you would be in for a surprise. For all the complaints about high taxes, our federal government's revenues as a percentage of GDP are much lower than many people realize. In fact, the rate is one of the lowest in the industrial world.

Tax Revenues as a % of GDP

France
Italy
U.K.
Canada
Germany
Japan
U.S.

55% 45% 35% 0%
'89 '91 '93 '95 1997

Source: *A Citizen's Guide to the Federal Budget, FY 2000*

Critical Thinking

1. **Analyzing Information** What is measured in the graph?
2. **Sequencing Information** Describe the pattern for Canada from 1991 to 1996.

CHAPTER 9: SOURCES OF GOVERNMENT REVENUE **247**

THE GLOBAL ECONOMY

High Taxes? Are You Sure? Individual income taxes are the main source of revenue for the Canadian government. Rates in Canada's progressive individual income tax system range from 6 percent to 34 percent. Another major source of revenue is the corporate income tax. Canadian corporations are supposed to pay 46 percent of their income in taxes but as a result of deferments and credits, seldom pay the full amount.

Answers:

1. *tax revenues as a percentage of GDP*
2. *Canada's rate increased slightly throughout the period.*

CRITICAL THINKING

Making Predictions Ask students if they have shopped at a factory outlet mall recently. Discuss the concept of outlet malls—manufacturers selling directly to the public through their own stores. **Ask:** How do you think a federal value-added tax would affect the trend of factory outlet malls? Would the number of such malls increase, decrease, or remain the same? On what do you base your prediction? *(Students may note that a value-added tax could increase the number of factory outlet malls. Outlet malls could sell products more cheaply because they circumvent the retailers' tax that increases prices.)*

ECONOMICS AT A GLANCE

Answer: *VAT tends to be regressive because persons with lower incomes tend to spend a larger percentage of their incomes on tax.*

The Concept of Value Added

The production of almost any good or service involves numerous steps. Consider wooden baseball bats. First, loggers cut the trees and sell the timber to lumber mills. Then the mills process the logs for sale to bat manufacturers. The manufacturers then shape the wood into baseball bats.

After the bats are painted or varnished, they are sold to a wholesaler. The wholesaler sells them to retailers, and retailers sell them to consumers. The whole process is illustrated in **Figure 9.10**. The first column of numbers shows the value added at each stage of production. With the VAT, the consumer ends up paying $11 for each bat.

Advantages of a VAT

As a way of raising revenue, the VAT has several advantages. First, it is hard to avoid because the tax collector levies it on the total amount of sales less the cost of inputs. Second, the tax incidence is widely spread, which makes it harder for a single firm to shift the burden of the tax to another group.

Third, the VAT is easy to collect because firms make their VAT payments to the government along with their regular tax payments. Consequently, even a relatively small VAT can raise a tremendous amount of revenue, especially when it is applied to a broad range of products.

ECONOMICS AT A GLANCE — Figure 9.10

The Value-Added Tax

		No Taxes		With a 10% Value-Added Tax	
		Value Added	Cumulative Value	Value Added with a 10% VAT	Cumulative Value with VAT
Step 1	Loggers fell trees and sell the timber to the mills for processing.	$1	$1	$1 + $.10 = $1.10	$1.10
Step 2	The mills cut the timber into blanks that will be used to make bats.	$1	$2	$1 + $.10 = $1.10	$2.20
Step 3	Bat manufacturers shape, paint, or varnish the bats and sell them to wholesalers.	$5	$7	$5 + $.50 = $5.50	$7.70
Step 4	The wholesalers sell the bats to retail outlets where consumers can buy them.	$1	$8	$1 + $.10 = $1.10	$8.80
Step 5	The retailers put the bats on the shelves and wait for the consumers.	$2	$10	$2 + $.20 = $2.20	$11.00
Step 6	The consumer buys the bat for:		$10.00		$11.00

Using Tables The VAT is like a national sales tax added to each stage of production. As a result, it is built into the final price of a product and is less visible to consumers. Is a VAT regressive, proportional, or progressive? Why?

INTERDISCIPLINARY CONNECTIONS ACTIVITY

History Show students that the fairness of income taxes has been debated for thousands of years by reading the following quote from Plato (circa 428–348 B.C.): "When there is an income tax, the just man will pay more and the unjust less on the same amount of income." **Ask:** Based on this quote, do you think Plato would prefer a flat tax on income or the current progressive income tax system? *(Students should mention that, under the present system, taxpayers can use loopholes to pay less than others with the same income. As a result, Plato would probably prefer the flat tax.)*

Finally, some supporters claim that the VAT would affect people's behavior in a manner that encourages them to save more than they do now. After all, if none of your money is taxed until it is spent, you might prefer to spend less—and save more—than you do now.

Disadvantages of a VAT

The main disadvantage of the VAT is that it tends to be invisible to consumers. In the baseball bat example, consumers may be aware that bat prices went from $10 to $11, but they might attribute this to a shortage of good wood, higher wages, or some other factor. In other words, consumers cannot be vigilant about higher taxes when they cannot see them.

Another difficulty is that the VAT would compete with state sales taxes. Because the VAT is a federal tax, adding a VAT is like adding a federal sales tax to already-existing state taxes. If some of these bats were sold in Indiana, Arizona, or Texas, would those states want to forgo their sales tax simply because a federal VAT was in place? Or would those states simply add their own sales taxes, thereby raising the price to $11.50 or even higher?

The Flat Tax

The concept of a **flat tax**—a proportional tax on individual income after a specified threshold has been reached—did not receive much attention until Republican candidate Steve Forbes and others raised the issue in the 1996 presidential elections. Supporters promoted the flat tax as a way to both simplify taxes and stimulate growth.

Advantages of the Flat Tax

The primary advantage of the flat tax is the simplicity it offers to the taxpayer. A person would still have to fill out an income tax return every year, but many current procedures, such as itemizing deductions, could be skipped.

A second advantage is that a flat tax closes or minimizes most tax loopholes. Under today's tax-code, for example, the donation of a single artwork can substantially reduce a millionaire's tax liability.

A third advantage is that a flat tax reduces the need for tax accountants, tax preparers, and even large portions of the IRS. The savings to everyone could be as high as $100 billion annually.

Disadvantages of the Flat Tax

The first disadvantage of the flat tax is that it removes many of the behavior incentives already built into the tax code. For example, the current tax code allows homeowners to deduct interest payments on home mortgages. Other incentives include deductions for donations to charitable organizations, and education and training.

Eliminating these incentives may encounter some resistance. For example, *Money Magazine* warned that a 15 percent flat tax would hurt homeowners because they could no longer deduct mortgage interest payments. The writer noted that, "under his own plan, multimillionaire Steve Forbes could see his personal tax bill cut by almost two-thirds." This, of course, highlights the second

---

Careers

Public Accountant

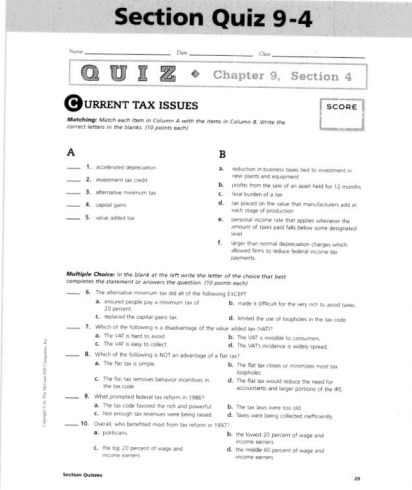

Accountants prepare, analyze, and verify financial reports that provide information to the general public and to business firms.

The Work

They check clients' financial records, ensuring that they conform to standard procedures for reporting. They give advice on tax advantages and disadvantages, on setting up an accounting system and on managing cash resources, and they prepare income tax statements.

Qualifications

Most firms require applicants to have, at the minimum, a bachelor's degree in accounting or some closely related field. Accountants must be good at mathematics, be able to compare, analyze, and to interpret numbers and facts, and to make sound judgments.

249

THE GLOBAL ECONOMY

Canadian Tax System The federal government of Canada collects a federal income tax and provincial income taxes for nine of its provinces. The provincial income tax from each province equals a percentage of its federal income tax. Only Quebec collects its own taxes according to its own rates.

③ ASSESS

Assign Section 4 Assessment as homework or as an in-class activity.

💾 Have students use **Interactive Tutor Self-Assessment Software** to review Section 4.

Section Quiz 9-4

QUIZ ◆ Chapter 9, Section 4

CURRENT TAX ISSUES

EXTENDING THE CONTENT

Steve Forbes is a newspaper and magazine publisher who sought the Republican nomination in the 1996 and 2000 presidential elections. His grandfather founded *Forbes,* the business magazine which is still owned by the Forbes family. Steve Forbes was born in Morristown, New Jersey, in 1947 and graduated from Princeton University in 1970. While still in college, Forbes started *Business Today,* a magazine that came out three times a year. In 1993 Forbes became chairman of Empower America, a research center dedicated to conservative principles. He supports a flat tax and an end to the federal government's progressive income tax.

Reteach

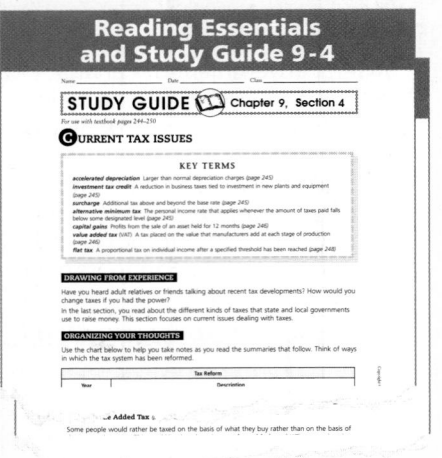

Enrich

Have students poll family members, neighbors, and friends on what they think are the major tax issues of the day. Ask students to combine the poll results and present their findings in a class report.

CLOSE

Ask: If there were one thing you could change in the tax laws, what would it be? Why?

---

problem with the flat tax—namely, it will benefit those with high incomes at the expense of lower-income individuals.

Would a flat tax stimulate economic growth? Critics point out that the extraordinary growth of the American economy in the 1990s, the longest period of peacetime prosperity in our history, sheds doubt on the claim that the current system hinders growth.

Second, no one knows exactly what rate is needed to replace the revenues already collected under the current system. Estimates by economists who proposed the tax, as well as estimates done by the United States Treasury, place the tax closer to 23 percent—which represents more of a burden on low-income earners.

The Inevitability of Future Reforms

There were more changes, additions, deletions, exceptions, and exclusions made to the tax code from 1981 to 2002 than at any time in our history. Several factors ensure further change.

First, the tax code is more complex now than ever—a fact that guarantees future attempts to simplify it. The flat tax movement, for example, has moved beyond the point of being a campaign strategy to the stage where some people in Congress seriously consider such a tax.

Second, there is no guarantee that economic growth will continue uninterrupted until 2010. If the economy falters so that tax collections fall, federal budget deficits could return. This is exactly what happened in mid–2001 when the economy unexpectedly slowed and federal revenues fell.

Third, unexpected political events may require additional, and unplanned, expenditures. Shortly after the September 11, 2001 terrorist attack on the World Trade towers in New York, for example, Congress voted to spend $40 billion to rebuild the city and restore confidence in our air traffic system.

Fourth, political change is not like economic change, which is gradual and generally evolutionary. Political change is more abrupt, with less continuity from one period to the next, as one party leaves office and another enters. New administrations often display a sense of urgency, a desire to finally do things the "right" way, or to clean up the excesses of their predecessors.

Finally, dramatic change is tempered by the reluctance of politicians to give up some of the power they currently exercise through the tax code—power vested in the ability to modify behavior, influence resource allocation, support pet projects, and grant concessions to special interest groups. As the editorial in the cover story aptly put it, "The tax code is the way it is because a majority of Congress wants it that way."

Section 4 Assessment

Checking for Understanding

1. **Main Idea** What is the purpose of tax reform?

2. **Key Terms** Define accelerated depreciation, investment tax credit, surcharge, alternative minimum tax, capital gains, value-added tax, flat tax.

3. **Describe** four major tax reform bills.

4. **Explain** the advantages and disadvantages of the VAT.

5. **Describe** the features of the flat tax.

6. **Identify** three forces that are likely to cause future revision of the tax code.

Applying Economic Concepts

7. **Flat Tax** What do you think might happen to donations to charitable organizations if there was a flat tax? If possible, support your answer with examples.

Critical Thinking

8. **Summarizing Information** What changes would you recommend in the federal tax code if you were in charge of revising it? Explain your answer.

Practice and **assess** key social studies skills with the *Glencoe Skillbuilder Interactive Workbook, Level 2.*

Section 4 Assessment Answers

1. to influence and reward behavior

2. All vocabulary terms are defined in the text.

3. Answers may describe Economic Recovery Tax Act of 1981, tax reform act of 1986, Omnibus Budget Reconciliation Act of 1993, Taxpayer Relief Act of 1997, and 2001 tax reform.

4. adv: hard to avoid, widely spread tax incidence, easy to collect, encourages savings; disadv: invisible to consumers, competes with state sales taxes

5. taxes all income at a specific rate, exempts some income from taxation, eliminates incentives and deductions

6. tax code is more complex now, strong economy of 1990s resulted in record tax collections, power shifts can trigger political change

7. While current tax policies allow tax deductions for charitable contributions, proposed flat tax policies would not.

8. Answers should be sound.

Section 1

The Economics of Taxation

(pages 223–229)

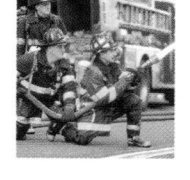

- Taxes affect the allocation of resources, behavior, and economic growth.

- The **incidence of a tax,** or final burden of a tax, is affected by elasticity—when demand for a product is elastic, less of the tax can be shifted to the buyer; more can be shifted when demand is inelastic.

- Equity, simplicity, and efficiency are the criteria used to judge the effectiveness of a tax.

- Two principles, the **benefit principle of taxation** and the **ability-to-pay principle of taxation,** have been used to help select the group or groups that bear the burden of the tax. Both involve value judgments, and both types of taxes are widely used today.

- Taxes can be placed into three groups—**proportional taxes, progressive taxes,** and **regressive taxes**—depending on the way in which the tax burden changes as income changes.

Section 2

The Federal Tax System (pages 231–236)

- The main source of revenue for the federal government is the **individual income tax.**

- **Indexing** is used to change the **marginal tax rates** to offset the effects of inflation.

- The second largest revenue source is the **FICA tax,** collected to cover Social Security and **medicare.**

- The **corporate income tax** is the third largest source of federal revenue.

- Other sources of federal revenue include **excise taxes, gift taxes, customs duties,** and **user fees,** which is a different name for a benefit tax.

Section 3

State and Local Tax Systems

(pages 238–242)

- **Intergovernmental revenues** are the largest source of state revenues.

- Local governments receive intergovernmental revenues from state and federal governments. Local governments also raise revenue from **property taxes,** utility and liquor store sales, sales taxes, and other sources.

- The **payroll withholding statement** attached to a person's weekly, biweekly, or monthly paycheck provides a summary of wages, taxes, and other withholdings.

Section 4

Current Tax Issues (pages 244–250)

- A **value added tax** (VAT) is a tax on consumption rather than income. It is built into a product's every stage of production.

- The Economic Recovery Tax Act of 1981 lowered marginal tax rates for all levels of income, and added **accelerated depreciation** and the **investment tax credit** for businesses.

- The 1986 tax reform law closed tax loopholes opened in 1981, and reduced the individual income tax code to two brackets.

- The Budget Deficit Reduction Act of 1993 added two marginal tax brackets, restoring the progressive nature of the tax removed in 1986.

- The Taxpayer Relief Act of 1997 provided the wealthy with long-term investment tax breaks, and provided modest tax relief for individuals with child and educational expenses.

- President Bush's 2001 tax plan is designed to cut taxes $1.35 billion over ten years.

- A **flat tax** is a proportional tax on individual income after a specified threshold has been reached.

Teacher's Notes / Internet Bookmarks

NIGHTLY BUSINESS REPORT

ECONOMICS & YOU

Chapter 15
Disc 1, Side 2

How the Government Spends, Collects, and Owes

Also available in VHS.

Using the Chapter 9 Summary

Use the Chapter 9 Summary to preview, review, condense, or reteach the chapter.

Preview/Review

Vocabulary PuzzleMaker CD-ROM reinforces Key Terms.

Interactive Tutor Self-Assessment Software provides a review of Chapter 9 content.

Condense

Have students listen to the Chapter 9 Audio Program. Spanish also available.

Assign the Chapter 9 Audio Program Activity and give students the Chapter 9 Audio Program Test.

Have students complete the Guided Reading Activities and Reading Essentials and Study Guides for Chapter 9.

Reteach

Have students complete Reteaching Activity 9 in the TCR. Spanish also available.

GLENCOE
TECHNOLOGY

Use **MindJogger Videoquiz** to review the Chapter 9 content.

Have students visit the Web site at epp.glencoe.com to review Chapter 9 and take the **Self-Check Quiz**.

Identifying Key Terms

1. **f**	8. **k**
2. **j**	9. **m**
3. **h**	10. **e**
4. **i**	11. **c**
5. **l**	12. **a**
6. **d**	13. **b**
7. **g**	

Reviewing the Facts

Section 1

1. A heavy tax can be imposed on a product to limit consumption of that product.
2. Answers should demonstrate understanding of supply and demand curves and incidence of a tax.
3. equity—taxes should be just and impartial; simplicity—tax laws should be easily understood; efficiency—taxes should be relatively easy to administer.
4. benefit principle, ability-to-pay principle

Section 2

5. It is a progressive tax on people's earnings, collected through payroll withholding system and sent directly to the government.
6. Social Security taxes, medicare
7. the tax a corporation pays on its profits
8. excise taxes—taxes on the manufacture or sale of certain items; estate taxes—levied on transfer of property

Self-Check Quiz Visit the *Economics: Principles and Practices* Web site at epp.glencoe.com and click on *Chapter 9—Self-Check Quizzes* to prepare for the chapter test.

Identifying Key Terms

On a separate sheet of paper, choose the letter of the term identified by each phrase below.

a. **ability-to-pay**	h. **progressive tax**
b. **corporate income tax**	i. **proportional tax**
c. **estate tax**	j. **regressive tax**
d. **excise tax**	k. **sales tax**
e. **FICA**	l. **sin tax**
f. **indexing**	m. **VAT**
g. **individual income tax principle**	

1. annual adjustment of tax brackets to keep pace with inflation
2. average tax per dollar decreases as taxable income increases
3. average tax per dollar increases as taxable income increases
4. average tax per dollar unchanged as taxable income rises
5. designed to discourage consumption of socially undesirable goods or services
6. tax on the manufacture or sale of certain items
7. largest source of revenue for the federal government
8. large source of revenue for state governments
9. national sales tax on value added at each stage of production
10. Social Security and medicare taxes
11. tax on the transfer of property when a person dies
12. tax paid by those who can most afford to pay
13. third largest source of income for the federal government

Reviewing the Facts

Section 1 (pages 223–229)

1. **Describe** how taxes can be used to affect people's behavior.
2. **Illustrate,** using supply and demand curves, how the burden of a tax can be shifted.
3. **Explain** the three criteria used to evaluate taxes.
4. **Name** the two principles of taxation.

Section 2 (pages 231–236)

5. **Describe** the main features of the individual income tax.
6. **Identify** the two components of FICA.
7. **Describe** the corporate income tax.
8. **Distinguish** between excise taxes, estate and gift taxes, and customs duties.

Section 3 (pages 238–242)

9. **Identify** the main sources of revenue for state governments.
10. **List** the main sources of revenue for local governments.
11. **Identify** the main types of taxes that are normally withheld from a worker's paycheck.

Section 4 (pages 244–250)

12. **Describe** the five major tax reform bills enacted since 1980.
13. **List** the advantages and disadvantages of a VAT.

when a person dies; gift taxes—levied on donations of money or wealth; customs duties—levied on goods brought in from other countries

Section 3

9. sales taxes, intergovernmental revenues, individual income taxes, employee retirement contributions
10. intergovernmental revenues, property taxes, utilities and liquor stores, sales taxes
11. federal income tax, state income tax, city income tax, FICA taxes

Section 4

12. Economic Recovery Tax Act of 1981, tax reform law of 1986, Omnibus Budget Reconciliation Act of 1993, Taxpayer Relief Act of 1997, and 2001 tax reform
13. adv: hard to avoid, incidence of tax widely spread, not visible to consumer, easy to collect, small tax can raise large revenue; disadv: invisible to consumers, might compete with state sales taxes
14. individuals with high incomes

14. Identify the income group that will receive the most benefit under a flat tax.

15. Explain why future tax reforms are inevitable.

Thinking Critically

1. **Synthesizing Information** If you were an elected official who wanted to increase tax revenues, which of the following taxes would you prefer to use: individual income, sales, property, corporate income, user fees, VAT, or flat? Provide reasons for your decision.

2. **Making Comparisons** Distinguish between the benefit and the ability-to-pay principles of taxation. Use a web like the one below to help you organize your answer.

Principles of taxation

Ability to pay ◄——► Benefit

Applying Economic Concepts

1. **User Fees** In your own words, prepare the rationale for a user fee that you think should be enacted.

2. **Sales Taxes** Some people object to state and local governments imposing sales and property taxes. What would you say to these people in defense of the two taxes?

3. **Flat Taxes** Evaluate the concept of a flat income tax using the three criteria for effective taxes. Write a brief summary of your support or opposition to such a proposal.

Math Practice

After deductions and exemptions, Mindy's unmarried brother had taxable income of $87,000 in 2002. According to the tax table in **Figure 9.5**, what will

he owe in federal income taxes? What did he pay in Social Security taxes? What did he pay in medicare taxes?

Thinking Like an Economist

Describe how an economist might go about analyzing the consequences of shifting from the individual income tax to a consumption tax like the VAT.

Technology Skill

Using a Database For one week, keep a journal of all taxes you hear about on television or read about in the newspaper. Classify your journal entries into three categories: Federal, State, and Local taxes.

Create a database that has a record for each of the articles you used to find your information. Each record should have a separate field for the following: Title; Author; Year of publication; Tax category (Federal, State, Local); Criteria of taxation (equity, simplicity, efficiency).

Using your computer's software, sort the records by tax category (Federal, State, Local). Create a hard copy of this report. Share your database with the rest of the class.

Building Skills

Classifying Information Make a list of five taxes, charges, or user fees that you pay in your community. Draw a matrix like the one below and classify each of your five taxes in the appropriate place.

	Ability-to-Pay Principle	Benefit Principle
Regressive		
Proportional		
Progressive		

 Practice and **assess** key social studies skills with the *Glencoe Skillbuilder Interactive Workbook, Level 2.*

Math Practice

He paid $20,675 in income tax, and a little more than 7 cents per dollar in Social Security and medicare taxes—roughly $6,100.

Thinking Like an Economist

Answers should address the differences between individual income taxes and value-added taxes.

Technology Skill

Check databases for accuracy.

Building Skills

Answers will vary. Student responses should show an understanding of the different kinds of taxes and of the ability-to-pay and benefit principles.

 Bonus Test Question

The government decides to fight air pollution by cutting back on the amount of gasoline used. A one-dollar-per-gallon tax is to be imposed on gasoline. Should this tax be placed on oil companies or consumers? Explain. *(Placing the tax on consumers has the best chance of reducing gasoline use. Producers could absorb some of the cost of the tax in order to keep sales up.)*

15. because of the complexity of the tax code, the record tax collections in the 1990s, the abruptness of political changes

Thinking Critically

1. Answers should consider the criteria and principles of taxation.
2. Webs should contain information from pages 227–229.

Applying Economic Concepts

1. Answers should show understanding of the user fee's burden on the individual.
2. The sales tax is relatively cheap to administer and raises huge revenue; many public services enable people to improve their property value, so that property should be taxed.
3. A flat tax is a proportional tax on individual income after a specified threshold has been reached; answers should consider equity, simplicity, and efficiency of a flat tax.

253

Chapter 10 Resource Manager

SECTION RESOURCES

Daily Objectives

Section 1
The Economics of Government Spending
1. Explain why and how government expenditures have grown since the 1940s.
2. Describe two kinds of government expenditures.
3. Describe how government spending impacts the economy.

Section 2
Federal Government Expenditures
1. Explain how the federal budget is established.
2. Describe the parts of the federal budget.

Section 3
State and Local Government Expenditures
1. Explain how state and local governments approve spending.
2. Identify the major categories of state government expenditures.
3. Identify the major categories of local government expenditures.

Section 4
Deficits, Surpluses, and the National Debt
1. Explain how the federal deficit is related to the federal debt.
2. Relate the impact of the federal debt on the economy.
3. Describe past attempts to eliminate the federal deficit.
4. Describe entitlements.

Reproducible Resources

Section 1
- Reproducible Lesson Plan 10-1
- Daily Lecture Notes 10-1
- Guided Reading Activity 10-1
- Reading Essentials and Study Guide 10-1
- Section Quiz 10-1*

Section 2
- Reproducible Lesson Plan 10-2
- Daily Lecture Notes 10-2
- Guided Reading Activity 10-2
- Reading Essentials and Study Guide 10-2
- Section Quiz 10-2*

Section 3
- Reproducible Lesson Plan 10-3
- Daily Lecture Notes 10-3
- Guided Reading Activity 10-3
- Reading Essentials and Study Guide 10-3
- Section Quiz 10-3*

Section 4
- Reproducible Lesson Plan 10-4
- Daily Lecture Notes 10-4
- Guided Reading Activity 10-4
- Reading Essentials and Study Guide 10-4
- Section Quiz 10-4*

Technology/Multimedia Resources

Section 1
- Daily Focus Transparency 74
- Interactive Tutor Self-Assessment Software
- ExamView® Pro Testmaker
- Presentation Plus!

Section 2
- Daily Focus Transparency 75
- NBR Economics & You Video Program
- Interactive Tutor Self-Assessment Software
- ExamView® Pro Testmaker
- Presentation Plus!

Section 3
- Daily Focus Transparency 67
- Interactive Tutor Self-Assessment Software
- ExamView® Pro Testmaker
- Presentation Plus!

Section 4
- Daily Focus Transparency 76
- NBR Economics & You Video Program
- Vocabulary PuzzleMaker CD-ROM
- Interactive Tutor Self-Assessment Software
- ExamView® Pro Testmaker
- Presentation Plus!

 Transparency   CD-ROM   Software   Blackline Master

 Videodisc   Audio Program   Videocassette

Also available in Spanish

Chapter 10 Resource Manager

TeacherWorks™ All-In-One Planner and Resource Center

- **Interactive Teacher Edition** Access your Teacher Wraparound Edition and your classroom resources with a few easy clicks.
- **Interactive Lesson Planner** Planning has never been easier! Organize your week, month, semester, or year with all the lesson helps you need to make teaching creative, timely, and relevant.

Use Glencoe's **Presentation Plus!** multimedia teacher tool to easily present dynamic lessons that visually excite your students. Using Microsoft PowerPoint® you can customize the presentations to create your own personalized lessons.

ACTIVITY

From the Classroom of...

**Bill Yee
Alhambra High School
Alhambra, CA**

Economic Plan for the Fiscal Year

Organize students into groups of four. Instruct each group to choose and answer two of the following questions:
1. Does the United States government create more jobs by increasing spending on highway and public transit projects?
2. Should Congress provide funding for job training or retraining in economically depressed areas?
3. Should Congress cut entitlement programs such as Social Security, medicare, and medicaid?
4. How many years would you take to balance the budget, and how would you reduce the federal debt?

After the groups have researched and answered their questions, they should prepare and make a presentation to the president as part of his team of economic advisers. The presentation may include charts, graphs, a PowerPoint presentation, and so on. Follow each presentation with a discussion of whether the recommended policies will benefit the economy of the United States.

National Council on Economic Education

THE **Economics**America AND **Economics**International PROGRAMS

Voluntary National Content Standards in Economics
Emphasized in Chapter 10

Content Standard 16

Content Standard 20

For a complete listing of NCEE Standards and entire text correlation, see Teacher pages in front of book.

Resources Available from NCEE
- Capstone: The Nation's High School Economics Course
- Civics and Government: Focus on Economics
- Economics at Work

To order these materials or to contact your state Council on Economic Education about workshops and programs, call 1-800-338-1192 or visit www.nationalcouncil.org

Chapter 10 Resource Manager

Economic Concept Transparency 12:
The Role of Government

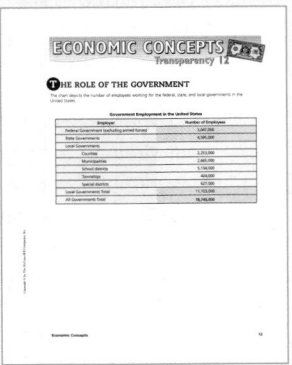

APPLICATION AND ENRICHMENT

Consumer Application
Activity 15

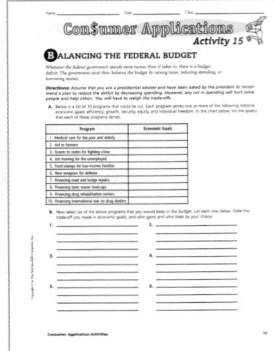

Free Enterprise
Activity 15

APPLICATION AND ENRICHMENT

Enrichment Activity 10

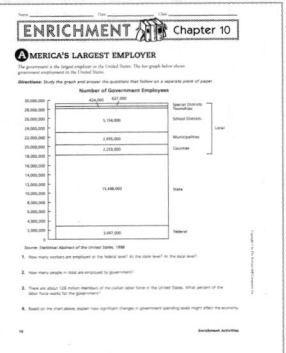

Cooperative Learning
Activity 15

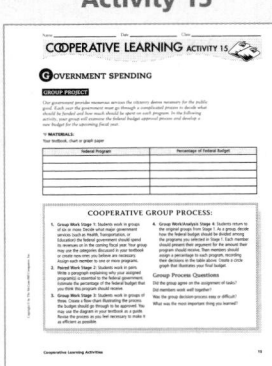

Math Practice
Activity 15

Economic Cartoon 15

Primary and Secondary
Source Reading 15

REVIEW AND REINFORCEMENT

Economic Vocabulary
Activity 10

Reteaching Activity 10

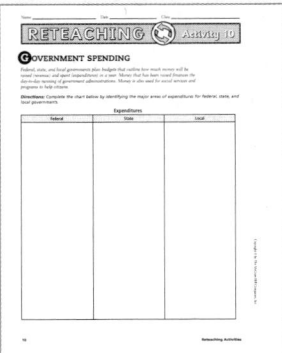

Critical Thinking
Activity 15

Reinforcing Economic
Skill 23

Chapter 10 Resource Manager

ASSESSMENT AND EVALUATION

Chapter 10 Test Form A

Chapter 10 Test Form B

Performance Assessment Activity 15

ExamView® Pro Testmaker

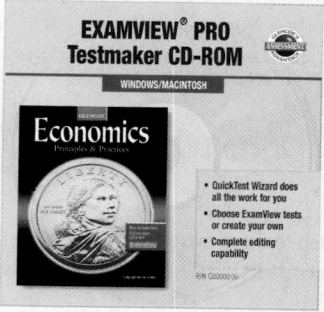

SPANISH RESOURCES

The following Spanish language materials are available in the Spanish Resources binder:

 Spanish Economic Vocabulary Activities

 Spanish Reteaching Activities

 Spanish Section Quizzes

 Spanish Economic Concepts Transparencies

Also available:

  Spanish Chapter 10 Audio Program Activity and Test

TECHNOLOGY/MULTIMEDIA

- Vocabulary PuzzleMaker CD-ROM
- Interactive Tutor Self-Assessment Software
- ExamView® Pro Testmaker
- Audio Program (English or Spanish)
- NBR Economics & You Video Program (English or Spanish)
- MindJogger Videoquiz
- Interactive Economics! CD-ROM
- Presentation Plus!
- TeacherWorks CD-ROM
- Glencoe Skillbuilder Interactive Workbook CD-ROM, Level 2

ECONOMICS Online

Use our Web site for additional resources. All essential content is covered in the Student Edition.

You and your students can visit epp.glencoe.com, the Web site companion to **Economics: Principles and Practices.** This innovative integration of electronic and print media offers your students a wealth of opportunities. The student text directs students to the Web site for the following options:

- **Chapter Overviews**
- **Student Web Activities**
- **Self-Check Quizzes**
- **Textbook Updates**

Answers are provided for you in the Web Activity Lesson Plan. Additional Web resources and interactive puzzles are also available.

Performance Assessment

Refer to Activity 15 in the *Performance Assessment Strategies and Activities* booklet.

 BLOCK SCHEDULING

 ECONOMICS *Online*

Introduce students to chapter content and key terms by having them access **Chapter Overview 10** at epp.glencoe.com

NIGHTLY BUSINESS REPORT

 ECONOMICS & YOU

Chapter 16
Disc 1, Side 2

Government Spending

After viewing this segment, students should be able to:
- Discuss how federal spending decisions are made.

 Also available in VHS.

GLENCOE TECHNOLOGY

Use **MindJogger Videoquiz** to preview the Chapter 10 content.

CHAPTER 10
Government Spending

Government expenditures are used to maintain transportation systems and protect the environment.

Economics & You

If you borrow money because you spend more than you earn, you run a deficit. In **Chapter 10,** you will learn how federal deficits and surpluses impact the U.S. economy. To learn more about government spending, view the Chapter 16 video lesson:

Government Spending

ECONOMICS *Online*

Chapter Overview Visit the *Economics: Principles and Practices* Web site at epp.glencoe.com and click on **Chapter 10—Chapter Overview** to preview chapter information.

✚ EXTRA CREDIT PROJECT

Ask students to make a weekly budget, noting expected income, categories into which these funds should be divided, the proposed spending on each category, and the actual spending. Have them report if they ran a deficit or surplus, and how they plan to adjust spending in the future.

The Economics of Government Spending

Study Guide

Main Idea
The role of the federal government has grown, making it a vital player in the economy.

Reading Strategy
Graphic Organizer As you read the section, complete a graphic organizer similar to this one by listing reasons for the increase in government spending since the 1940s.

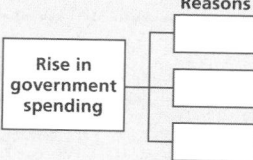

Reasons

Rise in government spending

Key Terms
per capita, public sector, private sector, transfer payment, grant-in-aid, distribution of income

Objectives
After studying this section, you will be able to:
1. **Explain** why and how government expenditures have grown since the 1940s.
2. **Describe** two kinds of government expenditures.
3. **Describe** how government spending impacts the economy.

Applying Economic Concepts
Transfer Payments Read to find out how transfer payments serve as one of the tools used to promote the goal of economic security.

FOCUS

Section Overview
This section gives background information on the growth of government spending.

BELLRINGER
Motivational Activity

 Project **transparency** and have students answer questions.

 Available as blackline master.

Daily Focus Transparency 74

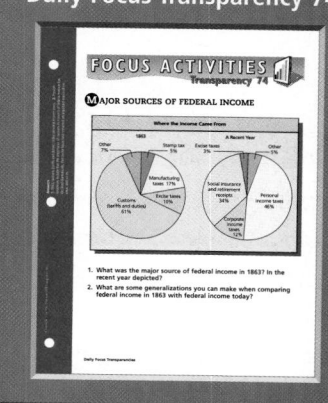

Cover Story

Raising the Stakes in the Budget Game

The $1.35 trillion tax cut Congress passed last month was supposed to leave ample room for such goodies as higher defense and education spending, a prescription drug benefit, and even some buybacks of government IOUs. It's quickly becoming clear, however, that the wish lists of the White House, Congress, and federal agencies may need a heavy edit.

House Budget chair, Rep. Jim Nussle

Congress is already on track to spend more than the White House wants: Last week, a Republican-controlled House Appropriations committee volunteered $150 million more for payments to apple farmers and an added $814 million for a natural resources bill. Meanwhile, a senate-passed education bill calls for $15 billion above the White House's request. . . .

—*U.S. News & World Report,* June 25, 2001

Government is big business in America. In fact, all levels of government in the United States spend more than all privately owned businesses combined. Government is a major player in our economy due to its enormous expenditures.

Government Spending in Perspective

In 2001, total expenditures by federal, state, and local governments collectively amounted to nearly $2.9 trillion. On a **per capita,** or per person, basis, this amounts to almost $10,300 for every man, woman, and child in the United States.

Spending in the **public sector**—the part of the economy made up of federal, state, and local governments—did not begin to rise significantly until the 1940s. Several reasons account for this increase. The first was the huge amount of spending required because of World War II. The second reason was the change in public opinion that gave government a larger role in everyday economic affairs. After the

CHAPTER 10: GOVERNMENT SPENDING **255**

Study Guide

Reading Strategy
Have students create the graphic organizer.
Answers to Graphic: *World War II, change in public opinion, success of public works projects*

Preteaching Vocabulary
Ask students to write, in their own words, definitions of the Key Terms.

RESOURCE MANAGER

📂 Reproducible Masters
- Reproducible Lesson Plan 10-1
- Daily Lecture Notes 10-1
- Guided Reading Activity 10-1
- Reading Essentials and Study Guide 10-1
- Section Quiz 10-1

🖥 Transparencies
- Daily Focus Transparency 74

Multimedia
- 💾 Interactive Tutor Self-Assessment Software
- 💿 ExamView® Pro Testmaker
- 💿 Presentation Plus!

2 TEACH

Daily Lecture Notes 10-1

Answer: *Yes; following World War II*

L2 Applying Ideas

Write the following headings on the board: *Allocation of Resources, Distribution of Income,* and *Competition with the Private Sector.* Call on volunteers to provide examples of how government spending affects each of the categories listed on the board. Note their responses on the board. Have students use this information to write a paragraph on the impact of government spending on the economy.

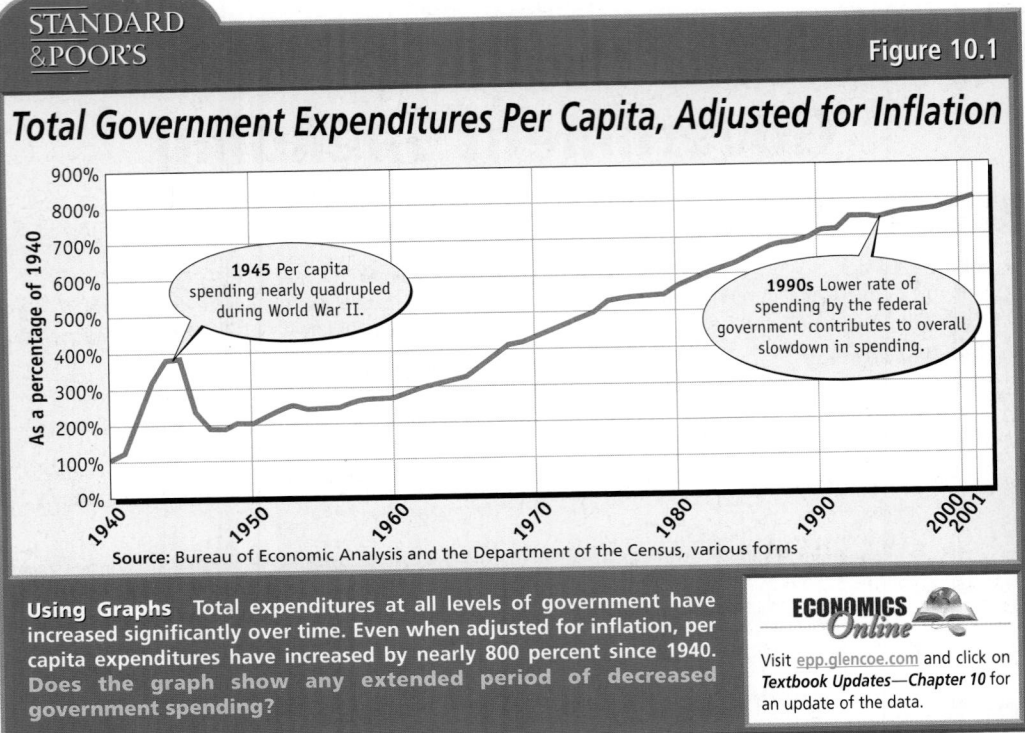

Total Government Expenditures Per Capita, Adjusted for Inflation

Figure 10.1

1945 Per capita spending nearly quadrupled during World War II.

1990s Lower rate of spending by the federal government contributes to overall slowdown in spending.

Source: Bureau of Economic Analysis and the Department of the Census, various forms

Using Graphs Total expenditures at all levels of government have increased significantly over time. Even when adjusted for inflation, per capita expenditures have increased by nearly 800 percent since 1940. Does the graph show any extended period of decreased government spending?

ECONOMICS *Online*

Visit epp.glencoe.com and click on **Textbook Updates—Chapter 10** for an update of the data.

Great Depression, government was called upon to regulate banks, public utilities, and many other activities.

A third reason was the success of large-scale public works projects like the TVA, which brought low-cost electricity to millions in the rural South during the mid-1930s. The events of the 1930s and early 1940s set the stage for the unprecedented growth of government spending shown in **Figure 10.1**.

Over time, many Americans have accepted increased government expenditures as the inevitable consequence of progress. Still, some people question how many goods and services government should provide—and, therefore, the level of revenue collection required to support these expenditures.

Others question what services the government should provide and what services the **private sector**—the part of the economy made up of private individuals and privately-owned businesses—should provide.

Two Kinds of Spending

In general, government makes two broad kinds of expenditures. The first is the purchase of goods and services. As **Figure 10.2** shows, all levels of government combined consume nearly one-third of the nation's output. The second is in the form of payments to disadvantaged Americans and other designated groups.

Goods and Services

The government buys many goods, such as tanks, planes, ships, and even space shuttles. It needs office buildings, land for parks, and capital goods for schools and laboratories. The government also needs to purchase supplies and hire people to work in its agencies and staff the military. Payments for these services include the wages and salaries paid to these workers.

MEETING SPECIAL NEEDS ACTIVITY

Learning Style: Kinesthetic Challenge kinesthetic learners to a game of "Spending Twister." On several plate-sized circles of cardboard, write the names of goods and services for which the government pays. Examples of goods are tanks, books, and buildings. Examples of services are military defense, medical research, and park maintenance. Tape circles to the floor and have each player place a hand or a foot on an appropriate circle when you call out "good" or "service." You may leave several circles unmarked. If a player uses the circle, he or she must give an example not already used.

Refer to *Inclusion for the Social Studies Classroom Strategies and Activities* in the TCR.

The government uses goods, services, and other resources to provide the public goods and services that most Americans enjoy. In general, the more the government provides, the more goods and services it consumes in the first place.

Transfer Payments

The second kind of government expenditure is a **transfer payment**—a payment for which the government receives neither goods nor services in return. Transfer payments to individuals include Social Security, welfare, unemployment compensation, and aid for people with disabilities. People normally receive these payments solely because they need assistance.

There are different kinds of transfer payments. A transfer payment one level of government makes to another is known as a **grant-in-aid.** Interstate highway construction programs are an example. The federal government grants money to cover the major part of the cost, while the states in which the highways will be built pay the rest. The construction of new public schools also can be financed through grants-in-aid.

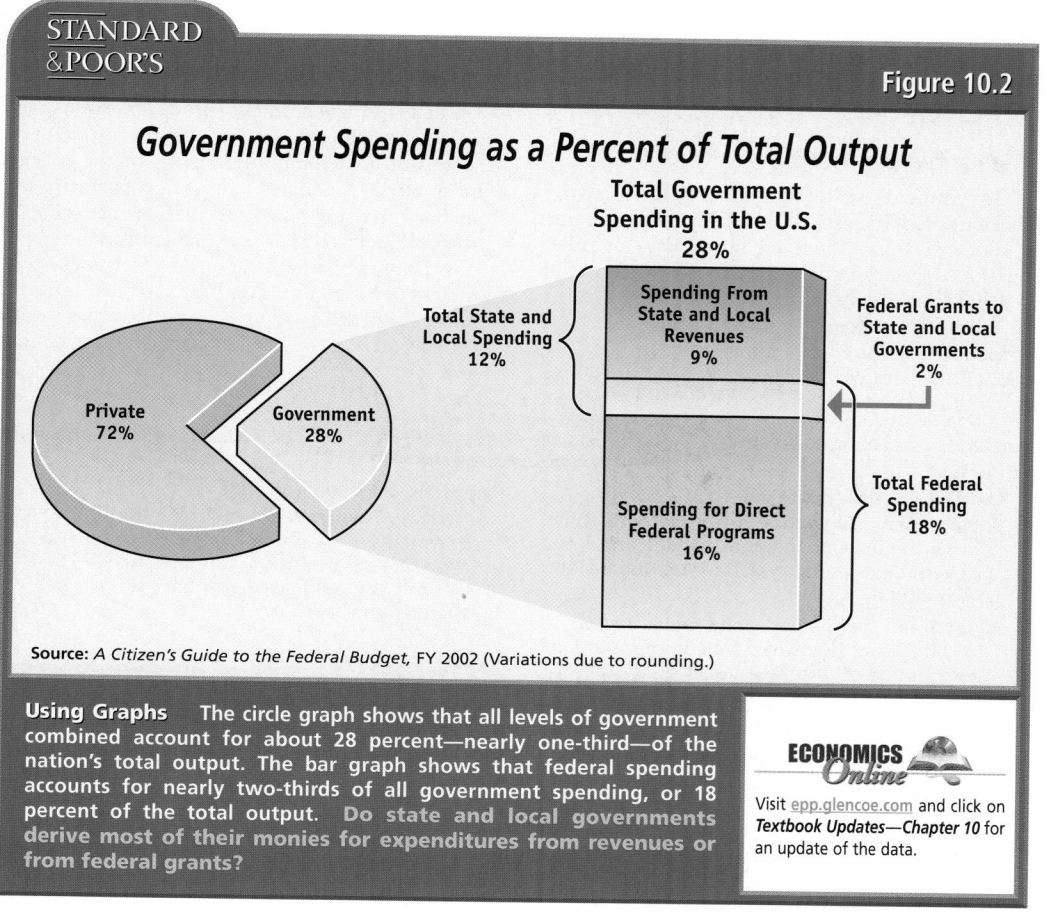

STANDARD &POOR'S

Figure 10.2

Government Spending as a Percent of Total Output

Total Government Spending in the U.S.
28%

Private **72%**
Government **28%**

Total State and Local Spending **12%**

Spending From State and Local Revenues **9%**

Federal Grants to State and Local Governments **2%**

Spending for Direct Federal Programs **16%**

Total Federal Spending **18%**

Source: *A Citizen's Guide to the Federal Budget*, FY 2002 (Variations due to rounding.)

Using Graphs The circle graph shows that all levels of government combined account for about 28 percent—nearly one-third—of the nation's total output. The bar graph shows that federal spending accounts for nearly two-thirds of all government spending, or 18 percent of the total output. **Do state and local governments derive most of their monies for expenditures from revenues or from federal grants?**

ECONOMICS *Online*

Visit epp.glencoe.com and click on *Textbook Updates—Chapter 10* for an update of the data.

CHAPTER 10: GOVERNMENT SPENDING **257**

STANDARD &POOR'S

Answer: *from revenues*

 ASSESS

Assign Section 1 Assessment as homework or as an in-class activity.

Have students use **Interactive Tutor Self-Assessment Software.**

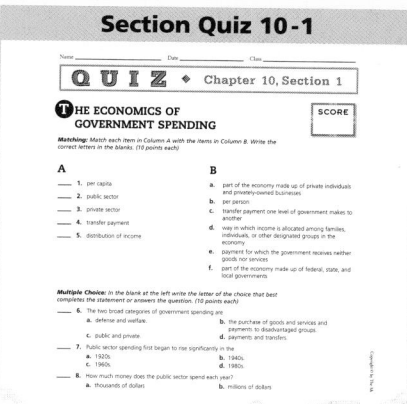
FREE ENTERPRISE ACTIVITY

Government spending is a frequent and critical target of conversation on the street and in the classroom. Ask students to write down three public goods and/or services for which they believe taxes should *not* be used. In a follow-up discussion, have students present and explain their choices. Note on the board the items most often selected. Then lead a discussion by **asking:** Would the items listed be better produced by the private sector? Why or why not? **BLOCK SCHEDULING**

Reteach

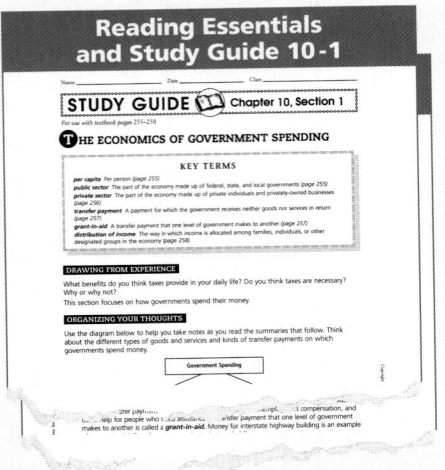

Enrich

Have students investigate and write a report on the changes in society—population growth, changes in employment, transportation, and communications, for example—that have led to increased government spending.

CLOSE

Have students discuss the economic impact of government spending in their community. **Ask:** How has spending by the school board affected our school?

258

Impact of Government Spending

 The enormous size of the public sector gives it the potential to affect people's daily lives in many ways. Several of these effects are examined below.

Affecting Resource Allocation

Government spending decisions directly affect how resources are allocated. If the government spends its revenues on projects such as missile systems in rural areas rather than on social welfare programs in urban areas, economic activity is stimulated in rural areas as resources are shifted there. The allocation of resources can be affected indirectly as well. In agriculture, the decision to support the prices of milk, grains, or peanuts keeps the factors of production working in those industries.

Redistributing Income

Government spending also influences the **distribution of income,** or the way in which income is allocated among families, individuals, or other designated groups in the economy. The incomes of needy families, for example, can be directly affected by increasing or decreasing transfer payments.

Incomes are affected indirectly when the government decides where to make expenditures. The decision to buy fighter planes from one factory rather than from another has an impact on the communities near both factories. Many businesses not linked to either company will feel the effects when workers are laid off or get new jobs and alter their spending habits. These situations are not merely hypothetical. The military base closings of the 1990s had a devastating impact on incomes in local communities that had come to depend on the military installations.

On the positive side, government can provide temporary income support for selective groups. In 1999, for example, the Department of Agriculture purchased millions of pounds of pork in an attempt to support low pork prices for farmers.

Competing With the Private Sector

When the government produces goods and services, it often competes with the private sector. In the area of higher education, many public colleges and universities compete with more expensive private ones. In many cases the cost difference is due to the subsidies received by the public institutions.

In the area of health care, the government runs a system of hospitals for military veterans. Taxpayer dollars fund these facilities, which compete with hospitals in the private sector that offer similar services.

Section 1 Assessment

Checking for Understanding
1. **Main Idea** Using your notes from the graphic organizer activity on page 255, describe why government spending during the Depression increased.
2. **Key Terms** Define per capita, public sector, private sector, transfer payment, grant-in-aid, distribution of income.
3. **Describe** the per capita growth in government spending since 1940.
4. **List** two kinds of government spending.
5. **Identify** three ways that government spending may impact the economy.

Applying Economic Concepts
6. **Transfer Payments** Do you think that transfer payments, such as unemployment compensation, are a successful or unsuccessful way to accomplish the goal of economic security? Defend your answer.

Critical Thinking
7. **Making Generalizations** Is government spending too much? Interview five people to learn their views on this question. Summarize their views in a short paper.

Practice and assess key social studies skills with the *Glencoe Skillbuilder Interactive Workbook, Level 2.*

258 UNIT 3 MACROECONOMICS: INSTITUTIONS

Section 1 Assessment Answers

1. because the government was called upon to regulate banks, public utilities, and many other activities
2. All vocabulary terms are defined in the text.
3. It grew dramatically during World War II and then fell back after the war. Since that time it has grown significantly.
4. purchase of goods and services; transfer payments to support incomes of disadvantaged persons
5. It can affect the allocation of resources, the distribution of income, and cause the government to compete with producers in the private sector.
6. They provide a minimum income for the poorest people.
7. Papers should summarize views.

TECHNOLOGY Skill

Using E-Mail

Electronic mail, or E-mail, refers to communicating at a distance through the use of a computer. A computer is ready to "talk" to other computers after two things are added to it: (a) a modem—or device that allows communication through a telephone line, and (b) communications software, which lets your computer prepare and send information to the modem.

Help our class!

Arial 12 **B** / U

To... UmbisaGusa@AOL.com

Cc...

Subject: Help our class!

Dear Umbisa,
    Hello! We know you are very happy being back home in Kenya. Your postcard was so cool. I would really like to see Mt. Kilimanjaro some day. Our class is researching government taxation. We would like to know about the tax system in Kenya. Do your parents pay an income tax? Do you pay sales taxes on the items you purchase? Reply as soon as you can because my report is due tomorrow! Thanks!
Your friend,
Dylan

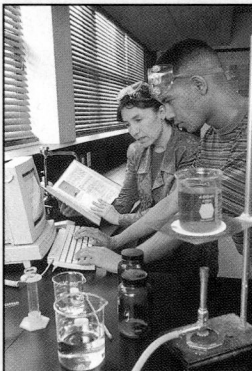

After you type in your message, you may send it, forward it, and even save it to a folder.

Learning the Skill

To send an E-mail message, complete the following steps:

- Select the "Message" function from your communications software.
- Type in your message, and proofread it for errors.
- Type in the E-mail address of the recipient and select the "Send" button.

The E-mail system places the message in the receiver's electronic mailbox. He or she may read the message at any time, and send you a return message. When you receive E-mail, the sender's address is on the message—add it to your electronic address book at that time.

Practicing the Skill

Select a current issue in economics to research. Possible topics include, What is the effect of the debt on the economy? and, What steps can be taken to reduce the debt? Then browse the Internet to obtain the E-mail address of a federal official concerned with the issue. E-mail the official, sharing opinions about the issue, asking questions about the issue, and requesting information.

Application Activity

E-mail a classmate. Forward the information you received from the government official concerning the issue above. Working together, write a summary of the E-mail correspondence with the official.

Technology Skill

Teaching Skills

Research on the Internet to find economics teachers in schools in other parts of the country, or from around the world. Contact the teachers and arrange for your classes to be E-mail pen pals. Students may simply exchange notes on what they are learning in economics, or solicit opinions on subjects such as government spending or the U.S. economy.

Additional Practice

Reinforcing Economic Skill 23

Reinforcing Economic Skills — Chapter 23

USING A DATABASE

	A	B	C
1	Field 1	Field 2	
2	3.5		
3			
4			

An electronic database is a collection of facts or statistics that are stored in a file on a computer. The information is organized into categories, called fields. For example, a field could contain the names or street addresses of your clients. It could also include the amount of money each client spent in the past year. A set of related fields is known as a record. Together, all of the records make up the database.

To create a database, think about what information you want to include. Then follow the instructions in your computer program to set up fields. Be sure to enter each item in the correct field. Then determine how you want to organize or sort the information in the database (chronologically, alphabetically, by zip code, or some other way).

Directions: Survey at least 10 of your classmates or other people you know on their shopping preferences. Then use a database program to create fields and records that include each person's name, address, and favorite retail clothing store. Be sure to place each piece of information in a separate field.

1. Which retail store was preferred by the largest number of people?
2. How many people who preferred the retail store in Question 1 live in the same zip code?
3. Print out an alphabetical list of all people in your database.
4. Print out an alphabetical list of all of the retail stores that appear in your database.
5. If you were about to open a clothing store in your area, how would you use the information in this database?
6. What other information might you want to include in the database?

Reinforcing Economic Skills   23

Answers to Practicing the Skill

Check that students have accurately followed E-mail procedures. Answers should reflect the opinions of the official responding to students' E-mail.

1 FOCUS

Section Overview
This section describes the process for establishing the federal budget and the major spending categories.

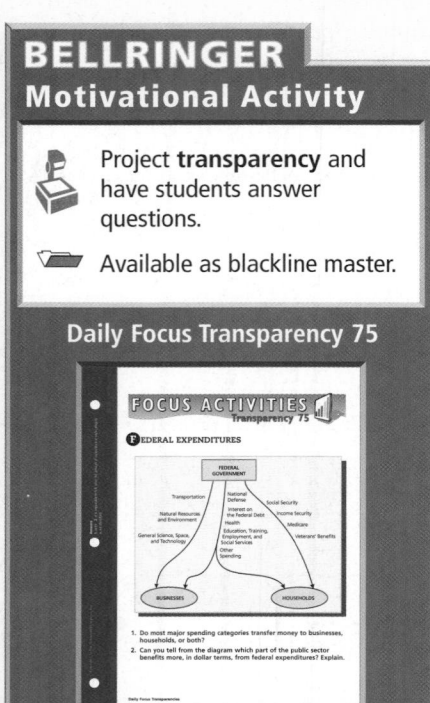

Study Guide

Reading Strategy
Have students create the graphic organizer.
Answers to Graphic: *mandatory: authorized by law, continues without annual congressional approval; discretionary: must receive annual authorization by Congress*

Preteaching Vocabulary
Call on students to read aloud the definitions of the Key Terms from the Glossary. Have volunteers use each term in a sentence.

Federal Government Expenditures

Study Guide

Main Idea
The federal government's budget supplies money for many services and programs.

Reading Strategy
Graphic Organizer As you read the section, complete a graphic organizer similar to the one below that describes the different types of government spending.

Key Terms
federal budget, mandatory spending, discretionary spending, fiscal year, federal budget surplus, federal budget deficit, appropriations bill, medicaid

Objectives
After studying this section, you will be able to:
1. **Explain** how the federal budget is established.
2. **Describe** the parts of the federal budget.

Applying Economic Concepts
Mandatory Spending Remember those FICA taxes deducted from your paycheck? The government does not save your FICA taxes until you retire. As soon as this money is collected from you, the government spends it as Social Security payments to others, which is why they are called transfer payments.

Cover Story

The Federal Budget

WASHINGTON— President Bush sent Congress a federal budget framework on Wednesday that would curtail and even reverse the growth of many domestic programs while plowing savings into tax relief and debt reduction.

President George W. Bush

Over a 10-year period, Bush pledged to slash the national debt by $2 trillion, set aside funds to protect Medicare, cut taxes by $1.6 trillion and establish a new reserve fund for unexpected needs.

Bush argued that his approach was "compassionate," "responsible" and "reasonable." The plan, he said, presumes "a federal government that is both active to promote opportunity and limited to preserve freedom."

—*The Los Angeles Times*, March 1, 2001

Taking action on spending bills is but one step in the preparation of the **federal budget**—an annual plan outlining proposed revenues and expenditures for the coming year.

Approximately two-thirds of the federal budget consists of **mandatory spending**—spending authorized by law that continues without the need for annual approvals of Congress. Mandatory spending includes interest payments on borrowed money, Social Security, and medicare. The remaining one-third of the budget deals with **discretionary spending**—programs that must receive annual authorization. Discretionary spending decisions include how much to spend on programs such as the military, the Coast Guard, and welfare.

Establishing the Federal Budget

 The federal budget is prepared for a **fiscal year**—a 12-month financial planning period that may or may not coincide with the calendar year. The government's fiscal year starts on October 1 of every calendar year and expires on September 30 of the following year.

RESOURCE MANAGER

Reproducible Masters
- Reproducible Lesson Plan 10-2
- Daily Lecture Notes 10-2
- Guided Reading Activity 10-2
- Reading Essentials and Study Guide 10-2
- Section Quiz 10-2

Transparencies
- Daily Focus Transparency 75

Multimedia
- 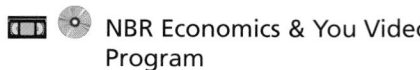 NBR Economics & You Video Program
- Interactive Tutor Self-Assessment Software
- ExamView® Pro Testmaker
- Presentation Plus!

Executive Formulation

The first step in the process of developing the budget is executive formulation. This means that the president establishes the general budget guidelines for a multiyear period, with the primary focus on the upcoming fiscal year.

As part of the preparation, the president confers with government agencies, other executive office units, and the Office of Management and Budget (OMB), the division of the executive branch primarily responsible for assembling the budget under presidential guidelines.

By law, the federal budget must be sent to Congress no later than early February. However, the budget pictured in **Figure 10.3** was presented to Congress in March, because of the change in administrations. The budget lists $2,192 billion of revenues and $1,961 billion of mandatory and discretionary spending. The budget also shows a **federal budget surplus**—an excess of revenues over expenditures—of $231 billion. If the budget had shown expenditures to be larger than revenues, then it would have been a **federal budget deficit** equal to the shortfall. Whether these numbers turn out to be accurate depends on a number of factors, including the health of the economy and, more importantly, the will of Congress.

Action by the House

The president's budget is only a request to Congress. Congress has the power to approve, modify, or disapprove the president's proposed budget—the most difficult and time-consuming part of the budget process. However, the House does not debate all budget expenditures, only the discretionary spending, which amounted to approximately $692 billion in that year.

First, the House sets initial budget targets for discretionary spending. For example, the House might decide that the projected expenditures for agriculture are too high and spending on international affairs is too low, and then set different targets.

Once the budget targets are set, the House assigns appropriations bills to various House subcommittees—effectively breaking the entire budget down into 13 smaller ones. An **appropriations bill** is an act of Congress that allows federal agencies to

spend money for specific purposes. House subcommittees hold hearings on each bill and debate the measure. If the bill is approved, it is sent to the full House Appropriations Committee. If it passes there, the bill is sent to the entire House for approval.

The deadline for completing this part of the process is September 15. However, individual appropriations bills are often delayed, or changed in a way that makes them incompatible with the overall budget targets. Part of the problem is that individuals in Congress often try to get appointed to specific budget appropriation committees so that they can secure funds to help their home districts.

Action by the Senate

The Senate receives the budget after the House approves it. The Senate may approve the bill as sent by the House, or it may draft its own version. If differences exist between the House and the Senate versions, a joint House-Senate conference committee tries to work out a compromise bill.

During this process, the House and the Senate often seek advice from several government bureaus and offices, including the Congressional Budget Office (CBO). The CBO is a congressional agency that evaluates the impact of legislation and projects future revenues and expenditures that will result from the legislation.

② TEACH

Daily Lecture Notes 10-2

DAILY LECTURE NOTES — Lesson 10-2

DID YOU KNOW?
In January 1999 President Clinton presented to Congress the federal budget for 2000, a balanced budget that anticipated a federal surplus. Clinton recommended that Congress spend the surplus on sustaining Social Security and improving medicare. He cited measurable signs that the nation's economy was strong and prosperous—17 million new jobs, the lowest rate of unemployment in 40 years, and the lowest number of people on welfare in 25 years. He acknowledged that, to streamline government, his administration had cut 365,000 civilians from the federal work force, making it the smallest federal workforce since 1933.

PAGES 260–262

I. Establishing the Federal Budget

A. The federal budget consists of (1) mandatory spending, which includes interest payments on borrowed money, Social Security, and medicare (two-thirds of the budget); and (2) discretionary spending, which includes programs that Congress must approve annually (one-third of the budget).

B. The government's fiscal year is from October 1 to September 30.

C. The first step toward adopting a budget is executive formulation—the president confers with his advisors and drafts a budget which he submits to Congress.

D. The second step is House action—Congress has the power to approve, modify, or disapprove the president's proposed budget. The House sets budget targets for each category of the discretionary budget, then assigns appropriations bills to various subcommittees where subcommittee members study and debate each bill. If the bill is approved in subcommittee, it is sent to the full House Appropriations Committee. If approved there, it goes to the entire House for a vote. All these congressional steps must be completed by September 15 each year.

L1 The Budget Process
Read aloud the description of the process of federal budget making. Note the following on the board: the president, OMB, House Appropriations subcommittees, House Appropriations Committee, joint conference committees, Congressional Budget Office. Have students use the items listed to construct a flowchart. **ELL**

NIGHTLY BUSINESS REPORT

ECONOMICS & YOU

Chapter 16
Disc 1, Side 2

Government Spending

Ask: What are three areas of government spending? *(national defense, interest on national debt, Social Security, and transfer payments)*

Guided Reading Activity 10-2

F.Y.I.

On average, the federal government spends about $3.2 million per minute.

L2 Constitutional Principles

Call on volunteers to explain how the budget process demonstrates the constitutional principle of checks and balances.

ECONOMICS
AT A GLANCE

Answer: *individual income tax*

Final Approval

If everything goes as planned, the House and the Senate approve the compromise bill and then send it to the president for signature. Because Congress literally took apart, rewrote, and put back together the president's budget, the final version may or may not resemble the original proposal.

If the budget was altered too much, the president can veto the bill and force Congress to come up with a budget closer to the president's original version. Or, if Congress fails to pass a budget in time for approval by the Senate, the government can shut down briefly—as it did in late 1995 and early 1996. However, it is more likely that Congress and the president would agree to continue to operate at the previous year's spending levels.

Once signed by the president, the budget becomes the official document for the next fiscal year that starts on October 1 and ends on September 30. The budget shown in **Figure 10.3** is called the fiscal year 2002 budget because nine of the 12 calendar months fall in that year.

Major Spending Categories

The thousands of individual expenditures in the federal budget can be grouped into the broad categories shown in **Figures 10.3** and **10.4.**

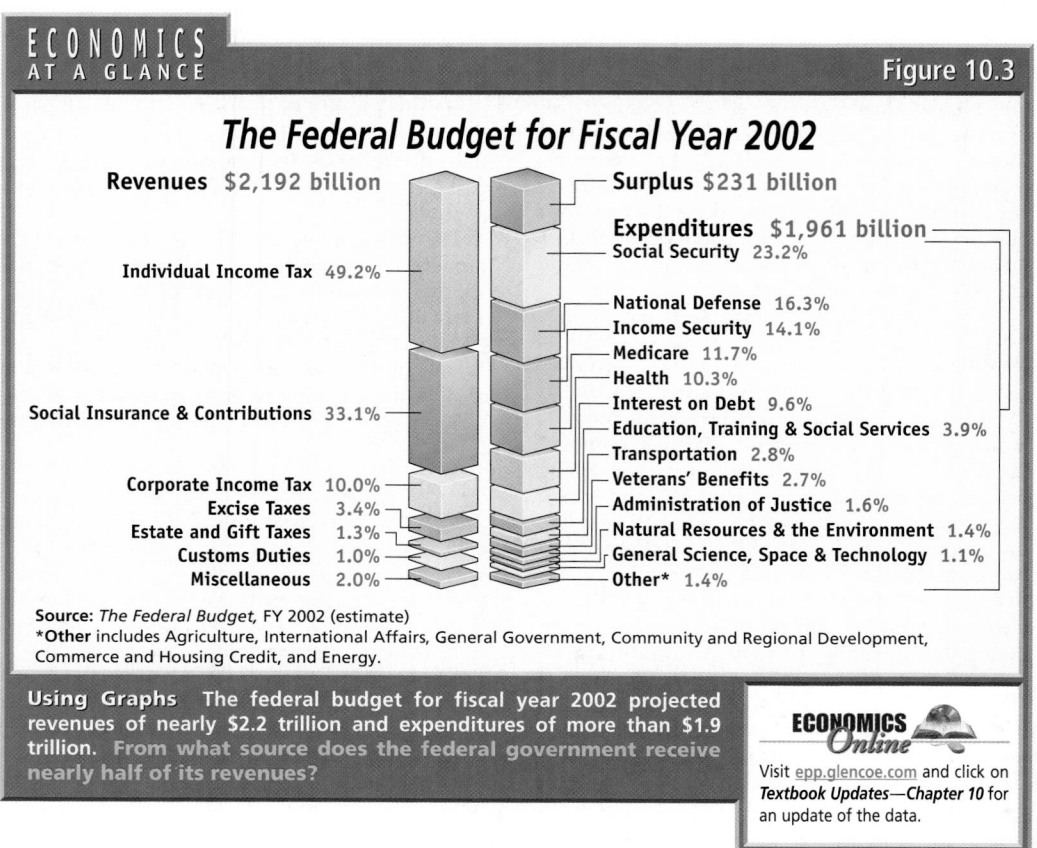

ECONOMICS
AT A GLANCE

Figure 10.3

The Federal Budget for Fiscal Year 2002

Revenues $2,192 billion

Surplus $231 billion

Expenditures $1,961 billion

Individual Income Tax 49.2%

Social Insurance & Contributions 33.1%

Corporate Income Tax 10.0%
Excise Taxes 3.4%
Estate and Gift Taxes 1.3%
Customs Duties 1.0%
Miscellaneous 2.0%

Social Security 23.2%
National Defense 16.3%
Income Security 14.1%
Medicare 11.7%
Health 10.3%
Interest on Debt 9.6%
Education, Training & Social Services 3.9%
Transportation 2.8%
Veterans' Benefits 2.7%
Administration of Justice 1.6%
Natural Resources & the Environment 1.4%
General Science, Space & Technology 1.1%
Other* 1.4%

Source: *The Federal Budget*, FY 2002 (estimate)
***Other** includes Agriculture, International Affairs, General Government, Community and Regional Development, Commerce and Housing Credit, and Energy.

Using Graphs The federal budget for fiscal year 2002 projected revenues of nearly $2.2 trillion and expenditures of more than $1.9 trillion. **From what source does the federal government receive nearly half of its revenues?**

ECONOMICS *Online*
Visit epp.glencoe.com and click on **Textbook Updates—Chapter 10** for an update of the data.

FREE ENTERPRISE ACTIVITY

Organize the class into five groups and explain that each group is a congressional subcommittee reviewing budget priorities. Ask subcommittees to discuss and rank the programs listed below in descending order with the highest priority first. Have subcommittee members try to reach consensus, although it is not absolutely necessary. After discussion is completed, ask representatives from each subcommittee to share their lists with the class and explain their reasoning.

1. national defense; **2.** health care; **3.** food for starving people in a nation involved in a civil war; **4.** research on the environment; **5.** space exploration; **6.** homes for the homeless in the U.S.; **7.** Food Stamps; **8** scholarships for needy students to attend college **BLOCK SCHEDULING**

Federal Government Expenditures, 1980–2002

1980

23.2%	Social Security
20.6%	
15.0%	
9.1 %	
5.6%	
5.3%	
4.0%	
3.7%	
3.7%	
1.9%	
1.0%	
6.9%	

1990

23.9%	
19.8%	
14.7%	
11.7%	
7.8%	
4.6%	
3.1%	
2.4%	
2.3%	
1.2%	
1.1%	
7.4%	

2002

23.2%	Social Security
16.3%	National Defense
14.1%	Income Security
11.7%	Medicare
10.3%	Health
9.6%	Net Interest on Debt / Education, Training, Employment & Social Services
3.9%	Transportation
2.8%	Veterans' Benefits
2.7%	General Science, Space & Technology
1.1%	International Affairs
1.1%	
3.2%	Other

Source: *Economic Report of the President,* various years

Using Graphs The major categories of federal government expenditures show some change from 1980 to 2002. The three largest federal spending categories in 2002 were Social Security, national defense, and income security. **How has spending for Social Security changed during the period from 1980 to 2002?**

ECONOMICS *Online*

Visit epp.glencoe.com and click on *Textbook Updates—Chapter 10* for an update of the data.

CHAPTER 10: GOVERNMENT SPENDING **263**

STANDARD &POOR'S

Answer: *Spending for Social Security changed very little between 1980 and 2002. It went from 20.6 percent in 1980, to 19.8 percent in 1990, to 23.2 percent in 2002.*

 CURRICULUM CONNECTION

History Congress established the National Aeronautics and Space Administration (NASA) in 1958 to oversee U.S. space-flights. Congress took this action largely in response to the Soviet Union's launching of the satellite *Sputnik* the previous year.

L2 Writing Letters

Direct students to identify a category discussed on pages 262–263 on which they think too much or too little is spent. Then have students write letters to their U.S. representatives or one of their senators challenging the spending of so much or so little on that particular category. Make sure that students explain the reasons for their challenge. Call on volunteers to read their letters to the class. Also have students share with the class any replies they receive.

CRITICAL THINKING

Determining Cause and Effect Ask students to identify the ways government expenditures impact their lives. Remind students to consider transfer payments as well as the public goods they enjoy. List their responses on the board, and have them use this information to write a brief paragraph titled "The Impact of Government Spending on Everyday Life." Call on volunteers to read and discuss their paragraphs.

THE GLOBAL ECONOMY

Government Spending
Another way of examining government spending in different countries is to compare how much each government spends per member of the population.

Answers:
1. *Japan, the U.S.*
2. *Yes. Spending percentage remained at 30.35% throughout the period and showed less variance than most of the other nations' spending.*

ASSESS

Assign Section 2 Assessment as homework or as an in-class activity.

💾 Have students use **Interactive Tutor Self-Assessment Software.**

Section Quiz 10-2

Payments to aged and disabled Americans through the Social Security program make up the largest category of federal spending. Retired persons receive benefits from the Old-Age and Survivors Insurance (OASI) program. Those unable to work receive payments from disability insurance (DI) programs.

Because Social Security is one of the mandatory spending categories, Congress simply takes the amount to be spent as a given that is dependent on the number of people eligible for Social Security payments.

For much of the late 1900s, national defense comprised the largest category of spending, although it is now second to Social Security. National defense includes military spending by the Department of Defense and defense-related atomic energy activities, such as the development of nuclear weapons and the disposal of nuclear wastes. This is the largest single discretionary category whose spending is approved annually.

Income security includes expenditures for retirement benefits to railroad workers and disabled coal miners, civil service retirement and disability programs, and retirement benefits for the military. Subsidized housing, child nutrition, and food programs for low-income families also fall under this category. Most of these expenditures are mandatory, and are therefore not authorized annually.

Medicare, a health-care program available to all senior citizens regardless of income, began in 1966. The program provides an insurance plan that covers major hospital costs. It also offers optional insurance that provides additional coverage for doctor and laboratory fees, outpatient services, and some equipment costs. This is another of the mandatory programs that does not require annual funding approval.

THE GLOBAL ECONOMY

GOVERNMENT SPENDING

Our government certainly spends a lot of money, but other nations spend even more. A comparison of the total government spending as a percentage of total output, or Gross Domestic Product, is shown in the graph.

Using this method, we can get a general impression of the size of the economic role of different governments. France and Italy are among the biggest spenders—with total government outlays exceeding 50 percent of their GDP. Germany and Canada are not far behind. During the time period shown on the graph, Japan and the United States generally spent between 30 and 40 percent.

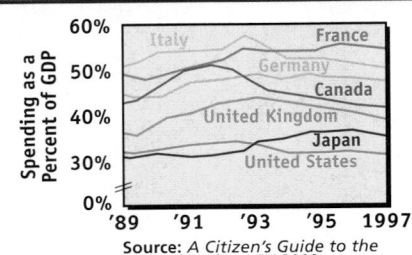

Source: *A Citizen's Guide to the Federal Budget, FY 2000*

Critical Thinking
1. **Analyzing Information** Which nations' expenditures stayed at a level between 30 and 40 percent of their GDP?
2. **Drawing Conclusions** Would you agree with the statement that government spending by the United States "follows a consistent trend?" Why or why not?

264 UNIT 3 MACROECONOMICS: INSTITUTIONS

EXTENDING THE CONTENT

Foreign Aid Although foreign aid accounts for only a small percentage of federal expenditures, it is often the subject of heated congressional debate. Some critics say that aid makes the recipient nation dependent on the United States to such a degree that its own economic development is stifled. Others contend that foreign aid is a form of bribery, used to gain the support of potentially unfriendly nations. Supporters of foreign aid say that a developing nation needs capital equipment in order to develop its economy and raise its standard of living. Foreign aid can help provide this equipment. Supporters also point out that foreign aid is humanitarian, because it provides help for countries and regions of the world troubled by war, famine, and disease.

When the federal government spends more than it collects in taxes and other revenues, it borrows money to make up the difference. Interest on the federal debt made up the sixth largest category of federal spending for fiscal year 2002. The amount of interest paid varies with changes in interest rates and is a mandatory expenditure.

Health-care services for low-income people, disease prevention, and consumer safety account for this part of the federal budget. One popular program in this category is **medicaid,** a joint federal-state medical insurance program for low-income persons. Another is the Occupational Safety and Health Administration (OSHA)—a federal agency that monitors occupational safety and health in the workplace. Still others include AIDS and breast cancer research, substance abuse treatment, and mental health service programs. Some programs such as medicaid are part of mandatory expenditures, although many others are considered to be discretionary.

Other broad categories of the federal budget include education, training, employment, and social services; transportation; veterans' benefits; administration of justice; and natural resources and the environment.

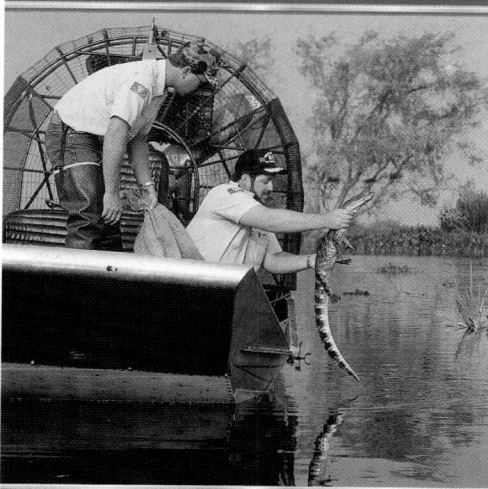

Federal Expenditures

Natural Resources Biologists and conservation specialists release a farm-raised alligator into wetlands. *What percentage of federal expenditures went to natural resources and the environment?*

Visual Instruction

Answer to Caption:
1.4 percent

Reteach

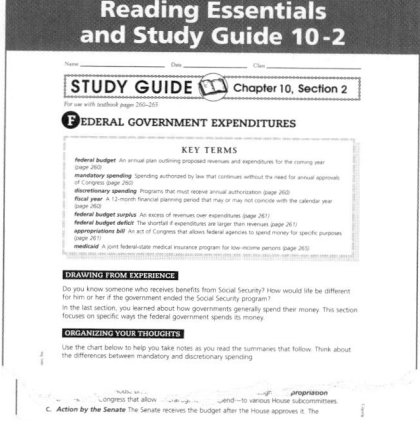

Reading Essentials and Study Guide 10-2

Enrich

Have students research one of the categories of government expenditures discussed on pages 262–265. Assign students a paper in which they use their research to answer the question, "What do the American people get from federal spending?" Papers should focus on total expenditures, programs provided, and important outcomes of the programs.

 CLOSE

Ask students to identify the category of federal spending they believe is most important and have them explain their choice.

Section 2 Assessment

Checking for Understanding

1. **Main Idea** Using your notes from the graphic organizer activity on page 260, write a definition of mandatory spending.

2. **Key Terms** Define federal budget, mandatory spending, discretionary spending, fiscal year, federal budget surplus, federal budget deficit, appropriations bill, medicaid.

3. **Describe** the three stages required to establish the federal budget.

4. **List** the five largest components of federal government spending.

Applying Economic Concepts

5. **Mandatory Spending** Contact your local Social Security office to find out about a person's eligibility to receive Social Security payments. Ask about the age, other eligibility requirements, and the amount of the Social Security payments.

Critical Thinking

6. **Understanding Cause and Effect** People are living longer, and families have fewer members. How will the combination of these two factors affect transfer payments, such as Social Security, in the future?

7. **Finding the Main Idea** When the federal government spends more than it collects, how does it make up the difference?

 Practice and **assess** key social studies skills with the *Glencoe Skillbuilder Interactive Workbook, Level 2.*

CHAPTER 10: GOVERNMENT SPENDING **265**

Section 2 Assessment Answers

1. Mandatory spending is authorized by law and continues without the need for annual approvals of Congress.

2. All vocabulary terms are defined in the text.

3. executive formulation, in which the president prepares budget and submits it to Congress; congressional action, during which Congress reviews, modifies, and approves budget; final approval, in which the president signs or vetoes the budget

4. Social Security, national defense, income security, medicare, net interest on the federal debt

5. Results should take form of written report.

6. There will be more older people receiving Social Security but fewer people making contributions; resulting shortfall corrected by cuts in benefits or increases in contributions

7. It borrows money to make up the difference.

Profiles in Economics

BACKGROUND

Although John Maynard Keynes earned his place in history as an economist, he was something of a Renaissance man. He was a logician, a renowned collector of art and of rare books, and a journalist. Keynes was also a member of the famous Bloomsbury Group, a group of English artists and writers who met regularly in the Bloomsbury section of London, and which included luminaries such as the writers Virginia Woolf and E. M. Forster, and the artists Roger Fry and Clive Bell. For many, Keynes remains the model of the English gentleman.

TEACH

Share this quotation from Keynes with students: "In the long run we are all dead. Economists set themselves too easy, too useless a task if in tempestuous seasons they can only tell us that when the storm is long past the ocean will be flat again." Challenge students to write paragraphs explaining the quotation, making references to classical economics, the Great Depression, and Keynes's influence on American fiscal policy.

Profiles in Economics

Economic Journal

A New Economics:
John Maynard Keynes
(1883–1946)

John Maynard Keynes is widely regarded as the most influential economist of the twentieth century. He wrote numerous books and articles that focused on short-run problems, instead of the long-run equilibrium solutions prevalent at the time. Keynes defended his short-run approach on the grounds that "in the long run, we are all dead."

His most famous and influential work is *The General Theory of Employment, Interest, and Money* (1936). The book, written during the depths of the Great Depression, offered new insights in the midst of a crisis. The policy recommendations derived from his theories soon took the world by storm.

ECONOMIST, TEACHER

Keynes attended Eton, and then Cambridge University. After graduation, Keynes returned to Cambridge as a lecturer. In addition he served, at various times, as editor of the famous *Economic Journal*, on the staff of the Treasury, and as a director of the Bank of England. He was instrumental in the planning of the World Bank. For his service to Great Britain, Keynes was knighted in 1942.

INFLUENCE

Keynes's *General Theory* divided the economy into four sectors—consumer, investment, government, and foreign. Keynes argued that the health of the economy is based on the total spending of all the sectors. He hypothesized that a fall in spending by the business sector could have a magnified impact on other sectors of the economy. Increased government spending could offset this process. These ideas stood in stark opposition to classical economics, which emphasize laissez-faire policies. They have been dubbed the New Economics, or, more frequently, Keynesian economics.

The theories were revolutionary and they provided much needed insight into the workings of a depression-era economy. Soon, the label *Keynesian economics* stood for any spending and taxing policies designed to stimulate the private sector.

The influence of Keynes was such that it led, in part, to the development of our national income and products accounts (NIPA) that are used to measure GDP and GNP.

Examining the Profile

1. **Synthesizing Information** Write a brief description of Keynesian economics and compare it with one of classical economics to explain why the former was labeled "the New Economics."

2. **For Further Research** Find out in what ways countries today follow Keynesian economic policies.

Answers to Examining the Profile

1. Answers will vary. Students should cite the activist role Keynes identified for government, contrast it with the laissez-faire principle of classical economics, note the fundamental difference in these two views, and recognize that the "New" in the term "New Economics" is a reference to this difference.

2. Answers will vary. Students should develop their answers through one of two research approaches: searching for articles that address the issue directly, or identifying national economies and governments by type and making a reasonable inference.

State and Local Government Expenditures

Study Guide

Main Idea
Like the federal government, state and local governments have budgets that provide money for many programs and services.

Reading Strategy
Graphic Organizer As you read the section, complete a graphic organizer similar to the one below by listing and describing the components of the categories that account for more than 10 percent of local spending.

10% or more

Key Terms
balanced budget amendment, intergovernmental expenditures

Objectives
After studying this section, you will be able to:
1. **Explain** how state and local governments approve spending.
2. **Identify** the major categories of state government expenditures.
3. **Identify** the major categories of local government expenditures.

Applying Economic Concepts
Human Capital is one of the most important investments we can make. Read to find out how state and local governments support this investment.

Cover Story

Hard Choices Await State Lawmakers

Gov. Gray Davis

The May revision of the governor's budget is due within the fortnight.

Lawmakers in Sacramento are waiting to see whether Gov. Gray Davis holds fast to the $104.7 billion plan he unveiled in January or proffers a truly revised budget that reflects that the state's economic outlook has taken a turn for the worst.

There are suggestions in the state capital that the looming budget problem is mostly attributable to California's electricity-supply crisis. Solve the electricity crisis, the argument goes, and the state's budget problem goes away.

– The San Diego Union-Tribune, May 9, 2001

State and local levels of government, like the federal government, also have expenditures. Like the federal government, these governments must approve spending before revenue dollars can be released. As the cover story shows, the budget process at the state and local levels can be just as complicated as it is at the federal level.

Approving Spending

Approving spending at the state level can take many forms. In most states, however, the process is loosely modeled after that of the federal government.

Some states have enacted a **balanced budget amendment**–a constitutional amendment that requires that annual spending not exceed revenues. Under these conditions, states are forced to cut spending when state revenues drop. A reduction in revenues may occur if sales taxes or state income taxes fall because of a decline in the general level of economic activity.

CHAPTER 10: GOVERNMENT SPENDING **267**

---

1 FOCUS

Section Overview
This section outlines state and local government spending.

BELLRINGER
Motivational Activity

Project **transparency** and have students answer questions.

Available as blackline master.

Daily Focus Transparency 67

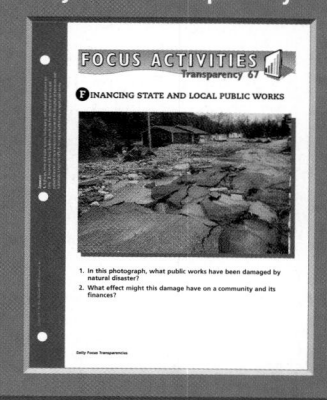

Study Guide

Reading Strategy
Have students create the graphic organizer.
Answers to Graphic: *elementary and secondary education, public utilities, other*

Preteaching Vocabulary
Ask students to explain what they think the term "balanced budget amendment" means.

RESOURCE MANAGER

Reproducible Masters
- Reproducible Lesson Plan 10-3
- Daily Lecture Notes 10-3
- Guided Reading Activity 10-3
- Reading Essentials and Study Guide 10-3
- Section Quiz 10-3

Transparencies
- Daily Focus Transparency 67

Multimedia
- Interactive Tutor Self-Assessment Software
- ExamView® Pro Testmaker
- Presentation Plus!

② TEACH

Daily Lecture Notes 10-3

L1 Statistical Table

Have students examine Figure 10.4 on page 263 and Figure 10.5 on page 269. Then direct students to use the information in Figure 10.5 to construct a statistical table comparing spending at the state and local levels.

 ### Math Practice

Per Capita State Aid Have students consult a recent almanac to find out how much their state receives in block grants each month for temporary assistance to the needy, and how many people in the state receive aid. Then ask students to divide the amount of money by the number of people to calculate the average amount of money available per person. For example, in one recent year, Alabama received $98,853,000 per month and has an average of 85,750 recipients. ($1,153)

At the local level, power to approve spending often rests with the mayor, the city council, the county judge, or some other elected representative or body. Generally, the amount of revenues collected from property taxes and other local sources limits the spending of local agencies. If state and local governments are unable to raise the revenue they need, they must deal with having inadequate resources to hire teachers, police officers, or other state and local workers.

State Government Expenditures

The major types of state government expenditures are shown in **Figure 10.5.** Seven of the most important categories, accounting for nearly 80 percent of all state spending, are examined next.

Careers

Budget Analyst

Are you good at analyzing and comparing data? Budget analysts develop financial plans and provide technical advice about budgeting.

The Work

Budget analysts research, analyze, develop, and execute annual budgets. Working with managers and department heads, they seek new ways to improve a company's efficiency and increase profits. Reviewing financial requests, examining past and current budgets, and researching developments that can have an effect on spending are additional responsibilities.

Qualifications

Budget analysts need strong analytical skills and must be knowledgeable in mathematics, statistics, and computer science. Because of their frequent interaction with others and the obligation to present budget proposals, budget analysts must possess strong oral and written communication skills.

268 UNIT 3 MACROECONOMICS: INSTITUTIONS

The largest category of state spending is **intergovernmental expenditures**—funds that one level of government transfers to another level for spending. These funds come from state revenue sources such as sales taxes, and they are distributed to towns and other local communities to cover a variety of educational and municipal expenditures.

The second largest category of state expenditures is public welfare. These payments take the form of cash assistance, payments for medical care, spending to maintain welfare institutions, and other miscellaneous welfare expenditures.

Many states have their own retirement funds and insurance funds for state employees. Money in these funds is invested until such time as people retire, become unemployed, or are injured on the job. Contributions to these funds make this category the third largest type of spending overall.

Generally a large category, higher education is a traditional responsibility of state governments with their networks of state colleges and universities. Local governments spend less in this area, usually to support community colleges and universities.

Highway construction and road improvement expenditures represent a significant portion of state expenditures. The federal government builds and maintains much of the interstate highway system, but states maintain state roads and other highways that generally link smaller communities with larger ones.

Local Government Expenditures

Local governments include counties, municipalities, townships, school districts, and other special districts. The largest categories of spending by local governments include elementary and secondary education, utilities, hospitals, police protection, interest on debt, public welfare, and highways.

Local governments have primary responsibility for elementary and secondary education. Expenditures in this category include teachers' and administrators' salaries, textbooks, and construction and maintenance of school buildings. This category accounts for more than one-third of local government spending.

Many public utilities, such as water and sanitation, serve local needs. For most local governments,

---

MEETING SPECIAL NEEDS ACTIVITY

Learning Style: Naturalist Have students visit a state park, or other local park, and develop a list of possible state/local expenditures involved in running the park. For example, students might note expenditures for maintaining the natural environment, and for upkeep of human-made structures such as lodges or picnic areas. Discuss students' lists as a class, noting some less obvious expenditures such as animal breeding and control, and the stocking of fisheries. If possible, invite a representative from the Department of Natural Resources to class to discuss expenditures and programs. Finally, have students write essays explaining whether they think expenditures for natural resources are well spent.

📁 Refer to *Inclusion for the Social Studies Classroom Strategies and Activities* in the TCR.

ECONOMICS AT A GLANCE

Figure 10.5

Expenditures by State and Local Governments

State: $894,132 million

Local: $836,577 million

State	Category	Local
29.6%	Intergovernmental Expenditure	
18.7%	Public Welfare	3.9%
10.6%	Insurance Trust	1.9%
	Elementary & Secondary Education	34.9%
10.1%	Higher Education	1.9%
5.5%	Highways	4.0%
3.2%	Hospitals	4.7%
2.9%	Interest on General Debt	4.3%
3.0%	Corrections	1.5%
3.1%	Governmental Administration	4.7%
2.5%	Health	2.4%
0.9%	Utilities	10.5%
	Fire Protection	2.3%
0.7%	Police Protection	4.9%
0.4%	Parks and Recreation	2.1%
	Housing & Community Development	2.5%
8.7%	Other	13.6%

Source: *Bureau of the Census*, June 2001 (Variations due to rounding)

Using Graphs   Education is the main expenditure for local government. What are the three largest spending categories for local governments? For state governments?

ECONOMICS Online

Visit epp.glencoe.com and click on **Textbook Updates—Chapter 10** for an update of the data.

CHAPTER 10: GOVERNMENT SPENDING   269

FREE ENTERPRISE ACTIVITY

Ask students to assume that they are members of the city council in a community with high unemployment and few jobs for recent high school graduates. At a city council meeting, members are notified that a company wants to locate a new manufacturing plant in the community. This would create 200 new jobs, but would also require additional spending for infrastructure repairs and construction and for increased police and fire protection. The company also wants some special tax advantages, including no property taxes or utility taxes for 12 years. Have students, as city council members, write a letter to the president of the company either agreeing or not agreeing to the relocation plan and explaining why.

Guided Reading Activity 10-3

ECONOMICS AT A GLANCE

Answer: *elementary and secondary education, utilities, police protection; intergovernmental expenditures, public welfare, insurance trust*

③ ASSESS

Assign Section 3 Assessment as homework or as an in-class activity.

📖 Have students use **Interactive Tutor Self-Assessment Software.**

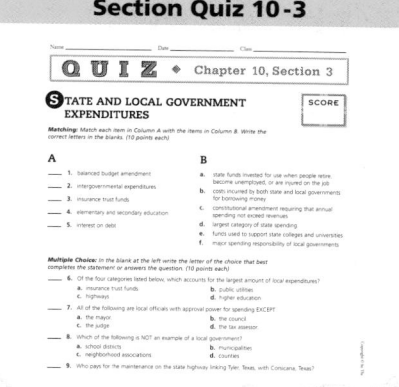

Section Quiz 10-3

Reteach

Reading Essentials and Study Guide 10-3

Enrich

Have students research the expenditures of their state, county, or city, township, or village. Suggest that they write a report that describes the budget-making process and lists the major categories of expenditures.

4 CLOSE

Ask students to identify the category of state spending and of local spending they believe is most important and why.

spending on utilities amounts to the second most important expenditure.

Many hospitals receive some of their funding from local governments. Some hospitals are entirely city- or municipal-owned, which makes them a modest budget item for local governments.

Most localities have a full-time, paid police force to protect their community. As a result, police protection is a cost for local governments. Because there are far fewer state than local police forces, state spending for police protection is much lower.

State and local governments, like the federal government, often borrow money to cover capital expenditures for highways, universities, and even government buildings. As with the federal government, interest expenses vary as interest rates go up and down.

Local governments, like state governments, face public welfare expenditures. Local governments, however, spend much less than state governments on this category.

Local governments also spend money on highways, roads, and street repairs. This expenditure category includes the repair of potholes, the installation and repair of street signs, snow removal, and other street-related items.

The remaining local government expenditures, approximately one-third of the total, are spread over a wide range of categories. Among the most important are housing and community development, fire protection, and parks and recreation.

Government Expenditures

Education Local government's largest spending category is primary and secondary education. *Which level of government has the major responsibility for higher education?*

Section 3 Assessment

Checking for Understanding

1. **Main Idea** What are some services that state and local governments provide for in their budgets?

2. **Key Terms** Define balanced budget amendment, intergovernmental expenditures.

3. **Describe** how state governments handle the spending approval process.

4. **List** seven major categories of state spending.

5. **Identify** the seven major categories of local government spending.

Applying Economic Concepts

6. **Human Capital** How does the market reward those who have invested in human capital—the acquired skills of an individual in the areas of education, training, and work habits? Cite specific examples from your community to support your answer.

Critical Thinking

7. **Finding the Main Idea** What is the purpose of a balanced budget amendment?

8. **Making Generalizations** If you were to argue for reduced spending at the state and local levels, which categories shown in **Figure 10.5** would you choose to cut back? Explain the reasons for your choices.

 Practice and **assess** key social studies skills with the *Glencoe Skillbuilder Interactive Workbook, Level 2.*

270 UNIT 3 MACROECONOMICS: INSTITUTIONS

Section 3 Assessment Answers

1. education, hospitals, public welfare, interest on debt, and highways

2. All vocabulary terms are defined in the text.

3. There are many different methods, but in most states the process is loosely modeled after that of the federal government.

4. intergovernmental expenditures, public welfare, insurance trust, higher education, highways, hospitals, interest on debt

5. elementary and secondary education, public utilities, police protection, hospitals, interest on debt, public welfare, highways

6. This investment results in more productive workers; greater productivity leads to more profits and higher pay.

7. to prevent annual spending from exceeding revenues

8. Answers should reflect an understanding of categories for state and local expenditures.

BusinessWeek

MARCH 15, 1999

Newsclip

Creative students are finding new ways to gain the financing needed to attend the college of their choice. As you read the article, think about why it is important for students to explore many options as they plan for how to finance their college educations.

Dialing for Dollars

Jonathan Piper, 18, applied to nine top-notch colleges and got into them all. The Cleveland native scored in the 95th percentile on his SATs and managed a 3.9 average at prep school while playing baseball, singing lead in musicals, and participating in an engineering society. He's also an African American. But getting accepted was just the first step. Next came the money.

Last spring, Piper made call after call to college financial-aid officers. His soft-spoken pitch: "I have no idea what I want to do, and I want to see the best that each of you can offer me." University of Pennsylvania and Princeton University didn't move much, but Wake Forest University in Winston-Salem, N.C., raised its annual aid offer from $8,000 to $26,000. A freshman there now, Piper is studying poetry with Maya Angelou and has no regrets. "It would have cost me $15,000 a year to go to Princeton, vs. nothing for Wake Forest," he says.

Colleges call it "dialing for dollars"—the time in March and April when parents and students phone them with better offers from other schools in hopes of coaxing more aid out of them. Rare a decade ago, negotiating is now so much a part of the picture that some colleges openly encourage it, while others are quietly putting away aid dollars for maneuvering at season's end.

The result is that a classroom now resembles an airplane. Three people sitting side-by-side could be paying different prices, and economic need has less to do with it than savvy. Nationally, about half of all students receive assistance. . . .

It pays to be astute. Tuition and fees have risen 94% since 1989, nearly triple the 32.5% increase in inflation, according to the Bureau of Labor Statistics. The sticker price—tuition, fees, and room and board—for a year of undergraduate education ranges from $33,000 at Ivy League schools down to $10,500 at state universities. . . .

Cash-strapped students are . . . saving thousands by enrolling at a public college and later transferring to a private college or starting at a junior college (average tuition of $1,500 a year) and moving on to a state university. . . .

Students are finding other creative ways to save. High school pupils who take advanced-placement courses can knock off several semesters of college. Some private colleges offer three-year bachelor's programs or five-year bachelor's-master's degrees. . . .

Examining the Newsclip

1. **Finding the Main Idea** What change does the writer discuss regarding financing college education?

2. **Synthesizing Information** What methods are students using to decrease the cost of college?

271

TEACH

Discuss with students how much tuition can be saved at a state university with state support. On the board, copy the following chart showing annual tuition paid at private and public universities in several states/areas:

Public Universities:

Georgia State University—$2,632
University of Texas—$2,520
University of the District of Columbia—$2,250
University of Massachusetts—$5,212

Private Universities:

Emory University, Georgia—$25,240
Rice University, Texas—$16,600
Georgetown, Washington, D.C.—$25,152
Harvard, Massachusetts—$23,457

Point out that the tuition at each state university applies only to residents of that state. Then have students use the information on the board to calculate how much more on the average students at the private universities pay in annual tuition. *($19,458)*

☞ Refer to **Business Week Focus on the New Economy** in the TCR for additional unit-based articles.

Answers to Examining the Newsclip

1. the new trend of parents and students phoning potential colleges with better offers from other schools in hopes of coaxing more aid out of them

2. negotiating with potential colleges, enrolling at a public college or junior college and transferring to a private college or university, taking advanced-placement classes in high school, opting for three-year bachelor's programs or five-year bachelor's-master's programs

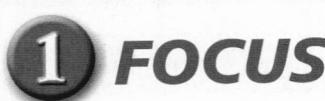

1 FOCUS

Section Overview
This section analyzes the relationship between the federal deficit and the federal debt.

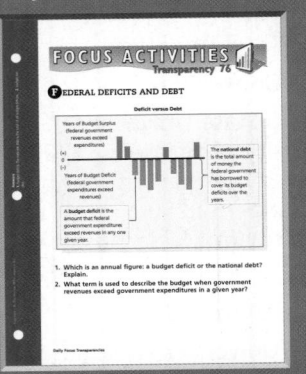
Study Guide

Reading Strategy
Have students create the graphic organizer.
Answers to Graphic: *Students should describe the debt, noting whether the measure used is constant dollars, chained, or on a per capita basis.*

Preteaching Vocabulary
Use the Vocabulary Puzzle-Maker to create crossword and word-search puzzles.

Deficits, Surpluses, and The National Debt

Study Guide

Main Idea
Deficit spending has helped create a national debt.

Reading Strategy
Graphic Organizer As you read the section, describe the growth of the debt before and after 1970.

Rise in national debt

Key Terms
deficit spending, federal debt, balanced budget, trust fund, crowding-out effect, pay-as-you-go provision, line-item veto, spending cap, entitlement

Objectives
After studying this section, you will be able to:
1. **Explain** how the federal deficit is related to the federal debt.
2. **Relate** the impact of the federal debt on the economy.
3. **Describe** past attempts to eliminate the federal deficit.
4. **Describe** entitlements.

Applying Economic Concepts
Deficit Spending When the government must borrow money to spend, deficit spending occurs. Read to learn why American taxpayers must pay the interest on that borrowed money.

Cover Story

Tax Cut Helps Drain Surplus

WASHINGTON – The new tax cut, coupled with falling corporate tax revenue, has gobbled up three-quarters of the projected federal budget surplus through 2004, a revised Congressional Budget Office estimate reveals.

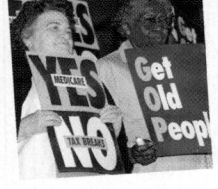

Older Americans protest possible Medicare cuts

As the surplus shrinks, budget experts from both parties now believe Congress and President Bush will have to tap funds reserved for Medicare to pay for the spending increases they want for the fiscal year that begins in October.

Only last January, budget forecasters had expected the surplus ... to total a record $489 billion from 2001 through 2004. That number has shrunk to $127 billion.

—*Chicago Sun-Times*, June 27, 2001

272

In 1998, the federal budget had its first surplus in 29 years, due in part to strong economic growth. While the surplus was due largely to the Social Security trust fund, it presented nevertheless a whole new range of possibilities and temptations for politicians.

From the Deficit to the Debt

Historically, the federal budget has been characterized by a remarkable amount of **deficit spending**—or spending in excess of revenues collected. Sometimes the government plans deficit spending. At other times, the government is forced to spend more than it collects because unexpected developments cause a drop in revenues or a rise in expenditures.

Figure 10.3 shows that the government projected a $231 billion surplus for fiscal year 2002. Budget projections are based partially on assumptions about the direction of the economy. If the economy has strong economic growth, the surplus

---

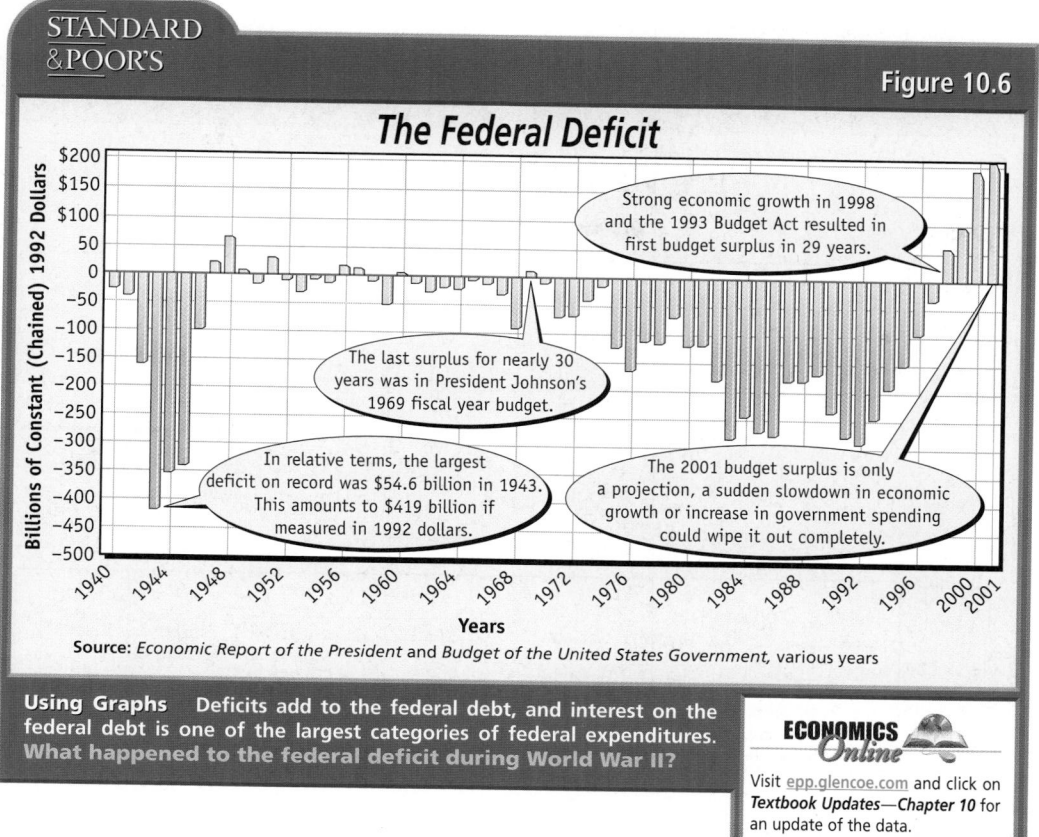

Figure 10.6

The Federal Deficit

Strong economic growth in 1998 and the 1993 Budget Act resulted in first budget surplus in 29 years.

The last surplus for nearly 30 years was in President Johnson's 1969 fiscal year budget.

In relative terms, the largest deficit on record was $54.6 billion in 1943. This amounts to $419 billion if measured in 1992 dollars.

The 2001 budget surplus is only a projection, a sudden slowdown in economic growth or increase in government spending could wipe it out completely.

Source: *Economic Report of the President* and *Budget of the United States Government,* various years

Using Graphs   Deficits add to the federal debt, and interest on the federal debt is one of the largest categories of federal expenditures. **What happened to the federal deficit during World War II?**

Visit epp.glencoe.com and click on **Textbook Updates—Chapter 10** for an update of the data.

2 TEACH

Daily Lecture Notes 10-4

DAILY LECTURE NOTES   Lesson 10-4

DID YOU KNOW?

The accounting system of the Bureau of the Public Debt, a part of the Department of the Treasury, announces the "public debt outstanding" at about 11:30 A.M. daily. The system takes into consideration 50 different reporting sources to determine how much the federal government owes on any particular day. The public can monitor the debt by checking the Bureau's Web site at www.publicdebt.treas.gov/opd/opdpenny.htm

PAGES 272-276

I. From the Deficit to the Debt

   A. Throughout United States history, the federal government has practiced deficit spending, or spending more than the revenues it collected. In 1998 the federal budget had its first surplus in 29 years.

   B. Historically, the largest federal deficits happened during World War II. The budget, however, had a surplus by 1947, which lasted until the 1980s, when the Reagan administration increased defense spending and cut taxes. It was not until after the Omnibus Budget Reconciliation Act of 1993 that the deficit began to shrink.

   C. When the budget runs a deficit, the Treasury Department sells bonds to the public to raise money. The federal debt is the total amount the government has borrowed from investors to finance its deficit spending over its long history.

   D. The total federal debt had grown to $5.6 trillion by 1999. About $1.9 trillion is trust fund money the government owes itself, which economists do not include in the total as economically significant.

   E. The federal debt differs from private debt because: (1) we owe most of the federal debt to ourselves, whereas private debt is owed to others; (2) private debt typically has a repayment deadline, but federal debt does not; the government just issues new bonds; (3) private debt means individuals give up their purchasing power as they pay down their debt; but when the federal government repays a debt, the funds transfer to others who gain purchasing power (unless payments are to foreign investors).

   ◆ Discussion Question
What is the difference between the federal deficit and the federal debt? *(The deficit is the shortage between revenues collected and federal expenditures any one fiscal year; the federal debt is the accumulated balance the government owes to investors for its many years of deficit spending.)*

Daily Lecture Notes   64

turn ▶

Answer: *The deficit increased.*

Thomas Jefferson feared that a growing government debt could pose a threat to liberty. "To preserve our independence, we must not let our rulers load us with perpetual debt," he said. "We must make our election between economy and liberty, or provision and servitude."

could grow larger. A downturn in the economy means less federal government revenues and a rise in expenditures such as unemployment compensation. **Figure 10.6** shows the history of federal budget deficits and surpluses since 1940, with numbers adjusted so that inflation does not distort year-to-year deficit comparisons.

Deficits Add to the Debt

When the federal government runs a deficit, it must finance the shortage of revenue by borrowing from others. It does this by having the Department of the Treasury sell bonds and other forms of government debt to the public. If we add up all outstanding federal bonds and other debt obligations, we have a measure of the **federal debt**—the total

amount borrowed from investors to finance the government's deficit spending.

The debt grows whenever the government spends more than it collects in revenues. If the federal government attains a **balanced budget**—an annual budget in which expenditures equal revenues—the federal debt will not change. If the federal budget generates a surplus, the federal debt will become smaller.

How Big Is the Debt?

The national debt has grown almost continuously since 1900, when the debt was $1.3 billion. By 1929 it had reached $16.9 billion, and by 1940 it was $50.7 billion. By mid-2001 the total federal debt was about $5,669 billion—or $5.7 trillion.

CHAPTER 10: GOVERNMENT SPENDING **273**

MEETING SPECIAL NEEDS ACTIVITY

Learning Disabled For students who have attention deficit hyperactivity disorder, paying attention in class can be difficult. Severe inattention problems call for special interventions in the classroom. One popular intervention is to give a time limit for a task. Ask students to read the subsections "Deficits Add to the Debt" and "How Big Is the Debt?," which are approximately 300 words long. Give students four minutes to read (enough time for average readers). **Ask:** Did the time limit help you pay attention? Discuss.

      Refer to *Inclusion for the Social Studies Classroom Strategies and Activities* in the TCR.

Guided Reading Activity 10-4

GUIDED READING Activity 10-4

For use with textbook pages 272–278

DEFICITS, SURPLUSES, AND THE NATIONAL DEBT

OUTLINING

Directions: Locate the heading in your textbook. Then use the information under the heading to help you write each answer. Use another sheet of paper if necessary.

I. From the Deficit to the Debt.
   A. From the Deficit to the Debt—What is deficit spending?

   B. Deficits Add to the Debt—What is the only way the annual budget can lower the federal debt?

II. Impact of the National Debt—What happens to the purchasing power of individuals as a consequence of the federal debt?

III. Taming the Deficit
   A. Omnibus Budget Reconciliation Act of 1993—What feature of this act helped account for the 1998 budget surplus?

   B. Balanced Budget Agreement of 1997—What is a spending cap?

   C. Reforming Entitlements—What is the connection between entitlements and mandatory spending in the federal budget?

Guided Reading Activities

STANDARD &POOR'S

Answer: *1991*

L2 Wall Display

Organize students into five groups and assign each group one of the following time periods: 1940s, 1950s, 1960s, 1970s, 1980s, 1990s through the present. Ask groups to research important events and legislation in their assigned time period related to the development of the federal debt. Then have groups develop annotated illustrations—photographs, cartoons, or drawings—of selected events and add them to a chronological wall display on the federal debt. Use the completed wall display as a starting point for a class discussion on the events that have had the most impact on the development of the federal debt. **ELL**

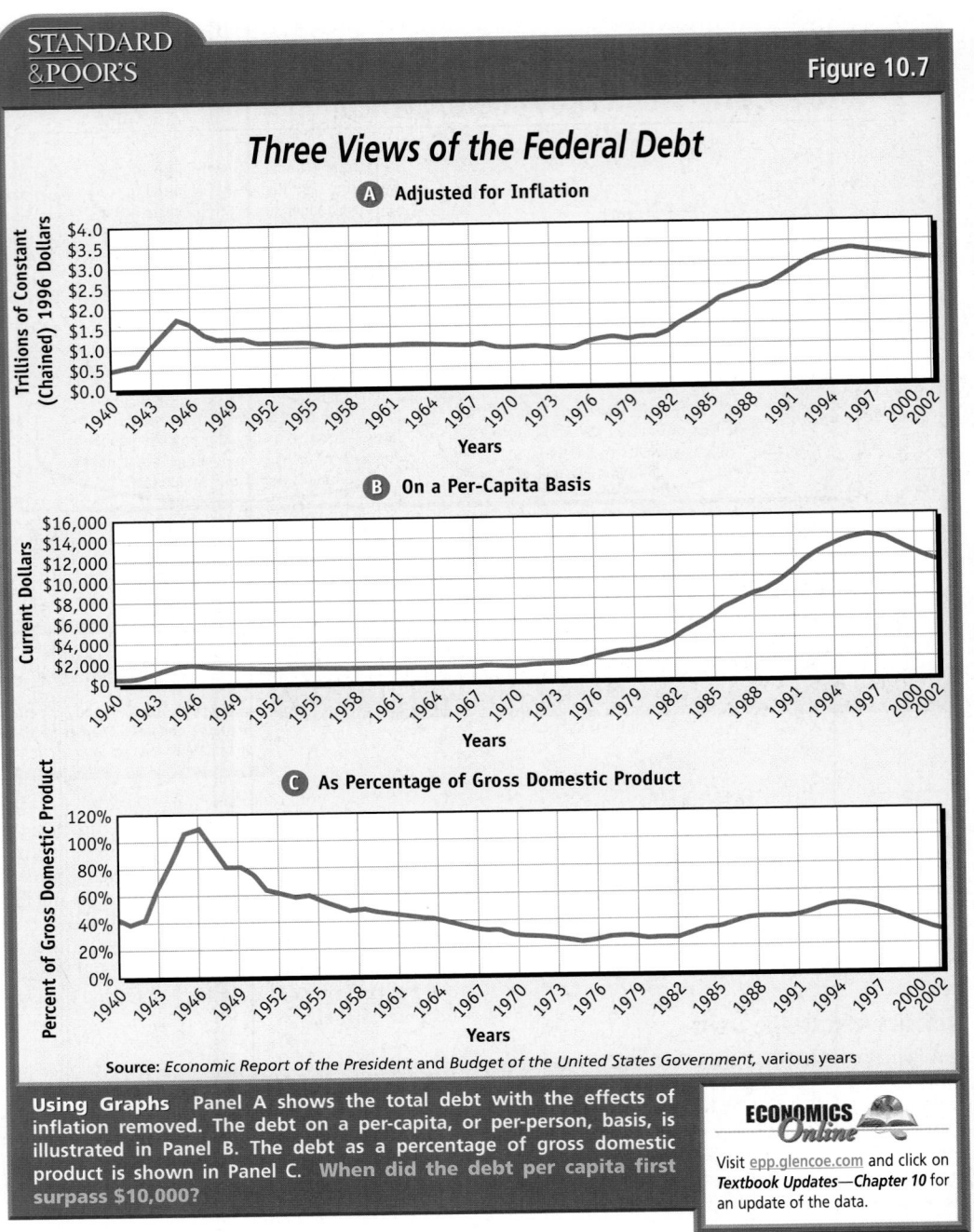

STANDARD &POOR'S

Figure 10.7

Three Views of the Federal Debt

A Adjusted for Inflation

B On a Per-Capita Basis

C As Percentage of Gross Domestic Product

Source: Economic Report of the President and Budget of the United States Government, various years

Using Graphs Panel A shows the total debt with the effects of inflation removed. The debt on a per-capita, or per-person, basis, is illustrated in Panel B. The debt as a percentage of gross domestic product is shown in Panel C. **When did the debt per capita first surpass $10,000?**

ECONOMICS *Online*
Visit epp.glencoe.com and click on **Textbook Updates—Chapter 10** for an update of the data.

FREE ENTERPRISE ACTIVITY

Organize students into groups of five. Have groups review Figure 10.3 on page 262 detailing the 2000 federal budget, and the discussion of federal government expenditure categories in Section 2. Then ask group members to discuss how they will balance the budget by considering questions such as: Should there be caps on the amount of spending for each category? Should expenditures be reduced? If so, should cuts be across the board or in certain categories only? Should taxes be increased? If so, which taxes should be raised? Instruct groups to thoroughly analyze the economic impact of their recommendations. Have representatives report their recommendations to the class. **BLOCK SCHEDULING**

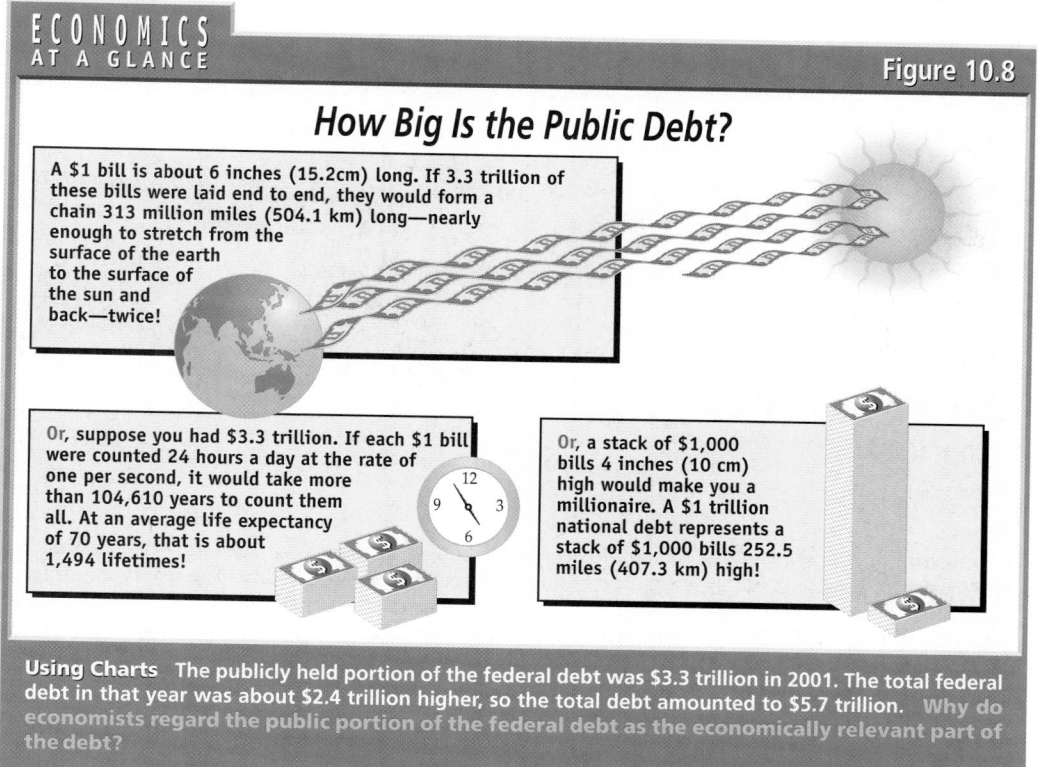

How Big Is the Public Debt?

A $1 bill is about 6 inches (15.2cm) long. If 3.3 trillion of these bills were laid end to end, they would form a chain 313 million miles (504.1 km) long—nearly enough to stretch from the surface of the earth to the surface of the sun and back—twice!

Or, suppose you had $3.3 trillion. If each $1 bill were counted 24 hours a day at the rate of one per second, it would take more than 104,610 years to count them all. At an average life expectancy of 70 years, that is about 1,494 lifetimes!

Or, a stack of $1,000 bills 4 inches (10 cm) high would make you a millionaire. A $1 trillion national debt represents a stack of $1,000 bills 252.5 miles (407.3 km) high!

Using Charts The publicly held portion of the federal debt was $3.3 trillion in 2001. The total federal debt in that year was about $2.4 trillion higher, so the total debt amounted to $5.7 trillion. Why do economists regard the public portion of the federal debt as the economically relevant part of the debt?

ECONOMICS
AT A GLANCE

Answer: *They tend to disregard the portion of the debt held in trust funds because the funds represent money the government owes to itself. Economists focus instead on the public portion of the debt.*

THE GLOBAL ECONOMY

Sweden Until the early 1990s, Sweden had a "welfare state" philosophy, in which Swedes counted on the state to provide for them. "In the past 50 years, we created in this country about the biggest welfare state ever seen. But it was done at the expense of the economic awareness of every citizen. People really had no idea of the cost of everything.

Government subsidies paid 60 percent of housing costs, leaving Swedes used to artificially low rents. The . . . government is gradually reducing housing subsidies, which are to be halted by 1999. A tax code that routinely claimed half of people's income . . . made it pointless for entrepreneurs to expand businesses. . . . "—Marc Fisher, "Sweden's Reagan Revolution" in *The Washington Post,* June 8–14, 1992.

Some of this debt is money that the government owes to itself. In 2001 approximately $2.4 trillion of this debt was held in government **trust funds**—special accounts used to fund specific types of expenditures such as Social Security and medicare. When the government collects the FICA or payroll tax, it puts the revenues in these trust accounts. The money is then invested in government securities until it is paid out.

Because trust fund balances represent money the government owes to itself, most economists tend to disregard this portion of the debt. Instead, they view the public portion of the debt—which amounted to $3.3 trillion in 2001—as the economically relevant part of the debt. **Figure 10.7** presents three views of the total federal debt held by the public. **Panel A,** which is adjusted for inflation, shows that the debt did not increase dramatically until the 1980s. **Panel B,** computed on a per capita basis, also shows a dramatic increase in the 1980s.

According to this view, the debt on a per capita basis was approximately $11,700 by the end of 2001.

Panel C shows the debt as a percentage of Gross Domestic Product (GDP)—the dollar value of all final goods, services, and structures (houses and commercial buildings) produced within a country during any one year. The debt peaked in 1946. By 2001 it was about 32 percent.

Public vs. Private Debt

How does the federal debt differ from private debt? A key difference is that we owe most of the federal debt to ourselves—whereas private debt is owed to others. The federal debt is also different from private debt in other ways.

One difference is repayment. When private citizens borrow money, they usually make plans to repay the debt by a specific date. When the federal

CHAPTER 10: GOVERNMENT SPENDING **275**

CRITICAL THINKING

Identifying Alternatives Ask students to consider the problem of reducing the federal deficit. Have them list the various attempts at controlling the deficit discussed in the text. Students should include the advantages and disadvantages to each plan, as well as the plan's level of success. Then ask students to identify alternative plans for reducing the deficit. They might list cuts in specific federal programs, or possible taxes, or tax reform. Again, have students determine the advantages and disadvantages for each plan. Discuss students' recommendations as a class. **BLOCK SCHEDULING**

CYBERNOMICS

Legislation on the Web Tell students to find out about the latest legislation related to the federal budget by using the following URL: www.whitehouse.gov/OMB and clicking on *Legislative Information*.

NIGHTLY BUSINESS REPORT

 ECONOMICS & YOU

 Chapter 15
Disc 1, Side 2

How the Government Spends, Collects, and Owes

Ask: What factors contributed to a budget surplus in the late 1990s? *(The president and Congress agreed to some spending restraints, and the economy grew faster, increasing tax revenue.)*

Federal Debt

Effects In the 1990s the federal debt surpassed $5 trillion. *How does the federal debt impact the economy?*

government borrows, it gives little thought to eventual repayment because it simply issues new bonds and uses the proceeds to pay off the old bonds.

Another difference has to do with purchasing power. When private individuals repay a debt, they give up purchasing power. They no longer have that money and so it cannot be used to buy more goods and services. When the federal government repays a debt, there is no loss of purchasing power because the taxes and revenue collected from some groups are simply transferred to others. The exception is 15 to 20 percent of the public debt owned by foreigners. When payments are made to investors outside the United States, some purchasing power is temporarily diverted from the American economy.

Impact of the National Debt

Even though we owe most of the federal debt to ourselves, it still affects the economy in ways that can harm the private sector.

The federal debt can have a significant impact on the distribution of income within the economy. If the government borrows money from the wealthy, and if the burden of taxes falls on the middle class and the poor, taxes would be transferred to the rich in the form of interest payments on the debt.

If the government borrows money from the middle class, and if the burden of taxes falls on the rich, those taxes would be used to make interest payments to the middle class. The federal tax structure, as much as the size of the debt itself, determines the distribution effects. Given the current progressive nature of the personal income tax, less is taken from the lower and middle income classes than would be the case under a less progressive, or flat tax.

Another consequence of the federal debt is that it causes a transfer of purchasing power from the private sector to the public sector. In general, the larger the public debt, the larger the interest payments and, therefore, the more taxes needed to pay them. When people pay more taxes to the government, they have less money to spend on their own needs.

A third impact is that the taxes needed to pay the interest can reduce the incentives to work, save, and invest. Individuals and businesses might feel

STANDARD & POOR'S INFOBYTE

Budget Deficits A deficit can be a negative catalyst in an economy. Some economists, however, will advocate deficit spending under certain conditions, such as a government spending its way out of a recession.

EXTENDING THE CONTENT

Government Securities The U.S. Treasury Department sells government securities (bonds, notes, and bills) to make up the difference between what the federal government takes in every year and what it spends. Government securities are also sold to refinance the debt as other securities mature. Securities may be purchased by individuals or organizations, such as banks and insurance companies. Government agencies also are permitted to purchase securities. An individual can purchase securities through a bank, but he or she must pay a small service charge. Federal Reserve banks (see Chapter 15) are another source for purchasing securities.

less inclined to work harder and earn extra income if higher taxes are placed on them.

Some people feel that the government spends taxpayers' money in a careless manner. A community, for example, may secure a federal grant to purchase expensive equipment that taxpayers in the community would never have approved. If people feel that their taxes are being squandered, they may have a reduced incentive to work.

When the government sells bonds to borrow money, it competes with the private sector for scarce resources. An example of this competition is the **crowding-out effect**—the higher-than-normal interest rates that heavy government borrowing causes.

This effect is illustrated in **Figure 10.9**. If the government runs a deficit and tries to raise funds by selling bonds, it will cause the interest rate paid by private borrowers to go up.

Taming the Deficit

Concern over the size of the federal deficit and the debt has led to a number of attempts to control it. Several of the more important attempts are described below.

Gramm-Rudman-Hollings

One of the first significant attempts to control the federal deficit took place when Congress tried to mandate a balanced budget by 1991. The legislation was formally called the Balanced Budget and Emergency Deficit Control Act of 1985, or Gramm-Rudman-Hollings (GRH) after its sponsors.

The key to GRH was to set federal deficit targets for Congress and the president to meet over a six-year period—targets that resulted in a zero deficit by 1991. Despite high hopes, GRH failed for two reasons. First, Congress discovered that it could get around the law by passing spending bills that took effect two or three years later. Second, the economy started to decline in July 1990—triggering a safety valve in the law that suspended automatic cuts when the economy was weak.

Budget Enforcement Act of 1990

In an effort to control future budgetary action, Congress passed the Budget Enforcement Act

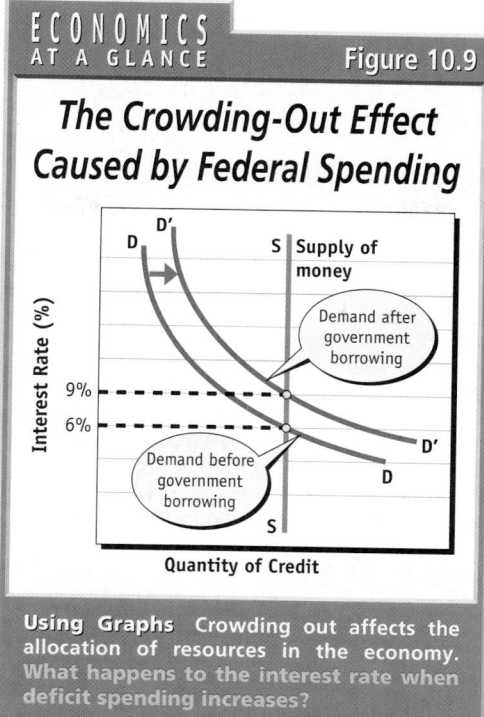

ECONOMICS AT A GLANCE   Figure 10.9

The Crowding-Out Effect Caused by Federal Spending

Using Graphs Crowding out affects the allocation of resources in the economy. What happens to the interest rate when deficit spending increases?

(BEA) in 1990. The BEA's main feature is a **"pay-as-you-go" provision**—a requirement that new spending proposals or tax cuts must be offset by reductions elsewhere. If no agreement on the reductions is reached, then automatic, across-the-board spending cuts are to be instituted.

The BEA also has limitations. For one, it applies only to discretionary spending. For another, the act can be suspended if the economy enters a low-growth phase or if the president declares an emergency.

Omnibus Budget Reconciliation Act of 1993

President Clinton's Omnibus Budget Reconciliation Act of 1993 was an attempt to trim $500 billion from the deficit over a five-year period. By 1993 the federal deficit had reached such enormous proportions that the act was intended to reduce only the rate of growth of the deficit, not the deficit itself.

CHAPTER 10: GOVERNMENT SPENDING **277**

ECONOMICS AT A GLANCE

Answer: *When the government runs a deficit and tries to raise funds by selling bonds, it will cause the interest rate paid by private borrowers to go up.*

(3) ASSESS

Assign Section 4 Assessment as homework or as an in-class activity.

Have students use **Interactive Tutor Self-Assessment Software** to review Section 4.

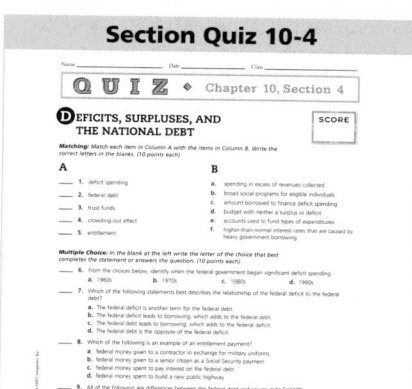

INTERDISCIPLINARY CONNECTIONS ACTIVITY

History Point out to students that the federal government has been paying off a debt since 1789. Most years, just the interest on the debt has been in the millions. Have volunteers consult an almanac to find out how much the federal government paid in interest on the debt for every tenth year between 1800 and 1900. Then have them use the information to create a time line for display in the classroom. *(1800: $3 million, 1810: $3 million, 1820: $5 million, 1830: $2 million, 1840: [information unavailable], 1850: $4 million, 1860: $3 million, 1870: $129 million, 1880: $96 million, 1890: $36 million, 1900: $40 million)* Also ask students to hypothesize about why the interest on the debt increased by 4300% between 1860 and 1870. *(Students will probably say that the debt increased considerably during the Civil War in the 1860s.)*

Reteach

Enrich

Have students clip magazine and newspaper articles about specific entitlements and use them to prepare a bulletin board display. In class discussion, review why entitlements have grown over the years.

4 CLOSE

Have students discuss whether they believe they will see the eradication of national debt within their lifetime. **Ask:** Is such a goal even desirable?

The act featured a combination of spending reductions and tax increases that made the individual income tax more progressive–especially for the wealthiest 1.2 percent of taxpayers.

Balanced Budget Agreement of 1997

Congress gave the president a **line-item veto**–the power to cancel specific budget items without rejecting the entire budget–in 1996, but the Supreme Court declared it unconstitutional. This was followed by the Balanced Budget Agreement of 1997, which featured rigid **spending caps**–legal limits on annual discretionary spending–to assure that Congress balanced the budget by 2002.

Like many bills in Congress, however, most of the painful consequences of the cap would arise in later years rather than right away. Also, the caps required politically unpopular cuts in many programs like health, science, and education.

Success at Last

After 29 consecutive years of budget deficits, the United States government finally achieved the 1998 budget surplus shown in **Figure 10.6**. There were two reasons for this. First, a strong economy led to record tax collections. Second, previous efforts to control the deficit led to a reduced rate of federal

spending. The budget surpluses were even projected to last until 2010 if the economy remained healthy and if federal spending was contained.

One of the problems the federal government still faces is the rapid growth of **entitlements**–broad social programs that use established eligibility requirements to provide health, nutritional, or income supplements to individuals. These programs are called *entitlements* because people are entitled to draw benefits if they meet the eligibility requirements. Entitlements make up most of the "mandatory" spending in the federal budget. While this ensures that annual spending authorizations are not needed, Congress can still decide to revise these programs. Congress is simply reluctant to revise them because these programs are very popular.

Did you know?

All Those Pages! George Washington was able to put all the figures for the national government's first budget on one large piece of paper. Today, the federal budget consumes thousands of pages.

Section 4 Assessment

Checking for Understanding
1. **Main Idea** What is the difference between the federal debt and the federal deficit?
2. **Key Terms** Define deficit spending, federal debt, balanced budget, trust fund, crowding-out effect, pay-as-you-go provision, line-item veto, spending cap, entitlement.
3. **Describe** how the federal deficit affects the debt.
4. **List** five ways the national debt can affect the economy.
5. **Identify** four recent attempts to bring the federal deficit under control.
6. **Identify** three entitlement programs.

Applying Economic Concepts
7. **Deficit Spending** Identify those benefits that are directly related to entitlement programs. If you were given the task of reducing entitlement programs, which ones would you select to reduce or alter? Provide reasons for your choices.

Critical Thinking

8. **Making Generalizations** Make a list of five ways that you or your family directly benefit from federal government expenditures.
9. **Understanding Cause and Effect** How can the federal debt affect worker incentive?

 Practice and **assess** key social studies skills with the *Glencoe Skillbuilder Interactive Workbook, Level 2.*

Section 4 Assessment Answers

1. federal deficit: the government's expenditures exceed its revenues in a given year; federal deficit adds to the federal debt
2. All vocabulary terms are defined in the text.
3. When the federal government runs a deficit, it must borrow to cover the shortage of revenue, adding to the total debt.
4. may reduce purchasing power of economy, affect the distribution of income, transfer

purchasing power from private to public sector, reduce the incentive to work, save, and invest, cause rise in interest rates
5. Balanced Budget and Emergency Deficit Control Act of 1985 (Gramm-Rudman-Hollings); Budget Enforcement Act of 1990; Omnibus Budget Reconciliation Act of 1993; Balanced Budget Agreement of 1997

6. Social Security, medicaid, medicare, agricultural price supports, federal employee retirement and health benefits, unemployment compensation, aid to the poor
7. health, nutritional, or income supplements
8. lists might include better education, health
9. If people feel that government spends their tax money carelessly, they may have reduced incentive to work.

Section 1

The Economics of Government Spending (pages 255–258)

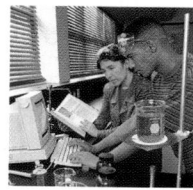

- Government spending takes the form of expenditures on goods and services, most of which are public goods, and on **transfer payments** such as **grants-in-aid** for which the government receives nothing in return.

- Government spending influences the **private sector** by affecting the allocation of resources, the **distribution of income,** and by competing with the private sector for scarce resources.

Section 2

Federal Government Expenditures

(pages 260–265)

- The president is responsible for developing the **federal budget** for the **fiscal year,** which begins on October 1. When the budget is complete, the budget is sent to the House of Representatives.

- The House only deals with **discretionary spending. Mandatory spending** is not part of the annual budget process, although Congress can deal with it separately.

- Discretionary spending is broken down for action by various committees that propose **appropriations bills.** The budget is reassembled and voted on by the House and the Senate.

- If differences between the House and the Senate emerge, a compromise bill is developed on which both vote.

- The largest components of the federal budget are Social Security, national defense, income security, medicare, net interest on the federal debt, and health.

Section 3

State and Local Government Expenditures (pages 267–270)

- State budgets go through an approval process that varies from state to state. The largest state spending categories are intergovernmental expenditures, public welfare, insurance trust, and higher education. Others include highways, hospitals, and interest on state debt.

- The largest single category of spending for local governments is elementary and secondary education. Public utilities, hospitals, police protection, interest on debt, public welfare, and highways follow.

Section 4

Deficits, Surpluses, and the National Debt (pages 272–278)

- Federal budget deficits existed from 1970 until 1998 when the budget finally had a surplus.

- Deficits add to the **federal debt,** and the total debt amounted to $5.7 trillion in fiscal year 2001, approximately $3.3 trillion of which is held by the public.

- The debt affects the economy in several ways: Taxes are needed to pay the interest on the debt; the **distribution of income** is altered; purchasing power is transferred from the **private sector** to the **public sector;** and incentives to work, save, and invest may also be altered.

- Despite recent budget surpluses, the overall federal budget would show a deficit if not for the surpluses in the Social Security Trust Fund.

- The rapid growth of **entitlements** are still a threat to future budget surpluses.

NIGHTLY BUSINESS REPORT

ECONOMICS & YOU

Chapter 16
Disc 1, Side 2

Government Spending

Also available in VHS.

Using the Chapter 10 Summary

Use the Chapter 10 Summary to preview, review, condense, or reteach the chapter.

Preview/Review

Vocabulary PuzzleMaker CD-ROM reinforces Key Terms.

Interactive Tutor Self-Assessment Software provides a review of Chapter 10 content.

Condense

Have students listen to the Chapter 10 Audio Program. Spanish also available.

Assign the Chapter 10 Audio Program Activity and give students the Chapter 10 Audio Program Test.

Have students complete the Guided Reading Activities and Reading Essentials and Study Guides for Chapter 10.

Reteach

Have students complete Reteaching Activity 10 in the TCR. Spanish also available.

Teacher's Notes / Internet Bookmarks

GLENCOE
TECHNOLOGY

 Use **MindJogger Videoquiz** to review the Chapter 10 content.

Self-Check Quiz Visit the *Economics: Principles and Practices* Web site at epp.glencoe.com and click on **Chapter 10—Self-Check Quizzes** to prepare for the chapter test.

Have students visit the Web site at epp.glencoe.com to review Chapter 10 and take the **Self-Check Quiz.**

Identifying Key Terms

Sentences may include:
1. Governments, or the **public sector,** buy goods and services from the **private sector.**
2. The **grant-in-aid** is one form of **transfer payment.**
3. **Deficit spending** has to be covered by borrowing, and this may affect the **distribution of income.**
4. The **federal budget** outlines proposed revenues and expenditures for the **fiscal year.**
5. A **balanced budget amendment** would limit the amount set aside through **appropriations bills.**
6. The total **federal debt** is the amount borrowed to finance government **deficit spending.**
7. To cover **deficit spending,** the government has to borrow, which may lead to the **crowding-out effect.**
8. Fast-growing **entitlement** programs make the establishment of a **balanced budget** very difficult.
9. The federal budget consists of **mandatory spending** and **discretionary spending.**
10. A **spending cap** can only help reduce or prevent a **federal budget deficit.**

Reviewing Key Terms

Write a sentence about each pair of terms below. The sentences should show how the terms are related.

1. public sector, private sector
2. transfer payment, grant-in-aid
3. distribution of income, deficit spending
4. federal budget, fiscal year
5. appropriations bill, balanced budget amendment
6. deficit spending, federal debt
7. deficit spending, crowding-out effect
8. entitlement, balanced budget
9. mandatory spending, discretionary spending
10. spending cap, federal budget deficit

Reviewing the Facts

Section 1 (pages 255–258)

1. **Describe** the growth of government spending since 1940.
2. **Identify** two kinds of government spending.
3. **Explain** three ways that government spending can impact the economy.

Section 2 (pages 260–265)

4. **Identify** the three stages of approval required to establish the federal budget.
5. **Identify** nine of the most important budget categories in the federal budget.

Section 3 (pages 267–270)

6. **Explain** how states model their budget approval process.
7. **Describe** three major categories of state spending.
8. **Describe** three major categories of local spending.

Section 4 (pages 272–278)

9. **Discuss** the relationship of the federal deficit to the federal debt.
10. **Describe** how the debt can affect the economy.
11. **List** four legislative attempts to deal with the problem of federal budget deficits.
12. **Cite** at least six examples of entitlement programs.
13. **Explain** why entitlements are so named.

Thinking Critically

1. **Classifying Information** Examine the major types of federal expenditures in **Figure 10.3** on page 262. Classify each as to whether they are entitlement or non-entitlement programs. Use a chart like the one below to answer the question.

Program	Entitlement	Non-Entitlement

2. **Making Comparisons** Compare the federal expenditures for the three years included in **Figure 10.4.** Identify at least three major differences in the expenditures. How do changes in spending reflect the priorities of the administration that develops the budget?

Reviewing the Facts

Section 1

1. It grew after 1940, declined briefly after WWII, and has continued to grow to the present day.
2. purchase of goods and services, transfer payments
3. It can affect the allocation of resources and the distribution of income, and cause the government to compete with producers in the private sector.

Section 2

4. executive formulation, congressional action, final approval
5. See graph, p. 262.

Section 3

6. modeled on that of the federal government
7. intergovernmental revenues, public welfare, and insurance trusts
8. elementary and secondary education, public utilities, and hospitals

Applying Economic Concepts

1. **Human Capital** Which of the categories in **Figure 10.4** reflect an investment in human capital?

2. **Deficit Spending** If you were a presidential adviser, what spending cuts would you suggest to balance the budget? Explain your reasoning.

3. **Budget Deficits** The federal government has made several attempts to deal with the problem of federal budget deficits. Identify three of the pieces of legislation discussed in the chapter, and outline their main features and weaknesses in a chart similar to the one below.

```
A. _____
    1. Features
    2. Weaknesses
B. _____
    1. Features
    2. Weaknesses
C. _____
    1. Features
    2. Weaknesses
```

Math Practice

A neighbor spent $20,000 a year for 10 years and had an annual income of $15,000 during this period. What is the neighbor's total debt?

Thinking Like an Economist

An economist likes to think in terms of trade-offs and opportunity costs. If you wanted to make changes to a balanced budget in any given year, what would be the opportunity cost of lowering taxes? Of increasing discretionary spending?

Technology Skill

Using a Spreadsheet Review the information on using a spreadsheet on page 29. If you need additional assistance to help you get started, read the information on page 348. Using the Internet, select one of the states of the United States and download or print its state budget. Using this information, create a spreadsheet to record and analyze the following categories.

- Name of State
- Budget Total
- Public Welfare
- Higher Education
- Insurance Contributions
- Highways
- Hospitals
- Interest on State Debt

Enter the information from the state's budget into the spreadsheet.

After entering the information, create a graph for the state's expenditures. What conclusions can you draw from your data? Where is the most money allocated? Compare the data for the state you are analyzing to **Figure 10.5,** which shows expenditures by all the states. Would you consider that state typical or atypical in where it spends its funds? Using a word processor, create a brief summary of your findings. Import your spreadsheet and graphs into the document. Print your results and share them with the class.

Building Skills

Using E-Mail Locate a Web site for your state's government on the Internet. Find out about current bills that your state legislature is considering. Using E-mail, compose a letter to your legislator requesting his or her opinion about current bills of interest to you that are being considered.

 Practice and **assess** key social studies skills with the *Glencoe Skillbuilder Interactive Workbook, Level 2.*

---

2. Students should provide valid responses. An increase indicates that particular category is a priority.

Applying Economic Concepts

1. education, medicare, health, and veterans' benefits
2. Encourage students to offer reasons for their answers
3. Students may use any three. A sample follows. GRH; 1. set federal deficit targets over a six-year period; automatic spending cuts went into effect; 2. could be circumvented by Congress; in weak economy automatic cuts could be suspended

Math Practice

$50,000

Thinking Like an Economist

lowering taxes: programs the government might have to cut; discretionary spending: taxes assessed to support the spending.

Technology Skill

Check for accuracy.

Building Skills

Check students' work for mastery of E-mail skills.

? Bonus Test Question

Describe the major change in priorities between the 1980 and 1998 budgets. *(decline in spending on national defense and increase in interest payments on the debt)*

Section 4

9. When the federal government runs a deficit, it must borrow to cover the shortage of revenue. This adds to the total federal debt.

10. The debt may reduce purchasing powers, affect the distribution of income, transfer purchasing power, cut down incentive to work, save, and invest, and cause interest rates to rise.

11. Balanced Budget and Emergency Deficit Control Act, Budget Enforcement Act, Omnibus Budget Reconciliation Act, Balanced Budget Agreement

12. Social Security, medicaid, medicare, federal employee retirement and health benefits, unemployment compensation

13. because individuals are entitled to draw on these programs if they meet eligibility requirements

Thinking Critically

1. Entitlements include Social Security, income security, medicare, veterans' benefits; the remainder are non-entitlements.

① FOCUS

Write "The Environment" on one side of the board and circle it. Invite the class to brainstorm words, phrases, and concepts that they associate with the term and record their responses by constructing a web diagram around the circle. Then write "The Economy" on the other side of the board, circle it, and construct another web diagram. Next, challenge the class to bridge the two diagrams by identifying shared topics. **Ask:** Why do discussions about the environment necessitate discussions about the economy? As students read the selections, have them consider how the environment forms the basis of all economic activity.

② TEACH

L1 Identifying Main Ideas and Details

Write "Brown and Flavin" and "Easterbrook" on the board as headings. Have volunteers provide concise statements of the main idea of each selection. Write them after the word "Position:" under each heading. Then have the class identify the specific evidence (as opposed to arguments) used in each selection to support each position. List the evidence in an abbreviated form under each heading. Discuss the similarities in argumentative approach, and challenge the class to find evidence cited by one position that contradicts evidence cited by the other.

A Case Study:

PROTECTING THE ENVIRONMENT: IS ENOUGH BEING DONE?

One of the sharpest debates of the last three decades has been over the state of the environment. Squaring off are business interests, who often view environmental regulations as unnecessary and costly, and environmental groups, who see such regulations as key to saving the planet.

Many analysts maintain that the earth is fragile, and that current economic activities are on the verge of damaging the planet in a fundamental way. Other analysts argue that economic activity always involves the exploitation of natural resources, resulting in some environmental impact. That impact, they claim, is negligible, especially in view of the many benefits of a thriving economy.

Who's right? As you read the selections, ask yourself: Is current economic activity putting the earth at risk?

PRO The World Environment Is Threatened

For us, the key limits [in the] twenty-first century are fresh water, forests, rangelands, oceanic fisheries, biological diversity, and the global atmosphere. Will we recognize the world's natural limits and adjust our economies accordingly, or will we proceed to expand our ecological footprint until it is too late to turn back? Are we headed for a world in which accelerating change outstrips our management capacity, overwhelms our political institutions, and leads to extensive breakdown of the ecological systems on which the economy depends? . . .

As world water use has tripled since mid-century, overpumping has led to falling water tables on every continent. . . .

Since mid-century, the demand for lumber has doubled, that for fuelwood has nearly tripled, while paper use has gone up nearly six times. In addition,

forestlands are being cleared for slash-and-burn farming by expanding populations and for commercial crop production and livestock grazing. . . .

[In] just the last half-century the oceanic fish catch increased nearly five times, doubling seafood availability per person for the world as a whole. [But] 11 of the world's 15 most important fishing areas and 70 percent of the major fish species are either fully or overexploited. . . .

[A]s with fisheries, overgrazing [of rangeland] is now the rule, not the exception. . . . Yet another of our basic support systems is being overwhelmed by continuously expanding human needs.

Perhaps the best single indicator of the earth's health is the declining number of species with which we share the planet. . . . [We] are now in the early stages of the greatest decimation of plant and animal life in 65 million years. . .

Even in a high-tech information age, human societies cannot continue to prosper while the natural world is progressively degraded.

—Lester R. Brown and Christopher Flavin, Worldwatch Institute

Behind the Viewpoints

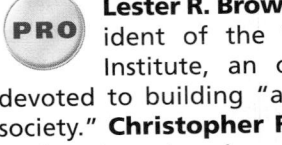

PRO **Lester R. Brown** is the president of the Worldwatch Institute, an organization devoted to building "a sustainable society." **Christopher Flavin** is the Institute's senior vice president for research.

CON **Gregg Easterbrook** is a well-known writer on environmental affairs, and the author of *A Moment in Time.*

CON The American Environment Is Improving

Twenty-five years ago, only one-third of America's lakes and rivers were safe for fishing and swimming; today two-thirds are, and the proportion continues to rise. Annual wetlands loss has fallen by 80 percent in the same period, while soil losses to agricultural runoff have been almost cut in half. Total American water consumption has declined nine percent in the past 15 years, even as the population expands. . . . Since 1970, smog has declined by about a third, even as the number of cars has increased by half; acid rain has fallen by 40 percent; airborne soot particles are down 69 percent, which is why big cities have blue skies again. . . . [Emissions] of CFCs, which deplete stratospheric ozone, have all but ended.

Other environmental measures are almost uniformly positive. Toxic emissions by industry declined 46 percent from 1988 to 1996, even as petrochemical manufacturers enjoyed record U.S. production and copious profits. . . . The forested acreage of the United States is expanding, with wildlife numbers up in most areas. . . . Since the Endangered Species Act was passed, only a few U.S. species have fallen extinct, not the thousands predicted, while species such as the bald eagle, gray whale, and peregrine falcon have recovered enough to no longer require full legal protection. Only two major U.S. environmental gauges are now negative: continuing inaction against greenhouse gases and continuing loss of wildlife habitats to urban expansion.

An important conceptual lesson is being learned: When pollution stops, natural recovery does not require ponderous geological time. . . .

[T]echnology has (for the moment, at least) entered a relatively benign phase in which products and industrial processes consume steadily fewer resources and produce steadily less waste. . . . Because the character of environmental progress is nonideological—reflecting well both on federal initiatives and on business—neither political camp knows how to extol what's happened. That no interest group sees itself as benefiting from public awareness of environmental success . . . [has] the effect of preventing commentators and voters from focusing on the locus of the real environmental emergencies—the developing world.

—Gregg Easterbrook, social issues analyst

Analyzing the Issue

1. What "important conceptual lesson" does Easterbrook refer to? How might this impact Brown and Flavin's argument?

2. Do the two selections address the same issues? Explain.

3. On what issue might Brown and Flavin agree with Easterbrook?

Issues in Free Enterprise

3 ASSESS

Have students answer the questions listed under **Analyzing the Issue**.

4 CLOSE

Have students evaluate the issue of the environment by having them write paragraphs that explore this topic: "The environment and the economy are inextricably connected."

LINKING PAST & PRESENT

Environmental Regulations
Regulations against certain types of environmental damage date to ancient times. The earliest cities faced pollution problems, and some of the earliest law codes (c. 2,000 years ago) specify punishments for certain acts of pollution. Yet pollution didn't garner truly widespread concern until the Industrial Revolution, which blackened the skies over many European cities. In the United States, it wasn't until the last half of the twentieth century that the matter achieved widespread attention.

Answers to Analyzing the Issue

1. Easterbrook refers to the idea that "when pollution stops, natural recovery does not require ponderous geological time." Its implication for Brown and Flavin's argument is that the damage they cite could be corrected in a relatively short amount of time, and so is not disastrous, as they maintain.

2. Brown and Flavin refer to the global environmental conditions, while Easterbrook focuses on American environmental conditions.

3. Easterbrook says that "the locus of the real environmental emergencies" is the developing world, with which Brown and Flavin might well agree.

Chapter 11 Resource Manager

SECTION RESOURCES

Daily Objectives	Reproducible Resources	Technology/Multimedia Resources
Section 1 **The Evolution of Money** 1. Explain the three functions of money. 2. Identify four major types of money used in early societies. 3. Describe the four characteristics of money.	Reproducible Lesson Plan 11-1 Daily Lecture Notes 11-1 Guided Reading Activity 11-1 Reading Essentials and Study Guide 11-1 Section Quiz 11-1*	Daily Focus Transparency 58 Interactive Tutor Self-Assessment Software ExamView® Pro Testmaker Presentation Plus!
Section 2 **Early Banking and Monetary Standards** 1. Explain the history of privately issued bank notes. 2. Describe an inconvertible money standard.	Reproducible Lesson Plan 11-2 Daily Lecture Notes 11-2 Guided Reading Activity 11-2 Reading Essentials and Study Guide 11-2 Section Quiz 11-2*	Daily Focus Transparency 59 NBR Economics & You Video Program Interactive Tutor Self-Assessment Software ExamView® Pro Testmaker Presentation Plus!
Section 3 **The Development of Modern Banking** 1. Relate the effects of Depression-era bank failures on deposit insurance creation. 2. Identify three other forms of depository institutions. 3. Describe the reasons for the S&L crisis in the 1980s.	Reproducible Lesson Plan 11-3 Daily Lecture Notes 11-3 Guided Reading Activity 11-3 Reading Essentials and Study Guide 11-3 Section Quiz 11-3*	Daily Focus Transparency 61 Vocabulary PuzzleMaker CD-ROM Interactive Tutor Self-Assessment Software ExamView® Pro Testmaker Presentation Plus!

*Also available in Spanish

Transparency CD-ROM Software Blackline Master

Videodisc Audio Program Videocassette

 OUT OF TIME?
Assign the Chapter 11 Audio Program activity and test.

 Block Schedule

Activities that are particularly suited to use within the block scheduling framework are identified throughout this chapter by the following designation: **BLOCK SCHEDULING**

KEY TO ABILITY LEVELS

Teaching strategies have been coded for varying learning styles and abilities.

L1 **BASIC** activities for all students

L2 **AVERAGE** activities for average to above-average students

L3 **CHALLENGING** activities for above-average students

ELL **ENGLISH LANGUAGE LEARNER** activities

Chapter 11 Resource Manager

Timesaving Tools

TeacherWorks™ All-In-One Planner and Resource Center

- **Interactive Teacher Edition** Access your Teacher Wraparound Edition and your classroom resources with a few easy clicks.
- **Interactive Lesson Planner** Planning has never been easier! Organize your week, month, semester, or year with all the lesson helps you need to make teaching creative, timely, and relevant.

Use Glencoe's **Presentation Plus!** multimedia teacher tool to easily present dynamic lessons that visually excite your students. Using Microsoft PowerPoint® you can customize the presentations to create your own personalized lessons.

ACTIVITY

From the Classroom of...

Dathan Cole
Brecksville-Broadview
Heights High School
Brecksville, OH

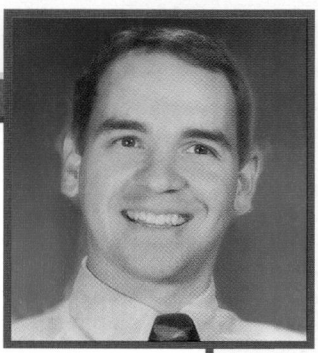

Barter

This activity demonstrates the shortcomings of barter and the functions of money. Organize students into five groups. Distribute different role cards and the appropriate trade slips to each group. The role cards state: *blacksmith* needs wood/has axes; *cattle rancher* needs corn/has hides; *corn farmer* needs wood/has corn; *lumberjack* needs axes/has wood; *shoemaker* needs hides/has shoes. The trade slips state: *Axes* can be traded for hides or corn, *hides* can be traded for axes or wood, *corn* can be traded for axes or shoes, *wood* can be traded for hides or shoes, and *shoes* can be traded for corn or wood.

Tell students they have five minutes to trade goods to acquire what they need. After trading, determine how many students were successful and ask what problems they encountered. Use their experiences to point out the difficulty of not being able to trade directly for what they needed. Ask students to imagine what trading would be like if they had to consider the relative value of the units.

Discuss the advantages of money as a medium of exchange, a measure of value, and a store of value.

National Council on Economic Education

THE **Economics**America AND **Economics**International PROGRAMS

Voluntary National Content Standards in Economics
Emphasized in Chapter 11

Content Standard 11

For a complete listing of NCEE Standards and entire text correlation, see Teacher pages in front of book.

Resources Available from NCEE
- Capstone: The Nation's High School Economics Course
- Civics and Government: Focus on Economics
- Economics at Work
- United States History: Eyes on the Economy

To order these materials or to contact your state Council on Economic Education about workshops and programs, call 1-800-338-1192 or visit www.nationalcouncil.org

Chapter 11 Resource Manager

Economic Concept Transparency 6:
Exchange, Money, and Interdependence

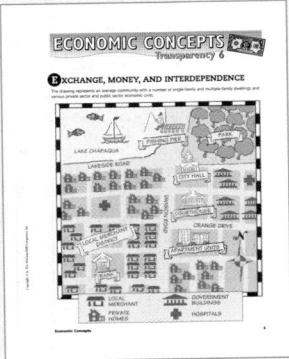

Consumer Application
Activity 16

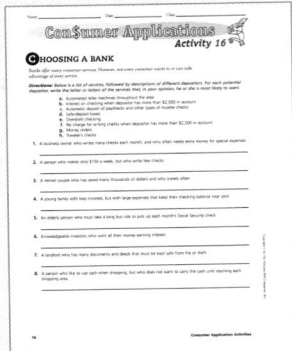

Free Enterprise
Activity 16

Enrichment Activity 11

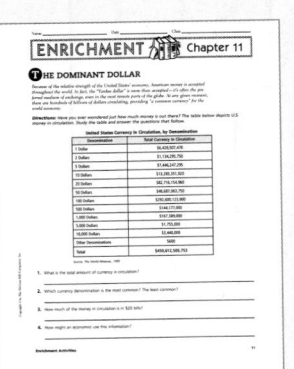

Cooperative Learning
Activity 16

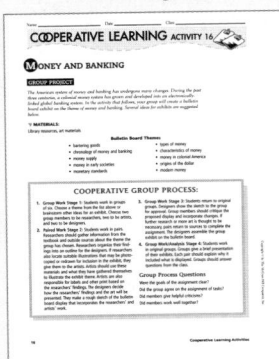

Math Practice
Activity 16

Economic Cartoon 16

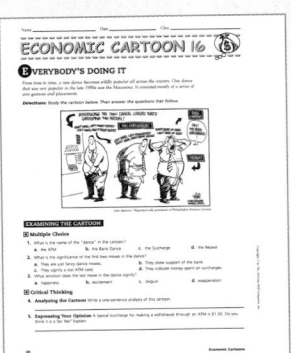

Primary and Secondary
Source Reading 16

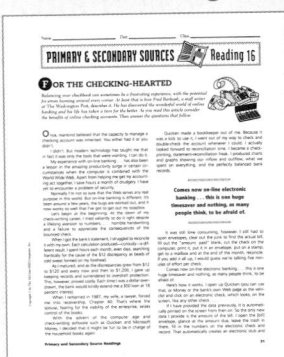

Economic Vocabulary
Activity 11

Reteaching Activity 11

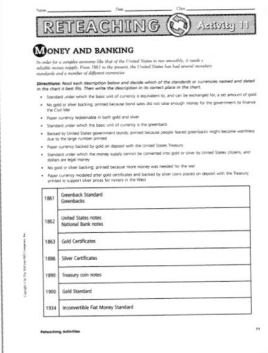

Critical Thinking
Activity 16

Reinforcing Economic
Skill 25

Chapter 11 Resource Manager

ASSESSMENT AND EVALUATION

Chapter 11 Test Form A

Chapter 11 Test Form B

Performance Assessment Activity 16

ExamView® Pro Testmaker

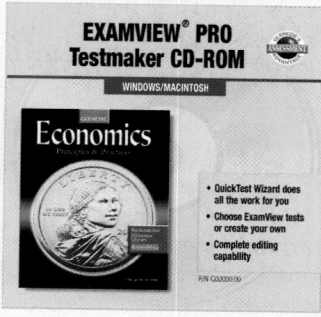

SPANISH RESOURCES

The following Spanish language materials are available in the Spanish Resources binder:

 Spanish Economic Vocabulary Activities

 Spanish Reteaching Activities

 Spanish Section Quizzes

 Spanish Economic Concepts Transparencies

Also available:

  Spanish Chapter 11 Audio Program Activity and Test

TECHNOLOGY/MULTIMEDIA

- Vocabulary PuzzleMaker CD-ROM
- Interactive Tutor Self-Assessment Software
- ExamView® Pro Testmaker
- Audio Program (English or Spanish)
- NBR Economics & You Video Program (English or Spanish)
- MindJogger Videoquiz
- Interactive Economics! CD-ROM
- Presentation Plus!
- TeacherWorks CD-ROM
- Glencoe Skillbuilder Interactive Workbook CD-ROM, Level 2

ECONOMICS Online

Use our Web site for additional resources. All essential content is covered in the Student Edition.

You and your students can visit epp.glencoe.com, the Web site companion to **Economics: Principles and Practices.** This innovative integration of electronic and print media offers your students a wealth of opportunities. The student text directs students to the Web site for the following options:

- **Chapter Overviews**
- **Student Web Activities**
- **Self-Check Quizzes**
- **Textbook Updates**

Answers are provided for you in the Web Activity Lesson Plan. Additional Web resources and interactive puzzles are also available.

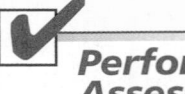

Performance Assessment

Refer to Activity 16 in the *Performance Assessment Strategies and Activities* booklet.

 BLOCK SCHEDULING

 ECONOMICS *Online*

Introduce students to chapter content and key terms by having them access **Chapter Overview 11** at epp.glencoe.com

 NIGHTLY BUSINESS REPORT

 ECONOMICS & YOU

Chapter 18
Disc 1, Side 2

Money and Banking
After viewing this segment, students should be able to:
• List some of the services offered by financial institutions.

 Also available in VHS.

GLENCOE TECHNOLOGY

 Use **MindJogger Videoquiz** to preview the Chapter 11 content.

CHAPTER 11
Money and Banking

Economics & You

Why do you accept money in exchange for a good or service? Why were so many different kinds of money used around the world? In **Chapter 11**, you will learn about the development of money. To learn more about how our money and banking system works, view the Chapter 18 video lesson:

Money and Banking

ECONOMICS *Online*

Chapter Overview Visit the *Economics: Principles and Practices* Web site at epp.glencoe.com and click on **Chapter 11—Chapter Overviews** to preview chapter information.

To carry out its economic functions, money must be acceptable, divisible, portable, and stable in value.

✚ EXTRA CREDIT PROJECT

Have students write a research paper on the role that banks—or a particular bank—play in the local economy. Encourage students to illustrate their papers with charts and graphs. Call on volunteers to read their papers to the class.

The Evolution of Money

Study Guide

Main Idea
Money is any substance that functions as a medium of exchange, a measure of value, and a store of value.

Reading Strategy
Graphic Organizer As you read the section, complete a graphic organizer similar to the one below that illustrates the characteristics of money.

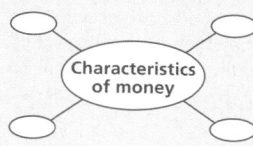

Characteristics of money

Key Terms
barter economy, money, medium of exchange, measure of value, store of value, commodity money, fiat money, specie, monetary unit

Objectives
After studying this section, you will be able to:
1. **Explain** the three functions of money.
2. **Identify** four major types of money used in early societies.
3. **Describe** the four characteristics of money.

Applying Economic Concepts
Money Did you trade items when you were younger? Read to find out more about trade and how the use of money makes it easier.

1 FOCUS

Section Overview
This section describes the development of money over time.

BELLRINGER
Motivational Activity

Project **transparency** and have students answer questions.

Available as blackline master.

Daily Focus Transparency 58

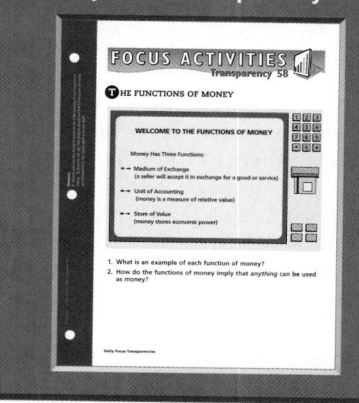

Study Guide

Reading Strategy
Have students create the graphic organizer.
Answers to Graphic: *portability, durability, divisibility, limited availability*

Preteaching Vocabulary
Direct students to the list of Key Terms. Have them use the words they know in sentences.

Cover Story

To the Colonies

The enterprising colonists being generally destitute of families, Sir Edward Sandys, the treasurer, proposed to the Virginia Company to send over a freight of young women to become wives for the planters. The proposal was applauded, and ninety girls, "young and uncorrupt," were sent over in the ships that arrived this year (1620) and the year following, sixty more, handsome and well recommended to the company for their virtuous education and demeanor. The [cost of transport] was one hundred pounds of tobacco; but as the number became scarce, [it] increased to one hundred and fifty pounds; the value of which in money was three shillings per pound. . . .

—*Holmes' American Annals*, 1620

Virginia Company insignia

It may seem odd to you that people once used a plant like tobacco as a form of money. Frequently, people used things that were easily available and valued by others as a form of money. Money is something we all take for granted, but without it—as we saw in the cover story—life would be quite different.

Think what life would be like in a **barter economy,** a moneyless economy that relies on trade. Without money, the exchange of goods and services would be greatly hindered because the products some people have to offer are not always acceptable or easy to divide for payment. For example, how could a farmer with a pail of milk obtain a pair of shoes if the cobbler wanted a basket of fish? Unless there is a "mutual coincidence of wants"—which means that two people want exactly what the other has and are willing to trade what they have for it—it is difficult for trade to take place.

Life is simpler in an economy with money. The farmer sells the milk for cash and then exchanges the cash for shoes. The cobbler takes the cash and looks for someone selling fish. Money, as it turns out, makes life easier for everybody in ways we may have never even thought about.

CHAPTER 11: MONEY AND BANKING **285**

RESOURCE MANAGER

Reproducible Masters
- Reproducible Lesson Plan 11-1
- Daily Lecture Notes 11-1
- Guided Reading Activity 11-1
- Reading Essentials and Study Guide 11-1
- Section Quiz 11-1

Transparencies
- Daily Focus Transparency 58

Multimedia
- Interactive Tutor Self-Assessment Software
- ExamView® Pro Testmaker
- Presentation Plus!

② TEACH

F.Y.I.

In the past, complex exchange arrangements among businesses allowed them to trade barter credits for goods and services. For example, a hotel might have paid a construction company "vacation time" for building work. Bartering helped companies stay busy even when they had uncertain cash flows from their regular operations.

L1 Applying Ideas

Call on students to name objects that might be used as money today if there were no dollar bills or coins. List about 10 responses on the board. Then organize students into groups of five and direct groups to apply the characteristics of money to the listed objects. Have groups select the object that would best serve as money based on their analysis. **ELL**

Functions of Money

Money can be any substance that serves as a medium of exchange, a measure of value, and a store of value. If it satisfies these three functions, it will be accepted and used by everyone in a society.

Medium of Exchange

For something to function as money, it must serve as a **medium of exchange**–something accepted by all parties as payment for goods and services. Throughout history, societies have used many materials as a medium of exchange, including gold, silver, and even salt. In ancient Rome, salt was so valuable that each soldier received an annual salt payment called a "salarium." The modern term for an annual income–or "salary"–is based on this Latin term.

Measure of Value

For something to serve as money, it must be accepted as a **measure of value,** a common denominator that can be used to express worth in terms that most individuals understand. This is what we observe whenever we see a price tag on something– a value that we can use to make comparisons with other products. In the United States, our measure of value is expressed in dollars and cents.

Store of Value

For something to function as money, it must also serve as a **store of value,** the property that allows purchasing power to be saved until needed. For example, goods or services can be converted into money, which is easily stored until needed. Money enables a period of time to pass between earning and spending an income.

CYBERNOMICS SPOTLIGHT

The Future of Money

As you have learned, money must have certain characteristics to perform its functions in the economy. Money must be accepted. This means that everyone in the economic system must agree that the money has value and be willing to take it as payment for debts. Money must also be divisible. This means that units of money can be divided into smaller units without losing their relative value. Money must be portable. This means that it must be possible to move the money from one place to another with ease. In addition, money must have a reasonably stable value. This means that a person will be able to buy about the same number or value of products today, next week, or next year.

Despite the widespread use and advantages of currency, some analysts predict that the use of electronic payments will grow tremendously. Have you heard of cybercurrency? Smart cards? Electronic money? One analyst defines cybercurrency as the use of microchip-based electronic money for financial transactions, via smart cards and the

Smart cards

Internet. Some economists and analysts contend that cybercurrency has the potential to assume an important place in domestic and worldwide payment systems.

Nobel Prize–winning economist Milton Friedman noted that paper and coin eventually will give way to electronic money. Walter Wriston, the former president of the financial institution Citicorp, estimates that in the not-too-distant future, one in every four Americans will have a smart card. Smart cards are wallet-sized plastic cards that serve three purposes: as data carriers, for identification,

286 UNIT 3 MACROECONOMICS: INSTITUTIONS

CYBERNOMICS SPOTLIGHT

Smart Cards Smart cards, similar to plastic credit cards, have been in development since the late 1970s and in use for over 10 years. A chip embedded in each card enables it to provide many services, most notably data portability, security, and convenience. Smart cards can carry 10 to 100 times more information than a magnetic-stripe card, and can serve multiple purposes: personal identification, credit card, automated teller machine card, telephone credit card, and medical information source. Smart card activities are growing at a rate of about 30 percent annually.

Smart cards are very popular in Europe, where they are commonly accepted in stores, vending machines, and pay phones, but they have not caught on as quickly in the United States. Of the

Money in Early Societies

The use of money developed because it makes life easier for people. Money comes in an incredible variety of forms, shapes, and sizes. Tea leaves compressed into "bricks" comprised money in ancient China, and compressed cheese was used in early Russian trade. The East African Masai used a currency made of miniature iron spears fastened together to form a necklace.

Today, this money would be classified as **commodity money**—money that has an alternative use as an economic good, or commodity. For example, the compressed tea leaves could be made into tea when not needed for trade. Other items became **fiat money**—money by government decree—such as the tiny, metallic coins used in Asia Minor in the seventh century B.C. These coins served as money largely because the government said they were money.

The use of money became accepted because it served everyone's best interests to do so. In this sense, money was then—and is now—a social convention, much like the general acceptance of laws and government.

Money in Colonial America

The money used by early settlers in America was similar to the money found in early societies. Some of it was commodity money, and some was fiat money.

Many products—including gunpowder, musket balls, corn, and hemp—served as commodity money. It could be used to settle debts and make purchases, or could even be consumed if necessary.

Did You Know?

Dollars and Cents The United States decimalized monetary system, based on dollars and cents, was adopted in 1784. The units of the monetary system were the mill (1/100th of a cent), cent, dime, dollar, and eagle ($10).

and for financial transactions. Wriston notes that "people will use an ATM or home computer to download the money from their bank accounts to the cards."

Features Do these new forms of money meet the characteristics of useful currency? Supporters say they do and, additionally, provide an added feature—transfer velocity—almost instantaneous transfer of funds from point to point. Another advantage is reduced transaction costs. Merchants pay credit card transaction fees, and those fees usually include a minimum that can erase profit margins on low-cost items. Research analyst Heather Aston says, "It doesn't make a lot of sense to have to process something that costs $2 the same way you process something that costs $50." Micropayment schemes eliminate the expensive step of asking the credit card issuer to confirm the card holder's ability to pay for each transaction. What is needed is confirmation that the encrypted serial number is valid.

Will Cybermoney Catch On? Some economists and analysts believe that the use of U.S. currency and credit cards is too deeply ingrained for new forms to displace them. While technological innovation may make cash less essential, public demand for it is strong. In addition, coin and paper money provide an advantage in privacy—you are in charge of your money and no one else needs to know. Will cybermoney lead the way to a cashless age? Only the future will tell.

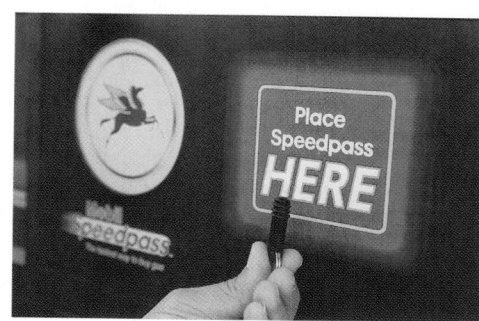

"Key" and sensing pad

962 million smart cards sold worldwide in 1997, less than 1 percent were sold in the United States. One obstacle is that the U.S. does not have standardized technology for reading smart cards. Many merchants are holding off buying a smart card reader until a single system becomes dominant. Some experts believe that Internet commerce will help usher in smart cards, since they are such a convenient way to pay for online purchases. Once that happens, they expect smart cards to become more widely accepted off-line as well. Others believe new and evolving markets will be forerunners in smart card use, as will companies that demand tight security. Discuss with students the possible need for additional rules and regulations if smart cards catch on. Do they believe paper money will become obsolete?

Guided Reading Activity 11-1

> **GUIDED READING** Activity 11-1
>
> For use with textbook pages 285–290
>
> ❶ THE EVOLUTION OF MONEY
>
> **RECALLING THE FACTS**
>
> **Directions:** Use the information in your textbook to answer the questions. Use another sheet of paper if necessary.
>
> 1. What is a barter economy?
>
> 2. What are the three functions of money? Define each term.
>   a.
>   b.
>   c.
>
> 3. What is commodity money?
>
> 4. What is fiat money?
>
> 5. In early America, what was used to "back" paper currency?
>
> 6. Why was specie considered the most desirable form of money?

CURRICULUM CONNECTION

Sociology The citizens of Yap, a tiny island in the South Pacific, use the dollar only at grocery stores and gas stations. For most of their purchases, they rely on the large limestone wheels that have been used as currency for nearly 2,000 years. The Yapese are accustomed to using the stones as payment for land, canoes, and even permission to marry. This currency system has several advantages: it is impossible to counterfeit, it is difficult to steal, and it is stable because a limited number of stone wheels exist on the island.

L2 Illustrating Ideas

On the board, write the three functions and the four characteristics of money. Have students look at a dollar bill, and call on volunteers to explain how it fulfills each function and exhibits each characteristic.

THE GLOBAL ECONOMY

Paper Money The first country to use paper money was China. From the early tenth century until the middle of the fifteenth century, China experimented with issuing different kinds of paper money. These experiments invariably failed as the Chinese authorities periodically succumbed to the temptation to print too much money. In 1020, for example, China printed a lot of paper money in order to buy off invaders from the north, resulting in inflation.

L3 Researching Money in Other Countries

Have students work in small groups to prepare research reports on the money of a selected country. Have groups focus on: **(1)** The historical evolution of money in the country selected; **(2)** How the historical development of money, and the money the country uses today, reflects the country's culture; **(3)** How successfully the country's money performs the three functions of money—as a medium of exchange, as a measure of value, and as a store of value; **(4)** How the country's money measures up to the four characteristics of money—portability, durability, divisibility, and limited availability. Have groups illustrate their reports with examples of past and present coin and paper money. Have groups present their completed reports to the class.

Barter Economy

Medium of Exchange As the cartoon shows, a barter economy can cause problems for those wanting to exchange goods for products they may use. *How does money function as a medium of exchange?*

A commonly accepted commodity money was tobacco, with a value set at three English shillings per pound by the governor of colonial Virginia in 1618. Two years later, as you read in the cover story, the colonists used some of this money to bring wives to the colonies.

Other colonies established fiat monies. In 1645 Connecticut set a monetary value for *wampum*—a form of currency the Narragansett Native Americans made out of white conch and black mussel shells. Because white shells were more plentiful than black ones, and because the Narragansett and the settlers used them in trade, one English penny was made equal to six white or three black shells. In 1648 the General Court of Massachusetts passed a law ordering the wampum to be "suitably strung" in lengths of 1, 3, and 12 pennies.

Paper Currency

As time passed, Americans used other forms of money. In some cases, state laws allowed individuals

to print their own paper currency. Backed by gold and silver deposits in banks, it served as currency for the immediate area.

Most states printed money in the form of tax-anticipation notes that could be redeemed with interest at the end of the year. State governments printed these notes and then used them to pay salaries, buy supplies, and meet other expenditures until taxes were received and the notes redeemed.

Paper money was issued to finance the Revolutionary War. In 1775, *Continental dollars,* a form of fiat paper currency with no gold or silver backing, were printed by the Continental Congress. By the end of the war, nearly one-quarter *billion* Continental dollars had been printed to pay soldiers and buy supplies—a volume so large that it was virtually worthless by the end of the revolution.

Specie

A modest amount of **specie**—or money in the form of coins made from silver or gold—was also used in the colonies. These included English

MEETING SPECIAL NEEDS ACTIVITY

Learning Disabled For students with attention deficit disorder, who are often distracted by movement and noise in the classroom, make a self-evaluation checklist of their classroom-attending behaviors by dividing a sheet of paper into two columns, one titled "On-task" and the other "Off-task." As they silently read any part of Section 1 (assign about 10 minutes of reading), call out "check" at intervals. They should put a check under the heading that describes their level of attention to the task. If they were "off-task," ask them if they know what interfered with their ability to concentrate.

Refer to *Inclusion for the Social Studies Classroom Strategies and Activities* in the TCR.

shillings, Austrian talers, and various European coins that immigrants brought to the colonies.

Coins were the most desirable form of money, not only because of their mineral content, but because they were in limited supply. By 1776, only $12 million in specie circulated in the colonies as compared to nearly $500 million in paper currency.

Origins of the Dollar

When George Washington became president in 1789, the most plentiful coin in circulation was the Spanish peso. Consequently, one of Washington's first challenges was to establish a money supply for the new country, a task he assigned to Benjamin Franklin and Secretary of the Treasury Alexander Hamilton.

Pesos in America

Long before the American Revolution had begun, the Spanish were mining silver in Mexico. They melted the silver into bullion—ingots or bars of precious metals—or minted it into coins for shipment to Spain. When the Spanish treasure ships stopped in the West Indies to buy fresh provisions, however, they often became victims of Caribbean pirates who spent their stolen treasure in America's southern colonies.

Meanwhile, the colonies engaged in a profitable exchange known as the triangular trade, which exported rum in exchange for enslaved people and molasses. Molasses from the West Indies was shipped to the colonies where it was made into rum. The rum was shipped across the Atlantic Ocean to Africa, where it was exchanged for enslaved Africans. The Africans were packed into ships and taken across the Atlantic to the West Indies where they were sold for molasses and pesos. The molasses, silver pesos, and some enslaved people were then returned to the colonies to begin the triangle again.

From "Talers" to "Dollars"

Pesos were known as "pieces of eight," because they were divided into eight sub-parts known as *bits*. Because the pesos resembled the Austrian talers, they were nicknamed talers, which sounds

Paper Currency

Characteristics Various forms of paper currency have been used in the United States. *What characteristics must money have to be a successful medium of exchange?*

like the word "dollars." This term became so popular that Franklin and Hamilton decided to make the dollar the basic **monetary unit,** or standard unit of currency, in the U.S. money system.

Rather than divide the dollar into eighths as the Spanish had done with the peso, Franklin and Hamilton decided to divide it into tenths, which was easier to understand. Even today, some of the terminology associated with the Spanish peso remains, as when people sometimes call a 25-cent coin—one quarter of a dollar—"two bits."

Characteristics of Money

The study of early money is useful because it helps us understand the characteristics that give money its value. To be successful, money must be portable, durable, divisible, and limited in supply.

CHAPTER 11: MONEY AND BANKING **289**

Visual Instruction

Answer to Caption:
portability, durability, divisibility, limited availability

 CURRICULUM CONNECTION

History The silver mined in Mexico by the Spanish in the 1500s and 1600s led to massive inflation in Spain after the silver was shipped there. The oversupply of money caused prices to go up and the value of money to fall.

3 ASSESS

Assign Section 1 Assessment as homework or as an in-class activity.

Have students use **Interactive Tutor Self-Assessment Software.**

Section Quiz 11-1

EXTENDING THE CONTENT

Have You Got a Buck? In the frontier areas during the colonial period, hunters often left their deerskins at trading posts until they could pick them up at a later date. As proof of ownership, the hunters would obtain a receipt, which they could exchange among themselves or use at the trading post for supplies. The receipts, worth about a dollar because of the value of the hides, were called "bucks"—and hence the common name for the dollar.

Reteach

Enrich

Have students investigate the steps taken by various countries to combat the counterfeiting of money. Have them present their findings in a written report.

4 CLOSE

Have students comment on the following statement: The American economy could not function without the dollar bill.

Portability

First, money must be portable, or easily transferred from one person to another, to make the exchange of money for products easier. Most money in early societies was very portable—including dog teeth, feather-stick money, wampum, tobacco, and compressed blocks of tea and cheese.

Durability

Money must also be reasonably durable so that it lasts when handled and does not deteriorate when being held as a store of value. Most colonial money was quite durable, especially monies like musket balls and wampum. Wampum, for example, did not require special care when being handled, and it lasted a long time. Even the fiat paper money of the colonial period had a type of durability in that it could be easily replaced by issuing new bills when old ones became worn.

Divisibility

Money should be easily divisible into smaller units, so that people can use only as much as needed for any transaction. Most early money was highly divisible. In the case of the Masai's iron spear currency, the necklace was untied and some of the spears removed. The blocks of tea or cheese were cut with a knife. Bundles of tobacco leaves were broken apart.

Limited Availability

Finally, if something is to serve as money, it must be available, but only in limited supply. The dog teeth of New Guinea, for example, were extracted from packs of wild dogs. Because the islanders hunted the dogs for their teeth, the wild dog population never grew large. Stones used as money on the Yap Islands were carried in open canoes from other islands 400 miles away. Because navigation was uncertain and the weather unpredictable, only one canoe in 20 completed the round-trip—circumstances that limited the supply of stone money.

Money—like almost everything else—loses its value whenever there is too much of it, a major problem for most types of commodity money. In Virginia, for example, the price of tobacco went from 36 pennies a pound to 1 penny a pound after everyone started growing their own money. Wampum even lost its value when settlers used industrial dyes to turn the white shells into black—thereby doubling its value.

Section 1 Assessment

Checking for Understanding

1. **Main Idea** How does money advance the exchange of goods and services?
2. **Key Terms** Define barter economy, money, medium of exchange, measure of value, store of value, commodity money, fiat money, specie, monetary unit.
3. **Describe** three functions of money.
4. **Name** four types of early money.
5. **Explain** how the dollar was adopted as the basic monetary unit.
6. **Identify** the four characteristics of money.

Applying Economic Concepts

7. **Money** Write a brief critique of the following statement: "Money is our servant, not our master. Those who treat money as the master rather than the servant do not really understand money."

Critical Thinking

8. **Drawing Conclusions** Suppose the color and shape of our currency was changed. How would these changes affect the role money played?

 Practice and **assess** key social studies skills with the *Glencoe Skillbuilder Interactive Workbook, Level 2.*

Section 1 Assessment Answers

1. Money allows people to buy directly what they need instead of waiting for a "mutual coincidence of wants."

2. All vocabulary terms are defined in the text.

3. It serves as a medium of exchange; as a measure of value; and as a store of value.

4. tea leaves, cheese, spears, various commodity money

5. Answers should reflect content on page 289.

6. portability, durability, divisibility, limited availability

7. Money is a tool that enables the economy to run smoothly.

8. As long as the new currency possesses the four characteristics and is readily accepted as a medium of exchange, its function would not change.

Profiles in Economics

A Fingertip Fortune:
Dineh Mohajer
(1973–)

It might be hard to believe that a multimillion dollar business started in a bathroom, but that's exactly where Dineh Mohajer's Hard Candy cosmetics company was born.

The year was 1995. Fed up with a life of hard study as a pre-med student, the 22-year-old Mohajer recalls making a conscious decision to make a change. "I used to stare out the window," she said, "and think, 'I wonder what the civilians are doing out there?' So that summer I told myself, this is my last summer of real life. I'm rebelling! I'm not going to do it!"

HARD CANDY

Mohajer took a job at a Los Angeles boutique. One night, she decided she needed nail polish to match a pair of sky-blue sandals. In her bathroom, she applied her knowledge of chemistry from her pre-med classes to mix up some nail polish. The unusual color was a hit with her friends, so Mohajer, at the urging of her sister Pooheh, took it to the boutique owner, who agreed to sell it. Mohajer mixed up several more colors of

nail polish, and called the line Hard Candy. The striking colors proved so popular that the boutique couldn't keep Hard Candy in stock. Mohajer took a loan from her parents and went into business full time. It was the start of something big.

RAPID SUCCESS

The colors Mohajer chose for her nail polishes, with hip names like "Tantrum," "Greed," and "Dork," were bold and hard-edged, unlike the more conservative colors available from the big cosmetics companies. They proved a hit with young, fashion-conscious women in Los Angeles. Hard Candy became the new, cool makeup among trend-setters, and its popularity was reported in national fashion magazines like *Vogue, Elle, Teen,* and *Seventeen.* Tens of thousands of young

women across the country, eager to stay in style, ordered bottles of the nail polish. Within six months, Hard Candy was grossing more than $70,000 a month. Within a year, annual sales had topped $10 million.

The fashion industry, by definition, is volatile: what's "in" today is likely to be "out" tomorrow, so the long-term fortunes of Hard Candy are hard to predict. But there can be no doubt that it has proved a multimillion dollar, overnight success, born in the bathroom of a young woman who parlayed her love of fashion into a big business.

Examining the Profile

1. **Identifying Cause and Effect** What factors made Hard Candy successful?

2. **For Further Research** Conduct research to determine Hard Candy's current condition. Report on its market share and immediate prospects.

CHAPTER 11: MONEY AND BANKING **291**

BACKGROUND

Dineh Mohajer's success has brought her a wealth of attention, including the notice of larger companies that would like to own the highly profitable Hard Candy as a subsidiary. Says Mohajer, "There have been offers, but not anything I'm interested in. It's important to me that it goes to the right person, someone who understands my vision and can execute it, not some vulture who will throw it into the mass market." Such commitment to her company is part of the reason for Hard Candy's success.

TEACH

Organize students into small groups and direct each group to brainstorm a list of ideas for businesses. Students should select the business they think would be most likely to succeed, and create an abbreviated business marketing plan that answers these questions: *What* is the business? *Who* would purchase the business's products or services? *How* would the business reach potential customers? *Where* are potential customers located? *Why* would the business be successful? Group representatives should share their plans with the class. Use the presentations as a springboard for discussion about the role of marketing in business growth.

Answers to Examining the Profile

1. Answers will vary. Students should at least cite the marked differences between the Hard Candy line of cosmetics and the existing products on the market, their adoption by fashion trendsetters, and the national press attention the company and its products received.

2. Answers will vary. Have students report how and where they located the information. Reward thoughtful researching techniques.

FOCUS

Section Overview
This section tracks the history of banking.

BELLRINGER
Motivational Activity

 Project **transparency** and have students answer questions.

 Available as blackline master.

Daily Focus Transparency 59

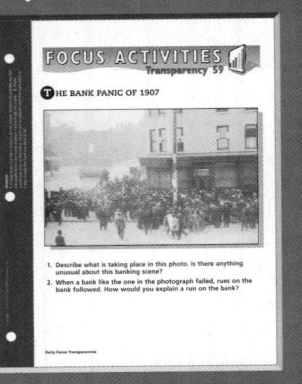

Study Guide

Reading Strategy
Have students create the graphic organizer.
Answers to Graphic: *1862: Legal Tender Act; 1886: silver certificates introduced; 1900: Gold Standard Act; 1934: adoption of incontrovertible fiat money standard; U.S. goes off gold standard*

Preteaching Vocabulary
Call on students to explain the meanings of the Key Terms in their own words. Have students check the accuracy of these definitions.

292

SECTION 2

Early Banking and Monetary Standards

 Study Guide

Main Idea
Although the monetary standard has changed throughout American history, an inconvertible fiat money standard is used today.

Reading Strategy
Graphic Organizer As you read the section, complete a time line similar to the one below by listing major events in American monetary history in the appropriate spaces.

1860	1880	1900	1920	1940
	↑	↑ ↑		↑
1862	**1886**	**1900**		**1934**

Key Terms
monetary standard, state bank, legal tender, United States note, national bank, National Bank note, national currency, gold certificate, silver certificate, Treasury coin note, gold standard, inconvertible fiat money standard

Objectives
After studying this section, you will be able to:
1. **Explain** the history of privately issued bank notes.
2. **Describe** an inconvertible money standard.

Applying Economic Concepts
Money Supply Managing the money supply is a difficult task. Read to see how we use different methods to keep the dollar strong.

Cover Story

Swiss Set to Abandon Gold Standard

Switzerland has always been regarded as a country that "understands" gold. It owns the world's fifth biggest gold reserves, its big banks still operate their own gold refineries, and the Swiss franc is the last currency still tied to gold.

However, this weekend the Swiss electorate is expected to do what would have been unthinkable a decade ago—abandon the gold standard. . . . [I]n law gold is still set at 142.9 Swiss francs per troy ounce.

The decision to sever the legal link between the Swiss franc and gold, is a reminder that [gold] has lost one of its biggest official cheer leaders. . . .

—*The Financial Times* (London) April 16, 1999

One-ounce gold bar

The week after the article in the cover story was published, the Swiss adopted a new constitution—and abandoned the gold standard. Fortunately, there are other ways to keep the money supply sound so that the economy functions smoothly.

A **monetary standard**—the mechanism designed to keep the money supply portable, durable, divisible, and limited in supply—helps with this task. The United States has had several monetary standards in its history.

Privately Issued Bank Notes

During the Revolutionary War, nearly 250 million Continental dollars were printed. After the Revolution, Continental currency was worthless, and people did not trust the government to issue anything except coin. Accordingly, Article 1, Section 8, of the United States Constitution states:

The Congress shall have the power
To coin money, regulate the value thereof, and of foreign coin, and fix the standard of weights and measures;

292

  RESOURCE MANAGER

📁 Reproducible Masters
- Reproducible Lesson Plan 11-2
- Daily Lecture Notes 11-2
- Guided Reading Activity 11-2
- Reading Essentials and Study Guide 11-2
- Section Quiz 11-2

🖥 Transparencies
- Daily Focus Transparency 59

Multimedia
- 📼 💿 NBR Economics & You Video Program
- 💾 Interactive Tutor Self-Assessment Software
- 💿 ExamView® Pro Testmaker
- 💿 Presentation Plus!

Monetary Standards

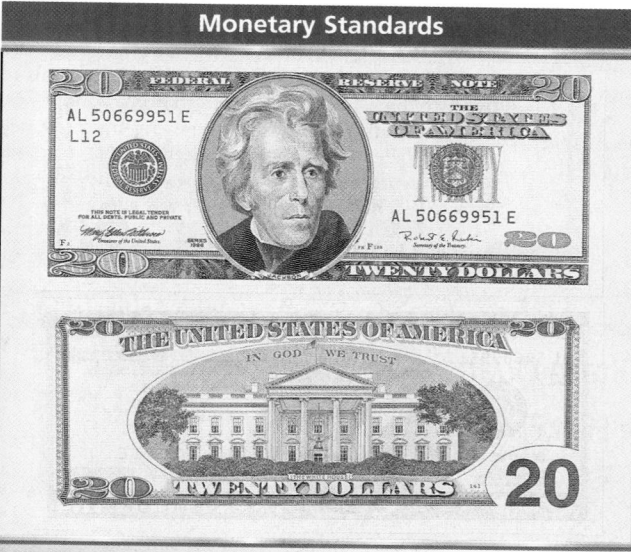

Fiat Money The paper money in our economy is "fiat" money: it is money partly because government says it is money. *What part of the Constitution gives Congress the right to coin money?*

To provide for the punishment of counterfeiting the securities and current coin of the United States; . . .

To make all laws which shall be necessary and proper for carrying into execution the foregoing powers, and all other powers vested by this Constitution in the government of the United States, or in any department or officer thereof.

Article 1, Section 10, further states:

No State shall . . . coin money; emit bills of credit; make anything but gold and silver coin a tender in payment of debts. . . .

Because of these clauses, the federal government did not print paper currency until the Civil War. Instead, the paper money supply was left for private banks to produce.

Growth of State Banking

Banks in the colonial period were allowed to issue their own paper money, a practice not prohibited by the new Constitution. As a result, banking grew in popularity, and by 1811 the country had about 100 **state banks**—banks that received their charter to operate from a state government.

State banks issued their own currency by printing their notes at local printing shops. The banks then put these notes in circulation with the assurance that people could exchange them for gold or silver if they ever lost faith in the bank or its currency.

Abuses in Banking

At first, most banks printed only the amount of currency they could reasonably back with their gold and silver reserves. Others, however, were not as honest and became known as wildcat banks—fraudulent banks that printed large amounts of currency in remote areas to make the redemption of their currency difficult. These banks got their name from people who claimed that you had to be a wildcat to get to them.

Problems With Currency

Even when banks were honest, problems with the currency arose. First, each bank issued its own currency in different sizes, colors, and denominations. As a result, hundreds of different kinds of notes could be in circulation in any given city.

Second, because a bank could print more money whenever it wanted, the temptation to issue too many notes always existed. Third, counterfeiting became a major problem. With so many different types of notes in circulation, many counterfeiters did not even bother to copy other notes. Instead, they just made up new notes.

By the Civil War, the United States had more than 1,600 banks issuing more than 10,000 kinds of paper currency. Each bank was supposed to have backing in the form of gold or silver, but this was seldom the case. As a result, when people tried to buy something, merchants would often check their notes against the latest listing of good and bad currencies before deciding which ones to accept in payment.

CHAPTER 11: MONEY AND BANKING **293**

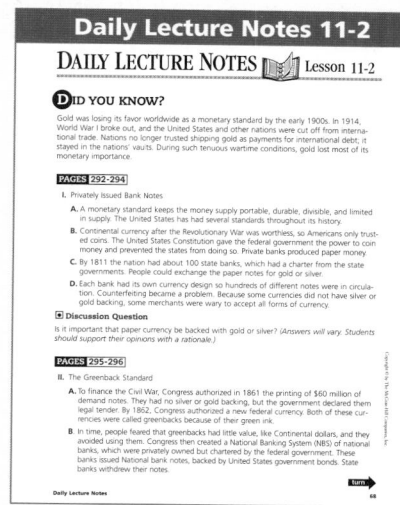

Daily Lecture Notes 11-2

Visual Instruction

Answer to Caption:
Article 1, Section 8

L1 Comparing Forms of Currency

Have students draw a simple chart to compare the various forms of currency discussed in this section: private bank notes, greenbacks, National Bank notes, gold and silver certificates, Treasury coin notes, and modern Federal Reserve notes. Students can compare the histories of the different currencies, any problems with the currencies, and the backing behind each form of currency.

MEETING SPECIAL NEEDS ACTIVITY

Learning Style: Logical/Mathematical When many private currencies were being used in the nineteenth century, merchants used "Bank Note Reporters," books that showed pictures of different currencies and how much they were worth. Notes from reputable banks were redeemed at face value, while those from less reputable banks were discounted by 1 percent to 50 percent. Have your class make its own Bank Note Reporter. First, have students design their own $1 bank notes on sheets of plain white paper. When they are finished, have them randomly draw slips of paper telling how much their currency is being discounted, then write their discount rates on the bottoms of their papers. Bind the papers into a book, then have students use the book to calculate how much of each kind of currency it would take to buy $10 worth of goods.

Refer to *Inclusion for the Social Studies Classroom Strategies and Activities* in the TCR.

L2 Applying Ideas

Call on volunteers to identify different forms of modern money—coins, paper currency, checking accounts, savings accounts, money market accounts, and so on—and note their responses down the left side of the board. Along the top of the board write the headings: *Portability, Durability, Divisibility,* and *Availability*. Then ask students to detail how each form of money conforms to each characteristic of money. **ELL**

ECONOMICS AT A GLANCE

Answer: *in the order in which the states were admitted to the union*

The Greenback Standard

By the 1850s, the paper currency component of the money supply was badly in need of overhaul. Politically powerful local bankers, however, resisted change until an event came along that was to change banking forever in America—the Civil War.

Greenbacks

When the Civil War erupted, both the Union and the Confederacy needed to raise enormous sums to finance the war. Congress tried to borrow money by selling bonds, but this did not raise as much money as the federal government needed. As a result, Congress decided to print paper currency for the first time since the Constitution was adopted.

ECONOMICS AT A GLANCE   Figure 11.1

The 50 State Quarter Program
The First Five Quarters:

The 10-Year Release Schedule:

Year	States	Year	States	Year	States	Year	States
1999	Delaware	2002	Tennessee	2005	California	2008	Oklahoma
	Pennsylvania		Ohio		Minnesota		New Mexico
	New Jersey		Louisiana		Oregon		Arizona
	Georgia		Indiana		Kansas		Alaska
	Connecticut		Mississippi		West Virginia		Hawaii
2000	Massachusetts	2003	Illinois	2006	Nevada		
	Maryland		Alabama		Nebraska		
	South Carolina		Maine		Colorado		
	New Hampshire		Missouri		North Dakota		
	Virginia		Arkansas		South Dakota		
2001	New York	2004	Michigan	2007	Montana		
	North Carolina		Florida		Washington		
	Rhode Island		Texas		Idaho		
	Vermont		Iowa		Wyoming		
	Kentucky		Wisconsin		Utah		

Using Charts The United States Mint is introducing 50 new quarters over a 10-year period to celebrate individual states' histories and traditions. In what order are the quarters being released?

FREE ENTERPRISE ACTIVITY

Have students experience monetary expansion, such as that which occurred with the issue of Continental currency or the issue of currency by state banks. Distribute play money of various denominations to the class. Place a number of items, such as a meal ticket, a candy bar, or a pen on the desk and sell a few of the items for the play money. Next, give students twice as much money as they received in the first distribution. Ask them if they are any better off now than they were when they received the first batch of money. Then sell the rest of the items, but at double the original price. Conclude by pointing out that increasing the supply of money means each dollar is actually worth less and will buy less. Although students had more money, they were not better off because their purchasing power had not increased.

In 1861, Congress authorized the printing of $60 million of demand notes. Although these notes had no gold or silver backing, they were declared **legal tender**–fiat currency that must be accepted in payment for debts. These new federal demand notes were soon dubbed greenbacks because both sides of the notes were printed with green ink to distinguish them from the state notes already in circulation.

In 1862, Congress passed the Legal Tender Act, authorizing the Union government to print $150 million of **United States notes,** a new federal fiat currency that also had no gold or silver backing. These new notes were also called greenbacks, and they accounted for half of the currency in circulation by 1863. Meanwhile, the Confederacy did essentially the same thing by printing large amounts of paper money to finance its war efforts.

National Currency

As the war dragged on, people feared that greenbacks–like the Continental dollars used to finance the Revolutionary War–might also become worthless. When the greenbacks did lose some of their value, people avoided using them, forcing Congress to find another way to finance the war.

The solution was to create a National Banking System (NBS) made up of **national banks**–privately owned banks that received their operating charters from the federal government. These banks issued **National Bank notes** or **national currency,** paper currency of uniform appearance that was backed by United States government bonds. The government hoped that rigorous bank inspections and other high standards would give people confidence in the new NBS and its currency.

This backing made the currency seem more secure to the public. It also generated a new demand for war bonds because any group that wanted to set up a national bank had to first purchase government bonds as part of the requirement to get the national charter. The bonds were then put on deposit with the United States Treasury as backing against the currency.

Initially, few state-chartered banks joined the system because it was easier for them to print their money at a local printer than to join the NBS.

Student Web Activity Visit the *Economics: Principles and Practices* Web site at epp.glencoe.com and click on *Chapter 11—Student Web Activities* for an activity on the new dollar coin.

Finally, in 1865 the federal government forced state banks to join the National Banking System by placing a 10 percent tax on all privately issued bank notes. Because state-chartered banks could not afford the tax, they withdrew their notes, leaving only the greenbacks and national currency in circulation.

As a result of the need to finance the Civil War, the makeup of the money paper supply shifted from being entirely privately-issued to being entirely publicly-issued.

Gold Certificates

The removal of more than 10,000 different sizes and denominations of state bank notes simplified the currency system. Before long, however, new types of federal currency appeared.

In 1863, the government issued **gold certificates**–paper currency backed by gold placed on deposit with the United States Treasury. At first, these certificates were printed in large denominations for banks to use when settling differences with each other at the end of the business day. In 1882, the government began printing gold certificates in smaller denominations for public use.

Silver Certificates

In 1886, the government introduced **silver certificates**–paper currency backed by silver dollars and bullion placed on reserve with the Treasury. Silver certificates were modeled after the highly popular gold certificates, but they were really designed to prop up sagging silver prices for western silver miners.

At the time, the government was already minting silver dollars. However, silver dollars were bulky and inconvenient to use, so the act was amended in 1886

CHAPTER 11: MONEY AND BANKING **295**

Objectives, goals, and answers to the student activity can be found in the **Web Activity Lesson Plan** feature at epp.glencoe.com

The move to the gold standard was made possible by the discovery of huge deposits of gold in South Africa and in the Klondike region of Canada.

L2 Creating Designs

Have students look at any coins and paper currency they have with them. **Ask:** Does the money look "modern"? Tell students that the government has decided to update the currency and give it the "look of the twenty-first century." Have students draw designs for at least two coins and two notes of this new money. Call on volunteers to present and explain their designs.

CRITICAL THINKING

Analyzing Information In recent years, there has been an increase in the use of "private" money in the United States. At Disney parks and stores, for example, visitors can exchange ordinary dollars for "Disney dollars," which they can use to buy food and souvenirs. For fundraisers, schools sometimes sell supermarket "scrip," which can be used like money at certain supermarkets. Airlines often issue "frequent flyer miles," which can be redeemed for air travel. Ask students to come up with other examples of private money. In an essay, have students discuss why it is advantageous for organizations to issue their own "currencies." Ask them to also discuss the problems that would arise if a large number of alternative currencies came into use.

CURRICULUM CONNECTION

History The election of 1896 pitted William Jennings Bryan against William McKinley. Bryan opposed the gold standard, while McKinley supported it. In accepting the Democratic nomination, Bryan gave his famous "Cross of Gold" speech, saying "You shall not press down upon the brow of labor this crown of thorns, you shall not crucify mankind upon a cross of gold."

L2 Common Currency

In 1999, eleven European countries began phasing out their own currencies in favor of a common one, the euro. They decided, as did the U.S. in the nineteenth century, that having a single unified currency would be beneficial. Have students discuss why Europe will benefit from having one currency rather than several.

NIGHTLY BUSINESS REPORT

ECONOMICS & YOU

Chapter 18
Disc 1, Side 2

Money and Banking

Ask: What is fiat money? *(money that has value solely because people agree to accept it in exchange for goods and services)*

 Also available in VHS.

---

to allow silver dollars to be used as backing for the new silver certificates. This appeased both the silver miners and the public who wanted an alternative to the generally unwanted silver dollars.

Treasury Coin Notes

In 1890, the federal government printed the fifth, and last, type of paper currency issued before the banking system was overhauled in 1913. The currency came in the form of **Treasury coin notes**—paper currency issued by the Treasury that was redeemable in both gold and silver. The law was repealed in 1893, and further issues of Treasury coin notes were ended.

The Gold Standard

 In 1900, Congress passed the Gold Standard Act, fixing the price of gold at $20.67 an ounce. For the first time, the United States was on a **gold standard**—a monetary standard under which the basic currency unit is equal to, and can be exchanged for, a specific amount of gold.

The Gold Standard Act did not affect the type of currency people used. People continued to use the same greenbacks, National bank notes, gold certificates, silver certificates, and Treasury coin notes as they did before. The difference was that these notes could now be exchanged for gold at the Treasury at any time.

Advantages of a Gold Standard

A gold standard has two major advantages. First, some people feel more secure about their money if they know it can be converted into gold.

Second, it is supposed to prevent the government from printing too much paper currency. In theory, the government promises to print only as much currency as can be backed by, or exchanged into, gold. This keeps the currency relatively scarce and helps to maintain its value.

In reality, the United States never did have enough gold to back all of its currency. This is normally the case whenever a country goes on a gold standard because it is unlikely that everyone will

want to convert all of their currency into gold at the same time. Consequently, it is usually sufficient to maintain the *appearance* of having enough gold to back the paper money.

Disadvantages of a Gold Standard

One disadvantage of a gold standard is that the gold stock may not grow fast enough to support a growing economy. If new gold supplies cannot be found, the money supply may not be able to expand, thereby restricting economic growth.

A second disadvantage is that people may suddenly decide to convert their currency into gold, thereby draining the government's gold reserves. This can easily happen if a government is trying to maintain the appearance of having enough gold—when in fact it does not.

Third, we know that the price of gold is likely to change dramatically over time if it is not fixed. For example, in Chapter 6 we saw that the price of gold fell from $850 an ounce in 1980 to $280 in early 1999. This means that any government that tries to "fix" the price of gold by buying and selling unlimited amounts at an official price will face—and must triumph over—tremendous market pressures.

Finally, there is always the political risk of failure. A government that announces an official price for gold looks ineffective and foolish if it cannot carry out its intentions. When the Swiss abandoned the gold standard, for example, the "official" price of an ounce of gold was 142.9 Swiss francs—or about $95. Clearly no one was going to sell gold to the Swiss at that price. Nor were the Swiss willing to sell their gold on the open market at that price.

Did you know?

Why the Notches? Why do dimes, quarters, and half-dollars have notched or reeded edges while pennies and nickels don't? The United States Mint notched the edges of coins containing gold and silver to hinder people from shaving off quantities of the precious metals. Since pennies and nickels contain cheaper metal, they have no notches.

EXTENDING THE CONTENT

Gresham's Law Thomas Gresham, a financial advisor to England's Queen Elizabeth I, formulated the principle that bad money tends to drive good money out of circulation. If two coins have the same face, for example, but the metallic content of one coin is more valuable, then the coin with lesser value—the "bad money"—will be used for transactions. The more valuable coin—the "good money"—will be taken out of circulation and saved. An example of Gresham's Law in operation occurred in 1965. Instead of silver, copper and nickel were used to mint dimes, quarters, and half dollars. As a result, the older, silver coins were hoarded, while the newer, cheaper coins remained in circulation.

THE GLOBAL ECONOMY

WHY ISN'T THERE JUST ONE CURRENCY?

Some frustrated American tourists who try to communicate in foreign lands by screaming English words at a hundred decibels may wish that everyone just spoke English and used the dollar. Wouldn't that make it easier for international trade? There would be no more standing in line at the bank window waiting for the teller to exchange currencies and take a cut off the top.

That might work well—except for three things. First, most people like their currency. The depictions on paper money and coins reinforce national icons and symbols. Why would the Brits want to trade in Queen Elizabeth's noble chin for George Washington's wooden-toothed grimace? Second, national currencies allow countries to manage their own banking system (though they cannot insulate themselves from the policies of trading partners).

Third, most countries are reluctant to surrender control of their macroeconomic policy to foreigners. Suppose Spain's 20 percent unemployment rate demands urgent attention in the form of lower interest rates, yet Portugal's higher inflation rate makes the authorities nervous about easier money. If Spain and Portugal shared a currency, they would have to share policy prescriptions. That would be like two patients in a doctor's waiting room agreeing to the same medication, even though they suffered from different ailments.

—*From Here to Economy* by Todd G. Buchholz, Dutton, 1995

Critical Thinking

1. **Analyzing Information** Why does the writer believe countries will not accept a common currency?

2. **Drawing Conclusions** Read to find out about the euro. Is the writer's argument that nations will not accept using the same currency valid? Why or why not?

Abandoning the Gold Standard

The gold standard remained in force until the Depression of the 1930s when banks began to fail in record numbers. Because of the uncertain times, and because people felt safer holding gold rather than paper currency, they began to cash in their dollars for gold. Foreign governments with large holdings of dollars began to do the same thing.

The federal government feared it could not continue to back the money supply with gold, so on August 28, 1933, President Franklin D. Roosevelt declared a national emergency. As part of the emergency, the government decreed that anyone holding more than $100 worth of gold or gold certificates must file a disclosure form with the United States Treasury.

Several months later, the Gold Reserve Act of 1934 was passed, which required citizens, banks, and businesses to turn their gold and gold certificates over to the United States government. Those who had filed a disclosure had no choice but to surrender their gold holdings. Others simply ignored the government and kept their gold. Regardless, the United States went off the gold standard in 1934 when it confiscated gold from private citizens.

The Inconvertible Fiat Money Standard

 Since 1934 the United States has been on an **inconvertible fiat money standard**—a monetary standard under which the fiat money supply cannot be converted into gold or silver by its citizens.

A Managed Money Supply

The money supply of the United States, like those of other major industrialized countries in the world, is a managed money supply. In other words,

CHAPTER 11: MONEY AND BANKING **297**

THE GLOBAL ECONOMY

Why Isn't There Just One Currency? Many countries are finding that the cost of having a national currency is unacceptably high. In Argentina, the U.S. dollar is already being used for many transactions, and President Carlos Menem has declared that "dollarizing" the Argentine economy is a top priority for his administration.

Answers:
1. *The depictions on currency reinforce national icons and symbols; countries are reluctant to surrender control of their own banking systems and macroeconomic policy.*
2. *Answers should relate information about the euro's acceptance.*

3 ASSESS

Assign Section 2 Assessment as homework or as an in-class activity.

Have students use **Interactive Tutor Self-Assessment Software**.

Section Quiz 11-2

INTERDISCIPLINARY CONNECTIONS ACTIVITY

Literature *The Wizard of Oz* by Frank Baum is not just an amusing children's story; economists read it as an allegory of the nineteenth century Populist effort to rid the country of the gold standard. In the book, Dorothy wears ruby slippers and goes along the yellow brick road (the gold standard) with a Scarecrow (representing farmers), the Tin Man (representing eastern laborers), and the Cowardly Lion (William Jennings Bryan) to the Emerald City (Washington, D.C.) to meet the Wizard (president) of Oz (the abbreviation for ounce, as in gold). Have students do reports on the history of the Populist movement. Next, have them view the film version of *The Wizard of Oz* and discuss the symbolism depicted. **BLOCK SCHEDULING**

Reteach

Enrich

Have students prepare an illustrated report on the operations of one of the two agencies that make American currency—the Bureau of the Mint and the Bureau of Engraving and Printing.

4 CLOSE

Ask students to speculate about what our modern money system would be like if the United States were still on the gold standard.

---

the government or its designated agent controls the quantity, composition, and even the quality of the money supply.

This task is somewhat easier now that a single currency issued by the Federal Reserve System has replaced the multiple currencies that appeared after the Civil War. National currency and Treasury coin notes were withdrawn from circulation in the 1930s, and gold certificates were confiscated in 1934. The last issue of United States notes (greenbacks) took place in 1968. Silver certificates were also retired, and the government stopped redeeming them for silver dollars in 1968. Americans have been allowed to own gold and silver certificates since 1975, but neither is officially part of the money supply.

Today, the tangible component of modern money consists of coins and Federal Reserve notes. Intangible components consists of traveler's checks along with checking and savings accounts. How well these substances function as money depends on how well the four characteristics of money are satisfied.

Characteristics of Modern Money

Although money has changed in shape, kind, and size over the years, modern money shares the same characteristics of early money. Modern money is *portable*. Currency is lightweight, convenient, and can be easily transferred from one person to another. The same applies to the use of checks.

Modern money is reasonably *durable*. Metallic coins last about 20 years under normal use. Paper currency also is reasonably durable, with a $1 bill lasting about 18 months in circulation. Even the introduction of the new Sacagawea dollar coin is part of an attempt to make the money supply more durable by replacing low-denomination currency with coins.

Modern money is *divisible*. The penny, which is the smallest denomination of coin, is small enough for almost any purchase. In addition, checks can be written for the exact amount.

If anything, modern money has an uneven track record when it comes to *limited availability* and stability in value. The money supply often grew at a rate of 10 to 12 percent a year in the early 1970s, which contributed greatly to the inflation of the period. It slowed considerably after that, contributing to the period of relative price stability in the 1990s.

In the end, the money supply can be managed, and price stability can be maintained—but only if the government and monetary authorities have the political courage to do so.

Section 2 Assessment

Understanding Key Terms

1. **Main Idea** What is the purpose of a monetary standard?

2. **Key Terms** Define monetary standard, state bank, legal tender, United States note, national bank, National Bank note, national currency, gold certificate, silver certificate, Treasury coin note, gold standard, inconvertible fiat money standard.

3. **Explain** how privately issued bank notes became part of the money supply.

4. **List** the five major currencies in use after the Civil War.

5. **Identify** the advantages and disadvantages of a gold standard.

6. **Describe** the inconvertible fiat money standard that the United States uses.

Applying Economic Concepts

7. **Money Supply** Suppose that Federal Reserve notes did not exist to serve as "legal tender." What else could be done to establish a suitable money supply?

Critical Thinking

8. **Making Comparisons** Some experts have proposed a return to the gold standard. Explain why you think this may or may not be a good idea.

   Practice and assess key social studies skills with the *Glencoe Skillbuilder Interactive Workbook, Level 2.*

Section 2 Assessment Answers

1. to keep the money supply portable, durable, divisible, and limited in supply

2. All vocabulary terms are defined in the text.

3. Before the Civil War, most of the money supply was paper currency issued by privately owned state-chartered banks.

4. greenbacks, national currency, gold certificates, silver certificates, Treasury coin notes

5. **adv:** some feel secure if they know money can be converted into gold, can prevent the government from printing too much paper currency; **disadv:** gold stock may not grow fast enough, drain on the government's gold reserves, the price of gold fluctuates, political risk of failure

6. It is a system under which the fiat money supply cannot be converted into gold or silver by its citizens.

7. Answers should consider the characteristics of money when establishing a money supp

8. **against:** the money supply would be tied to the amount of gold the country possessed, and a restricted money supply could impede economic growth; **for:** it would make certain that the value of money remained stable.

Developing Multimedia Presentations

Your economics teacher has assigned a presentation about how banks operate. You want to develop a presentation that really holds your classmates' attention. How do you go about it?

Learning the Skill

A multimedia presentation involves using several types of media, including photographs, videos, or sound recordings. The equipment can range from simple cassette players, to overhead projectors, to VCRs, to computers, and beyond.

Multimedia, as it relates to computer technology, is the combination of text, video, audio, and animation in an interactive computer program. You need certain tools to create multimedia presentations on a computer, including computer graphics tools and draw programs, animation programs, and authoring systems that tie everything together. Your computer manual will tell you which tools your computer can support.

Various equipment that can be used in multimedia presentations

Practicing the Skill

Plan and create a multimedia presentation on a topic found in the chapter, such as the development of money in colonial America. List three or four major ideas you would like to cover. Then think about how multimedia resources could enhance your presentation. Use the following questions as a guide when planning your presentation.

1. Which forms of media do I want to include? Video? Sound? Animation? Photographs? Graphics?

2. Which kinds of media equipment are available at my school or local library?

3. What types of media can I create to enhance my presentation?

4. Which of the media forms does my computer support?

Application Activity

Choose an economist from the twentieth century and create a multimedia presentation about his or her theories. Use as many multimedia materials as possible, and share your presentation with the members of your class.

Technology Skill

Teaching Skills

Before students prepare lengthy presentations, ask them to develop alternative ways of presenting a single fact or simple concept. You may wish to have students discuss their methods in small groups. Ask them to discuss what type of media would best present their simple subject matter. As other students make suggestions, have the presenter think about ways of broadening his or her presentation with multiple media.

Additional Practice

Reinforcing Economic Skill 25

Name _____ Date _____ Class _____

Reinforcing Economic Skills Chapter 25

① DEVELOPING MULTIMEDIA PRESENTATIONS

Multimedia computer presentations combine text, video, audio, and animation to create lively and visually appealing reports. To create a multimedia presentation on your computer, you will need a variety of programs depending on the type of media you intend to use. Make a list of the topics you want to cover in your presentation. Then identify the forms of media you would like to include and determine whether your computer can support them.

Directions: *Design a multimedia presentation on the euro, the new currency that will replace national currencies in 11 Western European countries beginning in 2002. To create your presentation, first research the euro using library resources or the World Wide Web. Then use the panels below to sketch storyboards or series of screenshots that outline what you will include in your presentation. For each storyboard indicate which media you plan to use.*

Answers to Practicing the Skill

Answers should demonstrate an understanding of multimedia resources and the chapter content.

1 FOCUS

Section Overview
This section focuses on modern banking and deregulation.

BELLRINGER
Motivational Activity

Project **transparency** and have students answer questions.

Available as blackline master.

Daily Focus Transparency 61

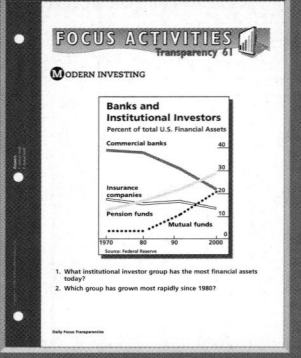

Study Guide

Reading Strategy
Have students create the graphic organizer.
Answers to Graphic: *commercial banks, thrift institutions, mutual savings banks, credit unions, savings and loan associations*

Preteaching Vocabulary
Use the Vocabulary Puzzle-Maker to create crossword and word-search puzzles.

The Development of Modern Banking

Main Idea
The Federal Reserve System serves the monetary needs of the federal government and controls the monetary system.

Reading Strategy
Graphic Organizer As you read the section, complete a graphic organizer similar to the one below by listing at least three kinds of depository institutions.

Institutions

Key Terms
Federal Reserve System, central bank, Federal Reserve note, run on the bank, bank holiday, commercial bank, demand deposit account (DDA), thrift institution, mutual savings bank (MSB), savings bank, NOW accounts, savings and loan association (S&L), credit union, share draft account, deregulation, creditor

Objectives
After studying this section, you will be able to:
1. **Relate** the effects of Depression-era bank failures on deposit insurance creation.
2. **Identify** three other forms of depository institutions.
3. **Describe** the reasons for the S&L crisis in the 1980s.

Applying Economic Concepts
Demand Deposit Accounts You may think that checking accounts are pretty useful. Read to find out how they replaced the carrying of large amounts of cash to make life easier for everyone.

Cover Story

Suspicious Internet Banking

More banks go online.

Today more and more banks are offering financial services via the Internet. While the vast majority of these are entirely legitimate, the sad fact is that a few unscrupulous people may take advantage of the anonymity of the Internet to perpetuate fraud. . . . [W]e [the FDIC] offer two items you may find helpful in determining . . . suspicious Web sites.

[The first is a] searchable database [that] will help you determine if an institution has a legitimate charter and is a member of the FDIC.

[The second is a] special alert financial institution letter . . . pertaining to unauthorized banking operations currently identified. . . .

—*FDIC*, June 10, 1999

300

Banks fulfill two distinct needs. They provide a safe place for people to deposit their money, and they lend excess funds to individuals and businesses temporarily in need of cash. This can only happen if the nation has a strong banking system.

Revising the Banking System

In 1863, the federal government strengthened the financial system by passing the National Banking Act. It set up a system of nationally chartered and inspected banks. Yet problems persisted as financial crises and recessions marked the next half century. Each crisis led to calls for reform, but when the crisis ended, the protests faded away. Finally, when consumer and commercial credit dried up during the panic of 1907, the need for reform could no longer be ignored. The government set up a commission to formulate a plan for a new system.

RESOURCE MANAGER

Reproducible Masters
- Reproducible Lesson Plan 11-3
- Daily Lecture Notes 11-3
- Guided Reading Activity 11-3
- Reading Essentials and Study Guide 11-3
- Section Quiz 11-3

Transparencies
- Daily Focus Transparency 61

Multimedia
- Vocabulary PuzzleMaker CD-ROM
- Interactive Tutor Self-Assessment Software
- ExamView® Pro Testmaker
- Presentation Plus!

The Federal Reserve System

Reform came in 1913 when Congress created the **Federal Reserve System,** or Fed, as the nation's first true central bank. A **central bank** is a bank that can lend to other banks in times of need.

To ensure membership in the Fed, all national banks were required, and all state-chartered banks were eligible, to become "members"—or part owners—of the Fed. Because the Fed was organized as a corporation, any bank that joined had to purchase shares of stock in the system, just as a private individual purchases shares in a regular corporation. As a result, privately-owned banks own the Federal Reserve System, not the government.

Despite its private ownership, the Fed is publicly controlled. The president appoints, subject to congressional approval, the Fed's Board of Governors and its chairperson.

Finally, **Federal Reserve notes**—paper currency issued by the Fed that eventually replaced all other types of federal currency—were added to the money supply. Federal Reserve notes were backed by gold when first issued in 1914, but became inconvertible fiat money after 1934.

Banking During the Great Depression

Despite the reforms many banks were only marginally sound during the 1920s. Part of the reason was the over-expansion in banking that took place between 1880 and 1921. Although some consolidation occurred between 1921 and 1929, the banking industry was overextended when the Great Depression began in 1929.

As **Figure 11.2** shows, the number of bank failures during the 1930s was staggering. At the start of the Depression, about 25,500 banks existed—none of which had deposit insurance for their customers. As a result, concern about the safety of bank deposits often caused a **run on the bank**—a rush by depositors to withdraw their funds from a bank before it failed. This made the situation even worse and caused more banks to fail.

To ease the situation, on March 5, 1933, President Roosevelt announced a **bank holiday**—a brief period during which every bank in the country was required to close. Several days later, after Congress passed legislation that strengthened banking, most banks were allowed to reopen. The Great Depression took its toll, however, and by 1934 more than 10,000 banks had closed or merged with stronger partners.

Federal Deposit Insurance

When banks failed during the Depression, depositors lost almost all their savings. The Banking Act of 1933, also known as the Glass-Steagall Act, was passed to strengthen the banking industry. The act also created the Federal Deposit

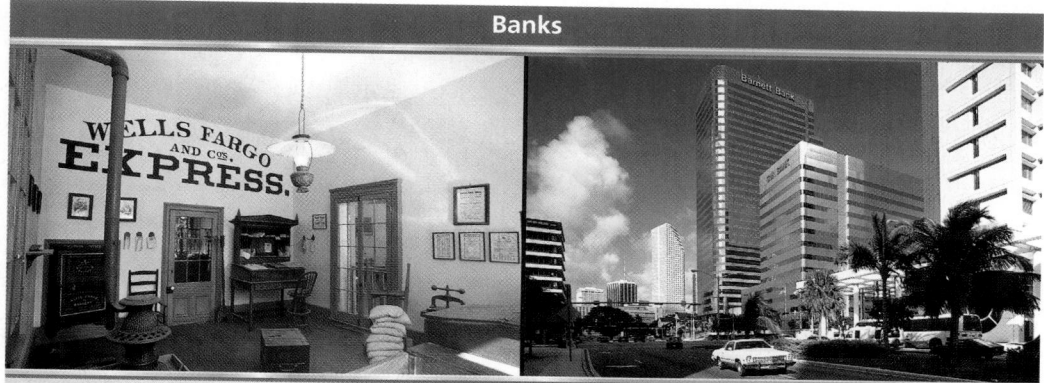

Banks

Purposes From early times on, banks provided safe storage facilities, interest payments on deposits, money transfers, and loans. *What is the purpose of the Federal Deposit Insurance Corporation?*

CHAPTER 11: MONEY AND BANKING **301**

 TEACH

CURRICULUM CONNECTION

History During the Great Depression, the money supply fell by about one-third, causing a nationwide shortage of currency. As a result, towns, counties, and even civic organizations printed their own private currency—known as Depression-era script.

Visual Instruction

Answer to Caption:
to insure customer deposits in event of bank failure

L3 Compare and Contrast

Have students prepare a chart comparing modern banking services with those of the early 1900s.

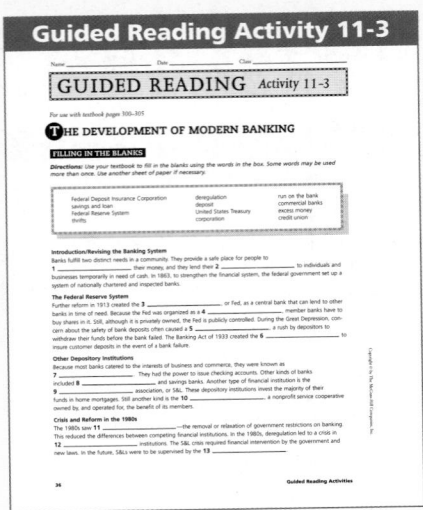
STANDARD
&POOR'S

Answer: *At present, there are almost two-thirds as many state banks as there are national banks.*

L1 Federal Reserve Banks

Currency is issued by 12 regional Federal Reserve Banks or FRBs. Have students identify the locations of these banks by looking at the paper money they have in their wallets. The name of the issuing bank is printed in a round stamp on the front of each bill. Have them find and mark the locations of these banks on a U.S. map. *(The banks are located in Boston, New York City, Philadelphia, Cleveland, Richmond, Atlanta, Chicago, St. Louis, Minneapolis, Kansas City, Dallas, and San Francisco.)*

STANDARD
&POOR'S

Figure 11.2

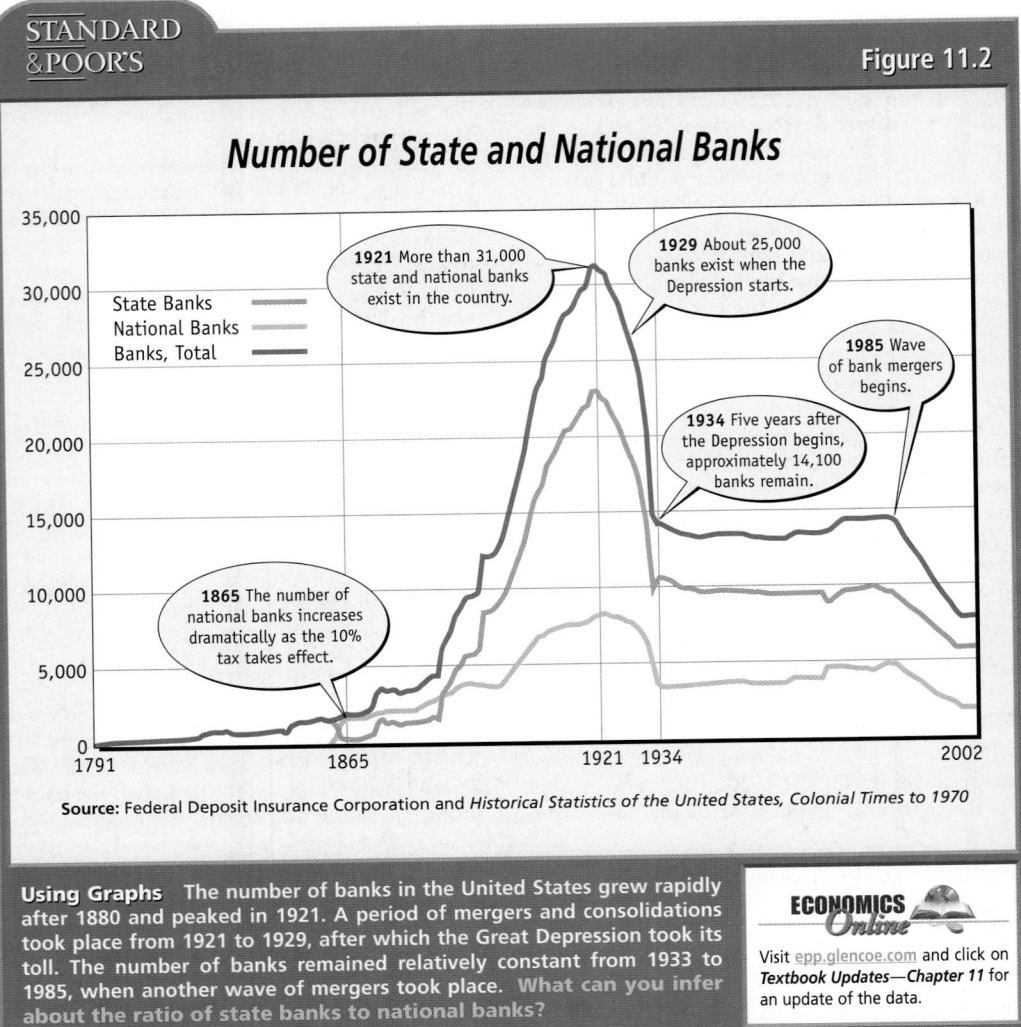

Number of State and National Banks

Source: Federal Deposit Insurance Corporation and *Historical Statistics of the United States, Colonial Times to 1970*

Using Graphs The number of banks in the United States grew rapidly after 1880 and peaked in 1921. A period of mergers and consolidations took place from 1921 to 1929, after which the Great Depression took its toll. The number of banks remained relatively constant from 1933 to 1985, when another wave of mergers took place. **What can you infer about the ratio of state banks to national banks?**

ECONOMICS
Online

Visit epp.glencoe.com and click on *Textbook Updates—Chapter 11* for an update of the data.

Insurance Corporation (FDIC) to insure customer deposits in the event of a bank failure. The initial coverage was only $2,500 per account, but it has since been increased to a maximum of $100,000 for one person at one bank.

The insurance did little for those who lost their savings before 1934, but it has provided a sense of security in banking ever since. After the FDIC was created, people worried less about the safety of their deposits, reducing the number of runs on a bank.

Today, protection provided by the FDIC goes far beyond deposit insurance. As you read in the cover story, the FDIC aggressively pursues ways to protect consumers against fraudulent banks—even those not insured by the FDIC.

302 UNIT 3 MACROECONOMICS: INSTITUTIONS

FREE ENTERPRISE ACTIVITY

Determine the number of financial institutions in your community, then assign small groups of students to visit each one to help determine how financial institutions affect households and businesses. Suggest that students get data such as: **(1)** Current interest paid on NOW accounts; **(2)** Interest paid on one-year certificates of deposit (CDs); **(3)** Interest rate charged for a used-car loan; and **(4)** Interest rate charged for a new-car loan. Have students research other information on these items, such as the minimum balance for NOW accounts and the amount of down payments for car loans. When groups have obtained the information, have them prepare a comparison chart for a bulletin-board display.

Other Depository Institutions

Most of the early U.S. banks were **commercial banks**—banks that catered to the interests of business and commerce. They had the power to issue checking accounts. Checking accounts are also called **demand deposit accounts (DDAs)**—accounts whose funds could be removed by simply writing a check without prior approval from the depository institution. Other financial institutions, called **thrift institutions,** or thrifts, accepted the deposits of small investors but did not have DDAs until the mid-1970s.

Savings Banks

One of the oldest thrift institutions in the United States is the **mutual savings bank (MSB),** a depositor-owned financial organization operated only for the benefit of its depositors. Later, many MSBs decided to sell stock to raise additional financial capital. These institutions then became **savings banks** because they were no longer mutually owned by depositors.

Mutual savings banks got their start in the late 1700s. At that time, commercial banks were not interested in the accounts of small wage earners. Savings banks emerged to fill that need and became very popular with consumers.

By the mid-1800s, commercial banks, along with the savings and loan associations, began to compete more heavily with the savings banks. As a result, savings banks did not spread beyond their foothold in the industrial northeast and the Pacific northwest.

STANDARD &POOR'S   INFOBYTE

Interest Rates Interest rates represent the time value of money. In other words, a dollar today is worth more than a dollar one year from now. To compensate investors for the risks of investment, interest rates must take into account inflation, liquidity, credit, and other risks.

Even so, savings banks had a powerful influence. In 1972, the Consumer's Savings Bank of Worcester, Massachusetts introduced Negotiable Order of Withdrawal, or **NOW accounts,** a type of checking account that pays interest. Because commercial banks held most checking accounts at the time, they strongly opposed NOW accounts. NOW accounts proved popular, however, and they were offered nationwide after 1980.

Savings and Loan Associations

Another type of financial institution is the **savings and loan association (S&L)**—a depository institution that invests the majority of its funds in home mortgages. S&Ls began as cooperative clubs for home-builders in the 1800s. The association's members promised to deposit a certain sum regularly into the association. Members then took turns borrowing money to build a home.

Later, in the 1930s, the Federal Home Loan Bank Board was created to supervise and regulate individual savings and loan associations. The Federal Savings and Loan Insurance Corporation (FSLIC), a federal government agency like the FDIC that serves commercial bankers, was also created to insure savings and loan deposits.

Credit Unions

A fourth type of depository institution is the **credit union**—a nonprofit service cooperative that is owned by, and operated for, the benefit of its members. Costs are generally low because a sponsor such as the members' place of employment often provides management, clerical help, and office facilities.

Because most credit unions are organized around an employer, contributions generally are deducted from a worker's paycheck. Credit unions have introduced **share draft accounts,** or interest-earning checking accounts, to compete with NOW accounts.

Crisis and Reform

Because of the massive banking failures during the Great Depression, financial institutions were closely regulated from 1933 through the 1970s. The regulations even applied to maximum

CYBERNOMICS

Cyberbanking Cyberbanking has become popular as many people reap the benefits of paying their bills on the Internet. Online account access and electronic bill payment are currently available free of charge or for a very small fee. By paying online, customers save time and paper, but they can also save money and keep better tabs on their bank accounts. One cyberbanking customer says that by periodically using the service to check her balance and fees, she avoids late charges and bounced checks.

L2 Identifying Trends

Have students write summaries of five recent magazine or newspaper articles on current banking issues. Use these as the starting point for a class discussion on the most pressing issues in banking today. Have students speculate on how these issues might be resolved.

Many people mistakenly believe that *each* account in a single bank is insured to the $100,000 maximum. This is not true. Point out to students that a person with separate checking and savings accounts in a single bank will only be insured for a maximum of $100,000, regardless of the balance in each account.

CRITICAL THINKING

Drawing Conclusions Deposit insurance was one of the major causes of the savings and loan crisis. Since depositors in U.S. banks are insured against losses, they have little incentive to avoid poorly managed banks. Knowing this, many banks in the 1980s made very risky loans and ultimately failed. To illustrate how insurance distorts incentives, ask students how their driving would change if they didn't have auto insurance. Next, have students list other kinds of insurance that people can buy. Break the students into groups and assign each group a kind of insurance from the list. Have each group discuss how the insurance distorts incentives among buyers. Have the groups share their conclusions with the entire class.

Math Practice

Calculating Weight and Height
A penny weighs 2.5 grams and is 1.55 mm thick. Have students calculate the weight of $10,000 worth of pennies. Also have them calculate the height of a single stack of $10,000 worth of pennies. *(2,500 kg; 1,550 m)*

3 ASSESS

Assign Section 3 Assessment as homework or as an in-class activity.

💾 Have students use **Interactive Tutor Self-Assessment Software** to review Section 3.

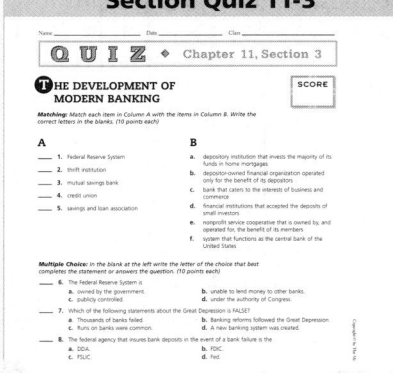

Section Quiz 11-3

QUIZ ◆ Chapter 11, Section 3

THE DEVELOPMENT OF MODERN BANKING

SCORE

Matching: Match each item in Column A with the items in Column B. Write the correct letters in the blanks. (10 points each)

A
___ 1. Federal Reserve System
___ 2. thrift institution
___ 3. mutual savings bank
___ 4. credit union
___ 5. savings and loan association

B
a. depository institution that invests the majority of its funds in home mortgages
b. depositor-owned financial organization operated only for the benefit of its depositors
c. bank that caters to the interests of business and commerce
d. financial institutions that accepted the deposits of small investors
e. nonprofit service cooperative that is owned by, and operated for, the benefit of its members
f. system that functions as the central bank of the United States

Multiple Choice: In the blank at the left write the letter of the choice that best completes the statement or answers the question. (10 points each)
___ 6. The Federal Reserve System is
a. owned by the government.
b. unable to lend money to other banks.
c. publicly controlled.
d. under the authority of Congress.
___ 7. Which of the following statements about the Great Depression is FALSE?
a. Thousands of banks failed.
b. Banking reforms followed the Great Depression.
c. Runs on banks were common.
d. A new banking system was created.
___ 8. The federal agency that insures bank deposits in the event of a bank failure is the
a. DDA.
b. FDIC.
c. FSLIC.
d. Fed.

---

rates of interest that could be paid on checking and savings accounts, as well as to restrictions on how and to whom the institutions could lend their funds.

By the late 1970s, most financial institutions were calling for relief from federal regulations. When Ronald Reagan was elected president in 1980, the political climate changed, allowing **deregulation**—the removal or relaxation of government restrictions on business.

Deregulation reduced the differences between competing financial institutions. First, the requirement that set maximum interest rates on savings accounts was phased out. This action eliminated the advantage that savings banks and S&Ls had over commercial banks when it came to paying higher interest rates on savings accounts.

Second, NOW accounts could be offered on a nationwide basis by any type of financial institution. This provision eliminated the advantage that commercial banks had with their check-issuing powers.

Careers

Bank Teller

When you go to a bank, a bank teller often handles your money. The bank teller's job is to process a customer's transactions.

The Work

Bank tellers handle a wide range of banking transactions, including cashing checks, accepting deposits and loan payments, and processing withdrawals. Bank tellers may sell savings bonds and traveler's checks, and handle foreign currencies or commercial accounts. They are trained to explain the various types of accounts and financial services the bank offers.

Qualifications

Tellers need an aptitude for using computers, and they must be quick, accurate, and honest. Good numerical, clerical, and communication skills are a must. A bank teller's job is an entry-level position. After a few years, a bank teller can be promoted to be a personal banker or into a management position.

304 UNIT 3 MACROECONOMICS: INSTITUTIONS

Third, all depository institutions could borrow from the Federal Reserve System in times of need, a privilege previously reserved for commercial banks. In return, all depository institutions were required to set aside a larger part of their customers' deposits in the form of reserves.

The Savings and Loan Crisis

An S&L crisis unfolded slowly but surely during the 1980s. In 1980 the United States had 4,600 S&Ls. By mid-1988, bankruptcies and mergers reduced the number to about 3,000. By the early 1990s, fewer than 2,000 institutions survived.

Deregulation was one of the reasons for the crisis. Savings and loan institutions were used to having the government set their interest rates and determine what types of loans they could make. Most S&Ls, therefore, were not well prepared to face real competition in the marketplace.

Another problem was high interest rates. Most S&Ls made long-term, low-interest loans to homeowners in the early 1970s. When interest rates reached record levels in the early 1980s, S&Ls ended up paying more on funds deposited with them than they earned on the loans they already made.

A third problem was the relatively small capital reserves kept by the S&Ls to absorb bad loans—reserves about half the size that commercial banks kept. This meant that several bad loans could force an S&L to go out of business, rather than be absorbed by the capital accounts.

Deregulation also resulted in fewer federal inspectors to make sure the rules and regulations were followed. As a result, a few institutions were able to engage in fraud on a scale seldom seen before.

Reforming the Thrift Industry

The Financial Institutions Reform, Recovery, and Enforcement Act (FIRREA) was passed in 1989. This act abolished the independence of the savings and loan industry and is regarded as the most significant financial legislation since the Depression.

Many S&Ls were profitable during the crisis. These institutions were allowed to continue operations, and many even kept the words *savings and loan association* in their titles. Others, however, chose to

---

EXTENDING THE CONTENT

Secondary Bank Functions In recent years, banking and financial institutions have taken on many secondary functions. One function may issue credit cards, such as Mastercard or Visa, which, in a sense, are short-term loans. Some larger banks process credit card payments for major credit card issuers, such as oil companies and large retail operations. In addition, a number of institutions accept utility payments as a convenience for their customers. Numerous banks provide trust services and investment and business counseling. Many banks also sell traveler's checks and money orders, rent safety deposit boxes, and provide foreign currency exchange. Banking officials believe that institutions must offer a variety of financial services in order to compete in the marketplace.

change their name to distance themselves from the crisis that had tarnished so many reputations.

Even so, the cost of the thrift crisis to taxpayers was enormous, amounting about $300 billion. This amounted to approximately $1,200 for every man, woman, and child in America.

Dealing With Failed Banks

Bank failures were also a problem in the 1980s. If a bank is in danger of collapse, the FDIC can seize the bank and either sell it to a stronger one or liquidate it and pay off the depositors. The forced sale or liquidation is done in secrecy to prevent panic withdrawals and to prevent shareholders from selling their worthless stock to unsuspecting investors.

Either way, depositors have little to fear because they are covered up to the $100,000 FDIC insurance limit. If an account has more than this, the depositor may go to court as a **creditor**—a person or institution to whom money is owed—and sue the bank's owners to recover the rest.

Banks fail for many reasons, but poor management is the primary cause. Some banks make loans without adequate collateral, others fail to keep expenses under control, and still others may be victims of a weak economy. The reforms instituted as a result of the S&L crisis, however, have made all financial institutions safer.

Return to Stability

The 1980s were so turbulent that caution became the watchword of the 1990s. The thrift crisis was largely over, and the surviving financial institutions adopted more conservative lending policies, which helped them return to profitability.

Along with stronger federal regulations, all financial institutions were required to strengthen their capital reserves. The FDIC, as we saw in the cover story, even provides innovative ways to help the public discover and prevent abuses by fraudulent financial institutions.

Two trends that emerged at the beginning of the decade were in full swing by the end of the century. One was the improving health of all financial institutions. The second was the continued erosion of historical differences among the commercial banks, savings banks, S&Ls, and credit unions.

Section 3 Assessment

Checking for Understanding

1. **Main Idea** Why was the Federal Reserve System created?

2. **Define** Federal Reserve System, central bank, run on the bank, bank holiday, commercial bank, demand deposit account (DDA), thrift institution, mutual savings bank (MSB), savings bank, NOW accounts, savings and loan association (S&L), credit union, share draft accounts, deregulation, creditor.

3. **Explain** why the National Banking System was created.

4. **Explain** why deposit insurance developed in the 1930s.

5. **Identify** three depository institutions.

6. **Describe** four factors contributing to the S&L crisis.

Applying Economic Concepts

7. **Demand Deposit Accounts** Adam Smith argued that a competitive economy functions best when everyone pursues his or her own best interests. Explain how the self-interest of state-chartered banks in 1865 led to the development of demand deposit accounts.

Critical Thinking

8. **Drawing Conclusions** The FDIC insures deposits up to $100,000. What would you do if you had $400,000 you wanted to deposit and insure?

9. **Summarizing Information** What is a demand deposit account?

Practice and assess key social studies skills with the *Glencoe Skillbuilder Interactive Workbook, Level 2.*

Section 3 Assessment Answers

1. to give the country a central bank that could lend to other banks in times of need

2. All vocabulary terms are defined in the text.

3. to bring the state banks under control and to help finance the Civil War

4. to strengthen banking and insure deposits

5. savings banks, savings and loan associations, credit unions

6. deregulation, high interest rates, inadequate financial reserves, fraud

7. Problems with different state bank currencies led to overhaul of paper currency component of money supply.

8. deposit funds in four different institutions

9. an account whose funds can be removed by writing a check

CHAPTER 11
Section 3, pages 300–305

Reteach

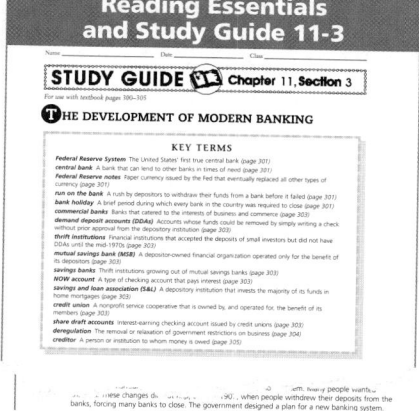

Enrich

Have students research the history and development of banking, or the history of a particular bank in the community. Encourage students to present their findings in an illustrated time line.

CLOSE

Have students interview a local banker and ask the following questions: Do you ever fear a "run on the bank"? Why or why not? Have students share the results of their interviews.

TEACH

Online bill collectors are able to make some money by "playing the float," or earning short-term interest on a transaction. When a customer pays a utility bill electronically, for example, the bill collector takes money out of the customer's account immediately, and then earns interest on the money until it is received by the utility company. But a much stronger incentive for online bill collectors is the potential to advertise on their Web sites. They have discovered that customers who pay electronically tend to have higher incomes, so the collectors are eager to pitch goods and services to them.

Refer to *Business Week Focus on the New Economy* in the TCR for additional unit-based articles.

BusinessWeek

JULY 19, 1999

Newsclip

Technology now exists for businesses to bill their customers over the Internet and for the customers to return payment over the Internet. Bankers are hoping that this electronic billing will allow banks to continue managing money for companies.

The Battle To Be Your Online Bill Collector

Every year, American business sends out 29 billion bills. And by any measure, the exercise isn't much fun. For companies, printing, processing and posting a typical consumer bill runs about 90¢. . . .

But for banks trying to make it on the Internet, bills are cool. Bankers see bills as surefire eyeball-grabbers in an environment where it's tough to command consumer attention—and a key to protecting their existing business managing cash for big companies. Increasingly, banks are battling high-tech competitors for control of Internet billing, or electronic-bill presentment, as it is called. . . .

The question is who will become the bill collector on the Net. Bankers reckon that if they can turn their Web sites into mailboxes for electronic bills, they can become key entry points on the Net—portals even. That would enable them to sell other financial services online. The fear is that existing portals, such

as Yahoo! or even America Online, will become centers of bill payment and, in turn, siphon off existing bank businesses. . . .

Banks have their advantages. They can offer customers simultaneous access to their bills and their money. Banks have long relationships with billers, such as utilities and retailers, and centuries of experience in protecting people's money. . . .

Big banks also are worried that technology companies offering bill presentment could muscle into one of their fastest-growing businesses—managing cash for big companies. After all, distributing and collecting bills is a close cousin to cash management. . . .

At this point, predicting how the industry will shake out is premature. Banks and technology companies already have formed several alliances aimed a[t] delivering bills on the Net. More combinations are likely. What's clear, though, is the banks know they are running out of time to get their Internet billing act together.

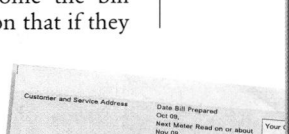

Examining the Newsclip

1. **Making Comparisons** What are some advantages that banks can offer customers compared to Internet companies?

2. **Analyzing Information** Why are banks concerned that Internet companies will become bill payment centers?

Answers to Examining the Newsclip

1. Banks can offer customers simultaneous access to their bills and their money, have long relationships with billers, and have centuries of experience in protecting people's money.

2. If Internet companies become bill payment centers, online banks would lose business.

Section 1

The Evolution of Money (pages 285–290)

- **Money** is any substance that serves as a medium of exchange, a measure of value, and a store of value.
- **Commodity money,** wampum, **specie,** and paper currency were used extensively in colonial America.
- The Continental Congress issued large amounts of **Continental dollars** to finance the American Revolution, but excessive issue made the money worthless by the end of the war.
- The U.S. dollar was based on the Spanish peso, which was imported from the West Indies.
- All successful monies have portability, durability, divisibility, and limited availability.

Section 2

Early Banking and Monetary Standards (pages 292–298)

- From the American Revolution to 1861, paper currency was issued by state-chartered, privately owned banks. The federal government issued coins but no paper currency.
- The variety of private notes eventually made the money supply difficult to use, and fraudulent wildcat banks often abused the privilege of printing currency.
- The government sold bonds and then printed **greenbacks** to finance the Civil War.
- In 1863 the National Banking System was set up to strengthen the banking system and to generate new demand for government bonds. Later, other federal currencies became popular, including **gold certificates, silver certificates,** and **Treasury coin notes.**
- The **gold standard** was adopted in 1900, which made all currencies, including **Federal Reserve notes,** convertible into gold on demand. However, the country left the gold standard in 1934 because gold stocks ran low during the Great Depression.

- After 1934 Americans could not convert dollars into gold.
- Today, most governments manage their currencies with respect to quality, size, composition, and availability. Most modern money functions well as a medium of exchange and is portable, durable, divisible, and reasonably stable in value.

Section 3

The Development of Modern Banking (pages 300–305)

- The National Banking System brought uniformity to banking. National banks also issued their own currency known as **National Bank notes.** State-chartered banks that chose not to join gave up printing currency in favor of **demand deposit accounts.**
- The **Federal Reserve System** (Fed) was established in 1913, giving the country a true **central bank.** All **national banks** were required to join the Fed, and all **state banks** were also invited to join.
- Despite the Fed, massive banking failures occurred during the Great Depression.
- Other depository institutions—mutual savings banks, credit unions, and savings and loan associations—appeared to cater to the small investor ignored by commercial banks.
- Deregulation, high interest rates, inadequate financial reserves, and fraud reduced the numbers of S&Ls by half in the 1980s.
- The financial crisis was largely over by the end of the decade, and the 1990s saw the continued growth of similarities between commercial banks, savings banks, and S&Ls.

CHAPTER 11: MONEY AND BANKING **307**

NIGHTLY BUSINESS REPORT

ECONOMICS & YOU

Chapter 18
Disc 1, Side 2

Money and Banking

Also available in VHS.

Using the Chapter 11 Summary

Use the Chapter 11 Summary to preview, review, condense, or reteach the chapter.

Preview/Review

Vocabulary PuzzleMaker CD-ROM reinforces Key Terms.

Interactive Tutor Self-Assessment Software provides a review of Chapter 11 content.

Condense

Have students listen to the Chapter 11 Audio Program. Spanish also available.

Assign the Chapter 11 Audio Program Activity and give students the Chapter 11 Audio Program Test.

Have students complete the Guided Reading Activities and Reading Essentials and Study Guides for Chapter 11.

Reteach

Have students complete Reteaching Activity 11 in the TCR. Spanish also available.

Teacher's Notes / Internet Bookmarks

GLENCOE
TECHNOLOGY

Use MindJogger Videoquiz to review the Chapter 11 content.

ECONOMICS Online

Have students visit the Web site at epp.glencoe.com to review Chapter 11 and take the Self-Check Quiz.

Identifying Key Terms

1. **c-e**	9. **c-f**
2. **b-f**	10. **b-f**
3. **a**	11. **c-f**
4. **e**	12. **e, f**
5. **c-f**	13. **b-f**
6. **c, d**	14. **c-e**
7. **c, d**	15. **a**
8. **d-f**	16. **c**

Reviewing the Facts

Section 1

1. medium of exchange, measure of value, store of value
2. Descriptions could include tea leaves compressed into "bricks," compressed cheese, miniature iron spears on necklaces, stones
3. portability, durability, divisibility, limited availability

Section 2

4. For the most part, state banks issued their own paper currency. By the Civil War, the U.S. had more than 1,600 banks issuing more than 10,000 different kinds of paper currency.
5. The greenback was the first paper currency printed by the government since the Constitution was adopted.
6. gold stock may not grow fast enough to support a growing economy, people may drain government's gold reserves by converting their

---

Chapter 11 Assessment and Activities

ECONOMICS Online

Self-Check Quiz Visit the *Economics: Principles and Practices* Web site at epp.glencoe.com and click on **Chapter 11—Self-Check Quizzes** to prepare for the chapter test.

Identifying Key Terms

On another sheet of paper, place each of the vocabulary terms in its correct historical period(s). Some terms will appear under more than one period.

Historical Periods:
a. **Colonial: 1607–1776**
b. **Pre-Civil War: 1789–1861**
c. **Civil War–Pre-Depression: 1861–1929**
d. **Depression: 1929–1939**
e. **World War II–FIRREA: 1940–1989**
f. **1989–present**

1. United States note _____
2. commercial bank _____
3. Continental dollar _____
4. deregulation _____
5. Federal Reserve System _____
6. gold certificate _____
7. gold standard _____
8. inconvertible fiat money standard _____
9. legal tender _____
10. mutual savings bank _____
11. national bank _____
12. NOW account _____
13. savings and loan association _____
14. silver certificate _____
15. specie _____
16. Treasury coin note _____

Reviewing the Facts

Section 1 (pages 285–290)

1. **List** the three functions of money.
2. **Describe** five types of early money.
3. **List** the four characteristics that give money its value.

Section 2 (pages 292–298)

4. **Describe** the paper currencies used from the period of the American Revolution to the time of the Civil War.
5. **Explain** the importance of the greenback during the Civil War.
6. **Describe** four disadvantages of a gold standard.
7. **Evaluate** modern money as a medium of exchange.

Section 3 (pages 300–305)

8. **Describe** the main difference between the Federal Reserve System and the National Banking System.
9. **Explain** why many banks failed during the Great Depression.
10. **Describe** two evolutionary trends in banking that emerged in the 1990s.

Thinking Critically

1. **Understanding Cause and Effect** How did high interest rates affect the S&L industry in the early 1980s?
2. **Making Comparisons** Why were coins a more desirable form of money than paper during the colonial period? Create a table like the one below to help you organize your answer.

Kinds of Money	Advantages	Disadvantages
Coins		
Paper		

---

currency into gold, the price of gold changes dramatically over time, political risk of failure

7. portable because coins, currency, and checks are easy to transport; durable because metallic coins last a long time, paper notes last at least a year, and checking accounts never wear out; divisible because the penny—the smallest coin—is small enough for any purchase, and checks can be written in any amount; a mixed record with respect to limited availability

Section 3

8. The Federal Reserve System acted as a central bank, lending to other banks in times of need. The National Banking System was not a central bank.
9. There was an overabundance of banks, none of which had deposit insurance. Customers removed their deposits before banks failed, leading to panic and then bank failure.
10. the improving health of all financial institutions, the continued erosion of historical

Applying Economic Concepts

1. **Money** Ask your friends, parents, and neighbors if they have any examples of old currency. If so, make a note of (a) the name of the currency (gold certificate, silver certificate, United States note, etc.); (b) the date on the currency; and (c) any mention of backing (silver certificates backed by silver dollars). Describe the role this money played in United States history.

2. **Barter** Assume that you live in a barter society. Organize a list of 10 items that you use frequently, and then identify alternate goods of comparable worth that you would be willing to trade for them.

Math Practice

The table below provides information on the number and total assets of FDIC-insured commercial banks. Study the data and then design a graph to present this information.

Total Assets	Number of Institutions
Less than $25 million	1,404
$25 to $50 million	2,107
$50 to $100 million	2,598
$100 to $300 million	2,937
$300 to $500 million	585
$500 to $1 billion	393
More than $1 billion	537
Total Institutions	**10,561**

Thinking Like an Economist

Over time different financial institutions—state banks, national banks, S&Ls, MSBs, and credit unions—have lost some of their individual identities and have become more and more like each other. Is this an outcome that could have been predicted by an economist?

Technology Skill

Using the Internet The money supply of the United States, much like that of the major industrialized countries, is a managed money supply. The government or its designated agent tries to control the quantity, composition, and even the quality of the money supply. The two agencies that make United States currency are the Bureau of the Mint and the Bureau of Engraving and Printing. What are the roles of these two agencies? Use the Internet to find out about the operations of one of these two currency-making institutions.

To begin, log on to the Internet and access a World Wide Web search engine. Search by selecting one of the listed categories or by typing in the subject you want to find, such as *Bureau of the Mint* or *Bureau of Engraving and Printing*. Next, enter words like the following to focus your search: *currency, United States Mint,* and *counterfeiting.*

Gather your findings. Using the findings, create a pamphlet that could be distributed by either bureau to describe its role in the creation of American currency.

Building Skills

Developing Multimedia Presentations
Examine the list of topics below. Choose one of the topics and explain how you would use at least three types of media in a presentation to best teach the topic to your class.

- Trade in colonial America
- Origins of the dollar
- Establishment of a national bank—Alexander Hamilton's view and Thomas Jefferson's view
- Currencies around the world
- Banking during the Civil War
- Roosevelt's bank holiday during the Great Depression

 Practice and **assess** key social studies skills with the *Glencoe Skillbuilder Interactive Workbook, Level 2.*

Math Practice

Graphs should represent data.

Thinking Like an Economist

Answers will vary. Students might focus on changes that strengthened similarities among institutions: more conservative lending policies, foreign stocks and currencies, federal regulations, strengthened capital reserves, programs to inform the public.

Technology Skill

Pamphlets should accurately describe one of the bureaus and its role.

Building Skills

Answers should show understanding of multimedia and content.

 Bonus Test Question

How is a commercial bank like other businesses? How is it different? *(Like: its aim is to make a profit. Different: it makes that profit by lending other people's money.)*

differences between the commercial banks, savings banks, S&Ls, and credit unions

Thinking Critically

1. Most S&Ls made long-term, low-interest loans to homeowners in the early 1970s. When interest rates reached record levels in the early 1980s, S&Ls had to pay more on funds deposited with them than they earned on the loans they already made.

2. In the nation's early years, coins were more desirable because of their mineral content and they were in limited supply.

Applying Economic Concepts

1. Examples should demonstrate an understanding of past currency and its role in U.S. history.
2. Lists should show understanding of barter system.

1 FOCUS

NIGHTLY BUSINESS REPORT

ECONOMICS & YOU

Chapter 11
Disc 1, Side 1

Buying the Necessities

 Also available in VHS.

2 TEACH

- Introduce the workshop activity by asking students what they understand "the American dream" to mean, and then isolating the economic elements of it. Point out that buying a house is, for most Americans, the largest purchase they will ever make, and so preparing for it properly is critical, and can literally save them tens of thousands of dollars.
- For Steps 1, 2, and 3 encourage students to be creative (but at least somewhat realistic). They may wish to model their scenarios on people they admire.
- For Step 4, encourage students to identify authoritative sources of free, and, importantly, *objective* information. Consider assigning one pair of students to obtain federal government pamphlets designed to educate home buyers.
- For steps 5 and 6, arrange to meet with student pairs after they have conducted their research in order to guide them in the preparation. They should plan and craft their reports carefully, and make necessary revisions.

ECONOMICS WORKSHOP IN ACTION

Buying a Home

From the classroom of . . .
Hal Kraynek
Valley High School
Santa Ana, California

The ability to buy a home is usually the result of proving to a lending institution that your salary is sufficient to make the monthly mortgage payments. Also, the lending institution will demand evidence that the amount you will pay for the house is a reasonable amount for the neighborhood, the size, and the condition of the house. Buying a home is usually a lengthy, complex process.

Select a partner to work with. Imagine that you and your partner have completed your education and successfully acquired jobs in your respective fields. You both have saved money all those years and are now ready to purchase a home. You will combine your salaries to buy this home.

Setting Up the Workshop

Prepare a report on the process you would follow to purchase a home. The report will be five pages long. This will include a cover sheet, three pages of text, and a bibliography on the fifth page. The outline of your report should be similar to the following:

I. Title page, including title, date, student's name, and class
II. Background
   A. Education
   B. Occupation
III. Price of house
   A. Payments
   B. Taxes
IV. Procedure followed and paperwork involved
V. Location of home
VI. Decisions
   A. Reason for home location
   B. Insurance choice
   C. Payment plan
VII. Bibliography, including names and titles of people who helped you, Internet Web sites, title companies, newspapers, banks, county tax collector, flyers, realtors, and so forth

The report will contain *at least* the following information:

REQUIRED:
- ❏ Occupation (both you and your partner)
- ❏ Salary (yours and partner's)
- ❏ Education (yours and partner's)
- ❏ Mortgage rates
- ❏ Loaning institute
- ❏ Taxes
- ❏ Loan amount
- ❏ Interest rate
- ❏ Down payment
- ❏ Type of loan
- ❏ Savings and loan companies, credit unions
- ❏ Number of years
- ❏ Procedure followed to acquire the loan

Participating in Economics

Home Buying in Your Community Most community newspapers have real estate sections that provide information such as median house costs in various areas, tips for home buyers, advertisements of homes for sale, and so on. Have the class read the real estate section of your local newspaper for at least one week and create annotated clippings files of articles and other features that would be useful to home buyers in your area.

- ❑ Qualifications needed for loan
- ❑ Examples of paperwork involved in the application process
- ❑ Location of home

OPTIONAL:
- ❑ Other interesting information
- ❑ Visual aids
- ❑ Pamphlets/brochures

Procedures

STEP 1

Establish your education and professions. List any specialized training, and degrees or certificates achieved.

STEP 2

Describe your job, city or locale of employment, what company, if you are self-employed, and your salary.

STEP 3

Based on your salaries and where you work, decide where you want to live, and what price range of house you can afford.

STEP 4

Compile places you might go for information and help. This might include Internet sites, title companies, friends, family, newspapers, and all types of lending institutions, and real estate advertising sources in your area.

STEP 5

Research to find out what is involved with purchasing a house: what papers are needed; time spent in escrow; fees; charges; interest rates for 15-, 20-, and 30-year mortgages; payment rates; types of homeowners' insurance; notes; differences in buying a new home or an older home; repair expenditures; landscape costs; location of schools and shopping; and the type of neighborhood you are interested in.

STEP 6

Write and submit your report, following the criteria outlined above.

Summary Activity

Discuss with the other groups what problems you encountered and how you solved them.

③ ASSESS

Lead a class discussion in which you name terms and processes associated with home buying, and call on individual students to identify them and explain how they fit into the overall home-buying process.

④ CLOSE

Invite students to share their visions of their dream houses, and how a knowledge of economics will help them realize these dreams.

Summary Activity Answers

To summarize the workshop, conduct a class discussion about the various experiences students had in compiling their reports. Guide students into identifying the basic steps that must be taken to purchase a home, and the order in which these steps must occur. Create a flowchart on the board to record these steps, and modify it as the class discussion evolves. When complete, the diagram will illustrate the steps in buying a home.

Chapter 12 Resource Manager

SECTION RESOURCES

Daily Objectives	Reproducible Resources	Technology/Multimedia Resources
Section 1 **Savings and the Financial System** 1. Explain why saving is important for capital formation. 2. Explain how the financial system works to transfer funds from savers to borrowers. 3. Understand the role of the major nondepository financial institutions in the financial system.	Reproducible Lesson Plan 12-1 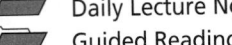 Daily Lecture Notes 12-1 Guided Reading Activity 12-1 Reading Essentials and Study Guide 12-1 Section Quiz 12-1*	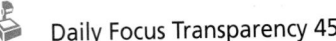 Daily Focus Transparency 45 Interactive Tutor Self-Assessment Software ExamView® Pro Testmaker Presentation Plus!
Section 2 **Investment Strategies and Financial Assets** 1. Identify four important investment considerations. 2. Describe the three characteristics of bonds. 3. Describe the characteristics of major financial assets. 4. Understand four views of markets for financial assets.	Reproducible Lesson Plan 12-2 Daily Lecture Notes 12-2 Guided Reading Activity 12-2 Reading Essentials and Study Guide 12-2 Section Quiz 12-2*	Daily Focus Transparency 46 Interactive Economics! Interactive Tutor Self-Assessment Software ExamView® Pro Testmaker Presentation Plus!
Section 3 **Investing in Equities, Futures, and Options** 1. Describe the major stock exchanges. 2. Explain how stock market performance is measured.	Reproducible Lesson Plan 12-3 Daily Lecture Notes 12-3 Guided Reading Activity 12-3 Reading Essentials and Study Guide 12-3 Section Quiz 12-3*	Daily Focus Transparency 43 Vocabulary PuzzleMaker CD-ROM Interactive Economics! Interactive Tutor Self-Assessment Software ExamView® Pro Testmaker Presentation Plus!

Also available in Spanish

 Transparency   CD-ROM   Software   Blackline Master

Videodisc   Audio Program   Videocassette

 0:00 OUT OF TIME?
Assign the Chapter 12 Audio Program activity and test.

 Block Schedule

Activities that are particularly suited to use within the block scheduling framework are identified throughout this chapter by the following designation: **BLOCK SCHEDULING**

KEY TO ABILITY LEVELS

Teaching strategies have been coded for varying learning styles and abilities.
L1 BASIC activities for all students
L2 AVERAGE activities for average to above-average students
L3 CHALLENGING activities for above-average students
ELL ENGLISH LANGUAGE LEARNER activities

Chapter 12 Resource Manager

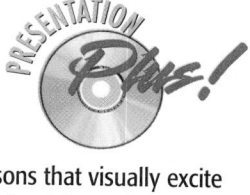
ACTIVITY

From the Classroom of...

Jerrie Glassman
Omaha Northwest
High School
Omaha, NB

Company/Stock Investment Term Paper

This project can be done over a number of weeks. Begin by giving students the outline shown below, and explaining that they need to select a company that is publicly traded. Have students follow the steps in the outline and conclude with the presentations in Step VII.

I.   Name of company and how long it has been publicly traded

II. Select one international political or social trend. Select one international or economic trend (unemployment, stock market, CPI, and so on). Do these trends affect your company?

III. Same as II, but identify national trends.

IV. Who makes up the competition? Where in the business cycle is the industry? Where is the company positioned in the industry?

V.   Fundamental analysis: brief company history; demographic makeup of leadership; legal considerations; other aspects to consider.

VI. Ratio analysis: liquidity, asset management, debt management, profitability; company ratio analysis compared with industry.

VII. Is this a good stock to buy—why or why not? "Be prepared to present this to the class in 5 minutes or less."

National Council on Economic Education

THE **Economics**America AND **Economics**International PROGRAMS

Voluntary National Content Standards in Economics
Emphasized in Chapter 12

Content Standard 10

For a complete listing of NCEE Standards and entire text correlation, see Teacher pages in front of book.

Resources Available from NCEE

- Economics and Entrepreneurship
- Entrepreneurship in the U.S. Economy
- Personal Decision Making: Focus on Economics
- Personal Finance Economics: Wallet Wisdom
- Capstone: The Nation's High School Economics Course
- Learning from the Market: Integrating the Stock Market Game™ Across the Curriculum

To order these materials or to contact your state Council on Economic Education about workshops and programs, call 1-800-338-1192 or visit www.nationalcouncil.org

Chapter 12 Resource Manager

Economic Concept Transparency 6:
Exchange, Money, and Interdependence

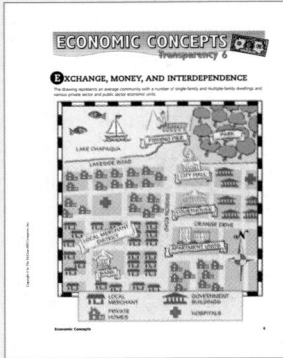

Consumer Application Activity 17

Free Enterprise Activity 17

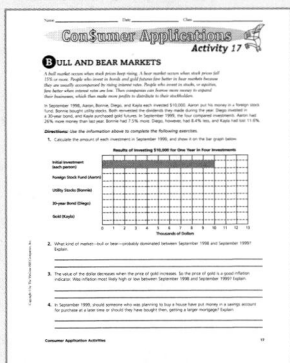

Enrichment Activity 12

Cooperative Learning Activity 17

Math Practice Activity 17

Economic Cartoon 17

Primary and Secondary Source Reading 17

Economic Vocabulary Activity 12

Reteaching Activity 12

Critical Thinking Activity 17

Reinforcing Economic Skill 18

Chapter 12 Resource Manager

ASSESSMENT AND EVALUATION

**Chapter 12 Test
Form A**

**Chapter 12 Test
Form B**

**Performance Assessment
Activity 17**

**ExamView® Pro
Testmaker**

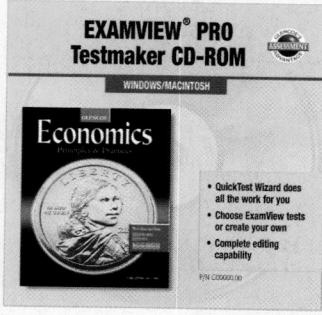

SPANISH RESOURCES

The following Spanish language materials are available in the Spanish Resources binder:

 Spanish Economic Vocabulary Activities

 Spanish Reteaching Activities

 Spanish Section Quizzes

 Spanish Economic Concepts Transparencies

Also available:

Spanish Chapter 12 Audio Program
Activity and Test

TECHNOLOGY/MULTIMEDIA

- Vocabulary PuzzleMaker CD-ROM
- Interactive Tutor Self-Assessment Software
- ExamView® Pro Testmaker
- Audio Program (English or Spanish)
- NBR Economics & You Video Program
  (English or Spanish)
- MindJogger Videoquiz
- Interactive Economics! CD-ROM
- Presentation Plus!
- TeacherWorks CD-ROM
- Glencoe Skillbuilder Interactive Workbook CD-ROM, Level 2

ECONOMICS Online

Use our Web site for additional resources. All essential content is covered in the Student Edition.

You and your students can visit epp.glencoe.com, the Web site companion to **Economics: Principles and Practices.** This innovative integration of electronic and print media offers your students a wealth of opportunities. The student text directs students to the Web site for the following options:

- **Chapter Overviews**
- **Student Web Activities**
- **Self-Check Quizzes**
- **Textbook Updates**

Answers are provided for you in the Web Activity Lesson Plan. Additional Web resources and interactive puzzles are also available.

SCHOOL OF EDUCATION
CURRICULUM LABORATORY
UM-DEARBORN

Introducing
CHAPTER 12

Performance Assessment

Refer to Activity 17 in the *Performance Assessment Strategies and Activities* booklet.

🔲 **BLOCK SCHEDULING**

ECONOMICS *Online*

Introduce students to chapter content and key terms by having them access **Chapter Overview 12** at epp.glencoe.com

NIGHTLY BUSINESS REPORT

 ECONOMICS & YOU

  Chapter 13 Disc 1, Side 1

Saving and Investing
After viewing this segment, students should be able to:
• Differentiate between low-risk and high-risk investments.

📼 Also available in VHS.

GLENCOE TECHNOLOGY

 Use **MindJogger Videoquiz** to preview the Chapter 12 content.

CHAPTER **12**

Financial Markets

BOLSA DE MADRID

Economics & You

Do you save your money? In **Chapter 12,** you will learn about the role that savings plays in the economy. To learn about investment strategies, view the Chapter 13 video lesson:

Saving and Investing

ECONOMICS *Online*

Chapter Overview Visit the *Economics: Principles and Practices* Web site at epp.glencoe.com and click on **Chapter 12—Chapter Overviews** to preview chapter information.

Financial investors daily buy and sell the stock of thousands of corporations.

➕ EXTRA CREDIT PROJECT

Have students create a television-viewing log for news items about the stock market presented on the nightly news. Suggest that some students watch national newscasts and others watch local newscasts. They should record the date, the subject of the item, and the length of time given to the item. When study of the chapter is completed, have students compare and discuss their logs.

Savings and the Financial System

Study Guide

Main Idea
The components of a financial system work together to transfer savings to investors.

Reading Strategy
Graphic Organizer As you read the section, complete a graphic organizer like the one below by identifying how saving and savings differ.

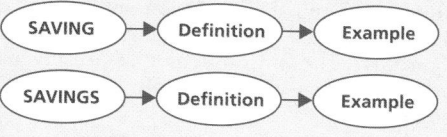

Key Terms
saving, savings, financial system, certificate of deposit, financial asset, financial intermediary, nonbank

financial institution, finance company, bill consolidation loan, premium, mutual fund, net asset value (NAV), pension, pension fund, real estate investment trust (REIT)

Objectives
After studying this section, you will be able to:
1. **Explain** why saving is important for capital formation.
2. **Explain** how the financial system works to transfer funds from savers to borrowers.
3. **Understand** the role of the major nondepository financial institutions in the financial system.

Applying Economic Concepts
Financial Assets Do you have a checking account, savings account, or government savings bond? If so, you have one or more financial assets.

Cover Story

The Golden Years

The Spirit of '76

Many people think of Boston as the birthplace of democracy in our country. They may not realize that it is also the birthplace of the democratization of investing. It was there, 75 years ago, that three stock salesmen created the first mutual fund and opened up what was once an exclusive province of the affluent to just about everyone.

When the Massachusetts Investors Trust made its debut in March 1924, it had $50,000 in assets and owned 45 stocks. . . . By pooling investments, the fund made shares in American companies accessible to a broader market . . . (the) true innovation was allowing investors to redeem shares upon request, at market value of the underlying stocks.

—*U.S. News & World Report*, April 5, 1999

F or an economic system to grow, it must produce capital—the equipment, tools, and machinery used in the process of production. To produce capital, people must be willing to save so that productive resources are released for use elsewhere. To the economist, **saving** means the absence of spending, while **savings** refers to the dollars that become available when people abstain from consumption. After all, there are only two things you can do with your income—spend it or save it.

Competitive markets are remarkably innovative, as the example in the cover story illustrates. The creation of the mutual fund industry is just one of many examples describing how our financial system evolves to meet the needs of savers and investors.

Saving and Capital Formation

 When people save, they make funds available. When businesses borrow these savings, they can produce new goods and services, build new plants and equipment, and create more jobs. Saving makes economic growth possible.

CHAPTER 12: FINANCIAL MARKETS **313**

1 FOCUS

Section Overview
This section discusses savings and the financial system.

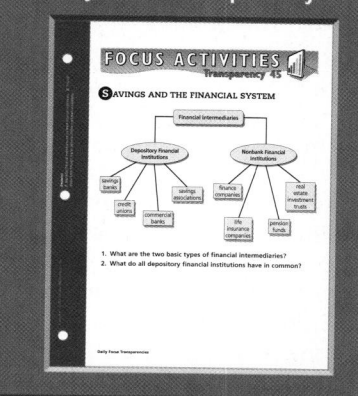
Study Guide

Reading Strategy
Have students create the graphic organizer.
Answers to Graphic: "Saving" *means not spending.* "Savings" *refers to the available dollars in the absence of consumption.*

Preteaching Vocabulary
Call on students to define the Key Terms in their own words.

TEACH

L1 Understanding Ideas

Write the following terms on the board: *savings, borrowing, growth.* Ask students to imagine that they have borrowed money to build a new home. Have students name others who would benefit from building the house. *(building contractors, suppliers, architects, and so on)* Mention that the money they borrowed benefited the economy as a whole, because it generated economic activity. Then point out that all this was made possible by others' savings. Conclude by asking students to write a generalization about the relationship between the three terms on the board. **ELL**

L2 Writing a Letter

Encourage students to imagine that they live in a country where people save very little. Have them write a letter to a friend detailing the economic problems the country faces because of the low level of savings.

Suppose two entrepreneurs want to set up their own businesses. Lisa wants to open a pet shop, while Juanita's lifelong dream is to run a photography studio. How do they go about it? Lisa saves her income, keeping her money in a bank account. When she saves enough money to invest, Lisa can set up her pet shop.

Eager to start her business immediately, Juanita decides to borrow the money she needs from a bank. If other people have been saving some of their income, like Lisa, the bank should have the funds to lend her. If people have been spending all of their income, however, the bank might not be able to give Juanita the loan even if it wanted to.

For investment to take place, someone in the economy must save. An individual can save as well as invest, as Lisa did. Or, a person may invest using money others have saved, as Juanita did. When people save, they provide money for others to borrow and use, making investments possible.

Financial Assets and the Financial System

For people to use the savings of others, the economy must have a **financial system**—a network of savers, investors, and financial institutions that work together to transfer savings to investors.

Financial Assets

People can save in a number of ways. They can open a savings account. They can purchase a **certificate of deposit**—a receipt showing that an investor has made an interest-bearing loan to a bank—or a government or corporate bond. In each case, the savers obtain receipts for the funds they save.

Economists call these receipts **financial assets**—claims on the property and the income of the borrower. These receipts are assets because they are property that has value. They represent claims on the borrower because they specify the amount loaned and the terms at which the loan was made.

Financial Intermediaries

You have just read about two of the main parts of the financial system. The first is the funds that the saver transfers to the borrower. The second is the financial assets or receipts that certify that the loans were made. The other parts of the financial system, illustrated in **Figure 12.1**, are the savers, borrowers, and institutions that bring the surplus funds and financial assets together.

Many surplus funds are placed with **financial intermediaries,** financial institutions that lend the funds that savers provide to borrowers. Financial intermediaries include depository institutions, life insurance companies, pension funds, and other institutions that channel savings from savers to borrowers. These institutions are especially helpful to small savers who have only limited funds to invest.

The Circular Flow of Funds

Figure 12.1 shows the circular flow that takes place when funds are transferred from savers to borrowers. Savers can provide their funds directly to the borrower or indirectly through the many financial intermediaries in the economy such as banks and credit unions. The borrowers then generate the financial assets, which return to the lender.

Any sector of the economy can supply savings, but households and businesses are the most important. As shown in **Figure 12.1,** savers provide some funds directly to borrowers, as when households or businesses purchase bonds directly from the government or businesses.

Any sector of the economy can borrow, but governments and businesses are the largest borrowers. If a corporation borrows directly from savers, or indirectly from savers through financial intermediaries, the corporation will issue a bond or other financial asset to the lender. Likewise, when the government borrows, it issues government bonds or other financial assets to the lender.

As a result, almost everyone participates in, and benefits from, the financial system. The smooth flow of funds through the system helps ensure that savers will have an outlet for their savings. Borrowers, in turn, will have a source of financial capital.

MEETING SPECIAL NEEDS ACTIVITY

Learning Disability For students who have trouble with writing, consider the following strategy. To help those students glean essential information from the text, provide the standard headings of *Who, What, Where, When,* and *Why* (or *What Happened)* to structure answers. Ask students to read the subsection "Financial Assets and the Financial System" and to write brief responses for each of the five questions. Assist the students with spelling and grammar.

Refer to *Inclusion for the Social Studies Classroom Strategies and Activities* in the TCR.

Overview of the Financial System

Using Charts Financial intermediaries help channel surplus funds from savers to borrowers, who put the money to work. **What do lenders receive in return for their funds?**

Guided Reading Activity 12-1

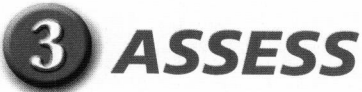

ECONOMICS
AT A GLANCE

Answer: *financial assets—claims on the property/income of borrower*

③ ASSESS

Assign Section 1 Assessment as homework or as an in-class activity.

💾 Have students use **Interactive Tutor Self-Assessment Software.**

Nonbank Financial Intermediaries

Savings banks, credit unions, commercial banks, and savings associations obtain funds when their customers or members make regular deposits. Another important group of financial intermediaries includes **nonbank financial institutions**—nondepository institutions that channel savings to borrowers. Finance companies, life insurance companies, pension funds, and real estate investment trusts are examples of nonbank financial institutions.

Finance Companies

A **finance company** is a firm that specializes in making loans directly to consumers and in buying installment contracts from merchants who sell goods on credit. Many merchants, for example, cannot afford to wait years for their customers to pay off high-cost items on an installment plan. Instead, the merchant sells the customer's installment contract to a finance company for a lump sum. This allows the merchant to advertise instant credit or easy terms without actually carrying the loan full term, absorbing losses for an unpaid account, or taking customers to court if they do not pay.

Some finance companies make loans directly to consumers. These companies generally check a consumer's credit rating and will make a loan only if the individual qualifies. Because they make some risky loans, and because they pay more for the funds they borrow, finance companies charge more than commercial banks for loans. Many consumer finance companies offer **bill consolidation loans.** This is a loan consumers use to pay off other bills.

Life Insurance Companies

Another financial institution that does not get its funds through deposits is the life insurance company. Although its primary purpose is to provide financial protection for survivors of the insured, it also collects a great deal of cash.

The head of a family, for example, purchases a life insurance policy to leave money for a spouse and children in case of his or her death. The **premium** is

CHAPTER 12: FINANCIAL MARKETS **315**

FREE ENTERPRISE ACTIVITY

Invite a local business entrepreneur to visit the class. Ask the entrepreneur to explain to students how he or she started the business, paying special attention to the procedures he or she followed to borrow money. Encourage students to ask questions about the role that borrowing plays in business start-ups and operations. Suggest that the entrepreneur conclude by discussing how savings and borrowing have played a role in his or her success in business.

Section Quiz 12-1

Reading Essentials and Study Guide 12-1

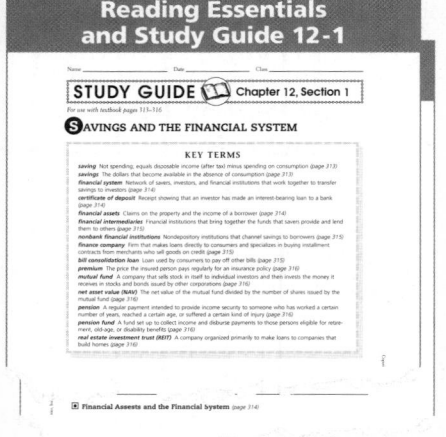

Enrich

Have students conduct an informal poll among family members, neighbors, and friends to discover how many save and for what reasons. Suggest that students combine their results and display them on a wall chart.

CLOSE

Have students design a symbol or logo that illustrates the relationship between savings and borrowing.

316

---

the price the insured pays for this policy and is usually paid monthly, quarterly, or annually for the length of the protection. Because insurance companies collect cash on a regular basis, they often lend surplus funds to others.

Mutual Funds

A **mutual fund** is a company that sells stock in itself to individual investors and then invests the money it receives in stocks and bonds issued by other corporations. Mutual fund stockholders receive dividends earned from the mutual fund's investments. Stockholders can also sell their mutual fund shares for a profit, just like other stocks.

Mutual funds allow people to play the market without risking all they have in one or a few companies. The large size of the typical mutual fund makes it possible to hire a staff of experts to analyze the securities market before buying and selling securities. Their large size also allows them to buy many different stocks and bonds.

The **net asset value (NAV)**—the net value of the mutual fund divided by the number of shares issued by the mutual fund—is the market value of a mutual fund share.

Pension Funds

Another nondepository financial institution is the pension fund. A **pension** is a regular payment intended to provide income security to someone who has worked a certain number of years, reached a certain age, or suffered a certain kind of injury. A **pension fund** is a fund set up to collect income and disburse payments to those persons eligible for retirement, old-age, or disability benefits.

In the case of private pension funds, employers regularly withhold a percentage of workers' salaries to deposit in the fund. During the 30- to 40-year lag between the time the savings are deposited and the time the workers generally use them, the money is usually invested in corporate stocks and bonds. Government pension funds are similar to private ones in that the government makes regular contributions to the fund that will pay benefits later.

Real Estate Investment Trusts

Still another nonbank financial institution is the **real estate investment trust (REIT)**—a company organized primarily to make loans to construction companies that build homes. REITs help provide billions annually for home construction.

Section 1 Assessment

Checking for Understanding

1. **Main Idea** Using your notes from the graphic organizer on page 313, describe the difference between saving and savings.

2. **Key Terms** Define saving, savings, financial system, certificate of deposit, financial asset, financial intermediary, nonbank financial institution, finance company, bill consolidation loan, premium, mutual fund, net asset value (NAV), pension, pension fund, real estate investment trust (REIT).

Reviewing Objectives

3. **Explain** why saving is required for capital formation.

4. **Describe** how the financial system works to transfer funds from savers to borrowers.

5. **Explain** the role of the major nondepository financial institutions in the financial system.

6. **Financial Assets** An I.O.U. that you draft and give to a friend in payment of a debt is an example of a financial asset. Explain why this is so.

Critical Thinking

7. **Understanding Cause and Effect** What is necessary before investment can take place?

8. **Making Generalizations** Why might an individual choose to borrow money from a finance company that charges higher interest rates than commercial banks do?

 Practice and **assess** key social studies skills with the *Glencoe Skillbuilder Interactive Workbook, Level 2.*

Section 1 Assessment Answers

1. Saving is not spending. Savings are dollars left over after you buy your necessities.

2. All vocabulary terms are defined in the text.

3. Savings make funds available for others to use in creating goods and services.

4. Savers can either provide their funds directly to the borrower or indirectly through financial intermediaries.

5. Nondepository institutions channel savings to borrowers.

6. It indicates that the friend has a claim on your property or income.

7. Someone in the economy must save so others can borrow.

8. The individual might be unable to get a loan from a commercial bank.

Profiles IN Economics

Managing Money:
Helen Young Hayes
(1962–)

Helen Hayes is the type of person people trust. In fact, people have entrusted her with more than $23 *billion* of their money.

Hayes is one of the most successful mutual fund managers in the world.

Picking the right stocks, especially foreign ones, takes research. But what sets Hayes apart, and is a key to her success, is her uncanny ability to read people. When she meets with corporate executives, for example, she pays a great deal of attention to body language, which she maintains can reveal as much, or more, about a company than what the executive says.

In her spare time, Hayes trains for and competes in triathlons—grueling races that combine swimming, bicycling, and running. She claims she's not very good, and

that she only competes against herself. But Hayes's gusto for athletics seems a clear reflection of the zeal she brings to bear in business.

Building a Business:
Edward T. Lewis
(1940–)

As chairman and CEO of Essence Communications, Inc. (ECI), Edward T. Lewis heads one of the largest African American businesses in the United States. His struggle to make *Essence* magazine a success shows determination and entrepreneurial skill.

In the late 1960s, Lewis, then a financial analyst for a bank, attended a conference held to encourage initiative in African American capitalism. One idea captured him: that someone could publish a magazine targeted at African American women.

Lewis launched the first issue of *Essence* in May 1970. The stylish magazine, which featured full-page color photos of African American models and cutting-edge articles, became a great success.

ECI is also a major investor in Amistad Press, a respected book publishing company that focuses on minority authors and titles. Essence Art Reproductions markets reproductions of fine art created by African American artists.

Lewis's success is the result of the age-old formula of good ideas combined with hard work. His legacy is ECI.

Examining the Profiles

1. **Making Comparisons** What similarities and differences do you see in Hayes's and Lewis's careers?

2. **For Further Research** Review several issues of *Essence* magazine. Write an analysis of the magazine's editorial policy.

Profiles IN Economics

BACKGROUND

The careers of Helen Hayes and Edward Lewis reflect a fundamental dichotomy in the U.S. market economy: the selling of goods or services. Hayes earns a living by selling a service: analyzing and choosing investments. Lewis earns a living primarily by selling goods: *Essence* magazine and merchandise.

TEACH

Have students create Venn diagrams to compare and contrast businesses that provide goods and businesses that provide services. Lead a class discussion about how marketing each type of economic product might affect the day-to-day work of business people.

School TO WORK

Selling Goods or Services Invite two community business owners to class, one of whom owns a service business and one of whom sells goods. Guide students in asking questions that help them develop a sense of the advantages and disadvantages of each basic type of business.

Answers to Examining the Profile

1. Answers will vary. Similarities include decisions to change careers early in life and inferred personal characteristics, such as intelligence and determination. Differences include that Hayes works for a company and provides a service, whereas Lewis runs a company and provides both goods and services.

2. Answers will vary. Reward thoughtful analyses.

FOCUS

Section Overview
This section discusses investment considerations and assets.

BELLRINGER
Motivational Activity

- Project **transparency** and have students answer questions.

- Available as blackline master.

Daily Focus Transparency 46

Study Guide

Reading Strategy
Have students create the graphic organizer.
Answers to Graphic: *certificates of deposit, corporate/municipal/government savings/treasury bonds, treasury bills, IRAs*

Preteaching Vocabulary
Call on volunteers to tell what they think each Key Term means. Have other students check the accuracy of these definitions by finding the terms in the text.

SECTION 2

Investment Strategies and Financial Assets

Study Guide

Main Idea
To invest wisely, investors must identify their goals and analyze the risk and return involved.

Reading Strategy
Graphic Organizer As you read the section, identify at least four financial assets.

Financial assets

Key Terms
risk, 401(k) plan, coupon, maturity, par value, current yield, municipal bond, tax-exempt, savings bond, Treasury note, Treasury bond, Treasury bill, Individual Retirement Account (IRA), Roth IRA, capital market, money market, primary market, secondary market

Objectives
After studying this section, you will be able to:
1. **Identify** four important investment considerations.
2. **Describe** the three characteristics of bonds.
3. **Describe** the characteristics of major financial assets.
4. **Understand** four views of markets for financial assets.

Applying Economic Concepts
Risk-Return Relationship Riskier projects must offer higher returns to be attractive.

Cover Story

Popular Plan Has Attracted $1 Trillion

In just 15 years, 401(k) has been transformed from an obscure section of the tax code into corporate America's most popular retirement benefit.

Today, 25 million people have about $1 trillion invested in 401(k) plans, triggering a revolution in retirement planning that's made money managers out of workers from the factory floor to the corner office.

But with 401(k)s now covering as many employees as traditional pensions, an . . . analysis of the 401(k)s at the nation's largest employers finds dramatic disparities in the plans' generosity.

For individuals, the difference could easily amount to hundreds of thousands of dollars. For society, they could further widen the gap between rich and poor.

The 401(k) provides a nest egg for millions.

—*USA Today*, April 23, 1999

318

Before you invest in a financial asset, it helps to have a basic understanding of investment considerations. Possessing this information will help you make your own investment goals and decide whether a plan like the 401(k) is right for you.

Basic Investment Considerations

It is important to consider several factors when you invest in financial assets. The first concerns the relationship between risk and return. The second has to do with the investor's personal investment goals. The third deals with avoiding some types of investments, and the last deals with the consistency of investing.

The Risk-Return Relationship

One of the most important relationships in the market is the relationship between risk and return. **Risk** is a situation in which the outcome is not certain, but probabilities for each possible outcome can be estimated. Investors realize that

---

RESOURCE MANAGER

Reproducible Masters
- Reproducible Lesson Plan 12-2
- Daily Lecture Notes 12-2
- Guided Reading Activity 12-2
- Reading Essentials and Study Guide 12-2
- Section Quiz 12-2

Transparencies
- Daily Focus Transparency 46

Multimedia
- Interactive Economics!
- Interactive Tutor Self-Assessment Software
- ExamView® Pro Testmaker
- Presentation Plus!

financial assets are risky. Assets such as notes, bills, and bonds may go up or down in price, or the agency that issued the asset may even fail to redeem it, leaving the lender with a loss. As a result, investors demand a higher return to compensate for higher risk. This relationship between risk and return is illustrated in **Figure 12.2,** which shows that riskier assets offer higher returns to attract investors.

As an investor, your first consideration should be the level of risk that you can tolerate. For example, if someone offers you a risky deal that doubles your money, it may be better to focus on the chances of getting your money back rather than on the size of the return. If you are uncomfortable with high levels of risk, then consider another investment.

Investment Objectives

Another factor to consider is the reason for investing. If your goal is to save for retirement, you might want to purchase assets that simply appreciate in value rather than generate current income. If your purpose is to accumulate reserves to fund a vacation or to cover living expenses during periods of unemployment, a strategy that focuses on the accumulation of assets that are highly liquid, or easily converted into cash, might be better.

The source of income used for investment may help determine which assets are purchased. If you receive a steady salary and almost no other income, a payroll deduction plan that puts money into a special retirement fund like a 401(k) or government bonds might be best. If you receive bonuses, royalties, or other occasional payments, corporate bonds or some other large-denomination financial asset might be preferable.

In the end, each investor must consider his or her own circumstances and personal investment goals. Investors have a large number of financial assets, equities, and other investments from which to choose. The investor's knowledge of his or her own needs is important in making these decisions.

Simplicity

Most analysts advise investors to stay with what they know. Thousands of investments are available, and many are complicated. Although you do not have to understand them all to be a good investor,

knowing a few fundamentals can help you make good choices.

One rule that many investors follow is this: If an investment seems too complicated, then ignore it and invest in something else. Another often-cited rule is that any investment that seems too good to be true probably is. A few investors do get lucky, but most build wealth because they invest regularly, and they avoid the investments that seem too far out of the ordinary.

Consistency

Most successful investors invest consistently over long periods of time. In many cases, the amount invested is not as important as investing on a regular basis.

Figure 12.3 shows how a small deposit of $10 per month would grow over a 5- to 30-year period at various interest rates. The balance in the account accumulates fairly quickly, even at modest interest rates. Because $10 is a small amount, imagine how

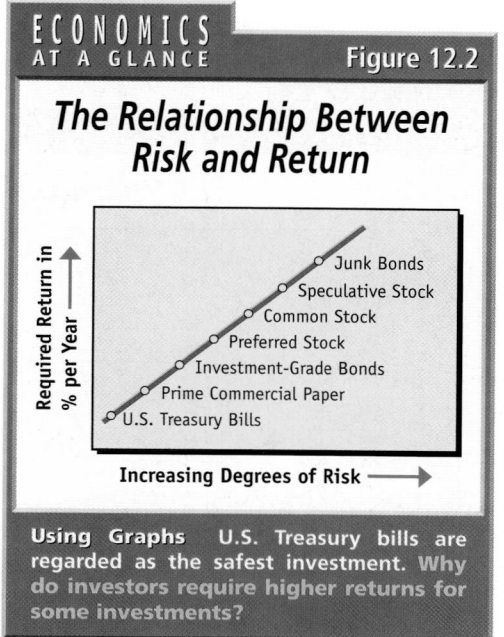

ECONOMICS
AT A GLANCE   Figure 12.2

The Relationship Between Risk and Return

Using Graphs U.S. Treasury bills are regarded as the safest investment. **Why do investors require higher returns for some investments?**

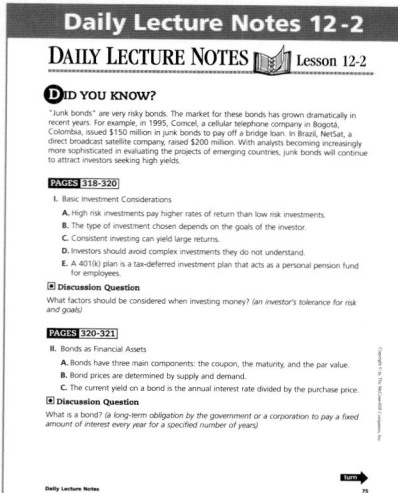

ECONOMICS
AT A GLANCE

Answer: *to compensate for greater risk*

THE GLOBAL ECONOMY

"Foreign" Mutual Funds A financial instrument gaining popularity among American investors is the mutual fund with assets that are largely foreign. These assets usually are in the emerging areas of the world—Latin America and Asia, for example. The fast-growing economies of these areas usually mean high returns for investors.

MEETING SPECIAL NEEDS ACTIVITY

English Language Learners Point out to students that there are a number of key or marker words in this section that will help them focus on listed items. The subsection titled "Bonds as Financial Assets" may be used to help students note key or marker words such as *When, In order to,* and *Therefore.* Discuss the use of these words in identifying main ideas and then have students write a short paragraph about one of the concepts covered in this section using key or marker words. **ELL**

Refer to *Inclusion for the Social Studies Classroom Strategies and Activities* in the TCR.

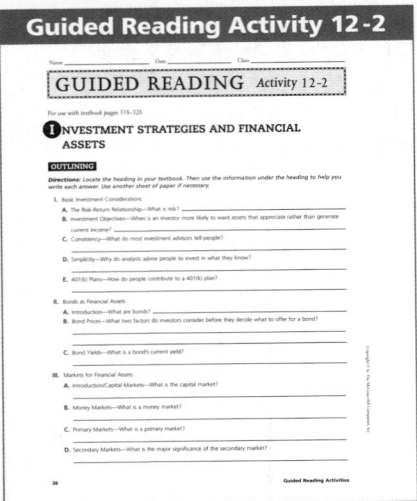

L1 Understanding Ideas

Have students select a block of five corporate bonds from the bond listings in *The Wall Street Journal* or in the business section of the local newspaper. Ask students to construct a chart using the information they have gathered about the bonds, complete with explanation and analysis. Point out that they may need to consult other sources to find full company names. Encourage students to display and discuss their completed charts. **ELL**

ECONOMICS
AT A GLANCE

Answer: *$439*

---

the account would grow if the deposit was for $25, $50, or even $100 a month! Many investment advisers tell people to save something every month, even if it is only a small sum.

401(k) Plans

A program that has become increasingly popular among investors is the **401(k) plan**—a tax-deferred investment and savings plan that acts as a personal pension fund for employees. To contribute to the plan, employees authorize payroll deductions, which are invested in mutual funds or other investments approved by their companies. Contributing to a plan lowers your taxable income because you don't have to pay income taxes on the money you contribute until you withdraw it. An added benefit of a 401(k) plan is that more than 80 percent of employers match an employee's contributions, by typically 25 percent to 100 percent. This explains why individual plans vary widely from company to company, as noted in the cover story.

Returns on a 401(k) are especially high when the employer provides matching funds. For example, if your employer matches your contribution at 50 cents on the dollar, you have an immediate 50 percent return on the investment—even before the funds are invested. **Figure 12.4** illustrates that an annual contribution of $2,000 with a 25 percent employer match can provide a substantial retirement fund in 30 years.

The 401(k) is popular because it provides a simple, consistent, and relatively safe way for employees to save—and you can take the 401(k) with you if you change jobs. In addition, you can borrow against the money before you retire at a substantially reduced rate. You will, however, have to pay taxes on the earnings when you withdraw the money at retirement.

Bonds as Financial Assets

When the government or firms need to borrow funds for long periods, they often issue bonds. Bonds are long-term obligations that pay a stated rate of interest for a specified number of years.

ECONOMICS
AT A GLANCE

Figure 12.3

The Power of Compound Interest

Annual Interest (in percent)	Value at End of Year					
	5	10	15	20	25	30
0	$600	$1,200	$1,800	$2,000	$2,500	$3,600
2	$630	$1,327	$2,097	$2,948	$3,888	$4,927
4	$663	$1,472	$2,461	$3,668	$5,141	$6,940
6	$698	$1,639	$2,908	$4,620	$6,930	$10,045
8	$735	$1,829	$3,460	$5,890	$9,510	$14,904
10	$774	$2,048	$4,145	$7,594	$13,268	$22,605
12	$817	$2,300	$4,996	$9,893	$18,788	$34,950

Using Tables This table shows the balance in an account if monthly deposits of $10 were compounded monthly. **How much interest is earned after the first 10 years at 6 percent?**

FREE ENTERPRISE ACTIVITY

Organize students into four groups to undertake further study of bonds. Ask one group to interview the school superintendent or another administrator to learn about bonds for schools. The second group could interview a finance official in city, county, or state government to ask about municipal bonds. The third group could interview the controller or president of a local corporation to find out about corporate bonds. The fourth group might interview a member of Congress or a staff employee of a member of Congress to learn about U.S. Treasury bonds. Have each group present its interview results to the class. Then have students discuss the similarities and differences among the various bonds.

BLOCK SCHEDULING

Bond Components

A bond has three main components: the **coupon**, or the stated interest on the debt; the **maturity**, or the life of the bond; and the **par value**–the principal or the total amount initially borrowed that must be repaid to the lender at maturity.

Suppose, for example, a corporation sells a 6 percent, 20-year, $1,000 par value bond that pays interest semiannually. The coupon payment to the holder is $30 semiannually (.06 times $1,000, divided by 2). When the bond reaches maturity after 20 years, the company retires the debt by paying the holder the par value of $1,000.

Bond Prices

The investor views the bond as a financial asset that will pay $30 twice a year for 20 years, plus a final par value payment of $1,000. Investors can offer $950, $1,000, $1,100, or any other amount for this future payment stream. Investors consider changes in future interest rates, the risk that the company will default, and other factors before they decide what to offer. Supply and demand will then establish the final price of the bonds.

Bond Yields

In order to compare bonds, investors usually compute the bond's **current yield,** the annual interest divided by the purchase price. If an investor paid $950 for the bond described above, the current yield would be $60 divided by $950, or 6.32 percent. If the investor paid $1,100 for the bond, the current yield would be $60 divided by $1,100, or 5.45 percent. Although it may appear as if the issuer fixes the return on a bond when the bond is first issued, the interest received and the price paid determine the actual yield on the bond.

Because the credit-worthiness, or financial health, of corporations and governments differ, all 6 percent, 20-year, $1,000 bonds will not cost the same. Bonds are not insured, and there are no guarantees that the issuer will be around in 20 years to redeem the bond. Therefore, investors will pay more for bonds issued by an agency with an impeccable credit rating. Investors will pay less for a similar bond if it is issued by a corporation with a low credit rating.

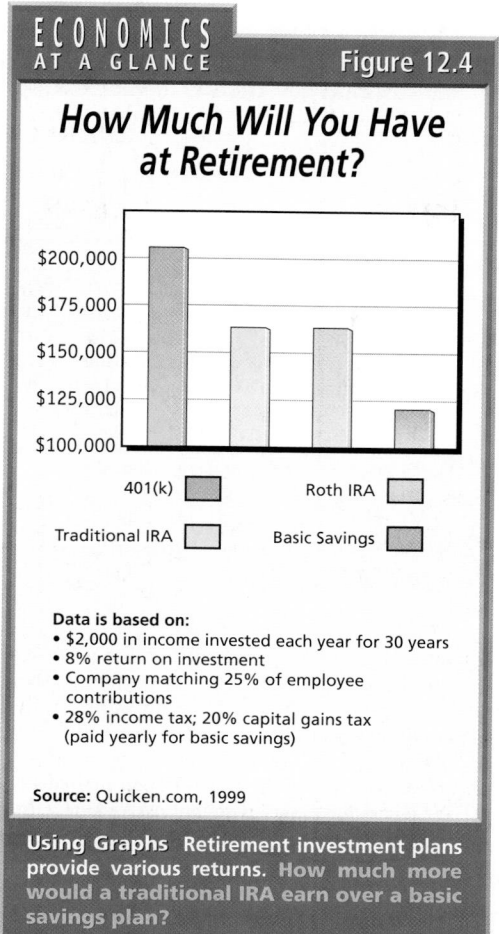

How Much Will You Have at Retirement?

- 401(k)
- Traditional IRA
- Roth IRA
- Basic Savings

Data is based on:
- $2,000 in income invested each year for 30 years
- 8% return on investment
- Company matching 25% of employee contributions
- 28% income tax; 20% capital gains tax (paid yearly for basic savings)

Source: Quicken.com, 1999

Using Graphs Retirement investment plans provide various returns. How much more would a traditional IRA earn over a basic savings plan?

Bond Ratings

 Fortunately, investors have a way to check the quality of bonds. Two major corporations, Standard & Poor's and Moody's, publish bond ratings. They rate bonds on a number of factors, including the basic financial health of the issuer, the ability to make the future coupon and principal payments, and the issuer's past credit history.

The bond ratings, shown in **Figure 12.5,** use letters scaled from AAA, which represents the highest investment grade, to D, which generally stands for

CHAPTER 12: FINANCIAL MARKETS **321**

ECONOMICS AT A GLANCE

Answer: *approximately $42,000*

CYBERNOMICS

Investments on the Web
People can check the value of their mutual funds online. Most mutual funds or mutual fund families have Web sites that offer the public general information about their funds. An investor in the mutual fund can use a password at the Web site to check the value of his or her investment in the fund.

INTERACTIVE ECONOMICS!

CD-ROM

PERSONAL FINANCE Have students click on "Basic Investment Considerations" in Lesson 10. **Ask:** What four things should an investor consider before purchasing financial assets? *(the risk-return relationship, the investor's personal investment goals, the importance of investing consistently, and the avoidance of complexity)*

Also available in disk format.

CRITICAL THINKING

Making Comparisons Have students work in groups of three or four to select three investment options and compare their levels of safety and returns. Students can develop visual symbols and make presentations to compare the information. They may consider any of the following: government or corporate bonds, equities, certificates of deposit, and treasury bills. Discuss group findings in class.   **BLOCK SCHEDULING**

CURRICULUM CONNECTION

Family and Consumer Science
The U.S. government created 401(k) plans in 1978. The plan gets its name from the section of the Internal Revenue Code that created it. One advantage of the plan is that it is portable—employees can change jobs and keep their 401(k) plans. Another advantage is that employees can decide how to invest the money in the plan. Before 401(k) plans became available, many employees had either pension plans or profit-sharing plans invested by their employers. If an employee left the job or was fired, rights to pensions or profit-sharing sometimes ceased.

ECONOMICS
AT A GLANCE

Figure 12.5

Bond Classifications

Standard & Poor's		Moody's	
Highest Investment Grade	AAA	Aaa	Best Quality
High Grade	AA	Aa	High Quality
Upper Medium Grade	A	A	Upper Medium Grade
Medium Grade	BBB	Baa	Medium Grade
Lower Medium Grade	BB	Ba	Possesses Speculative Elements
Speculative	B	B	Generally Not Desirable
Vulnerable to Default	CCC	Caa	Poor, Possibly in Default
Subordinated to Other Debt Rated CCC	CC	Ca	Highly Speculative, Often in Default
Subordinated to CC Debt	C	C	Income Bonds Not Paying Income
Bond in Default	D	D	Interest and Principal Payments in Default

Sources: Standard & Poor's Corporation, Moody's

Using Tables Standard & Poor's Corporation and Moody's publish bond ratings. Junk bonds, those with ratings of BB or Ba and lower, are generally the riskiest types of bonds. **How do bond ratings affect the price of bonds?**

default. If a bond is in default, the issuer has not kept up with the interest or the par value payments. These ratings are widely publicized, and investors can find the rating of any bond they plan to purchase.

Bonds with high ratings sell at higher prices than do bonds with lower ratings. A 6 percent, 20-year, $1,000 par value bond with an AAA-grade rating may sell for $1,100 and have a current yield of 5.45 percent. Another 6 percent, 20-year, $1,000 par value bond issued by a different company may have a BBB rating, and may therefore only sell for $950 because of the higher risk. The second bond, however, has a higher current yield of 6.32 percent. This points out the basic nature of the risk-return relationship—riskier investments require higher returns to offset the risk.

Financial Assets and Their Characteristics

 The modern investor has a wide range of financial assets from which to choose. These include certificates of deposit, bonds, treasury notes and bills, and individual retirement accounts. They vary in cost, maturity, and risk.

Certificates of Deposit

Certificates of deposit (CDs) are one of the most common forms of investments available. Many people think of them as just another type of account with a depository institution, but they are really loans investors make to financial institutions. Because banks and others count on the use of these funds for a certain time period, they usually impose penalties when people try to cash in their CDs early.

CDs are attractive to small investors because they can cost as little as $100. Investors can also select the length of maturity, giving them an opportunity to tailor the expiration date to future expenditures such as college tuition, a vacation, or some other expense.

Finally, CDs issued by commercial banks, savings banks, and savings associations are included in the $100,000 FDIC insurance limit. The National Credit Union Association insures most CDs issued by credit unions.

Corporate Bonds

Corporate bonds are an important source of corporate funds. Some individual corporate bonds have par values as low as $1,000, but par values of

EXTENDING THE CONTENT

Money Market Mutual Funds Money market mutual funds are in competition with commercial banks and savings institutions for the small investor. Therefore, they offer services similar to those provided by their competitors—checkbooks, for example. However, there often is a minimum amount for each check, usually about $500.

$10,000 are more common. The actual prices of the bonds are usually different from the par values because supply and demand for the bonds determine the price.

Investors usually decide on the highest level of risk they are willing to accept, and then they try to find a bond that has the best current yield. "Junk" bonds—exceptionally risky bonds with a Standard & Poor's rating of BB or lower, or a Moody's rating of Ba or lower—carry a high rate of return as compensation for the possibility of default.

Investors usually purchase corporate bonds as long-term investments, but they can also be liquidated, or quickly sold, if the investor needs cash for other purposes. The Internal Revenue Service considers the interest, or coupon, payments on corporate bonds as taxable income, a fact investors must consider when they invest in bonds.

Municipal Bonds

Municipal bonds (or "munis") are bonds issued by state and local governments. States issue bonds to finance highways, state buildings, and some public works. Cities issue bonds to finance baseball parks and football stadiums or to finance libraries, parks, and other civic improvements.

Municipal bonds are attractive investments for several reasons. First, they are generally regarded as safe because state and local governments do not go out of business. Because governments have the power to tax, it is generally presumed that they will be able to pay interest and principal in the future.

More importantly, municipal bonds are generally **tax-exempt,** meaning that the federal government does not tax the interest paid to investors. In some cases, the states issuing the bonds also exempt the interest payments from state taxes, which makes them very attractive to investors. The tax-exempt feature also allows the governmental agencies to pay a lower rate of interest on the bonds, thereby lowering their cost of borrowing.

Government Savings Bonds

The federal government generates financial assets when it sells savings bonds. **Savings bonds** are low-denomination, nontransferable bonds

THE GLOBAL ECONOMY

INVESTING GLOBALLY

Is it risky to invest in markets around the world? Some economists argue that investing a portion of your money in overseas markets is safe and profitable.

Many people think that there are too many uncertainties associated with investing in overseas markets. Governments can be unstable and economic information about the region may be sketchy. Countries can devalue their currencies or maintain poor accounting standards.

Economists, however, believe that investing a portion of one's money in Latin American, Asian, or European companies is a wise strategy, and many

mutual funds today exist for just that purpose. Even though the United States market has been prosperous, shifting some assets overseas can serve as a safety net if the United States market plunges. Stock markets around the world generally do not experience simultaneous highs and lows, so maintaining a level of profit making can be steady. Many overseas companies are restructuring to become more efficient, creating healthy investment opportunities for American investors.

Critical Thinking

1. **Analyzing Information** What are the arguments against investing in overseas markets?
2. **Making Generalizations** Why is it important to diversify investments throughout different regions rather than in investing in a single region?

CHAPTER 12: FINANCIAL MARKETS **323**

 Math Practice

CD Yields The interest rate on certificates of deposit (CDs) is usually expressed in two ways— the actual interest rate and the annual percentage yield. The interest rate differs among banks and at different times. Ask students to figure out the annual yield on $500 for a CD at an annual yield of 3.92 percent and a CD at an annual yield of 4.86 percent. *($19.60; $24.30)*

THE GLOBAL ECONOMY

Investing Globally In 1998, the total U.S. holding of foreign stocks was $1,407.1 billion. More than half the holdings ($959.8 billion) were invested in Western Europe.

Answers:
1. *Governments can be unstable; lack of economic information; countries can devalue their currencies or maintain poor accounting standards.*
2. *Stock markets around the world do not generally experience simultaneous highs and lows, so by diversifying investments, an investor doesn't stand to lose too much in any one market.*

INTERDISCIPLINARY CONNECTIONS ACTIVITY

Daily Life Many newspapers post interest rates for both corporate and government bonds. Televised financial shows also offer the interest rates daily. Ask students to select three bonds or types of bonds and follow their interest rates for a week. Students may make charts, graphs, or tables to present their findings.

L3 Advertising

Call on volunteers to identify and explain the factors that people should consider when investing. Note their responses on the board. Then organize students into small groups and ask them to develop a public-service advertising campaign that encourages sensible investment practices. Groups might create a print advertisement, a tape of a radio commercial, or storyboards for a television campaign. Have groups present their campaign ideas to the class.

CURRICULUM CONNECTION

History After the attack on Pearl Harbor, the government introduced savings bonds called war bonds to increase public funding for the war effort. Radio shows sponsored by the Treasury promoted the bonds. Department stores set up window displays with war bond themes and encouraged customers to accept war stamps in place of change. Even movie stars urged the public to buy more bonds.

issued by the United States government, usually through payroll-savings plans.

These bonds are usually available in denominations ranging from $50 to $10,000, and they are purchased at a discount from their redemption amount. For example, a new $50 savings bond may be obtained today for $25, but it could take up to 18 years before it could be redeemed for the full $50, depending on the interest rate. The government pays interest on these bonds, but it builds the interest into the redemption price rather than sending checks to millions of investors on a regular basis.

Savings bonds are attractive because they are easy to obtain and there is virtually no risk of default. They cannot be sold to someone else if the investor needs cash, but they can be redeemed early, with some loss of interest, if the investor must raise cash for other purposes. Most investors tend to hold long-term savings bonds, treating them as a form of automatic savings.

Careers

Stockbroker

Do you enjoy scouting financial trends and doing research? Then a career as a stockbroker might be the right one for you.

The Work

The stockbroker's duties include handling individual investment accounts and advising customers on the purchase or sale of securities. They must supply the latest price quotations on stocks and keep informed about the financial activities of corporations issuing stock. The ability to act quickly is helpful in building and keeping a strong customer base.

Qualifications

Stockbrokers are college graduates with sales ability and good communication skills. Many hold degrees in business administration, with a specialization in finance.

324 UNIT 3 MACROECONOMICS: INSTITUTIONS

Treasury Notes and Bonds

When the federal government borrows funds for periods longer than one year, it issues Treasury notes and bonds. **Treasury notes** are United States government obligations with maturities of two to 10 years, while **Treasury bonds** have maturities ranging from more than 10 to as many as 30 years. The only collateral that secures both is the faith and credit of the United States government.

Treasury notes and bonds come in denominations of $5,000 for maturities of two to three years, and denominations of $1,000 for maturities longer than four years. The government also keeps computerized records of its debt holders so that it can make periodic interest payments to those individuals.

Although these financial assets have no collateral or backing, they are popular because they are generally regarded as the safest of all financial assets. Due to the trade-off between risk and return, however, these assets also have the lowest returns of all financial assets.

Treasury Bills

Federal government borrowing generates other financial assets known as **Treasury bills.** A Treasury bill, also known as a T-bill, is a short-term obligation with a maturity of 13, 26, or 52 weeks and a minimum denomination of $10,000.

T-bills do not pay interest directly, but instead are sold on a discount basis, much like government savings bonds. For example, an investor may pay the auction price of $9,300 for a 52-week bill that matures at $10,000. The $700 difference between the amount paid and the amount received is the investor's return. The investor is receiving $700 on a $9,300 investment, for a return of $700 divided by $9,300, or 7.5 percent.

Individual Retirement Accounts

Individual Retirement Accounts (IRAs) are long-term, tax-sheltered time deposits that an employee can set up as part of a retirement plan. If the worker's spouse does not work outside the home, up to $2,000 per year can be deposited in a separate account for each spouse.

FREE ENTERPRISE ACTIVITY

Have students select a goal, such as saving for a college education or saving to buy a car. Then ask them to select one of the financial assets described in Section 2 as the best choice to reach their goal. Instruct students to write an essay explaining why they chose that asset, detailing the risk and return. Call on volunteers to read their essays to the class.

Treasury Bonds A Treasury bond refers to a Treasury security with a maturity greater than 10 years. The only difference between a Treasury bond and a Treasury note is the longer maturity of the bond. Coupon interest on a Treasury bond is paid semiannually. Treasury bond issuance was recently increased from two auctions per year to three, settling on the 15th of February, August, and November. The 30-year bond is considered the "benchmark" bond in determining interest rate trends.

The worker deducts this deposit from his or her taxable income at the end of the year, thereby sheltering the $2,000 from income taxes. Taxes on the interest and the principal will eventually have to be paid, but it gives the worker an incentive to save today, postponing the taxes until the worker is retired and in a lower tax bracket. IRAs are not transferable, and penalties exist if they are liquidated early.

Figure 12.4 on page 321 also shows a **Roth IRA**–an IRA whose contributions are made after taxes so that no taxes are taken out at maturity. This type of IRA may work well for someone who plans to retire in a high tax bracket.

Markets for Financial Assets

Investors often refer to markets according to the characteristics of the financial assets traded in them. These markets are not really separate entities, and many overlap to a considerable degree.

Capital Markets

When investors speak of the **capital market,** they mean a market where money is loaned for more than one year. Long-term CDs and corporate and government bonds that take more than a year to mature belong in this category. Capital market assets are shown in the right-hand column of **Figure 12.6.**

Money Markets

When investors speak of the **money market,** they mean a market where money is loaned for periods of less than one year. The financial assets that belong to the money market are shown in the left-hand column of **Figure 12.6.** Note that a person who owns a CD with a maturity of one year or less is involved in the money market. If the CD has a maturity of more than one year, the person is involved in the capital market as a supplier of funds.

Money market mutual funds are issued by stockbrokers and other institutions. These firms pool the deposits by their customers to purchase stocks or bonds. Mutual funds usually pay slightly higher interest rates than banks.

ECONOMICS AT A GLANCE

Figure 12.6

Financial Assets and Their Markets

	Money Market (less than 1 year)	Capital Market (more than 1 year)
Primary Market	Money market mutual funds Small CDs	Government savings bonds IRAs Money market mutual funds Small CDs
Secondary Market	Jumbo CDs Treasury bills	Corporate bonds International bonds Jumbo CDs Municipal bonds Treasury bonds Treasury notes

Using Charts If the length of maturity is important, the market is sometimes called a money or capital market. If the ability to sell the asset to someone other than the original issuer is important, the market may be described as being a primary or secondary market. **Why do some financial assets, like CDs, appear in more than one market?**

CHAPTER 12: FINANCIAL MARKETS **325**

---

③ ASSESS

Assign Section 2 Assessment as homework or as an in-class activity.

💾 Have students use **Interactive Tutor Self-Assessment Software** to review Section 2.

Section Quiz 12-2

L2 Identifying Alternatives

Have students identify responsible investment purchases, for both individuals and businesses. What criteria would they use in making their decision?

EXTENDING THE CONTENT

Savings Bonds U.S. government savings bonds are often given as gifts, especially EE bonds and I bonds. They can be bought and cashed in at banks and credit unions. A Social Security number is required to own bonds. The U.S. Treasury prints certificates for savings bonds. Many people also buy and keep savings bonds as a means of saving for an education. To find out more about savings bonds, log on to the U.S. Treasury Department's Web site at www.treas.gov

Reteach

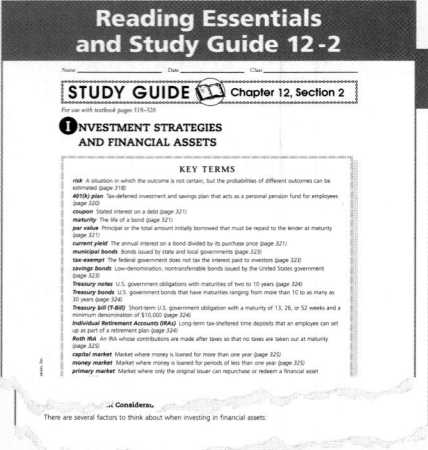

Reading Essentials and Study Guide 12-2

Enrich

Invite representatives of a bank and a brokerage firm to visit with the class and discuss the advantages and disadvantages of different types of financial assets.

④ CLOSE

Lead a discussion by asking: If you could give only one piece of advice on investing, what would it be?

Primary Markets

Another way to view financial markets is to focus on the liquidity of a newly created financial asset. One market for financial assets is the **primary market,** a market where only the original issuer can repurchase or redeem a financial asset. Government savings bonds and IRAs are in this market because they are both nontransferable. Small CDs are in the primary market because investors tend to cash them in early, rather than try to sell them to someone else, if they need cash.

Secondary Markets

If a financial asset can be sold to someone other than the original issuer it becomes part of the secondary market. The **secondary market** is a market in which existing financial assets can be resold to new owners.

The major significance of the secondary market is the liquidity it provides to investors. If a strong secondary market exists for a financial asset, investors know that, other than the fees paid to handle the transaction, the assets can be liquidated fairly quickly and without penalty.

Investment

"THE BAD NEWS IS OUR FUND LOST MILLIONS. THE GOOD NEWS IS NONE OF IT WAS OUR OWN MONEY."

Markets for Financial Assets Investing always includes some risk. *What is the difference between a capital market and a money market?*

Section 2 Assessment

Checking for Understanding
1. **Main Idea** What rules do many investors follow in regard to investment goals?
2. **Key Terms** Define risk, 401(k) plan, coupon, maturity, par value, current yield, municipal bond, tax-exempt, savings bond, Treasury note, Treasury bond, Treasury bill, Individual Retirement Account (IRA), Roth IRA, capital market, money market, primary market, secondary market.
3. **List** four important investment considerations.
4. **Identify** the three main characteristics of bonds.
5. **Describe** the characteristics of major financial assets.

6. **Differentiate** between the four markets of financial assets.

Applying Economic Concepts
7. **Risk-Return Relationship** If you had money to invest, in which financial asset(s), if any, would you choose to invest? Explain how you arrived at your answer.

Critical Thinking

8. **Making Generalizations** Review the four basic investment considerations. Which do you think is most important? Explain your answer.

 Practice and **assess** key social studies skills with the *Glencoe Skillbuilder Interactive Workbook, Level 2.*

Section 2 Assessment Answers

1. invest wisely and analyze the risk and return
2. All vocabulary terms are defined in the text.
3. risk and return, personal investment goals, consistency, simplicity
4. coupon, maturity, par value
5. Example: CDs cost as little as $100 and are a safe investment. Investors select the length of maturity. See pp. 322–324 for the characteristics of other assets.

6. A capital market grants longer-term loans than does a money market. In a primary market, only the original issuer can redeem a financial asset. In a secondary market, previously issued securities are sold.
7. Answers should reflect an understanding of all investment considerations.
8. Answers will vary. Students should provide valid reasons to support their answer.

BusinessWeek

SEPTEMBER 17, 2001 ——— Newsclip

When terrorists attacked the United States on September, 11, 2001, the U.S. financial markets were forced to close for four days. When the markets reopened, the trading system didn't buckle, and the losses could have been worse.

Members of New York's uniformed services open the New York Stock Exchange on September 17, 2001.

Dow Posts Record Point Loss

Nearly a week after terrorists attacked the heart of the world's financial community in lower Manhattan, U.S. stock markets reopened for business Sept. 17 and closed substantially lower, as expected. The blue-chip Dow Jones industrial average, which fell 7%, posted its biggest one-day point loss ever – 685 points.

The selling came despite an unprecedented move by the Federal Reserve to cut short-term interest rates by half a percentage point before the opening bell. Many U.S. companies also tried to stem the losses by announcing massive stock repurchase plans. But while a patriotic rally didn't materialize, many observers noted there was no panic selling, trading systems worked, and losses could have been much steeper. . . .

. . .[M]arket observers would not characterize Monday's selling as precursors to a global recession, as some on Wall Street fear. While stocks and indexes recorded fresh lows into the final hour of regular trading, the markets overall stabilized after expected widespread selling early in the session. Trading was active on record volume but for the most part orderly. . . .

Among the hardest hit stocks were shares of U.S. airlines, which plunged amid worries a sharp decline in air travel will mean layoffs, depressed earnings, perhaps even bankruptcy in some cases unless the feds step in with a bailout, which is expected. Shares of AMR Corp., the holding company of American Airlines, lost more than 39%. UAL Corp. that includes United Air Lines shed more than 43%. Boeing Co. was down more than 17%.

–Reprinted from September 17, 2001 issue of *Business Week* (online), by special permission, copyright © 2001 by The McGraw-Hill Companies, Inc.

Examining the Newsclip

1. **Analyzing Information** Why do you think companies were buying back their own stocks?

2. **Understanding Cause and Effect** Why were the airlines stocks the hardest hit when the market reopened?

TEACH

Ask: Why do you think so many people were anxious to sell off their stock when the market reopened?

Discuss with students the reasons for major drops in the stock market. Often, political instability can lead to sell-offs. Explain that the reason for this is that an uncertain political situation creates risk for investors. After a crisis, it is impossible to predict the future performance of certain companies, and thus impossible to predict the value of that company's stock. Uncertainty about a company's performance means a possible risk to investors. The greater the crisis, the more investors opt to sell their stocks and avoid the risk. Ask students to think of other examples of situations that create risk for investors.

Refer to ***Business Week Focus on the New Economy*** in the TCR for additional unit-based articles.

Answers to Examining the Newsclip

1. Many companies were repurchasing their own stocks as a way to show support for the company and the U.S. economy when the markets finally reopened. In addition, buying back stock provides a sort of reassuring base price for companies in a possible sell-off, and helps to raise stock price by reducing the number of shares available to the public.

2. After the events of September 11, it was clear there would be a decline in the airline and travel industries. Many airlines were already battling sinking stock prices, and the massive loss of business resulting from the terrorist attacks would cause many companies to lay off workers and some to shut down completely.

1 FOCUS

Section Overview
This section explains the stock exchanges and futures markets.

BELLRINGER
Motivational Activity

Project **transparency** and have students answer questions.

 Available as blackline master.

Daily Focus Transparency 43

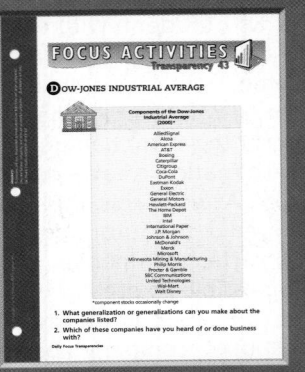

Study Guide

Reading Strategy
Have students create the graphic organizer.
Answers to Graphic: *New York Stock Exchange, American Stock Exchange, regional stock exchanges, global stock exchanges*

Preteaching Vocabulary
Use the Vocabulary Puzzle-Maker to create crossword and word-search puzzles.

Investing in Equities, Futures, and Options

Study Guide

Main Idea
Equities, or stocks, represent ownership of a corporation.

Reading Strategy
Graphic Organizer
As you read the section, list three different organized stock exchanges.

Stock exchanges

Key Terms
equities, Efficient Market Hypothesis (EMH), portfolio diversification, stockbroker, securities exchange, seat, over-the-counter market (OTC), Dow-Jones Industrial Average (DJIA), Standard & Poor's 500 (S&P 500), bull market, bear market, spot market, futures contract, futures market, option, call option, put option, options market

Objectives
After studying this section, you will be able to:
1. **Describe** the major stock exchanges.
2. **Explain** how stock market performance is measured.

Applying Economic Concepts
Futures Exchanges Have you ever negotiated to receive your allowance early, or asked to be paid right away for a service to be completed later? Read to find out how this corresponds to a futures market.

Cover Story

Rough Ride in Market after Attacks

We can all breathe easier that the stock market didn't crash when trading resumed on Sept. 17....

...The markets are likely in for a week of volatile trading after being shut down for the longest stretch since the Great Depression. For most people the smartest strategy will be to stay on the sidelines until emotions cool....

The terrorist attack that badly damaged the Pentagon and leveled the World Trade Center...will have a profound short-term effect on the markets. Virtually every company's results will feel the tragedy's impact in some way, says Chuck Hill, director of research at First Call.

Trader proclaims reopening of NYSE

—*BusinessWeek* (online), September 18, 2001

328

In addition to financial assets, investors may buy **equities.** These are stocks that represent ownership shares in corporations. The markets for equities are reasonably competitive because there are a large number of buyers and sellers, and investors possess reasonably good information.

Even so, investor confidence is important for market stability. After the attack on the World Trade Towers, for example, investor uncertainty caused a temporary 14 percent decline in overall stock prices.

Market Efficiency

Many things influence the price of equities. Some companies may have relatively few outstanding shares to be traded, while others have a large number. Some companies are profitable; others are not. Expectations are especially important. For example, two companies may be equal in all respects, but one may have far better prospects for growth.

As a result, stock prices can vary considerably from one company to the next. The difficulty

---

RESOURCE MANAGER

Reproducible Masters
- Reproducible Lesson Plan 12-3
- Daily Lecture Notes 12-3
- Guided Reading Activity 12-3
- Reading Essentials and Study Guide 12-3
- Section Quiz 12-3

Transparencies
- Daily Focus Transparency 43

Multimedia
- Vocabulary PuzzleMaker CD-ROM
- Interactive Economics!
- Interactive Tutor Self-Assessment Software
- ExamView® Pro Testmaker
- Presentation Plus!

Equities

A. BACALL

"We're expecting stocks to rally but we don't know which ones and when."

Price Factors Equities entitle the buyer to a certain part of the future profits and assets of the corporation selling the stock. *What factors influence the price of equities?*

facing the investor, then, is to decide which to buy—and which to avoid. Fortunately, the answer is simpler than you might imagine.

The **Efficient Market Hypothesis (EMH)**—the argument that stocks are always priced about right and that bargains are hard to find because they are followed closely by so many investors—is often used to help explain the pricing of equities. A leading expert on the topic explains how this might happen:

Essentially, the EMH states that there are some 100,000 or so full-time, highly trained, professional analysts and traders operating in the market and following some 3,000 major stocks. If each analyst followed only 30 stocks, there would still be 1,000 analysts following each stock. Further, these analysts work for organizations such as Merrill Lynch and Prudential Insurance, which have billions of dollars available with which to take advantage of bargains. As new information about a stock becomes available, these 1,000 analysts all receive and evaluate it at approximately the same time, so the price of the stock adjusts almost immediately to reflect new developments.

—from Eugene F. Brigham's *Fundamentals of Financial Management*

One implication for the investor is that if all stocks are priced about right, it does not matter which ones you purchase. You might be lucky and pick a stock about to go up, or you might get unlucky and pick a stock about to go down. Because of this, **portfolio diversification**—the practice of holding a large number of different stocks so that increases in some can offset unexpected declines in others—is a popular strategy.

There are different ways to purchase equities. Opening an Internet account with a discount brokerage firm is one means. The investor can then buy, sell, and monitor his or her stock portfolio from a personal computer. Or, the investor may enlist the assistance of a **stockbroker**—a person who buys or sells equities for clients. The broker arranges to have the stocks purchased at a stock exchange, or supplies the securities from an inventory, or buys them from some other broker.

Organized Stock Exchanges

A number of organized **securities exchanges** exist—places where buyers and sellers meet to trade securities. An organized exchange gets its name from the way it conducts business. Members pay a fee to join, and trades can only take place on the floor of the exchange.

The New York Stock Exchange

The oldest, largest, and most prestigious of the organized stock exchanges in the United States is the New York Stock Exchange (NYSE), located on Wall Street in New York City. This exchange, like most other organized exchanges, has certain rules for both its members and the corporations listed on the exchange.

ECONOMICS Online

Student Web Activity Visit the *Economics: Principles and Practices* Web site at epp.glencoe.com and click on *Chapter 12—Student Web Activities* for an activity on the New York Stock Exchange.

CHAPTER 12: FINANCIAL MARKETS **329**

② TEACH

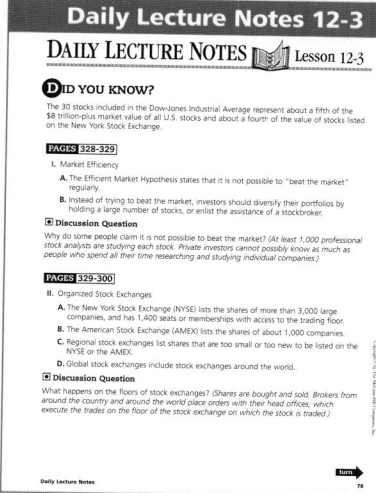

Daily Lecture Notes 12-3

DAILY LECTURE NOTES Lesson 12-3

① DID YOU KNOW?
The 30 stocks included in the Dow-Jones Industrial Average represent about a fifth of the $8 trillion-plus market value of all U.S. stocks and about a fourth of the value of stocks listed on the New York Stock Exchange.

PAGES 328-329
I. Market Efficiency
  A. The Efficient Market Hypothesis states that it is not possible to "beat the market" regularly.
  B. Instead of trying to beat the market, investors should diversify their portfolios by holding a large number of stocks, or enlist the assistance of a stockbroker.

☑ Discussion Question
Why do some people claim it is not possible to beat the market? *(At least 1,000 professional stock analysts are studying each stock. Private investors cannot possibly know as much as people who spend all their time researching and studying individual companies.)*

PAGES 329-300
II. Organized Stock Exchanges
  A. The New York Stock Exchange (NYSE) lists the shares of more than 3,000 large companies, and has 1,400 seats or memberships with access to the trading floor.
  B. The American Stock Exchange (AMEX) lists the shares of about 1,000 companies.
  C. Regional stock exchanges list shares that are too small or too new to be listed on the NYSE or the AMEX.
  D. Global stock exchanges include stock exchanges around the world.

☑ Discussion Question
What happens on the floors of stock exchanges? *(Shares are bought and sold. Brokers from around the country and around the world place orders with their head offices, which execute the trades on the floor of the stock exchange on which the stock is traded.)*

Daily Lecture Notes   76

Visual Instruction

Answer to Caption:
number of outstanding shares to be traded; company profitability; expectations

ECONOMICS Online

Objectives, goals, and answers to the student activity can be found in the **Web Activity Lesson Plan** feature at epp.glencoe.com

---

MEETING SPECIAL NEEDS ACTIVITY

Learning Style: Interpersonal Have students work in small groups to select three companies that produce products or services used by the students. Groups should use the Internet or newspapers to find the current stock price of those companies as well as the high and low for the year. Have each group present its three companies to the class. Ask the class as a whole to identify the two companies that would have been the best investments for the year. **BLOCK SCHEDULING**

Refer to *Inclusion for the Social Studies Classroom Strategies and Activities* in the TCR.

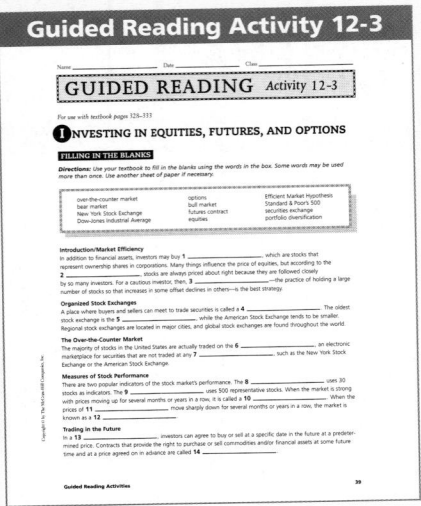

ECONOMICS
AT A GLANCE

Answer: *Ford Motor*

L1 Stock Listings

Before the lesson, make copies of a section of the NYSE listing and select about 12 companies in the listing. Distribute copies of the listing to the class. Announce each company in turn and call on a volunteer to provide an explanation of that company's listing. Direct students to follow one of the 12 companies. Select students to share the results with the class.

ECONOMICS
AT A GLANCE
Figure 12.7

The New York Stock Exchange

YTD % CHG	52 Weeks HI	52 Weeks LO	STOCK(SYM)	DIV	YLD %	PE	VOL 100S	LAST	NET CHG
+28.8	19.35	8.50	ExtndStayAm **ESA**		...	21	1183	16.55	-4.40
+1.0	95.44	75.13	ExxonMobile **XOM**	1.76	2	16	61224	87.80	-0.30
-0.8	49.85	33.25	FedExCp **FDX**		...	16	5398	39.64	-0.08
+6.6	49.51	21.69	FordMotor **F**	1.20	4.8	21	53049	24.99	+0.16

Reading the Financial Page Figure 12.7 shows examples of stocks traded on the New York Stock Exchange. The price of a share of stock generally goes up and down throughout the day as the conditions of supply and demand change. At the end of the business day, each stock has a closing price. **Of the stocks shown, which made the biggest gain on this particular day?**

The NYSE has about 1,400 **seats,** or memberships, that allow access to the trading floor. Large brokerage companies, such as Merrill Lynch, may own as many as 20 seats at any given time. The members may pay several million dollars for each seat. Members have the right to elect their own directors and vote on the rules and regulations that govern the exchange.

The NYSE lists stocks from more than 3,000 companies. The firms must meet requirements related to profitability and size, which virtually guarantee that the companies will be among the largest, most profitable publicly held companies. **Figure 12.7** shows how prices are listed on the NYSE.

During the last 12 months, Exxon sold for as much as $95.44 and as little as $75.13 a share. Its annual dividend (Div) is $1.76, which is paid in four equal installments. The yield (Yld) is the dividend divided by the closing price. The PE, or price-earnings ratio, is a stock's price divided by annual earnings of each share of common stock outstanding. Exxon closed at $.30 lower than the day before, as indicated by the Net Change (Net Chg) column.

The American Stock Exchange

Another prestigious national exchange is the American Stock Exchange (AMEX), which is also located in New York City. It has approximately 1,000 listed stocks.

For many years, the AMEX was the second largest organized exchange in the country behind the NYSE. Its growth then slowed, and some of the regional exchanges overtook the AMEX. Overall, the companies represented on the AMEX tend to be smaller and more speculative than those listed on the NYSE.

Regional Stock Exchanges

The regional exchanges include the Chicago, Pacific, Philadelphia, Boston, and Memphis exchanges, along with some smaller exchanges in other cities. Many of these exchanges originally listed corporations that were either too small or too new to be listed on the NYSE or the AMEX. Today, however, many stocks are listed on both the NYSE and a regional exchange. The regional stock exchanges also meet the needs of the smaller and middle-sized corporations in their regions.

Global Stock Exchanges

Stock exchanges can be found throughout the world. Exchanges operate in such cities as Sydney, Tokyo, Hong Kong, Singapore, Johannesburg, and Frankfurt. Developments in computer technology and electronic trading have linked these markets so that most major stocks can be traded around the clock, somewhere in the world.

FREE ENTERPRISE ACTIVITY

Have students select a major corporation and investigate the goods or services it produces, how many employees it has, where it is located, and what its prospects are for future growth. Instruct students to consult *Standard and Poor's, Moody's,* or *Value Line,* or contact a stockbroker for information. After students have studied the corporation and followed the stock, have them write a letter to a friend describing the stock from the viewpoint of a prospective investor interested in buying shares of the corporation. Call on students to read their letters to the class.

The Over-the-Counter Market

Despite the importance of the organized exchanges, the majority of stocks in the United States are not traded on exchanges. Instead, they are traded on the **over-the-counter market (OTC)**—an electronic marketplace for securities that are not traded on an organized exchange.

Securities traded over the counter are listed in a sophisticated computer network called the National Market System (NMS). The members of the OTC market belong to the National Association of Securities Dealers (NASD). The National Association of Securities Dealers Automated Quotation (NASDAQ), is the listing that provides information on stocks that this group trades. The main difference between a NASDAQ listing and the NYSE is that few OTC stocks pay dividends, mostly because they are issued by new firms.

The organized exchanges and the OTC market may differ, but this means little to investors. An investor who opens an Internet account with a brokerage firm may buy and sell stocks in both markets. When the investor places an order over the Internet to buy shares, the broker forwards the order to the exchange where the stock is traded and the purchase is made there—whether it be on the NYSE, AMEX, or OTC.

STANDARD & POOR'S

Figure 12.8

Tracking Stocks With the DJIA and the S&P 500

— DJIA (right axis)
— S&P 500 (left axis)

1994–1999: The strongest bull market of the century

October 1987: The worst bear market in 50 years

S&P 500 1941-43 = 100 (left axis: 300, 600, 900, 1,200, 1,500)

Dow-Jones Industrial Average (right axis: 0, 1,000, 2,000, 3,000, 4,000, 5,000, 6,000, 7,000, 8,000, 9,000, 10,000, 11,000, 12,000)

(x-axis: 1965, 1970, 1975, 1980, 1985, 1990, 1995, 2000)

Using Graphs The Dow-Jones Industrial Average and Standard & Poor's 500 are two indices used to track stock prices. **When did the DJIA first surpass 10,000?**

ECONOMICS Online

Visit epp.glencoe.com and click on *Textbook Updates—Chapter 12* for an update of the data.

STANDARD & POOR'S

Answer: *1999*

THE GLOBAL ECONOMY

Foreign Stocks An increasing number of foreign corporations are listing their stock on American stock exchanges. Today, for example, hundreds of major foreign corporations are listed on the New York Stock Exchange. These corporations include Daimler-Benz AG, the German manufacturer of the Mercedes-Benz, Pan American Beverages of Panama, and Grupo Tribasa SA, a Mexican construction company.

INTERACTIVE ECONOMICS!

CD-ROM

PERSONAL FINANCE Have students click on "Stocks, Stock Markets, and Mutual Funds" in Lesson 10. After students read the tutorial, have them draw a diagram explaining the process of buying and selling stocks. Ask students to share their diagrams with the class.

Also available in disk format.

CRITICAL THINKING

Synthesizing Information Have students use the information in this section to develop their own personal investment plans. The plan should be diversified. It need not name specific stocks or bonds, but it should indicate kinds of investment tools and discuss and compare the criteria students would use when judging investment opportunities. Each student should also consider his or her own risk/reward level of comfort. Have students explain their plans in essays.

L3 Research

Ask students to select one of the following—NYSE, AMEX, a regional stock exchange, or a global stock exchange—and conduct library research about their selected topic. Students should consider such items as the size of the exchange, its location, the kind of corporations that are listed on the exchange, and how trading operates on the exchange. Have students write reports to summarize their research.

Visual Instruction

Answer to Caption:
the Dow-Jones Industrial Average and Standard & Poor's 500

③ ASSESS

Assign Section 3 Assessment as homework or as an in-class activity.

📀 Have students use **Interactive Tutor Self-Assessment Software** to review Section 3.

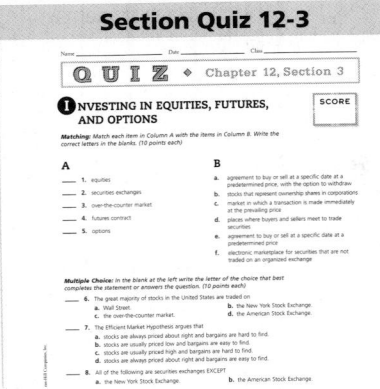

Section Quiz 12-3

Investment

"We put all our money in precious metal—we got braces for all the kids."

Performance Some investors take chances, while others prefer a safe investment. *What are the two most popular indicators of the market's performance?*

Measures of Stock Performance

Because most investors are concerned about the performance of their stocks, they often consult two popular indicators.

The Dow-Jones Industrial Average

The **Dow-Jones Industrial Average (DJIA),** shown in **Figure 12.8,** is the most popular and widely publicized measure of stock market performance on the NYSE. In 1884, the Dow-Jones corporation published the average closing price of 11 active stocks. In 1928, coverage was expanded to 30 stocks. Since then, some stocks have been added, and others deleted, but the sample remains constant at 30.

Because of these changes, the DJIA is no longer a mathematical average of stock prices. Also, the evolution of the DJIA has obscured the meaning of a "point" change in the index. At one time, a one "point" change in the DJIA meant that an average share of stock changed by $1. This is no

longer the case. Consequently, it is better to focus on the percentage change of the index rather than the number of points.

Standard & Poor's 500

Another popular benchmark of stock performance is the **Standard & Poor's 500 (S&P 500).** It uses the price changes of 500 representative stocks as an indicator of overall market performance. Because the sum of 500 stock prices would be very large, it is reduced to an index number. Unlike the Dow-Jones, the Standard & Poor's 500 reports on stocks listed on the NYSE, AMEX, and OTC markets.

Bull vs. Bear Markets

Investors often use colorful terms to describe which way the market is moving. For example, a **bull market** is a "strong" market with the prices moving up for several months or years in a row. One of the strongest bull markets in history began in 1995 when the DJIA broke 4,000—and then reached 12,000 in 2000.

A **bear market** is a "mean" market, with the prices of equities moving sharply down for several months or years in a row. In mid-1998, the DJIA passed the 9,000 level, and then lost nearly 1,200 points before it finally recovered. As you can see, these two terms take their names from the characteristics of the animals they are named after.

Trading in the Future

In **Figure 12.6** on page 325, markets are defined according to the life of the financial asset and whether or not it can be resold. Another attribute of a financial asset is time, which leads to a discussion of spot, futures, and options markets.

Spot and Futures Markets

A **spot market** is a market in which a transaction is made immediately at the prevailing price. The spot price of gold in London, for example, is the current price as it exists in that city. The term spot means "immediate" and is used to distinguish this market from two other markets that trade in the future.

EXTENDING THE CONTENT

Development of the NYSE Before 1792, no organized market for trading securities existed. In May of that year, individuals who wanted to trade in securities met in New York City, only a short walk from the present site of the NYSE. At first, only United States bonds and a few stocks were traded on the NYSE, but trading activity increased as the 1800s progressed, reflecting economic growth and expansion. In 1867 the NYSE introduced the stock ticker, a machine that records purchases and sales of stock. This innovation helped accommodate the growth brought about by the Industrial Revolution. Nearly 100 years later, electronic data processing automated a large part of the transfer of trading information. Today, it is not unusual for more than 500 million shares of stock worth billions of dollars to be traded on the NYSE in a single day.

Sometimes the exchange takes place later on, rather than right away. This can be arranged with a **futures contract**–an agreement to buy or sell at a specific date in the future at a predetermined price. For example, a buyer agrees to buy a specified amount of gold at $280 an ounce from a seller, who promises delivery in six months. When the settlement date arrives, the buyer takes possession of the gold and pays the seller $280–regardless of the market price.

Futures markets are the marketplaces in which futures contracts, or "futures," are bought and sold. Many of these markets are affiliated with the grain and livestock exchanges that originated in the Midwest. Futures markets include the New York Mercantile Exchange, the Chicago Board of Trade, the Chicago Mercantile Exchange, the New York Cotton Exchange, and the Kansas City Board of Trade.

Options Markets

Options are contracts that provide the right to purchase or sell commodities or financial assets at some point in the future at a price agreed upon today. Options are closely related to futures;

however, options give one of the parties the opportunity to back out.

For example, you may pay $5 today for a **call option**–the right to *buy* a share of stock at a specified price some time in the future. If the call option gives you the right to purchase the stock at $70, and if the price of the stock drops to $30, you tear up the option and buy the stock at the going price. If the price rises to $100, however, you can purchase the stock for $70. Either way, the $5 option gives you the right to make the choice in the future.

If you were interested in selling instead of buying, you would have purchased the **put option**–the right to *sell* a share of stock at a specified price in the future. If you pay $3 for the right to sell at $50, and if the price of the stock drops to $40, you can require the buyer to pay the contract price for the stock. You would then net $47 from the sale, the $50 contract price minus the $3 paid for the option. If the price rose to $80 instead, you would be better off to tear up the option and sell the stock for $80. Either way, the $3 option gives you the right to make the choice in the future.

Options markets are the markets in which options are traded. Most of the exchanges that offer futures also sell options.

Reteach

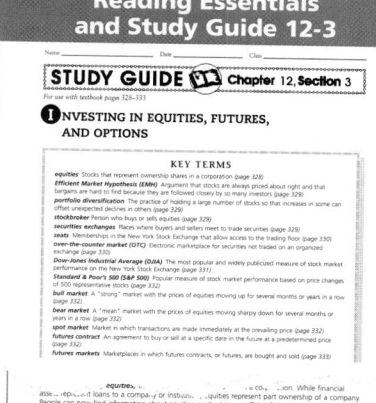

Reading Essentials and Study Guide 12-3

Enrich

Have students write to one of the futures markets listed in the section to obtain information on how this type of market functions.

4 CLOSE

Ask students to write a paragraph supporting or challenging the following statement: The best indicator of how the economy is performing is the stock market.

Section 3 Assessment

Understanding Key Terms

1. **Main Idea** If the price of a type of stock goes up, what does this suggest about the quantity of that stock being demanded and the quantity being supplied?

2. **Key Terms** Define equities, Efficient Market Hypothesis (EMH), portfolio diversification, stockbroker, securities exchange, seat, over-the-counter market (OTC), Dow-Jones Industrial Average (DJIA), Standard & Poor's 500 (S&P 500), bull market, bear market, spot market, futures contract, futures market, option, call option, put option, options market.

3. **Describe** the characteristics of the major organized stock exchanges in the United States.

4. **Discuss** two measures of stock market performance.

5. **Describe** how financial assets and equities can be traded in the future.

Applying Economic Concepts

6. **Futures exchanges** What is a futures contract? Would you ever invest in such a contract? Why or why not?

Critical Thinking

7. **Making Generalizations** Does the Efficient Market Hypothesis affect your view of playing the stock market? Explain.

Practice and **assess** key social studies skills with the *Glencoe Skillbuilder Interactive Workbook, Level 2.*

CHAPTER 12: FINANCIAL MARKETS **333**

Section 3 Assessment Answers

1. quantity demanded greater than quantity supplied

2. All vocabulary terms are defined in the text.

3. Answers include: where buyers and sellers meet; members pay fees; trades can take place only on exchange floors.

4. Both DJIA and the S&P 500 use price changes of representative stocks to measure stock performance.

5. Futures are contracts to buy or sell in the future at a price set today; options are similar but include the right to back out.

6. allows buying or selling in the future on a specific date at a predetermined price; students should provide reasons to support their view.

7. Answers should reflect an understanding of the effects of traders on investing.

Teaching Skills

Locate and photocopy a number of articles and opinion pieces dealing with the stock market, investing, or economics in general. Distribute the articles to students. Ask them to use one color of pen or highlighter to mark any words that indicate opinions. Have them use another color to denote facts within the article. Discuss with students how they recognized facts, and what sources they might use to verify those facts.

Additional Practice

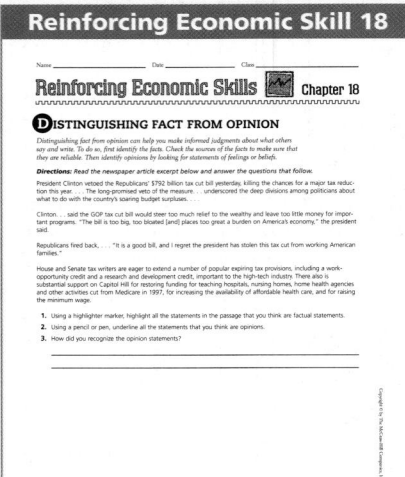

Reinforcing Economic Skill 18

Name _____ Date _____ Class _____

Reinforcing Economic Skills — Chapter 18

① DISTINGUISHING FACT FROM OPINION

Distinguishing fact from opinion can help you make informed judgments about what others say and write. To do so, first identify the facts. Check the sources of the facts to make sure that they are reliable. Then identify opinions by looking for statements of feelings or beliefs.

Directions: *Read the newspaper article excerpt below and answer the questions that follow.*

President Clinton vetoed the Republicans' $792 billion tax cut bill yesterday, killing the chances for a major tax reduction this year . . . The long-promised veto of the measure . . . underscored the deep divisions among politicians about what to do with the country's soaring budget surpluses. . . .

Clinton . . . said the GOP tax cut bill would steer too much relief to the wealthy and leave too little money for important programs. "The bill is too big, too bloated [and] places too great a burden on America's economy," the president said.

Republicans fired back, . . . "It is a good bill, and I regret the president has stolen this tax cut from working American families."

House and Senate tax writers are eager to extend a number of popular expiring tax provisions, including a work-opportunity credit and a research and development credit, important to the high-tech industry. There also is substantial support on Capitol Hill for restoring funding for teaching hospitals, nursing homes, home health agencies and other activities cut from Medicare in 1997, for increasing the availability of affordable health care, and for raising the minimum wage.

1. Using a highlighter marker, highlight all the statements in the passage that you think are factual statements.
2. Using a pencil or pen, underline all the statements that you think are opinions.
3. How did you recognize the opinion statements?

GLENCOE TECHNOLOGY

Glencoe Skillbuilder Interactive Workbook, Level 2

This interactive CD-ROM reinforces student mastery of essential social studies skills.

CRITICAL THINKING
Skill

Distinguishing Fact From Opinion

Being able to distinguish fact from opinion can help you make reasonable judgments about what others say and write. Facts can be proved by evidence such as records, documents, or historical sources. Opinions are based on people's differing values and beliefs.

Stockbrokers at work

Learning the Skill

The following steps will help you identify facts and opinions:

- Read or listen to the information carefully. Identify the facts. Ask: Can these statements be proved? Where would I find information to verify them?

- If a statement can be proved, it is factual. Check the sources for the facts. Often statistics sound impressive, but they may come from an unreliable source.

- Identify opinions by looking for statements of feelings or beliefs. The statements may contain words like *should, would, could, best, greatest, all, every,* or *always.*

Practicing the Skill

Read the excerpt that follows, then answer the questions.

The stock market has been good to America. In recent years, it has generated enormous wealth for individuals, financing for investment, jobs for people, and tax revenue for governments. Families now depend on it for retirement, the education of their children, and, increasingly, even consumption. Millions day-trade Internet stocks, and millions more actively manage their mutual funds and 401(k)s. Soon, people may be handling Social Security investment accounts. The stock market is insinuating itself into the everyday lives of ordinary Americans as never before. . . .

A few years ago, only a small percentage of the American population—the rich—would have been affected by this. No longer. A quarter of households earning $10,000 to $25,000 now own equities, either directly or through defined-contribution pension plans such as 401(k)s. Two-thirds of all households earning $50,000 to $99,000 hold equities. And some 84% of households earning over $100,000 own stocks.

—*Business Week*, December 21, 1998

1. Identify facts. How can you verify these statements?

2. Note opinions. What phrases alert you that these are opinions?

Application Activity

Record a television interview. List three facts and three opinions that were stated. Do the facts seem reliable? How can you verify the facts? What statements, if any, seemed to contain both fact and opinion?

 Practice and **assess** key social studies skills with the *Glencoe Skillbuilder Interactive Workbook, Level 2.*

Answers to Practicing the Skill

1. Statements can be verified with evidence such as records, documents, or historical sources.
2. Words such as *should, would, could, best, greatest, all, every,* or *always* note opinions.

Section 1

Savings and the Financial System

(pages 313–316)

- **Saving** is a process that makes **savings** available for others to invest.

- The economy has a **financial system** that transfers savings to investors.

- **Financial assets** are the receipts savers get when they loan funds to individuals, businesses, and governments.

- **Financial intermediaries** help facilitate the transfer of funds from savers to other investors.

- Financial intermediaries include finance companies, life insurance companies, **mutual funds, pension funds,** and **real estate investment trusts,** or **REITs.** These institutions are part of the financial system, even though they do not take deposits like commercial banks, savings banks, or credit unions.

- **Current yield** is a measure of return on bonds. Bond ratings are widely available and can be used as a measure of the bond's risk.

- Financial markets are named for the characteristics of the assets traded in them. **Capital markets** have financial assets with maturities of more than one year, while **money markets** have assets with maturities of less than one year.

- Assets traded in **primary markets** are those that have to be redeemed by the issuer.

Section 2

Investment Strategies and Financial Assets

(pages 318–326)

- Investors generally require larger returns to compensate for situations with greater **risk.**

- Successful investors analyze their goals, invest consistently, and avoid complexity.

- **401(k) plans** are popular investments that offer simplicity and relatively high returns.

- Bonds are popular financial assets. The three components of bonds are the **coupon,** the **maturity,** and the **par value.**

Section 3

Investing in Equities, Futures, and Options (pages 328–333)

- **Equities,** or stocks, are different from financial assets because equities represent ownership of a corporation rather than a loan to it.

- Because equity markets are reasonably efficient, most investors diversify their portfolio to protect against risk.

- Many stocks are traded on organized exchanges such as the NYSE, the AMEX, and a number of regional stock exchanges.

- The majority of stocks are traded in a computerized marketplace of organized dealers called the **over-the-counter market.** These stocks represent newer and sometimes smaller companies that could not get listed on the NYSE.

NIGHTLY BUSINESS REPORT

⊙ **ECONOMICS & YOU**

Chapter 13
Disc 1, Side 1

Saving and Investing

📼 Also available in VHS.

Using the Chapter 12 Summary

Use the Chapter 12 Summary to preview, review, condense, or reteach the chapter.

Preview/Review

🔵 Vocabulary PuzzleMaker CD-ROM reinforces Key Terms.

💾 Interactive Tutor Self-Assessment Software provides a review of Chapter 12 content.

Condense

🎧 📁 Have students listen to the Chapter 12 Audio Program. Spanish also available.

📁 📁 Assign the Chapter 12 Audio Program Activity and give students the Chapter 12 Audio Program Test.

📁 📁 Have students complete the Guided Reading Activities and Reading Essentials and Study Guides for Chapter 12.

Reteach

📁 📁 Have students complete Reteaching Activity 12 in the TCR. Spanish also available.

Teacher's Notes / Internet Bookmarks

_____

_____

_____

_____

_____

_____

_____

_____

GLENCOE
TECHNOLOGY

Use **MindJogger Videoquiz** to review the Chapter 12 content.

Have students visit the Web site at epp.glencoe.com to review Chapter 12 and take the **Self-Check Quiz.**

Identifying Key Terms

Students should incorporate chapter concepts in their paragraphs.

Reviewing the Facts

Section 1

1. Savings makes funds available for others to use. When businesses borrow these funds, they create new equipment and plants, employ more workers, and produce new goods and services.
2. People decide to save—by opening a savings account, for example—and receive some form of receipt in return. In this case, the receipt is a savings book. These receipts are financial assets.
3. finance companies, life insurance companies, mutual funds, pension funds, real estate investment trusts

Section 2

4. relationship between risk and return, investment objectives, consistency of investment, avoiding complex investments
5. Employees authorize payroll deductions, which are invested in investments approved by the employee's company.
6. Current yields are obtained by dividing annual interest by purchase price.
7. Corporate bonds usually have common par values of $10,000,

ECONOMICS
Online

Self-Check Quiz Visit the *Economics: Principles and Practices* Web site at epp.glencoe.com and click on *Chapter 12—Self-Check Quizzes* to prepare for the chapter test.

Reviewing Key Terms

For each of the investments below, write a brief paragraph that describes at least three of the term's principal characteristics.

1. Treasury bond
2. Treasury bill
3. equities
4. Treasury note
5. futures
6. Individual Retirement Account
7. 401(k)
8. Roth IRA
9. option
10. municipal bond

Reviewing the Facts

Section 1 (pages 313–316)

1. **Explain** the relationship between savings and capital formation.
2. **Describe** how financial assets are created in the free enterprise system.
3. **Describe** five nonbank financial intermediaries in the American economy.

Section 2 (pages 318–326)

4. **Name** four considerations important to investors.
5. **Explain** how a 401(k) plan works.
6. **Explain** how current yields are computed.

7. **Compare** four types of bonds that are commonly traded in the United States.

Section 3 (pages 328–333)

8. **Explain** what the Efficient Market Hypothesis means to investors.
9. **Compare** the NYSE to the other organized stock exchanges.
10. **Describe** the nature of the over-the-counter market.
11. **Compare** the similarities and differences between the Dow-Jones Industrial Average and the Standard & Poor's 500.
12. **Explain** how options contracts are different from futures contracts.

Thinking Critically

1. **Drawing Conclusions** If you contacted several local banks to get their rates paid on various CDs, you would find that rates vary only slightly from one institution to another. Do you think the similarities are caused by efficient markets or by other causes? Explain.

2. **Understanding Cause and Effect** Explain how each of the following will affect saving. Use a graphic organizer similar to the one below to answer the question.

   a. An increase in the federal personal income tax is instituted.
   b. The United States undergoes a prolonged period of inflation.

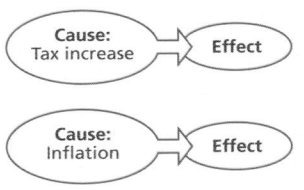

but their prices actually are set by supply and demand, and they can be resold. Interest on corporate bonds is taxable income. Municipal bonds are issued by state and local governments and are tax-exempt. Government savings bonds are low-denomination, nontransferable bonds issued by the U.S. government. International bonds are large-denomination bonds issued by foreign governments. Payments on these bonds often are made in foreign currency. Treasury bonds, issued by the federal government, have maturities of 10 to 30 years and come in denominations of $1,000.

Section 3

8. Bargains are hard to find.
9. NYSE is the oldest, largest, and most prestigious of all the organized stock exchanges.
10. It is an electronic marketplace for securities not listed on organized exchanges.
11. Dow-Jones Industrial Average uses 30 representative stocks listed on NYSE as indicator. S&P 500 uses price changes of 500 representative stocks listed on NYSE, AMEX, and OTC market as performance indicator.

Applying Economic Concepts

1. **Risk-Return Relationship** List five possible investments a person could make if funds were available. Rank the investments in order of how much risk each entails (from highest to lowest). Then rank the investments according to expected returns (from highest to lowest). What is the significance of the rankings to the risk-return relationship?

2. **Financial Assets** Visit a local bank or a nonbank financial institution. Ask for its free brochure that outlines the institution's investment opportunities such as savings accounts, certificates of deposit, money market accounts, and stock brokerage accounts. Write a brief report describing the financial assets the institution generates or trades.

3. **Market Efficiency** What does the Efficient Market Hypothesis mean to you as an investor, especially with respect to the composition of your stock portfolio?

Math Practice

Complete the following table by filling in the correct data in the blank spaces.

Total Income	Consumption	Saving
a. $2,000	$1,800	
b.	$2,500	$1,000
c. $7,000		-$500
d. $10,000	$10,000	
e. $12,500		$400

Thinking Like an Economist

How do you think the Internet will affect future competition among stockbrokers for individual investors' business?

Technology Skill

Using the Internet Scan the stock market listings in the business section of your local newspaper. Assume that you have $50,000 to invest in a stock portfolio, and select one or more stocks in which to invest. Study the information on reading the financial page in the Economics Handbook in the front of this book. Then, in your journal, track the progress of your stock(s) for one week or more. To help you keep track, use the following Internet sites:

The Dow Jones Industrial Averages®
http://averages.dowjones.com

The New York Stock Exchange
http://www.nyse.com

American Stock Exchange
http://www.amex.com

Chicago Board of Trade
http://www.cbot.com

After you have completed the activity, write a one-page paper in which you explain what types of information people should have before they invest in stocks. Share your results with the rest of the class.

Building Skills

Distinguishing Fact from Opinion Read the following statements. Identify each as a statement of fact or a statement of opinion. Then, explain the reasoning behind your answer.

1. A share of stock is a unit of ownership in a corporation.
2. Market analysts' predictions are of little value.
3. Junk bonds are excellent investments because they have high yields.
4. The United States is not the only government to sell bonds.
5. Financial intermediaries take part in every financial transaction.

 Practice and **assess** key social studies skills with the *Glencoe Skillbuilder Interactive Workbook, Level 2.*

Math Practice

a. $200 d. 0
b. $3,500 e. $12,100
c. $7,500

Thinking Like an Economist

Students may answer that the Internet will greatly affect future competition among stockbrokers. Investors may even choose to buy, sell, and monitor their stock portfolios from personal computers, thus eliminating the need for a stockbroker.

Technology Skill

Students' journals should accurately track the progress of stock(s).

Building Skills

1. fact, can be verified
2. opinion, expression of disapproval
3. opinion, generalization
4. fact, can be verified
5. opinion, generalization

? Bonus Test Question

Many workers own stock in the companies for which they work. Why do companies encourage this? *(Employers hope that employees will work harder to make the company successful.)* Why might a worker not want to hold stock in the company where he or she works? *(Workers may recognize discouraging trends in the quality of the company's product or management.)*

12. futures: a promise to buy or sell in future at a price set today; options: give investor option to buy or sell in future at price set today

Thinking Critically

1. efficient markets; because interest rates are set by the forces of supply and demand
2. increase: will decrease the amount of money a person has to put into a savings account; inflation: will also decrease the amount of money a person can put into a savings account

Applying Economic Concepts

1. Lists will vary. Refer students to Figure 12.2 on page 319 to establish risk and returns. There is a direct relationship between risk and return—the higher the risk, the greater the expected return.
2. Reports should show understanding of various financial assets.
3. It means that if all the stocks are priced right, it does not matter which ones you purchase. As a result, your portfolio will be greatly diversified.

Unit 4 Resource Manager

Materials listed may be used at any time during the study of the unit.

Economics Forms and Financial Pages Transparencies

Transparency 3
Personal Check

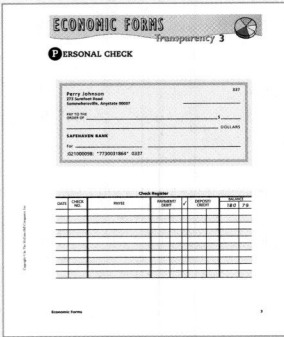

Transparency 14
Government Agency Issues

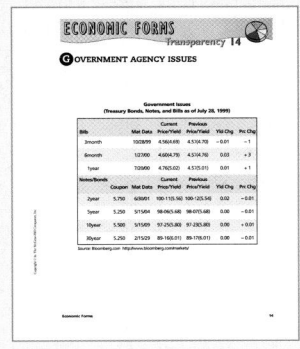

Transparency 15
Loan Amortization Schedule

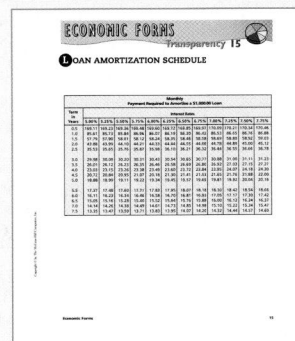

Economic Concepts Transparencies

Transparency 10
Income Distribution

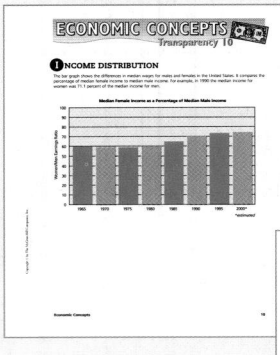

Transparency 13
Gross Domestic Product

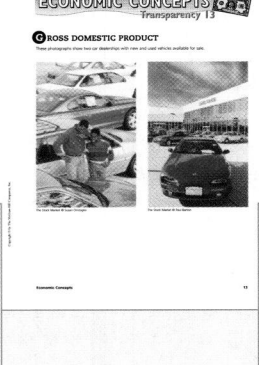

Transparency 17
Inflation and Deflation

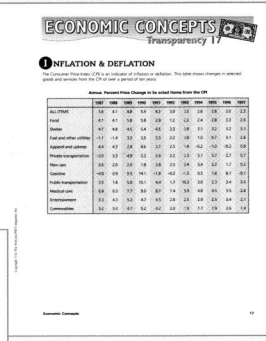

Transparency 18
Monetary Policy

Transparency 19
Fiscal Policy

REAL-WORLD ECONOMICS

*Have your students learn about investing and managing their financial future by participating in the exciting simulation **The Stock Market Game**™. See Teacher pages in front of book for more information.*

*Strengthen students' research, cooperation, presentation and critical-thinking skills by having them compete in the **Fed Challenge**. See Teacher pages in front of book for more information.*

Additional Glencoe Resources for This Unit:

- 🌐 **Interactive Economics!**
- 🌐 **Glencoe Skillbuilder Interactive Workbook, Level 2**
- 📼 💿 **Nightly Business Report Economics & You Video Program**
- 💲 **Economic Survival: A Financial Simulation**

Unit 4 Resource Manager

ASSESSMENT

Unit 4 Test

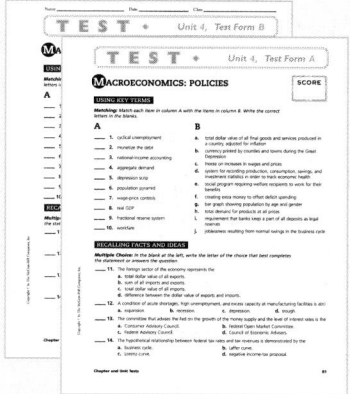

APPLICATION AND ENRICHMENT

Economics Laboratory 4

Unit 4 Business Week Focus on the New Economy

Use the following tools to easily assess student learning in a variety of ways:

- Performance Assessment Strategies and Activities
- Section Quizzes
- Chapter and Unit Tests
- Interactive Tutor Self-Assessment Software
- ExamView® Pro Testmaker
- MindJogger Videoquiz
- SAT I/II Test Practice
- epp.glencoe.com

*inter*NET CONNECTION

Economics: Principles and Practices
Visit the *Economics: Principles and Practices* Web site for economics overviews, activities, assessments, and updated charts and graphs.
epp.glencoe.com

Glencoe Social Studies
Visit the Glencoe Web site for social studies activities updates, and links to other sites.
socialstudies.glencoe.com

 Glencoe's Guide to Using the Internet
Provides an introduction to many of the current technologies on the Internet. Professional resources and teaching strategies included.

Business Week Online
Visit the *Business Week* Web site for up-to-date news and special reports.
www.businessweek.com

Our Web sites provide additional resources. All essential content is covered in the Student Edition.

BIBLIOGRAPHY

Readings for the Student

Hacker, Andrew, *Who Has How Much and Why*. New York: Scribner, 1998.

"Supply-Side Isn't Voodoo Anymore," by Paul Craig Roberts, *Business Week*, November 1, 1999.

Readings for the Teacher

Wolff, Edward N., *Top Heavy: The Increasing Inequality of Wealth in America and What Can Be Done About It*. New York: The New Press, 1996.

"How Most Economists Missed the Boat," by Michael J. Mandel, *Business Week*, November 15, 1999.

Multimedia Resources

Videocassette. *Money, Banks and the Role of Government.* Churchill Media. 1995. Available from Social Studies School Service, 10200 Jefferson Blvd., P.O. Box 802, Culver City, CA 90232-0802. Color video, 30 min. Part of the "Economics in a Changing World: Where Do I Fit In?" series. Emphasizes the connection between people and economics.

Unit Objectives

After studying this unit, students will be able to:

1. Discuss the different methods to measure economic performance.
2. Describe the phases of the business cycle and its possible causes.
3. Explain the organization and role of the Federal Reserve System.
4. Explain the social costs of economic instability.
5. Understand the purposes of monetary and fiscal policies.

Unit Overview

Unit 4 explains the measurement of the U.S. economy and policies designed to achieve economic growth and stability. **Chapter 13** focuses on the nation's economic performance and its Gross Domestic Product (GDP). **Chapter 14** discusses unemployment, inflation, and the distribution of poverty and income. **Chapter 15** describes the Federal Reserve System and its role as manager of the country's money supply. **Chapter 16** focuses on the goal of economic stability and the policies needed to achieve it.

UNIT 4

Macroeconomics: Policies

CHAPTER 13
Economic Performance

CHAPTER 14
Economic Instability

CHAPTER 15
The Fed and Monetary Policy

CHAPTER 16
Achieving Economic Stability

Why It's Important

As you read this unit, learn how the study of economics helps answer the following questions:

- Why is the price of a used car not added to the nation's gross domestic product?

- Why does your dollar buy less than six cents worth of the goods and services it bought 100 years ago?

In the United States, macroeconomi policies are used to stimulate the nation's overall economic growth.

MAKING IT RELEVANT

International Economics Ask each student to select a country and look up macroeconomic statistics about that country. Have them find real GDP, the population, the unemployment rate, and the inflation rate. On a long sheet of paper, draw a scale of per capita real GDP. Have students mark on the scale where their countries lie. On another large sheet of paper, draw a scaled graph with the inflation rate on the vertical axis and the unemployment rate on the horizontal. Have students mark the position of their countries on that graph. Discuss the differences among the country statistics.

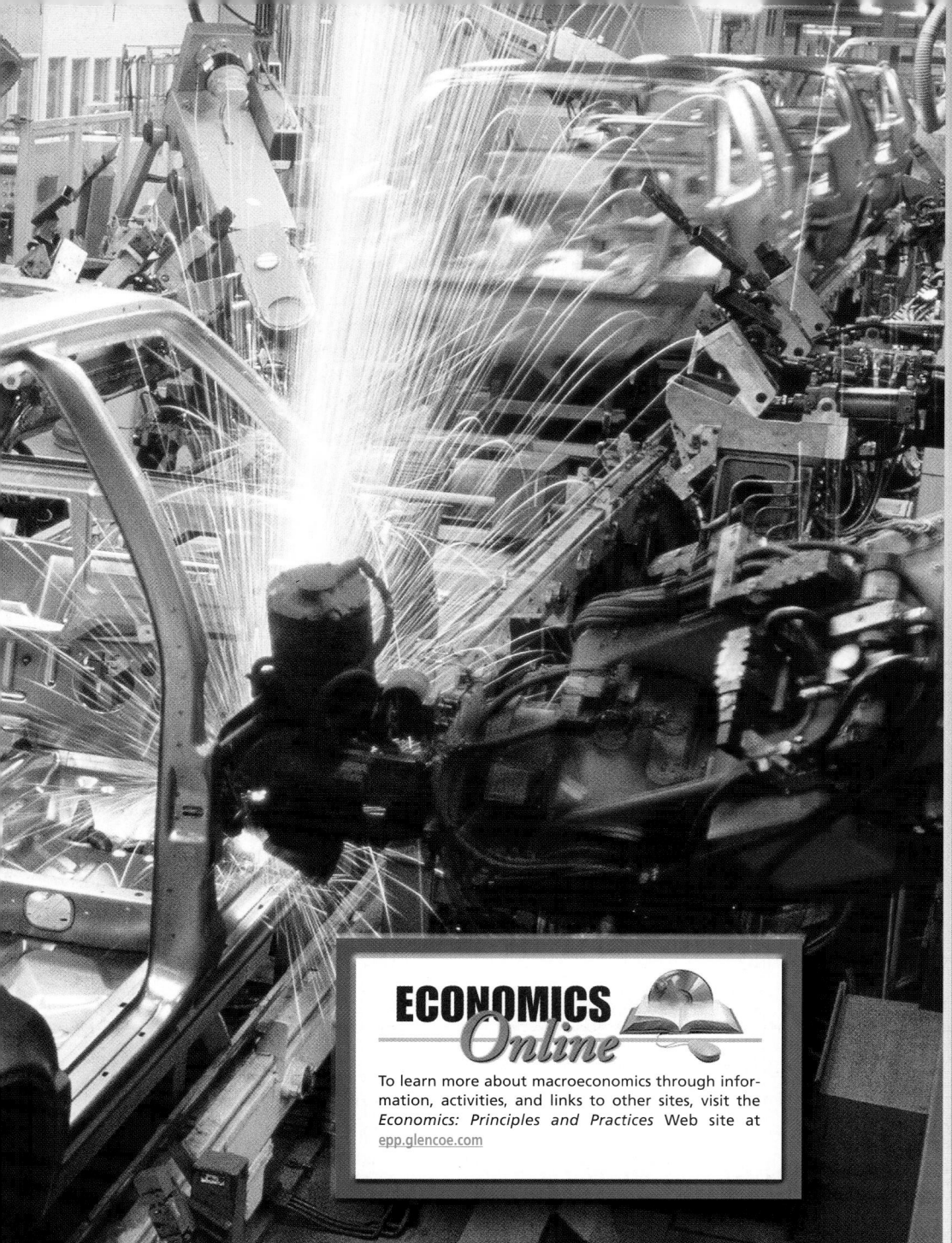

ECONOMICS
Online

To learn more about macroeconomics through information, activities, and links to other sites, visit the *Economics: Principles and Practices* Web site at epp.glencoe.com

Introducing the Unit

Ask students to summarize magazine and newspaper articles or television news reports on population growth and stability, inflation, unemployment, or poverty. Call on students to present and discuss their summaries. Then have students decide which of the situations addressed in the summaries affect them and their community directly. Have students explain their decisions.

Visual Instruction

As students study the photograph, ask them to consider the following questions: How does the photograph illustrate Gross Domestic Product (GDP)? How does the photograph illustrate economic growth? After completing study of the unit, have students return to the photograph and answer these questions. *(New automobiles are counted as part of GDP. Increasing productivity in the automobile industry contributes to economic growth.)*

ECONOMIC SURVIVAL
A FINANCIAL SIMULATION

To help students learn to manage their own finances, have them participate in the game **Economic Survival: A Financial Simulation** in which each student enters the workforce, rents an apartment, and deals with everyday events.

ECONOMICS
Online

To access the data, follow these steps:

1. Log on to the Woodrow Federal Reserve Bank of Minneapolis at http://woodrow.mpls.frb.fed.us/
Scroll down to the category for Federal Reserve System and under that, click on Monetary Policy. At this site you will see U.S. Monetary Policy: An Introduction; click on it.

What to Do When You Are There
Have students read about how the U.S. monetary policy affects different aspects of our economy. Have students use a search engine to access an online newspaper and choose an article that demonstrates an example of how monetary policy has influenced a current issue or situation. Discuss findings with your class. If students have limited access to the Internet, have them use other resources.

Chapter 13 Resource Manager

Daily Objectives	Reproducible Resources	Technology/Multimedia Resources
Section 1 Measuring the Nation's Output 1. Explain how Gross Domestic Product (GDP) is measured. 2. Describe the limitations of GDP. 3. Understand the importance of GDP.	Reproducible Lesson Plan 13-1 Daily Lecture Notes 13-1 Guided Reading Activity 13-1 Reading Essentials and Study Guide 13-1 Section Quiz 13-1*	Daily Focus Transparency 52 Interactive Tutor Self-Assessment Software ExamView® Pro Testmaker Presentation Plus!
Section 2 GDP and Changes in the Price Level 1. Explain how a price index is constructed. 2. Describe three price indices. 3. Understand the difference between real and current GDP.	Reproducible Lesson Plan 13-2 Daily Lecture Notes 13-2 Guided Reading Activity 13-2 Reading Essentials and Study Guide 13-2 Section Quiz 13-2*	Daily Focus Transparency 71 Interactive Tutor Self-Assessment Software ExamView® Pro Testmaker Presentation Plus!
Section 3 GDP and Population 1. Explain how population is estimated in the U.S. 2. Describe the factors affecting future population growth.	Reproducible Lesson Plan 13-3 Daily Lecture Notes 13-3 Guided Reading Activity 13-3 Reading Essentials and Study Guide 13-3 Section Quiz 13-3*	Daily Focus Transparency 53 Interactive Tutor Self-Assessment Software ExamView® Pro Testmaker Presentation Plus!
Section 4 Economic Growth 1. Describe how economists measure the growth of the United States economy. 2. Explain the importance of economic growth. 3. Outline the factors of economic growth. 4. Relate productivity to economic growth.	Reproducible Lesson Plan 13-4 Daily Lecture Notes 13-4 Guided Reading Activity 13-4 Reading Essentials and Study Guide 13-4 Section Quiz 13-4*	Daily Focus Transparency 56 Vocabulary PuzzleMaker CD-ROM NBR Economics & You Video Program Interactive Tutor Self-Assessment Software ExamView® Pro Testmaker Presentation Plus!

Transparency   CD-ROM   Software   Blackline Master

Videodisc   Audio Program   Videocassette

Also available in Spanish

0:00 OUT OF TIME?
Assign the Chapter 13 Audio Program activity and test.

Activities that are particularly suited to use within the block scheduling framework are identified throughout this chapter by the following designation: **BLOCK SCHEDULING**

Chapter 13 Resource Manager

ACTIVITY

From the Classroom of...

Diane Roberts
Neal F. Simeon
   Career Academy
Chicago, IL

GDP and the Quality of Life

Does a higher GDP automatically mean a better quality of life? Have students do research and compare GDP for three countries (the U.S. and any other two) in a given year. Students should then research the quality of life in these countries with a focus on health, industry, violence, and culture. Compare the countries with the highest and lowest GDPs.

Tell students to take into consideration the consumption of items such as tobacco and alcohol, as well as the ownership of material possessions. Is there a correlation between high consumption and family values, crime, and health issues? Are environmental hazards more prevalent in countries with a higher or lower GDP? Do these hazards lead to more government spending?

Other factors such as poverty, health care, senior care, child welfare, homelessness, and environmental factors should come into the discussion. The teacher may focus on any topics that spark the interest of students and lead to a better understanding of current economic issues.

National Council on Economic Education

THE **Economics**America AND **Economics**International PROGRAMS

Voluntary National Content Standards in Economics
Emphasized in Chapter 13

Content Standard 15

Content Standard 18

For a complete listing of NCEE Standards and entire text correlation, see Teacher pages in front of book.

Resources Available from NCEE
- Capstone: The Nation's High School Economics Course
- Focus: High School Economics
- Learning from the Market: Integrating the Stock Market Game™ Across the Curriculum
- Focus: International Economics
- Geography: Focus on Economics
- World History: Focus on Economics

To order these materials or to contact your state Council on Economic Education about workshops and programs, call 1-800-338-1192 or visit www.nationalcouncil.org

Chapter 13 Resource Manager

Economic Concept Transparency 13: Gross Domestic Product

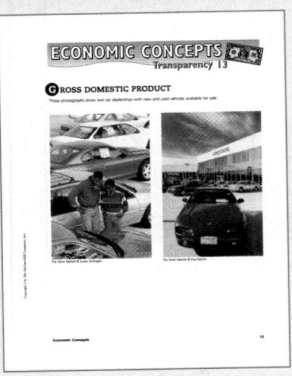

Consumer Application Activity 18

Free Enterprise Activity 18

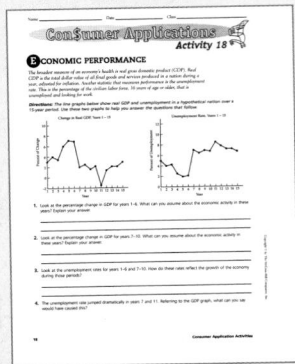

Enrichment Activity 13

Cooperative Learning Activity 18

Math Practice Activity 18

Economic Cartoon 18

Primary and Secondary Source Reading 18

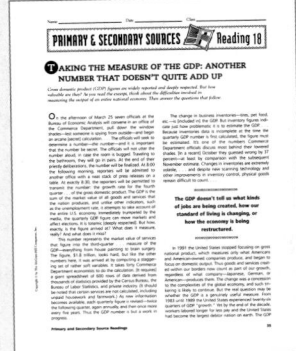

Economic Vocabulary Activity 13

Reteaching Activity 13

Critical Thinking Activity 18

Reinforcing Economic Skill 24

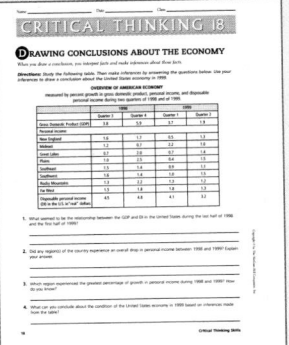

Chapter 13 Resource Manager

ASSESSMENT AND EVALUATION

Chapter 13 Test Form A

Chapter 13 Test Form B

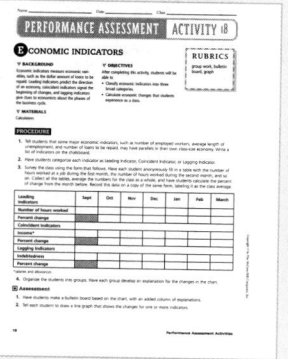

Performance Assessment Activity 18

ExamView® Pro Testmaker

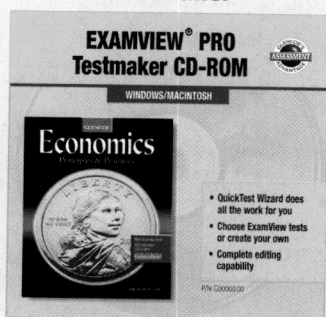

SPANISH RESOURCES

The following Spanish language materials are available in the Spanish Resources binder:

 Spanish Economic Vocabulary Activities

 Spanish Reteaching Activities

 Spanish Section Quizzes

 Spanish Economic Concepts Transparencies

Also available:

  Spanish Chapter 13 Audio Program Activity and Test

TECHNOLOGY/MULTIMEDIA

- Vocabulary PuzzleMaker CD-ROM
- Interactive Tutor Self-Assessment Software
- ExamView® Pro Testmaker
- Audio Program (English or Spanish)
- NBR Economics & You Video Program (English or Spanish)
- MindJogger Videoquiz
- Interactive Economics! CD-ROM
- Presentation Plus!
- TeacherWorks CD-ROM
- Glencoe Skillbuilder Interactive Workbook CD-ROM, Level 2

ECONOMICS Online

Use our Web site for additional resources. All essential content is covered in the Student Edition.

You and your students can visit epp.glencoe.com, the Web site companion to **Economics: Principles and Practices.** This innovative integration of electronic and print media offers your students a wealth of opportunities. The student text directs students to the Web site for the following options:

- **Chapter Overviews**
- **Student Web Activities**
- **Self-Check Quizzes**
- **Textbook Updates**

Answers are provided for you in the Web Activity Lesson Plan. Additional Web resources and interactive puzzles are also available.

Performance Assessment

Refer to Activity 18 in the *Performance Assessment Strategies and Activities* booklet.

 BLOCK SCHEDULING

ECONOMICS *Online*

Introduce students to chapter content and key terms by having them access **Chapter Overview 13** at epp.glencoe.com

NIGHTLY BUSINESS REPORT

 ECONOMICS & YOU

Chapter 20
Disc 1, Side 2

Measuring the Economy's Performance

After viewing the segment, students should be able to:
- Differentiate between leading and lagging economic indicators.

 Also available in VHS.

GLENCOE TECHNOLOGY

Use **MindJogger Videoquiz** to preview the Chapter 13 content.

CHAPTER **13**

Economic Performance

Economics & You

A growing economy means an expanding economy, one that continues to provide more people with what they want or need. In **Chapter 13,** you will learn how the nation's economic growth is the key to a better future for everyone. To learn how statistical measures are used to monitor the economy's performance, view the Chapter 20 video lesson:

Measuring the Economy's Performance

ECONOMICS *Online*

Chapter Overview Visit the *Economics: Principles and Practices* Web site at epp.glencoe.com and click on **Chapter 13—Chapter Overviews** to preview chapter information.

Any final product manufactured within the United States is included in the country's GDP.

✚ EXTRA CREDIT PROJECT

Ask students to develop an illustrated report titled "Analyzing the Economy," using the following three headings: "Measuring the Nation's Output," "Measuring the Nation's Income," and "Adjusting for Price Changes." Call on volunteers to present their reports to the class.

Measuring the Nation's Output

Study Guide

Main Idea
Gross Domestic Product (GDP) and Gross National Product (GNP) are two important measures of economic performance.

Reading Strategy
Graphic Organizer As you read the section, complete a graphic organizer similar to the one below by identifying what calculations are necessary to go from GDP to GNP.

GDP + _____ − _____ = GNP

Key Terms
Gross Domestic Product, national income accounting, intermediate products, secondhand sales, nonmarket transactions, underground economy, Gross National Product, net national product, national income, personal income, disposable personal income, household, unrelated individual, family, output-expenditure model, net exports of goods and services

Objectives
After studying this section, you will be able to:
1. **Explain** how Gross Domestic Product (GDP) is measured.
2. **Describe** the limitations of GDP.
3. **Understand** the importance of GDP.

Applying Economic Concepts
Gross Domestic Product Read to find out why GDP is the most important measure of overall economic performance.

1 FOCUS

Section Overview
This section explains how Gross Domestic Product is calculated.

BELLRINGER
Motivational Activity

Project **transparency** and have students answer questions.

Available as blackline master.

Daily Focus Transparency 52

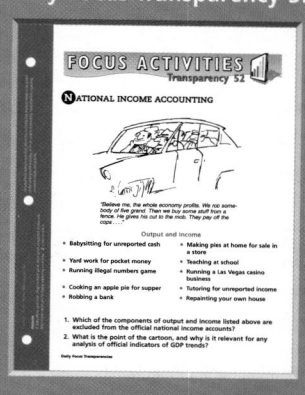

Cover Story

Economy Grew Less Than Previously Thought

WASHINGTON (AP) – The U.S. economy limped along in the first three months of the year at a pace slightly slower than the government previously thought. The biggest drag on growth came from companies struggling to get rid of their unsold goods.

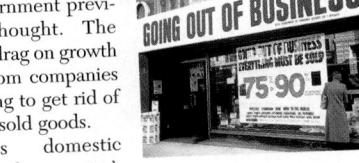

Going out of business sale

Gross domestic product–the country's total output of goods and services–grew at an annual rate of 1.2 percent from January to March, according to revised figures released by the Commerce Department Friday.

The weak economy and higher energy prices took a bite of U.S. companies' profits in the first quarter, which registered their biggest decline in three years.

—*The New York Times,* June 29, 2001

The report in the cover story may be of only passing interest to many people, but it is vitally significant news for economists. This is because **Gross Domestic Product (GDP)**—the dollar amount of all final goods and services produced within a country's national borders in a year–is the single most important measure of the economy's overall economic performance. When GDP does not do well, neither does the rest of the economy.

Economists devised **national income accounting**–a system of statistics and accounts that keeps track of production, consumption, saving, and investment–to track overall economic performance. This data becomes part of the National Income and Product Accounts (NIPA) kept by the U.S. Department of Commerce. The NIPA is like a statistical road map that tells Americans where they are and how they got there.

GDP—The Measure of National Output

  GDP is a measure of national output. This means that Japanese automobiles produced in Kentucky, Indiana, Ohio, or Tennessee count in GDP even if investors who own the

CHAPTER 13: ECONOMIC PERFORMANCE **341**

Study Guide

Reading Strategy
Have students create the graphic organizer.
Answers to Graphic: *all payments U.S. citizens receive from outside the U.S.; all payments made to foreign-owned resources in the U.S.*

Preteaching Vocabulary
Have volunteers skim the section to find each Key Term, read it in context, and paraphrase it.

RESOURCE MANAGER

Reproducible Masters
- Reproducible Lesson Plan 13-1
- Daily Lecture Notes 13-1
- Guided Reading Activity 13-1
- Reading Essentials and Study Guide 13-1
- Section Quiz 13-1

Transparencies
- Daily Focus Transparency 52

Multimedia
- Interactive Tutor Self-Assessment Software
- ExamView® Pro Testmaker
- Presentation Plus!

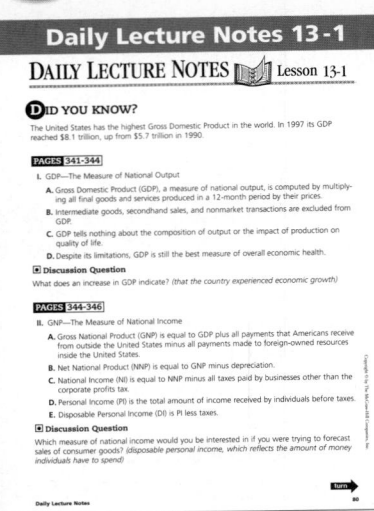

L1 Nonmarket Transactions

Over a weekend, have students list any nonmarket transactions they observe. Have them explain why they think each listed item is a nonmarket transaction. Call on students to share and discuss their lists and explanations. **ELL**

ECONOMICS
AT A GLANCE

Answer: *quantity multiplied by price per unit*

---

plants live outside the United States. On the other hand, production in U.S.-owned plants that are located in Mexico, Canada, or other countries is not counted in GDP.

Computing GDP

The measurement of GDP is fairly easy to grasp. Conceptually, we only have to multiply all of the final goods and services produced in a 12-month period by their prices, and then add them up to get the total dollar value of production.

Figure 13.1 provides an example. The first column contains three categories of products used in the NIPA. These are goods, services, and structures. The third category—structures—includes residential housing, apartments, and buildings for commercial purposes. In the second column, the final goods and services produced in the year are listed. The next two columns show the quantity produced and the average price of each product. To get GDP, multiply the quantity of each good by its price and then add the results, as is done in the last column of the table.

Government statisticians use scientific sampling techniques along with other methods to estimate both the quantity and the prices of the individual products. In addition, since the reporting process includes such extensive data, GDP estimates are made only quarterly, or every three months. The figures are revised for months after that, so it takes several months or years to discover how the economy actually performed.

ECONOMICS
AT A GLANCE

Figure 13.1

Estimating Gross Domestic Product

Product		Quantity (millions)	Price (per 1 unit)	Dollar Value (millions)
Goods	Automobiles	6	$20,000	$120,000
	Replacement Tires	10	$60	$600
	Shoes	55	$50	$2,750
	...*	...*	...*	...*
Services	Haircuts	150	$8	$1,200
	Income Tax Filings	30	$150	$4,500
	Legal Advice	45	$200	$9,000
	...*	...*	...*	...*
Structures	Single Family	3	$75,000	$225,000
	Multifamily	5	$300,000	$1,500,000
	Commercial	1	$1,000,000	$1,000,000
	...*	...*	...*	...*

Total Gross Domestic Product = $9 trillion

Note: *... other goods, services, and structures

Using Tables Gross Domestic Product is the dollar value of all final goods, services, and structures produced within a country's borders in a year. **How is the dollar value for each of the products on the table calculated?**

MEETING SPECIAL NEEDS ACTIVITY

Learning Style: Logical/Mathematical Have students make an extremely rough estimate of the GDP for their community using a chart like that in Figure 13.1. They should list the items, services, and structures produced by the community in the first column, the approximate quantity of each in the second column, and the approximate price per unit in the third column. Students should then multiply quantity by price to get the dollar value, which they should record in the fourth column. Have them calculate their community's GDP by adding the dollar value of each item.

Refer to *Inclusion for the Social Studies Classroom Strategies and Activities* in the TCR.

Underground Economy

Excluded From GDP Although there is no consensus on the size of the underground economy, estimates suggest that it is between 5 and 15 percent of the recorded GDP. *What activities make up the underground economy?*

Some Things Are Excluded

When the Department of Commerce analyzes production data, it faces several decisions concerning what should and what should not be included in GDP.

One case involves **intermediate products**—products used to make other products already counted in GDP. If you purchase replacement tires for your automobile, for example, these tires are counted in GDP. However, if you purchase a new car, the tires are not counted separately because their value is built into the price of the car.

Intermediate products are eliminated from GDP so they are not counted twice, which would make GDP seem larger than it actually is. Some goods such as flour, sugar, and salt *are* included in GDP if they are bought for final use by the consumer. For example, if you buy flour to make a pie, the flour counts in GDP. If you are a baker who buys the flour to make pies for sale, only the value of the pies are counted.

Another decision involves the exclusion of **secondhand sales**—the sales of used goods. When products already produced are transferred from one person or group to another, no new production is created. Although the sale of a used car, house, clothes, or compact disc player may give others cash that they can use on new purchases, only the original sale is included in GDP.

Nonmarket transactions—transactions that do not take place in the market—are excluded because they are so difficult to measure. GDP does not take into account the value of services when you mow your own lawn or perform your own home maintenance. These activities are counted only when they are done for pay outside the home. The largest group of nonmarket transactions excluded from GDP includes the services that homemakers provide. If homemakers received pay for the cooking, cleaning, laundering, child care, and other household chores they normally perform, billions of dollars would be spent every year for these services.

Many other activities take place in the market, but they are excluded from GDP because they are illegal and not reported. Unreported legal and illegal activities such as gambling, smuggling, prostitution, drugs, and counterfeiting are part of the so-called **underground economy.**

CHAPTER 13: ECONOMIC PERFORMANCE **343**

Visual Instruction

Answer to Caption:
illegal activities, such as gambling and smuggling; some legal activities not reported to avoid taxes

L2 Classifying Ideas

Draw a two-column chart on the board, using *Strengths of GDP* and *Weaknesses of GDP* as column headings. Call on volunteers to identify strengths of the GDP and enter responses under the appropriate heading. Do the same for weaknesses of the GDP. Then have students use information in the chart to write a paragraph on how the GDP, despite its weaknesses, is a valuable measure of economic performance and economic health.

FREE ENTERPRISE ACTIVITY

Remind students that the GDP might increase 10 to 15 percent if underground economic transactions were included. Then ask students to analyze ways to decrease the amount of activity in the underground economy. Note responses on the board. (*Responses may include: lower taxes, increased policing of underground economic activities, harsher penalties for those convicted of taking part in underground economic activities.*) Have students use the information on the board to write a letter to their member of Congress on ways to address the problem of the underground economy.

THE GLOBAL ECONOMY

GDP Bill Gates had an estimated net worth of $77 billion in 1999, making him the richest man in the world. An interest rate of 6 percent on his $77 billion would provide him with $4.6 billion a year of income. That income would exceed the annual GDP of several countries, including Burundi, with a population of 5.7 million, Somalia, with a population of over 7 million, and Liberia, with a population of almost 3 million.

L2 Comparing Graphs

Organize students into groups of five and provide groups with copies of data on GDP and the four sectors that make up GDP—consumer, investment, government, and foreign—for a 10-year period. Have each student construct a line graph for one of the five sets of statistics. Then have groups work together to draw up a brief report on trends and similarities and differences among the graphs.

L2 Analyzing Ideas

Randomly assign one of the five income measures to students until all students have an assignment. Have them write a "biography" of their assigned measure that answers the following: What does the measure show? What is added or subtracted to find the measure? To whom would this measure be most valuable? Why? Have volunteers read their biographies aloud.

STANDARD & POOR'S INFOBYTE

GDP Due to the increased level of globalization in the economy, the GDP calculation has replaced Gross National Product as the accepted measurement of national output. GDP differs from GNP in that GDP is an international measure of a country's annual *output* regardless of who owns the resources. GNP, on the other hand, is an international measure of a country's *income*, regardless of where the factors of production are located.

Limitations of GDP

Increases in GDP are desirable because they indicate that more people have jobs and earn an income. GDP alone, however, tells nothing about the *composition of output*. If GDP increases by $10 billion, for example, we know that production is growing and we likely would view the growth as a good thing. However, we might feel differently if we discover that the extra production took the form of military nerve gas stockpiles rather than schools, libraries, and parks.

Additionally, GDP tells little about the impact of that production on the *quality of life*. The construction of 10,000 new homes may appear to be good for the economy. However, if the homes threaten a wildlife refuge or destroy the natural beauty of an area, the value of the homes may be viewed differently. In practice, GDP does not take into account quality of life issues, so it is helpful to be aware of such matters to gain a better understanding of GDP.

An Overall Measure of Economic Health

Despite its limitations, GDP is still our best measure of overall economic health. Because it is a measure of the voluntary transactions that take place in the market—and because voluntary transactions are only made when both parties feel they are better off—a larger GDP indicates that more people are better off than before. If GDP does not grow, people may become unhappy and dissatisfied with government or its leaders.

344 UNIT 4 MACROECONOMICS: POLICIES

Presidential elections are often influenced by the health of the economy. In 1992, President George Bush lost a very close election to Bill Clinton, in part because people were still suffering from the short but sharp GDP downturn in 1991. Had the economy been healthy, many political analysts believe that Bush would have been reelected.

We can examine smaller parts of GDP—housing, consumer spending, and even the price increases detailed in the cover story—if we want more detail, but the total measure is the standard followed most closely. For these reasons, GDP is the single most important economic statistic compiled today.

GNP—The Measure of National Income

When economists measure income rather than output, they use **Gross National Product (GNP)**—the dollar value of all final goods, services, and structures produced in one year with labor and property supplied by a country's residents.

GNP is based on GDP, but there are differences between the two. While GDP measures the value of all the final goods and services produced within U.S. borders, for example, GNP measures the income of all Americans, whether the goods and services are produced in the United States or in other countries. To go from GDP to GNP, it is necessary to add all payments that Americans receive from outside the United States, then subtract all payments made to foreign-owned resources in the United States.

Figure 13.2 shows the relationship between GDP and GNP. Notice that GNP is the smaller of the two figures. This is because the United States paid out more income to factors of production from the rest of the world than it received; this is not the case for all countries. In a closed economy—one with no foreign sector—GDP equals GNP.

Net National Product

GNP is the first of five income measures included in the National Income and Product Accounts (NIPA). The second measure is **net national product (NNP)**, or GNP less depreciation. Depreciation represents the capital equipment that has worn out or become obsolete over the year.

CRITICAL THINKING

Recognizing Bias As a class, discuss the effects of economic indicators on political elections. Point out the example of the 1992 presidential election in the text, and **ask:** Can you can think of other elections, either local or national, in which economic issues played a role? Then have students do library research to find primary and secondary sources dealing with economic issues and an election. Have students search for bias in the reporting on economic factors; for example, are statistics presented in a fair manner, or are there vague references to the health of the economy? Hold another class discussion on students' findings. **BLOCK SCHEDULING**

The National Income and Product Accounts
(in billions of current dollars)

Gross Domestic Product (GDP)	**$10,226.8**
Plus: Payments to American citizens who employ resources outside the U.S.	+ 360.2
Less: Payments to foreign-owned resources employed inside the U.S.	- 367.2
Gross National Product (GNP)	**$10,219.8**
Less: Capital consumption allowances and adjustments (depreciation)	- 1,318.6
Net National Product (NNP)	**$8,901.2**
Less: Indirect business taxes and subsidies	- 736.2
National Income (NI)	**$8,165.0**
Plus: Transfer payments to persons, personal interest income, and Social Security receipts	+ 2,572.8
Less: Undistributed corporate profits, corporate income taxes, and Social Security contributions	- 2,183.6
Personal Income (PI)	**$8,554.2**
Less: Personal taxes and nontax payments	- 1,372.2
Disposable Personal Income (DI)	**$7,182.0**

Source: *Bureau of Economic Analysis*, June, 2001 (data for first quarter)

Using Tables The National Income and Product Accounts show the relationship between GDP and five measures of the nation's income. **What is the main difference between GDP and GNP?**

ECONOMICS
Online

Visit epp.glencoe.com and click on **Textbook Updates—*Chapter 13*** for an update of the data.

STANDARD
&POOR'S

Answer: *GDP does not count payments U.S. citizens receive from outside the country but does count payments made to foreign-owned resources employed within the U.S.*

L3 Summarizing

Direct students to locate an article on foreign trade from a current magazine or newspaper. Ask students to summarize the article in one or two paragraphs and then write a conclusion that analyzes the impact of U.S. imports and exports on the United States and the foreign country. Have students present their summaries to the class.

F.Y.I.

When an American tourist visits a foreign country, the money he or she spends there has the same effect on net foreign investment as a U.S. import.

National Income

The third measure is **national income (NI).** National income is the income that is left after all taxes except the corporate profits tax are subtracted from NNP. Examples of these taxes, also known as indirect business taxes, are excise taxes, property taxes, licensing fees, customs duties, and general sales taxes.

Personal Income

The fourth measure of the nation's total income is **personal income (PI)**—the total amount of income going to consumers before individual income taxes are subtracted. To go from national to personal income, four adjustments must be made.

First, income that does not go to the consumer must be subtracted from national income. One

CHAPTER 13: ECONOMIC PERFORMANCE **345**

EXTENDING THE CONTENT

Publishing GDP Data GDP estimates are made quarterly, and additional revisions are made as new data become available. The Bureau of Economic Analysis (BEA) in the U.S. Department of Commerce releases three estimates according to the following schedule: *Advance*—released in the first month after the end of quarter; *Preliminary*—released in the second month after the end of quarter; *Final*—released in the third month after the end of quarter.

Math Practice

Graphing Income In 1997, the lowest-earning 20% of American households received 3.6% of total income, the second 20% received 8.9%, the third 20% received 15%, the fourth 20% received 23.2%, and the highest 20% received 49.4%. Show this information in a circle graph. If total U.S. personal income in 1997 was $6.784 billion, calculate the personal income received by each quintile. Show the results in a bar graph.

CYBERNOMICS

Measuring GDP The Bureau of Economic Analysis (BEA), the government agency responsible for measuring GDP, has been criticized for not accurately measuring the impact of the information revolution on GDP. The BEA admits that it is hard to measure a rapidly changing economy. "We're like a tailor who's trying to take measurements for a suit from somebody who's running," says BEA spokesperson Larry Moran. For example, until 1999, the BEA counted software as a raw material, like oil or timber, so it was not included in GDP. Now the BEA considers software to be an investment in plant and equipment, and so it is included in GDP.

such type of income is retained earnings, also known as undistributed corporate profits. These are the profits that corporations keep to reinvest in new plants, offices, and equipment.

The second type of income that must be subtracted consists of corporate income taxes, which is a form of income to government. The third item subtracted is Social Security contributions from people's paychecks. After these three types of income have been subtracted from national income, transfer payments in the form of unemployment insurance, Social Security, medicaid, and several other forms of assistance must be added back in.

Disposable Personal Income

The fifth and smallest measure of income is **disposable personal income (DI)**—the total income the consumer sector has at its disposal after personal income taxes. This is an important measure because it reflects the actual amount of money the consumer sector is able to spend.

At the individual level, a person's disposable income is equal to the amount of money received from an employer after taxes and Social Security have been taken out. The $586.89 net pay on the check in **Figure 9.9** on page 241, plus the $3.20 of miscellaneous deductions, is disposable personal income.

The $3.20 is part of disposable income because the deduction was for something other than FICA or taxes. The wage earner could even choose to have more salary withheld to cover contributions to a credit union or charity or to buy savings bonds. However, these contributions would not lower a person's disposable personal income—they are merely one way of allocating disposable income.

Did you know?

A Growing Female Workforce The number of women in the labor force has virtually doubled since the early 1960s. From 1960 to 1997, the number of women in the workforce increased from 37.7 percent to 59.8 percent. The increase is a result of women having more education than ever before and delaying child rearing until they are established in their careers.

Economic Sectors and Circular Flows

It is useful to think of the economy as being made up of several different parts, or sectors. These sectors receive various components of the national income, and they use this income to purchase the total output. Sectors, described below and illustrated in **Figure 13.3**, are critical links in the circular flow of economic activity.

Consumer Sector

The largest sector in the macro economy is the consumer, or private, sector. Its basic unit, the **household,** is made up of all persons who occupy a house, apartment, or room that constitutes separate living quarters. A household includes related family members and all others—such as lodgers, foster children, and employees—who share the living quarters.

As long as the person or persons occupy a separate place of residence, a household also can consist of an **unrelated individual**—a person who lives alone even though he or she may have family living elsewhere. The concept of a household is broader than that of a **family**—a group of two or more persons related by blood, marriage, or adoption who are living together in a household.

All three definitions have value to the United States Bureau of the Census. The definition of the household is especially useful because the demand for durable goods, such as stoves, water heaters, furnaces, and refrigerators, is more closely tied to the number of households than to the number of families. Also, many households, even when made up of persons not related by blood, marriage, or adoption, tend to behave as a single economic unit.

Shown as **"C"** in **Figure 13.3**, the consumer sector receives its income in the form of disposable personal income. In a sense, the consumer sector receives the income that is left over after all of the depreciation, business taxes, and FICA payments are made, plus the income received in transfer payments that are added back in.

Investment Sector

The second sector of the macro economy is the business, or investment, sector, labeled **"I"** in

INTERDISCIPLINARY CONNECTIONS ACTIVITY

Daily Life Many students confuse income with wealth. Like GDP, income is a "flow variable," or a variable that measures a value over a period of time. Wealth is a "stock variable," or a variable that measures a value at one point in time. Have students find examples of other flow variables and stock variables that they encounter in their daily lives. *(Examples of flow variables are driving speeds, rainfall, and calorie consumption. Examples of stock variables are the size of a CD collection, the money in a wallet, and the weight of a desk.)*

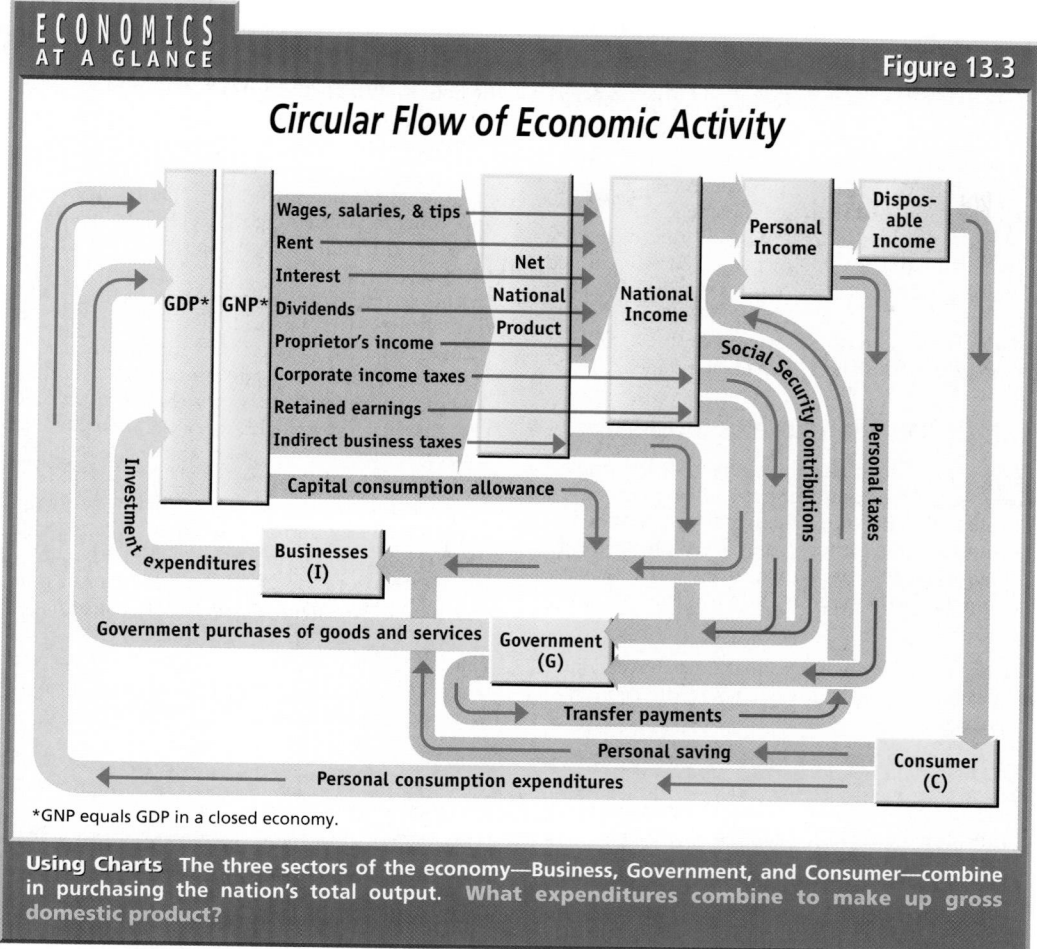

ECONOMICS
AT A GLANCE

Figure 13.3

Circular Flow of Economic Activity

*GNP equals GDP in a closed economy.

Using Charts The three sectors of the economy—Business, Government, and Consumer—combine in purchasing the nation's total output. **What expenditures combine to make up gross domestic product?**

ECONOMICS
AT A GLANCE

Answer: *personal consumption expenditures, government purchases of goods and services, and investment expenditures*

3 ASSESS

Assign Section 1 Assessment as homework or as an in-class activity.

💾 Have students use **Interactive Tutor Self-Assessment Software** to review Section 1.

Section Quiz 13-1

QUIZ ◆ Chapter 13, Section 1

MEASURING THE NATION'S OUTPUT   SCORE

Figure 13.3. It is made up of proprietorships, partnerships, and corporations. It is the productive sector responsible for bringing the factors of production together to produce output.

The income to the investment sector is the depreciation that is subtracted from GNP and the retained earnings subtracted from NI. The business sector can treat depreciation as a form of income because it is a non-cash expense that never leaves the firm.

Government Sector

The third sector is the public sector, which includes all local, state, and federal levels of government. Shown as **"G"** in **Figure 13.3,** the government sector receives its income from sources such as indirect business taxes, corporate income taxes, Social Security contributions, and personal income taxes from the consumer or household sector. If the figure had a foreign sector, then customs duties would also be part of the sector's income.

CHAPTER 13: ECONOMIC PERFORMANCE **347**

EXTENDING THE CONTENT

Three Kinds of Consumption National income accounting records three classifications of consumption in the consumer sector. Durable goods are goods with an average life of more than three years—automobiles, furniture, and appliances, for example. Nondurable goods are goods that have an average life of less than three years—shampoo, food products, gasoline, and clothing, for example. Services, such as financial or legal advice, health care, and haircuts, make up the final classification of consumption. In some instances, such classifications seem arbitrary. A well-made overcoat, for example, may last for 5 to 10 years. Even so, as an item of clothing it would be regarded as a nondurable good.

Reteach

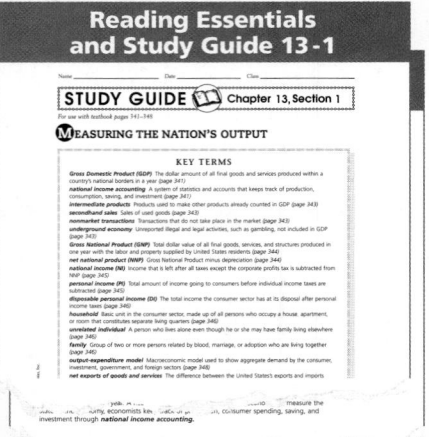

Reading Essentials and Study Guide 13-1

Enrich

Direct students to consult a recent copy of the *Statistical Abstract of the United States* to find a year in which GDP increased or decreased significantly. Have them conduct research to determine why GDP changed significantly and to note what economic policy changes, if any, were enacted.

 CLOSE

Ask students to list 10 factors not recorded directly in the GDP that affect the quality of life negatively or positively.

Foreign Sector

The fourth sector of the macro economy is the foreign sector, usually identified as **"F,"** but not shown in **Figure 13.3**. This sector includes all consumers and producers outside the United States. Unlike the other sectors, the international sector does not have a source of income specific to it.

Instead, this sector represents the difference between the dollar value of goods sent abroad and the dollar value of goods purchased from abroad. If the two are reasonably close, the foreign sector appears to be fairly small, even when there are large numbers of goods and services being traded.

The Output-Expenditure Model

The circular flow in **Figure 13.3** is complete when the output-expenditure model is introduced. The **output-expenditure model** is a macroeconomic model used to show aggregate demand by the consumer, investment, government, and foreign sectors. When this is written as

$$GDP = C + I + G + F$$

the equation becomes a formal output-expenditure model used to explain and analyze the economy's performance.

According to this model, the consumer sector spends its income on the goods and services used by households. These personal consumption expenditures include groceries, rent, books, automobiles, clothes, and almost anything else people buy.

The investment, or business, sector spends its income on plants, offices, equipment, inventories, and other investment goods. These expenditures represent the total value of capital goods created in the economy during the year.

The government sector spends its income on many categories, including national defense, income security, interest on the national debt, health care, roads, and education. The only major government expenditure not included in total output is transfer payments, because this money is used by others to buy goods and services that are part of total GDP.

The foreign sector also buys many goods and services—tractors, computers, airplanes, and agricultural products—that make up GDP. In return, it supplies such products as Japanese cars, Korean shirts, and Brazilian shoes to be consumed at home. For this reason, the foreign sector's purchases are called **net exports of goods and services,** a term that refers to the difference between the United States's exports and its imports.

Section 1 Assessment

Checking for Understanding

1. **Main Idea** Explain the difference between GDP and GNP.

2. **Key Terms** Define Gross Domestic Product, national income accounting, intermediate products, secondhand sales, nonmarket transactions, underground economy, Gross National Product, net national product, national income, personal income, disposable personal income, household, unrelated individual, family, output-expenditure model, net exports of goods and services.

Reviewing Objectives

3. **Describe** how GDP is measured.

4. **List** the limitations of GDP.

5. **Explain** the importance of GDP.

Applying Economic Concepts

6. **Gross Domestic Product** What effect do you think the computer industry has had on the GDP? Use examples, if available, to support your claim.

Critical Thinking

7. **Making Generalizations** What would be the effects of a decline in GDP?

8. **Summarizing Information** Why is GDP not a proper measure of the total income earned by U.S. citizens?

 Practice and **assess** key social studies skills with the *Glencoe Skillbuilder Interactive Workbook, Level 2.*

Section 1 Assessment Answers

1. GDP is the dollar amount of all final goods and services produced within a country's national borders in a year. GNP is the dollar value of all final goods, services, and structures produced with labor and property supplied by a country's residents.

2. All vocabulary terms are defined in the text.

3. Sampling techniques are used to estimate all the goods, services, and structures produced within national boundaries in a given year. The quantity of final goods and services is multiplied by their prices.

4. GDP tells nothing about the composition of output and tells little about the impact of production on the quality of life.

5. It is the best measure of economic health.

6. Computers allow greater amounts of work to be completed more quickly, so it has probably increased the GDP.

7. decline in manufacturing or spending or both

8. because it does not include payments Americans receive from outside the U.S.

TECHNOLOGY Skill

Using a Spreadsheet

People use electronic spreadsheets to manage numbers quickly and easily. Formulas may be used to add, subtract, multiply, and divide the numbers in the spreadsheet. If you make a change to one number, the totals are recalculated automatically for you.

Learning the Skill

To understand how to use a spreadsheet, read the following descriptions of several spreadsheet calculations:

- A spreadsheet is an electronic worksheet. It is made up of numbered cells that form rows and columns. Each column (vertical) is assigned a letter or number. Each row (horizontal) is assigned a number. Each point where a column and row intersect is called a *cell*. The cell's position on the spreadsheet is labeled according to its corresponding column and row—Column A, Row 1 (A10); Column B, Row 2 (B2) and so on. See the diagram below.

A1	B1	C1	D1	E1
A2	B2	C2	D2	E2
A3	B3	C3	D3	E3
A4	B4	C4	D4	E4
A5	B5	C5	D5	E5

- The computer highlights the cell you are in. The contents of the cell also appear on a status line at the top of the screen.

- Spreadsheets use *standard formulas* to calculate numbers. To create a formula, highlight the cell you want the results in. Type an equal sign (=) and then build the formula, step by step. If you type the formula =B4+B5+B6 in cell B7, the values in these cells are added together and the sum shows up in cell B7.

- To use division, the formula would look like this: =A5/C2. This divides A5 by C2. An asterisk (*) signifies multiplication: =(B2*C3)+D1 means you want to multiply B2 times C3, then add D1.

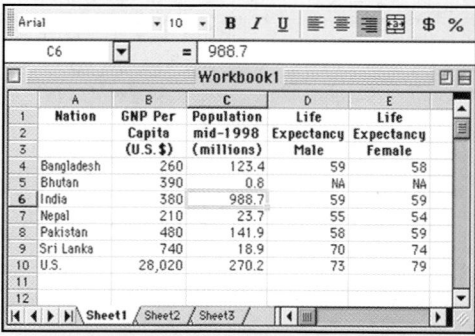

The computer highlights the cell you're working in.

Practicing the Skill

Study the spreadsheet on this page.

1. Which cell is highlighted? What information is found in the cell?

2. What formula would you type in which cell to calculate the average life expectancy of both males and females in Sri Lanka?

3. What formula would you type in which cell to find the total GNP per capita of the countries listed?

Application Activity

Use a spreadsheet to enter your test scores and your homework grades. At the end of the grading period, input the correct formula and the spreadsheet will calculate your average grade.

Technology Skill

Teaching Skills

Many spreadsheet programs provide built-in templates or sample spreadsheets. To find them, search for the keywords "template" or "samples" or "tutorial" in the program's help index. Have students practice with these existing spreadsheets before designing their own. If the programs at school do not have such a feature, ask the school treasurer or other local businesspeople to provide nonconfidential examples of spreadsheets for students to examine.

Additional Practice

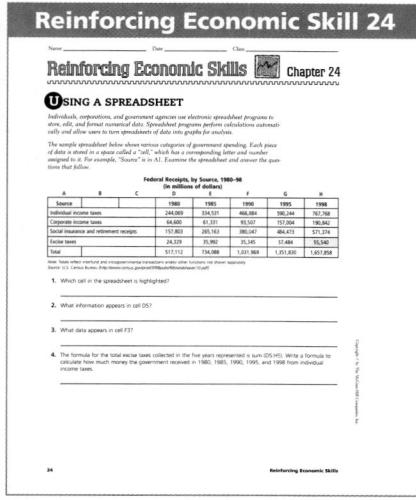

Answers to Practicing the Skill

1. C6; population mid-1998 (millions) for India
2. Highlight the cell you want the results in. Then type an equal sign and the formula (D9 + E9) ÷ 2.
3. Select the cell you want the results in. Type an equal sign and enter B4 + B5 + B6 + B7 + B8 + B9 + B10.

1 FOCUS

Section Overview

This section discusses price index and the difference between real and current GDP.

BELLRINGER
Motivational Activity

 Project **transparency** and have students answer questions.

Available as blackline master.

Daily Focus Transparency 71

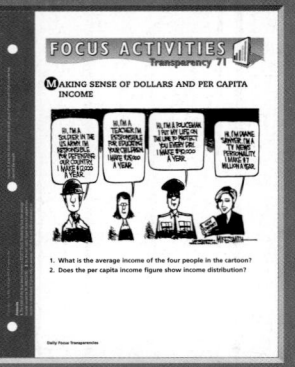

Study Guide

Reading Strategy

Have students create the graphic organizer.
Answers to Graphic: *Current GDP is not adjusted to remove the effects of inflation, but real GDP is.*

Preteaching Vocabulary

Randomly list the five measures of income on the board. Have students rank them in descending order from largest to smallest and explain the meaning of each.

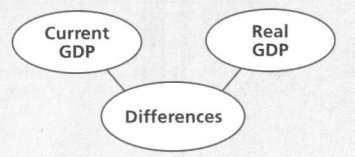

GDP and Changes in the Price Level

Study Guide

Main Idea
GDP is calculated at existing prices and adjusted for inflation to make comparisons over time.

Reading Strategy
Graphic Organizer As you read the section, complete a graphic organizer similar to the one below by explaining the ways in which these economic measures differ from one another.

Current GDP — Real GDP — Differences

Key Terms
inflation, price index, base year, market basket, consumer price index, producer price index, implicit GDP, price deflator, current GDP, real GDP, GDP in constant dollars

Objectives
After studying this section, you will be able to:
1. **Explain** how a price index is constructed.
2. **Describe** three price indices.
3. **Understand** the difference between real and current GDP.

Applying Economic Concepts
Market Basket Read to find out how economists use the market basket, consisting of items most frequently purchased by consumers, to construct the consumer price index.

Cover Story

Eyes on the Price

Trenton, N.J.—The hospital's finance director is relentlessly unhelpful, but she is still no match for Sabina Bloom, government gumshoe.

BLS keeps tabs

Mrs. Bloom wants to know the exact prices of some hospital services. "Nothing's changed," the woman says. "Well, do you have the ledger?" Mrs. Bloom asks. "We haven't changed any prices," the woman insists. Mrs. Bloom's fast talk finally pries the woman from behind her desk, and she gets the numbers. It turns out that a semi-private surgery recovery room now costs $753.80 a day—or four cents less than a month ago.

Chalk up another small success for Mrs. Bloom, one of about 300 Bureau of Labor Statistics employees who gather the information that is fed into the monthly Consumer Price Index.

—*The Wall Street Journal*, January 1, 1997

350

Most people are surprised to discover how hard the government works to collect and process data. The scene described in the cover story dealing with gathering information on inflation is just one such example.

Inflation is a rise in the general price level. It is important to track inflation because it distorts the economic statistics that we keep. To see how this happens, compare the GDP in **Figure 13.1** with the GDP in **Figure 13.4**. Assume that the second table was compiled one year after the first, and that the inflation rate during that year was 10 percent. The second and third columns in each table show that the product composition and quantity of output was the same for both years. In other words, there was no real change in the amount of goods and services produced.

The fourth and fifth columns in each table, however, do not match. Looking at columns 4 and 5, you'll notice that everything costs more in the second table than in the first one. This makes GDP rise by 10 percent, or $900 billion, revealing

---

RESOURCE MANAGER

Reproducible Masters
- Reproducible Lesson Plan 13-2
- Daily Lecture Notes 13-2
- Guided Reading Activity 13-2
- Reading Essentials and Study Guide 13-2
- Section Quiz 13-2

Transparencies
- Daily Focus Transparency 71

Multimedia
- Interactive Tutor Self-Assessment Software
- ExamView® Pro Testmaker
- Presentation Plus!

Figure 13.4

Estimating Gross Domestic Product

	Product	Quantity (millions)	Price (per 1 unit)	Dollar Value (millions)
Goods	Automobiles	6	$22,000	$132,000
	Replacement Tires	10	$70	$700
	Shoes	55	$55	$3,025
	...*	...*	...*	...*
Services	Haircuts	150	$10	$1,500
	Income Tax Filings	30	$160	$4,800
	Legal Advice	45	$220	$9,900
	...*	...*	...*	...*
Structures	Single Family	3	$80,000	$240,000
	Multifamily	5	$330,000	$1,650,000
	Commercial	1	$1,100,000	$1,100,000
	...*	...*	...*	...*
			Total Gross Domestic Product = $9.9 trillion	

*... other goods, services, and structures

Using Tables Inflation can distort the value of Gross Domestic Product from one year to the next. Compare the total gross domestic product in this chart to that in Figure 13.1. What accounts for the higher total?

the effects of inflation. The problem is that the dollar value of the final output appeared to go up without any changes in the quantity of goods and services produced.

Constructing a Price Index

To remove the distortions of inflation, economists construct a **price index**—a statistical series that can be used to measure changes in prices over time. A price index can be compiled for a specific product or for a range of items.

It is fairly easy to construct a price index. First, select a **base year**—a year that serves as the basis of comparison for all other years. The price index expresses the price of goods and services in a given year as a percentage of the price of those during the base year.

Second, select the **market basket**—a representative selection of commonly purchased goods and services. Then, record the price of each item in the market basket. Finally, total the prices. The total represents the base-year market basket price and is assigned a value of 100 percent.

Figure 13.5 shows a price index for a representative market basket with a large number of items. Because 1982–84 is used as the base period, the prices in the base-year column are lower than those today. The total of the market prices—$1,792.00—is assigned a value of 100 percent, which is the index number for that year.

In order to track inflation, we have to track the price of the goods and services in the market basket at regular intervals, and then compare them to the base year. In **Figure 13.5** for example, the cost of the market basket in 1998 is $2,920.96—or 163 percent

CHAPTER 13: ECONOMIC PERFORMANCE **351**

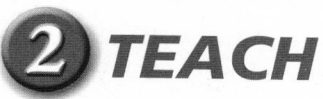
Daily Lecture Notes 13-2

DAILY LECTURE NOTES Lesson 13-2

DID YOU KNOW?

In 1999, classrooms around the country helped create a market basket of goods and services used by teenagers. The data was used to create a Teenage Consumer Price Index (TCPI).

PAGES 351-352

I. Constructing a Price Index

A. A price index is used to measure changes in prices over time.

B. A price index is created by selecting a base year and a representative market basket of goods.

Discussion Question

What do price indices show? (the change in price relative to a base year)

PAGES 352-353

II. Major Price Indices

A. The consumer price index (CPI) reports changes in the prices of 90,000 consumer goods and services.

B. The producer price index (PPI) reports changes in prices received by domestic producers for 3,000 commodities.

C. The GDP price deflator is an index of average prices for all goods and services.

Discussion Question

Why are price indices broken down into subcategories? (to give consumers and businesses a better idea of how prices in industry have changed)

ECONOMICS
AT A GLANCE

Answer: *inflation has changed the price per unit of each item*

CURRICULUM CONNECTION

History From December 1922 to November 1923, Germany experienced hyperinflation, an inflation rate greater than 50 percent per month. Prices rose by an astonishing 100 million percent. Carting their money in wheelbarrows and baby carriages, people rushed to spend their wages before prices rose even higher. The hyperinflation wiped out many families in Germany and planted the seeds for Hitler's rise to power.

MEETING SPECIAL NEEDS ACTIVITY

English Language Learners Have students locate unfamiliar words in Section 2. Assign each student several words. Have them research the meanings of their words in the text and in translation dictionaries. Have them write each word, its definition, and a picture or illustration on a sheet of paper. Ask students to present their pages to the class, then bind all of them together to create an illustrated dictionary of Section 2 words. **ELL**

 Refer to *Inclusion for the Social Studies Classroom Strategies and Activities* in the TCR.

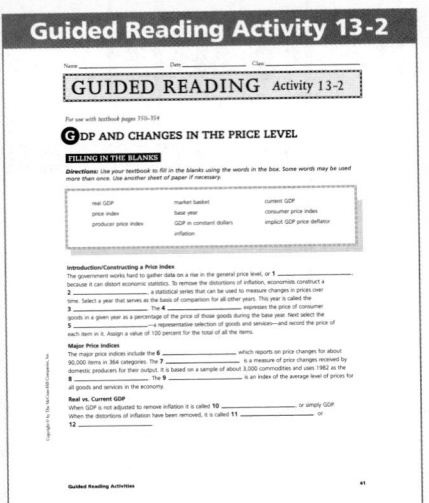

L2 Applying Concepts

Have students track price changes over the last five years for a few items they buy regularly. Then have them chart how their income—from allowances and/or wages for part-time jobs—has changed over the same period. Direct them to calculate the percentage change in prices and income. Ask them to write a paragraph showing how they have been affected by inflation.

STANDARD &POOR'S

Answer: *Subtract the price of the market basket for the base year from the price of the new market basket. Then divide the difference by the market basket price for the base period. The percentage is the change of the new market basket in relation to the base-period market basket.*

---

higher than in the base year. By April of 2001, prices had increased to 176.9 percent of base-year prices.

Major Price Indices

Price indices can be constructed for a number of different purposes. Some measure changes in the price of a single item. Some measure the price changes of imported goods, while others do the same for agricultural products. Different base years are often used for each, but this is not important since index numbers for an individual series are only compared with other numbers in the same series.

Consumer Price Index

The **consumer price index (CPI)** reports on price changes for about 90,000 items in 364 categories. Prices for the goods and services currently sampled are taken from 85 geographically distributed areas around the country and are compared to their 1982–84 base-year prices. Some of the items are surveyed in all the areas, while others are sampled in only a few.

Information on consumer price changes is collected by Bureau of Labor Statistics employees, as described in the cover story on page 350. The BLS compiles the index monthly and then publishes it for the economy as a whole. There also are separate indices for 28 selected areas across the nation.

Producer Price Index

The **producer price index** measures price changes paid by domestic producers for their inputs. It is based on a sample of about 100,000 commodities and uses 1982 as the base year. The Bureau of Labor Statistics reports the producer price index every month. Although it is compiled for all commodities, it also is broken down into various subcategories that include farm products, fuels, chemicals, rubber, pulp and paper, and processed foods.

STANDARD &POOR'S
Figure 13.5

Constructing the Consumer Price Index

Item	Description	Price Base Period (1982–84)	Price Second Period (1998)	Price April (2001)
1.	Toothpaste (7 oz.)	$1.40	$1.49	$2.25
2.	Milk (1 gal.)	1.29	1.29	1.79
3.	Peanut butter (2 lb. jar)	2.50	2.65	3.73
4.	Light bulb (60 watt)	.45	.48	.65
•••••	••••••	•••••	•••••	•••••
364.	Automobile engine tune-up	40.00	42.00	64.75
	Total Cost of Market Basket:	$1,792.00	$2,920.96	$3,170.05
	Index Number:	100%	163.0%	176.9%

Using Tables The Bureau of Labor Statistics measures items in terms of their 1982–84 base-period prices. As time goes by, prices change, giving the new market basket a different total value. **How is the new price index computed?**

ECONOMICS Online
Visit epp.glencoe.com and click on **Textbook Updates—Chapter 13** for an update of the data.

FREE ENTERPRISE ACTIVITY

Point out that, in part, the amount of free enterprise in the economy is related to the total expenditures in the government sector. Then organize students into six groups and assign each group an even-numbered, recent year. Have groups discover the size of the government sector in relation to the other sectors for their particular year. Next, have groups research government activity during that year. Finally, have groups write a brief report about the role of government in the economy for their year, citing government activities and any unusual rise or fall in government expenditures. **BLOCK SCHEDULING**

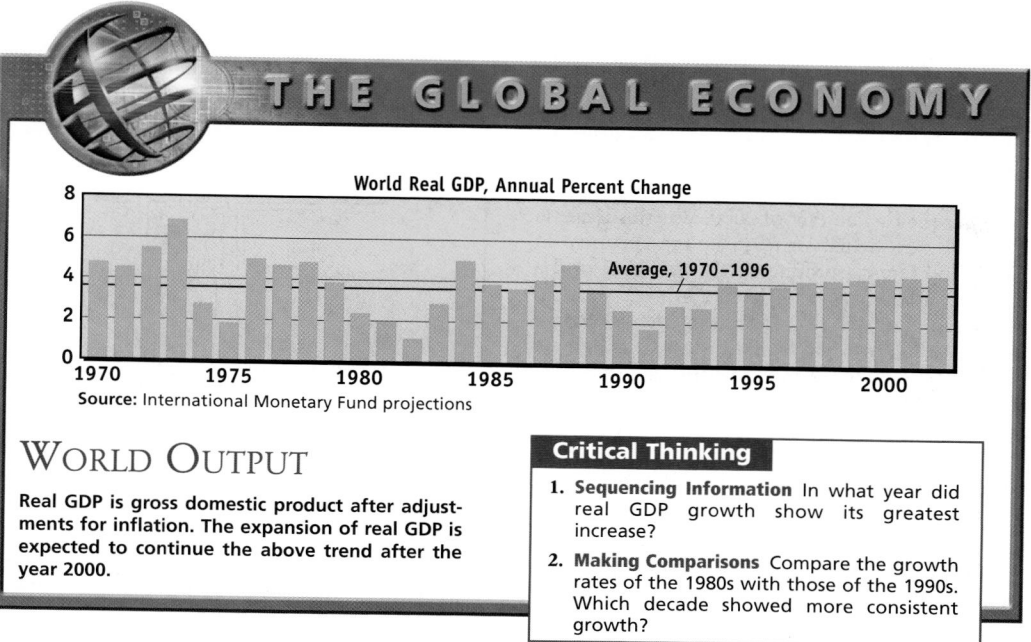

THE GLOBAL ECONOMY

World Real GDP, Annual Percent Change

Average, 1970–1996

1970   1975   1980   1985   1990   1995   2000

Source: International Monetary Fund projections

WORLD OUTPUT

Real GDP is gross domestic product after adjustments for inflation. The expansion of real GDP is expected to continue the above trend after the year 2000.

Critical Thinking

1. **Sequencing Information** In what year did real GDP growth show its greatest increase?

2. **Making Comparisons** Compare the growth rates of the 1980s with those of the 1990s. Which decade showed more consistent growth?

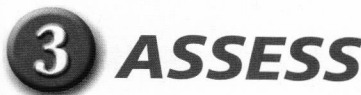

THE GLOBAL ECONOMY

World Output An apparent increase in the GDP can be caused by an increase in prices. To obtain the real value of growth in the GDP, the figures must be adjusted for inflation.

Answers:
1. *from 1975 to 1976*
2. *the 1990s; because from 1995 and on, growth consistently increased*

③ ASSESS

Assign Section 2 Assessment as homework or as an in-class activity.

■ Have students use **Interactive Tutor Self-Assessment Software** to review Section 2.

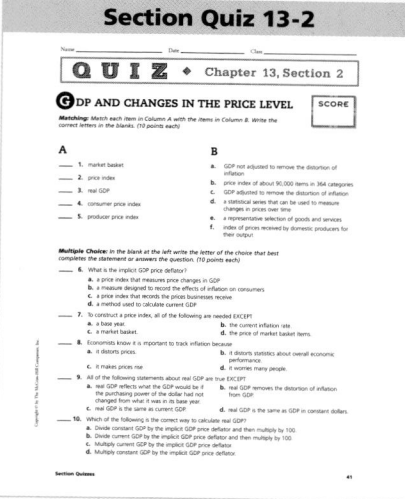

Implicit GDP Price Deflator

The **implicit GDP price deflator** is an index of average levels of prices for all goods and services in the economy. It is computed quarterly and has a base year of 1996.

Because GDP is a measure of the final output of goods and services and covers thousands of items instead of hundreds, many economists believe it is a good, long-run indicator of the price changes that consumers face. The deflator is only compiled quarterly, however, so it cannot be used to measure monthly changes in inflation.

Real vs. Current GDP

To compare GDP over time, you need to distinguish between changes in GDP because of the effects of inflation and changes in GDP that represent increases in production and income. When GDP is not adjusted to remove the effects of inflation, it is called **current GDP,** or simply GDP. When the distortions of inflation have been removed, it is called **real GDP** or **GDP in constant dollars.** This measure reflects what the GDP would have been if prices had not changed from what they were in the base year.

Converting GDP to Real Dollars

How would you convert current GDP to GDP in real (inflation-adjusted) dollars? First, divide the current GDP by the deflator, then multiply by 100 (since the deflator is really a percent). Or:

$$\text{Real GDP} = \frac{\text{GDP in current dollars}}{\text{implicit GDP price deflator}} \times 100$$

To illustrate, the GDP estimate for the first quarter of 2001 was $10,226.8 billion. The GDP deflator for that period was 108.53. In other words, prices in 2001 were 108.53 percent higher than in 1996. To calculate, divide current GDP by the deflator and multiply by 100:

$$\text{Real GDP} = \frac{\$10,226.8 \text{ billion}}{108.53} \times 100 = \$9,423.0 \text{ billion}$$

The amount of $9,423.0 billion, then, is the dollar value of all goods and services produced, if measured in 1996 prices.

CHAPTER 13: ECONOMIC PERFORMANCE **353**

CRITICAL THINKING

Analyzing Information Have your class create a price index that can be updated over time by future classes. Begin by having students design a market basket that represents goods and services that high school students typically buy, then determine the total cost of that market basket. Each semester, have students determine new prices for the market basket and use their data to update the price index. Keep records, too, of the wages your students receive at their jobs. Use the price index to convert their nominal wages into real wages and track the level of their real wages over time. Each year, have students analyze the updated index and prepare a paper or presentation about the changes.

Reteach

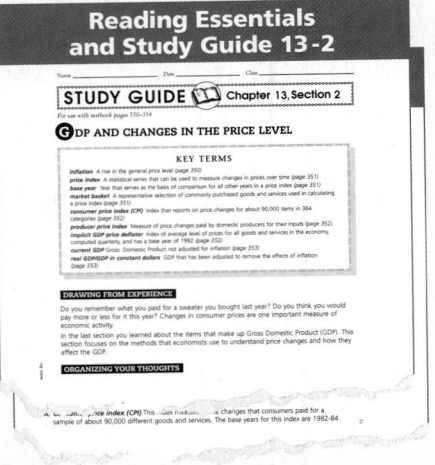

Reading Essentials and Study Guide 13-2

Enrich

Have students write an essay comparing GDP and GNP as measures of economic health and economic performance. Select students to read and discuss their essays.

4 CLOSE

Have students discuss the importance of inflation when discussing economic statistics. Ask them to name any familiar products that they believe have been affected by a rise in inflation.

Comparing GDP in Different Years

Converting current dollar amounts to real dollars is useful for making comparisons. For example, the $10,226.8 billion GDP estimate for the first quarter of 2001 was larger than the $9,752.7 billion GDP for the first quarter of 2000. Was this increase caused by an actual increase in the quantity of goods and services produced? Or was some of the increase in GDP caused by inflation?

We can find out by converting the 2000 first quarter GDP to 1996 dollars through the same procedure described above. The only change is that we have to use the GDP price deflator for the 2000 first quarter:

$$\text{Real GDP} = \frac{\$9,752.7 \text{ billion}}{106.10} \times 100 = \$9,192.0 \text{ billion}$$

In terms of constant 1996 dollars, real GDP in the first quarter of 2000 amounted to $9,192.0 billion. Because the 2001 real or constant dollar GDP amount of $9,423.0 billion was greater than the 2000 real dollar amount, there was a real increase in GDP that was not due to inflation.

Inflation

"The price may seem a little high, but you have to remember that's in today's dollars."

Comparing Prices As long as we have inflation, we must be careful when comparing prices from different eras. *How can we compare a price today with a price from an earlier period?*

Section 2 Assessment

Checking for Understanding

1. **Main Idea** Would there be a difference between the rate of growth in real GDP and the rate of growth in real GDP per person? Explain. (Real GDP per person includes adjustments for changes in the population.)

2. **Key Terms** Define inflation, price index, base year, market basket, consumer price index, producer price index, implicit GDP price deflator, current GDP, real GDP, GDP in constant dollars.

3. **Explain** why a market basket is used whenever a price index is constructed.

4. **List** three major price indices.

5. **Describe** the difference between real and current GDP.

Applying Economic Concepts

6. **Market Basket** If you were to construct a market basket of goods and services that high school students typically consume, what would you select?

Critical Thinking

7. **Making Comparisons** What do you think a typical market basket 20 years ago might have included that we do not use today? What do you think a future market basket might have that we do not include?

8. **Making Predictions** Suppose you were told that you would earn $60,000 a year in 2008. Explain why this information would tell you little about the standard of living you might enjoy. What other information would you need to have before you could evaluate how well you might live in 2008?

Practice and assess key social studies skills with the *Glencoe Skillbuilder Interactive Workbook, Level 2.*

Section 2 Assessment Answers

1. No. If adjustments are made for population growth, the rates should be the same.

2. All vocabulary terms are defined in the text.

3. representative of purchases

4. consumer price index, producer price index, implicit GDP price deflator

5. Current GDP is the GDP not adjusted to remove the effects of inflation. When the distortions of inflation have been removed, it is called real GDP.

6. commonly purchased goods and services

7. Lists will reflect changes caused by technological developments.

8. If you knew what the consumer price index was in relation to the base period you would have a better idea about how much $60,000 would buy in 2008.

Profiles IN Economics

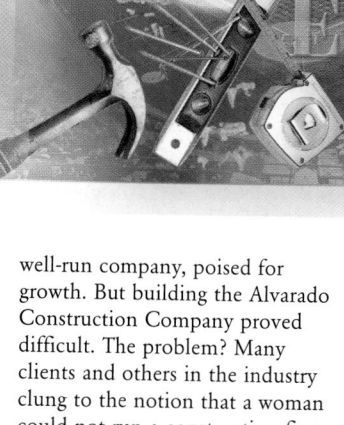

Succeeding in a "Man's" Business:
Linda Alvarado
(1951–)

"There are still too many doors that need opening for women and minorities," Linda Alvarado once said. "There's no lack of talent or ambition out there—just a lack of opportunity for women and minorities to try."

Alvarado knows all about talent and ambition—and the obstacles women and minorities face. She herself has become one of the most successful individuals in one of the most male-dominated industries in the country: construction.

SUCCESS IN BUSINESS

As a young woman, Alvarado became intrigued by the construction industry. While still a student, she took a part-time job with a development company. Her talent and ambition earned her a steady advancement, and she eventually struck out on her own.

Alvarado knew enough about the construction industry to make first-rate service and on-time delivery the top priorities of her Denver-based Alvarado Construction Company. An objective analysis would have revealed a strong,

well-run company, poised for growth. But building the Alvarado Construction Company proved difficult. The problem? Many clients and others in the industry clung to the notion that a woman could not run a construction firm. "There's a perception out there that buildings are built by guys—big guys, real men," Alvarado said.

Alvarado's first-rate work disproved this nonsense. Through perseverance, she brought Alvarado Construction to a leading position in the construction industry. Moreover, many international companies, eager for her insight, have sought her entrepreneurial and management talents. Alvarado is also an owner of the Colorado Rockies baseball team.

SUCCESS IN THE COMMUNITY

Alvarado shines when it comes to using her business success to

help others. Because of her own arduous personal experience, she is especially interested in the difficulties facing Hispanics and women and does what she can to help. She regularly meets with other women in business and mentors women who are just starting out. Many civic organizations have lauded her for her extensive contributions to the Hispanic community.

To many young people, therefore, Alvarado is a hero: a living example of how talent and ambition can open doors that long have been closed to women and minorities.

Examining the Profile

1. **Demonstrating Reasoned Judgment** Reread the first paragraph. Explain why you agree or disagree with Alvarado.

2. **Evaluating Information** Do you think successful businesspeople like Alvarado have a moral responsibility to contribute to their communities? Explain your answer.

BACKGROUND

Despite her economic success, Linda Alvarado continues to fight passionately on behalf of women and minorities. "In an ideal world, ability would count for everything, and gender and ethnicity wouldn't matter," she says. "We're making progress, but we aren't there yet." To help achieve that goal, Alvarado helped found the Denver Hispanic Chamber of Commerce and has served as its chairperson. She has also served as a commissioner for the White House Initiative on Educational Excellence for Hispanic Americans and is a nationally recognized advocate for diversity in the workplace.

TEACH

Point out to students that when Alvarado was starting out, there were no affirmative action programs of which she could take advantage. Have students write brief essays in which they evaluate this fact as evidence that supports arguments for or arguments against affirmative action.

School TO WORK

Construction Worker Have students consult the federal *Occupational Outlook Handbook* and other sources to learn about the prospects for various construction jobs (including skilled trades), pay rates, union and licensing requirements, and so on. Have them report what they learn in writing.

Answers to Examining the Profile

1. Students who agree with Alvarado might cite economic indicators that reveal the continuing discrepancy between the economic status of whites and males and that of minorities and women. Students who disagree with Alvarado might argue that discrimination is illegal and that equal opportunities exist for all.

2. Students who think that such people have a responsibility might argue that those who benefit from a system have a responsibility to "give something back." Students who think that such people do not have a responsibility may argue that success incurs no such responsibility since it was earned.

FOCUS

Section Overview
This section analyzes the U.S. population.

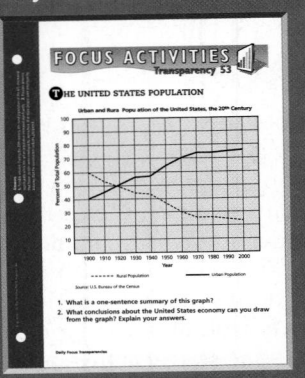
Study Guide

Reading Strategy
Have students create the graphic organizer.
Answers to Graphic: *was more than 3 percent until the Civil War, but has declined steadily and is now 0.9 percent; 5.8 people during colonial times, but has fallen to 2.6 today; current growth in West and South and losses in Northeast and Central Plains*

Preteaching Vocabulary
Call on volunteers to offer definitions for each of the Key Terms.

GDP and Population

Study Guide

Main Idea
Projected population trends can help determine the direction of economic developments.

Reading Strategy
Graphic Organizer As you read the section, complete a graphic organizer similar to the one below by identifying changes in the United States in the categories that are listed.

Key Terms
census, urban population, rural population, center of population, demographer, fertility rate, life expectancy, net immigration, baby boom, population pyramid, dependency ratio

Objectives
After studying this section, you will be able to:
1. **Explain** how population is estimated in the U.S.
2. **Describe** the factors affecting future population growth.

Applying Economic Concepts
Urban and Rural How do you define the words *rural* and *urban*? Read to find out how rural and urban are defined in economic terms.

Cover Story

Atlanta Pays Environmental Price for Fast Growth

Atlanta (CNN)—Atlanta, long known as "a city built in a forest," is becoming a concrete jungle as its trees disappear to make way for shopping malls, houses, and highways.

Busy thoroughfare in Atlanta

Metro Atlanta's population jumped from 3 million to 3.5 million between 1990 and 1996, . . . and the trend shows no sign of slowing.

The Atlanta area includes four of the nation's top 10 fastest-growing counties. Developers are clearing an average of 50 acres of tree-covered land per day, which amounts to an area larger than Manhattan each year.

Unemployment . . . hovers around 3 percent. But commuting times have risen along with the number of jobs. The average commute for the Atlanta area is now 35 miles round-trip per day!—longer than any other city's in the nation.

—*CNNInteractive*, March 19, 1999

356

The rate at which population grows influences GDP and economic growth in several ways. First, for an economy to grow, its factors of production must also grow or become more productive. One of the factors of production, labor, is closely tied to the size of the population.

Second, changes in population can distort some macroeconomic measures like GDP and GNP—which is why they are often expressed on a per capita, or per person, basis. If a nation's population grows faster than output, per capita output falls and the country could end up with more mouths than it can feed. Or, if a nation's population grows too slowly, there may not be enough workers to sustain economic growth.

Finally, population growth affects the quality of life, especially in fast-growing areas such as Atlanta. The study of population involves more than a simple total of people.

Population in the United States

The Constitution of the United States requires the government to periodically take a **census,** an official count of all people, including their place of residence. Because the

---

official census occurs every 10 years, it is called the *decennial census*. The nation's founders initiated the decennial census to apportion the number of representatives each state elects to Congress.

Counting the Population

The federal government conducted the first census in 1790. Throughout the 1800s, temporary agencies were created each decade to conduct the counts. In 1902, Congress permanently established the Census Bureau. Today, the Bureau works year-round, conducting monthly surveys relating to the size and other characteristics of the population.

When the Census Bureau conducts the decennial census, it uses the household as its primary survey unit. About five in every six households receive a "short form," which takes just a few minutes to fill out. The remaining households receive a "long form," which includes more questions and serves to generate a more detailed profile of the population. Bureau employees use different methods to count special groups, such as homeless persons, who do not normally conform to the household survey unit.

The Census Bureau tabulates and presents its data in a number of ways. One classification denotes the size of the **urban population**—people living in incorporated villages or towns with 2,500 or more inhabitants. The **rural population** makes up the remainder of the total population, including those persons who live in sparsely populated areas along the fringes of cities.

Historical Growth

The population of the United States has grown considerably since colonial times. The rate of growth, however, has steadily declined. Between 1790 and 1860, the population grew at a compounded rate of about 3.0 percent a year. From the beginning of the Civil War until 1900, the average fell to 2.2 percent. From 1900 to the beginning of World War II, the rate dropped to 1.4 percent. It declined slowly but steadily after that, and by 2002 the rate of population growth had fallen to approximately 0.9 percent.

The census also shows a steady trend toward smaller households. During colonial times, household size averaged 5.8 people. By 1960, the average

had fallen to 3.33 and then to approximately 2.60 people today. The figures reflect a worldwide trend toward smaller families in industrial countries where couples often view children as a financial liability. The figures also show that more individuals are living alone today than ever before.

Regional Change

An important population shift began in the 1970s, with a migration to the western and southern parts of the country. These regions have grown quite rapidly, while most of the older, industrial areas in the North and East have grown more slowly or even lost population. Many people have left the crowded, industrial Northeast for warmer, more spacious parts of the country. States such as Arizona, Nevada, and Florida have grown tremendously.

The Census Bureau also tracks changes in the geographic distribution of the population. **Figure 13.6** shows changes in population distribution for nine regions in 1988 and projected in 2010.

The projections show growth in the West and South and losses of population in the Northeast and Central Plains regions.

Center of Population

Another indicator of distribution shifts is the **center of population**—the point where the country would balance if it could be laid flat and all the people weighed the same. In 1790, the center was 23 miles east of Baltimore, Maryland. Since then, it has moved farther west. By the 2000 decennial census, the center of population had reached a point about 2.8 miles east of Edgar Springs, Missouri.

Student Web Activity Visit the *Economics: Principles and Practices* Web site at epp.glencoe.com and click on **Chapter 13—Student Web Activities** for an activity using international population data.

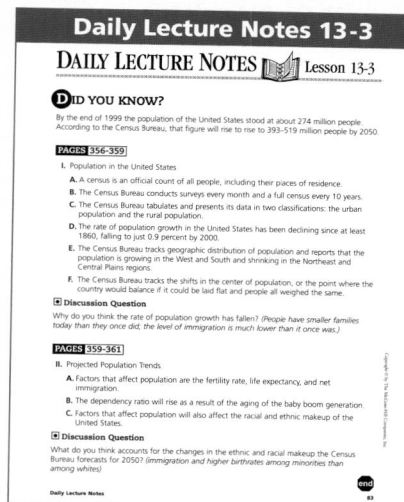

Daily Lecture Notes 13-3

L1 Writing a Letter

Have students write a letter to the Bureau of Census requesting information on how census information is gathered and analyzed. **ELL**

Objectives, goals, and answers to the student activity can be found in the **Web Activity Lesson Plan** feature at epp.glencoe.com

---

MEETING SPECIAL NEEDS ACTIVITY

Learning Disabled For students who have problems with reading, scanning a passage before reading can help develop a time frame for the events or ideas that are presented. Have students scan the subsection "Historical Growth" for time markers such as the words "Between 1790 and 1860." Note that many paragraphs contain these markers. Other examples are: "From the beginning of the Civil War . . ."; "From 1900 . . ."; and "During colonial times. . . ."

Refer to *Inclusion for the Social Studies Classroom Strategies and Activities* in the TCR.

Guided Reading Activity 13-3

GUIDED READING Activity 13-3

For use with textbook pages 356–361

GDP AND POPULATION

OUTLINING

Directions: Locate the heading in your textbook. Then use the information under the heading to help you write each answer. Use another sheet of paper if necessary.

I. Population in the United States
  A. Introduction—Why does the government periodically take a census?
  B. Counting the Population—What are the two classifications of population?
  C. Historical Growth—What has been the trend in the rate of population growth since colonial times?
  D. Regional Change—Which parts of the country are growing in population and which are showing losses?

II. Projected Population Trends
  A. Introduction—How do businesses use what they learn about population trends?
  B. Factors Affecting Population Growth—What are the three most important factors affecting the rate of population growth?

  C. Projections by Age and Gender
    1. What is the population pyramid?
    2. What is the dependency ratio?
  D. Projections by Race and Ethnic Origin
    1. What group currently is the largest component in the total population?
    2. What other racial/ethnic groups make up the total population?

Guided Reading Activities

L2 Identifying Trends

Have students review the section to identify the population trends that are mentioned. Then instruct students to write a brief essay that discusses how these trends will affect their lives in the future.

ECONOMICS
AT A GLANCE

Answer: *West North Central, East North Central, East South Central, New England, Middle Atlantic*

Projected Population Trends

Population trends are important to many groups. Political leaders, for example, closely watch population shifts to see how voting patterns may change. Community leaders are interested because increases or decreases in local population affect services such as sanitation, education, crime prevention, and fire protection. Businesses use census data to help determine new plant locations, markets for products, and sales territories.

Factors Affecting Population Growth

According to **demographers**—people who study growth, density, and other characteristics of population, the three most important factors affecting population growth are fertility, life expectancy, and net immigration levels.

The **fertility rate** is the number of births that 1,000 women are expected to undergo in their lifetime. A fertility rate of 2,110, for example, translates to 2.11 births per woman. The Bureau of the Census projects 2,119 as the most likely fertility rate for the United States. That rate is barely above the replacement population rate–the rate at which the number of births in a population just offsets the number of deaths.

This was not always the case. In the late 1800s and early 1900s, Americans tended to have large families. In the days before modern machines and appliances, the work of maintaining a home and family and earning a living was difficult and time-consuming. Children were needed to do household chores, work on family farms, and bring in additional money from outside jobs.

As modern life became more automated, and fewer people lived on farms, having large families became less important. As a result, the nation's birthrate dropped steadily throughout the 1990s.

The second factor, **life expectancy,** is the average remaining life span of people who reach a given

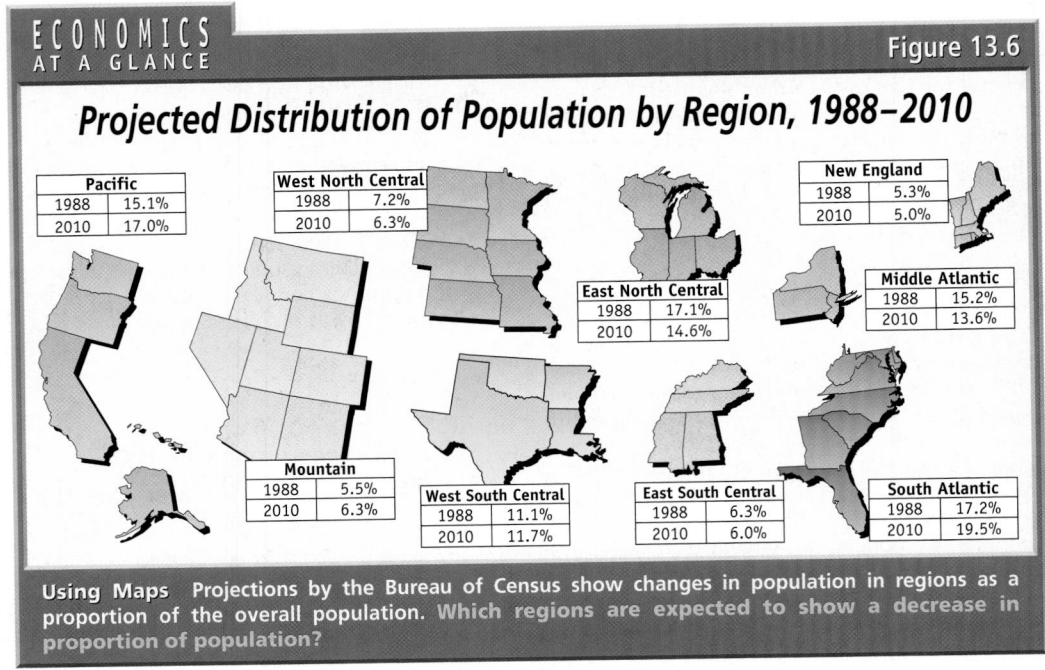

ECONOMICS
AT A GLANCE

Figure 13.6

Projected Distribution of Population by Region, 1988–2010

Pacific	
1988	15.1%
2010	17.0%

West North Central	
1988	7.2%
2010	6.3%

New England	
1988	5.3%
2010	5.0%

East North Central	
1988	17.1%
2010	14.6%

Middle Atlantic	
1988	15.2%
2010	13.6%

Mountain	
1988	5.5%
2010	6.3%

West South Central	
1988	11.1%
2010	11.7%

East South Central	
1988	6.3%
2010	6.0%

South Atlantic	
1988	17.2%
2010	19.5%

Using Maps Projections by the Bureau of Census show changes in population in regions as a proportion of the overall population. Which regions are expected to show a decrease in proportion of population?

358 UNIT 4 MACROECONOMICS: POLICIES

FREE ENTERPRISE ACTIVITY

Census information can be valuable to the small, private businesses that are so important to the growth and success of our free enterprise economy. Ask students to choose a particular small business, such as a restaurant. Then have students consult a *Statistical Abstract of the United States* or census data publications and look for trends in their region. Suggest that they do this by looking for answers to the following: Is population increasing? Is the number of businesses increasing? Is disposable personal income increasing? Is the volume of sales increasing? Have students write a paragraph, based on the data they collect, explaining why they would or would not advise a friend to enter their selected business.

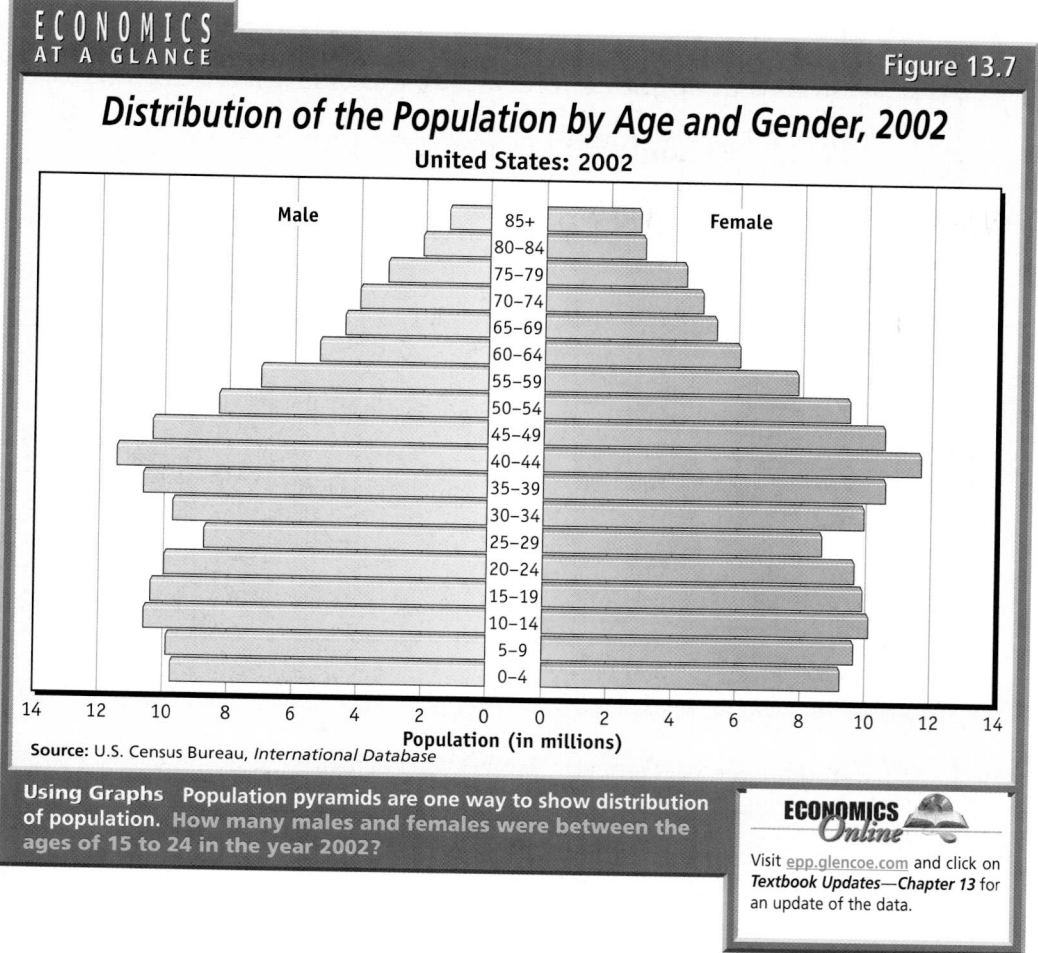

ECONOMICS
AT A GLANCE

Figure 13.7

Distribution of the Population by Age and Gender, 2002

United States: 2002

Male | Female

85+
80–84
75–79
70–74
65–69
60–64
55–59
50–54
45–49
40–44
35–39
30–34
25–29
20–24
15–19
10–14
5–9
0–4

14 12 10 8 6 4 2 0 0 2 4 6 8 10 12 14

Population (in millions)

Source: U.S. Census Bureau, *International Database*

Using Graphs Population pyramids are one way to show distribution of population. **How many males and females were between the ages of 15 to 24 in the year 2002?**

ECONOMICS *Online*

Visit epp.glencoe.com and click on **Textbook Updates—Chapter 13** for an update of the data.

CURRICULUM CONNECTION

Statistics In the year 2000, more people will live in urban areas than in rural ones, and most of this change will take place in developing countries. Cities in developed nations, for the most part, have stopped growing, whereas cities in developing countries continue to grow. If this trend continues, two-thirds of the world's population will live in urban areas by the year 2025.

In 1900 only 11 cities in the world had populations of 1 million. In 2000 there were approximately 300. In another 20 years there will be nearly 600. Many of these cities will be pushed to the breaking point as they try to accommodate large numbers of people who flock to urban areas in an effort to flee rural poverty.

age. The Bureau of the Census predicts that life expectancy at birth will go from about 75.9 years today to 82.1 years by 2050.

The third major factor is **net immigration**—the net change in population caused by people moving into and out of the country. The Bureau estimates a constant net immigration of about 880,000 per year. This figure is based on 1,040,000 *immigrants*—those entering the country—and 160,000 *emigrants*—those leaving the country—in the future.

Taking into account these three factors, analysts expect the rate of population growth in the United States to continue to decline. The growth rate is likely to fall to 0.82 percent between 2000 and 2005 and then continue to decrease until it reaches 0.49 percent by 2050. At that time, the resident United States population should be about 380 million people.

Projections by Age and Gender

In making its projections, the Census Bureau assumed that the aging baby boomer generation will drive many characteristics of the population.

CHAPTER 13: ECONOMIC PERFORMANCE **359**

CRITICAL THINKING

Synthesizing Information Refer students to Figure 13.8 on page 360. Direct them to research the latest figures for the racial and ethnic makeup of the United States, their state, their county, their school district, and their city, town, or village, using the same categories as those in the figure. Suggest that students consult the *Statistical Abstract of the United States*, county and community administrative offices, or Web sites. Instruct students to use their data to construct a bar graph showing the percentages of population by race and ethnic origin for the United States, the state, the county, the community, and the school district. Have students present their graphs. Discuss the differences in racial and ethnic makeup of the various populations shown in the graph. **BLOCK SCHEDULING**

ECONOMICS
AT A GLANCE

Answer: *Asians and Hispanics; Whites*

Graph Skills Practice
In approximately what year will the Asian population rise to about 5 percent of the total population? *(2010)* In approximately what year will the White population fall to about 60 percent of the total population? *(2030)*

Assign Section 3 Assessment as homework or as an in-class activity.

Have students use **Interactive Tutor Self-Assessment Software** to review Section 3.

ECONOMICS
AT A GLANCE

Figure 13.8

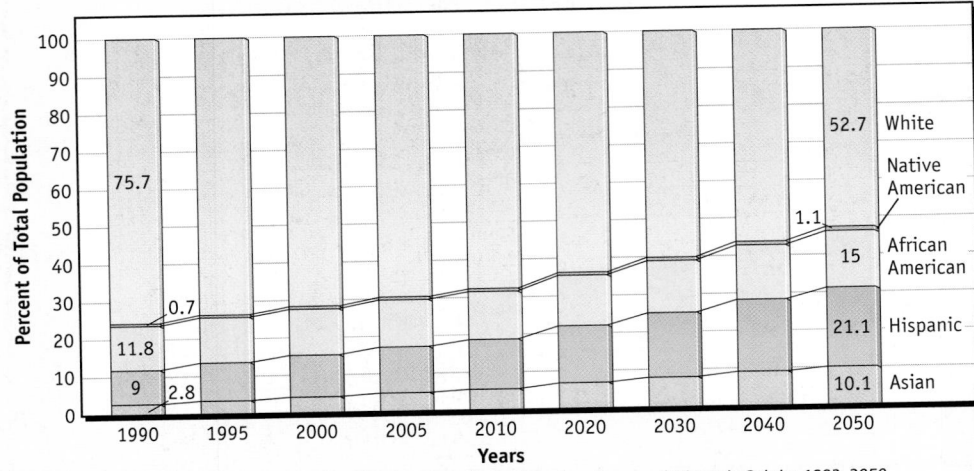

Projected Change in U.S. Population by Race and Ethnic Origin, 1990–2050

Source: *Population Projections in the United States, by Age, Sex, Race and Hispanic Origin: 1992–2050,* U.S. Bureau of the Census

Using Graphs The distribution of population by race is projected to change dramatically by the year 2050. Which ethnic components of the population are expected to make the largest gains? Which will incur the largest losses?

People born during the **baby boom,** the high birthrate years from 1946 to 1964, make up a sizeable portion of the population. As shown in **Figure 13.7** on page 359, people born during those years created a pronounced bulge in the **population pyramid,** a type of bar graph that shows the breakdown of population by age and gender.

The bulge in the middle of the pyramid represents the baby boomers. As years pass, more births add to the bottom of the pyramid and push earlier groups upward into higher age brackets.

Eventually, the baby boomers will reach their retirement years and want to collect pensions, Social Security, and medicare benefits. Because most of these payments are transfer payments,

they will place a heavy burden on the younger and relatively smaller working population. The burden becomes evident with changes in the **dependency ratio**—a ratio based on the number of children and elderly for every 100 persons in the working-age bracket of 18 through 64. The dependency ratio was 63.9 in 1998, but according to Census Bureau projections, it will rise to 67.5 by 2020, to 77.5 by 2030, and to 78.0 by the year 2040.

Finally, notice what the population pyramid indicates about gender. If you compare the left sides of the pyramid with the right, you will see that women tend to outlive men. Separate population pyramids can also be created for any racial or ethnic group.

360 UNIT 4 MACROECONOMICS: POLICIES

EXTENDING THE CONTENT

The Census and Economic Data In addition to counting the number of people, identifying population trends, and making projections, the Bureau of the Census also collects a significant amount of data that is of interest to private businesses. For example, the Census Bureau gathers information on farms, wholesale businesses, service industries, transportation, manufacturing, construction, and retailing. One of the many Bureau of the Census publications is called *Retail Trade: United States.*

Projections by Race and Ethnic Origin

Census Bureau projections for race and ethnic groups are shown in **Figure 13.8**. In 1990, Whites were the largest component of the total population. The numbers of African Americans, Hispanic Americans, Asian Americans, and Native Americans followed in that order.

Differences in fertility rates, life expectancies, and immigration rates will change racial statistics dramatically in the future. By 2050, the Asian component of the population will increase nearly five times, and the Hispanic component will almost double. The number of African Americans will also increase. Whites will remain a bare majority of the total population at 52.7 percent.

Population

Trends The makeup of the United States population by age, gender, and ethnic origin has changed and is expected to continue this trend. *What is the Hispanic percentage of the population projected to be in the year 2050?*

Section 3 Assessment

Checking for Understanding

1. **Main Idea** How does the rate of population growth affect economic growth?

2. **Key Terms** Define census, urban population, rural population, center of population, demographer, fertility rate, life expectancy, net immigration, baby boom, population pyramid, dependency ratio.

3. **Describe** how U.S. population is estimated.

4. **List** the three most important factors that determine future population growth.

Applying Economic Concepts

5. **Urban and Rural** What could happen to your community that might cause it to be classified as a rural community instead of urban, or urban instead of rural?

Critical Thinking

6. **Drawing Conclusions** At some point, the baby boomers will reach their retirement years. How will this development affect your generation? How do you think the baby boomers will feel about this?

7. **Understanding Cause and Effect** What special demands does a high birthrate put on a nation's economy?

 Practice and **assess** key social studies skills with the *Glencoe Skillbuilder Interactive Workbook, Level 2.*

Section 3 Assessment Answers

1. The size of the population directly affects the growth of one of the factors of production, labor.

2. All vocabulary terms are defined in the text.

3. census: every household receives a form to complete; other methods also used.

4. fertility, life expectancy, net immigration

5. an increase or decrease in population growth; increased or decreased economic development that would affect population; natural disasters or a discovery of resources that would cause people to move

6. dependency ratio will rise, which will place a burden on younger generation; boomers may be worried that the workforce cannot help support them.

7. growth of the dependency ratio and possible overcrowding

Visual Instruction
Answer to Caption:
21.1

Reteach

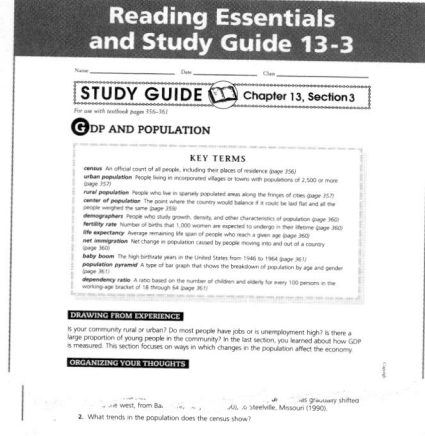

Reading Essentials and Study Guide 13-3

STUDY GUIDE — Chapter 13, Section 3

GDP AND POPULATION

Enrich

Invite an official from state or local government to visit the class and talk about how population projections affect government plans concerning raising revenue and allocating expenditures.

 CLOSE

Have students identify the population trend that they think will have the greatest impact on the nation and on their community in the next 25 years.

TEACH

Have students write a paper on a well-known immigrant, discussing his or her reasons for immigrating to the United States and contributions to our society. Examples of well-known immigrants include Albert Einstein, Bob Hope, Charlie Chaplin, Seiji Ozawa, Joseph Pulitzer, Felix Frankfurter, Jacob Riis, Enrico Fermi, Samuel Gompers, Madeline Albright, Elizabeth Blackwell, John J. Audubon, Wernher von Braun, Andrew Carnegie, Marlene Dietrich, Maura N. Donohue, E.L. Godkin, Cary Grant, Sonja Henie, Gianni Versace, Gabriela Mistral, and Alexander Hamilton.

☞ Refer to *Business Week Focus on the New Economy* in the TCR for additional unit-based articles.

BusinessWeek

Newsclip

AUGUST 31, 1998

Without immigrants, economic growth could decline by the year 2015, when the U.S. workforce is expected to shrink. Researchers predict that immigrants will help transform the economy in the twenty-first century.

Immigrants and the Job Market

During the next decade, barring a change in government policy, nearly a million immigrants are expected to arrive in the U.S. every year. Most, both legal and illegal, will continue to come from Latin America and Southeast Asia, but every foreign land will be represented. So will every level of skill, education, and talent: New arrivals will make up hotel beds, start their own shops, and pursue pathbreaking medical research.

And they'll play a critical role in providing the workers needed to keep the economy healthy. As baby boomers age and domestic birthrates stagnate, only foreign-born workers will keep the labor pool growing. By 2006, in fact, immigrants will account for half of all new U.S. workers; over the next 30 years, their share will rise to 60%.

Economic dynamism, in other words, will depend on a continuing stream of foreign-born workers. A limited labor supply "is going to affect growth," says Carol D'Amico, senior research fellow at the Hudson Institute; "if you fast-forward 10 years, it will be a real issue. . . ."

Just as crucial, the array of education and skills immigrants bring could fit neatly with the supply of jobs over the next decade. According to Linda Levine at the Congressional Research Service, a branch of the Library of Congress, 60% of the jobs created through 2005 will require some post-secondary education. But, she adds, low-skill jobs will still represent about half of total employment.

Compare that job market to the prospective immigrant labor force. Of recent arrivals, only 63% have finished high school. . . . Yet immigrants also are 50% more likely than Americans to have a graduate degree. . . .

Indeed, foreign-born workers have shown an extraordinary ability to assimilate and flourish. Certainly, some less skilled workers will remain at the bottom economic rung all their lives. Yet others will catch up quickly. Within a decade of their arrival, the well-educated go from making barely half that of native-born Americans in comparable work to nearly 90%.

Examining the Newsclip

1. **Analyzing Information** What role are immigrant workers expected to play in the U.S. economy during the twenty-first century?

2. **Making Predictions** Will immigrants' skills be needed in the twenty-first century job market? Explain your answer.

362

Answers to Examining the Newsclip

1. Immigrants will play a crucial role, accounting for half of all new U.S. workers by 2006.

2. Answers should note that immigrants' skills range from low to very high, and they will likely be needed in the twenty-first century job market.

SECTION 4

Economic Growth

Study Guide

Main Idea
The ability of an economy to produce output determines its growth.

Reading Strategy
Graphic Organizer As you read the section, complete a graphic organizer like the one below by explaining how saving influences economic growth.

Saving → Economic growth

Key Terms
real GDP per capita, growth triangle, standard of living, tax base, renewable resources, capital-to-labor ratio, labor productivity

Objectives
After studying this section, you will be able to:
1. **Describe** how economists measure the growth of the United States economy.
2. **Explain** the importance of economic growth.
3. **Outline** the factors of economic growth.
4. **Relate** productivity to economic growth.

Applying Economic Concepts
Standard of Living Read to find out why the standard of living is important in a free enterprise economy.

Cover Story

Computer Age Gains Respect of Economists

In a nation of technophiles, where Internet millionaires are minted daily, it seems heresy to question the economic payoff from information technology. . . . But for more than a decade, most of the nation's leading economists have been heretics.

Computers are having an impact on the marketplace.

"You can see the Computer Age everywhere," Robert Solow, a Nobel prizewinner from the Massachusetts Institute of Technology wrote a few years ago, "but in the productivity statistics."

For years, even as the computer revolutionized the workplace, productivity . . . stagnated, barely advancing 1 percent per year.

Yet today, even renowned skeptics . . . are having second thoughts. Productivity growth has picked up, starting in 1996, . . . [S]omething seems fundamentally different this time . . . computers (are) finally paying off.

—*The New York Times*, April 14, 1999

E conomic growth, one of the seven major goals of the United States economy, has the potential for improving everyone's lot in life. *Everyone* includes not only every American, but also people living in other countries.

Economic Growth in the United States

 One of the first things we need to know about economic growth is how to measure it. Two methods are equally important, and both make use of topics covered earlier in this chapter.

Measuring Growth

 When we measure economic growth in the short term—a period of one to five years—real GDP, or GDP adjusted to remove the distortions of inflation, is a fairly satisfactory gauge. Changes in real GDP on a quarterly or annual basis are the statistics we hear about most often in the news.

When it comes to the long run, however, real GDP does not tell the whole story. Because population also grows, **real GDP per capita**—the

CHAPTER 13: ECONOMIC PERFORMANCE **363**

1 FOCUS

Section Overview
This section discusses economic growth and how it relates to productivity.

BELLRINGER
Motivational Activity

Project **transparency** and have students answer questions.

Available as blackline master

Daily Focus Transparency 56

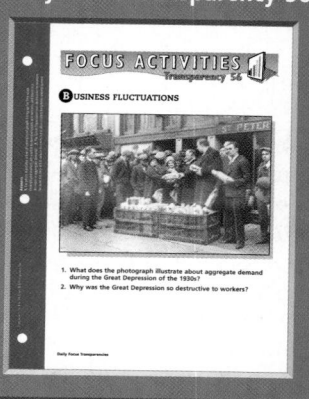

Study Guide

Reading Strategy
Have students create the graphic organizer.
Answers to Graphic: *Saving makes money available for investment in capital goods, which favors economic growth.*

Preteaching Vocabulary
Use the Vocabulary Puzzle-Maker to create crossword and word-search puzzles.

RESOURCE MANAGER

Reproducible Masters
- Reproducible Lesson Plan 13-4
- Daily Lecture Notes 13-4
- Guided Reading Activity 13-4
- Reading Essentials and Study Guide 13-4
- Section Quiz 13-4

Transparencies
- Daily Focus Transparency 56

Multimedia
- Vocabulary PuzzleMaker CD-ROM
- NBR Economics & You Video Program
- Interactive Tutor Self-Assessment Software
- ExamView® Pro Testmaker
- Presentation Plus!

2 TEACH

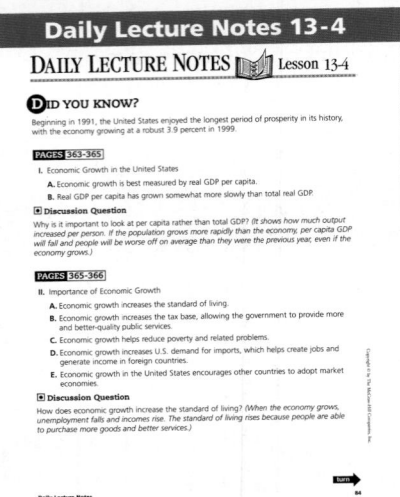

Daily Lecture Notes 13-4

DAILY LECTURE NOTES — Lesson 13-4

DID YOU KNOW?
Beginning in 1991, the United States enjoyed the longest period of prosperity in its history, with the economy growing at a robust 3.9 percent in 1999.

PAGES 363-365

I. Economic Growth in the United States
   A. Economic growth is best measured by real GDP per capita.
   B. Real GDP per capita has grown somewhat more slowly than total real GDP.

Discussion Question
Why is it important to look at per capita rather than total GDP? (It shows how much output increased per person. If the population grows more rapidly than the economy, per capita GDP will fall and people will be worse off on average than they were the previous year, even if the economy grows.)

PAGES 365-366

II. Importance of Economic Growth
   A. Economic growth increases the standard of living.
   B. Economic growth increases the tax base, allowing the government to provide more and better-quality public services.
   C. Economic growth helps reduce poverty and related problems.
   D. Economic growth increases U.S. demand for imports, which helps create jobs and generate income in foreign countries.
   E. Economic growth in the United States encourages other countries to adopt market economies.

Discussion Question
How does economic growth increase the standard of living? (When the economy grows, unemployment falls and incomes rise. The standard of living rises because people are able to purchase more goods and better services.)

Daily Lecture Notes

L1 Brainstorming

Organize students into several groups. Have groups brainstorm why economic growth is important to a high school student. Have a representative from each group share the results of their brainstorming session. List new reasons on the board as they are mentioned. Have students use the list to identify some of the signs of economic growth in their community.

STANDARD &POOR'S

Answer: *Real GDP is the dollar amount of final output for the whole economy; real GDP per capita is the dollar amount of real GDP produced per person.*

dollar amount of real GDP produced on a per-person basis—is a better measure. Most economists agree that it is the single most important measure of long-term growth because it adjusts for changes in both inflation and population.

Dividing real GDP by the population yields real GDP per capita. If the population grows faster than real GDP, the average amount of output produced for each person in the economy falls. If the population grows more slowly than real GDP, there will be more goods and services available for everyone.

The Historical Record

Figure 13.9 compares real GDP with real GDP per capita. The figure shows that the overall rate of economic growth is somewhat slower when population growth is taken into account. In addition, relatively slow periods of real GDP growth can actually become negative if population growth is taken into consideration, as in 1990–91.

Another way to examine growth is with a **growth triangle**—a table that shows annual compound rates of growth between selected periods of time. **Figure 13.10** shows that there was almost no

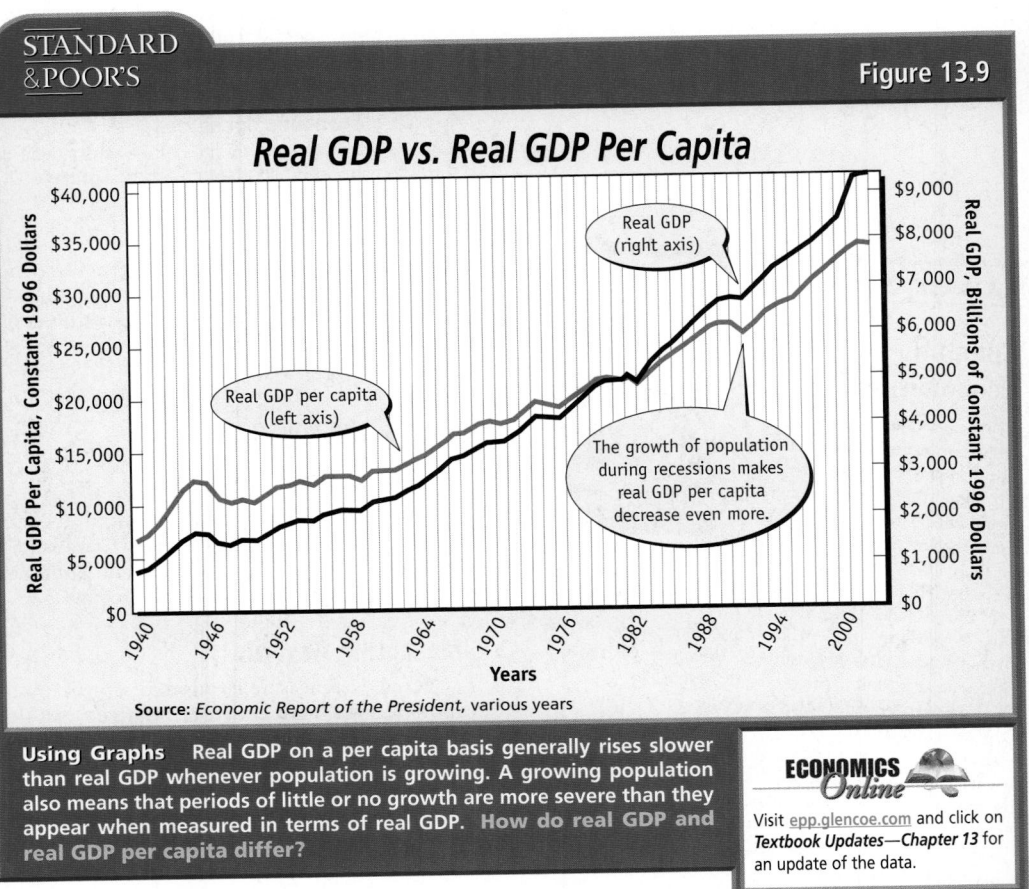

STANDARD &POOR'S

Figure 13.9

Real GDP vs. Real GDP Per Capita

Real GDP (right axis)

Real GDP per capita (left axis)

The growth of population during recessions makes real GDP per capita decrease even more.

Source: Economic Report of the President, various years

Using Graphs Real GDP on a per capita basis generally rises slower than real GDP whenever population is growing. A growing population also means that periods of little or no growth are more severe than they appear when measured in terms of real GDP. **How do real GDP and real GDP per capita differ?**

ECONOMICS Online

Visit epp.glencoe.com and click on *Textbook Updates—Chapter 13* for an update of the data.

MEETING SPECIAL NEEDS ACTIVITY

Learning Style: Intrapersonal Ask students to comment on their standard of living in a personal journal entry. How do they feel about their current standard of living? What indicators do they use to judge their standard of living? How do they think it compares to that of their parents when they were in high school? How would they like their standard of living to change? How will they work to change it?

 Refer to *Inclusion for the Social Studies Classroom Strategies and Activities* in the TCR.

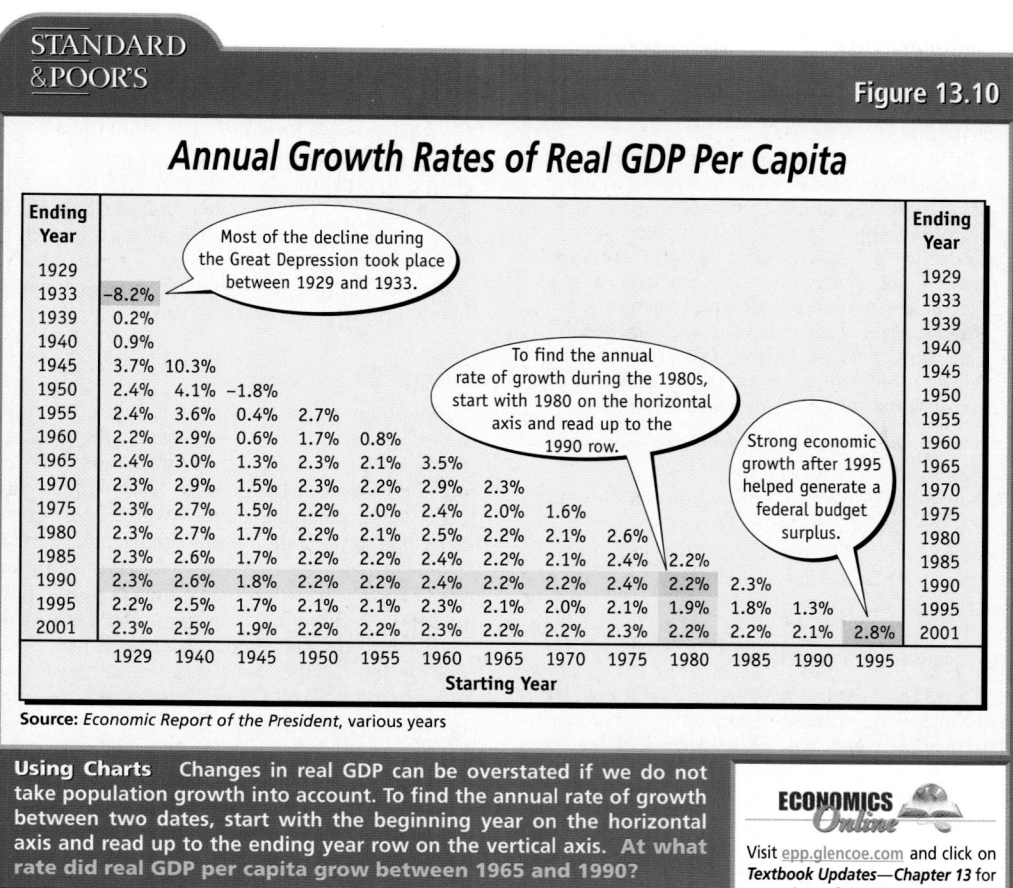

STANDARD &POOR'S

Figure 13.10

Annual Growth Rates of Real GDP Per Capita

Ending Year													Ending Year
1929													1929
1933	-8.2%												1933
1939	0.2%												1939
1940	0.9%												1940
1945	3.7%	10.3%											1945
1950	2.4%	4.1%	-1.8%										1950
1955	2.4%	3.6%	0.4%	2.7%									1955
1960	2.2%	2.9%	0.6%	1.7%	0.8%								1960
1965	2.4%	3.0%	1.3%	2.3%	2.1%	3.5%							1965
1970	2.3%	2.9%	1.5%	2.3%	2.2%	2.9%	2.3%						1970
1975	2.3%	2.7%	1.5%	2.2%	2.0%	2.4%	2.0%	1.6%					1975
1980	2.3%	2.7%	1.7%	2.2%	2.1%	2.5%	2.2%	2.1%	2.6%				1980
1985	2.3%	2.6%	1.7%	2.2%	2.2%	2.4%	2.2%	2.1%	2.4%	2.2%			1985
1990	2.3%	2.6%	1.8%	2.2%	2.2%	2.4%	2.2%	2.2%	2.4%	2.2%	2.3%		1990
1995	2.2%	2.5%	1.7%	2.1%	2.1%	2.3%	2.1%	2.0%	2.1%	1.9%	1.8%	1.3%	1995
2001	2.3%	2.5%	1.9%	2.2%	2.2%	2.3%	2.2%	2.2%	2.3%	2.2%	2.2%	2.1%	2.8%	2001
	1929	1940	1945	1950	1955	1960	1965	1970	1975	1980	1985	1990	1995

Starting Year

> Most of the decline during the Great Depression took place between 1929 and 1933.

> To find the annual rate of growth during the 1980s, start with 1980 on the horizontal axis and read up to the 1990 row.

> Strong economic growth after 1995 helped generate a federal budget surplus.

Source: Economic Report of the President, various years

Using Charts Changes in real GDP can be overstated if we do not take population growth into account. To find the annual rate of growth between two dates, start with the beginning year on the horizontal axis and read up to the ending year row on the vertical axis. **At what rate did real GDP per capita grow between 1965 and 1990?**

ECONOMICS Online

Visit epp.glencoe.com and click on **Textbook Updates—Chapter 13** for an update of the data.

growth in real GDP per capita between 1929 and 1939. From 1940 to 1970, the annual rate was 2.9 percent, but it then fell to 2.1 percent from 1970 to 1980. Between 1980 and 1990, the growth rate was 2.2 percent. Growth then plummeted in the early 1990s, only to rebound spectacularly by the end of the decade.

These are the types of numbers economists, businesspeople, politicians, and even the American public watch on a regular basis. They are far more noticeable—and even painful—when growth is slow, as President Bush discovered in the early 1990s, but they are nevertheless always important.

Importance of Economic Growth

Economic growth benefits a country in many ways. It raises the standard of living, eases the burden of government, and helps solve domestic problems. It can also boost the economies of foreign trade partners.

Standard of Living

A major feature of a free enterprise economy is its ability to increase real per capita output enough to allow people to raise their standard of living. The **standard of living** means the quality of life

CHAPTER 13: ECONOMIC PERFORMANCE **365**

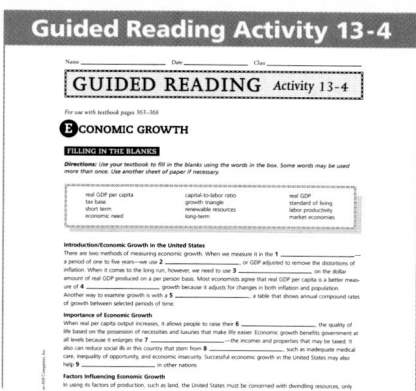

Guided Reading Activity 13-4

Name _____ Date _____ Class _____

GUIDED READING Activity 13-4

Ⓔ**CONOMIC GROWTH**

FILLING IN THE BLANKS

Directions: *Use your textbook to fill in the blanks using the words in the box. Some words may be used more than once. Use another sheet of paper if necessary.*

real GDP per capita	capital-to-labor ratio	real GDP
tax base	growth triangle	standard of living
short term	renewable resources	labor productivity
economic need	long-term	market economies

Introduction/Economic Growth in the United States

There are two methods of measuring economic growth. When we measure it in the **1** _____ a period of one to five years—we use **2** _____ or GDP adjusted to remove the distortions of inflation. When it comes to the long run, however, we need to use **3** _____ on the dollar amount of real GDP produced on a per person basis. Most economists agree that real GDP per capita is a better measure of **4** _____ growth because it adjusts for changes in both inflation and population. Another way to examine growth is with a **5** _____ a table that shows annual compound rates of growth between selected periods of time.

Importance of Economic Growth

When real per capita output increases, it allows people to raise their **6** _____ the quality of life based on the possession of necessities and luxuries that make life easier. Economic growth benefits government at all levels because it enlarges the **7** _____ the incomes and properties that may be taxed. It also can reduce social ills in this country that stem from **8** _____ such as inadequate medical care, inequality of opportunity, and economic insecurity. Successful economic growth in the United States may also help **9** _____ in other nations.

Factors Influencing Economic Growth

In using its factors of production, such as land, the United States must be concerned with dwindling resources, only

ECONOMICS AT A GLANCE

Answer: *2.2 percent*

L2 Constructing a Chart.

On the board draw a chart with *Positive Aspects* and *Negative Aspects* as horizontal headings, and *Land, Capital, Labor,* and *Entrepreneurship* as vertical headings. Have students review the discussion on factors influencing economic growth on pages 366–368. Then ask students to offer negative and positive aspects in the use of each of the four factors of production and enter their suggestions under the appropriate heading. Finally, have students choose the factor of production they believe has contributed most to economic growth in the United States and write a paragraph justifying their choices.

FREE ENTERPRISE ACTIVITY

Organize students into several groups and have each group brainstorm ways to increase the productivity of the United States. Then have groups select the method for increasing productivity that they agree, by consensus, is the best. Have groups present and explain their methods. In a follow-up class discussion, have students consider which methods would require some kind of government intervention and what the possible consequences of that intervention might be. **BLOCK SCHEDULING**

L3 Researching

Have students use outside resources to study daily life in another time period. Then ask students to write an essay comparing life for young people in their selected time period to life for young people today. Suggest that they focus on the standard of living in the two time periods. Call on volunteers to read their essays to the class.

NIGHTLY BUSINESS REPORT

 ECONOMICS & YOU

 Chapter 20
Disc 1, Side 2

Measuring the Economy's Performance

Ask: What is the difference between leading and lagging economic indicators? *(Leading economic indicators are statistics that predict economic changes. Lagging economic indicators are statistics that help economists interpret changes in economic activity that have already occurred.)*

 Also available in VHS.

CYBERNOMICS SPOTLIGHT

Population Centers
Washington, D.C. is becoming a hotbed for new high-tech communication and Internet companies. Technology workers now outnumber government employees in Washington, D.C. and the surrounding area. Companies have settled in the area for a practical reason: they are near the government, which makes it easier to get authorizations and licenses for their services. Washington, D.C., ranks as the third-largest high-tech center in the United States, after Silicon Valley and Boston.

---

based on the possession of necessities and luxuries that make life easier. A free enterprise system also increases people's free time, allowing them to devote more attention to families, hobbies, and recreational activities.

Government Spending

Economic growth benefits government at all levels by enlarging the **tax base**—the incomes and properties that may be taxed. An enlarged tax base increases government revenues, which helps finance the number and quality of public services. The economic growth and resulting budget surpluses of the late 1990s, for example, gave political leaders the option of increasing spending on highways, defense, and some social programs. It also gave them the opportunity to think about reducing tax rates on citizens.

Domestic Problems

Like most countries of the world, the United States faces varying degrees of poverty, inadequate medical care, inequality of opportunity, and economic insecurity. Most of these problems stem from economic need. Economic growth creates more jobs and income for more people, thus helping to alleviate social ills at their source.

Economic growth in the 1990s helped the United States lower its unemployment rate and reduce the number of people on welfare. Also, intense competition among firms for workers drove the industrial wage up.

366 UNIT 4 MACROECONOMICS: POLICIES

Helping Other Nations

Economic growth increases American demand for foreign-made products, which helps create jobs and generate income in those countries. These purchases, in turn, enable foreign citizens to buy more goods and services from the United States, which may also create new jobs here. Consumers in the United States and the countries with which it trades benefit from an increased variety of competitively priced goods and services.

Global Role Model

A number of emerging nations are forming their political and economic ideologies. These nations tend to copy the most successful economic systems of other nations. Many people in the United States believe that emerging nations will be best able to help themselves if they adopt a free market system.

In the past, the free world and the communist world each tried to influence the economic development of emerging countries. The competition ended with the fall of communism in Europe and the breakup of the Soviet Union. Successful economic growth in the United States may now help the market economies of all nations to grow.

Factors Influencing Economic Growth

A number of factors are important to economic growth—especially the quantity and quality of the factors of production. Also important is how efficiently these resources are used.

Land

The United States enjoys an abundance of natural resources. Unlike island nations such as Great Britain and Japan, it need not depend heavily on international trade for raw materials. Although some minerals must be imported, the United States is reasonably self-sufficient in many natural resources.

Even so, the United States needs to conserve its natural resources. Many of the natural resources most Americans take for granted—clean air and water, forests, and fertile land—are dwindling rapidly. Only some of these are **renewable resources,**

CRITICAL THINKING

Distinguishing Fact from Opinion Discuss as a class the relationship between economic growth and conservation. Students should recognize that those two goals are often at odds. Ask students how a balance between the two issues might be reached. Then have students contact both environmental groups and manufacturers and request literature dealing with their views on the subject. Students should examine the literature, identifying facts and opinions, bias, propaganda, and frame of reference. Have students report their findings to the class.

resources that can be replenished for future use. Reseeding, for example, can restore some—but not all—forests for use in the foreseeable future. Trees such as California redwoods and giant firs require centuries to grow to full size.

Capital

A growing supply of high-quality capital favors overall economic growth because it improves the **capital-to-labor ratio**—the total capital stock divided by the number of workers in the labor force. A high capital-to-labor ratio encourages economic growth because it enables individual workers to produce more than they could otherwise.

Because capital goods result from production, it is possible to influence their creation. The key is saving, and the key to saving is the consumer. When people cut back on consumption in order to save and invest, they free up factors of production to generate new capital.

Unfortunately, it is not always possible to reduce consumption so that more can be saved. In some countries, people are so poor and their incomes so low that they must spend everything they earn just to exist. In these countries, there is very little saving and, therefore, low investment in capital goods. Without capital goods, overall output remains low. People are trapped by circumstances. They are too poor to save, but their incomes can rise only if they have savings to invest in capital goods.

Labor

For any country's economy to grow, it needs a skilled and growing labor force. In general, the size of the labor force is dependent on the size of the population. If the rate of population growth declines, the size of the labor force might also decline. One way to offset a labor shortage is to hire workers from other countries. Another is to encourage new additions to the labor force, such as retirees and people who traditionally have stayed at home.

The American labor force is more educated and skilled today than in the past. In 1970, for example, the median number of school years workers

Answer: *Productivity grew at a compound annual rate of 2.9 percent.*

③ ASSESS

Assign Section 4 Assessment as homework or as an in-class activity.

💾 Have students use **Interactive Tutor Self-Assessment Software** to review Section 4.

Section Quiz 13-4

STANDARD &POOR'S

Figure 13.11

Labor Productivity, 1959–2002

1959–1973: Productivity grew at a compound annual rate of 2.9%.

1973–1995: Annual productivity growth rate fell to 1.1%.

1995–2002: Productivity rose to an annual growth rate of 2.8%.

Source: *Economic Report of the President,* various years and Bureau of Labor Statistics

Using Graphs Labor productivity is the rate of growth of output per unit of labor input. **How did the productivity index change between 1959 and 1973?**

ECONOMICS *Online*

Visit epp.glencoe.com and click on *Textbook Updates—Chapter 13* for an update of the data.

CHAPTER 13: ECONOMIC PERFORMANCE **367**

EXTENDING THE CONTENT

Zero GDP Growth Some economists are now expressing the view that economic growth is not necessary. This point of view, first presented in the 1970s when the U.S. was experiencing the effects of the OPEC oil embargo, suggested that the problem of oil shortages should be resolved by learning to live with less. Later, other economists pointed to problems associated with pollution and the depletion of natural resources as reasons for discarding economic growth as a major economic goal. However, critics argue that this viewpoint—often referred to as *zero GDP growth*—is contrary to the basic concept of economics—people's wants are unlimited. Increasing productivity, they suggest, is the only way to address this "economic truth."

Reteach

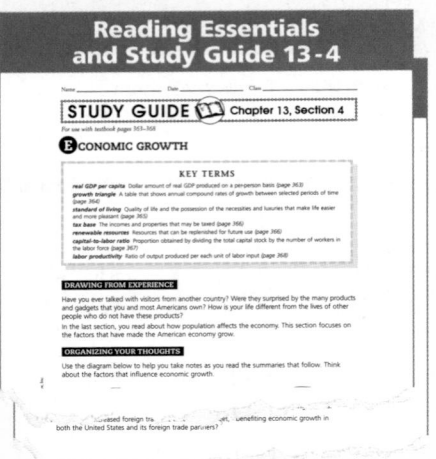

Reading Essentials and Study Guide 13-4

Enrich

Have students use library resources to find GDP statistics for five foreign countries. Then have them construct graphs similar to that in Figure 13.9 for each of their selected countries.

4 CLOSE

Discuss how a continued slow increase in productivity might affect students' future in the workforce.

---

had completed was 12.1. In 1991, the median number was 12.7. In 2000, it exceeded 13. This means that one-half of the labor force has a high school education plus at least one year of college or its equivalent.

Entrepreneurs

The entrepreneur's role as an agent of change qualifies him or her as being a key to economic growth. A country may possess the other growth potentials, but without entrepreneurs who are willing to innovate and take risks, economic growth is apt to lag.

As a group, entrepreneurs require little more than a business climate that allows them to succeed. Most entrepreneurs would favor a minimum of government regulation and an economic system that allows them to keep much of their profits. One of the most visible and successful entrepreneurial areas today is the Internet, which is affecting the way that virtually every company does business.

Productivity and Growth

 Productivity refers to the efficient use of productive inputs to create goods and services. Without productivity, economic growth is difficult to achieve. The official measure of

productivity is **labor productivity**—the amount of output produced per unit of labor input. Productivity goes up when this ratio goes up and down when it goes down.

Figure 13.11 on page 367 traces labor productivity in the U.S. economy since 1959. From 1959 to 1973, the productivity index increased from 54.3 to 80.8, for an annual compound growth rate of 2.9 percent. From 1973 to 1995, however, the productivity rate averaged only 1.1 percent per year.

Productivity rebounded in 1995, reaching an annual compound growth rate of 2.8 percent. As noted in the cover story, part of the increase is due to the personal computer's impact.

When productivity falters, the entire economy suffers. Declining labor productivity can even lead to a rise in the price level, making foreign-made goods cheaper than goods made at home. Eventually, unemployment in domestic industries rises.

When productivity grows, the entire economy benefits. Because people produce relatively more with the same amount of inputs, the prices of goods and services tend to stay low. Domestically produced goods become relatively less expensive than foreign-made ones, so employment at home expands to keep up with increased product demand.

Section 4 Assessment

Checking for Understanding

1. **Main Idea** Why is real GDP per capita considered the best measure of long-term economic growth?

2. **Key Terms** Define real GDP per capita, growth triangle, standard of living, tax base, renewable resources, capital-to-labor ratio, labor productivity.

3. **Describe** two measures of economic growth.

4. **Explain** why economic growth is important.

5. **Identify** the factors influencing economic growth.

6. **Explain** how productivity relates to economic growth.

Applying Economic Concepts

7. **Standard of Living** Identify your most valued material possession. Define the concept "standard of living" in your own words. Then, list the ways in which this possession enhances your standard of living.

Critical Thinking

8. **Determining Cause and Effect** Why is productivity important to a nation's standard of living?

9. **Finding the Main Idea** What does the capital-to-labor ratio measure?

   Practice and assess key social studies skills with the *Glencoe Skillbuilder Interactive Workbook, Level 2.*

Section 4 Assessment Answers

1. It adjusts for both inflation and population changes.

2. All vocabulary terms are defined in the text.

3. Real GDP is the dollar amount of output for the whole economy; real GDP per capita is the dollar amount of real GDP produced per person.

4. It raises the standard of living, eases the burden of government, helps solve domestic

problems, and can boost the economies of foreign trade partners.

5. land, capital, labor, entrepreneurs

6. Productivity is essential for economic growth. When productivity increases, the prices of goods and services tend to stay low, and domestic employment expands. When productivity decreases, prices can rise, and unemployment in domestic industries can rise.

7. Answers should demonstrate an understanding of the concept of standard of living.

8. It keeps the price levels down and industries running. Consumers continue to buy products and workers continue to earn wages and salaries that enable them to buy.

9. total capital stock divided by the number of workers

Section 1

Measuring the Nation's Output

(pages 341–348)

- **Gross Domestic Product (GDP)** is the most complete measure of total output.

- GDP excludes intermediate goods and secondhand sales, nonmarket activities, and unreported activities in the underground economy.

- **Gross National Product (GNP)** is the measure of the total income received by American citizens, regardless of where their productive resources are located.

- Other measures of income are **net national product, national income, personal income,** and **disposable personal income,** which appears as the take-home pay on paychecks.

- The four sectors of the macro economy are the consumer, investment, government, and foreign sectors.

- The **output-expenditure model,** GDP = C + I + G + F, is used to show how GDP is consumed by the four sectors of the economy.

Section 2

GDP and Changes in the Price Level (pages 350–354)

- A **price index** tracks price changes over time and can be used to remove the distortions of inflation from other statistics.

- The price index is computed by dividing the latest prices of the market basket items by the base-year prices and then multiplying by 100.

- Three popular indices are the **consumer price index,** the **producer price index,** and the **implicit GDP price deflator.**

- **Current GDP** is converted to **real GDP,** or constant dollar GDP, by dividing the unadjusted number by the price index and then multiplying by 100.

Section 3

GDP and Population (pages 356–361)

- The annual population growth was more than 3 percent until the Civil War, but it has declined steadily to the point where it is now about 0.9 percent annually.

- The factors that contribute to changing populations are the **fertility rate, life expectancy,** and **net immigration.**

- Projections by age and sex show the continuing influence of the baby boom, which will ultimately increase the **dependency ratio.**

- The racial and ethnic mix will change with population gains by Asian Americans, Hispanic Americans, and African Americans, so that the White component of the population will be a bare majority by the middle of the next century.

Section 4

Economic Growth (pages 363–368)

- Because of changes in population, long-term economic growth is usually measured in terms of **real GDP per capita.**

- Economic growth is important because it raises the **standard of living,** increases the **tax base,** increases employment, and helps the economies of other nations.

- Economic growth requires an ample supply of productive resources, especially entrepreneurs, to organize production and make the economy grow.

- When **labor productivity** is increasing, it helps in raising economic growth and improving living standards.

NIGHTLY BUSINESS REPORT

⊙ **ECONOMICS & YOU**

Chapter 20
Disc 1, Side 2

Measuring the Economy's Performance

📼 Also available in VHS.

Using the Chapter 13 Summary

Use the Chapter 13 Summary to preview, review, condense, or reteach the chapter.

Preview/Review

⑧ Vocabulary PuzzleMaker CD-ROM reinforces Key Terms.

💾 Interactive Tutor Self-Assessment Software provides a review of Chapter 13 content.

Condense

🎧 📁 Have students listen to the Chapter 13 Audio Program. Spanish also available.

📁 📁 Assign the Chapter 13 Audio Program Activity and give students the Chapter 13 Audio Program Test.

📁 📁 Have students complete the Guided Reading Activities and Reading Essentials and Study Guides for Chapter 13.

Reteach

📁 📁 Have students complete Reteaching Activity 13 in the TCR. Spanish also available.

Teacher's Notes / Internet Bookmarks

GLENCOE
TECHNOLOGY

Use **MindJogger Videoquiz** to review the Chapter 13 content.

Have students visit the Web site at epp.glencoe.com to review Chapter 13 and take the **Self-Check Quiz.**

Identifying Key Terms

Sentences will vary. Sample sentences are provided below.

1. **Base year** and **market basket** are both used in constructing a price index.
2. **Both** are used as a measure of the nation's economy.
3. A **household** may consist of **unrelated individuals.**
4. **Intermediate products** and **secondhand sales** are not counted in GDP.
5. The **underground economy** and **nonmarket transactions** are not counted in GDP.
6. **Both** measure price changes.
7. **Real GDP** and **GDP in constant dollars** are two terms for GDP adjusted for inflation.
8. **Demographers** study how far the **center of population** moves.
9. The **population pyramid** shows people born during the **baby boom** to be the most sizable portion of the population.
10. As **life expectancy** increases, **dependency ratio** increases.
11. Increased **labor productivity** leads to lower prices and more employment, allowing for a higher **standard of living.**

Economics Online

Self-Check Quiz Visit the *Economics: Principles and Practices* Web site at epp.glencoe.com and click on **Chapter 13—Self-Check Quizzes** to prepare for the chapter test.

Identifying Key Terms

Examine the pairs of words below. Then write a sentence explaining what each of the pairs have in common.

1. base year, market basket
2. Gross National Product, Net National Product
3. household, unrelated individuals
4. intermediate products, secondhand sales
5. underground economy, nonmarket transactions
6. consumer price index, producer price index
7. real GDP, GDP in constant dollars
8. demographer, center of population
9. baby boom, population pyramid
10. life expectancy, dependency ratio
11. standard of living, labor productivity

Reviewing the Facts

Section 1 (pages 341–348)

1. **Explain** why GDP is an important concept.
2. **Explain** the steps necessary to convert GDP into GNP.
3. **Describe** the three main sectors that make up the United States economy.
4. **Describe** the output-expenditure model.

Section 2 (pages 350–354)

5. **Explain** why price indices are used.
6. **Identify** three of the major price indices the federal government calculates.

7. **Explain** how the government uses the implicit GDP price deflator to convert current GDP to real GDP.

Section 3 (pages 356–361)

8. **Describe** the historical growth of population in the United States.
9. **Describe** how the population of the United States is expected to change by the year 2050.

Section 4 (pages 363–368)

10. **Trace** the record of real economic growth per capita in the United States.
11. **Name** the factors that are essential for economic growth.
12. **Describe** the relationship between productivity and economic growth.

Thinking Critically

1. **Expressing Problems Clearly** Why is GDP not a proper measure of the total income earned by American citizens?
2. **Predicting Consequences** Suppose that politicians wanted to examine the growth of real output over the last 10 years. What conclusions would they reach if they used GDP measured in current dollars? How would these conclusions be different if they examined GDP measured in real dollars? Use a chart like the one below to help you formulate your answers.

	Conclusions
GDP in Current Dollars	
GDP in Real Dollars	

Reviewing the Facts

Section 1

1. It is a reliable measure of the country's economic performance and health.
2. Add all payments Americans receive from outside the U.S., then subtract all payments made to foreign-owned resources in the U.S.
3. consumer sector, households in the U.S.; investment sector, business organizations; government sector, local, state, and federal governments

4. a macroeconomic model used to show aggregate demand by four sectors of the economy, GDP = C + I + G + F

Section 2

5. to reduce the distortions of inflation
6. consumer price index, producer price index, implicit GDP price deflator
7. Current GDP is divided by the implicit GDP price deflator and then multiplied by 100.

3. **Synthesizing Information** Suppose you were told that you would earn $75,000 in 2010. Explain why this information would tell you little about the standard of living you might enjoy. What other information would you need to have before you could evaluate how well you could live in 2010?

Applying Economic Concepts

1. **Economic Growth** Go to the World Wide Web to find a report on GDP. What are the implications of your report for the future of economic growth?

2. **Nonmarket Transactions** Explain what would happen to GDP if nonmarket transactions were included.

3. **Life Expectancy** How would an increase in life expectancy affect the rate of population growth in the country?

4. **Standard of Living** Under what circumstances, if any, do you think you might prefer economic security to a rise in standard of living?

Math Practice

Your uncle has been telling you how cheap gas was back in 1970 when it was $.35 a gallon. (Assume the price of gas is $1.30 a gallon today.) You know that the CPI was 38.8 in 1970 and that it is 170.0 today. Show how you would use this information to determine when gas was relatively cheaper.

Thinking Like an Economist

In your own words, explain why greater life expectancies and declining birthrates make some entitlements like Social Security and medicare more difficult to fund.

Technology Skill

Developing Multimedia Presentations For one week, clip articles from newspapers that refer to one of the following:

- consumer expenditures
- business expenditures
- government expenditures
- exports or imports

On a separate sheet of paper, log the expenditures under one of the four headings. Now imagine you must teach a younger class the differences among the four sectors that make up our economy. Using a camcorder, videotape examples of consumer expenditures, government expenditures, business or investment expenditures, and foreign expenditures (refer to pages 346 through 348 for examples). Explain on camera how all four sectors work together.

Building Skills

Using a Spreadsheet Use the following information to create a spreadsheet and then a bar graph showing real GDP per capita in the United States for four years.

Years	Population	Real GDP in $Billion
1960	179,323,000	$2,263
1970	203,302,000	$3,398
1980	226,542,000	$4,615
1990	248,710,000	$6,136

Remember to use the following equation to determine real GDP per capita:

$$\frac{\text{Real GDP}}{\text{Population}} = \text{Real GDP per capita}$$

You may find your calculations will be easier if you change GDP from billions of dollars to millions. When you complete your calculations, input the information onto a spreadsheet, then convert the numbers to a bar graph. Print out your completed graph.

 Practice and **assess** key social studies skills with the *Glencoe Skillbuilder Interactive Workbook, Level 2.*

Applying Economic Concepts

1. Answers should demonstrate understanding of relationship between GDP and economic growth.
2. The measurement would increase, but become less accurate.
3. It would cause an increase.
4. Economic security provides comfort in the short run, but a low standard of living may cause frustration in the long run.

Math Practice

Appropriate ratios should show that, in relative terms, gas at today's price ($.77 adjusted) is cheaper than at the 1970 price ($.90 adjusted).

Thinking Like an Economist

Greater life expectancy means baby boom generation will live longer in retirement, while declining birthrates mean smaller workforce to support it.

Technology Skill

Presentations should convey understanding of sectors.

Building Skills

Check for accuracy.

 Bonus Test Question

Write *yes* for items that would be included in the GDP, *no* for those that would not.

1. Automobiles produced by a Japanese-owned factory in Tennessee. *(yes, final product produced in U.S.)*
2. Leather bought by shoe factory. *(no, intermediate product)*

Section 3

8. Population has grown; rate of growth has steadily declined.
9. Rate of population growth is expected to decline as fertility declines.

Section 4

10. Refer students to Figure 13.10 to answer this question.
11. quantity and quality of land, capital, labor, entrepreneurs
12. Productivity fosters economic growth.

Thinking Critically

1. It does not consider changes in population.
2. By looking at current GDP, they would assume that GDP had shown marked growth. Using real GDP, the rise has not been so striking.
3. You would not know what prices would be in 2010; price indices.

① FOCUS

The purpose of this activity is to provide students with hands-on experience in the use of capital and other factors of production in the production process.

② TEACH

- Prepare by obtaining these materials for each group of students that will participate in the workshop activity: a ruler, a stapler, scissors, three colored markers, and a supply of construction paper.

- Begin the workshop by organizing students into groups of five or fewer. Distribute the materials to the groups and instruct them to consider them their capital goods.

- As students conduct the workshop activity, offer mini-lectures on the issues of diminishing returns and production process organization, and challenge students to explain, as they work, the fundamental economic difference between the paper and the other things they are using.

ECONOMICS
WORKSHOP
IN ACTION

Using Factors of Production

From the classroom of . . .
Linda Morrell
Rancocas Valley Regional High School
Mount Holly, New Jersey

One of the principle goals of an economic system is efficiency. How do we achieve efficiency in production? One key is operational innovation. This includes improving the methods of organizing production in order to reduce costs, improve quality, and meet the demands of the customers.

Setting Up the Workshop

In this workshop, you will experiment with a process that you design to produce paper baskets. You will produce as many baskets as you can, decorated as attractively as possible, within a period of 10 minutes.

Your teacher will provide you with one ruler, one stapler, three colored markers, and a supply of paper. These are your **capital goods,** the tools and equipment you will use to produce the baskets. Before you begin, decide on the design. Read the procedures that follow. Your teacher will tell you when to begin your production process and when to stop.

You are to work individually. Do not communicate with other students. The member of your class who makes the most will have the highest productivity. Only those products that are completed (finished goods) will be counted. Products that were started but not yet completed (goods in process) will count against your productivity (one less for each good in process). Your teacher or a student volunteer your teacher selects will serve as the quality control inspector, who will inspect the baskets and reject any that are not of acceptable quality.

Procedures

STEP 1

Divide, then cut, each sheet of paper into four equal strips.

STEP 2

Decorate the strips to make an attractive design for the basket.

STEP 3

Staple three of the strips so they make a basket. Use the fourth strip for a basket handle.

372 UNIT 4 MACROECONOMICS: POLICIES

Participating in Economics

A Production Process in Action Arrange a tour for your students of a local manufacturing plant or workshop. At appropriate points during the tour, challenge students to identify the factors of production (land, labor, capital) in use and to apply other economic concepts they have been studying. Upon your return, have students create flowcharts that depict the process they witnessed and annotate their flowcharts at appropriate points with concise descriptions of relevant economic concepts.

STEP 4

After time is called, count the number of baskets you produced and compare your total with that of the other students.

STEP 5

Discuss the results. Discuss what problems occurred due to a scarcity of resources.

STEP 6

Your teacher will place you in a team. Your task is the same as before—create as many baskets as you can. You will have a few minutes to plan your strategy before you begin.

STEP 7

Repeat the 10-minute production period. You are permitted to communicate with your team members as you work.

STEP 8

After time is called, do the following:
* Count the number of baskets your group produced.
* Compare your total with the total of the other groups.
* Describe to the other groups the production process you used.

Summary Activity

1. Why was the total class output higher when everyone worked in groups?
2. Discuss your group's productivity. In what ways could it be increased?
3. Devise a statistical measure to gauge the increase in productivity observed in the activity.
4. Economists use terms like factors of production and intermediate products when they talk about production. Provide examples of each.
5. What is the role of the entrepreneur in the production process?
6. What happens to a firm's productivity and its costs of production when efficiency improves? How do improvements in productivity affect the supply of products?

Economics in Action Workshop

F.Y.I.

"Production miracles"—outstanding feats of production—are not well-known to the general public but have at times served vital national interests. In World War II, for example, the Kaiser shipyards could completely construct a huge warship in just four days. This production miracle, like others, was not so much a result of mass effort, but of the careful and precise management of the factors of production: land, labor, and capital goods.

③ ASSESS

Have the class brainstorm a list of items they would likely find at an automobile factory. Then have each student write down the items he or she would classify as capital goods.

④ CLOSE

Challenge students to identify careers in which knowledge of the factors of production would be critical.

Summary Activity Answers

Student summaries will vary. Have students present their results in writing. Reward groups who address each of the five summary points thoroughly, in turn.

Chapter 14 Resource Manager

SECTION RESOURCES

Daily Objectives	Reproducible Resources	Technology/Multimedia Resources
Section 1 **Business Cycles and Fluctuations** 1. Explain the phases of the business cycle. 2. Identify five causes of business cycles.	Reproducible Lesson Plan 14-1 Daily Lecture Notes 14-1 Guided Reading Activity 14-1 Reading Essentials and Study Guide 14-1 Section Quiz 14-1*	Daily Focus Transparency 57 Interactive Tutor Self-Assessment Software ExamView® Pro Testmaker Presentation Plus!
Section 2 **Unemployment** 1. Explain how the Bureau of Labor Statistics determines if a person is employed. 2. Describe five kinds of unemployment.	Reproducible Lesson Plan 14-2 Daily Lecture Notes 14-2 Guided Reading Activity 14-2 Reading Essentials and Study Guide 14-2 Section Quiz 14-2*	Daily Focus Transparency 70 NBR Economics & You Video Program Interactive Tutor Self-Assessment Software ExamView® Pro Testmaker Presentation Plus!
Section 3 **Inflation** 1. Explain how inflation is measured. 2. Discuss five causes of inflation. 3. Analyze the destabilizing consequences of inflation.	Reproducible Lesson Plan 14-3 Daily Lecture Notes 14-3 Guided Reading Activity 14-3 Reading Essentials and Study Guide 14-3 Section Quiz 14-3*	Daily Focus Transparency 54 Interactive Tutor Self-Assessment Software ExamView® Pro Testmaker Presentation Plus!
Section 4 **Poverty and the Distribution of Income** 1. Explain how economists measure the distribution of income. 2. Discuss the reasons for the inequality of income. 3. Discuss antipoverty programs.	Reproducible Lesson Plan 14-4 Daily Lecture Notes 14-4 Guided Reading Activity 14-4 Reading Essentials and Study Guide 14-4 Section Quiz 14-4*	Daily Focus Transparency 71 Vocabulary PuzzleMaker CD-ROM Interactive Tutor Self-Assessment Software ExamView® Pro Testmaker Presentation Plus!

Also available in Spanish

 Transparency
 Videodisc
 CD-ROM
 Audio Program
 Software
Videocassette
Blackline Master

0:00 **OUT OF TIME?**
Assign the Chapter 14 Audio Program activity and test.

Activities that are particularly suited to use within the block scheduling framework are identified throughout this chapter by the following designation: **BLOCK SCHEDULING**

KEY TO ABILITY LEVELS

Teaching strategies have been coded for varying learning styles and abilities.
L1 BASIC activities for all students
L2 AVERAGE activities for average to above-average students
L3 CHALLENGING activities for above-average students
ELL ENGLISH LANGUAGE LEARNER activities

Chapter 14 Resource Manager

TeacherWorks™ All-In-One Planner and Resource Center

- **Interactive Teacher Edition** Access your Teacher Wraparound Edition and your classroom resources with a few easy clicks.
- **Interactive Lesson Planner** Planning has never been easier! Organize your week, month, semester, or year with all the lesson helps you need to make teaching creative, timely, and relevant.

Use Glencoe's **Presentation Plus!** multimedia teacher tool to easily present dynamic lessons that visually excite your students. Using Microsoft PowerPoint® you can customize the presentations to create your own personalized lessons.

ACTIVITY

From the Classroom of...

**Laronda Narcisse
Robert E. Lee
High School
Baton Rouge, LA**

Economic Instability

Organize students into groups of four to six individuals. Have them follow the steps listed below.
- Have each group conduct a brainstorming session to identify several costs of instability.
- Ask students to list ways that economic instability would affect their personal lives.
- Next have students think of possible solutions to eliminate or reduce economic instability.
- Ask students to write individual letters to their senators describing how economic instability is affecting their lives at the local, state, and national levels. Tell students to include in their letters the possible solutions their groups developed. Students may mail their letters if they wish.
- Have volunteers read their letters aloud. Discuss the different problems and solutions the students identified.
- Finally, as a class, compare the students' hypothetical situations with the current state of the U.S. economy.

National Council on Economic Education

THE **Economics**America AND **Economics**International PROGRAMS

Voluntary National Content Standards in Economics
Emphasized in Chapter 14

Content Standard 13

Content Standard 18

Content Standard 19

For a complete listing of NCEE Standards and entire text correlation, see Teacher pages in front of book.

Resources Available from NCEE
- Capstone: The Nation's High School Economics Course
- Civics and Government: Focus on Economics
- Economies in Transition: Command to Market
- Focus: High School Economics
- United States History: Eyes on the Economy
- Learning from the Market: Integrating the Stock Market Game™ Across the Curriculum

To order these materials or to contact your state Council on Economic Education about workshops and programs, call 1-800-338-1192 or visit www.nationalcouncil.org

Chapter 14 Resource Manager

Economic Concept Transparency 17:
Inflation and Deflation

Consumer Application Activity 19

Free Enterprise Activity 19

Enrichment Activity 14

Cooperative Learning Activity 19

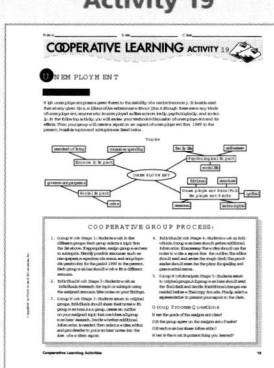

Math Practice Activity 19

Economic Cartoon 19

Primary and Secondary Source Reading 19

Economic Vocabulary Activity 14

Reteaching Activity 14

Critical Thinking Activity 19

Reinforcing Economic Skill 21

Chapter 14 Resource Manager

ASSESSMENT AND EVALUATION

Chapter 14 Test Form A

Chapter 14 Test Form B

Performance Assessment Activity 19

ExamView® Pro Testmaker

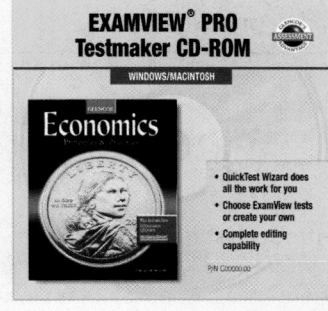

SPANISH RESOURCES

The following Spanish language materials are available in the Spanish Resources binder:

 Spanish Economic Vocabulary Activities

 Spanish Reteaching Activities

 Spanish Section Quizzes

 Spanish Economic Concepts Transparencies

Also available:

  Spanish Chapter 14 Audio Program Activity and Test

TECHNOLOGY/MULTIMEDIA

- Vocabulary PuzzleMaker CD-ROM
- Interactive Tutor Self-Assessment Software
- ExamView® Pro Testmaker
- Audio Program (English or Spanish)
- NBR Economics & You Video Program (English or Spanish)
- MindJogger Videoquiz
- Interactive Economics! CD-ROM
- Presentation Plus!
- TeacherWorks CD-ROM
- Glencoe Skillbuilder Interactive Workbook CD-ROM, Level 2

ECONOMICS Online

Use our Web site for additional resources. All essential content is covered in the Student Edition.

You and your students can visit epp.glencoe.com, the Web site companion to **Economics: Principles and Practices.** This innovative integration of electronic and print media offers your students a wealth of opportunities. The student text directs students to the Web site for the following options:

- **Chapter Overviews**
- **Student Web Activities**
- **Self-Check Quizzes**
- **Textbook Updates**

Answers are provided for you in the Web Activity Lesson Plan. Additional Web resources and interactive puzzles are also available.

Performance Assessment

Refer to Activity 19 in the *Performance Assessment Strategies and Activities* booklet.

 BLOCK SCHEDULING

Introduce students to chapter content and key terms by having them access **Chapter Overview 14** at epp.glencoe.com

ECONOMICS & YOU

Chapter 21
Disc 1, Side 2

Fighting Unemployment, Inflation, and Poverty
After viewing this segment, students should be able to:
- Describe the effects of inflation on businesses and individual consumers.

 Also available in VHS.

GLENCOE
TECHNOLOGY

 Use **MindJogger Videoquiz** to preview the Chapter 14 content.

CHAPTER 14

Economic Instability

Economics & You

Do you worry about the future? If you are concerned about getting a job, earning a decent income, or keeping up with inflation, the concept of economic stability is important to you. To learn more about the effects of unemployment and inflation, view the Chapter 21 video lesson:

Fighting Unemployment, Inflation, and Poverty

Downturns in the economy result in some businesses failing.

ECONOMICS Online

Chapter Overview Visit the *Economics: Principles and Practices* Web site at epp.glencoe.com and click on **Chapter 14—Chapter Overviews** to preview chapter information.

BANKRUPTCY LIQUIDATION

Contents of these Premises in Custody of

United States District Court

FOR THE

IN BANKRUPTCY

EXTRA CREDIT PROJECT

Have students monitor television newscasts, newspapers, and current affairs magazines for stories on unemployment, inflation, and poverty. Ask students to write a report summarizing these stories, paying special attention to the causes and solutions discussed.

Business Cycles and Fluctuations

Study Guide

Main Idea
The term "business cycle" refers to alternating increases and decreases in the level of economic activity.

Reading Strategy
Graphic Organizer As you read the section, complete a graphic organizer similar to the one below by listing factors that can cause changes in the business cycle.

Changes in the business cycle

Key Terms
business cycle, business fluctuation, recession, peak, trough, expansion, trend line, depression, depression scrip, econometric model, index of leading indicators

Objectives
After studying this section, you will be able to:
1. **Explain** the phases of the business cycle.
2. **Identify** five causes of business cycles.

Applying Economic Concepts
Economic Security Do you have a job and a paycheck on which you depend? Read to find out how economic instability can threaten your income.

Cover Story

Leading Indicators Decline

A key gauge of future U.S. economic activity declined 0.5% last month, as the Sept. 11 terrorist attacks in New York and Washington weakened an already troubled economy.

The Conference Board said Monday its index of leading economic indicators fell to 109.2 in September, . . . the largest one-month decline since January 1996. . . . The index indicates where the overall U.S. economy

Declining construction may signal a slowing economy

is headed in the next three to six months. . . .

The economy had been struggling for several months before the Sept. 11 attacks. Many economists have said they believe that a recession is unavoidable with the new uncertainties raised by the disaster.

—USAToday.com, October 22, 2001

Economic growth is something that is beneficial to almost everyone. However, we cannot take economic growth for granted. Sometimes economic growth is interrupted by **business cycles**—largely systematic ups and downs of real GDP. At other times economic growth is interrupted by **business fluctuations**—the rise and fall of real GDP over time in a nonsystematic manner.

Either way, economic growth—even the record-setting expansion that took place during the 1990s—always comes to a halt before it begins to take off again. The inevitable ups and downs of the economy are among the reasons why economists have developed tools like the monthly index of leading indicators featured in the cover story.

Business Cycles in the United States

Economic activity in the United States followed an irregular course throughout the twentieth century. The worst and most prolonged downturn was the Great Depression of the 1930s. The years since World War II have taken on a special pattern of their own.

CHAPTER 14: ECONOMIC INSTABILITY **375**

FOCUS

Section Overview
This section explains the business cycle and its causes.

BELLRINGER
Motivational Activity

- Project **transparency** and have students answer questions.
- Available as blackline master.

Daily Focus Transparency 57

Study Guide

Reading Strategy
Have students create the graphic organizer.
Answers to Graphic: *capital expenditures, inventory adjustments, innovation and imitation, monetary factors, external shock*

Preteaching Vocabulary
Have students create an annotated diagram of the business cycle using the following Key Terms as labels: *business cycle, business fluctuation, recession, peak, trough, expansion,* and *trend line.*

RESOURCE MANAGER

📁 Reproducible Masters
- Reproducible Lesson Plan 14-1
- Daily Lecture Notes 14-1
- Guided Reading Activity 14-1
- Reading Essentials and Study Guide 14-1
- Section Quiz 14-1

📑 Transparencies
- Daily Focus Transparency 57

Multimedia
- 💾 Interactive Tutor Self-Assessment Software
- 💿 ExamView® Pro Testmaker
- 💿 Presentation Plus!

② TEACH

Daily Lecture Notes 14-1

DAILY LECTURE NOTES 📖 Lesson 14-1

❓ DID YOU KNOW?
The average recession in the United States lasted 15 months and reduced output by 8.7 percent. The average expansion lasted 46 months and increased output by 22.5 percent.

PAGES 375-378
I. Business Cycles in the United States
   A. The business cycle consists of two phases: expansion and recession.
   B. Recession begins with a peak and ends with a trough.
   C. Expansion is the recovery from a recession.
   D. If a recession becomes very severe, it can turn into a depression.
   E. The worst depression in U.S. history was the Great Depression, which began in 1929.
   F. The Great Depression was caused by various factors, including excessive borrowing in the 1920s and global economic conditions.
   G. Since the Great Depression, the United States has experienced several recessions, but each was short compared with the recovery that followed.

⊞ Discussion Question
What happens during a depression? (Production slows, output declines, unemployment rises, and the standard of living falls.)

PAGES 378-379
II. Causes of the Business Cycle
   A. Businesses reduce their capital expenditures once they decide they have expanded enough.

ECONOMICS
AT A GLANCE

Answer: *the turnaround point where real GDP stops going down*

L1 Illustrating Ideas

To illustrate the impact of a downturn in business activity, point out that one person's spending is someone else's income. When spending does not take place, a chain reaction is set off that affects the whole economy. Provide students with the following scenario: Joe's Diner is a popular lunch spot with workers from Handmade Steel Products. In fact, Joe could not run the diner at a profit without the business from Handmade's workers. Handmade's management has just announced that the factory will close within weeks.

Have students construct an annotated flow diagram that illustrates the chain reaction set off by the closing of the factory. Display and discuss student diagrams.

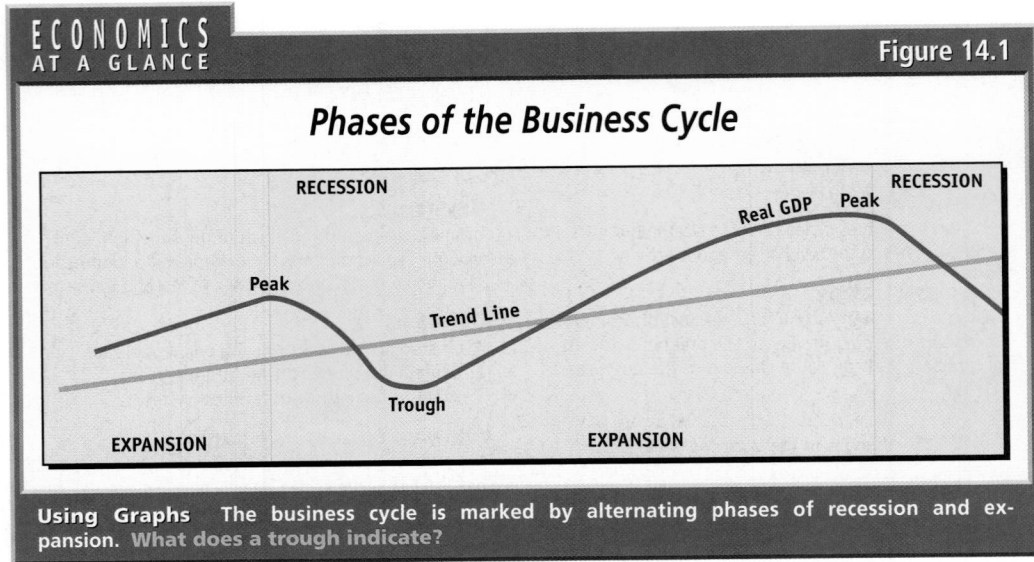

ECONOMICS
AT A GLANCE

Figure 14.1

Phases of the Business Cycle

Using Graphs The business cycle is marked by alternating phases of recession and expansion. **What does a trough indicate?**

Phases of the Business Cycle

The two phases of the business cycle are illustrated in **Figure 14.1.** The first phase is **recession,** a period during which real GDP declines for two quarters in a row, or six consecutive months. The recession begins when the economy reaches a **peak**—the point where real GDP stops going up. It ends when the economy reaches a **trough**—the turnaround point where real GDP stops going down.

As soon as the declining real GDP bottoms out, the economy moves into the second phase of the cycle, **expansion**—a period of recovery from a recession. Expansion continues until the economy reaches a new peak. If periods of recession and expansion did not occur, the economy would follow a steady growth path called a **trend line.** As **Figure 14.1** shows, the economy departs from, and then returns to, its trend line as it passes through phases of recession and expansion.

If a recession becomes very severe, it may turn into a **depression**—a state of the economy with large numbers of people out of work, acute shortages, and excess capacity in manufacturing plants.

376 UNIT 4 MACROECONOMICS: POLICIES

Most experts agree that the Great Depression of the 1930s was the only depression the United States has had in the twentieth century.

The Great Depression

The stock market crash on October 29, 1929, or "Black Tuesday," marks the beginning of the Great Depression. Between 1929 and 1933, GDP fell from approximately $103 to $55 billion—a decline of nearly 50 percent. At the same time, the number of people out of work rose nearly 800 percent—from 1.6 to 12.8 million. During the worst years of the Depression, one out of every four workers was jobless. Even workers who had jobs suffered. The average manufacturing wage, which had reached fifty-five cents an hour by 1929, plunged to five cents an hour by 1933.

Many banks across the country failed. The FDIC did not exist at the time, so depositors were not protected. To prevent panic withdrawals, the federal government declared a "bank holiday" in March of 1933. Every bank in the country closed for several days, and many banks never reopened.

MEETING SPECIAL NEEDS ACTIVITY

Learning Style: Verbal/Linguistic Encourage students who are verbal and linguistic learners to create "code words" that help them remember important ideas. For instance, causes of the Great Depression can be reduced to DIDOI (disparity in distribution of income), EAPC (easy and plentiful credit), and GEC (global economic conditions).

📁 Refer to *Inclusion for the Social Studies Classroom Strategies and Activities* in the TCR.

The money supply fell by one-third. Currency was in such short supply that towns, counties, chambers of commerce, and other civic bodies resorted to printing their own money, known as **depression scrip.** Several billion dollars of scrip was used to pay teachers, firefighters, police officers, and other municipal employees.

Causes of the Great Depression

Several factors contributed to the Great Depression. One was the disparity in the distribution of income. A great number of very poor and very rich people lived in America. The poor could not stimulate the economy with consumer spending because they had little or no income. The rich had the income, but often used it for such nonproductive activities as stock market speculation.

Easy and plentiful credit also appears to have played a role. Many people borrowed heavily in the late 1920s, which made them vulnerable to credit contractions, high interest rates, and even minor business fluctuations. When the crunch came, heavily indebted people had nothing to fall back on.

Global economic conditions also played a part. During the 1920s, public and private institutions in the United States made many foreign loans to help support a high level of international trade. Shortly before the Depression began in the United States, the private institutions withdrew many of these loans. Without the loans, some foreign nations could no longer buy American goods, so American exports fell sharply.

At the same time, high American tariffs on imports kept many countries from selling goods to the United States. Many countries that depended

Guided Reading Activity 14-1

Name _____ Date _____ Class _____

GUIDED READING Activity 14-1

For use with textbook pages 375–380

BUSINESS CYCLES AND FLUCTUATIONS

OUTLINING

Directions: Locate the heading in your textbook. Then use the information under the heading to help you write each answer. Use another sheet of paper if necessary.

I. Business Cycles in the United States
A. Phases of the Business Cycle—What is the difference between a recession and a depression?

B. The Great Depression—Why did the government declare a "bank holiday" in 1933?

C. Causes of the Great Depression—How did easy and plentiful credit contribute to the Great Depression?

II. Causes of the Business Cycle
A. Capital Expenditures—When do businesses invest heavily in capital goods?

B. Inventory Adjustments—What is an inventory adjustment?

C. Innovation and Imitation—What does an innovation usually trigger in industry?

D. Monetary Factors—What happens when the Fed follows an easy money policy?

E. External Shocks—Give an example of a positive and negative external shock.

III. Predicting Business Cycles
A. What is an econometric model?

B. What is the index of leading indicators?

44   Guided Reading Activities

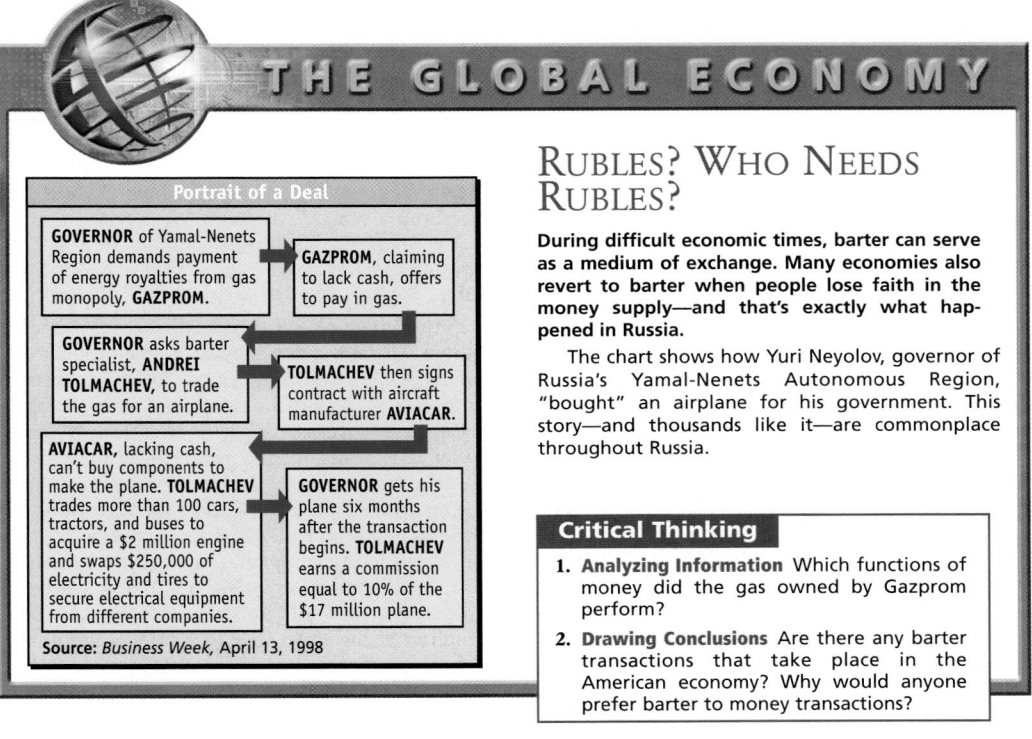

THE GLOBAL ECONOMY

RUBLES? WHO NEEDS RUBLES?

During difficult economic times, barter can serve as a medium of exchange. Many economies also revert to barter when people lose faith in the money supply—and that's exactly what happened in Russia.

The chart shows how Yuri Neyolov, governor of Russia's Yamal-Nenets Autonomous Region, "bought" an airplane for his government. This story—and thousands like it—are commonplace throughout Russia.

Portrait of a Deal

- **GOVERNOR** of Yamal-Nenets Region demands payment of energy royalties from gas monopoly, **GAZPROM.**
- **GAZPROM,** claiming to lack cash, offers to pay in gas.
- **GOVERNOR** asks barter specialist, **ANDREI TOLMACHEV,** to trade the gas for an airplane.
- **TOLMACHEV** then signs contract with aircraft manufacturer **AVIACAR.**
- **AVIACAR,** lacking cash, can't buy components to make the plane. **TOLMACHEV** trades more than 100 cars, tractors, and buses to acquire a $2 million engine and swaps $250,000 of electricity and tires to secure electrical equipment from different companies.
- **GOVERNOR** gets his plane six months after the transaction begins. **TOLMACHEV** earns a commission equal to 10% of the $17 million plane.

Source: *Business Week,* April 13, 1998

Critical Thinking

1. **Analyzing Information** Which functions of money did the gas owned by Gazprom perform?
2. **Drawing Conclusions** Are there any barter transactions that take place in the American economy? Why would anyone prefer barter to money transactions?

CHAPTER 14: ECONOMIC INSTABILITY **377**

THE GLOBAL ECONOMY

Rubles? Who Needs Rubles?
Across the world from Russia in a society that still subscribes to communist principles, Cubans carry on another form of barter. They cannot legally buy or sell a house or an apartment. If they want to move, they find other homeowners who will agree to swap accommodations.

Answers:
1. *Gas acted as payment for royalties.*
2. *Bartering is rarely done in the American economy, though some cultures such as the Native Americans still use the system. People prefer to barter when they lose faith in the money supply.*

FREE ENTERPRISE ACTIVITY

Write the following statement on the board: *Some economists have suggested that business cycles are the result of the clustering of new inventions and innovation.* **Ask:** How do new inventions and innovations stimulate growth of the economy? What happens to the land, labor, and capital when new production methods are employed? Then have students hypothesize about the effects of new production methods on the business cycle. As an example, point out that the economy was stimulated by the introduction of the personal computer in the late 1970s. Investment in the industry increased as the new product was copied, production increased, and employment grew. Conclude by asking students for examples of innovation and invention that have changed production methods in their or their parents' lifetimes.

L2 Summarizing

Tell students to locate a magazine or newspaper article that discusses the economy in a recession or an expansion. Have students summarize the main points of the article and present them to the rest of the class in an oral report.

L3 Writing a Report

Have students imagine that they are economic advisers to the president. Have them write a report noting what phase of the business cycle the economy is presently in and how the various factors that cause business cycles may have contributed to this position.

CURRICULUM CONNECTION

History Perhaps the most vivid description of the stock market crash appeared on the front page of the October 30, 1929, edition of the show-business newspaper, *Variety.* A banner headline blared: "WALL ST. LAYS AN EGG."

---

heavily on sales to the United States were soon faced with economic crises. As the Depression spread from country to country, world trade declined, and American exports dropped even further.

Business Cycles Since World War II

Massive government spending during World War II added a huge stimulant to the economy for most of the early 1940s. Recession returned in 1945, but it did not last. As soon as the war was over, consumers went on a buying binge that stimulated expansion again. The economy experienced several more recessions after that, but each downturn was short compared with the length of the recovery that followed. The average recession lasted about 11 months, while the average expansion lasted 43 months.

Figure 14.2 shows the recurring pattern of recessions and expansions since 1965. With few exceptions, most of the earlier recessions occurred on a fairly regular basis. After 1980, however, recessions occurred less frequently. The expansion that began in 1991 is the longest expansion in United States history.

Causes of the Business Cycle

No one theory seems to explain past business cycles, or serves as a way to predict future ones. In many cases, several factors are working together to create a cycle.

Capital Expenditures

Changes in capital expenditures are one cause of business cycles. When the economy is expanding,

STANDARD & POOR'S INFOBYTE

The Business Cycle The term "business cycle" describes economy-wide fluctuations in output, incomes, and employment. Generally, periods of expansion follow periods of low output.

378 UNIT 4 MACROECONOMICS: POLICIES

---

businesses expect future sales to be high, so they invest heavily in capital goods. Companies may build new plants or buy new equipment to replace older equipment in their plants. After a while, businesses may decide they have expanded enough. They begin to pull back on their capital investments, causing layoffs in the capital goods industries and, eventually, recession results.

Inventory Adjustments

Inventory adjustments, or changes in the level of business inventories, are a second possible cause of business cycles. Some businesses cut back on inventories at the first sign of an economic slowdown and then build them back up again at the first sign of an upturn. Either action causes investment expenditures—and therefore real GDP—to fluctuate.

The influence of inventory adjustments showed up clearly in the business cycle of the late 1940s. Right after World War II, businesses in the United States invested heavily in inventories to fill shelves depleted during the war years. By 1948 consumer demand caught up with the backlog and people stopped buying. Inventories built up on store shelves, so businesses stopped buying inventory. The resulting recession of 1949 lasted for about a year.

Innovation and Imitation

A third possible cause of business cycles is innovation. An innovation may be a new product or a new way of performing a task. When a business innovates, it often gains an edge on its competitors because its costs go down or its sales go up. In either case, profits increase, and the business grows. If other businesses in the same industry want to keep up, they must copy what the innovator has done or come up with something even better.

The imitating companies must invest heavily to do this, and an investment boom follows. After the innovation takes hold in the industry, however, the situation changes. Further investments are unnecessary, and economic activity may slow. Meanwhile, the fluctuation of investments has produced a business cycle.

CRITICAL THINKING

Determining Cause and Effect On the board, copy the chart below. Omit the answers in parentheses. Tell students to read page 378, and then ask volunteers to complete the chart.

CAUSES	EFFECTS
Businesses pull back on their capital investments.	(Layoffs occur in the capital goods industries and recession results.)
Businesses cut back or build up inventories.	(Investment expenditures and real GDP fluctuate.)
(A business innovates and gains an edge on its competitors.)	Profits increase and a business grows.

STANDARD &POOR'S

Figure 14.2

The Index of Leading Economic Indicators

On average, the index turns down 12 months before the recession begins.

On average, the index turns up 4 months before the recovery begins.

Occasionally, the index predicted a recession that never occurred.

Recession years

Source: The Conference Board

Using Graphs The index of leading indicators is one of the tools used to predict future economic activity. **How do economists use this index to predict recessions?**

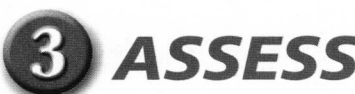

ECONOMICS *Online*

Visit epp.glencoe.com and click on *Textbook Updates—Chapter 14* for an update of the data.

Monetary Factors

A fourth possible cause of business cycles is the credit and loan policies of the Federal Reserve System. When "easy money" policies are in effect, interest rates are low and loans are easy to get. Easy money encourages the private sector to borrow and invest, which stimulates the economy for a short time. Eventually the increased demand for loans causes interest rates to rise, which in turn discourages new borrowers.

As borrowing and spending slow down, the level of economic activity declines. Lenders think twice about making new loans or renewing old ones, and the business cycle begins again.

External Shocks

A final potential cause of business cycles is external shocks, such as increases in oil prices,

wars, and international conflict. Some shocks drive the economy up, as when Great Britain discovered North Sea oil in the 1970s. Other shocks can be negative, as when high oil prices hit the United States in early 2001.

Predicting Business Cycles

Economists use a number of methods to predict business cycles. One popular technique involves macroeconomic modeling. Another makes use of statistical predictors.

An **econometric model** is a macroeconomic model that uses algebraic equations to describe how the economy behaves. Most models used today are based on some adaptation of the output-expenditure model we examined earlier:

$$GDP = C + I + G + F$$

CHAPTER 14: ECONOMIC INSTABILITY **379**

CHAPTER 14
Section 1, pages 375–380

STANDARD &POOR'S

Answer: *by measuring the beginning and the end of a business cycle*

3 ASSESS

Assign Section 1 Assessment as homework or as an in-class activity.

Have students use **Interactive Tutor Self-Assessment Software** to review Section 1.

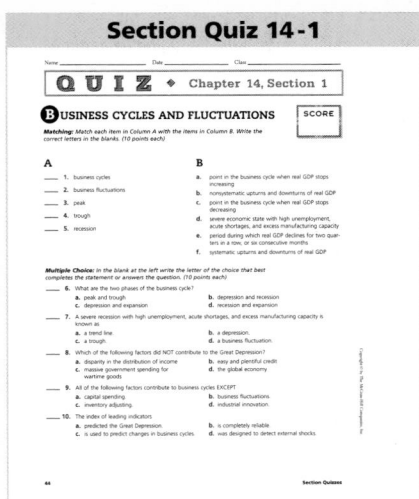

Section Quiz 14-1

EXTENDING THE CONTENT

Uncertainty and Predictions A careful economic forecaster knows that past data is not a certain predictor of future events. Even though there is an abundance of data about past economic activity, too many unknowns exist to predict the future with certainty. To begin with, there are too many variables to measure, and the variables affecting economic activity can change from one time period to another. For example, when the automobile was first developed, few people felt that it would have a long-lasting economic impact. However, it literally became the driving force of the entire economy.

Reteach

Enrich

Have students write a research paper on the stock market crash of 1987. Suggest that they compare the 1987 crash to that of 1929.

4 CLOSE

Ask: Are there any measures you can take to protect yourself from the ups and downs of the business cycle? If so, what are they?

For example, an economist might use X to stand for exports, and M for imports (instead of F for the foreign sector) to get:

$$GDP = C + I + G + (X - M)$$

Other equations in the model also may be substituted for some of the variables. Suppose that households annually spend a fixed amount of money, designated as **a,** along with 95 percent of their disposable personal income. In this case, **C = a + .95 (DI).** If this were substituted for the C in the output-expenditure model, the equation would read:

$$GDP = a + .95(DI) + I + G + (X - M)$$

The equation is then broken down into smaller and smaller components to the point where it may have as many as 1,000 variables.

To predict GDP, forecasters put in the latest figures for the variables on the right side of the equation. Because most econometric models are solved using a computer, little time is needed to obtain a solution.

As the quarter unfolds, actual changes in the economy are compared to the model's predictions. The model is then updated. Some models give reasonably good forecasts for up to nine months. Overall, short-term econometric models have proven their value and are used extensively.

Another tool used to predict the turning points of business cycles is the **index of leading indicators,** a monthly statistical series that usually turns down before real GDP turns down, and turns up before real GDP turns up. As we saw in the cover story, the index is widely used to predict the direction of future economic activity.

Some statistical indicators, such as the length of the average workweek—which tends to shrink just before a recession begins—are fairly good predictors of real GDP changes. Still, no single series has proven completely reliable. To resolve this problem, 10 individual series are combined into an overall index that closely patterns the behavior of real GDP, making the index of leading indicators a useful tool.

The behavior of the composite index can be seen in **Figure 14.2,** where the shaded areas represent recessions. As you can see, the average time between a dip in the index and the onset of recession is about 12 months. The average time between a rise in the index and an expansion is about four months. The information it supplies is used along with results from other econometric models. Together, the results generally let the forecaster predict how real GDP will behave in the short run.

Section 1 Assessment

Checking for Understanding
1. **Main Idea** Explain the difference between a business cycle and a business fluctuation.
2. **Key Terms** Define business cycle, business fluctuation, recession, peak, trough, expansion, trend line, depression, depression scrip, econometric model, index of leading indicators.
3. **Identify** the two main phases of a business cycle.
4. **Explain** how the Great Depression compared to other recessionary periods.
5. **List** five causes of business cycles.

Applying Economic Concepts
6. **Economic Security** Suppose you were the head of a household. How would you plan your spending for your family's needs if you had an accurate prediction of future business cycles? Include examples in your response to the question.

Critical Thinking
7. **Understanding Cause and Effect** If business inventories are falling, the average hours worked per week is going up, and there is an increase in the number of new building permits, we would expect the economy to be in an expansion phase of the business cycle. Explain why each of these indicators would show that the economy would grow in the near future.

Practice and assess key social studies skills with the *Glencoe Skillbuilder Interactive Workbook, Level 2.*

Section 1 Assessment Answers

1. Business cycles are systematic increases and decreases in real GDP; unsystematic changes are business fluctuations.

2. All vocabulary terms are defined in the text.

3. recession, expansion

4. The Great Depression was more severe than the other recessionary periods. It was the worst economic decline in U.S. history.

5. capital expenditures, inventory adjustments, innovation and imitation, monetary factors, external shocks

6. Answers will vary. If you knew a recession was coming, you might save more money.

7. Falling inventories = many items being produced and sold. An increasing number of hours worked = more work time needed to keep up with increased demand. An increasing number of building permits = companies forming and expanding.

Profiles
IN Economics

ECONOMIC FREEDOM

Championing
Economic Freedom:
Walter E. Williams
(1936–)

Walter E. Williams is an economist, author, and professor of economics at George Mason University. Williams's views are decidedly free market—and often controversial.

FREEDOM IS KEY

"Economic freedom" is the cornerstone of Williams's beliefs. He argues that economic freedom is the key to both economic growth and the fair distribution of wealth. Williams often points to Hong Kong, Korea, Taiwan, and Singapore as evidence of the spectacular economic growth that can be achieved when there is little government intervention. This has led him to become an outspoken critic of many popular government programs.

Many Americans, for example, support the minimum wage. To Williams, however, it is a cause of economic problems.

One example he cites involves a comparison between unemployment levels of African American and white teenagers: "In 1948, black teenage unemployment was less than that of whites. Compare it with today and it's the opposite," Williams explains. "You can't explain it by saying there was less racism in 1948 than there is today. You can't explain it by saying that blacks had more education than whites in 1948. You have to explain it by increases in both the level and coverage of the minimum wage law." The implication is that if employers had the freedom to pay lower wages, then more black teenagers would have jobs.

AFFIRMATIVE ACTION

Perhaps Williams's most controversial stand is his opposition to affirmative action. He views it as a violation of his cherished idea of economic freedom, and worse:

"I think many government programs have harmed blacks in making achievements less credible," he argues. "For example, whatever inspiration Harvard or the University of Virginia has in requiring so many articles in the law journals to be written by women or by minorities reduces the credibility of a black student or a female student having written for the law journal."

Examining the Profile

1. **Summarizing Information** Write a short paragraph that identifies and describes Williams's basic views.

2. **Applying the Writing Process** Write a response to what Williams said about unemployment levels among white and African American teenagers. Explain why you agree or disagree with his analysis.

CHAPTER 14: ECONOMIC INSTABILITY **381**

BACKGROUND

Walter Williams's syndicated column generates a great deal of correspondence, especially from African Americans. Some letters are harsh, accusing Williams of "giving aid and comfort to racism around the United States" (an allusion to treason), and of "pushing a white man's agenda." Other readers, however, have congratulated him for his "color-blind" and "even-handed" examination of issues that affect African Americans. Such controversy is typical of that which surrounds well-known African Americans who maintain conservative economic positions.

TEACH

Have students explore the concept of "economic freedom" by creating a web diagram on the board and inviting students to contribute to it. Relevant concepts to consider include laissez-faire, economic rights, economic responsibilities, political freedom, the minimum wage, and affirmative action.

Answers to Examining the Profile

1. Paragraphs will vary. Students should refer to economic freedom as intrinsic to Williams's views, his position that it can lead to growth and fair distribution of wealth, and his related opposition to the minimum wage and affirmative action.

2. Answers will vary. Students who agree might echo Williams's analysis, which seeks to eliminate other causes. Students who disagree might suggest that Williams argues in a vacuum by too easily dismissing racism and other social factors.

① *FOCUS*

Section Overview
This section describes the various kinds of unemployment.

BELLRINGER
Motivational Activity

- Project **transparency** and have students answer questions.
- Available as blackline master.

Daily Focus Transparency 70

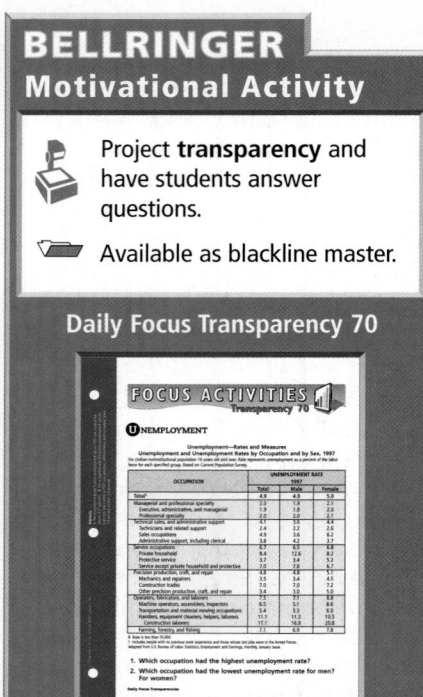

Study Guide

Reading Strategy
Have students create the graphic organizer.
Answers to Graphic: *changes in technology and changes in consumer tastes; changes in the way industries operate*

Preteaching Vocabulary
Ask students to write questions for which the Key Terms are the answers. Have students use their questions to test each other's understanding of the Key Terms.

SECTION 2

Unemployment

Study Guide

Main Idea
Frictional, structural, cyclical, seasonal, and technological are the general types of unemployment.

Reading Strategy
Graphic Organizer As you read the section, complete a graphic organizer similar to the one below by listing two ways that structural unemployment takes place.

Structural unemployment → [ ] [ ]

Key Terms
unemployed, unemployment rate, frictional unemployment, structural unemployment, cyclical unemployment, seasonal unemployment, technological unemployment, automation

Objectives
After studying this section, you will be able to:
1. **Explain** how the Bureau of Labor Statistics determines if a person is employed.
2. **Describe** five kinds of unemployment.

Applying Economic Concepts
Employment Did you work for at least one hour per week for pay or profit last month? Read to find out how your answer to this question determines your employment status.

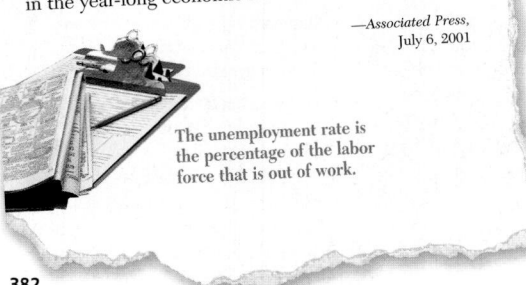

Cover Story

Unemployment Rate Rises to 4.5 Percent

Washington(AP)–The nation's unemployment rate rose to 4.5 percent in June as manufacturers continued to suffer heavy job losses and demand for workers in service industries fell to the lowest level in 10 months.

The Labor Department reported Friday that the jobless rate rose 0.1 percentage point from a 4.4 percent rate in May. The 4.5 percent level matched the unemployment rate in April with both months representing the highest level the jobless rate has reached in the year-long economic slowdown.

—*Associated Press,*
July 6, 2001

The unemployment rate is the percentage of the labor force that is out of work.

382

Nearly one-half of the population of the United States belongs to the civilian labor force, and at any given time millions of these people are without jobs. This issue is so important that full employment is one of the seven economic and social goals of the American economy.

Measuring Unemployment

To understand the severity of joblessness, we need to know how it is measured, as well as what the measure overlooks. The measure of joblessness is the unemployment rate, one of the most closely watched statistics in the economy.

The Unemployment Rate
In the middle of any given month, thousands of specialists from the Bureau of the Census begin their monthly survey of about 50,000 households in nearly 2,000 counties, covering all 50 states. Census workers are looking for the **unemployed**–people available for work who made a specific effort to find a job during the past month and who, during the most recent

---

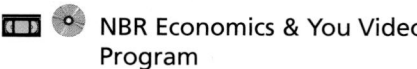
RESOURCE MANAGER

📁 Reproducible Masters
- Reproducible Lesson Plan 14-2
- Daily Lecture Notes 14-2
- Guided Reading Activity 14-2
- Reading Essentials and Study Guide 14-2
- Section Quiz 14-2

🖥 Transparencies
- Daily Focus Transparency 70

Multimedia
- 📀 NBR Economics & You Video Program
- 💾 Interactive Tutor Self-Assessment Software
- ⊛ ExamView® Pro Testmaker
- ⊛ Presentation Plus!

survey week, worked less than one hour for pay or profit. People are also classified as unemployed if they worked in a family business without pay for less than 15 hours a week.

After the Census workers collect their data, they turn it over to the Bureau of Labor Statistics for analysis and publication. This data is then published on a monthly basis.

Unemployment also is expressed in terms of the **unemployment rate,** the number of unemployed individuals divided by the total number of persons in the civilian labor force. As **Figure 14.3** shows, the unemployment rate tends to rise dramatically during recessions and then come down slowly afterward. With a civilian labor force of approximately 140 million people, a one-tenth of one percent rise

in the unemployment rate would mean that nearly 140,000 people had lost their jobs. This number is more than the population of cities such as Kansas City, Kansas; Tallahassee, Florida; Bridgeport, Connecticut; or Savannah, Georgia.

Limitations of the Unemployment Rate

It might seem that a measure as comprehensive as the unemployment rate would summarize the problem. If anything, however, the unemployment rate understates employment conditions for two reasons.

First, the unemployment rate does not count those who have become too frustrated or discouraged to look for work. These labor force "dropouts" may include nearly a million people

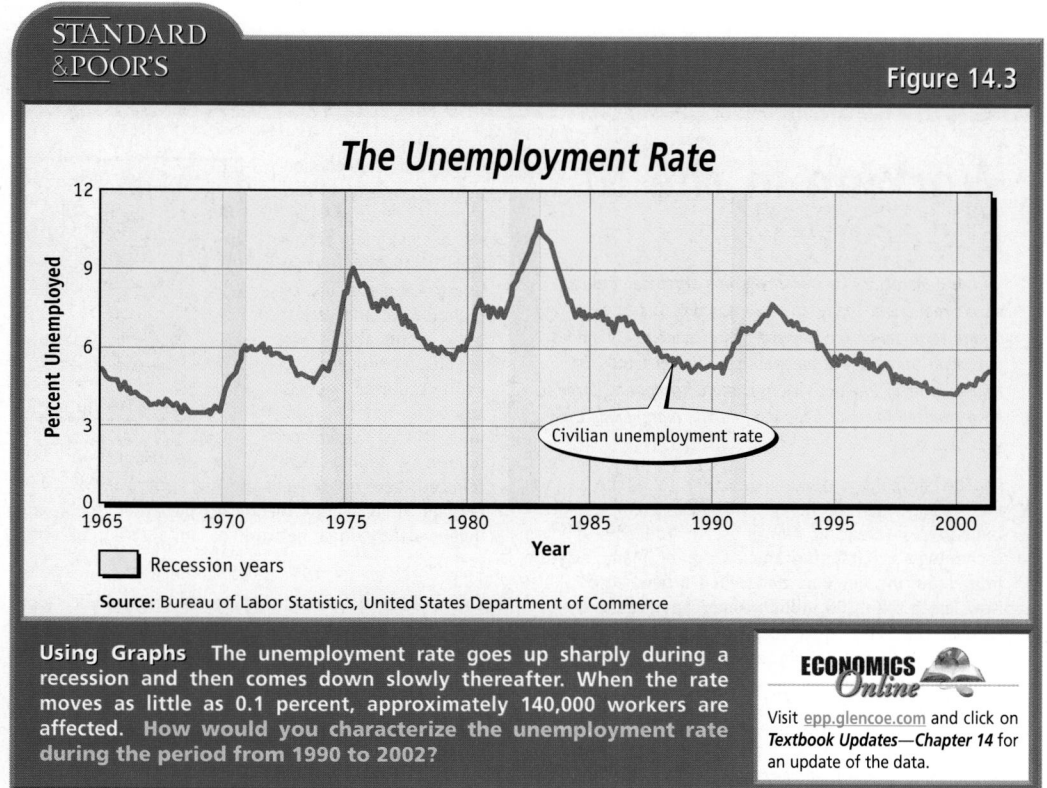

STANDARD &POOR'S

Figure 14.3

The Unemployment Rate

Civilian unemployment rate

Recession years

Source: Bureau of Labor Statistics, United States Department of Commerce

Using Graphs The unemployment rate goes up sharply during a recession and then comes down slowly thereafter. When the rate moves as little as 0.1 percent, approximately 140,000 workers are affected. **How would you characterize the unemployment rate during the period from 1990 to 2002?**

ECONOMICS *Online*

Visit epp.glencoe.com and click on **Textbook Updates—Chapter 14** for an update of the data.

MEETING SPECIAL NEEDS ACTIVITY

Learning Disabled For students who have problems with reasoning, consider helping them categorize information. To do this, use a framework for comparing the different types of unemployment discussed in this section. Develop categories for comparisons such as: Who does the unemployment affect? What is the nature of the unemployment? What is the cause of the unemployment? How does this type of unemployment differ from the other types? How is it similar? Direct students in searching for information that might be included in these categories.

Refer to *Inclusion for the Social Studies Classroom Strategies and Activities* in the TCR.

---

2 TEACH

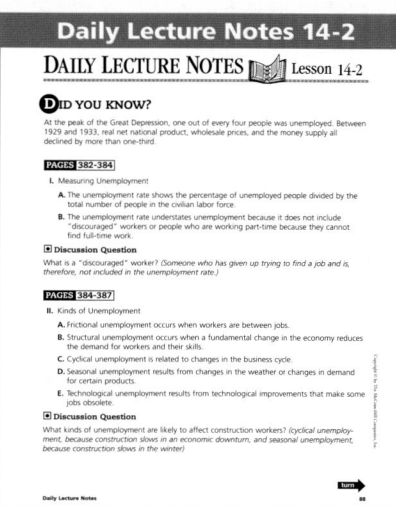

Daily Lecture Notes 14-2

DAILY LECTURE NOTES Lesson 14-2

DID YOU KNOW?
At the peak of the Great Depression, one out of every four people was unemployed. Between 1929 and 1933, real net national product, wholesale prices, and the money supply all declined by more than one-third.

PAGES 382-384
I. Measuring Unemployment
   A. The unemployment rate shows the percentage of unemployed people divided by the total number of people in the civilian labor force.
   B. The unemployment rate understates unemployment because it does not include "discouraged" workers or people who are working part-time because they cannot find full-time work.

Discussion Question
What is a "discouraged" worker? (Someone who has given up trying to find a job and is, therefore, not included in the unemployment rate.)

PAGES 384-387
II. Kinds of Unemployment
   A. Frictional unemployment occurs when workers are between jobs.
   B. Structural unemployment occurs when a fundamental change in the economy reduces the demand for workers and their skills.
   C. Cyclical unemployment is related to changes in the business cycle.
   D. Seasonal unemployment results from changes in the weather or changes in demand for certain products.
   E. Technological unemployment results from technological improvements that make some jobs obsolete.

Discussion Question
What kinds of unemployment are likely to affect construction workers? (cyclical unemployment, because construction slows in an economic downturn, and seasonal unemployment, because construction slows in the winter)

Daily Lecture Notes

L1 Understanding Ideas

List on the board the five types of unemployment. Ask students to write five sentences, with each sentence providing an example of one type of unemployment. **ELL**

STANDARD &POOR'S

Answer: *It rose dramatically around 1993, then came down slowly, and started to rise in 2001.*

THE GLOBAL ECONOMY

Responsible Tourism Americans can affect the levels of employment in other countries, according to a group called the Center for Responsible Tourism. Its members urge American visitors in foreign countries to patronize cafes and guest houses owned by indigenous peoples. In this way, tourists support native workers rather than international travel consortiums, which often exploit native workers by paying low wages. The center also advises "bargaining with compassion" when buying souvenirs from the local merchants.

---

during recessionary periods. Although they are not working, these people are not classified as unemployed because they did not try to find a job within the previous four-week period.

Second, people are considered employed even when they hold part-time jobs. Someone who has lost a high-paying job, but is working just one hour a week at a minimum-wage job, would still be considered employed. As a result, being employed is not the same as being fully employed.

Kinds of Unemployment

Economists have identified several different kinds of unemployment. The nature and cause of each affect how much unemployment can be reduced in the economy.

Frictional Unemployment

One kind of unemployment is **frictional unemployment**—unemployment caused by workers who are between jobs for one reason or another. These workers are short-term unemployed and will suffer little economic hardship from their lack of employment. With freedom to choose occupations, many choose to leave their old jobs to look for better work. Others have lost their jobs, but will quickly find others.

Some frictional unemployment is the result of new people moving into the labor force, particularly young workers searching for their first jobs. Unemployment of this nature is a minor problem that cannot be completely eliminated. It is necessary for workers to be able to move to the jobs where they are most needed. Because there are

---

CYBERNOMICS SPOTLIGHT

Working in the New Economy

For generations, the economy was organized around mass production. Today, the new economy is fast becoming a high-technology, service, and office economy. This does not mean that mass production is no longer important. Higher rates of productivity in manufacturing and farming have resulted in fewer people producing more goods than ever before.

As the shift from a manufacturing to a service and knowledge-based economy continues, the rise of new industries is creating new jobs. In addition, modern technology is changing the nature of many existing jobs, requiring new knowledge and a new set of skills. Now, more than 100 million Americans (nearly 80 percent of the total workforce) work in occupations that are service-related or information-related.

The Virtual Workplace As electronic commerce and Internet business grows, fewer people will work in central offices, retail stores and other facilities. Analysts believe that the virtual workplace, allowing employees to work from any location with a computer and Internet connection, will become more prevalent. Ideally, the virtual workplace makes use of technology and other work innovations to enable employees to work together across space and time. Workers in a virtual workplace require a highly customized set of skills,

More and more people are working at home.

ranging from highly technical specialties to working independently in a network or on a string of virtual teams.

Job Trends Jobs requiring postsecondary, vocational, or higher education are expected to grow as a share of total employment. Positions calling for individuals with at least an associate's degree are expected to increase from 31 percent of all jobs in 1996 to 32.4 percent in 2006. Along with an increase in the number of high-skilled jobs, the number of low-skilled jobs is expected to grow. Occupations predicted to show the largest

384 UNIT 4 MACROECONOMICS: POLICIES

CYBERNOMICS SPOTLIGHT

More About . . . Working in the New Economy A great source for information on employment trends is the *Occupational Outlook Handbook* printed by the Bureau of Labor Statistics. According to the Handbook, 246 industries employed 140,513,683 American workers in 1998. The ten industries with the most workers were education, public and private; self-employed workers; eating and drinking establishments; hospitals, public and private; local government, except education and hospitals; wholesale trade; personnel supply services; grocery stores; department stores; and state government, except education and hospitals. Together these industries employed about 54 million people.

The occupational outlook for the year 2008 is a little different. Supposedly, computer and data always some workers who are in the process of changing jobs, there will always be some frictional unemployment in the economy.

Structural Unemployment

Structural unemployment—unemployment that occurs when a fundamental change in the operations of the economy reduces the demand for workers and their skills—is a more serious type of unemployment.

Changes in technology and changes in consumer tastes often cause structural unemployment. Workers are structurally unemployed because their skills and the skills required by employers who are hiring workers do not match. In the early 1900s, for example, people reduced their demand for horses, buggies, and buggy whips in favor of domestic automobiles. Later, tastes changed in favor of foreign-made automobiles, causing considerable unemployment in Michigan, Ohio, and the industrial Northeast.

Industries may also change the way they operate. During the 1990–1991 recession, a series of mergers and cost reductions trimmed the white-collar labor force in the banking and computer industries. This change was sudden and left millions of highly skilled people out of work. Many of these workers had to develop new skills before they could find employment in other industries.

Sometimes the government contributes to structural unemployment when it changes the way it does business.

> ### Did You Know?
> **Job Trends** For the next few years, most of the new jobs will be in the services and retail trade industries. By 2005 these industries are expected to account for 16.2 million out of a total projected growth of 16.8 million wage and salary jobs.

increases include cashiers, janitors, retail salespersons, and restaurant workers. Low-skilled occupations are expected to account for 13 percent of all new job growth.

Job Skills in the Information Age

A survey of more than 400 of the fastest-growing U.S. firms over a five-year period points to the importance of education and training. Over one-half of the entry-level positions offered by the firms require a high school diploma and often at least two years of post-high school studies. Nearly 40 percent of the firms require a four-year college degree, and an additional 7 percent require completion of postgraduate studies. The companies' CEOs place great importance on math skills. "Mastering challenging mathematics is more important than ever before for our students," noted U.S. Secretary of Education Richard W. Riley. "Algebra is considered a new basic."

 ## Math Practice

Percentage Change In 1987 Americans bought 7,080,858 American-made cars and 3,195,751 imports. Ten years later, Americans bought 6,916,769 American-made autos and 1,355,305 imports. What was the percent of change in American purchases of imports? *(−14.7 percent)* How might this change have affected unemployment in the American automobile industry? *(Unemployment would have most likely decreased as Americans were buying relatively more American cars.)*

 NIGHTLY BUSINESS REPORT

 ECONOMICS & YOU

 Chapter 21
Disc 1, Side 2

Fighting Unemployment, Inflation, and Poverty

Ask: What problems are associated with unemployment? *(It is a sign of a troubled economy. It reduces living standards, and can disrupt families and reduce individuals' self-respect.)*

Also available in VHS.

processing services will replace grocery stores as the eighth largest employer in the nation. Also, hospitals will have more employees than local governments, and the need for doctors will increase more than the need for workers in state government. Why? Most likely because the population will be aging as well as becoming more technologically proficient.

③ ASSESS

Assign Section 2 Assessment as homework or as an in-class activity.

💾 Have students use **Interactive Tutor Self-Assessment Software** to review Section 2.

Section Quiz 14-2

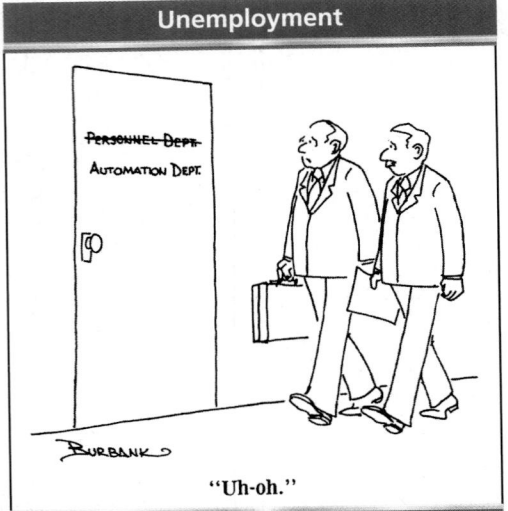

Unemployment

"Uh-oh."

Technological Unemployment When technological unemployment occurs, many workers find they have to learn new skills. *What causes technological unemployment?*

Congress's decision to close military bases in the 1990s is a prime example. Military bases are much larger than most private companies, and the impact of the base closings was concentrated in select regions and communities. Some areas were able to attract new industry that hired many of the unemployed workers, but most workers either developed new skills or moved to other regions.

Cyclical Unemployment

A third kind of unemployment is **cyclical unemployment**—unemployment directly related to swings in the business cycle. During a recession, for example, many people put off buying durable goods such as automobiles, refrigerators, washers, dryers, and new homes. As a result, some industries must lay off workers until the economy recovers.

Laid-off workers generally get their jobs back eventually when the economy improves. Accordingly, many try to wait out the recession by living on savings or by taking temporary jobs.

Seasonal Unemployment

A fourth kind of unemployment is **seasonal unemployment**—unemployment resulting from changes in the weather or changes in the demand for certain products. Many carpenters and builders, for example, have less work in the winter than during the spring and summer because some tasks, such as replacing a roof or digging a foundation, are harder to do when the weather is cold.

The difference between seasonal and cyclical unemployment relates to the period of measurement. Cyclical unemployment takes place over the course of the business cycle, which may last three to five years. Seasonal unemployment takes place every year, regardless of the general health of the economy.

Technological Unemployment

A fifth kind of unemployment is **technological unemployment**—unemployment caused when workers with less skills, talent, or education are replaced by machines and other equipment that do their jobs. Technological unemployment happens when workers face the threat of **automation**—production with mechanical or other processes that reduce the need for workers.

In some cases, automation results in a drastic reduction in the number of workers needed for production. Japan, for example, pioneered the use of large mechanized factories. Entire assembly lines in industries such as automobiles and steel are staffed by one-fifth of the workers needed in similar U.S. plants. In the United States, the use of automated teller machines by banks has reduced the need for bank tellers.

Did you know?

Employment Trends Every spring, the unemployment rate slightly rises as college graduates enter the labor force. The high unemployment rates in the mid-1980s were caused in part by the baby boomers who had graduated from college and were entering the work force.

FREE ENTERPRISE ACTIVITY

For more than 50 years, the *Occupational Outlook Handbook* has provided information about the world of work. Currently, the Handbook presents expected employment changes in nearly 250 occupations, including the qualifications that will be needed for them. Ask your students to list two or three occupations that interest them. Have them research these occupations in the Handbook and report to the class the occupations' salaries and qualifications.

The Concept of Full Employment

 Economists have long wrestled with the concept of full employment. Full employment does not mean zero unemployment. Instead, full employment is the lowest possible unemployment rate, with the economy growing and all factors of production being used as efficiently as possible.

While opinions may vary, it appears as if full employment is reached when the unemployment rate drops below 4.5 percent. Unemployment rates do, however, get much lower. In late 2000, the rate reached a record low of 3.9 percent and stayed there for two months.

Consistently low unemployment is difficult to maintain because of the business cycle. **Figure 14.3** shows that the 1969–1970 recession drove the unemployment rate to 6.1 percent. The 1974 recession drove the rate to 9.0 percent in 1975, and the 1981–1982 recession drove the rate to 10.8 percent. The rate declined thereafter, but the 1991 recession drove it back up to 7.8 percent.

ECONOMICS AT A GLANCE — Figure 14.4

The Fastest-Growing Occupations, 1998–2008

Occupation	Employment 1998	Employment 2008	% Increase 1998–2008
Computer engineers	299	622	108
Computer support specialists	429	869	102
Systems analysts	617	1,194	94
Database administrators	87	155	77
Desktop publishing specialists	26	44	73
Paralegals and legal assistants	136	220	62
Personal care and home health aides	746	1,179	58
Medical assistants	252	398	58
Social and human service assistants	268	410	53
Physician assistants	66	98	48

Source: Bureau of Labor Statistics (Number in thousands of jobs)

Using Tables These occupations are projected to be the 10 fastest-growing occupations from 1998 to 2008. Other than technology, in what fields are many of the fastest-growing jobs concentrated?

Section 2 Assessment

Checking for Understanding

1. **Main Idea** Why is structural unemployment a more difficult problem for the economy and for individual workers than other types of unemployment?

2. **Key Terms** Define unemployed, unemployment rate, frictional unemployment, structural unemployment, cyclical unemployment, seasonal unemployment, technological unemployment, automation.

3. **Describe** how the government collects monthly data on employment.

4. **Differentiate** between the five major kinds of unemployment.

Applying Economic Concepts

5. **Employment** Examine the similarities and differences between structural and technological unemployment. Give an example of each. Why are these kinds of unemployment serious problems for an economy?

Critical Thinking

6. **Drawing Inferences** What factors make it difficult to determine the unemployment rate?

7. **Categorizing Information** Make a list of three reasons that could cause a person to become a discouraged worker.

> **Practice** and **assess** key social studies skills with the *Glencoe Skillbuilder Interactive Workbook, Level 2.*

CHAPTER 14: ECONOMIC INSTABILITY **387**

ECONOMICS AT A GLANCE

Answer: *medical field, legal field*

Reteach

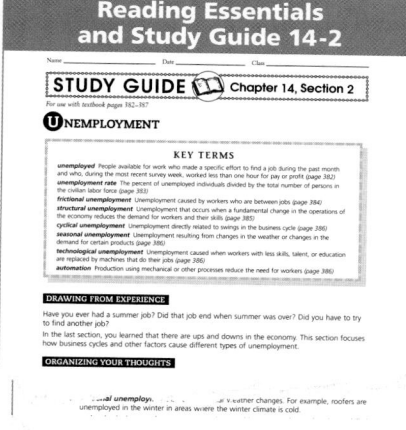

Reading Essentials and Study Guide 14-2

STUDY GUIDE — Chapter 14, Section 2

For use with textbook pages 382–387

UNEMPLOYMENT

KEY TERMS

Enrich

Have students write an essay detailing the social costs of long-term unemployment.

 CLOSE

Ask students to write a paragraph explaining the kind of unemployment that provides the greatest challenge for the economy and why.

Section 2 Assessment Answers

1. causes long-term unemployment; unemployed must learn new skills

2. All vocabulary terms are defined in the text.

3. The Census Bureau surveys and turns data over to the Bureau of Labor Statistics for analysis.

4. See pages 384–386.

5. Structural unemployment occurs when certain goods and services are no longer in demand. Technological unemployment results from a change in the means of production. Both forms of unemployment are long-term.

6. does not count part-time workers or those too discouraged to look for work

7. Students should provide valid reasons in their answers.

TEACH

Ask: Is the article saying that workers between 45 and 64 years of age generally make less than younger workers? *(No; the article points out that older workers are hit with pay declines while younger workers experience pay increases.)* Point out that a major reason young workers are given jobs and pay increases is that they command lower salaries than older workers. **Ask:** Why would a pay decrease pose a hardship for an older worker–even when the older worker earns more than a younger worker doing the same job? *(A possible answer is that the older worker has accrued more debt over a lifetime.)*

Refer to **Business Week Focus on the New Economy** in the TCR for additional unit-based articles.

BusinessWeek

DECEMBER 28, 1998

Newsclip

What do laid-off workers have to fear in today's labor market? For those severed after only a year or two on the job— especially younger workers—the issue may not be a burning one. But for many of those severed from more permanent jobs, it's compelling.

What Is the Impact of
Lay-Offs?

Looking at the 3.1 million workers who were laid off from full-time permanent jobs (held at least three years) from 1995 through 1997, the survey found that in many respects their fates were comparable to those found in [a] 1996 survey for workers laid off in 1993 and 1994. Specifically, in each case about 67% of workers were reemployed at full-time jobs, 14% to 16% were working part-time or at home, and 12% to 14% had dropped out of the labor force.

The main difference was that recent earnings declines were far less pronounced. Whereas 55% of reemployed full-timers in the earlier survey experienced pay drops, and 34% of them suffered cuts of more than 20%, the figures in the 1998 survey were 38% and 21%, respectively. And the median period between jobs fell from 8.3 to 5 weeks.

In addition, the reemployed full-time contingent's median weekly earnings were up about 2% in the 1998 survey, compared with a 14% decline in the prior survey.

However, all of the recent increases [went to] to younger workers. Those from ages 45 to 64 were still hit with pay declines averaging 10%.

In short, the severe earnings drops suffered by earlier groups of displaced full-time workers have diminished significantly as the expansion has continued. But with only two-thirds of those laid off in recent years back at full-time jobs, and nearly 40% of full-timers taking pay cuts, it's clear that many workers–particularly those over 45– continue to suffer considerable economic pain.

–Reprinted from December 28, 1998 issue of *Business Week*, by special permission, copyright © 1998 by The McGraw-Hill Companies, Inc.

Examining the Newsclip

1. **Analyzing Information** What percentage of workers who were laid off during the period from 1995 through 1997 found new, full-time jobs?

2. **Analyzing Information** What percentage either left the labor force or remained unemployed?

3. **Drawing Conclusions** What age group faced the most difficulty in obtaining employment? Why do you think this is so?

388 UNIT 4 MACROECONOMICS: POLICIES

Answers to Examining the Newsclip

1. 67 percent
2. 12–14 percent

3. older workers; younger workers can be hired for lower wages

Inflation

Study Guide

Main Idea
"Inflation" is a rise in the general level of prices.

Reading Strategy
Graphic Organizer As you read the section, complete a graphic organizer similar to the one below by identifying the steps in a wage-price spiral.

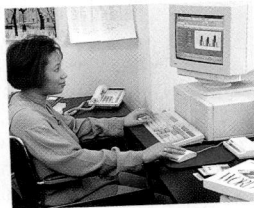

Step 1 → Step 2 → Higher prices

Key Terms
price level, deflation, creeping inflation, galloping inflation, hyperinflation

Objectives
After studying this section, you will be able to:
1. **Explain** how inflation is measured.
2. **Discuss** five causes of inflation.
3. **Analyze** the destabilizing consequences of inflation.

Applying Economic Concepts
Inflation Have you ever wondered if you should buy something before the price of the item goes up? Read to find out how inflation changes our spending habits.

1 FOCUS

Section Overview
This section considers the characteristics, causes, and destabilizing effects of inflation.

BELLRINGER
Motivational Activity

Project **transparency** and have students answer questions.

Available as blackline master.

Daily Focus Transparency 54

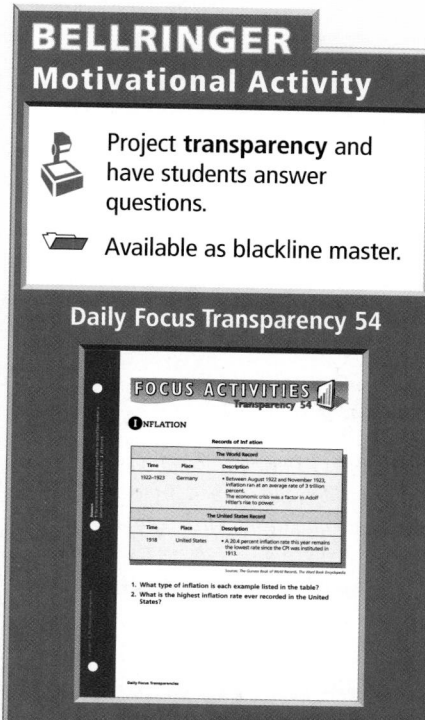

Cover Story

Shrinking Labor Pool Raises Fear of Wage Pressures and Higher Prices

Is the number of available but jobless workers in the United States shrinking to the point that employers may be forced to grant inflationary wage increases to attract new employees or keep the ones they have?

Are fewer workers available?

"Should labor markets continue to tighten, significant increases in wages, in excess of productivity growth, will inevitably emerge, absent the unlikely repeal of the law of supply and demand," [Federal Reserve Chairman Alan] Greenspan told Congress.

—*The Washington Post*, June 25, 1999

Inflation is a special kind of economic instability, one that deals with changes in the level of prices rather than the level of employment and output. Even so, as we saw in the cover story, changes in prices, employment, and output are all linked.

Inflation in the United States

To better understand inflation, we must first examine how it is measured. Then we can examine the causes of inflation and its consequences. In order to find inflation, we start with the **price level,** the relative magnitude of prices at one point in time.

Measuring Inflation

To measure the price level, economists select a market basket of goods. They then construct a price index such as the consumer price index (CPI), the producer price index, or the implicit GDP price deflator.

Inflation is reported in terms of annual rates of change of the price level. For example, if the CPI at the beginning of one year is 111, and if it reaches 115 by the beginning of the next, inflation would be computed as follows (with

CHAPTER 14: ECONOMIC INSTABILITY **389**

Study Guide

Reading Strategy
Have students create the graphic organizer.
Answers to Graphic: *Step 1: Higher prices force workers to ask for higher wages. Step 2: Higher wages make producers recover that cost through higher prices.*

Preteaching Vocabulary
Have volunteers use each Key Term correctly in a sentence.

RESOURCE MANAGER

Reproducible Masters
- Reproducible Lesson Plan 14-3
- Daily Lecture Notes 14-3
- Guided Reading Activity 14-3
- Reading Essentials and Study Guide 14-3
- Section Quiz 14-3

Transparencies
- Daily Focus Transparency 54

Multimedia
- Interactive Tutor Self-Assessment Software
- ExamView® Pro Testmaker
- Presentation Plus!

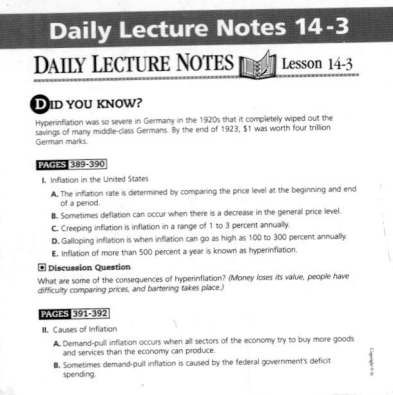

② TEACH

Daily Lecture Notes 14-3

DAILY LECTURE NOTES 📖 Lesson 14-3

❶ DID YOU KNOW?
Hyperinflation was so severe in Germany in the 1920s that it completely wiped out the savings of many middle-class Germans. By the end of 1923, $1 was worth four trillion German marks.

PAGES 389-390
I. Inflation in the United States
  A. The inflation rate is determined by comparing the price level at the beginning and end of a period.
  B. Sometimes deflation can occur when there is a decrease in the general price level.
  C. Creeping inflation is inflation in a range of 1 to 3 percent annually.
  D. Galloping inflation is when inflation can go as high as 100 to 300 percent annually.
  E. Inflation of more than 500 percent a year is known as hyperinflation.

⊟ Discussion Question
What are some of the consequences of hyperinflation? (Money loses its value, people have difficulty comparing prices, and bartering takes place.)

PAGES 391-392
II. Causes of Inflation
  A. Demand-pull inflation occurs when all sectors of the economy try to buy more goods and services than the economy can produce.
  B. Sometimes demand-pull inflation is caused by the federal government's deficit spending.

STANDARD & POOR'S

Answer: *During this period the rate started high but dipped a year later and remained level (between 2 and 4 percent).*

 Math Practice

Calculating Inflation Rates
If the price level stood at 154 last year and now is at 165, what is the rate of inflation? ([165 − 154] ÷ 154 × 100 = 7.14 percent)

Guided Reading Activity 14-3

GUIDED READING Activity 14-3

For use with textbook pages 389–392

❶ INFLATION

OUTLINING

Directions: Locate the heading in your textbook. Then use the information under the heading to help you write each answer. Use another sheet of paper if necessary.

I. Inflation in the United States
  A. Introduction/Measuring Inflation
    1. What is the price level?
    2. How is price level used in determining the rate of inflation?
  B. Degrees of Inflation
    1. What is the difference between creeping inflation and galloping inflation?
    2. What is hyperinflation?
II. Causes of Inflation
  A. In what way does excessive demand cause inflation?
  B. What happens when the federal budget has a surplus?
  C. How do labor costs affect inflation?
  D. What is the wage-price spiral?
  E. What is excessive monetary growth?
III. Consequences of Inflation

STANDARD & POOR'S

Figure 14.5

The Rate of Inflation

Source: Bureau of Economic Analysis, United States Department of Commerce

☐ Recession years

Using Graphs Inflation tends to increase at the end of expansions, and tends to decrease during periods of recession. How would you characterize the inflation rate during the period from 1990 to 2002?

ECONOMICS *Online*
Visit epp.glencoe.com and click on *Textbook Updates—Chapter 14* for an update of the data.

everything multiplied by 100 to convert the decimal to a percent):

$$\text{inflation rate} = \frac{\text{change in price level}}{\text{beginning price level}} \times 100$$

or,

$$\text{inflation rate} = \frac{(115 - 111)}{111} \times 100 = 3.6\%$$

Figure 14.5 shows the rate of inflation from 1965 to the present. As you can see, prices tend to rise faster during expansions and then slow down during recessions.

On rare occasions, unusual circumstances may cause **deflation,** or a decrease in the general price level. Only two significant deflations have taken place in the 1900s. One was during the post–World War I recession of the early 1920s. The other was during the Great Depression of the 1930s.

390 UNIT 4 MACROECONOMICS: POLICIES

Degrees of Inflation

Several terms describe the severity of inflation. One is **creeping inflation**–inflation in the range of 1 to 3 percent per year. Another is **galloping inflation,** a more intense form of inflation that can go as high as 100 to 300 percent. Many Latin American countries and many countries in the former communist bloc have experienced rates in this range in recent years. When inflation gets totally out of control, **hyperinflation**–inflation in the range of 500 percent a year and above–occurs. Hyperinflation, however, does not happen very often and generally is the last stage before a total monetary collapse.

The record for hyperinflation was set in Hungary during World War II, when huge amounts of currency were printed to pay the government's bills. By the end of the war, it was claimed that 828 octillion (828,000,000,000,000,000,000,000,000,000) pengös equaled 1 prewar pengö.

MEETING SPECIAL NEEDS ACTIVITY

English Language Learners Students learning English may have trouble decoding words that are unfamiliar or are used in unfamiliar ways. Demonstrate how they can use context clues or illustrations to find the meaning of such terms. Have students scan the paragraphs under the heading "Degrees of Inflation" for words that are unfamiliar to them. Have them write the words and then guess the meanings based on context or the graph on page 390. Some terms that may need definitions or review are *inflation, annual rate, communist bloc, currency,* and *pengö.* **ELL**

▭ Refer to *Inclusion for the Social Studies Classroom Strategies and Activities* in the TCR.

Causes of Inflation

Several explanations have been offered for the causes of inflation. Nearly every period of inflation is due to one of the following causes.

According to demand-pull theory, all sectors in the economy try to buy more goods and services than the economy can produce. As consumers, businesses, and governments converge on stores, shortages occur and prices go up. Thus prices are "pulled up" by excessive demand.

Another explanation involves the federal government's deficit. Basically, this explanation is a variant of the demand-pull theory. While demand-pull blames excess demand on all sectors of the economy, this explanation blames inflation only on the federal government's deficit spending.

A third explanation claims that rising input costs—especially labor—drive up the cost of products for manufacturers and cause inflation. This situation might take place, for example, when a strong national union wins a large wage contract, forcing producers to raise prices to recover the labor costs. Or, as noted in the cover story, labor costs could go up when labor markets are tight and the unemployment rate is exceptionally low.

An unexpected increase in the cost of nonlabor inputs also could cause the price level to rise. Such a price rise occurred during the 1970s when oil prices went from $5 to $35 a barrel.

Still another explanation says that no single group is to blame for inflation. According to this view, a self-perpetuating spiral of wages and prices begins that is difficult to stop.

Higher prices force workers to ask for higher wages. If they get the higher wages, producers try to recover that cost with higher prices. As each side tries to increase its relative position with a larger price hike than before, the rate of inflation keeps rising.

The final and most popular explanation for inflation is excessive monetary growth. This occurs when the money supply grows faster than real GDP. According to this view, any extra money that is created by the Federal Reserve System will increase some group's purchasing power. When this money is spent, it causes a demand-pull effect that drives up prices.

Advocates of this explanation point out that inflation cannot be maintained without a growing money supply to fuel it. For example, if the price of gas goes up sharply, and if the amount of money people have does not change, then they will simply have to buy less of something else. So, while the price of gas may rise, the prices of other things will fall, leaving the price level unchanged.

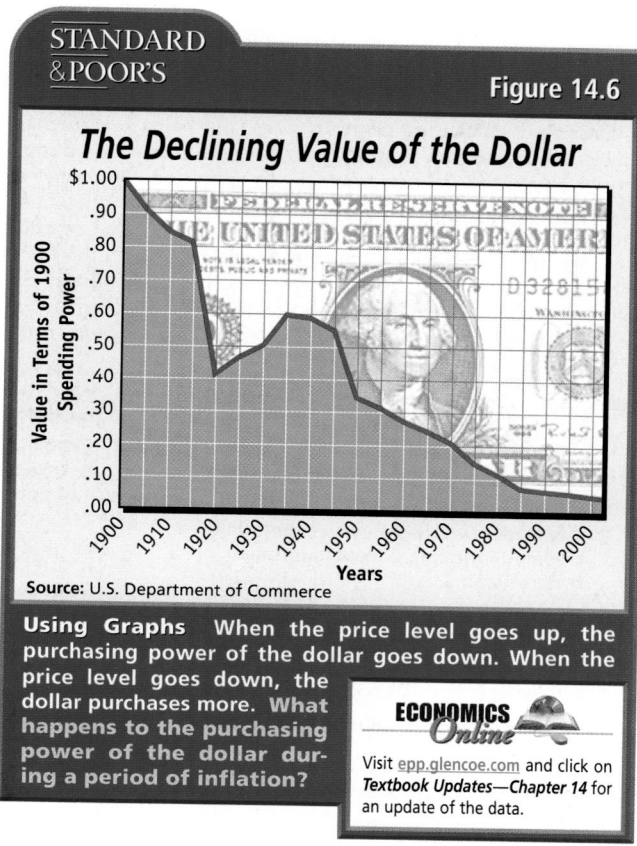

STANDARD & POOR'S

Figure 14.6

The Declining Value of the Dollar

Value in Terms of 1900 Spending Power (y-axis: $1.00, .90, .80, .70, .60, .50, .40, .30, .20, .10, .00)

Years (x-axis: 1900, 1910, 1920, 1930, 1940, 1950, 1960, 1970, 1980, 1990, 2000)

Source: U.S. Department of Commerce

Using Graphs When the price level goes up, the purchasing power of the dollar goes down. When the price level goes down, the dollar purchases more. What happens to the purchasing power of the dollar during a period of inflation?

ECONOMICS *Online*

Visit epp.glencoe.com and click on **Textbook Updates—Chapter 14** for an update of the data.

CHAPTER 14: ECONOMIC INSTABILITY **391**

STANDARD & POOR'S

Answer: *The dollar loses value during a period of inflation.*

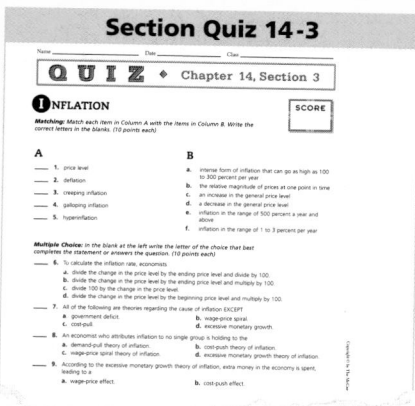

③ ASSESS

Assign Section 3 Assessment as homework or as an in-class activity.

💾 Have students use **Interactive Tutor Self-Assessment Software.**

Section Quiz 14-3

QUIZ ◆ Chapter 14, Section 3

❶ INFLATION

Matching: Match each item in Column A with the items in Column B. Write the correct letters in the blanks. (10 points each)

A
___ 1. price level
___ 2. deflation
___ 3. creeping inflation
___ 4. galloping inflation
___ 5. hyperinflation

B
a. intense form of inflation that can go as high as 100 to 300 percent per year
b. the relative magnitude of prices at one point in time
c. an increase in the general price level
d. a decrease in the general price level
e. inflation in the range of 500 percent a year and above
f. inflation in the range of 1 to 3 percent per year

Multiple Choice: In the blank at the left write the letter of the choice that best completes the statement or answers the question. (10 points each)

___ 6. To calculate the inflation rate, economists
   a. divide the change in the price level by the ending price level and divide by 100.
   b. divide the change in the price level by the ending price level and multiply by 100.
   c. divide 100 by the change in the price level.
   d. divide the change in the price level by the beginning price level and multiply by 100.
___ 7. All of the following are theories regarding the cause of inflation EXCEPT
   a. government deficit.   b. wage-price spiral.
   c. cost-pull.   d. excessive monetary growth.
___ 8. An economist who attributes inflation to no single group is holding to the
   a. demand-pull theory of inflation.   b. cost-push theory of inflation.
   c. wage-price spiral theory of inflation. d. excessive monetary growth theory of inflation.
___ 9. According to the excessive monetary growth theory of inflation, extra money in the economy is spent, leading to a
   a. wage-price effect.   b. cost-push effect.

FREE ENTERPRISE ACTIVITY

Have students evaluate how a sharp increase in inflation might affect the following people:
1. A person who has just withdrawn a considerable amount from a savings account. *(Money will have less value, or buying power, than when it was initially saved.)*
2. A doctor on staff at a large hospital. *(Work will be largely unaffected, because demand for medical services is relatively inelastic.)*
3. A retired autoworker on a fixed pension. *(Fixed incomes are susceptible to a loss of purchasing power.)*
4. A borrower about to repay a loan. *(The money paid back will have less value than that borrowed.)*

Reteach

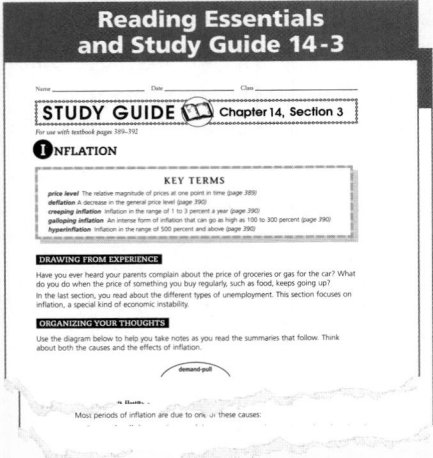

Enrich

Have students research a country that has experienced hyperinflation.

CLOSE

Ask students to debate the following: "In a free enterprise economy, economic growth automatically means rising prices."

Consequences of Inflation

 Inflation involves more than rapidly rising prices. When inflation is present, it can have a disruptive effect on an economy for several reasons.

The most obvious effect of inflation is that the dollar buys less. Because the purchasing power of the dollar falls as prices rise, a dollar loses value over time. **Figure 14.6** shows how the dollar lost its value as inflation eroded its purchasing power.

Decreased purchasing power is especially hard on retired people with fixed incomes because their money buys a little less each month. Those not on fixed incomes are better able to cope. They can increase their fees to secure additional income.

A second destabilizing effect is that inflation can cause people to change their spending habits, which disrupts the economy. For example, when prices went up in the early 1980s, interest rates—the price of borrowed money—also went up. This caused spending on durable goods, especially housing and automobiles, to fall dramatically.

To illustrate, suppose that a young couple wanted to borrow $60,000 over 20 years to buy a house. At an 8 percent interest rate, their monthly mortgage payment would be $501.86. At 14 percent, the payment would be $746.11. In 1981 some mortgage rates reached 18 percent, which meant a monthly payment of about $926 for the same loan! As a result, the housing industry almost collapsed.

A third destabilizing effect of inflation is that it tempts some people to speculate heavily in an attempt to take advantage of a higher price level. People who ordinarily put their money in reasonably safe investments begin buying luxury condominiums, diamonds and gemstones, and other exotic items that might be expected to increase in price.

Finally, inflation alters the distribution of income. During long inflationary periods, lenders are generally hurt more than borrowers. Loans made earlier are repaid later in inflated dollars.

Suppose, for example, that a person borrows money to buy bread that costs fifty cents a loaf. If the amount borrowed was $100, the person could buy 200 loaves of bread. If inflation set in, and if the price doubled by the time the loan was paid back, the lender would only be able to buy 100 loaves of bread. Inflation in the long run, then, favors debtors over creditors.

Section 3 Assessment

Checking for Understanding

1. **Main Idea** What is the difference between the price level and the rate of inflation?

2. **Key Terms** Define price level, deflation, creeping inflation, galloping inflation, hyperinflation.

3. **Describe** how the CPI is used to compute the inflation rate.

4. **List** five explanations for the causes of inflation.

5. **Identify** four ways inflation destabilizes the economy.

Applying Economic Concepts

6. **Inflation** What does an inflation rate of 4 percent mean?

Critical Thinking

7. **Categorizing Information** What kind of inflation might be described as "too many dollars chasing too few goods"?

8. **Understanding Cause and Effect** In 1974 the price of crude oil increased greatly. What type of inflation did this cause?

Practice and assess key social studies skills with the *Glencoe Skillbuilder Interactive Workbook, Level 2.*

Section 3 Assessment Answers

1. The price level is the relative magnitude of prices at one point in time and is the starting point for measuring the rate of inflation. The rate of inflation itself is the rate of change in the level of prices.

2. All vocabulary terms are defined in the text.

3. Change in the price level is divided by the beginning price level, then multiplied by 100.

4. demand-pull, government deficit, cost-push, wage-spiral, excessive monetary growth

5. The dollar buys less, spending habits change, speculation increases, and the distribution of income is altered.

6. The economy is experiencing more than creeping inflation.

7. Answers may include demand-pull or excessive monetary growth.

8. cost-push

TECHNOLOGY Skill

Using the Internet

To learn more about almost any topic imaginable, use the Internet—a global network of computers. Many features, such as E-mail, interactive educational classes, and shopping services are offered on the Net. To get on the Internet, you need three things: (a) a personal computer, (b) a modem (a device that connects your computer to a telephone line), and (c) an account with an Internet Service Provider (ISP). An ISP, such as America Online, is a company that enables you to log on to the Internet, usually for a fee.

Learning the Skill

After you are connected, the easiest way to access Internet sites is to use a "Web browser," a program that lets you view and explore information on the World Wide Web. The Web consists of many documents called "Web sites," each of which has its own address, or Uniform Resource Locator (URL). Many URLs start with the keystrokes *http://*

If you don't know the exact URL of a site, commercial "search engines" such as Yahoo! or AltaVista, can help you find information. Type a subject or name into the "search" box, then press Enter. The search engine lists available sites that may have the information you are looking for.

Practicing the Skill

Follow these steps to learn more about the inflation rate.

1. Log on to the Internet and choose a search engine to use.

2. Search by selecting one of the listed categories or by typing in the subject you want to find, such as "inflation" or "the inflation rate."

3. Continue your search by scrolling down the list that appears on your screen. When you select an entry, click on it to access the information. Sometimes the information you first access will not be exactly what you need. If so, continue searching until you find the information that you want.

4. If you get "lost" on the Internet, click on the back-arrow key at the top of the screen until you find a site that looks familiar.

5. Continue selecting sites until you have enough information to write a short report on inflation trends over the past three months.

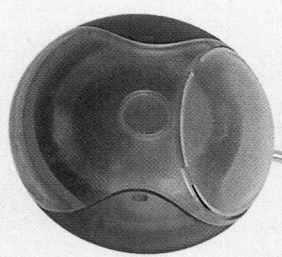

A search engine can help you quickly locate information on the World Wide Web.

Application Activity

Follow the above procedures to locate information about the population of your state. Use the information you gather to create a chart or graph depicting changes in population from 1960 to the present.

Technology Skill

Teaching Skills

Tell students that the Internet contains much inaccurate information. Students should research carefully and rely on Web sites by recognized authorities. These include government organizations, educational institutions, news media, reputable nonprofit organizations, and established business firms. Listed below are several examples of such sites. Ask students to visit one of these Web sites, find an interesting item about the economy, and report it to the class.

U.S. Bureau of Labor Statistics: www.bls.gov

The Ohio State University, Financial Data Finder: www.cob.ohio-state.edu/dept/fin/osudata.htm

Cable News Network-Financial (CNNfn): www.cnnfn.com

Environmental Defense Fund: www.edf.org

Additional Practice

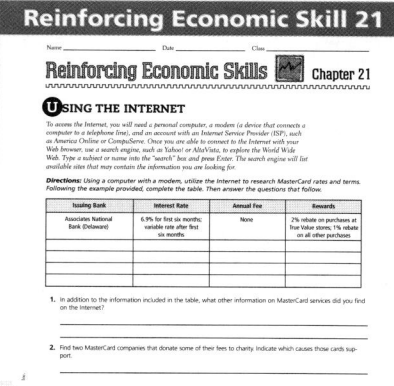

Answers to Practicing the Skill

Reports should demonstrate an understanding of both Chapter 14 content and Internet research procedures.

① FOCUS

Section Overview
This section discusses aspects of income.

BELLRINGER
Motivational Activity

Project **transparency** and have students answer questions.

Available as blackline master.

Daily Focus Transparency 71

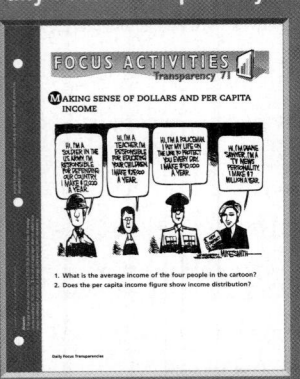

Study Guide

Reading Strategy
Have students create the graphic organizer.
Answers to Graphic: *structural change in the economy, growing gap between well-educated and poorly-educated workers, declining unionism, changing structure of families*

Preteaching Vocabulary
Use the Vocabulary Puzzle-Maker to create crossword and word-search puzzles.

SECTION 4

Poverty and the Distribution of Income

Study Guide

Main Idea
Reasons for income inequality include ability differences, education and training, and discrimination.

Reading Strategy
Graphic Organizer As you read the section, complete a graphic organizer similar to the one below by listing three explanations for a growing income gap.

Key Terms
Lorenz curve, poverty guidelines, welfare, food stamps, Earned Income Tax Credits (EITC), enterprise zone, workfare, negative income tax

Objectives
After studying this section, you will be able to:
1. **Explain** how economists measure the distribution of income.
2. **Discuss** the reasons for the inequality of income.
3. **Discuss** antipoverty programs.

Applying Economic Concepts
Distribution of Income Do you compare what you make to the earnings of others? Read to find out more about how income is distributed in the United States.

Cover Story

From Welfare to Work

When United Parcel Service of America started hiring welfare recipients to sort packages 25 years ago, the company had no idea of what it was getting itself into.

What UPS got was a pool of adept employees in it for the long haul.

Work-hire program a plus for UPS

In fact, of the 10,000 welfare recipients the company has hired since January 1996, the shipping giant estimates about 70 percent stay.

"Our experience has proven that welfare-to-work hires are excellent hires," said . . . a spokeswoman for UPS.

—*CNNfn*, August 5, 1998

394

I n the United States, as in other parts of the world, people do not all have the same income. A large number of people live in poverty despite the efforts of programs such as the one featured in the cover story.

The Distribution of Income

To evaluate the distribution of income, the incomes of all families are ranked from highest to lowest. The ranking is then divided into quintiles, or fifths, for examination. The table in **Panel A** of **Figure 14.7** shows family income quintile data for two different years. Only money income is counted; other aid such as food stamps, medicaid, or subsidized housing is excluded. Using a recent year as our example, the percent of income earned by each quintile is added to the lower quintiles and plotted as a Lorenz curve. The **Lorenz curve**—a curve that shows how much the actual distribution of income varies from an equal distribution—appears in **Panel B.**

RESOURCE MANAGER

Reproducible Masters
- Reproducible Lesson Plan 14-4
- Daily Lecture Notes 14-4
- Guided Reading Activity 14-4
- Reading Essentials and Study Guide 14-4
- Section Quiz 14-4

Transparencies
- Daily Focus Transparency 71

Multimedia
- Vocabulary PuzzleMaker CD-ROM
- Interactive Tutor Self-Assessment Software
- ExamView® Pro Testmaker
- Presentation Plus!

To illustrate, the 4.3 percent of total income received by the lowest quintile is plotted in **Panel B** as point **a**. This amount is combined with the income the next quintile earns and then plotted as point **b**. This process continues until the cumulative values of all quintiles are plotted.

If all families received exactly the same income—so that 40 percent of the families would earn 40 percent of the total income and so on—the Lorenz curve would appear as a diagonal line running from one corner of the graph to the other. Because all families do not receive the same income, however, the Lorenz curve is not a diagonal. As you can see in the figure, the distribution of income recently has become more unequal than it was in 1980.

Reasons for Income Inequality

A number of reasons explain why the incomes of various groups may be different. They include education, wealth, discrimination, ability, and monopoly power.

Education

Some people have higher incomes than others because they have more education. Although exceptions exist, there is generally a strong relationship between median income and level of education. Education puts people in a better position to get the higher-paying jobs that require a higher level of skills.

Wealth

Income also varies because some people hold more wealth than others—and the distribution of wealth is even more unequal than the distribution of income. When wealth holders are ranked from highest to lowest, the top fifth has 75 percent of all the wealth in the country. The bottom two-fifths, which is 40 percent of the people in the country, have less than 2 percent of the total wealth.

This inequality has an impact on people's ability to earn income. Wealthy families can send their children to expensive colleges and universities. The wealthy can also afford to set their children up in businesses where they can earn a better income. Even if the wealthy choose not to work, they can make investments that will bring them income.

CHAPTER 14: ECONOMIC INSTABILITY **395**

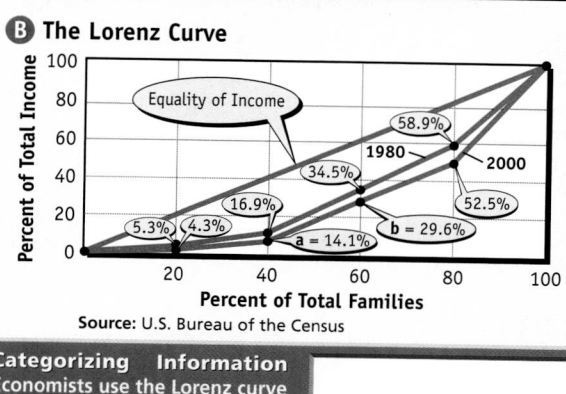

ECONOMICS AT A GLANCE   Figure 14.7

The Distributions of Income by Families

A Family Income Ranked by Quintiles

	1980	2000	
	Quintiles	Quintiles	Cumulative
Lowest Fifth	5.3%	4.3%	4.3%
Second Fifth	11.6%	9.8%	14.1%
Third Fifth	17.6%	15.5%	29.6%
Fourth Fifth	24.4%	22.9%	52.5%
Highest Fifth	41.1%	47.5%	100%
Top 5 Percent	14.6%	20.8%	

B The Lorenz Curve

Source: U.S. Bureau of the Census

Categorizing Information Economists use the Lorenz curve to contrast the distribution of income at different points in time. What percentage of income is received by the richest quintile in 1980? In 2000?

ECONOMICS Online
Visit epp.glencoe.com and click on *Textbook Updates—Chapter 14* for an update of the data.

②TEACH

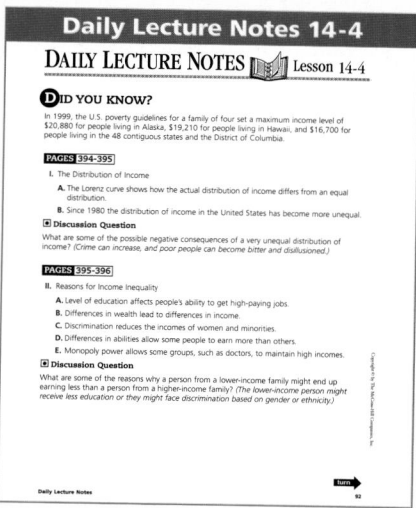

Daily Lecture Notes 14-4

DAILY LECTURE NOTES   Lesson 14-4

①DID YOU KNOW?
In 1999, the U.S. poverty guidelines for a family of four set a maximum income level of $20,880 for people living in Alaska, $19,210 for people living in Hawaii, and $16,700 for people living in the 48 contiguous states and the District of Columbia.

PAGES 394-395
I. The Distribution of Income
   A. The Lorenz curve shows how the actual distribution of income differs from an equal distribution.
   B. Since 1980 the distribution of income in the United States has become more unequal.

✦ Discussion Question
What are some of the possible negative consequences of a very unequal distribution of income? (Crime can increase, and poor people can become bitter and disillusioned.)

PAGES 395-396
II. Reasons for Income Inequality
   A. Level of education affects people's ability to get high-paying jobs.
   B. Differences in wealth lead to differences in income.
   C. Discrimination reduces the incomes of women and minorities.
   D. Differences in abilities allow some people to earn more than others.
   E. Monopoly power allows some groups, such as doctors, to maintain high incomes.

✦ Discussion Question
What are some of the reasons why a person from a lower-income family might end up earning less than a person from a higher-income family? (The lower-income person might receive less education or they might face discrimination based on gender or ethnicity.)

Daily Lecture Notes   turn ➤

ECONOMICS AT A GLANCE

Answer: *1980: 41.1%; 2000; 47.5%*

CYBERNOMICS

Interactive Economics
Northwestern Mutual Life Insurance has set up a Web site (themint.org) for high school students. The site has several interactive sections. Visitors to Learning and Earning, for example, learn about how finishing high school helps them to get ahead financially.

MEETING SPECIAL NEEDS ACTIVITY

Learning Style: Verbal/Linguistic To help build discussion skills, have students work in groups to create class presentations or hold panel discussions about the Lorenz curve—how it is constructed, how cumulative percentages are arrived at, and what a "wider" curve means. Each student should play an active role in the presentation or panel discussion. Be sure students limit the focus of the discussion and take into account the class time allowed.

📁 Refer to *Inclusion for the Social Studies Classroom Strategies and Activities* in the TCR.

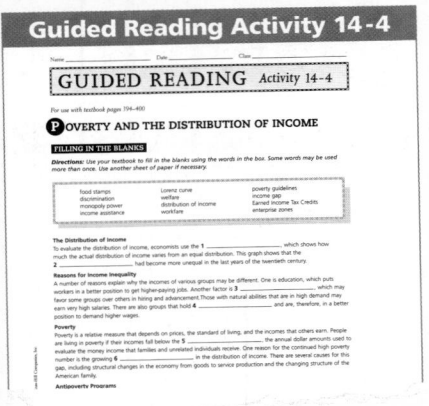
L2 Conducting an Interview

Have students investigate which local government agencies provide assistance for low-income families in the community. Then have students interview an official at one of these agencies to determine the answers to the following: What assistance programs does the agency oversee? Who is eligible for benefits? How much is given in benefits? Is some form of work required of benefit recipients who are capable of working? Are there any restrictions on those receiving benefits? In your opinion, what are the strengths and weaknesses of your assistance programs? Have students report their findings to the rest of the class.

Some European countries, worried by rising unemployment rates, have called for the institution of a four-day workweek. Although it would mean a cut in workers' wages, many unions support the idea. In Italy, unions are campaigning with the slogan: "Work less, and everyone works."

Discrimination

Discrimination is another factor influencing income. Women may not be promoted to executive positions in some companies because male executives simply are not accustomed to women in roles of power. Some unions may deny immigrants or ethnic minorities membership on the grounds that they "don't belong" in the professions.

Although discrimination is illegal, it still takes place. When it does occur, discrimination causes women and minority groups to be crowded into other labor markets where oversupply drives down wages.

Ability

Some people earn more income because they have certain natural abilities, such as professional athletes who sometimes earn millions of dollars every year. Such athletes as Shaquille O'Neal and Alex Rodriguez earn high incomes because they have unique abilities or talents. The same is true of popular performers such as Oprah Winfrey, Jim Carrey, and Harrison Ford.

Monopoly Power

Another factor is the degree of monopoly power that some groups hold. Recall from Chapter 8 that unions have been able to obtain higher wages for their members. Some white-collar workers—clerical, business, or professional workers who generally are salaried—also hold a degree of monopoly power. The American Medical Association, for example, has been successful in limiting the number of people in its profession by limiting enrollments in medical schools. More recently, the AMA voted to unionize in order to be in a better position to deal with the health maintenance organizations (HMOs) that employ them.

Poverty

Poverty is a relative measure that depends on prices, the standard of living, and the incomes that others earn. Poverty is a major problem in America—and one that is extremely difficult to resolve. Families and individuals are defined as living in poverty if their incomes fall below certain levels. **Poverty guidelines** are annual dollar amounts used to evaluate the money income that families and unrelated individuals receive. In 2001, poverty was defined as having an income of less than $17,650 for a family of four.

People in Poverty

Poverty in the United States is more extensive than most people realize. According to recent statistics, nearly 33 million Americans live in poverty—or approximately 13 percent of the total population.

As **Figure 14.8** shows, even the record economic expansions of the 1980s and 1990s failed to make a significant dent in the percent of Americans living in poverty. In fact, the proportion of the population living in poverty was about the same in the late 1960s and 1970s as it is today.

Of those in poverty, slightly more than two-thirds are white and approximately one-quarter are African American. Finally, children of all races make up approximately 38 percent of the people in poverty even though they account for only 26 percent of the total population.

The Growing Income Gap

One reason for the continued high poverty numbers is the growing gap in the distribution of income. According to the Census Bureau, the growing spread that has taken place since 1980 has several causes.

The first involves a structural change in the economy as industry changes from goods production to service production. Because wages are typically lower in the service industries such as fast-food chains, movie theaters, and entertainment parks, weekly paychecks tend to be lower.

The second reason for the spread in income distribution is the growing gap between well-educated and poorly educated workers. During the 1990s, wages for the highly skilled soared, while wages for the less skilled remained about the same.

A third reason—declining unionism (especially among low-skilled workers)—is adding to the growing differential. The decline of unions means that many low-skilled workers have to work elsewhere for less pay.

FREE ENTERPRISE ACTIVITY

Tell students that only about one-third of the poor people in the nation benefit from the federal government's system of welfare. Even so, less than 50 percent of the people who are poor today will still be poor a year from now, and less than 10 percent will remain poor for five years or more. However, the proportion of the population that is poor stays about the same because as people rise out of poverty, others sink into it. Ask students to calculate about how many of the 34.5 million people who were poor in 1999 will still be poor in 2005. *(less than 3,450,000)*

The fourth reason for the income gap concerns the changing structure of the American family. The shift from two-parent families to single-parent families and other nonfamily household living arrangements tends to lower average family income. All of these factors contribute to the trend of the rich getting richer and the poor getting poorer.

Antipoverty Programs

Over the years, the federal government has instituted a number of programs to help the needy. Most come under the general heading of **welfare**—economic and social programs that provide regular assistance from the government or private agencies because of need.

Income Assistance

Programs that provide direct cash assistance to those in need fall into the category of income assistance. One such program is the Temporary Aid to Needy Families (TANF), which replaced the Aid to Families with Dependent Children (AFDC) in 1996. Although provisions and benefits vary from state to state, many families are able to receive cash payments because of the death, continuous absence, or permanent disability of a parent.

Another income assistance program is the Supplemental Security Income (SSI), which makes cash payments to blind or disabled persons age 65 and older. Originally, the states administered the program because benefits varied so much from state to state. The federal government took it over in 1979 to assure more uniform coverage.

General Assistance

Programs that assist poor people but do not provide direct cash assistance fall into the category of general assistance. One example is the food stamp program that serves millions of Americans. **Food stamps** are government-issued coupons that can be redeemed for food. They may be given or sold to eligible low-income persons. If, for example, a person pays 40 cents for a

$1 food stamp, that person is getting a dollar's worth of food for a fraction of its cost. The program, which began in 1961 and became law in 1964, is different from other programs because eligibility is based solely on income.

Another general assistance program is medicaid—a joint federal-state medical insurance program for low-income people. Under the program, the federal government pays a majority of health-care

---

Poverty in the United States: Total Number and Rate

Source: U.S. Bureau of the Census

Using Graphs The dividing line between those officially considered poor and those not officially considered poor is the poverty line. Was the percentage of the population below the poverty line greater in the 1990s than in the 1980s?

ECONOMICS *Online*

Visit epp.glencoe.com and click on **Textbook Updates—Chapter 14** for an update of the data.

ECONOMICS AT A GLANCE

Answer: *greater in the 1990s*

L2 Applying ideas

Organize students into groups of four. Explain that each group represents a family of four living on the 1997 poverty threshold—an annual income of $16,050, or roughly $310 per week. Have each group develop a weekly family budget, making certain that their budget balances. In a follow-up class discussion, have the groups share and evaluate their budgets and discuss the difficulties of living at the poverty threshold.

L3 Writing a News Article

Write the following on the board: *education, wealth, discrimination, ability, monopoly power.* Tell students that these factors are the major topics for a newspaper article on income inequality. Call on volunteers to suggest how the listed factors might help to explain income inequality. Note responses under the appropriate factor. Then ask students to use information on the board to write the news article. Select students to read their articles to the class.

CRITICAL THINKING

Drawing Conclusions Have students reread the paragraphs under "People in Poverty" and "The Growing Income Gap." Then ask them to identify the reason for poverty that most likely explains why 40 percent of poor people are children. *(Answers may vary. A possible answer is that the changing structure of the American family leaves many children with the financial support of only one parent rather than two.)*

Before the establishment of many antipoverty programs in the 1960s, more than 20 percent of all Americans lived in poverty.

L3 Writing a Report

Organize students into six groups and assign each group one of the types of antipoverty programs discussed in the section. Have groups prepare a report that outlines the history and development of their assigned program and evaluates its effectiveness in combating poverty. Direct groups to choose representatives to present their reports to the class. Then discuss if government rules and regulations are the best way to combat poverty.

L3 Generating Solutions

Have students write down at least three ideas for reducing poverty. Call on students to share their lists with the class and note on the board the most frequently mentioned solutions. Lead a class discussion on the economic and social costs and benefits of the solutions. Finally, have students decide which idea they think is the best and write letters to the editor of the local newspaper proposing this solution to the problem of poverty.

costs, and the state governments pay the rest of the cost. Medicaid serves millions of Americans, including children, the visually impaired, and the disabled.

Social Service Programs

Over the years, the individual states have developed a variety of social service programs to help the needy. These include such areas as child abuse prevention, foster care, family planning, job training, child welfare, and day care.

Although the states control the kinds of services the programs provide, the federal government matches part of the cost. To be eligible for matching funds, a state must file an annual service plan. If the plan is approved, the state is free to select social issues it wishes to address, set the eligibility requirements for the programs, and decide how the programs are to be carried out.

Careers

Urban Planners

Most urban and regional planners work for community, county, and city governments.

The Work

Planners develop comprehensive plans for the development and rebuilding of communities. Planners recommend strategies on how to effectively utilize land and resources to meet the needs of the community. They also take part in decisions about transportation systems, resource development, and protection of the environment. Planners often specialize in a single area such as transportation, demography, housing, or urban design.

Qualifications

Most jobs in government agencies require a master's degree in urban or regional planning or urban design.

398 UNIT 4 MACROECONOMICS: POLICIES

Tax Credits

Many working low-income Americans qualify for special tax credits. The most popular is the **Earned Income Tax Credit (EITC)** which provides federal tax credits and sometimes cash to low-income workers. The credit was created in 1975 to partially offset the payroll tax burden on working families. The credit is applied first to federal income taxes, but low-income workers can take the remainder of the credit in cash if the credit is larger than the taxes owed. The credit has proved to be popular, with approximately 20 million working families receiving nearly $30 billion annually.

Enterprise Zones

Special **enterprise zones** are areas where companies can locate free of some local, state, and federal tax laws and other operating restrictions. Many enterprise zones are established in run-down or depressed areas. This benefits area residents because they can find work without worrying about transportation, thereby helping depressed areas to grow again.

Nearly everyone agrees that a healthy and growing economy helps alleviate poverty. The enterprise zone concept is an attempt to focus some of that growth directly in the areas that need it most, making more employment opportunities available.

Workfare Programs

Because of rising welfare costs, many state and local governments require those individuals who receive welfare to provide labor in exchange for benefits. **Workfare** is a program that requires welfare recipients to exchange some of their labor for benefits. People on workfare often assist law enforcement officials or sanitation and highway crews, or perform other types of community service work.

Most states that have workfare programs require almost everyone except for the disabled, the elderly, and those with very young children to work. If the workfare assignments are well designed, then recipients have a valuable opportunity to learn new skills that will eventually help them get other jobs.

EXTENDING THE CONTENT

Distribution of Poverty Poverty is not evenly distributed across the country. In 1996, for example, Washington D.C., Mississippi, Louisiana, and New Mexico had the highest rates of poverty. In contrast, the lowest poverty rates were found in New Hampshire, Utah, Indiana, and Alaska. Refer students to Figure 14.9 on page 399 and point out that, in general, there is an inverse relationship between poverty rates and income. In other words, states with high income levels tend to have lower poverty rates.

ECONOMICS
AT A GLANCE

Figure 14.9

Per Capita Personal Income by State

A.

States listed top to bottom: CT, MA, DC, NJ, NY, MD, NH, CO, CA, IL, MN, WA, DE, VA, NV, AK, RI, US, MI, PA, OH, OR, WI, HI, FL, GA, TX, NE, KS, MO, WY, NC, IN, VT, IA, TN, SD, ME, AZ, ND, SC, KY, ID, UT, OK, AL, LA, MT, AR, NM, WV, MS

Per Capita Personal Income (in $1,000s)

x-axis: 0 5 10 15 20 25 30 35 40
U.S. Average Annual Per Capita Personal Income

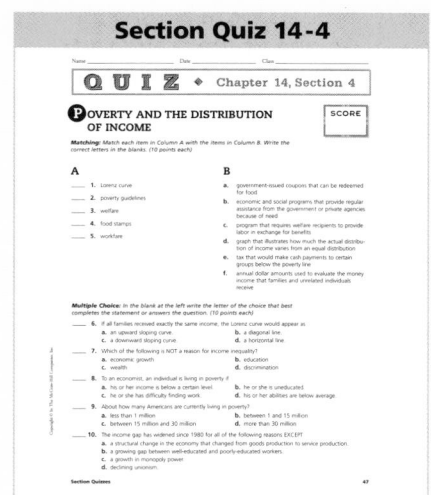

B. Per Capita Personal Income, 2000

$0–$23,999	$28,000–$29,999
$24,000–$25,999	$30,000–$32,999
$26,000–$27,999	$33,000 and up

C. Average Annual Percentage Growth of Real Per Capita Personal Income, 1990–2000

Negative growth	1.25%–1.49%
0%–0.99%	1.50%–1.74%
1.0%–1.24%	1.75%–1.99%
	2.0%+%

Source: *Survey of Current Business*, various issues

Using Graphs and Maps Average per capita personal income varies considerably from state to state, ranging from a low of $20,993 to a high of $40,640. The average rate of growth, after adjusting for inflation, amounted to 1.42 percent. One state—Hawaii—had a negative annual rate of growth from 1990 to 2000. In what range was the per capita personal income in your state?

CHAPTER 14: ECONOMIC INSTABILITY **399**

ECONOMICS
AT A GLANCE

Answer: *Check to make sure students have answered correctly for their state.*

3 ASSESS

Assign Section 4 Assessment as homework or as an in-class activity.

💾 Have students use **Interactive Tutor Self-Assessment Software** to review Section 4.

Section Quiz 14-4

QUIZ ♦ Chapter 14, Section 4

POVERTY AND THE DISTRIBUTION OF INCOME

SCORE

Matching: Match each item in Column A with the items in Column B. Write the correct letters in the blanks. (10 points each)

A
1. Lorenz curve
2. poverty guidelines
3. welfare
4. food stamps
5. workfare

B
a. government-issued coupons that can be redeemed for food
b. economic and social programs that provide regular assistance from the government or private agencies because of need
c. program that requires welfare recipients to provide labor in exchange for benefits
d. graph that illustrates how much the actual distribution of income varies from an equal distribution
e. tax that would make cash payments to certain groups below the poverty line
f. annual dollar amounts used to evaluate the money income that families and unrelated individuals receive

Multiple Choice: In the blank at the left write the letter of the choice that best completes the statement or answers the question. (10 points each)

6. If all families received exactly the same income, the Lorenz curve would appear as
 a. an upward sloping curve.   b. a diagonal line.
 c. a downward sloping curve.   d. a horizontal line.

7. Which of the following is NOT a reason for income inequality?
 a. economic growth   b. education
 c. wealth   d. discrimination

8. To an economist, an individual is living in poverty if
 a. his or her income is below a certain level.   b. he or she is uneducated.
 c. he or she has difficulty finding work.   d. his or her abilities are below average.

9. About how many Americans are currently living in poverty?
 a. less than 1 million   b. between 1 and 15 million
 c. between 15 million and 30 million d. more than 30 million

10. The income gap has widened since 1980 for all of the following reasons EXCEPT
 a. a structural change in the economy that changed from goods production to service production.
 b. a growing gap between well-educated and poorly-educated workers.
 c. a growth in monopoly power.
 d. declining unionism.

Section Quizzes   47

INTERDISCIPLINARY CONNECTIONS ACTIVITY

Geography Distribute copies of outline maps of the United States with each state labeled. Have students divide the map into quadrants—the northwest, the southwest, the northeast, and the southeast. Next, tell them to use the bar graph on page 399 to determine the ten states with the highest per capita income. Then, ask students to make a generalization about the location of most states with the highest per capita income. *(Most states with the highest per capita income are in the northeastern quadrant of the United States.)* **Ask:** What state is an exception to this generalization? *(Colorado)*

Reteach

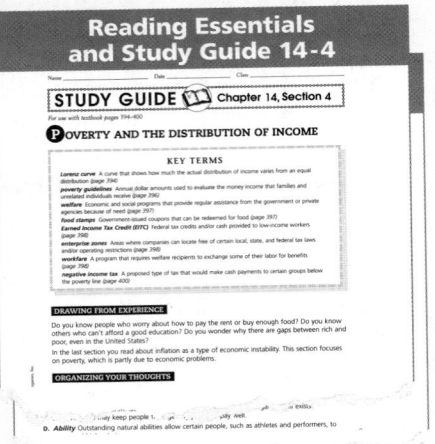

Reading Essentials and Study Guide 14-4

Enrich

Have students write a research paper on one of the antipoverty programs established during the administrations of Presidents Kennedy and Johnson.

CLOSE

Encourage students to imagine that they are designing a time capsule to be opened in the year 2100. Have them select 12 items to include in the capsule that would tell people of the future about unemployment, inflation, and poverty in the 1990s and 2000s.

Many welfare-to-work programs, like the UPS program discussed in the cover story, have had promising results. In many cases, companies can even earn federal tax credits when they hire workers directly from the welfare rolls, making the employment a win-win situation for both employer and employee.

Negative Income Tax

The **negative income tax** is a proposed type of tax that would make cash payments to certain groups below the poverty line. These cash payments would take the place of existing welfare programs rather than supplement them. Also, everyone would qualify for the program, not just working people as with the EITC.

Under the negative income tax, the federal government would set an income level below which people would not have to pay taxes. Then, the government would pay a certain amount of money to anyone who earned less than that amount.

For example, suppose that an individual's tax liability was computed using the following formula:

$$\text{taxes} = (25\% \text{ of income}) - \$8{,}000$$

Under this formula a person with no income would have a tax of minus $8,000—which is another way of saying that the person will *receive* $8,000 from the government. Or, if the person earned exactly $12,000, then the person would receive an additional $5,000 under the formula for a total of $17,000. Under this formula, a person would have to make $32,000 before any taxes were actually paid.

The negative income tax is different from other antipoverty programs in two respects. First, it is a market-based program designed to encourage people to work. The object of the negative income tax is to make the minimum payment large enough to be of some assistance, yet small enough to encourage people to work. Then, when people do go to work, the taxes they actually pay need to be small enough so as not to discourage them from working.

Second, the negative income tax would be cost-effective because it would take the place of other costly welfare programs. In the end, individuals would have money to spend as they saw fit. Government would also save because it would have fewer welfare programs and administrative costs than it does currently. Although the negative income tax is currently not used, many economists believe it would be a reasonable alternative to the existing welfare structure.

Section 4 Assessment

Checking for Understanding

1. **Main Idea** Using your notes from the graphic organizer activity on page 394, list the reasons for the growing income gap.

2. **Key Terms** Define Lorenz curve, poverty guidelines, welfare, food stamps, Earned Income Tax Credit (EITC), enterprise zone, workfare, negative income tax.

3. **Describe** how the distribution of income is measured.

4. **List** the five main reasons for inequality of income.

5. **Identify** the major programs and proposals designed to alleviate the problem of poverty.

Applying Economic Concepts

6. **Distribution of Income** What would happen to the Lorenz curve if nonfinancial aid such as food stamps and medicaid were treated as income? Explain why this would occur.

Critical Thinking

7. **Analyzing Information** Some people have said that "the rich got richer" in the 1990s. What factors can you cite to explain that what actually happened was more complex than this simple statement?

 Practice and **assess** key social studies skills with the *Glencoe Skillbuilder Interactive Workbook, Level 2.*

Section 4 Assessment Answers

1. structural change in the economy as industry changes from goods production to service production; gap between well-educated and poorly educated workers; declining unionism; changing structure of families

2. All vocabulary terms are defined in the text.

3. Incomes are ranked by families from lowest to highest, then divided into quintiles. Quintile data is then plotted as a Lorenz curve.

4. education, wealth, discrimination, ability, monopoly power

5. TANF; SSI; food stamps; medicaid; social service programs such as child abuse prevention, foster care, family planning; enterprise zones; workfare

6. It would move closer to the 45-degree diagonal, with less area between it and the diagonal line. The aid would increase the income total for the lower income families making for a more even overall distribution of income.

7. Students may note the reasons for income inequality and the gap in the income-to-poverty ratio.

Section 1

Business Cycles and Fluctuations

(pages 375–380)

- **Business cycles** are systematic increases and decreases in real GDP; unsystematic changes are **business fluctuations.**

- The two phases of the cycle are **recession** and **expansion;** a **peak** is when the expansion ends, while a **trough** is when the recession ends.

- The Great Depression of the 1930s was the worst economic decline in U.S. history; income distribution inequalities, risky credit practices, weak international economic conditions, and tariff wars all contributed to the Depression.

- Several short, mild recessions have occurred since WWII.

- Business cycles are caused by changes in capital and inventory spending by businesses, stimuli supplied by innovations and imitations, monetary factors, and external shocks.

- **Econometric models** and the **index of leading indicators** are used to predict changes in future economic activity.

Section 2

Unemployment (pages 382–387)

- Unemployed persons are identified monthly by the Census Bureau. The number of **unemployed** is divided by the civilian labor force to arrive at the unemployment rate.

- The **unemployment rate** does not count dropouts, nor does it distinguish between full- and part-time employment.

- **Frictional, structural, cyclical, seasonal,** and **technological** are different forms of unemployment.

Section 3

Inflation (pages 389–392)

- Inflation is the rate of change in the **price level** as measured by the CPI.

- Terms used to describe the severity of inflation are **creeping inflation, galloping inflation,** and **hyperinflation.**

- Generous credit conditions and excessive growth of the money supply allow demand-pull, deficit spending, cost-push, and wage-price spiral inflation to take place.

- Inflation erodes the value of the dollar, makes life difficult for people on fixed incomes, changes the spending habits of consumers and businesses, and alters the distribution of income in favor of debtors.

Section 4

Poverty and the Distribution of Income (pages 394–400)

- The distribution of income is measured by ranking family incomes from lowest to highest and then dividing the ranking into quintiles. The income earned by each quintile is then compared to other quintiles.

- The **Lorenz curve** shows that incomes are not evenly distributed, and that they are becoming less equal.

- Factors accounting for the unequal distribution of income include educational levels, wealth, discrimination, ability, and monopoly power.

- Poverty is determined by comparing the amount of income earned by families to measures called the **poverty guidelines.**

- The growing income gap is due to the increased importance of the service industry, the widening workers' skills gap, the decline of union influence, and the changing composition of the American family.

NIGHTLY BUSINESS REPORT

○ **ECONOMICS & YOU**

Chapter 21
Disc 1, Side 2

Fighting Unemployment, Inflation, and Poverty

▭ Also available in VHS.

Using the Chapter 14 Summary

Use the Chapter 14 Summary to preview, review, condense, or reteach the chapter.

Preview/Review

Vocabulary PuzzleMaker CD-ROM reinforces Key Terms.

Interactive Tutor Self-Assessment Software provides a review of Chapter 14 content.

Condense

Have students listen to the Chapter 14 Audio Program. Spanish also available.

Assign the Chapter 14 Audio Program Activity and give students the Chapter 14 Audio Program Test.

Have students complete the Guided Reading Activities and Reading Essentials and Study Guides for Chapter 14.

Reteach

Have students complete Reteaching Activity 14 in the TCR. Spanish also available.

Teacher's Notes / Internet Bookmarks

GLENCOE
TECHNOLOGY

Use **MindJogger Videoquiz** to review the Chapter 14 content.

Have students visit the Web site at epp.glencoe.com to review Chapter 14 and take the **Self-Check Quiz.**

Identifying Key Terms

1.	f	9. n
2.	d	10. a
3.	j	11. h
4.	m	12. g
5.	l	13. k
6.	b	14. i
7.	e	15. o
8.	p	16. c

Reviewing the Facts

Section 1

1. It was the worst economic decline in U.S. history, resulting in income distribution inequalities, risky credit practices, weak international economic conditions, and tariff wars.
2. depression: phase of business cycle characterized by high unemployment, acute shortages, and excess capacity in plants; recession: phase of business cycle that occurs when the real GDP declines for two consecutive quarters
3. econometric models, index of leading indicators

Section 2

4. It is the number of unemployed individuals divided by the total number of persons in the civilian labor force.
5. frictional, structural, cyclical, seasonal, technological
6. It is reached when the unemployment rate drops below 4.5 percent.

Self-Check Quiz Visit the *Economics: Principles and Practices* Web site at epp.glencoe.com and click on *Chapter 14—Self-Check Quizzes* to prepare for the chapter test.

Identifying Key Terms

Write the letter of the key term that best matches each definition below.

a. **trend line**
b. **cyclical unemployment**
c. **unemployed**
d. **food stamps**
e. **frictional unemployment**
f. **peak**
g. **trough**
h. **inflation**
i. **Lorenz curve**
j. **poverty guidelines**
k. **price level**
l. **seasonal unemployment**
m. **structural unemployment**
n. **technological unemployment**
o. **recession**
p. **workfare**

1. marks the end of a recession
2. an example of a welfare program
3. annual benchmark used to evaluate the money income that families receive
4. caused by a shift in demand or a change in the way the economy operates
5. caused by annual changes in weather and holiday seasons
6. caused by periodic swings in business activity

7. caused by workers who are "between jobs" for short periods
8. describes the requirement that welfare recipients exchange labor for benefits
9. happens when workers face the threat of automation
10. growth path in absence of recession or expansion
11. measured by changes in the CPI
12. lowest point of the business cycle
13. measured by the CPI
14. shows how much the actual distribution of income differs from an equal distribution
15. real GDP declines two consecutive quarters
16. works less than one hour per week for pay or profit

Reviewing the Facts

Section 1 (pages 375–380)

1. **Describe** the Great Depression.
2. **Distinguish** between depressions and recessions.
3. **Analyze** two methods economists use to predict business cycles.

Section 2 (pages 382–387)

4. **Describe** how the unemployment rate is computed.
5. **Identify** the major types of unemployment.
6. **Analyze** what is meant by full employment.

Section 3 (pages 389–392)

7. **Compare** the difference between the price level and inflation.
8. **Identify** the five causes of inflation.
9. **List** four destabilizing effects of inflation.

Section 3

7. The price level refers to the relative magnitude of prices at one point in time. Inflation is a rise in the general price level and is generally reported in terms of annual rates of change.
8. demand-pull, the government deficit, cost-push, wage-price spiral, and excessive monetary growth
9. The dollar buys less, spending habits change, speculation increases, and the distribution of income is altered.

Section 4

10. the way income is distributed among individuals, families, households, and other groups
11. education, wealth, discrimination, ability, and monopoly power
12. Family incomes are ranked from lowest to highest, then the ranking is divided into quintiles. This information, plotted as a Lorenz curve, shows how much the actual distribution of income varies from an equal distribution.
13. income assistance, general assistance, social service programs, tax credits, enterprise zones,

Section 4 (pages 394–400)

10. **Explain** what is meant by the distribution of income.

11. **Identify** five major reasons for inequality in the distribution of income.

12. **Explain** how the Lorenz curve is used to show the inequality of income distribution.

13. **Name** seven antipoverty programs.

Thinking Critically

1. **Analyzing Information** Why is it important to understand the impact of business cycles?

2. **Drawing Conclusions** Why might a government statistic about the number of employed people be misleading?

3. **Understanding Cause and Effect** Explain the effect that inflation has on the financial positions of borrowers and lenders. Use a chart similar to the one below to help you organize your answer. If you managed a bank, what interest rate would you charge to overcome the disadvantage of long-term inflation?

Cause: Inflation → Effect:

Applying Economic Concepts

1. **Unemployment rate** If we were to enter a period of recession, what would likely happen to the unemployment rate? The inflation rate? The poverty rate?

2. **Inflation** Explain why inflation cannot take place without an expansion of the money supply.

3. **Lorenz curve** Suppose that a new government program reduced the level of poverty in the country. How would this affect the Lorenz curve?

Math Practice

Use the following information to determine real GDP per capita for each of the following years.

Year	Population	Real GDP in $billion
1960	179,323,000	$2,263
1970	203,302,000	$3,398
1980	226,542,000	$4,615
1990	248,710,000	$6,136

Thinking Like an Economist

Why is an economist likely to prefer a program like negative income tax over other welfare programs?

Technology Skill

Sending E-Mail Write a topic sentence about income to research. Examples include: "Is income rising above or below the rate of inflation?" "Is there an income gap between men's and women's wages? And if so, "Is the income gap widening?"

Then browse the Internet or call the government to obtain the E-mail address of a federal agency concerned with this issue. E-mail the federal agency, sharing your topic and requesting information.

Building Skills

Using the Internet Search for information on trends in inflation and unemployment rates from the following sites on the Internet: the Census Bureau, the Bureau of Labor Statistics, and the Economic Statistics Briefing Room.

Search for recent articles discussing unemployment, inflation, or poverty. Download at least two recent press releases from each of the above sites. Summarize the articles and share your findings with other members of the class.

 Practice and **assess** key social studies skills with the *Glencoe Skillbuilder Interactive Workbook, Level 2.*

---

people to purchase more products, which results in higher prices.

3. Reduction of poverty would raise the left side of the Lorenz curve, which shows the percentage of total income received by families in the lowest quintiles.

Math Practice

1960: $12,600; 1970: $16,700; 1980: $20,300; 1990: $24,600

Thinking Like an Economist

because the negative income tax would be cost-effective and would encourage people to work

Technology Skill

Students should demonstrate an understanding of Chapter 14 concepts and E-mail procedures.

Building Skills

Check students' answers for accuracy of research.

Bonus Test Question

Have students answer the following problem: *Find the unemployment rate under the following circumstances: The civilian labor force numbers 15,000; there are 945 people available and looking for work; 20 of these people worked more than 3 hours last week; another 10 worked more than 15 hours last week in a family business. ([945 − 20 − 10] ÷ 15,000 × 100 = 6.10)*

---

workfare programs, and any specific programs under these general headings

Thinking Critically

1. Answers should note that understanding the impact of business cycles enables us to predict and prepare for changes in the economy.

2. Answers will vary. For example, it does not distinguish between full-time and part-time employment.

3. Lenders need to raise interest rates, leading to borrowers borrowing less; borrowers generally benefit because the money they pay back is worth less.

Applying Economic Concepts

1. inflation would fall, others rise

2. If the money supply stayed the same, people would buy the same amount of products, and prices would remain at their equilibrium. The money supply must expand for inflation to occur. An expanding money supply causes

Issues in Free Enterprise

Issues in Free Enterprise are case studies that allow students to investigate opposing views of economic issues. The case study contains background information about a current topic related to economics. Two differing opinions are presented that debate the issue and how it should be resolved. Students answer questions that evaluate their understanding of the arguments. They are then asked to identify which opinion they agree with, and explain the reason for their decision.

 FOCUS

Remind students of the meaning of the term *median,* and ask them what they think the median annual income in the United States is today. Tell them that the actual figure is approximately $39,000 per household. Point out that for every person who makes more than that, there is someone who makes less. Challenge them to explain *why* income varies, from nothing to millions of dollars a year, and list their reasons on the board. **Ask:** Regardless of the reason(s), is it *fair* that some people make much more than others? As students read the selections, have them consider how income inequality fits with the American ideal of economic equity.

A Case Study:

IS INCOME INEQUALITY REALLY A PROBLEM?

Not everyone in the United States makes the same amount of money. Some people make a great deal, some make very little, and most make something in between. Economists call this situation, quite simply, income or wage inequality. Others call it the income gap.

An income gap is inevitable in a free market economy. First, the market gives different values to different activities, and second, some people work more than others. So the existence of some income inequality, in and of itself, doesn't generally cause concern.

But some analysts express concern that, if the gap widens, it will be more and more difficult to close. In other words, the rich will get richer and the poor will get poorer.

> As you read the selections, ask yourself: Is the income gap a serious economic problem, or are fears about it overblown?

 PRO The Gap is Widening

Income inequality has been worsening in the United States since the early 1970s. Before 1973, all groups enjoyed healthy income gains, particularly the middle class. However, since 1979, the rich have gained far more than the middle class, while the income of the poor has fallen in absolute terms. A recent study found that the richest one percent of families (average annual income: $800,000 for a family of four) captured 70 percent of the total rise in family income in the United States between 1977 and 1989.

America has always been considered a land of opportunity, where parents believe in the possibility of a "better life" for their children. Does upward mobility mean growing inequality is unimportant, since, with effort and a bit of luck, those at the bottom can still move toward the top?

Not exactly. First of all, we know that historically high rates of mobility in the United States resulted from fast economic growth that was shared across the board. Today, growth benefits the wealthy far more than the middle class, let alone the poor.

404 UNIT 4 MACROECONOMICS: POLICIES

Behind the Viewpoints

 PRO **Nancy Birdsall** is the executive vice-president of the Inter-American Development Bank.

 PRO **George F. Will** is a nationally syndicated columnist and commentator.

Second, although many families do move from one income category to another over time, individuals have suffered larger downward, and smaller upward, income changes since the 1970s—with the exception of the rich, whose earnings have jumped dramatically.

Third, though education has always been seen as the great leveler, it now reinforces initial advantages instead of compensating for initial handicaps. [Schools] no longer effectively make up for deep inequalities among children. . . .

So, if America is to remain the land of opportunity, elementary and secondary education must work for the poor. Otherwise, inequality of income will come to reflect not just differences in motivation, work effort, and sheer luck among players in a fair game, but different rules for rich and poor.

—Nancy Birdsall, Executive Vice-President, Inter-American Development Bank

The Problem is Exaggerated

That we are rapidly becoming richer is clear. People who deny that equality is increasing are fixated on the recent small increase in income inequality. That increase, the subject of an unceasing journalistic drumbeat, is, [Chris DeMuth, president of American Enterprise Institute] argues, a small incongruity in the long-term "leveling of material circumstances" that has been underway for three centuries and is accelerating.

Since 1700, the average life span in Western societies has doubled. Today material necessities—food, shelter—are so universally available that the problem of poverty, understood as material scarcity, has been solved. Poverty, DeMuth notes,

now is a problem of individual behavior, social organization and policy, not of society's material scarcities.

Two centuries ago land was the essential source of wealth. One century ago, physical capital was. Today, human capital—knowledge, cognitive skill—is, and such capital is widely distributed by nature and is augmented by universal education. Furthermore, sexual equality has advanced so far that young men and women of comparable education and training now earn essentially equal incomes.

As societies become more wealthy, DeMuth argues, money income becomes a less informative measure of individual welfare, as is demonstrated by this fact: Western democracies have become so wealthy that, for the first time in history, "voluntary reduction in time spent at paid employment has become a major social and economic phenomenon." This reduction appears in expanded education of the young and, even more, in longer retirement of the elderly. . . .

The modern age's expansion of individual autonomy . . . frees individuals for admirable and improving pursuits—and for unworthy and self-destructive behavior. With the growth of wealth, freedom and equality has come an equally astounding explosion of social pathologies, from family disintegration and illegitimacy to drug abuse and vulgar popular entertainment. . . .

Citizens are turning their attention, as individuals and as members of civic and religious groups, to the question: What is freedom for? The question is itself among the luxuries of a wealthy, free and equal society.

—George F. Will, *Washington Post* Writers Group

Analyzing the Issue

1. Summarize Birdsall's argument.

2. What does Will mean by calling income inequality (quoting DeMuth) "a small incongruity"?

3. Will calls America "a wealthy, free and equal society." Considering Birdsall's argument, do you agree? Explain.

TEACH

L1 Making Connections

Challenge students to link any of the factors they listed during the Focus activity to elements of Birdsall's and Will's arguments.

L2 Displaying Information Visually

Have students pair off to create timelines that visually depict the temporal references made by Birdsall and by Will. When they have finished their timelines, have pairs develop a statement (perhaps three sentences) that juxtaposes the two arguments in terms of time.

ASSESS

Have students answer the Analyzing the Issue questions.

CLOSE

Remind students that "economic equity" is one of the fundamental economic and social goals of the United States. Have them address the issue of income inequality in terms of this goal, and write paragraphs that argue that the current income distribution in the United States is or is not in keeping with the goal of economic equity.

Answers to Analyzing the Issue

1. Summaries will vary. Sample: Income inequality has been worsening in the United States, and mobility of poorer individuals toward higher levels of wealth is stymied by unequal economic growth, smaller upward and larger downward income changes, the failure of education to make up for inequalities, and the loss of market value of a high school diploma.

2. DeMuth, via Will, is placing current concerns about income inequality in a larger historical context; compared to the overall social and economic improvements of the last 300 years, current inequalities are extremely minor.

3. Answers will vary, but should be explained.

SECTION RESOURCES

Daily Objectives	Reproducible Resources	Technology/Multimedia Resources

Daily Objectives

Section 1
The Federal Reserve System
1. Describe the structure of the Federal Reserve System.
2. Explain the major regulatory responsibilities of the Fed.

Section 2
Monetary Policy
1. Describe the use of fractional reserves.
2. Understand the tools used to conduct monetary policy.

Section 3
Monetary Policy, Banking, and the Economy
1. Explain how monetary policy affects interest rates in the short run.
2. Relate monetary expansion to inflation in the long run.
3. Identify the two major definitions of money.
4. Describe how interest rates are affected by political pressure.

Reproducible Resources

Section 1
- Reproducible Lesson Plan 15-1
- Daily Lecture Notes 15-1
- Guided Reading Activity 15-1
- Reading Essentials and Study Guide 15-1
- Section Quiz 15-1*

Section 2
- Reproducible Lesson Plan 15-2
- Daily Lecture Notes 15-2
- Guided Reading Activity 15-2
- Reading Essentials and Study Guide 15-2
- Section Quiz 15-2*

Section 3
- Reproducible Lesson Plan 15-3
- Daily Lecture Notes 15-3
- Guided Reading Activity 15-3
- Reading Essentials and Study Guide 15-3
- Section Quiz 15-3*

Technology/Multimedia Resources

Section 1
- Daily Focus Transparency 63
- Interactive Economics!
- Interactive Tutor Self-Assessment Software
- ExamView® Pro Testmaker
- Presentation Plus!

Section 2
- Daily Focus Transparency 64
- Interactive Economics!
- Interactive Tutor Self-Assessment Software
- ExamView® Pro Testmaker
- Presentation Plus!

Section 3
- Daily Focus Transparency 62
- Vocabulary PuzzleMaker CD-ROM
- Interactive Economics!
- Interactive Tutor Self-Assessment Software
- ExamView® Pro Testmaker
- Presentation Plus!

Also available in Spanish

- Transparency
- Videodisc
- CD-ROM
- Audio Program
- Software
- Videocassette
- Blackline Master

0:00 OUT OF TIME?
Assign the Chapter 15 Audio Program activity and test.

Block Schedule

Activities that are particularly suited to use within the block scheduling framework are identified throughout this chapter by the following designation: **BLOCK SCHEDULING**

KEY TO ABILITY LEVELS

Teaching strategies have been coded for varying learning styles and abilities.
L1 BASIC activities for all students
L2 AVERAGE activities for average to above-average students
L3 CHALLENGING activities for above-average students
ELL ENGLISH LANGUAGE LEARNER activities

Timesaving Tools

TeacherWorks™ **All-In-One Planner and Resource Center**

- **Interactive Teacher Edition** Access your Teacher Wraparound Edition and your classroom resources with a few easy clicks.

- **Interactive Lesson Planner** Planning has never been easier! Organize your week, month, semester, or year with all the lesson helps you need to make teaching creative, timely, and relevant.

Use Glencoe's **Presentation Plus!** multimedia teacher tool to easily present dynamic lessons that visually excite your students. Using Microsoft PowerPoint® you can customize the presentations to create your own personalized lessons.

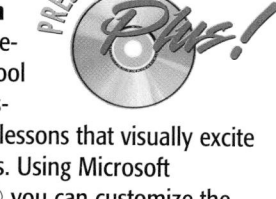

ACTIVITY

From the Classroom of...

**Tina Page
Edmond Memorial H.S.
Edmond, OK**

Monetary Blues

If consumer spending *(C)* and investment spending *(I)* are going down in a recession, what can the Fed do about monetary policy to raise them? Lower the discount rate (d.r.), lower the reserve requirement (r.r), and buy bonds.

If consumer spending and investment spending are going up in an inflationary spiral, what can the Fed do with monetary policy to lower them? Raise the discount rate, raise the reserve requirement, and sell bonds.

Draw the following diagrams on the board to illustrate what you just explained:

If $C\downarrow$ and $I\downarrow$, to raise them:	If $C\uparrow$ and $I\uparrow$, to lower them:
Boost money supply by	Shrink money supply by
1. d.r.$\downarrow$	1. d.r.$\uparrow$
2. r.r$\downarrow$	2. r.r.$\uparrow$
3. buy bonds	3. sell bonds

Organize the class into groups and have each group devise lyrics, making a song out of the information in the diagrams.

National Council on Economic Education

THE **Economics**America AND **Economics**International PROGRAMS

Voluntary National Content Standards in Economics
Emphasized in Chapter 15

Content Standard 12

Content Standard 20

For a complete listing of NCEE Standards and entire text correlation, see Teacher pages in front of book.

Resources Available from NCEE

- Capstone: The Nation's High School Economics Course
- Focus: High School Economics
- Civics and Government: Focus on Economics
- United States History: Eyes on the Economy

To order these materials or to contact your state Council on Economic Education about workshops and programs, call 1-800-338-1192 or visit www.nationalcouncil.org

Chapter 15 Resource Manager

Economic Concept Transparency 18: Monetary Policy

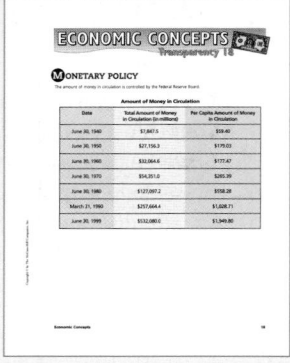

Consumer Application Activity 20

Free Enterprise Activity 20

Enrichment Activity 15

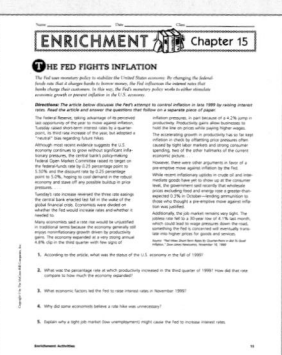

Cooperative Learning Activity 20

Math Practice Activity 20

Economic Cartoon 20

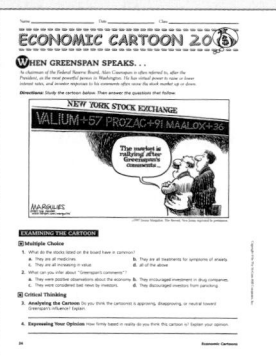

Primary and Secondary Source Reading 20

Economic Vocabulary Activity 15

Reteaching Activity 15

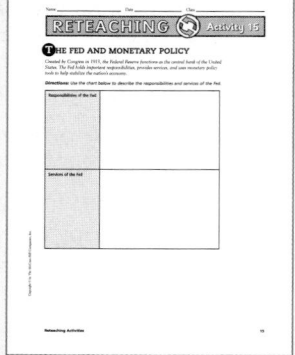

Critical Thinking Activity 20

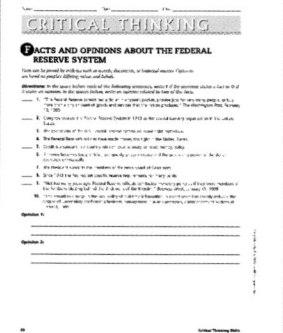

Reinforcing Economic Skill 14

Chapter 15 Resource Manager

ASSESSMENT AND EVALUATION

Chapter 15 Test Form A

Chapter 15 Test Form B

Performance Assessment Activity 20

ExamView® Pro Testmaker

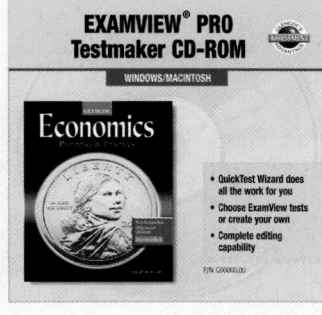

SPANISH RESOURCES

The following Spanish language materials are available in the Spanish Resources binder:

 Spanish Economic Vocabulary Activities

 Spanish Reteaching Activities

 Spanish Section Quizzes

 Spanish Economic Concepts Transparencies

Also available:

  Spanish Chapter 15 Audio Program Activity and Test

TECHNOLOGY/MULTIMEDIA

- Vocabulary PuzzleMaker CD-ROM
- Interactive Tutor Self-Assessment Software
- ExamView® Pro Testmaker
- Audio Program (English or Spanish)
- NBR Economics & You Video Program (English or Spanish)
- MindJogger Videoquiz
- Interactive Economics! CD-ROM
- Presentation Plus!
- TeacherWorks CD-ROM
- Glencoe Skillbuilder Interactive Workbook CD-ROM, Level 2

ECONOMICS Online

Use our Web site for additional resources. All essential content is covered in the Student Edition.

You and your students can visit epp.glencoe.com, the Web site companion to **Economics: Principles and Practices.** This innovative integration of electronic and print media offers your students a wealth of opportunities. The student text directs students to the Web site for the following options:

- **Chapter Overviews**
- **Student Web Activities**
- **Self-Check Quizzes**
- **Textbook Updates**

Answers are provided for you in the Web Activity Lesson Plan. Additional Web resources and interactive puzzles are also available.

Performance Assessment

Refer to Activity 20 in the *Performance Assessment Strategies and Activities* booklet.

 BLOCK SCHEDULING

Introduce students to chapter content and key terms by having them access **Chapter Overview 15** at epp.glencoe.com

NIGHTLY
BUSINESS
REPORT

 ECONOMICS & YOU

|||||| Chapter 22
Disc 1, Side 2
The Federal Reserve System and Monetary Policy

After viewing this segment, students should be able to:
- Compare and contrast tight and loose monetary policies.

 Also available in VHS.

GLENCOE
TECHNOLOGY

 Use **MindJogger Videoquiz** to preview the Chapter 15 content.

CHAPTER
15

The Fed and Monetary Policy

Economics & You

One important requirement of money is that it be worth about the same amount from one year to the next. In **Chapter 15,** you will learn that money must have stability in value to function as it should. To learn more about how the Federal Reserve System controls the money supply, view the Chapter 22 video lesson:

The Federal Reserve System and Monetary Policy

ECONOMICS Online

Chapter Overview Visit the *Economics: Principles and Practices* Web site at epp.glencoe.com and click on **Chapter 15—Chapter Overviews** to preview chapter information.

The Federal Reserve System controls the supply of money in the economy.

EXTRA CREDIT PROJECT

Direct students to prepare a four-page, illustrated report on the Federal Reserve System, focusing on the Fed's structure and the major services it provides to the banking industry and to the government. Call on students to present and discuss their reports.

The Federal Reserve System

Study Guide

Main Idea
The Federal Reserve works to strengthen and stabilize the nation's monetary system.

Reading Strategy
Graphic Organizer As you read this section, complete a graphic organizer similar to the one below by listing the components that make up the Federal Reserve System.

The Federal Reserve System

Key Terms
member bank, bank holding company, Regulation Z, currency, coins

Objectives
After studying this section, you will be able to:
1. **Describe** the structure of the Federal Reserve System.
2. **Explain** the major regulatory responsibilities of the Fed.

Applying Economic Concepts
Truth-in-Lending Laws Have you or your parents ever bought anything on credit? Read to find out how the Fed influences the type of information you receive from the lender.

Cover Story

Design by Sculptor of Vietnam Women's Memorial Selected for Coin

A rendering of Sacagawea by the New Mexico sculptor who created the Vietnam Women's Memorial will appear in millions of Americans' pockets starting in 2000.

Rendering of Sacagawea used for the coin

After sorting through more than 90,000 comments delivered via the Internet, U.S. Mint officials [selected a design by] Glenna Goodacre of Santa Fe. . . . It will depict the Shoshone teenager who accompanied explorers Meriwether Lewis and William Clark to the Pacific Ocean in 1805. . . . Just 16 when she accompanied the explorers, Sacagawea acted as an interpreter and go-between with tribes along the way. . . .

Officials weren't sure Americans would accept the nontraditional look, . . . but Internet responses overwhelmingly favor the mother and child theme and the realistic portrayal.

—*CNNInteractive*, December 17, 1998

On December 23, 1913, Congress created the Federal Reserve System, or "Fed," as the central bank of the United States. Today, the Fed provides financial services to the government, regulates financial institutions, maintains the payments system, enforces consumer protection laws, and conducts monetary policy. Even the new Sacagawea dollar coin featured in the cover story is warehoused and distributed by the Fed. Because everyone uses money, and because interest rates affect the overall level of economic activity, the Fed's activities affect us all.

Structure of the Fed

Figure 15.1 outlines the main organizational structure of the Federal Reserve System. The Fed's main components have remained practically unchanged since the Great Depression of the 1930s.

Private Ownership

One of the unique features of the Fed is that it is privately owned by its **member banks**—commercial banks that are members of, and hold

CHAPTER 15: THE FED AND MONETARY POLICY **407**

① FOCUS

Section Overview
This section describes the Federal Reserve System structure.

BELLRINGER
Motivational Activity

- Project **transparency** and have students answer questions.
- Available as blackline master.

Daily Focus Transparency 63

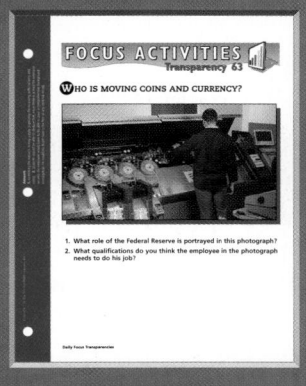

Study Guide

Reading Strategy
Have students create the graphic organizer.
Answers to Graphic: *Board of Governors, Federal Open Market Committee, Federal Advisory Council, 12 district banks, member banks, advisory councils*

Preteaching Vocabulary
Ask students to find each Key Term and read it in context.

RESOURCE MANAGER

📁 Reproducible Masters
- Reproducible Lesson Plan 15-1
- Daily Lecture Notes 15-1
- Guided Reading Activity 15-1
- Reading Essentials and Study Guide 15-1
- Section Quiz 15-1

✎ Transparencies
- Daily Focus Transparency 63

Multimedia
- 🔘 Interactive Economics!
- 💾 Interactive Tutor Self-Assessment Software
- 🔘 ExamView® Pro Testmaker
- 🔘 Presentation Plus!

TEACH

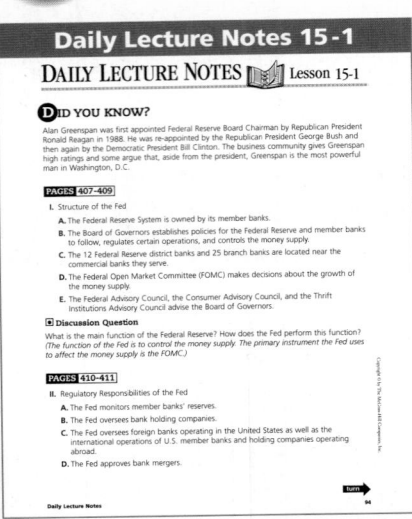

Daily Lecture Notes 15-1

L1 Understanding Ideas

Make a number of flash cards that detail some aspect of the Federal Reserve System. Next, review with students the discussion on the structure of the Fed on pages 407–410 and have students study Figure 15.1 on page 408. Then hold up the flash cards, one at a time, and call on students to identify what aspect of the Fed is being described. **ELL**

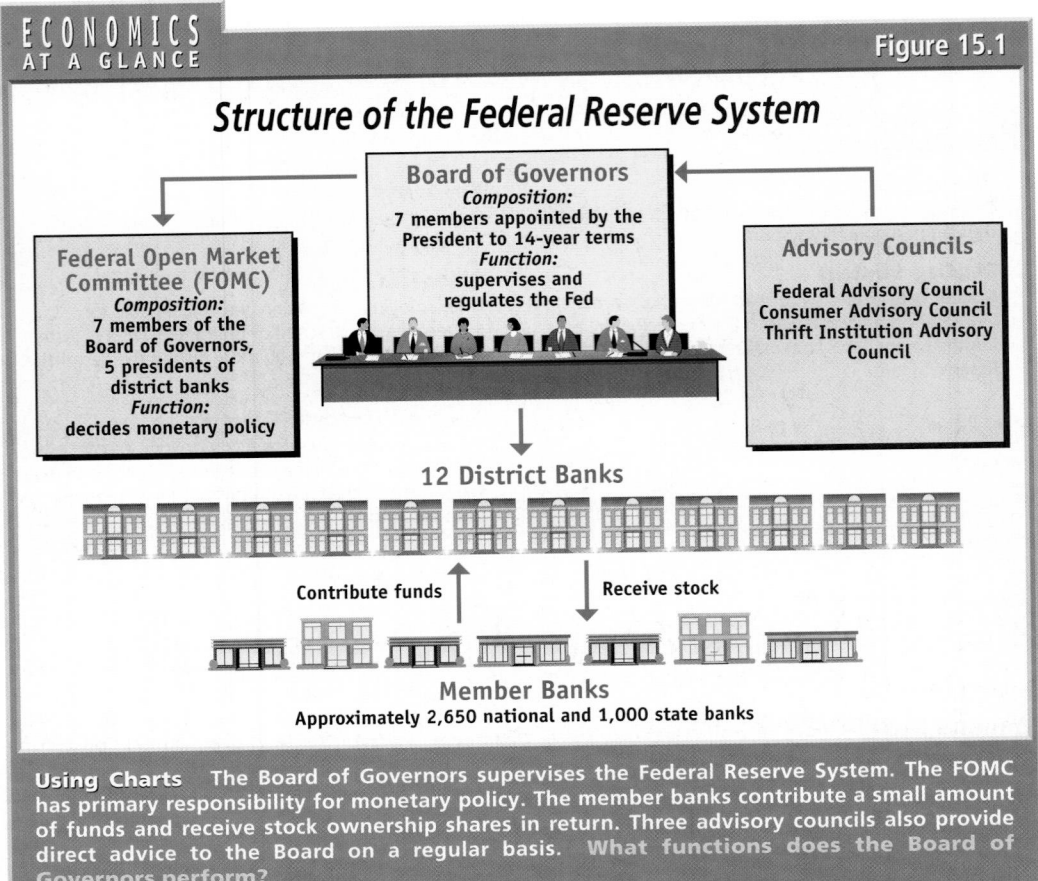

Figure 15.1

Structure of the Federal Reserve System

Board of Governors
Composition:
7 members appointed by the President to 14-year terms
Function:
supervises and regulates the Fed

Federal Open Market Committee (FOMC)
Composition:
7 members of the Board of Governors, 5 presidents of district banks
Function:
decides monetary policy

Advisory Councils
Federal Advisory Council
Consumer Advisory Council
Thrift Institution Advisory Council

12 District Banks

Contribute funds   Receive stock

Member Banks
Approximately 2,650 national and 1,000 state banks

Using Charts The Board of Governors supervises the Federal Reserve System. The FOMC has primary responsibility for monetary policy. The member banks contribute a small amount of funds and receive stock ownership shares in return. Three advisory councils also provide direct advice to the Board on a regular basis. **What functions does the Board of Governors perform?**

stock in, the Fed. When the Fed was established in 1913, it was organized as a corporation that issued shares of stock, just like any other corporation. Individual banks may or may not belong to the Fed. National banks—those chartered by the national government—*must* belong. Those chartered by state governments have the choice to belong or not.

When privately owned banks joined the Fed, they were required to purchase some of its shares. This made them part owners of the Fed, just as someone might own shares in IBM, Ford Motor, or Microsoft. Only member banks can own shares.

Private individuals can only own shares indirectly by owning shares of stock in a Fed-member bank. Today, Fed membership consists of all national banks and some state banks.

Board of Governors

In 1935 Congress established a seven-member Board of Governors for the Federal Reserve System. Each member is appointed by the president and approved by the Senate to serve a 14-year term of office. These appointments are staggered, so that one

408 UNIT 4 MACROECONOMICS: POLICIES

MEETING SPECIAL NEEDS ACTIVITY

Learning Disabled For students who have problems listening, keep in mind that they may look like they are not paying attention. Actually, however, they get "lost" in the confusion of language unless certain classroom modifications are made. To help students listen effectively, cue them when you are coming to an important point.

Refer to *Inclusion for the Social Studies Classroom Strategies and Activities* in the TCR.

appointment becomes vacant every two years. As a result, there are always experienced people on the board.

The Board is primarily a regulatory and supervisory agency. It sets general policies for Federal Reserve and member banks to follow, regulates certain operations of state-chartered member banks, and conducts some aspects of monetary policy. It also makes a report each year to Congress and puts out a monthly bulletin that reports on national and international monetary matters.

Federal Reserve District Banks

When the Fed was established in 1913, it was intended to operate as a system of 12 independent and equally powerful banks. Each reserve bank was responsible for a district, and Federal Reserve notes even carried the name of the district bank on the seal to the left of the portrait. Restructuring minimized, and later eliminated, the Fed's regional nature. The new Fed seal does not incorporate any mention of the district banks.

Today, the 12 Federal Reserve district banks and 25 additional branch banks are strategically located so that they can be near the commercial banks they serve. While each of the 12 banks has its own president and board of directors, the Reserve banks are supervised by the Federal Reserve Board in Washington, D.C. The Federal Reserve banks carry out the same functions for banks and thrift institutions as those institutions carry out for people. The district banks accept the deposits of and make loans to banks and thrift institutions, just as banks perform these functions for the public.

Federal Open Market Committee

The Federal Open Market Committee (FOMC) makes decisions about the growth of the money supply and the level of interest rates. It has 12 members: seven members from the Board of Governors, the president of the New York district Fed, and four district Federal Reserve bank presidents who serve one-year rotating terms.

The committee meets eight times a year in Washington, D.C., to review the country's economy and to make decisions about the cost and availability of credit. Most decisions are made in private but are announced almost immediately. The FOMC is the Fed's primary monetary policy-making body.

Advisory Committees

The Fed has three advisory committees that advise the Board of Governors directly. The first is the Federal Advisory Council, which consists of representatives from each of the 12 district banks. It provides advice to the Federal Reserve on matters concerning the overall health of the economy.

The second committee is the Consumer Advisory Council. The council's 30 members meet with the Board three times a year on consumer credit laws.

Board of Governors

Responsibilities The Board of Governors supervises the entire Federal Reserve System. *What role does the Fed play in mergers of member banks?*

Guided Reading Activity 15-1

GUIDED READING Activity 15-1

For use with textbook pages 407–413

THE FEDERAL RESERVE SYSTEM

RECALLING THE FACTS

Directions: Use the information in your textbook to answer the questions. Use another sheet of paper if necessary.

1. What banks must belong to the Fed and what others have a choice whether to belong?

2. What are the main functions of the Board of Governors?

3. What are the functions of the Federal Open Market Committee (FOMC)?

4. What are the three advisory committees that advise the Board of Governors? Explain briefly what each one does.
   a.
   b.
   c.

5. What are two key uses for the reserves that depository institutions must maintain?
   a.
   b.

6. What is a bank holding company and how is it different from a bank?

Visual Instruction

Answer to Caption:
If the surviving bank is a state member bank, it approves the merger.

INTERACTIVE ECONOMICS!

CD-ROM

MONETARY POLICY Have students click on "An Introduction to Monetary Policy" in Lesson 8. After students read the tutorial, **ask:** Who makes up the Federal Open Market Committee? *(the Board of Governors, along with five presidents from the 12 district Fed banks)* What do they discuss at their monthly meetings? *(whether interest rates are too high or too low)*

💾 Also supplied in disk format.

FREE ENTERPRISE ACTIVITY

On the board, write the following responsibilities of the Fed: *State Member Bank Supervision, Holding Companies, International Operations, Mergers, Check Clearing, Consumer Legislation, Currency,* and *Margin Requirements.* (Call the Federal Reserve Board in Washington, D.C., to obtain a list of stocks eligible for margin loans.) Ask students to give an example of each Fed responsibility, and note responses on the board under the appropriate heading. Then organize the class into a number of groups of equal size and have group members discuss which of the Fed's responsibilities they believe is most important to the U.S. economy and why. Call on group representatives to report and explain their group's decision. 📦 **BLOCK SCHEDULING**

L2 Drawing a Cartoon

Direct students to draw a cartoon illustrating one of the responsibilities of the Federal Reserve System. Suggest that students make an editorial point with their cartoons— for example, indicating whether they think the selected responsibility is one the Fed should fulfill. Call on volunteers to display and explain their cartoons.

THE GLOBAL ECONOMY

Central Banks Many of the world's nations have central banks, but each country's banks operate on their own system. After the breakup of the Soviet Union in 1990, most of the newly independent countries had to set up their own central banks with their own rules and currency.

Visual Instruction

Answer to Caption:
conducts nationwide auctions of Treasury bills, bonds, and notes; issues, services, and redeems these securities on behalf of the Treasury; maintains the equivalent of numerous demand deposit accounts for the Treasury and clears checks drawn on those accounts; processes savings bonds; maintains accounts for IRS; issues federal agency checks

---

Members include educators, consumer legal specialists, and representatives from consumer and financial industry groups.

The third advisory group is the Thrift Institutions Advisory Council. On the council are representatives from savings and loan associations, savings banks, and credit unions. It meets with the Board annually to advise on matters pertaining to the thrift industry.

Regulatory Responsibilities

The Federal Reserve System has a broad range of responsibilities ranging from member bank supervision to enforcing consumer legislation.

State Member Banks

All depository institutions—including commercial banks, savings banks, savings institutions, and credit unions—must maintain reserves against their customers' deposits. The Fed is responsible for monitoring the reserves of its state-chartered member banks, while other federal agencies monitor the reserves of nonmember banks and other depository institutions.

While reserves were originally a matter of prudent banking practice, they fulfill two key roles today. First, the banks use reserves to clear checks. Second, the Fed uses reserves to control the size of the money supply.

Bank Holding Companies

The Fed also has broad legislative authority over **bank holding companies**—corporations that own one or more banks. Holding companies, unlike banks, do not accept deposits or make loans. When individuals buy stock in a bank today, they generally purchase the stock of the holding company, which in turn owns one or more individual banks.

This arrangement may seem unusual, but it can be traced to the many restrictions placed on banks after many of them failed during the Great Depression. At the time, bankers tried to sidestep the restrictions by setting up holding companies that would not be subject to banking laws because they were not banks in the traditional sense. Later, Congress gave the Fed the power to regulate the activities of the holding companies so that they could not evade restrictions.

Today about 6,000 holding companies control approximately 7,000 commercial banks. In many cases, the holding company structure has resulted in even more regulation and supervision. For example, the FDIC may inspect and regulate three nonmember state banks that a single holding company owns, while the Fed regulates the holding company itself.

Financial Services

Managed Money Because nations no longer back their money with gold, they rely on central banks, like the Fed, to manage the amount of money in circulation. *What financial services does the Fed provide to the government?*

CRITICAL THINKING

Demonstrating Reasoned Judgment Remind students that legislation establishing the Federal Reserve System with its 12 Federal Reserve District Banks was passed in 1913. Have students work in groups to make a map showing the locations of the 12 district banks. Then have them decide how they would change the 12 districts and in which cities they would recommend locating the Federal Reserve District Banks today. Call on the groups to present and explain their changes to the class. **BLOCK SCHEDULING**

International Operations

Foreign banks have a large presence in the economy. Banks from 60 different countries operate about 500 branches and agencies in the United States. In addition, foreign banks own shares of many large United States banks. In all, foreign banks control about 20 percent of all banking assets in the United States.

The Fed has broad authority to supervise and regulate these foreign banks. Branches and agencies of these banks are examined annually, and the Fed even has the power to terminate the domestic operations of foreign banks.

In addition, the Fed authorizes and supervises the international operations of United States member banks and holding companies. Currently, Fed member banks operate about 800 branches in foreign countries.

Member Bank Mergers

A merger of two or more banks requires the approval of the appropriate federal banking authority. If the surviving bank is a state member bank, the Fed must approve the merger.

Other banking authorities approve other mergers. If two national banks merge, the Comptroller of the Currency, a Treasury Department official, must approve the merger. If two nonmember state banks merge, the FDIC must approve the merger.

Other Federal Reserve Services

The Federal Reserve has other responsibilities as well. These include clearing checks, enforcing consumer legislation, maintaining currency and coins, and providing financial services to the government.

One major service the Fed performs is that of clearing checks, a process that makes extensive use of the reserves in the banking system. In general, the deposits that member banks keep with the Fed are shifted from one bank to another, depending on the way checks are written on the member banks.

Figure 15.2 illustrates the check-clearing process. The person in the example writes a $5 check. As the check is processed through the banking system,

Bank Mergers

"For credit-card information, press one; for a current statement, press two; for the bank's present owner, press three."

The Fed's Role   Mergers are a fact of economic life. *What is the Federal Reserve's role in bank mergers?*

funds are moved from one member bank's account to another until the check returns to the issuer. The money is then removed from the issuer's checking account.

The Fed clears millions of checks at any given time by using the latest high-speed check-sorting equipment available. In some cases banks gather information from a check when it is deposited, and then transfer the information to computer files. These files are sent to the Fed, which uses the information to adjust member banks' accounts. In this way, the member bank's balance can be adjusted without the check having to go through the entire system.

The Fed is also responsible for some consumer legislation, primarily the federal Truth in Lending Act that requires sellers to make complete and accurate disclosures to people who buy on credit. Under **Regulation Z,** the Fed has the authority to

CHAPTER 15: THE FED AND MONETARY POLICY   **411**

Visual Instruction

Answer to Caption:
has role in merger of state member banks; not in mergers between nonmember or national banks

L3 Research

Have students research and prepare an illustrated report on the operations of one of the two agencies that make U.S. money. *(the Bureau of the Mint and the Bureau of Engraving and Printing)*

Among the 25 largest corporate mergers in the United States by the end of 1999, four involved banks, some with other banks and others with other financial institutions. By 1999, Citicorp was the largest bank in the U.S. and the third-largest bank in the world.

CYBERNOMICS

The End of Paper Checks?
Some experts believe that debit cards and online banking will eventually make written checks obsolete. The U.S. government has already switched from paper checks to electronic deposits for Social Security payments.

EXTENDING THE CONTENT

Truth-in-Savings On June 21, 1993, the Truth-in-Savings Act became law. This legislation makes it possible for savers to compare interest rates in much the same way borrowers have been able to compare interest rates. Banks are required to disclose the Annual Percentage Yield—or APY—which, in effect, means all banks must standardize the way they compute interest on savings accounts, NOW accounts, and certificates of deposit (CDs). Prior to this act, one bank might use the term "effective yield," and another "annualized yield." These terms confused customers. Further, some banks paid interest quarterly, others semi-annually, and still others annually; yet all might have reported the same interest rate. The APY is the interest percentage that all banks must use.

Point out that most checks are cleared in two days. This is a remarkably short period of time considering that the Fed deals with about 20 billion checks each year.

③ ASSESS

Assign Section 1 Assessment as homework or as an in-class activity.

💾 Have students use **Interactive Tutor Self-Assessment Software** to review Section 1.

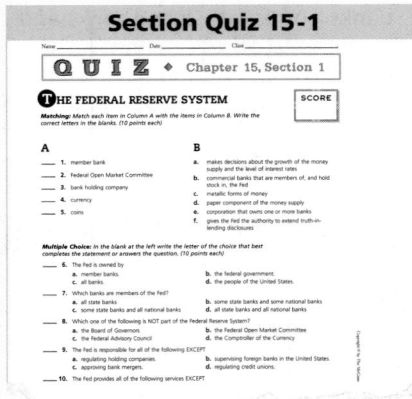

Section Quiz 15-1

Name _____ Date _____ Class _____

Q U I Z ◆ Chapter 15, Section 1

ⓣHE FEDERAL RESERVE SYSTEM   SCORE ____

Matching: Match each item in Column A with the items in Column B. Write the correct letters in the blanks. (10 points each)

A
____ 1. member bank
____ 2. Federal Open Market Committee
____ 3. bank holding company
____ 4. currency
____ 5. coins

B
a. makes decisions about the growth of the money supply and the level of interest rates.
b. commercial banks that are members of, and hold stock in, the Fed
c. metallic forms of money
d. paper component of the money supply
e. corporation that owns one or more banks
f. gives the Fed the authority to extend truth-in-lending disclosures

Multiple Choice: In the blank at the left write the letter of the choice that best completes the statement or answers the question. (10 points each)

____ 6. The Fed is owned by
a. member banks.   b. the federal government.
c. all banks.   d. the people of the United States.

____ 7. Which banks are members of the Fed?
a. all state banks   b. some state banks and some national banks
c. some state banks and all national banks d. all state banks and all national banks

____ 8. Which one of the following is NOT part of the Federal Reserve System?
a. the Board of Governors   b. the Federal Open Market Committee
c. the Federal Advisory Council   d. the Comptroller of the Currency

____ 9. The Fed is responsible for all of the following EXCEPT
a. regulating holding companies.   b. supervising foreign banks in the United States.
c. approving bank mergers.   d. regulating credit unions.

____ 10. The Fed provides all of these services EXCEPT

Figure 15.2

Clearing a Check

Anna	
DDA $~~100~~	
95	

The check is returned to Anna.

Bank X

Bank X then returns Anna's check to her at the end of the month, along with any others she wrote during the same period. When Anna gets the canceled checks, she balances her checkbook to make sure her records agree with the bank's.

Bank X learns of Anna's check only when it arrives from the Fed. The bank then makes up for the loss of the $5 in its MBR account by reducing Anna's DDA by $5.

Bank X	
MBR $~~10~~	Anna's DDA $~~100~~
5	95

Bank X has its MBR reduced, and receives Anna's check.

The process begins with Anna, who has a $100 demand deposit account (DDA) with Bank X. Anna writes a check for $5, which she gives to Nathan. At the same time, she records the amount in her checkbook to show a new balance of $95. (Note that only the accounts affected by the $5 check are shown in this figure.)

Nathan	
DDA $~~100~~	
105	

Nathan deposits the check.

Bank Y

Nathan, who banks at Bank Y, now has the check. If he decides to cash it, he will have $5 in currency in addition to his DDA of $100. If he decides to make a deposit, his DDA will rise to $105. Either way, Bank Y ends up with the check written by Anna.

Because the check is drawn on Bank X, Bank Y gets payment for it by sending the check to the district Federal Reserve Bank. The Fed then processes the check by transferring $5 from Bank X's MBR account to Bank Y's MBR account. The Fed then sends Anna's check to Bank X.

Bank Y	
MBR $~~10~~	Nathan's DDA $~~100~~
15	105

Bank Y sends the check to the Fed district bank for payment.

District Federal Reserve System Bank	
MBR Bank X $~~10~~	5
MBR Bank Y $~~10~~	15

INTERDISCIPLINARY CONNECTIONS ACTIVITY

Technology Many countries' bills feature a variety of colors, larger portraits, and watermarks that are visible when the bill is held to the light. All these features thwart counterfeiters. Discuss with students how computers have made counterfeiting easier. Then ask them to find out how the U.S. has been changing its money to make it more difficult to counterfeit. Have them share with the class their findings and any suggestions for making changes.

extend truth-in-lending disclosures to millions of individuals who purchase or borrow from corporations, retail stores, automobile dealers, banks, and lending institutions.

If you buy furniture or a car on credit, for example, you will discover that the seller must explain several items before you make the purchase. These items include the size of the down payment, the number and size of the monthly payments, and the total amount of interest over the life of the loan.

Today's **currency,** the paper component of the money supply, is made up of Federal Reserve notes—fiat paper money issued by Federal Reserve banks and printed at the Bureau of Engraving and Printing. This currency, issued in amounts of $1, $2, $5, $10, $20, $50, and $100, is distributed to the Fed district banks for storage.

The Bureau of the Mint produces **coins**—metallic forms of money—such as pennies, nickels, dimes, quarters, and the new Sacagawea dollar coin. After the coins are minted, they are shipped to the Fed district banks for storage. When member banks need additional coins or currency, they contact the Fed to fulfill their needs.

When banks come across coins or currency that are mutilated or cannot be used for other reasons, they return it to the Fed for replacement. The Fed then destroys the old money so that it cannot be put back into circulation.

Did you know?

Commercial Banks Commercial banks are the largest financial institutions in the country and are the main sources for exchanging money. The first commercial bank in the United States was founded in 1782 in Philadelphia. Today, commercial banks hold about two-thirds of the nation's money deposits.

One of the Fed's important functions involves the financial services it provides to the federal government and its agencies. For example, the Fed conducts nationwide auctions of Treasury bills, bonds, and notes. It also issues, services, and redeems these securities on behalf of the Treasury. In the process, it maintains the equivalent of numerous demand deposit accounts for the Treasury and clears all checks drawn on those accounts. Other accounts are used to process the tens of millions of dollars of U.S. savings bonds that are sold and redeemed annually.

The Fed also maintains accounts for the IRS, which holds federal taxes paid by individuals and businesses. In fact, any check written to the United States Treasury is deposited in the Fed. Any federal agency check, such as a monthly Social Security payment, comes from accounts held at the Fed. In essence, the Fed serves as the federal government's bank.

CHAPTER 15
Section 1, pages 407–413

Reteach

Reading Essentials and Study Guide 15-1

STUDY GUIDE Chapter 15, Section 1

For use with textbook pages 407–413

❶ THE FEDERAL RESERVE SYSTEM

KEY TERMS

member banks Commercial banks that are members of, and hold stock in, the Federal Reserve System (page 407)
bank holding company A corporation that owns one or more banks (page 413)
Regulation Z Federal regulation under which the Federal Reserve has the authority to extend truth-in-lending disclosures to millions of individuals who purchase or borrow from corporations, retail stores, automobile dealers, banks, and lending institutions (page 413)
currency The paper component of the money supply (page 413)
coins Metallic forms of money (page 413)

DRAWING FROM EXPERIENCE

If you have a checking account, have you ever wondered what happens after you write a check? Do you know what happens to paper money that is worn out? This section focuses on the different responsibilities of the Federal Reserve.

ORGANIZING YOUR THOUGHTS

Use the diagram below to help you take notes as you read the summaries that follow. Think about the various ways the Fed affects people's daily lives.

Enrich

Have students write an essay comparing the central banking system of a foreign country to the Federal Reserve System.

❹ CLOSE

Ask: How might things be different if the chairman of the Fed and the Board of Governors were elected rather than appointed?

Section 1 Assessment

Checking for Understanding

1. **Main Idea** What is the purpose of the Federal Reserve?

2. **Key Terms** Define member bank, bank holding company, Regulation Z, currency, coins.

3. **Describe** the structure of the Fed.

4. **List** eight areas in which the Fed has responsibility.

Applying Economic Concepts

5. **Truth-in-Lending Laws** Visit any local store that sells goods on credit—appliances, cars, or furniture, for example. Ask the owner or manager about the type of information that the store is required to disclose when the sale is made. Obtain copies of the disclosure forms and share them with your classmates.

Critical Thinking

6. **Synthesizing Information** One of the responsibilities of the Fed is to approve or disapprove mergers between state member banks. Explain how the mergers of two such banks would be classified according to the discussion of mergers in Chapter 3.

💿 **Practice** and **assess** key social studies skills with the *Glencoe Skillbuilder Interactive Workbook, Level 2.*

Section 1 Assessment Answers

1. to provide financial services to the government, regulate financial institutions, maintain the payments system, enforce consumer protection laws, and conduct monetary policy

2. All vocabulary terms are defined in the text.

3. Member banks contribute a small amount of funds to the Fed, for which they receive ownership shares in return. Member banks also select directors for each of the 12 district banks. Overall supervision of Fed is in the hands of a seven-member Board of Governors appointed by the president and confirmed by the Senate. The Board also dominates the Federal Open Market Committee, which makes monetary policy. Member banks can advise the Board through the Federal Advisory Council, which has one representative for each district bank.

4. state member bank supervision, holding companies, international operations, mergers, check clearing, consumer legislation, currency, margin requirements, maintain currency and coin

5. Materials gathered by students will differ.

6. horizontal merger, because both produce banking services

Profiles
IN
Economics

BACKGROUND

Texas Representative Frank Ikard once described Alan Greenspan in this way: "He is the kind of person who knows how many thousands of flat-headed bolts were used in a Chevrolet and what it would do to the national economy if you took out three of them." Ikard's respect for Greenspan's economic knowledge reflects the respect that a great many individuals, both in and out of government and business, hold for Greenspan.

TEACH

Assign pairs of students the following tasks: obtain a political cartoon that depicts Greenspan, obtain an article that profiles Greenspan, analyze Greenspan's presence on the Internet (number of sites, and so on), and identify references to Greenspan in the popular media (radio and television news reports and newspaper articles and editorials) within the past month. Have the pairs summarize or otherwise present their findings to the class. In a class discussion, integrate these presentations with students' answers to question 2 in Examining the Profile.

Enormous Power:

Alan Greenspan

(1926–)

The FED

interest rates

In some ways, Alan Greenspan is like many other people in government today—a longtime public servant, a respected administrator, and a fiscally conservative theorist with a Ph.D. in economics. What sets him apart, however, is that he is widely regarded as being the second most powerful person in America, after the president.

Greenspan is chairman of the Federal Reserve System's Board of Governors. As such, his views on the economy are closely monitored by almost everyone in the business community.

MOVING MARKETS

In late 1996, when stocks were setting record highs during a bull market, Greenspan asked publicly if prices weren't being propelled by the "irrational exuberance" of investors. The reaction to his remarks was almost instantaneous: investors, fearing that the Fed chairman was about to implement restrictive monetary policies that would drive stock prices down, began to sell. Within hours, stock exchanges around the world lost 2 percent of their value, and the Dow-Jones Industrial Average fell 145 points. Such is the power of Greenspan.

FISCAL CONSERVATISM

Greenspan is a longtime conservative. Early in his career, he was even a staunch advocate of the gold standard, which he saw as a way to assure monetary stability and fiscal responsibility by government. In his career he has worked as an economic consultant to private industry and served on a number of corporate and industry boards. Greenspan served from 1974 to 1977 as chair of the president's Council on Economic Advisors during the Ford administration. From 1981 to 1983, he chaired the National Commission on Social Security Reform, leading to the reform of the nation's Social Security system.

Greenspan joined the Fed in 1987 and was appointed chair of the Fed's Board of Governors by Presidents Reagan, Bush, and Clinton. Greenspan continues to be a strong supporter of the free market and an opponent of government intervention in the economy. As the second most powerful person in America, people will continue to scrutinize his every statement.

Examining the Profile

1. **Synthesizing Information** Explain how Greenspan's position as chairman of the Federal Reserve System's Board of Governors makes him extremely influential.

2. **Evaluating Information** Do you think Greenspan has too much power? Explain your answer.

Answers to Examining the Profile

1. Answers will vary. Students should note the basic responsibilities and powers of the Federal Reserve Board, and how Fed policies ripple through the economy.
2. Answers will vary. Students who think that Greenspan has too much power might find it at odds with a free market economy and a democracy. Students who think Greenspan does not have too much power might argue that such influence is unavoidable given the Fed's structure and position, and that it enables the government to help the economy as a whole.

Monetary Policy

Study Guide

Main Idea
Federal Reserve actions intended to stabilize the economy make up what is called monetary policy.

Reading Strategy
Graphic Organizer As you read the section, complete a graphic organizer similar to the one below.

Cause: The Fed raises the reserve requirement. → Effect:

Key Terms
monetary policy, fractional reserve system, legal reserves, reserve requirement, excess reserves, liabilities, assets, balance sheet, net worth, liquidity, savings account, time deposit, member bank reserve, easy money policy, tight money policy, open market operations, discount rate, margin requirement, moral suasion, selective credit controls

Objectives
After studying this section, you will be able to:
1. **Describe** the use of fractional reserves.
2. **Understand** the tools used to conduct monetary policy.

Applying Economic Concepts
Fractional Bank Reserves Did you know that most of our money supply exists in the form of intangible computer entries? Read to find out how the fractional reserve system works.

Cover Story

Fed Slashes Interest Rates

WASHINGTON—Federal Reserve policymakers cut their short-term interest rate target an aggressive half-point to 2% Tuesday.... This cut was the Fed's 10th attempt this year to shore up the U.S. economy, which is still

Interest rate cut to 2.0%

weakening after the Sept. 11 attacks. The moves represent some of the most furious rate-cutting in Fed history. . . . Fed officials have now pushed the rate banks charge each other for overnight loans to its lowest level since 1961. . . .

Major banks lowered the prime rate in [lockstep] with the Fed, bringing it down to 5% from 5.5%. That translates into lower rates for home-equity loans, business loans, and some credit cards.

—*USA Today*, November 7, 2001

O ne of the Federal Reserve System's most important responsibilities is that of monetary policy. **Monetary policy** is the expansion or contraction of the money supply in order to influence the cost and the availability of credit. The Fed, as you read in the cover story, does not hesitate to change interest rates whenever the economy's health is threatened.

Monetary policy is a structured process. In order to understand it better, it helps to understand the fractional reserve system that our banking system is based on.

Fractional Bank Reserves

The United States has a **fractional reserve system,** which requires banks and other depository institutions to keep a fraction of their deposits in the form of legal reserves. **Legal reserves** consist of coins and currency that depository institutions hold in their vaults, plus deposits with Federal Reserve district banks. Under this system, banks are subject to a **reserve requirement,** a rule stating that a percentage of every deposit be set aside as legal reserves.

CHAPTER 15: THE FED AND MONETARY POLICY **415**

1 FOCUS

Section Overview
This section explains fractional reserves and how commercial banks operate.

BELLRINGER
Motivational Activity

Project **transparency** and have students answer questions.

Available as blackline master.

Daily Focus Transparency 64

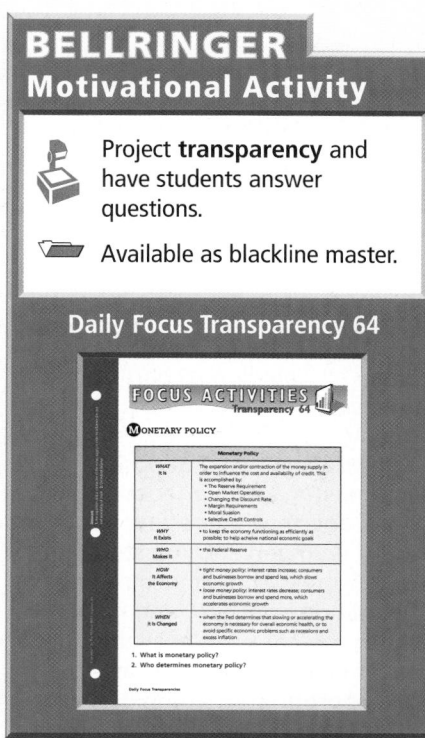

Study Guide

Reading Strategy
Have students create the graphic organizer.
Answers to Graphic: *Banks have less money to lend, and interest rates tend to increase.*

Preteaching Vocabulary
Call on volunteers to define the Key Terms.

RESOURCE MANAGER

📁 Reproducible Masters
- Reproducible Lesson Plan 15-2
- Daily Lecture Notes 15-2
- Guided Reading Activity 15-2
- Reading Essentials and Study Guide 15-2
- Section Quiz 15-2

🖥 Transparencies
- Daily Focus Transparency 64

Multimedia
- Interactive Economics!
- Interactive Tutor Self-Assessment Software
- ExamView® Pro Testmaker
- Presentation Plus!

2 TEACH

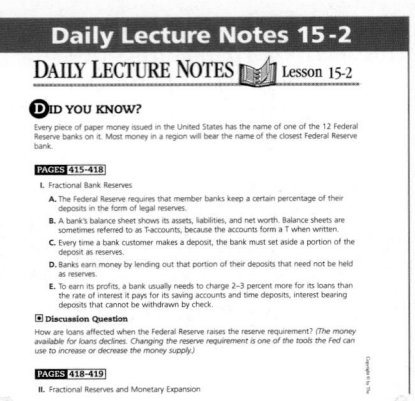

Daily Lecture Notes 15-2

DAILY LECTURE NOTES 📖 Lesson 15-2

❶ DID YOU KNOW?

Every piece of paper money issued in the United States has the name of one of the 12 Federal Reserve banks on it. Most money in a region will bear the name of the closest Federal Reserve bank.

PAGES 415-418

I. Fractional Bank Reserves

A. The Federal Reserve requires that member banks keep a certain percentage of their deposits in the form of legal reserves.

B. A bank's balance sheet shows its assets, liabilities, and net worth. Balance sheets are sometimes referred to as T-accounts, because the accounts form a T when written.

C. Every time a bank customer makes a deposit, the bank must set aside a portion of the deposit as reserves.

D. Banks earn money by lending out that portion of their deposits that need not be held as reserves.

E. To earn its profits, a bank usually needs to charge 2–3 percent more for its loans than the rate of interest it pays for its saving accounts and time deposits, interest bearing deposits that cannot be withdrawn by check.

❒ Discussion Question

How are loans affected when the Federal Reserve raises the reserve requirement? *(The money available for loans declines. Changing the reserve requirement is one of the tools the Fed can use to increase or decrease the money supply.)*

PAGES 418-419

II. Fractional Reserves and Monetary Expansion

L1 Monetary Expansion

Draw a two-column chart on the board, using *Reserve Requirement* and *Money Created* as headings. Tell students that a deposit of $100 has been made in a federal member bank and that the reserve requirement is 20 percent. Ask students to determine how much must be held in reserve *($20)* and how much the bank has available for loans *($80)*. Record responses in the appropriate column. Have students copy the chart into their notebooks and record the loans that could be made until the initial $100 is depleted. Ask students to note how much remains in reserve and how much money has been created. *($100 in reserve, $500 created)* **ELL**

Objectives, goals, and answers to the student activity can be found in the **Web Activity Lesson Plan** feature at epp.glencoe.com

---

To illustrate, the banking system today operates with a 12 percent reserve requirement against demand deposit accounts. That means that whenever someone deposits $100 to open a checking account, $12 must be set aside as vault cash or kept as a deposit at the Fed. The other $88 is called **excess reserves**—legal reserves in excess of the reserve requirement. The excess reserves are the funds the bank can lend to others who may want a loan.

How Banks Operate

To understand how a bank operates, it helps to examine the bank's liabilities and assets. Its **liabilities** are the debts and obligations to others. Its **assets** are the properties, possessions, and claims on others. Liabilities and assets generally are put together in the form of a **balance sheet**—a condensed statement showing all assets and liabilities at a given time. The balance sheet also reflects **net worth**—the excess of assets over liabilities, which is a measure of the value of a business.

Organizing a Bank

Suppose someone obtains a charter to start the hypothetical State Bank of Highland Heights. The bank is organized as a corporation, and the owners supply $20 so that the bank can obtain buildings and furniture before it opens for business. In return for this investment, the owners receive stock, which shows as net worth or equity. **Panel A** in **Figure 15.3** shows how the balance sheet of the bank might look as soon as it is organized.

The balance sheet shows the assets on the left and the liabilities and net worth on the right. To see why

Student Web Activity Visit the *Economics: Principles and Practices* Web site at **epp.glencoe.com** and click on *Chapter 15—Student Web Activities* for an activity on the Fed's monetary policy.

---

net worth is placed on the right side of the balance sheet, rearrange the definition of net worth from

Assets − Liabilities = Net Worth
to
Assets = Liabilities + Net Worth

The balance sheet in the figure is sometimes called a *T-account* because of its appearance, separating the assets from the liabilities and net worth the same way the equal sign does in the above equation. The T-account also works like an equal sign in that the entries on the left must always be equal to the entries on the right.

Accepting Deposits

Suppose that now a customer walks in and opens a checking account with $100 in currency. This transaction, shown in **Panel B** of **Figure 15.3**, is reflected on the balance sheet in two ways.

First, to indicate that the money is owed to the depositor, the $100 checking account (or demand deposit) is carried as a liability. Second, to indicate that the cash is the property of the bank, it also appears as an asset on the balance sheet. Actually, the $100 appears in two places on the asset side—$90 appears as cash, and $10 appears as required reserves. The size of the reserve is determined by the reserve requirement, which is assumed to be 10 percent in this example. If the requirement was 15 percent, $15 would be set aside.

Making Loans

Now that the bank has some cash on hand, it can make loans. Specifically, it is free to loan out $90 of excess reserves, the cash and currency not needed to fulfill the reserve requirement.

If another person enters the bank and borrows an amount equal to the excess reserves, the $90 is moved from the cash line to the loans, or accounts receivable, line in the balance sheet. These changes appear in **Panel C.** Note that there is no change in total assets, only in their distribution—a change from a noninterest-earning asset (cash) to an interest-earning one (a consumer loan).

If the bank charged 12 percent interest on the new loan, it would earn 12 percent of $90, or

---

MEETING SPECIAL NEEDS ACTIVITY

Learning Style: Logical/Mathematical Share with students copies of annual reports from banks or other large corporations. Ask them to locate the balance sheets in the annual reports and to identify the assets, liabilities, and net worth of each company as shown on each balance sheet they examine.

📁 Refer to *Inclusion for the Social Studies Classroom Strategies and Activities* in the TCR.

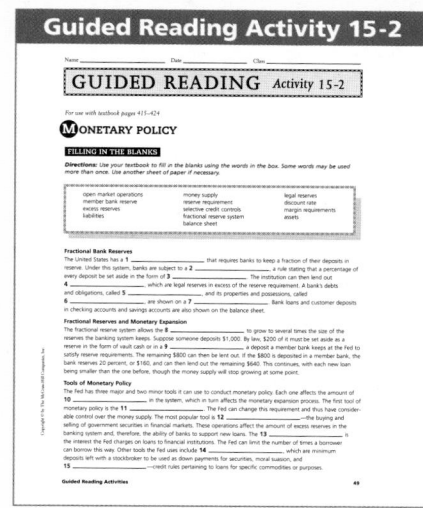

Guided Reading Activity 15-2

Answer: *$80*

Chart Skills Practice

If the reserve requirement was five percent, how much could the bank loan? *($95)* How would that change the bank's net worth? *(It would not.)*

L2 Understanding Ideas

Ask students to write a brief explanation of liquidity and how it might apply to the following kinds of bank accounts: demand deposit account, certificate of deposit, savings account, time deposit.

FREE ENTERPRISE ACTIVITY

Conduct the following simulation of open market operations. Organize students into two groups to represent the public and the Fed. Give 10 slips of paper, each representing $1,000, to each member of the public. Count and record on the board the total amount of money in circulation. Next, give 10 whole sheets of paper, each one depicting a $1,000 bond, to each person representing the Fed. Announce that a new issue of bonds is available for purchase at a good interest rate from the Fed, and have the public buy some. Count and record the money in circulation. Ask the class what happened to the money supply. *(decreased)* Next, have the Fed buy back some of the bonds. Count and record the money now in circulation among buyers. Ask students what has happened to the money supply. *(increased)* **BLOCK SCHEDULING** profit if it can maintain a 2- to 3-percent spread between the rate it charges on its loans and the rate it pays for borrowed funds in the form of CDs, savings accounts, and time deposits. If a bank pays 6 percent interest on money it receives, for example, it must loan money at a minimum of 8 or 9 percent to make enough income to pay expenses.

Fractional Reserves and Monetary Expansion

The fractional reserve system allows the money supply to grow to several times the size of the reserves the banking system keeps. **Figure 15.4** uses a reserve requirement of 20 percent to show how this can happen.

Banks as Businesses

Services to Customers Banks provide a source of loans for individuals and businesses that need to borrow money. Banks also provide safety and interest income for their depositors' money. *What are time deposits?*

Loans and Monetary Growth

In the figure, a depositor named Fred opens a demand deposit account (DDA) on Monday by depositing $1,000 cash in a bank. By law, $200 of Fred's deposit must be set aside as a reserve in the form of vault cash or in a **member bank reserve (MBR)**—a deposit a member bank keeps at the Fed to satisfy reserve requirements. The remaining $800 of excess reserves represents the bank's lending power.

On Tuesday, the bank lends its excess reserves of $800 to Bill. Bill can take the loan either in cash or in the form of a DDA with the bank. If he decides to take the DDA, the money never leaves the bank. Instead, it is treated as a new deposit, and 20 percent, or $160, is set aside as a reserve. The remaining $640 are excess reserves that can be lent to someone else.

On Wednesday, Maria enters the bank and borrows $640. She, too, can take the loan in cash or a DDA. If she elects to do the latter, the bank has a new $640 deposit, 20 percent of which must be set aside as a required reserve, leaving $512 of excess reserves.

By Wednesday, Fred has a $1,000 DDA, Bill has an $800 DDA, and Maria has either $640 in cash or a $640 DDA. This amounts to $2,440 in the hands of the nonbank public by the end of the business day—a process that began on Monday with the $1,000 deposit. As long as the bank continues to have excess reserves, the lending process can continue.

Reserves and the Money Supply

Because each new loan is smaller than the one before, the money supply will stop growing at some point. A mathematical relationship exists between the dollar amount of reserves, the reserve requirement, and the size of the money supply. For example, if the total dollar amount of reserves equals 20 percent of the money supply, we could write:

Total Reserves = .20 (Money Supply)
or,
$1,000 ÷ .20 = Money Supply
Therefore, $5,000 = Money Supply

This shows that $1,000 of total reserves, given a 20 percent reserve requirement, will result in a money supply of $5,000. This amount is the final outcome of the example in **Figure 15.4,** after Fred made his initial deposit.

After the money supply has reached its full size, further changes in the amount of total reserves can still affect it. Using the symbol Δ, meaning *change in*, we see that:

Δ Reserves = .20 (Δ Money Supply)
or,
Δ Reserves ÷ .20 = Δ Money Supply

Someone, for example, might withdraw $5 from the bank and keep it permanently in a wallet. The money supply would then change by:

Δ Reserves ÷ .20 = Δ Money Supply
or,
−$5 ÷ .20 = −$25

In other words, the money supply would shrink by $25, from $5,000 to $4,975.

Tools of Monetary Policy

 The Fed has three major and two minor tools it can use to conduct monetary policy. Each tool affects the amount of excess reserves in the system, which in turn affects the monetary expansion process described above. The outcome of monetary policy is to influence the cost and availability of credit. The direction of change depends on the objectives of the Federal Reserve System.

Under an **easy money policy,** the Fed allows the money supply to grow and interest rates to fall, which normally stimulates the economy. When interest rates are low, people tend to buy on credit.

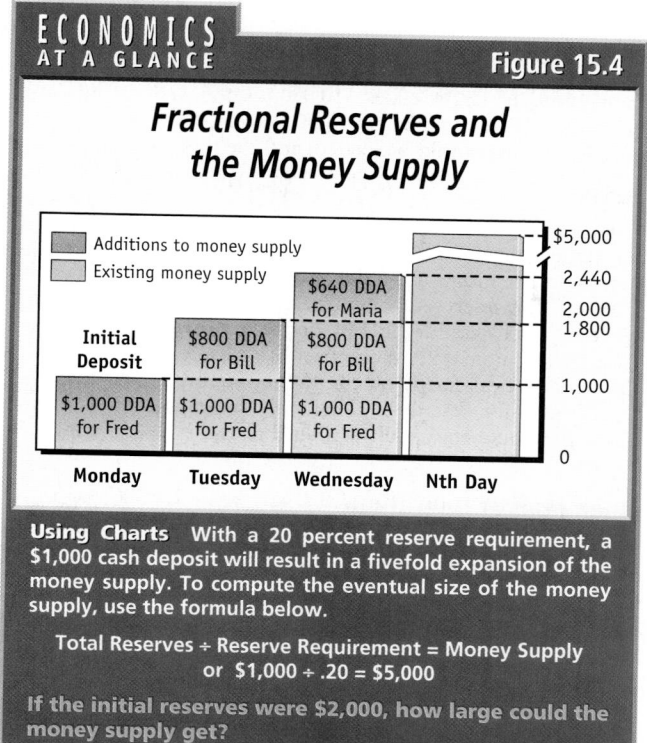

ECONOMICS AT A GLANCE

Figure 15.4

Fractional Reserves and the Money Supply

Using Charts With a 20 percent reserve requirement, a $1,000 cash deposit will result in a fivefold expansion of the money supply. To compute the eventual size of the money supply, use the formula below.

Total Reserves ÷ Reserve Requirement = Money Supply
or $1,000 ÷ .20 = $5,000

If the initial reserves were $2,000, how large could the money supply get?

ECONOMICS AT A GLANCE

Answer: *$10,000*

Chart Skills Practice
What would be the eventual size of the money supply if there was a 25 percent reserve requirement? *($1,000 ÷ 0.25 = $4,000)* A 15 percent reserve requirement? *($1,000 ÷ 0.15 = $6,666.67)*

L2 Applying Ideas
Organize students into several groups to role-play members of the Federal Reserve Board of Governors. Tell half the groups they must decide on a policy to expand the money supply, and the other half to develop a policy to restrict the growth of the money supply. Have groups consider the following: What tools of monetary policy should be used? How should they be used? Why should they be used? Call on group representatives to explain their plans to the class.

F.Y.I.
The limits within which the Fed can adjust the reserve requirement were set by the Depository Institution's Deregulation and Monetary Control Act of 1980. The present reserve requirement is in the current edition of the *Federal Reserve Bulletin.*

This encourages sales at stores and production at factories. Businesses also tend to borrow and then invest in new plants and equipment when money is cheap. Under a **tight money policy,** the Fed restricts the growth of the money supply, which drives interest rates up. When interest rates are high, consumers and businesses borrow and spend less, which slows economic growth.

Reserve Requirement

The first tool of monetary policy is the reserve requirement. Within limits that Congress sets, the Fed can change this requirement for all checking, time, or savings accounts in the country.

This tool gives the Fed considerable control over the money supply. For instance, suppose the Fed lowers the reserve requirement in the previous

CHAPTER 15: THE FED AND MONETARY POLICY **419**

EXTENDING THE CONTENT

The Fed and Consumer Credit In 1980 the Fed imposed restraints on consumer borrowing in an effort to restrict the money supply. Banks were required to make a deposit with the Federal Reserve Banks equal to 15 percent of any increase in total outstanding credit in the form of credit card purchases or unsecured personal loans. Because this special deposit earned no interest, it would increase the cost of making loans and, therefore, discourage the expansion of credit and the money supply.

THE GLOBAL ECONOMY

The Euro: Today and in the Future
Initially 11 nations adopted the euro, which has a new currency symbol, €.
The designs of bills and coins were carefully chosen to reflect a generalized European heritage without specific references to any country. Shops in many euro countries started posting prices in both their own currency and in euros, even before the latter was in circulation. People throughout the world will have to add the euro symbol to their computers and typewriters.

Answers:
1. *to have a single currency that people in European countries can use in their own and other European countries without worrying about currency fluctuations*
2. *adapting computers to bill and pay people in euros; converting business transactions between subsidiaries into euros; changing over payroll, benefits, and tax payments into euros*
3. *Answers might note that it will be hard for some people to get used to euros and a single currency. Others might say it will be confusing to have more than one system going at the same time.*

example from 20 to 10 percent. More money could be loaned to Bill, Maria, and others, and the money supply could reach $10,000. If the Fed raises the reserve requirement to 40 percent, however, less money would be loaned, and the money supply would be smaller. The effects of different reserve requirements are shown in **Figure 15.5.**

Historically, the Fed has been reluctant to use the reserve requirement as a policy tool, in part because other monetary policy tools work better. Even so, the reserve requirement can be a very powerful tool should the Fed decide to use it. **Figure 15.6** summarizes the impact of a change in the reserve requirement on the money supply in the manner just described, along with the impact of the other monetary tools described below.

Open Market Operations

The second and most popular tool of monetary policy is **open market operations**—the buying and selling of government securities in financial markets. Open market operations are one of the methods the Federal Reserve can use to influence short-term interest rates. Open market operations involve the purchase or sale of government securities by the Federal Reserve. When the Fed purchases government securities, it increases the supply of money, putting downward pressure on interest rates. When the Fed sells government securities, it decreases the supply of money, putting upward pressure on interest rates. Open market operations affect the amount of excess reserves in the banking system and, therefore, the ability of banks to support new loans.

Suppose the Fed decides to increase the money supply. To do so, it buys government securities from a dealer who specializes in large-volume transactions of those securities. The Fed pays for the securities by writing a check drawn on itself. The dealer then deposits the check with his or her bank. The bank forwards the check to the Fed for payment. At this

THE GLOBAL ECONOMY

THE EURO: TODAY AND IN THE FUTURE

European industry is transferring to a single currency, the euro. Monetary union means that industries can build plants, sell products, and raise capital in other European markets without worrying about currency fluctuations.

Retooling is costly, however. Most multinational corporations will need to invest millions of dollars. Some are converting their entire operations to the *euro* system immediately. Other companies are instituting the changes in phases. In step 1, for example, companies adapt their computers to bill customers and pay suppliers in euros. At the same time, they will maintain dual accounting in euros and national currencies. Step 2 includes converting transactions such as budget allocations and payments between subsidiaries into euros. Step 3 includes the changeover of human resource functions, including payroll and benefits and paying taxes in eurodollars.

What does the changeover mean for consumers? The old currency units won't disappear until mid-2002, and many consumers may use them till the last minute. Even if consumers aren't yet using euro notes and coins, their bank accounts, retirement funds, and in many cases paychecks will be expressed in euros.

—*Business Week*, December 14, 1998

Critical Thinking
1. **Analyzing Information** What is the purpose of the euro?
2. **Sequencing Information** What steps are involved in the transition to the euro?
3. **Drawing Conclusions** What might be drawbacks that Europe could face during the changeover?

420 UNIT 4 MACROECONOMICS: POLICIES

INTERDISCIPLINARY CONNECTIONS ACTIVITY

Geography Ask students to use a map to plan a trip through the 11 countries that originally adopted the euro. (The countries are Austria, Belgium, Germany, Finland, France, Ireland, Italy, Luxembourg, the Netherlands, Portugal, and Spain.) Ask students to draw a route map for their trip. Have them also find out the names of each country's original currency and identify the countries' capital cities. Then ask students to use reference materials to list one product they might like to buy in each of the 11 countries.

BLOCK SCHEDULING

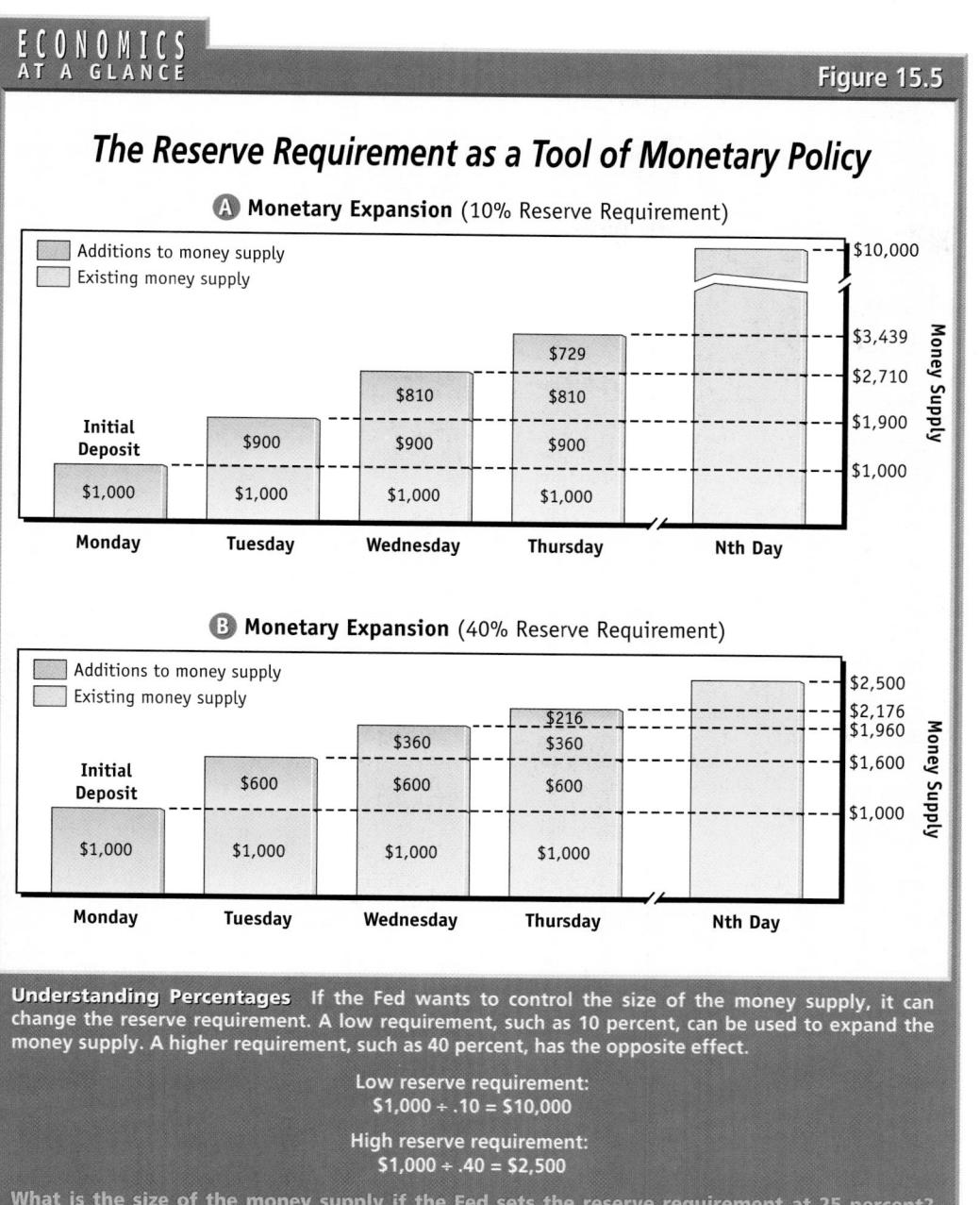

The Reserve Requirement as a Tool of Monetary Policy

A Monetary Expansion (10% Reserve Requirement)

B Monetary Expansion (40% Reserve Requirement)

Understanding Percentages If the Fed wants to control the size of the money supply, it can change the reserve requirement. A low requirement, such as 10 percent, can be used to expand the money supply. A higher requirement, such as 40 percent, has the opposite effect.

Low reserve requirement:
$1,000 ÷ .10 = $10,000

High reserve requirement:
$1,000 ÷ .40 = $2,500

What is the size of the money supply if the Fed sets the reserve requirement at 25 percent?

CHAPTER 15: THE FED AND MONETARY POLICY **421**

ECONOMICS
AT A GLANCE

Answer: $4,000

Chart Skills Practice

What would be the addition to the money supply if the Fed set the reserve requirement at 20 percent? ($5,000)

L3 Illustrating Ideas

Encourage students to draw cartoons or other forms of visual images that illustrate easy money policy and tight money policy. Offer the following examples: for tight money policy—an accordion player (the Fed) squeezing an accordion (money supply); for easy money policy—an accordion player easing pressure on an accordion.

CYBERNOMICS

The Fed Online The Federal Reserve has the Web site, the "National Information Center" (NIC), that offers information to the public about banks and other financial institutions. Information is available on both domestic and foreign institutions and can be researched by the location or the name of the institution.

EXTENDING THE CONTENT

Buying Treasury Securities Some individual investors in Treasury securities prefer to buy through their own commercial banks; however, other investors, in order to avoid the fee that banks charge, deal directly with a regional Federal Reserve Bank or one of its branches. Interested investors must make an offer for the amount of securities they wish to purchase. This offer must be submitted on the appropriate forms and accompanied by payment, either currency or a certified personal check. Investors consider Treasury securities an attractive investment. These securities are safe because they are backed by the federal government and can be sold prior to the maturity date on the Treasury securities market. (Buying securities is covered in Chapter 13.)

CURRICULUM CONNECTION

The Arts The back of the $1 bill shows both the front and back of the Great Seal of the United States. On the front of the seal, an eagle holds an olive branch, which symbolizes peace. It has 13 berries and 13 leaves. In the eagle's other talon are 13 arrows, symbolizing war. The 13 units represent the 13 colonies. The eagle's head is turned toward the olive branch, symbolizing a desire for peace. The pyramid on the reverse of the seal stands for permanence and strength. It is unfinished, representing future U.S. growth and the goal of perfection.

F.Y.I.

The FDIC currently covers losses up to $100,000. If you have several accounts under one name—$90,000 in a CD, $50,000 in a savings account, and $35,000 in a checking account—the maximum you can collect is $100,000.

Tools of the Federal Reserve

FOX TROT

Changes in Interest The most important job of the Federal Reserve System is to maintain a stable supply of money for the economy. The Fed uses several basic tools to carry out this responsibility. *How do changes in the discount rate affect other interest rates?*

---

point, the Fed "pays" the check by increasing the bank's MBR with the Fed.

The result is that whenever the Fed writes a check, more reserves are pumped into the banking system. Because only some of these additional reserves are needed to back existing deposits, the excess reserves can be loaned out, thus increasing the money supply.

If the Fed wants to contract the money supply, it can sell billions of dollars of government securities back to dealers. Dealers pay for the securities with checks drawn on their own banks. The Fed then processes the checks by reducing the MBRs of dealers' banks. With fewer reserves in the banking system, fewer loans are made and the money supply contracts—driving interest rates up.

The Federal Open Market Committee (FOMC) conducts open-market operations. Normally the FOMC decides if interest rates and monetary growth are too high, too low, or just right. After the committee votes to set targets, officials at the trading desk take over. The trading desk is the physical location at the Fed's New York district bank where the buying and selling actually takes place. The officials at the desk buy and sell bonds daily to maintain the targets set by the FOMC. The desk is permanently located in New York to be close to the nation's financial markets.

422 UNIT 4 MACROECONOMICS: POLICIES

Discount Rate

As a central bank, the Fed makes loans to othe depository institutions. The **discount rate**—th interest the Fed charges on loans to financial insti tutions—is the third major tool of monetary policy

Private individuals and businesses cannot bo row from the Fed. Banks can, and frequently do If the discount rate goes up, fewer banks will wan to borrow from the Fed. This will reduce th amount of money these banks have available t loan to their customers and will force interes rates up. Changes in the discount rate usuall result in similar changes in other interest rates.

A bank might obtain a loan from the Fed for tw reasons. First, it could have an unexpected drop i its MBRs, which would shrink its excess reserves. I this case, the bank could go to the Fed and arrang a short-term loan to cover the shortfall.

Second, a bank could be faced with seasona demands for loans. A bank in an agricultural are for example, might face a heavy demand for loan during the planting season. In that case, it woul need additional MBRs to support the loans mad in the spring.

Most institutions can borrow from the Feder Reserve, including member and nonmembe banks, savings institutions, and even cred unions. The Fed, however, views borrowing as

---

INTERDISCIPLINARY CONNECTIONS ACTIVITY

Literature Have students read selections from personal stories of the Great Depression, such as *Hard Times: An Oral History of the Great Depression* by Studs Terkel. Some of the personal histories in the book are about people who lost all their savings during the Depression. Interested students can read the entire work, or read novels that deal with the effects of the Great Depression. Have students prepare reports to share with the class that identify common characteristics found in the various pieces they read.

privilege rather than a right. As a result, the Fed may limit the number of times a borrower can borrow from the Fed.

Margin Requirements

Before the Great Depression, people speculated wildly in the stock market. Easy credit in the form of **margin requirements,** minimum deposits left with a stockbroker to be used as down payments to buy other securities, made much of the speculation possible.

For example, with a margin requirement as low as 10 percent, a person only had to deposit $100 with a stockbroker to purchase $1,000 worth of stocks. The stockbroker would supply the remaining $900. If the stock rose to $1,300, it could be sold and the investor would net $400 after repaying $900 to the broker. If, however, the stock dropped to $900, the broker would sell the stock to protect his or her own loan if the investor could not come up with additional money.

Because credit was easily obtained and because margins were so low, the margins were easy to forfeit when modest declines in stock prices occurred. In fact, many investors lost everything they had when stock prices crashed in 1929. Today, most margin requirements are set at 50 percent, meaning an investor has to put up at least half the money needed to buy eligible stocks and bonds. The Federal Reserve sets the margin requirement and also monitors activity on the stock market. It also publishes a list of stocks that are eligible for margin loans.

The Fed seldom uses margin requirements as an active tool of monetary policy. Instead, it uses them very selectively to dampen or stimulate spending on equities in the stock market.

Other Tools

The Fed may also use two other methods to control the money supply. These are moral suasion and selective credit controls.

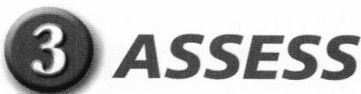

Answer: *expands; contracts*

3 ASSESS

Assign Section 2 Assessment as homework or as an in-class activity.

Have students use **Interactive Tutor Self-Assessment Software** to review Section 2.

ECONOMICS AT A GLANCE

Figure 15.6

Summary of Monetary Policy Tools

Tool	Fed Action	Effect on Excess Reserves	Money Supply
Reserve Requirement	Lower	Frees excess reserves because fewer are needed to back existing deposits in the system.	Expands
	Raise	More reserves are required to back existing deposits. Excess reserves contract.	Contracts
Open Market Operations	Buy bonds	Checks written by the Fed add to excess reserves in the system.	Expands
	Sell bonds	Checks written by buyers are subtracted from reserves. Excess reserves in the system contract.	Contracts
Discount Rate	Lower	Additional reserves can be obtained at lower cost. Excess reserves expand.	Expands
	Raise	Additional reserves through borrowing are now more expensive. Excess reserves are not added.	Contracts

Using Charts The key to monetary policy is to see how the excess reserves in the system are affected. What happens to the money supply when the Fed increases excess reserves? When it decreases excess reserves?

CHAPTER 15: THE FED AND MONETARY POLICY **423**

EXTENDING THE CONTENT

The 1933 Bank Holiday The importance of people's confidence in banks became apparent on March 1, 1933, when six states declared a "bank holiday" that closed banks to prevent depositors from making a run on the banks to withdraw their money. Bank panics peaked a few days later. By March 13, banks around the country began to reopen, and by the end of March, three-fourths of the nation's banks had reopened. In June, Congress passed the Banking Act of 1933, which established the Federal Deposit Insurance Corporation (FDIC).

Visual Instruction

Answer to Caption:
minimum deposits left with a stockbroker to be used as down payments to buy other securities

Reteach

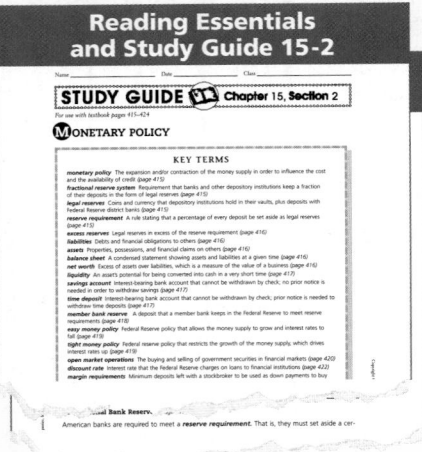

Reading Essentials and Study Guide 15-2

Enrich

Have students investigate the most recent action taken by the Fed on monetary policy. Have them report their findings to the class.

4 CLOSE

Have students state which of the tools of monetary policy is the most effective in controlling the money supply. Ask them to offer explanations for their selections.

Tools of the Federal Reserve

Margin Requirements Depositors besiege a merchant bank in Passaic, New Jersey, following the Wall Street crash in 1929. During the 1920s, the common practice of buying on margin attracted thousands of people to pour their savings into stocks. *What are margin requirements?*

Moral suasion is the use of persuasion such as announcements, press releases, articles in newspapers and magazines, and testimony before Congress. Moral suasion works because bankers often try to anticipate changes in monetary policy.

Suppose that the chairperson of the Fed is called before Congress to give his or her view on the state of the economy. Assume also that the chair states that interest rates seem somewhat low, and that it might be good for the economy if they were raised. These statements might lead bankers to expect a tighter money policy in the next few weeks. As a result, they might be less willing to loan their excess reserves, and they might even raise their interest rates by a small amount. In the end, the money supply might contract just slightly, even if the Fed did no more than offer its views.

A second method is **selective credit controls**—credit rules pertaining to loans for specific commodities or purposes. These controls took the form of minimum down payments on cars and other consumer goods during World War II and the Korean War. Selective credit controls during those periods were imposed to free factories to produce war materials.

Section 2 Assessment

Checking for Understanding

1. **Main Idea** What is the purpose of monetary policy?

2. **Key Terms** Define monetary policy, fractional reserve system, legal reserves, reserve requirement, excess reserves, liabilities, assets, balance sheet, net worth, liquidity, savings account, time deposit, member bank reserve, easy money policy, tight money policy, open market operations, discount rate, margin requirement, moral suasion, selective credit controls.

3. **Explain** how fractional reserves are used.

4. **Describe** the relationship between the reserve requirement, reserves, and the size of the money supply.

5. **Describe** the three major tools of monetary policy.

Applying Economic Concepts

6. **Fractional Bank Reserves** Your local national bank is required to keep its reserves in the form of vault cash and member deposits with the Fed. Why do you suppose that other assets, such as common stocks or real estate, are not suitable reserves?

Critical Thinking

7. **Drawing Conclusions** At times, someone with a good credit rating may not be able to get a loan. When this happens, the potential customer may be told to try again in the near future. What does this tell you about the bank's reserves? How should the customer react to a situation like this?

 Practice and **assess** key social studies skills with the *Glencoe Skillbuilder Interactive Workbook, Level 2.*

Section 2 Assessment Answers

1. to influence the cost and availability of credit; to keep the economy healthy

2. All vocabulary terms are defined in the text.

3. They are used to control the supply of money.

4. The reserve requirement determines the amount of legal reserves a bank has to keep, which then determines how much money a bank can lend and the size of the money supply.

5. Answers should describe reserve requirements, open market operations, and the discount rate.

6. They have a low degree of liquidity.

7. The bank is fully loaned out (temporarily has no excess reserves). This is not unusual; customers should not be offended.

JULY 20, 1998

───Newsclip

Bank mergers are becoming more common. Supporters and nonsupporters of bank mergers debate whether these consolidations benefit customers.

Bank Mergers:
Who Benefits?

Although the number of commercial banks in the U.S. fell from 13,123 in 1988 to 9,215 in 1997, there's still no end in sight to the banking industry's rapid consolidation. But is the merger wave beneficial to consumers?

Advocates claim that mergers produce efficiencies that lower costs and thus permit better service to customers. Skeptics worry that mergers allow banks to cut services because they now face less competition. A recent study by Katerina Simons and Joanna Stavins of the Federal Reserve Bank of Boston tends to support the latter view.

Drawing on nationwide data covering some 500 banks from 1985 to 1995, the two economists looked at how market concentration and mergers affected interest rates on customers' deposits. They found that merged banks actually tend to lower deposit rates in the wake of a merger (but only in the first year following the merger). More important, while rivals of newly merged

banks initially boost interest rates after the merger–presumably to gain customers–they subsequently lower rates even more. Thus, their depositors lose out over the long term.

Why don't the merged banks follow the lead of their unmerged competitors by lowering their interest rates over the

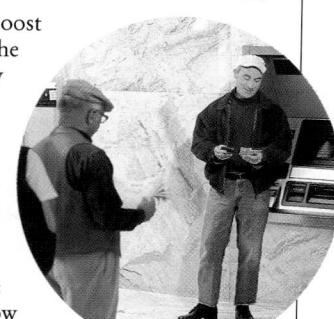

Questions remain as to whether bank mergers benefit or hurt the customer.

long term? The authors speculate that service declines so much after a merger that merged banks have to pay slightly higher interest rates than their rivals to retain customers.

In any case, the study's overall conclusion is that banks tend to pay lower interest rates in markets that become more concentrated. And that, say the authors, is something that antitrust regulators need to look at more closely.

–Reprinted from July 20, 1998 issue of *Business Week*, by special permission, copyright © 1998 by The McGraw-Hill Companies, Inc.

Current Mortgage Offerings

RATE %		APR %
7.375	1 Year ARM 1-4 Family	9.880
9.375	5 Year ARM 1-4 Family	10.01
9.625	7 Year ARM 1-4 Family	10.14
10.00	30 Year Fixed 1-4 Family	10.37

WE'RE A **NYCE** BANK

Examining the Newsclip

1. **Analyzing Information** Describe how advocates and skeptics view mergers between banks.

2. **Understanding Cause and Effect** How are interest rates on customer deposits affected by bank mergers?

CHAPTER 15: THE FED AND MONETARY POLICY **425**

TEACH

Help students clarify the arguments in favor of bank mergers and those against mergers. Work with the class to draw up a chart with a "for" side and an "against" side. Ask them to list the specific arguments given in the newsclip. Ask students to make a list of the banks in their local community and to analyze the choices that bank customers do or do not have. Students may also interview parents and other adults to find out what banks they used in the past and what happened to them.

Refer to ***Business Week Focus on the New Economy*** in the TCR for additional unit-based articles.

Answers to Examining the Newsclip

1. Advocates say mergers result in greater efficiency that, in turn, allows the merged banks to lower costs and therefore provide better services to customers. Skeptics say that merged banks take advantage of the fact that there is less competition by cutting services.

2. In the short term, they go up, and in the long term, they go down.

① FOCUS

Section Overview
This section discusses monetary policy and its effects.

BELLRINGER
Motivational Activity

- Project **transparency** and have students answer questions.

- Available as blackline master.

Daily Focus Transparency 62

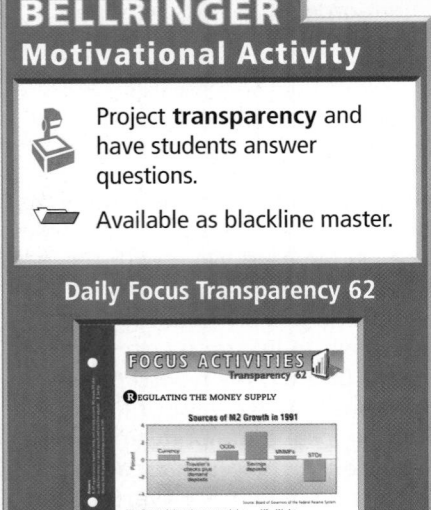

Study Guide

Reading Strategy
Have students create the graphic organizer.
Answers to Graphic: *M1: travelers' checks, coins, currency, demand deposits, other checkable deposits; M2: M1, small denomination time deposits, savings deposits, money market funds*

Preteaching Vocabulary
Use the Vocabulary Puzzle-Maker to create crossword and word-search puzzles.

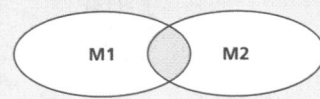

Monetary Policy, Banking, and the Economy

Study Guide

Main Idea
Changes in the money supply affect the interest rate, the availability of credit, and the price level.

Reading Strategy
Graphic Organizer As you read the section, complete a graphic organizer similar to the one below by listing the components of M1 and M2.

M1   M2

Key Terms
prime rate, quantity theory of money, monetizing the debt, real rate of interest, M1, M2

Objectives
After studying this section, you will be able to:
1. **Explain** how monetary policy affects interest rates in the short run.
2. **Relate** monetary expansion to inflation in the long run.
3. **Identify** the two major definitions of money.
4. **Describe** how interest rates are affected by political pressure.

Applying Economic Concepts
Money Where do you keep your money? On your person? In a savings or checking account? Read to find out why the answers to these questions make the definition of money more complicated than it seems.

Cover Story

Fed Worried About Future Inflation

WASHINGTON (AP)—Members of the Federal Reserve expressed concerns about future inflation at their May meeting, leading them to vote unanimously for a policy directive leaning toward an increase in interest rates, according to minutes of the meeting released Thursday.

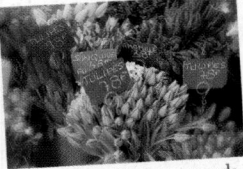

Inflation can affect many goods.

While the FOMC members agreed that recent improvements in the nation's productivity allowed more room for noninflationary economic growth, they worried that growth, which came in at a 4.3 percent annual rate in the first quarter, was still too rapid to keep inflation under control. . . .

—*The Washington Post*, July 1, 1999

426

The impact of monetary policy on the economy is complex. In the short run, monetary policy affects interest rates and the availability of credit. In the long run, it affects inflation which—as we saw in the cover story—is one of the Fed's major concerns. In addition, no one can be sure how long it will take for the effects of monetary policy to impact the economy.

Short-Run Impact

In the short run, an increase or a decrease in the money supply affects the interest rate, which is the price of credit. When the Fed expands the money supply, the cost of credit goes down. When the Fed contracts the money supply, the cost of credit goes up.

This short-run relationship between money and interest rates is shown in **Figure 15.7.** The demand curve for money has the usual shape which shows that more money will be demanded

---

RESOURCE MANAGER

Reproducible Masters
- Reproducible Lesson Plan 15-3
- Daily Lecture Notes 15-3
- Guided Reading Activity 15-3
- Reading Essentials and Study Guide 15-3
- Section Quiz 15-3

Transparencies
- Daily Focus Transparency 62

Multimedia
- Vocabulary PuzzleMaker CD-ROM
- Interactive Economics!
- Interactive Tutor Self-Assessment Software
- ExamView® Pro Testmaker
- Presentation Plus!

when the price of credit is low. The supply curve, however, does not have its usual shape. Instead, it is vertical, indicating that the supply of money is fixed at any given time.

Before the market is disturbed, the interest rate, as shown in **Panel A**, is at 10 percent. If the Fed expands the money supply to **S¹S¹**, the interest rate falls to 8 percent. A contraction of the money supply, as shown in **Panel B**, increases the rate from 10 to 12 percent.

Although the Fed tries to do what it thinks is best for the economy, people do not always agree with its decisions. In 1981, for example, the Fed was criticized for allowing interest rates to get too high. In that year, the **prime rate**—the best or lowest interest rate commercial bankers charge their customers—reached 21.5 percent. Critics felt that the economy would have been better off if the Fed had expanded the money supply, thus lowering interest rates. Supporters, however, understood that these policies were necessary to achieve long-run goals.

Long-Run Impact

In the long run, changes in the supply of money affect the general level of prices. This relationship, formally known as the **quantity theory of money,** has been demonstrated repeatedly in history.

Historical Precedents

When the Spanish brought gold and silver back to Spain from the Americas in the 1700s, the increase in the money supply started inflation that lasted for 100 years. When the Continental Congress issued $250 million of currency during the Revolutionary War, the economy suffered severe inflation. A similar thing happened during the Civil War when nearly $500 million of greenbacks were printed.

Monetizing the Debt

When the federal government financed the Vietnam War with deficit spending in the 1960s, interest rates started to rise. To keep the rates from going up too high, the Fed decided to **monetize the debt**—create enough extra money to offset the

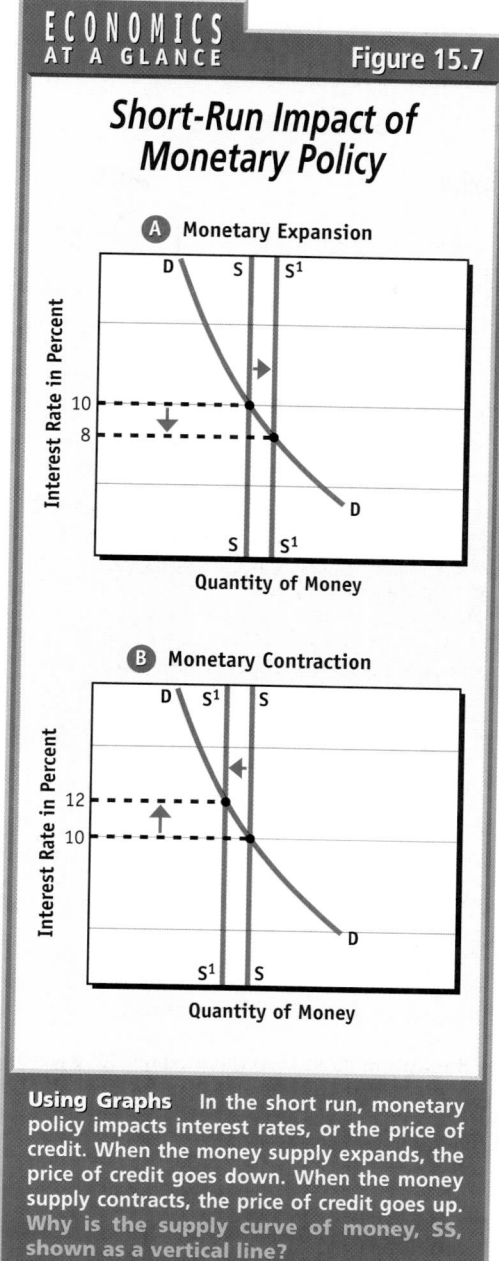

ECONOMICS
AT A GLANCE   Figure 15.7

Short-Run Impact of Monetary Policy

A Monetary Expansion

B Monetary Contraction

Using Graphs In the short run, monetary policy impacts interest rates, or the price of credit. When the money supply expands, the price of credit goes down. When the money supply contracts, the price of credit goes up. Why is the supply curve of money, SS, shown as a vertical line?

CHAPTER 15: THE FED AND MONETARY POLICY **427**

2 TEACH

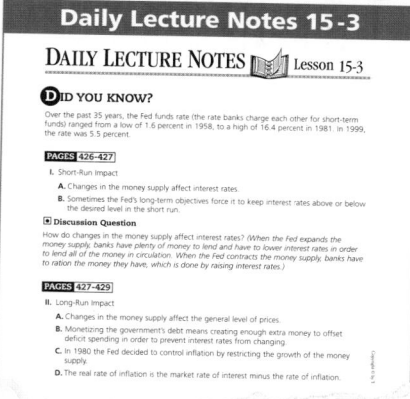

Daily Lecture Notes 15-3

DAILY LECTURE NOTES — Lesson 15-3

DID YOU KNOW?
Over the past 35 years, the Fed funds rate (the rate banks charge each other for short-term funds) ranged from a low of 1.6 percent in 1958, to a high of 16.4 percent in 1981. In 1999, the rate was 5.5 percent.

PAGES 426-427
I. Short-Run Impact
   A. Changes in the money supply affect interest rates.
   B. Sometimes the Fed's long-term objectives force it to keep interest rates above or below the desired level in the short run.

Discussion Question
How do changes in the money supply affect interest rates? (When the Fed expands the money supply, banks have plenty of money to lend and have to lower interest rates in order to lend all of the money in circulation. When the Fed contracts the money supply, banks have to ration the money they have, which is done by raising interest rates.)

PAGES 427-429
II. Long-Run Impact
   A. Changes in the money supply affect the general level of prices.
   B. Monetizing the government's debt means creating enough extra money to offset deficit spending in order to prevent interest rates from changing.
   C. In 1980 the Fed decided to control inflation by restricting the growth of the money supply.
   D. The real rate of inflation is the market rate of interest minus the rate of inflation.

L1 Class Project

Most Fed district banks shred old money when they take it out of circulation. Have volunteers call your local Fed bank and ask if your class can have some shredded money for a class project or fund-raiser. The shredded money is usually free if you can specify the use of the currency—filler for paperweights, bookmarks, and so on.

ECONOMICS
AT A GLANCE

Answer: *to indicate that it is fixed at any given time*

Graph Skills Practice

Ask: Explain why the price of credit falls when the money supply increases. *(The price of credit—the interest rate—is like any other price; it goes down when supply increases.)*

MEETING SPECIAL NEEDS ACTIVITY

Learning Disabled For students who have trouble with writing, it will be helpful to modify instructional and evaluative procedures used in class. These students may find taking notes virtually impossible. Appoint three or four students to be "scribes," and provide them with either carbon paper or carbonless copy paper. As the class discusses Section 3, have the scribes take complete notes, which they can later share with those who need them. Have poorer note takers write only key words.

Refer to *Inclusion for the Social Studies Classroom Strategies and Activities* in the TCR.

ECONOMICS
AT A GLANCE

Answer: *inflation*

Graph Skills Practice

Ask: Explain the crowding-out effect. *(higher-than-normal interest rates that result from heavy government borrowing)*

THE GLOBAL ECONOMY

Turkey Inflation has been a serious problem in Turkey, which worked to bring down its level of inflation from nearly 100 percent in 1997 to 70 percent in 1998. A public debt of 42 percent of government spending made it difficult to fight inflation. In addition, a series of earthquakes in 1999 had major negative effects on Turkey's economy.

ECONOMICS
AT A GLANCE
Figure 15.8

Monetizing the Debt

Using Graphs When the government borrows to cover a debt in the federal budget, interest rates tend to rise because of the increased demand for credit. This raises the possibility of crowding out. If the Fed expands the money supply just enough to offset the borrowing, interest rates may remain unchanged. **What are the long-run effects of monetizing the debt?**

deficit spending in order to keep interest rates from changing. The process of monetizing the debt is illustrated in **Figure 15.8,** where **DD** and **SS** represent the initial demand and supply of money.

Suppose that the government borrows $25 billion, shifting the demand curve for money from **DD** to **D¹D¹.** If the Fed does not take any action, the interest rate would rise from 8 to 10 percent. If the Fed wants to keep the interest rate from rising, it could increase the money supply from **SS** to **S¹S¹** and push interest rates back down to their original level.

In the short run, then, the Fed can increase the money supply just enough to keep the interest rate from rising. This procedure is effective if done infrequently. Repeated short-run attempts to keep rates low, however, result in a long-term

expansion of the money supply, making inflation worse.

Taming Inflation

Much of the federal debt was monetized from the late 1960s until the late 1970s. During this period, the money supply grew at rates of 12 percent or more for several years in a row. As inflation worsened, the price of most goods and services—including interest rates—also went up. Attempts by the Fed to keep interest rates low by increasing the supply of money worked at first, but eventually the policy intensified inflation.

By 1980 the Fed realized that it had to choose between interest rates and inflation—and it chose to control inflation by restricting the growth of the money supply. When this happened, the prime rate rose and by 1981 reached 21.5 percent. Most people did not like the high interest rates at the time, but today they recognize that the tight money policies were necessary to bring down inflation.

Because inflation distorts our economic statistics, it is useful to consider the **real rate of interest**—the market rate of interest minus the rate of inflation. To illustrate, the 21.5 percent interest rate in 1981 was not as bad as it seemed when you consider that the inflation rate was 10.5 percent. Subtracting the

STANDARD & POOR'S   INFOBYTE

The Prime Rate The prime rate is a loan rate charged by banks to their best or "prime" customers. The rate is determined by general trends in interest rates. As rates decline, the prime rate will also move lower. However, it does not typically move on a day-by-day basis. Prime-rate changes are usually led by major money center banks. Normally, the prime rate will move in steps and then remain constant until a major rate change has been made. This usually happens when the Federal Reserve makes major changes in monetary policy.

FREE ENTERPRISE ACTIVITY

Invite a local bank official to visit the class to make a presentation on the status of the banking industry today. Suggest that the speaker cover such topics as the reasons banks fail, the steps government agencies take to deal with failed banks, and the safeguards the industry and the federal government have put in place to prevent further failures. After the presentation, have students write short essays summarizing the major points made by the guest speaker. 📦 **BLOCK SCHEDULING** inflation rate from the interest rate results in an 11.0 percent real rate of interest for that year.

Other Monetary Policy Issues

When the Fed conducts monetary policy, it has several other issues to consider. The first issue involves the timing and burden of monetary policy.

Timing and Burden

Sometimes a tight money policy will show results in six months. At other times, the impact might not be felt for two years. The same happens when the Fed follows an easy money policy. Such variations in timing make it difficult to use monetary policy to fine-tune the economy.

A second problem is that monetary policy has an uneven impact on the economy. If the Fed follows a tight money policy to control inflation, interest rates go up. This increase hurts some industries like homebuilding and auto manufacturing more than others because of higher borrowing costs. If the Fed follows an easy monetary policy, interest rates may go down—thereby benefiting homebuilding and auto making more than other industries.

Present vs. Future Allocation

The Fed also realizes that interest rates and inflation affect the allocation of scarce resources between present and future uses. When interest rates are low, people find it easier to finance the purchase of a car, house, or college education right away. When people spend more today, however, they end up saving less—and therefore they consume less in the future.

High interest rates have the opposite effect. When rates are high, some purchases are delayed until rates come down or until people have saved enough to buy the products they desire. As a result, people have more money to spend in the future, and so the use of some resources shifts from the present to the future.

Inflation also makes a difference in investment decisions. For example, if people expect prices to go up, they may try to make certain purchases right

away, before prices get even higher. Or, if they feel that prices are likely to remain stable or go down, they may put off some spending until later. Either way, expectations about inflation affect the allocation of resources between present and future uses.

Defining Money

With so many financial institutions offering different ways for people to deposit or hold their money, the Fed has had to develop some new definitions to keep track of it.

Figure 15.9 lists a number of components of the money supply, or ways that people have chosen to keep money. The Fed groups these together according to function and gives them names. The first is **M1,** which represents the transactional components of the money supply, or the components of the money supply that most closely match money's role as a medium of exchange. This definition of money includes traveler's checks, coins, currency, demand

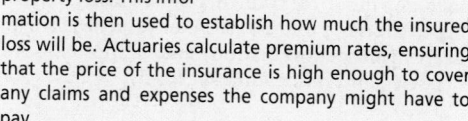

Careers

Actuary

Actuaries design insurance and pension plans.

The Work

Actuaries gather and analyze statistics on death, sickness, injury, disability, unemployment, retirement, and property loss. This information is then used to establish how much the insured loss will be. Actuaries calculate premium rates, ensuring that the price of the insurance is high enough to cover any claims and expenses the company might have to pay.

Qualifications

Actuaries must be knowledgeable in subjects that can affect insurance practices, including general economic, social, health, and legislation trends. Many actuaries hold a degree in mathematics or statistics and they must pass actuarial examinations.

429

CHAPTER 15
Section 3, pages 426–431

L2 Journalism

Have students write newspaper headlines that encapsulate an action of the Fed and that action's short-run and long-run impact. Call on volunteers to read their headlines.

F.Y.I.

Traveler's checks are different from other kinds of checks because a person buys them in specific denominations and spends the money at the time of purchase. They are more like bills than like checks. Other kinds of checks are written for specific sums, and the check writer's account is debited when the check is cleared. Traveler's checks are available in U.S. denominations as well as in the denominations of other national currencies.

INTERACTIVE ECONOMICS!

CD-ROM

MONETARY POLICY Have students click on the Advanced Topic "The Federal Discount Rate" in Lesson 8. Then have them apply what they learned about the federal discount rate to the graphs shown on page 427.

Also supplied in disk format.

CRITICAL THINKING

Demonstrating Reasoned Judgment Have students review the discussion of the politics of interest rates on pages 430–431. Next have them consider the following: "The Federal Reserve System's Board of Governors should be nationally elected officials." Allow students to do further research on the subject. Then ask them to write an essay supporting or challenging the resolution. Hold a class discussion on students' views.

Answer: *savings deposits*

CYBERNOMICS

Interest Rates on the Internet
Many banks post their interest rates for time deposits as well as some interest rates for loans on their Web sites. There are also some Web sites that post comparisons of different banks' interest rates.

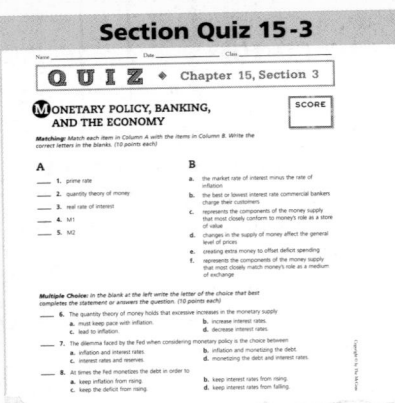

3 ASSESS

Assign Section 3 Assessment as homework or as an in-class activity.

💾 Have students use **Interactive Tutor Self-Assessment Software** to review Section 3.

Section Quiz 15-3

QUIZ ◆ Chapter 15, Section 3

MONETARY POLICY, BANKING, AND THE ECONOMY   SCORE

Matching: Match each item in Column A with the items in Column B. Write the correct letters in the blanks. (10 points each)

A
1. prime rate
2. quantity theory of money
3. real rate of interest
4. M1
5. M2

B
a. the market rate of interest minus the rate of inflation
b. the best or lowest interest rate commercial bankers charge their customers
c. represents the components of the money supply that most closely conform to money's role as a store of value
d. changes in the supply of money affect the general level of prices
e. creating extra money to offset deficit spending
f. represents the components of the money supply that most closely match money's role as a medium of exchange

Multiple Choice: In the blank at the left write the letter of the choice that best completes the statement or answers the question. (10 points each)

6. The quantity theory of money holds that excessive increases in the monetary supply
 a. must keep pace with inflation.   b. increase interest rates.
 c. lead to inflation.   d. decrease interest rates.

7. The dilemma faced by the Fed when considering monetary policy is the choice between
 a. inflation and interest rates.   b. inflation and monetizing the debt.
 c. interest rates and reserves.   d. monetizing the debt and interest rates.

8. At times the Fed monetizes the debt in order to
 a. keep inflation from rising.   b. keep interest rates from rising.
 c. keep the deficit from rising.   d. keep interest rates from falling.

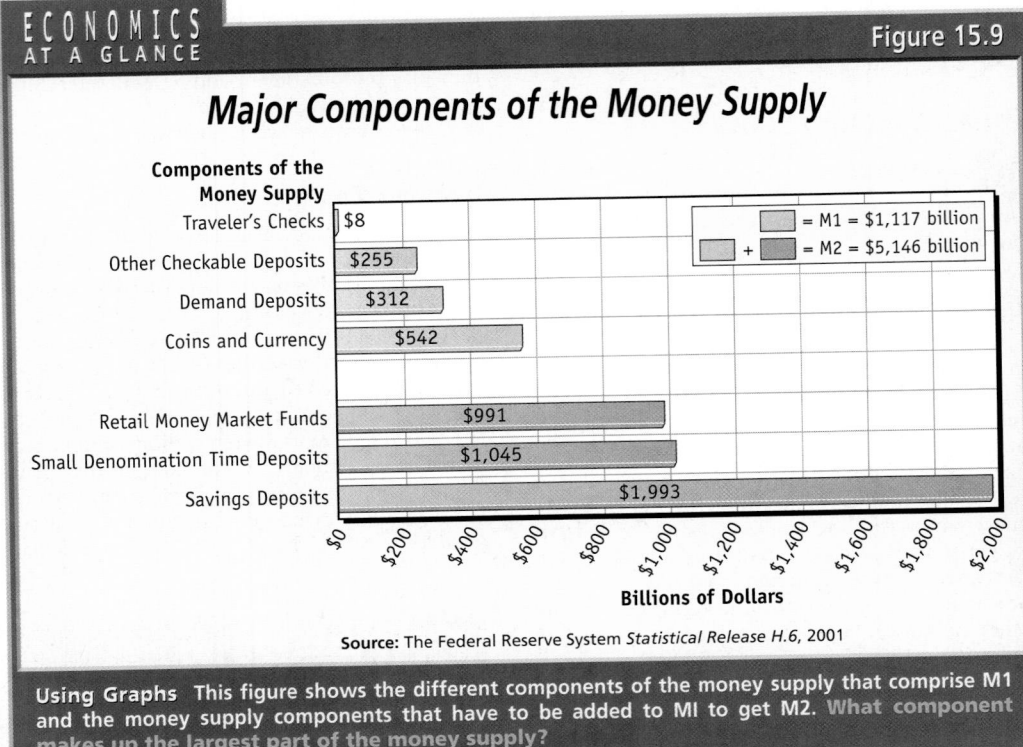

Major Components of the Money Supply

Components of the Money Supply

Component	Amount
Traveler's Checks	$8
Other Checkable Deposits	$255
Demand Deposits	$312
Coins and Currency	$542
Retail Money Market Funds	$991
Small Denomination Time Deposits	$1,045
Savings Deposits	$1,993

Billions of Dollars ($0 – $2,000)

= M1 = $1,117 billion
+ = M2 = $5,146 billion

Source: The Federal Reserve System *Statistical Release H.6*, 2001

Using Graphs This figure shows the different components of the money supply that comprise M1 and the money supply components that have to be added to M1 to get M2. What component makes up the largest part of the money supply?

---

deposits, and other checkable deposits such as NOW accounts and credit union share drafts.

The simple M1 definition includes only items directly and immediately useable as a medium of exchange. A second and broader definition of money is M2. **M2** is a measure of money that includes those components most closely conforming to money's role as a store of value. M2 includes M1, small denomination time deposits, savings deposits, and money market funds.

The Politics of Interest Rates

Because the Fed is privately owned by its member banks, and because the members of the Board of Governors have 14-year terms of office, the Fed is widely regarded as being an independent

monetary authority. Even so, the Fed often comes under political pressure because it has the ability to move interest rates one way or the other.

The president or members of Congress up for reelection may call for low interest rates to stimulate the economy. Incumbent politicians know that their reelection chances are better if voters are happy—and voters normally prefer lower interest rates to higher ones.

The president and Congress can gain some influence over monetary policy by appointing new members to the Board of Governors as existing terms expire. After new appointments are made, however, the Board of Governors usually conducts monetary policy as it sees fit.

Sometimes, political leaders have tried to influence monetary policy by criticizing the Fed or by threatening to introduce legislation to make the

430 UNIT 4 MACROECONOMICS: POLICIES

EXTENDING THE CONTENT

Disposable Credit Credit cards are not included in the money supply because, although many people use them to make purchases, they are not really money. Rather, they are an easy method of obtaining a short-term loan from the institution that issued the card. A variation of the credit card, however, may cause the Fed to reassess its definition of the money supply once again. This card is prepaid and disposable. In other words, the consumer decides how much he or she wants to spend and then buys a card for that amount. As the card is used, value is reduced until the card is used up. The consumer then simply throws the card away. The card is designed to be used at automatic teller machines (ATMs) to draw cash. In the future, however, consumers will be able to make purchases at retail stores, as they can do now with regular credit cards.

Fed less independent. Fortunately, no such laws have been passed.

The Fed is usually reluctant to accommodate demands for lower interest rates in the short term because of the long-run fear of inflation. Unlike many politicians, who frequently focus on interest rates and thereby take a short-term view of monetary policy, the Fed is more concerned about the long-run health of the economy.

People tend to use the interest rate, like the unemployment rate, as a measure of the overall health of the economy. In particular, they think the economy is healthy when interest rates are low, and unhealthy when rates are high. This makes it more difficult for the Fed to raise interest rates, especially during election years when incumbents want voters to think that they are doing a good job with the economy. As a result, the Fed is always conscious of its unique role in the economy and often goes to great lengths to avoid political confrontations that could threaten its independence.

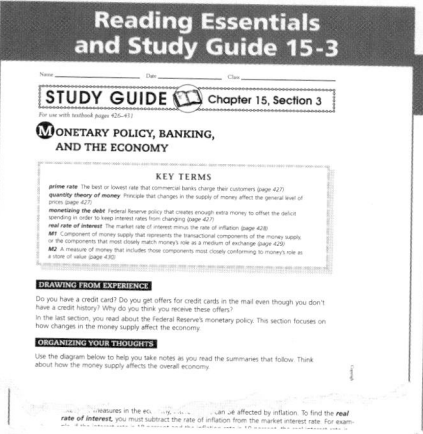

The Fed

OH, WHAT A BEAUTIFUL MORNING, OH, WHAT A BEAUTIFUL DAY, I'VE GOT A BEAUTIFUL FEELING THAT...

...EVERYTHING'S GOING ASTRAY.

U.S. ECONOMY

GREENSPAN

OMIGOD! INFLATION!

Political Pressure While the president and Congress largely control taxation and spending, they have little control over the Fed. *How can the president and Congress influence monetary policy?*

Section 3 Assessment

Checking for Understanding
1. **Main Idea** How do changes in the money supply affect the cost of credit?
2. **Key Terms** Define prime rate, quantity theory of money, monetizing the debt, real rate of interest, M1, M2.
3. **Describe** the short-run impact of monetary policy.
4. **Explain** the long-run impact of monetary policy.
5. **Describe** the two definitions of money.
6. **Describe** the political nature of interest rates.

Applying Economic Concepts
7. **Money** Our money supply, as well as the different forms or ways to hold it, has changed considerably over the years. Describe one or two ways you think United States money might change even more in the future.

Critical Thinking
8. **Making Generalizations** Historically, expansions in money supply have set off inflation. Something similar might have happened to you. Identify a period in your life when you had a little more money than usual. How did you spend the extra cash? Were prices as important to you then as they were at times when you did not have as much to spend? Why do prices tend to increase faster when more money is available?

 Practice and **assess** key social studies skills with the *Glencoe Skillbuilder Interactive Workbook, Level 2.*

CHAPTER 15: THE FED AND MONETARY POLICY **431**

Section 3 Assessment Answers

1. They affect the interest rate and the availability of credit, and then the price level.
2. All vocabulary terms are defined in the text.
3. It affects interest rates and the availability of credit.
4. It affects inflation.
5. money as a medium of exchange (M1) and money as a store of value (M2)
6. Political pressure is often applied to influence Fed.
7. Remind students of the point made in "Extending the Content" on page 430.
8. Price seems less of an issue when people have more money than usual. As the supply of money increases, the buying power decreases.

Visual Instruction

Answer to Caption:
The president and Congress can control the money supply by raising or lowering taxes—the higher the taxes, the smaller the money supply. Congress can also control the money supply by setting limits for the reserve requirements within which the Fed operates.

Reteach

Reading Essentials and Study Guide 15-3

STUDY GUIDE — Chapter 15, Section 3

MONETARY POLICY, BANKING, AND THE ECONOMY

KEY TERMS

Enrich

Have students select a past monetary policy action taken by the Fed. Ask them to describe the short-run and long-run impact of this action.

4 CLOSE

Discuss: "The answer to the nation's debt problem is simply to monetize future deficit spending."

Teaching Skills

Have students each choose a subsection of Section 3 to examine. Have them follow the steps outlined in the feature for that subsection. Students should note on a piece of paper what they believe the subject matter to be, any related facts and examples within the subsection, and any similarities between the identified facts and examples. Ask students to explain how the similarities support the general idea of the subsection. You may wish to have students practice further with articles on economic topics you have collected from newspapers or magazines.

Additional Practice

Reinforcing Economic Skill 14

Name _____ Date _____ Class _____

Reinforcing Economic Skills Chapter 14

Ⓜ MAKING GENERALIZATIONS

Generalizations are judgments that are usually true, based on the facts at hand. To make a valid generalization, first, identify the subject matter. Next, gather related facts and examples and identify similarities among these facts. Finally, use the similarities to form some general ideas about the subject.

Directions: Study the information below and answer the questions that follow.

Rate of Unemployment in Selected Countries (1999)

Country	Percentage of Unemployment
Argentina	12.0
Belgium	8.4
Bolivia	11.4
Brazil	8.5
Ecuador	12.0
France	11.6
Germany	9.1
Liechtenstein	1.6
Luxembourg	3.0
Spain	17.8
Switzerland	3.6
United States	4.3

Read each generalization below. If it is valid based on the information in the chart, write V. If it is invalid write I.

1. Unemployment is high throughout Europe. _____
2. Unemployment in English-speaking countries is lower than in other countries. _____
3. Latin American countries are less concerned with unemployment than some other countries. _____

CRITICAL THINKING
Skill

Making Generalizations

Generalizations are judgments that are usually true, based on the facts at hand. If you say, "We have a great soccer team," you are making a generalization. If you also say that your team is undefeated, you are providing evidence to support your generalization.

Learning the Skill

To make a valid generalization, you must first collect factual information relevant to the topic. Follow these steps:

- Identify the subject matter.
- Gather related facts and examples.
- Identify similarities among these facts.
- Use these similarities to form some general ideas about the subject.

Practicing the Skill

Read the excerpt below, then complete the activity that follows.

The Fed has a strong say in how banks do business.

Federal Reserve actions that are intended to stabilize the economic system make up what is called monetary policy. The Fed uses open market operations most frequently to carry out monetary policy. For example, if the Fed wanted banks to have more money to lend, it would buy government securities. This would add more money to the expansion process and increase the ability of banks to make loans.

During its history, the Fed has had different objectives for its monetary policy. In World War II it tried to keep interest rates low to help the government pay for the war. In the mid-1960s it tried to reduce the amount of money banks had available in order to fight inflation. *In the early 1980s, Federal Reserve actions helped force interest rates to very high levels. These high interest rates contributed to the recession of 1981–82, but eventually helped to reduce the high rate of inflation.*

Some politicians and economists feel the Fed has made many mistakes. Others feel that it has done a good job most of the time. It is clear at least that the Federal Reserve is an important power in our economic system.

Based on the information presented above, identify whether each of the generalizations stated below is valid.

1. Raising interest rates is the Fed's most important goal.

2. There is disagreement over the proper role of the Federal Reserve System.

3. Monetary policy is intended to help keep our economic system from going into a recession or from having inflation.

4. The largest part of spending in this country is done with checks.

Application Activity

For one week, read the editorials in your local newspaper. Then write a list of generalizations about the newspaper's position on issues such as unemployment or the environment.

 Practice and **assess** key social studies skills with the *Glencoe Skillbuilder Interactive Workbook, Level 2.*

Answers to Practicing the Skill

1. not valid
2. valid
3. valid
4. not valid

Section 1

The Federal Reserve System

(pages 407–413)

- The Federal Reserve System was established as the nation's central bank in 1913.

- The Fed is unique in that it is owned by private **member banks** rather than by the government.

- Today, the Fed regulates financial institutions, maintains the payments system, enforces consumer protection laws, provides services to the government, and conducts monetary policy.

- The Fed supervises its state member banks, and it has broad authority over **bank holding companies,** the international operations of all commercial banks, some mergers, check clearing, consumer truth-in-lending laws, and the maintenance of the nation's **currency.**

Section 2

Monetary Policy (pages 415–424)

- Modern banks operate on a **fractional reserve system.** Under this system **excess reserves** can be loaned out to other customers.

- Commercial banks charge interest on their loans and use the income to pay expenses, keeping the remainder as profit.

- The size of the money supply is determined by the **reserve requirement** and the reserves in the system. An increase in the reserve requirement will shrink the money supply. A decrease in the requirement will expand the money supply.

- **Monetary policy** affects the size of the money supply, and therefore the level of interest rates.

- The tools of monetary policy include: a change in the reserve requirement; **open market operations,** which involves the buying and selling of government bonds; and a change in the **discount rate.**

- Two lesser tools include **moral suasion** and **selective credit controls** such as **margin requirements.**

Section 3

Monetary Policy, Banking, and the Economy (pages 426–431)

- Monetary policy affects interest rates in the short run and inflation in the long run–forcing the Fed into a trade-off between lower interest rates today and more inflation later on.

- The impact of monetary policy varies, sometimes affecting the economy sooner, and sometimes later. Monetary policy also affects some sectors of the economy differently than others.

- The interest rate affects the allocation of resources between present and future uses. Expectations of inflation also affect the allocation of resources between present and future uses.

- The interest rate is one of the most visible and politically sensitive prices in the economy. For political reasons, the Fed is often pressured to keep interest rates low, even at the expense of future inflation.

NIGHTLY BUSINESS REPORT

ECONOMICS & YOU

Chapter 22
Disc 1, Side 2

The Federal Reserve System and Monetary Policy

Also available in VHS.

Using the Chapter 15 Summary

Use the Chapter 15 Summary to preview, review, condense, or reteach the chapter.

Preview/Review

Vocabulary PuzzleMaker CD-ROM reinforces Key Terms.

Interactive Tutor Self-Assessment Software provides a review of Chapter 15 content.

Condense

Have students listen to the Chapter 15 Audio Program. Spanish also available.

Assign the Chapter 15 Audio Program Activity and give students the Chapter 15 Audio Program Test.

Have students complete the Guided Reading Activities and Reading Essentials and Study Guides for Chapter 15.

Reteach

Have students complete Reteaching Activity 15 in the TCR. Spanish also available.

Teacher's Notes / Internet Bookmarks

433

GLENCOE
TECHNOLOGY

Use **MindJogger Videoquiz** to review the Chapter 15 content.

ECONOMICS
Online

Have students visit the Web site at epp.glencoe.com to review Chapter 15 and take the **Self-Check Quiz**.

Identifying Key Terms

1. **b**
2. **e**
3. **i**
4. **f**
5. **o**
6. **m**
7. **j**
8. **l**
9. **g**

Reviewing the Facts

Section 1

1. It is privately owned by commercial banks that are members of and hold stock in the Fed.
2. Board of Governors: seven members appointed by president to 14-year terms; FOMC: seven Board members and five district bank presidents
3. state member bank supervision, holding companies, international operations, mergers, check clearing, consumer legislation, currency, coins, providing financial service

Section 2

4. The fractional reserve system requires banks to keep only a fraction of their deposits on reserve. They are free, within legal limits, to use the rest as they see fit.
5. When a customer opens an account, the bank must keep a required percentage of the deposit

ECONOMICS
Online

Self-Check Quiz Visit the *Economics: Principles and Practices* Web site at epp.glencoe.com and click on **Chapter 15—Self-Check Quizzes** to prepare for the chapter test.

Identifying Key Terms

Write the key term that best completes the following sentences.

a. balance sheet
b. Board of Governors
c. certificate of deposit
d. Regulation Z
e. easy money policy
f. excess reserves
g. FOMC
h. holding company
i. legal reserves
j. M1
k. M2
l. monetary policy
m. monetizing the debt
n. moral suasion
o. open market operations
p. selective credit controls

1. The main governing body of the Fed is the _____ .
2. A(n) _____ would expand the money supply and tend to lower interest rates.
3. _____ are the funds that banks use to satisfy the reserve requirement.
4. If a bank has _____ , it is able to make additional loans to customers.
5. The most popular and effective tool of monetary policy is that of _____ .
6. When the Fed increases the money supply to offset the effects of government borrowing, it is _____ .
7. The transactional component of the money supply is _____ .
8. One of the most important responsibilities of the Fed is _____ .
9. The part of the Fed that buys and sells government bonds as part of monetary policy is the _____ .

Reviewing the Facts

Section 1 (pages 407–413)

1. **Describe** the ownership of the Fed.
2. **Identify** the membership of the Board of Governors and the FOMC.
3. **Identify** the most important regulatory responsibilities of the Fed.

Section 2 (pages 415–424)

4. **Explain** how banks operate under a fractional reserve system.
5. **Identify** the conditions that enable a bank to make new loans.
6. **Describe** the three major tools of monetary policy.

Section 3 (pages 426–431)

7. **Identify** the major short-run impact of monetary policy.
8. **Explain** how the long-run impact of monetary policy differs from its short-run impact.
9. **Explain** how M1 differs from M2.
10. **Explain** why the level of interest rates is politically sensitive.

Thinking Critically

1. **Understanding Cause and Effect** What are the effects of the Federal Reserve instituting an easy money policy? Complete a graphic organizer similar to the one below to answer to the question.

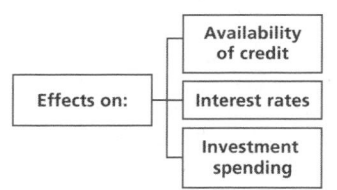

Easy Money Policy

Effects on: → Availability of credit / Interest rates / Investment spending

---

in reserve. The remaining amount of money is free to be used as loans.

6. reserve requirement—by requiring banks to hold more in reserve, Fed can restrict money supply; by requiring less, it can increase money supply; open market operations—by buying or selling government securities, Fed can restrict or increase money supply; discount rate—by raising or reducing interest rate it charges on loans to financial institutions, Fed affects cost of borrowing, thus restricting or increasing money supply

Section 3

7. Short-run impact affects interest rates and the availability of credit.
8. Long-run impact affects inflation rather than interest rates.
9. M1 represents the parts of the money supply that are used to complete transactions, where money is used as a medium of exchange. This would include, for example, coins, currency, and traveler's checks. M2, while it includes the components of M1, represents the role of money

2. Drawing Conclusions Defend or refute the following statement: The independence of the Federal Reserve System is essential to the health of the economy.

Applying Economic Concepts

1. **Money** Ask your parents how they keep their money (CDs, traveler's checks, savings accounts, time deposits, banks, etc.). How many categories mentioned in this chapter do they use?

2. **Balance Sheet** Make a list of all your assets and all your liabilities. Then, prepare a balance sheet that shows your assets, liabilities, and net worth.

Math Practice

Assume that total reserves in the banking system amount to $1,000 and that the fractional reserve requirement is 15 percent. If all banks are fully loaned out, and if the Fed sells an additional $100 of bonds to investors, how large will the money supply be?

Thinking Like an Economist

If the Fed were to expand the money supply, it would face a trade-off between lower interest rates today and higher inflation later on. Explain how an economist would use cost-benefit analysis to examine the implications of these outcomes.

Technology Skill

Using a Database For one week, analyze the currency that comes into your possession. In your journal, keep track of the features that appear on the front and back of each bill, noting the similarities and differences among the various currencies.

Create a database for foreign visitors that describes the specific features and purposes of each United States

bill and coin. Create fields such as the following: portrait, paper/coin, value, Federal Reserve Bank seal, and so on. Arrange the fields and text in an appealing way, including clip art, decorative fonts, and color. Use words that will easily be understood by someone with limited knowledge of the English language, or translate the database into another language if possible. Distribute a copy of your databank to your local visitor's center or Chamber of Commerce.

┌ *Building Skills* ┐

Making Generalizations Read the following passage and answer the questions.

Although there are effective checks and balances on powers held by the Congress and the president, there are few checks on the monetary power of the Federal Reserve System's Board of Governors. Under current law, the Board is free to act within broad limits established by Congress and the president.

Actions taken by the Fed are important to the success of government economic policy, yet there is no guarantee that members of the Board of Governors will cooperate with Congress and the president in implementing economic plans. Some political leaders have suggested that the powers of the Fed's Board of Governors should be limited, or that the Board should be made responsible to the president.

Supporters of controlling the Fed believe such a policy would assure the country of a unified economic policy. Some argue that it is wrong for people with so much power not to be elected by the people.

Identify each generalization below as valid or invalid based on the information presented.

1. Politicians are too slow to act, and therefore monetary power should remain with the Federal Reserve System.

2. Some people criticize the Fed because it holds a great deal of power without having to answer to the voters.

3. The powers of the Fed should be limited.

 Practice and **assess** key social studies skills with the *Glencoe Skillbuilder Interactive Workbook, Level 2.*

Math Practice

$6,000

Thinking Like an Economist

Answers should include the idea of listing the costs and the benefits and then weighing one against the other to make a decision.

Technology Skill

Check students' databanks for accuracy and readability.

Building Skills

1. not valid
2. valid
3. not valid

Bonus Test Question

Have students classify the following as easy money policy actions or tight money policy actions.

1. Fed raises reserve requirement. *(tight money policy)*
2. Fed buys government securities. *(easy money policy)*
3. Fed lowers the discount rate. *(easy money policy)*
4. Fed sells government securities. *(tight money policy)*

as a store of value. It includes, for example, savings deposits and money market funds.

10. Because people use low interest rates as an indicator of economic health, many politicians want the Fed to lower interest rates in election years. The Fed, however, may want interest rates to rise because it is concerned with the long-run health of the economy.

Thinking Critically

1. availability of credit: grows; interest rates: fall; investment spending: increases

2. Answers may vary. As guidance, point out that some politicians disagree on this issue, but the vast majority of economists would argue strongly for the independence of the Fed.

Applying Economic Concepts

1. Answers will vary. Suggest that students present their findings in chart form.

2. Balance sheets will vary. Have students discuss whether they were surprised by their findings. Students should not talk about their personal information unless they want to.

Chapter 16 Resource Manager

SECTION RESOURCES

Daily Objectives	Reproducible Resources	Technology/Multimedia Resources

Section 1
The Cost of Economic Instability
1. Explain the economic costs of instability.
2. Describe the social costs of instability.

Reproducible Lesson Plan 16-1
Daily Lecture Notes 16-1
Guided Reading Activity 16-1
Reading Essentials and Study Guide 16-1
Section Quiz 16-1*

Daily Focus Transparency 73
Interactive Economics!
Interactive Tutor Self-Assessment Software
ExamView® Pro Testmaker
Presentation Plus!

Section 2
Macroeconomic Equilibrium
1. Explain the concept of aggregate supply.
2. Describe the importance of aggregate demand.
3. Examine the nature of macro-economic equilibrium.

Reproducible Lesson Plan 16-2
Daily Lecture Notes 16-2
Guided Reading Activity 16-2
Reading Essentials and Study Guide 16-2
Section Quiz 16-2*

Daily Focus Transparency 14
Interactive Tutor Self-Assessment Software
ExamView® Pro Testmaker
Presentation Plus!

Section 3
Stabilization Policies
1. Explain the operations and impact of fiscal policy.
2. Distinguish between supply-side economics and fiscal policy.
3. State the basic assumptions of monetary policy.

Reproducible Lesson Plan 16-3
Daily Lecture Notes 16-3
Guided Reading Activity 16-3
Reading Essentials and Study Guide 16-3
Section Quiz 16-3*

Daily Focus Transparency 77
Interactive Economics!
Interactive Tutor Self-Assessment Software
ExamView® Pro Testmaker
Presentation Plus!

Section 4
Economics and Politics
1. Explain why monetary policy sometimes conflicts with other economic policies.
2. Recognize that economists have differing views.
3. Understand the way that poli-tics and economics interact.

Reproducible Lesson Plan 16-4
Daily Lecture Notes 16-4
Guided Reading Activity 16-4
Reading Essentials and Study Guide 16-4
Section Quiz 16-4*

Daily Focus Transparency 78
Vocabulary PuzzleMaker CD-ROM
Interactive Tutor Self-Assessment Software
ExamView® Pro Testmaker
Presentation Plus!

 Transparency   CD-ROM   Software   Blackline Master

 Videodisc   Audio Program   Videocassette

Also available in Spanish

Block Schedule
Activities that are particularly suited to use within the block scheduling framework are identified throughout this chapter by the following designation: **BLOCK SCHEDULING**

KEY TO ABILITY LEVELS

L1 BASIC activities for all students
L2 AVERAGE activities for average to above-average students
L3 CHALLENGING activities for above-average students
ELL ENGLISH LANGUAGE LEARNER activities

Chapter 16 Resource Manager

Timesaving Tools

TeacherWorks™ All-In-One Planner and Resource Center

- **Interactive Teacher Edition** Access your Teacher Wraparound Edition and your classroom resources with a few easy clicks.
- **Interactive Lesson Planner** Planning has never been easier! Organize your week, month, semester, or year with all the lesson helps you need to make teaching creative, timely, and relevant.

Use Glencoe's **Presentation Plus!** multimedia teacher tool to easily present dynamic lessons that visually excite your students. Using Microsoft PowerPoint® you can customize the presentations to create your own personalized lessons.

PRESENTATION Plus!

ACTIVITY

From the Classroom of...

Lynn Meyer
Howard County R-11
School District
Glasgow, MO

"What If?"

One game that I have my students play is called the "What If?" game. I present a number of different events and have students provide the effects of the event on the economy and on economic stability. For example, I might ask, "What if Russia made a large purchase of wheat from the United States?" How might this affect GDP? What effect might this eventually have on the misery index? How might this impact unemployment? Inflation? Government policies? The next presidential election? Other questions I ask students might be "What if there was a 5 percent rise in excise tax on gasoline?" or "What if war broke out in the Middle East?"

You can take the same information and format it into the kinds of questions that are used on the TV game show "Who Wants to Be a Millionaire?"—only in this case it's "Who Wants to Be an Economist?" Other game show formats may also lend themselves to this activity.

National Council on Economic Education

THE **Economics**America AND **Economics**International PROGRAMS

Voluntary National Content Standards in Economics
Emphasized in Chapter 16

Content Standard 12

Content Standard 18

Content Standard 20

For a complete listing of NCEE Standards and entire text correlation, see Teacher pages in front of book.

Resources Available from NCEE
- Capstone: The Nation's High School Economics Course
- Focus: High School Economics
- Civics and Government: Focus on Economics
- United States History: Eyes on the Economy

To order these materials or to contact your state Council on Economic Education about workshops and programs, call 1-800-338-1192 or visit www.nationalcouncil.org

Chapter 16 Resource Manager

TEACHING TRANSPARENCY

Economic Concept Transparency 19: Fiscal Policy

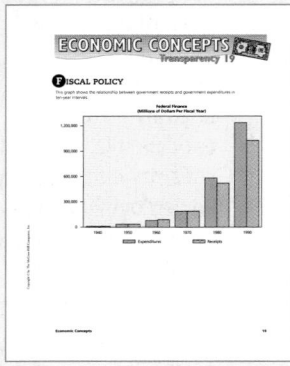

APPLICATION AND ENRICHMENT

Consumer Application Activity 21

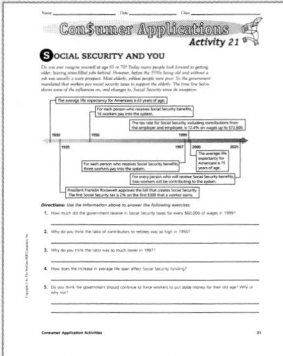

Free Enterprise Activity 21

APPLICATION AND ENRICHMENT

Enrichment Activity 16

Cooperative Learning Activity 21

Math Practice Activity 21

Economic Cartoon 21

Primary and Secondary Source Reading 21

REVIEW AND REINFORCEMENT

Economic Vocabulary Activity 16

Reteaching Activity 16

Critical Thinking Activity 21

Reinforcing Economic Skill 29

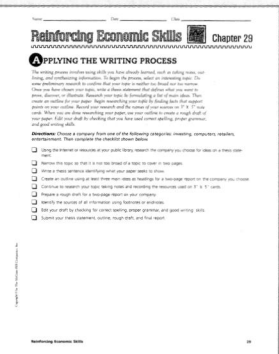

Chapter 16 Resource Manager

ASSESSMENT AND EVALUATION

**Chapter 16 Test
Form A**

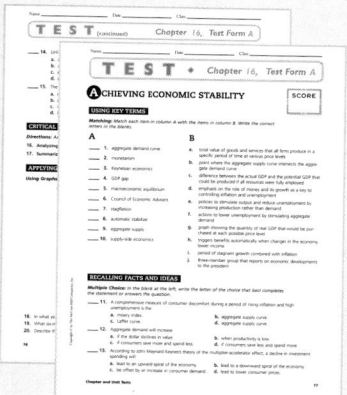

**Chapter 16 Test
Form B**

**Performance Assessment
Activity 21**

**ExamView® Pro
Testmaker**

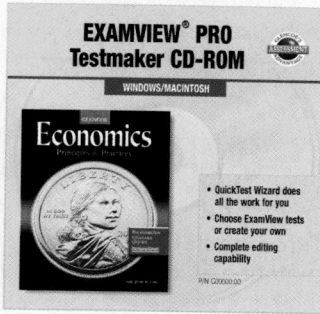

SPANISH RESOURCES

**The following Spanish language materials
are available in the Spanish Resources binder:**

 Spanish Economic Vocabulary Activities

 Spanish Reteaching Activities

 Spanish Section Quizzes

 Spanish Economic Concepts Transparencies

Also available:

  Spanish Chapter 16 Audio Program
Activity and Test

TECHNOLOGY/MULTIMEDIA

- Vocabulary PuzzleMaker CD-ROM
- Interactive Tutor Self-Assessment Software
- ExamView® Pro Testmaker
- Audio Program (English or Spanish)
- NBR Economics & You Video Program
  (English or Spanish)
- MindJogger Videoquiz
- Interactive Economics! CD-ROM
- Presentation Plus!
- TeacherWorks CD-ROM
- Glencoe Skillbuilder Interactive Workbook CD-ROM, Level 2

ECONOMICS Online

*Use our Web site for additional resources. All essential
content is covered in the Student Edition.*

You and your students can visit epp.glencoe.com, the
Web site companion to **Economics: Principles and Practices.**
This innovative integration of electronic and print
media offers your students a wealth of opportunities.
The student text directs students to the Web site for
the following options:

- **Chapter Overviews**
- **Student Web Activities**
- **Self-Check Quizzes**
- **Textbook Updates**

Answers are provided for you in the Web Activity Lesson
Plan. Additional Web resources and interactive puzzles
are also available.

Performance Assessment

Refer to Activity 21 in the *Performance Assessment Strategies and Activities* booklet.

 BLOCK SCHEDULING

 ECONOMICS *Online*

Introduce students to chapter content and key terms by having them access **Chapter Overview 16** at epp.glencoe.com

  NIGHTLY BUSINESS R E P O R T

◉ ECONOMICS & YOU

||||| Chapter 23
Disc 1, Side 2

Economic Growth and Stability
After students have viewed this segment, they should be able to:
- Compare and contrast boom and bust situations in the business cycle.
- Also available in VHS.

GLENCOE TECHNOLOGY

Use **MindJogger Videoquiz** to preview the Chapter 16 content.

CHAPTER 16

Achieving Economic Stability

Economics & You

One of our nation's most important goals is to create an economic environment favorable to growth and stability. In **Chapter 16,** you will learn about the policies and factors that influence our economic stability. To learn about theories for controlling economic cycles, view the Chapter 23 video lesson:

Economic Growth and Stability

ECONOMICS *Online*

Chapter Overview Visit the *Economics: Principles and Practices* Web site at epp.glencoe.com and click on **Chapter 16—Chapter Overviews** to preview chapter information.

The mental and social health of society is an important concern for economists.

✚ EXTRA CREDIT PROJECT

Have students write a report outlining the present administration's fiscal policies and the current monetary policies followed by the Fed. Call on volunteers to present and discuss their reports.

The Cost of Economic Instability

Study Guide

Main Idea
Economic instability leads to social as well as economic problems.

Reading Strategy
Graphic Organizer As you read the section, use a graphic organizer similar to the one below to describe the GDP gap.

> GDP Gap
> ↓
> What causes the GDP gap to fluctuate?

Key Terms
stagflation, GDP gap, misery (discomfort) index

Objectives
After studying this section, you will be able to:
1. **Explain** the economic costs of instability.
2. **Describe** the social costs of instability.

Applying Economic Concepts
Misery Index Do you know someone who has suffered from the problems associated with unemployment and inflation at the same time? Many people do, which is why economists have invented a measure called the *misery index*. Read to find out how the misery index got its name.

Cover Story

Inflation Fears Punish Dow

NEW YORK (CNNfn)—U.S. stocks opened with a tumble Friday after one of the market's worst fears materialized—inflation at the consumer level posted its biggest increase in more than eight years in April.

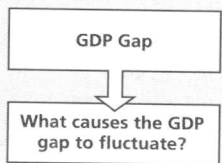

At around 10 A.M. the Dow-Jones Industrial Average lost 128.58, or 1.1 percent, to 10,987.61 as investors exited the market in droves amid surging bond yields and intensifying speculation that official interest rates could soon head higher as well.

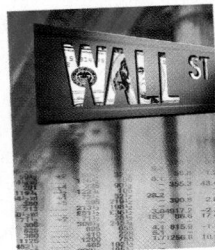

Instability can affect the stock market.

Losers overwhelmed gainers on the New York Stock Exchange, with 2,035 stocks falling and 435 rising. . . .

—*CNNfn*, May 14, 1999

Recession, high unemployment, and inflation are forms of economic instability that hinder long-term economic growth. Sometimes the economy experiences these problems separately, and sometimes they occur at the same time. In the early 1970s, for example, the economy experienced **stagflation**—a period of stagnant growth combined with inflation.

Even when the economy is relatively healthy, or when there is a hint of problems on the horizon, as you just saw in the cover story, we still worry about inflation—and even our worries have real consequences. These fears are not unfounded, because economic instability carries an enormous cost—one that can be measured in human as well as economic terms.

The Economic Costs

 On one level, unemployment and inflation are simply numbers that are collected, reported in the press, or plotted on a graph. At another level, they represent enormous economic failures that waste the resources of the nation and its people.

CHAPTER 16: ACHIEVING ECONOMIC STABILITY **437**

1 FOCUS

Section Overview
This section describes the economic and social costs of instability.

BELLRINGER
Motivational Activity

- Project **transparency** and have students answer questions.
- Available as blackline master.

Daily Focus Transparency 73

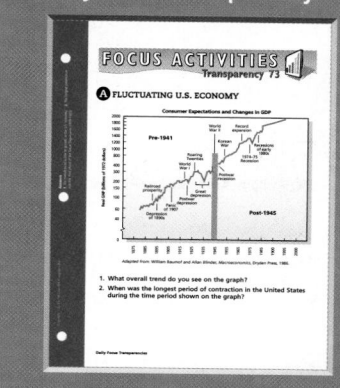

Study Guide

Reading Strategy
Have students create the graphic organizer.
Answers to Graphic: *the normal business cycle will cause changes in the size of the GDP gap*

Preteaching Vocabulary
Have students locate the meanings of the Key Terms in the Glossary.

RESOURCE MANAGER

Reproducible Masters
- Reproducible Lesson Plan 16-1
- Daily Lecture Notes 16-1
- Guided Reading Activity 16-1
- Reading Essentials and Study Guide 16-1
- Section Quiz 16-1

Transparencies
- Daily Focus Transparency 73

Multimedia
- Interactive Tutor Self-Assessment Software
- ExamView® Pro Testmaker
- Presentation Plus!

② TEACH

Daily Lecture Notes 16-1

DAILY LECTURE NOTES 📖 Lesson 16-1

ⓓ DID YOU KNOW?

The "misery index" (the sum of inflation plus the unemployment rate) in the United States was below 8 percent at the end of the twentieth century, far lower than the 14 percent rate in Israel or the 22 percent rate in Spain.

PAGES 437-438

I. The Economic Costs

A. The GDP gap measures the difference between actual GDP and the GDP that could have been achieved had all resources been fully employed.

B. The misery index is the sum of monthly inflation and unemployment rates.

C. Uncertainty increases when real GDP declines.

⊞ Discussion Question

Do you think the GDP gap is large today? (Answers will vary but should indicate students' awareness that the economy is growing rapidly and that unemployment is below the full employment rate.)

PAGES 439-440

II. The Social Costs

A. Economic instability results in wasted labor, capital, and natural resources.

B. Economic instability can lead to political instability.

C. Economic instability is associated with increased crime, lower levels of police protection and municipal services, and less willingness by companies to hire disadvantaged people or provide on-the-job training.

ECONOMICS
AT A GLANCE

Answer: *It falls.*

L1 Understanding Ideas

On the board, write "Economic Instability." Underneath, draw a two-column chart with the headings "Economic Costs" and "Social Costs." Have students decide the two most important economic and social costs of economic instability. **ELL**

INTERACTIVE
ECONOMICS!

💿 CD-ROM

OPPORTUNITY COSTS Have students click on "The Cost of Unemployed Resources" in Lesson 1. **Ask:** What does a point inside the production possibilities frontier show? *(the opportunity cost measured in terms of output NOT produced because some resources were not working to their fullest potential)*

💾 Also supplied in disk format.

The GDP Gap and the Production Possibilities Frontier

Using Graphs The GDP gap is the difference between the actual production at point a and the potential production as indicated by points b, c, or d. What happens to production when some resources are idle or are not employed efficiently?

The GDP Gap

One measure of the cost of stagnation is the **GDP gap**—the difference between the actual GDP and the potential GDP that could be produced if all resources were fully employed. In other words, the gap is a type of opportunity cost—a measure of output not produced because of unemployed resources.

The GDP gap, illustrated in **Figure 16.1,** shows the production possibilities curve in the classic guns-versus-butter example. The output not produced because of idle resources can be measured in either guns, butter, or a combination of the two items.

In a more dynamic sense, business cycles or fluctuations cause the size of this gap to vary over time. The scale of GDP is such that if GDP declines even a fraction of a percentage point, the amount of lost production and income can be enormous.

In 2001, for example, the GDP of the United States economy was approximately $10.2 trillion. If a $10.2 trillion economy declines just one-fourth of one percentage point, *$25.7 billion* of production would be lost. This amount is more than the federal government spent on agriculture or general science, space, and technology during the entire 2001 fiscal budget year.

Described in other terms, this amount would be equal to 850,000 workers losing jobs that paid $30,000 each for an entire year. In practice, the effects of a decline in GDP generally are spread out over a large area rather than being concentrated in just one spot, but they are still enormous by any measure.

The Misery Index

The **misery index,** sometimes called the **discomfort index,** is the sum of the monthly inflation and unemployment rates. **Figure 16.2** shows the misery index for a period beginning in 1965.

Although it is not an official government statistic, the misery index is a comprehensive measure of consumer suffering during periods of high inflation and unemployment. The index is relevant only over long periods because of the wide month-to-month swings in some of the numbers.

Uncertainty

When the economy is unstable, a great deal of uncertainty exists. A worker may not buy something because of concern over his or her job. This uncertainty translates into purchases that are not made, causing some unemployment to rise and jobs to be lost.

The worker is not the only one the uncertainty affects. For example, the owner of a business producing at capacity may decide against an expansion although new orders are arriving daily. Instead, the producer may try to raise prices, which increases inflation.

MEETING SPECIAL NEEDS ACTIVITY

Learning Disabled For students who have trouble with reading, it is often helpful to have a specific purpose presented by the teacher. Focused reading exercises help in two ways: they present a limited goal, and they make the reader more active, requiring judgments to be made about the applicability of the material to the question. Have students read "The Social Costs" on pages 439–440. Ask them to find examples in their daily lives of the various types of social costs listed.

📁 Refer to *Inclusion for the Social Studies Classroom Strategies and Activities* in the TCR.

The Social Costs

The cost of instability can be measured in dollars rather easily, but it is harder to measure in terms of human suffering. In human terms, the costs are almost beyond comprehension. Because of these social costs, everyone agrees that stability must be achieved. Economists are interested not only in society's production, but in its mental and social health as well.

Wasted Resources

Human suffering during periods of instability goes beyond not having more goods and services that raise the standard of living. The labor resource is wasted, with people wanting work but not being able to find it. When this happens, the economy fails to satisfy the basic human need to be a useful and productive member of society. This labor situation is particularly acute in inner cities where unemployment rates run high among minority groups.

Wasted resources are not limited to just human resources. Idle factories waiting to be utilized are another wasted resource. Natural resources may also lie unused or go to waste.

Political Instability

Politicians also suffer from the consequences of economic instability. When times are hard, voters are dissatisfied, and incumbents are often thrown out of office. For example, most experts agree that Bill Clinton's victory over President George Bush in 1992 was due in part to the 1991 recession.

ECONOMICS AT A GLANCE

Figure 16.2

The Misery Index

(Graph: Annual Percentage Rate (y-axis, 0 to 25) vs. Year (x-axis, 1965 to 2000). Recession years shaded.)

☐ Recession years

Source: Bureau of Economic Analysis, United States Department of Commerce

Using Graphs The misery index is the sum of the monthly inflation and unemployment rates. When did the misery index reach its highest point?

ECONOMICS Online
Visit epp.glencoe.com and click on *Textbook Updates—Chapter 16* for an update of the data.

CHAPTER 16: ACHIEVING ECONOMIC STABILITY **439**

CHAPTER 16
Section 1, pages 437–440

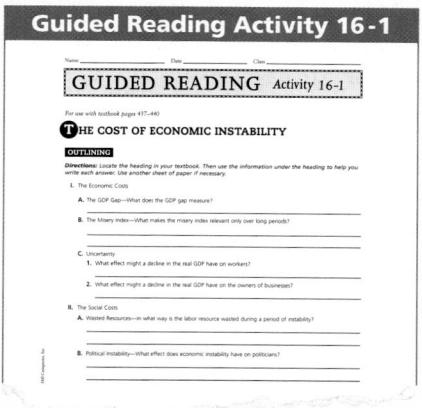

Guided Reading Activity 16-1

GUIDED READING Activity 16-1

For use with textbook pages 437–440

THE COST OF ECONOMIC INSTABILITY

OUTLINING

Directions: Locate the heading in your textbook. Then use the information under the heading to help you write each answer. Use another sheet of paper if necessary.

I. The Economic Costs
   A. The GDP Gap—What does the GDP gap measure?
   B. The Misery Index—What makes the misery index relevant only over long periods?
   C. Uncertainty
      1. What effect might a decline in the real GDP have on workers?
      2. What effect might a decline in the real GDP have on the owners of businesses?
II. The Social Costs
   A. Wasted Resources—In what way is the labor resource wasted during a period of instability?
   B. Political Instability—What effect does economic instability have on politicians?

ECONOMICS AT A GLANCE

Answer: *1980*

③ ASSESS

Assign Section 1 Assessment as homework or as an in-class activity.

💾 Have students use **Interactive Tutor Self-Assessment Software.**

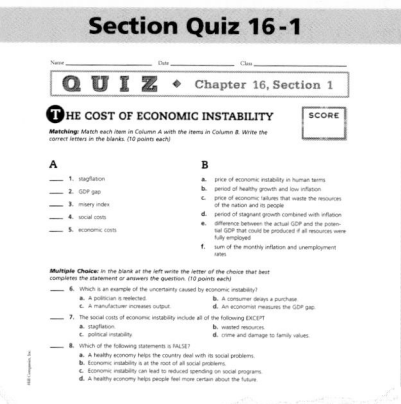

Section Quiz 16-1

QUIZ ◆ Chapter 16, Section 1

THE COST OF ECONOMIC INSTABILITY SCORE

Matching: Match each item in Column A with the items in Column B. Write the correct letters in the blanks. (10 points each)

A	B
___ 1. stagflation	a. price of economic instability in human terms
___ 2. GDP gap	b. period of healthy growth and low inflation
___ 3. misery index	c. price of economic failures that waste the resources of the nation and its people
___ 4. social costs	d. period of stagnant growth combined with inflation
___ 5. economic costs	e. difference between the actual GDP and the potential GDP that could be produced if all resources were fully employed
	f. sum of the monthly inflation and unemployment rates

Multiple Choice: In the blank at the left write the letter of the choice that best completes the statement or answers the question. (10 points each)

___ 6. Which is an example of the uncertainty caused by economic instability?
   a. A politician is reelected.   b. A consumer delays a purchase.
   c. A manufacturer increases output.   d. An economist measures the GDP gap.

___ 7. The social costs of economic instability include all of the following EXCEPT
   a. stagflation.   b. wasted resources.
   c. political instability.   d. crime and damage to family values.

___ 8. Which of the following statements is FALSE?
   a. A healthy economy helps the country deal with its social problems.
   b. Economic instability is at the root of all social problems.
   c. Economic instability can lead to reduced spending on social programs.
   d. A healthy economy helps people feel more certain about the future.

FREE ENTERPRISE ACTIVITY

Remind students that the cost of economic instability includes wasted resources, political instability, and crime. Organize students into several groups, and have each group propose and discuss possible ways to reduce the social costs of economic instability. Call on groups to offer their solutions. Classify solutions into two categories—those that require significant government intervention and those that require little or no government intervention. Select a few solutions and discuss their feasibility. 📦 **BLOCK SCHEDULING**

Visual Instruction

Answer to Caption:
Resources are wasted less, political stability is present, and people feel more positive about the future in general.

Reteach

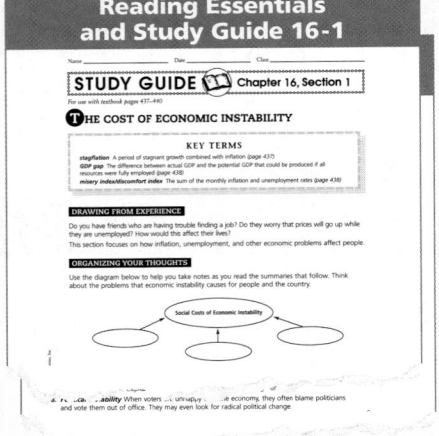

Reading Essentials and Study Guide 16-1

Enrich

Have students locate unemployment and inflation figures for their state or local area over the last 20 years. Have them use these statistics to construct a state or local misery index.

CLOSE

Have students discuss how economic instability has affected their community.

If too much economic instability exists, as during the Great Depression of the 1930s, voters are often willing to vote for radical change. As a result, economic stability adds to the political stability of our nation.

Crime and Family Values

High crime rates, too few economic and social opportunities for minorities, the loss of individual freedoms, and the lack of economic stability for many Americans are all grounds for concern. Many people believe that some of these social ills cannot be cured without the help of a strong and stable economy.

When the economy is healthy, the citizens of a society can more easily deal with its social problems. People have jobs and can provide for themselves and their families. Communities can take advantage of higher tax collections, which can be used to increase police protection and other municipal services. Companies are more willing to hire disadvantaged persons and provide on-the-job training.

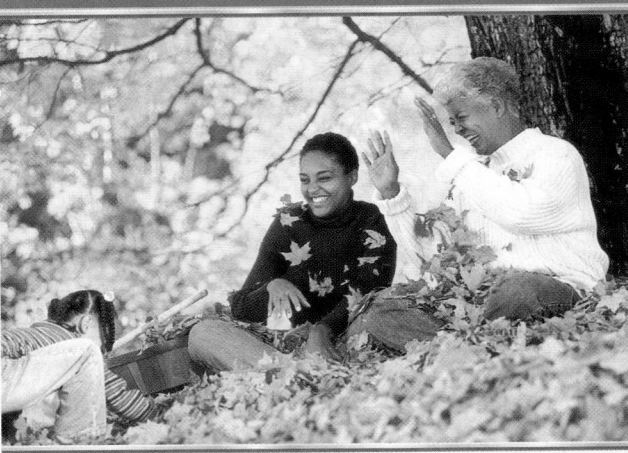

Economics and Society

Family Values A vibrant economy means that people will be more certain of their ability to provide for themselves and their families. *What are some benefits of a healthy economy?*

A healthy economy means that people will be more certain of their ability to provide for themselves and their families. When people can do this, they are more positive about the future in general.

Section 1 Assessment

Checking for Understanding

1. **Main Idea** Using your notes from the graphic organizer activity on page 437, explain what the GDP gap measures.

2. **Key Terms** Define stagflation, GDP gap, misery (discomfort) index.

3. **Explain** how economists measure the economic cost of instability.

4. **Describe** the social cost of instability.

Applying Economic Concepts

5. **Misery Index** How might the psychological strains that many people feel in difficult economic times help prolong an economic downturn? Provide at least one example with your answer.

Critical Thinking

6. **Making Generalizations** If the GDP gap in a given year rose dramatically, what do you think would happen to unemployment and inflation?

7. **Making Comparisons** How does stagflation differ from the traditional business cycle?

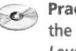 **Practice** and **assess** key social studies skills with the *Glencoe Skillbuilder Interactive Workbook, Level 2.*

440 UNIT 4 MACROECONOMICS: POLICIES

Section 1 Assessment Answers

1. The GDP gap measures the difference between the actual GDP and the potential GDP that could be produced if all resources were fully employed.

2. All vocabulary terms are defined in the text.

3. They use the GDP gap and the misery index to measure this cost.

4. wasted resources, including labor; political instability; increases in crime

5. Workers who have been laid off may not spend money after being rehired because they lived with uncertainty. This keeps manufacturers from producing and keeps some jobs from getting filled.

6. Unemployment would rise and inflation would taper off.

7. The economy experiences stagnant growth and inflation at the same time.

Applying the Writing Process

Researching and writing allows you to organize your ideas in a logical manner. The writing process involves using skills you have already learned, such as taking notes, outlining, and synthesizing information.

Learning the Skill

Use the following guidelines to help you apply the writing process.

- Select an interesting topic. As you identify possible topics, focus on resources that would be available. Do preliminary research to determine whether your topic is too broad or too narrow.

- Write a thesis statement that defines what you want to prove, discover, or illustrate in your writing. This will be the focus of your entire paper.

- Prepare and do research on your topic. First formulate a list of main idea questions; then do research to answer those questions. Prepare note cards on each main-idea question, listing the source information.

- Organize your information by building an outline or another kind of organizer. Then follow your outline or organizer in writing a rough draft of your report.

- A report should have three main parts: the introduction, the body, and the conclusion. The introduction briefly presents the topic and gives your topic statement. In the body, follow your outline to develop the important ideas in your argument. The conclusion summarizes and restates your findings.

- Each paragraph should express one main idea in a topic sentence. Additional sentences support or explain the main idea by using details and facts.

- Revise the draft into a final report. Wait for a day, then reread and revise it.

Practicing the Skill

Suppose you are writing a report on the role political turmoil plays in economic instability. Answer the following questions about the writing process.

1. How could you narrow this topic?

2. Write a thesis statement.

3. What are three main ideas?

4. What are three possible sources of information?

A systematic approach facilitates the writing process.

Application Activity

Use research resources in your library to find information on political instability during the Great Depression. Write a short report on the topic.

 Practice and **assess** key social studies skills with the *Glencoe Skillbuilder Interactive Workbook, Level 2.*

Answers to Practicing the Skill

Answers should reflect an understanding of the writing process and the appropriate economic concepts.

Teaching Skills

In small groups have students imagine that they have been assigned to write a five-page report on a subject of their choice from this unit. Have group members develop two short lists; the first should contain subjects that are either too broad or too narrow for the length of the report; the second list should contain feasible subjects. Ask groups to choose one of the possible subjects and come up with five or six main-idea questions related to that subject. Discuss how groups recognized if a subject was too broad or too narrow for the report. Also discuss how groups formulated the main-idea questions.

Additional Practice

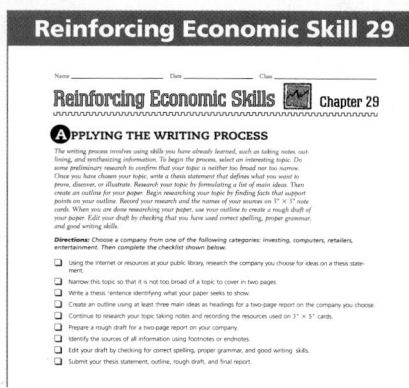

Reinforcing Economic Skill 29

GLENCOE
TECHNOLOGY

 Glencoe Skillbuilder Interactive Workbook, Level 2

This interactive CD-ROM reinforces student mastery of essential social studies skills.

FOCUS

Section Overview
This section examines the nature of macroeconomic equilibrium.

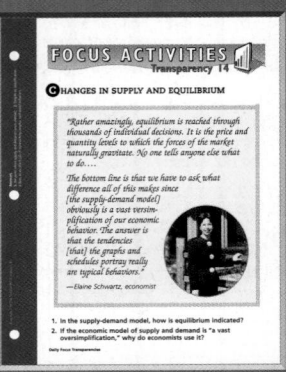
Study Guide

Reading Strategy
Have students create the graphic organizer.
Answers to Graphic: *discovery of less expensive resources, lower prices for inputs, lower interest rates, increases in labor productivity, liberalized immigration laws, decreased regulation, lower taxes*

Preteaching Vocabulary
Have students use the Key Terms in a short paragraph.

Macroeconomic Equilibrium

Study Guide

Main Idea
Aggregate *supply* is the total quantity of goods and services produced at different price levels. Aggregate *demand* is the total quantity purchased at different price levels.

Reading Strategy
Graphic Organizer As you read the section, complete a graphic organizer similar to the one below by listing at least three factors that could lower production costs leading to an increase in aggregate supply.

Cause
Cause
Cause
Effect: Increase in aggregate supply

Key Terms
aggregate supply, aggregate supply curve, aggregate demand, aggregate demand curve, macroeconomic equilibrium

Objectives
After studying this section, you will be able to:
1. **Explain** the concept of aggregate supply.
2. **Describe** the importance of aggregate demand.
3. **Examine** the nature of macroeconomic equilibrium.

Applying Economic Concepts
Equilibrium Have you ever experienced one of those rare moments when you feel completely satisfied and do not want to change anything that you are doing? This is called a state of *equilibrium*. Read to find out how the economy, too, reaches a state of equilibrium occasionally.

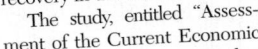

Cover Story

Report Sees Economy Recovering

WASHINGTON (Reuters) - Conditions in the U.S. economy are improving and favor a recovery by the start of next year, a congressional report released Tuesday said.

"Currently, several forces making for a near-term slow-down have reversed themselves or are on the wane and moving in the right direction," the report said. "At this time, therefore, the odds appear to favor a recovery in the near-term."

Economy improving

The study, entitled "Assessment of the Current Economic Environment", was put together by the Joint Economic Committee of the U.S. Congress.

But the study warns that there are still risks in the economy and encourages policy makers to continue to take the necessary actions to get the economy back on track.

—*Excite News* (online), July 3, 2001

442

From a historical perspective, sustained strong economic growth is relatively rare. We would like to see this prevail more often, but something always seems to happen to prevent it. As a result, economists study markets in an attempt to find out how they work, and how they can be made to work even better.

Aggregate Supply

When we study markets, we often use the tools of supply and demand to show how the equilibrium price and quantity of output are determined. When we study the economy as a whole, we can use the concepts of supply and demand in much the same way.

One approach is to study **aggregate supply,** the total value of goods and services that all firms would produce in a specific period of time at various price levels. If the period was exactly one year, and if production took place within a country's borders, then aggregate supply would be the same as GDP.

The Aggregate Supply Curve

The concept of aggregate supply assumes that the money supply is fixed and that a given price level prevails. However, if prices should change, then individual firms would adjust their profit-maximizing quantities of output, producing a slightly different level of GDP. If it were somehow possible to keep adjusting the price level to see how total output changed, we could then construct an **aggregate supply curve,** which shows the amount of real GDP that could be produced at various price levels.

Figure 16.3 shows how an aggregate supply curve, **AS,** for the whole economy might look. It is shown as upward sloping, but with a horizontal as well as vertical range. The horizontal range represents various levels of output that coexist with large amounts of unemployed resources. If the economy is producing at point **a,** for example, output could be expanded to point **b** by putting some unemployed resources to work, without causing any change in the general price level.

However, any expansion of real GDP beyond point **b,** which has an output of Q_1, is not possible without some increase in the price level. By the time the economy has reached point **c,** the price level has risen to P_1, because firms have been competing for increasingly scarce resources. Q_2 is the level of output where all resources are fully employed, because firms merely drive up prices if they try to expand production beyond point **c.**

The aggregate supply curve, like the supply curve of the individual firm, can increase or decrease. Most of the increases in aggregate supply are tied to the cost of production for the individual firm. If the cost goes down for some or all firms, aggregate supply increases, which shows as a shift to the right.

Factors that tend to increase the cost of production for an individual firm tend to decrease aggregate supply. These factors include higher prices for foreign oil, higher interest rates, and lower labor productivity. Any increase in cost that causes firms to offer fewer goods and services for

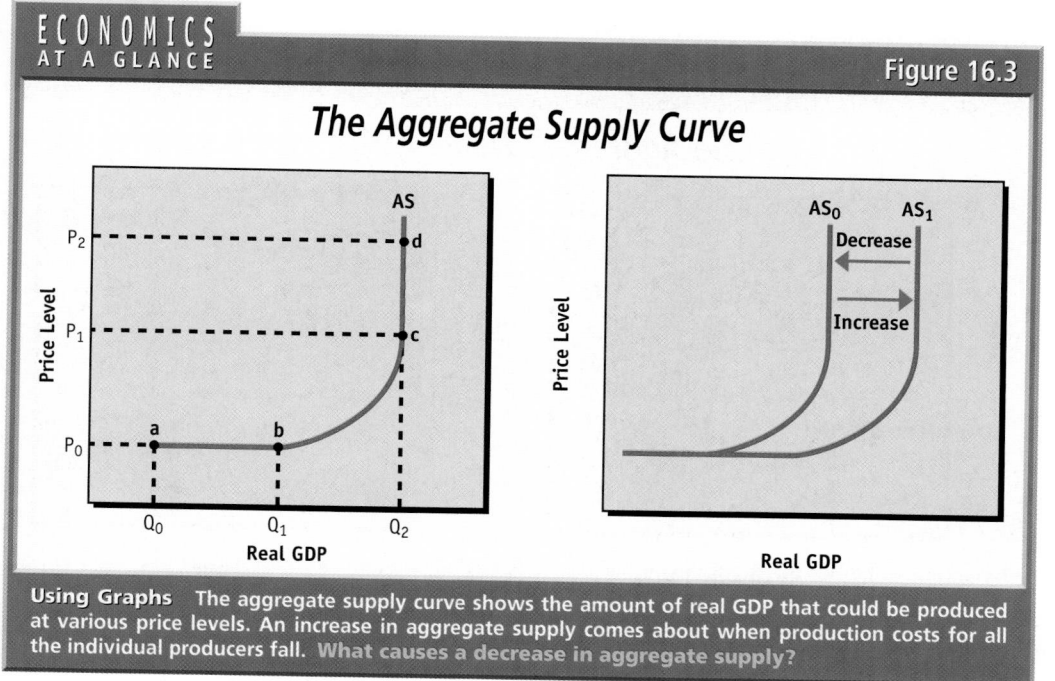

ECONOMICS AT A GLANCE

Figure 16.3

The Aggregate Supply Curve

Using Graphs The aggregate supply curve shows the amount of real GDP that could be produced at various price levels. An increase in aggregate supply comes about when production costs for all the individual producers fall. **What causes a decrease in aggregate supply?**

CHAPTER 16: ACHIEVING ECONOMIC STABILITY **443**

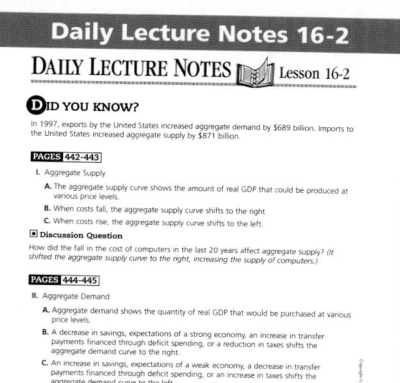

Daily Lecture Notes 16-2

DAILY LECTURE NOTES 📖 Lesson 16-2

❶ DID YOU KNOW?
In 1997, exports by the United States increased aggregate demand by $689 billion. Imports to the United States increased aggregate supply by $871 billion.

PAGES 442-443
I. Aggregate Supply
   A. The aggregate supply curve shows the amount of real GDP that could be produced at various price levels.
   B. When costs fall, the aggregate supply curve shifts to the right.
   C. When costs rise, the aggregate supply curve shifts to the left.

❷ Discussion Question
How did the fall in the cost of computers in the last 20 years affect aggregate supply? *(It shifted the aggregate supply curve to the right, increasing the supply of computers.)*

PAGES 444-445
II. Aggregate Demand
   A. Aggregate demand shows the quantity of real GDP that would be purchased at various price levels.
   B. A decrease in savings, expectations of a strong economy, an increase in transfer payments financed through deficit spending, or a reduction in taxes shifts the aggregate demand curve to the right.
   C. An increase in savings, expectations of a weak economy, a decrease in transfer payments financed through deficit spending, or an increase in taxes shifts the aggregate demand curve to the left.

ECONOMICS AT A GLANCE

Answer: *any factors that tend to increase the cost of production for an individual firm*

L1 Understanding Ideas

Write the following on the board: *Increase in Aggregate Supply, Decrease in Aggregate Supply, Increase in Aggregate Demand, Decrease in Aggregate Demand.* Call on students to identify factors that would cause these four situations to occur and note their responses under the appropriate heading. Then ask students to select one factor from each heading and illustrate the shift of the curve graphically. **ELL**

MEETING SPECIAL NEEDS ACTIVITY

Learning Style: Logical/Mathematical Economists have observed that there is often a trade-off between inflation and unemployment. Have students use the aggregate supply and aggregate demand model to show how inflation can rise if the unemployment rate falls, and how inflation can fall if the unemployment rate rises. Have them also use the model to show how both inflation and unemployment can rise or fall at the same time.

📁 Refer to *Inclusion for the Social Studies Classroom Strategies and Activities* in the TCR.

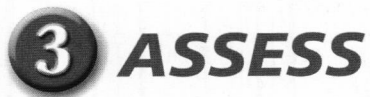

ECONOMICS
AT A GLANCE

Answer: *the amount of money people save, taxes, transfer payments*

3 ASSESS

Assign Section 2 Assessment as homework or as an in-class activity.

💾 Have students use **Interactive Tutor Self-Assessment Software.**

Section Quiz 16-2

---

sale at each and every price would shift the aggregate supply curve to the left.

Aggregate Demand

Aggregate demand is the total quantity of goods and services demanded at different price levels. It is like aggregate supply in that it is a summary measure of all demand in the economy; it can be represented in the form of a graph; and it can either increase or decrease over time.

The Aggregate Demand Curve

Figure 16.4 illustrates the **aggregate demand curve,** a graph showing the quantity of real GDP that would be purchased at each possible price level in the economy. This curve, labeled **AD,** represents the sum of consumer, business, and government demands at various price levels. It slopes downward and to the right like the demand curve for individuals, but for entirely different reasons.

The primary reason for the negative slope is the underlying assumption that the economy can have only one money supply at a time. The size of this supply is fixed and has a different purchasing power at every possible price level. When prices are very high, a given money supply will purchase a limited amount of output, such as that represented by point **a.** When prices are much lower, everyone will be able to buy relatively more GDP, putting output purchased at point **b.** If the price level dropped further, even more GDP could be purchased, which is why the curve tends to slope downward and to the right.

The aggregate demand curve, like the aggregate supply curve, can increase or decrease depending on certain conditions. One factor that affects the aggregate demand curve is a change in the amount of money that people save. If consumers collectively save less and spend more, the increase in consumer spending would increase aggregate demand, shifting the aggregate demand curve to the right.

ECONOMICS
AT A GLANCE

Figure 16.4

The Aggregate Demand Curve

Using Graphs The aggregate demand curve shows the amount of real GDP the economy would demand at all possible price levels. **What causes the aggregate demand curve to shift?**

444 UNIT 4 MACROECONOMICS: POLICIES

FREE ENTERPRISE ACTIVITY

Point out that underemployment is a growing problem for the U.S. economy. In this situation, workers are employed, but they have jobs that demand fewer skills and less training than they possess. Examples of underemployed workers include carpenters or bricklayers who work as servers at fast-food restaurants, and taxicab drivers who have doctoral degrees. Ask students to give examples of underemployment in their community and explain the impact that it has on aggregate supply. (*Examples will vary. Aggregate supply will decrease because resources are not fully utilized.*)

A decrease in aggregate demand can be caused by the same factors behaving in an opposite fashion. For example, an increase in saving–leaving consumers less money to spend–will cause the aggregate demand curve to shift to the left.

Higher taxes and lower transfer payments could also reduce aggregate spending. Such decisions shift the aggregate demand curve to the left because all sectors of the economy collectively buy less GDP at all price levels.

Macroeconomic Equilibrium

Macroeconomic equilibrium is the level of real GDP consistent with a given price level, as determined by the intersection of the aggregate supply and demand curves. This equilibrium is shown in **Figure 16.5** where **Q** is the level of real GDP that is consistent with the price level **P**. This is a static equilibrium because it represents a situation at a particular point in time.

If the economy is growing, the price level may or may not change, depending on changes in productivity and the money supply. This is one of the dilemmas facing economic policy makers–how to make real GDP grow without unduly increasing the price level and thereby the rate of inflation.

Aggregate supply and demand curves are useful concepts, providing a framework for analyzing equilibrium, economic growth, and price stability. They can be used to give an idea of the way and direction

that things will change, but they do not yield exact predictions. Even so, they are becoming increasingly important when analyzing macroeconomic issues.

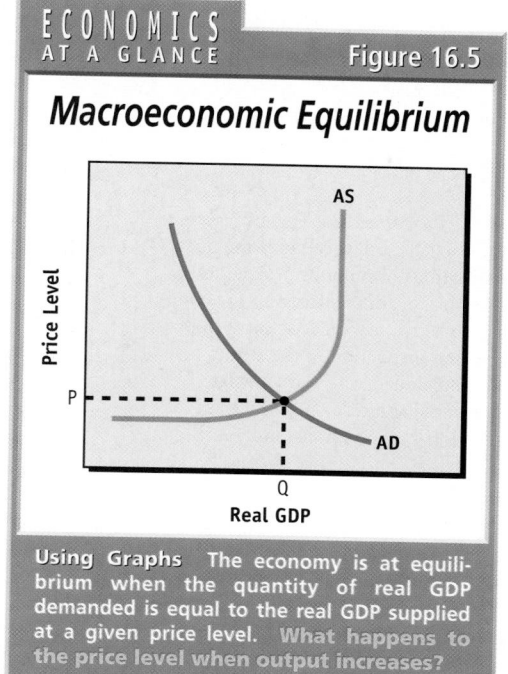

ECONOMICS AT A GLANCE   Figure 16.5

Macroeconomic Equilibrium

Using Graphs The economy is at equilibrium when the quantity of real GDP demanded is equal to the real GDP supplied at a given price level. What happens to the price level when output increases?

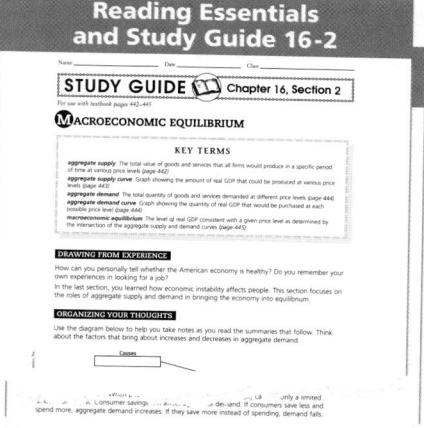

ECONOMICS AT A GLANCE

Answer: *The price level will increase.*

Reteach

Reading Essentials and Study Guide 16-2

STUDY GUIDE   Chapter 16, Section 2

MACROECONOMIC EQUILIBRIUM

Enrich

Direct students to scan the business pages of the newspaper for stories that detail conditions that might cause a change in aggregate supply or demand. Have students summarize the articles they find, focusing on how aggregate supply or aggregate demand will change.

CLOSE

Encourage students to write a riddle, poem, or proverb that explains macroeconomic equilibrium.

Section 2 Assessment

Checking for Understanding
1. **Main Idea** What factors might cause aggregate demand to increase?
2. **Key Terms** Define aggregate supply, aggregate supply curve, aggregate demand, aggregate demand curve, macroeconomic equilibrium.
3. **Describe** the concept of aggregate supply.
4. **Explain** the importance of aggregate demand.
5. **Describe** the nature of macroeconomic equilibrium.

Applying Economic Concepts
6. **Equilibrium** Define macroeconomic equilibrium, then discuss how a decrease in business investments would affect the macroeconomic equilibrium.

Critical Thinking
7. **Analyzing Information** What kind of effect would higher taxes have on aggregate supply? Explain your reasoning.

   Practice and **assess** key social studies skills with the *Glencoe Skillbuilder Interactive Workbook, Level 2.*

CHAPTER 16: ACHIEVING ECONOMIC STABILITY   **445**

Section 2 Assessment Answers

1. increased spending, expectations about future conditions, increased transfer payments, decreased taxes
2. All vocabulary terms are defined in the text.
3. Aggregate supply is the total value of goods and services that all firms would produce at a specific period of time at various price levels.
4. It is the total quantity of goods and services demanded at different price levels.
5. level of GDP consistent with a price level
6. See p. 445 for definition. It would cause workers to lose jobs and spend less. Aggregate demand would decrease, real GDP would fall, and the price level decline.
7. Higher taxes would decrease aggregate supply because the cost of production would rise.

BACKGROUND

What makes the companies profiled here all the more remarkable is that the overwhelming majority of businesses in the United States—estimates reach as high as three out of four—fail within their first year. Many that survive the difficult first few years still fail soon thereafter. Businesses still existing five or ten years down the road may remain small, or grow to moderate size. It is a truly tiny percentage of business ventures that reach the gigantic proportions and financial success of a DuPont, Heinz, or Hershey's.

TEACH

Organize students into groups. Have each group select a major company with which they are familiar. The group should conduct library and Internet research to create a profile or brief history of their selected company.

Profiles IN Economics

HEINZ

DU PONT

From Rags to Riches

Rags to riches. The expression is cliché, but it captures the imaginations of millions of Americans who dream of success in the country's free market economy. They find inspiration in the stories of individuals who started what would some day become giant global corporations—individuals, perhaps, not unlike themselves.

E.I. DU PONT

The DuPont Company is a multi-*billion* dollar enterprise, one of the largest corporations in the world. It has about 125 plants in the United States and elsewhere, manufacturing more than 40,000 distinct products. Most are chemical products—anything from polyester to pesticides to camera film. In addition, DuPont controls many subsidiaries, including Conoco, the petroleum giant.

DuPont's official name is E.I. DuPont de Numours & Company, a tribute to Èleuthère Irénée du Pont (1771–1834), its founder. At 17, du Pont was a worker at the French royal gunpowder works. At 19, he and his family were forced by the revolution to come to the United States. Noting the poor quality of American gunpowder, he thought he could succeed by making one of higher quality. In 1802, he constructed a small powder works on Brandywine Creek near Wilmington, Delaware. From these humble beginnings, the DuPont giant grew.

HENRY JOHN HEINZ

The J. Heinz Company markets 5,000 varieties of food in 200 countries. The company is named for its founder, Henry John Heinz. Heinz was born in Pittsburgh in 1844. He started his selling career at age 12, hawking produce from his family's garden. At 25, he sold his mother's grated horseradish. He called it "pure and superior," and sold it in clear glass jars to prove his claim. The company went bankrupt after a few years, but Heinz persevered.

He started a food company, selling ketchup, pickles, jams, jellies and condiments. Clever marketing ("It's not so much what you say," said Heinz, "but how, when and where.") and aggressive sales were key to company growth. By 1896, when Heinz was 52, his company had made him a millionaire. Its growth since then has been even more impressive.

Examining the Profile

1. **Making Comparisons** How are the individuals profiled alike? How are they different?

2. **Synthesizing Information** Explain why you think the companies du Pont and Heinz founded are typical or atypical.

Answers to Examining the Profile

1. Answers will vary. Similarities: both men became entrepreneurs at a young age and by selling a higher quality product; Differences: products created, Heinz persevered after bankruptcy and diversified his business.

2. Answers will vary. Students should identify them as atypical in terms of longevity and size.

Stabilization Policies

Study Guide

Main Idea
Government can promote economic growth through demand-side and supply-side policies.

Reading Strategy
Graphic Organizer As you read the section, complete graphic organizers similar to the ones below by describing the role of government under demand-side and supply-side policies.

Key Terms
fiscal policy, Keynesian economics, multiplier, accelerator, automatic stabilizer, unemployment insurance, supply-side economics, Laffer curve, monetarism, wage-price controls

Objectives
After studying this section, you will be able to:
1. **Explain** the operations and impact of fiscal policy.
2. **Distinguish** between supply-side economics and fiscal policy.
3. **State** the basic assumptions of monetary policy.

Applying Economic Concepts
Automatic Stabilizers You may know someone who collects unemployment insurance, Social Security, or medicare. Read to find out why these programs are some of the key fiscal policy measures used today.

① FOCUS

Section Overview
This section explains the operations and impact of fiscal policy.

BELLRINGER
Motivational Activity

- Project **transparency** and have students answer questions.
- Available as blackline master.

Daily Focus Transparency 77

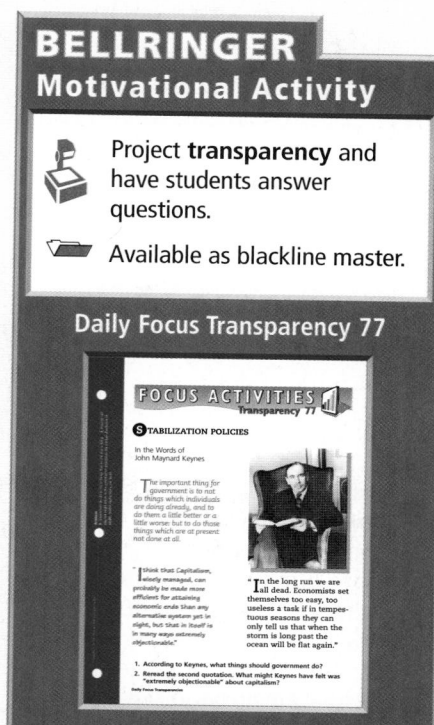

Cover Story

Hard to Find the Funny Side of Gridlock

Even by the high standards of acrimony common in Washington, the legislative agenda has fallen prey to particularly bitter wrangling over the government's big budget surpluses—projected at $3,000 billion over the next 10 years.

Both Republican and Democratic leaders are under pressure from rank-and-file members to avoid compromises this year.

Many candidates for Congress and the presidency would prefer to run on party-defining issues, unclouded by messy compromises or cross-over votes. As a result, Democrats and Republicans have been unable—or are unwilling—to reach agreement on many routine bills.

Congress in session

—*The Financial Times, August 6, 1999*

conomic growth, full employment, and price stability are three of the seven major economic goals of the American people. In order to reach these goals, sound economic policies must be designed and implemented.

Economic stability can be achieved in several ways. Some people favor policies that stimulate aggregate demand, while others favor ones that stimulate aggregate supply. While these two approaches have their supporters, Congressional gridlock, as we just saw in the cover story, makes them increasingly more difficult to implement. As a result, a third approach that favors monetary policy has filled the void.

Demand-Side Policies

Demand-side policies are federal policies designed to increase or decrease total demand in the economy by shifting the aggregate demand curve to the right or to the left. One approach is known as **fiscal policy**—the federal government's attempt to stabilize the economy through taxing and government spending.

CHAPTER 16: ACHIEVING ECONOMIC STABILITY **447**

Study Guide

Reading Strategy
Have students create the graphic organizer.
Answers to Graphic: *demand-side policies: to stabilize the economy through taxing and government spending; supply-side policies: lower taxes and decrease regulation to stimulate production*

Preteaching Vocabulary
Have volunteers explain in their own words the meaning of the Key Terms.

RESOURCE MANAGER

Reproducible Masters
- Reproducible Lesson Plan 16-3
- Daily Lecture Notes 16-3
- Guided Reading Activity 16-3
- Reading Essentials and Study Guide 16-3
- Section Quiz 16-3

Transparencies
- Daily Focus Transparency 77

Multimedia
- Interactive Economics!
- Interactive Tutor Self-Assessment Software
- ExamView® Pro Testmaker
- Presentation Plus!

TEACH

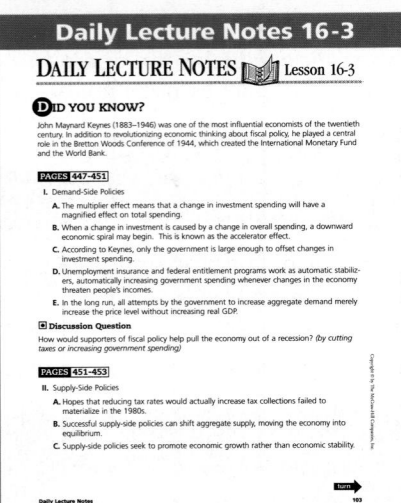

Daily Lecture Notes 16-3

DAILY LECTURE NOTES Lesson 16-3

DID YOU KNOW?
John Maynard Keynes (1883–1946) was one of the most influential economists of the twentieth century. In addition to revolutionizing economic thinking about fiscal policy, he played a central role in the Bretton Woods Conference of 1944, which created the International Monetary Fund and the World Bank.

PAGES 447–451

I. Demand-Side Policies
A. The multiplier effect means that a change in investment spending will have a magnified effect on total spending.
B. When a change in investment is caused by a change in overall spending, a downward economic spiral may begin. This is known as the accelerator effect.
C. According to Keynes, only the government is large enough to offset changes in investment spending.
D. Unemployment insurance and federal entitlement programs work as automatic stabilizers, automatically increasing government spending whenever changes in the economy threaten people's incomes.
E. In the long run, all attempts by the government to increase aggregate demand merely increase the price level without increasing real GDP.

Discussion Question
How would supporters of fiscal policy help pull the economy out of a recession? *(by cutting taxes or increasing government spending)*

PAGES 451–453

II. Supply-Side Policies
A. Hopes that reducing tax rates would actually increase tax collections failed to materialize in the 1980s.
B. Successful supply-side policies can shift aggregate supply, moving the economy into equilibrium.
C. Supply-side policies seek to promote economic growth rather than economic stability.

Daily Lecture Notes 103

Visual Instruction

Answer to Caption:
Government deficits are unfortunate but necessary to stop further declines in economic activity. When the economy improves, the government will collect a surplus and pay down the debt.

L2 Debate

Have students indicate by a show of hands whether they favor demand-side or supply-side economics. Organize students into two groups according to their votes. Then have the two groups debate the following: "To ensure economic stability in the U.S., the policy known as supply-side economics must be instituted and maintained."

Keynesian Economics

The Role of Government
According to Keynesian economics, economic activity will be stimulated if the federal government invests in projects such as hydroelectric plants. *What is the role of government deficits according to Keynesian theory?*

Fiscal policies are derived from **Keynesian economics,** a set of actions designed to lower unemployment by stimulating aggregate demand. John Maynard Keynes put forth these theories in 1936 and they dominated the thinking of economists until the 1970s.

The Keynesian Framework

Keynes provided the basic framework with the output-expenditure model, $GDP = C + I + G + F$. According to this model, any change in GDP on the left side of the equation could be traced to changes on the right side of the equation. The question was, which of the four components caused the instability?

According to Keynes, the net impact of the foreign sector (F) was so small that it could be ignored. The government sector (G) was not the problem either, because its expenditures were normally stable over time. Spending by the consumer sector (C), stated Keynes, was the most stable of all. Ruling out F, G, and C, it then appeared that the business, or investment, sector (I) was to blame for the instability.

In Keynes's theory, investment sector spending was not only unstable, but had a magnified effect on other spending. If investment spending declined by $50 billion, for example, many workers would lose

their jobs. These workers in turn would spend les and pay fewer taxes. Soon, the amount of spendin by all sectors in the economy would be down b more than the initial decline in investment. Thi effect is called the **multiplier,** and it says that change in investment spending will have a magni fied effect on total spending. The multiplier i believed to be about 2 in today's economy, so i investment spending goes down by $50 billion, th decline in overall spending could reach $100 billior

Conditions are likely to be made even worse b the **accelerator**—the change in investment spendin caused by a change in total spending. After a declin in overall spending begins, it causes investmen spending to be reduced even further. Before long the economy is trapped in a downward spiral. Th combined multiplier-accelerator effect is importar because it contributes to the instability of GDP.

The Role of Government

Keynes argued that only the government was bi enough to step in and offset changes in investmen sector spending. The government could take direct role and undertake its own spending to off set the decline in spending by businesses. Or, i could play an indirect role by lowering taxes an

---

MEETING SPECIAL NEEDS ACTIVITY

English Language Learners For students with language problems, restating is difficult. These students often have trouble finding synonyms for words in the text. Explain that the point of restating in their own words is for them to use common language and not to make it sound like the textbook. In the subsection "The Role of Government," have students look for words that might be somewhat complex and restate them in their own words. **ELL**

Refer to *Inclusion for the Social Studies Classroom Strategies and Activities* in the TCR.

enacting other measures to encourage businesses and consumers to spend more.

Suppose the government wanted to take direct steps quickly to offset a $50 billion decline in business spending. To do this, it could spend $10 billion to build a dam, give $20 billion in grants to cities to fix up poor neighborhoods, and spend another $20 billion in other ways. Thus, the $50 billion that business does not spend would be replaced by the $50 billion the government spends. Thus, the overall sum of C + I + G + F would remain unchanged.

Or, instead of spending the $50 billion, the government could reduce tax rates by that amount and give investors and consumers more purchasing power. If the $50 billion not collected in taxes were spent, the initial decline in investment spending would be offset, and the sum for C + I + G + F again would remain the same.

Either way, the government would run the risk of a growing federal deficit. In Keynes's view, the deficit was unfortunate, but necessary to stop further declines in economic activity. When the economy recovered, tax collections would rise, the government would run a surplus, and the debt could be paid back. The justification for *temporary* federal deficits was one of the lasting contributions of Keynesian economics, and a major departure from the economic thinking of the time.

Automatic Stabilizers

Another key component of fiscal policy is the role of **automatic stabilizers,** programs that automatically trigger benefits if changes in the economy

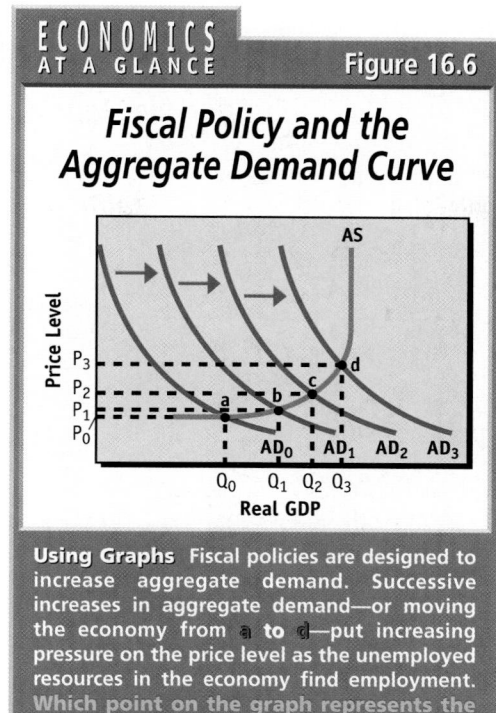

ECONOMICS AT A GLANCE

Figure 16.6

Fiscal Policy and the Aggregate Demand Curve

Using Graphs Fiscal policies are designed to increase aggregate demand. Successive increases in aggregate demand—or moving the economy from **a** to **d**—put increasing pressure on the price level as the unemployed resources in the economy find employment. Which point on the graph represents the lowest aggregate demand?

threaten income. Three important stabilizers are unemployment insurance, federal entitlement programs, and the progressive income tax.

Unemployment insurance is insurance that workers who lose their jobs through no fault of their own can collect for a limited amount of time. Unemployment insurance cannot be collected by people who are fired because of misconduct or who quit their jobs without good reason.

Federal entitlement programs and many social welfare programs designed to provide minimum health, nutritional, and income levels for selected groups of people also work as automatic stabilizers. They include federal programs such as welfare, government pensions, medicare, medicaid, and Social Security. The availability of these programs is a guarantee that economic instability or some other factor will not cause demand to fall below a certain level for selected individuals.

CHAPTER 16: ACHIEVING ECONOMIC STABILITY **449**

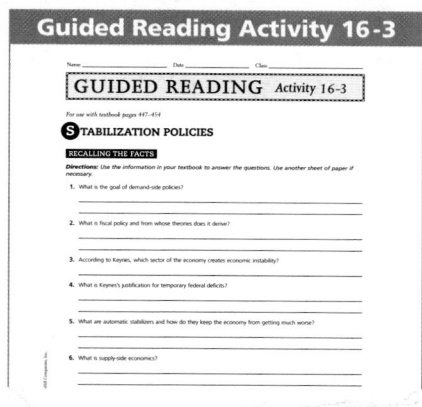

ECONOMICS AT A GLANCE

Answer: *point a*

L2 Applying Ideas

Have students discuss what they believe are the most important macroeconomic problems today. List problems on the board as they are identified. Organize students into several small groups, randomly assigning a macroeconomic problem to each group. Encourage groups to imagine they are the President's Council of Economic Advisers or the Fed Board of Governors. Have them develop a policy recommendation to tackle their assigned macroeconomic problem. Have group representatives present and discuss their recommendations.

FREE ENTERPRISE ACTIVITY

Provide students with the following scenario: The United States is experiencing a severe recession. Nationwide unemployment is at 10 percent, but in some regions it stands at 25 percent. Inflation, however, is running at an annual rate of 3 percent. Consumer and business spending are down. GDP has fallen 5 percent over the last 3 quarters, and government revenues have declined. Have students analyze the scenario above and select an economic policy—demand-side, supply-side, or monetarism—to bring the United States out of the recession. Direct students to write a brief report detailing and justifying the actions they would take.

L2 Creating Cartoons

Direct students to create three cartoons that support or oppose the use of demand-side policies, supply-side policies, or monetary policies in establishing economic stability. Call on students to display and explain their cartoons. **ELL**

ECONOMICS
AT A GLANCE

Answer: *Under supply-side there is less government intervention and lower taxes.*

L3 Television News Report

Organize students into two groups, assigning one group the topic "Demand-Side Economic Policies" and the other the topic "Supply-Side Economic Policies." Have each group prepare a five-minute television news report on its assigned topic. Reports should provide answers to the following questions: What is the goal of the policy? How or by whom was the policy developed? When and by whom has the policy been practiced? What is government's role in the policy? What are the immediate and long-term consequences of the policy? Have each group "broadcast" its news report for the rest of the class.

ECONOMICS
AT A GLANCE

Figure 16.7

Supply-Side and Demand-Side Economics

Supply-Side Policies

Stimulate production (supply) to spur output

Cut taxes and government regulations to increase incentives for businesses and individuals

Businesses invest and expand, creating jobs; people work, save, and spend more

Increasing investment and productivity lead to increased output

Demand-Side Policies

Stimulate consumption of goods and services (demand) to spur output

Cut taxes or increase federal spending to put money into people's hands

With more money, people buy more

Businesses increase output to meet growing demand

With output increasing, the economy grows and unemployment goes down

Making Comparisons Supply-side policies and demand-side policies have the same goal: continuous and stable economic growth without price inflation. How does the role of government differ under supply-side and demand-side policies?

The progressive income tax is the third automatic stabilizer. For example, if someone loses his or her job, or ends up working fewer hours because of cutbacks, that person will earn less. If the reduction in income is significant, that person is likely to fall into a lower tax bracket, which cushions the decline in income.

Fiscal Policy and Aggregate Demand

The impact of fiscal policies can be illustrated with the aggregate demand curve **AD. Figure 16.6**

shows a single aggregate supply curve and several aggregate demand curves. When aggregate demand is very low, as during the Great Depression or other periods of severe economic downturn, the economy would be at point **a** where AD_0 intersects **AS.** Increases in government spending—public works projects, transfer payments, or even tax reductions—could be used to increase aggregate demand to AD_1. Because many resources are not employed, the movement of the economy from **a** to **b** causes very little price inflation.

450 UNIT 4 MACROECONOMICS: POLICIES

CRITICAL THINKING

Identifying Central Issues Have students debate in a one-page essay the positive and negative aspects of increasing unemployment insurance benefits. On the positive side, they might note that increasing benefits would help stabilize the economy, provide help for families in need, and allow workers to search longer for jobs that best use their skills. On the negative side, they might argue that increased benefits would be costly and that they would encourage higher unemployment.

Further attempts to increase aggregate demand to **AD₂** and **AD₃** produce successively less output with increasingly higher price levels. Eventually, all attempts the government sector makes to increase aggregate demand only increase the price level without increasing the production of real GDP.

Limitations of Fiscal Policy

Keynes envisioned the role of government spending as a counterbalance to changes in investment spending. Ideally, the government would increase its spending to offset declines in business spending, and conversely government would decrease spending whenever business spending recovered. In practice, however, the federal government has been generally unable to bring its spending under control, even when it ran enormous budget deficits in the 1980s.

As a result, the most effective counter-cyclical fiscal policies used today are the automatic stabilizers. The advantage of the stabilizers is that spending approval or tax reduction is not needed when the economy enters a recession, or when people lose jobs and need unemployment insurance coverage.

Supply-Side Policies

 Supply-side economics are policies designed to stimulate output and lower unemployment by increasing production rather than demand. The supply-side view gained support in the late 1970s because demand-side policies did not seem to be controlling the nation's growing unemployment and inflation. In the 1980s, supply-side policies became the hallmark of President Reagan's administration.

The differences between supply-side economics and demand-side economics are smaller than most people realize. Both policies, which are summarized in **Figure 16.7**, have the same goal—that of increasing production and decreasing unemployment without increasing inflation.

Answer: *Revenues went up.*

Before the advent of supply-side economics, demand-side policies were primarily known as Keynesian economics. Remind students that Keynes was the subject of the Chapter 13 Profile in Economics (see page 355).

Math Practice

Unemployment Benefits
When determining unemployment benefits, government agencies typically find an average week's wage for the unemployed person based on a certain number of past weeks' wages. The unemployed person then receives a percentage of that average week's pay as unemployment insurance. If a worker's average weekly wages were $638, benefits are equal to 50 percent of the average weekly wage, and the benefits can be paid for a maximum of 26 weeks, what is the greatest amount of benefits the unemployed worker could receive? *($8,294)*

ECONOMICS
AT A GLANCE

Figure 16.8

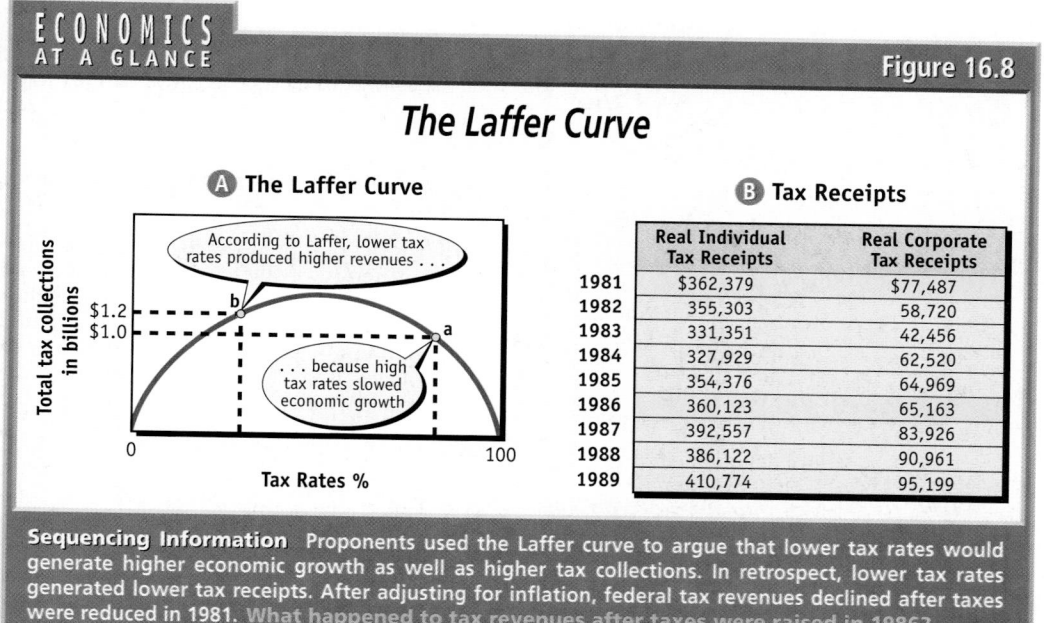

The Laffer Curve

A The Laffer Curve

According to Laffer, lower tax rates produced higher revenues . . .

. . . because high tax rates slowed economic growth

Total tax collections in billions

$1.2
$1.0

0   100

Tax Rates %

B Tax Receipts

	Real Individual Tax Receipts	Real Corporate Tax Receipts
1981	$362,379	$77,487
1982	355,303	58,720
1983	331,351	42,456
1984	327,929	62,520
1985	354,376	64,969
1986	360,123	65,163
1987	392,557	83,926
1988	386,122	90,961
1989	410,774	95,199

Sequencing Information Proponents used the Laffer curve to argue that lower tax rates would generate higher economic growth as well as higher tax collections. In retrospect, lower tax rates generated lower tax receipts. After adjusting for inflation, federal tax revenues declined after taxes were reduced in 1981. What happened to tax revenues after taxes were raised in 1986?

CHAPTER 16: ACHIEVING ECONOMIC STABILITY **451**

EXTENDING THE CONTENT

Demand-Side Policies During a recession, demand-side economics calls for an expansionary fiscal policy. This involves increased government spending, or tax cuts, or a combination of both. This approach would tend to move the government's budget toward a deficit. In times of high inflation, demand-side economics calls for a contractionary fiscal policy. This would mean government spending cuts, or tax increases, or a mix of the two. This approach would tend to move the government's budget toward a surplus.

ECONOMICS
AT A GLANCE

Answer: *Price levels go down.*

INTERACTIVE ECONOMICS!

CD-ROM

MACROECONOMIC EQUILIBRIUM Have students go to the Advanced Topics menu and click on "Fiscal Policy, Monetary Policy, and Macroeconomic Equilibrium" in Lesson 6. After reading the tutorial, have students write several paragraphs summarizing which policy they believe has the most impact on the economy.

💾 Also supplied in disk format.

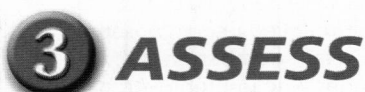

3 ASSESS

Assign Section 3 Assessment as homework or as an in-class activity.

💾 Have students use **Interactive Tutor Self-Assessment Software** to review Section 3.

Smaller Role for Government

A key issue for supply-siders is that of reducing government's role in the economy. One way to do this is to reduce the number of federal agencies. Another way to make government's role smaller is through deregulation—removing established regulations with which industries must comply.

Deregulation is a major objective of supply-siders and is favored by some demand-siders as well. Under the administration of President Jimmy Carter, major steps were taken to deregulate the energy, airline, and trucking industries. The Reagan administration continued deregulation efforts in the savings and loan industry, hoping to bring about more competition.

Lower Federal Taxes

Another target of supply-siders is the federal tax burden on individuals and businesses. They believe that if taxes are too high, people will not want to work, and businesses will produce less. Lower tax rates, they argue, allow individuals and businesses to keep more of the money they earn, which encourages them to work harder. This would give workers more money to spend in the long run. Government would also gain as total tax collections go up because of the extra activity.

In the 1980s, somewhat optimistic supply-siders even argued that lower tax rates would stimulate the economy so much that eventually even more taxes could be collected than before. This was formalized in the **Laffer curve**—a hypothetical relationship between federal tax rates and tax revenues—shown in **Panel A** of **Figure 16.8**. This proposition was the basis for President Reagan's 1981 tax cut, which reduced income taxes 25 percent over a three-year period.

As it turned out, either the interpretation or the assumptions of the Laffer curve were invalid, as the increased revenue collections never materialized. As **Panel B** in **Figure 16.8** shows, after adjusting for inflation, both individual income tax receipts and corporate tax receipts were lower in 1986 than they were in 1981. Because tax collections never went up the federal budget showed a deficit instead. In fact real tax collections did not surpass their 1981 level until after the 1986 tax revisions took effect in 1987.

Supply-Side Policies and Aggregate Supply

The impact of supply-side policies can be illustrated in terms of the aggregate supply and demand curves shown in **Figure 16.9**. When aggregate supply is very low, the economy would be at point **a,** where **AS₀** intersects **AD.** If supply side policies were successfully instituted, the aggregate supply curve would shift to **AS₁,** moving the point of macroeconomic equilibrium to **b** Without any corresponding change in aggregate demand, real output would grow, and the price level would come down.

Further attempts to increase aggregate supply to move the economy to **c** has even less impact on the price level. If the aggregate supply curve does have a horizontal range then the price level could never be reduced below **P₀.**

ECONOMICS
AT A GLANCE
Figure 16.9

Supply-Side Policies and the Aggregate Supply Curve

Analyzing Graphs Supply-side policies are designed to increase aggregate supply. What happens to the price level when the aggregate supply curve shifts to the right?

INTERDISCIPLINARY CONNECTIONS ACTIVITY

History Have students draw graphs showing the relative size of the role of government in the U.S. economy since 1790. Have them plot the ratio of government spending to GDP (or GNP) on the vertical axis, and time on the horizontal axis. When students' graphs are drawn, ask them to explain any sudden increases in the role of government. **Ask:** Why do you think the role of government has been increasing? Good sources of historical data are the *Economic Report of the President, Historical Statistics of the United States: Colonial Times to 1970,* and the *Datapedia of the United States, 1790-2000.*

THE GLOBAL ECONOMY

STABILIZING EFFORTS IN AFRICA

Beginning in the 1970s, droughts, growing populations, lack of capital, and falling world prices for their exports weakened many African economies.

Relying on foreign help to remedy these problems, African countries south of the Sahara took on $130 billion worth of debt by the 1980s. African leaders increasingly realized that they would have to find answers to Africa's problems without much outside help. To break their reliance on foreign countries, some African nations formed regional associations to promote trade and economic cooperation. Governments that had once adopted socialist policies increasingly encouraged free enterprise.

Critical Thinking

1. **Analyzing Information** What policies helped create the large debt?
2. **Analyzing Information** Why did many African nations form regional associations?

Limitations of Supply-Side Policies

One limitation of supply-side policies is a lack of enough experience with them to know how they affect the economy. Even the concepts of aggregate supply and aggregate demand are largely conceptual, making it difficult to predict, based on the shapes of the two curves, the exact consequence of any particular supply-side policy.

In the case of the Laffer curve, total tax collections, when adjusted for inflation, actually declined after the 1981 tax reductions were implemented. The result was that one of the main foundations of the supply-side school was found to be invalid. Even so, policies that promote productivity, reduce unnecessary paperwork, or otherwise allow the economy to grow to its maximum potential are certainly worthwhile. Almost everyone, including demand-siders, favors these policies.

Finally, supply-side economic policies are designed more to promote economic growth rather than to remedy economic instability. No matter how fast or slow the economy grows, it seems to have a tendency to fluctuate around its trend line. Supply-side policies during the Reagan presidency tended to weaken the automatic stabilizers by making the federal tax structure less progressive and by reducing many of the "safety net" programs.

Monetary Policies

Both demand-side economics and supply-side economics are concerned with stimulating production and employment. Neither policy assigns much importance to the money supply. A doctrine called **monetarism,** however, places primary importance on the role of money and its growth.

Monetarists believe that fluctuations in the money supply can be a destabilizing element that leads to unemployment and inflation. Because of this, they favor policies that lead to stable, long-term monetary growth at levels low enough to control inflation.

Interest Rates and Inflation

In the short run, expansionist monetary policy can lower interest rates. This action would reduce the cost of consumer and business borrowing and shift the aggregate supply curve to the right. Real GDP would tend to increase, but so would the possibility of future inflation. The money supply can grow over time, but how fast should the money supply be allowed to grow?

Most monetarists believe that inflation can be controlled if the money supply is allowed to grow at a slow but steady rate. The rates of growth of real GDP and productivity would determine the

CHAPTER 16: ACHIEVING ECONOMIC STABILITY **453**

THE GLOBAL ECONOMY

Stabilizing Efforts in Africa
The latest crisis in Africa has been the AIDS epidemic. Only 10 percent of the world's population lives in African countries south of the Sahara, but as of 1998, an estimated 83 percent of all AIDS deaths occurred in that region. South African president Thabo Mbeiki said in 1998, "Now we face the danger that half of our youth will not reach adulthood. Their education will be wasted. The economy will shrink. There will be a large number of sick people whom the healthy will not be able to maintain. Our dreams as a people will be shattered."

Answers:
1. *reliance on foreign countries, socialist policies*
2. *to promote local trade and economic cooperation*

Section Quiz 16-3

EXTENDING THE CONTENT

The Tax Wedge Supply-side economists argue that increases in taxes—most notably sales, excise, and Social Security taxes—are eventually incorporated into business costs and, therefore, result in higher prices. Taxes, they continue, act as a "wedge" between the actual costs of productive resources and the prices charged for products. Higher prices lead to a decrease in demand, which, in turn, leads to a cutback in production. The tax wedge, supply-siders conclude, causes a decrease in aggregate supply.

Reteach

Enrich

Have students read about current macroeconomic issues and policies in another nation, and write an essay comparing the current macroeconomic issues and policies of their selected country with those of the U.S.

4 CLOSE

Discuss the following statement: "Economic policymakers are about as skillful at predicting outcomes of their policies as meteorologists are at forecasting the weather."

rate at which the money supply grows. For example, if the rate of growth of real GDP were 3 percent, and that of productivity 1 percent, the money supply would grow at about 4 percent without causing inflation. At this rate, there would be just enough extra money each year to buy the additional goods and services the economy produces.

This approach to inflation control is in sharp contrast to those tried earlier. In the early 1970s, for example, President Richard Nixon tried to stop inflation by imposing **wage-price controls**—regulations that make it illegal for businesses to give workers raises—or to raise prices without the explicit permission of the government. Most monetarists at the time said the controls would not work. The economy ultimately proved the economists correct: the controls did little to stop inflation.

Monetary Policy and Unemployment

Monetarists argue that attempts to cut unemployment by expanding the money supply provide only temporary relief. They argue that excessive rates of monetary growth eventually drive up prices and interest rates.

When rates eventually do go up, the cost of borrowing for businesses increases, which shifts the aggregate supply curve to the left. The larger money supply also shifts the aggregate demand curve to the right. The result is that real GDP would fall back to its original level—but at a different and much higher price level. The final result would appear as if the aggregate supply and demand curves shifted up together.

An overly expansionist monetary policy, then, will only cause long-term inflation. Monetary policy is not a long-term cure for unemployment.

CYBERNOMICS SPOTLIGHT

Deregulation and New Growth
The deregulation of the telecommunications industry and the breakup of AT&T have helped turn the telephone into an important component of the economy. The telephone is responsible for helping Sioux Falls, South Dakota, and Omaha, Nebraska, become major centers for the credit-card processing and telemarketing industries.

Section 3 Assessment

Checking for Understanding
1. **Main Idea** Compare the views of supply-side economists and demand-side economists regarding the role of government in the economy.
2. **Key Terms** Define fiscal policy, Keynesian economics, multiplier, accelerator, automatic stabilizer, unemployment insurance, supply-side economics, Laffer curve, monetarism, wage-price controls.
3. **Describe** the objectives of demand-side policies.
4. **Identify** the main assumptions of supply-side policies.
5. **Explain** how monetary policy could be destabilizing.

Applying Economic Concepts
6. **Automatic Stabilizers** Fiscal policy is one of the tools designed to stabilize the economy. First, define fiscal policy in your own words. Then, explain its role in shifting the aggregate demand curve.

Critical Thinking
7. **Making Comparisons** How do demand-side policies and supply-side policies differ from one another?
8. **Analyzing Information** According to monetarists, how do fluctuations in the money supply affect the economy?

 Practice and **assess** key social studies skills with the *Glencoe Skillbuilder Interactive Workbook, Level 2.*

454 UNIT 4 MACROECONOMICS: POLICIES

Section 3 Assessment Answers

1. Supply-siders advocate smaller role.
2. All vocabulary terms are defined in the text.
3. to achieve steady economic growth by affecting aggregate demand
4. Lower taxes and less government will raise production and employment.
5. causes inflation in long-term
6. Fiscal policy is the government's attempt to stabilize the economy through taxing and government spending. Increases in government spending can increase aggregate demand.
7. See pages 447–452.
8. Fluctuations in the money supply can be destabilizing and lead to unemployment and inflation.

BusinessWeek

MARCH 29, 1999 ——————Newsclip

Wages are determined basically the same way other prices are—by demand and supply. People work and earn money. The amount they earn usually depends on the value of their labor. Those who possess a unique skill or ability may receive very high wages.

Unequal Pay Strikes Out

Economists and psychologists who have studied the impact of pay differentials on corporate performance seem to be of two minds on the subject. Some experts argue that unequal pay is beneficial—inspiring greater individual effort and productivity. Others claim that large pay differences often generate dissatisfaction and poorer quality work.

Both views may be valid, depending on the degree of inequality and the nature of a business and its workers. But in a team sport such as baseball, unequal pay doesn't seem to pay off. That's the finding of an intriguing study in the *Academy of Management Journal* by Matt Bloom of Purdue University.

Using two measures of pay dispersion, Bloom analyzed how they affected both individual player performance and final team standings for 29 teams from 1985 to 1993. Adjusting for such factors as past performance, age, experience, and pay levels, he found that unequal pay distributions translated into poorer stats for lower-paid players on a number of performance measures—and into lower standings for their teams.

The proof of the pudding: Bloom notes that three of [1998's] division winners, the New York Yankees, the San Diego Padres, and the Cleveland Indians, each had one of the smallest pay spreads in their respective leagues.

Successful teams like the San Diego Padres and Cleveland Indians tend to have relatively smaller pay spreads.

—Reprinted from March 29, 1999 issue of *Business Week*, by special permission, copyright © 1999 by The McGraw-Hill Companies, Inc.

Examining the Newsclip

1. **Synthesizing Information** What are the two theories presented in the article regarding large pay differentials?

2. **Finding the Main Idea** Which theory does the Bloom theory support?

3. **Drawing Conclusions** In your opinion, are the study's findings valid? Explain your reasoning.

CHAPTER 16: ACHIEVING ECONOMIC STABILITY **455**

TEACH

Many economists are concerned about the growing disparity in pay between managers and workers. In 1980, the average pay of a chief executive officer (CEO) of a major corporation was 42 times that of a factory worker. In 1998, the average pay of a CEO was 419 times that of a factory worker. Ask students to debate whether they believe such large differences in pay undermine the sense of teamwork within a corporation.

Refer to *Business Week Focus on the New Economy* in the TCR for additional unit-based articles.

Answers to Examining the Newsclip

1. Pay differentials inspire greater individual effort and productivity, or they foster dissatisfaction and poor work.

2. Bloom supports the theory that unequal pay is harmful to productivity.

3. Answers should demonstrate understanding of the Newsclip and chapter content.

FOCUS

Section Overview
This section discusses the inter-relationship of economics and politics.

BELLRINGER
Motivational Activity

Project **transparency** and have students answer questions.

Available as blackline master.

Daily Focus Transparency 78

Study Guide

Reading Strategy
Have students create the graphic organizer.
Answers to Graphic: *discretionary, passive, structural*

Preteaching Vocabulary
Use the Vocabulary Puzzle-Maker to create crossword and word-search puzzles.

SECTION 4

Economics and Politics

Study Guide

Main Idea
Monetary policy is becoming more important because discretionary fiscal policy is difficult to implement.

Reading Strategy
Graphic Organizer As you read the section, complete a graphic organizer similar to the one below by identifying and describing the different kinds of fiscal policy.

Key Term
Council of Economic Advisers

Objectives
After studying this section, you will be able to:
1. **Explain** why monetary policy sometimes conflicts with other economic policies.
2. **Recognize** that economists have differing views.
3. **Understand** the way that politics and economics interact.

Applying Economic Concepts
Diversity of Opinion Well-meaning friends often disagree over how something should be done. Read to find out why the same thing happens to economists.

Cover Story

Slew of New Issues Await Congress

WASHINGTON—Members of Congress return to work this week in a city still shaken by last week's terrorist attacks [on the World Trade Center].

Priorities that once commanded Congress' attention—prescription drugs, a new farm bill and health-care reform—have been squeezed aside by a pending military confrontation overseas, the financial crisis of U.S. airlines and a desire to provide sustenance to the nation's ailing economy.

The sharply partisan tones of appropriations season in Washington have been replaced by bipartisanship unknown in recent history.

Lawmakers already are working out the details of an economic assistance package for the airline industry. Defense budgets are expected to grow. And intelligence-gathering agencies seem destined for a big boost in funding.

Defense spending may increase

—*Omaha World-Herald,* September 20, 2001

456

As we look at the economic history of the United States, it is clear that times are better now than at any time in our past. Inflation is largely under control and the economy is larger and more productive than ever. Recessions still occur, of course, but business cycles have generally turned into fluctuations, and economic expansions are longer than ever.

Major political events such as the one mentioned in the cover story can temporarily interrupt the economy, but democratic market economies have a remarkable ability to cope with adversity. If anything, the task before us is to manage our prosperity in a way that improves our economic health, and in a way that benefits everyone.

The Changing Nature of Economic Policy

As you know, fiscal policy is the federal government's attempt to stabilize the economy through taxing and government spending. Fiscal policy involves planning a budget that has either surpluses or deficits that are intended to maintain a steady level of total spending in the economy.

RESOURCE MANAGER

Reproducible Masters
- Reproducible Lesson Plan 16-4
- Daily Lecture Notes 16-4
- Guided Reading Activity 16-4
- Reading Essentials and Study Guide 16-4
- Section Quiz 16-4

Transparencies
- Daily Focus Transparency 78

Multimedia
- Vocabulary PuzzleMaker CD-ROM
- Interactive Tutor Self-Assessment Software
- ExamView® Pro Testmaker
- Presentation Plus!

Fiscal policy can be either *discretionary, passive,* or *structural.* Discretionary fiscal policy is policy that someone must *choose* to implement. It requires an action by either the Congress and the president, or by an agency of government, to take effect. Passive fiscal policy does not require new or special action to go into effect. It reacts automatically when the economy changes. Structural fiscal policy includes plans and programs put in operation to strengthen the economy in the long run.

The Decline of Discretionary Fiscal Policy

Discretionary fiscal policy is used less today for several reasons. The first is the "recognition lag." This lag is the time between the beginning of a recession or a period of inflation and the awareness that it is actually happening. Most people do not believe that a recession is imminent until it actually occurs. Meanwhile, the economic problem may grow more severe than it would have if the situation had been recognized and dealt with sooner. This recognition lag is often followed by an "implementation lag," which is the amount of time it takes to do something once the problem is identified.

In November of 1973, for example, the American economy entered a severe recession that was to last for 16 months. At the time, it was considered the worst recession since the 1930s. To stimulate the economy, Congress approved a $100 income tax refund. However, the refunds were not mailed until the second quarter of 1975—shortly after the recession *ended.*

A third reason contributing to the decline of discretionary fiscal policy is the relatively short duration of recessions—about 11 months on average. To illustrate, when the 1990 recession began, political leaders waited for it to end rather than enact any programs to stimulate the GDP. The Fed used monetary policy to help move the economy out of the recession, but recovery was weak.

The fourth reason contributing to the decline of fiscal policy is the gridlock that has characterized our government since the 1990s. In both 1995 and 1996, Congress shut the federal government down when the parties could not agree on the federal budget. When Republicans and Democrats deadlocked in 1999 over a $792 billion

tax cut proposal, the federal government could not use fiscal policy to shape the economy.

Fifth, Congress imposed budget caps designed to limit federal government spending. The caps gave Congress little leeway to pursue discretionary policies. As a result, some spending for agriculture, military operations in Kosovo, and even routine expenditures such as those required to carry out the 2000 census, were classified as "emergency expenditures" to get around the budget caps.

Of course, discretionary fiscal policies are still possible, but it takes an event like the one discussed in the cover story to spur Congress to action. For all these reasons, discretionary fiscal policies are losing ground to passive fiscal policies.

The Importance of Passive Fiscal Policies

Despite the declining use of discretionary fiscal policies, several passive fiscal programs contribute to the stability of the American economy.

All of the automatic stabilizers—unemployment insurance, social security, and other programs dis-

Careers

Credit Manager

Credit managers decide whether to extend credit to clients—either companies or individuals.

The Work

Credit managers' duties include analyzing financial reports submitted by client companies and reviewing credit agency reports on their promptness in paying bills. Credit managers also draw up credit policies to be met by individuals applying for credit. They set up office procedures and oversee other employees in the credit department.

Qualifications

To succeed in their work, credit managers must be able to analyze detailed information, draw conclusions, and speak and write effectively. A degree in business administration is a must.

457

②TEACH

Daily Lecture Notes 16-4

DAILY LECTURE NOTES 📖 Lesson 16-4

🅓 DID YOU KNOW?

Martin Feldstein, former chair of the Council of Economic Advisers writes that people are frequently surprised to learn how small the Council actually is. They hear the word "council" and think of a dozen or more people sitting around a conference table when, in fact, the CEA has only a chairman and two additional members. Talking with senior economic officials from around the world, Feldstein also discovered that the institutionalized appointment of a professional economist to a country's president or leader is rare. In other countries economists rarely have direct and regular access to the head of the government, nor are they able to participate as an equal in all cabinet-level discussions.

PAGES 456-458

I. The Changing Nature of Economic Policy

  A. For a variety of reasons, discretionary fiscal policy is used less today than it once was.

  B. Passive fiscal policy, like automatic stabilizers and a progressive income tax, contribute to the stability of the American economy.

  C. Structural fiscal policies are designed to strengthen the economy in the long run rather than deal with temporary problems, such as unemployment or inflation.

  D. Declining discretionary fiscal policy has increased the influence of monetary policy.

  E. Though often the target of criticism, most members of Congress believe that the power to create money should remain with an independent agency, not elected officials.

🅔 Discussion Question

Why is it difficult to use fiscal policy to deal with short-term changes in the economy? *(Fiscal policy cannot be implemented quickly. By the time a tax cut or an increase in government spending is approved, the economy may already be recovering.)*

L1 Fiscal Policy Jeopardy

Have students develop Jeopardy-style questions for the section titled "The Changing Nature of Economic Policy." For example, if the answer is "Policies not designed to deal with temporary problems such as recession and unemployment," the required question would be "What are structural fiscal policies?" Have students develop enough questions for a short review game.

L2 Making Comparisons

Call on students to identify similarities and differences between the Fed and the Council of Economic Advisers. Note suggestions on the board. Then have students use this information to write a comparative essay on these two bodies.

MEETING SPECIAL NEEDS ACTIVITY

Learning Style: Interpersonal Ask students to survey adults about their economic values. Have them include the following questions, along with others they develop, in their survey: What is your political affiliation? Do you think the federal government is too large or too small? Do you think the federal government should cut taxes? On what programs, if any, should the government increase spending? Have students summarize the survey data and identify any differences in attitudes among Democrats, Republicans, and members of other political parties.

📂 Refer to *Inclusion for the Social Studies Classroom Strategies and Activities* in the TCR.

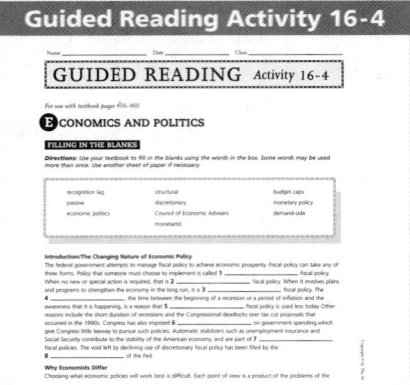

CYBERNOMICS

Forecasting Economic Change
Economists use computers to create models predicting the future of the economy. These models are actually systems of equations that describe the economy. Economists use computers and historical data to estimate the value of any constants (like *a* and *b*) in the model. They then use the model to forecast changes in economic variables.

THE GLOBAL ECONOMY

Preparing for the Euro
The euro is the new European currency that is gradually replacing the currencies of 11 nations. Before adopting the euro, the 11 countries involved had to align their fiscal and monetary policies in a process called "convergence." Now these countries are allowing a new European Central Bank (ECB) in Frankfurt to conduct monetary policy on their behalf.

cussed on page 449—protect consumers and the economy if economic conditions worsen. Other programs, such as the progressive individual income tax, discussed on page 450, provide the same relief.

For example, if the economy slows down, workers earn less and drop into lower tax brackets, which helps offset their lost income. On the other hand, if the economy accelerates, as it did in the late 1990s, workers earn more and move into higher tax brackets. The higher tax brackets help put a break on over-expansion, and generate substantial tax revenues in the process. These surpluses can then be used to repay money that was previously borrowed—as the Democrats suggested in 1999. Or, they can be returned to the American people in the form of lower taxes—as the Republicans preferred to do.

Structural Fiscal Policies

Structural fiscal policies are policies designed to strengthen the economy in the long run. They are not designed to deal with temporary problems such as recession and unemployment.

One example of a structural program is the national health-care program President Clinton proposed in the early 1990s. Another is the 1996 welfare overhaul that replaced the Aid to Families with Dependent Children (AFDC) with the Temporary Aid to Needy Families (TANF). Proposals to strengthen the banking system with better inspection and insurance even come under this heading. Finally, there is President Bush's $1.35 billion tax cut that passed in mid-2001.

Did you know?

Private Property Early Americans believed so strongly in the right to private property that they incorporated this right into law. The first Congress proposed the Fifth Amendment, which was ratified in 1791. The amendment states that private property shall not be taken for public use without just compensation. The Fourteenth Amendment prevents any state from depriving people of their property without due process of law.

Finally, because structural policies are designed to deal with long-term problems, they do not need short-term attention once they are put in place.

The Dominance of Monetary Policy

The declining use of discretionary fiscal policy left a void filled by the Federal Reserve System (Fed), which conducts monetary policy. The abandonment of discretionary fiscal policy also means that monetary and fiscal policies are less likely to clash—although monetary policy is still subject to criticism by political leaders.

Such a situation occurred during the 1992 presidential election campaign. Because of the threat of inflation, the Fed was pursuing a tighter monetary policy than President Bush wanted. The high interest rates caused by the Fed's policy also contributed to the length of the 1991 recession. Eventually, the high interest rates and the recession during the election year—along with President Bush's broken promise not to raise taxes—paved the way for Bill Clinton's narrow election victory.

Of course, the Fed is not above criticism. For example, the Fed's efforts to prevent inflation by raising interest rates several times in 2000 may have caused the 2001 slowdown. The Fed then reversed itself and lowered interest rates ten times in a row in 2001 to stimulate growth. Even so, Congress has not been willing to make the Fed less independent. Most members of Congress continue to believe that the power to create money should remain with an independent agency rather than with elected officials.

Why Economists Differ

Choosing which economic policies will work best is difficult. The proposals economists offer often seem contradictory, which adds to the difficulty. These differences, however, are smaller than most people realize.

Different Criteria

Economists who choose one policy over another normally do so because they think that some problems are more critical than others. For

---

FREE ENTERPRISE ACTIVITY

Have students review business and economics periodicals from previous years for several articles that make predictions about the economy. Ask students to summarize what economists predicted, the extent to which predictions agreed, and the accuracy of the predictions.

example, one economist might think that unemployment is the crucial issue, while another believes that inflation is. If you were to survey all economists on the best way to deal with a specific problem, their recommendations would be much more consistent.

Different Eras

Another reason economists differ is that most economic explanations and theories are a product of the problems of the times. The unemployment and other problems that occurred during the Great Depression of the 1930s, for example, influenced demand-side economists. Because the government sector was so small at the time, supply-side policies designed to make government's role even smaller probably would not have helped much.

The Monetarist Point of View

The monetarist point of view emerged in the 1960s and 1970s when inflation soared. Because demand-side economic policies were not designed to deal with inflation, new solutions were needed. The problem with the monetarist view, however, was that it offered long-term solutions but little short-term relief.

Supply-Side Policies

Supply-side policies eventually grew out of frustration with stagflation and the failure of demand-siders and monetarists to address this issue. Again, changing times led to changing problems, and so something new and different seemed to be needed.

For the most part, economists do not normally define their positions as being purely demand-side, supply-side, or monetarist. Many demand-siders are monetarists when it comes to controlling inflation. Many monetarists are supply-siders when it comes to agreeing on the potential burden of the tax structure. Most economists take a middle road that incorporates many points of view.

As long as society keeps changing, new problems will continue to arise. From each new set of problems, new theories—and advocates for those theories—are bound to emerge.

Economic Policy

Hang In There!

"ECONOMISTS. ONE'S A KEYNESIAN...THE OTHER ISN'T."

Difference of Opinion Although economists do not come to blow like the ones in this cartoon, they often do not agree on economic policies. *Why do economists differ in their policies?*

Economic Politics

In the 1800s, the science of economics was known as "political economics." After a while, economists broke away from the political theorists and tried to establish economics as a science in its own right.

In recent years, the two fields have merged again. This time, however, they have done so in a way best described as "economic politics." Today, politicians are concerned with the economic consequences of what they do. Most of the major debates in Congress, for example, are over spending, taxes, or other budgetary matters.

Council of Economic Advisers

Generally, economists and politicians work together fairly closely. The president relies on a

CHAPTER 16: ACHIEVING ECONOMIC STABILITY **459**

Visual Instruction

Answer to Caption:
because they feel some problems are more crucial than others; theories are a product of the times

3 ASSESS

Assign Section 4 Assessment as homework or as an in-class activity.

Have students use **Interactive Tutor Self-Assessment Software.**

Section Quiz 16-4

CRITICAL THINKING

Recognizing Ideologies As a class, discuss the concept of economic politics. **Ask:** Why must politicians be concerned with economics? How important are economic matters to voters? Then locate a number of newspaper and magazine articles dealing with political debates on economic policy. Copy the articles and distribute them to students. Ask them to read the articles and write an essay describing the economic views of the major political parties. Students should include quotes and examples from the articles to support their conclusions. **BLOCK SCHEDULING**

ECONOMICS *Online*

Objectives, goals, and answers to the student activity can be found in the **Web Activity Lesson Plan** feature at epp.glencoe.com

Reteach

Reading Essentials and Study Guide 16-4

STUDY GUIDE — Chapter 16, Section 4

For use with textbook pages 456–460

E CONOMICS AND POLITICS

KEY TERMS

Council of Economic Advisers A three-member group of presidential advisers who report on economic developments and suggest strategies (page 459)

DRAWING FROM EXPERIENCE

Have you ever had a serious disagreement with a friend over money? Did you disagree over how to earn it or spend it?

In the last section, you read about the different views for achieving economic stability. This section focuses on how politics and economics work together to make policies.

ORGANIZING YOUR THOUGHTS

Use the table below to help you take notes as you read the summaries that follow. Think about why discretionary fiscal policy is used less today than it previously was.

Reasons Why Discretionary Policy is Not Often Used
1.
2.
3.
4.
5.

...economists often suggest policies ...em very different from one another. But these differences may not be as large as they seem. Many economists actually agree with some parts of

Enrich

Have students write a research paper on an election year in which fiscal and monetary policy were at odds.

4 CLOSE

Discuss playwright George Bernard Shaw's comment that if you laid all the economists end to end, they still would not reach a conclusion.

Council of Economic Advisers, a three-member group that reports on economic developments and proposes strategies. The economists basically are the advisers, while the politicians direct or implement the policies. In its role as "the president's intelligence arm in the war against the business cycle," the council gathers information and makes recommendations.

The president listens to the economists' advice, but may not be willing or able to follow it. To illustrate, if the president advocates a balanced budget, the economic advisers may recommend raising taxes to achieve this goal. If one of the president's campaign pledges was not to raise taxes, however, the president might reject the advisers' suggestion.

Increased Understanding and Awareness

Despite disagreeing on some points, economists have had considerable success in the description, analysis, and explanation of economic activity. They have developed many statistical measures of the economy's performance. Economists also have constructed models that are helpful in the tasks of economic analysis and explanation.

In the process, economists have helped the American people become more aware of the workings of the economy. This awareness has benefited everyone, from the student just starting out to the politician who must answer to the voters.

Today, economists know enough about the economy to prevent a depression like the one in the 1930s. It is doubtful that economists know enough—or can persuade others that they know enough—to avoid minor recessions. They can, however, devise policies to stimulate growth, help disadvantaged groups when unemployment rises or inflation strikes, and generally make the American economy more successful.

ECONOMICS *Online*

Student Web Activity Visit the *Economics: Principles and Practices* Web site at epp.glencoe.com and click on **Chapter 16—Student Web Activities** for an activity on the Council of Economic Advisers.

Section 4 Assessment

Checking for Understanding

1. **Main Idea** Using your notes from the graphic organizer activity on page 456, explain the difference between automatic and discretionary fiscal policy. List examples of each in your answer.

2. **Key Term** Define Council of Economic Advisers.

3. **Describe** monetary policy and its goals. Then explain how monetary policy can sometimes conflict with economic policy.

4. **List** several reasons economists differ over policies and issues.

5. **Explain** what "economic politics" means in your own words.

Applying Economic Concepts

6. **Diversity of Opinion** Why do monetary and fiscal policies often operate at cross-purposes? What impact does this conflict have on the economy?

Critical Thinking

7. **Making Inferences** Suppose that, in an election year, Congress passes a massive tax cut even though inflation is at 9 percent. What actions might the Fed take in response during such economic times?

8. **Analyzing Information** Why might monetary and fiscal policy be at odds during an election year?

 Practice and **assess** key social studies skills with the *Glencoe Skillbuilder Interactive Workbook, Level 2.*

460 UNIT 4 MACROECONOMICS: POLICIES

Section 4 Assessment Answers

1. Discretionary is chosen. Automatic is self-acting.

2. All vocabulary terms are defined in the text.

3. to promote economic growth and price stability by controlling the amount of money in circulation; To control inflation, monetary policy may increase interest rates; however, politicians often do not want higher rates.

4. They view different problems as most critical; different time periods face different problems.

5. Politicians are concerned with the economic consequences of what they do.

6. Elected officials may not agree with Fed policies. Differences may lead to delay of policies.

7. They may raise interest rates to slow the growth of money and reduce inflation.

8. because fiscal policy is controlled by politicians, and monetary policy is controlled by an independent body

CHAPTER 16
Summary

Section 1

The Cost of Economic Instability

(pages 437–440)

- Low economic growth and economic instability in the form of inflation and high unemployment rates have both economic and social costs.

- The economic costs can be measured with the **misery index** or the **GDP gap.**

- The social costs include unemployment, wasted resources, potential political instability, increased crime, and damage to family financial security.

- Strong economic growth is more than an economic ideal. It is one of the foundations of a healthy society.

Section 2

Macroeconomic Equilibrium

(pages 442–445)

- **Macroeconomic equilibrium** is similar to equilibrium in individual markets. It can be analyzed with the help of **aggregate supply curves** and **aggregate demand curves.**

- Most of the factors that influence the individual supply and demand curves also affect the aggregate curves. They shift to the right to represent an increase, and to the left to represent a decrease.

- The intersection of aggregate supply and aggregate demand determines **macroeconomic equilibrium.** This equilibrium is defined in terms of a certain amount of real GDP being produced at a specific price level.

Section 3

Stabilization Policies (pages 447–454)

- Demand-side policies, or **fiscal policies,** are policies designed to affect the aggregate demand curve through federal spending and taxing decisions. Fiscal policies are derived from **Keynesian economics,** which assigns the government a key role in offsetting fluctuating spending by the business sector.

- **Automatic stabilizers** are an important part of demand-side economics.

- Supply-side economics recommends a smaller role for governments and a lower federal tax structure.

- The outcome of monetary policy is a change in the size of the money supply that, in turn, affects the cost and availability of credit.

- The short-run impact of monetary policy is on interest rates. The long-run impact is on the rate of inflation.

Section 4

Economics and Politics (pages 456–460)

- Discretionary policy is increasingly difficult to execute due to recognition lags, implementation lags, Congressional gridlock, the brevity of recessions, and conservative budget caps.

- Passive fiscal policy in the form of automatic stabilizers still provides much stability, but monetary policy has filled the void and has become dominant.

- The fields of economics and politics are closely intertwined. The president has a **Council of Economic Advisers** but, for political reasons, may not always be able to follow the Council's advice.

CHAPTER 16: ACHIEVING ECONOMIC STABILITY 461

NIGHTLY BUSINESS REPORT

⊙ **ECONOMICS & YOU**

Chapter 23
Disc 1, Side 2

Economic Growth and Stability

▭ Also available in VHS.

Using the Chapter 16 Summary

Use the Chapter 16 Summary to preview, review, condense, or reteach the chapter.

Preview/Review

Vocabulary PuzzleMaker CD-ROM reinforces Key Terms.

Interactive Tutor Self-Assessment Software provides a review of Chapter 16 content.

Condense

Have students listen to the Chapter 16 Audio Program. Spanish also available.

Assign the Chapter 16 Audio Program Activity and give students the Chapter 16 Audio Program Test.

Have students complete the Guided Reading Activities and Reading Essentials and Study Guides for Chapter 16.

Reteach

Have students complete Reteaching Activity 16 in the TCR. Spanish also available.

Teacher's Notes / Internet Bookmarks

GLENCOE
TECHNOLOGY

Use **MindJogger Videoquiz** to review the Chapter 16 content.

Have students visit the Web site at epp.glencoe.com to review Chapter 16 and take the **Self-Check Quiz.**

Identifying Key Terms

1. d-s	4. d-s	8. d-s
2. s-s	5. s-s	9. s-s
3. d-s	6. d-s	10. m
	7. d-s	

Reviewing the Facts

Section 1

1. the GDP gap, the misery index
2. wasted resources, political instability, high crime rates, increase in bankruptcy

Section 2

3. aggregate supply curve: the amount of GDP that could be produced at different price levels; supply curve for an individual firm: the amount the firm is willing to supply at different prices.
4. decrease in savings, increase in consumer spending, improved expectations, increase in government spending and transfers, and a decrease in taxes
5. when the quantity of real GDP demanded is equal to the real GDP supplied at a given price level

Section 3

6. spending and/or taxation policies to influence economic activity; automatic stabilizers such as unemployment insurance; entitlements

462

Identifying Key Terms

Classify each of the terms below into one of the following categories:

- **supply-side policies**
- **demand-side policies**
- **monetary policies**

1. aggregate demand curve
2. aggregate supply curve
3. automatic stabilizer
4. multiplier
5. deregulation
6. entitlements
7. fiscal policy
8. Keynesian economics
9. Laffer curve
10. wage-price controls

Reviewing the Facts

Section 1 (pages 437–440)

1. **List** two measures used to describe the problems of growth and economic instability.
2. **Name** some of the social costs of instability.

Section 2 (pages 442–445)

3. **Describe** the difference between the supply curve of a firm and the aggregate supply curve.

4. **Identify** the factors that would cause the aggregate demand curve to increase.
5. **Discuss** what is meant by macroeconomic equilibrium.

Section 3 (pages 447–454)

6. **Identify** the major tools of fiscal policy.
7. **List** the main assumptions of supply-siders.
8. **Describe** the short-term and long-term impacts of monetary policy.

Section 4 (pages 456–460)

9. **Explain** why discretionary fiscal policy is so difficult to use.
10. **Explain** why new problems will arise in the economy, even as old ones are solved.
11. **State** an example of how politics sometimes overrides sound economic policies.

Thinking Critically

1. **Drawing Conclusions** Why is the misery index a more personal measure of the social costs of instability than other concepts, such as the GDP gap?
2. **Making Comparisons** How do aggregate supply and demand differ from simple supply and demand? Use a chart similar to the one below to answer the question.

	Description
Demand	
Aggregate Demand	
Supply	
Aggregate Supply	

7. Deregulation and lower taxes will give businesses and consumers more incentive to produce and spend, thus increasing revenue collections because of the extra activity.
8. In the short term, monetary policy can affect interest rates and perhaps unemployment. In the long run, expansionist monetary policy can cause inflation.

Section 4

9. recognition lag, implementation lag, short duration of recessions, gridlock, budget caps
10. Society and the economy keep changing.

11. Answers may cite the refusal of the president and Congress to raise taxes, even when economic advisors recommend it.

Thinking Critically

1. It measures inflation and unemployment while the GDP gap simply measures the output not produced.
2. demand: the desire, ability, and willingness to buy a product; supply: schedule of quantities offered for sale at all possible prices in a market; aggregate demand: total quantity of goods and services demanded at different price levels;

3. Making Comparisons Analyze the use of discretionary fiscal policy and monetary policy to offset the effects of a short recession. Which policy would you choose? Include reasons to support your choice.

Applying Economic Concepts

1. Automatic Stabilizers What automatic stabilizers have benefited you or your family in the recent past? Could you have managed without them?

2. Multiplier Provide an example of how a $100,000 expenditure in your community would have a magnified effect as described by the multiplier.

3. Diversity of Opinion Some economists favor policies that stimulate demand, while others favor those that stimulate the supply of goods and services. Still other economists prefer policies based on the growth of the money supply. With which group of economists do you agree? Provide reasons to support your choice.

4. Monetary Policy The Federal Reserve System conducts monetary policy. At one time or another, most presidents have complained about the independence of the Fed. Do you think this independence should be maintained, or that elected officials should have more control over monetary policy? Support your answer.

Math Practice

According to Keynesian economics, what action should government take if business investment fell by $20 billion? Show your findings using the output-expenditure model:

$$GDP = C + I + G + F$$

Thinking Like an Economist

Both demand-side and supply-side policies are designed to ensure stable economic growth. The approaches differ, however, on what should be done to achieve this goal. Assume that real GDP growth was negative during the last quarter. Make a two-column chart. In the left column, list the policies that demand-side economists would follow to help the economy. Place the supply-side solution in the right column. How do they differ?

Technology Skill

Using the Internet Log on to the Internet. Then, using a search engine, type in the following key words:

- John Maynard Keynes
- Unemployment
- Stabilization policies
- Inflation
- Fiscal policy

Print out (or download) any articles or reports on these topics. Using the information you retrieved, prepare a two-paragraph report on each topic listed above—defining the terms and summarizing their significance to economic security. Add a list of Web sites and bibliography entries at the end of your report.

Building Skills

Applying the Writing Process Go to a library to look up advertisements for airfares from 19 years ago. Find out what the current airfares are when traveling to the same locations. Write an essay that explains the effect these price changes may have had on consumers. What might they have to do with the deregulation of the airline industry?

 Practice and **assess** key social studies skills with the *Glencoe Skillbuilder Interactive Workbook, Level 2.*

Math Practice

The government should spend $20 billion or increase transfers by $20 billion.

Thinking Like an Economist

demand-side: enlarged government role, automatic stabilizers; supply-side: reduced government role, lower federal tax structure; major difference: role of government

Technology Skill

Reports and lists of Web sites should be appropriate and informative. Have students present the results of their "surfing" to the class.

Building Skills

Essays should explain the effects of airfare changes on consumers and relate the changes to the deregulation of the airline industry.

 Bonus Test Question

Have students identify the impact on aggregate supply or aggregate demand of each of the following:
1. OPEC decides to double its output. *(Oil prices fall; aggregate supply will increase.)*
2. Income tax rates are increased 10 percent. *(People have less money to spend; aggregate demand will decline.)*
3. People expect the next set of economic indicators to show a sharp economic decline. *(Unfavorable expectations; aggregate demand will decline.)*

aggregate supply: total value of goods and services that all firms would produce in a specific period of time at various price levels
3. Choices and supporting details should demonstrate knowledge of chapter content, especially fiscal and monetary policies.

Applying Economic Concepts

1. Answers should include one or more examples of unemployment insurance, federal entitle-

ment programs, or progressive income tax. Students should provide details and demonstrate knowledge of chapter content.
2. Examples should describe the magnified effect and demonstrate knowledge of chapter content.
3. Choices should include supporting details and should demonstrate knowledge of economic policies.
4. Answers should include supporting details and demonstrate knowledge of the Fed and monetary policy.

Unit 5 Resource Manager

Materials listed may be used at any time during the study of the unit.

TEACHING TRANSPARENCIES

Economics Forms and Financial Pages Transparencies

Transparency 6
Circle Graph

Transparency 7
Bar Graph

Transparency 13
Currency Exchange Rates

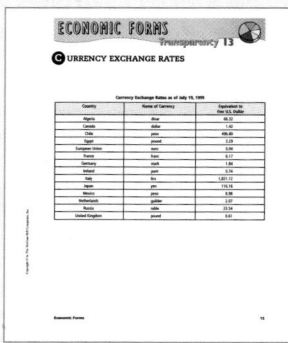

Economic Concepts Transparencies

Transparency 20 Absolute and Comparative Advantage

Transparency 21 Exchange Rates and Balance of Payments

Transparency 22 International Aspects of Growth and Stability

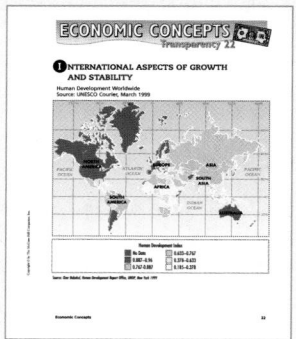

REAL-WORLD ECONOMICS

*Have your students learn about investing and managing their financial future by participating in the exciting simulation **The Stock Market Game**TM. See Teacher pages in front of book for more information.*

*Strengthen students' research, cooperation, presentation and critical-thinking skills by having them compete in the **Fed Challenge**. See Teacher pages in front of book for more information.*

Additional Glencoe Resources for This Unit:

- **Interactive Economics!**
- **Glencoe Skillbuilder Interactive Workbook, Level 2**
- **Nightly Business Report Economics & You Video Program**
- **Economic Survival: A Financial Simulation**

Unit 5 Resource Manager

ASSESSMENT

Unit 5 Test

APPLICATION AND ENRICHMENT

Economics Laboratory 5

Unit 5 Business Week Focus on the New Economy

Use the following tools to easily assess student learning in a variety of ways:

- Performance Assessment Strategies and Activities
- Section Quizzes
- Chapter and Unit Tests
- Interactive Tutor Self-Assessment Software
- ExamView® Pro Testmaker
- MindJogger Videoquiz
- SAT I/II Test Practice
- epp.glencoe.com

*inter*NET CONNECTION

Economics: Principles and Practices
Visit the *Economics: Principles and Practices* Web site for economics overviews, activities, assessments, and updated charts and graphs.
epp.glencoe.com

Glencoe Social Studies
Visit the Glencoe Web site for social studies activities updates, and links to other sites.
socialstudies.glencoe.com

 Glencoe's Guide to Using the Internet
Provides an introduction to many of the current technologies on the Internet. Professional resources and teaching strategies included.

Business Week Online
Visit the *Business Week* Web site for up-to-date news and special reports.
www.businessweek.com

Our Web sites provide additional resources. All essential content is covered in the Student Edition.

BIBLIOGRAPHY

Readings for the Student

Pomeranz, Kenneth, and Steven Topik. *The World That Trade Created: Society, Culture, and the World Economy, 1400–the Present.* Armonk, NY: M.E. Sharpe, 1998.

"What Price Pollution? Leave that to a Global Market," by Gary S. Becker, *Business Week*, Oct.18, 1999.

Readings for the Teacher

Ohmae, Kenichi. *A Borderless World: Power and Strategy in the Interlinked Economy.* New York: HarperBusiness, 1999.

"Whose World Is It, Anyway?" by Paul Manusson and Aaron Bernstein, *Business Week*, Dec. 20, 1999.

Multimedia Resources

Simulation. *International Cutthroat: A Simulation of Global Competition and Cooperation.* Active Learning Consultants. Available from Social Studies School Service, 10200 Jefferson Boulevard, P.O. Box 802, Culver City, California 90232-0802.

`0:00` OUT OF TIME?

If time does not permit teaching each chapter in this unit, you may use the Audio Program that includes a one-page activity and a one-page test for each chapter.

Unit Objectives

After studying this unit, students will be able to:

1. Recognize the importance of international trade, foreign exchange, and the interdependence among nations.
2. Compare major economic systems of the world to capitalism.
3. Analyze the problems of economically developing countries.
4. Describe significant global economic challenges.

Unit Overview

Unit 5 examines economics from a global perspective. **Chapter 17** examines international trade. **Chapter 18** presents the spectrum of economic systems and traces the rise and fall of the Soviet Union. **Chapter 19** discusses the problems faced by developing countries. **Chapter 20** reviews the economic challenges the world faces.

UNIT 5
International and Global Economics

Why It's Important

As you read this unit, learn how the study of economics helps answer the following questions:

- Why do imported goods sometimes cost more than domestically produced goods?
- Why did capitalism triumph over communism?
- How do population growth rates on the other side of the world affect you?

464 UNIT 5 INTERNATIONAL AND GLOBAL ECONOMICS

MAKING IT
activity
RELEVANT

An Economic Challenge Recycling is an important economic as well as environmental challenge. For instance, each year discarded electronic equipment accounts for 75,000 tons of solid waste in Massachusetts. A state-sponsored program transforms old and obsolete computers into asphalt and uses it to fill potholes. At several different times during the study of this unit, have students examine the contents of a school trash can and brainstorm ideas for products that might be made from the different kinds of garbage.

International trade—both the importing and exporting of goods—is essential to the U.S. economy.

Introducing the Unit
In this unit, students will discover the importance of economic interdependence and examine economic issues on a global scale. Write the following questions on the board: Why do nations trade? How do other economic systems differ from our own? What are some of the problems of developing nations, and what can be done to foster their economic development? What types of global economic challenges face all nations? Direct students to write the questions and their answers in their notebooks. Have students check and adjust their answers as they study the unit.

Visual Instruction

Have students discuss how international trade allows nations to specialize, increase the productivity of their resources, and obtain more goods and services. Nations, like individuals and regions of a nation, can gain by specializing in products they can produce efficiently and by trading for goods they cannot produce as efficiently.

ECONOMICS Online

To learn more about global economics through information, activities, and links to other sites, visit the *Economics: Principles and Practices* Web site at epp.glencoe.com

ECONOMICS Online

To access the information, follow these steps:

1. Log on to the **Economics: Principles and Practices** Web site at epp.glencoe.com
2. From the options on the opening screen, select Web Resources.
3. Select the World Bank.

Click on Regions & Countries. Select a country and click on it.

What to Do When You Are There
Browse through the various topics about the country you selected. In particular, read about the different projects, assistance strategies, and financial initiatives that the World Bank is involved in to improve that country's living standards and alleviate poverty. After you have read the information, write a brief summary describing how the World Bank's efforts are helping this particular country.

Chapter 17 Resource Manager

SECTION RESOURCES

Daily Objectives	Reproducible Resources	Technology/Multimedia Resources

Section 1
Absolute and Comparative Advantage
1. Explain the importance of international trade in today's economy.
2. Describe the basis for international trade.
3. Explain why total world output increases when countries specialize to engage in trade.

 Reproducible Lesson Plan 17-1
Daily Lecture Notes 17-1
Guided Reading Activity 17-1
Reading Essentials and Study Guide 17-1
 Section Quiz 17-1*

 Daily Focus Transparency 79
Interactive Economics!
Interactive Tutor Self-Assessment Software
ExamView® Pro Testmaker
Presentation Plus!

Section 2
Barriers to International Trade
1. Explain how international trade can be restricted to protect special interests.
2. Cite the main argument used in support of protection.
3. Relate the history of the free trade movement.

 Reproducible Lesson Plan 17-2
Daily Lecture Notes 17-2
Guided Reading Activity 17-2
Reading Essentials and Study Guide 17-2
 Section Quiz 17-2*

 Daily Focus Transparency 81
  NBR Economics & You Video Program
Interactive Tutor Self-Assessment Software
ExamView® Pro Testmaker
Presentation Plus!

Section 3
Financing and Trade Deficits
1. Explain how foreign currency is used in trade.
2. Describe the problem of a trade deficit and the main solution to the problem.

 Reproducible Lesson Plan 17-3
Daily Lecture Notes 17-3
Guided Reading Activity 17-3
Reading Essentials and Study Guide 17-3
 Section Quiz 17-3*

 Daily Focus Transparency 80
Vocabulary PuzzleMaker CD-ROM
Interactive Tutor Self-Assessment Software
ExamView® Pro Testmaker
Presentation Plus!

 Transparency   CD-ROM   Software   Blackline Master   *Also available in Spanish*

 Videodisc   Audio Program   Videocassette

0:00 OUT OF TIME?
Assign the Chapter 17 Audio Program activity and test.

 Block Schedule

Activities that are particularly suited to use within the block scheduling framework are identified throughout this chapter by the following designation: **BLOCK SCHEDULING**

KEY TO ABILITY LEVELS

Teaching strategies have been coded for varying learning styles and abilities.
L1 BASIC activities for all students
L2 AVERAGE activities for average to above-average students
L3 CHALLENGING activities for above-average students
ELL ENGLISH LANGUAGE LEARNER activities

Timesaving Tools

TeacherWorks™ All-In-One Planner and Resource Center

- **Interactive Teacher Edition** Access your Teacher Wraparound Edition and your classroom resources with a few easy clicks.
- **Interactive Lesson Planner** Planning has never been easier! Organize your week, month, semester, or year with all the lesson helps you need to make teaching creative, timely, and relevant.

Use Glencoe's **Presentation Plus!** multimedia teacher tool to easily present dynamic lessons that visually excite your students. Using Microsoft PowerPoint® you can customize the presentations to create your own personalized lessons.

PRESENTATION Plus!

ACTIVITY

From the Classroom of...

**Jack L. Gallegos
Englewood High School
Englewood, CO**

Foreign Exchange Rate and Strength of U.S. Dollar

Have students choose a newspaper ad for a consumer good made in the United States. The ad must contain the price of the good. **Ask:**
1. What is the consumer good?
2. What is the price of the good in U.S. dollars?

Have students use available newspapers to find a list of exchange rates. Tell them to pick a foreign country of their choice. **Ask:**
1. What is the name of the country you chose?
2. What is the country's monetary unit?
3. What is the exchange rate? One U.S. dollar = ?
4. What would the price of the good be if it were exported from the United States and purchased in the foreign country using that country's currency?

Ask the class: If it takes fewer of a foreign country's currency to buy a U.S. dollar, would you expect the sales of the consumer good exported to the foreign country to increase or decrease? Why? Would the U.S. dollar be described as weak or strong against that foreign currency? What would likely happen to sales in the foreign country if it takes more of a foreign country's currency to buy a U.S. dollar? In this case, would the U.S. dollar be considered weak or strong against the foreign currency? How does a strong U.S. dollar impact our economy? A weak dollar?

National Council on Economic Education

THE **Economics**America AND **Economics**International PROGRAMS

Voluntary National Content Standards in Economics
Emphasized in Chapter 17

Content Standard 5

Content Standard 6

Content Standard 7

Content Standard 17

For a complete listing of NCEE Standards and entire text correlation, see Teacher pages in front of book.

Resources Available from NCEE
- Capstone: The Nation's High School Economics Course
- Focus: International Economics
- Civics and Government: Focus on Economics
- Geography: Focus on Economics
- World History: Focus on Economics
- The Great Economic Mysteries Book

To order these materials or to contact your state Council on Economic Education about workshops and programs, call 1-800-338-1192 or visit www.nationalcouncil.org

Chapter 17 Resource Manager

TEACHING TRANSPARENCY

Economic Concept Transparency 20:
Absolute and Comparative Advantage

APPLICATION AND ENRICHMENT

Consumer Application
Activity 22

Free Enterprise
Activity 22

APPLICATION AND ENRICHMENT

Enrichment Activity 17

Cooperative Learning
Activity 22

Math Practice
Activity 22

Economic Cartoon 22

Primary and Secondary
Source Reading 22

REVIEW AND REINFORCEMENT

Economic Vocabulary
Activity 17

Reteaching Activity 17

Critical Thinking
Activity 22

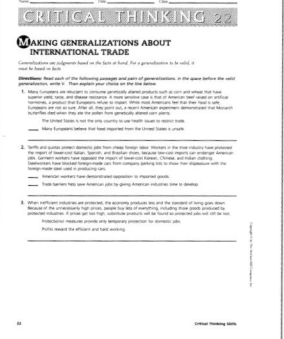

Reinforcing Economic
Skill 16

Chapter 17 Resource Manager

ASSESSMENT AND EVALUATION

Chapter 17 Test Form A

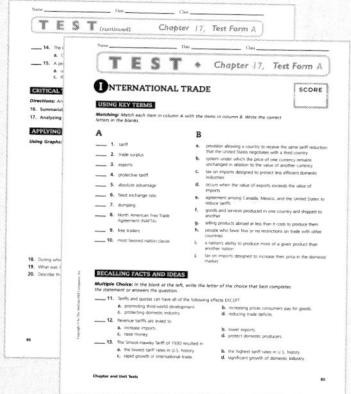

Chapter 17 Test Form B

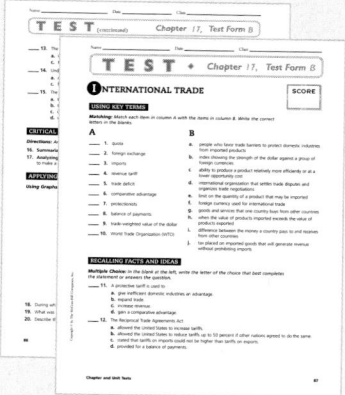

Performance Assessment Activity 22

ExamView® Pro Testmaker

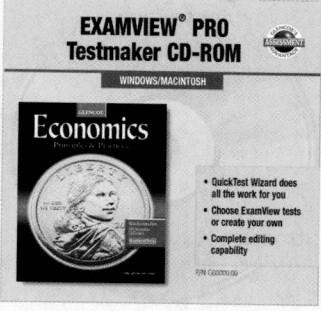

SPANISH RESOURCES

The following Spanish language materials are available in the Spanish Resources binder:

 Spanish Economic Vocabulary Activities

 Spanish Reteaching Activities

 Spanish Section Quizzes

 Spanish Economic Concepts Transparencies

Also available:

  Spanish Chapter 17 Audio Program Activity and Test

TECHNOLOGY/MULTIMEDIA

- Vocabulary PuzzleMaker CD-ROM
- Interactive Tutor Self-Assessment Software
- ExamView® Pro Testmaker
- Audio Program (English or Spanish)
- NBR Economics & You Video Program (English or Spanish)
- MindJogger Videoquiz
- Interactive Economics! CD-ROM
- Presentation Plus!
- TeacherWorks CD-ROM
- Glencoe Skillbuilder Interactive Workbook CD-ROM, Level 2

ECONOMICS Online

Use our Web site for additional resources. All essential content is covered in the Student Edition.

You and your students can visit epp.glencoe.com, the Web site companion to **Economics: Principles and Practices.** This innovative integration of electronic and print media offers your students a wealth of opportunities. The student text directs students to the Web site for the following options:

- **Chapter Overviews**
- **Student Web Activities**
- **Self-Check Quizzes**
- **Textbook Updates**

Answers are provided for you in the Web Activity Lesson Plan. Additional Web resources and interactive puzzles are also available.

Performance Assessment

Refer to Activity 22 in the *Performance Assessment Strategies and Activities* booklet.

 BLOCK SCHEDULING

Introduce students to chapter content and key terms by having them access **Chapter Overview 17** at epp.glencoe.com

 ECONOMICS & YOU

 Chapter 24
Disc 1, Side 2

International Trade
After viewing this segment, students should be able to:
• Differentiate between a trade surplus and a trade deficit.

 Also available in VHS.

GLENCOE
TECHNOLOGY

 Use **MindJogger Videoquiz** to preview the Chapter 17 content.

CHAPTER 17

International Trade

Economics & You

Look at the labels on your clothes, in your shoes, on food products you buy, or even on the car you drive—and you see why international trade is important to everyone. In **Chapter 17,** you will learn about the role international trade plays in the American economy. To learn more about global commerce, view the Chapter 24 video lesson:

International Trade

ECONOMICS Online

Chapter Overview Visit the *Economics: Principles and Practices* Web site at epp.glencoe.com and click on **Chapter 17—Chapter Overviews** to preview chapter information.

Tourism is an important part of the global economy.

✚ EXTRA CREDIT PROJECT

Have students write essays on the role that international trade plays in the American economy. Suggest that they illustrate their essays with examples, charts, and graphs. Call on volunteers to present and discuss their essays.

Absolute and Comparative Advantage

Study Guide

Main Idea
Nations trade according to the theory of comparative advantage.

Reading Strategy
Graphic Organizer As you read the section, complete graphic organizers similar to the ones below by defining each term and providing an example of each.

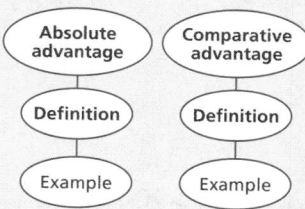

Key Terms
exports, imports, absolute advantage, comparative advantage

Objectives
After studying this section, you will be able to:
1. **Explain** the importance of international trade in today's economy.
2. **Describe** the basis for international trade.
3. **Explain** why total world output increases when countries specialize to engage in trade.

Applying Economic Concepts
Comparative Advantage When you do the chores around the house, you are probably better at some than others. Read to find out how the concept of comparative advantage helps everyone become more productive.

① FOCUS

Section Overview
This section describes the importance of international trade in today's economy.

BELLRINGER
Motivational Activity

- Project **transparency** and have students answer questions.
- Available as blackline master.

Daily Focus Transparency 79

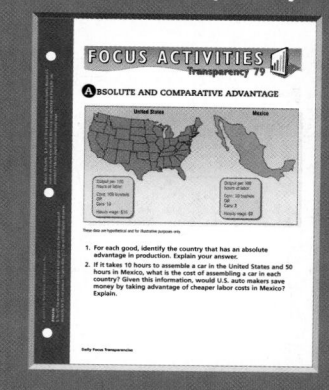

Cover Story

Study: U.S. Still Biggest Arms Provider

WASHINGTON—Worldwide demand is slumping, but that hasn't kept the USA out of the arms business, a congressional study finds. In 1998, the USA led in new arms deals, with $7.1 billion—up from $5.7 billion the year before. Germany ranked second, with $5.5 billion in new sales, and France third, with $3 billion. The value of all new arms sales worldwide was $23 billion, up from $21.4 billion the year before. However, the report said that the trend in terms of arms sales has generally been downward, particularly among developing nations, which are the biggest buyers of weapons.

U.S. warship at sea

—*USA Today*, August 6, 1999

The key to trade—whether among people, states, or countries—is specialization. Some people specialize in cutting hair. Others specialize in fixing computers. These people exchange their services for money, which they then use to buy the specialized goods and services they need from others.

Different regions of a country specialize in certain economic activities in much the same way. New York, for example, is a center of the U.S. financial industry, and Detroit specializes in automobiles. The Midwest and High Plains areas are known for wheat farming. Texas is recognized for oil and cattle, while Florida and California are famous for citrus fruit. All of these states trade with one another so that people in one area can consume the goods and services that workers in other areas offer.

If you want to find out what a country specializes in, look at its **exports**—the goods and services that it produces and then sells to other nations.

CHAPTER 17: INTERNATIONAL TRADE **467**

Study Guide

Reading Strategy
Have students create the graphic organizer.
Answers to Graphic: *absolute: a country's ability to produce more of a product than another country; comparative: a country's ability to produce a product relatively more efficiently than another country.*

Preteaching Vocabulary
Have students explain the difference between absolute and comparative advantage.

RESOURCE MANAGER

📁 Reproducible Masters
- Reproducible Lesson Plan 17-1
- Daily Lecture Notes 17-1
- Guided Reading Activity 17-1
- Reading Essentials and Study Guide 17-1
- Section Quiz 17-1

📽 Transparencies
- Daily Focus Transparency 79

Multimedia
- 💿 Interactive Economics!
- 💾 Interactive Tutor Self-Assessment Software
- 💿 ExamView® Pro Testmaker
- 💿 Presentation Plus!

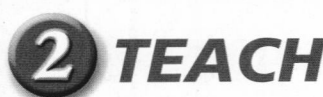

② TEACH

Daily Lecture Notes 17-1

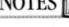

DAILY LECTURE NOTES 📖 Lesson 17-1

❶ DID YOU KNOW?

As the Industrial Revolution spread across Europe, its nations began to build colonial empires in Asia and Africa so that they would have a reliable supply of the raw materials they needed for their factories. Former colonies had to end European colonialism in order to benefit from the exportation of their own natural resources.

PAGES 468-469

I. The U.S. and International Trade

  A. The sheer volume of exports and imports indicates that international trade is beneficial.

  B. Nations trade because they believe the products they receive (imports) are worth more than the products they sell (exports).

  C. Without international trade, many products would not be available on the world market.

  D. Many imports to the United States are necessities that would be unavailable without trade.

❷ Discussion Question

Think about what would happen if the United States could not obtain oil on the world market. What would the United States have to do in order to get more oil? *(The country's industries would either have to find a domestic source, find an equally useful substitute, or stop producing certain products. Whatever the scenario, there would probably be increased production costs and a reduction in supply.)*

PAGES 469-470

II. The Basis for Trade

ECONOMICS
AT A GLANCE

Answer: *Western Europe*

L2 Analyzing Information

Refer students to Figure 17.1 and **ask:** What would happen if the U.S. were no longer able to import materials from these areas? **Have students write a paragraph about the importance of international trade to daily life in the U.S.**

INTERACTIVE ECONOMICS!

💿 CD-ROM

INTERNATIONAL TRADE Have students go to the Introduction menu and click on "Finding Comparative Advantage" in Lesson 9. Ask students to read through the tutorial and find the comparative advantage for both Alpha and Beta.

💾 Also supplied in disk format.

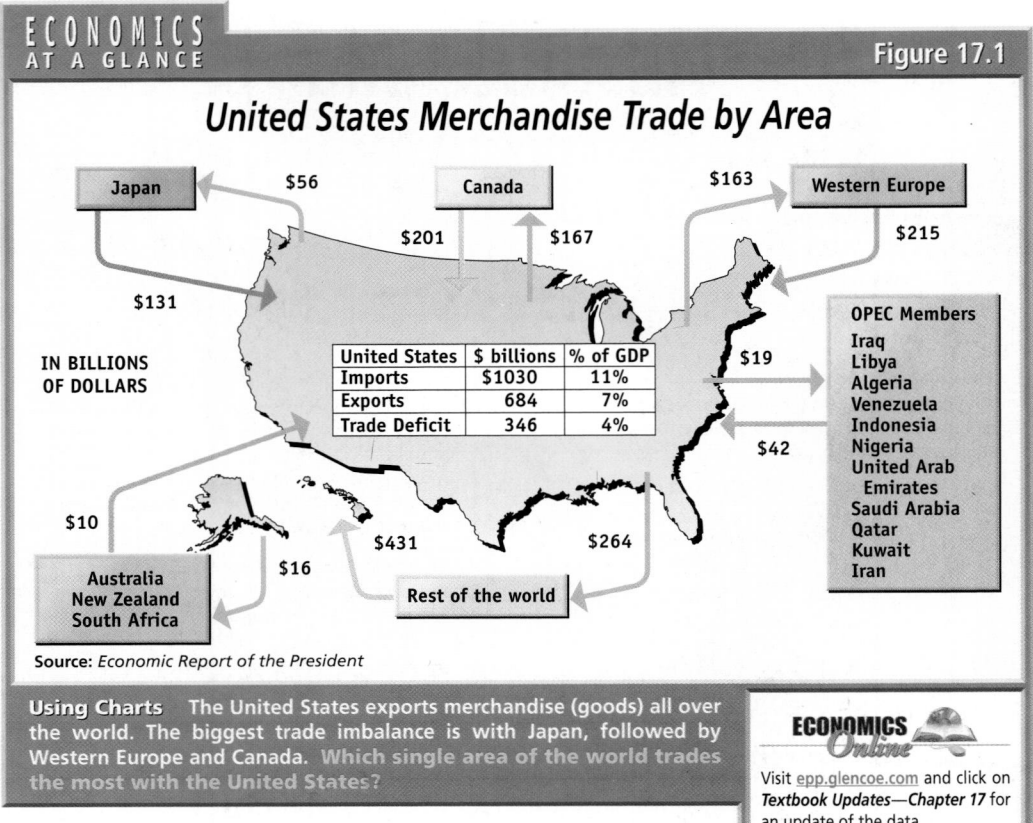

United States Merchandise Trade by Area

United States	$ billions	% of GDP
Imports	$1030	11%
Exports	684	7%
Trade Deficit	346	4%

IN BILLIONS OF DOLLARS

Japan — $56
Canada — $201 / $167
Western Europe — $163 / $215
$131
$19
$42
OPEC Members: Iraq, Libya, Algeria, Venezuela, Indonesia, Nigeria, United Arab Emirates, Saudi Arabia, Qatar, Kuwait, Iran
$10
$16
Australia New Zealand South Africa
$431
$264
Rest of the world

Source: *Economic Report of the President*

Using Charts The United States exports merchandise (goods) all over the world. The biggest trade imbalance is with Japan, followed by Western Europe and Canada. **Which single area of the world trades the most with the United States?**

ECONOMICS *Online*

Visit epp.glencoe.com and click on ***Textbook Updates—Chapter 17*** for an update of the data.

The U.S. and International Trade

International trade is important to all nations, even a country as large as the United States. Most of the products exchanged are goods, although services, such as insurance and banking, are being bought and sold in increasing numbers.

In 2001, **imports**—goods and services that one country buys from other countries—amounted to about $1,486 billion. This number corresponds to nearly $5,230 for every person in the country, and it has grown steadily over the years.

Figure 17.1 shows the merchandise trade patterns for the United States and the rest of the world. As large as these numbers are, they would be even bigger if we counted the value of services in addition to the merchandise, or goods, shown in the figure. The sheer volume of trade between nations of such different geographic, political, and religious characteristics is proof that trade is beneficial.

In fact, nations trade for the same reasons that individuals do—they trade because they believe that the products they receive are worth more than the products they give up.

Without international trade, many products would not be available on the world market. Bananas, for example, would not leave Honduras, nor would coffee beans leave Colombia or Brazil. Some people may think of international trade as a way to obtain exotic products and fancy consumer

468 UNIT 5 INTERNATIONAL AND GLOBAL ECONOMICS

MEETING SPECIAL NEEDS ACTIVITY

Learning Style: Visual/Spatial Have students create a large, wall-size map of the world. Students should re-create on their map the import arrows into the United States as shown in Figure 17.1 on page 468, drawing the arrows back to their countries of origin. Then have students collect photos or draw pictures of items imported by the United States and paste the pictures in their places of origin. Students should find pictures of finished products, raw materials, and agricultural products. Discuss any patterns in U.S. trade that are apparent on the map.

📁 Refer to *Inclusion for the Social Studies Classroom Strategies and Activities* in the TCR.

goods, but trade is much more than that. Many imports are necessities, such as crude oil, clothing, and shoes. In the United States, many minerals, metals, and raw materials that are not available must be imported.

The Basis for Trade

In many cases, it may be cheaper for a country to import a product than to manufacture it. This becomes clear when we examine the difference between absolute and comparative advantage.

Absolute Advantage

A country has an **absolute advantage** when it is able to produce more of a given product than another country can. Consider, for example, the hypothetical case of two countries—Alpha and Beta—which are the same size in terms of area, population, and capital stock. Only their climate and soil fertilities differ. In each country, only two crops can be grown—coffee and cashew nuts.

Figure 17.2 shows the production possibilities frontiers for Alpha and Beta. Note that if both countries devote all of their efforts to producing coffee, Alpha could produce 40 million pounds and Beta six million—giving Alpha an absolute advantage in the coffee production. However, if both countries devote all their efforts to the production of cashew nuts, Alpha could produce eight million pounds and Beta six million. Alpha, then, also has an absolute advantage in the production of cashew nuts because it can produce more than Beta.

For years, people thought that absolute advantage was the basis for trade because it enabled a country to produce enough of a good to consume domestically while leaving some for export. However, the concept of absolute advantage did not explain how a country with a large output like Alpha could trade with a country having a smaller output like Beta—and yet have both countries benefit from the exchange.

Comparative Advantage

Even when one country enjoys an absolute advantage in the production of all goods—as in the case of Alpha above—trade between it and another

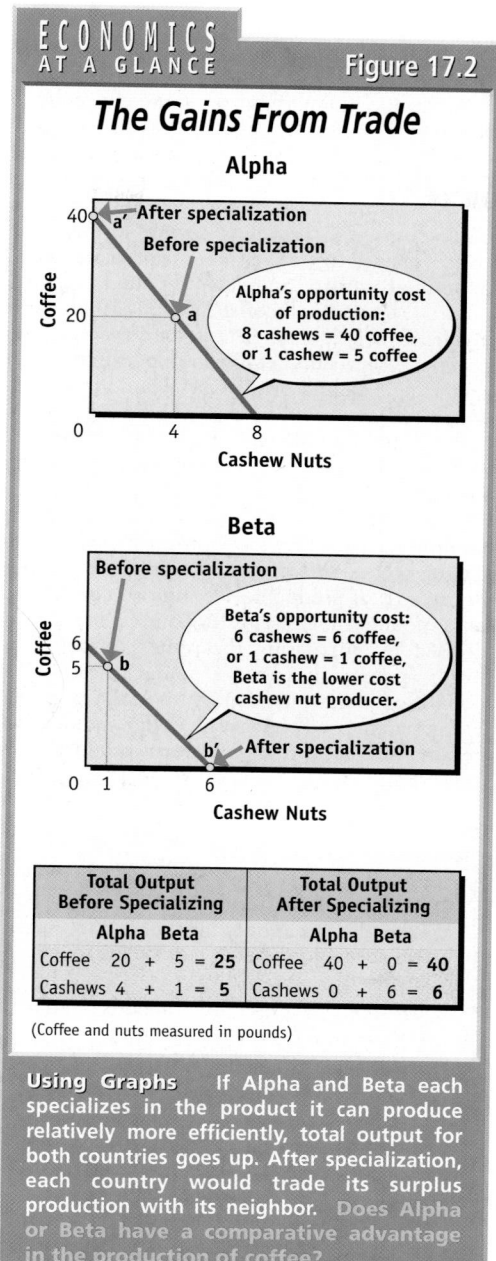

ECONOMICS AT A GLANCE · Figure 17.2

The Gains From Trade

Alpha

Coffee (vertical axis): 400, 20
Cashew Nuts (horizontal axis): 0, 4, 8

a′ After specialization
Before specialization

Alpha's opportunity cost of production:
8 cashews = 40 coffee,
or 1 cashew = 5 coffee

Beta

Coffee (vertical axis): 6, 5
Cashew Nuts (horizontal axis): 0, 1, 6

Before specialization

Beta's opportunity cost:
6 cashews = 6 coffee,
or 1 cashew = 1 coffee,
Beta is the lower cost cashew nut producer.

b′ After specialization

	Total Output Before Specializing		Total Output After Specializing	
	Alpha	Beta	Alpha	Beta
Coffee	20 +	5 = 25	Coffee 40 +	0 = 40
Cashews	4 +	1 = 5	Cashews 0 +	6 = 6

(Coffee and nuts measured in pounds)

Using Graphs If Alpha and Beta each specializes in the product it can produce relatively more efficiently, total output for both countries goes up. After specialization, each country would trade its surplus production with its neighbor. Does Alpha or Beta have a comparative advantage in the production of coffee?

CHAPTER 17: INTERNATIONAL TRADE **469**

ECONOMICS AT A GLANCE

Answer: *Alpha*

③ ASSESS

Assign Section 1 Assessment as homework or as an in-class activity.

Have students use **Interactive Tutor Self-Assessment Software.**

FREE ENTERPRISE ACTIVITY

Point out that geographic factors have an enormous influence on international trade. The climate, weather, topography, soil fertility, and natural resources all affect what a nation is able to produce and export. Have students select a product that a particular nation exports and write a paragraph explaining how geographic factors, such as location, influence the production of that item.

Reteach

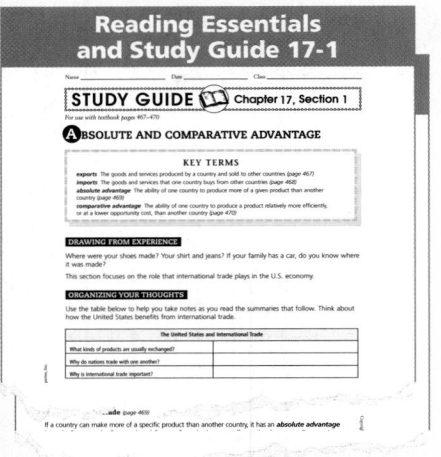

Enrich

Have students write two questions for each major heading in the section. Collect questions and use them to test students' understanding.

4 CLOSE

Have students discuss the following: "International trade is the life-blood of the economy."

---

country is still beneficial. This happens whenever a country has a **comparative advantage**—the ability to produce a product *relatively* more efficiently, or at a lower opportunity cost.

To illustrate, because Alpha can produce either 40 pounds of coffee or 8 pounds of cashew nuts, the opportunity cost of producing 1 pound of cashew nuts is 5 pounds of coffee (40 pounds of coffee divided by 8). At the same time, Beta's opportunity cost of producing 1 pound of cashew nuts is 1 pound of coffee (6 pounds of coffee divided by 6). Clearly, Beta is the lower-cost producer of cashew nuts because its opportunity cost of producing 1 pound of nuts is 1 pound of coffee—whereas Alpha would have to give up 5 pounds of coffee to produce the same amount of cashews.

If Beta has a comparative advantage in producing cashews, then Alpha must have a comparative advantage in coffee production. Indeed, if we try to find each country's opportunity cost of producing coffee, we would find that Alpha's opportunity cost of producing 1 pound of coffee is $1/5$ of a pound of cashews (8 pounds of cashews divided by 40). Using the same computations, Beta's opportunity cost is 1 pound of cashews (6 pounds of cashews divided by 6). Alpha, then, has a comparative advantage in coffee production, because its opportunity cost of production is lower than Beta's.

The Gains From Trade

 The concept of comparative advantage is based on the assumption that everyone will be better off producing the products they produce relatively best. This applies to individuals, companies, states, and regions as well as to nations. The final result is that specialization and trade increases total world output, just as in the case of Alpha and Beta.

This explains the nature of trade between the United States and a country such as Colombia. The United States has excellent supplies of iron and coal. It also has the capital and the labor that are needed to produce tractors and farm machinery efficiently. Colombia, in contrast, does not have as much capital or skilled labor. It does, however, have the land, labor, and climate to produce coffee efficiently. Because the United States has a comparative advantage in the production of farm machinery, it will trade these products for Colombian coffee. Because Colombia has a comparative advantage in the production of coffee, it will export coffee and import farm equipment.

For similar reasons, a country like Saudi Arabia produces more crude oil than it can consume—enabling it to export the surplus. The United States, in turn, produces more military aircraft than it consumes—allowing it to sell aircraft to Saudi Arabia in exchange for oil.

Section 1 Assessment

Checking for Understanding

1. **Main Idea** What does the theory of comparative advantage offer as a guideline to countries?

2. **Key Terms** Define exports, imports, absolute advantage, comparative advantage.

3. **Explain** why international trade is important in today's economy.

4. **Explain** the concepts of absolute advantage and comparative advantage.

5. **Explain** why total world output increases as countries specialize to engage in trade.

Applying Economic Concepts

6. **Comparative Advantage** If you were to open a business with two of your best friends, how would you divide the work to be done? Would your decisions regarding who does what reflect comparative advantage? Explain.

Critical Thinking

7. **Making Generalizations** Do you know of a product for which your state has a comparative advantage? Explain how this might affect trade with another state.

   Practice and **assess** key social studies skills with the *Glencoe Skillbuilder Interactive Workbook, Level 2.*

Section 1 Assessment Answers

1. A country should produce the products that it produces relatively best.

2. All vocabulary terms are defined in the text.

3. Many essential raw materials not available in the United States must be imported.

4. absolute advantage: when a country is able to produce more of a given product than another; comparative advantage: when a country has the ability to produce a product relatively more efficiently/at a lower opportunity cost

5. When each nation focuses on the product(s) it can produce relatively more efficiently, total world output goes up.

6. Tasks may be based on each person's strengths, reflecting comparative advantage.

7. Answers should show understanding of comparative advantage and effect on trade.

Profiles IN Economics

Marketing Savvy:
Bill Gates
(1955–)

One unavoidable fact about Bill Gates, cofounder of Microsoft, is that with a net worth of billions of dollars, he is one of the richest men in the world.

Gates is matter-of-fact about the reason for his wealth. "Our success," he says, "is based on only one thing: good products. It's not very complicated." To his many critics, however, the story is not so simple.

A TEENAGE WIZARD

While in high school, Gates designed a class scheduling program so that he could take courses with the prettiest girls in his school. He also started Traf-O-Data, a computer traffic analysis company.

At age 19, Gates dropped out of Harvard University to pursue his interest in computers. He and his friend Paul Allen developed a condensed operating-system language, which they licensed to a computer manufacturer. Based on this success, Gates and Allen established Microsoft Corporation in 1975.

INTO THE BIG LEAGUES

In 1980 computer industry giant IBM asked Gates to develop an operating system for its new personal computer. Gates bought an operating system from a small company, revamped it, and licensed it to IBM. The system was called MS-DOS, for Microsoft Disk Operating System. The key fact is that Gates licensed MS-DOS to IBM—he didn't sell it to them. Because he retained ownership of MS-DOS, he was able to market it to other companies. In 1981 IBM unveiled its PC, setting off the personal computer boom. MS-DOS became the dominant operating system in the market, and propelled Gates to wealth.

When Microsoft went public in 1986, Gates, who owned 45 percent of the company, became a millionaire several hundred times over.

CONTROVERSIAL SUCCESS

By 1993 Microsoft operating systems ran nearly 90 percent of the world's PCs. Much of Gates's success came from his unique combination of technological expertise and an understanding of the computer needs of the average user. But not everyone attributes Gates's success to know-how and marketing. Many view Gates's Microsoft as an industry bully, forcing would-be competitors out of the market. In fact, the Justice Department and many states have pursued antitrust legislation against Microsoft.

Examining the Profile

1. **Predicting Consequences** How might the Microsoft story have been different if Gates had sold MS-DOS to IBM rather than licensing it?

2. **For Further Research** Report the current status of the lawsuits against Microsoft.

BACKGROUND

Bill Gates's phenomenal economic success is a result of many factors, among them aggressive business decisions, absolute dedication, and exploiting a fundamental development in the American economy. Another key to his success was his dedication to his studies during his high school years. He attended Lakeside School in Seattle, an institution known for its high academic standards. He became "completely engrossed," his father recalled, in the school's computer lab. Gates and two of his friends (one of whom would become co-founder of Microsoft) formed the Lakeside Programming Group, and spent most of their free time learning about computers. While still in high school, Gates told one of his teachers that his interest in computers and his hard work in high school would someday make him a millionaire.

TEACH

Have students write brief papers that compare and contrast one of the following aspects of Gates's career with that of another business giant (e.g., John D. Rockefeller): net worth, how fortune was achieved, philanthropy, conflict/cooperation with federal government, or impact on society.

In 1986 Bill Gates became the youngest billionaire in United States history. He was 31 years old.

Answers to Examining the Profile

1. Answers will vary. Students should note that licensing MS-DOS instead of selling it enabled Gates and Microsoft to market it to other companies and so build a fortune.

2. Answers will vary. Students should be able to find reports of the status in newspaper and magazine articles. Suggest that they consult the *Readers' Guide to Periodical Literature,* or conduct Internet research.

FOCUS

Section Overview

This section discusses trade barriers and the debate on free trade.

BELLRINGER
Motivational Activity

Project **transparency** and have students answer questions.

Available as blackline master.

Daily Focus Transparency 81

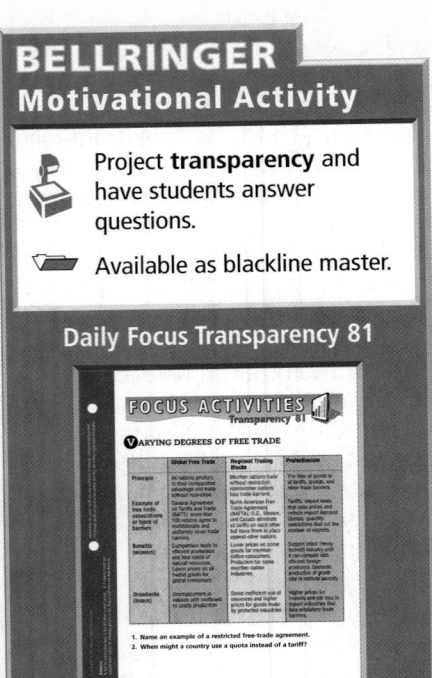

Study Guide

Reading Strategy

Have students create the graphic organizer.
Answers to Graphic: *tax placed on imports to increase their price in the domestic market; limit placed on the quantities of a product that can be imported*

Preteaching Vocabulary

Organize students into pairs. Have one student read aloud a term and its meaning from the text. Then have the other student explain the meaning of the term in his or her own words. Switch roles.

Barriers to International Trade

Study Guide

Main Idea
Tariffs and quotas are two restrictions on international trade.

Reading Strategy
Graphic Organizer As you read the section, complete a graphic organizer similar to the one below by describing the differences between a tariff and a quota.

Tariff/Quota → Differences

Key Terms
tariff, quota, protective tariff, revenue tariff, dumping, protectionists, free traders, infant industries

argument, balance of payments, most favored nation clause, World Trade Organization (WTO), North American Free Trade Agreement (NAFTA)

Objectives
After studying this section, you will be able to:
1. **Explain** how international trade can be restricted to protect special interests.
2. **Cite** the main argument used in support of protection.
3. **Relate** the history of the free trade movement.

Applying Economic Concepts
Quotas Do you think the prices of some goods are too high? Read to find out how international trade can help keep some prices low.

Cover Story

US Gets Go-Ahead for European Sanctions

The World Trade Organization yesterday authorized the US to impose trade sanctions on European Union goods in retaliation for the EU's ban on hormone-treated beef.

French delicacies subject to U.S. duties

From July 29, the US will impose punitive 100 percent duties on imports from the EU, including delicacies such as foie gras, truffles, and Roquefort cheese as well as beef, pork, canned tomatoes and mustard.

US officials said last week the sanctions, worth a total of $116.8 [million] would target goods from France, Germany, Italy and Denmark as these were the countries most influential in preserving the 10-year-old beef hormone ban.

—*The Financial Times*, July 27, 1999

472

Although international trade can bring many benefits, some people object to it because it can displace selected industries and groups of workers in the United States. The European ban on American hormone-treated beef discussed in the cover story is just one example of attempts to restrict trade.

Restricting International Trade

Historically, trade has been restricted in two major ways. One is through a **tariff**—a tax placed on imports to increase their price in the domestic market. The other is with a **quota**—a limit placed on the quantities of a product that can be imported.

Tariffs

Governments levy two kinds of tariffs—protective and revenue. A **protective tariff** is a tariff high enough to protect less-efficient domestic industries. Suppose, for example, that it costs $1 to produce a mechanical pencil in the United States. The exact

---

RESOURCE MANAGER

Reproducible Masters
- Reproducible Lesson Plan 17-2
- Daily Lecture Notes 17-2
- Guided Reading Activity 17-2
- Reading Essentials and Study Guide 17-2
- Section Quiz 17-2

Transparencies
- Daily Focus Transparency 81

Multimedia
- NBR Economics & You Video Program
- Interactive Tutor Self-Assessment Software
- ExamView® Pro Testmaker
- Presentation Plus!

ame product, however, can be imported for 35 cents from another country. If a tariff of 95 cents is placed on each imported pencil, the cost climbs to $1.30—more than the cost of the American-made one. The result is that a domestic industry is protected from being undersold by a foreign one.

The **revenue tariff** is a tariff high enough to generate revenue for the government without actually prohibiting imports. If the tariff on imported mechanical pencils were 40 cents, the price of the imports would be 75 cents, or 25 cents less than the American-made ones. As long as the two products are identical, people would prefer the imported one because it was less expensive—so the tariff would raise revenue rather than protect domestic producers from foreign competition.

Traditionally, tariffs were used more for revenues than for protection. Before the Civil War, tariffs were the chief source of revenue for the federal government. From the Civil War to 1913, tariffs provided about one-half of the government's total revenue. In 1913 the federal income tax was passed, which gave the government a new and more lucrative source of revenue. Modern tariffs—also called customs duties—only account for a small portion of total government revenue, as shown in **Figure 9.4** on page 232.

Quotas

Foreign goods sometimes cost so little that even a high tariff on them may not protect the domestic market. In such cases, the government can use a quota to keep foreign goods out of the country. Quotas can even be set as low as zero to keep a product from ever entering the country. More typically, quotas are used to reduce the total supply of a product to keep prices high for domestic producers.

In 1981, for example, domestic automobile producers faced intense competition from lower-priced Japanese automobiles. Rather than lower their own prices, domestic manufacturers wanted President Ronald Reagan to establish import quotas on Japanese cars. The Reagan administration told the Japanese to voluntarily restrict auto exports, and they reluctantly agreed. As a result, Americans had fewer cars from which to choose, and the prices of all cars were higher than they would otherwise have been.

During the Bush administration, "voluntary" import quotas were imposed on steel. The quotas protected jobs in the domestic steel industry, but at the cost of higher steel prices for the rest of the

Protectionism

Jobs These citizens are protesting the loss of manufacturing jobs in the face of competition from other countries. *What is the purpose of a protective tariff?*

CHAPTER 17: INTERNATIONAL TRADE **473**

Daily Lecture Notes 17-2

DAILY LECTURE NOTES Lesson 17-2

DID YOU KNOW?
International trade benefits port cities—those with harbors—as well as cities with extensive industry. Ports in Louisiana, Texas, New York, and New Jersey together handle over 109 million tons of exports, based on 1997 figures.

PAGES 472-475
I. Restricting International Trade
   A. Two major ways of restricting trade are through a tariff, or tax placed on imports, and a quota, a limit on the quantities of a product that can be imported.
   B. A protective tariff is one that is high enough to protect less efficient domestic industries.
   C. A revenue tariff is one high enough to generate revenue.
   D. Most quotas are used to reduce the supply of a product and keep prices high for domestic producers.
   E. Other barriers to trade include overly rigorous health inspections and difficult licensing requirements.

■ **Discussion Question**
Current trade agreements give country A the right to retaliate with trade barriers if country B restricts country A products. Do you think that's a good idea? Why or why not? *(Answers will vary. It does provide a mechanism for enforcement, however, and could lead to further barriers. Mediation is sometimes a more effective response.)*

PAGES 475-478
II. Arguments for Protection
   A. Protectionists are people who favor trade barriers that protect domestic industries and offer various arguments to defend their position.
   B. According to one argument, a country could become so specialized that it would end up being dependent enough on other countries that it would affect national defense.
   C. The infant-industries argument is the belief that new industries should be protected from foreign competition.
   D. Some argue that tariffs and quotas protect domestic jobs from cheap foreign labor.
   E. The argument for keeping the money at home claims that limiting imports will keep American money in the United States.

Daily Lecture Notes

Visual Instruction

Answer to Caption: *to protect less-efficient domestic industries*

Math Practice

Per Capita Imports During a recent year, U.S. companies imported more than one billion garments made in China. Ask students to calculate how many Chinese-made garments were imported for each American consumer. Have them divide one billion by 270 million, the U.S. population at the time, and round the answer to the nearest whole number. *(about 4 garments per person)*

MEETING SPECIAL NEEDS ACTIVITY

English Language Learners One way to motivate students to read is to have them make predictions about the content beforehand and then evaluate their predictions after they read. Ask students to predict what might happen if harsh trade restrictions were erected between all nations of the world. Then have students read the section, helping them as necessary. After students have finished reading, have them review their predictions to see if they were correct. **ELL**

📁 Refer to *Inclusion for the Social Studies Classroom Strategies and Activities* in the TCR.

L2 Applying Ideas

Provide students with the following scenario: You (the student) are the president of a nation with a relatively healthy economy. However, one of your major industries—computer parts—is in decline, largely because of foreign competition. Members of your political party who represent districts where computer parts are the main industry want a high tariff on imported computer parts. In addition, workers in the computer parts industry have launched a huge publicity campaign in support of a tariff increase. At the same time, many people are calling for no tariff because they want to be able to buy inexpensive computer parts.

Have students explain what they, as leaders, intend to do and why. Have them write their decision in the form of a speech to be made to the nation.

country. A trade crisis emerged in mid-1997 when charges of **dumping,** or selling products abroad at less than it cost to produce them at home, were levied against Japan and Russia.

Other Barriers

Tariffs and quotas are not the only barriers to trade. Many imported foods are subject to health inspections far more rigorous than those given to domestic foods. For years this tactic was used to keep beef grown in Argentina out of the United States. Another tactic is to require a license to import. If the government is slow to grant the license, or if the license fees are too high, international trade is restricted.

The United States is not the only country to use health issues to restrict trade. Many Europeans are reluctant to consume corn, wheat, and other crops that have been genetically altered for superior yield, taste, and disease resistance. A more sensitive case is that of American beef raised on artificial hormones, a product that Europeans refuse to import. While most Americans feel that their food is safe, Europeans are not so sure. After all, they point out, an experiment by U.S. scientists demonstrated that Monarch butterflies died when they ate the pollen from genetically altered corn plants.

Nationalism and culture often play a role in these debates, with Europeans frequently claiming that they prefer regional and traditional foods to genetically altered ones. While these may or may not be legitimate arguments, they do restrict trade between nations.

Did you know?

A Safety Net To minimize the price changes caused by the Arab oil embargoes of the 1970s, the United States in 1977 created the Strategic Petroleum Reserve, to store millions of barrels of oil. The reserve can be used as an emergency supply of oil in case of a complete oil embargo. The reserve holds enough oil to provide a normal level of petroleum use in the United States for 60 days.

Arguments for Protection

Freer international trade has been a subject of debate for many years. Some people, known as **protectionists,** favor trade barriers that protect domestic industries. Others, known as **free traders,** favor fewer or even no trade restrictions. The debate between the two groups usually centers on the five arguments for protection discussed below.

National Defense

The first argument for trade barriers centers on national defense. Protectionists argue that without trade barriers, a country could become so specialized that it would end up becoming too dependent on other countries.

During wartime, protectionists argue, a country might not be able to get critical supplies such as oil and weapons. As a result, even some smaller countries such as Israel and South Africa have developed large armaments industries for such crises. They want to be sure they will have a domestic supply if hostilities break out or other countries impose economic boycotts.

Free traders admit that national security is a compelling argument for trade barriers. They believe, however, that the advantages of having a reliable source of domestic supply must be weighed against the disadvantages that the supply will be smaller and possibly less efficient than it would be with free trade. The political problem of deciding which industries are critical to national defense and which are not must also be considered. At one time, the steel, auto, ceramic, and electronics industries all have argued that they are critical to national defense and so should receive protection.

Promoting Infant Industries

The **infant industries argument**—the belief that new or emerging industries should be protected from foreign competition—is also used to justify trade barriers. Protectionists claim that these industries need to gain strength and experience before they can compete against developed industries in other countries. Trade barriers would give them the time they need to develop. If infant

FREE ENTERPRISE ACTIVITY

Organize students into three groups. Assign two groups the pro or con position on the following proposition: U.S. industries should be protected from foreign competition. Have the two groups research and debate the proposition. Have the third group act as judges and keep track of major points and arguments made during the debate.   **BLOCK SCHEDULING** industries compete against foreign industries too soon, they argue, they might fail.

Many people are willing to accept the infant industries argument, but only if protection will eventually be removed so that the industry is forced to compete on its own. The problem is that industries used to having some protection are normally unwilling to give it up—making for difficult political decisions later on.

To illustrate, some Latin American countries have used tariffs to protect their own infant automobile industries, with tariffs as high as several hundred percent. In some cases, the tariff raised the price of used American-made cars to more than double the cost of new ones in the United States. In spite of this protection, no country in Latin America has been able to produce a competitive product on its own. To make matters worse, governments have come to rely on the revenue supplied by tariffs, so prices for automobiles remain high for their citizens.

Protecting Domestic Jobs

A third argument—and one used most often—is that tariffs and quotas protect domestic jobs from cheap foreign labor. Workers in the shoe industry, for example, have protested the import of lower-cost Italian, Spanish, and Brazilian shoes. Garment workers have opposed the import of lower-cost Korean, Chinese, and Indian clothing. Steelworkers have blocked foreign-made cars from company parking lots to show their displeasure with the foreign-made steel used in producing the cars.

In the short run, protectionist measures provide temporary protection for domestic jobs. This is especially attractive to people who want to work in the communities where they grew up. In the long run, however, industries that find it hard to compete today will find it even harder to compete in the future unless they change the way they are doing things. As a result, most free traders believe that it is

International Trade

Expansion With the great expansion of trade, many U.S. companies set up operations in other countries. Protectionists favor trade barriers that protect domestic industries. *What is the assumption behind the infant industries argument?*

best not to interfere, and thereby keep pressure on threatened industries to modernize and improve.

When inefficient industries are protected, the economy produces less and the standard of living goes down. Because of unnecessarily high prices, people buy less of everything, including those goods produced by protected industries. If prices get too high, substitute products will be found and protected jobs will still be lost. Free traders argue that the profit-and-loss system is one of the major features of the American economy. Profits reward the efficient and hard working, while losses eliminate the inefficient and weak.

Keeping the Money at Home

Another argument for trade barriers claims that limiting imports will keep American money in the United States instead of allowing it to go abroad. Free traders, however, point out that the American dollars that go abroad generally come back again.

CHAPTER 17: INTERNATIONAL TRADE **475**

Visual Instruction

Answer to Caption:
Trade barriers would give them the time they need to develop.

L3 History
Organize students into several groups and assign each group a particular period in U.S. history. Have groups research and evaluate international trade during the assigned periods to determine the primary countries with which the U.S. traded, the extent of the trade, the benefits of the agreements, any trade restrictions or legislation passed, and the effect of such restrictions on American markets. Have groups report to the rest of the class.

NIGHTLY BUSINESS REPORT

 ECONOMICS & YOU

 Chapter 24
Disc 1, Side 2

International Trade

Ask: What factors affect the demand for American products in other countries? *(A country's demand for American products will be affected by the current strength of its economy and the going exchange rate between its currency and the American dollar.)*

 Also available in VHS.

CRITICAL THINKING

Expressing Problems Clearly Inform students that, although Wal-Mart is a U.S.-based company, relatively few of the products it sells in Argentina or in the United States are made in the United States. Wal-Mart's goods come from factories all over the world. At one such factory in Nicaragua, workers receive $1.84 for a 12-hour workday—too little to meet even one-third of a Nicaraguan's basic needs. Ask students how a supporter of protectionism might use this information to defend trade restrictions. *(Students' answers may vary. A possible reply would be that supporters of protectionism might insist that the U.S. government ban imports from such factories because paying starvation wages is an abuse of human rights.)*

THE GLOBAL ECONOMY

The Art of Communication

In Japan, gift giving is considered good business. When doing business with the Japanese, Americans should keep in mind several gift-giving tips: **1.** Use both hands to give or receive gifts. This gesture shows respect and humility. **2.** Always wrap the gift, but do not use white paper because in Japan, white is the color of death. **3.** Never give four of anything, such as a set of four drinking glasses. Like the color white, *shi,* the Japanese word for four, is associated with death.

Answers:
1. *one's personal space; how close a person approaches when conversing with another*
2. *that you need to allow more space when dealing with an American than with an Arab or Russian*
3. *to show respect and to avoid inadvertently insulting a business partner*

CURRICULUM CONNECTION

Literature In 1999 concerned Americans picketed a meeting of the World Trade Organization in Seattle. They protested, among other issues, the WTO's failure to insist that member countries protect the human rights of workers, including children. David L. Parker's *Stolen Dreams: Portraits of Working Children* (Lerner, 1998) describes why and how millions of the world's children are forced to work.

THE GLOBAL ECONOMY

THE ART OF COMMUNICATION

With the globalization of business, it is necessary to understand and to adjust to the communication style of other cultures.

Only in the Germanic countries will the people be as eager to get down to business as in the United States of America. Almost anywhere else in the world, but especially in Asian and Latin countries, it's important to first get to know the person with whom you're dealing to build a bond of trust. Three f's of business in Asian cultures are family, friends and favors. If you're not part of an extended Asian family or if you don't have close Asian chums from your school days, find the time to develop a friendship with a well-connected intermediary [agent]. Relationships, once formed, are long lasting bonds of loyalty that must be respected. . . .

Space is one of those seemingly inconsequential aspects of human interaction that can have major consequences elsewhere. The American personal bubble of space is much greater than that of an Arab or a Russian, but smaller than that of a Briton. Infringing upon another's personal space or inadvertently backing away when someone enters your bubble can send unintended negative messages. Touching someone—a hand on the forearm, an arm around the shoulder, or a pat on the back—is one of the easiest ways to violate personal space.

—Etiquette International

Critical Thinking

1. **Analyzing Information** What does the writer mean by "space"? Explain the concept in your own words.
2. **Summarizing Information** What does it mean to say that "the American bubble of space is much greater than that of an Arab or Russian"?
3. **Drawing Conclusions** Why is it important to understand the values of another culture when doing business?

The Japanese, for example, use the dollars they receive for their automobiles to buy American cotton, soybeans, and airplanes. These purchases benefit American workers in those industries.

The same is true of the dollars used to buy oil from the Middle East. The money comes back to the United States when oil-wealthy foreigners buy American-made oil technology. Keeping the money home also hurts those American industries that depend on exports for their jobs.

Helping the Balance of Payments

Another argument involves the **balance of payments**—the difference between the money a country pays out to, and receives from, other nations when it engages in international trade. Protectionists argue that restrictions on imports help the balance of payments by restricting the amount of imports.

What protectionists overlook, however, is that the dollars return to the United States to stimulate

employment in other industries. As a result, most economists do not believe that interfering with free trade can be justified on the grounds of helping the balance of payments.

The Free Trade Movement

The use of trade barriers to protect domestic industries and jobs works only if other countries do not retaliate with their own trade barriers. If they do, all countries suffer because they have neither the benefits of efficient production nor access to less costly products and raw materials from other nations.

Tariffs During the Great Depression

In 1930 the United States passed the Smoot-Hawley Tariff, one of the most restrictive tariffs in history. It set import duties so high that the price

EXTENDING THE CONTENT

The Smoot-Hawley Tariff Act The Smoot-Hawley Tariff Act of 1930 increased duties on raw agricultural materials from 38 to 49 percent and on other goods from 31 to 34 percent. This raised the prices of imported goods so much that tariff revenues represented 45 percent of the total value of all imports. Just 10 years before, the figure was 16 percent. Many experts argue that this tariff made the Great Depression even worse.

Organize students into small groups and assign each group a U.S. trading partner. Have students research and analyze the impact of imports and exports on both the U.S. and its trading partner.

of many imported goods rose nearly 70 percent. When other countries did the same, international trade nearly came to a halt.

Before long, most countries realized that high tariffs hurt more than they helped. As a result, in 1934 the United States passed the Reciprocal Trade Agreements Act, which allowed it to reduce tariffs up to 50 percent if other countries agreed to do the same. The act also contained a **most favored nation clause**—a provision allowing a country to receive the same tariff reduction that the United States negotiates with a third country.

Suppose, for example, that the United States and China have a trade agreement with a most favored nation clause. If the United States then negotiates a tariff reduction with a third country, the reduction would also apply to China. This clause is very important to China, because its goods will then sell at an even lower price in the American market.

The World Trade Organization

In 1947, 23 countries signed the General Agreement on Tariffs and Trade (GATT). The GATT extended tariff concessions and worked to do away with import quotas. Later, the Trade Expansion Act of 1962 gave the president of the United States the power to negotiate further tariff reductions. As a result of this legislation, more than 100 countries had agreed to reduce the average level of tariffs by the early 1990s.

More recently, the GATT was replaced by the **World Trade Organization (WTO)**—an international agency that administers previous GATT trade agreements, settles trade disputes between governments, organizes trade negotiations, and provides technical assistance and training for developing countries. As you read in the cover story, the WTO agreed that Europe was discriminating against the United States by banning hormone-treated beef. While the WTO normally opposes retaliatory measures, it approved the U.S. measures because the European Union ignored earlier WTO demands to drop American beef restrictions.

Because so many countries have been willing to reduce tariffs and quotas under GATT and the WTO, international trade is flourishing. Tariffs that once nearly doubled the price of many goods now increase prices by a small percentage, while other tariffs have been dropped altogether. As a result,

CYBERNOMICS

Trade and Keeping Time The first oceangoing timepiece accurate enough to determine a merchant ship's position in rough weather was spring operated. The clock's time was off by only five seconds after six and a half weeks at sea. Two hundred years later, physicists developed the cesium atomic clock. It uses the movement of atoms instead of springs to mark the time. This clock will lose only one second every 1.4 million years. Today, captains of super-tankers carrying oil from the Middle East depend on cesium clocks to find their way to market.

Trade

Protectionism vs. Free Trade Free traders argue that reducing tariffs and quotas allows consumers to choose from a variety of both domestic and foreign products. *What arguments do protectionists use in support of trade restrictions?*

CHAPTER 17: INTERNATIONAL TRADE **477**

INTERDISCIPLINARY CONNECTIONS ACTIVITY

Geography Many consumer goods that Americans buy come from somewhere else. Each year, imports make up 60 percent of Americans' clothing purchases, 80 percent of their toy and sporting good purchases, and 90 percent of their shoe purchases. Have students check the insides of their shoes to find out where each pair was made. List the countries on the board and then have students locate these places on a map of the world. Do the same for other articles of clothing and any classroom objects/accessories that are marked with a country of origin.

ECONOMICS
AT A GLANCE

Answer: *imports*

Map Skills Practice

What is the per capita GDP of Canada? Mexico? *($23,067/person; $8,616/person)*

3 ASSESS

Assign Section 2 Assessment as homework or as an in-class activity.

■ Have students use **Interactive Tutor Self-Assessment Software.**

Section Quiz 17-2

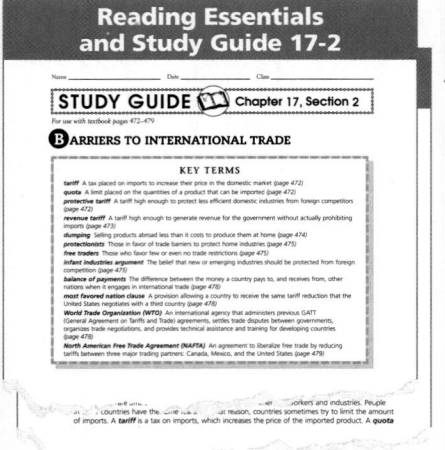

Reteach

Reading Essentials and Study Guide 17-2

ECONOMICS AT A GLANCE
Figure 17.3

The North American Free Trade Agreement

THE NORTH AMERICAN FREE TRADE AREA, 2000
Population 407.3 million
GDP $10.8 trillion
Two-Way Trade $658 billion

CANADA
Population 31.3 million
GDP $722 billion

U.S.-CANADA TRADE
U.S. exports to Canada $175 billion
U.S. imports from Canada $229 billion

CANADIAN-MEXICAN TRADE
Canadian exports to Mexico $1.3 billion
Canadian imports from Mexico $8.5 billion

UNITED STATES
Population 275.6 million
GDP $9.3 trillion

U.S.-MEXICO TRADE
U.S. exports to Mexico $109 billion
U.S. imports from Mexico $135 billion

MEXICO
Population 100.4 million
GDP $865 billion

Source: *CIA Fact Book*

Using Maps The North American Free Trade Agreement (NAFTA) makes up the second largest free-trade area in the world, after the European Union. After NAFTA was implemented, trade between the three nations began to grow by 10 to 15 percent annually. **Do imports or exports comprise the larger portion of Mexico's trade with Canada and the United States?**

ECONOMICS Online
Visit epp.glencoe.com and click on **Textbook Updates—Chapter 17** for an update of the data.

EXTENDING THE CONTENT

NAFTA and Traditional Culture Some Mexicans have expressed concern about the cultural impact of NAFTA. The increased exchange between the U.S. and Mexico, they suggest, will result in Mexican tradition being swamped by American technology and culture. The biggest impact will come in rural areas, where traditional Native American culture still flourishes. Most rural people make a living from farming small plots of land and will not be able to compete with American farmers. As a result, many will simply abandon their farms and head for the cities. "We could be looking at the loss of our cultural environment," a Mexican sociologist predicted.

stores are able to offer a wide variety of industrial and consumer goods from all over the world.

NAFTA

The **North American Free Trade Agreement (NAFTA)** is an agreement to liberalize free trade by reducing tariffs among three major trading partners: Canada, Mexico, and the United States. It was proposed by the Bush administration and concluded by the Clinton administration in 1993.

Before NAFTA, United States goods entering Mexico faced an average tariff of 10 percent. At the same time, approximately half of the goods entering the United States from Mexico were duty-free, while the other half faced an average tax of only 4 percent. Exceptions did exist, however. A 32 percent tariff on brooms imported from Mexico protected approximately 3,000 broom makers in southern Illinois.

Free trade is good in general, but it is not painless. NAFTA was controversial specifically because some workers would be displaced when trade barriers were lowered. Opponents predicted that some high-paid American jobs would be lost to Mexico—including those held by broom makers who will

find their protective tariff reduced to zero over a 15-year period. Proponents predicted that trade among all three nations would increase dramatically, stimulating growth and bringing a wider variety of lower-cost goods to everyone, protectionists and free traders alike.

The case for freer trade is a classic case of cost-benefit analysis. Some of the costs and benefits identified during the NAFTA debate actually occurred, but not to the extent originally predicted. Trade among the three countries has grown dramatically since NAFTA was created. In the end, freer trade allowed the NAFTA partners to capitalize on their comparative advantages for everyone's benefit.

Student Web Activity Visit the *Economics: Principles and Practices* Web site at epp.glencoe.com and click on *Chapter 17—Student Web Activities* for an activity on the World Trade Organization.

Objectives, goals, and answers to the student activity can be found in the **Web Activity Lesson Plan** feature at epp.glencoe.com

Enrich

Have students write to their U.S. senator or representative to request copies of recent testimony about some aspect of international trade, such as the effects of free trade or trade barriers.

④ CLOSE

Have students discuss the benefits and costs of NAFTA.

Section 2 Assessment

Checking for Understanding

1. **Main Idea** Explain why protectionists favor tariffs and quotas.

2. **Key Terms** Define tariff, quota, protective tariff, revenue tariff, dumping, protectionists, free traders, infant industries argument, balance of payments, most favored nation clause, World Trade Organization (WTO), North American Free Trade Agreement (NAFTA).

3. **Describe** three barriers to international trade.

4. **List** five arguments that are commonly used to support the protectionist argument.

5. **Identify** two attempts to facilitate the growth of international trade.

Applying Economic Concepts

6. **Quotas** Explain how a quota on a good or service produced in your community can protect the jobs in a particular industry. Then explain how the same quota might be harmful to consumers.

Critical Thinking

7. **Drawing Conclusions** If you were a member of Congress approached by a delegation of autoworkers seeking additional tariff or quota protection, how would you respond? Defend your response.

8. **Analyzing Information** Explain the infant industries argument.

 Practice and assess key social studies skills with the *Glencoe Skillbuilder Interactive Workbook, Level 2.*

CHAPTER 17: INTERNATIONAL TRADE **479**

Section 2 Assessment Answers

1. to protect domestic industries

2. All vocabulary terms are defined in the text.

3. tariffs to protect less efficient domestic industries and to raise money; quotas to keep foreign goods out; health inspections on imported foods, requiring license to import

4. maintain national defense, protect infant industries, protect domestic jobs, keep the money home, help the balance of payments

5. GATT, NAFTA

6. Quotas favor domestic producers by restricting competition; consumers may pay higher price for product.

7. Answers should reflect an understanding of protectionist policies.

8. New companies should be protected from foreign competition until they are ready to compete against foreign developed industries.

TEACH

Tell students that other countries in Southeast Asia and Eastern Europe are "aggressively courting" multinational corporations. These countries offer tax breaks and other incentives to foreign companies building factories abroad. Meanwhile, Mexico has historically refused to offer these tax breaks and incentives.

Ask students what they think the benefits are to producing in these countries—for the corporations, and for the countries themselves. Then ask students what they think Mexico needs to do to stay competitive. *(Answers may include tax breaks, lower wages, better trained and more educated workers, better infrastructure, and less bureaucracy and corruption.)*

📁 Refer to *Business Week Focus on the New Economy* in the TCR for additional unit-based articles.

BusinessWeek

AUGUST 6, 2001

Newsclip

The North American Free Trade Agreement (NAFTA) is a free trade pact among Canada, the United States, and Mexico. NAFTA has created one of the world's most productive economic blocs, rivaled only by the European Union and by Japan.

Workers at an electronics assembly plant in Mexico

Is the Magic Fading?

It's not quite Silicon Valley, but it's as close as you'll get in Mexico. Over the past 25 years, dozens of technology companies, including IBM and Hewlett-Packard Co., have flocked to Guadalajara....Those companies built factories to churn out everything from celluar phones to Palm Pilots, plus all manner of electronics components. The city's attractions: its proximity to the U.S. and its abundance of cheap labor.

But Guadalajara's appeal as a high-tech hub is losing some of its luster....[H]igh-tech companies have begun shifting production of such price-sensitive products as printed circuit boards and low-end printers from Mexico to China and Malaysia.

What have these countries got that Mexico doesn't? Plenty, it turns out: wages as low as 60 cents an hour, tax incentives, and less red tape....It's certainly not the image Mexico boosters like to paint. They depict an economy that has grown 28% in the past seven years, thanks in large part to the North American Free Trade Agreement, which is eliminating all tariffs on trade between Mexico, the U.S., and Canada. Since the agreement has been in effect, Mexico's exports have tripled, to $166.4 billion, and foreign investment has tallied $85 billion.

Yet Mexico may be reaching its day of reckoning. The country has long suffered from problems of its own making—poor schools, rampant corruption, and outmoded infrastructure, just to name a few....

Some top Mexican officials are keenly aware that the country is at a crossroads. Says Eduardo Sojo, [President Vicente] Fox's chief economic stratagist, "We have to identify the niches that allow us to stand apart from other emerging markets." That may mean watching some industries wither while nurturing others....

–Reprinted from August 6, 2001 issue of *Business Week*, by special permission, copyright © 2001 by The McGraw-Hill Companies, Inc.

Examining the Newsclip

1. **Analyzing Information** Why are some technology companies shifting the production of price-sensitive products out of Mexico?

2. **Drawing Conclusions** What can the Mexican government do to keep a good relationship with the technology companies?

480 UNIT 5 INTERNATIONAL AND GLOBAL ECONOMICS

Answers to Examining the Newsclip

1. Other countries, like China and Malaysia, have lower wages, tax incentives, and less red tape.

2. The Mexican government needs to identify and focus on the industries that will help them stand apart from other countries. In addition, solutions need to be created for problems like poor schools, corruption, and insufficient infrastructure.

Financing and Trade Deficits

Study Guide

Main Idea
A long-lasting trade deficit affects the value of a nation's currency and the price and volume of its exports and imports.

Reading Strategy
Graphic Organizer As you read the section, complete a graphic organizer similar to the one below by describing the effects of a long-lasting trade deficit.

Cause: Trade deficit → Effect, Effect, Effect

Key Terms
foreign exchange, foreign exchange rate, fixed exchange rate, flexible exchange rate, trade deficit, trade surplus, trade-weighted value of the dollar

Objectives
After studying this section, you will be able to:
1. **Explain** how foreign currency is used in trade.
2. **Describe** the problem of a trade deficit and the main solution to the problem.

Applying Economic Concepts
Foreign Exchange Do you have any souvenir foreign currency such as pesos, pounds, or yen? Read to find out how this foreign exchange is used to finance international trade.

① FOCUS

Section Overview
This section explains foreign exchange and the trade deficit.

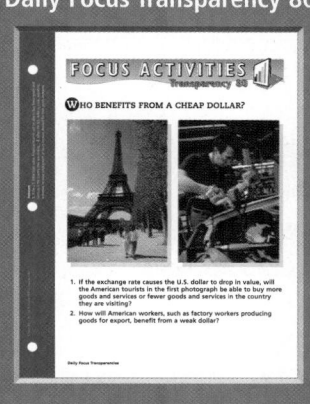
Cover Story

Quaking Before the Fed

No place has more to fear from every twitch of U.S. monetary policy than Hong Kong. Its currency is rigidly pegged to the U.S. dollar, and when U.S. interest rates go up, Hong Kong's must follow. With the economy in its worst recession in half a century, Hong Kong can ill afford higher rates, although the Federal Reserve is now leaning in that direction....

[In Hong Kong, the] grinding process of deflation continues. Property prices are down about 50% from their mid-1997 peak... the government expects consumer prices to fall 2.5% for all of 1999... real interest rates [are] more than 8%... the benchmark Hang Seng stock index is ... 26% below its August 1997, peak, and higher interest rates could knock [the current modest] recovery off track.

—*Business Week*, June 21, 1999

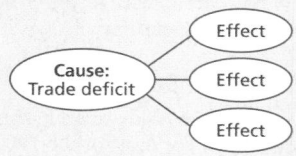

Boeing 747 flies over Kowloon peninsula

Trade between nations is similar to exchange between individuals. The major difference is that each country has its own monetary system, which makes the exchange more complicated. The value of some currencies, like the Hong Kong dollar in the cover story, is tied to the value of the U.S. dollar in the hope of simplifying international trade.

Financing International Trade

Scenarios like the following occur every day across the globe. A clothing firm in the United States wants to import business suits from a company in Great Britain. Because the British firm pays its bills in a currency called "pound sterling," it wants to receive payment in sterling. Therefore, the American firm must exchange its dollars for British pounds.

Foreign Exchange

In the field of international finance, **foreign exchange**—foreign currencies used to facilitate international trade—are bought and sold in the

CHAPTER 17: INTERNATIONAL TRADE **481**

Study Guide

Reading Strategy
Have students create the graphic organizer.
Answers: *value of currency is reduced on foreign exchange markets; unemployment rises in import industries; unemployment goes down in export industries.*

Preteaching Vocabulary
Use the Vocabulary Puzzle-Maker to create puzzles.

RESOURCE MANAGER

📂 Reproducible Masters
- Reproducible Lesson Plan 17-3
- Daily Lecture Notes 17-3
- Guided Reading Activity 17-3
- Reading Essentials and Study Guide 17-3
- Section Quiz 17-3

🖥 Transparencies
- Daily Focus Transparency 80

Multimedia
- Vocabulary PuzzleMaker CD-ROM
- Interactive Tutor Self-Assessment Software
- ExamView® Pro Testmaker
- Presentation Plus!

TEACH

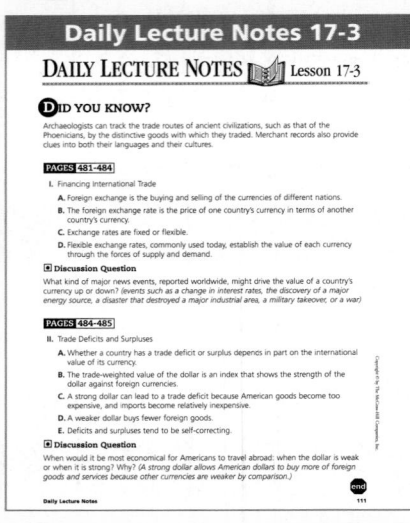

Daily Lecture Notes 17-3

DAILY LECTURE NOTES 📖 Lesson 17-3

DID YOU KNOW?
Archaeologists can track the trade routes of ancient civilizations, such as that of the Phoenicians, by the distinctive goods with which they traded. Merchant records also provide clues into both their languages and their cultures.

PAGES 481–484

I. Financing International Trade
  A. Foreign exchange is the buying and selling of the currencies of different nations.
  B. The foreign exchange rate is the price of one country's currency in terms of another country's currency.
  C. Exchange rates are fixed or flexible.
  D. Flexible exchange rates, commonly used today, establish the value of each currency through the forces of supply and demand.

Discussion Question
What kind of major news events, reported worldwide, might drive the value of a country's currency up or down? (events such as a change in interest rates, the discovery of a major energy source, a disaster that destroyed a major industrial area, a military takeover, or a war)

PAGES 484–485

II. Trade Deficits and Surpluses
  A. Whether a country has a trade deficit or surplus depends in part on the international value of its currency.
  B. The trade-weighted value of the dollar is an index that shows the strength of the dollar against foreign currencies.
  C. A strong dollar can lead to a trade deficit because American goods become too expensive, and imports become relatively inexpensive.
  D. A weaker dollar buys fewer foreign goods.
  E. Deficits and surpluses tend to be self-correcting.

Discussion Question
When would it be most economical for Americans to travel abroad: when the dollar is weak or when it is strong? Why? (A strong dollar allows American dollars to buy more of foreign goods and services because other currencies are weaker by comparison.)

Daily Lecture Notes   111

ECONOMICS
AT A GLANCE

Answer: *120.05*

L1 Illustrating Ideas

Ask each student to select a country and investigate its exchange rates over the last year. Have them graph the monthly change in rates. Call on students to share their graphs with the class.

L2 Analyzing Ideas

Ask students to clip articles from newspapers and magazines that deal with foreign trade and trade imbalances. Call on students to summarize their articles for the class.

---

foreign exchange market. This market includes banks that help secure foreign currencies for importers, as well as banks that accept foreign currencies from exporters.

Suppose that one pound sterling, £1, is equal to $1.42. If the business suits are valued at £1,000 in London, the American importer can go to an American bank and buy a £1,000 check for $1,420 plus a small service charge. The American firm then pays the British merchant, and the suits are imported.

American exporters sometimes accept foreign currency or checks written on foreign banks for their goods. They deposit the payments in their own banks, which helps the American banking system build a supply of foreign currency. This currency then can be sold to American firms that want to import goods from other countries. As a result, both the importer and the exporter end up with the currency they need.

The **foreign exchange rate** is the price of one country's currency in terms of another country's currency. The rate can be quoted in terms of the United States dollar equivalent, as in $1.42 = £1, or in terms of foreign currency per United States dollar, as in £0.7042 = $1. The rate is reported both ways, as shown in the foreign currency listings in **Figure 17.4.**

Fixed Exchange Rates

Today, two major kinds of exchange rates exist—fixed and flexible. For most of the 1900s, the world depended on **fixed exchange rates**—a system under which the price of one currency is fixed in terms of another so that the rate does not change.

Fixed exchange rates were popular when the world was on a gold standard. Gold served as the common denominator that allowed comparisons of currencies, and it also kept exchange rates in line. For example, suppose that a country allowed its money supply to grow too fast and that some of the money was spent on imports. Under a gold standard, the countries receiving the currency had the right to demand that it be converted into gold. Because no country wanted to lose its gold, each country worked to keep its money supply from growing too fast.

ECONOMICS
AT A GLANCE   Figure 17.4

Foreign Exchange Rates

Exchange Rates
May 29, 2001

Country	U.S. $ equiv.	Currency per U.S. $
Argentina (Peso)	1.0001	0.9999
Australia (Dollar)	0.5167	1.9355
Britain (Pound)	1.4200	0.7042
Canada (Dollar)	0.6501	1.5383
Chile (Peso)	0.001641	609.35
China (Renminbi)	0.1208	8.2768
Czech. Rep. (Koruna)		
Commercial rate	0.02499	40.014
Equador (US Dollar)	1.0000	1.0000
Israel (Shekel)	0.2424	4.1250
Japan (Yen)	0.008330	120.05
Mexico (Peso)		
Floating rate	0.1098	9.1080
Poland (Zolty)	0.2475	4.0400
Russia (Ruble)	.03439	29.081
South Korea (Won)	0.0007755	1289.50
Taiwan (Dollar)	0.02941	34.000
Euro	0.9100	1.0989

Reading the Financial Page Exchange rates are set according to the demand and supply of different types of money. **About how many Japanese yen equal one U.S. dollar?**

482   UNIT 5 INTERNATIONAL AND GLOBAL ECONOMICS

CYBERNOMICS SPOTLIGHT

Economic Espionage
Economic espionage is increasing as trade grows between countries. Economic espionage is the stealing of technology secrets. In order to be competitive, many countries are tempted to steal the secrets of another to avoid paying the high costs of research and development. Fax machines, cellular phones, and the Internet make it easier than ever to commit economic espionage.

MEETING SPECIAL NEEDS ACTIVITY

Learning Style: Verbal/Linguistic Ask students to imagine that they were requested to teach the materials in Section 3 to middle school students. Direct half of the class to individually prepare lectures covering the subsection titled "Financing International Trade." The other half of the class should individually prepare lectures covering the subsection titled "Trade Deficits and Surpluses." Tell students their lectures should be thorough but simple. Students should prepare simple outlines for their lectures that can be shared with listeners. As a review, pair students with the different subsections and have them present their lectures, and lecture notes, to one another.

📁 Refer to *Inclusion for the Social Studies Classroom Strategies and Activities* in the TCR.

Flexible Exchange Rates

Figure 17.5

A The Foreign Exchange Market for Dollars

B The Foreign Exchange Market for Marks

Using Graphs The value of foreign exchange, like the value of most other products, is determined by supply and demand. When investors sell one currency to buy another, what happens to the value of the currency that is sold?

This practice worked until the early 1960s when the United States developed a huge appetite for imports. During that time, it bought large quantities of foreign goods with dollars. At first, foreign countries willingly held dollars because they were acceptable as an international currency, so only a portion of these dollars came back when other countries bought American exports.

As dollars began to pile up in the rest of the world, many countries wondered if the United States could honor its promise that the dollar was "as good as gold." Eventually France and several other countries started redeeming their dollars, which drained U.S. gold reserves. As a result, President Richard Nixon announced that the United States would no longer redeem foreign-held dollars for gold in 1971. This action saved the gold stock, but it also angered many foreign governments that were planning to cash their American dollars into gold.

Flexible Exchange Rates

When the United States stopped redeeming foreign-held dollars for gold, the world monetary system went to a floating or flexible rate system. Under flexible exchange rates, also known as floating exchange rates, the forces of supply and demand establish the value of one country's currency in terms of another country's currency.

Figure 17.5 shows how flexible exchange rates work. In 1971, for example, the price of the dollar was four German marks (DM) as shown in **Panel A.** Alternatively, we could say that the price of one DM was $0.25 as shown in **Panel B.**

Suppose now that an American car dealer wanted to purchase Volkswagens that could be bought for 12,000 DMs in Germany. To obtain a single car, the American importer would have to sell $3,000 in the foreign exchange market to obtain the 12,000 DMs needed to buy the

CHAPTER 17: INTERNATIONAL TRADE **483**

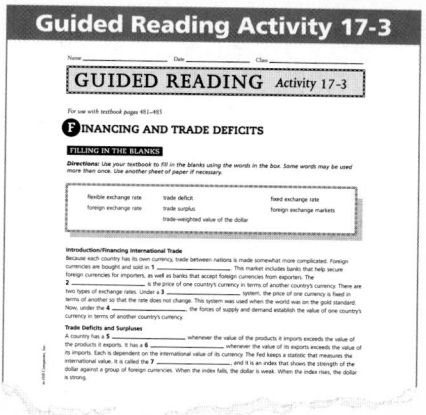

Guided Reading Activity 17-3

GUIDED READING Activity 17-3

FINANCING AND TRADE DEFICITS

Answer: *it decreases*

In recent years, the trade deficit has attracted almost as much attention as the federal budget deficit. Unlike the latter, however, the trade deficit has the potential to be self-correcting.

CYBERNOMICS

Exchange Rates on the Internet What is the current value of the U.S. dollar in pesos, shekels, or yen? To find out, click on the "Currency Calculator" at www.bloomberg.com

FREE ENTERPRISE ACTIVITY

Write the following exchange rate problems on the board and have students solve them:

1. A television set sells for ¥52,500 in Tokyo. How much would it cost in U.S. dollars if the exchange rate was ¥110 = $1.00? *(52,500 ÷ 110 = $477.27)*

2. A clock in London sells for £200. How much would it cost in U.S. dollars if the exchange rate was £1 = $1.62? *(200 x 1.62 = $324)*

3. A pair of blue jeans costs $29.99 in Los Angeles. How much would this item cost in Canadian dollars if the exchange rate was $1.00 Canadian = $0.76 U.S.? *(29.99 ÷ 0.76 = $39.46 Canadian)*

THE GLOBAL ECONOMY

The Dollar in Russia Because the ruble fell so much in value during the 1990s, the U.S. dollar became Russia's second currency. The most popular note was the new $100 bill introduced in the United States in 1996. To meet demand, planeloads of currency were flown into Russia, and Russian banks even charged their citizens $2 to exchange old U.S. currency for the new $100 bills.

3 ASSESS

Assign Section 3 Assessment as homework or as an in-class activity.

💾 Have students use **Interactive Tutor Self-Assessment Software** to review Section 3.

Section Quiz 17-3

QUIZ ◆ Chapter 17, Section 3

FINANCING AND TRADE DEFICITS SCORE

Matching: Match each item in Column A with the items in Column B. Write the correct letters in the blanks. (10 points each)

A
1. foreign exchange rate
2. floating exchange rate
3. trade deficit
4. trade surplus
5. trade-weighted value of the dollar

B
a. system under which the forces of supply and demand establish the value of one country's currency in terms of another country's currency
b. system under which the price of one currency is fixed in terms of another
c. occurs when the value of imported products exceeds the value of exported products
d. index showing the strength of the dollar against a group of foreign currencies
e. occurs when the value of exported products exceeds the value of imported products
f. the price of one country's currency in terms of another country's currency

Multiple Choice: In the blank at the left write the letter of the choice that best completes the statement or answers the question. (10 points each)

6. Foreign exchange is necessary in international trade because
   a. each country has its own monetary system.
   b. the United States went off the gold standard.
   c. international trade is conducted in foreign markets.
   d. it prevents a devaluation of the currency.

7. For most of the 1900s, the world depended on
   a. fixed exchange rates.
   b. floating exchange rates.
   c. the gold standard.
   d. flexible exchange rates.

8. The trade-weighted value of the dollar explains that when the dollar is strong,
   a. the trade deficit decreases.
   b. the trade deficit is not affected.

Volkswagen. This would simultaneously increase the supply of dollars shown in **Panel A** and the demand for DM in **Panel B**. Eventually the continuing American demand for foreign products would push the value of the dollar down to 2 DM, and its reciprocal, the price of the DM, up to $0.50.

When the dollar reaches 2 DMs, the price of the Volkswagen is much less competitive. This is because the importer now has to pay $6,000 to obtain the 12,000 DMs needed to purchase the car. Excessive imports thus cause the value of the dollar to decline, making imports cost more.

This may be bad news for U.S. importers, but it is good news for exporters. A German firm that bought American soybeans at $6 a bushel before 1971, for example, would have paid 24 DMs for each bushel. After the value of the dollar fell, it had to pay only 12 DMs for each bushel. As a result, soybeans were cheaper, and more could be sold abroad.

The system of flexible exchange rates has worked relatively well. More importantly, the

Careers

Sociologist

Sociologists study the development, interaction, and behavior of organized groups as well as various social, religious, and business organizations.

The Work

Sociologists may work for the government, universities and colleges, and in private business. Duties include gathering firsthand information from people. They prepare reports to be used in comparative studies of similar programs in other communities. Sociologists derive conclusions about the effectiveness of programs that can lead to formulating policy.

Qualifications

Sociologists must be skilled in research and analysis and possess the ability to communicate ideas clearly. A master's degree in sociology is a requirement.

484

---

switch to flexible rates did not interrupt the growth in international trade as many people had feared. More countries trade with one another today than ever before.

Trade Deficits and Surpluses

A country has a **trade deficit** whenever the value of the products it imports exceeds the value of the products it exports. It has a **trade surplus** whenever the value of its exports exceeds the value of its imports. Each is dependent on the international value of its currency.

The International Value of the Dollar

Ever since floating rates became standard in 1971, the Federal Reserve System has kept a statistic that measures the international value of the dollar. Called the **trade-weighted value of the dollar,** it is an index showing the strength of the dollar against a group of foreign currencies. When the index falls, the dollar is weak in relation to other currencies. When the index rises, the dollar is strong.

When the dollar reached strong levels in 1985, foreign goods became less expensive, and American exports became more costly for the rest of the world. As a result, imports rose, exports fell, and the United States suffered record trade deficits in 1986 and 1987. The value of the dollar remained relatively stable throughout the early 1990s, and then rose late in the decade when the rest of the world, especially countries in Asia, experienced an economic downturn. The stronger dollar led to another record trade deficit in early 2001.

The Effect of a Trade Deficit

A persistent trade imbalance tends to reduce the value of a country's currency on foreign exchange markets. The devalued currency then causes a chain reaction that affects income and employment in that country's industries.

To illustrate, the large deficit in the United States balance of payments in the mid-1980s and late 1990s flooded the foreign exchange markets with dollars. An increase in the supply of dollars, as illustrated by the supply and demand curves in **Figure 17.5,** causes the dollar to lose some of its

---

CRITICAL THINKING

Analyzing Cause and Effect On the board, copy the following diagram, omitting the answers in parentheses. Have students complete the diagram with facts from page 484.

CAUSE	EFFECT
(a persistent trade imbalance)	the reduction of the value of a country's currency on foreign exchange markets
reduction of the value of a country's currency on foreign exchange markets	*(income and employment in the country's industries)*

value. The weaker dollar causes unemployment to rise in import industries as imports become more expensive, and it causes unemployment to go down in export industries as their goods become more competitive.

Eventually the dollar will get strong again as foreigners sell their currency in order to buy dollars—thereby reversing the patterns of unemployment. As the dollar gets stronger, export industries will have a more difficult time and import industries will begin to recover. The economy may adjust slowly to changes in the value of the dollar, but the adjustments do take place.

As a result, the shift in employment between import and export industries is one of the biggest problems with a trade deficit. In the automobile industry, for example, Japanese cars once undercut the price of cars being produced in Detroit, causing severe unemployment for both domestic autoworkers and domestic car dealerships. As the Japanese yen rose against the dollar in the early 1990s, however, the price of Japanese cars increased, making domestic automobiles more attractive and restoring some of the employment in that industry.

Under flexible exchange rates, trade deficits tend to automatically correct themselves through the price system. A strong currency generally leads to a deficit in the balance of payments and a subsequent decline in the value of the currency. A

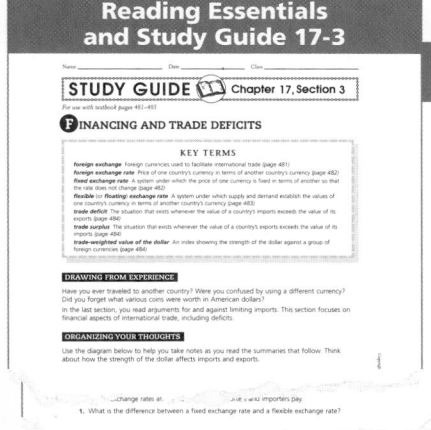

The Global Economy

Value of Currency Exchange When the value of the dollar goes up, American exports go down and imports rise. *What causes the value of the dollar to fluctuate?*

weak currency tends to cause trade surpluses, which eventually pull up the value of the currency. As a result, the United States and many other countries no longer design economic policies just to improve their trade position.

Visual Instruction

Answer to Caption:
the demand for foreign imports by the U.S. and the demand for U.S. exports

Reteach

Reading Essentials and Study Guide 17-3

Enrich

Invite the international officer from a local bank to speak to the class about foreign exchange. Ask the guest to discuss the difference between fixed and flexible exchange rates as well as any special problems of foreign exchange.

 CLOSE

Have students analyze the following statement: "A strong dollar resulted in a greater than expected trade deficit last month."

Section 3 Assessment

Checking for Understanding

1. **Main Idea** What is the relationship between the international value of the dollar and foreign trade?

2. **Key Terms** Define foreign exchange, foreign exchange rate, fixed exchange rate, flexible exchange rate, trade deficit, trade surplus, trade-weighted value of the dollar.

3. **Describe** how foreign exchange is used in trade.

4. **Explain** how trade deficits correct themselves under flexible exchange rates.

Applying Economic Concepts

5. **Foreign Exchange** How does a weak American dollar affect you as a consumer? How does a strong dollar affect you?

Critical Thinking

6. **Making Generalizations** How do exchange rates influence international trade?

7. **Making Comparisons** Explain the difference between a fixed exchange rate and a flexible exchange rate.

   Practice and assess key social studies skills with the *Glencoe Skillbuilder Interactive Workbook, Level 2.*

CHAPTER 17: INTERNATIONAL TRADE **485**

Section 3 Assessment Answers

1. When the dollar's value increases, foreign goods become less expensive, U.S. exports become more expensive, and vice versa.

2. All vocabulary terms are defined in the text.

3. It is used in trade to determine the relative value of different currencies.

4. through the price system

5. A weak dollar means consumers will pay more for foreign products, and vice versa.

6. When a country's currency is weak, other countries will import more of that country's products. When a country's currency is strong, it will export less.

7. The price of one currency is fixed in terms of another; supply and demand establish the value.

Teaching Skills

Read aloud the following passage from Part I of the United Auto Workers (UAW) Action program, *Reforming America's Trade Policy:*

Under NAFTA and GATT, decision making, instead of being based on one person/one vote, is based on market power: one dollar/one vote. Political democracy and the interests of the working class are overwhelmed by the economic interests of the largest industrial and financial corporations.

Then ask students to complete the following statements based on inferences that they make from the passage:

1. Members of the UAW believe that NAFTA and GATT are
   a. anti-capitalistic
   b. undemocratic *(b)*
2. The author probably supports
   a. protectionism
   b. free trade *(a)*

Additional Practice

Reinforcing Economic Skill 16

Name _____ Date _____ Class _____

Reinforcing Economic Skills Chapter 16

DRAWING INFERENCES AND CONCLUSIONS

Drawing inferences involves "reading between the lines," or drawing conclusions that are not stated directly in the text. To draw inferences and make conclusions, read the information carefully and list the important facts. Then apply related information from other sources as well as your own knowledge and insight to develop some conclusions about these facts.

Directions: *Study the tables below and answer the questions that follow.*

Country	Infant Deaths per 1,000 Live Births	Number of Television Sets per 1,000 People	Private Consumption per capita (dollars)
Bangladesh	79	7	1,049
Finland	5	519	11,431
Morocco	55	145	2,454
United States	8	776	18,507

Country	Health Spending (percent of GNP)	People per Hospital Bed	Gross National Product per capita (millions of dollars)
Bangladesh	2.4	5,479	240
Finland	8.3	93	20,580
Morocco	3.4	775	3,340
United States	14.3	221	26,980

Source: World Development Indicators

1. Using these tables, what inference can you make about why infant mortality is high in Bangladesh?

CRITICAL THINKING

Skill

Drawing Inferences and Conclusions

To *infer* means to evaluate information and arrive at a conclusion. When you make inferences, you "read between the lines," or draw conclusions that are not stated directly in the text. You must use the available facts *and* your own knowledge and experience to form a judgment or opinion about the material.

International flags, airport display

Learning the Skill

Use the following steps to help draw inferences and make conclusions:

- Read carefully for stated facts and ideas.
- Summarize the information and list the important facts.
- Apply related information that you may already know to make inferences.
- Use your knowledge and insight to develop some conclusions about these facts.

Practicing the Skill

Read the passage below, then answer the questions that follow.

From its beginnings until the mid-1860s, the United States encouraged trade with other nations, protecting only a few industries from foreign competition. We encouraged the world to buy American agricultural products and traded for manufactured goods. *Beginning in the 1860s, Northern industrial interests in control of the government passed high protective tariffs to prevent foreign competition from threatening our young industries. With some fluctuations, these tariffs remained high until the 1930s, when President Franklin Roosevelt tried to increase trade by lowering tariffs and encouraging our trading partners to do the same.*

When World War II ended, the United States knew it would be necessary to help Europe rebuild its economy. The government did this through the Marshall Plan, which provided the resources needed to reconstruct European economies. Along with other nations, the United States set up a World Bank for Reconstruction and Development from which all nations could borrow. The United States also led the development of the International Monetary Fund, so that nations could borrow foreign currencies in short-term loans in order to trade. Finally, the United States helped organize the General Agreement on Tariffs and Trade (GATT). Under this agreement, nations meet regularly to discuss mutual tariff policies.

1. What events does the writer describe?
2. What facts are presented?
3. What can you infer about the effects of the Marshall Plan on relations between the United States and Europe today?
4. What conclusion can you make about U.S. trade policy?

Application Activity

Study the statistics in Figure 17.1 on page 468. From the data, what can you infer about U.S. trade with Canada? Why does this relationship exist?

 Practice and **assess** key social studies skills with the *Glencoe Skillbuilder Interactive Workbook, Level 2.*

Answers to Practicing the Skill

1. trade between the U.S. and foreign countries
2. facts on tariffs, European rebuilding, and the World Bank
3. Answers include: facilitated trade; indebted Europe to the U.S.
4. With the exception of the period of time between the 1860s and the 1930s, the United States has encouraged trade with other nations.

Section 1

Absolute and Comparative Advantage (pages 467–470)

- The United States is extensively involved in international trade, with the average American spending more than $4,200 per year for **imports** in the form of goods and services.
- **Absolute advantage** means that a country can produce more of a good than another country can.
- The basis for trade today is **comparative advantage.** If people and countries specialize in the things they produce relatively more efficiently, and if they engage in trade to secure the things they do not produce, then total world output will increase.

Section 2

Barriers to International Trade

(pages 472–479)

- Barriers to trade include **tariffs, quotas,** licensing, health certifications, and voluntary quotas, all of which have been used to restrict the free flow of products.
- **Protectionists** support trade barriers on the grounds of national defense, **infant industries,** protecting domestic jobs, keeping the money at home, and helping the **balance of payments.**
- **Free traders** believe that all of these arguments are flawed, with the possible exception of the infant industries argument.
- High tariffs were one of the causes of the Great Depression, although the world has moved toward freer trade since then.

- The **most favored nation clause** is important to many countries because it gives them the same tariff reductions that the United States negotiates with other trading nations.
- The GATT was established in 1947 and has evolved into the **World Trade Organization (WTO),** which administers GATT agreements, promotes freer trade, and helps settle disputes between governments.

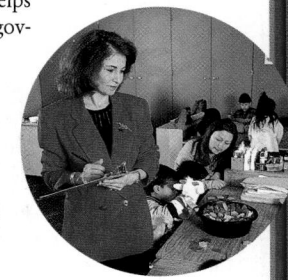

- The **North American Free Trade Agreement (NAFTA)** will eventually remove all trade barriers among Canada, Mexico, and the United States.

Section 3

Financing and Trade Deficits

(pages 481–485)

- **Foreign exchange** is the lifeblood of international trade; its value is determined in foreign exchange markets where currencies are bought and sold.
- Most countries use a system of **floating** or **flexible exchange rates,** meaning that supply and demand determine the currency's value.
- Some smaller countries also use a system of **fixed exchange rates,** which ties the value of their currency to a major currency like the U.S. dollar.
- The large **trade deficits** in the United States in the mid-1980s were partially caused by a strong dollar, resulting in unemployment in the export industries; the country would have had a **trade surplus** if the value of its exports had exceeded the value of its imports.
- Because deficits tend to be self-correcting, most nations no longer design economic policies just to improve the balance of payments.

CHAPTER 17: INTERNATIONAL TRADE **487**

Teacher's Notes / Internet Bookmarks

CHAPTER 17
Summary

ECONOMICS & YOU

Chapter 24
Disc 1, Side 2

International Trade

Also available in VHS.

Using the Chapter 17 Summary

Use the Chapter 17 Summary to preview, review, condense, or reteach the chapter.

Preview/Review

Vocabulary PuzzleMaker CD-ROM reinforces Key Terms.

Interactive Tutor Self-Assessment Software provides a review of Chapter 17 content.

Condense

Have students listen to the Chapter 17 Audio Program. Spanish also available.

Assign the Chapter 17 Audio Program Activity and give students the Chapter 17 Audio Program Test.

Have students complete the Guided Reading Activities and Reading Essentials and Study Guides for Chapter 17.

Reteach

Have students complete Reteaching Activity 17 in the TCR. Spanish also available.

Use **MindJogger Videoquiz** to review the Chapter 17 content.

Have students visit the Web site at epp.glencoe.com to review Chapter 17 and take the **Self-Check Quiz.**

Identifying Key Terms

Sentences may vary. Sample sentences are provided below.

1. The country that can produce the most of a product has an **absolute advantage,** but the country that can produce that same product relatively more efficiently has a **comparative advantage.**

2. A **trade deficit** is a deficit in the "goods" component of the **balance of payments.**

3. **Flexible exchange rates** help countries automatically correct deficits or surpluses in their **balance of payments.**

4. When the value of the products a country imports exceeds the value of the products it exports, there is a **trade deficit.** When the value of the exports exceed the value of the imports, it is a **trade surplus.**

5. Under a system of **flexible exchange rates,** the value of **foreign exchange** is measured in terms of another country's currency.

6. A **protectionist** wants **infant industries** protected from foreign competition.

7. A **protective tariff** and a **revenue tariff** are taxes levied on foreign imports.

8. **Tariffs** and **quotas** are barriers to free trade.

9. When the **trade-weighted value of the dollar** rises, the **trade deficit** increases.

488

Self-Check Quiz Visit the *Economics: Principles and Practices* Web site at epp.glencoe.com and click on **Chapter 17—Self-Check Quizzes** to prepare for the chapter test.

Identifying Key Terms

For each of the pairs of terms below, write a sentence or short paragraph showing how the two are related.

1. **absolute advantage**
   comparative advantage
2. **balance of payments**
   trade deficit
3. **balance of payments**
   flexible exchange rates
4. **trade deficit**
   trade surplus
5. **foreign exchange**
   flexible exchange rates
6. **protectionist**
   infant industries
7. **protective tariff**
   revenue tariff
8. **tariff**
   quota
9. **trade deficit**
   trade-weighted value of the dollar

Reviewing the Facts

Section 1 (pages 467–470)

1. **Describe** the extent of United States involvement in world trade.

2. **Describe** a case in which the United States might have an absolute advantage over another country in the production of a good.

3. **Explain** how applying comparative advantage makes trade between countries of different sizes possible.

Section 2 (pages 472–479)

4. **Name** three barriers to international trade.

5. **Describe** five protectionist arguments.

6. **Describe** the role of the WTO in the free trade movement.

Section 3 (pages 481–485)

7. **Differentiate** between fixed and flexible exchange rates.

8. **Explain** how deficits can be self-correcting when currency values are flexible.

Thinking Critically

1. **Drawing Conclusions** Do you favor protection as a national trade policy? Why or why not?

2. **Making Comparisons** What is the difference between a protective tariff and a revenue tariff? Use a graphic organizer similar to the one below to help you organize your answer.

Tariffs	
Protective	Revenue

3. **Analyzing Information** Some people feel the United States should return to a system of fixed exchange rates. Defend or oppose this view. Cite examples to support your position.

4. **Understanding Cause and Effect** Does the protection of inefficient industries hurt an economy? Why or why not?

5. **Making Comparisons** How might the issue of protectionism differ for a worker and a consumer? Use examples to support your argument.

Reviewing the Facts

Section 1

1. In 1999 imports of goods and services amounted to about $1,150 billion.
2. The U.S. would have an absolute advantage if it could produce more of a product.
3. When it can make a product relatively more efficiently, a smaller country can compete.

Section 2

4. tariffs, quotas, inspections
5. See pages 474–476.

6. settles trade disputes, organizes trade negotiations, and provides training

Section 3

7. fixed: currency is fixed in terms of gold or another currency; flexible: value determined by supply and demand
8. allows for the value of currency to rise and fall; self-correcting through the price system

Thinking Critically

1. Students may cite or reject protectionist arguments.

Applying Economic Concepts

1. **Comparative Advantage** Think of a project you recently completed with a friend. How could you have completed the project more efficiently, applying the principle of comparative advantage? Explain.

2. **Quotas** You have just started a business manufacturing toothbrushes. Would you favor a quota on imported toothbrushes? Why or why not?

3. **Foreign Exchange** Explain how doubling the $400 tax-free limit on goods brought in from abroad by American citizens would affect the balance of payments.

4. **Interdependence** How does the lack of certain raw materials force nations to become interdependent?

Math Practice

Suppose you are planning a trip to Russia and plan to bring $500 in spending money. If the exchange rates in **Figure 17.4** prevail at the time of your departure, how many rubles would you have after you exchanged your dollars for rubles? If you spent 5,000 rubles while you were there, and if you converted the rest of the rubles back to dollars when you came home, how many dollars would you have?

Thinking Like an Economist

Assume that the country is running a large trade deficit. What predictions would you make about future changes in the value of the dollar in the foreign exchange markets? Would these developments be a matter of concern?

Technology Skill

Using E-Mail During the course of one day, make a note of at least 10 manufactured items you handle, such as your clothing and the cafeteria trays used in your school. Find out where each item is produced, and make a log of the items, noting whether each is domestic or foreign made.

Next, write a persuasive argument explaining your opinion on international trade. In writing a persuasive argument, it is important to state the issue clearly and to give your position on it.

Use the evidence you gathered in your log notes to support your position and to refute any opposing position. Use other sources to identify evidence that will help you establish your claim. Conclude your argument by restating your position and summing up the evidence.

Finally, e-mail your argument to the editor of a newspaper or magazine. One day soon, you may see your argument in print!

Building Skills

Drawing Inferences and Conclusions Read the following passage about U.S. trade with other nations. Use the stated facts and your own knowledge to answer the questions that follow.

In the early 1980s, American producers found it increasingly difficult to sell their products to other countries. At least part of this problem was the result of the high value of the dollar. To buy American products, foreign nations must trade their currency for dollars. When the dollar's value is too high, foreign nations receive fewer dollars in exchange for their money. Beginning in the mid-1980s, the value of the dollar declined in relation to foreign currencies. That was like putting American products on sale to foreign buyers. U.S. exports increased sharply.

1. What is the main topic of the passage?
2. What facts are presented?
3. From this passage, what can you infer about fluctuations in U.S. trade?
4. What fact(s) or observations helped you make this inference?

 Practice and **assess** key social studies skills with the *Glencoe Skillbuilder Interactive Workbook, Level 2.*

Math Practice

12,275 rubles; $296.33

Thinking Like an Economist

A future weak dollar should eventually encourage exports and discourage imports thereby increasing the trade deficit.

Technology Skill

Students' arguments should refer to evidence gathered in their logs and reflect an understanding of international trade.

Building Skills

1. trade and the dollar's value
2. American producers found it difficult to sell products to other countries; the value of the dollar decreased and exports increased.
3. The fluctuations are based on the value of the American dollar.
4. When the dollar's value was too high, American producers had difficulty selling their products.

? Bonus Test Question

Arcania can produce 6,000 televisions or 4,000 radios per month. Esoterica can produce 4,000 televisions and 3,000 radios per month. Arcania specializes in televisions and Esoterica specializes in radios. Explain why. *(Arcania is applying its comparative advantage in televisions because it does a relatively better job of producing televisions. Esoterica has a comparative advantage in radios.)*

2. Revenue tariff: raises money; a protective tariff: protects less efficient domestic industries.
3. Students' answers should reflect an understanding of fixed and flexible exchange rates.
4. Students may say that inefficient industries use resources that might be used more profitably elsewhere.
5. People, as consumers, want to buy products at low prices; therefore they may oppose protectionism. As workers, they want their jobs protected.

Applying Economic Concepts

1. Students may cite strengths and weaknesses to assess how the project could have been completed more efficiently.
2. A quota on imported toothbrushes would lessen foreign competition, or quotas will push up the price of the product.
3. would increase imports thereby increasing the trade deficit
4. Trade is the only way to obtain essential raw materials.

Chapter 18 Resource Manager

SECTION RESOURCES

Daily Objectives	Reproducible Resources	Technology/Multimedia Resources
Section 1 **The Spectrum of Economic Systems** 1. Explain the advantages and disadvantages of capitalism. 2. Describe the differences among the doctrines of socialism, capitalism, and communism. 3. Compare the features of communism to other types of economic systems.	Reproducible Lesson Plan 18-1 Daily Lecture Notes 18-1 Guided Reading Activity 18-1 Reading Essentials and Study Guide 18-1 Section Quiz 18-1*	Daily Focus Transparency 82 Interactive Tutor Self-Assessment Software ExamView® Pro Testmaker Presentation Plus!
Section 2 **The Rise and Fall of Communism** 1. Explain the rise of the Soviet economy under Lenin and Stalin. 2. Describe the complexities of a centrally planned economy. 3. Understand the forces that brought about the collapse of communism as an economic system.	Reproducible Lesson Plan 18-2 Daily Lecture Notes 18-2 Guided Reading Activity 18-2 Reading Essentials and Study Guide 18-2 Section Quiz 18-2*	Daily Focus Transparency 83 Interactive Tutor Self-Assessment Software ExamView® Pro Testmaker Presentation Plus!
Section 3 **The Transition to Capitalism** 1. List four problems encountered when an economy makes the transition to capitalism. 2. Recognize the major countries and regions that are making the transition to capitalism.	Reproducible Lesson Plan 18-3 Daily Lecture Notes 18-3 Guided Reading Activity 18-3 Reading Essentials and Study Guide 18-3 Section Quiz 18-3*	Daily Focus Transparency 84 NBR Economics & You Video Program Interactive Tutor Self-Assessment Software ExamView® Pro Testmaker Presentation Plus!
Section 4 **The Various Faces of Capitalism** 1. Explain the factors that encouraged economic growth in Japan. 2. Rank the "Asian Tigers" according to per capita GNP. 3. Describe Sweden's retreat from socialism.	Reproducible Lesson Plan 18-4 Daily Lecture Notes 18-4 Guided Reading Activity 18-4 Reading Essentials and Study Guide 18-4 Section Quiz 18-4*	Daily Focus Transparency 85 Vocabulary PuzzleMaker CD-ROM Interactive Tutor Self-Assessment Software ExamView® Pro Testmaker Presentation Plus!

 Transparency   CD-ROM   Software   Blackline Master   *Also available in Spanish*

 Videodisc   Audio Program   Videocassette

Chapter 18 Resource Manager

TeacherWorks™ All-In-One Planner and Resource Center

- **Interactive Teacher Edition** Access your Teacher Wraparound Edition and your classroom resources with a few easy clicks.
- **Interactive Lesson Planner** Planning has never been easier! Organize your week, month, semester, or year with all the lesson helps you need to make teaching creative, timely, and relevant.

Use Glencoe's **Presentation Plus!** multimedia teacher tool to easily present dynamic lessons that visually excite your students. Using Microsoft PowerPoint® you can customize the presentations to create your own personalized lessons.

PRESENTATION Plus!

ACTIVITY

From the Classroom of...

**Sharon Owens
Westerville
    City Schools
Westerville, OH**

Shake Hands or Bow?

As nations around the world move to a market economy, American businesses are interacting more and more with different cultures in other countries. Have students write or e-mail an American company that conducts business in a foreign country to discover any cultural or business practices the company has incorporated into its operations. For example, businesspeople in Japan greet each other by bowing. Failure to honor such traditional courtesies may have a negative impact on a company's efforts to do business.

In addition, students can select a specific country and research its culture in relation to business protocol. Then have students work in groups to make videotapes demonstrating the various procedures and key words one should know in order to properly conduct business in their chosen country. Students can show their completed videos to the class.

National Council on Economic Education

THE **Economics**America AND **Economics**International PROGRAMS

Voluntary National Content Standards in Economics
Emphasized in Chapter 18

Content Standard 3

Content Standard 16

For a complete listing of NCEE Standards and entire text correlation, see Teacher pages in front of book.

Resources Available from NCEE
- Capstone: The Nation's High School Economics Course
- Focus: High School Economics
- Focus: International Economics
- Civics and Government: Focus on Economics
- Economies in Transition: Command to Market
- From Plan to Market
- Economics and Entrepreneurship, Teaching Strategies

To order these materials or to contact your state Council on Economic Education about workshops and programs, call 1-800-338-1192 or visit www.nationalcouncil.org

Chapter 18 Resource Manager

TEACHING TRANSPARENCY

Economic Concept Transparency 22:
International Aspects of Growth and Stability

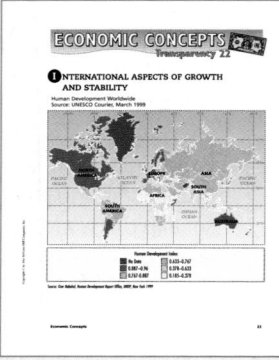

APPLICATION AND ENRICHMENT

Consumer Application
Activity 23

Free Enterprise
Activity 23

APPLICATION AND ENRICHMENT

Enrichment Activity 18

Cooperative Learning
Activity 23

Math Practice
Activity 23

Economic Cartoon 23

Primary and Secondary
Source Reading 23

REVIEW AND REINFORCEMENT

Economic Vocabulary
Activity 18

Reteaching Activity 18

Critical Thinking
Activity 23

Reinforcing Economic
Skill 23

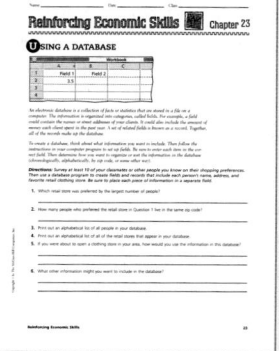

Chapter 18 Resource Manager

Chapter 18 Test Form A

Chapter 18 Test Form B

Performance Assessment Activity 23

ExamView® Pro Testmaker

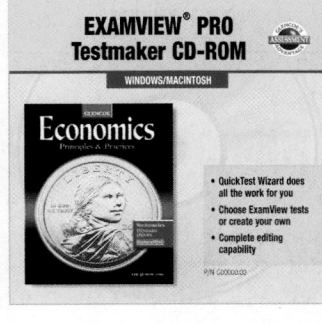

SPANISH RESOURCES

The following Spanish language materials are available in the Spanish Resources binder:

 Spanish Economic Vocabulary Activities

 Spanish Reteaching Activities

 Spanish Section Quizzes

 Spanish Economic Concepts Transparencies

Also available:

  Spanish Chapter 18 Audio Program Activity and Test

TECHNOLOGY/MULTIMEDIA

- Vocabulary PuzzleMaker CD-ROM
- Interactive Tutor Self-Assessment Software
- ExamView® Pro Testmaker
- Audio Program (English or Spanish)
- NBR Economics & You Video Program (English or Spanish)
- MindJogger Videoquiz
- Interactive Economics! CD-ROM
- Presentation Plus!
- TeacherWorks CD-ROM
- Glencoe Skillbuilder Interactive Workbook CD-ROM, Level 2

ECONOMICS Online

Use our Web site for additional resources. All essential content is covered in the Student Edition.

You and your students can visit epp.glencoe.com, the Web site companion to **Economics: Principles and Practices.** This innovative integration of electronic and print media offers your students a wealth of opportunities. The student text directs students to the Web site for the following options:

- **Chapter Overviews**
- **Student Web Activities**
- **Self-Check Quizzes**
- **Textbook Updates**

Answers are provided for you in the Web Activity Lesson Plan. Additional Web resources and interactive puzzles are also available.

Performance Assessment

Refer to Activity 23 in the *Performance Assessment Strategies and Activities* booklet.

BLOCK SCHEDULING

ECONOMICS *Online*

Introduce students to chapter content and key terms by having them access **Chapter Overview 18** at epp.glencoe.com

NIGHTLY BUSINESS REPORT

ECONOMICS & YOU

Chapter 25
Disc 1, Side 2

Comparative Economic Systems

After viewing this segment, students should be able to:
* Describe the challenges faced by state-owned industries.

Also available in VHS.

GLENCOE TECHNOLOGY

Use **MindJogger Videoquiz** to preview the Chapter 18 content.

CHAPTER 18

Comparative Economic Systems

Economics & You

The freedom to use your own tools and labor in pursuit of profits is one of the primary features of capitalism. In **Chapter 18**, you will learn that capitalism is more than an ideology. It is the way we live and the way the world is headed. To learn more about the different systems of economics, view the Chapter 25 video lesson:

Comparative Economic Systems

ECONOMICS *Online*

Chapter Overview Visit the *Economics: Principles and Practices* Web site at epp.glencoe.com and click on **Chapter 18—Chapter Overviews** to preview chapter information.

This scene of the city of Jaipur in northwest India shows a blend of traditional and modern life.

 EXTRA CREDIT PROJECT

Have students work individually or in small groups to create a three-part bulletin board display illustrating the three economic systems discussed in Chapter 18. Suggest that students use photographs, sketches, tables, charts, and graphs—accompanied by captions—to illustrate the three systems.

The Spectrum of Economic Systems

Study Guide

Main Idea
Capitalism, socialism, and communism are historically three popular economic systems.

Reading Strategy
Graphic Organizer As you read the section, complete a graphic organizer similar to the one below by listing six advantages of capitalism and providing an example of each.

Capitalism

Advantages	Examples

Key Terms
capitalism, socialism, communism

Objectives
After studying this section, you will be able to:
1. **Explain** the advantages and disadvantages of capitalism.
2. **Describe** the differences among the doctrines of socialism, capitalism, and communism.
3. **Compare** the features of communism to other types of economic systems.

Applying Economic Concepts
Surplus Value Have you ever felt that the value of your work was much more than your wage? If so, you have something in common with Karl Marx, who founded communism and introduced the concept of surplus value that is extracted from labor.

Cover Story

Sweden Pays the Price of High Taxes

STOCKHOLM—Electrolux AB, the big Swedish appliance maker, scoured the globe for a person to set up a new data-processing division last year before finding Stephan Carlquist, a Swede and senior executive at ABB Asea Brown Boveri in the United States.

Stephan Carlquist

Persuading him to jump to Electrolux was no problem, but bringing him to Sweden, home of the industrialized world's highest tax rates, was another matter. Instead, Mr. Carlquist set up shop in London, where taxes are lighter. . . .

Over the next year, he plans to build a multinational team of as many as 50 people—few of them Swedes. . . . "It's very hard to attract skilled, international people to Sweden." Mr. Carlquist said.

—International Herald Tribune, March 16, 1999

Throughout most of the 1900s, the world's developed nations fell into three categories of economic systems—communism, socialism, and capitalism. Communist countries were closely associated with command economies, capitalist countries were most similar to market economies, and socialist countries had a combination of both command and market economies. Sweden is an example of a country with a strong socialist tradition, and—as you read in the cover story—the high taxes that go along with it.

The three basic types of economic systems are shown in **Figure 18.1.** At the far left is communism, in which a strong central government influences almost every economic decision. At the far right is capitalism, in which government has a limited role. As one moves from left to right along the spectrum, both the ownership of resources and the degree of government involvement in the operation of the economy change.

CHAPTER 18: COMPARATIVE ECONOMIC SYSTEMS **491**

Section Overview
This section compares the characteristics of each of the three major economic systems.

BELLRINGER
Motivational Activity

 Project **transparency** and have students answer questions.

 Available as blackline master.

Daily Focus Transparency 82

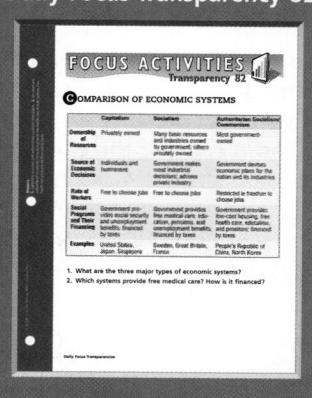

Study Guide

Reading Strategy
Have students create the graphic organizer.
Answers to Graphic: *efficiency, freedom, decentralization, smaller role of government in economy, consumer satisfaction, flexibility to accommodate change*

Preteaching Vocabulary
Write the Key Terms *socialism* and *communism* on the board. Call on students to explain how these terms differ from each other.

RESOURCE MANAGER

📁 Reproducible Masters
- Reproducible Lesson Plan 18-1
- Daily Lecture Notes 18-1
- Guided Reading Activity 18-1
- Reading Essentials and Study Guide 18-1
- Section Quiz 18-1

📽 Transparencies
- Daily Focus Transparency 82

Multimedia
- 💾 Interactive Tutor Self-Assessment Software
- 💿 ExamView® Pro Testmaker
- 💿 Presentation Plus!

TEACH

L1 Analyzing Ideas

Conduct a class discussion concerning the ways in which people are motivated to produce goods and services in each of the three types of economic systems. Conclude by asking students what they consider to be the good and bad aspects of each system. **ELL**

No lines separate communism, socialism, and capitalism. They appear on the spectrum as having a greater or lesser degree of government involvement and private ownership of resources.

Capitalism

Under **capitalism,** the means of production are privately owned. Supply and demand determine prices, and businesses are free to direct resources into activities that promise the greatest profits.

Advantages of Capitalism

One of the main advantages is efficiency. If there are many buyers and sellers, if resources are reasonably mobile, and if buyers and sellers are reasonably well informed, then resources will be directed to their most profitable and efficient use.

Another advantage is freedom, which gives consumers the opportunity to purchase the goods and services that best satisfy their preferences. Producers also have the freedom to direct productive resources into activities that consumers demand most. Producers have the incentive to do so because of the profit motive, and because private property rights allow them to keep the fruits of their efforts.

A third advantage is that capitalism is highly decentralized. Consumers and producers jointly answer the WHAT, HOW, and FOR WHOM questions all societies face. This is made possible because of the price system, which sends signals to both producers and consumers. The decentralized nature of decision making leads to the fourth advantage. Specifically, the role of government in the economy is much smaller.

The fifth advantage is the high degree of consumer satisfaction that comes from the variety of products that are produced to satisfy consumer demands. The sixth advantage is the flexibility to accommodate change. When consumer preferences change, or when the price of resources changes, signals are sent through the price system and everyone adjusts accordingly.

The most visible result of these advantages is the enormous amount of wealth that capitalist nations have accumulated. With few exceptions, the countries that have the highest living standards and per-capita incomes today are ones with market-based capitalist economies.

Disadvantages of Capitalism

Capitalism has its disadvantages. Although it is efficient in satisfying the demands of consumers, it does not always satisfy everyone's needs. At a collective level, capitalism ignores the production of many public goods such as roads, public schools, a system of justice, and national defense. Instead, the market produces private goods and services—items that can be withheld if people refuse to pay for them.

At an individual level, capitalism produces only for those who have demand, which means the ability and willingness to pay. A system of pure capitalism would ignore poor people, the unemployed, and less productive members of society like the elderly.

Socialism

Socialism is an economic system in which government owns and runs some of the basic productive resources in order to distribute output in ways deemed to be in the best interest of society. Most socialist societies are democracies in which elected officials direct the allocation of resources in key industries.

Advantages of Socialism

Socialism addresses the FOR WHOM question directly. Those who are not fortunate or productive enough to earn a competitive income still share in the benefits of society. Although the government owns the majority of productive resources in a socialist society, people use their electoral power to influence many of the WHAT, HOW, and FOR WHOM questions.

Disadvantages of Socialism

Socialism is normally less efficient than capitalism. If workers receive government guarantees of jobs, more workers will be hired than are necessary, driving up the cost of production. The

---

MEETING SPECIAL NEEDS ACTIVITY

English Language Learners Students who are still learning the English language can benefit by reading selections with a partner. Pair students in the class and have one student listen as his or her partner reads. Then the pair should discuss the reading, exchanging ideas and questions about what the passage means. **ELL**

Refer to *Inclusion for the Social Studies Classroom Strategies and Activities* in the TCR.

ECONOMICS
AT A GLANCE

Figure 18.1

The Spectrum of Economic Systems

COMMUNISM	SOCIALISM	CAPITALISM
Directed by Command		Directed by the Free Market

Ownership of Resources

All productive resources are government owned and operated.	Basic productive resources are government owned and operated; the rest are privately owned and operated.	Productive resources are privately owned and operated.

Allocation of Resources

Centralized planning directs all resources.	Government plans ways to allocate resources in key industries.	Capital for production is obtained through the lure of profits in the market.

Role of Government

Government makes all economic decisions.	Government directs the completion of its economic plans in key industries.	Government may promote competition and provide public goods.

Using Charts The distinguishing feature of economic systems is the ownership of the factors of production and the role of government in deciding WHAT, HOW, and FOR WHOM to produce. **How is capital for production acquired under capitalism?**

government also has an incentive to keep these workers employed—even if they are not all needed—to show that the government is providing jobs for everyone.

Because the government provides a broader range of services such as health care, education, and welfare, taxes are generally higher in socialist countries. This often causes the type of labor mobility problems discussed in the cover story—where workers may be reluctant to work in countries with such high taxes.

Communism

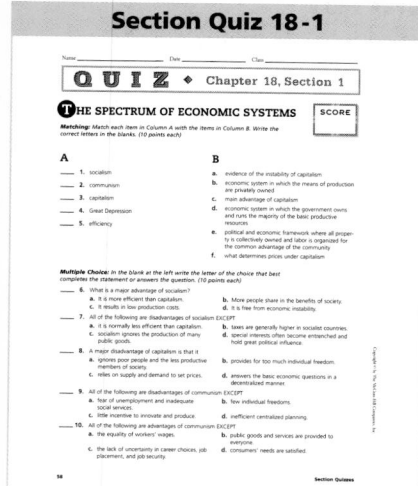 In its purest form, **communism** is a political and an economic framework where all property is collectively owned, labor is organized for the common advantage of the community, and everyone consumes according to their needs.

To date, no modern country has achieved the ideal of pure communism. Countries such as Cuba, North Korea, and the former Soviet Union instead developed rigid command-type economies where

CHAPTER 18: COMPARATIVE ECONOMIC SYSTEMS **493**

CHAPTER 18
Section 1, pages 491–494

ECONOMICS
AT A GLANCE

Answer: *through the lure of profits in the market*

③ ASSESS

Assign Section 1 Assessment as homework or as an in-class activity.

💾 Have students use **Interactive Tutor Self-Assessment Software** to review Section 1.

Section Quiz 18-1

QUIZ ◆ Chapter 18, Section 1

THE SPECTRUM OF ECONOMIC SYSTEMS SCORE

Matching: Match each item in Column A with the items in Column B. Write the correct letters in the blanks. (10 points each)

A
____ 1. socialism
____ 2. communism
____ 3. capitalism
____ 4. Great Depression
____ 5. efficiency

B
a. evidence of the instability of capitalism
b. economic system in which the means of production are privately owned
c. main advantage of capitalism
d. economic system in which the government owns and runs the majority of the basic productive resources
e. political and economic framework where all property is collectively owned and labor is organized for the common advantage of the community
f. what determines prices under capitalism

Multiple Choice: In the blank at the left write the letter of the choice that best completes the statement or answers the question. (10 points each)

____ 6. What is a major advantage of socialism?
  a. It is more efficient than capitalism.   b. More people share in the benefits of society.
  c. It results in low production costs.   d. It is free from economic instability.
____ 7. All of the following are disadvantages of socialism EXCEPT
  a. it is normally less efficient than capitalism.   b. taxes are generally higher in socialist countries.
  c. socialism ignores the production of many public goods.   d. special interests often become entrenched and hold great political influence.
____ 8. A major disadvantage of capitalism is that it
  a. ignores poor people and the less productive members of society.   b. provides for too much individual freedom.
  c. relies on supply and demand to set prices.   d. answers the basic economic questions in a decentralized manner.
____ 9. All of the following are disadvantages of communism EXCEPT
  a. fear of unemployment and inadequate social services.   b. few individual freedoms.
  c. little incentive to innovate and produce.   d. inefficient centralized planning.
____ 10. All of the following are advantages of communism EXCEPT
  a. the equality of workers' wages.   b. public goods and services are provided to everyone.
  c. the lack of uncertainty in career choices, job placement, and job security.   d. consumers' needs are satisfied.

58   *Section Quizzes*

FREE ENTERPRISE ACTIVITY

Organize students into three groups and assign each group one of the three economic systems. Direct groups to organize a furniture factory in accordance with their assigned economic system. Have groups consider and answer the following questions: How will you get the money to begin production? Where will the factors of production come from? How will workers be paid? How much will be produced? How will production be organized? How will the furniture be distributed? Have group representatives share their responses with the class. 📦 **BLOCK SCHEDULING**

493

Reteach

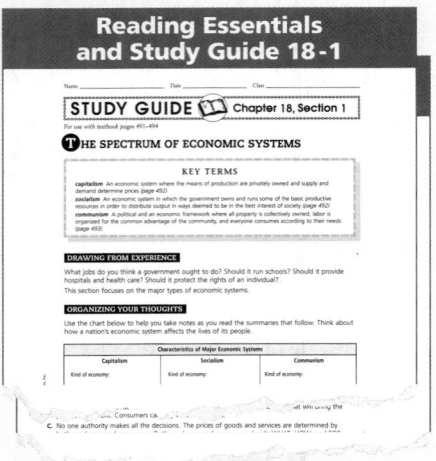

Reading Essentials and Study Guide 18-1

Enrich

Have students select one of the countries mentioned in the section and write a paragraph showing how that country's economic system compares to the pure form of capitalism, socialism, or communism.

CLOSE

Have students work individually or in small groups to develop logos or symbols for capitalism, socialism, and communism. Call on volunteers to display and explain their logos or symbols.

---

the state—usually represented by a single authoritarian party—claims the ideal of pure communism as its eventual goal.

Advantages of Communism

One of the main advantages of communism, from the typical worker's point of view, is that of equality. Because everyone is theoretically equal, the wages of workers from the assembly line in the factory to the surgeon in the hospital are nearly identical.

To make up for the lack of purchasing power, the state provides a broad range of public goods such as health care, transportation, education, and a military defense system. These services are normally supplied at little or no cost.

A third advantage is the lack of uncertainty concerning careers and job security. This is because the state directs workers into their jobs, and workers are not fired or dismissed as they could be in other societies.

A fourth advantage is that the centralized control allows the economy to shift directions in a relatively short period of time. In the case of the former Soviet Union, the entire economy changed from a relatively underdeveloped agrarian nation to an advanced industrial one in the course of a few short decades.

Disadvantages of Communism

One of the first disadvantages of communism is that individual freedom is lost. People have little or no say in their jobs, and economic planners determine even the choice of occupation.

Communism also lacks effective incentives that encourage people to work hard. Most people receive the same pay regardless of how hard they work.

Communism generally fails to meet the needs and wants of consumers, primarily because the WHAT to produce question is determined by central planners. Most communist states place a high priority on military preparedness, resulting in the neglect of consumer goods that are highly prized in other parts of the world.

One of the biggest drawbacks to communism is the inefficiency of centralized planning. The resources needed to execute the planning, and the overwhelming obstacles to effective execution, are serious problems that countries encounter after reaching a certain size. Finally, communist economies, like most command economies, lack the flexibility to deal with day-to-day changes.

Section 1 Assessment

Checking for Understanding

1. **Main Idea** Identify the three broad economic systems of the last century.

2. **Key Terms** Define capitalism, socialism, communism.

3. **List** the advantages and disadvantages of capitalism.

4. **Explain** how capitalism, socialism, and communism are different.

5. **Describe** how communism differs from other types of economic systems.

Applying Economic Concepts

6. **Surplus Value** According to Karl Marx, employers take advantage of their employees by paying them less than they are worth in order to make a larger profit. Do you think Marx's opinion is valid in the United States today? Why or why not?

Critical Thinking

7. **Making Comparisons** How does the role of the individual differ under capitalism, socialism, and communism? Explain your reasoning.

8. **Finding the Main Idea** What people does pure capitalism tend to ignore? Explain why this is the case.

 Practice and **assess** key social studies skills with the *Glencoe Skillbuilder Interactive Workbook, Level 2.*

Section 1 Assessment Answers

1. capitalism, socialism, communism

2. All vocabulary terms are defined in the text.

3. advantages: efficiency, freedom, decentralization, consumer satisfaction, flexibility; disadvantages: production of public goods, produces only for those who have demand

4. Capitalism offers individual freedom and little government control. Communism offers no individual freedom and complete government control. Socialism falls in between the other two systems.

5. The government makes economic decisions, and all property is collectively owned.

6. Students' answers should be supported by valid examples.

7. differs in freedom and role in economy

8. the poor, the unemployed, and the less productive members of society

TECHNOLOGY Skill

Using a Database

A computerized database program can help you organize and manage a large amount of information. After entering data in a database table, you can quickly locate the information according to key words.

Learning the Skill

An electronic database is a collection of facts that are stored in a file on the computer. The information is organized into categories called *fields*. For example, one field may be the names of your clients. Another field may be the street addresses of your clients. All the related fields make up a record. Together, all the records make up the database.

A database can be organized and reorganized in any way that is useful to you. By using a database management system (DBMS)—or special software developed for record keeping—you can easily add, delete, change, or update information. When you want to retrieve information, the computer searches the files, finds the information, and displays it on the screen.

Practicing the Skill

Follow these steps to build a database on economic reform in China.

1. Determine what facts you want to include in your database and research to collect that information.

Glencoe PuzzleMaker

Economics: Principles and Practices

Word	Clue	Set
noncompeting	___ labor grades; broad ...	Chapter 8
picket	demonstration before a ...	Chapter 8
professional	___ labor; workers with a ...	Chapter 8
rate	wage ___; prevailing pay ...	Chapter 8
real	___ dollars; dollar amounts ...	Chapter 8
right	___-to-work law; state law ...	Chapter 8
seizure	temporary government ...	Chapter 8
semiskilled	___ labor; workers who can ...	Chapter 8
seniority	length of time a person has ...	Chapter 8
skilled	___ labor; workers who can ...	Chapter 8
strike	union-organized work ...	Chapter 8
tier	two-___ wage system; wage ...	Chapter 8
traditional	___ theory of wage ...	Chapter 8
union	___ shop; arrangement under ...	Chapter 8
unskilled	___ labor; workers not ...	Chapter 8
voluntary	___ arbitration; agreement ...	Chapter 8

Selected: 236 of 578   Sorted by: Set

Using a database can help organize population statistics, clients' names and addresses, and even baseball card collections.

2. Follow the instructions in the DBMS that you're using to set up fields. Then enter each item of data in its assigned field.

3. Determine how you want to organize the facts in the database—chronologically by the date, alphabetically, or by some other category.

4. Follow the instructions in your computer program to sort the information in order of importance.

5. Verify that all the information in your database is correct. If necessary, add, delete, or change information or fields.

Application Activity

Research and build a database that organizes information about U.S. trade with countries in Asia. Explain why the database is organized the way it is and how it might be used in this class.

Technology Skill

Teaching Skills

On the board, copy the following excerpt from a database on baseball cards.

PLAYER	CARD YEAR	VALUE
Musial, Stan	1948 R*	$750
Williams, Ted	1950	$700
Mantle, Mickey	1951 R*	$5,250
Mays, Willie	1951 R*	$2,500
Mantle, Mickey	1952	$16,000
Banks, Ernie	1954 R*	$695
R* = rookie, or first year		

Ask students what fields are used in the database. *(player, card year, and value)* Ask how the information is organized. *(chronologically)* Have students name at least two other ways in which the information might be organized. *(alphabetically or according to value)*

Additional Practice

Reinforcing Economic Skill 23

495

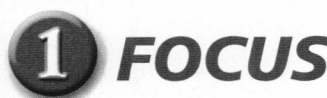

1 FOCUS

Section Overview
This section traces the economic history of the former Soviet Union.

BELLRINGER
Motivational Activity

Project **transparency** and have students answer questions.

Available as blackline master.

Daily Focus Transparency 83

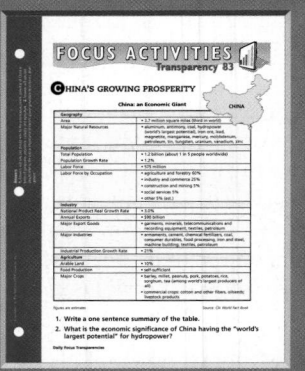

Study Guide

Reading Strategy
Have students create the graphic organizer.
Answers to Graphic: *government decides which products are made, by whom, and how many; government decides who works where and controls means of production through quotas and piecework; everyone receives products according to need*

Preteaching Vocabulary
Have students define each of the Key Terms.

The Rise and Fall of Communism

Main Idea
Communism is an economic system that has both centralized control of the means of production and of the political system.

Reading Strategy
Graphic Organizer As you read the section, complete a graphic organizer similar to the one below by explaining how the economic system in the former Soviet Union answered the basic economic questions.

Soviet Union
What — How — For whom

Key Terms
Five-Year Plan, collectivization, Gosplan, state farm, collective farm, piecework, storming, perestroika

Objectives
After studying this section, you will be able to:
1. **Explain** the rise of the Soviet economy under Lenin and Stalin.
2. **Describe** the complexities of a centrally planned economy.
3. **Understand** the forces that brought about the collapse of communism as an economic system.

Applying Economic Concepts
Perestroika Have you ever thought that some aspects of the economy should be changed from top to bottom? If so, read to find out more about perestroika, which is the Russian term for "restructuring."

Cover Story

Kiev to Pay Russian Debts with Bombers

Russia has agreed to accept bomber aircraft as payment for part of Ukraine's huge debt to Russia for natural gas . . . according to Russian figures and $1bn according to Ukrainian figures . . . Russia has agreed to take eight Tu-160 Blackjack bombers in payment from Ukraine.

Blackjack bomber

Ukraine owes Russia $1.8bn

Ukraine typically pays for gas in barter, with nominal prices set at around three times the market price for the goods . . . [but] Ukraine and Russia are constantly at loggerheads over gas debts.

Russia in the past has shut off gas supplies in Ukraine due to non-payment, but Ukraine has then simply stolen Russian gas bound for Europe instead. All of Russia's gas exports to Europe travel through Ukrainian pipelines.

—*The Financial Times*, August 9, 1999

496

In the absence of pure communism, the former Soviet Union is the most frequently cited example of a communist economic system. The early Soviet economy showed the main advantage of a command system—that it could mobilize resources and change direction in a short period of time. The sudden disintegration of the Soviet economy in the late 1980s, however, demonstrated the essential flaws of communism.

The Economy Under Lenin and Stalin

In 1917 a revolutionary named Vladimir Ilyich Ulyanov, or Lenin, overthrew the government of Russia. In its place, he set up a communist government. Lenin was a strong believer in theoretical communism, and he quickly took steps to develop a communist society. Large estates were taken from the rich, and the land was divided up and given to the peasants. Lenin also outlawed private property and turned the country's few factories over to the workers.

RESOURCE MANAGER

Reproducible Masters
- Reproducible Lesson Plan 18-2
- Daily Lecture Notes 18-2
- Guided Reading Activity 18-2
- Reading Essentials and Study Guide 18-2
- Section Quiz 18-2

Transparencies
- Daily Focus Transparency 83

Multimedia
- Interactive Tutor Self-Assessment Software
- ExamView® Pro Testmaker
- Presentation Plus!

The workers, however, did not have the skills to manage the factories. Before long, production fell and the economy began to disintegrate. People lost faith in the money supply, and a system of barter emerged. The government sent armed forces to the farms to confiscate surplus food for the hungry city dwellers and industrial workers. The angry farmers retaliated by reducing their production so there would be no surplus crops.

By 1927, many changes had taken place. Russia had become the Soviet Union, and the country was under Communist Party control. Lenin had died, and Joseph Stalin was the new leader. Stalin wanted to transform the Soviet economy from agriculture to industry.

To accomplish this goal, he introduced the government's first **Five-Year Plan**—a comprehensive, centralized economic plan designed to achieve rapid industrialization.

Under Stalin's leadership, the process of **collectivization**—the forced common ownership of all agricultural, industrial, and trading enterprises—began. Not surprisingly, many people opposed the reforms. Peasants even destroyed their livestock and sabotaged their equipment rather than turn their property over to the collective farms.

Stalin's retaliation was brutal. Millions of people were killed or imprisoned. Ukrainian grain stores were seized in the winter of 1932, causing the starvation of more than five million peasants. The suffering in the cities was nearly as harsh. Workers were forced to work in heavy industry, and the standard of living deteriorated drastically.

Although the first Five-Year Plan did not achieve all of its goals, the government continued with more planning. The plans that followed concentrated heavily on defense industries, heavy manufacturing, and some consumer goods.

The Soviet Economy After Stalin

Stalin's brutal regime ended in 1953. By then the Soviet economy had successfully completed its transition from a backward agrarian economy to a major industrial power. The Soviet government and its comprehensive system of planning dominated the Soviet economy, but the real force was the ruling Communist Party.

Complexities of Central Planning

In the Soviet economy, the **Gosplan** was the central planning authority that devised the Five-Year Plans. As the Soviet economy grew, however, this process became increasingly complex.

Consider the difficulties in a single industry such as shoes. First, the planners have to decide how many shoes should be produced in any given year. This amount would depend on the population and the number of pairs that each person, on average, would need. The planners would then have to decide how many pairs to make of each style, including colors, sizes, and widths.

Next, the various sizes, grades, and amounts of leather, dye, metal eyelets, thread, glue, and other materials needed to produce the shoes had to be estimated. After the central planners developed this data, individual factories were given monthly and annual quotas. Even a factory that produced thread would be told how much thread of every diameter and color to produce for use in shoes.

Similar decisions had to be made for all industries, including clothing, farm implements, stationery, and military goods. The planners detailed everything that would be needed in the economy right down to nails and paper clips. Even these minor items required the planners to make estimates of iron ore, coal, coke, blast furnaces, mining equipment, trains, and ore cars.

To ensure the growth of the economy from one year to the next, all the planners had to do—or so they thought—was to increase the quotas given to the factories. In short, the central planners determined almost everything beforehand.

Difficulties With Agriculture

The situation was similar in agriculture, where food was raised on state, collective, and peasant farms. The **state farms** were large farms entirely owned and operated by the state. Workers on the state farms were paid for the number of items they produced. All output was turned over to the government at prices fixed by the government.

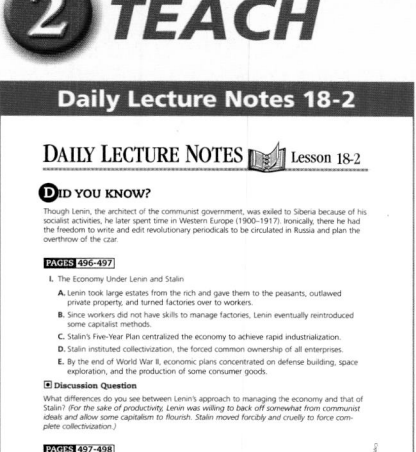

② TEACH

Daily Lecture Notes 18-2

DAILY LECTURE NOTES 📖 Lesson 18-2

DID YOU KNOW?
Though Lenin, the architect of the communist government, was exiled to Siberia because of his socialist activities, he later spent time in Western Europe (1900–1917). Ironically, there he had the freedom to write and edit revolutionary periodicals to be circulated in Russia and plan the overthrow of the czar.

PAGES 496–497
I. The Economy Under Lenin and Stalin
   A. Lenin took large estates from the rich and gave them to the peasants, outlawed private property, and turned factories over to workers.
   B. Since workers did not have skills to manage factories, Lenin eventually reintroduced some capitalist methods.
   C. Stalin's Five-Year Plan centralized the economy to achieve rapid industrialization.
   D. Stalin instituted collectivization, the forced common ownership of all enterprises.
   E. By the end of World War II, economic plans concentrated on defense building, space exploration, and the production of some consumer goods.

Discussion Question
What differences do you see between Lenin's approach to managing the economy and that of Stalin? (For the sake of productivity, Lenin was willing to back off somewhat from communist ideals and allow some capitalism to flourish. Stalin moved forcibly and cruelly to force complete collectivization.)

PAGES 497–498

L1 Understanding Ideas

Organize students into three groups and assign each group one of the section's main headings— "The Economy Under Lenin and Stalin," "The Soviet Economy after Stalin," and "The Soviet Economy Collapses." Have group members identify the most important ideas in their assigned topics. Then have groups team-teach the important ideas to the rest of the class. **ELL**

L2 Time Line

Have students research and construct an annotated time line of the Soviet Union's economic policies from 1917 to its collapse. Have them incorporate Lenin's policies, various five-year plans of Lenin's successors, and Gorbachev's efforts at reform under perestroika.

MEETING SPECIAL NEEDS ACTIVITY

Learning Style: Verbal/Linguistic With students, create a television talk show with the topic "What is your opinion of the current state of the Russian economy?" Organize students into four groups and assign each group a time period in Russian history (1917–1926, 1927–1953, 1953–1985, 1985–present). Have each student play the role of a leader, a worker, or a peasant and discuss how that character might react to the current Russian economy. After students have had time to brainstorm, ask for a leader, worker, and peasant representative from each group to appear on the panel for the talk show. Then hold a discussion on the question, using a talk-show format, with the teacher serving as host. **BLOCK SCHEDULING**

Refer to *Inclusion for the Social Studies Classroom Strategies and Activities* in the TCR.

Guided Reading Activity 18-2

3 ASSESS

Assign Section 2 Assessment as homework or as an in-class activity.

💾 Have students use **Interactive Tutor Self-Assessment Software** to review Section 2.

Section Quiz 18-2

Peasant families worked **collective farms,** small private farms collected into large units for joint operation. The land, buildings, tools, livestock, and machines belonged to the government, which bought a certain amount of produce per acre. Peasant families were allowed to keep their homes and household goods, and a small plot of land.

Despite its efforts, the government was not able to make agriculture as efficient as that of many capitalist countries. In the mid-1980s, before the collapse of the Soviet Union, nearly 25 percent of the workforce was in agriculture. In the United States at the time, only 3 percent of the workforce was in agriculture.

The Soviet Economy Collapses

 The Soviet Union made considerable progress with industrialization, but it never caught up to the United States. Despite its larger population and land area, the Soviet Union's GNP never exceeded two-thirds of that of the United States.

Careers

Customs Inspector

Do you like detailed work? Are you able to accept responsibility and deal with people in a firm but friendly manner?

The Work

Customs inspectors are part of the Treasury Department. Duties include examining baggage at airports or seaports to ensure that all merchandise is declared and that duties are paid. Commercial and noncommercial cargoes are inspected to determine admissibility and the amount of tax due.

Qualifications

Customs inspectors need training in laws governing imports and exports and in inspection procedures. A college degree is preferred. Passage of a civil service exam is required.

498

To offset low morale in the factories, a number of incentive programs were attempted. One involved the use of **piecework,** meaning that workers are paid for each piece of output they produce rather than for the number of hours they work.

Although this system may seem like a good idea, piecework quotas often were set at unrealistically high levels. This led to **storming,** the practice of rushing production at the end of the month to make up for the slower pace at the beginning of the month. The rush at the end often affected the quality of the products. Because of storming, knowledgeable Soviet shoppers often avoided buying goods made at the end of the month.

Other incentives included patriotic and emotional appeals. Workers who had outstanding records or did something special were awarded hero medals, such as the Order of Lenin and the Hero of Social Labor. Some of these medals brought rewards such as free public housing or vacations.

Production Quotas

As with incentives, quotas also failed at the factory level. During the 1950s, the Soviet economy had a reputation for producing some of the world's poorest consumer and industrial goods. Shoe factories, for example, were given quotas in terms of millions of pairs of shoes. Because small shoes could be made fastest, more were made than were needed. When the quotas were changed to measure production in the amount of shoe leather consumed, the result was shoes with some of the thickest soles in the world.

Production of Consumer Goods

Another major problem was the inadequate supply of consumer goods. After World War II, the Soviet people were asked to make sacrifices so their children might have a better life. Many willingly did so. In the 1970s and 1980s, those children were adults. When they were asked to make sacrifices so their children could have a better life, they were not as willing as their parents had been. The new generation had not suffered from the ravages of war and they were aware of the standards of living in other parts of the world. As a result, they were impatient for more consumer goods.

FREE ENTERPRISE ACTIVITY

Ask students to prepare an outline of a five-year plan for their own lives. Point out that they should address not only where they want to be and what they want to be doing five years from now, but also how they are going to get there. For example, how are they going to get the education and training necessary for the job they choose? Call on volunteers to share their plans. Then have students discuss what problems they faced in drawing up their plans. Conclude by having students compare their problems with those that would face a nation preparing a five-year plan.

Perestroika

When Mikhail Gorbachev assumed power in 1985, the Soviet economy was weaker than anyone imagined. The main cause was the burden imposed by centralized planning. The economy had become too complex and too large to be managed in the traditional manner.

Plant managers were under increasing pressure to meet or exceed quotas. Glitches in planning, however, were creating shortages and other problems. To facilitate the process, "fixers" called *tolkachi* were employed to resolve shortages or dispose of excess inventories. The *tolkachi* soon became indispensable to producers who wanted to fulfill their quotas. At the same time, they also caused problems for other plants whenever they rerouted a shipment or otherwise interrupted the master plan of the central planners.

To solve these problems, Gorbachev introduced a policy of **perestroika**, the fundamental restructuring of the economy and government. Under the restructuring, Five-Year Plans were retained, but the various ministries of production were to be converted to efficient, state-owned enterprises that would compete in a market economy. Plant managers were given more freedom to buy and sell in pursuit of profits, and small business was encouraged.

Perestroika represented a halfway point between a market economy and centralized planning. Gorbachev, however, did not remain in power long enough to see his plans realized. Those in industry who opposed Gorbachev's reforms allowed shortages and other problems to persist, and then used these problems as proof that the reforms were failing. Gorbachev's successor, Boris Yeltsin, faced similar opposition. Ultimately, the collapse of the economy, the collapse of the political leadership, and the stresses of ethnic diversity and unrest combined to cause the downfall and breakup of the Soviet Union.

Did you know?

Frozen Treasures Siberia covers 75 percent of Russia. It has the largest supply of mineral resources in the country, including gold, diamonds, and coal. Siberia remains mostly undeveloped because of its harsh climate and few transportation routes.

Section 2 Assessment

Checking for Understanding

1. **Main Idea** Using your notes from the graphic organizer activity on page 496, describe how the former Soviet Union's economic system functioned.

2. **Key Terms** Define Five-Year Plan, collectivization, Gosplan, state farm, collective farm, piecework, storming, perestroika.

3. **Explain** how the Soviet economy developed under Lenin and Stalin.

4. **Identify** several complexities of central planning.

5. **Describe** how central planning contributed to the breakdown of the economy of the Soviet Union.

Applying Economic Concepts

6. **Perestroika** Since the mid-1980s, the former Soviet Union has undergone tremendous changes, some of which led to hyperinflation. Why would this hyperinflation hinder the movement toward capitalism?

Critical Thinking

7. **Making Predictions** Based upon recent changes, is the former Soviet Union moving toward capitalism or away from capitalism? Give evidence to support your conclusions.

8. **Summarizing Information** What did Soviet planners think they had to do to ensure economic growth?

 Practice and assess key social studies skills with the *Glencoe Skillbuilder Interactive Workbook, Level 2.*

Section 2 Assessment Answers

1. Collective ownership; lack of incentive led to poor products; government made economic decisions

2. All vocabulary terms are defined in the text.

3. A barter system emerged after Lenin gave land to workers. Stalin devised plans to achieve industrialization and collective agriculture.

4. decide on product's size, color, and so on; anticipate inputs; set quotas

5. Central planning on such a massive scale was too complex to be effective. Poor decisions by planners compounded problems.

6. Hyperinflation makes money worthless. The economy reverts to barter, making exchange and other market activities difficult.

7. Students should cite specific changes.

8. restructure government and the economy, increase quotas given to the factories

Reteach

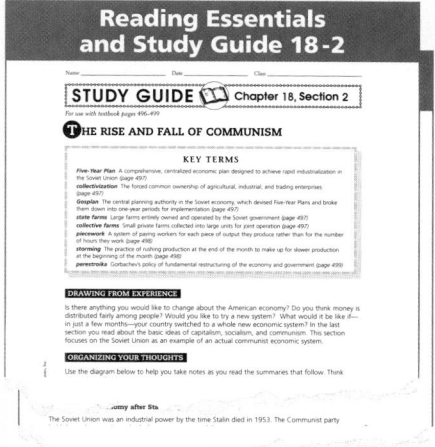

Reading Essentials and Study Guide 18-2

STUDY GUIDE — Chapter 18, Section 2

For use with textbook pages 496-499

THE RISE AND FALL OF COMMUNISM

KEY TERMS

Five-Year Plan A comprehensive, centralized economic plan designed to achieve rapid industrialization in the Soviet Union (page 497)
collectivization The forced common ownership of agricultural, industrial, and trading enterprises (page 497)
Gosplan The central planning authority in the Soviet economy, which devised Five-Year Plans and broke them down into one-year periods for implementation (page 497)
state farms Large farms entirely owned and operated by the Soviet government (page 497)
collective farms Small private farms collected into large units for joint operation (page 497)
piecework A system of paying workers for each piece of output they produce rather than for the number of hours they work (page 498)
storming The practice of rushing production at the end of the month to make up for slower production at the beginning of the month (page 498)
perestroika Gorbachev's policy of fundamental restructuring of the economy and government (page 499)

DRAWING FROM EXPERIENCE

Is there anything you would like to change about the American economy? Do you think money is distributed fairly among people? Would you like to try a new system? What would it be like if—in just a few months—your country switched to a whole new economic system? In the last section you read about the basic nature of capitalism, socialism, and communism. This section focuses on the Soviet Union as an example of an actual communist economic system.

ORGANIZING YOUR THOUGHTS

Use the diagram below to help you take notes as you read the summaries that follow. Think

...omy after Sta...
The Soviet Union was an industrial power by the time Stalin died in 1953. The Communist party

Enrich

Have students write a biographical sketch of Lenin, Stalin, or Gorbachev that focuses on that individual's economic policies. Call on students to read their sketches to the class.

 CLOSE

Have students identify what they feel was the major factor in the collapse of the Soviet economy. Call on volunteers to explain their answers.

BACKGROUND

Twentieth-century communist countries, such as the Soviet Union and its satellites in Eastern Europe, claimed to be based on the ideas of Karl Marx. However, many of their features had little in common with Marx's actual views. Marx, for example, believed that capitalism's overthrow would bring about a classless society and the "withering away" of the state. Instead, communist leaders formed themselves into a new ruling class and developed powerful governments that controlled economies and the lives of millions of people. History also proved Marx wrong in another way. Far from collapsing, capitalism prospered in the West by increasing productivity and improving the lives of workers. In fact, the world's first communist state did not arise, as Marx had predicted, in Germany or Britain, highly industrialized lands with large working classes. Instead, it emerged in Russia, a relatively backward, agricultural country. Despite his failure as a prophet, however, Marx was a powerful thinker. He profoundly influenced modern political and social thought, especially in his analysis of the economic struggle among social classes. Marx also inspired many of the revolutionary movements that swept the world during the course of the twentieth century.

TEACH

Draw students' attention to Marx's claim that "the history of . . . society is the history of class struggle." Lead a class discussion on the concept of class struggle in the world today. **Ask:** Is class struggle ongoing in the United States? In other countries? Among countries? Challenge students to identify the implications of their answers.

500

Profiles IN Economics

Reshaping the World:
Karl Marx
(1818–1883)

Workers of the World UNITE!

Marx was an economic historian and a social scientist. He earned his doctorate in philosophy and history from the University of Berlin, but because of his radical views, he could not get a teaching position.

Throughout the 1840s, he wandered from Cologne to Paris to Brussels. He joined with socialist and radical groups. Persecuted by Prussian and Parisian authorities, Marx fled to London in 1849 where he began a life of exile and, eventually, died in poverty.

MARX'S WORKS

Marx is best known for *The Communist Manifesto*, published in 1848, and *Das Kapital*, the first volume of which was published in 1867. In these works, Marx argues that "the history of all hitherto existing society is the history of class struggles." In each era, one class was pitted against another: master against slave, lord against serf, capitalist against worker—the "oppressor and oppressed."

HIS IDEAS

Marx argued that the oppressed of his day was the proletariat—people who must work for others because they have no means of production of their own. Their oppressors? The capitalists or bourgeoisie—people who own the means of production.

Marx argued that labor was exploited in a capitalist society. He gave the name "surplus value" to the difference between the wage paid to the worker and the market value of the worker's output. He believed this value was unfairly kept by capitalists as profits.

Marx argued that each cycle of prosperity would add to the suffering of the proletariat and the wealth and power of the capitalists. Eventually, he said, oppressed workers would rise up in a violent revolution. "Let the ruling classes tremble at a communist revolution," he wrote. "The proletarians have nothing to lose but their chains. They have a world to win. Working men of all countries, unite!" During the transition, the proletariat would, Marx argued, have to depend on a strong government: a "Dictatorship of the Proletariat." Thus, authoritarian Communism as practiced in the Soviet Union and other countries was born.

Marx believed that eventually the dictatorship would be replaced by a "classless society," without government, in which people would produce to the best of their abilities and consume to the extent of their needs.

Examining the Profile

1. **Analyzing Information** According to Marx, through what stages must society go before it can reach the ideal state of communism?

2. **For Further Research** Annotate a world map to show the extent of Marxist economies in the world today.

Answers to Examining the Profile

1. Society would experience repeated cycles of prosperity, each of which would add to the wealth and power of the capitalists and the suffering of the proletariat. The conflict would lead to a violent revolution by the proletariat, who would then set up a dictatorship of the proletariat to achieve the transition to the classless society of communism.

2. Maps should be logically highlighted and annotated. Reward thorough research and clean presentations.

The Transition to Capitalism

Study Guide

Main Idea
Reforms in the former Soviet Union, China, and many Latin American and eastern European nations have moved these economies toward more capitalistic, market-oriented systems.

Reading Strategy
Graphic Organizer As you read the section, complete a graphic organizer similar to the one below by selecting a country and describing how it is making the transition to capitalism.

Country — Action / Action / Action / Action → Capitalism

Key Terms
privatization, Solidarity, black market, Great Leap Forward

Objectives
After studying this section, you will be able to:
1. **List** four problems encountered when an economy makes the transition to capitalism.
2. **Recognize** the major countries and regions that are making the transition to capitalism.

Applying Economic Concepts
Privatization Do you value and take care of the things you own? Read to see why private ownership is essential if countries are to make the transition to capitalism.

1 FOCUS

Section Overview
This section describes problems facing countries in transition, as they move toward capitalism.

BELLRINGER
Motivational Activity

Project **transparency** and have students answer questions.

Available as blackline master.

Daily Focus Transparency 84

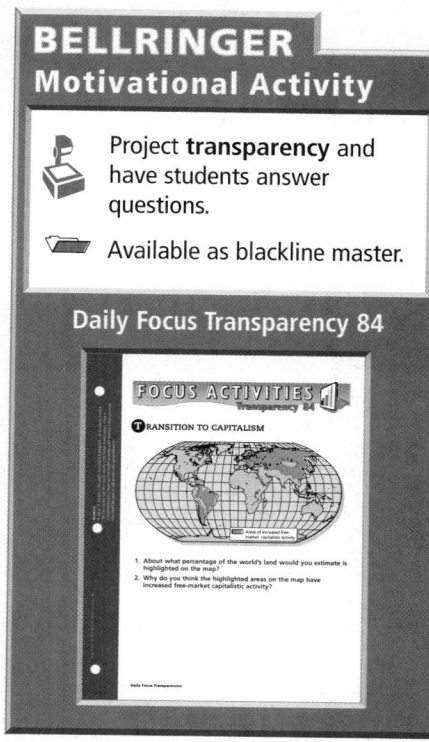

Cover Story

Rubles From the Ruins: A Russian Success

NIZHNY NOVGOROD, Russia—In general, the Russian economy is a mess: Industrial production is half what it was in 1991, the transition to a market economy has gone badly, the ruble has collapsed, and many giant enterprises are in desperate straits, unemployment and poverty are ubiquitous.

And yet, some Russian businesses are actually making money, some are thriving. . . .

Although criminals and corrupt government officials frustrate entrepreneurs all over the country, some manage to evade or ignore them. The experiences of the few who are succeeding provide some powerful lessons in why that hope remains so remote.

Consider the adventures of Andrei Mladentsev. . . .

Russian currency

—International Herald Tribune, July 20, 1999

Andrei Mladentsev, the Russian entrepreneur featured in the cover story, now runs one of the largest and most modern pharmaceutical companies in Russia. At age 26 he used the funds he accumulated trading stocks to engineer a takeover of the 75-year-old pharmaceutical factory in Nizhny Novgorod. He is, however, the exception rather than the norm—as the problems of transition are truly daunting.

Problems of Transition

Historically, communism and capitalism have been viewed as two opposing political and economic structures. The collapse of communism, however, does not mean that the transition to capitalism will be smooth, or that it will be made at all. An examination of the problems of transition will show why.

Privatization

A key feature of capitalism is private property—especially capital, which is sometimes referred to as the means of production. Because communist

CHAPTER 18: COMPARATIVE ECONOMIC SYSTEMS **501**

Study Guide

Reading Strategy
Have students create the graphic organizer.
Answers to Graphic: *Answers should reflect section content.*

Preteaching Vocabulary
Have students use the Key Terms in sentences.

 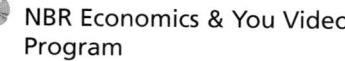
RESOURCE MANAGER

Reproducible Masters
- Reproducible Lesson Plan 18-3
- Daily Lecture Notes 18-3
- Guided Reading Activity 18-3
- Reading Essentials and Study Guide 18-3
- Section Quiz 18-3

Transparencies
- Daily Focus Transparency 84

Multimedia
- NBR Economics & You Video Program
- Interactive Tutor Self-Assessment Software
- ExamView® Pro Testmaker
- Presentation Plus!

2 TEACH

Daily Lecture Notes 18-3

DAILY LECTURE NOTES Lesson 18-3

DID YOU KNOW?
Where once the Soviet empire was shut off from the free flow of information, now many of its former republics have their own sites on the World Wide Web. Most up-to-date almanacs include those countries' Web sites.

PAGES 501-503
I. Problems of Transition
   A. Privatization in some transitional states has been accomplished using vouchers, and by selling state-owned companies to foreign corporations.
   B. Where vouchers worked, the Communist Party leaders lost power; in other nations, the old ruling group retained their power.
   C. Nations in transition have yet to develop the automatic stabilizers and social welfare nets that cushion the instabilities of capitalism.
   D. Transitional countries will have to learn to live with a whole new set of incentives.

Discussion Question
What are the costs to individual workers of making the transition from a command economy to a capitalist one? (Their jobs will not be guaranteed. The enterprises they work for will have to compete in the marketplace and will not have the support of the government. If an enterprise is inefficient, it will fail, and workers will have to seek other work.)

PAGES 503-507
II. Countries and Regions in Transition
   A. Privatization in Russia is well underway.
   B. Poland, Hungary, the Czech Republic, and the Baltic states are moving toward

THE GLOBAL ECONOMY

The World's Largest Cities by 2015 Point out that, of the 15 largest cities in the world, only one—Beijing, China—is located in a communist country. Also note that only four of the world's largest cities—Tokyo, New York, Los Angeles, and Osaka—are located in industrially developed countries. All the rest are in developing countries. The city with the largest percentage of projected growth is Lagos, Nigeria. In 1995 its population was about 10,287,000. By 2015 the number of people there will have increased 140 percent.

Answers:
1. *four*
2. *The number of jobs, and therefore the number of people, in cities continues to grow because large cities have an industrial infrastructure already in place, making growth easier.*

---

governments owned the means of production, **privatization,** or the conversion of state-owned factories and property to private ownership, has to be accomplished. Privatization is important because people tend to take better care of the property they actually own. Private property is also important for entrepreneurial activity, especially if the entrepreneurs are allowed to keep the fruits of their labor.

In Poland, Hungary, and the Czech Republic, this transition was accomplished using vouchers. Vouchers were certificates either given to people or sold at very low prices, depending on the country. As the vouchers were distributed, the government drew up a list of companies to be privatized and then organized the companies as corporations. The corporate shares were auctioned, and people would bid for the shares using their vouchers for payment. As people exchanged their vouchers for shares, ownership of the previously state-owned enterprises transferred to private hands.

In other cases, the transition governments simply sold state-owned companies to foreign corporations. The government then used the funds to pay other bills or make other purchases. These transactions bypassed the citizens and transferred ownership to foreign investors.

Loss of Political Power

Under communism, the Communist party was the ruling class. The transition to capitalism stripped the Communist party of its political power and transferred it to the new class of entrepreneurs and capitalists.

In countries where the Communists were literally thrown out—as in Poland, Czechoslovakia, and Hungary—the Communist leaders lost their power before industry was privatized. In these countries, the voucher system worked reasonably well.

In other countries, former Communist leaders grabbed a large share of vouchers, and thus a large portion of ownership in many privatized companies. In the most blatant cases, some of which occurred in Russia following the collapse of the Soviet Union, the ownership of companies was simply transferred to politicians who were influential during the transition period. Former political

THE WORLD'S LARGEST CITIES BY 2015

Rank	City, Country	Projected Population (in millions)
1	Tokyo, Japan	28.88
2	Bombay (Mumbai), India	26.22
3	Lagos, Nigeria	24.64
4	São Paulo, Brazil	20.32
5	Mexico City, Mexico	19.18
6	Shanghai, China	17.97
7	New York, New York USA	17.60
8	Calcutta, India	17.31
9	Delhi, India	16.86
10	Beijing, China	15.57

Source: *The Shape of Things to Come,* by Richard W. Oliver, McGraw-Hill, 1999

Most of the world's population lives in urban areas. Projections show that this trend will continue. Today's five largest cities are more populous than most countries. Cities are rapidly becoming the key economic units of global market analysis.

Critical Thinking

1. **Categorizing Information** How many cities are projected to surpass 20 million in population by the year 2015?

2. **Understanding Cause and Effect** What do you think are the economic reasons that the largest cities continue to grow?

MEETING SPECIAL NEEDS ACTIVITY

English Language Learners Have students practice using the text to locate information by playing a form of the popular game show Jeopardy. Name a place, date, person, or concept important to Section 3. Ask students to use the text to locate the term. Then, using context clues, have them formulate a question for which the term is the answer. Have the first student to find the term show the other students its location. If necessary, have students help each other write appropriate questions. **ELL**

Refer to *Inclusion for the Social Studies Classroom Strategies and Activities* in the TCR.

leaders traded their political power for economic power in the form of resource ownership—so that the old ruling group simply became the new ruling group.

The Discipline of Capitalism

Many countries that desire a capitalist structure have focused on the benefits to be obtained, not the costs. However, the costs can hinder or even discourage a country from making the transition.

The disadvantages of capitalism made apparent during the Great Depression included instability, unemployment, and social unrest. At that time, the United States did not have the fiscal policies, the automatic stabilizers, and the social welfare nets needed to lessen the devastation of the Depression. Now that such assistance exists, most economists agree that another Great Depression will not occur in the United States.

The same cannot be said for the nations in transition. They have not yet developed the automatic stabilizers and the social welfare nets that cushion the instabilities of capitalism. During the transition phase, nations will most likely experience the instabilities of early capitalism—the unemployment, the inflation, and the lost production—long before they experience the benefits.

Responding to New Incentives

Finally, countries that make the transition to capitalism have to learn to live with a whole new set of incentives. For generations, the government in the former Soviet Union told its people what to do. Under capitalism, people must learn how to make decisions on their own. They must learn how to take the initiative, how to interpret prices, and how to fend for themselves because the government no longer guarantees their jobs, nor does it keep prices artificially low.

These adjustments will be enormous, perhaps even prohibitive, for some people. Many will even long for the past when life was simpler. These people may not want to go through the adjustments and submit to the discipline of capitalism. Impatience for the end result may be a major obstacle to the transition.

New and Emerging Stock Markets

NUMBER OF LISTED COMPANIES		NUMBER OF LISTED COMPANIES	
Country		Country	
Argentina	138	Morocco	48
Brazil	543	Nigeria	180
Chile	296	Pakistan	778
China	763	Peru	247
Colombia	163	Philippines	222
Egypt	668	Poland	159
Greece	231	Portugal	143
Honduras	111	Russia	222
Hungary	50	South Korea	776
India	5,853	Sri Lanka	240
Indonesia	287	Taiwan	408
Israel	648	Thailand	431
Jamaica	46	Turkey	262
Malaysia	722	Venezuela	91
Mexico	198	Zimbabwe	64

Source: *Emerging Stock Markets Factbook,* 1998

Using Charts New and emerging stock markets are now found all over the world, and more are still to come. Why is the corporate form of organization a necessary component of capitalism?

ECONOMICS *Online*

Visit epp.glencoe.com and click on *Textbook Updates—Chapter 18* for an update of the data.

Countries and Regions in Transition

Despite the transitional problems, the rise of capitalism is one of the most remarkable phenomena of the late twentieth century. Today, nations and regions all over the globe are making the transition.

CHAPTER 18: COMPARATIVE ECONOMIC SYSTEMS **503**

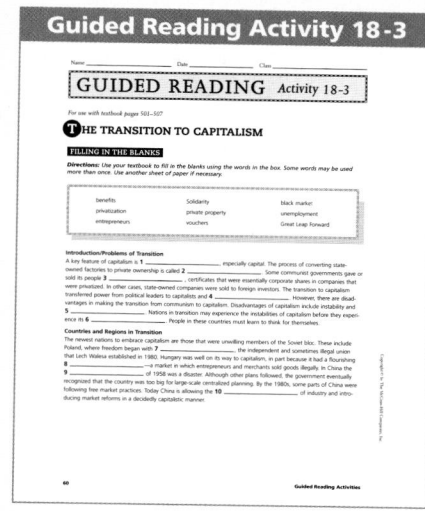

Guided Reading Activity 18-3

GUIDED READING Activity 18-3

THE TRANSITION TO CAPITALISM

L1 Changing Boundaries

Have students locate Poland, Hungary, the Czech Republic, and Russia on a map of the world. Point out that the Czech Republic was part of the former Czechoslovakia and that Russia was part of the former Soviet Union. With a pointer, outline the boundaries of these former countries on the map.

E C O N O M I C S
AT A GLANCE

Answer: *In a free enterprise economy, companies may be so large that the only way to develop capital is through the sale of private stock.*

FREE ENTERPRISE ACTIVITY

Review with students the four problems associated with the transition to capitalism. Then organize students into several groups. Have group members use their knowledge of the American economic system to brainstorm ways that these problems might be overcome. Direct groups to use these ideas to write an editorial on how this transition might be made successfully. Call on group representatives to read their editorials to the class.

L3 News Report

Organize students into several groups and have groups prepare a five-minute television or radio news report on the progress that the former communist countries are making in their transition to capitalism. Groups might focus on the Commonwealth of Independent States and Eastern Europe or on one particular country. Have students "broadcast" their reports to the class. If audio or video equipment is available, have groups record their news reports to play for other classes.

THE GLOBAL ECONOMY

Railroads Nearly all of Russia's state-run businesses have been privatized, but the government still runs the railway system. Although railroads in the U.S. are decreasing in importance, trains in Russia carry 50 percent of the nation's passenger traffic and 70 percent of its freight.

CURRICULUM CONNECTION

Geography The major mining industry in Estonia is based on a type of stone called oil shale.

L3 Analyzing Ideas

Encourage students to research current news reports about the economies of the countries discussed in the section. Have students use this information to speculate which of these countries will be most successful in the transition to capitalism.

504

Russia

Privatization in Russia is well underway, despite the continued resistance of hard-liners. Some privatization took place under Gorbachev, and President Boris Yeltsin accelerated the process when he signed a 1992 decree requiring that state-owned enterprises be converted to privately owned ones.

Many conversions took place when the government printed and distributed vouchers to its people. The people then used the vouchers to purchase shares of stock in the newly converted companies.

Smaller businesses were also being privatized at a rapid rate. Soon more than half of the restaurants and shops in the major cities were in private hands. Eventually Russia opened a stock market so that individuals could buy and sell shares. The widespread ownership of the means of production by individuals is now a reality in a country that once preached the evils of private ownership.

Eastern Europe

The nations of eastern Europe, especially those that were unwilling members of the Soviet bloc, are the newest nations to embrace capitalism. The struggle for freedom began in Poland with **Solidarity,** the independent and sometimes illegal union that Lech Walesa established in 1980. Solidarity was influential in securing a number of political freedoms in Poland. Eventually, the Communist party lost power, and interest in capitalism grew. Political reform slowed privatization plans at first, but capitalism finally appeared to be under way again in the face of progress by Poland's neighbors.

Hungary is another country well on the way to capitalism. Hungary was often regarded as the most

CYBERNOMICS SPOTLIGHT

An Emerging Latin American Market

Historically, the economies of most Latin American countries depended on agriculture. Beginning in the mid-nineteenth century, these Latin American economies began to change. Countries exported raw materials, such as oil, so that they could import machinery to build factories for manufacturing goods. As a result of the growth of the manufacturing sector, service industries such as banking and insurance took on new importance. An educated middle class emerged, consisting of lawyers, doctors, entrepreneurs, government employees, and skilled office and factory workers.

As Latin America moves into the twenty-first century, economies in the region are changing once again. Technology is affecting how business is done. Many groups in Latin America see e-commerce as a means to becoming more economically efficient and competitive.

Internet Users in Latin America Consumers, businesses, and governments are beginning to see the value of Internet commerce. Online supermarkets and retail

Changes in Latin America's business

shopping are becoming more popular with consumers. Technology is being developed in Brazil to develop an online-only grocery store, where consumers will be able to purchase products such as soap and oatmeal using a catalog and a bar-code scanner. Businesses use the Internet to link their factories with suppliers to cut costs. They can track product shipments and check on the status of an invoice. The government is also beginning to post government contracts online so that public and private companies can bid on them. Companies can get information about competing bids and contest decisions using the Internet.

504 UNIT 5 INTERNATIONAL AND GLOBAL ECONOMICS

CYBERNOMICS SPOTLIGHT

More About . . . E-commerce Companies in the United States are eagerly investing in the flourishing e-commerce trade in Latin America. StarMedia, the largest Spanish-language online service, has teamed with Hewlett-Packard, the Dell Computer Corporation, Netscape Communications, Fox Sports Latin America, eBay, and other companies in order to bring news, sports, searching capabilities, and purchasing power to Latin America. StarMedia and its affiliates were banking on analysts' predictions that the number of Internet users in Latin America would go from 15 million in 1999 to 34 million in 2000, and that revenues from e-commerce would soar from $240 million in 1998 to $8 billion by 2003.

"western" of the Eastern bloc countries. It also had a flourishing **black market**—a market in which entrepreneurs and merchants sold goods illegally. Hungary's experience with these markets helped ease the transition to capitalism.

The Czech Republic is another country in transition. By early 1998, more than 60 percent of the economy was in private hands. Progress accelerated after the separation of the Czech and Slovak Republics, a separation based in part on the Slovakian concern about adopting the capitalist ways of the West. The Czechs, who were strongly influenced by the economic success of the former West Germany, are now more able to pursue reforms.

The Baltic states of Estonia, Latvia, and Lithuania are also making great strides toward capitalism. Latvia and Lithuania have their own stock markets to help facilitate the transition. Estonia has made so much progress that it—along with the Czech Republic, Hungary, and Poland—will be considered for membership in the European Union between 2002 and 2006.

Latin America

In the past, many Latin American countries followed a path of economic development that combined socialism and isolationism based on the infant industries argument. Mexico accelerated the move to capitalism and open markets in 1989 as it made plans to restructure its economy for the North American Free Trade Agreement (NAFTA). Under President Salinas de Gortari, the government sold thousands of state-owned companies and cut back on the government bureaucracy.

Did You Know?

On The Net Even though fewer people in Latin America have access to the Internet than in the United States, those who use it spend many hours online. Latin American Internet users spend about 10.4 hours online a week, a figure up from 8.2 hours spent online per week in 1998.

Getting Online Several problems are hindering the growth of e-commerce in Latin America. Only one in ten people have a phone line. Because the average gross domestic product per capita is less than $4,000, the ability to buy a personal computer and get online is out of reach for many people. Few people in Latin America use credit cards; many are reluctant to give out credit card numbers online. Custom regulations and import duties can delay the arrival of goods or make them too expensive to buy.

Industry experts agree that these problems will be less troublesome in the future. It is expected that within a period of five to seven years the number of phone lines will double, to two per 10 people. Personal computer prices are expected to fall as the number of sales increases. Smart cards are becoming more popular, giving consumers a better sense of security for buying online. Internet companies are beginning to inform shoppers at the time of purchase how much they will owe for duties and other taxes, and it is expected that tariffs will be removed as more countries form regional trading blocs.

E-commerce grows

CHAPTER 18: COMPARATIVE ECONOMIC SYSTEMS **505**

Math Practice

Emerging Stock Markets Ask students which country listed in Figure 18.2 on page 503 has the greatest number of companies listed on a stock market. *(India)* Then challenge students to determine ten countries for which the total number of companies comes within five of India's total. *(Students' answers may vary. One possible combination is Brazil, China, Egypt, Honduras, Israel, Malaysia, Pakistan, South Korea, Taiwan, and Thailand. Their stock markets equal 5,848 companies.)*

NIGHTLY BUSINESS REPORT

 ECONOMICS & YOU

 Chapter 25
Disc 1, Side 2

Comparative Economic Systems

Ask: What is the main reason some state-owned businesses become inefficient? *(Since state-owned businesses do not have competition, they do not have to continually improve their operations to maintain a level of high efficiency.)*

Also available in VHS.

Competition in the Internet Market Although StarMedia has agreements with powerful U.S. companies, other online providers are equally successful. A Latin American network called El Sitio hosts a shopping channel, a search engine, free E-mail, and chat rooms. Televisa, a media company in Mexico, is spending $80 million to launch an Internet channel and hinted that it might eventually join with Microsoft or Mexico's national telephone company. Latin American networks have ample funding for new channels, services, and other innovations from a $100 million pledge to the Latin American Internet market from Softbank Corporation, a Japanese Internet investor.

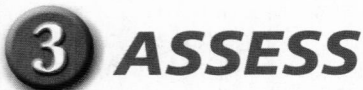

ASSESS

Assign Section 3 Assessment as homework or as an in-class activity.

■ Have students use **Interactive Tutor Self-Assessment Software** to review Section 3.

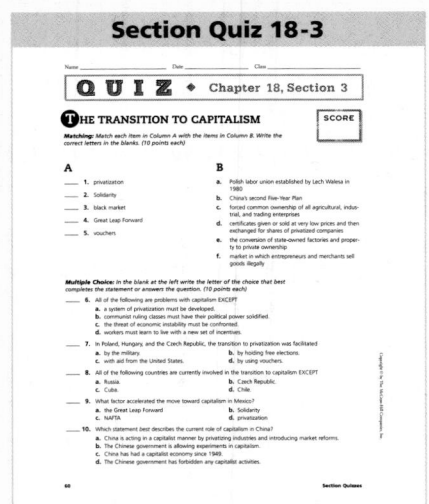

Section Quiz 18-3

Economic Change

Retreat From Socialism Once state-owned, many companies in Mexico are now under private ownership. *How is Argentina reducing the role of government in the economy?*

Chile has also taken major steps to foster the growth of capitalism. It has privatized airlines, telephone services, and utilities. Chile even used the billions deposited in its pension funds to supply capital to new entrepreneurs. As a result, the country exports copper, lumber, fruit, and even software to the rest of the world. Chile's markets include the United States, which imports millions of popsicle sticks, and Japan, which imports chopsticks.

Argentina has similarly embarked on a crash program to remove government from the everyday business of running the economy. The country has sold oil fields, petrochemical plants, and a number of other formerly state-owned businesses.

China

The People's Republic of China became a communist economy in 1949. That year, the Chinese Communists, under the leadership of Mao Zedong, gained control of the country. Over the years, China modeled itself after the Soviet Union, adopting a series of Five-Year Plans to manage its growth.

In 1958 the **Great Leap Forward** was instituted. This was the second Five-Year Plan that tried to institute a system of pure communism along with an industrial and agricultural revolution almost overnight. Industrialization was pushed and, at the same time, collectivization of agriculture was intensified. Farmers were forced off their land and made to live and work on large, state-owned farms.

The Great Leap Forward was a disaster. The agricultural experiment failed, and the economy never came close to achieving the planned degree of industrialization. Even the gains made during the first Five-Year Plan were lost.

Other plans followed but, by the late 1970s, the government decided that the country no longer could follow the models of either the Soviet Union or other command-type economies. China and its population were too big for large-scale centralized planning. Industrializing the cities enough to provide jobs for nearly one-fourth of the world's population would be nearly impossible.

By the early 1980s, the influence of other successful market economies in Asia—Taiwan, South Korea, Hong Kong, and Singapore—was too much for China to ignore. One of China's provinces,

Privatization

Changes in Chile Chile has privatized telephone services and airlines. *What is Chile hoping to accomplish through privatization?*

CRITICAL THINKING

Making Comparisons Copy this chart on the board, omitting the answers in parentheses. Have students complete the chart with facts from the section.

COUNTRY	STEPS TOWARD CAPITALISM
Mexico	1. *(sold thousands of state-owned companies)* 2. *(cut back on government bureaucracy)*
Chile	1. *(privatized airlines, telephone services, utilities)*

As a class, discuss the similarities in the countries' plans to achieve capitalism.

the Guangdong Province just north of Hong Kong, copied many of the free market practices of the region and was even allowed to officially experiment with capitalism. At one time Guangdong was an embarrassment to the official communist dogma, but it was later touted as an economic role model for the rest of the nation.

China was also influenced by the eventual reunification with Hong Kong, which took place in 1997. The city of Shanghai, in particular, embarked on a program of reforms and expansion in an attempt to become China's "first city" after the reunification.

Today China is no longer experimenting with capitalism. It is instead privatizing industries, introducing market reforms, and otherwise acting in a decidedly capitalistic manner. China still has a long way to go, and the government still directs most major economic activity. Its economy has evolved, however, into what former President Jiang Zemin once called "socialism with Chinese characteristics"—loosely translated as free market capitalism.

Reform and Expansion

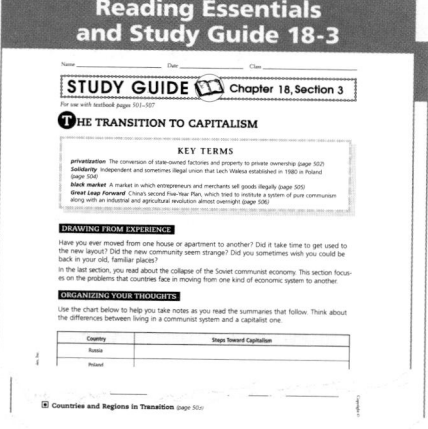

Shanghai Reform has resulted in strong economic growth for China. *Why did China stray from centralized planning?*

Visual Instruction
Answer to Caption:
China and its population were too large for centralized planning.

Reteach

Reading Essentials and Study Guide 18-3

STUDY GUIDE — Chapter 18, Section 3

THE TRANSITION TO CAPITALISM

Enrich

Have students imagine that they are writing an article for a newspaper in a former communist country. Their articles should explain how capitalism works, using the U.S. economy as an example.

 CLOSE

Ask: What is the greatest challenge facing nations making the transition to capitalism? Why?

Section 3 Assessment

Checking for Understanding

1. **Main Idea** What is privatization? Describe two ways in which transition economies handled privatization.

2. **Key Terms** Define privatization, Solidarity, black market, Great Leap Forward.

3. **List** the problems a country is likely to encounter when converting to capitalism.

4. **Identify** two major countries that are making the transition to capitalism.

5. **Trace** the economic policy changes in China.

Applying Economic Concepts

6. **Privatization** Explain why capital stock and other property is expected to last longer when it is privatized rather than collectively owned.

Critical Thinking

7. **Finding the Main Idea** Suppose you are visiting one nation in eastern Europe adopting a market economy. What questions would you ask local officials to determine whether they are successfully moving toward capitalism?

Practice and assess key social studies skills with the *Glencoe Skillbuilder Interactive Workbook, Level 2.*

Section 3 Assessment Answers

1. Privatization is the conversion of state-owned factories and property to private ownership; through vouchers, sale of state-owned companies, by decree

2. All vocabulary terms are defined in the text.

3. privatization, loss of political power, discipline of capitalism, responding to new incentives

4. Answers may include: Russia, Poland, Hungary, Mexico, Chile, others.

5. See pages 506–507.

6. People tend to take better care of the property they actually own. Also, entrepreneurs are rewarded with the fruits of their labor.

7. Questions should make reference to elements of capitalism, such as who owns the factors of production, how prices are established, how capital is obtained for production, and what role government plays in the economy.

BusinessWeek

TEACH

Most analysts expect the Chinese Internet market to be huge and profitable. According to a 1999 study by the China Internet Network Information Center (CNNIC), the number of Chinese residents using the Internet doubled from 1 million to 2 million from July to December 1998, and doubled again to 4 million from January to June 1999. Although Internet Service Providers (ISPs) from the United States are taking advantage of the growing Chinese market, Chinese ISPs are also reaping benefits. SINA.com has become the top portal in China. China.com, of which AOL is a 10 percent stockholder, is the first Asian ISP listed on a U.S. stock index. Ask students why the strength of Chinese ISPs is important for the future. *(Remind them that China may limit foreign ISPs.)* Also discuss with them why the affiliation between China.com and AOL is advantageous for both companies.

☞ Refer to *Business Week Focus on the New Economy* in the TCR for additional unit-based articles.

AUGUST 2, 1999

In 1949, communist forces won the civil war in China. The communists then established absolute control over the government and the economy. Today, however, technology is reshaping the communist state.

China's
Web Masters

Anyone who assumes the Internet is still a novelty in China has been asleep at the mouse. The communist giant's state-owned factories and political system may seem frozen in another era. But when it comes to cyberindustry, China is moving at net speed. Driven by soaring computer sales, rapid expansion of China's telecom networks, and the encouragement of reformist leaders, Internet use is growing explosively. . . .

The impact will be revolutionary, both on China's economy and society. A new class of entrepreneur is emerging because the government is allowing the private sector wide latitude to develop Web business—remarkable for an industry Beijing regards as strategic. The rapid spread of e-commerce could transform China's stodgy retail and banking sectors. It may also boost efficiency of Chinese industry by allowing old-line factories to streamline supply chains. . . .

To encourage development of Chinese content, Beijing makes it surprisingly easy for foreign companies. While they cannot own equity in mainland telecom operators, they can own majority control of Net companies. And although Beijing guards its monopoly on traditional media, it lets entrepreneurs publish on the Web. . . .

. . . The government limits what Chinese Net users can see by telling them to block portals run by dissident and human-rights groups. Determined surfers can go through offshore services. But because Beijing prohibits imported encryption technology, state snoops can easily eavesdrop on traffic. . . .

The Net's success could breed its own problems. As it grows more lucrative, bureaucrats may not be able to keep their hands off. Beijing is usually happy to accept foreigners' investment dollars at first. Then it often changes the rules to the advantage of state-run rivals once a sector gets hot. The same could happen with the Internet.

Examining the Newsclip

1. **Analyzing Information** How is technology changing China's economy and society?
2. **Making Predictions** What problems could arise as Internet use increases?

Answers to Examining the Newsclip

1. A new entrepreneur class is emerging, retail and banking sectors are changing, industries are becoming more efficient, and entrepreneurs may publish on the Web.

2. Bureaucrats may want to control the Internet.

The Various Faces of Capitalism

Study Guide

Main Idea
Many countries have moved toward capitalism, although its exact form varies from country to country.

Reading Strategy
Graphic Organizer As you read the section, complete a graphic organizer similar to the one below by selecting one of the nations discussed in the section and describing what role the government plays in its economy.

Country → Government and the economy

Key Terms
capital-intensive, keiretsu, infrastructure, collateral, transparency

Objectives
After studying this section, you will be able to:
1. **Explain** the factors that encouraged economic growth in Japan.
2. **Rank** the "Asian Tigers" according to per capita GNP.
3. **Describe** Sweden's retreat from socialism.

Applying Economic Concepts
Economic Growth Have you ever looked at the labels inside your clothes? If so, you may have noticed that many of them were made in Korea, Hong Kong, or Taiwan. Read to find out how different economies experienced economic growth.

Cover Story

Breaking the Border

If President George W. Bush and [Mexican President] Vicente Fox needed an emblem of their vision of a blurred US-Mexican border, Citigroup has just provided it. The bank's $12.5 billion purchase of Banacci, the leading Mexican bank, is as important for its symbolism as for its size.

The US financial services group does not just have Mexican customers in its sights. It also wants to use Banacci's brand, Banamex, in the US to attract Hispanics through its doors.... That a US institution should go to Mexico for help to penetrate its home market shows how far things have come since the launch of NAFTA in 1994.

Banamex and Citigroup merge

— *Financial Times*, May 23, 2001

Capitalism is a force sweeping the world. It is also a force that has many different faces. The common element of capitalism is that the factors of production are privately owned and controlled; there are, however, many variations on this theme.

The sharp financial crisis that swept Asia in the fall of 1997 also demonstrates another feature of capitalism—that the welfare of most capitalist economies is increasingly entwined. The interdependence we often see at the local and national level is beginning to become a feature of the global economy. These are some of the forces that are causing capitalism in places such as Japan to continue to evolve and expand.

Japan

Japan, like the United States, has a capitalist economy based on markets, prices, and the private ownership of capital. Unlike the United States, however, Japan's government is very involved in the day-to-day activities of the private sector.

CHAPTER 18: COMPARATIVE ECONOMIC SYSTEMS **509**

RESOURCE MANAGER

📂 Reproducible Masters
- Reproducible Lesson Plan 18-4
- Daily Lecture Notes 18-4
- Guided Reading Activity 18-4
- Reading Essentials and Study Guide 18-4
- Section Quiz 18-4

📖 Transparencies
- Daily Focus Transparency 85

Multimedia
- 💿 Vocabulary PuzzleMaker CD-ROM
- 💾 Interactive Tutor Self-Assessment Software
- 💿 ExamView® Pro Testmaker
- 💿 Presentation Plus!

1 FOCUS

Section Overview
This section deals with the economies of Japan, the "Asian Tigers," and Sweden.

BELLRINGER
Motivational Activity

🖨 Project **transparency** and have students answer questions.

📂 Available as blackline master.

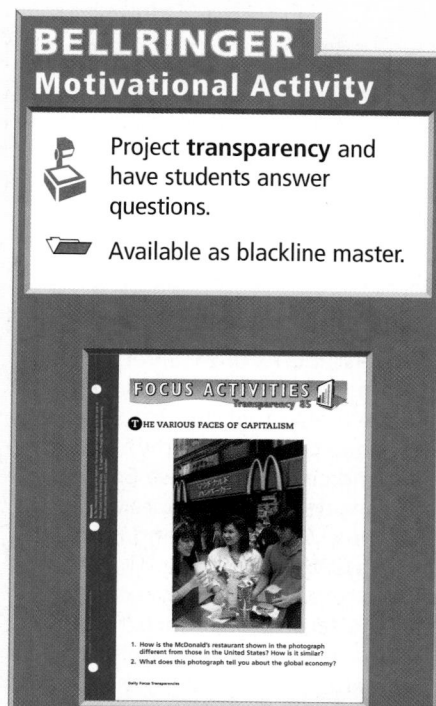

FOCUS ACTIVITIES 1
Transparency 85

THE VARIOUS FACES OF CAPITALISM

1. How is the McDonald's restaurant shown in the photograph different from those in the United States? How is it similar?
2. What does this photograph tell you about the global economy?

Daily Focus Transparency

Study Guide

Reading Strategy
Have students create the graphic organizer.
Answers to Graphic: *Answers should reflect section content.*

Preteaching Vocabulary
🔵 Use the Vocabulary Puzzle-Maker to create puzzles.

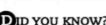

② TEACH

Daily Lecture Notes 18-4

DAILY LECTURE NOTES 📖 Lesson 18-4

ⅅID YOU KNOW?

Competition in an open marketplace has extended even to sports. Japan, where baseball is very popular, has developed many top players. Some have even been hired away by teams in the United States eager to improve their chances of winning.

PAGES 509–512

I. Japan

A. The government is very involved in the day-to-day activities of the private sector.

B. Japan's recent economic crisis has severely tested the historically close employee-employer relationship, which was one of the reasons for Japan's early success.

C. Another reason for Japan's success was its ability and willingness to develop new technology.

D. Government has worked closely with businesses to limit foreign competition in the domestic market.

E. Japan's economy is partially closed to the products of foreign producers.

F. Protectionism in Japan does not help consumers, who pay high costs for many products.

G. The Ministry of International Trade and Industry identifies promising export markets and then subsidizes industries so that they can be competitive in this area.

H. In the 1990s a banking crisis resulting from bad loans was part of the reason for Japan's poor economic performance.

I. Japan needs to institute reforms that redefine the government's role in the economy and to restructure how firms produce and compete with each other.

L1 Comparing and Contrasting

Have students draw a Venn diagram (two overlapping circles). Have them label the first circle "United States Economy" and the second circle "Japanese Economy." Ask students to list characteristics of the U.S. economy and record them in the first circle. They should then reread Section 4, recording in the second circle facts they find about the Japanese economy. Have students relocate items that appear in both circles to the overlapping center section. Discuss with students how this diagram shows the similarities and differences between the two economies.

Visual Instruction

Answer to Caption:
high level of capital investment; government assistance to business, willingness to develop new technology

At the end of World War II, Japan was a devastated country. Today, it is the second largest industrial nation in the world, with a GNP about 79 percent of that of the United States. In the 1970s and 1980s, the Japanese economy was one of the fastest growing in the world. However, it stalled in the 1990s. Slower growth, a currency crisis in 1995, and recession from 1998–2001 added to the economy's woes—factors that convinced the Japanese that further restructuring was necessary.

Reasons for Success

One of the reasons for Japan's early success was the workers' intense loyalty to their employers. Many workers joined large companies for life. In return, the company supplied benefits such as wedding halls, private schools, and even vacation resorts.

Japanese workers traditionally take great pride in the quality of their work. It is not unusual for a company's entire workforce to arrive early to take part in group calisthenics and meditation exercises.

Japan's recent economic crisis has severely tested the historically close employee-employer relationship. Some firms have actually laid off workers, and some no longer guarantee lifetime employment. Whether or not these changes will become widespread depends in large part on the speed and strength of the Japanese recovery.

Another reason for Japan's success is the ability and willingness of the Japanese to develop new technology. Because of their relatively small population, they have worked to boost productivity by developing methods that are **capital-intensive**—techniques that use a large amount of capital for every person employed. Today, the Japanese are recognized as the world leader in the area of industrial robots. As a result, most factories require only a fraction of the workers that similar factories in other countries need.

Most large Japanese firms also belong to a **keiretsu** (ky • reht • soo) This is a tightly knit group of firms governed by an external board of directors from potential competitors. The role of the governing board is to ensure that competition does not get so fierce that individual firms are threatened. A similar agreement in the United States among competing firms would be illegal under our antitrust laws.

The Role of Government

Historically, Japan's public sector was relatively small. Spending on **infrastructure**—the highways, mass transit, communications, power, water, sewerage and other public goods needed to support a large population—was low. The government also had a modest military capability and was not burdened with welfare spending. As a result, taxes were low, which

Japan

Worker Attitudes Japan's economic success is due in part to its workers' loyalty and pride in their products. *What other factors have contributed to Japan's success?*

MEETING SPECIAL NEEDS ACTIVITY

Learning Style: Intrapersonal Have students read the information under "Reasons for Success." Then ask them to summarize the reasons for Japan's economic success. *(workers' intense loyalty, pride in their work, the ability and willingness to develop new technology, and governing boards that ensure that competition does not get too fierce)* Have students write a journal entry in which they comment on the employer-employee relationship in Japan. Do students find such a relationship attractive? Ask them to explain whether they would want to work in a system in which the worker has many benefits and guaranteed employment, but pledges a lifetime of work to the company. Have students also discuss in their journal entries what they believe to be the characteristics of a good employer and a good employee.

📁 Refer to *Inclusion for the Social Studies Classroom Strategies and Activities* in the TCR.

allowed people to save their money or spend it on consumer goods.

The Japanese government also worked closely with businesses to limit foreign competition in the domestic market. Even today the Japanese government is more closely allied with businesses than consumers, often aiding efforts to keep foreign goods out of the country in order to protect domestic producers.

Some of this has changed with the recent economic downturn. In order to stimulate economic growth, the government introduced a number of Keynesian-type spending packages in 1998 and 1999 to stimulate the economy. As a result, the government sector now spends more than ever.

A Closed Economy

Despite Japan's success in international trade, their economy is partially closed to the products of foreign producers. When foreign companies try to sell their goods in Japan, many encounter numerous obstacles ranging from delayed government permission to huge amounts of paperwork.

Until recently, Japan was even reluctant to import rice, a food staple, in order to protect domestic rice producers. As a result, the cost of rice to the Japanese consumer is several times higher than it would be if Japan imported rice from the world markets.

The High Cost of Living

Protectionism in Japan may help certain segments of the economy such as the rice farmers, but it does not help the consumer. Because foreign competitors supply so few goods, products are generally expensive. Citrus fruits cost four to six times more in Japan than they do in the United States. Clothing costs two to three times as much, and even cameras and electronics cost more in Japan than elsewhere.

For years, the Japanese have been making electronic consumer goods and selling them abroad. Recently, Japanese citizens discovered they could purchase their own goods cheaper in Hawaii than they can in their own country. As a result, Japanese cameras, radios, and other electronic

Student Web Activity Visit the *Economics: Principles and Practices* Web site at epp.glencoe.com and click on *Chapter 18—Student Web Activities* for an activity on the governments and economies of nations.

equipment are among the most popular items Japanese visitors bring back from trips abroad.

Reliance on Manufacturing and Trade

Japan must actively engage in international trade because it is an island nation with few natural resources. Consequently, it must import most of its oil as well as a number of other critical materials. For the most part, the Japanese paid for their imports with revenues from the sale of cars, cameras, and other consumer products.

Much of Japan's trade success has been attributed to the direction that provides its Ministry of International Trade and Industry (MITI). This is a government ministry that identifies promising export markets, and then subsidizes industries so that they can be competitive in this area.

Stagnation and Recession

Despite Japan's economic successes, it experienced stagnation and recession for most of the 1990s. Industrial production peaked in 1991 and then declined until 1994. It recovered to its 1991 level in 1997, but then went into its worst recession since World War II.

Part of the reason for the poor economic performance was the banking crisis in the 1990s. When Japan was growing exceptionally fast several years earlier, land values soared. Many borrowers pledged their land as **collateral**—property or other security used to guarantee repayment of a loan—against loans that ultimately went bad. Banks had so many bad loans—estimates ranged as high as one in four—that banks simply stopped lending in 1996 and 1997. To make matters worse, banks had been so secretive about their loans that

CHAPTER 18: COMPARATIVE ECONOMIC SYSTEMS **511**

Guided Reading Activity 18-4

GUIDED READING Activity 18-4

For use with textbook pages 509–514

THE VARIOUS FACES OF CAPITALISM

RECALLING THE FACTS

Directions: Use the information in your textbook to answer the questions. Use another sheet of paper if necessary.

1. In what major way is Japan's capitalist economy different from that of the United States?

2. What factor forced Japan to boost productivity by developing capital-intensive industries?

3. What is a keiretsu? Explain its purpose.

4. How has the Japanese government helped to limit foreign competition in the domestic market?

5. In what way have Japanese consumers suffered from the government's actions?

6. What led to the banking crisis in the 1990s?

7. What did the government do in response to this crisis?

8. What four countries are known as the "Asian Tigers"?

9. What was the reason behind Sweden's economic restructuring?

Guided Reading Activities

Objectives, goals, and answers to the student activity can be found in the **Web Activity Lesson Plan** feature at epp.glencoe.com

CYBERNOMICS

Camera Advancements Japan is well known for its advancements in consumer electronics. For example, Japan's Casio Computer Company has introduced a digital camera that is worn like a wristwatch. The camera weighs only 32 grams, but stores up to 100 photos. Users employ infrared signals to transfer the photos to their personal computers.

FREE ENTERPRISE ACTIVITY

Ask students to list the similarities and differences between the U.S. economic system and the economic systems of the six countries discussed in Section 4. Then have students write a paragraph answering the following: What, in your opinion, are the most essential characteristics of the U.S. economic system? Do the six countries' economic systems have these essential characteristics? Are there any characteristics of these other countries' economic systems that you think the U.S. should adopt? Why or why not?

Each of the four Asian Tigers has opened textile and garment plants in Central America, taking advantage of cheap labor and more favorable U.S. import quotas.

L2 Making Comparisons

On the board, list the six countries discussed in Section 4. Call on volunteers to identify the major characteristics of these countries' economies. Note their responses next to the appropriate country name. Then have students use the information on the board to write a comparative essay on the economies of Japan, the Asian Tigers, and Sweden.

L3 Economics and Culture

Have each student select one of the nations mentioned in the chapter. Direct students to gather either current or historical information about the economic system of their selected nation. Then have students investigate their chosen nation's cultural heritage. Finally, ask students to collate their findings in a report, showing direct relationships between the country's societal values and characteristics of its economic system. Call on students to present their reports to the class.

STANDARD &POOR'S INFOBYTE

International Bonds An international bond is a bond that is issued in one country on behalf of borrowers that live in another country. An example would be a Japanese-issued corporate bond being offered for sale on the New York bond market.

banking regulators did not even know who received the loans, making default by the borrowers relatively easy.

The banking situation made it difficult for qualified borrowers to get loans, and many industries, including construction, came to a halt. Unemployment rose; the government tried to stimulate the economy with a number of programs, including "employee adjustment grants" designed to subsidize employee wages. In 1999 alone, the government used ¥61.1 billion ($532 million) to pay two-thirds of the salaries of nearly 2.5 million workers in 300 industries. Despite these subsidies, Japan's unemployment reached record-high levels in late 1999.

Restructuring and Reform

Another problem facing Japan is that it can no longer rely exclusively on basic manufacturing because many of its neighbors can now produce the same products at a lower cost. Also, the cozy relationship between government and industry makes it difficult for incremental change to take place—one of the features of capitalism. This inflexibility is made more difficult by the keiretsu, whose purpose is to maintain relationships and to ensure that competition does not become detrimental to its members. Finally, there is the issue of **transparency,** or the need to make business dealings more visible to everyone, especially government regulators. Without more transparency, it will be difficult to prevent another crippling banking crisis.

According to its Ministry of International Trade and Industry, Japan needs to institute supply-side reforms. These reforms would redefine government's role in the economy and restructure the way firms produce and compete with one another. This is an ironic turn of events because the world looked to Japan as the very model of growth in the 1980s. Today, Japan looks to the United States for guidance on restructuring so that it can resume its previous growth.

The Asian Tigers

Three other Asian countries—Singapore, Taiwan, and South Korea—have made striking economic progress during the last 50 years. The British colony of Hong Kong also experienced explosive growth before it was reunified with China. Despite setbacks during the Asian financial crisis of 1997, the four are called the "Asian Tigers." Each has based its growth on capitalism, but each has taken a slightly different path.

Hong Kong

When Hong Kong was still a British colony, it was recognized as the most free market economy in the world, one with virtually no government interference. Entrepreneurs in Hong Kong developed a manufacturing-based economy that used technology other countries had already developed. Their major industrial products included textiles, clothing, electronic games, radios, telephones, watches, electronic components, and toys.

At the time of unification in 1997, Hong Kong's per capita GNP was nearly 90 percent of the United States's, and nearly 40 times that of China. Other factors, however, were beginning to change. Financial services and tourism had caught up with manufacturing, and the Asian crisis had thrust the economy into a deep recession. Furthermore, China's promise not to interfere with Hong Kong markets for a period of 50 years seemed to be in jeopardy. In mid-1999, Hong Kong's chief executive Tung Chee-hwa announced plans to pour billions of dollars into high-tech computer industries, marking a sharp departure from the laissez-faire capitalism that once characterized Hong Kong.

CRITICAL THINKING

Formulating Questions Have students read the paragraphs under "The Asian Tigers" on pages 512 and 513. As they read, copy the following phrases on the board:
1. Hong Kong's chief executive made plans to spend billions on computer industries.
2. The government offered generous tax breaks, subsidies, and employee training.
3. telecommunications, consumer electronics, aerospace, and pharmaceuticals
4. a small number of powerful business families
When students complete their reading, ask them to formulate a question for each of the above answers. (e.g., 1. What occasion marked a departure from the laissez-faire capitalism that once characterized Hong Kong?)

Singapore

The second Asian Tiger is Singapore, an island nation about 3.5 times larger than Washington, D.C., with a per capita GNP about 80 percent of that of the United States. More than 1,000 multinational firms have been attracted to Singapore with the lure of generous tax breaks, government subsidies, and government-sponsored training of employees. Unlike Hong Kong, Singapore made a determined effort to develop its own technologies through extensive spending on research and development.

The government of Singapore is trying to develop a few select industries, including telecommunications services, software, and biotechnology. The government has spent millions on laboratories, attracting top scientists from all over the world. The biotechnology industry has scored some original successes, one of which is the transfer of firefly genes to orchids to make them glow in the dark.

Taiwan

The Republic of China, also known as Taiwan, is an island about the size of West Virginia located off the coast of the People's Republic of China. Taiwan's population is about 22 million, and the per capita GNP is almost half that of the United States.

Planning was always a feature of the Taiwanese economy. The most recent plan identified 10 industries to receive government assistance—these include telecommunications, consumer electronics, semiconductors, precision machinery, aerospace, pharmaceuticals, and others.

Taiwan was one of the early economic powers in Asia, but some people wonder if the centralized planning process will hamper future economic growth. Another concern is the looming presence of the People's Republic of China, which regards Taiwan as a "renegade province" and vows eventual unification. Despite its early start, the per capita GNP in Taiwan has fallen far behind those of Hong Kong and Singapore.

South Korea

South Korea, a country slightly larger than Indiana, has the smallest per capita GNP of the Asian Tigers, at about 45 percent of the United States's. In the past, a group of technocrats governed Korea with the help of the military. The factors of production were privately owned, but a small number of powerful business families dominated the private economy through conglomerates.

South Korea was hit hard by the 1997 Asian financial crisis, but it was also one of the first nations to recover. Many reforms have been undertaken since, but South Korea's future economic growth still depends on whether the private economy can adapt to competition and rely less on its relationship with the political sector.

Sweden

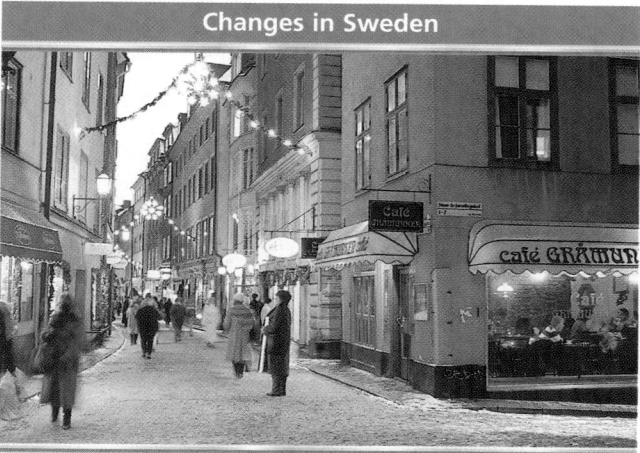 Sweden is a mature industrial nation, once regarded as the "socialist state that works." The reputation was apt because Sweden provided a broader range of social welfare programs for its citizens than did any other free-world country. Some

Changes in Sweden

Restructuring Many government-owned businesses in Sweden were privatized in the early 1990s. *What led to the ouster of Sweden's Socialist party?*

CHAPTER 18: COMPARATIVE ECONOMIC SYSTEMS **513**

 Visual Instruction

Answer to Caption:
heavy tax burden, additional costs of a welfare state, growing inflation, massive government deficit

③ ASSESS

Assign Section 4 Assessment as homework or as an in-class activity.

💾 Have students use **Interactive Tutor Self-Assessment Software** to review Section 4.

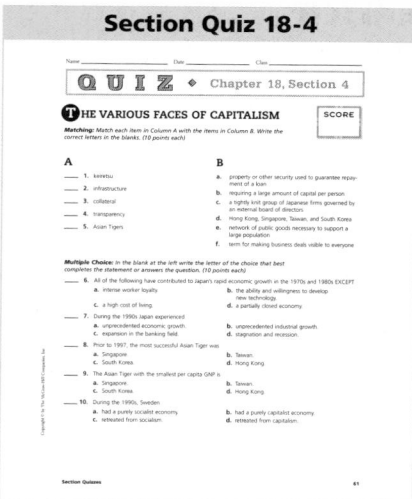
Section Quiz 18-4

EXTENDING THE CONTENT

Lifetime Employment In Japan, "lifetime employment" means that a person will have a job with the same firm for the rest of his or her life. These jobs often go to graduates of the best universities. To gain admission to these institutions, it is necessary to score high on the comprehensive examinations given in high school. In other words, a person's job is directly related to success in education. With lifetime employment, an individual can move up or down within the same firm depending on his or her success at each level. For example, unproductive workers may be assigned to unimportant jobs. Even when corporations go through tough times, many have tried to avoid layoffs, preferring instead to reassign employees.

Reteach

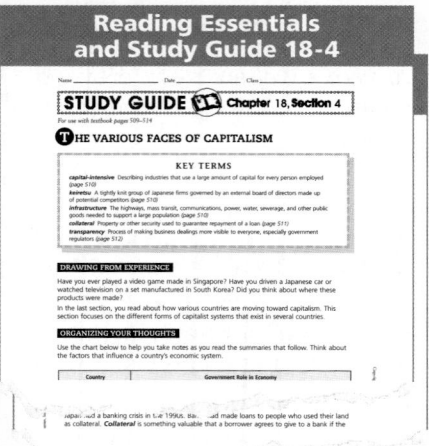

Reading Essentials and Study Guide 18-4

Enrich

Invite a guest speaker who has visited or lived in Sweden, Japan, or one of the Asian Tigers to talk about that country's standard of living, its main industries, and how culture influences the economy.

4 CLOSE

Have students use information from the section to comment on the following statement: Capitalist economies have more differences than similarities.

---

of the basic industries were nationalized, but Sweden also had a considerable amount of private enterprise. The country, therefore, was not a model of pure socialism in the traditional sense.

The Welfare State

Many worker benefits were instituted during the 44-year rule of the Socialist party. During this time, wages were high, jobs were easy to find, and unemployment was in the 1- to 3-percent range. The Swedish economy—with its generous maternity, education, disability, and old-age benefits—was thought to be the model of European socialism.

Because government owned some basic industries, and because many of these industries were not profitable, the government relied on steep taxes to pay for the welfare state benefits. In the mid-1980s, tax receipts were about 50 percent of GNP. In some cases, additional income that Swedish citizens earned was taxed at an 80 percent rate, meaning that a person who earned an additional $100 would keep only $20. Some individuals even left the country to avoid high taxes. When tennis star Bjorn Borg was at the peak of his career, he resided outside of Sweden to avoid paying high taxes.

Many others devised ways to avoid paying taxes. Some craft workers resorted to barter. A carpenter who built some cabinets for an auto mechanic, for example, might be paid with repair work on the family car.

Restructuring

Eventually, the heavy tax burden and the additional costs of the welfare state began to cut into Sweden's economic growth. Growing inflation added to the problems, as did a massive government deficit. Growing discontent with conditions finally led to the defeat of the Socialist party in 1976.

A free-market government was elected in 1991, and by 1993 the role of the public sector had been reduced, although current revenues by all levels of government exceed 60 percent of GNP. Taxes on individuals and corporations are also lower, although they are still high by U.S. standards. Many government-owned businesses have been privatized, and more are scheduled to be converted.

European nations such as Sweden were relatively unaffected by the Asian crisis, so economic growth was positive in the decade of the 1990s. Real GNP growth rates have been lower than those of the Asian tigers, however, leaving Sweden with a real GNP per capita about two-thirds of that in the United States.

Section 4 Assessment

Checking for Understanding

1. **Main Idea** Discuss how the approaches to economic growth differ in Taiwan and South Korea.

2. **Key Terms** Define capital-intensive, keiretsu, infrastructure, collateral, transparency.

3. **Describe** significant factors that contribute to economic growth and development in Japan.

4. **Rank** the "Asian Tigers" according to per capita GNP.

5. **Explain** how Sweden's retreat from socialism affected the nation's tax rates.

Applying Economic Concepts

6. **Economic Growth** How has Sweden's transition from socialism to capitalism helped promote economic growth?

Critical Thinking

7. **Making Predictions** How might continued economic growth in Asia affect industries in the United States?

8. **Making Comparisons** What type of help is provided to Japanese businesses by their government that the American government does not give to its businesses?

 Practice and **assess** key social studies skills with the *Glencoe Skillbuilder Interactive Workbook, Level 2.*

514 UNIT 5 INTERNATIONAL AND GLOBAL ECONOMICS

Section 4 Assessment Answers

1. Taiwan: centralized planning that provides government assistance to certain industries; South Korea: a number of powerful families controlled the private economy through conglomerates

2. All vocabulary terms are defined in the text.

3. worker and corporate loyalty, technology, low taxes

4. Hong Kong (89 percent of that in the U.S.), Singapore (81 percent), Taiwan (50 percent), South Korea (45 percent)

5. The retreat allowed taxes to be cut.

6. The transition to capitalism reduced the heavy tax burden and the high costs of the welfare state. Privatization of government-owned business has enabled the government to eliminate some of its massive debt.

7. Some students may indicate that continued economic growth in Asia could be beneficial to U.S. industries because Asian industries may import more products from the U.S. Others may indicate that it could be detrimental because they will create more competition for U.S. industries.

8. The Japanese government limits foreign competition in the domestic market.

Section 1

The Spectrum of Economic Systems (pages 491–494)

- The world's three main types of economic systems are capitalism, socialism, and communism.

- Under capitalism, productive resources are privately owned and operated; capital is obtained through profits in the market; supply and demand determine prices; and the role of government is limited to promoting competition and providing public goods.

- Under **socialism,** many of the basic resources are government owned and operated, with prices playing a major role in the allocation of resources.

- Under **communism,** all productive resources are government owned and operated; centralized planning directs all resources; and labor is organized for the common advantage of the community.

Section 2

The Rise and Fall of Communism

(pages 496–499)

- In 1917 revolutionists overthrew the government of Russia and instituted a communist system.

- Utilizing a series of **Five-Year Plans,** Stalin wanted to achieve rapid industrialization. The plans included the **collectivization** of agriculture and the transformation of industry.

- When Stalin's brutal regime ended in 1953, the Soviet Union had successfully completed its transition to a major industrial power.

- The command economy ultimately proved to be a miserable failure. Low productivity and the lack of incentives led Mikhail Gorbachev to attempt **perestroika,** the fundamental restructuring of the economy and the government. The restructuring was not completed, however, and in the early 1990s, the Soviet economic system collapsed.

Section 3

The Transition to Capitalism

(pages 501–507)

- The former communist systems face several challenges–including the **privatization** of capital resources–as they try to move toward capitalism.

- These challenges include privatization, the shift in political power from Communists to elected officials, and the new incentives of a capitalist economy.

- Russia and Eastern Europe have had varying amounts of success in this transition to capitalism.

- Many countries in Latin America and even China are also moving toward a capitalist economy.

Section 4

The Various Faces of Capitalism

(pages 509–514)

- Japan achieved phenomenal economic growth with a combination of worker and corporate loyalty, technology, and low taxes until the early 1990s.

- Despite Japan's economic success, it experienced stagnation and recession during the 1990s.

- The economies of the "Asian Tigers"–Singapore, Taiwan, Hong Kong (before reunification with China), and South Korea–also owe much of their remarkable success to capitalism.

- Sweden, once regarded as the "socialist state that works," has restructured in an attempt to move away from socialism.

CHAPTER 18: COMPARATIVE ECONOMIC SYSTEMS **515**

NIGHTLY BUSINESS REPORT

⊙ ECONOMICS & YOU

Chapter 25
Disc 1, Side 2

Comparative Economic Systems

Also available in VHS.

Using the Chapter 18 Summary

Use the Chapter 18 Summary to preview, review, condense, or reteach the chapter.

Preview/Review

Vocabulary PuzzleMaker CD-ROM reinforces Key Terms.

Interactive Tutor Self-Assessment Software provides a review of Chapter 18 content.

Condense

Have students listen to the Chapter 18 Audio Program. Spanish also available.

Assign the Chapter 18 Audio Program Activity and give students the Chapter 18 Audio Program Test.

Have students complete the Guided Reading Activities and Reading Essentials and Study Guides for Chapter 18.

Reteach

Have students complete Reteaching Activity 18 in the TCR. Spanish also available.

Teacher's Notes / Internet Bookmarks

GLENCOE
TECHNOLOGY

Use **MindJogger Videoquiz** to review the Chapter 18 content.

Have students visit the Web site at epp.glencoe.com to review Chapter 18 and take the **Self-Check Quiz.**

Identifying Key Terms

1. e
2. f
3. h
4. a
5. i
6. g
7. c
8. b
9. d
10. j

Reviewing the Facts

Section 1

1. Government may promote competition and provide public goods.
2. through the price system and the voting process
3. the state, as governed by a single authoritarian party

Section 2

4. He implemented collectivization and started the first Five-Year Plan.
5. set unrealistically high quotas, which led to the production of shoddy goods; failed to specify quotas succinctly enough, which led to excesses in some products and shortages in others; failed to establish effective incentives for workers
6. It allowed some industries to compete, allowed managers to pursue profits, encouraged small businesses.

Section 3

7. privatization, loss of political power, discipline of capitalism, responding to new incentives
8. Answers may include Russia, Poland, Hungary, the Czech

Republic, Estonia, Latvia, Lithuania, Mexico, Chile, Argentina, China.

Section 4

9. It keeps taxes low and works with businesses to limit foreign competition in domestic market.
10. Singapore: government provides tax breaks, subsidies, and sponsors training of employees; trying to develop a few select industries; South Korea: factors of production are privately owned; powerful businesses dominate the powerful economy.

Self-Check Quiz Visit the *Economics: Principles and Practices* Web site at epp.glencoe.com and click on **Chapter 18—Self-Check Quizzes** to prepare for the chapter test.

Identifying Key Terms

Write the key term that best completes the following sentences.

a. state farm
b. socialism
c. black market
d. capital-intensive
e. privatization
f. Five-Year Plan
g. collective farm
h. communism
i. perestroika
j. storming

1. In most former communist countries, state-owned enterprises are being converted to private ownership, a process known as _____ .
2. To direct production, Soviet planners adopted a _____ .
3. Under _____ , the government owns all the means of production.
4. In the Soviet agricultural system, the state owned and operated each _____ .
5. Soviet leader Mikhail Gorbachev introduced a policy of _____ , the fundamental restructuring of the economy and government.
6. In the Soviet Union, groups of peasant families, each of which was allowed to keep their home and household goods, a few cattle, and a small plot of land, worked each _____ .
7. Most nations of Eastern Europe had a flourishing _____ , where entrepreneurs and merchants sold goods illegally.
8. Under _____ , the government owns many, but not all, of the basic productive resources.

9. In _____ industries, a large amount of capital is used for every person employed in manufacturing.
10. Piecework quotas often led to _____ , where workers worked slowly until the last week of the month and then sped up to meet the unrealistically high quota.

Reviewing the Facts

Section 1 (pages 491–494)

1. **Explain** the role of the government in a capitalist economic system.
2. **Describe** how the people in a socialist economy help allocate the use of resources.
3. **Describe** who answers the basic economic questions in a communist system.

Section 2 (pages 496–499)

4. **Describe** Stalin's efforts to implement centralized planning.
5. **Describe** the problems that central planning caused in the Soviet economy.
6. **Explain** the impact that perestroika had on the Soviet economy.

Section 3 (pages 501–507)

7. **List** the problems that nations may face as they try to make the transition from communism to capitalism.
8. **Name** the nations that are currently trying to adapt to a market economy and describe the specific problems they are facing in their transition.

Section 4 (pages 509–514)

9. **Explain** the role that the government plays in Japan's economy.
10. **Describe** how the approaches to economic growth differ in South Korea and Singapore.

Thinking Critically

1. The extensive role of government in five-year plans would probably ensure that they would not be accepted in the U.S.
2. fiscal policies, automatic stabilizers, social welfare nets
3. While under a socialist economy, wages were high, unemployment was low, and workers had many benefits, but the people paid very high taxes. Eventually, growing inflation and a large deficit led to the defeat of the Socialist party in 1976. In 1991, a free-market government was

Thinking Critically

1. **Evaluating Information** Do you think five-year plans could work in the United States? Why or why not?

2. **Drawing Conclusions** What safeguards are in place to ensure that the United States will not face an economic downturn as severe as the Great Depression? List the safeguards on a graphic organizer like the one below.

3. **Sequencing Information** Trace Sweden's transition from socialism to capitalism.

4. **Drawing Conclusions** The Communists promised people that their system would lead to workers' paradises throughout the world. By the early 1990s, however, communist systems and their command economies in most countries had collapsed. Why do you think communism was such a failure?

Applying Economic Concepts

1. **Capitalism** Many nations are attempting to switch from communism or socialism to capitalism. Often, the transition has been quite difficult. What suggestions would you make to the leaders of these nations to help ease the transition to capitalism?

2. **Economic Growth** The "Asian Tigers" have experienced rapid economic growth and development. Do you think they can sustain this growth rate? Why or why not?

3. **Economic Change** Why have many countries chosen to change the mix of socialism and capitalism in their economies in recent years?

Math Practice

Assume that your salary is 500 rubles per month. The government-controlled price of bread is 10 rubles, and you buy five loaves each month. What percentage of your income do you spend on bread? After the government deregulates prices, bread costs 25 rubles. What percentage of your income goes to buy bread? How does the inflation affect your standard of living?

Thinking Like an Economist

Explain why firms in the former Soviet Union could make low-quality products and continue to exist year after year. What would happen to such a firm in the United States economy?

Technology Skill

Using a Computerized Card Catalog For one week, summarize in your journal news articles you read about events in eastern Europe and other former Soviet bloc nations. Focus on articles that relate to those regions working to convert from a command economy to a market economy.

Using a computerized card catalog, find other sources describing economic events in these areas. Compose a journal article analyzing current developments in either of those regions of the world. Include quotes from the sources you found using the computerized card catalog.

━ *Building Skills* ━

Building a Database Review recent issues of newsmagazines and current newspapers. Using the steps described on page 495, build a database of information about current world developments concerning capitalism and socialism that the newspapers or the news magazines mention. Explain to a partner why the database is organized the way it is and how it might be used in class.

 Practice and **assess** key social studies skills with the *Glencoe Skillbuilder Interactive Workbook, Level 2.*

CHAPTER 18: COMPARATIVE ECONOMIC SYSTEMS **517**

Thinking Like an Economist

Although producing poor quality products, firms in the Soviet Union were state supported and there was limitation of imports. Poor quality products could be sold because little competition existed. In the U.S. economy, such a firm would not make money because people would buy products of better quality, forcing the firm to close.

Technology Skill

Products should show understanding of card catalog and chapter content.

Building Skills

Databases should demonstrate technical and content knowledge.

 Bonus Test Question

Compare differences in motivation for the following in communist and capitalist economic systems:

a. for workers to put forth their best effort *(Communist: there is little motivation to put forth best effort since people receive same pay regardless of how hard they work. Capitalist: workers who work hardest may receive pay increases and promotion.)*

b. for managers to make careful business decisions *(Communist: quotas used to judge production, so managers may work only to meet quota rather than to improve quality. Capitalist: managers who make wise decisions and cut costs or improve product are often rewarded.)*

elected. Taxes were lowered and many businesses were privatized.

4. Lack of individual freedom undermined the efforts of communism; incompetence and inefficiency of central planning on a large scale led to the downfall of communism.

Applying Economic Concepts

1. Advice should target problems most often encountered in transition.

2. Answers should show knowledge of the economic growth and development of the Asian Tigers.

3. The high taxes and lack of individuality made the people living in socialist systems dissatisfied; capitalism allows for larger incomes and economic growth, more freedom and efficiency.

Math Practice

10 percent; 25 percent; After the price increase, people will have less to spend on other items, so their standard of living will probably decrease.

① FOCUS

The purpose of this activity is to provide students with hands-on experience in mock international trade in order to assess the strengths and weaknesses of each basic type of economy on the international market.

② TEACH

- Prepare by obtaining the following items: 8 tea bags, 15 packets of sugar, 24 cotton balls, and 12 cans of tuna or chicken.

- Begin the workshop by organizing students into four groups. Separate the groups into different areas of the room. Assign each group the role of a country with one type of economy (command, market, traditional, or mixed).

- After students have completed Step 2, have them read Step 3. Review with the class some "norms of international trade" —class rules—that will govern how trades are to be completed. Before trading begins in earnest, direct students from each group to model a transaction to ensure student understanding of the exercise.

ECONOMICS WORKSHOP IN ACTION

Simulating Trade in Various Economies

From the classroom of . . .
Danielle Dressler
Mifflinburg High School
Mifflinburg, Pennsylvania

The world contains various types of economic systems. Some countries have market economies, some command economies, some traditional, and still others have mixed economies. Each type of economy poses its own challenges when it comes to international trade. In this workshop, you will organize into groups and attempt to trade your products for goods produced in another country.

Setting Up the Workshop

Your teacher will separate you into groups and provide you with your products. Your group will represent a command, market, traditional, or mixed economic system. Read the instructions for your economic system. Then, read the steps of the procedures and begin the activity.

Procedures

STEP 1

Your group has all the "goods" your country produces (for example, the command economy has all the sugar packets). Later, you will use your goods to trade for the staples you need that are produced in the other countries.

STEP 2

When your group trades, keep in mind that the trade value of the products are: 100 lbs of sugar = 100 lbs of tea = 50 lbs of cotton = 25 lbs of meat.

STEP 3

Begin trading with the other "countries," paying careful attention to your restrictions on imports and exports. To satisfy the needs of its population, the goal of each country is to trade its product in such a way that it comes as close as possible to achieving the following mix of goods:

- 75 lbs of meat
- 250 lbs of cotton
- 500 lbs of sugar
- 300 lbs of tea

Participating in Economics

The World In Your Hands Hold up a wooden pencil for the class. Tell students that it is a good symbol of international trade and challenge them to explain why this is so. After a brief discussion, explain that factors of production from every inhabited continent are employed to make this simple and common good: zinc from Australia; zinc, crude oil, and graphite from Asia; copper and castor oil from Africa; zinc and crude oil from Europe; copper from South America; and zinc, crude oil, carbon, and black clay from North America, where the pencil was also manufactured. Have students choose another simple and common good and cooperate to conduct research to discover its international trading origins.

Command Economy

You are citizens of a country under a command economy. Your country has 1,500 pounds of **sugar** to trade. Your government has placed many regulations on both imports and exports. Three regulations are required during sugar production in order for sugar to be exported. Also, three regulations protecting your citizens need to be met in order for products to come into the country. Before you begin, organize your society (government officials, farmers, etc.) and list your regulations on imports and exports.

Traditional Economy

You are members of a society that has a traditional economic system. Your country has 800 pounds of **tea** to trade. You must decide in what quantities and with what countries you want to trade your tea, which is in very low supply. Before you begin, describe the characteristics of your society (climate, organization, leaders, etc.) and organize your group so that each member has a part in the economy.

Mixed Economy

You are members of a country that has a mixed economic system. You have 400 pounds of **cotton** to trade. Your government does not have complete control over the economy, but it places two regulations on the export of the cotton produced in your country and two regulations on imported products. Before you begin, organize your society (government officials, producers, etc.) and list your country's regulations on imports and exports.

Market Economy

You are a member of a country that has a market economic system. Your main export is **meat**—300 pounds in total. (Every member has an equal share.) You are free to compete in trade against one another. Your task is to export the meat from your country by competing with the other members of your group. Before you begin, describe the characteristics of your society and decide if you want to implement regulations on imports and exports.

Summary Activity

When the trading has been completed, discuss the following questions.

1. Which "country" came closest to the optimal mix of products? What factors of the economic system made this possible?

2. Which types of economies were least able to achieve a good mix of products? Why do you think this is so?

F.Y.I.

Most international trade goods are carried by ship. In fact, 95 percent of the world's freight travels on the sea, carried by some 75,000 merchant ships. Most follow sea lanes—standard navigational routes. In the sea lanes, the ocean is hardly a remote place. On a voyage from North America to Europe, for example, a sailor might typically encounter at least one other ship every day of the voyage. Such is the volume of the international sea trade.

3 ASSESS

Have students write paragraphs in which they evaluate the simulation. **Ask:** How realistic was it? Students should base their evaluations on their understanding of the real-world international market performance of countries with various types of economies.

4 CLOSE

Ask students to discuss the truth of this statement: "International trade always enhances the wealth of the trading nation."

Summary Activity Answers

All answers will vary. For question 1, focus students' attention on the factors of the economic system that made the mock country so successful. For question 2, focus students' attention on the factors of the economic system that made the mock country so unsuccessful. Reward students who draw logical conclusions about the causal relationship between economic systems and success in international trade.

Chapter 19 Resource Manager

SECTION RESOURCES

Daily Objectives	Reproducible Resources	Technology/Multimedia Resources
Section 1 **Economic Development** 1. State the concern for the plight of developing countries. 2. Identify the obstacles to economic development. 3. Compare per capita GNP among various countries and regions.	Reproducible Lesson Plan 19-1 Daily Lecture Notes 19-1 Guided Reading Activity 19-1 Reading Essentials and Study Guide 19-1 Section Quiz 19-1*	Daily Focus Transparency 88 Interactive Tutor Self-Assessment Software ExamView® Pro Testmaker Presentation Plus!
Section 2 **A Framework for Development** 1. Explain the stages of economic development. 2. Describe the steps industrialized countries can take to help developing countries. 3. Describe the steps developing countries can follow to help themselves.	Reproducible Lesson Plan 19-2 Daily Lecture Notes 19-2 Guided Reading Activity 19-2 Reading Essentials and Study Guide 19-2 Section Quiz 19-2*	Daily Focus Transparency 87 Interactive Tutor Self-Assessment Software ExamView® Pro Testmaker Presentation Plus!
Section 3 **Financing Economic Development** 1. Describe one internal and two external sources of funds for economic development. 2. Explain the role of international lending and developing agencies. 3. Explain how regional cooperation can assist economic growth.	Reproducible Lesson Plan 19-3 Daily Lecture Notes 19-3 Guided Reading Activity 19-3 Reading Essentials and Study Guide 19-3 Section Quiz 19-3*	Daily Focus Transparency 86 Vocabulary PuzzleMaker CD-ROM Interactive Tutor Self-Assessment Software ExamView® Pro Testmaker Presentation Plus!

 Transparency   CD-ROM   Software   Blackline Master   *Also available in Spanish*

Videodisc   Audio Program   Videocassette

0:00 OUT OF TIME?
Assign the Chapter 19 Audio Program activity and test.

Block Schedule
Activities that are particularly suited to use within the block scheduling framework are identified throughout this chapter by the following designation: **BLOCK SCHEDULING**

KEY TO ABILITY LEVELS

Teaching strategies have been coded for varying learning styles and abilities.
L1 **BASIC** activities for all students
L2 **AVERAGE** activities for average to above-average students
L3 **CHALLENGING** activities for above-average students
ELL **ENGLISH LANGUAGE LEARNER** activities

Chapter 19 Resource Manager

Timesaving Tools

TeacherWorks™ All-In-One Planner and Resource Center

- **Interactive Teacher Edition** Access your Teacher Wraparound Edition and your classroom resources with a few easy clicks.
- **Interactive Lesson Planner** Planning has never been easier! Organize your week, month, semester, or year with all the lesson helps you need to make teaching creative, timely, and relevant.

Use Glencoe's **Presentation Plus!** multimedia teacher tool to easily present dynamic lessons that visually excite your students. Using Microsoft PowerPoint® you can customize the presentations to create your own personalized lessons.

ACTIVITY

From the Classroom of...

Tom Glaser
School for Advanced Studies–Wolfson
Miami, FL

Infrastructure, Development, and the Decline of Socialism

Discuss what happens when a developing nation tries to compete with more established nations. **Ask:** What resources might a developing nation be lacking for it to be successful when doing business? What elements make up a country's infrastructure? (e.g., *good roads, bridges*). List these on the board. Discuss the effects of a lack of a good infrastructure on economic development.

Tell students that Marx thought that socialism would eventually win over capitalism, and that a command economy would give way to universal cooperation. What actually happens is that socialism, having served its purpose in forming an infrastructure, withers away, leaving capitalism as the system chosen by all free peoples, as it is the only system that deals with people as they are, not as someone may wish them to be.

Have students choose China, Russia, or another former socialist country, and write about its progress under and after socialism. Ask students if they believe the country they wrote about now has a strong enough infrastructure to compete with established nations.

National Council on Economic Education

THE **Economics**America AND **Economics**International PROGRAMS

Voluntary National Content Standards in Economics
Emphasized in Chapter 19

Content Standard 15

Content Standard 18

For a complete listing of NCEE Standards and entire text correlation, see Teacher pages in front of book.

Resources Available from NCEE
- Capstone: The Nation's High School Economics Course
- Focus: International Economics
- Geography: Focus on Economics
- World History: Focus on Economics

To order these materials or to contact your state Council on Economic Education about workshops and programs, call 1-800-338-1192 or visit www.nationalcouncil.org

Chapter 19 Resource Manager

TEACHING TRANSPARENCY

Economic Concept Transparency 22:
International Aspects of Growth and Stability

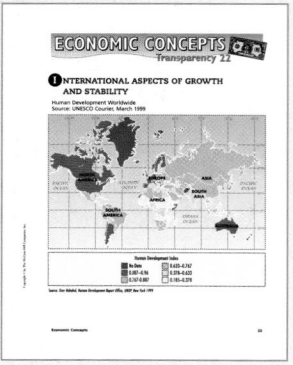

APPLICATION AND ENRICHMENT

Consumer Application Activity 24

Free Enterprise Activity 24

APPLICATION AND ENRICHMENT

Enrichment Activity 19

Cooperative Learning Activity 24

Math Practice Activity 24

Economic Cartoon 24

Primary and Secondary Source Reading 24

REVIEW AND REINFORCEMENT

Economic Vocabulary Activity 19

Reteaching Activity 19

Critical Thinking Activity 24

Reinforcing Economic Skill 13

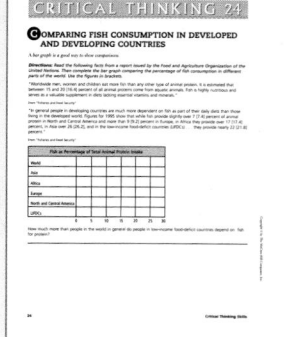

Chapter 19 Resource Manager

ASSESSMENT AND EVALUATION

Chapter 19 Test Form A

Chapter 19 Test Form B

Performance Assessment Activity 24

ExamView® Pro Testmaker

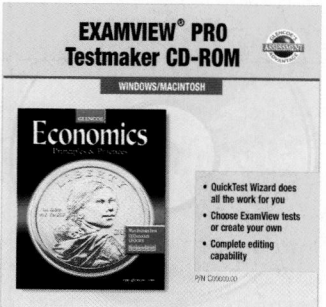

SPANISH RESOURCES

The following Spanish language materials are available in the Spanish Resources binder:

 Spanish Economic Vocabulary Activities

 Spanish Reteaching Activities

 Spanish Section Quizzes

 Spanish Economic Concepts Transparencies

Also available:

  Spanish Chapter 19 Audio Program Activity and Test

TECHNOLOGY/MULTIMEDIA

- Vocabulary PuzzleMaker CD-ROM
- Interactive Tutor Self-Assessment Software
- ExamView® Pro Testmaker
- Audio Program (English or Spanish)
- NBR Economics & You Video Program (English or Spanish)
- MindJogger Videoquiz
- Interactive Economics! CD-ROM
- Presentation Plus!
- TeacherWorks CD-ROM
- Glencoe Skillbuilder Interactive Workbook CD-ROM, Level 2

ECONOMICS Online

Use our Web site for additional resources. All essential content is covered in the Student Edition.

You and your students can visit epp.glencoe.com, the Web site companion to **Economics: Principles and Practices.** This innovative integration of electronic and print media offers your students a wealth of opportunities. The student text directs students to the Web site for the following options:

- **Chapter Overviews**
- **Student Web Activities**
- **Self-Check Quizzes**
- **Textbook Updates**

Answers are provided for you in the Web Activity Lesson Plan. Additional Web resources and interactive puzzles are also available.

Performance Assessment

Refer to Activity 24 in the *Performance Assessment Strategies and Activities* booklet.

 BLOCK SCHEDULING

ECONOMICS
Online

Introduce students to chapter content and key terms by having them access **Chapter Overview 19** at epp.glencoe.com

NIGHTLY
BUSINESS
R E P O R T

 ECONOMICS & YOU

 Chapter 26
Disc 1, Side 2

Developing Countries
After viewing this segment, students should be able to:
• Describe the general characteristics of developing countries' economies.

 Also available in VHS.

GLENCOE
TECHNOLOGY

Use **MindJogger Videoquiz** to preview the Chapter 19 content.

CHAPTER 19

Developing Countries

Economics & You

Read to find out how developing countries are working to increase their production and raise the standard of living of their people. To learn more about the economic challenges facing many nations, view the Chapter 26 video lesson:

Developing Countries

ECONOMICS
Online

Chapter Overview Visit the *Economics: Principles and Practices* Web site at epp.glencoe.com and click on **Chapter 19—Chapter Overviews** to preview chapter information.

Buyers and sellers meet at a produce market in the Vietnamese river town of Hoi An.

✚ EXTRA CREDIT PROJECT

Have students create a two-part data bank on the industrialized world and the developing world. Suggest that they include statistics on such topics as GDP, population growth, health and life expectancy, natural resources, education and technology, and so on. Have students compare their data banks, and analyze the effects of their topics on the economy (ie. productivity, marketing, manufacturing, and distribution).

Economic Development

Study Guide

Main Idea
Developing countries face a number of obstacles that make economic growth extremely difficult.

Reading Strategy
Graphic Organizer As you read the section, complete a graphic organizer similar to the one below by providing at least two reasons why it would probably be more difficult to bring about change in a traditional economic system than in a developed country.

> The difficulty of change in a traditional economy → ☐ ☐

Key Terms
developing country, crude birthrate, life expectancy, zero population growth (ZPG), external debt, default, capital flight, International Monetary Fund, World Bank

Objectives
After studying this section, you will be able to:
1. **State** the concern for the plight of the developing countries.
2. **Identify** the obstacles to economic development.
3. **Compare** per capita GNP among various countries and regions.

Applying Economic Concepts
Life Expectancy Are there any downsides to longer life expectancies? Read to find out how a longer life expectancy affects the quality of life in developing countries.

① FOCUS

Section Overview
This section identifies the obstacles to economic development.

BELLRINGER
Motivational Activity

Project **transparency** and have students answer questions.

Available as blackline master.

Daily Focus Transparency 88

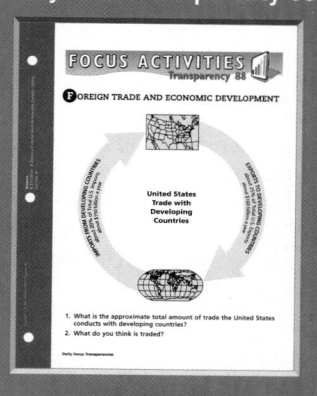

Cover Story

The Casualties Don't Stop When the War Does

Anti-personnel (AP) land mines have become the world's largest source of war-related injuries. According to the International Committee of the Red Cross, mines kill 800 people every month and another 1,200 are maimed—a total of 2,000 victims a month—one person every 20 minutes.

Mine detecting in Cambodia

Low cost and easy availability have made anti-personnel land mines the weapons of choice in the developing world. The United Nations estimates that there are currently tens of millions of anti-personnel land mines buried in more than 70 countries . . . approximately one mine for every 50 people on earth. . . .

Land mines cost as little as $3 (U.S.) to produce and up to $1,000 to remove. For every 5,000 mines cleared, one de-miner is killed and two are injured.

—*PALM Physicians Against Land Mines*, August, 1999

Most of the people in the world today live in **developing countries**—countries whose average per capita GNP is a fraction of that in more industrialized countries. Most developing countries are located in Africa, Asia, and Latin America.

In many ways, developing economies are similar to other economies of the world. The major difference is that their problems are much greater. Some problems faced by developing countries, such as the residual effects of war highlighted in the cover story, are so serious that some developing nations may never reach their potential.

Interest in Economic Development

Economists know that all nations are better off when they produce and trade the products in which they have a comparative advantage. Even so, the international community's concern for the developing countries is humanitarian as well as economic and political.

CHAPTER 19: DEVELOPING COUNTRIES **521**

Study Guide

Reading Strategy
Have students create the graphic organizer.
Answers to Graphic: *population growth, limited natural resources, lack of education and technology, external debt, capital flight, corruption, war and its aftermath*

Preteaching Vocabulary
Direct students to find definitions of the Key Terms in the Glossary.

RESOURCE MANAGER

📂 Reproducible Masters
- Reproducible Lesson Plan 19-1
- Daily Lecture Notes 19-1
- Guided Reading Activity 19-1
- Reading Essentials and Study Guide 19-1
- Section Quiz 19-1

🖨 Transparencies
- Daily Focus Transparency 88

Multimedia
- 💾 Interactive Tutor Self-Assessment Software
- 💿 ExamView® Pro Testmaker
- 💿 Presentation Plus!

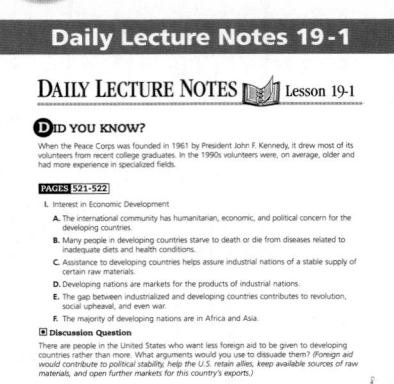
L1 Obstacles to Development

Have students help create a web to organize the obstacles to development discussed in this section. Place the phrase "obstacles to development" in a circle on the board, then draw lines away from it connecting to more circles, each containing an obstacle. Have students volunteer to fill in the circles. Discuss each obstacle as it is included in the web.

L2 Applying Ideas

Refer students to Figure 19.1 and have each student select a developing nation. Students should conduct research to discover the most problematic obstacles to economic development for their selected nation. Suggest that students present their findings in a brief written report.

Concern for Developing Countries

Industrialized countries of the world often believe it is their moral responsibility to help those who have less than they do. Assistance to developing countries helps assure the industrial nations of a stable supply of critical raw materials. In turn, developing countries also provide markets for the products of industrial nations.

Politics are also important. Despite the dramatic failure of communism in some countries, various political ideologies wage a continuing struggle for the allegiance of developing countries.

Per Capita Income

Today more than 1.2 billion people exist on an income of less than $1 a day. According to **Figure 19.1**, the majority of these people are in Africa and Asia. The map contrasts the income of the industrialized nations and the developing nations, scaling each country to show the size of its total GNP. Recall that GNP is a measure of *income*, while GDP is a measure of output relative to other countries. Thus, the United States, which has the largest total income in the world, is the largest area on the map. Countries with smaller GNPs are scaled accordingly.

The map is also color coded to show countries with similar per capita GNPs. When viewed this way, the contrast is clearly shown between the industrialized economies of North America, Western Europe, and Japan, and the developing countries of South America, the Caribbean, Africa, and Asia. The gap between industrialized and developing countries is enormous. If anything, the gap is getting larger, rather than smaller.

Obstacles to Development

Before examining some of the possible solutions to the plight of developing countries, we need to take a closer look at some common problems and challenges.

Population Growth

One obstacle to economic development is population growth. The populations of most developing

ECONOMICS AT A GLANCE

Greenland

Canada

United States

Bermuda

Barbado

Mexico

Bahamas — Aruba

Virgin Islands (US)

Belize — Trinidad and Tobago — Cuba — Dominican Republic — Puerto Rico (US

Honduras — Jamaica

Guatemala — Nicaragua — Netherlands — Haiti

El Salvador — Costa Rica — Antilles

Guyana — Grenada

Panama — Venezuela — Suriname

Colombia — French Guiana

Ecuador — Brazil — St. Vincent

St. Lucia

Peru — Martinique (Fr)

Uruguay — Dominica

Bolivia — Paraguay — Guadeloupe

Chile — Antigua and Barbuda

Argentina — St. Kitts and Nevis

GNP Per Capita

$27,000 +	$1,500 to $3,500
$23,000 to $27,000	$500 to $1,500
$15,000 to $23,000	under $500
$6,000 to $15,000	no data
$3,500 to $6,000	

Source: *The World Bank Atlas*

Figure 19.1

CHAPTER 19
Section 1, pages 521–526

Gross National Product and Gross National Product Per Capita

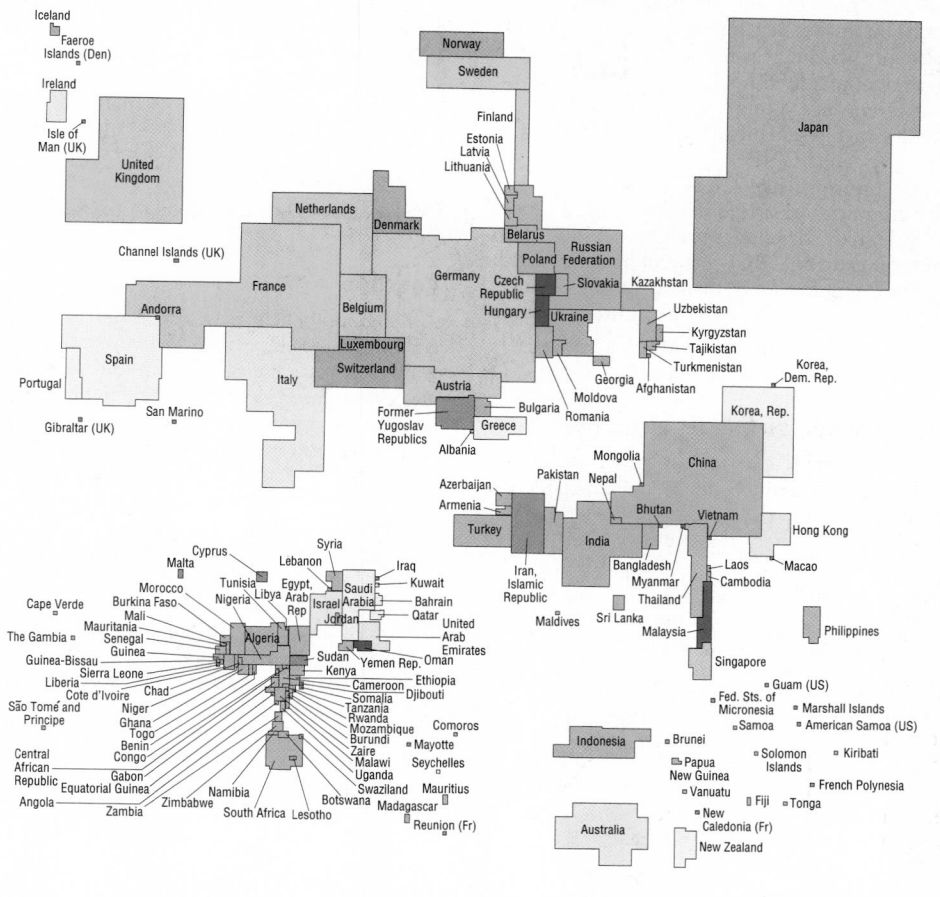

Reading Maps If every nation's land area were proportional to its Gross National Product, the world would look like the map in this figure. When GDP is computed on a per capita basis, we get another view of a nation's productivity. **Which nations have a per capita GNP equal to or larger than that of the United States?**

CHAPTER 19: DEVELOPING COUNTRIES **523**

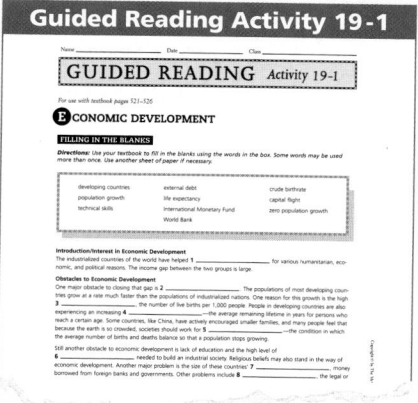

ECONOMICS AT A GLANCE

Answer: *Norway, Denmark, Iceland, Switzerland, Japan, Luxembourg*

THE GLOBAL ECONOMY

Distance Learning Developing countries must provide higher education in order to stimulate growth and raise per capita GNP, but often they cannot afford the cost of establishing and maintaining college campuses. Distance education, conducted through television, videotape, the Internet, E-mail, listservs, teleconferences, and traditional print correspondence, is a solution many developing countries have embraced. These nations have found that distance education is economically advantageous, facilitates lifelong learning, and fosters globalization.

FREE ENTERPRISE ACTIVITY

Have students imagine that they are successful entrepreneurs in the U.S. and that they wish to expand and establish a branch of their business in a developing country. Encourage these entrepreneurs to prepare a business plan that discusses the opportunities and obstacles presented by opening a business in that developing nation. Select students to present and explain their plans to the class.

CURRICULUM CONNECTION

History Initially, the purpose of the World Bank was to assist in the reconstruction of Europe. Although that task was accomplished with the Marshall Plan, the World Bank soon became the leading development aid agency.

L3 Capital Flight

China and Russia have both experienced capital flight recently as a result of foreign investments. China has profited, experiencing rapid growth in its foreign ventures, while Russia has not. Russia's foreign investments are growing slowly. Have students use the Internet to research the economic reasons and results of capital flight in these two nations. Then have them present their findings to the class using visual aids such as graphs and charts.

F.Y.I.

Nine of every 10 children born today are born in developing nations. In the last 20 years of the twentieth century, the number of people 20 to 40 years of age increased by an estimated 630 million in developing nations, compared to about 20 million in industrialized nations.

countries grow at a rate much faster than the populations of industrialized countries. One reason for this growth is the high **crude birthrate**—the number of live births per 1,000 people.

People in many developing countries are also experiencing an increasing **life expectancy**—the average remaining lifetime in years for persons who reach a certain age. Longer life expectancies, coupled with a high crude birthrate, make it difficult to increase per capita GNP.

Some countries, like China, have encouraged lower birth rates and smaller families. Some people even feel that societies should work for **zero population growth (ZPG)**—the condition in which the average number of births and deaths balance. Others feel efforts to disrupt population growth are wrong from both moral and religious perspectives.

Natural Resources and Geography

Another obstacle to economic growth is limited natural resources, which includes unproductive land and harsh climates. A shortage of natural and energy sources needed for industry also hinder growth.

In some cases, countries with limited natural resources can make up for the deficiency by engaging in international trade, as Japan has done. However, if a country is landlocked, trade is much more difficult. It is no accident that all of the major economic powers today have long had coastal cities with access to major trade routes.

Education and Technology

Still another obstacle to economic development is a lack of appropriate education and technology. Many developing countries do not have a highly literate population nor do they have the high level of technical skills needed to build an industrial society. In addition, most do not have money to train engineers and scientists.

Many developing countries cannot afford to provide free public education for school-age children. In those that can, not everyone is able to take advantage of it because children must work to help feed their families.

Religion

Religious beliefs may also stand in the way of economic development. While almost everyone realizes that capital investment and new technologies can help economic growth, some people may not be interested for religious reasons. In the United States, for example, many Mennonites have long rejected these advances on religious grounds.

In Asia, most Hindus and Buddhists believe that life is governed by a fate called karma; they believe that people are caught up in an eternal cycle of life, death, and rebirth. The Hindus believe that the eternal cycle can be broken, in part, by purifying the mind and body through living a simple and austere lifestyle. The Buddhists believe that the way to break the cycle is to extinguish desire and reject the temptations of the material world. Consequently, many Hindus and Buddhists—representing approximately 20 percent of the world's population—have little motivation to improve their material well-being.

The teachings of Catholicism, Protestantism, and Judaism are much more compatible with the concept of economic growth and material improvement, while the Islamic world is in between the Christians and the Hindus. We must realize, however, that some cultures may not be as interested in the Western concept of economic growth and development as we imagine.

External Debt

Another major problem facing the developing nations today is the size of their **external**

CRITICAL THINKING

Identifying Alternatives Many natural resources are being depleted as the world's population grows. In the past thirty years, the world's forests have decreased from 4.4 to 2.8 square miles per 1,000 people. Similarly, 25 percent of the world's fishes have been depleted. Many of these resources are found in developing nations. Have students identify ways a developing nation might benefit from continued, uncontrolled use of resources, and ways such nations might be harmed. Then have them write a brief essay detailing the problem and examining alternative actions that might allow continued economic growth with less harm to the world's resources.

debt—money borrowed from foreign banks and governments. Some nations have borrowed so much they may never be able to repay loans.

Today a number of developing countries—Bulgaria, Cameroon, the Ivory Coast, Ethiopia, Honduras, Jordan, Madagascar, Syria, and Tanzania—all have external debts larger than their GNP. Sudan and Zambia have external debts more than twice their GDP, and Angola's external debt is *three* times larger than its GDP.

When debts get this large, countries have trouble even paying interest on the loans. As a result, some developing nations have teetered on the brink of **default**, or not repaying borrowed money. Even this strategy is dangerous, however, because a country that defaults on its loans may not be able to borrow again.

Capital Flight

Another problem for developing nations is **capital flight**—the legal or illegal export of a nation's currency and foreign exchange. Capital flight occurs because people lose faith in their government or in the future of their economy. When capital flight occurs, businesses and even the government often face a cash shortage. At a minimum, capital flight limits the funds available for domestic capital investment.

Even private citizens can contribute to capital flight. Suppose that someone in Moscow wants to turn rubles into dollars. First, the person would go to several banks and purchase traveler's checks. Next, the individual would destroy the checks and then fly to New York. Third, the checks would be declared as being lost or stolen so that they can be redeemed in the U.S. for dollars.

Corruption

Corruption at any level of government is an obstacle to economic development. Sometimes corruption takes the form of minor officials requiring modest bribes to get even the smallest things done. At other times, corruption occurs on a massive scale.

When Ferdinand Marcos was president of the Philippines, foreign investors poured billions into the country's economy. Years later, however, the majority of Filipinos still lived in poverty. Officials later charged that Marcos had stolen at least $500 million from the nation and deposited the money in personal Swiss bank accounts.

When the Soviet Union began to collapse in the late 1980s and early 1990s, the Communist party took billions of dollars out of its own accounts, government-owned enterprises, and even its own central bank and deposited the money in various Swiss, European, and American banks. At the time, the Soviet secret police used a sophisticated network of trade delegations, central bank offices, and even Soviet embassies to move the money abroad—money that could have been used to modernize the Russian economy after the fall of communism.

War and Its Aftermath

Unfortunately, many of the developing nations of the world—Angola, Afghanistan, Egypt, Ethiopia, Cambodia, Somalia, and Vietnam to name just a few—were the scenes of bloody civil wars in the late 1900s. The immediate impact of war is the devastating loss of lives and property, not to mention the damage to the country's infrastructure.

Education

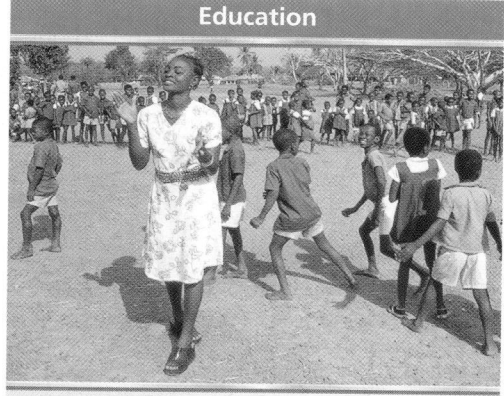

Developing Nations Although enrollment in schools, and the literacy rate, are improving in developing nations, many lack basic educational tools. *What is the status of free public education in developing countries?*

CHAPTER 19: DEVELOPING COUNTRIES **525**

Visual Instruction

Answer to Caption:
Many developing countries cannot afford to offer free public education, and many children cannot take advantage of available education because they need to work to help feed their families.

③ ASSESS

Assign Section 1 Assessment as homework or as an in-class activity.

💾 Have students use **Interactive Tutor Self-Assessment Software** to review Section 1.

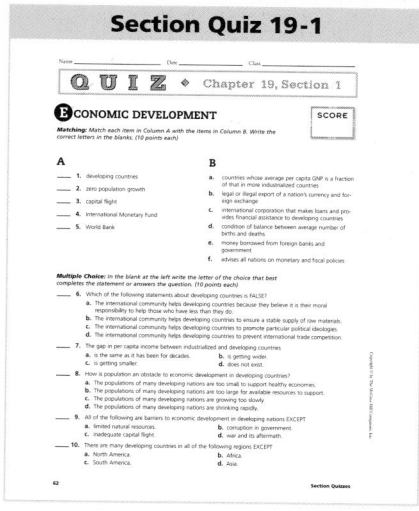

EXTENDING THE CONTENT

Using GNP Instead of GDP For purposes of international comparisons, economists like to use GNP rather than GDP. GNP is a measure of the total *income* earned by all citizens in a country, whereas GDP is a measure of total *output* produced within national boundaries. If GDP were used instead of GNP, then relatively poor countries with large foreign-owned investments would appear to be more prosperous than they really are.

Objectives, goals, and answers to
the student activity can be found
in the **Web Activity Lesson Plan**
feature at epp.glencoe.com

Reteach

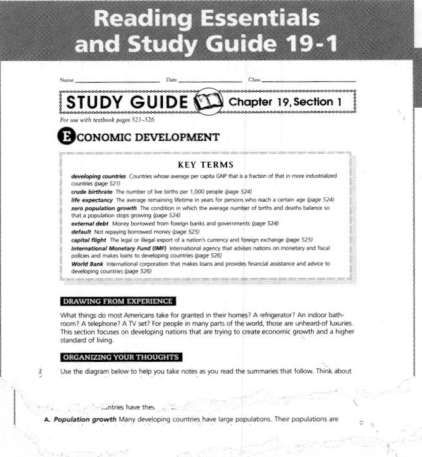

Enrich

Have students write either a pro
or con essay on the following
statement: Encouraging economic
growth in developing nations can
help economic growth in the
U.S. Call on students from both
positions to read their essays to
the class.

CLOSE

Ask students to identify and explain
which of the obstacles discussed in
the section they think constitutes
the greatest barrier to economic
development.

526

The aftermath of war can linger for decades. Poland lost virtually all of its *intelligentsia*–its scientists, engineers, and even most of its merchant class–to the gas chambers and concentration camps in World War II. The loss of this talent contributed to the slow recovery of the Polish economy after the war, and even hindered its economic development after the fall of communism.

The widespread use of chemical weapons and land mines make simple activities like farming extremely difficult in many areas. Moreover, many of the people injured by these weapons, such as children playing in fields, were not participants in the war in the first place. The weapons of war–as discussed in the cover story–often impede economic development long after the war is over.

International Agencies

The problems of the developing countries have not gone unnoticed by the more successful countries of the world. Two agencies, in particular, work directly with developing nations to solve their problems.

The **International Monetary Fund (IMF)** offers advice to all nations on monetary and fiscal policies. It also helps support the currency of some developing nations with loans so that the countries can compete in an open market and attract foreign investors.

Another important international lending and development agency is the World Bank Group, more commonly known as the **World Bank.** The World Bank is an international corporation that makes loans and provides financial assistance and advice to developing countries. The World Bank is owned by IMF member nations, but it operates as a separate organization.

Recently, the World Bank has undertaken projects to control the desert locust in East Africa. It also has funded projects to develop inland water transportation in Bangladesh, rural transportation systems in Vietnam, and even tax modernization in Kazakhstan.

Student Web Activity Visit the *Economics: Principles and Practices* Web site at epp.glencoe.com and click on *Chapter 19—Student Web Activities* for an activity on the International Monetary Fund.

Section 1 Assessment

Checking for Understanding
1. **Main Idea** Describe what a developing country is and some of the economic problems it may experience.
2. **Key Terms** Define developing country, crude birthrate, life expectancy, zero population growth, external debt, default, capital flight, International Monetary Fund, World Bank.
3. **List** three reasons why there is concern for the plight of developing countries.
4. **List** eight factors that may be obstacles to economic development.
5. **Compare** the per capita GNP of Algeria with that of Argentina.

Applying Economic Concepts
6. **Life Expectancy** Explain why an official of a developing nation would have both positive and negative views of increasing life expectancy.

Critical Thinking
7. **Identifying Alternatives** Suppose you are an official in charge of economic development in a developing country. Choose the first two obstacles to economic development that you would address. Then tell why you would tackle them first.

 Practice and **assess** key social studies skills with the *Glencoe Skillbuilder Interactive Workbook, Level 2.*

Section 1 Assessment Answers

1. a country whose average GNP is a fraction of that in more industrialized countries; economic problems more severe
2. All vocabulary terms are defined in the text.
3. humanitarian, economic, and political
4. population growth, limited natural resources, lack of appropriate education and technology, external debt, capital flight, government that changes often, religious beliefs, corrupt governments, war and its aftermath
5. Argentina's is higher.
6. Increasing life expectancy leads to a larger workforce and may increase productivity. However, an increased population requires more food, shelter, and clothing; decreases the per capita GNP; and costs the government more for elderly health care and social services.
7. Answers should show understanding of problems hindering economic development.

Profiles IN Economics

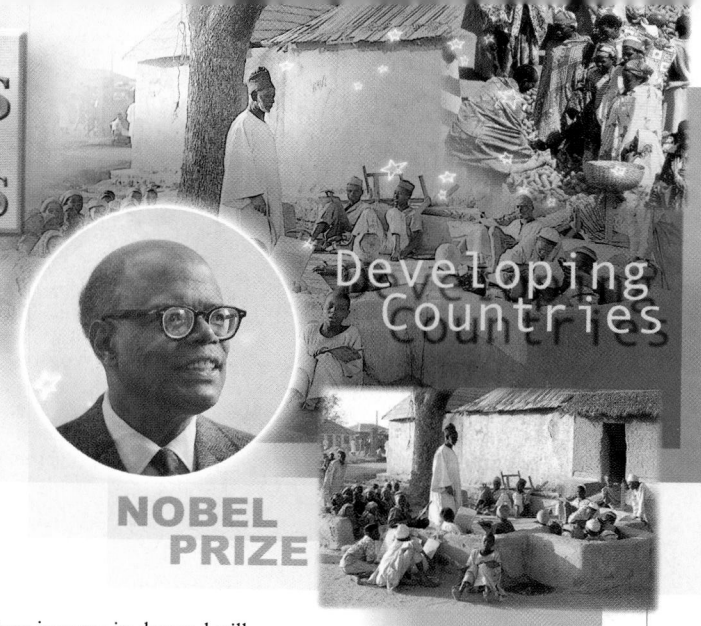

Opening Doors:
W. Arthur Lewis
(1915–1991)

Economist Sir W. Arthur Lewis achieved many firsts. After attending school in his native St. Lucia, he earned a scholarship to attend the London School of Economics (LSE) where, in 1937, he graduated first in his class. Soon after, while working on a Ph.D. in economics, he became the first black to receive an assistant lectureship at the LSE. In 1979 he became the first black to win the Nobel Prize in economics (jointly with Theodore Schultz). Lewis's prize-winning work focused on the economic problems of developing nations.

INSIGHT INTO DEVELOPING NATIONS

In particular, Lewis challenged the prevailing view that the supply of labor in developing nations is upward sloping, so that an increase in the demand for labor results in an increase in wages. Real wages, noted Lewis, tend to stay at low levels in many developing nations regardless of the increases in demand for labor. The only solution, he reasoned, is that the supply curve for labor has to be perfectly elastic—or horizontal rather than upward sloping—so

that an increase in demand will leave wages unchanged. His theory explains why countries such as Sri Lanka are still underdeveloped, although they have been developing for nearly 100 years.

Lewis did not claim to have solved the problems of the developing countries. His contributions, however, have made existing economic models and theory more applicable to realistic conditions.

"HOW I CONDUCT MYSELF"

Lewis explained how he felt about his illustrious career:

"I had never meant to be an economist. . . . What was this economics? I had never heard of it before, and nobody in St. Lucia knew what it was . . . ," he recalled. "Looking backward . . . I have lived through a period of transition. . . . I have been subject to all the usual disabilities—refusal of accommodations, denial of jobs for which I had

been recommended, generalized discourtesy, and the rest of it. All the same, some doors that were supposed to be closed opened as I approached them. I have got used to being the first black to do this or that, which gets to be more difficult as the transition opens up new opportunities. Having to be a role model is a bit of a strain, but I try to remember that others are coming after me, and that whether the door will be shut in their faces as they approach will depend to some small extent on how I conduct myself."

Examining the Profile

1. **Demonstrating Reasoned Judgment** Why might an increase in demand for labor not increase the wage rate in developing countries?

2. **Drawing Conclusions** What does Lewis mean by "the usual disabilities" he faced?

Profiles IN Economics

BACKGROUND

To many people, the economic problems faced by developing countries top the list of problems that face the world today. These economic problems are at the root of widespread human suffering. The magnitude of the suffering is difficult for many people in the wealthy United States to imagine. Thus, the contributions of economists like W. Arthur Lewis are more than abstract ideas. They can and do have real-world results that improve and sometimes literally save the lives of millions of people. Lewis, then, is known not only as an economist, but also as a humanitarian.

TEACH

Write the following terms on the board: *nationality, race, historical period, economic status.* Have students identify Lewis according to these categories, and then lead a discussion of Lewis's accomplishments in light of his circumstances. Challenge students to connect Lewis's background with that of the people he helped through his economic analysis.

Answers to Examining the Profile

1. According to Lewis, the supply of labor is perfectly elastic—in graphic terms, a horizontal line rather than an upward sloping line. Therefore, wages would remain at the same level, unchanged, regardless of the demand for labor.

2. Answers will vary. Lewis refers to "refusal of accommodations, denial of jobs . . . , generalized discourtesy. . . ." He is referring to racism.

① FOCUS

Section Overview

This section provides a framework for economic development in developing countries.

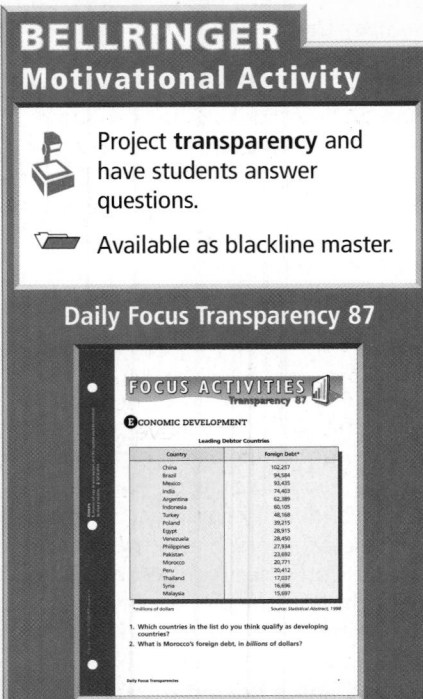

Study Guide

Reading Strategy

Have students create the graphic organizer.
Answers to Graphic: *primitive equilibrium, transition, takeoff, semidevelopment, high development*

Preteaching Vocabulary

Direct students to locate the Key Terms in the text. Then have them use each term in a sentence.

A Framework for Development

Study Guide

Main Idea
Economists suggest that developing nations have several ways of achieving their economic growth.

Reading Strategy
Graphic Organizer As you read the section, complete a graphic organizer similar to the one below by listing the stages of economic development. Then describe what occurs during each of the stages.

Key Terms
primitive equilibrium, takeoff

Objectives
After studying this section, you will be able to:
1. **Explain** the stages of economic development.
2. **Describe** the steps industrialized countries can take to help developing countries.
3. **Describe** the steps developing countries can follow to help themselves.

Applying Economic Concepts
Primitive Equilibrium Have you ever had a day during which nothing much was attempted and nothing much got done? Read to find out why this type of equilibrium is a stage that developing economies sometimes go through.

Cover Story

Easing the Debt Burden

COLOGNE, Germany—Leaders from the Group of Seven industrial nations agreed Friday to cut the debt burden of the world's poorest countries in what they described as a decisive push to alleviate poverty.

President Jacques Chirac of France said the relief, mainly for African countries, could total about $65 billion . . . [but] the amount could approach $90 billion if other creditors joined the initiative.

Some loans—about $15 billion worth—would be canceled outright, and mechanisms would be put in place to evaluate the countries for other forms of debt relief, based on future economic reforms.

Market in Burundi

—*The New York Times*, June 19, 1999

528

Because the problems of the developing nations are so great, economic development is a formidable task. Many approaches have been tried, and others, such as the one described in the cover story, have much promise.

Stages of Economic Development

Some economists have suggested that developing countries normally pass through several stages on their way to economic development. Others argue that the process is not uniform for all countries. Even so, it is helpful to think of economic development as occurring in stages, even if the boundaries between these stages are not always clear-cut.

Primitive Equilibrium

The first stage toward economic development is **primitive equilibrium.** It is "primitive" in the sense that the society has no formal economic organization. An example would be the Inuit of

---

RESOURCE MANAGER

📁 Reproducible Masters
- Reproducible Lesson Plan 19-2
- Daily Lecture Notes 19-2
- Guided Reading Activity 19-2
- Reading Essentials and Study Guide 19-2
- Section Quiz 19-2

🖥 Transparencies
- Daily Focus Transparency 87

Multimedia
- 💾 Interactive Tutor Self-Assessment Software
- ⊙ ExamView® Pro Testmaker
- ⊙ Presentation Plus!

Did you know?

Population Explosion Over the next 30 years, almost 98 percent of population growth is projected to take place in developing countries.

the past century, who shared the spoils of the hunt with other families in the village.

A people—or country—in primitive equilibrium often have no monetary system and may not be economically motivated. No capital investment takes place, and the society is in equilibrium because nothing changes. Rules are handed down from one generation to the next, and culture and tradition direct economic decision making.

Transition

The second stage of economic development is one of transition. It consists of a break with primitive equilibrium and a move toward economic and cultural changes. The break may be brief and sudden, or it may take years. A country does not grow economically in this transition stage, but old customs begin to crumble. People begin to question their traditions, and they try new patterns of living.

Takeoff

The third stage of development—**takeoff**—is not reached until the barriers of primitive equilibrium are overcome. A country in the takeoff stage begins to grow more rapidly than before. One reason is that customs have been put aside, and people have begun to seek new and better ways of doing things. Another reason is that the people have begun to imitate the new or different techniques that outsiders have brought into the country. Still another reason is that an industrial nation may be providing financial, educational, or military aid.

During the takeoff stage, a country starts to save and invest more of its national income. New industries grow rapidly, and profits are reinvested in them. Industry uses new production techniques, and agricultural productivity greatly improves.

Semidevelopment

The fourth stage is semidevelopment. In it, the makeup of the country's economy changes. National income grows faster than population, which leads to higher per capita income. At the same time, the core of the country's industry is built. The nation spends heavily on capital investment, and technological advances are made.

High Development

The final stage of development is high development. In this stage, efforts to obtain food, shelter, and clothing are more than successful. Most people have their basic needs and wants met. They turn their attention to services and consumer goods such as washing machines, refrigerators, and video equipment.

The nation no longer emphasizes industrial production. Instead, it increases services and provides more public goods. Mature service and

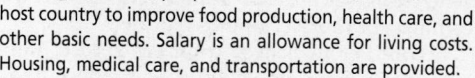

Careers

Peace Corps Volunteer

Are you willing to work for minimal pay in unfamiliar surroundings? Are you a dedicated individual who can work effectively with people?

The Work

Peace Corps volunteers take on two-year assignments overseas. They receive eight to 14 weeks of training in the history, culture, and language of the country in which they will serve. Duties include working with the people of the host country to improve food production, health care, and other basic needs. Salary is an allowance for living costs. Housing, medical care, and transportation are provided.

Qualifications

College training is not required, but assignments may be made on the basis of the volunteer's experience and skills. Volunteers must be U.S. citizens and at least 18 years old.

CHAPTER 19: DEVELOPING COUNTRIES **529**

Daily Lecture Notes 19-2

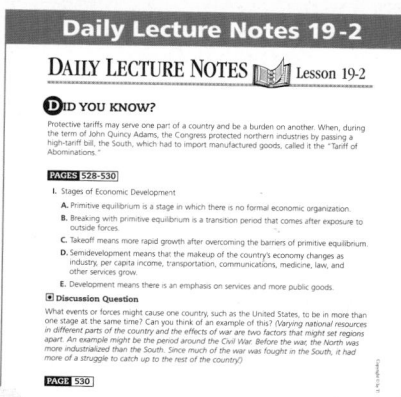

DAILY LECTURE NOTES Lesson 19-2

DID YOU KNOW?
Protective tariffs may serve one part of a country and be a burden on another. When, during the term of John Quincy Adams, the Congress protected northern industries by passing a high-tariff bill, the South, which had to import manufactured goods, called it the "Tariff of Abominations."

PAGES 528–530

I. Stages of Economic Development
   A. Primitive equilibrium is a stage in which there is no formal economic organization.
   B. Breaking with primitive equilibrium is a transition period that comes after exposure to outside forces.
   C. Takeoff means more rapid growth after overcoming the barriers of primitive equilibrium.
   D. Semidevelopment means that the makeup of the country's economy changes as industry, per capita income, transportation, communications, medicine, law, and other services grow.
   E. Development means there is an emphasis on services and more public goods.

Discussion Question
What events or forces might cause one country, such as the United States, to be in more than one stage at the same time? Can you think of an example of this? (Varying national resources in different parts of the country and the effects of war are two factors that might set regions apart. An example might be the period around the Civil War. Before the war, the North was more industrialized than the South. Since much of the war was fought in the South, it had more of a struggle to catch up to the rest of the country.)

PAGE 530

L2 Publicity Campaign

Call on students to identify the priorities for industrialized countries and for developing countries in promoting economic development. Have students work in small groups to develop a publicity campaign to inform industrialized and developing countries about the steps they should take to encourage development. Have groups present their campaigns.

Guided Reading Activity 19-2

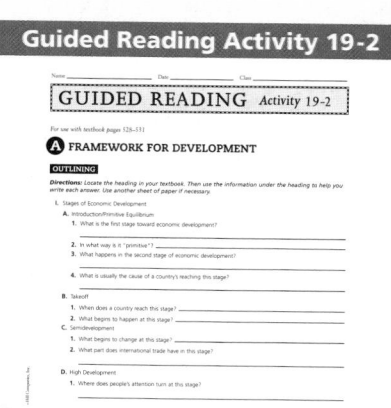

GUIDED READING Activity 19-2

For use with textbook pages 528–531

A FRAMEWORK FOR DEVELOPMENT

OUTLINING

Directions: Locate the heading in your textbook. Then use the information under the heading to help you write each answer. Use another sheet of paper if necessary.

I. Stages of Economic Development
   A. Introduction/Primitive Equilibrium
      1. What is the first stage toward economic development?
      2. In what way is it "primitive"?
      3. What happens in the second stage of economic development?
      4. What is usually the cause of a country's reaching this stage?
   B. Takeoff
      1. When does a country reach this stage?
      2. What begins to happen at this stage?
   C. Semidevelopment
      1. What begins to change at this stage?
      2. What part does international trade have in this stage?
   D. High Development
      1. Where does people's attention turn at this stage?

MEETING SPECIAL NEEDS ACTIVITY

Learning Disabled For students with attention deficit disorder, keep in mind that inattention is sometimes caused by the difficulty of the material that confronts the students. It is easier for a student to pay attention if he or she is working at an appropriate instructional level (only 5 to 10 percent of the material is new). Have students preview Section 2 to assess components that might be difficult for them. Discuss with them what factors might affect their ability to maintain attention.

Refer to **Inclusion for the Social Studies Classroom Strategies and Activities** in the TCR.

The New Peace Corps More than one thousand Peace Corps volunteers serve in business-related positions in more than fifty countries. Their work includes advising and developing small businesses, nongovernmental organizational development, and urban and regional planning.

Answers:

1. *It is becoming more diversified and attracting volunteers who want to obtain skills to further their own careers as well as to help others.*

2. *to gain experience in the business world before obtaining a job in the U.S. and to help the world*

 ASSESS

Assign Section 2 Assessment as homework or as an in-class activity.

💾 Have students use **Interactive Tutor Self-Assessment Software** to review Section 2.

Section Quiz 19-2

THE GLOBAL ECONOMY

THE NEW PEACE CORPS

On March 1, 1961, President Kennedy signed an executive order establishing the Peace Corps. Since then, tens of thousands of volunteers have served in the villages, towns, and cities of more than 130 countries.

In the past, it was easy to spot Peace Corps volunteers. They wore Birkenstocks and loose-fitting, gauzy garb. They often had wide-eyed notions of saving the world. To many of them, "capitalism" was a four-letter word.

No more. Today's Peace Corps volunteers—80 percent of whom are in their 20s—still want to help the world, but they also want to help themselves. Many volunteers have business degrees and view the Peace Corps as a two-year internship, culminating with a return home to a job with a top company.

What better way to gain experience than by helping a developing nation get its corporate feet on the ground?

"I'm definitely joining to improve my skills for a better job," said Beth Atkinson, 22, who recently received a bachelor's degree in business administration from Indiana Wesleyan University. Next month, she heads for Mali in West Africa to help craftsmen and entrepreneurs form businesses. "You hear a lot of talk about global business, and I thought there's no better way to go than this," she said.

—*The New York Times,* July 18, 1999

Critical Thinking

1. **Analyzing Information** According to the article, in what way is the Peace Corps changing?

2. **Understanding Cause and Effect** For what reasons are young people joining the Peace Corps?

---

manufacturing sectors are signs of a highly developed economy.

Priorities for Industrialized Nations

The World Bank has become a powerful force in economic development because it often requires that countries actually make market reforms as a condition for obtaining a loan. Because of its considerable experience with developing nations, the World Bank has a list of recommendations for both developing and industrialized countries.

First, trade barriers, especially nontariff barriers, need to be reduced or eliminated. The World Bank has estimated that eliminating trade barriers would generate as much as $50 billion annually in export earnings for the developing countries.

Second, industrialized countries need to implement macroeconomic policies that reduce budget deficits, lower interest rates, and stabilize inflation and foreign currency fluctuations. This would help the economic development of all types of economies. When industrialized economies grow,

their increased international trade often includes, and benefits, the developing economies.

Third, the industrialized nations need to provide more external financing to the developing countries. This financing could be direct aid, or it could be indirect aid to international agencies.

Fourth, the industrial economies need to support the economic development of developing countries. Traditionally, the majority of United States foreign aid has been granted to achieve political aims. Between one-half and two-thirds of all U.S. foreign aid has been used for military supplies and training, either directly or indirectly.

Priorities for the Developing Countries

As mentioned earlier, the World Bank also has a list of recommendations for the developing countries. The developing countries face the responsibility for directing their own economic development and future.

FREE ENTERPRISE ACTIVITY

Ask students to imagine that they have been hired as economic consultants to a developing country that is in the takeoff stage of economic development. Have students use the World Bank recommendations as the basis for a plan that would encourage economic growth and development in the country. Call on students to share and explain their plans.

First, governments in developing countries need to invest more in people—education, family planning, nutrition, and health care. The wealth of any nation, as Adam Smith wrote, resides in the strength and vitality of its people.

Second, improve the climate of free enterprise. Many price controls, subsidies, and other regulations that restrict the free development of markets should be removed. The World Bank suggests that competitive markets—not politicians—make the WHAT, HOW, and FOR WHOM allocation decisions.

Third, open economies to free trade. Many developing economies have quotas, tariffs, and other barriers that are used to protect domestic jobs and infant industries. At the same time, however, the trade barriers protect inefficient industries and depress a country's standard of living. Countries that open their markets to the world will benefit from comparative advantage and will ultimately develop competitive specialties of their own.

Fourth, developing countries, like the industrialized ones, need to follow policies that curb

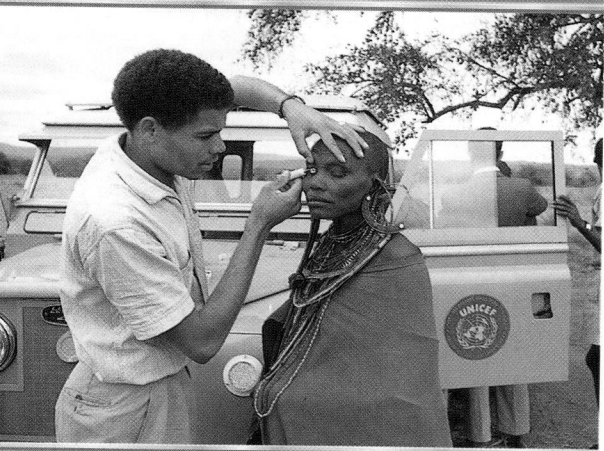

Investment in People

Priorities Investment in basic health care is an important priority for developing nations. *What is the reasoning for investing in people?*

inflation, reduce borrowing, and decrease deficits. Their policies also must allow market incentives such as profits, so that the economies can begin to sustain their own growth.

Visual Instruction

Answer to Caption:
The wealth of any nation resides in the strength and vitality of its people.

Reteach

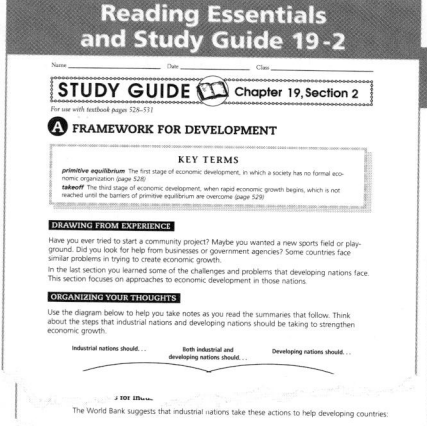

Reading Essentials and Study Guide 19-2

Enrich

Have students write a book report on W. W. Rostow's *The Stages of Economic Growth* (Cambridge University Press, 1971). Suggest that they focus their report on a comparison between Rostow's stages and the stages described in this section.

CLOSE

Have students discuss the most important steps the U.S. can take to encourage economic growth in developing nations.

Section 2 Assessment

Checking for Understanding

1. **Main Idea** Describe the nature of economic development. Does development happen all at once? Explain.

2. **Key Terms** Define primitive equilibrium, takeoff.

3. **List** the stages of economic development.

4. **Describe** what actions industrialized countries can take to help developing countries.

5. **Describe** recommendations that the World Bank has for developing countries.

Applying Economic Concepts

6. **Primitive Equilibrium** Imagine that a society is in primitive equilibrium—nothing is changing internally to begin economic development. Describe an event that could be a potential source of change.

Critical Thinking

7. **Making Inferences** The International Bank for Reconstruction and Development was organized near the end of World War II. For what purpose do you think it was founded?

Practice and **assess** key social studies skills with the *Glencoe Skillbuilder Interactive Workbook, Level 2.*

CHAPTER 19: DEVELOPING COUNTRIES **531**

Section 2 Assessment Answers

1. a process by which traditional economies evolve to more fully provide for people's wants and needs; transition passes through many stages

2. All vocabulary terms are defined in the text.

3. primitive equilibrium, transition, takeoff, semidevelopment, high development

4. reduce trade barriers; reform macroeconomic policy; increase financial support for developing nations; support market policy reform

5. invest more in education, basic health care; remove regulations that restrict the free development of markets; open economies to international trade; reduce borrowing, decrease deficits, and allow for market incentives

6. missionaries and tourists, war, business ventures

7. to help countries recover from WWII

TEACH

Tell students that ten years ago, many multinationals in search of new markets began expanding their markets into developing countries. Point out that many of the ventures failed, due to factors like local competition, lack of consumer interest, and community uprising. Ask students what makes the approach of companies like Whirlpool different. Discuss the importance of market research and how it can not only save company resources, but also develop products consumers actually need.

In addition, talk about the way Whirlpool and many other companies are working with the local population to get their products distributed and sold. Discuss with students how this approach is ultimately more beneficial to the population of the developing country, not only in terms of the products sold, but also in terms of the local jobs provided, the skills learned, and the influx of business for local transportation and retail companies.

Refer to **Business Week Focus on the New Economy** in the TCR for additional unit-based articles.

BusinessWeek

AUGUST 27, 2001

Newsclip

With American companies doing more buisness in developing countries, it is important to learn that being first and biggest in an emerging market isn't always the best way to conquer it. A better tactic is to learn local cultures and build a presence carefully.

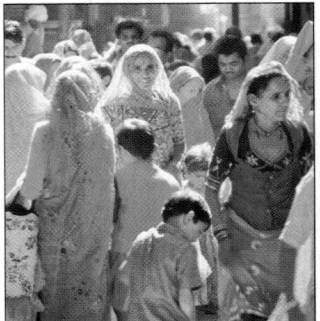

Smart Globalization

A television ad running these days in India shows a mother lapsing into a daydream: Her young daughter is in a beauty contest dressed as Snow White, dancing on a stage. Her flowing gown is an immaculate white. The garments of the other contestants, who dance in the background, are a tad gray. Snow White, no surprise, wins the blue ribbon. The mother awakes to the laughter of her adoring family—and glances proudly at her Whirlpool White Magic washing machine.

The TV spot is the product of 14 months of research by Whirlpool Corp. into the psyche of the Indian consumer. Among other things, the Benton Harbor (Mich.) company learned Indian homemakers prize hygiene and purity, which they associate with white. The trouble is, white garments often get discolored after frequent machine washing in local water. Besides appealing to this love of purity in its ads, Whirlpool custom-designed machines that are especially good with white fabrics.

Whirlpool hasn't stopped there. It uses generous incentives to get thousands of Indian retailers to stock its goods. To reach every cranny of the vast nation, it uses local contractors con-

versant in India's 18 languages to collect payments in cash and deliver appliances by truck, bicycles, even oxcart. Since 1966, Whirlpool's sales in India have leapt 80%—and should hit $200 million this year. Whirlpool now is the leading brand in India's fast-growing market for fully automatic washing machines....

...[A]s Whirpool and other savvy U.S. companies such as Kodak, Citigroup, and Hewlett-Packard are proving, investing time and energy to understand societies in developing nations can pay rich returns. Rather than swinging for the fences, with megaprojects or costly takeovers, the smarter approach is to methodically build a presence from the ground up....

Examining the Newsclip

1. **Making Predictions** What may have occurred if Whirlpool had not conducted research about Indian culture?
2. **Analyzing Information** How do you think Whirlpool's research helped it discover methods of distributing its washing machines throughout India?

Answers to Examining the Newsclip

1. Not likely. Not only are the washing machines tailored to local conditions, but the distribution channels are set up using local contractors. Without research, Whirlpool would not have known about the value Indian consumers place on white garments, for example.

2. Through research, Whirlpool was able to learn what types of distribution work best in each area of a vast country. Using local contractors also allows the company to overcome any language barriers, and ensure products are stocked in the right kinds of stores.

Financing Economic Development

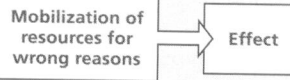

Main Idea
Economists suggest that developing countries can make progress by encouraging foreign direct investment, building human capital, and encouraging regional cooperation.

Reading Strategy
Graphic Organizer As you read the section, complete a graphic organizer similar to the one below by describing what may result if resources are mobilized for the wrong reasons.

Mobilization of resources for wrong reasons → Effect

Key Terms
expropriation, soft loan, free-trade area, customs union, European Union (EU), euro, ASEAN, cartel, population density

Objectives
After studying this section, you will be able to:
1. **Describe** one internal and two external sources of funds for economic development.
2. **Explain** the role of international lending and developing agencies.
3. **Explain** how regional cooperation can assist economic growth.

Applying Economic Concepts
Growth and Development Do you think you would buy more products if you didn't have to pay tariffs? Read to find out why free-trade areas are helping developing nations today.

FOCUS

Section Overview
This section discusses sources of capital for financing economic development.

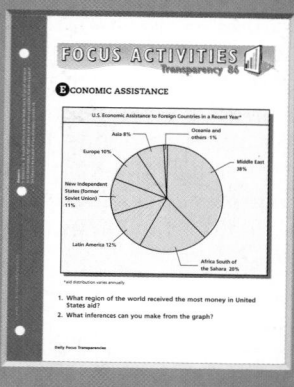

Cover Story

Dollarization in Latin America

Tired of spending precious vacation time searching for a place to change money? In what has been dubbed "dollarization," a growing number of Latin American countries are accepting the dollar as an official or de facto currency....

The latest country to see green: El Salvador, which kicked off the new year by making the U.S. dollar an official currency. The move comes less than a year after Ecuador, fed up with runaway inflation, eliminated its currency, the sucre, in favor of the dollar …

Salvadoran currency

—*USA TODAY*, April 27, 2001

For a developing country to foster industries in which it has a comparative advantage, it needs capital. Funds may be needed, for example, to provide irrigation for farms or heavy equipment for mining. Capital is also needed to build roads and highways for bringing products to ports for shipment to the rest of the world.

Financial capital generally can come from different sources, but it is always hard to obtain unless the developing countries have a certain degree of financial stability. One interesting attempt to achieve financial stability, as you read in the cover story, involves the use of the United States dollar in place of existing domestic currencies.

Development With Internal Funds

Internal funds are an important source of capital. In many cases, they may be the only source of capital for a developing country. To generate these internal funds from savings, an economy must produce more than it consumes.

CHAPTER 19: DEVELOPING COUNTRIES **533**

②TEACH

Daily Lecture Notes 19-3

DAILY LECTURE NOTES 📖 Lesson 19-3

ⒹID YOU KNOW?

Wampum, made from seashells strung as beads or woven into belts, was used not only as a medium of exchange but also to record diplomatic relationships among Indian tribes. The word wampum comes from the word Wampumpeag, a Massachusetts Indian language that used different color shells for recording important matters such as treaties. The purple or white wampum beads were carefully woven into patterns that would serve as a visual reminder of a treaty and the arrangements agreed upon.

PAGES 533-534

I. Development with Internal Funds
   A. Internal funds are an important source of capital.
   B. To generate internal funds, an economy must produce more than it consumes.
   C. In a market economy, these savings, in turn, produce financial capital.
   D. In a command economy, governments are able to force savings on the economy.

Ⓓ Discussion Question

What kinds of long-term incentives can governments use to encourage individuals to save? (They can give tax benefits such as deductions for retirement savings; reduce taxes on interest paid for savings; and defer taxation on long-term savings.)

PAGES 534-535

II. Development with External Funds
   A. Developing countries can try to attract private investment.
   B. They can ask for assistance from industrialized countries.

L2 Time Line

Have students research economic development in South Korea. Direct students to use their findings to construct a time line showing South Korea's economic growth from the end of the Korean War to the present day. Have students compare their time lines. **ELL**

Math Practice

Global Loans A developing nation receives an interest-free soft loan of 11.5 million dollars from an external source. The following year they are able to repay 1 million dollars, and in each subsequent year the size of their annual payment doubles. How many years will it take them, from the year they begin repayment, to repay the entire loan? *(Repayment would take four years. year one—1 million is paid; year two—2 million is paid; year three—4 million is paid, reducing the total to 4.5 million; year four—8 million available for payment, so nation can pay off the balance of 4.5 million.)*

Savings in a Market Economy

If a developing country is modeled after a market economy, the incentive to save stems from the profit motive. Firms often try to borrow funds for various projects, and banks charge interest rates on savings that are set by the forces of supply and demand. If the demand for money is high, the rate will rise, and more saving will be encouraged. Saving, in turn, produces financial capital.

One economy that developed in this way was Hong Kong. Before reunification with China, government interfered very little, and people were free to pursue almost any economic activity they desired. By 2000, Hong Kong's per capita GNP was about 70 percent of that of the United States, and more than 6 times greater than China's.

Savings in a Command Economy

Other developing countries, such as Cuba, the Dominican Republic, and Uganda, had command economies at one time or another. However, because the citizens were also poor, they had no ability to save on their own. Despite the poverty, their governments were still able to force savings on the economy. This was done by forcing people to work on farms, roads, or other projects the government thought were needed for economic development.

Unfortunately, history shows that although command economies can mobilize resources, they do not always use them to promote economic growth. More often, resources are mobilized for political reasons or personal gain. In addition, nearly all forced mobilizations fail to instill long-term incentives or work ethics in the people. When resources are mobilized for the wrong reasons, the cost in personal, economic, and political freedoms is higher than most people want to pay.

Development With External Funds

No matter what system of government a less developed country has, it is never easy to develop an economy with internal funds alone. Therefore, some developing countries try to obtain external funds. There are three ways they can do this.

One way a country can obtain external funds is to attract private funds from foreign investors who

STANDARD & POOR'S   INFOBYTE

Brady Bonds Brady bonds provide developing nations a way to restructure their sovereign debt obligations to foreign commercial banks. In a Brady restructuring, a portion of the developing country's debt is forgiven with the balance being exchanged for various series of bonds. The maturity of these new obligations is extended, reducing the country's annual debt service requirements. To attract investors, Brady bonds are often backed by U.S. Treasury securities and offer investors attractive yields.

might be interested in the country's natural resources. This happened in the Middle East with its abundance of oil, in Chile with its abundance of copper, and in Asia with its abundance of mahogany and teakwood.

If foreign investments are to work, the arrangement must be beneficial to both the investor and the host country. Many investors are unwilling to take major risks unless they are sure that the developing country is politically stable. Developing countries that follow a policy of **expropriation**— the taking over of foreign property without some sort of payment in return—make it harder for all developing nations to attract foreign capital.

Another way to obtain external funds is through borrowing from foreign governments. The United States and other industrialized countries, including Canada and those in Western Europe, grant some aid to developing countries.

The former Soviet bloc also gave economic assistance to developing countries. More than 50 percent of its aid, however, went to allies such as Cuba, Ethiopia, Afghanistan, and Iraq. Like most other foreign aid, it was given mostly to promote political, rather than economic, ends.

A third way a country can get external financial assistance is by obtaining a loan from an international agency. The International Bank for Reconstruction and Development—part of the World Bank Group—helps developing countries

---

MEETING SPECIAL NEEDS ACTIVITY

Learning Style: Interpersonal Organize students into small groups. Ask each group to draw a table with *Internal Funds, External Funds,* and *Regional Cooperation* as vertical headings, and *Advantages* and *Disadvantages* as horizontal headings. Have students identify the advantages and disadvantages of the three sources of financial capital for development and record their responses in the table. Ask for volunteers to share their tables with the class. Then lead the class in a discussion about which methods of financing economic development are most efficient.

📂 Refer to *Inclusion for the Social Studies Classroom Strategies and Activities* in the TCR.

with loans and guarantees of loans from private sources. In the past, many of the loans have been for projects such as dams, roads, and factories. More recently, loans have been made to developing nations in an effort to get them to change their economic policies.

Another part of the World Bank Group is the International Finance Corporation (IFC), an agency that invests in private businesses and other enterprises. The International Development Association (IDA) makes **soft loans**—loans that may never be paid back—to the neediest countries. The rates on IDA loans are interest-free and may be for periods of 35 or 40 years.

Countries can also get help from the IMF. After the Berlin Wall came down and the Soviet Union collapsed, a number of former Soviet bloc countries wanted to trade their currencies on global exchanges. The IMF provided loans to help with the conversion. Today, such currencies as the Hungarian *forint,* the Polish *zloty,* and the Czech Republic's *koruna* are listed on world markets. This is important because investors must be able to purchase the currencies of these countries to conduct international trade with them.

Regional Cooperation

Some countries have joined together to form a **free-trade area**—an agreement in which two or more countries reduce trade barriers and tariffs among themselves. The free-trade area does not try to set uniform tariffs for nonmembers. Other countries have formed a **customs union**—an agreement in which two or more countries abolish tariffs and trade restrictions among themselves and adopt uniform tariffs for nonmember countries.

The European Union

The most successful example of regional cooperation in the world today is the **European Union (EU).** The EU, formerly known as the European Community, started out as a customs union and now consists of the 15 member nations shown in **Figure 19.2** on page 536.

In January 1993, the EU became the single largest unified market—in terms of population and output—in the world, although the United States has since caught up in terms of GNP. The EU is a single market because there are no internal barriers regulating the flow of workers, financial capital, or goods and services. Citizens of the EU hold common passports, can vote in European elections, and can travel anywhere in the EU to work, shop, save, and invest.

The final stage of European integration is scheduled for 2002 when the EU introduces a single currency—the **euro**—to replace the majority of individual national currencies now issued by the member nations.

ASEAN

The economic success of the EU has encouraged other nations to try regional cooperation. In 1967 five nations—Indonesia, Malaysia, Singapore, the Philippines, and Thailand—formed the Association for Southeast Asian Nations, or ASEAN.

Today, **ASEAN** is a ten-nation group working to promote regional peace and stability, accelerate economic growth, and liberalize trade policies in order to become a free-trade area by 2008.

Development

External Funds This hydroelectric dam is part of the Uribante-Caparo development in the Venezuelan Andes. *Through what agencies can developing countries borrow money to finance projects?*

CHAPTER 19: DEVELOPING COUNTRIES **535**

Guided Reading Activity 19-3

GUIDED READING Activity 19-3

For use with textbook pages 533–537

FINANCING ECONOMIC DEVELOPMENT

RECALLING THE FACTS

Directions: Use the information in your textbook to answer the questions. Use another sheet of paper if necessary.

1. What makes internal funds important to a developing country?

2. What makes it difficult for a developing country to produce financial capital from savings?

3. In what three ways can a developing country obtain external funds?
   a.
   b.
   c.

4. What are two forms that regional cooperation between countries can take? Explain each one briefly.
   a.   b.

5. In what way is the European Union (EU) a single market?

6. What is ASEAN and what are its goals?

CYBERNOMICS

Bioengineered Foods Bioengineering refers to new methods of plant breeding that involve introducing a copy of a gene for a specific desired trait from another plant, animal, or microbe. This type of breeding allows scientists to develop new food varieties more quickly, and to make existing foods more nutritious, more resilient, better tasting, and resistant to pests and diseases. However, concerns exist about the safety of bioengineered foods. Consumers in Europe and Japan refuse to purchase bioengineered foods, and those in the U.S. who are worried about the possibility of harmful substances in the foods want them to be labeled. Thus, companies such as Gerber and Heinz will not use any genetically modified foods.

FREE ENTERPRISE ACTIVITY

Have students write an essay comparing and contrasting the three sources of capital for developing countries with sources of capital for industrialized countries. Call on volunteers to read their essays to the class. Then discuss as a class why it is easier for industrialized countries to raise financial capital for development. **BLOCK SCHEDULING**

Visual Instruction

Answer to Caption:
International Bank for Reconstruction and Development, IFC, IDA, IMF

ECONOMICS
AT A GLANCE

Answer: *No internal barriers regulate workers, financial capital, or goods and services; EU citizens have free access to other EU member nations and can vote in European elections.*

③ ASSESS

Assign Section 3 Assessment as homework or as an in-class activity.

💾 Have students use **Interactive Tutor Self-Assessment Software** to review Section 3.

Section Quiz 19-3

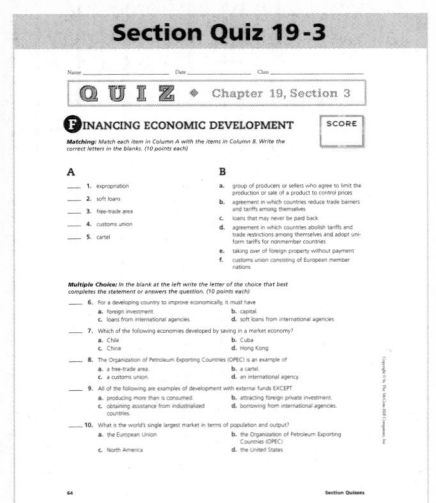

ECONOMICS
AT A GLANCE

Figure 19.2

The European Union

15 existing members:

Austria	1955
Belgium	1952
Denmark	1973
Finland	1995
France	1952
Germany	1952
Greece	1981
Ireland	1973
Italy	1952
Luxembourg	1952
Netherlands	1952
Portugal	1986
Spain	1986
Sweden	1995
United Kingdom	1973

Currently being considered for membership after 2004

Bulgaria
Cyprus
Czech Republic
Estonia
Hungary
Latvia
Lithuania
Malta
Poland
Romania
Slovakia
Slovenia

Reading Maps The 15 members of the European Union currently make up the largest single market in the world, with more than 370 million people. What are the benefits of membership in the EU?

OPEC

A number of oil-producing nations have joined to form a **cartel**—a group of producers or sellers who agree to limit the production or sale of a product to control prices. OPEC's (Organization of Petroleum Exporting Countries) members were able to take advantage of a natural monopoly and push up world oil prices. Since it was organized in 1960, OPEC has transferred trillions of dollars from the industrialized nations to the OPEC members as a result of higher prices paid for oil. Even with all this financial capital, however, the growth rates of most OPEC nations were low by most standards. In

Iran, revolution interrupted the development of the domestic economy. After Iraq invaded Kuwait, Iraq suffered huge losses during the Persian Gulf War. Overproduction by OPEC also pushed oil prices down.

The South Korean Success Story

One of the most successful developing nations is South Korea. In the early 1950s, South Korea was one of the poorest nations in Asia. It had the highest **population density**—number of

EXTENDING THE CONTENT

Agricultural Developments The "Green Revolution" refers to various efforts to increase and diversify crop yields in developing countries. U.S. scientist Norman Borlaug, who is credited with beginning the revolution, won the 1970 Nobel Peace Prize for his contribution to the development of high-yield grains. Borlaug used genetics and biology to develop a hybrid strain of wheat that is prolific and disease-resistant. He then put the strain into production in developing nations, with spectacular results. In only a few years, Mexico's grain production tripled, and southern Asia's wheat yields jumped 50 percent. However, high-yield grains are controversial because they require more fertilizers and irrigation, and large, industrialized farms.

people per square mile of land area—in the world. It also had a war-torn economy that had to be rebuilt.

The South Korean government opened its markets to world trade. In addition, the government focused only on a few industries so that its people could gain experience producing and exporting for world markets. Businesses in the South Korean economy first began to produce inexpensive toys and consumer goods for the world market. Next, they moved into textiles such as shirts, dresses, and sweaters. Then they invested in heavy industry, such as shipbuilding and steel manufacturing. Later, South Korea produced consumer and electronic goods such as radios, televisions, microwave ovens, and home computers. Most recently, the country has been making a strong bid as a leading producer of automobiles. The South Korean experience shows that a country can change a war-damaged economy to a well-developed, highly industrial one.

Economic Development

South Korea The Republic of Korea, also know as South Korea, overcame overwhelming odds to become the second largest economic power in Asia and the eleventh largest in the world. *What plans did South Korea implement to bring about economic growth?*

Visual Instruction

Answer to Caption:
opened its market to world trade and focused on fewer industries

Reteach

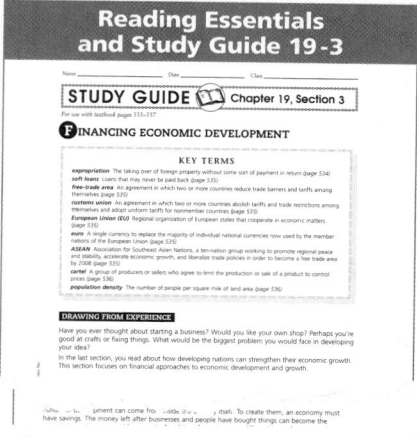

Reading Essentials and Study Guide 19-3

Enrich

Ask students to write a research paper on the development of either the EU or OPEC.

CLOSE

Have students write on index cards three questions about sources of funds for economic development. Collect and shuffle the cards, then randomly select students to answer the questions.

Section 3 Assessment

Checking for Understanding

1. **Main Idea** What can a country do to encourage economic development?

2. **Key Terms** Define expropriation, soft loan, free-trade area, customs union, European Union (EU), euro, ASEAN, cartel, population density.

3. **Describe** one internal and two external sources of funds for economic development.

4. **Describe** the role of international lending and developing agencies.

5. **Explain** how regional cooperation aids economic growth.

Applying Economic Concepts

6. **Growth and Development** Provide an example to support the following statement: Economic growth in developing nations is often slowed by the internal political problems and external political goals of industrialized nations.

Critical Thinking

7. **Drawing Conclusions** Developing countries often need capital from foreign investors. What economic and political conditions serve to encourage this kind of investment?

 Practice and **assess** key social studies skills with the *Glencoe Skillbuilder Interactive Workbook, Level 2.*

CHAPTER 19: DEVELOPING COUNTRIES **537**

Section 3 Assessment Answers

1. encourage savings, attract foreign investors, seek grants or loans from foreign governments, obtain a loan from an international agency, regional cooperation

2. All vocabulary terms are defined in the text.

3. internal: savings; external: private funds from foreign investors, grants or borrowing from other countries, borrowing from an international agency such as the World Bank

4. helping developing countries with loans and guarantees of loans from private sources

5. Such cooperation often consists of the reduction or elimination of barriers and tariffs.

6. Examples may note internal political problems or external political goals.

7. strong economic development opportunities that address saving, investment, and worker incentives, and a stable political climate

Teaching Skills

To help students grasp the concept of summarizing, have them read an article from a periodical and rewrite it as a children's book. Remind them that books for children are simplified and concise, and usually contain illustrations, diagrams, or photographs. When the children's books have been completed, discuss with students the process of turning a full-length article into a book for children. Show them that they were actually summarizing the adult version to make it accessible to children. Have students present their children's books to the class.

Additional Practice

Reinforcing Economic Skill 13

Reinforcing Economic Skills — Chapter 13

S UMMARIZING INFORMATION

Summarizing information helps you to remember the main ideas and important facts contained in a long reading selection. To write a summary, rewrite the main ideas of the reading selection in your own words. Do not copy sentences or phrases from the text. Make sure your summary is much shorter than the reading selection, but captures the selection's main ideas.

Directions: Read the remarks below from the chairman of the Federal Reserve Board, Alan Greenspan. Then, on a separate sheet of paper, answer the questions that follow.

1. What is the main idea of this passage?

2. What facts does the author provide to support the main idea?

3. Write a short paragraph summarizing this passage.

Summarizing Information

Have you ever read something and just a short time later forgotten what it was all about? Summarizing information—reducing many sentences to just a few well-chosen phrases—helps you remember the main ideas and important facts contained in a longer reading selection.

Learning the Skill

To summarize information, follow these guidelines:

- Your summary should be much shorter than the reading selection.

- Your summary should contain the main ideas of the reading selection.

- Your summary should not contain your opinion. It should contain only the opinion of the person who wrote the selection.

- Your summary sentences and phrases should not be copied word for word from the selection. Write a summary in your own words to be sure that you understand the main ideas of the selection.

Memorial sculpture, Hiroshima Peace Park

Practicing the Skill

Read the selection below, then answer the questions that follow.

During the 1950s, foreign aid from industrialized countries was considered absolutely necessary for the economic growth of developing nations. European countries and Japan, just beginning to recover from the massive destruction of World War II, were unable to provide aid during that period. The United States, which had helped with Japan's and Europe's recovery, provided the largest share of aid to developing nations during that decade. When Europe and Japan became richer, the distribution burden shifted. From 1960 to 1990, the United States's percentage of total aid supplied by the

Western nations to developing countries dropped from 60 percent to 17 percent.

1. What is the main idea of this paragraph?

2. What are the supporting details of the main idea?

3. Write a short summary that will help you remember what the paragraph is about.

Application Activity

Spend fifteen minutes reading and summarizing two articles on the front page of today's newspaper. Circle the articles and have a classmate ask you questions about them. How much were you able to remember after summarizing the information?

Practice and **assess** key social studies skills with the *Glencoe Skillbuilder Interactive Workbook, Level 2.*

538

Answers to Practicing the Skill

1. In the 1950s aid was necessary because of World War II destruction. As other Western countries have become richer, the percentage of the total aid that the U.S. provides to developing countries has diminished.

2. Europe and Japan could not provide aid after WWII; the United States provided the largest share of aid during the 1950s; in 1960 the U.S. provided 60 percent of the aid given by Western nations; in 1990 the U.S. provided 17 percent of the aid.

3. Answers should include the main idea.

CHAPTER 19
Summary

Section 1

Economic Development (pages 521–526)

- **Developing countries** have the same problems that industrialized countries have, only their problems are much larger.

- With more than 1.2 billion people in the world existing on an income of less than $1 a day, concern for developing countries is humanitarian as well as political.

- Developing countries face numerous obstacles, including population pressures from high **crude birthrates** and increasing **life expectancies.**

- A shortage of natural resources, limited education and technology, religion, large **external debts, capital flight,** corruption, and the aftermath of war all add to the problems of developing countries.

- The **IMF** and the **World Bank** are two international agencies that help with development.

Section 2

A Framework for Development

(pages 528–531)

- It helps to think of economic development as proceeding in stages, even if this does not always describe the pattern experienced by every nation.

- The stages include **primitive equilibrium,** breaking with primitive equilibrium, **takeoff,** semidevelopment, and high development.

- The World Bank recommends that developed nations reduce trade barriers, reform macroeconomic policies, increase financial support, and support the policy reforms of the developing countries.

- The World Bank also recommends that the developing countries themselves invest in people, improve the climate for enterprise, open their economies to international trade, and revise their macroeconomic policies.

Section 3

Financing Economic Development

(pages 533–537)

- Developing countries need to encourage saving to secure a domestic source of investment funds. Command economies often try to force saving by mobilizing resources in a manner that restricts individual freedoms.

- Attempts to secure capital through **expropriation** usually backfire because foreign investors become fearful of investing.

- External funds are sometimes available from foreign governments and banks; the World Bank and the IMF also provide considerable assistance.

- Some countries have been able to help themselves through regional cooperation in the form of a **free-trade area,** or a **customs union** such as the **European Union.**

- The ten ASEAN countries are working to develop a free-trade area by 2008.

- The oil-producing nations also organized a **cartel,** called OPEC, to increase the price of oil.

- South Korea is a striking example of a developing nation having achieved success: it has developed from a poor war-torn economy to the eleventh-largest economy in the world.

NIGHTLY BUSINESS REPORT

💿 **ECONOMICS & YOU**

Chapter 26
Disc 1, Side 2

Developing Countries

📼 Also available in VHS.

Using the Chapter 19 Summary

Use the Chapter 19 Summary to preview, review, condense, or reteach the chapter.

Preview/Review

🌐 Vocabulary PuzzleMaker CD-ROM reinforces Key Terms.

▪ Interactive Tutor Self-Assessment Software provides a review of Chapter 19 content.

Condense

🎧 📂 Have students listen to the Chapter 19 Audio Program. Spanish also available.

📂 📂 Assign the Chapter 19 Audio Program Activity and give students the Chapter 19 Audio Program Test.

📂 📂 Have students complete the Guided Reading Activities and Reading Essentials and Study Guides for Chapter 19.

Reteach

📂 📂 Have students complete Reteaching Activity 19 in the TCR. Spanish also available.

Teacher's Notes / Internet Bookmarks

539

GLENCOE
TECHNOLOGY

Use **MindJogger Videoquiz** to review the Chapter 19 content.

ECONOMICS
Online

Have students visit the Web site at epp.glencoe.com to review Chapter 19 and take the **Self-Check Quiz.**

Identifying Key Terms

1. h	6. c
2. g	7. j
3. b	8. e
4. i	9. f
5. d	10. a

Reviewing the Facts

Section 1

1. moral responsibility to help those who have less; to ensure a stable supply of raw materials; to gain allies and attain political strength
2. zero population growth
3. the World Bank and the International Monetary Fund

Section 2

4. People become dissatisfied with the way things are, old customs crumble, traditions are questioned, and new patterns of living arise.
5. A country starts to save and invest more of its income. New industries grow rapidly. Industry uses new production techniques. Agricultural productivity greatly improves.
6. invest more in people; improve climate of free enterprise; open economies to free trade; institute reforms that curb inflation, reduce borrowing, and decrease deficits

Section 3

7. savings, foreign investment, borrowing from foreign governments or international agencies

540

ECONOMICS
Online

Self-Check Quiz Visit the *Economics: Principles and Practices* Web site at epp.glencoe.com and click on *Chapter 19—Self-Check Quizzes* to prepare for the chapter test.

Identifying Key Terms

Write the key term that best completes the following sentences.

a. **population density**	f. **expropriation**
b. **customs union**	g. **free-trade area**
c. **primitive equilibrium**	h. **cartel**
d. **external debt**	i. **crude birthrate**
e. **capital flight**	j. **takeoff**

1. A(n) _____ is the formal arrangement to limit the production of a product.
2. A cooperative trade arrangement among nations that does not set uniform tariffs for nonmembers is called a(n) _____ .
3. A(n) _____ is a cooperative trade arrangement among nations that sets uniform tariffs for nonmembers.
4. A developing country may have a very high _____ , contributing to rapid population growth.
5. When _____ becomes too large, countries have difficulty paying the interest.
6. The least developed stage in economic development is called _____ .
7. The third stage of economic development is the _____ .
8. The problem of _____ occurs when corrupt officials take money out of the country and deposit it abroad.

9. When _____ takes place, it is harder for developing nations to attract foreign capital from industrialized countries.
10. The number of people per square mile of land is a measure of _____ .

Reviewing the Facts

Section 1 (pages 521–526)

1. **Identify** three reasons why industrialized countries are concerned about the problems of developing nations.
2. **Name** the condition in which the average number of births and deaths are approximately equal.
3. **Identify** two agencies that help developing economies.

Section 2 (pages 528–531)

4. **Describe** what happens in a developing country in the stage of breaking with primitive equilibrium.
5. **Identify** four changes that take place in the takeoff stage of economic development.
6. **List** the four World Bank recommendations for developing nations.

Section 3 (pages 533–537)

7. **Name** three sources of financial capital for development.
8. **Explain** how a developing country can attract foreign capital.
9. **List** three international agencies that provide funds for economic development.

Thinking Critically

1. **Predicting Consequences** What do you think would happen if industrialized nations and international agencies chose to withdraw support for developing nations?

8. It can attract private funds from foreign investors interested in the country's natural resources, secure grants or loans from industrialized nations that want political gains, or borrow from international agencies with a promise to change its economic policies.
9. World Bank, International Monetary Fund, International Finance Corporation, International Development Association

Thinking Critically

1. Developing countries might be unable to change their economic situations because they would not have capital necessary to institute agricultural or industrial changes or to build roads for trade; might contribute to political instability
2. offers advice to all nations on fiscal or monetary policies; helps support the currency of some developing nations with loans
3. If the U.S. increased aid to a country in turmoil, political leadership could change frequently or a war could begin, and the developing nations would not benefit fully from the aid.

2. **Summarizing Information** What are the functions of the IMF? Use a graphic organizer similar to the one below to help answer the question.

Functions of the IMF

3. **Demonstrating Reasoned Judgment** Would it be effective policy for the United States to increase financial aid to developing nations, regardless of their internal political conditions or economic policies? Explain the reasoning behind your answer.

4. **Making Generalizations** Studies indicate that, in general, landlocked nations tend to have lower per capita income levels than surrounding nations that are bordered by oceans and seas. Why do you think this is the case?

Applying Economic Concepts

1. **Growth and Development** How will the economic growth and development of developing countries affect you in the future?

2. **Primitive Equilibrium** Why is it increasingly unlikely that countries in the world today will remain in the primitive equilibrium stage of economic development?

3. **Drawing Conclusions** Developing nations often need capital from foreign investors. What economic and political conditions serve to encourage this kind of investment?

Math Practice

Suppose that a small country has a per capita GNP of $20,000 and a population of 1,000,000. How large is the total GNP? If population is expected to grow by 20 percent in the next ten years, and if total GNP is only expected to be 10 percent larger, what will be the per capita GNP in 10 years?

Thinking Like an Economist

What advice would you give a developing nation that was trying to decide between a command-type economy and a market-based economy?

Technology Skill

Using E-Mail For one week, keep a journal of all the economic problems of developing nations that you hear reported in the news. List the countries in one column and their problems in a second column.

Using the information you collected, write a plan detailing how the United States could assist in alleviating some of the economic problems of a specific country. E-mail your plan to your local representative or legislator. Be sure to support your proposal with statistics, facts, quotes, and historical events.

Building Skills

Summarizing Information A summary is a list of the major points or themes of something. To summarize is to present those points or themes briefly and without details. Read the following excerpt, then summarize the main points.

A problem for many developing countries is a lack of infrastructure. Infrastructure refers to the physical developments necessary for efficient production and distribution of goods and services. Such things as roads, ports, electric generators, telephones, and sewers are considered infrastructure. Without these things, it is difficult for an economic system to function efficiently. The lack of infrastructure makes it impossible for such countries to compete successfully with more developed nations. Building an infrastructure is very expensive. Many developing nations cannot afford to invest in these improvements.

 Practice and **assess** key social studies skills with the *Glencoe Skillbuilder Interactive Workbook, Level 2.*

Math Practice

$20 billion; $18,333

Thinking Like an Economist

Although command-type economies can mobilize resources, they are often used for political reasons, not to promote economic growth. Also, command economies fail to instill long-term incentives in the people.

Technology Skill

Answers may suggest that a market economy encourages saving through the profit motive, leading to the capital necessary for economic development.

Building Skills

A lack of infrastructure presents a roadblock to development, and that many developing countries cannot afford to invest in improving infrastructure.

? Bonus Test Question

How would an entrepreneur in a developing country be affected by each of the following?
a. lack of capital *(makes it difficult for an entrepreneur to borrow money to start a business)*
b. foreign control of large businesses within the developing country *(Foreign businesses might be unwilling to work with the entrepreneur; would compete for labor)*
c. governmental control of the economy *(Government might be unwilling to relinquish control of any business; make it difficult for businesses to start up)*

---

4. International trade is more difficult for countries without easy access to ports.

Applying Economic Concepts

1. Economic growth and development of developing countries should have a positive impact because international trade will increase.
2. Improvements in communication and travel, along with heightened social conscience, have enabled people and information to go into areas in the primitive equilibrium stage and expose them to different ways of living.
3. Strong economic development opportunities that address saving, investments, and worker incentives, and a stable political climate encourage foreign investment.

Issues in Free Enterprise

Issues in Free Enterprise are case studies that allow students to investigate opposing views of economic issues. The case study contains background information about a current topic related to economics. Two differing opinions are presented that debate the issue and how it should be resolved.

1 FOCUS

Present students with this scenario: A senator proposes a bill that would allow anyone four years old or older to work full time. **Ask:** How would such a proposal be received? Why would so many Americans object so vehemently to it? Is American opposition to child labor based on economic, social, or moral grounds, or on something else? Should Americans extend their objections overseas? Have students consider these questions as they read the selections.

2 TEACH

L2 Expressing Problems Differently

Point out the line in the introduction that states that there are as many as 200 million working children under the age of 12 in the world today. Have students conduct research to locate estimates of the *total* number of children under the age of 12 in the world, and convert the 200-million figure into a percentage. Have them write paragraphs that explore the advantages and disadvantages of expressing the figure in each way. Discuss whether each expression of these figures makes child labor appear more or less prevalent.

A Case Study:

SHOULD CHILD LABOR BE ABOLISHED?

Although it may surprise many Americans, child labor is prevalent in many parts of the world today, especially in developing countries. The estimates vary, but perhaps 200 million children under the age of 12 work regularly instead of going to school. Sometimes, the children start to work as soon as they are able; some of the youngest workers are just three years old.

Should the United States take steps to end child labor? Many people answer that question with a resounding "Yes!" They hold that child labor is immoral. The children, they say, are virtual slaves. Many are treated harshly, even cruelly—forced to work 12-hour days at mind-dulling yet dangerous tasks. These activists have put forth a variety of proposals aimed at eliminating child labor throughout the world.

Other people, however, oppose any such action. While deploring any mistreatment of children, they emphasize the contexts in which the children live. The cultures in many developing countries, they point out, support children working, while the state of the economies of these countries often requires it. Westerners, they say, may oppose child labor, but are in no position to force their beliefs onto other countries.

> As you read the selections, ask yourself: Should the United States work to abolish child labor in developing countries?

 PRO Child Labor Is "Reprehensible"

[There is] an unmistakable trend . . . toward convergence on global condemnation of child labor. . . .

However, . . . global child labor continues to flourish. The movement toward convergence in law seems strangely detached from everyday experience. Because it is illegal almost everywhere, child labor remains largely a hidden phenomenon, confined to the back channels and informal sectors of many economies, including advanced economies. The simple fact that child labor remains widespread would seem to belie any convergence of global

sentiment around its eradication. The sheer magnitude of the problem suggests a movement in law quite divergent from plain reality. The gross dimensions of the problem provide alarming support for the conclusion that cultural relativism may be prevailing—that local exceptionalism may dominate over convergent trends.

542 UNIT 5 INTERNATIONAL AND GLOBAL ECONOMICS

Behind the Viewpoints

PRO **Hugh D. Hindman** is an associate professor in the Management Department at Appalachian State University.

Charles G. Smith is an associate professor in the College of Business Administration at Niagara University.

CON **Bonnie Erbe** is a co-creator of *To The Contrary,* a news analysis series featuring women panelists. She also writes a newspaper column for Scripps Howard.

But examination of the history of child labor in advanced economies brings the argument full circle. While it can be argued that use of child labor is particular to a nation's current stage of economic development (a relativist argument), it also appears to be true, in the main, that advanced nations, always and everywhere, have grown beyond their heavy reliance on child labor and, thus, every nation should eventually be expected to do so (a universalist argument). When the debate is shifted in this way, the relevant question becomes: is heavy reliance on child labor necessary to economic development? We have shown that it is not; that it has always been economically inefficient and injurious. . . .

Child labor is inappropriate because, first, it is (or will come to be seen as) morally reprehensible and, second, it is economically inefficient and injurious. Case closed.

—Hugh D. Hindman and Charles G. Smith, *Journal of Business Ethics*

"Cultural Interference Is Not the Answer"

Ah, America! Thy commandeering ways!

We, the self-styled world's policeman, are seeing the error in our authoritarianism, our imposition of U.S. values on foreign cultures, our self-righteous yet mistaken belief that our way is the best way, indeed, the only way. . . . I'm talking about child labor. . . .

Even the previously unbending International Labor Organization has recognized the validity of not trying to force other cultures to adopt Western ideals. Several years ago it amended its broad-brush policy against all child labor after hearing from children in a variety of cultures at an international conference on child labor. . . .

Americans are finding out our lush economy provides luxuries to American families and children not afforded in many other countries, particularly poor ones. Most developing countries rely heavily on child labor. . . .

In developing countries, children are considered economic commodities. Parents love their children, of course, but they rely on them to help support the family and that is considered normal. As a result, the more children a poor family has, the greater a labor pool it possesses.

Former Pakistani Prime Minister Benazir Bhutto once told me that her country, one of the worst offenders, has passed laws that ban child labor. But every time she would try to enforce them, hundreds of thousands of parents would storm her residence. . . .

Every American would tell you our goal is to wipe out child labor completely: to bring developing nations on par with us economically so they no longer need to make 6-year-olds toil.

But . . . the fear is cultural, not economic, extinction. . . .

[W]e'll just have to learn to watch and worry, because, as we are just beginning to recognize, cultural interference is not the answer.

—Bonnie Erbe, *Journal of Commerce*

Analyzing the Issue

1. What are two basic objections that Hindman and Smith raise against child labor?

2. Would Hindman and Smith consider Erbe's argument "relativist" or "universalist"? Explain.

3. Do you think the United States should take steps to end child labor in developing countries? Explain your position.

L3 Creating an Economic Map

Have students conduct research to identify the countries where child labor is prevalent, and highlight and annotate a world map to depict their findings. Have students use their maps to draw conclusions about child labor.

③ ASSESS

Have students answer the Analyzing the Issue questions.

④ CLOSE

Have students share their answers to question 3 of "Analyzing the Issue" and use their answers as the basis for a class debate.

LINKING PAST & PRESENT

Child Labor has been a fact of life for most cultures for most of human history. The idea of childhood as a time of innocence is a relatively recent development. During the American Industrial Revolution most people thought little of sending children to work in factories; it seemed to them a natural extension of the work children had for generations done on farms. It was, in fact, the squalid working conditions of the new factories that led many to first speak out against "child labor"—a term that wasn't even used until the 1870s.

Answers to Analyzing the Issue

1. Hindman and Smith argue that child labor is "morally reprehensible" and "economically inefficient."

2. Hindman and Smith would consider Erbe's argument relativist, since she maintains that child labor is critical to the economies of developing nations and that the U.S. should not impose its values on foreign cultures.

3. Answers will vary. Students should provide cogent explanations for their positions.

543

Chapter 20 Resource Manager

SECTION RESOURCES

Daily Objectives	Reproducible Resources	Technology/Multimedia Resources
Section 1 **The Global Demand for Resources** 1. Explain Malthus's views on population growth. 2. Explain the importance of conserving nonrenewable resources. 3. List ways that people are using renewable energy resources to conserve scarce resources. 4. Identify other resources endangered by population growth.	Reproducible Lesson Plan 20-1 Daily Lecture Notes 20-1 Guided Reading Activity 20-1 Reading Essentials and Study Guide 20-1 Section Quiz 20-1*	Daily Focus Transparency 90 NBR Economics & You Video Program Interactive Tutor Self-Assessment Software ExamView® Pro Testmaker Presentation Plus!
Section 2 **Economic Incentives and Resources** 1. Explain how the price system helps conserve water, natural gas, and oil. 2. Describe government efforts to limit pollution. 3. State the importance of using resources wisely.	Reproducible Lesson Plan 20-2 Daily Lecture Notes 20-2 Guided Reading Activity 20-2 Reading Essentials and Study Guide 20-2 Section Quiz 20-2*	Daily Focus Transparency 91 Interactive Tutor Self-Assessment Software ExamView® Pro Testmaker Presentation Plus!
Section 3 **Applying the Economic Way of Thinking** 1. Describe the reasoned approach to economic decision making. 2. Understand how our market economy will be able to cope with the future.	Reproducible Lesson Plan 20-3 Daily Lecture Notes 20-3 Guided Reading Activity 20-3 Reading Essentials and Study Guide 20-3 Section Quiz 20-3*	Daily Focus Transparency 92 Vocabulary PuzzleMaker CD-ROM Interactive Tutor Self-Assessment Software ExamView® Pro Testmaker Presentation Plus!

 Transparency   CD-ROM   Software   Blackline Master

 Videodisc   Audio Program   Videocassette

Also available in Spanish

 OUT OF TIME?
Assign the Chapter 20 Audio Program activity and test.

Activities that are particularly suited to use within the block scheduling framework are identified throughout this chapter by the following designation: **BLOCK SCHEDULING**

KEY TO ABILITY LEVELS

Teaching strategies have been coded for varying learning styles and abilities.
L1 BASIC activities for all students
L2 AVERAGE activities for average to above-average students
L3 CHALLENGING activities for above-average students
ELL ENGLISH LANGUAGE LEARNER activities

Chapter 20 Resource Manager

TeacherWorks™ All-In-One Planner and Resource Center

- **Interactive Teacher Edition** Access your Teacher Wraparound Edition and your classroom resources with a few easy clicks.

- **Interactive Lesson Planner** Planning has never been easier! Organize your week, month, semester, or year with all the lesson helps you need to make teaching creative, timely, and relevant.

Use Glencoe's **Presentation Plus!** multimedia teacher tool to easily present dynamic lessons that visually excite your students. Using Microsoft PowerPoint® you can customize the presentations to create your own personalized lessons.

PRESENTATION Plus!

ACTIVITY

From the Classroom of...

Jay Grenawalt
George Washington
High School
Denver, CO

Foreign Investment

Increasingly, new factories are being constructed outside of national boundaries. In such an environment, nations will have to compete for foreign companies just as U.S. cities and states do today. **Ask:** What factors might lead a firm to build a factory in Country A instead of Country B? *(Some factors that might provide incentives/disincentives include wages, skilled labor, political stability, transportation and communication systems, import-export restrictions, government regulations, cultural and linguistics factors, and the size of the foreign country's market.)* Have students discuss the factors, ranking them from most to least important in their opinions. Students may also contribute other factors they believe apply.

Present students with a hypothetical situation. Suppose a company wants to build an automobile plant. Organize students into groups and ask each group to pick five nations that represent a diversity of development and regions. Using current encyclopedias, the *World Development Report*, *The Index of Economic Freedom*, and magazine and newspaper articles, have groups compile brief overviews of each economy using the above criteria. The students in each group should discuss and reach a consensus about which country would be their choice for the plant. As a class, tabulate the votes of the groups and lead a discussion about the choices.

National Council on Economic Education

THE **Economics**America AND
EconomicsInternational PROGRAMS

Voluntary National Content Standards in Economics
Emphasized in Chapter 20

Content Standard 1

Content Standard 4

Content Standard 8

Content Standard 16

For a complete listing of NCEE Standards and entire text correlation, see Teacher pages in front of book.

Resources Available from NCEE
- Focus: International Economics
- Economics and the Environment
- Geography: Focus on Economics
- The Great Economics Mysteries Book

To order these materials or to contact your state Council on Economic Education about workshops and programs, call 1-800-338-1192 or visit www.nationalcouncil.org

Chapter 20 Resource Manager

**Economic Concept Transparency 22:
International Aspects of Growth and Stability**

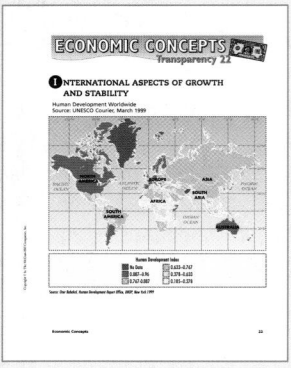

**Consumer Application
Activity 25**

**Free Enterprise
Activity 25**

Enrichment Activity 20

**Cooperative Learning
Activity 25**

**Math Practice
Activity 25**

Economic Cartoon 25

**Primary and Secondary
Source Reading 25**

**Economic Vocabulary
Activity 20**

Reteaching Activity 20

**Critical Thinking
Activity 25**

**Reinforcing Economic
Skill 15**

Chapter 20 Resource Manager

ASSESSMENT AND EVALUATION

Chapter 20 Test Form A

Chapter 20 Test Form B

Performance Assessment Activity 25

ExamView® Pro Testmaker

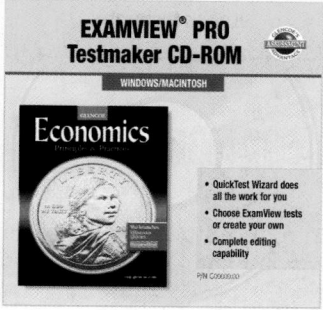

- QuickTest Wizard does all the work for you
- Choose ExamView tests or create your own
- Complete editing capability

SPANISH RESOURCES

The following Spanish language materials are available in the Spanish Resources binder:

 Spanish Economic Vocabulary Activities

 Spanish Reteaching Activities

 Spanish Section Quizzes

 Spanish Economic Concepts Transparencies

Also available:

  Spanish Chapter 20 Audio Program Activity and Test

TECHNOLOGY/MULTIMEDIA

- Vocabulary PuzzleMaker CD-ROM
- Interactive Tutor Self-Assessment Software
- ExamView® Pro Testmaker
- Audio Program (English or Spanish)
- NBR Economics & You Video Program (English or Spanish)
- MindJogger Videoquiz
- Interactive Economics! CD-ROM
- Presentation Plus!
- TeacherWorks CD-ROM
- Glencoe Skillbuilder Interactive Workbook CD-ROM, Level 2

ECONOMICS Online

Use our Web site for additional resources. All essential content is covered in the Student Edition.

You and your students can visit epp.glencoe.com, the Web site companion to **Economics: Principles and Practices.** This innovative integration of electronic and print media offers your students a wealth of opportunities. The student text directs students to the Web site for the following options:

- **Chapter Overviews**
- **Student Web Activities**
- **Self-Check Quizzes**
- **Textbook Updates**

Answers are provided for you in the Web Activity Lesson Plan. Additional Web resources and interactive puzzles are also available.

CHAPTER

20

Global
Economic Challenges

Economics & You

In order to accomplish economic development, the nations of the world have to overcome the problems that hinder their economic growth and they must make use of their resources effectively. To learn more about the challenges and opportunities of a global economy, view the Chapter 27 video lesson:

Global Economic Challenges

Dish-shaped solar power reflectors at a solar power station

The Global Demand for Resources

Study Guide

Main Idea
Worldwide economic challenges include overpopulation, food shortages, resource depletion, and environmental pollution.

Reading Strategy
Graphic Organizer As you read the section, complete a graphic organizer similar to the one below by explaining the difference between renewable and nonrenewable energy resources and providing two examples of each.

Key Terms
subsistence, nonrenewable resources, embargo, gasohol, aquifer

Objectives
After studying this section, you will be able to:
1. **Explain** Malthus's views on population growth.
2. **Explain** the importance of conserving nonrenewable resources.
3. **List** ways that people are using renewable energy resources to conserve scarce resources.
4. **Identify** other resources endangered by population growth.

Applying Economic Concepts
Scarcity Have you ever had a water shortage in your area? Read to find out how the price system works to solve this problem.

Cover Story

Six Billion People on Earth

WASHINGTON (AP)—Chances are it will be a boy born in the Third World on Oct. 12 [1999], but no one will know exactly which child pushes the world's population to 6 billion.

Earth's population surpassed 6 billion in 1999.

It took most of the age of humanity to mark the first billion in 1804 and more than a century to mark the second. But now the world is adding a billion every dozen years or so.

Demographers believe growth will slow down, [but] . . . median U.N. projections say it will take 14 years to add another billion people . . . . That's calculated from the yearly rate of population increase of about 1.4 percent . . .

—*The Cincinnati Post*, June 19, 1999

S carcity has been defined as the fundamental economic problem. You experience scarcity at the personal level, and scarcity is also a problem at the national level, even for relatively prosperous nations such as the United States. At the global level, scarcity reveals itself through food, energy, and other resource shortages—all of which are compounded as world population grows.

The world population has now surpassed 6 billion, and, as you read in the cover story, the next billion will be here before long. In many respects, the earth is a very small planet, and it seems to be getting smaller every day.

The Global Population Issue

 Population growth has fascinated the world ever since Thomas Malthus published his *Essay on the Principles of Population* in 1798. His views, published over 200 years ago, are still relevant because of the earth's growing population and its demand for resources.

1 FOCUS

Section Overview
This section discusses population, and nonrenewable/renewable energy sources.

BELLRINGER
Motivational Activity

- Project **transparency** and have students answer questions.
- Available as blackline master.

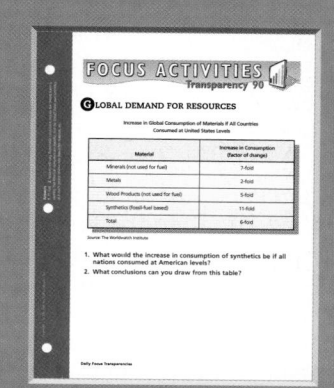

Study Guide

Reading Strategy
Have students create the graphic organizer.
Answers to Graphic: *renewable: hydroelectric power, biomass, and wind power, can be replenished; nonrenewable: petroleum, coal, and nuclear energy, cannot be replenished*

Preteaching Vocabulary
Call on volunteers to define the Key Terms.

RESOURCE MANAGER

Reproducible Masters
- Reproducible Lesson Plan 20-1
- Daily Lecture Notes 20-1
- Guided Reading Activity 20-1
- Reading Essentials and Study Guide 20-1
- Section Quiz 20-1

Transparencies
- Daily Focus Transparency 90

Multimedia
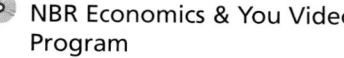
- NBR Economics & You Video Program
- Interactive Tutor Self-Assessment Software
- ExamView® Pro Testmaker
- Presentation Plus!

2 TEACH

Daily Lecture Notes 20-1

DAILY LECTURE NOTES — Lesson 20-1

DID YOU KNOW?
The three most densely populated states are in the Northeast. New Jersey has 1,094 residents per square mile, with runners-up being Rhode Island (946) and Massachusetts (784). Though the West's population shows the most rapid growth, it has the three states with the lowest density: Alaska with 1, Wyoming with 5, and Montana with 6.

PAGES 545–546
I. The Global Population Issue
A. The views of Thomas Malthus on population, published in 1798, are still relevant today because of Earth's growing population and its demand for resources.
B. Malthus argued that population would grow faster than its ability to feed itself and eventually be reduced to a condition of subsistence.
C. Malthus did not foresee advances in productivity and family choice.
D. The annual worldwide population growth rate is approximately 1.4 percent a year.

Discussion Question
Which countries are feeling the greatest pressures from a population increase, the developing or the industrialized nations? *(Developing nations especially feel the pressure because much of their populations lives at subsistence level. However, industrialized nations also feel the pressure as people from the developing nations move across borders, legally or otherwise, to look for work.)*

PAGES 546–548
II. Nonrenewable Energy Sources

CURRICULUM CONNECTION

Technology Scientists in Japan and many other nations are investigating the use of methane hydrate as a power source. Methane hydrate, a crystalline combination of natural gas and water that burns when ignited, is found under the ocean floor and under permafrost in polar regions. The problem with this resource is that no one has yet developed an affordable way to extract natural gas from the methane hydrate.

F.Y.I.

Natural pressures in new oil fields often force oil through the rock pores, into fractures, and into production wells that lead to the surface. After days, months, or years, the reservoir loses pressure, the natural flow of oil decreases, and oil companies use pumps to bring the oil to the surface.

Malthus: Views on Population

Thomas Malthus argued that population would grow faster than its ability to feed itself. The problem, he stated, was that population tended to grow geometrically, as in the number sequence 1, 2, 4, 8, 16, 32, 64, and so on. The ability of the earth to feed people, however, would grow at a slower and more constant rate, such as 1, 2, 3, 4, 5, and so on. Eventually, according to Malthus, the masses of the world would be reduced to a condition of **subsistence**—the state in which a population produces only enough to support itself.

In many countries—especially in the larger cities of the developing world—poverty is widespread. The Indian city of Calcutta, for example, has about 14 million people. Calcutta is one of the poorest and most crowded cities in the world. Hundreds of thousands of street dwellers beg and search for food in the city dumps and refuse piles. At night they sleep in the streets. Similar conditions exist in other parts of the world. In these places, the Malthusian prediction of a subsistence standard of living is a cruel reality.

Was Malthus Wrong?

In many other parts of the world, conditions are much better. Malthus did not foresee the enormous advances in productivity that have allowed an increasing standard of living to accompany a growing population. He also did not foresee that families might choose to have fewer children. In some countries, such as Japan, for example, the population is actually shrinking.

Malthus's predictions may not have been entirely accurate for the industrialized countries, but they still have long-term consequences for all nations. Today, for example, population pressures in other parts of the world are causing problems for many industrialized countries, including the United States, which is besieged by illegal immigrants from China, Mexico, and Haiti. As a result, many experts argue that it is in everyone's interest to control global population growth.

World Population Trends

Comparative world population growth rates are shown in **Figure 20.1.** For the world as a whole, the annual growth is approximately 1.4 percent a year. Although this may not seem very fast, the consequences can be enormous over time. Every year, the population increase is almost the equivalent of adding another Mexico to the world. If the population keeps growing at this rate, it will reach about 8 billion by 2020, and nearly 12 billion by 2050. At this rate, the population of the world will almost double from the time you graduate from high school until you retire at age 65.

Nonrenewable Energy Resources

Population pressure adds to the depletion of many important resources, and energy is one of these resources. Energy is necessary for production, and energy makes our lives more comfortable. In the form of gasoline, it powers cars. In the form of gas and electricity, it heats and cools homes.

Most of the energy we use comes from **nonrenewable resources**—resources that cannot be replenished once they are used. The major nonrenewable resource category—fossil fuels—is being consumed at an alarming rate and may only last for a few more generations at current consumption levels.

Oil

Oil is the biggest category of nonrenewable energy in use today—primarily because it was so inexpensive during much of the 1900s. Oil was also much more convenient to use than natural gas or coal. Because it could be refined into low-cost gasoline, automobiles were large, heavy, and usually got poor gas mileage.

The low cost of oil even affected living habits. People moved to the suburbs and then spent hours traveling to and from their jobs. Gasoline was so inexpensive that trains and city busses never became as important as the automobile.

In 1973, however, the oil-producing countries of the Middle East placed an **embargo**—a restriction on the export or import of a commodity in trade—on oil sales to the West. The embargo caused energy shortages in many parts of the world, driving the price of oil from $5 to more than $35 a barrel. Prices came

---

MEETING SPECIAL NEEDS ACTIVITY

English Language Learners Students who are learning the English language may experience frustration if they are asked to read *and* take notes. For them, it may be easier to finish reading and then review the text and take notes. Have these students read Section 1. As they read, have them use a signal—removable highlighting tape, for example—to mark important points. Then have them review the text and take notes. **ELL**

 Refer to *Inclusion for the Social Studies Classroom Strategies and Activities* in the TCR.

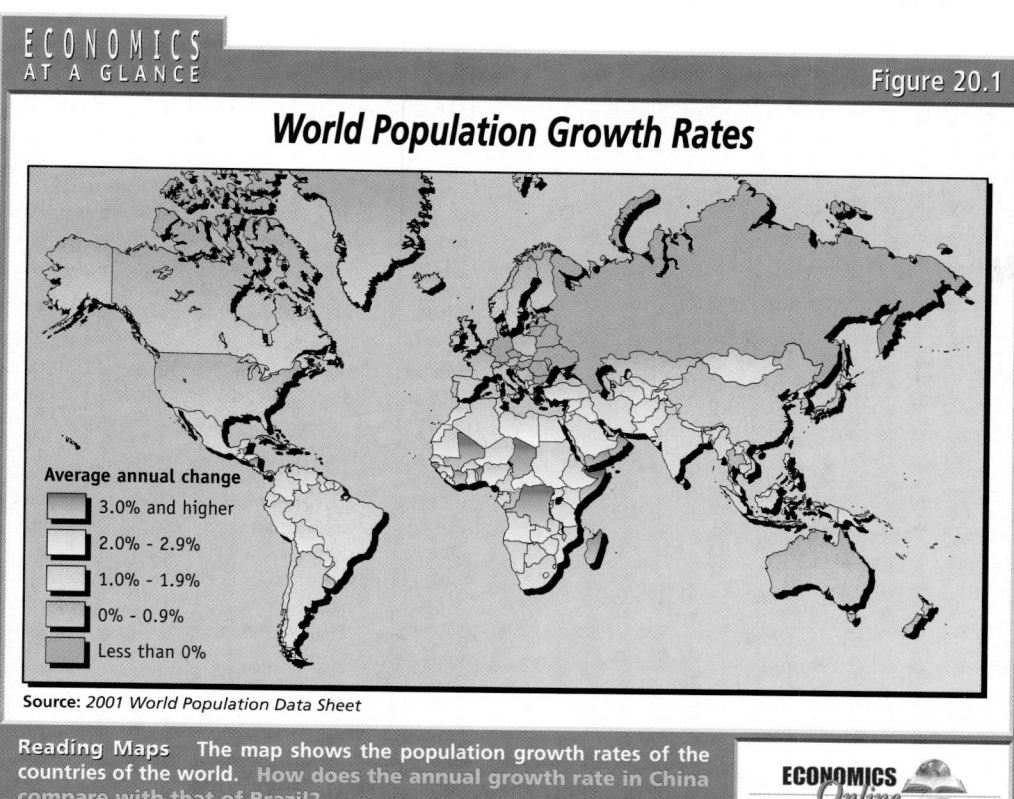

ECONOMICS AT A GLANCE

Figure 20.1

World Population Growth Rates

Average annual change
- 3.0% and higher
- 2.0% - 2.9%
- 1.0% - 1.9%
- 0% - 0.9%
- Less than 0%

Source: *2001 World Population Data Sheet*

Reading Maps   The map shows the population growth rates of the countries of the world.   How does the annual growth rate in China compare with that of Brazil?

ECONOMICS *Online*

Visit epp.glencoe.com and click on *Textbook Updates—Chapter 20* for an update of the data.

down slowly after that, reaching their inflation-adjusted pre-embargo levels in the mid-1990s. In late 1998, the price of oil even dropped below $9 a barrel, although it has since rebounded.

With the exception of the 20 years following the oil embargo, the world was flooded with, and grew up on, cheap oil. The oil was eagerly consumed and, because it is a nonrenewable resource, is gone forever.

Natural Gas

This category constitutes our second most important energy source, accounting for nearly 25 percent of energy consumption in the United States.

Historically, natural gas was more difficult to transport and use than oil, and so it did not become an important energy source until much later. Eventually inexpensive natural gas became popular as an industrial fuel, and so many factories and industrial technologies were built around it.

Coal

Coal is the third-largest nonrenewable resource used in the United States. While it was the first nonrenewable resource to be used on a large scale, oil and natural gas soon displaced it because they are more convenient to use.

CHAPTER 20: GLOBAL ECONOMIC CHALLENGES **547**

CHAPTER 20
Section 1, pages 545–550

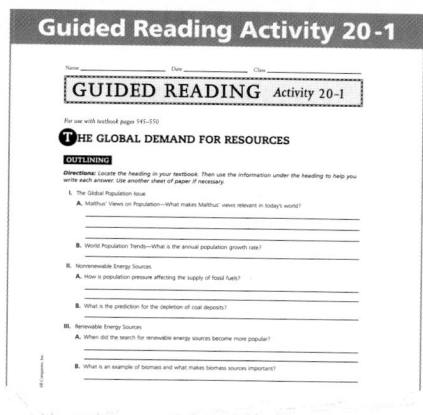

Guided Reading Activity 20-1

GUIDED READING Activity 20-1

For use with textbook pages 545–550

THE GLOBAL DEMAND FOR RESOURCES

OUTLINING

Directions: Locate the heading in your textbook. Then use the information under the heading to help you write each answer. Use another sheet of paper if necessary.

I. The Global Population Issue
   A. Malthus' Views on Population—What makes Malthus' views relevant in today's world?

   B. World Population Trends—What is the annual population growth rate?

II. Nonrenewable Energy Sources
   A. How is population pressure affecting the supply of fossil fuels?

   B. What is the prediction for the depletion of coal deposits?

III. Renewable Energy Sources
   A. When did the search for renewable energy sources become more popular?

   B. What is an example of biomass and what makes biomass sources important?

ECONOMICS AT A GLANCE

Answer: *Brazil, 1–1.9; China, 0–0.9*

L2 Analyzing Ideas

Have students review Thomas Malthus's views about population growth. Then write the following statement on the board: *Malthus was both right and wrong.* Ask students to discuss how this statement applies to Malthus's predictions about population and the supply of food. **Ask:** How do Malthus's views apply directly to poorer countries? How do these views apply directly to industrialized countries? Might rapid population growth have an indirect impact on the industrialized world? Have students write a brief essay titled "Thomas Malthus: Right and Wrong?"

FREE ENTERPRISE ACTIVITY

Have students survey business owners and managers in the community to discover what measures they are taking to conserve resources. Suggest that students ask such questions as: What types of resources are you conserving? What conservation methods are you using? What methods might you adopt in the future? Why are you taking steps to conserve resources? Have students summarize their findings and present them to the class.

L3 Library Research

Have students prepare an illustrated report on one of the following energy resources: oil, coal, natural gas, solar power, hydroelectric power, wind power, nuclear energy, or gasohol. Suggest that students focus their reports on such topics as history and development, reserves, and possible future use. Have students share their reports with the class.

THE GLOBAL ECONOMY

Solar Energy and the Developing World The use of solar energy is growing rapidly in developing nations. Developing countries have been some of the biggest buyers of solar energy equipment sold by American companies. Solar stations supply power to homes and schools as well as to telecommunications systems, water pumping stations, and refrigerators for medical supplies. The governments of Guatemala, Panama, El Salvador, and Mexico are among those that recognize the advantages of solar power.

Visual Instruction

Answer to Caption:
petroleum, natural gas, coal, nuclear power

Today, nearly two-thirds of the world's known coal reserves are in the United States, Russia, and China. Coal is the most plentiful fossil fuel in the world, but even these supplies will eventually run out. Estimates based on the present rate of consumption indicate that the reserves will last about 200 years.

Nuclear Energy

Nuclear energy is the newest and fourth largest source of nonrenewable energy, accounting for nearly 8 percent of all energy used in the United States. The future of nuclear power is uncertain, however, for a number of reasons.

One of the reasons is cost. Nuclear reactors are expensive to build and maintain. Second, nuclear energy produces highly hazardous byproducts, the safe disposal of which poses a major problem.

Finally, there is always some chance that a nuclear plant will fail, or that another accident would happen like the 1979 near-meltdown at Three Mile Island in Pennsylvania. The 1986 meltdown of the reactor in Chernobyl, Ukraine, served as another reminder of the nuclear power hazards.

Renewable Energy Resources

Before 1973, the low price of oil gave everyone very little incentive to develop alternative energy sources. Renewable energy resources became more popular after the oil embargo, but today they still account for a small portion of the total energy we consume.

Hydroelectric Power

Historically, hydropower was used to power the mills and factories of the Northeast in the 1800s. The power was reliable, and its source—water—was free at the time. Later, a number of larger generators at the Hoover Dam and the Tennessee Valley Authority were completed to generate power on a much larger scale. Aside from these newer projects, most dams were small and could not distribute power very efficiently to other locations.

When oil was obtained cheaply from the Middle East, hydroelectric power became less important. By the late 1950s, many of the commercial power dams in the United States had been abandoned. When oil became more expensive, however, steps

Natural Resources

Energy Demand for scarce resources is one of the most pressing problems facing all nations. *What are nonrenewable energy resources?*

CRITICAL THINKING

Distinguishing Fact From Opinion Nuclear power has been used for over 40 years, but it still faces strong opposition. Organize students into groups. Have groups use the Internet and the library to obtain primary and secondary sources on the positive and negative aspects of nuclear power. Ask each group to record ten interesting things they learned through their research. Then have them determine if the information is factual by finding material in a second source to prove or disprove the information. Have groups present their findings to the class, explaining which items on their list were based on fact and which were based on opinion.
Ask: Did any particular words or phrases alert you that the information you were considering might be an opinion? Explain. **BLOCK SCHEDULING**

were taken to bring some of the dams back into use. Today, hydroelectricpower is our most important renewable energy source, accounting for half of all renewable energy consumed in the United States.

Biomass

Energy made from biomass—wood and wood waste, peat, municipal solid waste, straw, corn, tires, landfill gasses, fish oils, and other waste—is the second most important category of renewable energy sources. While relatively new, this category accounts for approximately 40 percent of all renewable energy consumed in the United States today.

Ethanol is grain alcohol made from corn. Ethanol is used to make **gasohol**—a fuel that is a mixture of 90 percent unleaded gasoline and 10 percent ethanol. Although gasohol has not been accepted as quickly as supporters first hoped, it still has a small share of the market in some areas.

Other, lesser-known alternatives are also being used. Major food firms have made progress in converting chicken waste to fuel in the form of methane gas. This gas can then be recycled for industrial and commercial use. Over 100 cities are currently recovering and using methane gas generated in municipal landfills when the landfill waste decomposes.

Solar Energy

Solar power is the third largest source of renewable energy. Solar power has never been effectively harnessed, however, and it did not get much attention at first. After the oil embargo, the federal government began issuing grants to researchers to find ways to reduce the cost of solar energy. While solar power holds much promise, it only accounts for a fraction of the renewable energy used today.

Wind Power

The fourth-largest category of renewable energy sources is wind-generated electricity. In the early 1980s many wind farms were built, each of which produced enough electricity to power a medium-sized city. California is the largest producer of wind-generated energy, but it can also be found in Texas, Minnesota, Vermont, Hawaii, and Iowa.

The Most Dangerous Nuclear Reactors

Kola
RUSSIA
Sosnovy Bor
Novovoronezh
Baltic Sea
Smolensk
LITHUANIA
Ignalina
Kursk
Bohunice
Chernobyl
UKRAINE
SLOVAKIA
Graphite-moderated reactors
Kozloduy
Black Sea
Pressurized water reactors
BULGARIA

Reading Maps Nuclear reactors serve three general purposes. Civilian reactors generate energy for electricity and sometimes also steam for heating. Military reactors create materials that can be used in nuclear weapons. Research reactors are used to develop weapons or energy production technology. How many nuclear power plants are located in the former Soviet Union and Eastern Europe?

While this is still a small category, wind-generated electricity is an important source of power in areas such as islands or remote peninsulas where it is difficult to obtain other forms of energy.

Other Resources

 Resources other than those used to generate energy—water and land in particular—may also be in danger. In the past, American concern with water focused mainly on the pollution of the

CHAPTER 20: GLOBAL ECONOMIC CHALLENGES **549**

ECONOMICS
AT A GLANCE

Answer: *nine*

NIGHTLY BUSINESS REPORT

 ECONOMICS & YOU

 Chapter 27
Disc 1, Side 2
Global Economic Challenges

Ask: Why do companies from one country produce and sell products in other countries? *(They look for the most efficient and cost-effective places to make their products.)*

③ ASSESS

Assign Section 1 Assessment.

💾 Have students use **Interactive Tutor Self-Assessment Software**.

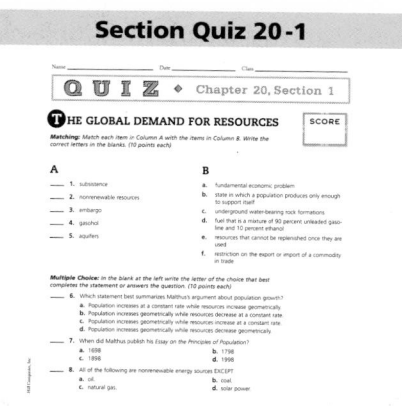
Section Quiz 20-1

EXTENDING THE CONTENT

U.S. Department of Energy The Department of Energy was created in 1977 primarily as a response to the 1973 embargo that forced up the price of oil. The purpose of the department is to plan energy policy and research and to develop new energy technology. The goal of the department is to reduce the country's vulnerability to future disruptions in oil markets.

Reteach

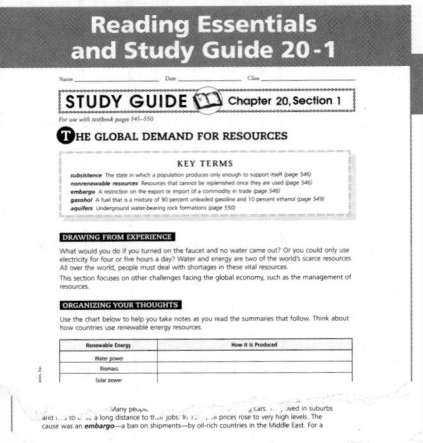

Reading Essentials and Study Guide 20-1

Enrich

Direct students to research the locations of major reserves of non-renewable energy sources. Have them record their findings on an outline map of the world. Remind students that their maps will need a title, labels, and a key. Call on volunteers to display their maps.

CLOSE

Have students discuss the problem of dwindling energy resources. **Ask:** What are we doing about this problem? What should we do about this problem?

CYBERNOMICS SPOTLIGHT

Science
Biotechnology is making an impact in the world economy. Genetic engineering allows researchers to place a gene into a plant in order to create a new plant that can grow twice as fast. Agricultural experts estimate that within the next 40 years the world population will increase by 50 percent, which means farmers will need to produce more crops than ever before. To sustain economic growth in the developing world, experts believe that food productivity improvements must be made using this type of biotechnology.

country's waterways. Today, however, the focus has shifted to the availability of water and the realization that water is in critical supply in many parts of the country.

More than 80 percent of the water consumed in the United States is used in agriculture, and most of this water is used in surface irrigation, which has a high evaporation rate. As a result, much water is lost into the atmosphere.

Farmers have been able to tap large sources of water from rivers, streams, ponds, and **aquifers**—underground, water-bearing rock formations.

Aquifers supply nearly 40 percent of the water that farmers use and are also the source of fresh water for many communities.

One of the largest aquifers in the country is the Ogallala Aquifer, which supplies water to the High Plains states from Texas to Nebraska. So much water has been pumped out, however, that the aquifer's water table has been dropping about three feet a year. Some experts even predict that the Ogallala Aquifer will run out of water in the next 40 or 50 years.

The water shortage is also a problem in southern California. Over the years, plans have been proposed and projects have been undertaken to bring in water from areas hundreds of miles away.

Land is another valuable natural resource subject to the demands of a growing world population. Land, however, is different from other resources because there is only a fixed supply that cannot be moved from one place to another.

A growing population has the effect of reducing the amount of land available for agriculture. As communities grow, factories, roads, and houses are built on the fertile land near the rivers. The development of this land forces the farmers to move to the outskirts. The phenomenon, now known as urban sprawl, has claimed some of our finest farmland—covering fertile fields with expressways, shopping centers, and housing developments.

Section 1 Assessment

Checking for Understanding
1. **Main Idea** How does population growth affect world resources?
2. **Key Terms** Define subsistence, nonrenewable resources, embargo, gasohol, aquifer.
3. **Describe** how Malthus believed population growth would affect the future of the planet.
4. **Identify** the importance of conserving nonrenewable resources.
5. **List** the major renewable resources today.
6. **Describe** the effects that a growing population has on scarce resources such as aquifers.

Applying Economic Concepts
7. **Scarcity** During the oil embargo, many people openly advocated nonprice gasoline rationing. Some favored allowing each automobile owner to use 10 gallons per week. What are the pros and cons of such a mandatory rationing program?

Critical Thinking
8. **Making Comparisons** How do renewable resources differ from nonrenewable resources?

 Practice and **assess** key social studies skills with the *Glencoe Skillbuilder Interactive Workbook, Level 2.*

Section 1 Assessment Answers

1. Population growth increases the demand for limited resources.
2. All vocabulary terms are defined in the text.
3. Malthus believed that population would grow geometrically but that the ability of the earth to feed people would grow at a slower, constant rate, eventually leading to worldwide starvation.
4. Nonrenewable resources cannot be replaced once they are used.
5. solar power, hydroelectric power, wind power, biomass
6. It quickly depletes scarce resources.
7. Pros: forces conservation of a nonrenewable resource; decreases pollution. Cons: opens door for black market trading; government interference; people whose careers depend on travel need special consideration.
8. nonrenewable: will run out; renewable: can be reused, grown, replaced, or regenerated

Profiles IN Economics

Population

A Classical Economist:
Thomas Malthus
(1766–1834)

Thomas Malthus was an English economist, sociologist, and member of the clergy who pioneered modern population study. He was a kind, gentle person dedicated to his father and his church. He was also the economist who is credited with giving economics the title of "the dismal science."

EDUCATION

Malthus was born to wealthy parents and was educated at home by his father and by private tutors. At age 18 he enrolled at Jesus College, Cambridge, to study mathematics and the classics.

While he was away from home, Malthus and his father often exchanged letters debating the popular issues of the day. At one point, the elder Malthus became fascinated with a popular utopian vision that promised eventual peace, prosperity, and equality for all. Malthus attacked the argument in a 50,000-word letter to his father. The elder Malthus was so impressed that he encouraged Thomas to publish the treatise

for others to read. The result was *An Essay on the Principle of Population as It Affects the Future Improvement of Society,* published in 1798.

POPULATION THEORY

The book was an instant success that was to change forever the way people viewed population. In it, Malthus argued that poverty and distress would be the eventual fate of people, not the popular utopian vision. He reasoned that population would increase at a geometric rate (1, 2, 4, 8, 16, . . .), while food supplies would increase at an arithmetic rate (1, 2, 3, 4, 5, . . .).

According to this progression, population growth would eventually outstrip the available food supply, resulting in famine, misery, and a subsistence standard of living for the masses.

At first, Malthus thought only three factors could check the growth of population: war, famine, and disease. Several years later, as

he refined his ideas, he added a fourth check: moral restraint. Separately or together, these factors could raise the death rate, lower the birthrate, or both. In Malthus's view, however, these restraints on population growth would not be enough to prevent most of the world from forever remaining at the subsistence level. Despite his considerable accomplishments in other aspects of economics, Malthus is best remembered for his pessimistic views on population.

Examining the Profile

1. **Evaluating Information** Do you agree or disagree with Malthus's predictions about population? Why or why not?

2. **For Further Research** Find out what Malthus's other contributions to economics were.

CHAPTER 20: GLOBAL ECONOMIC CHALLENGES **551**

BACKGROUND

The work of Malthus has had long-term, far-reaching, and fundamental effects. It was Malthus who first brought the problem of overpopulation to the attention of scholars, and his ideas have served as the basis for modern attempts to control population growth, especially in poor, developing nations. Malthus influenced David Ricardo, who based his theory—that overpopulation would keep wages near subsistence levels—on Malthus's work. This theory was also fundamental to Karl Marx's theory of surplus value. Malthus even influenced Charles Darwin, who read Malthus's *Essay on the Principle of Population,* and wrote that it helped him formulate his theory of natural selection. Malthus has had a significant role in influencing some of the most important intellectual and historical developments of the last 200 years.

TEACH

Challenge students to critique Malthus's essential argument that a geometric increase in population outstrips the arithmetic increase in food supply, dooming people to a subsistence level. Have them consider such things as advances in technology, genetic plant science, population control, and so forth.

Answers to Examining the Profile

1. Answers will vary. Students who agree might cite the population pressures and poverty that afflict developing countries. Students who disagree might cite population control programs and improvements in agriculture.

2. Answers will vary. Malthus wrote *Principles of Political Economy* and other books.

FOCUS

Section Overview
This section describes the role of market prices in the conservation of resources.

BELLRINGER
Motivational Activity

Project **transparency** and have students answer questions.

Available as blackline master.

Daily Focus Transparency 91

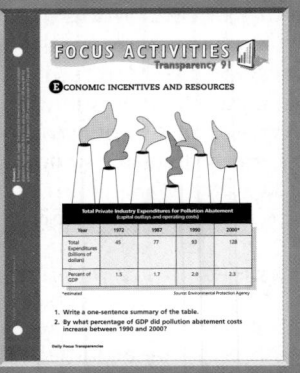

Study Guide

Reading Strategy
Have students create the graphic organizer.
Answers to Graphic: *legislated limits, taxes on pollution, tradable pollution permits*

Preteaching Vocabulary
Call on volunteers to provide the meaning of each Key Term. Have students check these meanings by finding the terms in the Glossary.

SECTION 2

Economic Incentives and Resources

Study Guide

Main Idea
Incentives help preserve scarce resources.

Reading Strategy
Graphic Organizer As you read the section, complete a graphic organizer similar to the one below by providing examples of ways to curtail the incentive to pollute.

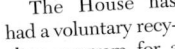

Methods to curtail the incentive to pollute

Example   Example

Key Terms
glut, pollution, acid rain, pollution permit

Objectives
After studying this section, you will be able to:
1. **Explain** how the price system helps conserve water, natural gas, and oil.
2. **Describe** government efforts to limit pollution.
3. **State** the importance of using resources wisely.

Applying Economic Concepts
Markets and Prices Have you ever traveled to different gasoline stations to get the cheapest price for a gallon of gas? Read to find out how markets and prices operate in the free enterprise system.

Cover Story

Lawmakers Can Recycling in House

Recycling area

WASHINGTON (AP)—The House of Representatives has rejected mandatory recycling for its offices.

The House has had a voluntary recycling program for a decade. But the Associated Press reported last month that most congressional offices were still mixing aluminum cans, bottles and different grades of paper. Many federal agencies and local governments separate their trash and sell recyclable material.

—*The Washington Post*, June 11, 1999

552

Economic systems require incentives to make them work smoothly. In a market economy, incentives such as the profit motive and prices can be used to preserve scarce resources.

Economic incentives are important because they tend to encourage more widespread and lasting results than other programs that rely on conscience, patriotism, or other motivations. Those who create them, as you read in the cover story, often abandon voluntary conservation programs.

The Price System

With resources becoming increasingly scarce, it is important to see how the price system contributes to the conservation—or lack—of scarce resources. The examples that follow illustrate this influence.

The higher price for oil after 1973 dramatically affected the production of oil. When oil was priced below $5 a barrel, few countries were

---

RESOURCE MANAGER

Reproducible Masters
- Reproducible Lesson Plan 20-2
- Daily Lecture Notes 20-2
- Guided Reading Activity 20-2
- Reading Essentials and Study Guide 20-2
- Section Quiz 20-2

Transparencies
- Daily Focus Transparency 91

Multimedia
- Interactive Tutor Self-Assessment Software
- ExamView® Pro Testmaker
- Presentation Plus!

willing to devote large resources to retrieve it. When the price increased to $35 and more, many countries increased their production almost overnight. At the same time, interest in alternative energy sources soared, and countries poured billions into energy-research projects ranging from shale oil to solar power.

By 1981, however, prices began to fall because of a worldwide **glut**—a substantial oversupply—of oil. A decline in demand caused by a recession contributed to the worldwide oversupply. People had also learned to conserve energy, which further reduced the demand for oil.

The collective impact of the increase in world supply and the decline in demand caused OPEC to lose some of its ability to control the supply of oil. This control slipped even further after the Persian Gulf War, when some OPEC members increased oil production to replenish their financial reserves depleted during the war. Finally, oil prices reached their pre-embargo levels in the mid-1990s.

Lower oil prices had several consequences. First, the search for alternative energy sources began to wane. Second, the exploration for new oil slowed dramatically because companies already had enough oil. Third, consumers changed their spending habits again. New houses became large once more, and consumers opted for low-mileage, sport utility vehicles instead of fuel-efficient economy cars.

In the end, the very mechanism that encouraged people to conserve energy when oil prices were high—the price system—did exactly the opposite when oil prices went down again.

When farmers pump water out of the ground to water their crops, they use pumps driven by electricity or natural gas. When water tables fall because of pumping, it costs more to pump the water. The increased cost of pumping encourages everyone to use it more efficiently, thus conserving a scarce resource.

In time, the falling water table makes some of the shallow wells useless, requiring deeper and more costly wells to be drilled. At this point, the price system will affect farming decisions again. Deeper wells will be dug for the most profitable crops, while marginal and unprofitable crops will be abandoned.

Ultimately, the price system works to establish an equilibrium between the rising cost of obtaining water and the profitability of the crops grown with the water. Although some crops and fields will be abandoned, they are likely to be the ones that were the least productive in the first place. As a result, the actual amount of lost agricultural output will not be that large.

When the price of natural gas was low in the 1960s, the quantity demanded was high. Because government regulated the price, however, producers had little incentive to increase its production.

Congress then tried to stimulate gas discovery and production by lifting the price controls on deep gas-pockets of natural gas, 15,000 feet or more below the earth's surface. The price of this gas then rose to three or four times its previous level, causing even more exploration for deep gas. Later, all gas price controls were removed, which encouraged even more production.

Conservation

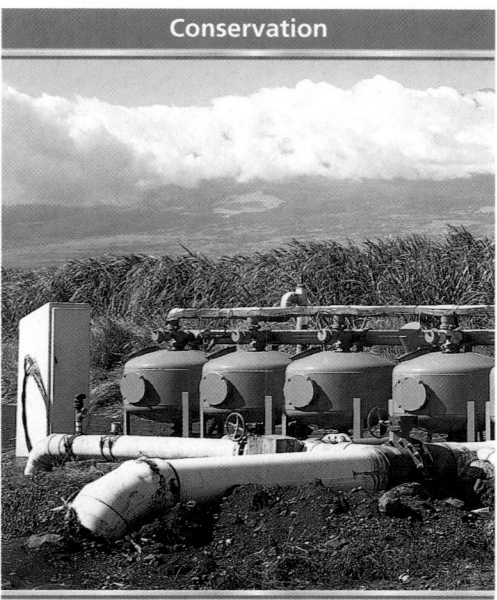

The Price System Surface irrigation systems are fairly common in the United States. *How does the price system affect farming decisions?*

CHAPTER 20: GLOBAL ECONOMIC CHALLENGES **553**

2 TEACH

Daily Lecture Notes 20-2

DAILY LECTURE NOTES 📖 Lesson 20-2

DID YOU KNOW?
Acid rain is in part due to efforts to reduce the effects of the Industrial Revolution. When smokestacks are short, the pollutants released hug the ground, causing local health problems. When smokestack heights were increased, the pollutants reached higher into the atmosphere, creating acid rain.

PAGES 552-554
I. The Price System
  A. The price system contributes to whether scarce resources are conserved.
  B. Interest in alternative energy sources surged when there was an oil embargo and waned when there was a glut.
  C. The price system works to establish an equilibrium between the rising cost of obtaining water and the profitability of the crops grown with water.
  D. The Law of Supply led gas producers to produce more of deregulated deep gas when its price went up.

Discussion Question
Why might a country choose to regulate the price of energy sources? (Possibilities might include preventing monopolies from charging very high prices; equalizing the access of various industries to energy sources; and promoting the use of one source over another.)

PAGES 554-556
II. Pollution and Economic Incentives
  A. Pollution will be less of a problem when the incentive to pollute is removed.
  B. The setting of legislated standards is one way to control pollution; another is through

📐 Math Practice

Oil Reserves In 1999 the known global reserves of oil amounted to 1,053 billion barrels. If the current consumption of oil is about 26.3 billion barrels per year, approximately how many years will those reserves last? *(about 40 years)*

Visual Instruction

Answer to Caption:
Farmers abandon marginal and unprofitable crops in favor of the more profitable crops when the cost of water increases.

MEETING SPECIAL NEEDS ACTIVITY

Learning Style: Intrapersonal Ask students to write a short essay that describes their personal thoughts and feelings about pollution. In their essays, students should identify sources of pollution within their own community. Students should also discuss their personal commitment to conservation and to preventing pollution. Then, as a class, discuss what individuals can do to reduce pollution both within the community and worldwide.
Ask: What can you do to help end pollution within your community?

 Refer to *Inclusion for the Social Studies Classroom Strategies and Activities* in the TCR.

L2 Analyzing Ideas

Discuss with students the different ways pollution might be controlled, focusing on the tax incentive alternative. Then randomly assign the following roles to students until every student has a role: a business owner whose factory pollutes, an environmentalist, an official from a state environmental protection agency, an economist, and a person who lives near the factory. Have students write a paragraph explaining how a person in their role might view the pollution tax. Have representatives of each role read their paragraphs to the class.

CYBERNOMICS

Cost-Benefit Analysis Online

Organizations used to visit professional economists for cost-benefit analysis, but now many are finding this service online. Consumers are now able to purchase software or download programs that provide the services they need for economic decision making. These programs are generally convenient, accurate, easy to use, equipped with professionally formatted software, and capable of creating charts, reports, and statistics.

The lack of interest in drilling for shallow gas was consistent with the law of supply, which maintains that the lower the price paid to producers, the less will be brought to market. Also consistent with the law of supply was the effort by producers to produce more of the deregulated deep gas when its price went up.

Pollution and Economic Incentives

Pollution is the contamination of air, water, or soil by the discharge of poisonous or noxious substances. Pollution is a problem that most countries face today.

Careers

EPA Inspector

The Environmental Protection Agency (EPA) is the federal agency responsible for protecting the environment. It employs thousands of inspectors to supervise enforcement of pollution control laws and regulations.

The Work

EPA inspectors examine air, water, and soil for evidence of pollution. Investigating the cause and scope of pollution requires inspectors to visit sites where pollution might occur, test for pollutants, and collect samples for analysis. They monitor the air quality of major cities and of industrial sites. After completing their examination, EPA inspectors put together reports of their findings and initiate action to stop further pollution.

Qualifications

EPA inspectors generally have a college education with a specialization in environmental or biological science, plus several years of experience in the field. As with most government jobs, EPA applicants must pass a civil service examination.

554

The Incentive to Pollute

Pollution does not occur on its own: it occurs because people and firms have an incentive to pollute. If that incentive can be removed, pollution will be less of a problem.

For years, factories have located along the banks of rivers so they could dump their refuse into the moving waters. Some factories that generated smoke and other air pollutants located farther from the water, but their tall smokestacks still blew the pollutants long distances. Others tried to avoid the problem by digging refuse pits on their property and burying their toxic wastes.

In all three situations, factory owners were trying to lower production costs by using the environment as a giant waste-disposal system. From an economic point of view, the reasoning was sound. Firms get ahead when they lower production costs. Those who produce the most at the least cost make the most profits.

The cost of pollution to society as a whole, however, is huge. For example, **acid rain**—a mixture of water and sulfur dioxide that makes a mild form of sulfuric acid—falls over much of North America, damaging countless rivers and streams. Fertilizer buildup and raw sewage runoff poison ecosystems in other areas. The damage caused by pollution is extensive, but it can be controlled. One way to control pollution is through legislated standards. Another way is through economic incentives.

Controlling Pollution

Legislated standards include laws that specify the minimum standards of purity for air, water, and auto emissions. Congress, for example, has declared that all automobiles sold in the United States must meet certain pollution standards.

Legislated standards can be effective, but they are generally inflexible. Once a standard is set, a firm has to meet it or cease production. Because of this, many firms lobby extensively to exempt their industry from the pollution controls.

Another method of controlling pollution is to have companies pay taxes on the amount of pollutants they release. The size of the tax would depend on the severity of the pollution and the quantity of toxic substances being released.

FREE ENTERPRISE ACTIVITY

Select about 10 students and organize them into two teams. Have the teams take opposite sides and debate the following statement: "Limits on pollution should be established by market forces, not by government legislation." Have students not directly involved in the debate act as judges and list the major arguments presented in the debate. At the conclusion of the debate, call on a number of judges to share their lists with the class. Then have students use this information to write a short paper supporting or opposing the proposal.

 BLOCK SCHEDULING

Fighting Pollution

The Incentive to Pollute Pollution is one of the painful by-products of modern life. Damage caused by pollution is extensive. *What methods are used to hinder the incentive to pollute?*

Suppose a community wants to reduce air pollution caused by four factories, each of which releases large quantities of coal dust. A $50 tax on every ton of coal dust released into the air would be applied to each factory. Devices attached to the top of the factory's smokestacks would measure the amount of dust released during a given period, and the factory would be billed accordingly.

Each company would then have the choice of paying the tax or removing the pollutants themselves. This tax approach does not try to remove all pollution. It does, however, allow individual companies freedom of choice. It also provides flexibility that legislated standards lack—and may even prevent some plants from closing entirely.

Some firms would rather pay the tax than clean up their own pollution. These firms, however, help fund the pollution clean-up campaign. Consumers will not have to fund these efforts out of their income, sales, or property taxes.

Pollution Permits

The Environmental Protection Agency (EPA) currently uses a similar system to reduce sulfur dioxide emissions at coal-burning electric utilities. Sulfur dioxide emissions from the burning of coal and oil react with water and oxygen to form compounds that fall to the earth as acid rain. The EPA's target is to ultimately reduce sulfur dioxide emissions to a level of nine million tons per year.

Student Web Activity Visit the *Economics: Principles and Practices* Web site at epp.glencoe.com and click on *Chapter 20—Student Web Activities* for an activity on the Environmental Protection Agency.

CHAPTER 20: GLOBAL ECONOMIC CHALLENGES **555**

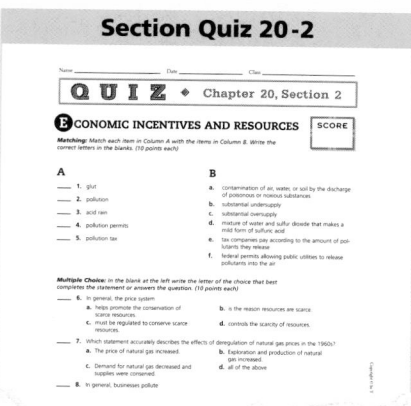
CRITICAL THINKING

Expressing Problems Clearly In January 2000, a district court judge ordered the EPA to set pollution limits on Louisiana's waters. The ruling judge said she was requiring the EPA's involvement because the state was slow to set its own water pollution limits. Over the next seven years, limits are to be set first in coastal waters, then in each basin across the state. Have students research the problem and solution on the Internet. Ask them to create a news report about the situation. News reports should clearly state details of the problem and the solution. Students should also note the current status of the EPA's efforts to set water pollution limits in Louisiana.

Reteach

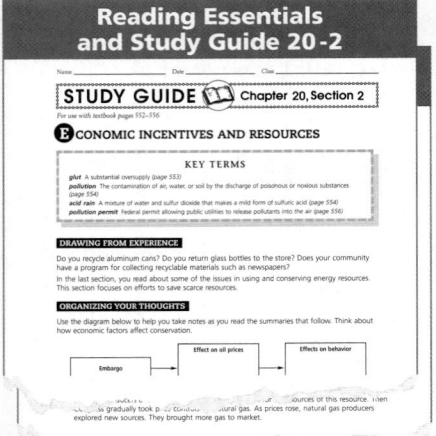

Reading Essentials and Study Guide 20-2

Enrich

Have students work individually or in small groups to create a four-page pictorial essay on the economic aspects of pollution. Display essays on the bulletin board.

4 CLOSE

Have students discuss, from an economic perspective, the following statement made by Ralph Waldo Emerson: "We do not inherit the earth from our ancestors, we borrow it from our children."

Issuing Permits

The EPA started its program by issuing sulfur dioxide **pollution permits**—federal permits allowing public utilities to release pollutants into the air—in 1993. Utilities are not allowed to operate without them, but if a utility has more permits than it needs, it can sell them in one-ton increments. Thus, utilities that want to spend money on emissions cleanup could sell their permits, and use the cash to clean up their emissions. Those who prefer to purchase and use the permits can do so.

The first set of pollution permits went on sale in March 1993 at the Chicago Board of Trade. The one-ton permits brought prices ranging from $122 to $450 each. The EPA issued additional permits in successive years, but fewer permits will be issued as time goes on, making them scarcer and more expensive. Ultimately, the utilities will either have to pay very high prices for the permits, or they will have to buy additional antipollution devices.

Advantages

The system also has advantages for environmentalists who wanted utilities to reduce pollution at even faster rates. Several environmental groups purchased the pollution permits with their own funds, making them scarcer and therefore more expensive, for the utilities.

Did you know?

Global Warming Most climatologists agree that the earth is likely to warm by as much as 2° to 9° F over the next 50 to 60 years. Human activities have released gasses that trap in the sun's rays and heat the earth. Scientists believe that polar caps will begin to melt, raising sea levels from at least a foot to as much as 6.6 feet in the next century. An estimated one-third of the world's population who live within 40 miles of the sea could be facing severe flooding and depletion of their freshwater sources.

Using Resources Wisely

The resource challenge is vital to a growing global economy. Resources become scarce when the quantity demanded for them is greater than the quantity supplied. In a market economy, the price system plays a major role in the allocation of resources. It tells consumers when resources are scarce. It also helps decision makers allocate resources more wisely.

Economists who understand the workings of a market economy are optimistic about the future, especially if the price system is allowed to function and fulfill its role in the economy. As long as the price "system" is allowed to operate, we will never suddenly run out of an endangered resource.

Section 2 Assessment

Checking for Understanding
1. **Main Idea** What are two incentives that can be used to preserve scarce resources in a market economy?
2. **Key Terms** Define glut, pollution, acid rain, pollution permit.
3. **Describe** how the price system helps conserve water, natural gas, and oil.
4. **Identify** the ways that the government tries to limit pollution.
5. **Explain** why resources should be used wisely.

Applying Economic Concepts
6. **Markets and Prices** Suppose that the demand for natural gas increases sharply because of a series of extremely harsh winters. How would a price increase affect gas usage as well as research efforts by natural gas companies?

Critical Thinking
7. **Making Comparisons** How do legislated standards and economic incentives differ in regard to pollution control?

 Practice and **assess** key social studies skills with the *Glencoe Skillbuilder Interactive Workbook, Level 2.*

Section 2 Assessment Answers

1. taxes and tradable permits
2. All vocabulary terms are defined in the text.
3. As the supply decreases, the price increases, lowering the quantity demanded.
4. legislated standards, pollution taxes, tradable pollution permits
5. Resources are limited; if used foolishly, there will not be enough for future.
6. People would limit their use, companies would find ways to increase production.
7. standards: specify minimum standards of purity for air, water, and auto emissions, are inflexible about compliance; incentives: include pollution taxes and pollution permits, offer choices in compliance

SEPTEMBER 11, 2000

— Newsclip

Foreign plants and animals are invading North America as a result of increased global trade and tourism, costing the U.S. billions of dollars each year. No longer hindered by time and distance, disease can strike any species, anywhere.

Bioinvasion

When reptile dealer Wayne Hill brought an ailing leopard tortoise into the veterinary clinic at the University of Florida at Gainsville in 1997, he was in for a big surprise. His pet, it turned out, had stowaways. Discreetly hidden beneath the animal's "armpits" were thumbnail-size African ticks, *Amblyomma marmoreum*. These critters can harbor a bacterium that causes heartwater, an animal disease that is endemic in sub-Saharan Africa but has spread to the Caribbean.

In the U.S., where cattle, sheep, deer, and elk have no immunity to the disease, heartwater could wipe out whole herds. . . .The tick that spreads heartwater is just the latest in a long list of foreign diseases that threaten ranch and farm economies throughout the world. . . .

The cattle industry could be affected by a bioinvasion.

Scientists and environmentalists have dubbed this phenomenon "bioinvasion." And the telltale signs of it are found all over the world. . . .In Mexico, just 200 miles from the Texas border,

nearly 14 million chickens were slaughtered this spring because of a highly contagious virus called Exotic Newcastle Disease. A virus called Nipah has destroyed the Malaysian pork industry and killed 105 people. In North America, veterinarians are fighting a deadly parasitic disease called leishmaniasis. . . .

Experts blame the spread of these and other pests on an explosion in world trade, business travel, and tourism. Global trade policies aggravate the problem by putting strict limits on countries' abilities to ban animal trade. Meanwhile, in the U.S., years of flat budgets for border inspectors and disease researchers have left populations of animals—and humans—doubly exposed.

Such oversights can incur appalling costs. Even in the U.S., which has been spared the worst of the recent plagues, the price tag for battling agricultural blights ran to $9 billion last year, according to a Cornell University study. . . .

Examining the Newsclip

1. **Understanding Cause and Effect** How have trade policies contributed to bioinvasion?

2. **Analyzing Information** What role have U.S. budget decisions played in this bioinvasion?

CHAPTER 20: GLOBAL ECONOMIC CHALLENGES **557**

BusinessWeek ONLINE

Visit the Business Week Web site at www.businessweek.com for up-to-date news, analysis on the economy, editorials, special reports, market updates, book reviews, personal finance information, and an archive of past articles.

TEACH

One of the newest species to invade U.S. waters is a tiny crustacean known as a fishhook flea. The fleas, which derive their name from their shape, clump together and clog fishing nets and lines in New York's Finger Lakes, and are working their way into the Great Lakes. Have students research to learn about fishhook fleas and other invasive aquatic species, such as zebra mussels. Have them answer questions such as "Where did the species originate?" "How did the species enter the U.S.?" "How much damage has been caused?" and "What action can be taken to prevent the spread of the species?" Have students use library resources and the Internet for their research.

☞ Refer to **Business Week Focus on the New Economy** in the TCR for additional unit-based articles.

Answers to Examining the Newsclip

1. Global trade policies limit countries' ability to ban animal trade, and it is difficult to prove which species may present a threat. In addition, insufficient budgets for border inspection in the U.S. make it easier for harmful diseases to spread.

2. The U.S. budget has not increased to help fund border inspectors and disease researchers. With more money for research and inspection, the U.S. would be more informed about the effects of different species on the animal and human population, and have the funding to search out and prevent possibly harmful species from entering the country.

SECTION 3

Applying the Economic Way of Thinking

1 FOCUS

Section Overview
This section describes the reasoned approach to economic decision making.

BELLRINGER
Motivational Activity

Project **transparency** and have students answer questions.

Available as blackline master.

Daily Focus Transparency 92

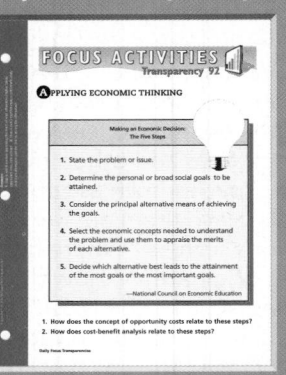

Study Guide

Reading Strategy
Have students create the graphic organizer.
Answers to Graphic: *1930s: provided only for those who had enough to buy the necessities of life; had little room for the elderly, ill, or incapacitated. Today: modified to satisfy the seven economic goals*

Preteaching Vocabulary
Use the Vocabulary Puzzle-Maker to create crossword and word-search puzzles.

Study Guide

Main Idea
Economics provides a foundation for analyzing choices and making decisions.

Reading Strategy
Graphic Organizer As you read the section, complete a graphic organizer similar to the one below by describing how American capitalism has changed.

```
         American capitalism
        /                    \
  Capitalism              Capitalism
  of the 1930s            today
```

Key Terms
cost-benefit analysis, modified free enterprise economy

Objectives
After studying this section, you will be able to:
1. **Describe** the reasoned approach to economic decision making.
2. **Understand** how our market economy will be able to cope with the future.

Applying Economic Concepts
Cost-Benefit Analysis Have you ever decided not to do something because the cost of doing it was greater than the benefits that would be received? Economists call this cost-benefit analysis—and they use this analysis often. If you think the same way, perhaps you are starting to think like an economist.

Cover Story

The Outlook—Pushing Adam Smith Past the Millennium

WASHINGTON—If Adam Smith were to visit the U.S. at the millennium's end, he would like what he saw. . . . Today, the invisible hand is more limber and supple than ever.

Free market idea grows

In the past two decades, globalization has forced American companies to compete on a worldwide scale, and the collapse of communism has extended capitalistic principles to every corner of the globe. Deregulation has injected market forces into areas long insulated from them . . . [and] the Internet has helped better-informed buyers find legions of new sellers, and sellers find far-flung buyers. . . .

—*The Wall Street Journal*, June 6, 1999

558

As a science, economics is concerned with the way in which people cope with scarcity. Because scarcity is a universal problem, the study of economics is important to everyone.

The economic system based on capitalism and free enterprise has, as you just read in the cover story, done quite well. There is also every likelihood that it will continue to do well in the future—although we also expect some evolution and modifications as we deal with new challenges and opportunities.

A Framework for Decision Making

Through the study of economics, you learn that choices must be made. You begin to discover different ways to analyze a problem, and that alternatives must be considered. The late economist Kenneth Boulding observed that economics has evolved to the point that it has now become a generalized theory of choice.

RESOURCE MANAGER

Reproducible Masters
- Reproducible Lesson Plan 20-3
- Daily Lecture Notes 20-3
- Guided Reading Activity 20-3
- Reading Essentials and Study Guide 20-3
- Section Quiz 20-3

Transparencies
- Daily Focus Transparency 92

Multimedia
- Vocabulary PuzzleMaker CD-ROM
- Interactive Tutor Self-Assessment Software
- ExamView® Pro Testmaker
- Presentation Plus!

THE GLOBAL ECONOMY

THE INFORMATION REVOLUTION

In this era, not only is capitalism global but so is the Information Revolution. As powerful data networks spread, the developing nations are being drawn into the borderless information economy.

Inside a gleaming computer center in Taipei, a young engineer labors late into the night. Connected by the Internet to some of the best software writers in the U.S., he is helping design a digital phone system that will match anything the U.S. or Europe can muster.

In China's northern boomtown of Tianjin, an auto worker pores over documents on how to arrange a low-interest mortgage on a modern condominium. In Mexico City, a working couple plows savings into a mutual fund, all to put two children through private school.

Ingenuity, new prosperity, middle-class striving—familiar Western values are appearing on the frontiers of capitalism. Multiply these scenes by the millions, and you see the shape of a revolution that will transform the global economy well into the next century. Already, capitalism is flourishing in regions as diverse as communist Asia and the former dictatorships of Latin America. Affluence is lifting millions out of poverty, giving many the chance to purchase their first Fiats and Toyotas as well as their first Apple computers and Panasonic VCRs. And inflation is brought to heel in even the most wayward economies.

The implications are huge for rich and poor alike. Hundreds of millions of peasants are leaving ancient ways of life for the factory. Cities such as Guangzhou and Bangalore teem with new inhabitants. Many are living poorly, of course, but just as many are thriving.

—*Business Week*, December 14, 1998

Critical Thinking

1. **Summarizing Information** What is the main point of the article? Write a thesis sentence in your own words explaining the main point.

2. **Drawing Conclusions** "The Information Revolution will draw economies from different parts of the world closer." Do you agree or disagree with this statement? Explain your answer.

Economics provides a framework for decision making that helps people to become better decision makers. The future will be different than the past, or even the present for that matter, but some things in economics—the way we think about problems—are likely to remain the same.

A Reasoned Approach

Economic decision making requires a careful, reasoned approach to problem solving. The National Council on Economic Education, an organization dedicated to the improvement of economic literacy in the United States, recommends five steps. These steps provide useful guidelines to decision making.

1. State the problem or issue.
2. Determine the personal or broad social goals to be attained.
3. Consider the principal alternative means of achieving the goals.
4. Select the economic concepts needed to understand the problem and use them to appraise the merits of each alternative.
5. Decide which alternative best leads to the attainment of the most goals or the most important goals.

—*A Framework for Teaching the Basic Concepts*, 1996

Life is full of trade-offs, but you will be better equipped to deal with the future if you know how to analyze the problems you will encounter.

CHAPTER 20: GLOBAL ECONOMIC CHALLENGES **559**

---

2 TEACH

Daily Lecture Notes 20-3

DAILY LECTURE NOTES 📖 Lesson 20-3

❶ DID YOU KNOW?
Though the Nobel Prizes were first distributed in 1901, the one for Economic Science was first awarded in 1969. While the money for the other prizes is drawn from the interest on the $9 million left by Alfred B. Nobel (1833–1896), inventor of dynamite, the economics prize is funded by the central bank of Sweden.

PAGES 558-560
I. A Framework for Decision Making
  A. Economic decision making requires a careful, reasoned approach to problem solving. The steps are:
    1. State the problem.
    2. Determine the goal to be obtained.
    3. Consider the alternatives needed to reach the goal.
    4. Choose an economic concept and use it to evaluate the alternatives.
    5. Decide which alternative leads to the achievement of the goal.
  B. Cost-benefit analysis involves comparing the costs of an action to its benefits.
  C. These costs include both opportunity and monetary costs.

❷ Discussion Question
Why is the mission of the National Council on Economic Education, to improve economic literacy in the United States, an important one for the future? *(While the economy and the kinds of economic decisions to be made might change, it makes sense to understand how to apply logic to analyze the problems that do arise.)*

THE GLOBAL ECONOMY

The Information Revolution
In 1999 the Global Technology Corps became the first public-private partnership program designed to provide technology and telecommunications to developing nations. Among the countries scheduled to benefit from the program were Albania and Macedonia.

Answers:
1. *Answers may include that the worldwide spread of capitalism is improving the standard of living for many people in developing countries.*
2. *Answers should be supported with sound reasoning.*

MEETING SPECIAL NEEDS ACTIVITY

Learning Style: Visual/Spatial Have students develop a visual display titled "The Triumph of Capitalism" based on the subsection of the same name and other knowledge they have gained from this course. Students should choose a theme, such as "U.S. Capitalism in the 1930s and Now," "Capitalism versus Communism," "Capitalism and Developing Countries," or "Famous Economists and Capitalism." They should then create a poster using pictures cut from magazines or newspapers, headlines, charts and graphs, and containing short paragraphs that they themselves write to explain their theme. Display and discuss students' posters within the context of the future of capitalism. 📦 **BLOCK SCHEDULING**

📁 Refer to *Inclusion for the Social Studies Classroom Strategies and Activities* in the TCR.

Guided Reading Activity 20-3

③ ASSESS

Assign Section 3 Assessment as homework or as an in-class activity.

💾 Have students use **Interactive Tutor Self-Assessment Software** to review Section 3.

Decision Making at the Margin

Economists use a number of tools to help them analyze and make decisions. Some of these tools include production possibilities curves, supply and demand curves, production functions, and even the National Income and Product Accounts.

One of the most important decision-making tools is the concept of marginal analysis. For example, when a firm makes a decision to produce additional output, it compares the extra cost of production with the extra benefits to be gained. If the benefits outweigh the costs, the firm decides to continue with the additional production. If the costs outweigh the benefits, the firm decides not to produce the additional output.

This process—**cost-benefit analysis**—involves comparing the costs of an action to its benefits. Firms use cost-benefit analysis when they make decisions to produce or purchase additional capital equipment. Many government agencies use it when they evaluate programs. Individuals also use it when they make decisions. Cost-benefit analysis is even used to make choices among economic goals. Some choices will work against one goal while favoring

STANDARD & POOR'S INFOBYTE

Economic Forecasts An economic forecast is a projection regarding the future direction of all or part of the economy. Economists analyze economic data to identify trends, and perform statistical evaluations to build their forecasts. Economists are like scientists in that they study phenomena by making observations based on collected data. The purpose of their studies is to uncover relationships between economic events and variables. An economist may, for example, study trends in the price and sales behavior of the domestic automobile market to arrive at a prediction of future auto sales. Businesses and governments rely on such forecasts for policy-making and goal-setting purposes. Individuals rely on these forecasts for their spending and investing decisions.

another, but evaluating the costs and benefits of each choice helps in making decisions.

Finally, we must remember that the economist uses a very broad definition of costs—that of opportunity costs. This ensures that we account for all of the costs of a decision, not just the monetary ones.

Coping With the Future

Everyone wants to know what will happen to the economy in the future. How will it adjust and what course will it take? Part of the answer can be found by examining the way markets work.

Markets and Prices

Our **modified free enterprise economy**—a free enterprise economy with some government involvement—is one that allows buyers and sellers to freely make the decisions that satisfy their wants and needs. The forces of supply and demand interact to establish prices in a market. Prices, in turn, act as signals, helping producers and consumers to make or even alter their spending decisions.

Prices also influence the allocation of resources across markets. The high price of oil in the 1970s made other energy sources competitive. In the 1980s, the high prices of personal computers attracted producers. Competition soon lowered prices and made the same computers affordable to mass markets.

A market economy has many advantages, including the ability to adjust to change gradually without the need for government intervention. As long as the forces of supply and demand are allowed to function, they will send producers and consumers the signals needed to reallocate resources. Although no one knows what the future will bring, capitalism has demonstrated its ability to adapt in the past, and it is likely to do so again in the future.

The Triumph of Capitalism

During the 1930s, the forces of socialism and communism were sweeping the world, while capitalist countries were in economic depression. Communism in the Soviet Union had considerable

FREE ENTERPRISE ACTIVITY

Organize students into several groups and have them discuss the question: "What course will the economy take in the future?" Have students consider the different factors that affect the economy, including technology and the Internet. Direct groups to predict what the state of the economy will be in five years, twenty-five years, and fifty years. Call on group representatives to read their predictions to the class.

impact upon the world, and socialist parties were on the rise in the European colonies in Africa.

Since then, communism in the former Soviet Union has collapsed under the weight of its own inefficiencies. Many socialist countries have embraced capitalism and the discipline of the market system. In addition, many developing countries have chosen capitalism as their economic system. Many emerging economic powers—including Singapore, South Korea, and Taiwan—owe much of their remarkable growth to capitalism.

Capitalism is now the dominant economic force in the world, but it is not the laissez-faire capitalism of the past. Capitalism has changed because people have addressed some of the weaknesses that Karl Marx and others identified many years ago.

The capitalism of the 1930s was ruthlessly efficient in that it provided only for those who produced or earned enough to buy the necessities of life. Early capitalism had little room for the elderly, the ill, or the incapacitated. Many economies today, including that of the United States, have a modified free enterprise economy, or modified private enterprise system. This is a free-market economy based on capitalism, yet modified by its people to satisfy the economic goals of freedom, efficiency, equity, security, full employment, price stability, and economic growth.

Capitalism has evolved over the years, and it shows every sign of continuing to do so in the future. In this respect, capitalism adjusts to change

the same way a market adjusts to small changes in supply and demand—incrementally, with adjustments so small that they are hardly noticed in the short run. This ability to evolve, and to adjust to the demands placed on it, are strengths of capitalism that will continue to ensure its success.

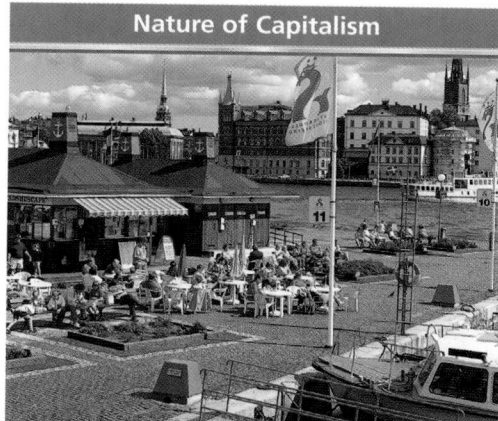

Nature of Capitalism

Adaptability In many industrial countries, capitalism is the prevailing economic system. Capitalism is based on private ownership of the means of production and on individual economic freedom. *How was the capitalism of the past different from the capitalism of today?*

Section 3 Assessment

Checking for Understanding

1. **Main Idea** How does cost-benefit analysis affect the decision-making process?

2. **Key Terms** Define cost-benefit analysis, modified free enterprise economy.

3. **Explain** the reasoned approach to economic decision making.

4. **Describe** how a market economy adapts to change.

5. **Explain** how marginal analysis assists in decision making.

Applying Economic Concepts

6. **Cost-Benefit Analysis** Think of a decision you must make in the next few days. How will you use your estimates of the costs and benefits to make your decision?

Critical Thinking

7. **Synthesizing Information** Provide an example of how prices act as a signal to you as a buyer and as a seller.

 Practice and **assess** key social studies skills with the *Glencoe Skillbuilder Interactive Workbook, Level 2.*

Section 3 Assessment Answers

1. It provides a logical basis for decision making, weighing the positive outcomes of a course of action against the negative.

2. All vocabulary terms are defined in the text.

3. It involves the five steps put forth by NCEE as guidelines to decision making.

4. Supply and demand adjust to cause price changes, which signal producers and consumers, causing them to reallocate resources.

5. Marginal analysis compares the cost of producing one additional unit of goods or services with the expected benefit.

6. Answers should reflect an understanding of cost-benefit analysis.

7. Low prices encourage buyers to buy more. Higher prices encourage sellers to produce more.

Visual Instruction

Answer to Caption:
Capitalism provided only for those who produced or earned enough to buy the necessities of life. Today, capitalism has evolved to better satisfy the economic goals of freedom, efficiency, equity, security, full employment, price stability, and economic growth.

Reteach

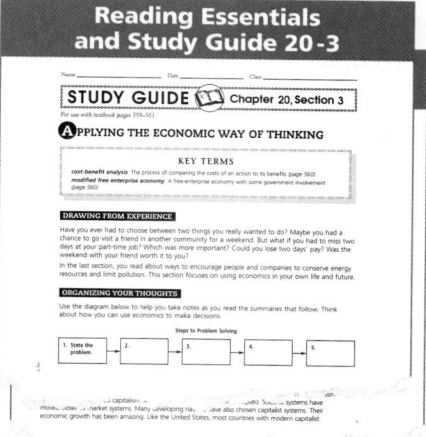

Enrich

Invite the manager of a local business to explain to the class how he or she uses cost-benefit analysis in his or her job.

 CLOSE

Have students develop a one-sentence description of economics. As an example, suggest: Economics is simply the study of choices.

Critical Thinking Skill

Teaching Skills

Have students use their understanding of the skill to make fact-based predictions for major economic indicators such as unemployment, inflation, and the stock market for the coming year. Students should use information gathered from library resources, newspapers and magazines, and the Internet to make their predictions. Ask students to photocopy or print all the material that they used. Have them present their predictions to the class and answer the question "How likely is this to occur?" after each one.

Additional Practice

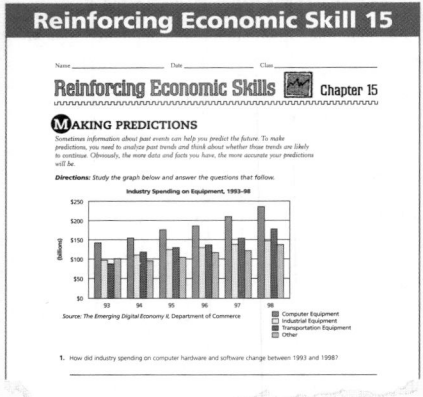

Reinforcing Economic Skill 15

GLENCOE
TECHNOLOGY

Glencoe Skillbuilder Interactive Workbook, Level 2
This interactive CD-ROM reinforces student mastery of essential social studies skills.

CRITICAL THINKING
Skill

Making Predictions

Predicting future events is obviously difficult and sometimes risky. The more information you have, however, the more accurate your predictions will be.

Learning the Skill

Follow these steps to help you analyze information in order to make predictions.

- Gather information about the decision or action.
- Use your knowledge of history and human behavior to identify what consequences could result.
- Analyze each of the consequences by asking: How likely is it that this will occur?

Practicing the Skill

Study the following passage, then answer the questions that follow.

Market scene, Peru

In 1950, only 42 percent of Latin Americans were city dwellers; today almost 73 percent live in cities, according to the United Nations. This compares with 34 percent in Africa and 33 percent in Asia. Despite oppressive poverty, Peruvians seeking a better life, for example, have been fleeing the countryside for Lima at the rate of more than a thousand a day and building settlements that seem like a never-ending expanse of small straw huts next to a noisy highway. The trend has created megacities throughout the continent.

The equation is similar in many countries. The major city attracts one-quarter to one-third of the country's population, with many living in squalid slums . . . encircling the affluent city. Experts say that by the year 2010, Rio de Janeiro and Sao Paulo will be one continuous megalopolis 350 miles long with almost 40 million people.

—by John L. Petersen, *The Road to 2015*

1. What trend does the passage show?
2. Do you think the trend the writer describes is likely to continue?
3. On what do you base this prediction?
4. What occurrences might have an effect on changing the trend?
5. What are three possible consequences or outcomes of this trend?

Application Activity

Analyze three articles in the business section of the newspaper. Predict three consequences of the actions in each of the articles. On what do you base your predictions?

 Practice and **assess** key social studies skills with the *Glencoe Skillbuilder Interactive Workbook, Level 2.*

562

Answers to Practicing the Skill

1. In Latin America, the cities are rapidly growing as many people move away from the countryside.
2. Answers should reflect an understanding of economic growth in developing countries.
3. Answers should note that the process of industrialization typically involves urban migration.
4. Higher prices for agricultural goods, lower wages in the city, or increased urban unemployment might change this trend.
5. Answers may include increased crime and disease, unemployment, and loss of a traditional way of life or cultural heritage.

Section 1

The Global Demand for Resources (pages 545–550)

- Over 200 years ago, Thomas Malthus predicted many of the population problems some developing nations face today–high birthrates, famine, and the threat of a **subsistence** standard of living.

- Malthus did not foresee advances in technology or that some birthrates would fall and some populations cease to grow.

- Many **nonrenewable resources** such as oil, natural gas, and coal are threatened today.

- The oil **embargo** of the early 1970s raised oil prices and encouraged Americans to seek alternative energy sources, along with alternative and renewable energy sources.

- Some renewable energy resources–hydroelectric power, biomass, solar power, wind power–have been developed, including **gasohol,** a combination of unleaded gasoline and grain alcohol.

- Other resources like water and land are also coming under pressure because of population growth.

Section 2

Economic Incentives and Resources (pages 552–556)

- During the oil embargo of the 1970s, high gas prices provided an incentive to preserve resources. When prices came back down, conservation efforts waned.

- As the population has grown and used more energy resources, people have become concerned about pollution.

- The traditional response to pollution is to have the government pass legislated standards prohibiting it.

- Economists argue that pollution cannot be controlled until the economic incentives to pollute are removed.

- Programs including pollution taxes and **pollution permits** are designed to give firms the incentive to not pollute.

- Markets have the flexibility to adjust to change–an adjustment that affects prices and the allocation of resources.

Section 3

Applying the Economic Way of Thinking (pages 558–561)

- Economics has become a generalized theory of choice and a framework for decision making.

- The National Council on Economic Education has recommended a five-point approach to decision making; the final step involves **cost-benefit analysis,** which compares the cost of a decision to the benefits gained.

- A fundamental knowledge of economics helps people cope with the future, especially now that capitalism has emerged as the dominant type of economic organization in the world today.

- Modern capitalism is not the ruthlessly efficient version of the 1930s; modern capitalism has been modified to suit the economic goals of their people.

- In the markets of the world today, supply and demand establish prices, and prices serve as signals to both producers and consumers.

- The flexibility markets provide enables the modern **modified free enterprise economy** to better deal with the unforeseen events of the future.

Teacher's Notes / Internet Bookmarks

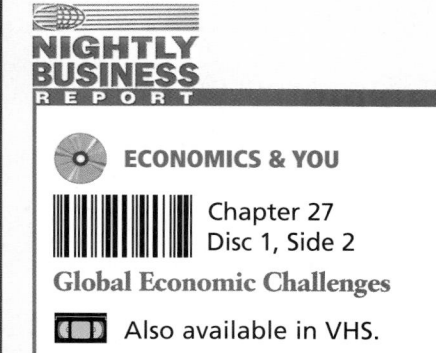

Using the Chapter 20 Summary

Use the Chapter 20 Summary to preview, review, condense, or reteach the chapter.

Preview/Review

Vocabulary PuzzleMaker CD-ROM reinforces Key Terms.

Interactive Tutor Self-Assessment Software provides a review of Chapter 20 content.

Condense

Have students listen to the Chapter 20 Audio Program. Spanish also available.

Assign the Chapter 20 Audio Program Activity and give students the Chapter 20 Audio Program Test.

Have students complete the Guided Reading Activities and Reading Essentials and Study Guides for Chapter 20.

Reteach

Have students complete Reteaching Activity 20 in the TCR. Spanish also available.

GLENCOE
TECHNOLOGY

Use **MindJogger Videoquiz** to review the Chapter 20 content.

ECONOMICS
Online

Have students visit the Web site at epp.glencoe.com to review Chapter 20 and take the **Self-Check Quiz**.

Identifying Key Terms

1. subsistence
2. modified free enterprise economy
3. embargo
4. gasohol
5. aquifer
6. biomass

Reviewing the Facts

Section 1

1. He did not foresee advances in productivity, which have allowed an increasing standard of living to accompany a growing population. He also did not foresee that some families would decide to have fewer children.
2. in many of the countries that have the lowest standard of living
3. oil, natural gas, coal, nuclear energy
4. It produces highly hazardous by-products, which are difficult to dispose of safely.

Section 2

5. Consumers consumed less, and the automobile industry started making smaller, more energy-efficient cars.
6. The law of supply maintains that the lower the price for a product, the less will be brought to market. Shallow gas was inexpensive, so producers had no economic incentive to produce more.
7. They hope eventually to make the permits scarce enough to be

ECONOMICS
Online

Self-Check Quiz Visit the *Economics: Principles and Practices* Web site at epp.glencoe.com and click on *Chapter 20—Self-Check Quizzes* to prepare for the chapter test.

Identifying Key Terms

Write the term that best completes the following sentences.

a. pollution permits	f. pollution
b. biomass	g. aquifer
c. modified free enterprise economy	h. embargo
	i. gasohol
d. glut	j. subsistence
e. acid rain	

1. The state in which the population produces barely enough to support itself is _____ .
2. The United States has a(n) _____ , a system that has been altered by its people to satisfy economic goals.
3. A restriction on the export or import of a commodity in trade is a(n) _____ .
4. _____ is a mixture of 90 percent unleaded gasoline and 10 percent grain alcohol.
5. An underground water-bearing rock formation is a(n) _____ .
6. The second largest source of renewable energy is _____ .

Reviewing the Facts

Section 1 (pages 545–550)

1. **Describe** why, despite Malthus's predictions, certain parts of the world have enjoyed steadily increasing standards of living.
2. **Explain** where the most rapid rates of population growth are found.

3. **List** the four major nonrenewable energy resources.
4. **Describe** the major drawback of nuclear energy.

Section 2 (pages 552–556)

5. **Explain** how American consumers and the automobile industry reacted to the oil price increases of the 1970s.
6. **Explain** how the reluctance of oil and gas producers to drill for shallow gas was consistent with the law of supply.
7. **Describe** what the EPA hopes to accomplish by issuing pollution permits.
8. **State** how the price system in a market economy helps ensure that resources are used wisely.

Section 3 (pages 558–561)

9. **List** the steps involved in economic decision making.
10. **State** the importance of cost-benefit analysis.
11. **Explain** why adapting to change is important for an economic system.

Thinking Critically

1. **Making Comparisons** If you had to decide to use legislated standards or a pollution tax to reduce pollution, which would you choose? In your reasoning, explain the pros and cons of each approach. Use a graphic organizer similar to the one below to organize your answer.

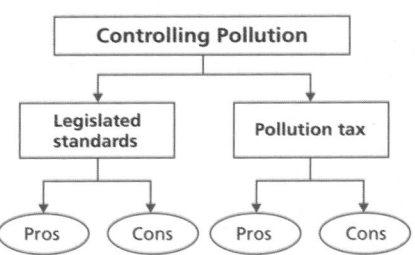

cost-prohibitive, forcing industries to choose to clean up their own pollution.
8. The price system tells consumers when resources are scarce and helps decision makers allocate resources more wisely.

Section 3

9. 1. State the problem. 2. Determine the goals to be attained. 3. Consider principal alternative means of achieving the goals. 4. Select the economic concepts needed to understand the problem and use them to appraise the alternatives. 5. Decide which alternative best leads to

the attainment of the most goals or the most important goals.
10. Cost-benefit analysis is based on marginal analysis, a comprehensive approach that compares the extra cost of doing something with the extra benefits to be gained. It enables firms, governments, and individuals to make better economic decisions.
11. Adapting to change allows an economic system to survive in a changing world and continue to be successful.

2. Making Predictions In what ways can Americans ensure the wise use of resources? How might the world be different in 50 years if we do not use resources wisely today?

Applying Economic Concepts

1. **Scarcity** Scarce natural resources are a problem that concerns citizens throughout the world. What can you personally do to help conserve resources?

2. **Modified Free Enterprise Economy** The United States has a modified free enterprise economy in which the government regulates some industries. Do you think the government should play a smaller or larger role in regulating the American economy? Give reasons to support your answer.

Math Practice

Many people all over the world recycle their aluminum cans in order to help our environment. The graph below shows the percentage of aluminum cans that have been recycled over the years. Study the information presented in the graph, then answer the questions.

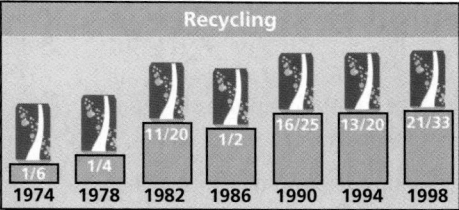

Recycling

1/6	1/4	11/20	1/2	16/25	13/20	21/33
1974	1978	1982	1986	1990	1994	1998

Source: The Aluminum Association, Inc.

1. During which year was the largest percentage of aluminum cans recycled?

2. In 1974, 2.3 billion cans were recycled. Write a formula to show the total number of cans consumed during that year.

Thinking Like an Economist

Renewable energy resources only account for a small portion of our total energy production. Explain the changes that would have to take place in order for people to make greater use of renewable energy resources.

Technology Skill

Using a Database Create a database on recycling centers in your community. Look in the telephone book to locate the nearest recycling centers. Find out the name, address, phone number, and operation hours of each service, and what services each provides. Use this information to create a database, making separate fields for the materials, the locations, and the rebates paid for recycled items. Print and distribute your database to the rest of the class.

▸Building Skills

Making Predictions The table below depicts the median inflation rate for advanced economies, developing countries, and countries in transition for selected years. Study the table, then answer the questions that follow.

	1997	1998	1999	1980–89	1990–99
Countries in Transition	14.8	11.0	7.7	1.2	165.6
Developing Countries	5.6	4.8	4.1	9.9	8.4
Advanced Economies	1.7	2.1	2.1	6.9	2.8

Source: *World Economic Outlook*

1. Which economies do you predict to maintain a relatively low rate of inflation? Why do you think this is the case?

2. If trends continue, do you project the median inflation rate for developing countries to rise, decrease, or stay at about the same level? Why?

 Practice and **assess** key social studies skills with the *Glencoe Skillbuilder Interactive Workbook, Level 2.*

CHAPTER 20: GLOBAL ECONOMIC CHALLENGES **565**

Math Practice

1. 1994
2. $\dfrac{1}{6} = \dfrac{2.3 \text{ billion}}{x}$

Thinking Like an Economist

Prices for nonrenewable resources would have to rise sharply, providing an incentive for the development and use of renewable energy resources.

Technology Skill

Check databases for accuracy.

Building Skills

1. Advanced economies normally maintain lower rates of inflation because they know approximately where their equilibrium prices should be. Advanced economies are generally more economically stable.

2. They will tend to both increase and decrease until the equilibrium price is found.

? Bonus Test Question

Remind students that in Chapter 7, pollution was identified as an externality, or something that is not reflected in the price mechanism between buyers and sellers. Ask students how pollution taxes might internalize the cost of pollution. *(Taxes, or purchasing new, nonpolluting equipment to avoid taxes, are counted as costs by sellers and will be reflected in the prices buyers pay.)*

Thinking Critically

1. Students should explain why they chose either legislated standards or a pollution tax to reduce pollution and explain the pros and cons of each approach.

2. Answers will vary. Americans can conserve resources, lowering the demand and encouraging the wise use of resources. In 50 years, forced restrictions might be in place, some resources might be at dangerously low levels, or alternative energy sources might be very costly.

Applying Economic Concepts

1. Students should cite specific examples such as turning off the lights that are not being used, turning off the water while they brush their teeth, taking short showers instead of baths, walking instead of driving, wearing clothing until it is worn out, and recycling aluminum, newspaper, glass, and plastic.

2. Students should support their answers with examples and logical arguments.

Contents

HONORING AMERICA

Flag Etiquette

Over the years, Americans have developed rules and customs concerning the use and display of the flag. One of the most important things every American should remember is to treat the flag with respect.

- The flag should be raised and lowered by hand and displayed only from sunrise to sunset. On special occasions, it may be displayed at night, but it should be illuminated.

- The flag may be displayed on all days, weather permitting, particularly on national and state holidays and on historic and special occasions.

- No flag may be flown above the American flag or to the right of it at the same height.

- The flag should never touch the ground or floor beneath it.

- The flag may be flown at half-staff by order of the president, usually to mourn the death of a public official.

- The flag may be flown upside down only to signal distress.

- When the flag becomes old and tattered, it should be destroyed by burning. According to an approved custom, the Union (stars on blue field) is first cut from the flag; then the two pieces, which no longer form a flag, are burned.

★ ★ ★ ★ ★ ★ ★ ★

The Star-Spangled Banner

O! say can you see, by the dawn's early light,
What so proudly we hail'd at the twilight's last gleaming,
Whose broad stripes and bright stars through the perilous fight,
O'er the ramparts we watched, were so gallantly streaming?
And the Rockets' red glare, the Bombs bursting in air,
Gave proof through the night that our Flag was still there;
O! say, does that star-spangled banner yet wave
O'er the Land of the free and the home of the brave!

The Pledge of Allegiance

I pledge allegiance to the Flag of the United States of America and to the Republic for which it stands, one Nation under God, indivisible, with liberty and justice for all.

REFERENCE ATLAS

NATIONAL GEOGRAPHIC

ATLAS KEY

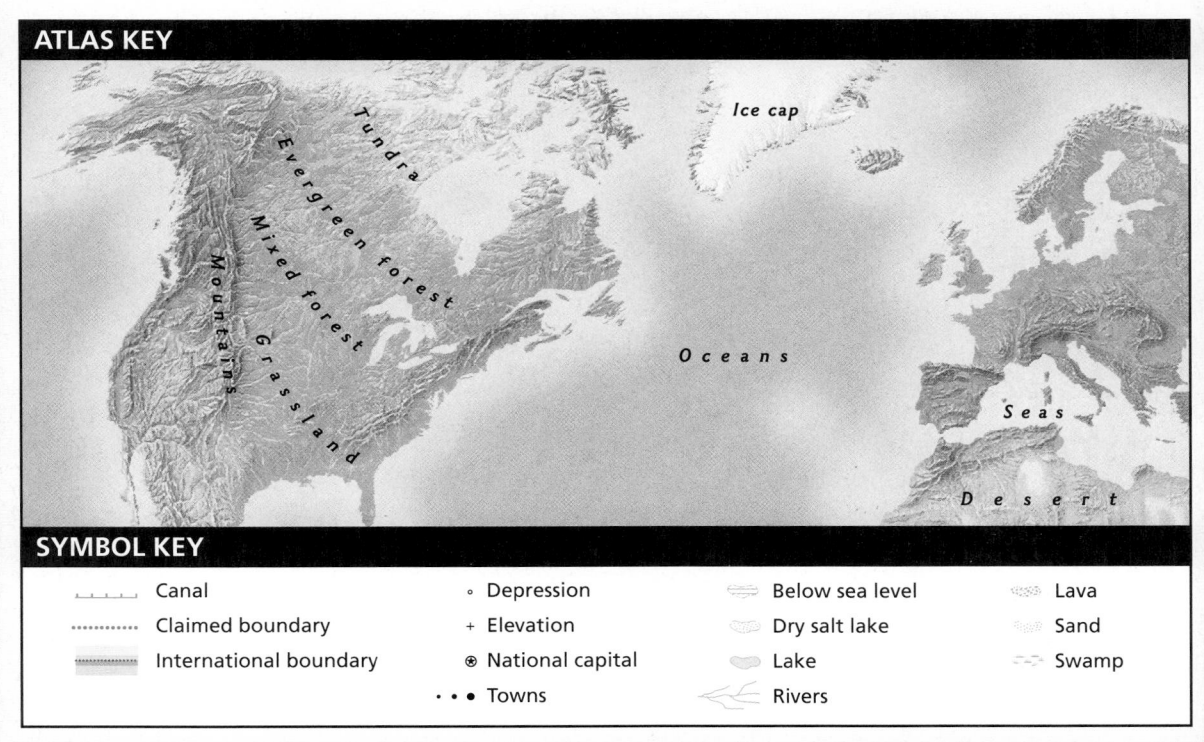

Ice cap

Tundra

Evergreen forest

Mixed forest

Mountains

Grassland

Oceans

Seas

Desert

SYMBOL KEY

Canal	∘ Depression	Below sea level	Lava
Claimed boundary	+ Elevation	Dry salt lake	Sand
International boundary	⊛ National capital	Lake	Swamp
	• • • Towns	Rivers	

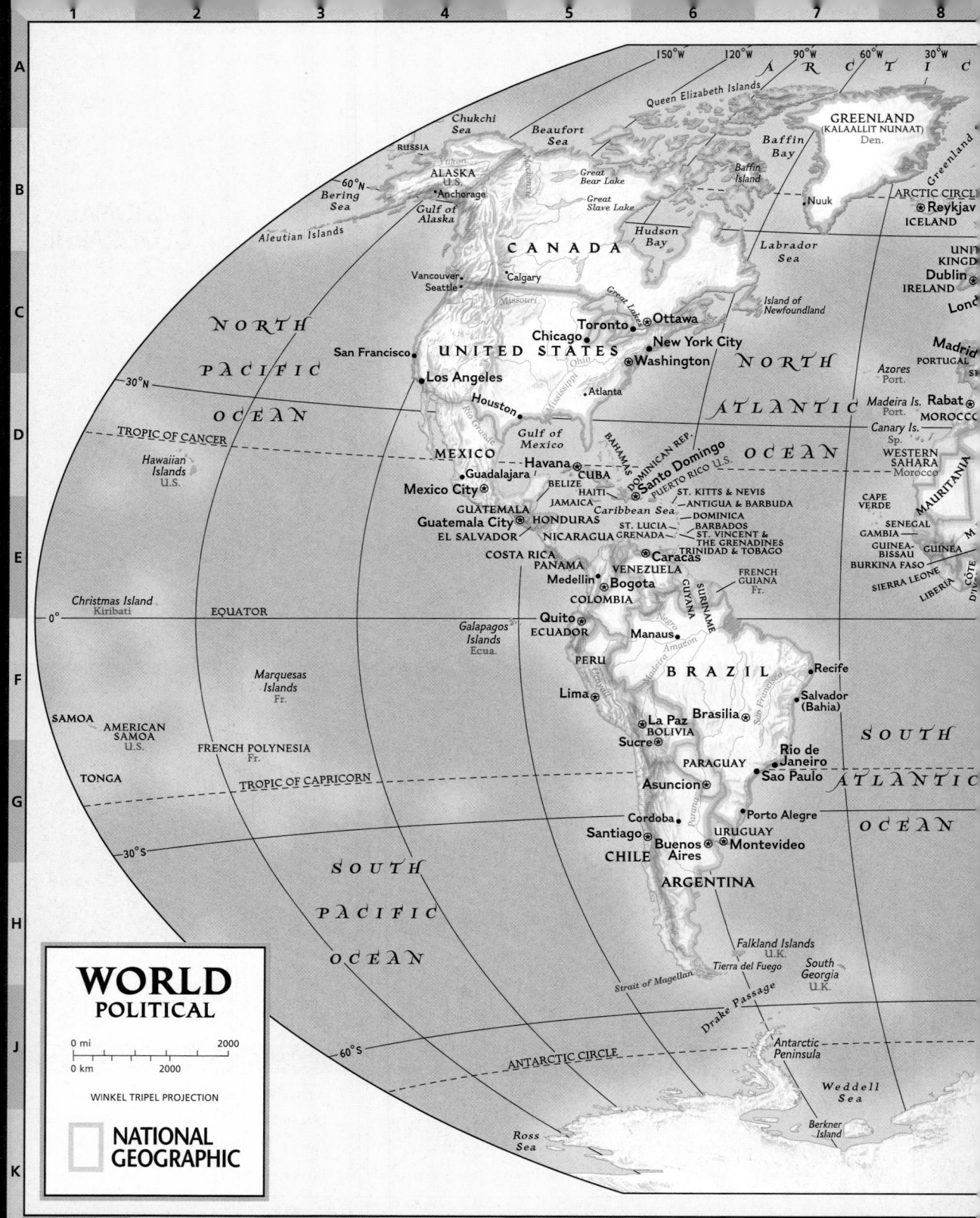

WORLD
POLITICAL

0 mi 2000
0 km 2000

WINKEL TRIPEL PROJECTION

NATIONAL
GEOGRAPHIC

A
B
C
D
E
F
G
H
J
K

30°E 60°E 90°E 120°E 150°E

Svalbard
Nor.
Barents
Sea
Novaya
Zemlya
Franz Josef
Land
Severnaya
Zemlya
New Siberian
Islands
Laptev Sea
East
Siberian Sea
Kara
Sea

O C E A N

RUSSIA

NORWAY
SWEDEN
FINLAND

EST.
LATVIA
LITH.

St. Petersburg
Moscow
Samara
Yekaterinburg
Omsk
Novosibirsk
Astana
Yakutsk
60°N
Bering
Sea
Sea of
Okhotsk
Kamchatka
Peninsula
Sakhalin
Hokkaido
Sapporo
Honshu

KAZAKHSTAN
Aral Sea
Almaty
Tashkent
UZBEKISTAN
Bishkek
KYRGYZSTAN
Ulaanbaatar
MONGOLIA
Harbin
Shenyang
Beijing
Tianjin
NORTH
KOREA
Pyongyang
Seoul
SOUTH
KOREA
JAPAN
Tokyo
Osaka
Kyushu

NORTH

PACIFIC

OCEAN

30°N

Lake
Baikal

POLAND
BELARUS
KIEV
UKRAINE

CZECH
REP.
SLOVAKIA
HUNG.
MOLD.
CROAT.
ROMANIA
AZERBAIJAN
GEORGIA
ARMENIA
TURKMENISTAN
Ashgabat
Dushanbe
TAJIKISTAN

BULGARIA
GREECE
TURKEY
Ankara
SYRIA
Tehran
IRAN
Baghdad
AFGHANISTAN
Islamabad
Lahore
Delhi
New
Delhi

CHINA
Chengdu
Wuhan
Shanghai

The People's Republic
of China claims Taiwan
as its 23rd province.

Taipei
TAIWAN
Hong Kong
Philippine
Sea

NORTHERN
MARIANA
ISLANDS
U.S.

Mediterranean Sea
CYPRUS
LEBANON
ISRAEL
Tripoli
Cairo
JORDAN
IRAQ
KUWAIT
BAHRAIN
QATAR
U.A.E.
Riyadh
SAUDI
ARABIA
Muscat
OMAN
PAKISTAN
Karachi
Mumbai
Hyderabad
INDIA
Bangalore
NEPAL
BHUTAN
Guangzhou
Dhaka
BANGLADESH
Kolkata
MYANMAR
(BURMA)
LAOS
Hanoi
VIETNAM
Hainan
South
China
Sea
Luzon
Manila
PHILIPPINES
Mindanao

LIBYA
EGYPT
Red Sea
Sanaa
YEMEN
DJIBOUTI
Socotra
Yemen
Arabian
Sea
Brahmaputra
Yangon
THAILAND
Bangkok
Phnom
Penh
CAMBODIA
Ho Chi Minh
City
BRUNEI
PALAU
FEDERATED STATES
OF MICRONESIA
MARSHALL
ISLANDS

CHAD
ERITREA
Khartoum
SUDAN
N'Djamena
Addis Ababa
ETHIOPIA
SOMALIA
Colombo
SRI
LANKA
Chennai
Bay
of
Bengal
MALDIVES
EQUATOR
Kuala
Lumpur
MALAYSIA
SINGAPORE
Borneo
NAURU
KIRIBATI

NIGER
Niamey
NIGERIA
Lagos
CENTRAL
AFRICAN
REPUBLIC
Bangui
CAMEROON
EQ.
GUINEA
GABON
SAO
TOME
PRINCIPE
Ang.
CABINDA
DEM. REP.
OF THE
CONGO
Kinshasa
Brazzaville
CONGO
UGANDA
KENYA
Nairobi
RWANDA
BURUNDI
Dodoma
Dar es Salaam
TANZANIA
SEYCHELLES
INDONESIA
Jakarta
Java
Surabaya
New
Guinea
PAPUA
NEW GUINEA
SOLOMON
ISLANDS
TUVALU

Luanda
ANGOLA
ZAMBIA
Lusaka
MALAWI
MOZAMBIQUE
COMOROS
Harare
ZIMBABWE
Antananarivo
MADAGASCAR
MAURITIUS
Reunion
Fr.
INDIAN
OCEAN
EAST
TIMOR
Arafura Sea
Darwin
Port
Moresby
Coral
Sea
VANUATU
FIJI
ISLANDS

NAMIBIA
Windhoek
BOTSWANA
Gaborone
Pretoria
Maputo
SWAZILAND
Bloemfontein
SOUTH
AFRICA
LESOTHO
Cape Town
Orange
New Caledonia
Fr.
AUSTRALIA
Brisbane
Perth
SOUTH
PACIFIC
OCEAN

Kerguelen Islands
Fr.
Sydney
Melbourne
Canberra
Tasman
Sea
Tasmania
North
Island
Auckland
NEW ZEALAND
Wellington
South
Island
Darling
Murray

60°S

ANTARCTICA
Ross Sea

ABBREVIATIONS

AUST.	AUSTRIA
B.&H.	BOSNIA & HERZEGOVINA
BELG.	BELGIUM
CROAT.	CROATIA
CZECH REP.	CZECH REPUBLIC
DEM. REP. OF THE CONGO	DEMOCRATIC REPUBLIC OF THE CONGO
EQ. GUINEA	EQUATORIAL GUINEA
EST.	ESTONIA
HUNG.	HUNGARY
LITH.	LITHUANIA
MACED.	MACEDONIA
MOLD.	MOLDOVA
NETH.	NETHERLANDS
SLOV.	SLOVENIA
SWITZ.	SWITZERLAND
U.A.E.	UNITED ARAB EMIRATES
YUG.	YUGOSLAVIA

ALGERIA
TUNISIA
Algiers
ITALY
Rome
Paris
GERMANY
DENMARK
Oslo
Norwegian
Sea
Baltic Sea
AUST.
SWITZ.
SLOV.
B.&H.
MACED.
ALBANIA
YUG.
Black Sea
Caspian Sea
Volga
Ob
Ural
Irtysh
Yenisey
Lena
Amur
Yangtze
Nile
Indus
Ob

A   B   C   D   E   F   G   H   J   K

1   2   3   4   5   6   7   8

170°E   50°N   180°   170°W   RUSSIA   70°N   160°W   150°W

St. Lawrence Island   Bering Strait   Point Barrow   ARCTIC OCEAN

Seward Peninsula   Brooks Range   Beaufort Sea

Norton Sound   Yukon

40°N   Nunivak Island   ALASKA

Aleutian Islands   Alaska Range   Fairbanks

180°   Bristol Bay   Anchorage

Alaska Peninsula   Kodiak I.

Gulf of Alaska

Alexander Archipelago   Juneau

P A C I F I C

170°W   30°N   O C E A N

Tacoma   Seattle   Spokane

Olympia   WASH.

Portland   Salem   OREGON   Boise

Eugene   IDAHO   Bu

Great Salt Lake   Salt Lake City

Reno   Carson City

Sacramento   NEVADA   UT

San Francisco   CALIFORNIA   Sierra Nevada

Las Vegas   ARIZO

20°N   Honolulu   Los Angeles

160°W   HAWAII   San Diego   Phoenix

Hilo   TROPIC OF CANCER   Tucson

10°N

150°W   140°W   130°W   120°W

1   2   3   4   5   6   7   8

A4   REFERENCE ATLAS

UNITED STATES
POLITICAL

0 mi 600
0 km 600

OBLIQUE AZIMUTHAL EQUIDISTANT PROJECTION

**NATIONAL
GEOGRAPHIC**

GREENLAND
(KALAALLIT NUNAAT)
Den.

ARCTIC CIRCLE

C A N A D A

MEXICO

MONTANA

NORTH
DAKOTA

MINNESOTA

Lake Superior

MICHIGAN

Lake Huron

MAINE

Augusta

Helena

Billings

SOUTH
DAKOTA

Bismarck

Minneapolis

St. Paul

WISCONSIN

Lansing

L. Michigan

Montpelier

NEW
YORK

Portland

Concord, N.H.

Pierre

Milwaukee

Madison

Lake
Ontario

Albany

V.T.

Boston, MASS.

WYOMING

Casper

Sioux City

IOWA

Chicago

Toledo

Detroit

L. Erie

Buffalo

Cleveland PA.

Providence, R.I.

Cheyenne

Des Moines

ILLINOIS

IND.

Columbus

OHIO

Pittsburgh

Harrisburg

New York City

Hartford, CONN.

NEBRASKA

Omaha

Indianapolis

Dayton W. VA.

Baltimore

Philadelphia

Trenton, N.J.

Denver

Lincoln

Springfield

Cincinnati

Washington, D.C.

Dover, DEL.

COLORADO

Kansas City

Topeka

MISSOURI

St. Louis

Louisville

Frankfort

VIRGINIA

Richmond

Annapolis, MD.

Santa Fe

KANSAS

Jefferson City

KENTUCKY

Raleigh

Virginia Beach

Nashville

NORTH CAROLINA

Oklahoma City

Tulsa

ARKANSAS

Memphis

TENNESSEE

Charlotte

SOUTH
CAROLINA

Columbia

Albuquerque

OKLAHOMA

Little Rock

Atlanta

Charleston

NEW
MEXICO

Birmingham

MISS.

ALABAMA

GEORGIA

Savannah

Fort
Worth

Dallas

LOUISIANA

Jackson

Montgomery

Tallahassee

Jacksonville

El Paso

TEXAS

Austin

Baton Rouge

New Orleans

FLORIDA

Tampa

San Antonio

Houston

Gulf of
Mexico

Miami

ATLANTIC OCEAN

Bermuda Is.
U.K.

BAHAMAS

CUBA

Straits of Florida

Caribbean

Sea

JAMAICA

HAITI

DOMINICAN
REPUBLIC

PUERTO
RICO
U.S.

San Juan

DOMINICA

ANTIGUA
& BARBUDA

ST. KITTS
& NEVIS

Rio Grande

Missouri

Mississippi

Arkansas

ROCKY MOUNTAINS

APPALACHIAN MTS.

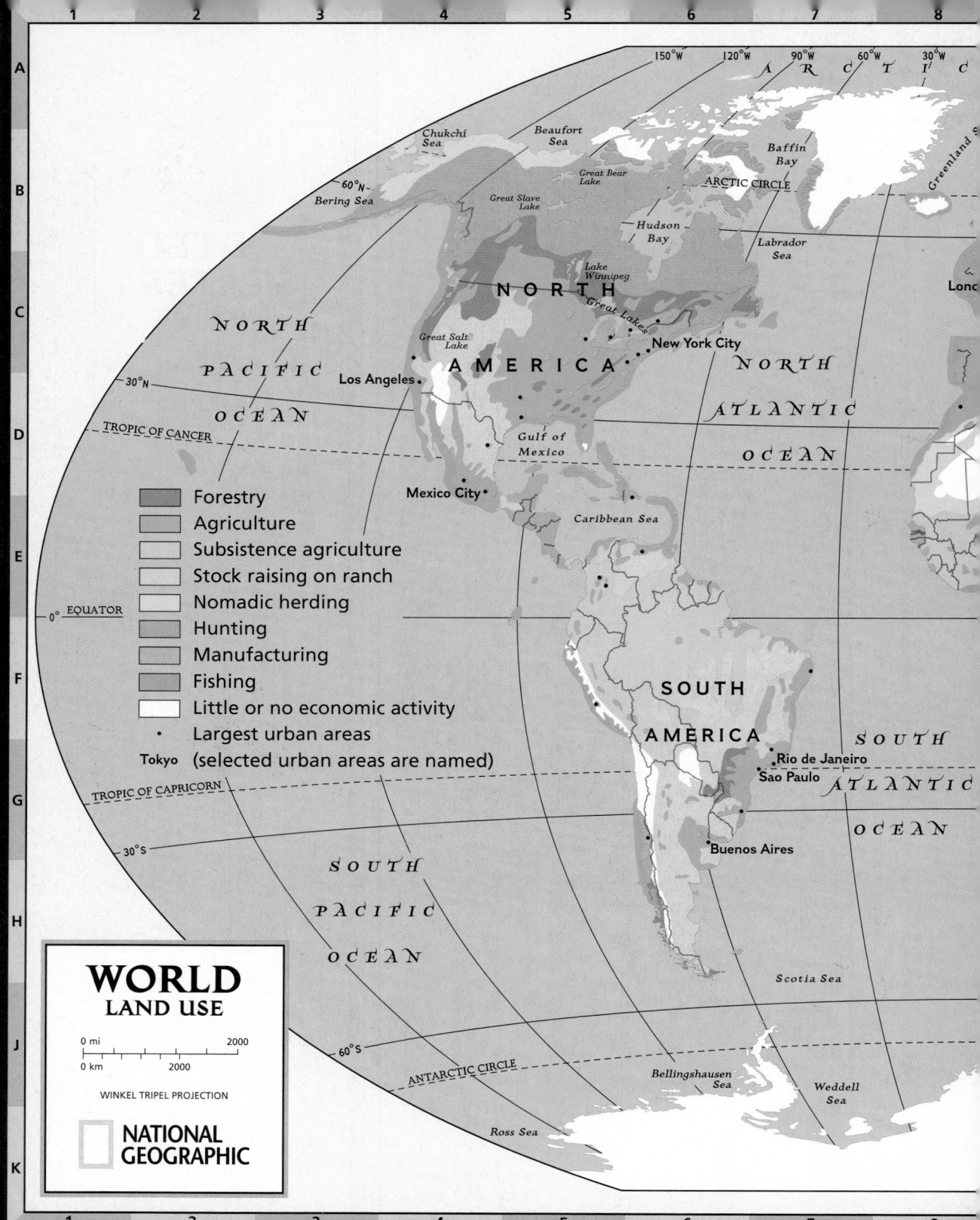

WORLD
LAND USE

Forestry
Agriculture
Subsistence agriculture
Stock raising on ranch
Nomadic herding
Hunting
Manufacturing
Fishing
Little or no economic activity
• Largest urban areas
Tokyo (selected urban areas are named)

0 mi   2000
0 km   2000

WINKEL TRIPEL PROJECTION

NATIONAL
GEOGRAPHIC

150°W   120°W   90°W   60°W   30°W

ARCTIC

Chukchi Sea
Beaufort Sea
Baffin Bay
Greenland S
ARCTIC CIRCLE
60°N
Bering Sea
Great Bear Lake
Great Slave Lake
Hudson Bay
Labrador Sea
Lake Winnipeg
London
NORTH
Great Lakes
NORTH
PACIFIC
Great Salt Lake
AMERICA
New York City
NORTH
30°N
Los Angeles
ATLANTIC
OCEAN
TROPIC OF CANCER
OCEAN
Gulf of Mexico
Mexico City
Caribbean Sea
0° EQUATOR
SOUTH
AMERICA
SOUTH
TROPIC OF CAPRICORN
ATLANTIC
Rio de Janeiro
Sao Paulo
30°S
OCEAN
SOUTH
Buenos Aires
PACIFIC
OCEAN
Scotia Sea
60°S
ANTARCTIC CIRCLE
Bellingshausen Sea
Weddell Sea
Ross Sea

9 10 11 12 13 14 15 16

30°E 60°E 90°E 120°E 150°E

O C E A N

Kara Sea

Laptev Sea

East Siberian Sea

Barents Sea

weglian Sea

60°N

Bering Sea

Baltic Sea

Moscow

Sea of Okhotsk

E U R O P E

A S I A

Lake Baikal

ris

Caspian Sea

Aral Sea

Black Sea

Sea of Japan

Seoul Tokyo

diterranean Sea

Yellow Sea

N O R T H

Cairo

Shanghai

East China Sea

P A C I F I C

30°N

TROPIC OF CANCER

Red Sea

O C E A N

Mumbai

Kolkata

Philippine Sea

A F R I C A

Arabian Sea

Bay of Bengal

Gulf of Aden

South China Sea

Andaman Sea

agos

f of nea

Lake Victoria

EQUATOR

0°

Kinshasa

Lake Tanganyika

Arafura Sea

Coral Sea

I N D I A N

TROPIC OF CAPRICORN

AUSTRALIA

O C E A N

S O U T H

P A C I F I C

Sydney

O C E A N

Tasman Sea

60°S

A N T A R C T I C A

Ross Sea

9 10 11 12 13 14 15 16

1	
2	
3	
4	
5	
6	
7	
8	

C A N A D A

WASHINGTON
- Seattle
- Olympia⊙ •Tacoma
- •Spokane
- Portland•
- Salem⊙
- Eugene•

Columbia

OREGON

IDAHO
- ⊙Boise

Snake

MONTANA
- Helena⊙

Missouri

NORTH DAKOTA
- ⊙Bismarck

SOUTH DAKOTA
- ⊙Pierre
- Sioux Falls

WYOMING
- Cheyenne⊙

N. Platte

NEBRASKA
- Lincoln

NEVADA
- Reno•
- ⊙Carson City

CALIFORNIA
- Sacramento⊙
- San Francisco•• Oakland
- San Jose•
- Fresno•
- Bakersfield•

UTAH
- Salt Lake City⊙

COLORADO
- ⊙Denver
- •Colorado Springs

KANSAS
- Wichita•

Arkansas

PACIFIC OCEAN
- Las Vegas•
- Los Angeles•
- •San Bernardino
- San Diego•

Colorado

ARIZONA
- Phoenix⊙
- •Tempe
- •Tucson

NEW MEXICO
- ⊙Santa Fe
- •Albuquerque

- Amarillo•

OKLAHOMA
- Oklahoma City⊙
- •Lubbock

Red

- Abilene•

Brazos

- Dallas
- Fort Worth
- Waco•

TEXAS
- Austin•
- San Antonio•
- •El Paso

Rio Grande

- Corpus Christi•
- •Laredo

M E X I C O

Alaska inset

ARCTIC OCEAN

Chukchi Sea

Beaufort Sea

RUSSIA

Bering Strait ARCTIC CIRCLE

Yukon

CANADA

ALASKA

Bering Sea

Bristol Bay

- Anchorage•

Gulf of Alaska

- Juneau⊙

PACIFIC OCEAN

ALASKA
| 0 mi | 300 |
| 0 km | 300 |

68°N
180°
172°W
60°N
52°N
164°W
156°W
148°W
140°W
132°W
68°N
60°N
52°N
30°N
110°W
60°N

Legend

▨	Forestry
▨	Agriculture
▨	Forestry and Agriculture
▨	Stock raising on ranch
▨	Wetlands
▨	Urban land
▨	Fishing
▨	Tundra
☐	Little or no economic activity

130°W 50°N 120°W 110°W 100°W
40°N
120°W

UNITED
STATES
LAND USE

| 0 mi | 300 |
| 0 km | 300 |

ALBERS CONIC EQUAL-AREA PROJECTION

NATIONAL
GEOGRAPHIC

PRINCIPAL HAWAIIAN
ISLANDS
| 0 mi | 100 |
| 0 km | 100 |

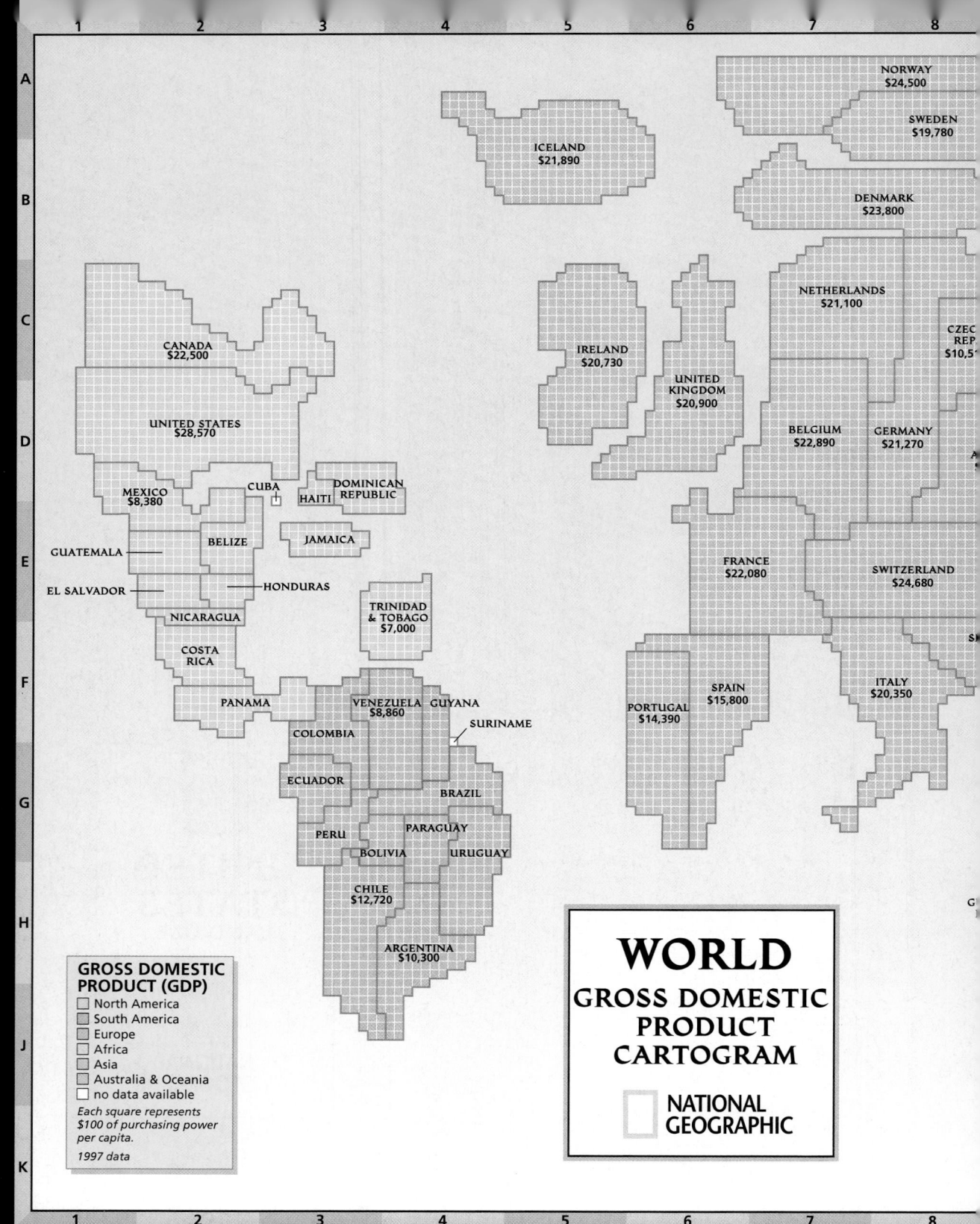

A

B

C

D

E

F

G

H

J

K

1 2 3 4 5 6 7 8

NORWAY
$24,500

SWEDEN
$19,780

ICELAND
$21,890

DENMARK
$23,800

NETHERLANDS
$21,100

CZEC
REP
$10,5

CANADA
$22,500

IRELAND
$20,730

UNITED
KINGDOM
$20,900

BELGIUM
$22,890

GERMANY
$21,270

UNITED STATES
$28,570

MEXICO
$8,380

CUBA

DOMINICAN
REPUBLIC

HAITI

GUATEMALA

BELIZE

JAMAICA

FRANCE
$22,080

SWITZERLAND
$24,680

EL SALVADOR

HONDURAS

NICARAGUA

TRINIDAD
& TOBAGO
$7,000

COSTA
RICA

ITALY
$20,350

PANAMA

VENEZUELA
$8,860

GUYANA

PORTUGAL
$14,390

SPAIN
$15,800

SURINAME

COLOMBIA

ECUADOR

BRAZIL

PERU

PARAGUAY

BOLIVIA

URUGUAY

CHILE
$12,720

ARGENTINA
$10,300

**GROSS DOMESTIC
PRODUCT (GDP)**

☐ North America
☐ South America
☐ Europe
☐ Africa
☐ Asia
☐ Australia & Oceania
☐ no data available

*Each square represents
$100 of purchasing power
per capita.*

1997 data

WORLD
GROSS DOMESTIC
PRODUCT
CARTOGRAM

☐ **NATIONAL
GEOGRAPHIC**

9 10 11 12 13 14 15 16

A

B

FINLAND
$20,150

ESTONIA

LITHUANIA

LATVIA

C

BELARUS

AZERBAIJAN

TAJIKISTAN

MONGOLIA BHUTAN NORTH
KOREA

JAPAN
$24,080

SLOVAKIA

UKRAINE

RUSSIA

KAZAKHSTAN

CHINA

GEORGIA

ARMENIA

KYRGYZSTAN

NEPAL LAOS

SOUTH
KOREA
$13,670

MOLDOVA

UZBEKISTAN

PAKISTAN

INDIA

CAMBODIA

D

HUNGARY

TURKMENISTAN

BANGLADESH

MYANMAR
(BURMA)

VIETNAM

ROMANIA

TURKEY

AFGHANISTAN

IRAN

SRI
LANKA

THAILAND
$6,790

PHILIPPINES

BULGARIA

IRAQ

CROATIA

SYRIA

ALBANIA

LEBANON

KUWAIT
$16,980

E

MACEDONIA

MALAYSIA
$8,410

GREECE
$12,490

INDONESIA

OSLAVIA

ISRAEL
$18,070

JORDAN

SNIA &
RZEGOVINA

UNITED
ARAB
EMIRATES
$19,180

F

SINGAPORE
$25,770

SAUDI
ARABIA

OMAN
$9,890

SOLOMON
ISLANDS

G

TUNISIA

PAPUA
NEW GUINEA

MOROCCO

ALGERIA

LIBYA

EGYPT

YEMEN

MAURITANIA

MALI

NIGER

CHAD

CENTRAL AFRICAN
REPUBLIC

FIJI
ISLANDS
$4,130

SENEGAL

ERITREA

GAMBIA

NIGERIA

SUDAN

GUINEA

GHANA

BENIN

CAMEROON

SOMALIA

H

SIERRA
LEONE

TOGO

KENYA

ETHIOPIA

LIBERIA

TANZANIA

BURKINA
FASO

EQUATORIAL
GUINEA

UGANDA

DEM. REP. OF
THE CONGO

NEW
ZEALAND
$17,410

CÔTE
D'IVOIRE

GABON

RWANDA

BURUNDI

MOZAMBIQUE

CONGO

MALAWI

ZAMBIA

ANGOLA

MADAGASCAR

J

ZIMBABWE

AUSTRALIA
$20,430

NAMIBIA

BOTSWANA

MAURITIUS

SWAZILAND

SOUTH
AFRICA

LESOTHO

K

9 10 11 12 13 14 15 16

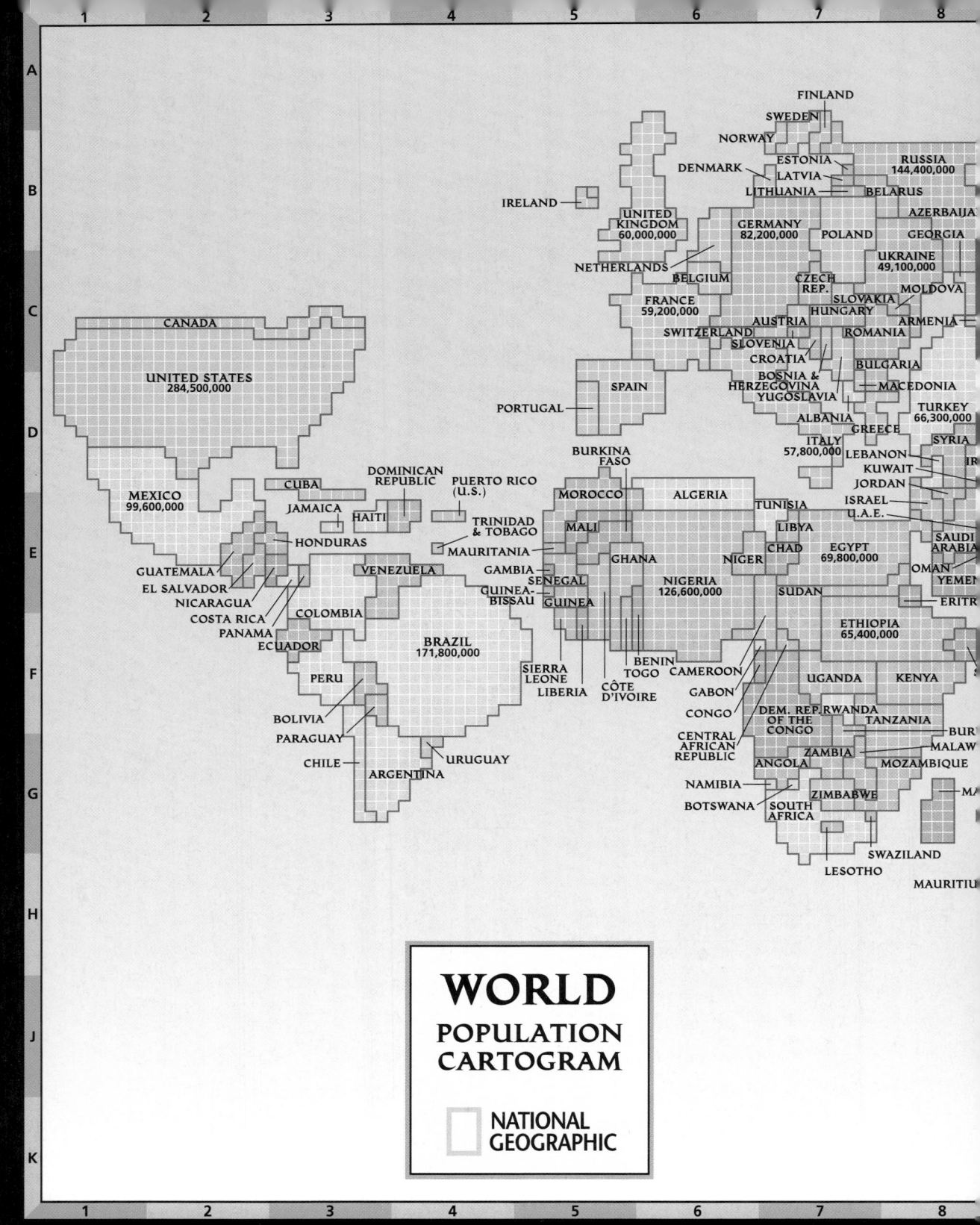

1   2   3   4   5   6   7   8

A

FINLAND
SWEDEN
NORWAY
DENMARK   ESTONIA   RUSSIA
IRELAND   LATVIA   144,400,000
LITHUANIA   BELARUS
B
UNITED   AZERBAIJAN
KINGDOM   GERMANY   GEORGIA
60,000,000   82,200,000   POLAND
NETHERLANDS   UKRAINE
BELGIUM   49,100,000
CZECH   MOLDOVA
REP.
FRANCE   SLOVAKIA
C   59,200,000   AUSTRIA   HUNGARY   ARMENIA
SWITZERLAND   ROMANIA
SLOVENIA
CROATIA   BULGARIA
SPAIN   BOSNIA &   MACEDONIA
HERZEGOVINA
PORTUGAL   YUGOSLAVIA   TURKEY
ALBANIA   66,300,000
ITALY   GREECE
D   57,800,000   LEBANON   SYRIA
BURKINA   KUWAIT   IR
FASO   JORDAN
DOMINICAN   PUERTO RICO   ISRAEL
REPUBLIC   (U.S.)   MOROCCO   ALGERIA   TUNISIA   U.A.E.
CUBA   SAUDI
JAMAICA   TRINIDAD   MALI   LIBYA   ARABIA
HAITI   & TOBAGO   EGYPT   OMAN
MEXICO   MAURITANIA   GHANA   NIGER   CHAD   69,800,000   YEMEN
E   99,600,000   HONDURAS   GAMBIA   ERITR
GUATEMALA   VENEZUELA   SENEGAL   NIGERIA
EL SALVADOR   GUINEA-   126,600,000   SUDAN
NICARAGUA   BISSAU   GUINEA
COSTA RICA   COLOMBIA   ETHIOPIA
PANAMA   BENIN   65,400,000
ECUADOR   BRAZIL   TOGO   CAMEROON   UGANDA   KENYA
F   171,800,000   SIERRA   GABON
PERU   LEONE   CÔTE   CONGO
LIBERIA   D'IVOIRE   DEM. REP. RWANDA
BOLIVIA   CENTRAL   OF THE   TANZANIA
PARAGUAY   AFRICAN   CONGO   BUR
CHILE   ARGENTINA   URUGUAY   REPUBLIC   ZAMBIA   MALAW
G   NAMIBIA   ANGOLA   MOZAMBIQUE
BOTSWANA   ZIMBABWE   MA
SOUTH
AFRICA
SWAZILAND
LESOTHO   MAURITIU
H

J

WORLD

POPULATION
CARTOGRAM
K
■ NATIONAL
GEOGRAPHIC

1   2   3   4   5   6   7   8

9　10　11　12　13　14　15　16

A
B
C
D
E
F
G
H
J
K

MONGOLIA

NORTH
KOREA

SOUTH
KOREA

JAPAN
127,100,000

KAZAKHSTAN — KYRGYZSTAN
UZBEKISTAN — TAJIKISTAN
TURKMENISTAN

AFGHANISTAN

CHINA
1,280,600,000

IRAN
100,000

NEPAL

PAKISTAN
145,000,000

TAIWAN

VIETNAM
78,700,000

MYANMAR
(BURMA)

BANGLADESH
133,500,000

LAOS

THAILAND
62,400,000

CAMBODIA

PHILIPPINES
77,200,000

INDIA
1,033,000,000

CAR

MALAYSIA
SINGAPORE

PAPUA
NEW GUINEA

I N D O N E S I A
206,100,000

SRI
LANKA

AUSTRALIA

NEW
ZEALAND

**POPULATION
GROWTH RATE**
(excluding effects
of migration)

3% and above

2-2.9%

1-1.9%

0-.9%

Population loss

*Each square represents
one million people.*

2000 data

STANDARD &POOR'S DATABANK

The data and forecasts for the graphs, tables, and charts in the Databank are based on information from Standard & Poor's. View the epp.glencoe.com Web site for data updates.

The American People

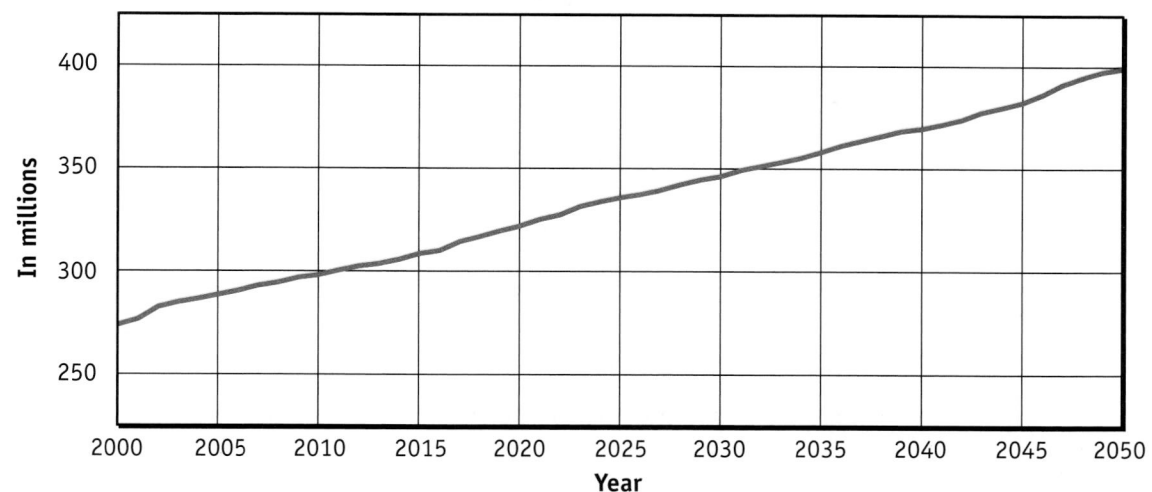

U.S. Population Projections, 2000–2050

Source: U.S. Bureau of the Census

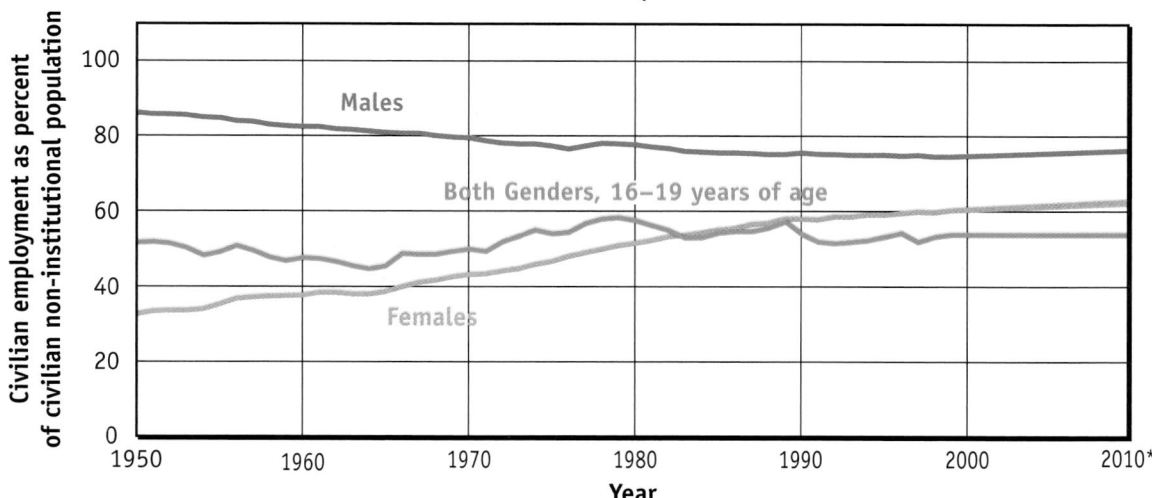

Civilian Labor Force, 1950–2010

Source: Department of Labor, Bureau of Labor Statistics
*Estimate

The American People

Hours and Earnings in Private Industries, 1960–2000

A Average Weekly Hours

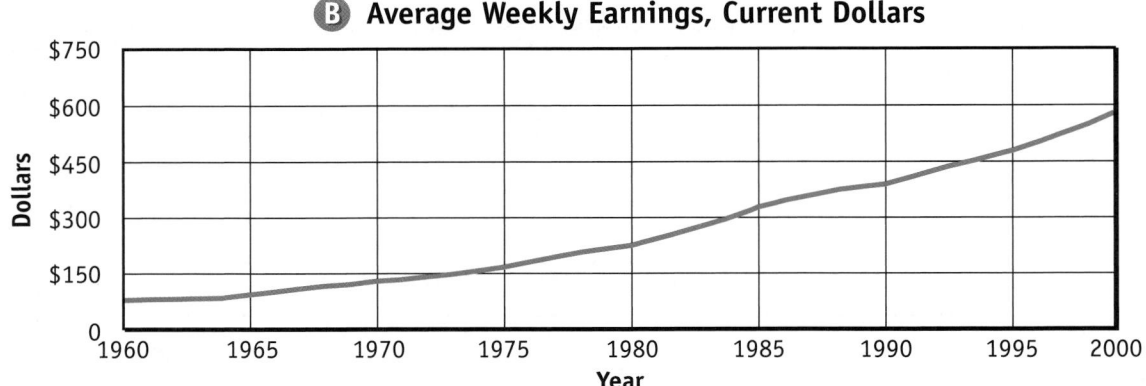

B Average Weekly Earnings, Current Dollars

C Average Weekly Earnings, 1982 Dollars

Source: Bureau of Labor Statistics

Visit epp.glencoe.com and click on **Textbook Updates—Databank** for an update of the data.

The U.S. Economy

Gross Domestic Product, 1950–2000

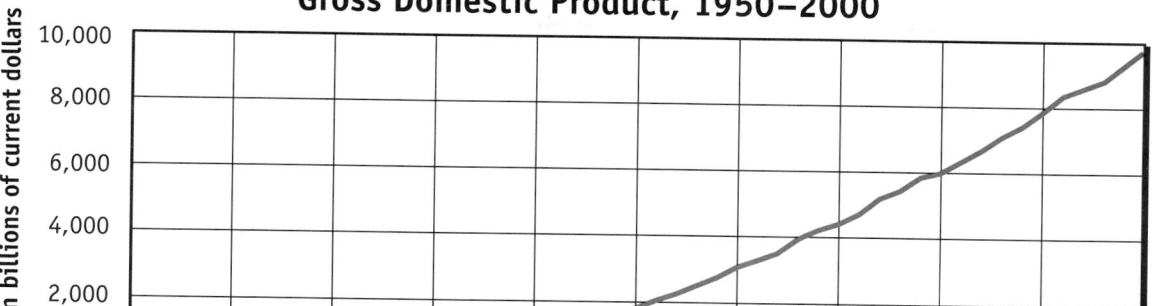

Source: U.S. Department of Commerce

A Look At Market History (S&P 500)

US launches air war against Iraq
January 17, 1991

Iraq invades Kuwait
August 8, 1990

Iran hostage crisis
November 4, 1979

Arab oil embargo
October 5, 1973

President Kennedy assassinated
November 22, 1963

Cuban Missile Crisis
October 22, 1962

South Korea invaded
June 25, 1950

Pearl Harbor bombed
December 7, 1941

WTC/Pentagon
terrorist attacks
September 11, 2001

ECONOMICS *Online*

Visit epp.glencoe.com and click on **Textbook Updates—Databank** for an update of the data.

The U.S. Economy

Personal Consumption Expenditures, 1960–2000

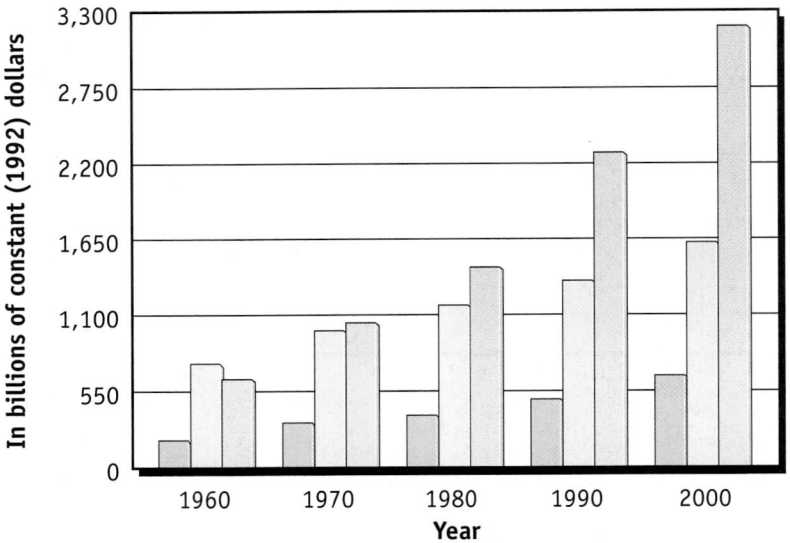

Source: Department of Commerce, Bureau of Economic Analysis

Personal Consumption Expenditures, Nondurable Goods, 1960–2000

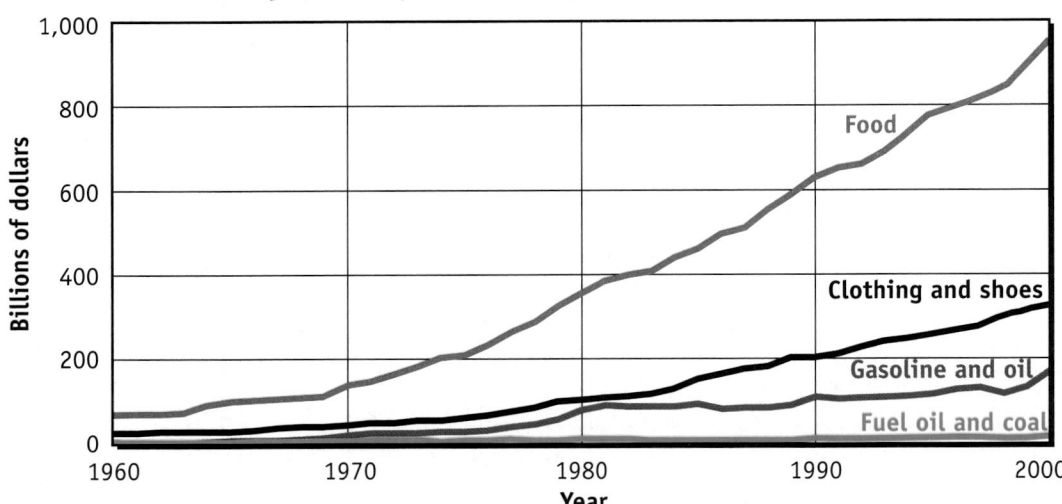

Source: Department of Commerce, Bureau of Economic Analysis

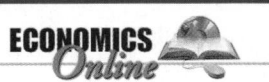

Visit epp.glencoe.com and click on **Textbook Updates—Databank** for an update of the data.

The U.S. Economy

Average Prices of Selected Goods, 1989–2001

Chart 1
Price
- $0.55
- $0.45
- $0.35
- $0.25
- $0.15

Electricity per 500 KWH

Utility natural gas, 40 therms
(1 therm = 100,000 British thermal units)

Year: 1989, 1991, 1993, 1995, 1997, 1999, 2001

Chart 2
Price
- $1.75
- $1.60
- $1.45
- $1.30
- $1.15
- $1.00
- $ .85

Gasoline, all types, per gallon

Gasoline, unleaded regular, per gallon

Year: 1989, 1991, 1993, 1995, 1997, 1999, 2001

Chart 3
Price
- $2.25
- $1.50
- $0.75
- $ .00

Ground chuck, 100% beef, per pound

Eggs, 1 dozen large

Chicken, per pound

White bread, per pound

Year: 1989, 1991, 1993, 1995, 1997, 1999, 2001

Chart 4
Price
- $2.00
- $1.50
- $1.00
- $0.50
- $ .00

Milk, 1/2 gal. whole

Tomatoes, per lb.

Apples, red delicious, per lb.

Bananas, per lb.

Year: 1989, 1991, 1993, 1995, 1997, 1999, 2001

Source: Bureau of Labor Statistics
U.S. city average prices for July

Visit epp.glencoe.com and click on
Textbook Updates—Databank for
an update of the data.

The U.S. Economy

Annual Changes in Consumer Price Indexes, 1940–2000

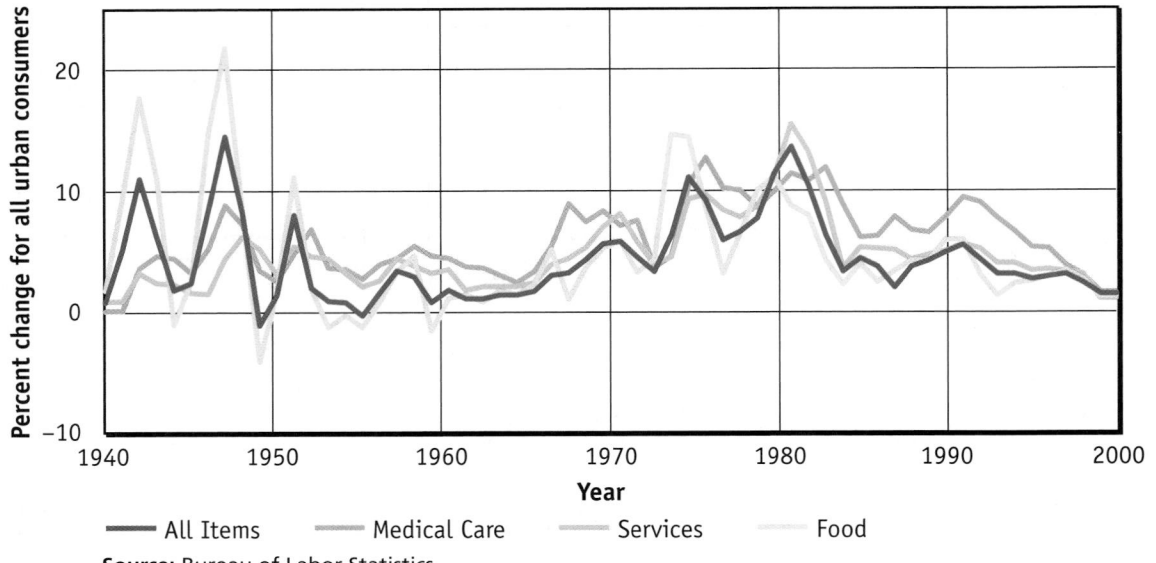

All Items — Medical Care — Services — Food

Source: Bureau of Labor Statistics

Inflation in Consumer Prices, 1915–2000

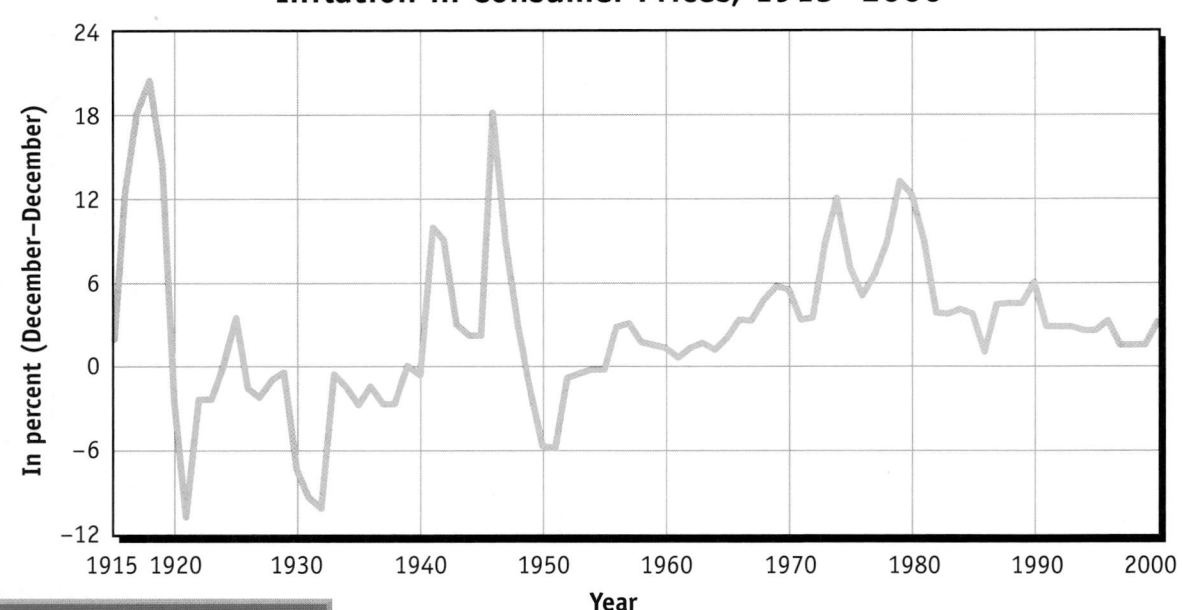

Source: Department of Commerce

ECONOMICS *Online*

Visit epp.glencoe.com and click on **Textbook Updates—Databank** for an update of the data.

The Government Sector

Federal Government Expenditures, 1949–2000

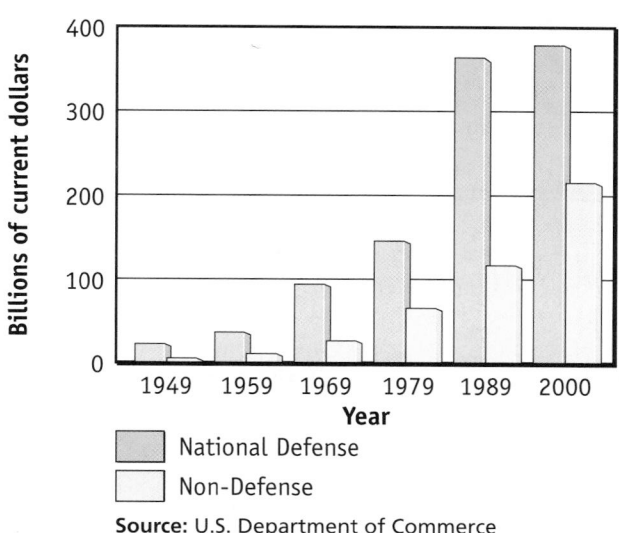

Source: U.S. Department of Commerce

Total Government Expenditures, 1949–2000

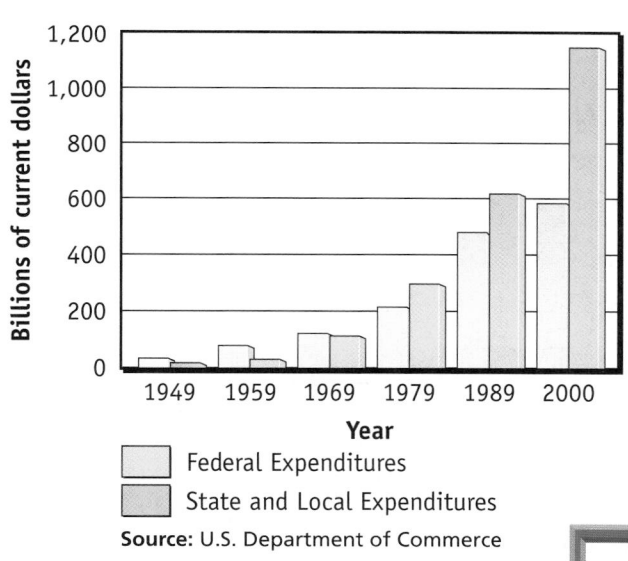

Source: U.S. Department of Commerce

ECONOMICS
Online

Visit epp.glencoe.com and click on
Textbook Updates—Databank for
an update of the data.

The Government Sector

Federal Government Total Receipts and Total Outlays, 1950–2000

In billions of dollars

2,500
2,000
1,500
1,000
500
0

1950   1960   1970   1980   1990   2000*

Outlays
Receipts

Year

Source: *Economic Report of the President*
*Estimate

Federal Debt, Total Outstanding, 1960–2000*

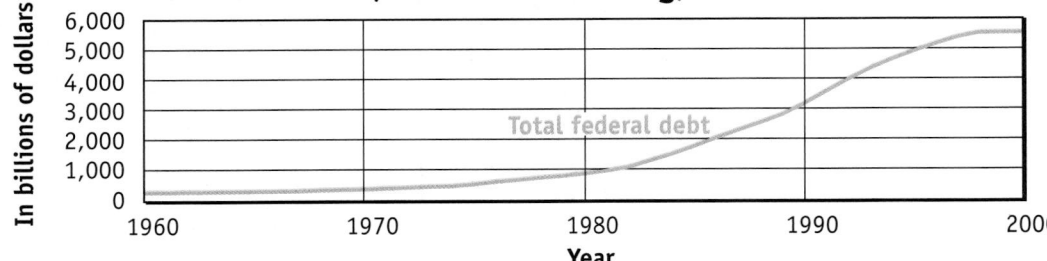

In billions of dollars

6,000
5,000
4,000
3,000
2,000
1,000
0

1960   1970   1980   1990   2000

Total federal debt

Year

Source: *Economic Report of the President,* various editions
*Includes federal debt held by the public and by the federal government

National Debt Per Capita, 1940–2000*

Year

2000
1990
1980
1970
1960
1950
1940

0   2   4   6   8   10   12   14   16   18   20   22

In thousands of dollars

Sources: U.S. Bureau of the Census; U.S. Bureau of Public Debt
*Includes federal debt held by the public and by the federal government

ECONOMICS *Online*

Visit epp.glencoe.com and click on
Textbook Updates—Databank for
an update of the data.

The Government Sector

Federal Budget Receipts, 1980–1999

A Federal Budget Receipts

B Individual Income Taxes

C Employment Taxes

D Corporate Income Taxes

E Excise Taxes

F Other Receipts

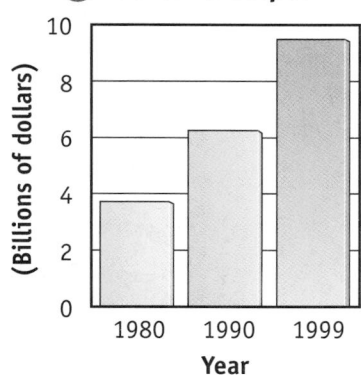

Percentage of Total Receipts

G 1980
13% 47% 14% 26%

H 1990
10% 11% 45% 34%

I 1999
9% 10% 49% 32%

Legend:
- Individual Income Taxes
- Employment Taxes
- Corporate Income Taxes
- Other Receipts

Source: *Economic Report of the President,* various editions

ECONOMICS Online

Visit epp.glencoe.com and click on **Textbook Updates—Databank** for an update of the data.

The Financial Sector

Interest Rates, 1929–2000

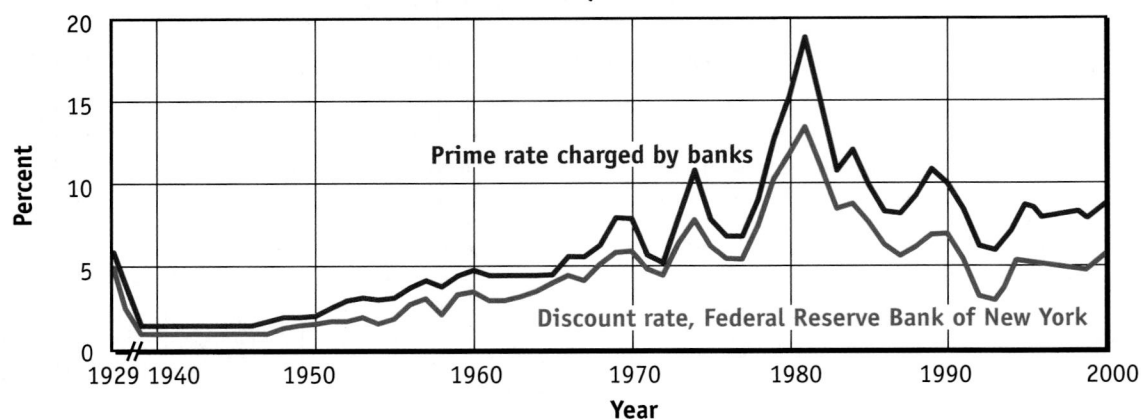

Prime rate charged by banks

Discount rate, Federal Reserve Bank of New York

Sources: *Economic Report of the President*, 2001; The Financial Forecast Center

Consumer Credit Outstanding, 1980–2000

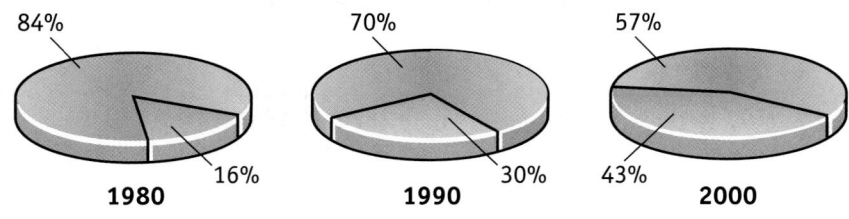

Total Consumer Credit	
1980	$350.1 billion
1990	$789.3 billion
2000	$1,531.5 billion

84%
16%
1980

70%
30%
1990

57%
43%
2000

Total Consumer Credit

Nonrevolving (includes loans for vacations, education, automobiles, etc.)

Revolving (includes credit card, check credit)

Source: Board of Governors of the Federal Reserve System

ECONOMICS Online

Visit epp.glencoe.com and click on **Textbook Updates—Databank** for an update of the data.

The Financial Sector

Personal Saving, 1960–2000

Source: U.S. Department of Commerce, Bureau of Economic Analysis

Money Stock, 1970–2000

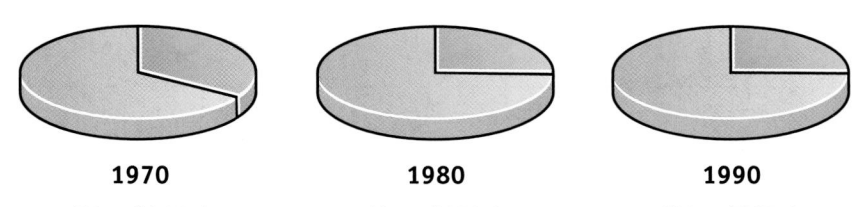

1970	1980	1990	2000
M1 = $214.4	M1 = $408.9	M1 = $825.8	M1 = $1,104.1
M2 = $626.5	M2 = $1,601.1	M2 = $3,279.6	M2 = $4,804.8

In billions of dollars

M1 consists of all currency and checkable deposits.

M2 consists of M1 plus noncheckable savings accounts, money market deposit accounts, time deposits, and money market mutual funds.

Source: Board of Governors of the Federal Reserve System

ECONOMICS Online

Visit epp.glencoe.com and click on **Textbook Updates—Databank** for an update of the data.

The Global Economy

Economic Groups: Population, Exports, and GDP, 2000

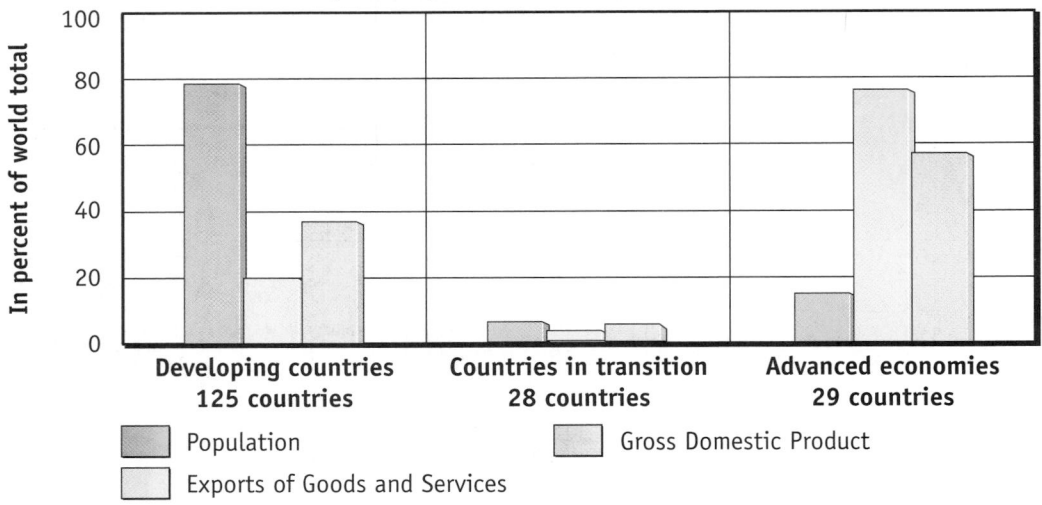

Source: International Monetary Fund

Growth Rates in Real GDP, 1990–2000

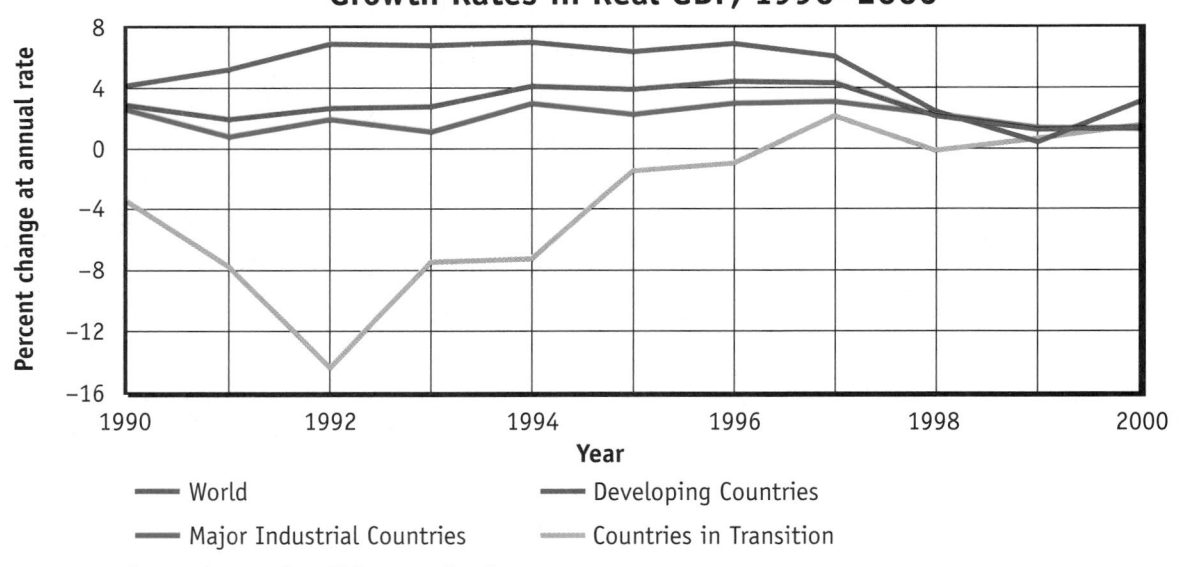

Source: International Monetary Fund

ECONOMICS Online

Visit epp.glencoe.com and click on *Textbook Updates—Databank* for an update of the data.

The Global Economy

World Population by Age, 2000–2050

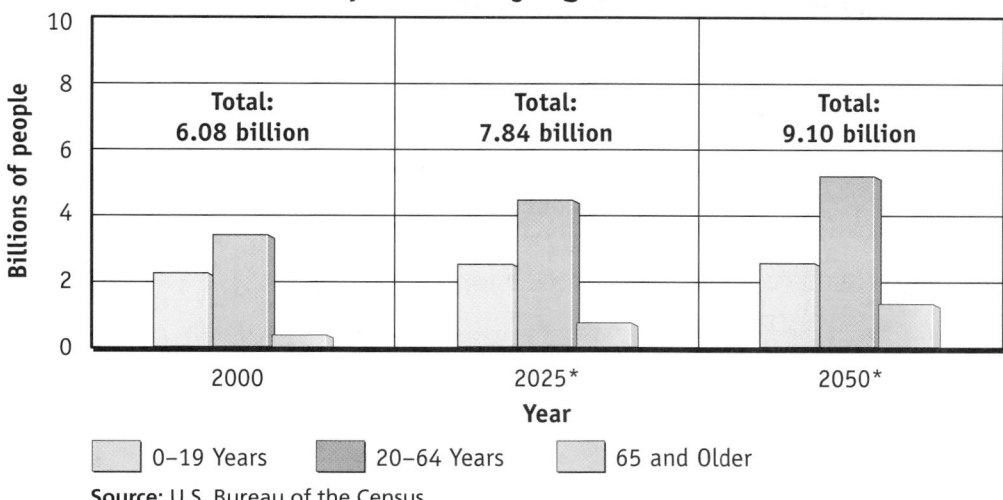

Billions of people

	2000	2025*	2050*
Total:	6.08 billion	7.84 billion	9.10 billion

Year

☐ 0–19 Years   ☐ 20–64 Years   ☐ 65 and Older

Source: U.S. Bureau of the Census
*Estimate

Countries Ranked by Population, 2000 and 2050

Country	Year 2000		Year 2050*	
	Population (in millions)	Rank	Population (in millions)	Rank
China	1,261	1	1,470	(2)
India	1,014	2	1,620	(1)
United States	276	3	404	(3)
Indonesia	224	4	338	(4)
Brazil	173	5	207	(7)
Russia	146	6	118	(14)
Pakistan	142	7	268	(6)
Bangladesh	129	8	205	(8)
Japan	127	9	101	(16)
Nigeria	123	10	304	(5)
Mexico	100	11	153	(12)

Source: U.S. Bureau of the Census
*Estimate

ECONOMICS *Online*

Visit epp.glencoe.com and click on **Textbook Updates—Databank** for an update of the data.

The Global Economy

Aging Index in Selected Nations of the Americas, 2000 and 2025

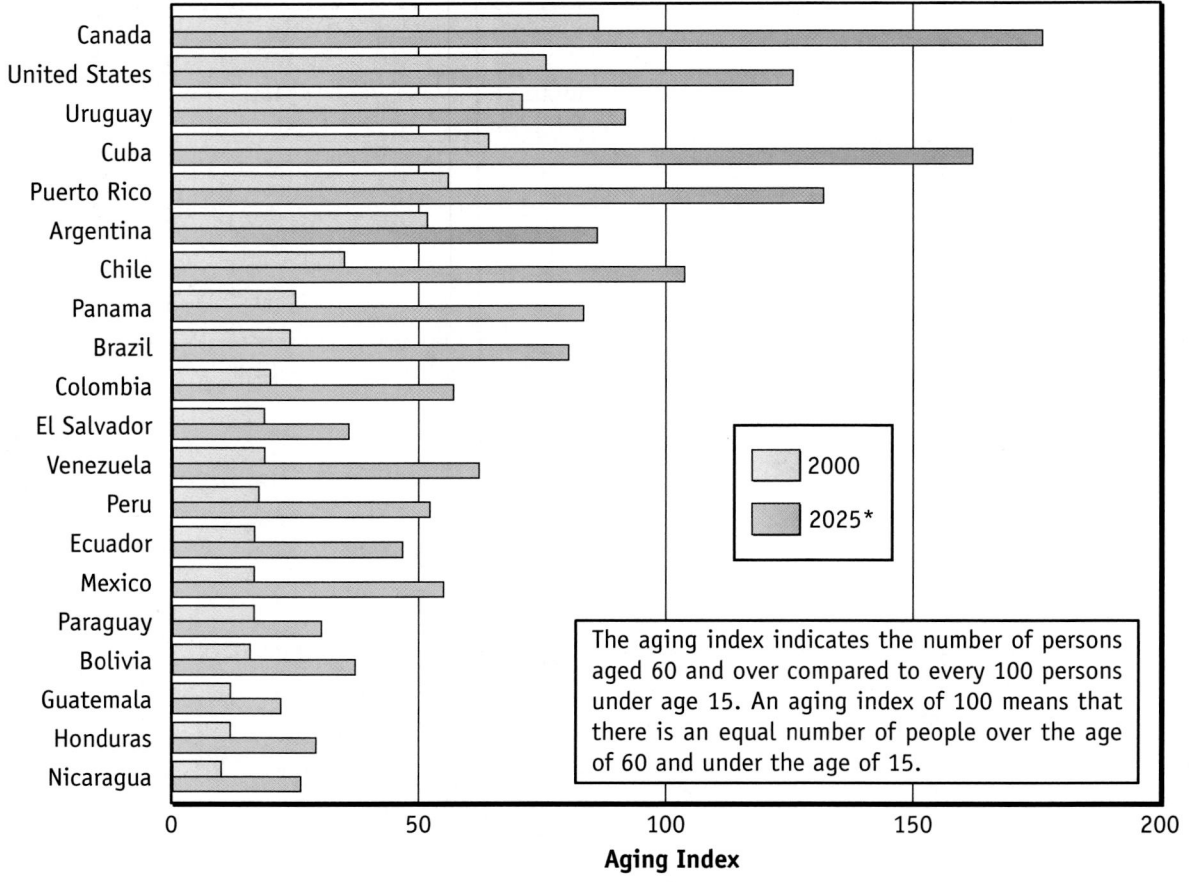

Canada
United States
Uruguay
Cuba
Puerto Rico
Argentina
Chile
Panama
Brazil
Colombia
El Salvador
Venezuela
Peru
Ecuador
Mexico
Paraguay
Bolivia
Guatemala
Honduras
Nicaragua

2000
2025*

Aging Index
0   50   100   150   200

The aging index indicates the number of persons aged 60 and over compared to every 100 persons under age 15. An aging index of 100 means that there is an equal number of people over the age of 60 and under the age of 15.

Median Age, World, 1975–2025

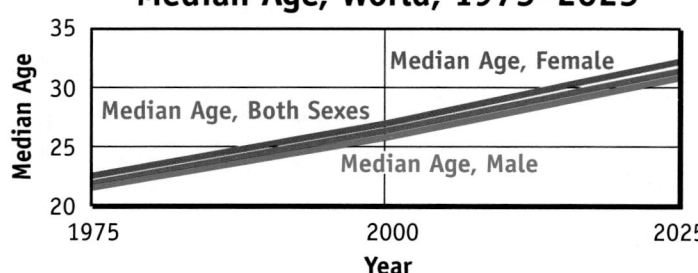

Median Age, Female
Median Age, Both Sexes
Median Age, Male

Median Age
35
30
25
20

1975   2000   2025*
Year

Source: U.S. Bureau of the Census
*Estimate

ECONOMICS *Online*

Visit epp.glencoe.com and click on **Textbook Updates—Databank** for an update of the data.

The Global Economy

U.S. Exports and Imports, 1950–2000

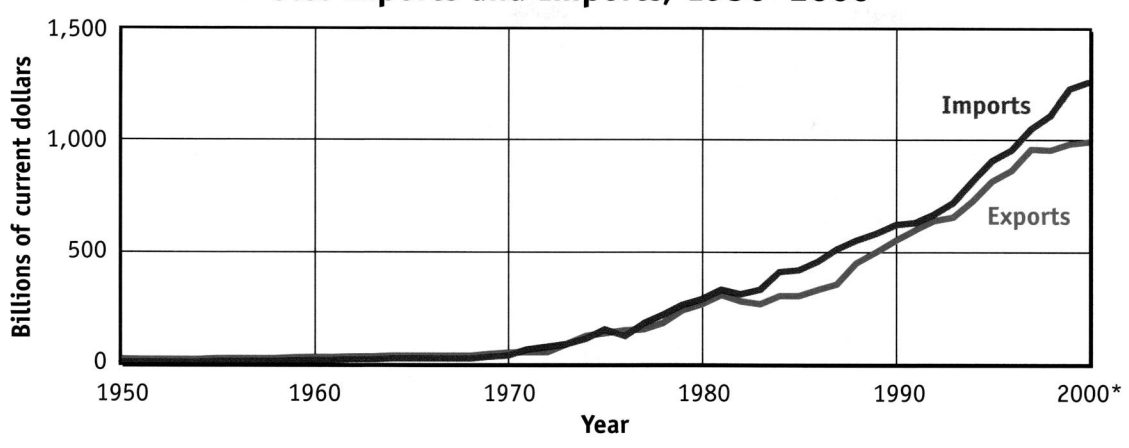

Billions of current dollars

1,500
1,000
500
0

Imports

Exports

1950 1960 1970 1980 1990 2000*

Year

*Estimate

Employment and Unemployment, Selected Economies

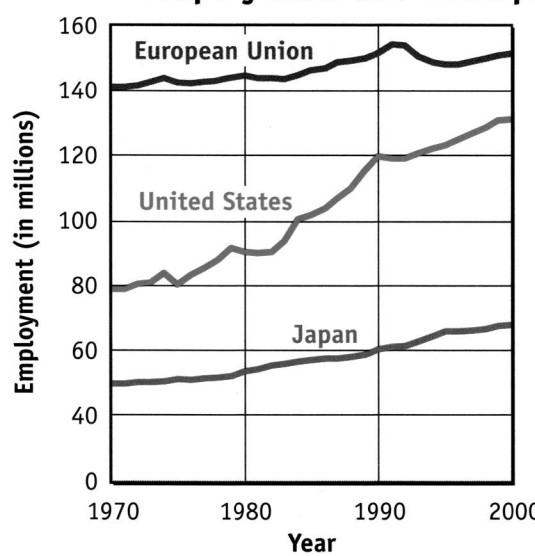

Employment (in millions)

160
140
120
100
80
60
40
0

European Union

United States

Japan

1970 1980 1990 2000

Year

Source: Bureau of Labor Statistics

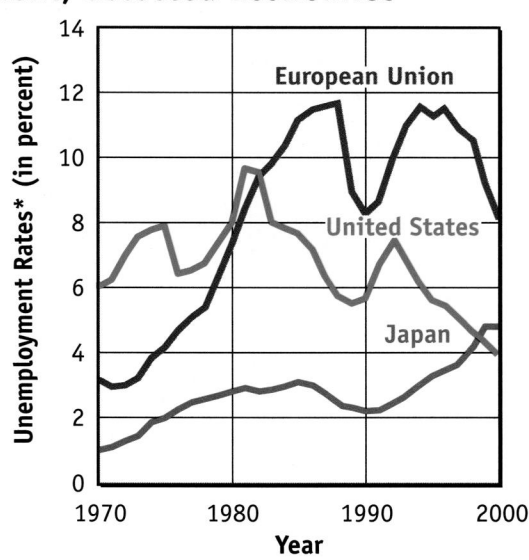

Unemployment Rates* (in percent)

14
12
10
8
6
4
2
0

European Union

United States

Japan

1970 1980 1990 2000

Year

Source: International Monetary Fund
*Based on national definitions

ECONOMICS
Online

Visit epp.glencoe.com and click on
Textbook Updates—Databank for
an update of the data.

Life Skills

F.Y.I.

A recent news magazine article listed the following as the fastest-growing jobs, 1996–2006:
- Database engineer
- Computer engineer
- Systems analyst
- Personal/home aide
- Physical-therapy assistant
- Home health aide
- Medical assistant
- Desktop publisher
- Physical therapist
- Occupational therapist

CYBERNOMICS

Demand for Jobs In today's ever-changing economy, there is huge demand for high-paying jobs that didn't exist just a few years ago. Among these jobs are:
- Chief information officer
- Wireless engineer
- Software-Development Manager
- Computer-systems architect
- Database manager
- Director of e-commerce
- Webmaster

Planning Your Career

Whether you plan to attend college after high school or begin working immediately, now is a good time to start thinking about what you want to do when you finish your high school education.

Thinking About What You Want From a Career Choosing a career depends on many factors, including your interests and skills, your level of education and training, and the opportunities available. To help you think about what kind of career you would like to pursue, use this checklist to identify skills, weaknesses, and interests.

Self-Assessment Checklist
- What are my interests?
- What are my strengths?
- What are my goals?
- Do I like working with people, or do I prefer working alone?
- Do I like working in an office, or do I prefer working outdoors?

Researching Job Opportunities Once you identify your strengths, weaknesses, and interests, you will want to try to identify what kinds of jobs could make use of those interests and skills. Several sources can help you learn about different types of jobs. These government publications are particularly helpful:
- *The Occupational Outlook Handbook* provides detailed information on hundreds of occupations. Included are job duties, working conditions, levels and places of employment, education and training requirements, job trends, and average earnings.
- *The Dictionary of Occupational Titles* lists 20,000 different jobs and is a good source for finding out about jobs you never knew about. The *Dictionary* provides detailed explanations of

job responsibilities, but it does not provide information on education or training requirements.
- *The Guide for Occupational Exploration* focuses on career interests and indicates the kinds of jobs that match different interests. It also offers guidelines on how to prepare for a career and find a job in a particular field.

Other good sources of information are schools and libraries, which often have career resource centers, and the Internet, which has many useful Web sites. Many schools also have computerized guidance programs that you can use to find out about different careers.

Finding a Job Once you have identified the kind of job you would like, you need to find out what opportunities are available in your community. You can find out about jobs by
- talking to people you know, including your guidance counselor.
- checking the classified ads in your local newspaper.
- contacting an employment agency.
- using the Internet.

Applying Life Skills

Identify three fields that interest you. Use resources available to you to learn as much as you can about jobs in these fields. In particular, find out what educational requirements are necessary, what the projected future demand for these jobs is, and what kind of salaries these jobs offer. Prepare a one-page report of your findings.

Answers to Applying Life Skills

Students should use the resources available to complete their research. Encourage students to visit the education department at a nearby college. Suggest that they call ahead to make an appointment with a professor in the field they are researching. Students should ask the professor about the field, the requirements, the future outlook of the field, and different opportunities.

Financing Your College Education

College costs have risen steadily in recent years. If you need financial aid, regardless of the reason, start researching for aid in your junior year or early in your senior year of high school. Check with your guidance counselor about federal aid and state, military, ethnic, and fraternal grants.

Financial Aid Financial aid comes in three basic forms: loans, which must be repaid; scholarships and grants, which need not be repaid; and jobs. Most financial-aid sponsors distribute their money through colleges. Therefore, contact the financial aid office of the college(s) of your choice. Because most colleges send out financial aid applications only upon request, you should obtain these forms early and then file them with your application for admission. Missing the appointed deadline will reduce your chances for aid.

Loans There are four major types of student loans.

1. The *National Direct Student Loan* is granted only to needy students. The funds come from the federal government, but individual colleges choose the students who receive them. The loan is interest-free while you are in school. After graduating, you have 10 years to repay the loan at low interest.

2. The *Government Guaranteed Student Loan* is made by financial institutions, and is guaranteed by the federal government to be repaid. While you are in school, the government pays the interest, which is generally 9 percent. After you graduate, you have 10 years to repay the loan.

3. A *bank loan* requires you or your parents to begin repayment while you are still in college. Although interest rates vary on this type of loan, they generally are higher than the rates on government loans.

4. A *special student loan* is one offered by colleges, civic and professional groups, and other organizations. The interest rates vary on these loans.

Scholarships and Grants Scholarships provide another source of financial aid and do not have to be repaid. In most cases, income plays no part in eligibility. Some available scholarships are *national, state, and college merit scholarships,* awarded on the basis of academic excellence, and *Reserve Officers' Training Corps scholarships,* awarded to students willing to spend four years in the armed forces after graduation. Grants also are available, but they generally are based on need. For those who qualify, *Pell Grants* can be used at any accredited college, vocational school, nursing school, and the like.

Work and Study The third basic kind of financial aid is in the form of a job. One is the *College Work-Study Program* sponsored by the federal government. To be eligible, you must be a full-time student who would not be able to afford school without the job.

If you are seeking financial aid for college, keep the following in mind:

- *Start your investigation early.*
- *Apply for every scholarship or grant for which you may qualify.*
- *You can borrow from more than one program.*

Applying Life Skills

1. If you need financial aid for college, when should you begin your search?
2. What are three forms of financial aid?
3. What kinds of scholarships are available?

LIFE SKILLS **A31**

Answers to Applying Life Skills

1. in your junior year or early in your senior year
2. loans, scholarships, grants, and jobs
3. Kinds of scholarships include: national, state, college, merit, and Reserve Officers' Training Corps scholarships.

F.Y.I.

The resume is a required element of most job applications, but a good resume alone doesn't guarantee a job offer. Rather, a resume piques the interest of an employer and is instrumental in getting the job applicant a personal interview. Most employers want to know whether the applicant can do the job the employer has available. They look for information in the resume that describes experience and aptitude that fit the position. In a personal interview, the employer determines whether the applicant has the communication skills necessary for the position.

Preparing a Resume

One of the most critical parts of finding a job is preparing a resume. A good resume provides a brief history of your accomplishments along with a description of your strengths and abilities. A prospective employer's decision to interview you often depends on his or her reaction to your resume.

Before You Begin Before writing your resume, conduct an inventory of your strengths and weaknesses by asking yourself questions such as:

* What kinds of skills and talents do I have?
* What is my work history?
* How much formal education have I had?
* What are my goals?
* What kind of work do I want?
* What salary would I be willing to accept?

Writing Your Resume When you have answered these questions, organize the entries on your resume.

* Begin with your name, address, telephone number, and e–mail address.
* Indicate the position or kind of position you are seeking.
* List all your relevant work experience, beginning with your most recent job. Include the dates of your employment, the names of the companies for which you have worked, and the positions you have held.
* List the schools you have attended. Include any special honors or awards you have received and any activities in which you have been or are involved.
* Provide at least three references, all of whom know you well enough to vouch for your abilities or strengths. Do not use relatives as references, and do not use more than two teachers.

Keep in mind that you may adjust the format of your resume to highlight the most relevant information.

Writing a Cover Letter When you send a resume, it should be accompanied by a cover letter. A cover letter identifies and explains anything you are sending to someone. It may be as short as two sentences or as long as several paragraphs. Follow these guidelines when you write your cover letter:

* State briefly what is enclosed, but include enough information to make the reader want to look at the attached resume.
* Mention why you are sending the resume.
* Indicate any response you are expecting or any future action you will be taking, such as a follow-up phone call.
* All cover letters should be typed on good quality paper.
* Address the person by name (instead of using "To Whom It May Concern").
* Sign each letter individually.

Applying Life Skills

Directions: View the Renssalaer Polytechnic Institute's *Preparing a Resume* Web page. Print a hard copy or read the article, and answer the following questions:
1. What is the purpose of a resume?
2. What are the steps in preparing a resume?
3. What type of information is included in a resume?
4. A cover letter should accompany the resume. Describe important items to include in this letter.

Answers to Applying Life Skills

1. A prospective employer's decision to interview you often depends on his or her reaction to your resume.
2. Before you begin, conduct an inventory of your strengths and weaknesses. Ask yourself: What kinds of skills and talents do I have? What are my goals? What kind of work do I want? What salary would I be willing to accept? Organize the entries on your resume.
3. Include the position you are seeking, your work experience, your education, and references.
4. A cover letter should state briefly what is enclosed and mention why you are sending the resume.

Preparing a Budget

	Jan	Feb	Mar	April	May	June	July	Aug	Sept	Oct	Nov	Dec
Net Income												
Rent												
Auto												
Telephone												
Utilities												
Cable												
Food												
Clothing												
Entertainment												
Miscellaneous												

To increase your wealth, financial planners recommend that you control your expenditures to live within your means. You can accomplish this by making a **budget**—a plan that matches expenditures with income. Budgeting can help you manage your money better and prevent you from buying goods and services that you do not really need or cannot afford.

Organizing Your Information
The first step in setting up a budget is to obtain a **spreadsheet**—a large sheet of paper with columns for weeks and months, and rows for different categories of expenditures. You can buy spreadsheets in an office supply store, make one of your own using pencil and paper, or use a computer software program designed for this purpose.

Next, decide whether you want to set up your budget on a weekly, monthly, or yearly basis. If you get paid every two weeks, you might want to set up an annual budget with 26 biweekly columns. If you get paid monthly, you might prefer to set up an annual budget with 12 monthly columns.

The first row of your budget should consist of the income you expect to have for each period. Be sure to record your **net income**—the income received after taxes have been taken out. The remainder of the rows should be used to list your expenditures.

List your monthly expenditures, such as rent and utility bills. Then list miscellaneous expenditures, such as clothing or gifts. Because you do not know how many unexpected expenditures you will have, allow 5 to 10 percent of your net income for this category. Keep in mind that it is more efficient and sometimes easier to spread larger expenditures across time.

Keeping Track
Monitor your budget to make sure that the amounts you have allotted for each expenditure are reasonable. If you find that a category does not reflect your actual spending, adjust it. One benefit of a budget is that it can show you where you need to increase or decrease your spending.

Applying Life Skills

1. Why is making a budget important?
2. What are the steps involved in making a budget?
3. What does it mean to monitor a budget?

NIGHTLY BUSINESS REPORT

  ECONOMICS & YOU

  Chapter 9
Disc 1, Side 1

Your Role as a Consumer

Ask: What is the difference between disposable income and discretionary income?
(disposable: the money left after taxes that is spent on such basics as food, clothing, and housing; discretionary: the money that is left over for things that are not considered essential, such as CDs or jewelry)

▶ Also available in VHS.

ECONOMIC SURVIVAL
A FINANCIAL SIMULATION

To help students learn to manage their own finances, have them participate in the game **Economic Survival: A Financial Simulation** in which each student enters the workforce, rents an apartment, and deals with everyday events.

Answers to Applying Life Skills

1. to increase your wealth, manage your money better, and prevent you from buying goods and services you do not really need or cannot afford
2. obtain a spreadsheet; organize your budget on a specific time basis, such as when you receive your paycheck; list your net income and monthly expenditures; monitor your budget by category
3. analyzing and adjusting your spending to make sure your allotments for each expenditure are reasonable and obtainable

Maintaining a Checking Account

Properly maintaining a checking account takes time and effort. Checking accounts generally are not free unless you are able to deposit—and not use—a minimum sum of money, which generally varies from $500 to $1,000. If you do not maintain the required minimum, you may have to pay a monthly fee, which can vary from one bank to another.

Comparing Terms Contact several banks to compare the terms of their checking accounts. After you've selected a bank, it will provide you with checks printed with your full name, current address, and telephone number. When you write checks, make all figures and amounts legible. Write the amount in the box on the extreme right and on the line on the left, using all the space available so that no one can change the amount. Be sure to date the checks correctly and sign them clearly and accurately. Immediately record in your checkbook the date the check was written, to whom it was written, and the amount for which it was written.

Balancing Your Checkbook You should balance your checkbook every month after receiving a statement from the bank. The statement will tell you which checks the bank has received and which deposits it has recorded. It will also tell you

what the balance of your account is at the time the statement was issued. It is your responsibility to reconcile your account with the bank's balance. To reconcile your account, follow these steps:

1. In your checkbook, mark each check entry listed on your bank statement with a checkmark to show that the check has been processed. As you do this, make sure the amount of each check recorded in your checkbook matches the amount on the statement.
2. List the checks you wrote but that have not been processed. Total the amounts of these checks, then add the total to the balance you have written in your checkbook.
3. Subtract any fees or charges indicated on the bank statement, such as a monthly service charge or a charge for new checks.
4. Subtract any cash withdrawals you made from automatic teller machines (ATMs).
5. Subtract any charges made using your debit card for purchases.
6. Compare this balance with the balance on your bank statement. If no mistakes were made, your balance should match the bank's. If the two balances do not match, look for mistakes. If you cannot clear up the error immediately, call the bank. The error may carry over to the next month and make balancing your checkbook even more difficult. If the balance gets too far out of line, a check may "bounce" (be returned for insufficient funds), which will cost you a penalty of $10, $20, or more.

Applying Life Skills

1. Why is having a checking account convenient for many consumers?
2. How do you balance a checkbook?
3. What does it mean when a check bounces?

Answers to Applying Life Skills

1. Answers will vary but might include the following: Most consumers do not feel comfortable carrying large amounts of cash. Most consumers pay their bills through the mail, and checks are much safer to mail than cash.
2. Mark each entry you made against the bank's statement. Total the amount of checks you wrote but that were not processed. Subtract any fees, charges, or ATM withdrawals. Compare your balance with the bank's.
3. It is returned because the check writer did not have sufficient funds in his or her account.

Filing an Income Tax Return

If you work, you probably have to file income tax forms with the federal government and, in some cases, with the state and/or city in which you live or work. The first step in filing income tax forms is to fill out a withholding statement for your employer. The federal withholding form, known as a W-4, asks for such information as your name and address, social security number, marital status, and any special allowances for disabilities or dependents. This form is shown here. The purpose of the W-4 is to help your employer determine how much money to withhold from each of your paychecks for income taxes. If you do not complete the form properly, your employer may not withhold enough money, and you will have to pay additional taxes at the end of the year.

Keeping Track Keep your pay stubs and the receipts for your expenditures together in a safe place. By law, every January your employer must provide you with a W-2 form, which summarizes your earnings for the year. You should check the information on your pay stubs against the information on the W-2. Some expenditures are tax deductible and will save you money by lowering your taxes. You must be able to prove, however, that you actually made the expenditures. Your proof is the receipts that you have saved.

Deductions Depending on the current tax laws, deductible expenses may include mortgage interest, medical bills and pharmaceutical expenses, child-care expenses, charitable contributions, such work-related expenses as union dues or uniforms, and uninsured losses from theft or natural disasters.

Tax Forms At the beginning of each year, the Internal Revenue Service sends out tax forms with detailed instructions on how to complete them. You can find the same forms at most post offices, public libraries, or banks. You may complete the forms yourself or have them completed by a

professional tax preparer. The fee for this service varies according to the complexity of your tax return and the amount of time it takes to prepare it. You generally must file the completed forms by midnight, April 15.

Applying Life Skills

1. What is a W-4 form? What is its purpose?
2. In preparing to file an income tax return, why are receipts important?
3. What are some examples of tax deductible expenses?

LIFE SKILLS **A35**

Jean-Baptist Colbert described taxation as "the art of [plucking] the goose without making it squawk."

Math Practice

Income Taxes Obtain current federal income tax materials, including tax booklets and forms, and distribute them to the class. Familiarize students with some of the terms used on the forms, such as *schedule, exemptions, adjusted gross income, taxable income,* and *deductions.* Then present the following hypothetical situation: Don and Jane Smith have a combined adjusted gross taxable income of $35,416. They have two children, ages 12 and 10. They have no additional income or deductions to claim. During the course of the year, Don and Jane had $5,312 withheld from their income for federal taxes.

Have students fill out a current income tax form for Don and Jane Smith. Then ask students if the Smiths are entitled to a tax refund or if they have to pay more. Invite a professional tax preparer to class to evaluate students' answers.

Answers to Applying Life Skills

1. a federal tax withholding form that allows your employer to withhold and send to the government a certain amount of taxes
2. They can be used to prove that you made the expenditures you claim.
3. mortgage, interest, medical bills, pharmaceutical expenses, spending for child care, charitable contributions, some work-related expenses, and uninsured losses from theft or natural disasters

Life Skills

NIGHTLY BUSINESS REPORT

🔘 **ECONOMICS & YOU**

‖‖‖‖‖‖‖‖ Chapter 10
Disc 1, Side 1

Going into Debt

Ask: How does a credit card work? *(When a credit card is used for a purchase, the owner receives a monthly statement. If the entire bill is paid immediately, no interest is charged. If the bill is not paid in full, interest charges begin to accumulate on the balance.)*

📼 Also available in VHS.

Activity

Finding the Best Credit Bargain

Organize the class into four groups. Tell them they will need to borrow $5,000 to furnish an apartment with a refrigerator, stove, dishwasher, and furniture. Assign each group to research how much it will cost to borrow the money from one of the following: commercial bank, savings and loan association, credit union, and consumer finance company. Have each group report their findings. Compare the four institutions' payment periods, amount of monthly payments, interest rates, finance charges, and total costs of the loans.

Borrowing Money

When you borrow money, you assume some risks. Being in debt can be dangerous and can even lead to personal bankruptcy. Before you decide to borrow money, keep the following factors in mind:

1. Do not borrow so much that if you become ill or lose your job, you no longer will be financially stable.
2. Stagger your debts. Spread out your payments so they are not all due at the same time.

If you have a legitimate need to borrow money, you might consider asking a family member or a friend for a loan. Life insurance companies, savings institutions, credit unions, commercial banks, retail organizations, and finance companies also lend money. The many types of loans that are available to consumers include the following:

- **Installment sales credit,** the most common type of loan available, is generally taken out to buy merchandise such as a major appliance. The consumer makes an initial deposit on the goods and agrees to pay the balance, plus interest and service charges, in equal installments over a period of time.
- **Installment cash credit** is a direct cash loan often used for vacations, home improvements, or other personal expenses. No down payment is required, but the loan, plus interest and other charges, must be repaid in equal installments over a specified period of time.
- **Single lump-sum credit** is a direct cash loan requiring that the amount borrowed plus interest be repaid on a specified day.
- **Open-ended or revolving credit** allows consumers to purchase goods and services from merchants on credit, often without a down payment. In some cases, the consumer may repay the entire balance within 30 days without any interest charges. Monthly payments are required thereafter, with interest being computed on the outstanding balance.

A36 LIFE SKILLS

- **Credit card loans** are loans made through the use of a bank credit card. The payment plans for this type of loan vary widely. In some cases, the consumer pays an annual fee for the use of the card. In other cases, the consumer may have to pay the balance in full at the end of the month or make monthly installment payments.

Costs of the Loan Regardless of the type of loan you obtain, you are entitled by law to receive information about the cost of credit. First, you are entitled to know the **finance charge**–the total dollar amount the credit will cost, including interest charged plus any carrying or service charge. Second, you are entitled to know the **annual percentage rate (APR)**–the interest cost of the loan on a yearly basis. Because repayment schedules differ, the APR is your guide to the true cost of the loan.

To obtain a loan, you must be a good credit risk. The lender checks on your character, your ability to repay the loan, and your capital assets. To determine your creditability, lenders often check with a **credit bureau**–an agency that collects credit information on consumers. If your **credit rating**–a record of debt and payment history–is not good or is in doubt, you probably will be denied credit. Thus, to maintain a good credit rating, you should pay debts on time.

Applying Life Skills

1. Analyze the factors involved when acquiring credit.
2. What kinds of loans are available for consumers?
3. What is a credit rating? Why is it important to maintain a good one?

Answers to Applying Life Skills

1. Answers will vary, but might include: do not borrow too much and spread out your payments.
2. installment sales credit, installment cash credit, single lump-sum credit, open-ended or revolving credit
3. A credit rating is a record of your debt and payment history. You may be denied credit if you do not maintain a good credit rating.

Buying Insurance

Almost everyone needs some kind of insurance. Your parents, for example, may have several types of insurance: homeowners or renters insurance in case of theft, fire, or natural disaster; automobile insurance in case of accident or disability; and health insurance to cover their expenses if they are hospitalized.

How much and what kind of insurance you need depends on your lifestyle, your job, your age, and many other factors. Most people need enough insurance to protect their belongings and potential income, but not so much that paying for it strains their budget.

Types of Insurance There are six major types of insurance that you should consider:

- **Whole life insurance,** sometimes called ordinary life insurance, pays money to your survivors in the event of your death. It also carries a provision for savings against which you can borrow. You may collect the savings in one lump sum when you retire.

- **Term insurance** offers one type of coverage only—payment to your survivors in the event of your death.

- **Health insurance** covers medical and hospital bills if you become ill. Some health insurance policies also cover medication. A standard policy covers approximately 80 percent of medical expenses with some restrictions.

- **Automobile insurance** can provide several different kinds of coverage: **Liability** coverage protects you from claims and lawsuits if you cause an accident. **Collision** covers damage to your automobile if another vehicle hits it.

- **Homeowners insurance** covers a homeowner when his or her home or property has been damaged. Mortgage lenders generally insist that a homeowner carry this type of insurance until his or her mortgage has been paid in full.

- **Property liability** protects renters and homeowners against claims of negligence filed by others when an accident occurs on the renter's or homeowner's property.

Deciding exactly what insurance to buy can be confusing. Different insurance companies often offer the same type of insurance under separate names, which makes it difficult to know if the insurance companies are talking about the same kind of policy. In addition, the product—coverage—is invisible. The consumer cannot always tell how much the policy will pay until something happens for which he or she wants to collect payment on a claim.

When you are buying insurance, keep the following factors in mind:

1. "Group" policies—offered to a group of people, generally through an employer or organization—tend to be less expensive than individual policies purchased from an insurance agent.

2. Always consult more than one agent before buying a policy. Describe your needs carefully to each agent, and ask each to recommend a policy and provide a written list of benefits and estimates of costs—usually in the form of a monthly premium. Inform each agent that you are consulting other agents and intend to compare costs and benefits before making any decision. Base your decision to buy a policy on the results of your comparison.

Applying Life Skills

1. Why do consumers need insurance?
2. What are six major types of insurance?
3. Analyze the factors involved when buying insurance?

LIFE SKILLS **A37**

Answers to Applying Life Skills

1. Consumers need insurance to protect themselves, their belongings, and potential income.
2. Types of insurance include whole life, term, health, automobile, homeowners, and property liability.
3. Answers include: group policies vs. individual policies; consulting more than one agent before buying a policy; comparing costs and benefits.

Life Skills

NIGHTLY BUSINESS REPORT

 ECONOMICS & YOU

Chapter 13
Disc 1, Side 1

Saving and Investing

Ask: How does inflation affect long-range savings goals?
(In setting long-range savings goals, the potential for inflation to decrease the value of the dollars saved must be taken into account so that enough dollars are available at the time they need to be spent.)

Also available in VHS.

Activity

Tracking Market Performance

Have students work in pairs to follow the performance of selected stocks and bonds. Direct the pairs to graph the performance of both the individual stocks and bonds they chose and their "holdings" as a whole. After they complete the graphs, have the student teams report on the strongest and weakest performers among their chosen stocks and bonds. Students might want to include in their reports some background information about the strongest and weakest performers.

Analyzing Your Saving and Investing Options

Economists define saving as the nonuse of income for a period of time so that it can be used later. You may already be setting aside some of your income for some future use, such as continuing your education.

The Decision to Save Any saving that you do now may be only for purchases that require more money than you usually have at one time. When you are self-supporting and have more responsibilities, you will probably save for other reasons. For example, you may save to have money in case of emergencies, such as losing your job, and for your retirement. Most Americans who save do so for these reasons. Saving evens out a person's ability to spend throughout his or her lifetime.

Analyzing Your Options Generally, when people think of saving, they think of putting their money in a savings bank or a similar institution where it will earn interest. However, you have many options of places and ways to invest your savings. The most common places are commercial banks, savings and loan associations, savings banks, and credit unions. Before depositing money, investigate the different types of financial institutions in your area and the services they offer. Each institution usually has several types of savings plans, each paying a different interest rate. In comparison shopping for the best savings plan for you, you need to consider the trade-offs. Some savings plans allow immediate access to your money but pay a low rate of interest. Others pay higher interest and allow immediate use of your money, but require a large minimum balance.

Saving and Investing People usually distinguish between saving and investing. People have savings plans because they want a sure, fixed rate of interest. If people are willing to take a chance on earning a higher rate of return, however, they can invest their money in other ways, such as

A38 LIFE SKILLS

stocks and bonds. Nevertheless, it is usually impossible to get a higher rate of return without taking some risk. Of course, the very nature of risk implies that some investment may yield a lower rate of interest, too.

Deciding How Much to Save and Invest Saving involves a trade-off like every other activity. The more you save today, the more you can buy and consume a year from now, 10 years from now, or 30 years from now. You will, however, have less to spend today. Deciding what percentage of income to save depends on several factors:

- How much do you spend on your fixed expenses?
- What are your reasons for saving?
- How much interest can you earn on your savings and, therefore, how fast will they grow?
- How much income do you think you will be earning in the future?

If you expect to make a much higher income tomorrow, you have less reason to save a large percentage of today's income. In this case, it would be better to wait to start a large savings plan. It is a good idea, however, to have some sort of savings plan.

Applying Life Skills

Write down a list of short-term saving goals, such as saving to buy a new bicycle. Make a list of typical ways in which you can save for such a purchase. Then make a list of long-term saving goals, such as saving for a house or retirement. Then, describe the different ways you can go about achieving your goals. What is the major difference between the two ways of saving?

Answers to Applying Life Skills

Students should compile a viable list of long-term savings goals. Goals might include saving regularly and contacting banks and credit unions in the community to analyze their current interest rates on savings accounts and certificates of deposit. Differences include: saving vs. investing; safer investment vs. riskier investment; saving a larger or smaller amount; short-term vs. long-term.

Renting an Apartment

If you decide to rent an apartment, take time to choose wisely. Determine the best location in terms of getting back and forth from work or school and convenience for shopping. Decide if you want a furnished or an unfurnished apartment. Consider how much space you need to have adequate storage and be comfortable. Most importantly, determine how much rent you can afford to pay. Monthly rent plus related expenses should not be more than one week's take-home pay.

Carrying Out the Search To find an apartment, consult the classified section of newspapers, ask friends for recommendations, search the Internet, or hire a rental agent. Never agree to rent an apartment until you have personally seen it. The best time to do this is during an evening or on a weekend, which will reveal the surrounding noise level and what the neighbors are like. If possible, talk to some of the people in the apartment complex to learn the advantages and disadvantages of moving into the area.

Inspect the apartment and the surrounding area carefully for the following:

1. Is the building well-built, well-maintained, and well-lit?
2. Is the apartment the right size? Does it have a convenient floor plan, enough wall space for your furniture, and adequate lighting and electrical outlets?
3. How many windows are there? Do they open and close easily? Are there screens and storm windows?
4. Is the apartment air-conditioned? Does it have its own heating and cooling controls?
5. Are major appliances, such as a stove and refrigerator, in good working condition?
6. If there is carpeting, is it clean? Are there drapes, blinds, or shades for the windows?
7. Does the building have fire walls? Smoke alarms?
8. Are laundry equipment and storage facilities available?
9. Is there trash collection or disposal? Where? How often? By whom? Who pays for it?
10. What kind of burglary protection is there?
11. What are the parking facilities?

The Lease After you have selected the apartment you want, you probably will have to sign a lease, a written agreement between you and the landlord that states the major terms of your occupancy. It generally includes a description of the rental property; the amount of rent to be paid and when it is due; how much deposit is required, what it covers, and under what conditions it may be forfeited; and how long the lease is in force and under what conditions it may be renewed. The lease also should include the terms for rent increases; who pays for specific utilities and repairs; what alterations you can make on the property; how much notice you must give before moving; whether you can rent the apartment to someone else; and whether children, pets, or roommates are allowed.

Before signing a lease, inspect the apartment with the landlord. Point out and write down any damage to walls, floors, appliances, and fixtures. Attach a copy of this list to the lease so that you cannot be held responsible for damage done before you moved into the apartment. Check to see if a security deposit is required in addition to the rental deposit. If it is, determine the amount and under what conditions it will be returned.

Applying Life Skills

1. What are some things to consider if you decide to rent an apartment?
2. When is the best time to look for an apartment?
3. What is a lease? What does it include?

ECONOMIC SURVIVAL
A FINANCIAL SIMULATION

To help students learn to manage their own finances, have them participate in the game **Economic Survival: A Financial Simulation** in which each student enters the workforce, rents an apartment, and deals with everyday events.

Activity

Conducting a Survey

Have students work in pairs to conduct a survey of housing arrangements or transportation arrangements used by their classmates. The survey should list the type of housing or transportation used by classmates and the advantages and disadvantages students perceive. After the surveys are completed, have student teams report on the most popular types of housing and transportation among the families of their classmates. Students might report their findings in an illustrated table.

Answers to Applying Life Skills

1. location, furnished or unfurnished, space you need for storage and to be comfortable, how much rent you can afford to pay
2. during an evening or on a weekend
3. A lease is a written agreement between you and the owner or manager that states the major terms of your occupancy. It includes: the amount of rent to be paid and when it is due; the amount of deposit, if required; the conditions of the deposit; the length of the lease; terms for rent increases; who pays for utilities and repairs; what alterations you can make to the apartment, and so on.

ability-to-pay principle of taxation   belief that taxes should be paid according to level of income regardless of benefits received (p. 228)

absolute advantage   country's ability to produce more of a given product than can another country (p. 469)

accelerated depreciation   schedule that spreads depreciation over fewer years than normal to generate larger tax reductions (p. 245)

accelerator   change in investment spending caused by a change in overall spending (p. 448)

acid rain   pollution in form of rainwater mixed with sulfur dioxide, a mild form of sulfuric acid (p. 554)

agency shop   arrangement under which non-union members must pay union dues (p. 201)

aggregate demand   the total quantity of goods and services demanded at different price levels (p. 444)

aggregate demand curve   hypothetical curve showing different levels of real GDP that could be purchased at various price levels (p. 444)

aggregate supply   the total value of goods and services that all firms would produce in a specific period of time at various price levels (p. 442)

aggregate supply curve   hypothetical curve showing different levels of real GDP that could be produced at various price levels (p. 443)

alternative minimum tax   personal income tax rate that applies to cases where taxes would otherwise fall below a certain level (p. 245)

appropriations bill   legislation earmarking funds for certain purposes (p. 261)

aquifer   underground water-bearing rock formation (p. 550)

arbitration   see voluntary arbitration and/or compulsory arbitration (p. 202)

ASEAN   group of ten Southeast Asian nations working to promote regional cooperation, economic growth, and trade (p. 535)

assets   properties, possessions and claims on others; usually listed as entries on a balance sheet (p. 416)

automatic stabilizer   program that automatically provides benefits to offset a change in people's incomes; unemployment insurance, entitlement programs (p. 449)

automation   production with mechanical or other processes that reduces the need for workers (p. 386)

average tax rate   total taxes paid divided by the total taxable income (p. 229)

baby boom   historically high birthrate years in the United States from 1946 to 1964 (p. 360)

balance of payments   difference between money paid to, and received from, other nations in trade; balance on current account includes goods and services, merchandise trade balance counts only goods (p. 478)

balance sheet   condensed statement showing assets, liabilities, and net worth of an economic unit (p. 416)

balanced budget   annual budget in which expenditures equal revenues (p. 273)

balanced budget amendment   constitutional amendment requiring government to spend no more than it collects in taxes and other revenues, excluding borrowing (p. 267)

bank holiday   brief period during which all banks or depository institutions are closed to prevent bank runs (p. 301)

bankruptcy   court-granted permission to an individual or business to cease or delay payment on some or all debts for a limited amount of time (p. 62)

barter economy   moneyless economy that relies on trade or barter (p. 285)

base year   year serving as point of comparison for other years in a price index or other statistical measure (p. 218, 351)

bear market   period during which stock market prices move down for several months or years in a row (p. 332)

benefit principle of taxation   belief that taxes should be paid according to benefits received regardless of income (p. 227)

Better Business Bureau   business-sponsored nonprofit organization providing information on local companies to consumers (p. 78)

bill consolidation loan   popular type of consumer loan used to pay off multiple existing loans (p. 315)

black market   market in which economic products are sold illegally (p. 505)

bond   formal contract to repay borrowed money and interest on the borrowed money at regular future intervals (p. 64)

boycott   protest in the form of a refusal to buy, including attempts to convince others to join (p. 195)

break-even point   production needed if the firm is to recover its costs; production level where total cost equals total revenue (p. 131)

bull market   period during which stock market prices move up for several months or years in a row (p. 332)

business cycle   systematic changes in real GDP marked by alternating periods of expansion and contraction (p. 375)

business fluctuation   changes in real GDP marked by alternating periods of expansion and contraction that occur on a less than systematic basis (p. 375)

call option   contract giving investors the option to buy commodities, equities, or financial assets at a specific future date using a price agreed upon today (p. 333)

capital   tools, equipment, and factories used in the production of goods and services; one of four factors of production (p. 7)

capital flight   legal or illegal export of a nation's currency and foreign exchange (p. 525)

capital gains   profits from the sale of an asset held for 12 months (p. 246)

capital good   tool, equipment, or other manufactured good used to produce other goods and services; a factor of production (p. 12)

capital-intensive   production method requiring relatively large amounts of capital relative to labor (p. 510)

capital market   market in which financial capital is loaned and/or borrowed for more than one year (p. 325)

capitalism   economic system in which private citizens own and use the factors of production in order to generate profits (p. 46, 492)

capital-to-labor ratio   measure obtained by dividing the total capital stock by the labor force (p. 367)

cartel   group of sellers or producers acting together to raise prices by restricting availability of a product; OPEC (p. 536)

cash flow   total amount of new funds the business generates from operations; broadest measure of profits for a firm, includes both net income and non-cash charges (p. 69)

cease and desist order   ruling requiring a company to stop an unfair business practice that reduces or limits competition (p. 179)

census   complete count of population, including place of residence (p. 356)

center of population   point where the country would balance if it were flat and everyone weighed the same (p. 357)

central bank   bank that can lend to other banks in times of need, a "bankers' bank" (p. 301)

certificate of deposit   receipt showing that an investor has made an interest-bearing loan to a financial institution (p. 314)

chamber of commerce   nonprofit organization of local businesses whose purpose is to promote their interests (p. 78)

change in demand   consumers demand different amounts at every price, causing the demand curve to shift to the left or the right (p. 96)

change in quantity demanded   movement along the demand curve showing that a different quantity is purchased in response to a change in price (p. 95)

change in quantity supplied   change in amount offered for sale in response to a price change; movement along the supply curve (p. 115)

change in supply   different amounts offered for sale at each and every possible price in the market; shift of the supply curve (p. 116)

charter   written government approval to establish a corporation; includes company name, address, purpose of business, number of shares of stock, and other features of the business (p. 63)

civilian labor force   non-institutionalized part of the population, aged 16 and over, either working or looking for a job (p. 193)

closed shop   illegal arrangement under which workers must join a union before they are hired (p. 200)

coins   metallic forms of money such as pennies, nickels, dimes, and quarters (p. 413)

collateral   property or other security used to guarantee repayment of a loan (p. 511)

collective bargaining   process of negotiation between union and management representatives over pay, benefits, and job-related matters (p. 77)

collective farm   small farms in the former Soviet Union owned by the state, but operated by families who shared in some of the profits (p. 498)

collectivization   forced common ownership of factors of production; used in the former Soviet Union in agriculture and manufacturing under Stalin (p. 497)

collusion   agreements, usually illegal, among producers to fix prices, limit output, or divide markets (p. 168)

command economy   economic system characterized by a central authority that makes most of the major economic decisions (p. 35)

commercial bank   depository institution that, until the mid-1970s, had the exclusive right to offer checking accounts (p. 303)

commodity money   money that has an alternative use as a commodity; gunpowder, flour, corn (p. 287)

communism   economic and political system in which factors of production are collectively owned and directed by the state; theoretically classless society in which everyone works for the common good (p. 493)

company union   union organized, supported, and even financed by an employer (p. 195)

comparable worth   doctrine stating that equal pay should be given for jobs of comparable difficulty (p. 215)

comparative advantage   country's ability to produce a given product relatively more efficiently than another country; production at a lower opportunity cost (p. 470)

competition   the struggle among sellers to attract consumers while lowering costs (p. 48)

complements   products that increase the value of other products; products related in such a way that an increase in the price of one reduces the demand for both (p. 98)

conglomerate   firm with four or more businesses making unrelated products, with no single business responsible for a majority of its sales (p. 71)

constant dollars   dollar amounts or prices that have been adjusted for inflation; same as real dollars (p. 218)

consumer good   good intended for final use by consumers rather than businesses (p. 12)

consumer price index   index used to measure price changes for a market basket of frequently used consumer items (p. 352)

Glossary

consumer sovereignty role of consumer as ruler of the market when determining the types of goods and services produced (p. 50)

cooperative nonprofit association performing some kind of economic activity for the benefit of its members (p. 76)

corporate income tax tax on corporate profits (p. 235)

corporation form of business organization recognized by law as a separate legal entity with all the rights and responsibilities of an individual, including the right to buy and sell property, enter into legal contracts, sue and be sued (p. 62)

cost-benefit analysis way of thinking that compares the cost of an action to its benefits (p. 24)

Council of Economic Advisers three-member group that devises strategies and advises the President of the United States on economic matters (p. 460)

coupon stated interest on a corporate, municipal or government bond (p. 321)

craft union labor union whose workers perform the same kind of work; same as trade union (p. 194)

credit union nonprofit service cooperative that accepts deposits, makes loans, and provides other financial services (p. 76, 303)

creditor person or institution to whom money is owed (p. 305)

creeping inflation relatively low rate of inflation, usually 1 to 3 percent annually (p. 390)

crowding-out effect higher than normal interest rates and diminished access to financial capital faced by private investors when government increases its borrowing in financial markets (p. 277)

crude birthrate number of live births per 1,000 people (p. 524)

currency paper component of the money supply, today consisting of Federal Reserve notes (p. 413)

current dollars dollar amounts or prices that are not adjusted for inflation (p. 218)

current GDP Gross Domestic Product measured in current prices, unadjusted for inflation (p. 353)

current yield bond's annual coupon interest divided by purchase price; measure of a bond's return (p. 321)

customs duty tax on imported products (p. 236)

customs union group of countries that have agreed to reduce trade barriers (p. 535)

cyclical unemployment unemployment directly related to swings in the business cycle (p. 386)

default the act of not repaying borrowed money (p. 525)

deficiency payment cash payment making up the difference between the market price and the target price of an agricultural crop (p. 153)

deficit spending annual government spending in excess of taxes and other revenues (p. 272)

deflation decrease in the general level of the prices of goods and services (p. 390)

demand combination of desire, ability, and willingness to buy a product (p. 89)

demand curve graph showing the quantity demanded at each and every possible price that might prevail in the market at a given time (p. 91)

demand deposit account (DDA) account whose funds can be removed by writing a check and without having to gain prior approval from the depository institution (p. 303)

demand elasticity measure of responsiveness relating change in quantity demanded (dependent variable) to a change in price (independent variable) (p. 101)

demand schedule listing showing the quantity demanded at all possible prices that might prevail in the market at a given time (p. 90)

demographer person who studies growth, density, and other characteristics of the population (p. 358)

dependency ratio ratio of children and elderly per 100 persons who are in the 18–64 working age bracket (p. 361)

depreciation gradual wear on capital goods during production (p. 69)

depression state of the economy with large numbers of unemployed, declining real incomes, overcapacity in manufacturing plants, general economic hardship (p. 376)

depression scrip currency issued by towns, chambers of commerce, and other civic bodies during the Great Depression of the 1930s (p. 377)

deregulation relaxation or removal of government regulations on business activities (p. 304)

developing country country whose average per capita income is only a fraction of that in more industrialized countries (p. 521)

diminishing marginal utility decreasing satisfaction or usefulness as additional units of a product are acquired (p. 93)

diminishing returns stage of production where output increases at a decreasing rate as more units of variable input are added (p. 125)

discomfort index unofficial statistic that is the sum of monthly inflation and the unemployment rate; same as misery index (p. 438)

discount rate interest rate that the Federal Reserve System charges on loans to the nation's financial institutions (p. 422)

discretionary spending spending for federal programs that must receive annual authorization (p. 260)

disposable personal income personal income less individual income taxes; total income available to the consumer sector after income taxes (p. 346)

distribution of income way in which the nation's income is divided among families, individuals, or other designated groups (p. 258)

dividend check paid to stockholders, usually quarterly, representing portion of corporate profits (p. 63)

division of labor division of work into a number of separate tasks to be performed by different workers; same as specialization (p. 16)

DJIA see Dow-Jones Industrial Average (p. 331)

double taxation feature of taxation that allows stockholders' dividends to be taxed both as corporate profit and as personal income (p. 65)

Dow-Jones Industrial Average (DJIA) statistical series of 30 representative stocks used to monitor price changes on the New York Stock Exchange (p. 332)

easy money policy monetary policy resulting in lower interest rates and greater access to credit; associated with an expansion of the money supply (p. 419)

e-commerce electronic business or exchange conducted over the Internet (p. 129)

econometric model macroeconomic model using algebraic equations to describe how the economy behaves and is expected to perform in the future (p. 379)

economic growth sustained period during which a nation's total output of goods and services increases (p. 15)

economic interdependence economic activities in one part of the country or world affect what happens elsewhere (p. 17)

economic model set of assumptions in a table, graph, or equations used to describe or explain economic behavior (p. 143)

economic product good or service that is useful, relatively scarce, and transferable to others (p. 12)

economic system organized way a society provides for the wants and needs of its people (p. 33)

economics social science dealing with the study of how people satisfy seemingly unlimited and competing wants with the careful use of scarce resources (p. 6)

economies of scale increasingly efficient use of personnel, plant, and equipment as a firm becomes larger (p. 170)

economy see economic system (p. 33)

Efficient Market Hypothesis (EMH) argument that stocks are always priced about right, and that bargains are hard to find because they are closely watched by so many investors (p. 329)

elastic type of elasticity where the percentage change in the independent variable (usually price) causes a more than proportionate change in the dependent variable (usually quantity demanded or supplied) (p. 102)

elasticity a measure of responsiveness that tells us how a dependent variable such as quantity responds to a change in an independent variable such as price (p. 101)

embargo prohibition on the export or import of a product (p. 546)

entitlement program or benefit using established eligibility requirements to provide health, nutritional, or income supplements to individuals (p. 278)

entrepreneur risk-taking individual in search of profits; one of four factors of production (p. 8)

equilibrium price price where quantity supplied equals quantity demanded; price that clears the market (p. 144)

equilibrium wage rate wage rate leaving neither a surplus nor a shortage in the market (p. 207)

equities stocks that represent ownership shares in corporations (p. 328)

estate tax tax on the transfer of property when a person dies (p. 235)

euro single currency of European Union (p. 535)

European Union successor of the European Community established in 1993 by the Maastricht Treaty (p. 535)

excess reserves financial institution's cash, currency, and reserves not needed to back existing loans; potential source of new loans (p. 416)

excise tax general revenue tax levied on the manufacture or sale of selected items (p. 235)

expansion period of growth of real GDP; recovery from recession (p. 376)

exports the goods and services that a nation produces and then sells to other nations (p. 467)

expropriation government confiscation of private- or foreign-owned goods without compensation (p. 534)

external debt borrowed money that a country owes to foreign countries and banks (p. 525)

externality economic side effect that affects an uninvolved third party (p. 175)

fact-finding agreement between union and management to have a neutral third party collect facts about a dispute and present non-binding recommendations (p. 202)

factor market market where productive resources are bought and sold (p. 14)

factors of production productive resources that make up the four categories of land, capital, labor, and entrepreneurship (p. 7)

family two or more persons living together that are related by blood, marriage, or adoption (p. 346)

federal budget annual plan outlining proposed expenditures and anticipated revenues (p. 260)

federal budget deficit excess of federal expenditures over tax and revenue collections (p. 261)

federal budget surplus federal budget that shows a positive balance after expenditures are subtracted from revenues (p. 261)

federal debt total amount of money the federal government has borrowed from others (p. 273)

Federal Reserve note currency issued by the Fed that eventually replaced all other types of federal currency (p. 301)

Federal Reserve System privately owned, publicly controlled, central bank of the United States (p. 301)

fertility rate number of births that 1,000 women are expected to undergo in their lifetime (p. 358)

fiat money money by government decree; has no alternative value or use as a commodity (p. 287)

FICA Federal Insurance Contributions Act; tax levied on employers and employees to support Social Security and medicare (p. 233)

finance company firm that makes loans directly to consumers and specializes in buying installment contracts from merchants who sell on credit (p. 315)

financial asset document that represents a claim on the income and property of the borrower; CDs, bonds, Treasury bills, mortgages (p. 314)

financial capital money used to buy the tools and equipment used in production (p. 7)

financial intermediary institution that channels savings to investors; banks, insurance companies, savings and loan associations, credit unions (p. 314)

financial system network of savers, investors, and financial institutions that work together to transfer savings to investment uses (p. 314)

fiscal policy use of government spending and revenue collection measures to influence the economy (p. 447)

fiscal year 12-month financial planning period that may not coincide with the calendar year; October 1 to September 30 for the federal government (p. 260)

Five-Year Plan comprehensive centralized economic plan used by the Soviet Union and China to coordinate development of agriculture and industry (p. 497)

fixed cost cost of production that does not change when output changes (p. 127)

fixed exchange rate system under which the value of currencies were fixed in relation to one another; the exchange rate system in effect until 1971 (p. 482)

fixed income income that does not increase even though prices go up (p. 42)

flat tax proportional tax on individual income after a specified threshold has been reached (p. 249)

flexible exchange rate system that relies on supply and demand to determine the value of one currency in terms of another; exchange rate system in effect since 1971, same as floating exchange rate (p. 483)

floating exchange rate see flexible exchange rate (p. 483)

floor price see price floor (p. 152)

food stamps government-issued coupons that can be exchanged for food (p. 397)

foreign exchange foreign currencies used by countries to conduct international trade (p. 481)

foreign exchange rate price of one country's currency in terms of another currency (p. 482)

401(k) plan a tax-deferred investment and savings plan that acts as a personal pension fund for employees (p. 320)

fractional reserve system system requiring financial institutions to set aside a fraction of their deposits in the form of reserves (p. 415)

free enterprise economy in which competition is allowed to flourish with a minimum of government interference; term used to describe the American economy (p. 46)

free enterprise economy market economy in which privately owned businesses have the freedom to operate for a profit with limited government intervention; same as private enterprise economy (p. 24)

free-trade area group of countries that have agreed to reduce trade barriers among themselves, but lack a common tariff barrier for nonmembers (p. 535)

free trader individual who favors fewer or even no trade restrictions (p. 474)

frictional unemployment unemployment caused by workers changing jobs or waiting to go to new ones (p. 384)

fringe benefit benefit received by employees in addition to wages and salaries; includes paid vacations, sick leave, retirement, insurance (p. 57)

futures contracts to buy or sell commodities or financial assets at a specific future date, using a price agreed upon today (p. 333)

futures contract an agreement to buy or sell at a specific date in the future at a predetermined price (p. 333)

futures market market where futures contracts are bought and sold (p. 333)

galloping inflation relatively intense inflation, usually ranging from 100 to 300 percent annually (p. 390)

gasohol mixture of 90 percent unleaded gasoline and 10 percent grain alcohol (p. 549)

GDP gap difference between what the economy can and does produce; annual opportunity cost of unemployed resources (p. 438)

GDP in constant dollars Gross Domestic Product after adjustments for inflation; also called GDP in constant (chained) dollars; same as real GDP (p. 353)

general partnership see partnership (p. 60)

geographic monopoly market situation where a firm has a monopoly because of its location or the small size of the market (p. 170)

gift tax tax on donations of money or wealth that is paid by the donor (p. 235)

giveback wage, fringe benefit, or work rule given up when renegotiating a contract (p. 212)

glass ceiling seemingly invisible barrier hindering advancement of women and minorities in a male-dominated organization (p. 214)

glut substantial oversupply of a product (p. 553)

gold certificate paper currency backed by gold; issued in 1863 and popular until recalled in 1934 (p. 295)

gold standard monetary standard under which a country's currency is equivalent to, and can be exchanged for, a specified amount of gold (p. 296)

good tangible economic product that is useful, relatively scarce, transferable to others; used to satisfy wants and needs (p. 12)

Gosplan central planning authority in former Soviet Union that devised and directed Five-Year plans (p. 497)

government monopoly monopoly created and/or owned by the government (p. 170)

grant-in-aid transfer payment from one level of government to another not involving compensation (p. 257)

Great Depression greatest period of economic decline in United States history, lasting from approximately 1929 to 1939 (p. 196)

Great Leap Forward China's disastrous second five-year plan begun in 1958 that forced collectivization of agriculture and rapid industrialization (p. 506)

grievance procedure contractual provision outlining the way future disputes and grievance issues will be resolved (p. 202)

Gross Domestic Product (GDP) dollar value of all final goods, services, and structures produced within a country's national borders during a one-year period (p. 9, 341)

Gross National Product (GNP) total dollar value of all final goods, services, and structures produced in one year with labor and property supplied by a country's residents, regardless of where the production takes place; largest measure of a nation's income (p. 344)

growth triangle table showing the rates of growth of a statistical series between any two dates (p. 364)

H

horizontal merger combination of two or more firms producing the same kind of product (p. 71)

household basic unit of consumer sector consisting of all persons who occupy a house, apartment, or separate living quarters (p. 346)

human capital sum of peoples' skills, abilities, health, and motivation (p. 16)

hyperinflation abnormal inflation in excess of 500 percent per year; last stage of a monetary collapse (p. 390)

I

imperfect competition market structure where all conditions of pure competition are not met; monopolistic competition, oligopoly, and monopoly (p. 166)

implicit GDP price deflator index used to measure price changes in Gross Domestic Product (p. 353)

imports the goods and services that a nation buys from other nations (p. 468)

incidence of a tax final burden of a tax (p. 225)

income effect that portion of a change in quantity demanded caused by a change in a consumer's real income when the price of a product changes (p. 96)

income statement report showing a business's sales, expenses, and profits for a certain period, usually three months or a year (p. 68)

inconvertible fiat money standard fiat money that cannot be exchanged for gold or silver; Federal Reserve notes today (p. 297)

independent union labor union not affiliated with the AFL-CIO (p. 198)

index of leading indicators composite index of 11 economic series that move up and down in advance of changes in the overall economy; statistical series used to predict business cycle turning points (p. 380)

indexing adjustment of tax brackets to offset the effects of inflation (p. 233)

individual income tax tax levied on the wages, salaries, and other income of individuals (p. 226)

Individual Retirement Account (IRA) retirement account in the form of a long-term time deposit, with annual contributions of up to $2,000 per year not taxed until withdrawn during retirement (p. 324)

industrial union labor union whose workers perform different kinds of work (p. 195)

inelastic type of elasticity where the percentage change in the independent variable (usually price) causes a less than proportionate change in the dependent variable (usually quantity demanded or supplied) (p. 102)

infant industries argument argument that new and emerging industries should be protected from foreign competition until they are strong enough to compete (p. 474)

inflation rise in the general level of prices (p. 42, 350)

infrastructure the highways, mass transit, communications, power, water, sewerage and other public goods needed to support a population (p. 510)

injunction court order issued to prevent a company or union from taking action during a labor dispute (p. 203)

interest payment made for the use of borrowed money; usually paid at periodic intervals for long-term bonds or loans (p. 64)

intergovernmental expenditures funds that one level of government transfers to another level for spending (p. 268)

Glossary

intergovernmental revenue   funds one level of government receives from another level of government (p. 238)

intermediate products   products directly excluded from GDP because they are components of other final products included in GDP; new tires and radios for use on new cars (p. 343)

Internal Revenue Service (IRS)   branch of Treasury Department that collects taxes (p. 232)

International Bank for Reconstruction and Development   see World Bank (p. 526)

International Monetary Fund (IMF)   international organization that offers advice and financial assistance to nations so that their currencies can compete in open markets (p. 526)

inventory   stock of goods held in reserve; includes finished goods waiting to be sold and raw materials to be used in production (p. 59)

investment tax credit   tax credit given for purchase of equipment (p. 245)

keiretsu   independently owned group of Japanese firms joined and governed by an external board of directors in order to regulate competition (p. 510)

Keynesian economics   government spending and taxation policies suggested by John Maynard Keynes to stimulate the economy; synonymous with fiscal policies or demand-side economics (p. 448)

labor   people with all their abilities and efforts; one of four factors of production, does not include the entrepreneur (p. 8)

labor mobility   ability and willingness of labor to relocate, usually for higher wages (p. 209)

labor productivity   growth rate of total output per unit of labor input; measure of productive efficiency (p. 368)

labor union   organization that works for its members' interests concerning pay, working hours, health coverage, fringe benefits, other job related matters (p. 76)

Laffer curve   graph showing that lower tax rates will supposedly stimulate higher tax revenues (p. 452)

laissez-faire   philosophy that government should not interfere with business activity (p. 163)

land   natural resources or "gifts of nature" not created by human effort; one of four factors of production (p. 7)

Law of Demand   rule stating that more will be demanded at lower prices and less at higher prices; inverse relationship between price and quantity demanded (p. 91)

Law of Supply   rule stating that more will be offered for sale at high prices than at lower prices (p. 113)

Law of Variable Proportions   rule stating that short-run output will change as one input is varied while others are held constant (p. 122)

legal reserves   currency and deposits used to meet the reserve requirement (p. 415)

legal tender   fiat currency that must be accepted for payment by decree of government (p. 295)

liabilities   debts and obligations owed to others; usually listed as entries on a balance sheet (p. 416)

life expectancy   average remaining life span in years for persons who attain a given age (p. 358)

limited life   situation in which a firm legally ceases to exist when an owner dies, quits, or a new owner is added; applies to sole proprietorships and partnerships (p. 59)

limited partnership   form of partnership where one or more partners are not active in the daily running of the business, and whose liability for the partnership's debt is restricted to the amount invested in the business (p. 62)

line-item veto   power to cancel specific budget items without rejecting the entire budget (p. 278)

liquidity   potential for being readily convertible into cash or other financial assets (p. 417)

lockout   management refusal to let employees work until company demands are met (p. 195)

long run   production period long enough to change amount of variable and fixed inputs used in production (p. 122)

Lorenz curve   curve showing how much the actual distribution of income differs from an equal distribution (p. 394)

luxury good   good for which demand increases faster than income when income rises (p. 235)

M1   money supply components conforming to money's role as medium of exchange; coins, currency, checks, other demand deposits, traveler's checks (p. 429)

M2   money supply components conforming to money's role as a store of value; M1, savings deposits, time deposits (p. 430)

macroeconomic equilibrium   level of real GDP consistent with a given price level; intersection of aggregate supply and aggregate demand (p. 445)

macroeconomics   that part of economic theory dealing with the economy as a whole and decision making by large units such as governments and unions (p. 193)

mandatory spending   federal spending authorized by law that continues without the need for annual approvals of Congress (p. 260)

margin requirement   minimum deposits left with a stockbroker to be used as partial payment on other securities (p. 423)

marginal analysis   decision making that compares the extra cost of doing something to the extra benefits gained (p. 131)

marginal cost   extra cost of producing one additional unit of production (p. 129)

marginal product   extra output due to the addition of one more unit of input (p. 124)

marginal revenue   extra revenue from the sale of one additional unit of output (p. 130)

marginal tax rate   tax rate that applies to the next dollar of taxable income (p. 229)

marginal utility   satisfaction or usefulness obtained from acquiring one more unit of a product (p. 93)

market   meeting place or mechanism allowing buyers and sellers of an economic product to come together; may be local, regional, national, or global (p. 14)

market basket   representative collection of goods and services used to compile a price index (p. 351)

market demand curve   demand curve that shows the quantities demanded by everyone who is interested in purchasing a product (p. 91)

market economy   economic system in which supply, demand, and the price system help people make decisions and allocate resources; same as free enterprise economy (p. 36)

market equilibrium   condition of price stability where the quantity demanded equals the quantity supplied (p. 143)

market failure   market where any of the requirements for a competitive market—adequate competition, knowledge of prices and opportunities, mobility of resources, and competitive profits—are lacking (p. 174)

market structure   market classification according to number and size of firms, type of product, and type of competition (p. 164)

market supply curve   supply curve that shows the quantities offered at various prices by all firms that sell the product in a given market (p. 114)

maturity   life of a bond or length of time funds are borrowed (p. 321)

measure of value   one of the three functions of money that allows it to serve as a common denominator to measure value (p. 286)

mediation   process of resolving a dispute by bringing in a neutral third party (p. 202)

medicaid   joint federal-state medical insurance program for low-income people (p. 265)

medicare   federal health-care program for senior citizens, regardless of income (p. 233)

medium of exchange   money or other substance generally accepted in exchange; one of the three functions of money (p. 286)

member bank   bank belonging to the Federal Reserve System (p. 407)

member bank reserves   reserves kept by member banks at the Fed to satisfy reserve requirements (p. 418)

merger   combination of two or more business enterprises to form a single firm (p. 68)

microeconomics   branch of economic theory that deals with behavior and decision making by small units such as individuals and firms (p. 89)

minimum wage   lowest legal wage that can be paid to most workers (p. 152, 216)

misery index   unofficial statistic that is the sum of monthly inflation and the unemployment rate; same as discomfort index (p. 438)

mixed economy   see modified private enterprise economy (p. 51)

modified free enterprise economy   free enterprise system with some government involvement; same as modified private enterprise economy (p. 560)

modified private enterprise economy   free enterprise market economy where people carry on their economic affairs freely, but are subject to some government intervention and regulation (p. 51)

modified union shop   arrangement under which workers have the option to join a union after being hired (p. 201)

monetarism   school of thought stressing the importance of stable monetary growth to control inflation and stimulate long-term economic growth (p. 453)

monetary policy   actions by the Federal Reserve System to expand or contract the money supply in order to affect the cost and availability of credit (p. 415)

monetary standard   mechanism that keeps a money supply durable, portable, divisible, and stable in value; gold standard, silver standard, fiat money standard (p. 292)

monetary unit   standard unit of currency in a country's money supply; American dollar, British pound (p. 289)

monetize the debt   process of creating enough additional money to offset federal borrowing so that interest rates remain unchanged (p. 427)

money   anything that serves as a medium of exchange, a measure of value, and a store of value (p. 286)

money market   market in which financial capital is loaned and/or borrowed for one year or less (p. 325)

monopolistic competition   market structure having all conditions of pure competition except for identical products; form of imperfect competition (p. 166)

monopoly   market structure characterized by a single producer; form of imperfect competition (p. 169)

moral suasion   Federal Reserve System's use of persuasion to accomplish monetary policy; congressional testimony, press releases (p. 424)

most favored nation clause   trade law allowing a third country to enjoy the same tariff reductions the United States negotiates with another country (p. 477)

multinational   corporation producing and selling without regard to national boundaries and whose business activities are located in several different countries (p. 72)

multiplier   change in overall spending caused by a change in investment spending (p. 448)

municipal bond bond, often tax exempt, issued by state and local governments; known as munis (p. 323)

mutual fund company that sells stock in itself and uses the proceeds to buy stocks and bonds issued by other companies (p. 316)

mutual savings bank depositor-owned savings institution operated for the benefit of depositors (p. 303)

NAFTA see North American Free Trade Agreement (p. 479)

national bank commercial bank chartered by the National Banking System; member of the Fed (p. 295)

National Bank note currency backed by government bonds, issued by national banks starting in 1863 and generally disappearing from circulation in the 1930s (p. 295)

national currency see National Bank note (p. 295)

national income net national product less indirect business taxes; measure of a nation's income (p. 345)

national income accounting system of accounts used to track the nation's production, consumption, savings, and income statistics (p. 341)

natural monopoly market where average costs are lowest when all output is produced by a single firm (p. 170)

need basic requirement for survival; includes food, clothing, and/or shelter (p. 6)

negative externality harmful side effect that affects an uninvolved third party; external cost (p. 175)

negative income tax tax system that would make cash payments in the form of tax refunds to individuals when their income falls below certain levels (p. 400)

Negotiable Order of Withdrawal (NOW) type of checking account that pays interest (p. 303)

net asset value (NAV) the market value of a mutual fund share determined by dividing the value of the fund by the number of shares issued (p. 316)

net exports of goods and services net expenditures by the output-expenditure model's foreign sector (p. 348)

net immigration net population change after accounting for those who leave as well as enter a country (p. 359)

net income measure of business profits determined by subtracting all expenses, including taxes, from revenues (p. 68)

net national product (NNP) Gross National Product minus depreciation charges for wear and tear on capital equipment; measure of net annual production generated with labor and property supplied by a country's citizens (p. 344)

net worth excess of assets over liabilities, usually listed as a separate summary on a balance sheet; measure of the value of a business (p. 416)

nominal GDP see current GDP (p. 353)

nonbank financial institution nondepository institution that channels savings to investors; finance companies, insurance companies, pension funds (p. 315)

noncompeting labor grades broad groups of unskilled, semiskilled, skilled, and professional workers who do not compete with one another (p. 206)

nonmarket transaction economic activity not taking place in the market and, therefore, not included in GDP; services of homemakers, work around the home (p. 343)

nonprice competition competition involving the advertising of a product's appearance, quality, or design, rather than its price (p. 166)

nonprofit organization economic institution that operates like a business but does not seek financial gain; schools, churches, community service organizations (p. 75)

nonrecourse loan agricultural loan that carries neither a penalty nor further obligation to repay if not paid back (p. 153)

nonrenewable resource resource that cannot be replenished once it is used (p. 546)

North American Free Trade Agreement (NAFTA) agreement signed in 1993 to reduce tariffs between the United States, Canada, and Mexico (p. 479)

NOW Account see Negotiable Order of Withdrawal (p. 303)

oligopoly market structure in which a few large sellers dominate and have the ability to affect prices in the industry; form of imperfect competition (p. 167)

open market operations monetary policy in the form of U.S. treasury bills or bond sales and purchases, or both (p. 420)

opportunity cost cost of the next best alternative use of money, time, or resources when one choice is made rather than another (p. 20)

option contract giving investors an option to buy or sell commodities, equities, or financial assets at a specific future date using a price agreed upon today (p. 333)

options markets markets where options, including put options and call options, are traded (p. 333)

output-expenditure model macroeconomic model describing aggregate demand by the consumer, investment, government, and foreign sectors; GDP = C + I + G + F (p. 348)

overhead broad category of fixed costs that includes interest, rent, taxes, and executive salaries (p. 127)

over-the-counter market (OTC) electronic marketplace for securities not listed on organized exchanges such as the New York Stock Exchange (p. 331)

par value principal of a bond or total amount borrowed (p. 321)

paradox of value apparent contradiction between the high value of nonessentials and low value of essentials (p. 13)

partnership unincorporated business owned and operated by two or more people who share the profits and have unlimited liability for the debts and obligations of the firm; same as general partnership (p. 60)

part-time worker worker who regularly works fewer than 35 hours per week (p. 216)

"pay-as-you-go" provision requirement that new spending proposals or tax cuts must be offset by reductions elsewhere (p. 277)

payroll tax tax on wages and salaries to finance Social Security and medicare costs (p. 233)

payroll withholding statement document attached to a paycheck summarizing pay and deductions (p. 242)

payroll withholding system system that automatically deducts income taxes from paychecks on a regular basis (p. 232)

peak point in time when real GDP stops expanding and begins to decline (p. 376)

pension regular allowance for someone who has worked a certain number of years, reached a certain age, or who has suffered from an injury (p. 316)

pension fund fund that collects and invests income until payments are made to eligible recipients (p. 316)

per capita per person basis; total divided by population (p. 255)

perestroika fundamental restructuring of the Soviet economy; policy introduced by Gorbachev (p. 499)

perfect competition market structure characterized by a large number of well-informed independent buyers and sellers who exchange identical products (p. 164)

personal income total amount of income going to the consumer sector before individual income taxes are paid (p. 345)

picket demonstration before a place of business to protest a company's actions (p. 195)

piecework compensation system that pays workers for units produced, rather than hours worked (p. 498)

pollution contamination of air, water, or soil by the discharge of a poisonous or noxious substance (p. 554)

pollution permit federal permit allowing a public utility to release pollutants into the air; a form of pollution control (p. 556)

population density number of people per square mile of land area (p. 536)

population pyramid diagram showing the breakdown of population by age and sex (p. 360)

portfolio diversification strategy of holding several investments to protect against risk (p. 329)

positive externality beneficial side effect that affects an uninvolved third party (p. 176)

premium monthly, quarterly, semiannual, or annual price paid for an insurance policy (p. 315)

price monetary value of a product as established by supply and demand (p. 137)

price ceiling maximum legal price that can be charged for a product (p. 151)

price discrimination illegal practice of charging customers different prices for the same product (p. 179)

price-fixing agreement, usually illegal, by firms to charge a uniform price for a product (p. 168)

price floor lowest legal price that can be charged for a product (p. 152)

price index statistical series used to measure changes in the price level over time (p. 351)

price level relative magnitude of prices at a given point in time as measured by a price index (p. 389)

primary market market in which only the original issuer will repurchase a financial asset; government savings bonds, IRAs, small CDs (p. 326)

prime rate best or lowest interest rate commercial banks charge their customers (p. 427)

primitive equilibrium first stage of economic development during which the economy is static (p. 528)

principal amount borrowed when getting a loan or issuing a bond (p. 64)

private enterprise economy see free enterprise economy (p. 24)

private property rights fundamental feature of capitalism, which allows individuals to own and control their possessions as they wish; includes both tangible and intangible property (p. 47)

private sector that part of the economy made up of private individuals and businesses (p. 256)

privatization conversion of state-owned factories and other property to private ownership (p. 502)

producer price index index used to measure prices received by domestic producers; formerly called the wholesale price index (p. 352)

product differentiation real or imagined differences between competing products in the same industry (p. 166)

product market market where goods and services are offered for sale (p. 14)

production process of creating goods and services with the combined use of land, capital, labor, and entrepreneurship (p. 8)

production function graphic portrayal showing how a change in the amount of a single variable input affects total output (p. 123)

production possibilities frontier diagram representing maximum combinations of goods and/or services an economy can produce when all productive resources are fully employed (p. 21)

productivity degree to which productive resources are used efficiently; normally refers to labor, but can apply to all factors of production (p. 15)

professional association   nonprofit organization of professional or specialized workers seeking to improve working conditions, skill levels, and public perceptions of its profession (p. 77)

professional labor   workers with a high level of professional and managerial skills (p. 206)

profit   extent to which persons or organizations are better off at the end of a period than they were at the beginning; usually measured in dollars (p. 48)

profit-maximizing quantity of output   level of production where marginal cost is equal to marginal revenue (p. 131)

profit motive   driving force that encourages people and organizations to improve their material well-being; characteristic of capitalism and free enterprise (p. 48)

progressive tax   tax where percentage of income paid in tax rises as level of income rises (p. 229)

property tax   tax on tangible and intangible possessions such as real estate, buildings, furniture, stocks, bonds, and bank accounts (p. 241)

proportional tax   tax in which percentage of income paid in tax is the same regardless of the level of income (p. 229)

proprietorship   see sole proprietorship (p. 57)

protectionist   person who would protect domestic producers with tariffs, quotas, and other trade barriers (p. 474)

protective tariff   tax on an imported product designed to protect less efficient domestic producers (p. 472)

public disclosure   requirement forcing a business to reveal information about its products or its operations to the public (p. 181)

public good   economic product that is consumed collectively; highways, national defense, police and fire protection (p. 176)

public sector   that part of the economy made up of the local, state, and federal governments (p. 255)

public utility   company providing essential services such as water and electricity to consumers, usually subject to some government regulations (p. 79)

put option   contract giving investors the option to sell commodities, equities, or financial assets at a specific future date using a price agreed upon today (p. 333)

quantity supplied   amount offered for sale at a given price; point on the supply curve (p. 115)

quantity theory of money   hypothesis that the supply of money directly affects the price level over the long run (p. 427)

quota   limit on the amount of a good that can be allowed into a country (p. 472)

ration coupon   certificate allowing holder to receive a given amount of a rationed product (p. 139)

rationing   system of allocating goods and services without prices (p. 139)

raw materials   unprocessed natural resources used in production (p. 123)

real dollars   see constant dollars (p. 218)

real estate investment trust (REIT)   company organized to make loans to homebuilders (p. 316)

real GDP   Gross Domestic Product after adjustments for inflation; same as GDP in constant dollars (p. 353)

real GDP per capita   Gross Domestic Product adjusted for inflation and divided by the total population; total dollar amount of all final output produced for every person in the country after compensating for inflation (p. 363)

real rate of interest   the market rate of interest minus the rate of inflation (p. 428)

rebate   partial refund of the original price of a product (p. 140)

recession   decline in real GDP lasting at least two quarters or more (p. 376)

regressive tax   tax where percentage of income paid in tax goes down as income rises (p. 229)

Regulation Z   provision extending truth-in-lending disclosures to consumers (p. 411)

renewable resources   natural resources that can be replenished for future use (p. 366)

reserve requirement   formula used to compute the amount of a depository institution's required reserves (p. 415)

revenue tariff   tax placed on imported goods to raise revenue (p. 473)

right-to-work law   state law making it illegal to require a worker to join a union (p. 197)

risk   situation in which the outcome is not certain, but the probabilities can be estimated (p. 318)

Roth IRA   individual retirement account in which contributions are made after taxes so that no taxes are taken out at maturity (p. 325)

run on the bank   sudden rush by depositors to withdraw all deposited funds, generally in anticipation of bank failure or closure (p. 301)

rural population   those persons not living in urban areas (p. 357)

S&P 500   see Standard & Poor's 500 (p. 332)

sales tax   general state or city tax levied on a product at the time of sale (p. 226)

saving   absence of spending that frees resources for use in other activities or investments (p. 313)

savings   the dollars that become available for investors to use when others save (p. 313)

savings account   interest-bearing deposit not requiring prior notice before making a withdrawal (p. 417)

savings and loan association (S&L)   depository institution that historically invested the majority of its funds in home mortgages (p. 303)

savings bank   publicly-held depository institution that competes with other banks for customer deposits (p. 303)

savings bond   low-denomination, non-transferable bond issued by the federal government, usually through payroll-savings plans (p. 323)

scarcity   fundamental economic problem facing all societies that results from a combination of scarce resources and people's virtually unlimited wants (p. 5)

seasonal unemployment   unemployment caused by annual changes in the weather or other conditions that prevail at certain times of the year (p. 386)

seat   membership in a stock exchange such as the New York Stock Exchange (p. 330)

secondary market   market in which all financial assets can be sold to someone other than the original issuer; corporate bonds, government bonds (p. 326)

secondhand sales   sales of used goods; category of activity not included in GDP computation (p. 343)

securities exchange   physical place where buyers and sellers meet to exchange securities (p. 329)

seizure   temporary government takeover of a company to keep it running during a labor-management dispute (p. 203)

selective credit controls   rules pertaining to loans for specific commodities or purchases such as margin requirements for common stock (p. 424)

semiskilled labor   workers who can operate machines requiring a minimum amount of training (p. 206)

seniority   length of time a person has been on a job (p. 208)

service   work or labor performed for someone; economic product that includes haircuts, home repairs, forms of entertainment (p. 13)

set-aside contract   guaranteed contract or portion thereof reserved for a targeted, usually minority, group (p. 215)

share draft account   checking account offered by a credit union (p. 303)

shareholder   see stockholder (p. 63)

short run   production period so short that only variable inputs can be changed (p. 122)

shortage   situation where quantity supplied is less than quantity demanded at a given price (p. 144)

signaling theory   theory that employers are willing to pay more for people with certificates, diplomas, degrees, and other indicators of superior ability (p. 208)

silver certificate   paper currency backed by, and redeemable for, silver from 1886 to 1968 (p. 295)

sin tax   relatively high tax designed to raise revenue and discourage consumption of a socially undesirable product (p. 224)

skilled labor   workers who can operate complex equipment and require little supervision (p. 206)

Social Security   federal program of disability and retirement benefits that covers most working people (p. 42)

socialism   economic system in which government owns some factors of production and has a role in determining what and how goods are produced (p. 492)

soft loan   loan that may never be paid back; usually involves loan to developing countries (p. 535)

sole proprietorship   unincorporated business owned and run by a single person who has rights to all profits and unlimited liability for all debts of the firm; most common form of business organization in the United States (p. 57)

Solidarity   independent Polish labor union founded in 1980 by Lech Walesa (p. 504)

specialization   assignment of tasks so that each worker performs fewer functions more frequently; same as division of labor (p. 16)

specie   money in the form of gold or silver coins (p. 288)

spending cap   limits on annual discretionary spending (p. 278)

spot market   market in which a transaction is made immediately at the prevailing price (p. 332)

stages of production   phases of production—increasing, decreasing, and negative returns (p. 125)

stagflation   combination of stagnant economic growth and inflation (p. 437)

Standard & Poor's 500 (S&P 500)   statistical series of 500 stocks used to monitor prices on the NYSE, American Stock Exchange, and OTC market (p. 332)

standard of living   quality of life based on ownership of necessities and luxuries that make life easier (p. 24, 365)

state bank   bank that receives its charter from the state in which it operates (p. 293)

state farm   large farms owned and operated by the state in the former Soviet Union (p. 497)

stock   certificate of ownership in a corporation; common or preferred stock (p. 63)

stock certificate   see stock (p. 63)

stockbroker   person who buys or sells securities for investors (p. 329)

stockholder   person who owns a share or shares of stock in a corporation; same as shareholders (p. 63)

store of value   one of the three functions of money allowing people to preserve value for future use (p. 286)

storming   Soviet practice of rushing production at month's end to fulfill quotas, often resulting in production of shoddy goods (p. 498)

strike   union organized work stoppage designed to gain concessions from an employer (p. 195)

Glossary

structural unemployment   unemployment caused by a fundamental change in the economy that reduces the demand for some workers (p. 385)

structures   category in the national income and product accounts that includes residential structures, apartments, and commercial buildings (p. 341)

subsidy   government payment to encourage or protect a certain economic activity (p. 117)

subsistence   state in which a society produces barely enough to support itself (p. 546)

substitutes   competing products that can be used in place of one another; products related in such a way that an increase in the price of one increases the demand for the other (p. 98)

substitution effect   that portion of a change in quantity demanded due to a change in the relative price of the product (p. 96)

supply   schedule of quantities offered for sale at all possible prices in a market (p. 113)

supply curve   graphical representation of the quantities produced at each and every possible price in the market (p. 114)

supply elasticity   responsiveness of quantity supplied to a change in price (p. 118)

supply schedule   tabular listing showing the quantities produced or offered for sale at each and every possible price in the market (p. 114)

supply-side economics   economic policies designed to increase aggregate supply or shift the aggregate supply curve to the right (p. 451)

surcharge   additional tax or charge added to other charges already in place (p. 245)

surplus   situation where quantity supplied is greater than quantity demanded at a given price (p. 144)

takeoff   third stage of economic development during which barriers of primitive equilibrium are overcome (p. 528)

target price   agricultural floor price set by the government to stabilize farm incomes (p. 153)

tariff   tax placed on an imported product (p. 472)

tax assessor   person who examines and values property for tax purposes (p. 241)

tax base   incomes and properties that are potentially subject to tax by local, state, or federal governments (p. 366)

tax-exempt   income from a bond or other investment not subject to tax by federal or state governments (p. 323)

tax loophole   exception or oversight in the tax law allowing taxpayer to avoid taxes (p. 226)

tax return   annual report filed with local, state, or federal government detailing income earned and taxes owed (p. 232)

technological monopoly   market situation where a firm has a monopoly because it owns or controls a manufacturing method, process, or other scientific advance (p. 170)

technological unemployment   unemployment caused by technological developments or automation that make some worker's skills obsolete (p. 386)

theory of negotiated wages   explanation of wage rates based on the bargaining strength of organized labor (p. 208)

theory of production   theory dealing with the relationship between the factors of production and the output of goods and services (p. 122)

thrift institution   savings & loan associations, mutual savings banks, and other depository institutions historically catering to savers (p. 303)

tight money policy   monetary policy resulting in higher interest rates and restricted access to credit; associated with a contraction of the money supply (p. 419)

time deposit   interest-bearing deposit requiring prior notice before a withdrawal can be made, even though the requirement may not always be enforced (p. 417)

total cost   variable plus fixed cost; all costs associated with production (p. 128)

total product   total output or production by a firm (p. 123)

total revenue   total receipts; price of goods sold times quantity sold (p. 130)

trade deficit   balance of payments outcome when spending on imports exceeds revenues received from exports (p. 484)

trade-offs   alternatives that must be given up when one is chosen rather than another (p. 19)

trade surplus   situation occurring when the value of a nation's exports exceeds the value of its imports (p. 484)

trade union   see craft union (p. 195)

trade-weighted value of the dollar   index showing strength of the United States dollar against a market basket of other foreign currencies (p. 484)

traditional economy   economic system in which the allocation of scarce resources and other economic activity is the result of ritual, habit, or custom (p. 34)

traditional theory of wage determination   explanation of wage rates relying on theory of supply and demand (p. 207)

transfer payment   payment for which the government receives neither goods nor services in return (p. 257)

transparency   making business dealings more visible to everyone, especially government regulators (p. 512)

Treasury bill   short-term United States government obligation with a maturity of one year or under in denominations of $10,000 (p. 324)

Treasury bond   United States government bond with maturity of 10 to 30 years (p. 324)

Treasury coin note   paper currency printed from 1890 to 1893, redeemable in both gold and silver (p. 296)

Treasury note   United States government obligation with a maturity of 2 to 10 years (p. 324)

trend line growth path the economy would follow if it were not interrupted by alternating periods of recession and recovery (p. 376)

trough point in time when real GDP stops declining and begins to expand (p. 376)

trust illegal combination of corporations or companies organized to hinder competition (p. 178)

trust fund special account used to hold revenues designated for a specific expenditure such as Social Security, medicare, or highways (p. 275)

two-tier wage system wage scale paying newer workers a lower wage than others already on the job (p. 212)

underground economy unreported legal and illegal activities that do not show up in GDP statistics (p. 343)

unemployed state of working for less than one hour per week for pay or profit in a non-family owned business, while being available and having made an effort to find a job during the past month (p. 382)

unemployment insurance government program providing payments to the unemployed; an automatic stabilizer (p. 449)

unemployment rate ratio of unemployed individuals divided by total number of persons in the civilian labor force, expressed as a percentage (p. 383)

union shop arrangement under which workers must join a union after being hired (p. 201)

unit elastic elasticity where a change in the independent variable (usually price) generates a proportional change of the dependent variable (quantity demanded or supplied) (p. 103)

United States note paper currency with no backing, first printed by the United States government in 1862 to finance the Civil War (p. 295)

unlimited liability requirement that an owner is personally and fully responsible for all losses and debts of a business; applies to proprietorships, general partnerships (p. 58)

unrelated individual person living alone or with nonrelatives even though that person may have relatives living elsewhere (p. 346)

unskilled labor workers not trained to operate specialized machines and equipment (p. 205)

urban population those persons living in incorporated cities, towns, and villages with 2,500 or more inhabitants (p. 357)

user fee fee paid for the use of good or service; form of a benefit tax (p. 236)

utility ability or capacity of a good or service to be useful and give satisfaction to someone (p. 13)

value worth of a good or service as determined by the market (p. 13)

value-added tax tax on the value added at every stage of the production process (p. 247)

variable cost production cost that varies as output changes; labor, energy, raw materials (p. 128)

vertical merger combination of firms involved in different steps of manufacturing or marketing (p. 71)

voluntary arbitration see arbitration (p. 202)

voluntary exchange act of buyers and sellers freely and willingly engaging in market transactions; characteristic of capitalism and free enterprise (p. 47)

wage-price controls policies and regulations making it illegal for firms to give raises or raise prices (p. 454)

wage rate prevailing pay scale for work performed in a given area or region (p. 207)

want way of expressing or communicating a need; a broader classification than needs (p. 6)

wealth sum of tangible economic goods that are scarce, useful, and transferable from one person to another; excludes services (p. 14)

welfare government or private agency programs that provide general economic and social assistance to needy individuals (p. 397)

wholesale price index see producer price index (p. 352)

workfare program requiring welfare recipients to provide labor in exchange for benefits (p. 398)

World Bank international agency that makes loans to developing countries; formally the International Bank for Reconstruction and Development (p. 526)

World Trade Organization (WTO) international agency that administers trade agreements, settles trade disputes between governments, organizes trade negotiations, and provides technical assistance and training for developing countries (p. 477)

zero population growth condition in which the average number of births and deaths balance so that population size is unchanged (p. 524) ability-to-pay principle of taxation/principio de tributación sobre la solvencia   creencia que los impuestos se deben pagar de acuerdo al nivel de ingresos sin considerar los beneficios recibidos (p. 228)

absolute advantage/ventaja absoluta   habilidad de un país para producir más de un producto en particular que los otros países (p. 469)

accelerated depreciation/depreciación acelerada   programa que extiende la depreciación a lo largo de menos años de lo normal para generar mayores reducciones de impuestos (p. 245)

accelerator/acelerador   cambio en el gasto causado por un cambio en el gasto global (p. 448)

acid rain/lluvia ácida   contaminación en la forma de agua-lluvia mezclada con dióxido de sulfuro, forma leve de ácido sulfúrico (p. 554)

agency shop/taller gremial   arreglo bajo el cual miembros que no son de la unión   tienen que pagar cuotas de unión (p. 201)

aggregate demand/demanda agregada   cantidad total de bienes y servicios demandados en varios precios (p. 444)

aggregate demand curve/curva de demanda global   curva hipotética que muestra distintos niveles del PIB real que se podrían producir a distintos niveles de precio (p. 444)

aggregate supply/oferta agregada   valor total de bienes y servicios que todas las empresas producirán durante un período específico en varios precios (p. 442)

aggregate supply curve/curva de oferta global   curva hipotética que muestra distintos niveles del PIB real que se podrían producir a distintos niveles de precio (p. 443)

alternative minimum tax/impuesto mínimo alternativo   índice de impuesto sobre la renta que se aplica a casos en que los impuestos de otro modo caerían por debajo de cierto nivel (p. 245)

appropriations bill/proyecto de ley para asignación de fondos   legislación para asignar fondos para ciertos propósitos (p. 261)

aquifer/acuífero   formación subterránea rocosa que contiene agua (p. 550)

arbitration/arbitraje   negociación en la cual los partidos opositores de un debate acuerdan arreglar sus diferencias ante un tercer partido cuya decisión será aceptada como determinación atadura y final (p. 202)

articles of partnership/contrato de asociación   documento legal que especifica formalmente los acuerdos entre socios, incluyendo la forma en que se han de dividir las ganancias y las pérdidas (p. 60)

ASEAN   (siglas en inglés) grupo de diez naciones asiáticas que trabajan para promover la cooperación, crecimiento económico y comercio regional (p. 535)

assets/haberes   propiedades, posesiones y demandas a otras personas; generalmente, aparecen anotadas como asiento en el estado de cuentas (p. 416)

automatic stabilizer/estabilizador automático   programa que automáticamente provee beneficios para compensar por un cambio en los ingresos de la gente; seguro de desempleo, programas de derecho a gratificación (p. 449)

automation/automatización   producción, tanto mecánica como de otros procesos, que reduce la necesidad de trabajadores (p. 386)

average tax rate/tasa impositiva media   total de impuestos pagados divididos por el total de renta imponible (p. 229)

baby boom/auge de bebés   años en Estados Unidos, entre 1946 y 1964, en que hubo una alta tasa de natalidad (p. 360)

balance of payments/balanza de pagos   diferencia entre dinero que se paga o que se recibe de otras naciones en actividad comercial; balance de cuenta corriente incluye bienes y servicios, balanza comercial de mercancía toma en cuenta sólo los bienes (p. 478)

balance sheet/estado de cuentas   extracto de cuenta que muestra el activo y el pasivo y el valor neto de una unidad económica (p. 416)

balanced budget/presupuesto balanceado   presupuesto anual en el que los gastos están a la par con los ingresos (p. 273)

balanced budget amendment/enmienda al presupuesto balanceado   enmienda constitucional estatal o federal que requiere que el gobierno no gaste más de lo que recauda en impuestos y otros ingresos, a exclusión de préstamos (p. 267)

bank holiday/cierre bancario   breve período durante el cual todos los bancos o instituciones de depósitos cierran para evitar los pánicos bancarios (p. 301)

bankruptcy/quiebra   permiso que concede la corte a una persona o a un negocio   para cesar o aplazar pago de algunas o todas las deudas durante un tiempo limitado (p. 62)

barter economy/economía de trueque   economía sin dinero que depende del comercio o trueque (p. 285)

base year/año base   año que sirve como punto de comparación para otros años en un índice de precios u otra estadística (p. 218, 351)

bear market/mercado en descenso   período durante el cual los precios de la bolsa bajan por varios meses o años seguidos (p. 332)

benefit principle of taxation/principio de tributación acerca de beneficios   creencia de que los impuestos se deben pagar de acuerdo con los beneficios que se reciban independiente del nivel de ingreso (p. 227)

Better Business Bureau   organización sin fines de lucro patronizada por el comercio la cual provee al consumidor información acerca de las compañías locales (p. 78)

bill consolidation loan/préstamo para la consolidación de cuenta   tipo popular de préstamo al consumidor que se usa para saldar múltiples préstamos en existencia (p. 315)

black market/mercado negro   mercado en que se venden productos económicos ilegalmente (p. 505)

bond/fianza   contrato formal para devolver el dinero y los intereses sobre dinero prestado durante intervalos sistemáticos en el futuro (p. 64)

boycott/boicot   protesta en la forma de rehusar a comprar, que incluye el esfuerzo para convencer a otras personas a tampoco comprar (p. 195)

break-even point/punto muerto   producción necesaria si la firma ha de recuperar sus costos; nivel de producción en que el costo total equivale al ingreso total (p. 131)

bull market/mercado en ascenso   período durante el cual los precios de la bolsa suben por varios meses o años seguidos (p. 332)

business cycle/ciclo comercial   cambios sistemáticos en el PIB real acentuados por periodos alternantes de expansión y contracción (p. 375)

business fluctuation/fluctuación comercial   cambios en el PIB acentuados por períodos alternantes de expansión y contracción que ocurren en una base menos que sistemática (p. 375)

call option/opción de compra   contrato que da a los inversionistas la opción de comprar productos, acciones o bienes financieros en una fecha específica en el futuro y usando el precio que se acordó hoy (p. 333)

capital/capital   implementos, equipo y fábricas que se usan en la producción de bienes y servicios; uno de cuatro factores de producción (p. 7)

capital flight/fuga de capitales   exportación legal o ilegal de la moneda y las divisas de una nación (p. 525)

capital gains/ganancias del capital   ganancias de la venta de un activo después de haberlo tenido por 12 meses (p. 246)

capital good/bienes de capital   implemento, equipo u otros bienes fabricados que se emplean para producir otros bienes y servicios; un factor de producción (p. 12)

capital-intensive/con gran intensidad de capital   método de producción que requiere relativamente grandes cantidades de capital con relación a la mano de obra (p. 510)

capital market/mercado de capital   mercado en el que el capital financiero se presta por más de un año (p. 325)

capitalism/capitalismo   economía mercantil en la cual los factores de producción son de propiedad privada (p. 46, 492)

capital-to-labor ratio/relación capital-trabajo   medida obtenida al dividir el total de las acciones de capital por la fuerza de trabajo (p. 367)

cartel/cartel   grupo de vendedores o productores que obran conjuntamente para subir los precios al restringir la disponibilidad de un producto; OPEC (p. 536)

cash flow/flujo de efectivo   cantidad total de nuevos fondos que el negocio genera por sus operaciones; la medida más comprensiva de las utilidades de una compañía que incluye el ingreso neto y cargos no al contado (p. 69)

cease and desist order/orden de cesar y desistir   fallo que ordena que una compañía pare una práctica comercial injusta que reduce o limita la competencia (p. 179)

census/censo   cuenta completa de la población, incluyendo el lugar de residencia (p. 356)

center of population/centro de población   punto donde el país se equilibraría si fuera plano y todo el mundo pesara lo mismo (p. 357)

central bank/banco central   banco que le presta a otros bancos en momentos de necesidad, el "banco de los banqueros" (p. 301)

certificate of deposit/certificado de depósito   recibo que indica que un inversionista ha hecho un préstamo con intereses a una institución financiera (p. 314)

chamber of commerce/cámara de comercio   organización sin fines de lucro cuyo propósito es promover los intereses comunes de los negocios locales (p. 78)

change in demand/cambio en demanda   los consumidores demandan distintas cantidades en cada precio, haciendo que la curva de demanda cambie hacia la izquierda o la derecha (p. 96)

change in quantity demanded/cambio en cantidad demandada   un movimiento en la curva de relación entre demanda y precio que demuestra que se está comprando una cantidad distinta debido a un cambio de precio (p. 95)

change in quantity supplied/cambio en la cantidad suplida   cambio en la cantidad que se ofrece a la venta en respuesta a un cambio de precio; movimiento a lo largo de la curva de abastecimiento (p. 115)

change in supply/cambio en abastecimiento   distintas cantidades ofrecidas a la venta a todos los precios posibles del mercado; cambio en la curva de abastecimiento (p. 116)

charter/carta constitucional   aprobación escrita del gobierno para establecer una corporación; incluye el nombre de la compañía, la dirección, propósito del negocio, número de acciones y otros aspectos del negocio (p. 63)

civilian labor force/fuerza de trabajo civil   parte de la población no institucionalizada, entre los 16 y 65 años, que está trabajando o buscando trabajo (p. 193)

closed shop/taller cerrado   arreglo ilegal bajo el cual los trabajadores tienen que ser miembros de una unión antes de que los emplee (p. 200)

coins/monedas   formas metálicas de dinero tal como el centavo, las monedas de cinco, diez y de 25 centavos (p. 413)

collateral/fianza   propiedad u otra seguridad que se usa para garantizar el pago de un préstamo (p. 511)

collective bargaining/negociación colectiva   proceso de negociación entre la unión y los representantes administrativos acerca de pago, beneficios y asuntos relacionados al trabajo (p. 77)

collective farm/granja colectiva en la antigua Unión Soviética, pequeñas granjas de propiedad del estado, pero operadas por familias que participaban en algunas de las ganancias (p. 498)

collectivization/colectivización propiedad común forzada de los factores de producción; se usó en la antigua Unión Soviética en la agricultura y en la industria manufacturera bajo Stalin (p. 497)

collusion/colusión acuerdos, por lo general ilegales, entre los productores para fijar los precios, limitar la producción o dividir los mercados (p. 168)

command economy/economía de mando sistema económico que se caracteriza por una autoridad central que hace la mayoría de las decisiones económicas (p. 35)

commercial bank/banco comercial institución depositoria que, hasta mediados de los años 70, tenía el derecho exclusivo de ofrecer cuentas de cheques (p. 303)

commodity money/dinero como producto dinero que tiene un uso alternativo como producto; pólvora, harina, maíz (p. 287)

communism/comunismo sistema económico y político en el que los factores de producción son de propiedad colectiva y dirigidos por el estado; teóricamente, una sociedad sin clases en que todos trabajan para el bien común (p. 493)

company union/sindicato de empresa unión organizada, sostenida y hasta financiada por el patrón (p. 195)

comparable worth/valor comparable doctrina que declara que se debe pagar lo mismo por trabajos de comparable dificultad (p. 215)

comparative advantage/ventaja comparativa habilidad del país de producir un cierto producto con relativamente más eficiencia que otro país; la oportunidad de producción al costo más bajo (p. 470)

complements/complementos productos que aumentan la utilidad o valor de otros productos; productos relacionados de tal modo que el aumento del precio de uno reduce la demanda de ambos (p. 98)

conglomerate/conglomerado de empresas firma con cuatro o más negocios que hacen productos no relacionados, sin ningún negocio en particular que sea responsable de la mayoría de sus ventas (p. 71)

constant dollars/dólares constantes las cantidades o precios al que se ajusta el dólar debido a la inflación; igual que dólares reales (p. 218)

consumer cooperative/cooperativa de consumidor asociación sin fines de lucro que compra bienes de consumidor en grandes cantidades para que así sus miembros puedan comprar a precios por debajo de los que cobran los negocios regulares (p. 76)

consumer good/bienes del consumidor bienes cuyo fin está dirigido a los consumidores en vez del comercio (p. 12)

consumer price index/índice de precios de consumidor índice que se usa para medir los cambios de precio de la cesta de compra de los productos que el consumidor usa con más frecuencia (p. 352)

consumer sovereignty/soberanía del consumidor papel del consumidor como soverano del mercado a la hora de determinar los tipos de bienes y servicios que se producen (p. 50)

co-op ver cooperativa (p. 76)

cooperative/cooperativa asociación sin fines de lucro que lleva a cabo algún tipo de actividad económica para el beneficio de sus miembros; incluye las cooperativas de consumidor, de servicios y de productores (p. 76)

corporate income tax/impuesto sobre la renta de corporación impuesto que pagan las corporaciones sobre sus ganancias de corporación (p. 235)

corporation/corporación una forma de organización comercial reconocida por la ley como una entidad legal independiente con todos los derechos y responsabilidades de individuo, inclusive el derecho de comprar y vender propiedad, entrar en contratos legales, demandar y ser demandada (p. 62)

cost-benefit analysis/análisis de costo-ventajas forma de pensar que compara el costo de una acción con sus ventajas (p. 24)

Council of Economic Advisers/Consejo de Asesores Económicos grupo de tres miembros que idea estrategias y aconseja al Presidente de los Estados Unidos acerca de asuntos económicos (p. 460)

coupon/cupón interés declarado de un bono corporativo, municipal o gubernamental (p. 321)

craft union/sindicato de artesanos gremio laboral cuyos trabajadores llevan a cabo el mismo tipo de trabajo; igual que un sindicato gremial (p. 194)

credit union/cooperativa de crédito cooperativa de servicios sin fines de lucro que acepta depósitos, hace préstamos y provee otros servicios financieros (p. 76, 303)

creditor/acreedor persona o institución a quien se le debe dinero (p. 305)

creeping inflation/inflación reptante índice de inflación bajo, generalmente de 1 a 3 por ciento anualmente (p. 390)

crowding-out effect/efecto de exclusión tasas de interés más altas de lo normal y disminución del acceso al capital financiero a que se enfrentan los inversionistas privados cuando el gobierno aumenta sus préstamos en los mercados financieros (p. 277)

crude birth rate/tasa de natalidad bruta número de nacimientos por 1,000 personas (p. 524)

currency/efectivo componente de papel del abastecimiento de dinero, hoy consiste en billetes de la Reserva Federal (p. 413)

current dollars/dólares corrientes cantidades o precios del dólar que no han sido ajustados para reflejar la inflación (p. 218)

current GDP/PIB imperante Producto Interno Bruto que se mide por los precios imperantes, sin ajustarlos para reflejar la inflación (p. 353)

current yield/rendimiento imperante el interés anual del cupón de un bono dividido por el precio de compra; medida de las ganancias de un bono (p. 321)

customs duty/derechos aduaneros

e-commerce/comercio electrónico

customs duty/derechos aduaneros impuestos sobre productos importados (p. 236)

customs union/unión aduanera grupo de países que han acordado reducir las barreras de intercambio comercial entre sí y han adoptado barreras comerciales uniformes para los países que no son miembros (p. 535)

cyclical unemployment/desempleo cíclico desempleo directamente relacionado a oscilaciones en el ciclo económico (p. 386)

default/incumplimiento acto de no pagar dinero prestado. (p. 525)

deficiency payment/aportación para enjugar un déficit aportación en efectivo para alcanzar la diferencia entre el precio del mercado y el precio indicativo de una cosecha agrícola (p. 153)

deficit spending/gastos deficitarios gastos anuales del gobierno en exceso de los impuestos y otros ingresos (p. 272)

deflation/deflación disminución en el nivel general de los precios (p. 390)

demand/demanda combinación de deseo, habilidad y voluntad de comprar un producto (p. 89)

demand curve/curva de demanda gráfica que ilustra la cantidad que se demanda a cada precio que puede prevalecer en el mercado en cualquier momento dado (p. 91)

demand deposit account/cuentas de depósito a la vista (CDV) cuentas cuyos fondos pueden retirarse al escribirse un cheque y sin la previa aprobación de la institución depositoria (p. 303)

demand elasticity/elasticidad de demanda medida de responsividad que relaciona el cambio en la cantidad demandada (variable dependiente) a un cambio en precio (variable independiente) (p. 101)

demand schedule/programa de demanda lista que indica la cantidad demandada a todos los precios posibles que pueden prevalecer en el mercado en cualquier momento dado (p. 90)

demographer/demógrafo persona que estudia el crecimiento, la densidad y otras características de la población (p. 358)

dependency ratio/relación de dependencia relación de niños a envejecientes por 100 personas dentro de la categoría de trabajo de las edades entre los 18-64 años (p. 361)

depreciation/depreciación desgaste gradual de los bienes de capital durante la producción (p. 69)

depression/depresión estado de la economía con grandes números de desempleados, disminución de ingresos reales, exceso de capacidad en las plantas manufactureras, dificultades económicas generales (p. 376)

depression scrip/vale de depresión moneda emitida por los pueblos, las cámaras de comercio y otras entidades cívicas durante la Gran Depresión de los años 30 (p. 377)

deregulation/eliminación de restricciones relajamiento o eliminación de los reglamentos del gobierno sobre las actividades comerciales (p. 304)

developing country/país en desarrollo país cuyo promedio de ingresos per cápita es tan sólo una fracción del de los países más industrializados (p. 521)

diminishing marginal utility/utilidad marginal decreciente satisfacción o utilidad decreciente a medida que se van adquiriendo unidades adicionales de un producto (p. 93)

diminishing returns/rendimientos decrecientes etapa de producción en la que el rendimiento aumenta a un ritmo disminuyente a medida que se añaden más unidades de insumo variable (p. 125)

discomfort index/índice de incomodidad estadística no oficial de la suma de la inflación mensual y el índice de desempleo; igual al índice de miseria (p. 438)

discount rate/tasa de descuento tasa de interés que el Sistema de Reserva Federal cobra a las instituciones financieras por los préstamos (p. 422)

discretionary spending/gasto discrecional gastos para programas federales que deben recibir autorización anual (p. 260)

disposable personal income/ingreso personal disponible el ingreso personal menos los impuestos personales; todo el ingreso disponible al sector consumidor después de los impuestos (p. 346)

distribution of income/distribución de ingresos modo por el cual los ingresos de la nación se dividen entre familias, individuos u otros grupos designados (p. 258)

dividend/dividendo cheque que se paga a los accionistas, por lo general trimestralmente, representa una porción de las ganancias de la corporación (p. 63)

division of labor/división de trabajo división de trabajo en un número de tareas separadas para llevarse a cabo por distintos trabajadores; igual que especialización (p. 16)

DJIA ver Dow-Jones Industrial Average (p. 332)

double taxation/doble impuesto característica de impuestos que permite que los dividendos de los accionistas sean gravados como utilidades de la corporación tanto como ganancias personales (p. 65)

Dow-Jones Industrial Average (DJIA) serie de estadísticas representativas de 30 acciones que se usan para seguir los cambios de precio en la New York Stock Exchange (p. 332)

dumping/inundación del mercado vender productos fuera del país a menos del costo de producirlos en casa (p. 474)

easy money policy/política de dinero abundante política monetaria que resulta en tasas de interés más bajas y mayor acceso a crédito; se asocia con la expansión del abastecimiento de dinero (p. 419)

e-commerce/comercio electrónico negocio o intercambio electrónico conducido por medio de Internet (p. 129)

econometric model/modelo econométrico modelo macro-económico que usa ecuaciones algebraicas para describir cómo la economía se conduce y cómo se espera que se conduzca en el futuro (p. 379)

economic growth/crecimiento económico período sostenido durante el cual se aumenta el rendimiento total de una nación en bienes y servicios (p. 15)

economic interdependence/interdependencia económica las actividades económicas en una parte del país o del mundo afectan lo que sucede en otro lugar (p. 17)

economic model/modelo económico conjunto de suposiciones en una tabla, gráfica o ecuaciones que se usan para describir o explicar la conducta económica (p. 143)

economic product/producto económico bienes o servicios útiles, relativamente escasos y transferibles a otras personas (p. 12)

economic system/sistema económico manera organizada de una sociedad proveer las necesidades de sus integrantes (p. 33)

economics/economía ciencia social que trata acerca del estudio de cómo la gente satisface los aparentemente ilimitados y competitivos deseos mediante el uso cuidadoso de escasos recursos (p. 6)

economies of scale/economías de escala aumento de la eficacia del uso del personal, la planta y el equipo a medida que la empresa aumenta de tamaño (p. 170)

Efficient Market Hypothesis/Hipótesis de Mercado Eficiente (HME) argumento acerca de que las acciones siempre tienen el precio adecuado, y que las rebajas son difíciles de hallar porque muchísimos inversionistas siempre las están vigilando (p. 329)

elastic/elástico tipo de elasticidad en que el cambio de porcentaje en la variable independiente (generalmente el precio) causa un cambio más que proporcionado en la variable dependiente (generalmente la cantidad demandada u ofrecida) (p. 102)

elasticity/elasticidad medida que nos dice cómo una variable dependiente, tal como cantidad, responde a un cambio en una variable independiente, tal como precio (p. 101)

embargo/embargo prohibición de la exportación o importación de un producto (p. 546)

entitlement/titularidad programa o beneficio que usa los requerimientos de la eligibilidad establecida para proveer suplementos de salud, de alimentación o de ingresos a individuos (p. 278)

entrepreneur/empresario individuo arriesgado en busca de ganancias; uno de cuatro factores de producción (p. 8)

equilibrium price/precio de equilibrio precio en que la cantidad ofrecida equivale a la cantidad demandada; precio que aprueba el mercado (p. 144)

equilibrium wage rate/índice del equilibrio salarial índice salarial que no deja ni exceso ni escacez en el mercado (p. 207)

equities/capital accionario acciones que representan acciones de propiedad en las corporaciones (p. 328)

estate tax/impuesto sucesorio impuesto por el traspaso de propiedad cuando una persona muere (p. 235)

European Union/Unión Europea la sucesora de la Comunidad Europea que estableció el Tratado de Maastricht en noviembre del 1993 (p. 535)

excess reserves/reservas excesivas dinero efectivo, divisas y reservas de una institución financiera que no se necesitan para respaldar préstamos en existencia; fuente potencial de nuevos préstamos (p. 416)

excise tax/impuesto sobre el consumo impuesto sobre ingresos generales recaudado sobre la manufactura o venta de objetos selectos (p. 235)

expansion/expansión periodo de crecimiento del PIB real; recuperación de la recesión (p. 376)

exports/exportaciones bienes y servicios que una nación produce y después vende a otras naciones (p. 467)

expropriation/expropiación cuando el gobierno confisca bienes de propiedad privada o extranjera sin compensación (p. 534)

external debt/deuda externa dinero prestado que un país debe a países y bancos extranjeros (p. 525)

externality/factores externos efecto secundario de la economía que afecta a un tercero que no está envuelto (p. 175)

fact-finding/indagación de los hechos acuerdo entre la unión y la empresa de pedirle a un tercero recoja los hechos acerca de una disputa y presente recomendaciones sin obligaciones (p. 202)

factor market/mercado de factor mercado en que se venden y se compran recursos productivos (p. 14)

factors of production/factores de producción recursos productivos que componen las cuatro categorías de tierra, capital, trabajo y espíritu empresarial (p. 7)

family/familia dos o más personas que viven juntas y que están vinculadas por sangre, matrimonio o adopción (p. 346)

federal budget/presupuesto federal plan anual que traza los gastos propuestos y las ganancias que se anticipan (p. 260)

federal budget deficit/déficit del presupuesto federal exceso de gastos federales sobre la recaudación de impuestos e ingresos (p. 261)

federal budget surplus/superávit del presupuesto federal presupuesto federal que muestra un balance positivo después de restar los gastos de los ingresos (p. 261)

federal debt/deuda federal cantidad total de dinero que el gobierno federal ha pedido prestado de los demás (p. 273)

Federal Reserve note/vale de la Reserva Federal moneda emitida por la Reserva Federal que con el tiempo sustituyó a todos los otros tipos de moneda federal (p. 301)

Federal Reserve System/Sistema de Reserva Federal banco central de los Estados Unidos, de propiedad privada y cuyo control es público (p. 301)

fertility rate/tasa de fecundidad número de alumbramientos que se espera que 1,000 mujeres experimenten en sus vidas (p. 358)

fiat money/moneda fiduciaria dinero por decreto del gobierno; no tiene valor alternativo ni uso como producto básico (p. 287)

FICA Acta de Contribuciones del Seguro Federal; gravamen impuesto sobre los patrones y empleados para sostener al Seguro Social y al Medicare (p. 233)

finance company/compañía financiera firma que hace préstamos directamente a los consumidores y que se especializa en la compra de contratos a plazos de los comerciantes que venden a crédito (p. 315)

financial asset/haber financiero documento que representa un derecho a los ingresos y la propiedad del prestatario; CDs, bonos, letras del Tesoro, hipotecas (p. 314)

financial capital/capital financiero dinero que se usa para comprar implementos y equipo que se usa en la producción (p. 7)

financial intermediary/intermediario financiero institución que canaliza los ahorros a los inversionistas; bancos, compañías de seguro, sociedades de ahorro y préstamo, cooperativas de crédito (p. 314)

financial system/sistema financiero red de personas que ahorran, inversionistas e instituciones financieras que colaboran para transferir los ahorros a usos de inversión (p. 314)

fiscal policy/política fiscal el uso de las medidas que usa el gobierno para gastos y recaudación de ingresos para influenciar la economía (p. 447)

fiscal year/año fiscal periodo de 12 meses para la planificación financiera que no necesariamente coincide con el año civil; del 1 de octubre al 30 de septiembre para el gobierno federal (p. 260)

Five-Year Plan/Plan de Cinco Años plan económico centralizado y abarcante que usó la Unión Soviética y la China para coordinar el desarrollo de la agricultura y la industria (p. 497)

fixed cost/costo fijo costo de producción que no cambia cuando cambia la producción (p. 127)

fixed exchange rate/cotización de divisa fija sistema bajo el cual el valor de una divisa se fijó en relación al de las otras; sistema de cotización que estuvo en efecto hasta el 1971 (p. 482)

fixed income/renta fija renta que no aumenta aunque los precios suban (p. 42)

flat tax/impuesto fijo impuesto proporcional sobre el ingreso individual después de haber alcanzado el ingreso especificado (p. 249)

flexible exchange rate/cotización de divisa flexible sistema que depende de oferta y demanda para determinar el valor de una moneda en términos de otra; sistema de cotización en efecto desde el 1971, igual a la cotización flotante (p. 483)

floating exchange rate/cotización flotante ver cotización de divisa flexible (p. 483)

floor price/precio mínimo precio legal más bajo que se puede cobrar por un producto (p. 152)

food stamps/sellos para la compra de alimentos cupones que emite el gobierno y que se canjean por alimentos (p. 397)

foreign exchange/divisas divisas que usan los países para conducir comercio internacional (p. 481)

foreign exchange rate/cotización de divisas precio de la moneda de un país en relación a la moneda de otro país (p. 482)

401(k) plan/plan 401(k) plan de ahorros e impuestos diferidos que actúa como una pensión personal para empleados. (p. 320)

fractional reserve system/sistema de reserva fraccionada sistema que dicta que las instituciones financieras aparten una fracción de sus depósitos en la forma de reservas (p. 415)

free enterprise/empresa independiente economía en la cual se permite prosperar la competencia con la mínima intervención gubernamental; término usado para describir la economía americana (p. 46)

free enterprise economy/economía de libre empresa economía de mercado en la que los comercios privados tienen la libertad de operar para obtener ganancias con intervención limitada del gobierno; lo mismo que economía de empresa privada (p. 24)

free-trade area/zona de comercio libre grupo de países que han acordado reducir las barreras comerciales entre sí, pero que carecen de una barrera arancelaria para los países no miembros (p. 535)

free traders/comerciantes libres individuos a favor de poca o hasta ninguna restricción sobre el comercio (p. 474)

frictional unemployment/desempleo friccional desempleo causado por trabajadores cuando cambian de trabajo o al esperar ir a nuevos empleos (p. 384)

futures/futuros contratos para comprar o vender mercancías o bienes financieros a una fecha específica en el futuro, usando un precio que se acordó hoy (p. 333)

futures contract/contrato de futuros acuerdo para comprar o vender en una fecha específica en el futuro a un precio predeterminado (p. 333)

futures market/mercado de futuros mercado donde se compran y se venden los contratos de futuros (p. 333)

galloping inflation/inflación galopante inflación relativamente intensa, generalmente alcanza desde 100 a 300 por ciento anualmente (p. 390)

gasohol mezcla de 90 por ciento gasolina sin plomo y 10 por ciento alcohol de grano (p. 549)

GDP gap/laguna del PIB diferencia entre lo que la economía puede producir y lo que, de hecho, produce; costo de oportunidad anual de los recursos desempleados (p. 438)

Glosario

GDP in constant dollars/PIB en dólares constantes

GDP in constant dollars/PIB en dólares constantes   el Producto Interno Bruto considerando la inflación; es igual al PIB (p. 353)

general partnership/asociación general   ver asociación (p. 60)

geographic monopoly/monopolio geográfico   situación del mercado en la que una firma tiene un monopolio debido al sitio en que está situada o a la pequeñez del mercado (p. 170)

gift tax/impuesto sobre donaciones y legados   impuesto sobre donaciones de dinero o riquezas que tiene que pagar el donante (p. 235)

giveback/devolución de beneficios   en la renegociación de un contrato, sueldo, beneficio complementario o regla de trabajo que se pierde (p. 212)

glass ceiling/techo de cristal   barrera aparentemente invisible que impide que las mujeres y las minorías avancen en una organización dominada por los hombres (p. 214)

glut/abarrotamiento   superabundancia de un producto (p. 553)

gold certificate/certificado de oro   billete de banco respaldado por oro; emitido en 1863 y popular hasta que fue retirado en 1934 (p. 295)

gold standard/patrón de oro   patrón monetario bajo el cual la moneda de un país equivale a, y se puede cambiar por, una cantidad específica de oro (p. 296)

good/bien   producto económico tangible y útil, relativamente escaso, transferible a otras personas; se usa para satisfacer necesidades y deseos (p. 12)

Gosplan   autoridad central de planificación en la antigua Unión Soviética que ideó y dirigió los planes de Cinco Años (p. 497)

government monopoly/monopolio fiscal   monopolio creado por/o de la propiedad del gobierno (p. 170)

grant-in-aid/donativo del gobierno   transferencia de pago desde un nivel del gobierno a otro y que no incumbe compensación (p. 257)

Great Depression/Gran Depresión   el periodo de mayor disminución económica en la historia de los Estados Unidos, duró aproximadamente desde 1929 hasta 1939 (p. 196)

Great Leap Forward/Gran Salto Adelante   el segundo desastroso plan de cinco años de la China iniciado en 1958, forzó la colectivización de la agricultura y la rápida industrialización (p. 506)

grievance procedure/procedimiento para la presentación de reclamaciones   provisión contractual que delínea la forma en que se resolverán futuras disputas y asuntos de quejas (p. 202)

Gross Domestic Product/Producto Interno Bruto (PIB)   valor en dólar de todos los productos, servicios y estructuras finales dentro de las fronteras nacionales de un país durante el periodo de un año (p. 9, 341)

Gross National Product/Producto Nacional Bruto (PNB)   valor total en dólar de todos los productos, estructuras y servicios finales producidos en un año con la mano de

index of leading indicators/índice de indicadores anticipados

obra y la propiedad suplidas por los residentes de un país, sin importar donde toma lugar la producción; la mayor medida de los ingresos de una nación (p. 344)

growth triangle/triángulo de crecimiento   tabla que muestra los índices de crecimiento de una serie estadística entre dos fechas cualquiera (p. 364)

horizontal merger/fusión horizontal   combinación de dos o más empresas que producen el mismo producto (p. 71)

household/unidad familiar   unidad básica del sector del consumidor que consiste de todas las personas que ocupan una casa, apartamento o vivienda separada (p. 346)

human capital/capital humano   suma de las destrezas, habilidades, salud y motivación (p. 16)

hyperinflation/hiperinflación   inflación anormal en exceso de 500 por ciento por año; última etapa de un colapso monetario (p. 390)

imperfect competition/competencia imperfecta   estructura mercantil en la que no se satisfacen todas las condiciones de competencia pura; competencia monopolística, olipolio y monopolio (p. 166)

implicit GDP price deflator/deflactor implícito del precio PIB   índice que se usa para medir los cambios de precio del Producto Interno Bruto (p. 353)

imports/importaciones   bienes y servicios que una nación compra de otras naciones (p. 468)

incidence of a tax/incidencia de un impuesto   carga final de un impuesto (p. 225)

income effect/efecto de ingreso   aquella porción de un cambio en cantidad demandada causada por un cambio en el ingreso real de un consumidor cuando el precio de un producto cambia (p. 96)

income statement/declaración de ingreso   informe que muestra las ventas, gastos y utilidades de un negocio por un período determinado, usualmente de tres meses o un año (p. 68)

inconvertible fiat money standard/estándar inconvertible de la moneda fiduciaria   moneda fiduciaria que no se puede cambiar por oro o plata; los vales de la Reserva Federal de hoy en día (p. 297)

independent union/unión independiente   gremio no afiliado con la AFL-CIO (p. 198)

index of leading indicators/índice de indicadores anticipados   índice compuesto de 11 series económicas que suben y bajan en anticipo a cambios en la economía global; series estadísticas que se usan para predecir los puntos críticos del ciclo comercial (p. 380)

indexing/indización ajuste de las escalas de impuestos para contrarrestar los efectos de la inflación (p. 233)

individual income tax/impuesto sobre la renta personal impuesto sobre jornales, salarios y otros ingresos de las personas (p. 226)

Individual Retirement Account (IRA) cuenta de retiro personal, cuenta de retiro en la forma de depósito a largo plazo, con contribuciones anuales de hasta $2,000 exemptas de impuestos hasta que se saquen durante el retiro (p. 324)

industrial union/unión industrial gremio cuyos trabajadores llevan a cabo distintos tipos de trabajo (p. 195)

inelastic/no elástica tipo de elasticidad en el cual el porcentaje de cambio en la variable independiente (usualmente el precio) causa un cambio menos que proporcionado en la variable dependiente (usualmente la cantidad demandada u ofrecida) (p. 102)

infant industries argument/argumento de las industrias nacientes argumento de que a las industrias nuevas que están surgiendo se las debe proteger de la competencia extranjera hasta que estén lo suficiente fuertes para competir (p. 474)

inflation/inflación aumento en el nivel general de los precios (p. 42, 350)

infrastructure/infraestructura las carreteras, tránsito público, comunicaciones, electricidad, agua, alcantarillado y otros servicios públicos necesarios para apoyar a una población (p. 510)

injunction/mandato judicial orden de la corte dictada para evitar que una compañía o unión tome acción durante una disputa laboral (p. 203)

interest/interés pago que se hace por el uso de dinero prestado; usualmente se paga a intervalos periódicos para bonos o préstamos de largo plazo (p. 64)

intergovernmental expenditures/gastos intergubernamentales fondos para gastos que un nivel de gobierno transfiere a otro. (p. 268)

intergovermental revenue/ingresos intergubernamentales fondos, que en el gobierno, se reciben de un nivel a otro (p. 238)

intermediate products/productos intermediarios productos directamente excluidos de las computaciones del PIB ya que son componentes de otros productos finales incluidos en el PIB; llantas y radios nuevos para usarse en autos nuevos (p. 343)

Internal Revenue Service (IRS)/Servicio de Rentas Internas rama del Departamento de Tesorería que recauda impuestos (p. 232)

International Bank for Reconstruction and Development/Banco Internacional para Reconstrucción y Desarrollo ver World Bank (p. 526)

International Monetary Fund (IMF)/Fondo Monetario Internacional (FMI) organización internacional que ofrece asesoría y asistencia financiera a naciones para que su moneda pueda competir en el mercado abierto. (p. 526)

inventory/inventorio abastecimiento de bienes en reserva; incluye bienes terminados esperando venderse y materias primas que se usan en producción (p. 59)

investment tax credit/crédito impositivo de inversión crédito impositivo que se da para la compra de equipo (p. 245)

keiretsu grupo de firmas japonesas de propiedad privada unidas y gobernadas por una junta directiva exterior para poder regular la competencia (p. 510)

Keynesian economics/economía keynesiana políticas del gobierno para gastos e impuestos sugeridas por John Maynard Keynes para estimular la economía; sinónimo de las políticas fiscales o de la economía del lado de la demanda (p. 448)

labor/trabajo la gente con todas sus habilidades y esfuerzos; uno de los cuatro factores de producción, no incluye al empresario (p. 8)

labor mobility/mobilidad laboral habilidad y voluntad laboral de reubicarse, por lo general por sueldos más altos (p. 209)

labor productivity/productividad laboral índice de crecimiento del rendimiento total por unidad de insumo; medida de la eficiencia de productividad (p. 368)

labor union/sindicato obrero organización que obra en beneficio de los intereses de sus miembros respecto a pago, horas de trabajo, seguro médico, beneficios complementarios y otros asuntos relacionados al trabajo (p. 76)

Laffer curve/curva Laffer gráfica que muestra que las tasas impositivas más bajas supuestamente estimulan mayores recaudaciones impositivas (p. 452)

laissez-faire/liberalismo filosofía de que el gobierno no debe interferir con las actividades comerciales (p. 163)

land/tierra recursos naturales o "dones de la naturaleza" no creados por el esfuerzo humano; uno de cuatro factores de producción (p. 7)

Law of Demand/Ley de Demanda regla que dicta que se demanda más a precios bajos y menos a precios altos; relación inversa entre precio y cantidad demandada (p. 91)

Law of Supply/Ley de Oferta regla que dicta que se ofrece más a la venta a precios altos que a precios bajos (p. 113)

Law of Variable Proportions/Ley de Proporciones Variables regla que dicta que la producción a corto plazo cambia a medida que un insumo es variado mientras otros se mantienen constante (p. 122)

legal reserves/reservas legales moneda y depósitos que se usan para cumplir con los requisitos de reserva (p. 415)

legal tender/moneda legal   moneda fiduciaria que por decreto del gobierno hay que aceptar por pago (p. 295)

liabilities/compromisos   deudas y obligaciones que se le deben a otras personas; usualmente anotadas como partidas en el estado de cuentas (p. 416)

life expectancy/expectativa de vida   promedio de la duración de vida restante en años para personas que logran una cierta edad (p. 358)

limited life/vida limitada   situación en la cual una firma deja de existir legalmente al morir o renunciar un dueño o al agregarse uno nuevo; se aplica a propietarios únicos y a sociedades (p. 59)

limited partnership/sociedad limitada   forma de sociedad en la que uno o más socios no participan activamente en el funcionamiento diario del negocio y cuyas responsabilidad por la deuda de la sociedad se limita a la cantidad invertida en el negocio (p. 62)

line-item veto/veto de artículo particular   el poder para cancelar artículos específicos en el presupuesto sin rechazar el presupuesto entero (p. 278)

liquidity/liquidez   potencial para conversión rápida a efectivo u otros bienes financieros (p. 417)

lockout/cierre patronal   rehuso patronal de dejar que los empleados trabajen hasta que se cumplan las demandas de la compañía (p. 195)

long run/largo plazo   periodo de producción lo bastante largo para cambiar la cantidad de insumos variables y fijos que se usan en la producción (p. 122)

Lorenz curve/curva de Lorenz   curva que muestra cuánto la distribución en sí de los ingresos varía de una distribución igual (p. 394)

luxury good/bienes de lujo   bienes cuya demanda aumenta mucho más rápido de lo que aumentan los ingresos (p. 235)

M1   componentes del abastecimiento de dinero que se conforman al papel del dinero como medio de intercambio; monedas, divisas, cheques, otros depósitos a la vista, cheques de viajeros (p. 429)

M2   componentes del abastecimiento de dinero que se conforman al papel del dinero como fuente de valor; M1, depósitos de ahorros, depósitos a plazo (p. 430)

macroeconomic equilibrium/equilibrio macroeconómico   nivel de PIB consistente con un nivel de precio dado; intersección de oferta y demanda globales (p. 445)

macroeconomics/macroeconomía   esa parte de la teoría económica que trata con la economía como un total y con la adopción de decisiones por grandes unidades como los gobiernos y las uniones (p. 193)

mandatory spending/gasto obligatorio   gastos federales autorizados por ley que continúan sin necesidad de aprobación anual del Congreso (p. 260)

margin requirement/requerimiento marginal   depósitos mínimos que se quedan con el corredor para usarlos como pago parcial de otros valores (p. 423)

marginal analysis/análisis marginal   adopción de decisión que compara el costo extra de hacer algo con los beneficios extras que se obtienen (p. 131)

marginal cost/costo marginal   costo extra de producir una unidad de producción adicional (p. 129)

marginal product/producto marginal   producción extra debida a adición de una unidad más de insumo (p. 124)

marginal revenue/ingreso marginal   ingreso extra de la venta de una unidad de producto adicional (p. 130)

marginal tax rate/tasa impositiva marginal   tasa impositiva que se aplica al próximo dólar de ingreso sujeto a impuesto (p. 229)

marginal utility/utilidad marginal   satisfacción o utilidad que se obtiene de adquirir una unidad más de un producto (p. 93)

market/mercado   lugar de encuentro o mecanismo que permite que los compradores y vendedores de un producto económico se reunan; puede ser local, regional, nacional o global (p. 14)

market basket/cesta de mercado   colección representativa de los bienes y servicios que se usan para compilar un índice de precios (p. 351)

market demand curve/curva de demanda mercadera   curva de demanda que muestra las cantidades demandadas por todos que están interesados en comprar un producto (p. 91)

market economy/economía de mercado   sistema económico en el cual la oferta y la demanda y el sistema de precios ayudan a la gente a tomar decisiones y a asignar los recursos; lo mismo que economía de libre comercio (p. 36)

market equilibrium/equilibrio del mercado   condición de la estabilidad del precio en que la cantidad demandada es igual a la cantidad ofrecida (p. 143)

market failure/fallo del mercado   mercado que carece de cualquiera de los requisitos de un mercado competidor, como competencia adecuada, conocimiento de precios y oportunidades, mobilidad de recursos y ganancias competitivas (p. 174)

market structure/estructura del mercado   clasificación del mercado de acuerdo al número y tamaño de las firmas, tipo de producto y tipo de competición (p. 164)

market supply curve/curva de oferta mercadera curva   de oferta que muestra las cantidades de un producto ofrecidas en varios precios por todas las empresas que lo venden en un mercado indicado. (p. 114)

maturity/vencimiento   plazo de un bono (p. 321)

measure of value/medida de valor   una de las tres funciones del dinero que le permite servir como denominador común para medir el valor (p. 286)

mediation/mediación   proceso de resolver un conflicto al incluir a un tercero neutral (p. 202)

medicaid   programa de seguro médico del gobierno federal y el estado para personas de ingresos bajos (p. 265)

medicare programa federal de cuidados de salud para enve-jecientes, que no toma en cuenta sus ingresos (p. 233)

medium of exchange/medio de cambio dinero u otra sustancia generalmente aceptada en intercambio; una de las tres funciones del dinero (p. 286)

member bank/banco miembro banco que pertenece al Sistema de Reserva Federal (p. 407)

member bank reserves/reservas de banco miembro reservas que mantienen los bancos miembros en la Reserva Federal para satisfacer los requisitos de reserva (p. 418)

merger/fusión combinación de dos o más empresas comerciales para formar una sóla firma (p. 68)

microeconomics/microeconomía rama de la teoría de la economía que trata con la conducta y las decisiones que adoptan las pequeñas unidades tales como los individuos y las firmas (p. 89)

minimum wage/sueldo mínimo sueldo legal más bajo que se le puede pagar a la mayoría de trabajadores (p. 152, 216)

misery index/índice de miseria estadística no oficial que es la suma de la inflación mensual y la tasa de desempleo; igual al índice de incomodidad (p. 438)

mixed economy/economía mixta ver economía de empresa privada modificada (p. 51)

modified free enterprise economy/economía de libre empresa modificada sistema de libre empresa con un poco de participación del gobierno; igual que economía de empresa privada modificada (p. 560)

modified private enterprise economy/economía de empresa privada modificada economía de mercado de libre empresa donde la gente lleva a cabo sus asuntos económicos libremente, pero están sujetos a algunas intervenciones y regulaciones del gobierno (p. 51)

modified union shop/empresa de exclusividad gremial modificada arreglo bajo el cual los trabajadores tienen la opción de unirse a una unión luego de habérseles empleado (p. 201)

monetarism/monetarismo escuela de pensamiento que enfatiza la importancia del crecimiento monetario estable para controlar la inflación y estimular el crecimiento económico de largo plazo (p. 453)

monetary policy/política monetaria acciones que toma el Sistema de Reserva Federal para ampliar o reducir el abastecimiento de dinero para afectar el costo y disponibilidad de crédito (p. 415)

monetary standard/estándar monetario mecanismo que mantiene un abastecimiento de dinero, durable, portátil, divisible y estable en valor; el estándar del oro, el estándar de la plata, el estándar de la moneda fiduciaria (p. 292)

monetary unit/unidad monetaria unidad monetaria estándar del abastecimiento monetario de un país; el dólar americano, la libra británica (p. 289)

monetizing the debt/monetización de la deuda proceso de crear suficiente dinero adicional para contrarrestar los préstamos del gobierno de modo que las tasas de interés permanezcan sin cambiar (p. 427)

money/dinero cualquier cosa que sirva como medio de intercambio, una medida de valor y un abastecimiento de valor (p. 286)

money market/mercado monetario mercado en el cual el capital financiero se ha prestado por un año o menos (p. 325)

monopolistic competition/competición monopolística estructura mercantil que posee todas las condiciones de competición pura a excepción de tener productos idénticos; una forma de competición imperfecta (p. 166)

monopoly/monopolio estructura mercantil caracterizada por un solo productor; una forma de competición imperfecta (p. 169)

moral suasion/persuasión moral el uso que el Sistema de Reserva Federal hace de la persuasión para lograr política monetaria; testimonio congresional, comunicados de prensa (p. 424)

most favored nation clause/cláusula de la nación más favorecida derecho mercantil que permite a un país tercero disfrutar las mismas rebajas de tarifas que los Estados Unidos negocia con otro país (p. 477)

multinational/multinacional corporación que produce y vende sin importarle las fronteras nacionales y cuyas actividades comerciales están situadas en varios países diferentes (p. 72)

multiplier/multiplicador cambio en el gasto global causado por un cambio en el gasto de inversión (p. 448)

municipal bond/bono municipal bono, a menudo exempto de impuestos, emitido por el gobierno estatal o local; conocido como munis (p. 323)

mutual fund/fondo mutuo compañía que vende acciones de sí misma y usa las ganancias para comprar acciones y bonos emitidos por otras compañías (p. 316)

mutual savings bank/banco mutualista de ahorro institución de ahorro de propiedad de los depositantes que opera para beneficio de ellos (p. 303)

NAFTA ver Acuerdo Norteamericano de Comercio Libre (p. 479)

national bank/banco nacional un banco comercial establecido por el Sistema Bancario Nacional; miembro del Fed (p. 295)

National Bank Note/billete del Banco Nacional moneda respaldada por bonos del gobierno, emitida por bancos nacionales comenzando en 1863 y que por lo general desaparecio de circulación alrededor de los años 30 (p. 295)

national currency/moneda nacional ver billete del Banco Nacional (p. 295)

national income/ingresos nacionales   producto nacional neto menos los impuestos comerciales indirectos; medida de los ingresos de una nación (p. 345)

national income accounting/contabilidad de los ingresos nacionales   sistema de cuentas que se usa para seguir la producción, el consumo, los ahorros, las estadísticas de los ingresos de la nación (p. 341)

natural monopoly/monopolio natural   mercado en que los costos promedios son más bajos cuando toda la producción la produce una sola firma (p. 170)

need/necesidad   requisito básico para supervivencia; incluye comida, ropa y/o albergue (p. 6)

negative externality/factores externos negativos   efectos secundarios negativos que afectan a un tercero no partícipe; costo externo (p. 175)

negative income tax/impuesto negativo sobre la renta   sistema de impuestos que hace pagos efectivos en la forma de reembolsos de impuestos cuando los ingresos de las personas caen por debajo de ciertos niveles (p. 400)

Negotiable Order of Withdrawal (NOW)   orden negativa de retiro, tipo de cuenta de cheques que paga intereses (p. 303)

net asset value/valor neto del activo   (NAV, siglas en inglés) valor en el mercado de una acción de un fondo mutualista de inversión determinado dividiendo el valor del fondo por el número de acciones emitidas (p. 316)

net exports of goods and services/exportaciones netas de bienes y servicios   gastos netos según el modelo de producción-gastos del sector extranjero (p. 348)

net immigration/inmigración neta   carga de población neta después de tomar en cuenta las personas que salen o entran del país (p. 359)

net income/ingreso neto   justificación de las utilidades de un negocio determinada substrayendo de la renta todos los gastos incluso los impuestos (p. 68)

net national product/producto interno neto (PIN)   Producto Interno Bruto menos los cargos de depreciación por uso y desgaste del equipo capital; medida de la producción anual neta generada con la mano de obra y la propiedad suplida por los ciudadanos de un país (p. 344)

net worth/valor neto   exceso de bienes por encima de las responsabilidades, usualmente anotados como un resumen separado en el estado de cuentas; medida del valor de un negocio (p. 416)

nominal GDP   ver PIB imperante (p. 353)

nonbank financial institution/institución financiera no bancaria   institución no depositoria que canaliza los ahorros a los inversionistas; compañías financieras, compañías de seguro, fondos de pensiones (p. 315)

noncompeting labor grades/grados de mano de obra no competitivos   amplios grupos de trabajadores no calificados, semicalificados, calificados y profesionales que no compiten entre sí (p. 206)

nonmarket transaction/transacción fuera del mercado   actividad económica que no toma lugar en el mercado y, por lo tanto, no está incluída en el PIB; los servicios de las amas de casa, trabajo del hogar (p. 343)

nonprice competition/competición sin precio   competición que implica la publicidad de la apariencia de un producto, su calidad o diseño en vez de su precio (p. 166)

nonprofit organization/organización sin fines de lucro   institución económica que opera como un negocio pero que no busca ganancias; escuelas, iglesias, organizaciones de servicios para la comunidad (p. 75)

nonrecourse loan/préstamo sin recurso   préstamo de agricultura que no lleva ni penalidad ni demás obligaciones de pago (p. 153)

nonrenewable resources/recursos no renovables   recursos que no pueden ser reemplazados una vez que hayan sido usados (p. 546)

North American Free Trade Agreement/Tratado Norteamericano de Libre Comercio (NAFTA)   tratado firmado en 1993 para reducir las tarifas entre los Estados Unidos, Canadá y México (p. 479)

NOW accounts/cuentas NOW   (siglas en inglés) clase de cuenta de cheques que genera interés (p. 303)

oligopoly/oligarquía   estructura mercantil en la que unos cuantos vendedores grandes dominan la industria y tienen la habilidad de afectar los precios; forma de competición imperfecta (p. 167)

open market operations/operaciones de mercado abierto   política monetaria en la forma de compra y venta de bonos en el mercado de bonos (p. 420)

opportunity cost/costo de oportunidad   cuando se hace una elección en lugar de otra, el costo de la mejor alternativa que sigue para el uso del dinero, tiempo o recursos (p. 20)

options/opciones   contratos que dan al inversionista una opción de comprar o vender bienes, capitales o bienes financieros a una fecha específica en el futuro usando el precio acordado hoy (p. 333)

options market/mercado de opciones   mercados donde las opciones, incluso las opciones de venta y de compra, se intercambian (p. 333)

output-expenditure model/modelo de producción-gastos   modelo macroeconómico que describe la demanda total del consumidor, la inversión, gobierno y los sectores extranjeros; $PIB = C + I + G + SE$ (p. 348)

overhead/gastos generales   categoría amplia de gastos fijos que incluyen intereses, alquiler, impuestos y salarios de ejecutivos (p. 127)

over-the-counter market (OTC)   mercado electrónico extrabursátil para valores no anotados en casas de cambio organizadas como la New York Stock Exchange (p. 331)

par value/valor a la par

private property rights/derechos de propiedad privada

par value/valor a la par capital de un bono o la cantidad total pedida en préstamo (p. 321)

paradox of value/paradoja de valores contradicción aparente entre el alto valor de objetos no esenciales y el bajo valor de los esenciales (p. 13)

partnership/sociedad negocio no incorporado operado por dos o más dueños quienes comparten las ganancias y que tienen responsabilidad ilimitada por las deudas y obligaciones de la firma; igual que sociedad colectiva (p. 60)

part-time workers/trabajadores de tiempo parcial trabajadores que generalmente trabajan menos de 35 horas por semana (p. 216)

"pay-as-you-go" provision/provisión de "pagar según vayas surgiendo" requerimiento que nuevas propuestas de gasto o reducción de impuestos deben ser igualados por reducciones en otras partes del presupuesto (p. 277)

payroll taxes/impuesto sobre nómina de pago impuestos en pagos y salarios para financiar el Seguro Social y costos de atención médica (medicare) (p. 233)

payroll withholding statement/estado de cuenta de retención de nómina documento adherido al cheque de pago que resume el pago y las deducciones (p. 242)

payroll withholding system/sistema de retención de nómina sistema periódico que automáticamente deduce del cheque de pago los impuestos sobre la renta (p. 232)

peak/apogeo punto en el tiempo cuando el PIB cesa de aumentar y comienza a declinar (p. 376)

pension/pensión pago regular para alguien que ha trabajado cierto número de años, ha alcanzado cierta edad o ha sufrido algún daño (p. 316)

pension fund/fondo de pensiones fondo que recauda e invierte ingresos hasta que se hacen pagos a los titulares que tienen derecho (p. 316)

per capita/per cápita en base a persona; el total dividido por la población (p. 255)

perestroika reestructuramiento fundamental de la economía soviética; política introducida por Gorbachev (p. 499)

perfect competition/competencia perfecta estructura del mercado que se caracteriza por un gran número de compradores y vendedores independientes bien informados que intercambian productos idénticos (p. 164)

personal income/ingresos personales cantidad total de ingresos que van al sector del consumidor antes de que se paguen los impuestos sobre la renta (p. 345)

picket/piqueteo demostración ante un establecimiento comercial para protestar las acciones de una compañía (p. 195)

piecework/trabajo por pieza sistema de compensación que paga a los trabajadores por las unidades producidas, en vez de las horas trabajadas (p. 498)

pollution/polución contaminación del aire, agua o tierra por la descarga de una sustancia venenosa o nociva (p. 554)

pollution permit/permiso de polución permiso federal que permite que las empresas de servicios públicos liberen polutantes en el aire; una forma de controlar la contaminación (p. 556)

population density/densidad demográfica número de personas por milla cuadrada de área de terreno (p. 536)

population pyramid/pirámide demográfica diagrama que muestra la distribución de la población por edad y sexo (p. 360)

portfolio diversification/diversificación de cartera estrategia de retener varias inversiones para protección contra riesgos (p. 329)

positive externality/factores externos positivos efectos secundarios beneficiosos que afectan a un tercero no involucrado (p. 176)

premium/prima precio que se paga mensualmente, trimestralmente, semianual o anual por una póliza de seguro (p. 315)

price/precio valor monetario de un producto establecido por la oferta y la demanda (p. 137)

price ceiling/precio máximo máximo precio legal que se puede cobrar por un producto (p. 151)

price discrimination/descriminación de precio práctica ilegal de cobrarle a los clientes distintos precios por el mismo producto (p. 179)

price-fixing/fijación de precios acuerdo, usualmente ilegal, que hacen las compañías para cobrar un precio uniforme por un producto (p. 168)

price floor/precio mínimo precio legal más bajo que se puede cobrar por un producto (p. 152)

price index/índice de precios serie estadística que se usa para medir cambios en el nivel de los precios a lo largo del tiempo (p. 351)

price level/nivel de precios magnitud relativa de los precios en un momento determinado según los mide un índice de precios (p. 389)

primary market/mercado primario mercado en que sólo el emisor original volverá a comprar un haber financiero; bonos de ahorros del gobierno, los IRA, pequeños CD (p. 326)

prime rate/tasa preferencial tasa de interés mejor o más baja que los bancos comerciales cobran a sus clientes (p. 427)

primitive equilibrium/equilibrio primitivo primera etapa del desarrollo económico durante la cual la economía está estática (p. 528)

principal/capital cantidad que se pide prestada cuando se obtiene un préstamo o se emite un bono (p. 64)

private enterprise economy/economía de empresa privada ver economía de empresa libre (p. 24)

private property rights/derechos de propiedad privada característica fundamental del capitalismo la cual permite a los individuos a poseer y controlar sus propiedades como lo deseen, incluso las propiedades tangibles e intangibles (p. 47)

private sector/sector privado aquella parte de la economía compuesta por personas privadas y negocios (p. 256)

privatization/privatización conversión de factorías y otras propiedades del gobierno a propiedad privada (p. 502)

producer cooperative/cooperativa de productores asociación sin fines de lucro de productores que ayuda a sus miembros a vender o mercadear sus productos; mayormente se halla en la agricultura (p. 76)

producer price index/índice de precios de productor índice que se usa para medir los precios recibidos de los productores domésticos; anteriormente denominado índice de precios al por mayor (p. 352)

product differentiation/diferenciación de precios diferencias reales o imaginadas entre productos que compiten en la misma industria (p. 166)

product market/mercado de productos mercado donde se ponen a la venta los bienes y servicios (p. 14)

production/producción proceso de crear bienes y servicios con el uso combinado de tierra, capital, mano de obra y espíritu empresarial (p. 8)

production function/función de producción rendimiento gráfico que muestra cómo un cambio en la cantidad de una sola variable de insumo afecta la producción total (p. 123)

production possibilities frontier/frontera de posibilidades de producción diagrama que representa el máximo de combinaciones de bienes y/o servicios que una economía puede producir cuando se emplean a plenitud todos los recursos (p. 21)

productivity/productividad grado hasta cual los recursos productivos se usan eficientemente; normalmente se refiere a mano de obra, pero puede aplicarse a todos los factores de producción (p. 15)

professional association/asociación profesional organización sin fines de lucro de trabajadores profesionales o especializados que buscan mejorar las condiciones de trabajo, los niveles de habilidades y la percepción pública de su profesión (p. 77)

professional labor/trabajo profesional trabajadores con un alto nivel de habilidades profesionales y gerenciales (p. 206)

profit/ganancias nivel al que personas y organizaciones mejoran al cabo de un periodo de lo que estaban al principio; usualmente se mide en dólares (p. 48)

profit-maximizing quantity of output/cantidad de producto para el máximo de ganancias nivel de producción en que el costo marginal equivale al ingreso marginal (p. 131)

profit motive/motivo de ganancia fuerza motriz que anima a la gente y organizaciones a mejorar su bienestar material; característica del capitalismo y el libre comercio (p. 48)

progressive tax/tributación progresiva tributación en que un porcentaje del ingreso que se paga en impuestos sube al subir el nivel de ingreso (p. 229)

property tax/impuesto sobre los bienes impuesto sobre posesiones tangibles e intangibles como bienes raices, edificios, muebles, acciones, bonos y cuentas bancarias (p. 241)

proportional tax/impuesto proporcional tributación en que un porcentaje de los ingresos que se paga en impuestos es igual sin importar el nivel de ingreso (p. 229)

proprietorship/patrimonio ver patrimonio personal (p. 57)

protectionist/proteccionista persona que proteje a los productores domésticos con tarifas, cuotas y otras barreras comerciales (p. 474)

protective tariff/arancel proteccionista impuesto sobre un producto importado diseñado para proteger a los productores domésticos menos eficientes (p. 472)

public disclosure/revelación pública requisito que fuerza a un negocio a que revele al público información acerca de sus productos u operaciones (p. 181)

public good/bien público producto económico que se consume colectivamente; autopistas, defensa nacional, protección de la policía y de los bomberos (p. 176)

public sector/sector público esa parte de la economía compuesta de los gobiernos locales, estatales y federales (p. 255)

public utility/empresa de servicios públicos compañía que provee servicios esenciales como el agua y la electricidad a los consumidores, usualmente sujeta a algunas regulaciones del gobierno (p. 79)

put option/opción de venta contrato que da a los inversionistas la opción de vender productos, valores o bienes finacieros a una fecha específica en el futuro usando el precio que se acordó hoy (p. 333)

quantity supplied/cantidad ofrecida cantidad ofrecida en venta a un precio dado; punto en la curva de oferta (p. 115)

quantity theory of money/teoría de la cantidad del dinero hipótesis de que a largo plazo el abastecimiento de dinero afecta directamente el nivel del precio (p. 427)

quota/cuota límite de cantidad de bienes que se pueden permitir en un país (p. 472)

ration coupon/cupón de raciones certificado que permite al portador recibir una cantidad específica de un producto racionado (p. 139)

rationing/racionamiento sistema de distribución de bienes y servicios sin precios (p. 139)

raw materials/materias brutas recursos naturales sin procesar que se usan en la producción (p. 123)

real dollars/dólares reales ver dólares constantes (p. 218)

real estate investment trust/compañía fiduciaria de inversiones en bienes raíces compañía organizada para hacer préstamos a los constructores de casas (p. 316)

real GDP/PIB real Producto Interior Bruto después de ajustes para la inflación; igual que PIB en dólares constantes (p. 353)

real GDP per capita/PIB real per cápita   Producto Interior Bruto ajustado para la inflación y dividido por la población total; cantidad total de dólar de todo producto final producido para cada persona en el país después de compensar por la inflación (p. 363)

real rate of interest/tasa de interés real   la tasa de interés en el mercado menos la tasa de inflación (p. 428)

rebate/descuento   devolución parcial del precio original de un producto (p. 140)

recession/recesión   reducción en el PIB real que dura al menos dos trimestres o más (p. 376)

regressive tax/impuesto regresivo   impuesto en que un porcentaje del ingreso que se paga en imposiciones baja cuando los ingresos suben (p. 229)

Regulation Z/Regulación Z   provisión que extiende a los consumidores revelaciones de veracidad de préstamos (p. 411)

renewable resources/recursos renovables   recursos naturales que se pueden reabastecer para uso futuro (p. 366)

reserve requirement/requisito de reserva   fórmula que se usa para calcular la cantidad de reservas que requiere una institución depositoria (p. 415)

revenue tariff/tarifa de ingresos   impuesto sobre bienes importados para recaudar fondos (p. 473)

right-to-work law/ley de derecho al trabajo   ley estatal que hace ilegal el requerir que un trabajador sea miembro de una unión (p. 197)

risk/riesgo   situación en la cual el resultado no es cierto, pero las probabilidades se pueden estimar (p. 318)

Roth IRA/IRA Roth   cuenta individual de pensión en la cual las contribuciones están hechas después de impuestos así que ningún impuesto es tomado al vencimiento (p. 325)

run on the bank/pánico bancario   prisa repentina de los depositantes por sacar todos sus fondos, generalmente en anticipación al fallo o cierre del banco (p. 301)

rural population/población rural   aquellas personas que no viven en áreas urbanas (p. 357)

S&P 500   ver Standard & Poor 500 (p. 332)

saving/ahorrar   ausencia de gastos que libera los recursos para usarlos en otras actividades o inversiones (p. 313)

savings/ahorros   los dólares que se hacen disponibles para que los inversionistas los usen cuando otras personas ahorran (p. 313)

savings account/cuenta de ahorros   depósito que paga interés y que no requiere aviso previo antes de retirarse (p. 417)

savings and loan association/sociedad de ahorro y préstamo   institución depositoria que históricamente invierte la mayoría de sus fondos en hipotecas de casas (p. 303)

savings bank/banco de ahorros   institución de ahorros propiedad de los accionistas en vez de los depositantes (p. 303)

savings bond/bono de ahorros   bono, no transferible, de baja denominación emitido por el gobierno federal, usualmente a través de planes de ahorros de nómina (p. 323)

scarcity/escasez   problema económico fundamental que enfrentan todas las sociedades como resultado de una combinación de escasos recursos y las necesidades ilimitadas de la gente (p. 5)

seasonal unemployment/desempleo estacional   desempleo causado por cambios anuales en el clima y otras condiciones que prevalecen durante ciertas épocas del año (p. 386)

seat/asiento   afiliación en una bolsa de valores como la New York Stock Exchange (p. 330)

secondary market/mercado secundario   mercado en el que todos los bienes finacieros se pueden vender a alguien excepto al emisor original; bonos de empresa privada, bonos del gobierno (p. 326)

secondhand sales/ventas de segunda mano   venta de bienes usados; categoría de actividad no incluida en la computación del PIB (p. 343)

securities exchange/bolsa de valores   lugar físico donde los compradores y los vendedores se reunen para intercambiar valores (p. 329)

seizure/incautación   cuando el gobierno toma temporáneamente una compañía para mantenerla operando durante un conflicto obrero-patronal (p. 203)

selective credit controls/controles de crédito selectivo   reglas que atañen a préstamos para productos específicos o compras como requisitos marginales para acciones ordinarias (p. 424)

semiskilled labor/mano de obra semientrenada   trabajadores que pueden operar máquinas que requieren la mínima cantidad de entrenamiento (p. 206)

seniority/antigüedad   cantidad de tiempo que una persona ha estado en un puesto de trabajo (p. 208)

service/servicio   obra o trabajo efectuado por alguien; producto económico que incluye cortes de pelo, reparaciones del hogar, formas de entretenimiento (p. 13)

service cooperative/cooperativa de servicio   sociedad de consumidores sin fines de lucro que trata con servicios en vez de con bienes; incluye las cooperativas de crédito y algunas agencias de seguro y de crédito (p. 76)

set-aside contract/contrato de destinación especial   contrato o parte de un contrato garantizado reservado para un grupo señalado, usualmente un grupo minoritario (p. 215)

share draft/giro de acción   cuenta de cheques ofrecida por una cooperativa de crédito (p. 303)

shareholder/accionista   persona que es dueña de acciones en una corporación (p. 63)

short run/corto plazo   periodo de producción tan corto que sólo se pueden cambiar los insumos variables (p. 122)

shortage/escasez   situación donde la cantidad ofrecida es menor que la cantidad demandada a un precio dado (p. 144)

Glosario

signaling theory/teoría de señalización   teoría de que los empleadores estarán dispuestos a pagar más a personas con certificados, diplomas, postgrados y otros indicadores de destrezas superiores (p. 208)

silver certificate/certificado de plata   papel moneda respaldado y redimible con plata desde 1886 hasta 1968 (p. 295)

sin tax/impuesto de pecado   impuesto relativamente alto diseñado para recaudar ingresos y desanimar el consumo de productos socialmente indeseables (p. 224)

skilled labor/mano de obra adiestrada   trabajadores que pueden operar equipo complejo y que requieren poca supervisión (p. 206)

Social Security/Seguro Social   programa federal de beneficios de invalidez y retiro que cubre a la mayoría de las personas que trabajan (p. 42)

socialism/socialismo   sistema económico en el cual el gobierno es dueño de algunos factores de producción y tiene un papel en la determinación de qué bienes se producirán y cómo (p. 492)

soft loans/préstamos indulgentes   préstamos que tal vez nunca serán pagados, muchas veces hechos a países en desarrollo (p. 535)

sole proprietorship/propietario contable único de empresa   negocio no incorporado de la propiedad y operación de una sóla persona quien tiene el derecho a todas las ganancias y responsabilidades sin límite por todas las deudas de la firma; la forma más común de organización comercial en los Estados Unidos (p. 57)

Solidarity/Solidaridad   gremio obrero independiente de Polonia fundado en 1980 por Lech Walesa (p. 504)

specialization/especialización   asignación de tareas para que cada trabajador haga menos funciones más frecuentemente; igual que división de trabajo (p. 16)

specie/especie   dinero en la forma de monedas de oro o plata (p. 288)

spending caps/límites de gastos   límites en gastos discrecionales anuales (p. 278)

spot market/mercado de entrega immediata   mercado en el cual se hace una operación inmediatamente al precio imperante (p. 332)

stages of production/etapas de producción   fases de producción—aumento, disminución y rendimiento negativo (p. 125)

stagflation   combinación de estancamiento del crecimiento económico y la inflación (p. 437)

Standard & Poor's 500/Las 500 de Standard & Poor (S&L 500)   serie estadística de las 500 acciones que se usan para observar los precios en la bolsa de valores de la NYSE, American Stock Exchange y el mercado extrabursátil (p. 332)

standard of living/estándar de vida   calidad de vida basada en la propiedad de necesidades y lujos que hacen la vida más fácil (p. 24, 365)

state bank/banco del estado   banco que recibe su escritura de constitución del estado en que opera (p. 293)

state farm/granja del estado   granjas enormes de la propiedad y operación del estado en la antigua Unión Soviética (p. 497)

stock/acción   certificado de propiedad en una corporación; acciones preferidas y ordinarias (p. 63)

stockbroker/agente de bolsa   persona que compra y vende valores para los inversionistas (p. 329)

stockholder/accionista   La persona dueña de acciones de una corporación (p. 63)

store of value/fuente de valor   una de las tres funciones del dinero que permite a las personas que preserven el valor para uso futuro (p. 286)

storming/tempestear   práctica soviética de apresurar la producción al final del mes para cumplir las cuotas, con frecuencia resultando en la producción de chapucería (p. 498)

strike/huelga   paro del trabajo organizado por la unión diseñado para obtener concesiones del patrón (p. 195)

structural unemployment/desempleo estructural   desempleo causado por un cambio fundamental en la economía que reduce la demanda de algunos trabajadores (p. 385)

subsidy/subsidio   pago del gobierno para animar o proteger cierta actividad económica (p. 117)

subsistence/subsistencia   estado en que una sociedad escasamente produce lo suficiente para sostenerse (p. 546)

substitutes/sustitutos   productos de competición que se pueden intercambiar; productos relacionados de tal forma que un aumento en el precio de uno aumenta la demanda por los otros (p. 98)

substitution effect/efecto de sustitución   esa porción de un cambio en la cantidad de la demanda debido a un cambio en el precio relativo del producto (p. 96)

supply/oferta   curva de cantidades que se ofrecen a la venta a todos los precios posibles del mercado (p. 113)

supply curve/curva de oferta   gráfica de las cantidades producidas en cada uno de los precios del mercado (p. 114)

supply elasticity/elasticidad de oferta   sensibilidad de la cantidad ofrecida al cambio de precio (p. 118)

supply schedule/tabla de oferta   tabla que muestra las cantidades producidas u ofrecidas a la venta a cada precio del mercado (p. 114)

supply-side economics/economía de oferta   política económica diseñada para aumentar la oferta global o para desplazar la curva de oferta global hacia la derecha (p. 451)

surcharge/sobretasa   impuesto adicional o carga que se añade a otros cargos ya establecidos (p. 245)

surplus/superávit   situación en que la cantidad ofrecida es mayor que la cantidad demandada a un precio dado (p. 144)

takeoff/despegue   tercer etapa de desarrollo económico durante el cual las barreras de equilibrio primitivo se han vencido (p. 528)

target price/precio indicativo   precio más bajo de agricultura fijado por el gobierno para estabilizar los ingresos agrarios (p. 153)

tariff/tarifa   impuesto sobre productos importados (p. 472)

tax assessor/tasador de impuestos   persona que examina y evalúa propiedades para propósitos de impuestos (p. 241)

tax base/base impositiva   ingresos y propiedades que están potencialmente sujetas a impuestos locales, estatales y del gobierno federal (p. 366)

tax-exempt/exento de impuestos   ingresos de bonos u otras inversiones no sujetas a impuestos por el gobierno del estado y el federal (p. 323)

tax loophole/laguna tributaria   excepción o descuido en la ley de impuestos que permite que los contribuyentes eviten impuestos (p. 226)

tax return/declaración de impuestos   reporte anual que se registra con el gobierno local, el estatal o el federal y que detalla los ingresos que se ganaron y los impuestos que se deben (p. 232)

technological monopoly/monopolio tecnológico   situación mercantil en que una firma tiene el monopolio porque es propietaria de/o controla un método o un proceso de manufactura u otro adelanto científico (p. 170)

technological unemployment/desempleo tecnológico   desempleo causado por desarrollos tecnológicos o automatización que hace que las destrezas de algunos trabajadores sean obsoletas (p. 386)

theory of negotiated wages/teoría de salarios negociados   explicación de las escalas de salarios basada en la fuerza de negociación del movimiento sindical (p. 208)

theory of production/teoría de producción   teoría que trata con la relación entre los factores de producción y la producción de bienes y servicios (p. 122)

thrift institution/institución de pequeños ahorros   sociedades de ahorros y préstamo, bancos mutualista de ahorro y otras instituciones depositorias que históricamente han provisto a los ahorradores (p. 303)

tight money policy/política de dinero escaso   política monetaria que resulta en tasas de interés más altas y acceso restringido al crédito; se asocia con la contracción del abastecimiento de dinero (p. 419)

time deposit/depósito a plazo   depósito que paga intereses y que requiere previo aviso antes de poder sustraerlo, aunque no siempre se cumple el requisito (p. 417)

total cost/costo total   costo variable y costo fijo; todos los gastos asociados a la producción (p. 128)

total product/producto total   rendimiento o producción total de una firma (p. 123)

total revenue/ingreso total   total de recibos; precio de los bienes vendidos por la cantidad vendida (p. 130)

trade deficit/déficit comercial   resultados de la balanza de pagos cuando los gastos de las importaciones exceden los ingresos recibidos de las exportaciones (p. 484)

trade-offs/compensación   alternativas a las que hay que renunciar cuando se escoge una en lugar de otra (p. 19)

trade surplus/superávit de intercambio   la situación que ocurre cuando el valor de las exportaciones de una nación excede al valor de sus importaciones (p. 484)

trade union/sindicato gremial   ver sindicato de artesanos (p. 195)

trade-weighted value of the dollar/valor del dólar ponderado según el comercio exterior   índice que indica la fuerza del dólar americano contra la cesta de mercado de otras divisas (p. 484)

traditional economy/economía tradicional   sistema económico en el que la distribución de escasos recursos y otra actividad económica es el resultado de rito, hábito o costumbre (p. 34)

traditional theory of wage determination/teoría tradicional de determinación de salario   explicación del índice salarial basado en la teoría de oferta y demanda (p. 207)

transfer payment/transferencia de pago   pago por el cual el gobierno no recibe ni bienes ni servicios de vuelta (p. 257)

transparency/transparencia   hacer los negocios comerciales más visibles para todos, especialmente para los reguladores gubernamentales (p. 512)

Treasury bill/letra del Tesoro   bono de corto plazo del gobierno de los Estados Unidos que madura al año o menos, en denominaciones de \$10,000 (p. 324)

Treasury bond/bono del Tesoro   bono del gobierno de los Estados Unidos que madura entre 10 y 30 años (p. 324)

Treasury coin note/pagaré del Tesoro en moneda   papel moneda emitido desde 1890 hasta 1893, redimible tanto en oro o plata (p. 296)

Treasury note/pagaré del Tesoro   obligación del gobierno de los Estados Unidos que madura entre 2 a 10 años (p. 324)

trend line/tendencia   rumbo de crecimiento que seguiría la economía si no se interrumpiera por periodos alternantes de recesión y recuperación (p. 376)

trough/sima   punto en el tiempo cuando el PIB real deja de declinar y comienza a ensanchar (p. 376)

trust/sociedad fiduciaria   combinación ilegal de corporaciones o compañías que se organizan para impedir la competición (p. 178)

trust fund/fondo fiduciario   cuenta especial que se usa para retener ingresos designados para un gasto específico como el Seguro Social, medicare o las autopistas (p. 275)

two-tier wage system/sistema de salario de dos niveles   escala de salario que paga a los nuevos trabajadores un sueldo más bajo que a los que ya estaban trabajando (p. 212)

underground economy/economía subterránea   actividades ilegales sin reportar que no aparecen en las estadísticas del PIB (p. 343)

Glosario

unemployed/desempleado condición de trabajar por menos de una hora por semana por paga o provecho en un negocio que no es de la familia, en tanto que se está disponible y se ha hecho el esfuerzo de hallar trabajo durante el mes pasado (p. 382)

unemployment insurance/seguro de desempleo programa de gobierno que provee pagos a los desempleados; un estabilizador automático (p. 449)

unemployment rate/índice de desempleo relación de personas desempleadas dividida por el número total de personas en la fuerza de trabajo civil, expresado como un porcentaje (p. 383)

union shop/empresa de exclusividad gremial arreglo bajo el cual los trabajadores tienen que unirse a una unión tras ser empleados (p. 201)

unit elastic/elasticidad de la unidad elasticidad en que un cambio en la variable independiente (usualmente el precio) genera un cambio proporcional de la variable dependiente (cantidad demandada u ofrecida) (p. 103)

United States note/pagaré de los Estados Unidos papel moneda sin respaldo, emitida por el gobierno de los Estados Unidos inicialmente en 1862 para financiar la Guerra Civil (p. 295)

unlimited liability/responsabilidad sin límite requisito de que un propietario es personal y plenamente responsable por todas las pérdidas y deudas de un negocio; se aplica a propietarios, sociedades generales (p. 58)

unrelated individual/individuo no relacionado persona que vive sola o con personas que no son sus parientes aunque esa persona tenga parientes que vivan en otro lugar (p. 346)

unskilled labor/mano de obra no adiestrada trabajadores no entrenados para operar máquinas y equipo especializados (p. 205)

urban population/población urbana aquellas personas que viven en ciudades incorporadas, pueblos y aldeas con 2,500 ó más habitantes (p. 357)

user fee/tarifas para el usuario tarifa que se paga por usar unos bienes o servicios; forma de un impuesto de beneficio (p. 236)

utility/utilidad habilidad o capacidad de un bien o de un servicio para ser útil y darle satisfacción a alguien (p. 13)

value/valor valor de un bien o servicio según lo determina el mercado (p. 13)

value-added tax/impuesto de valor agregado impuesto sobre el valor agregado a cada etapa del proceso de producción (p. 247)

variable cost/costo variable costo de producción que varía según cambia la producción; la mano de obra, la energía, la materia prima (p. 128)

vertical merger/fusión vertical combinación de firmas envueltas en distintos pasos de la manufactura o el mercadeo (p. 71)

voluntary exchange/intercambio voluntario hecho en el cual los compradores y los vendedores participan libre y voluntariamente en operaciones mercantiles; característica del capitalismo y el libre comercio (p. 47)

wage-price controls/controles de salario-precio políticas y regulaciones que hacen ilegal el que las firmas den aumento o suban los precios (p. 454)

wage rate/escala de salarios escala de pago prevalente para trabajo efectuado en una cierta área o región (p. 207)

want/carencia modo de expresar o comunicar una necesidad; una clasificación más amplia que necesidades (p. 6)

wealth/riquezas suma de los bienes económicos tangibles que son escasos, útiles y transferibles de una persona a otra; excluye servicios (p. 14)

welfare/asistencia social programas del gobierno o de las agencias privadas que proveen asistencia económica y social a personas necesitadas (p. 397)

wholesale price index/índice de precios al por mayor ver índice de precio de productor (p. 352)

workfare programa que requiere que los beneficiarios de asistencia social provean trabajo en cambio por los beneficios (p. 398)

World Bank/Banco Mundial agencia internacional que hace préstamos a países en vías de desarrollo; antiguamente el Banco Internacional para Reconstrucción y Desarrollo (p. 526)

World Trade Organization (WTO)/Organización Mundial del Comercio (OMC) agencia internacional que administra convenios de comercio, arregla disputas comerciales entre gobiernos, organiza negociaciones de comercio, y proporciona asistencia técnica y entrenamiento para los países en desarrollo (p. 477)

zero population growth/crecimiento demográfico nulo condición en la que el número promedio de nacimientos y muertes se equilibran de modo que el tamaño de la población no cambia (p. 524)

¿Qué es la economía?

Sección 1

La escasez y la ciencia de la economía (páginas 5–10)

- El problema económico básico de la **escasez** es debido a la combinación de los deseos sin límites de la gente y los relativamente pocos recursos.
- En el mundo de pocos recursos, no hay tal cosa como una comida gratis (TINSTAAFL, siglas en inglés).
- Debido a la escasez la sociedad tiene que decidir QUÉ, CÓMO, y PARA QUIÉN producir.
- Tierra, capital, mano de obra, y empresarios son los cuatro **factores de producción** requeridos para producir las cosas que la gente usa. Los empresarios son individuos que aceptan riesgo para entrar al negocio con el fin de ganar beneficios. Los empresarios organizan los otros factores de producción.
- La economía tiene que ver con la descripción, análisis, explicación, y predicción.

Sección 2

Conceptos económicos básicos (páginas 12–17)

- Consumidores usan bienes y servicios para satisfacer sus deseos y necesidades.
- Algo tiene valor cuando tiene utilidad y es relativamente escaso.
- El caudal consiste de productos que son escasos, útiles, y transferibles a otros, pero el caudal no incluye servicios los cuales son intangibles.
- Los mercados unen los individuos con los negocios en el corriente circular de actividad económica. Los factores de producción son intercambiados en mercados de factores. **Bienes** y **servicios** son intercambiados en mercados de productos.
- La **productividad** y las inversiones en capital humano ayudan el crecimiento económico. Las inversiones en **capital humano** se cuentan entre las más beneficiosas de todas las inversiones.
- Aumentos en la especialización y la división de labor causan más interdependencia económica.

Sección 3

Opciones económicas y la toma de decisiones (páginas 19–25)

- El **costo de oportunidad** en hacer algo es la mejor alternativa próxima que pierdes, es decir el trueque.
- Una cuadrícula para tomar decisiones puede ser usada para ayudar en evaluar alternativas.
- Una **frontera de posibilidades de producción** muestra las varias posibles combinaciones de producción cuando todos los recursos son usados a lo máximo. La producción adentro de la frontera ocurre cuando algunos recursos quedan desempleados o no son usados a su capacidad máxima. Cuando ocurre el crecimiento económico, la frontera de posibilidades de producción se mueve para afuera. Así indica que más productos son producidos que antes.
- Pensar de manera económica significa la simplificación con la construcción de modelos, **el análisis de costos y beneficios** para evaluar alternativas, y la toma de decisiones en incrementos.
- Estudiando la economía te harás más capaz de tomar decisiones y te ayudarás entender tu mundo alrededor. Pero el estudio de la economía no te indicará qué decisiones tomar.

Sistemas económicos y adopción de decisiones

Sección 1
Sistemas económicos (páginas 33–39)

- Cada sociedad tiene una **economía** o sistema económico, una manera de distribuir bienes y servicios para responder a las preguntas de QUÉ, CÓMO, y PARA QUIÉN.
- En una **economía tradicional**, las decisiones económicas principales son tomadas según el costumbre. La vida en estas economías tiende a ser duradera, previsible, y constante.
- En una **economía por mandato**, el gobierno toma las decisiones económicas principales. Las economías por mandato pueden cambiar su dirección drásticamente en poco tiempo enfocándose a lo que sea que el gobierno quiere promover.
- Las economías por mandato tienden a tener poca libertad económica, pocos bienes para consumidores, y poco incertidumbre.
- En una **economía mercadera** las decisiones no son tomadas de manera centralizada. La gente y los negocios operan según sus propios intereses.
- Una economía mercadera se ajusta poco a poco a los cambios, tiene gran medida de libertad individual con poca interferencia gubernamental, es poca centralizada, y ofrece una gran variedad de bienes y servicios que ayudan a satisfacer los deseos y necesidades de los consumidores.

Sección 2
Evaluar la actuación económica (páginas 41–44)

- Las metas sociales y económicas de la sociedad estadounidense incluyen la libertad económica, eficiencia económica, equidad económica, seguridad económica, pleno empleo, estabilidad de precios, y crecimiento económico.
- Cuando las metas chocan, la sociedad evalúa el costo y el beneficio de cada meta para promover una meta sobre la otra. Muchos debates durante las elecciones reflejan estos conflictos y opciones.

Sección 3
El capitalismo y la libertad económica (páginas 46–51)

- El **capitalismo** es un sistema económico competitivo en el cual los ciudadanos privados son dueños de los factores de producción.
- Las cuatro características del capitalismo son **libertad económica**, **intercambio voluntario**, **derechos de propiedad privada**, y **el motivo de ganancias**. El empresario es el individuo que organiza tierra, capital, y mano de obra para la producción con la esperanza de ganancias. El motivo de ganancias es la fuerza conductora del capitalismo.
- La soberanía del consumidor dice que el consumidor es él que decide QUÉ bienes y productos producir.
- El gobierno nacional toma el papel de protector, proveedor, consumidor, regulador, y promotor de metas económicas.
- Estados Unidos tiene una economía mixta, es decir una **economía modificada de empresa privada**, en la cual sus ciudadanos conducen sus actividades económicas libremente pero con alguna intervención y reglamentación gubernamental.

Organizaciones comerciales

Sección 1

Formas de organización comercial (páginas 57–66)

- **Compañías de propiedad exclusiva** son pequeñas empresas con un solo dueño que son fáciles de manejar. Son relativamente numerosas y lucrativas. Las desventajas incluyen levantar capital financiero y atraer empleados cualificados.
- **Asociaciones comerciales** tienen dos dueños o más. Su tamaño mayor hace más fácil atraer capital financiero y trabajadores cualificados. Las desventajas incluyen la responsabilidad sin límite de cada socio general por las actividades de los otros socios, la duración limitada de la asociación comercial, y la posibilidad de conflicto entre los socios.
- **Sociedades anónimas** son de propiedad de los accionistas. Los accionistas votan para elegir la mesa directiva. Los accionistas llevan responsabilidad limitada y no son responsables por las actividades o las deudas de la corporación. El tamaño grande de la sociedad anónima permite las funciones especializadas y la producción a gran escala dentro de la compañía. Las desventajas de las sociedades anónimas incluyen el costo de obtener estatutos, la influencia limitada de los accionistas sobre la póliza de la corporación, y las reglamentaciones gubernamentales.
- La sociedad anónima es reconocida como una entidad legal independiente así que tiene que pagar impuestos sobre los ingresos que las compañías de propiedad exclusiva y las asociaciones comerciales no tienen que pagar.

Sección 2

Crecimiento y extensión comercial (páginas 68–73)

- Los negocios pueden crecer reinvertiendo su flujo de efectivo en la planta, el equipo, y nuevas tecnologías.
- Los negocios pueden crecer también por fusiones. Muchas fusiones se llevan a cabo porque los negocios quieren hacerse más grandes o eficientes, adquirir un producto nuevo, alcanzar o eliminar un competidor, o cambiar su identidad corporativa.
- Una **fusión horizontal** ocurre cuando se unen dos empresas semejantes. Una **fusión vertical** ocurre cuando se unen dos o más empresas de diferentes etapas de producción o mercadeo.

- Un **conglomerado** es un gran negocio que incluye a lo menos cuatro empresas diferentes ninguna de las cuales es responsable de la mayoría de las ventas. Un **negocio multinacional** puede ser una corporación regular o un conglomerado que tiene operaciones de producción o servicio en varios países. Los negocios multinacionales introducen nuevas tecnologías, crean empleos, y producen renta por medio de impuestos para los países anfitriones.

Sección 3

Otras organizaciones e instituciones (páginas 75–79)

- Muchas escuelas, instituciones de atención médica, e iglesias operan como organizaciones sin fin lucrativo. Estas organizaciones funcionan como negocios, pero no con el motivo de ganancias, para adelantar una causa o el bienestar de sus miembros.
- La **cooperativa** es una de las más importantes organizaciones sin fin lucrativo. La cooperativa puede ser organizada para proveer bienes y servicios o para ayudar a los productores.
- Asociaciones profesionales trabajan para mejorar las condiciones de trabajo, el nivel de destrezas, y la opinión pública de su profesión. Los negocios muchas veces forman una cámara de comercio o una agencia de mejores negocios (en inglés, Better Business Bureau) para promover sus intereses colectivos.
- El gobierno toma un papel directo en la economía cuando ése provee bienes y servicios directamente al consumidor. Toma un papel indirecto cuando provee la **Seguridad Social**, beneficios a veteranos, compensaciones para el desempleo, y asistencia financiera a los estudiantes universitarios, o cuando reglamenta el negocio.

Demanda

Sección 1
¿Qué es la demanda? (páginas 89–93)

- Tú expresas una **demanda** para un producto cuando estás listo y capaz de comprarlo.
- La demanda puede ser resumida en un inventario de demanda que muestra las varias cantidades que serían compradas en todos los precios posibles que pudieran prevalecer en el mercado.
- La demanda también puede ser mostrada gráficamente como una curva de demanda con inclinación hacia abajo.
- La **Ley de Demanda** refiere a la relación inversa entre el precio y la cantidad demandada.
- **Las individuales curvas de demanda** para los productos específicos pueden ser agregadas para obtener la curva de demanda mercadera. La utilidad decreciente del margen indica que la satisfacción disminuye con cada unidad adicional.

Sección 2
Factores que afectan la demanda (páginas 95–99)

- La demanda puede cambiar en dos maneras, un cambio en la cantidad demandada o un cambio en la demanda.
- Un **cambio en la cantidad demandada** quiere decir que la gente compra una cantidad diferente de un producto cuando cambia el precio del mismo. Este cambio se representa como movimiento a lo largo de la curva de demanda.
- Un **cambio en la demanda** quiere decir que la gente ha cambiado su opinión sobre la cantidad que querría comprar a cada precio. Este cambio se representa como un desplazamiento lateral de la curva de demanda hacia la derecha o izquierda.
- Un cambio de los ingresos, gustos, o expectativas de los consumidores junto con el cambio del precio de bienes relacionados tales como substituciones y complementos causan el cambio de la demanda.
- La curva de demanda mercadera cambia cuando unos consumidores entran o salen del mercado o cuando cambia la curva de demanda de un individuo.

Sección 3
Elasticidad de demanda (páginas 101–107)

- La **elasticidad** es una medida general que relaciona cambios en una variable dependiente tal como cantidad con cambios en una variable independiente tal como precio.
- La **elasticidad de demanda** relaciona cambios en la cantidad demandada con cambios en el precio.
- Si un cambio en el precio causa un cambio relativamente más pequeño en la cantidad demandada la demanda es inelástica.
- La demanda tiene elasticidad de unidad si un cambio en el precio causa un cambio proporcional en la cantidad demandada.
- La prueba del total de gastos puede ser usada para averiguar la elasticidad de demanda.
- La elasticidad de demanda es influenciada por la capacidad de posponer una compra, por las substituciones disponibles, y por la proporción de ingresos requerida por la compra.

Oferta

Sección 1
¿Qué es oferta? (páginas 113–120)

- La **oferta** es la cantidad de producción que los productores sacarán al mercado en cada precio. La oferta puede ser representada en un inventario de oferta o gráficamente como una curva de oferta.
- La **Ley de Oferta** establece que las cantidades de un producto económico ofrecido en venta varían directamente con su precio. Si los precios están altos, los proveedores ofrecerán cantidades más grandes para vender. Si los precios están bajos, ofrecerán cantidades más pequeñas para vender.
- La **curva de oferta mercadera** es la agregación de las individuales curvas de oferta.
- Un cambio en la cantidad ofrecida se representa por movimiento a lo largo de la curva de oferta.
- Un cambio en la oferta es un cambio en la cantidad que será ofrecida en cada precio. Un incremento en la oferta se representa gráficamente como un desplazamiento lateral en la curva de oferta hacia la derecha, y un decremento en la oferta aparece como un desplazamiento lateral en la curva de oferta hacia la izquierda.
- Los cambios en la oferta pueden ser causados por un cambio del costo de los factores de producción, productividad, nuevas tecnologías, impuestos, subsidios, expectativas, reglamentaciones gubernamentales, y el número de vendedores. La elasticidad de oferta describe cómo un cambio en la cantidad de producción responde a un cambio de precios.

Sección 2
La teoría de producción (páginas 122–125)

- La **teoría de producción** tiene que ver con la relación entre los factores de producción y la producción de bienes y servicios.
- La teoría de producción tiene que ver con el **corto plazo,** un período de producción tan corto que sólo el factor variable (generalmente la mano de obra) puede ser cambiado. Esto contrasta con el **largo plazo,** un período de producción bastante largo para que todos los factores inclusive el capital puedan variar.

- La **Ley de Proporciones Variables** establece que la cantidad de la producción variará de acuerdo con el incremento de las unidades de un solo factor. Esta ley se representa gráficamente en la forma de una función de producción. Las dos medidas más importantes de producción son el producto total y el producto marginal, la producción adicional que se obtiene agregando una unidad de uno de los factores.
- Las tres **etapas de producción**—utilidad creciente, utilidad decreciente, y utilidad negativa—muestran cómo cambia el producto marginal cuando adicionales factores variables son agregados. La producción se lleva a cabo en la segunda etapa bajo las condiciones de utilidad decreciente.

Sección 3
Oferta y el papel del costo (páginas 127–131)

- Existen cuatro medidas importantes del costo: **costo total** que es la suma del **costo fijo** y **costo variable**, y **costo marginal** que es el incremento en el costo total causado por una unidad adicional de producción. La mezcla de costos variables y fijos que tiene un negocio afecta la forma en que el negocio opera.
- La medida clave de ingresos es **ingreso marginal** que es el cambio del **ingreso total** cuando una unidad más de producción es vendida. El **análisis marginal** es una manera de tomar decisiones que compara los beneficios adicionales de una acción con sus costos adicionales.
- La **cantidad de producción para máxima ganancia** sucede cuando el costo marginal es exactamente igual al ingreso marginal. Puede ser que otras cantidades de producción proporcionan la mismas ganancias pero ninguna proporciona más.

Los precios y la toma de decisiones

Sección 1
Los precios como señales (páginas 137–140)
- Los **precios** sirven como señales para productores y consumidores. Así ayudan a decidir las tres preguntas básicas que todas las sociedades encaran, las de QUÉ, CÓMO, y PARA QUIÉN.
- Los altos precios son señales a los negocios para producir más y a los consumidores para comprar menos. Los bajos precios son señales a los negocios para producir menos y a los consumidores para comprar más. Los precios tienen las ventajas de neutralidad, flexibilidad, eficiencia, y claridad.
- Pueden ser usados otros métodos de reparto no relacionados al precio tal como el racionamiento. Bajo tal sistema la gente recibe cupones de racionamiento que son similares a boletos o recibos que dan derecho a comprar cierta cantidad de un producto.
- Sistemas de reparto no relacionados al precio sufren de problemas de imparcialidad, altos costos administrativos e incentivos disminuidos para trabajar y producir.
- Una economía mercadera es elaborada de muchos diferentes mercados y diferentes precios prevalecen en cada uno de ellos. Un cambio en el precio en uno de los mercados afecta más que el reparto de recursos en ese mercado. También afecta el reparto de recursos entre los mercados.

Sección 2
El sistema de precios trabajando (páginas 142–148)
- Los economistas a menudo usan un **modelo económico** para analizar actuación y predecir resultados. Los modelos de mercados económicos se representan frecuentemente por curvas de oferta y demanda para examinar el concepto **de equilibrio del mercado**, una situación en la cual los precios son relativamente estables y la cantidad de producción ofrecida es igual a la cantidad demandada.
- En un mercado competitivo, los precios son establecidos por las fuerzas de oferta y demanda. Si el precio es muy alto, un superávit temporal aparece hasta que el precio baja. Si el precio es muy bajo, un déficit temporal aparece hasta que el precio sube. Eventualmente el mercado alcanza el **precio de equilibrio** donde no existe ni déficit ni superávit.

- Un cambio del el precio puede ser causado por un cambio de la oferta o un cambio de la demanda. El tamaño del cambio del precio está afectado por la elasticidad de ambas curvas. Cuanto más elásticas son las curvas, tanto más pequeño es el cambio en el precio. Cuanto menos elásticas las curvas, tanto más grande es el cambio en el precio.
- La **teoría del precio competitivo** representa un conjunto de condiciones y resultados ideales. La teoría sirve como modelo para medir la actuación de otros mercados menos competitivos así que la pura y absoluta competencia no es necesaria para que la teoría de precios competitivos sea práctica.

Sección 3
Metas sociales contra la eficiencia del mercado (páginas 150–155)
- Algunas veces los gobiernos fijan precios en niveles arriba y debajo del precio del equilibrio para completar las metas sociales de equidad y seguridad.
- Si el precio fijado es un límite al precio como controles de alquiler, generalmente ocurre una escasez mientras el precio permanezca fijo bajo el precio del equilibrio.
- El apoyo a los precios agrícolas fue introducido durante los años 1930 para apoyar a los ingresos de los agricultores. Programas de préstamos sin recurso permitían a los agricultores tomar préstamos usando las cosechas como prenda y luego quedarse con el dinero perdiendo la cosecha si los precios del mercado estuvieran bajos.
- Más tarde pagos de deficiencia fueron usados para dar a los agricultores un cheque para la diferencia entre el precio objetivo y el precio recibido por el producto.
- El Congreso aprobó la ley FAIR (siglas en inglés) en 1996 con el motivo de dejar la agricultura más sensible a las fuerzas mercaderas. Los pagos bajo esta ley están para terminar en el año 2002.

Estructuras del mercado

Sección 1

La competencia y las estructuras mercaderas
(páginas 163–171)

- La **competencia perfecta** es una estructura mercadera con grandes números de compradores y vendedores, productos económicos idénticos, acciones independientes por los compradores y los vendedores, participantes bien informados, y libertad para que las empresas entren y salgan del mercado.
- La competencia perfecta es una situación teórica usada como modelo para evaluar otras estructuras mercaderas. Las situaciones del mercado que faltan una o más de estas condiciones son llamadas competencia imperfecta.
- La **competencia monopolista** tiene todas las características de la competencia perfecta salvo los productos idénticos.
- El **oligopolio** es una estructura mercadera dominada por unas pocas empresas muy grandes. Las actividades de una de ellas afectan el bienestar de las otras.
- El **monopolista** es un solo productor con el mayor control sobre la oferta y el precio. Varias formas de monopolio incluyen el monopolio natural, el monopolio geográfico, el monopolio tecnológico, y el monopolio gubernamental.
- Todas las empresas privadas sin importar la estructura del mercado dan máximas ganancias produciendo al nivel en el cual el costo marginal es igual al ingreso marginal.

Sección 2

Fallas del mercado (páginas 173–176)

- Las **fallas del mercado** suceden cuando se llevan a cabo grandes desviaciones de una o más de las condiciones requeridas para la competencia perfecta.
- Tres de las cinco fallas comunes del mercado incluyen competencia inadecuada, información inadecuada, e inmovilidad de recursos.
- Las **externalidades**, es decir los efectos económicos hacia otros partidos, son la cuarta falla del mercado. Una externalidad negativa es un efecto dañoso y una externalidad positiva es un efecto beneficioso.
- Las externalidades se entienden como fallas del mercado porque no se reflejan en los precios mercaderos de las actividades que causaron los efectos.

- Finalmente, una economía mercadera a menudo falla para proveer bienes públicos tales como la defensa nacional y la educación publica porque éstos no pueden negarse a aquellos que se rehusan a pagar.

Sección 3

El papel del gobierno (páginas 178–183)

- La Ley Anticártel de Sherman de 1890 fue aprobada para prohibir cárteles, monopolios y otros arreglos que restringen la competencia. La Ley Anticártel de Clayton fue aprobada en 1914 para prohibir la **discriminación de precios**. La Ley de Robinson y Patman de 1936 fue aprobada para reforzar las cláusulas de la Ley Anticártel de Clayton en contra de la discriminación de precios.
- Las declaraciones públicas son usadas como instrumento para promover la competencia. Toda corporación que vende sus acciones públicamente es requerida para proveer reportes financieros periódicos a sus inversionistas y a la SEC (siglas en inglés).
- Los bancos operan bajo adicionales leyes de declaración pública y se reportan a varias agencias federales.
- Hoy día el gobierno participa en los asuntos económicos para promover y fomentar la competencia así que la economía moderna es una mezcla de diferentes estructuras mercaderas, diferentes formas de organización comercial, y alguna reglamentación gubernamental.

Empleo, mano de obra y salarios

Sección 1
El movimiento laboral (páginas 193–198)
- Gremios y sindicatos industriales fueron establecidos para el final de la Guerra Civil.
- Existían desfavorables actitudes públicas hacia la mano de obra. La Ley Anticártel de Sherman fue usado en contra de la mano de obra y hasta las cortes ignoraron la Ley de Clayton.
- Las actitudes cambiaron a favor de la mano de obra durante la **Gran Depresión** con la aprobación de la Ley de Norris y LaGuardia, la Ley de Wagner, y la Ley de Normas Justas para Trabajadores.
- La opinión pública volvió a cambiar en contra de la mano de obra después de la Segunda Guerra Mundial. La Ley de Taft y Hartley en 1947 limitó la actividad de los sindicatos y permitió a los estados a aprobar leyes de derecho al trabajo.
- El movimiento sindical fue dominado por la AFL y la CIO, las cuales eventualmente se unieron para formar la AFL-CIO en 1955.

Sección 2
Resolución de disputas entre los sindicatos y la dirección (páginas 200–203)
- El **taller cerrado** (ahora ilegal) requiere que los patrones contratan solamente a miembros del sindicato seleccionados por el sindicato. **El taller sindical** requiere que un empleado se una al sindicato poco después de haber sido contratado. El taller sindical modificado da al empleado la opción para unirse a la unión después de haber sido contratado. La taller de agencia requiere que los trabajadores paguen su cuota al sindicato sin requerirlos hacerse miembros aunque el sindicato representa a todos los trabajadores.
- Cuando falla la **negociación colectiva**, varios otros métodos están disponibles para resolver debates laborales incluso la mediación, el arbitraje, la investigación de hechos, los mandatos judiciales y las incautaciones.

Sección 3
Mano de obra y salarios (páginas 205–209)
- Las cuatro clases laborales son **mano de obra no entrenada**, **mano de obra semientrenada**, **mano de obra entrenada**, y **mano de obra profesional**. Éstas no compiten una contra la otra.
- Generalmente los trabajadores encuentran dificultades para cambiar a un grupo de mayor ingresos por causa del costo de educación y entrenamiento, la falta de oportunidades de educación y entrenamiento y la falta de iniciativa individual.
- La **teoría tradicional de determinación de salarios** usa las fuerzas mercaderas de oferta y demanda para explicar el índice de salarios. La **teoría de salarios negociados** establece que la fuerza de un sindicato es un factor. La teoría de señalización dice que certificados y diplomas son señales de capacidad.
- Los salarios también difieren por la movilidad de la mano de obra, el costo de vida, y atractivos lugares de trabajo.

Sección 4
Asuntos y tendencias de empleo (páginas 211–218)
- La membrecía sindical ha disminuido por causa de las actividades antisindicalistas de las compañías, nuevas adiciones a la fuerza laboral con poca lealtad hacia el sindicato, y sindicatos que han demandado salarios muy altos para el mercado.
- Medidas correctivas incluyen leyes de antidiscriminación, el principio de va lor comparativo, y contratos apartados.
- Los empleos de tiempo parcial están incrementando y proveen a los empleadores opciones flexibles de costo bajo.
- **El salario mínimo** ha perdido mucho de su poder adquisitivo por causa de la inflación. También se queda atrás midiéndose como porcentaje del salario promedio de manufactura.

Fuentes de renta gubernamental

Sección 1
La economía de los impuestos (páginas 223–229)
- Los impuestos afectan el reparto de recursos, la actuación y el crecimiento económico.
- La **incidencia de un impuesto**, es decir la carga final del impuesto, es afectada por la elasticidad. Cuando la demanda para un producto es elástica, menos del impuesto puede ser cargado al comprador. Cuando la demanda es inelástica, más del impuesto puede ser cargado al comprador.
- La equidad, la simplicidad y la eficiencia son los criterios usados para juzgar la efectividad de un impuesto.
- Dos principios han sido usados para seleccionar el grupo o grupos que se hacen cargo del impuesto: el principio del beneficio del impuesto y el principio de la capacidad de pagar el impuesto. Ambos principios involucran el juicio y ambos clases de impuestos son ampliamente usados hoy en día.
- Los impuestos pueden ser clasificados en tres grupos-impuestos proporcionales, impuestos progresivos e impuestos regresivos. La clasificación depende de la forma en que la carga del impuesto cambia mientras los ingresos cambian.

Sección 2
El sistema federal de impuestos (páginas 231–236)
- La fuente principal de renta para el gobierno federal es el impuesto sobre ingresos individuales.
- La regulación es usada para cambiar las tarifas marginales de los impuestos para compensar los efectos de la inflación.
- La segunda fuente de renta es el impuesto FICA (siglas en inglés) recaudado para pagar el Seguro Social y la asistencia médica (medicare). El impuesto sobre ingresos corporativos es la tercer fuente de renta federal.
- Otras fuentes de renta federal incluyen impuestos indirectos, impuestos sobre regalos, tributos aduanales y la cuota al usuario que es otro nombre para un impuesto sobre beneficios.

Sección 3
Sistemas de impuestos estatales y locales (páginas 238–242)
- **Renta intergubernamental** es la fuente más grande de rentas estatales.
- Los gobiernos locales reciben renta intergubernamental de los gobiernos estatales y federal. Los gobiernos locales también recaudan rentas por medio de impuestos sobre propiedad, servicios públicos, licores, ventas, y otras fuentes.
- El estado de cuenta de deducciones del salario adjunto a un cheque de pago de salario semanal, quincenal o mensual incluye un resumen del salario, impuestos y otras deducciones aplicadas.

Sección 4
Reforma y asuntos de impuestos (páginas 244–250)
- El **impuesto al valor agregado** (VAT, siglas en inglés) es un impuesto sobre el consumo más bien que el ingreso. Está calculado en cada etapa de producción.
- La Ley de Impuestos para la Recuperación Económica de 1981 bajó las tarifas marginales de impuestos para todos los niveles de ingresos, proporcionó la depreciación acelerada y el crédito al impuesto por inversiones para negocios.
- La ley de reforma de impuestos de 1986 cerró los pretextos que fueron abiertos en 1981 y redujo el código del impuesto sobre ingresos individuales a dos categorías.
- La Ley de Reducción del Déficit Presupuestario de 1993 agregó dos categorías marginales de impuestos, así restaurando la característica progresiva del impuesto removida en 1986.
- La Ley de Alivio al Contribuyente de 1997 proporcionó a los ricos una baja de impuestos por inversiones a largo plazo y proporcionó algún alivio de los impuestos para gente con gastos educacionales y niños.
- La ley de impuestos de 2001 de Presidente Bush proporciona una baja de $1.35 millones sobre un período de 10 años.
- Un **impuesto fijo** es un impuesto proporcional sobre el ingreso individual después de haber alcanzado el ingreso especificado.

Gastos gubernamentales

Sección 1

La economía de gastos gubernamentales
(páginas 255–258)
- Gastos gubernamentales toman la forma de desembolsos sobre productos y servicios, de los cuales la mayoría son bienes públicos, y sobre pagos de transferencia tales como otorgamientos por los cuales el gobierno no recibe nada a cambio.
- Gastos gubernamentales influyen el sector privado afectando el reparto de recursos, la distribución de ingresos y compitiendo contra el sector privado por recursos escasos.

Sección 2

Desembolsos del gobierno federal (páginas 260–265)
- El presidente es responsable para desarrollar el **presupuesto federal** para el año fiscal que comienza en octubre. Cuando el presupuesto está listo es enviado a la Cámara de Representantes.
- La Cámara solamente trata los gastos discrecionales. **Gastos obligatorios** no son parte del proceso presupuestario anual, pero el Congreso puede tratarlos aparte.
- **Gastos discrecionales** son desglosados para que los varios comités propongan leyes de apropiación. Entonces las partes del presupuesto son reunidas y el presupuesto es votado por la Cámara y el Senado. Si surgen diferencias entre la Cámara y el Senado, un ley de compromiso es desarrollada en la cual ambos votan.
- Los componentes más grandes del presupuesto federal son el Seguro Social, la defensa nacional, seguridad de ingresos, asistencia médica, interés neto sobre la deuda federal, y la salud.

Sección 3

Desembolsos de gobiernos estatales y locales
(páginas 267–270)
- Los presupuestos estatales pasan un proceso de aprobación que es diferente de un estado al otro. Las categorías más grandes de gastos estatales son desembolsos intergubernamentales, beneficios públicos, fideicomiso de seguros, y educación superior. Otros gastos incluyen carreteras, hospitales, e intereses sobre la deuda estatal.

- La categoría más grande de gastos de gobiernos locales es la educación primaria y secundaria. Siguen los servicios públicos, hospitales, protección policiaca, intereses sobre la deuda, beneficios públicos, y carreteras.

Sección 4

Déficits federales y la deuda nacional
(páginas 272–278)
- Los déficits del presupuesto federal existían desde 1970 hasta 1998 cuando el presupuesto finalmente tuvo superávit.
- Los déficits se agregan a la deuda federal y el total de la deuda alcanzó $5.7 trillones en el año fiscal de 2001, de los cuales aproximadamente $3.3 trillones son retenidos por el público.
- La **deuda nacional** es diferente de la deuda privada en lo que es dinero que nos lo debemos a nosotros mismos. La excepción es el 15 al 20 por ciento de la deuda que es retenida por los inversionistas extranjeros. La deuda afecta a la economía de varias maneras. Los impuestos son necesarios para pagar el interés de la deuda. La distribución de ingresos es alterada. El poder de compra es transferido desde el sector privado hacia el sector público. Los incentivos para trabajar, para ahorrar, y para invertir también pueden ser alterados.
- Las tasas de interés pueden subir cuando el gobierno compite contra el sector privado por fondos.
- La Ley de Reconciliación Presupuestaria de 1993, el fuerte crecimiento económico a mediados de los años 1990 y los límites de gastos de 1997 causaron un superávit presupuestario en 1998.
- A pesar de los recientes superávits presupuestarios, el presupuesto federal total mostraría un déficit si no por los superávits en el Fondo Fideicomisario del Seguro Social.
- El crecimiento rápido de los derechos financieros es todavía una amenaza para los futuros superávits presupuestarios. Estos programas son considerados gastos obligatorios, pero pueden ser revisados si el Congreso lo decide así.

El dinero y la banca

Sección 1
La evolución del dinero (páginas 285–290)
- El dinero es cualquier substancia que sirve como **medio de intercambio**, **medida de valor**, y **depósito de valor**.
- Trueque de mercancía, wampum, metálico, y papel moneda expedida por gobiernos e individuos privados fueron usados ampliamente en la América colonial.
- El Congreso Continental expidió grandes cantidades de dólares continentales para financiar la Revolución Americana. Por la expedición excesiva el dinero quedó sin valor para el final de la guerra.
- El dólar estadounidense fue basado en el peso español el cual fue importado de las Indias Occidentales.
- Todos las monedas exitosas son portátiles y tienen durabilidad, divisibilidad, y disponibilidad limitada.

Sección 2
La primera banca y normas monetarias (páginas 292–298)
- Desde la Revolución Americana hasta 1861, el papel moneda fue expedido por bancos privados regulados por el estado. El gobierno federal expidió monedas pero no papel moneda.
- Eventualmente la variedad de billetes privados hizo difícil el uso del abasto de moneda. Los bancos ilícitos y fraudulentos a menudo abusaron el privilegio de la impresión de la moneda.
- El gobierno vendió bonos y entonces imprimió billetes verdes para financiar la Guerra Civil.
- En 1863 el Sistema Nacional de la Banca fue establecido para fortalecer el sistema bancario y para generar nuevas demandas para bonos gubernamentales. Más tarde, otros tipos de monedas federales se hicieron populares, incluso los certificados de oro, certificados de plata, y pagarés de monedas de la Tesorería.
- El patrón oro fue adoptado en 1900. Entonces todas las monedas fueron convertibles en oro a su presentación inclusive billetes de la Reserva Federal. Sin embargo, el país abandonó el patrón oro en 1934 porque las reservas de oro bajaron durante la Gran Depresión.

- Después de 1934 los americanos no podían convertir los dólares en oro. Hoy en día, muchos gobiernos manejan la calidad, tamaño, composición, y disponibilidad de su moneda. La mayoría de monedas modernas funcionan bien como medio de intercambio y son portátiles, duraderas, divisibles, y bastante estables en su valor.

Sección 3
El desarrollo de la banca moderna (páginas 300–305)
- El **Sistema Nacional de la Banca** trajo uniformidad a la banca. Los bancos nacionales también expidieron su propia moneda conocida como billetes del Banco Nacional. Los bancos regulados por los estados que decidieron no unirse a este sistema abandonaron la impresión de moneda a favor de cuentas de depósito a la vista.
- El **Sistema de Reserva Federal** (Fed) fue establecido en 1913, dando al país un verdadero banco central. Todos los bancos nacionales fueron requeridos a unirse con la Reserva Federal y todos los bancos estatales también fueron invitados a unirse.
- A pesar de la Reserva Federal, durante la Gran Depresión ocurrieron quiebras masivas de la banca.
- Otras instituciones depositarias, es decir, bancos de ahorros mutuos, asociaciones de crédito, y asociaciones de préstamos y ahorros, aparecieron para servir a los pequeños inversionistas ignorados por los bancos comerciales.
- En los años 1980 el quite de reglamentaciones, las altas tasas de interés, las reservas financieras inadecuadas, y el fraude redujeron el número de asociaciones de préstamos y ahorros hasta que quedaron la mitad de las que antes había.
- La crisis financiera había terminado para el final de la década. En los años 1990 se vio el continuo crecimiento de las semejanzas entre los bancos comerciales, bancos de ahorros, y asociaciones de préstamos y ahorros.

Mercados financieros

Sección 1
El ahorro y el sistema financiero (páginas 313–316)
- El **ahorro** es un proceso que hace los **ahorros** disponibles para que otros los inviertan.
- La economía tiene un sistema financiero que transfiere los ahorros a los inversionistas.
- Los activos financieros son generados por el proceso y son expedidos por individuos, empresas, y gobiernos.
- Los **intermediarios financieros** ayudan a facilitar las transferencias de fondos desde los ahorradores hacia otros inversionistas. Los intermediarios financieros incluyen compañías financieras, compañías de seguros de vida, fondos mutualistas, fondos de pensión, y garantías de inversiones de bienes raíces (REITs, siglas en inglés). Estas instituciones son parte del sistema financiero aunque no aceptan depósitos como bancos comerciales, bancos de ahorros, o asociaciones de crédito.

Sección 2
Estrategias de inversión y haberes financieros (páginas 318–326)
- Los inversionistas generalmente requieren mayores ganancias para compensar las situaciones con más **riesgo**.
- Los inversionistas exitosos analizan sus objetivos, invierten consistentemente, y evitan la complejidad.
- Los planes **401(k)** son inversiones populares que ofrecen la simplicidad y ganancias bastante altas.
- Los bonos son activos financieros populares. Los tres componentes de los bonos son el rendimiento del cupón, el vencimiento, y el valor a la par. El rendimiento corriente es una medida de ganancias de los bonos. Las solvencias de los bonos son también ampliamente disponibles y pueden ser usados como medida del riesgo del bono.
- Los **mercados financieros** son nombrados por las características de los activos que son intercambiados en los mismos. Los **mercados de capital** tienen activos financieros con vencimientos de más de un año. Los mercados de dinero tienen activos con vencimientos de menos de un año.
- Los activos intercambiados en mercados primarios son aquellos que tienen que ser pagados por el expedidor.

Sección 3
Inversiones en acciones, futuros, y opciones (páginas 328–333)
- Las acciones son diferentes de los activos financieros porque ésas representan la propiedad de una corporación más bien que un préstamo a la misma.
- Como la bolsa es bastante eficiente, la mayoría de los inversionistas diversifican su portafolio para protegerse en contra de los riesgos. Muchas acciones son intercambiadas en bolsas organizadas tales como NYSE, AMEX, y varias bolsas regionales.
- La mayoría de las acciones son intercambiadas en un mercado computarizado compuesto de vendedores organizados llamado el mercado de acciones no cotizadas. Estas acciones representan las compañías nuevas o pequeñas que no pudieron inscribirse en NYSE.

Actuación económica

Sección 1

Medición del ingreso y el producto de la nación (páginas 341–348)

- El **producto doméstico bruto** (GDP, siglas en inglés) es la medida más completa del producto total.
- El GDP no incluye productos intermedios y ventas de segunda mano, actividades fuera del mercado y actividades de la economía clandestina que no son reportadas.
- El **producto nacional bruto** (GNP) es la medida del ingreso total recibido por los ciudadanos americanos sin importar dónde sean localizados los recursos productivos.
- Otras medidas de ingresos son el producto nacional neto, ingreso nacional, ingreso personal, e ingreso personal disponible que aparece como el pago final en los cheques de pago.
- Los cuatro sectores de la macroeconomía son el consumidor, la inversión, el gobierno, y los sectores en extranjero.
- El modelo de producción y gastos, GDP = C + I + G + F, es utilizado para mostrar cómo GDP es consumido por los cuatros sectores de la economía.

Sección 2

GDP y cambios en el nivel de precios (páginas 350–354)

- El **índice de precios** analiza los cambios de los precios a través del tiempo y elimina de las otras estadísticas las distorsiones de inflación. El índice de precios es calculado dividiendo los precios actuales de la canasta básica del mercado por los precios del año base y multiplicando el resultado por 100.
- Tres índices populares son el **índice de precios al consumidor**, el **índice de precios al productor**, y el **desvalorizador de precios implícito de GDP**. GDP actual es convertido a GDP real, o GDP del dólar constante, dividiendo del número sin ajustar por el índice de precios y multiplicando el resultado por 100.

Sección 3

GDP y la población (páginas 356–361)

- El crecimiento anual de la población fue más del 3 por ciento hasta la Guerra Civil, pero ha disminuido sin interrupción hasta el 0.9 por ciento anual de hoy.
- Los factores que contribuyen al cambio de la población son la tasa de natalidad, la expectativa de vida, y la inmigración neta.
- La mezcla racial y étnica cambiará con incrementos de los americanos asiáticos, los hispanoamericanos, y los afroamericanos de manera que el componente anglo de la población apenas será la mayoría para mediados del siglo.

Sección 4

Crecimiento económico (páginas 363–368)

- **GDP real per cápita** es utilizado para medir el crecimiento económico a largo plazo.
- El crecimiento económico aumenta la norma de vida, aumenta la base para impuestos, aumenta el empleo, y ayuda a las economías de otras naciones. El crecimiento económico requiere un amplio abasto de recursos productivos especialmente empresarios para organizar la producción y hacer crecer la economía.
- **La productividad laboral** está incrementando de nuevo, así ayudando a elevar el crecimiento económico y la norma de vida.

Inestabilidad económica

Sección 1

Fluctuaciones y ciclos comerciales (páginas 375–380)

- Los **ciclos comerciales** son incrementos y decrementos sistemáticos en GDP real. Las fluctuaciones comerciales son incrementos y decrementos no sistemáticos.
- Las dos fases del ciclo son la recesión y la expansión. El máximo ocurre cuando la expansión termina, y el mínimo ocurre cuando la recesión termina.
- La Gran Depresión de los años 1930 fue la peor caída económica en la historia de Estados Unidos. La desigualdad de la distribución del ingreso, prácticas arriesgadas de crédito, débiles condiciones económicas internacionales, y guerras de tarifas contribuyeron a la Depresión. Varias recesiones cortas y no severas han ocurrido desde la Segunda Guerra Mundial.
- Los ciclos comerciales son causados por cambios en gastos de capital e inventario por las empresas, estímulos proporcionados por innovaciones e imitaciones, factores monetarios, y choques externos.
- Los modelos econométricos y el índice de indicadores mayores son utilizados para predecir cambios en la actividad económica futura.

Sección 2

El desempleo (páginas 382–387)

- Las personas desempleadas son identificadas mensualmente por el Departamento del Censo. El número de desempleados es dividido por la fuerza laboral civil para expresar el desempleo como un porcentaje.
- El **índice de desempleo** no cuenta los retiros ni distingue empleo de tiempo parcial de empleo de tiempo completo.
- Diferentes formas de desempleo son el desempleo friccional, estructural, cíclico, temporal, y tecnológico.
- Plena empleo se alcanza cuando el índice de desempleo baja a menos del 4.5 por ciento.

Sección 3

La inflación (páginas 389–392)

- La **inflación** es el porcentaje de cambio en el nivel de precios como se ha medido por CPI. El desvalorizador de precios implícito de GDP y el índice de precios al productor también pueden ser utilizados para medir la inflación. La inflación lenta, la inflación rápida, y la hiperinflación son términos usados para describir la severidad de la inflación.

- Las condiciones generosas de crédito y el excesivo crecimiento del abastecimiento de la moneda permiten la influencia por la demanda, gastos déficits, presión sobre costos, e inflación espiral de precios y salarios.
- La inflación desgasta el valor del dólar, hace la vida difícil para la gente de ingresos fijos, cambia los costumbres de gastos de consumidores y empresas y altera la distribución del ingreso a favor de los deudores.

Sección 4

La pobreza y distribución del ingreso (páginas 394–400)

- La distribución del ingreso es medida categorizando los ingresos familiares desde los más bajos hasta los más altos y dividiendo el resultado entre quintiles. El ingreso ganado por cada quintil es entonces comparado.
- La **curva de Lorenz** muestra que los ingresos no son distribuidos con igualdad, y que han llegado a ser menos iguales a través del tiempo.
- Los factores responsables de la distribución desigual del ingreso incluyen el nivel de educación, la riqueza, la discriminación, la capacitación, y el poder de monopolio.
- La pobreza está determinada comparando el índice de la pobreza con el ingreso familiar.
- La creciente desigualdad del ingreso se debe a la mayor importancia de la industria de servicio, la creciente desigualdad de capacitación de trabajadores, la caída del sindicalismo, y la composición cambiante de la familia americana.

La Reserva Federal y la póliza monetaria

Sección 1

El Sistema de la Reserva Federal (páginas 407–413)

- El **Sistema de la Reserva Federal** fue establecido como el banco central de la nación en 1913.
- Fed es único en lo que los propietarios son miembros bancos privados más bien que el gobierno.
- Hoy día, Fed regula las instituciones financieras, mantiene el sistema de pagos, refuerza las leyes de protección al consumidor, provee servicios al gobierno, y conduce la póliza monetaria.
- Fed supervisa sus miembros bancos estatales y lleva amplia autoridad sobre las compañías tenedoras bancarias, operaciones internacionales de todos los bancos comerciales, algunas fusiones, compensación de cheques, leyes para proteger al consumidor al tomar préstamos, y el mantenimiento de la moneda de la nación.

Sección 2

Política monetaria (páginas 415–424)

- Los bancos modernos operan sobre un sistema fraccional de reserva. Bajo este sistema las reservas excesivas pueden ser prestadas a otros clientes. Los **bancos comerciales** cargan intereses sobre sus préstamos. Utilizan los ingresos para pagar gastos y guardan los excedentes como ganancias.
- El magnitud del abasto monetario está determinado por el requerimiento de reserva y las reservas en el sistema. Un incremento en el requerimiento de reserva encogerá el abasto monetario. Un decremento en el requerimiento de la reserva expandirá el abasto monetario.
- La **póliza monetaria** afecta la magnitud del abasto monetario y en consecuencia el nivel de las tasas de interés.
- Las herramientas de la póliza monetaria incluyen un cambio en el requerimiento de reserva, operaciones en mercados abiertos las cuales involucran la compra y venta de bonos gubernamentales, y un cambio en la tasa de descuento.
- Dos herramientas menores incluyen la persuasión moral y controles de crédito selectivos tales como requerimientos de margen.

Sección 3

La póliza monetaria, la banca, y la economía (páginas 426–431)

- La póliza monetaria afecta las tasas de interés a corto plazo y la inflación a largo plazo. Esto requiere que Fed encara la opción de bajos intereses hoy con mayor inflación más tarde.
- El impacto de la póliza monetaria varía. Algunas veces afecta la economía más pronto, algunas veces más tarde. La póliza monetaria también afecta algunos factores de la economía diferentemente que afecta otros.
- La tasa de interés afecta al reparto de recursos entre el uso en el presente y en el futuro. Las expectativas de la inflación también afectan el reparto de recursos entre el uso en el presente y en el futuro.
- La tasa de interés es una de los precios más visibles y políticamente sensibles en la economía. Por razones políticas, a menudo Fed se encuentra bajo presión de conservar bajas tasas de interés aunque causará la inflación en el futuro.

Logrando la estabilidad económica

Sección 1
El costo de la inestabilidad económica
(páginas 437–440)
- El bajo crecimiento e inestabilidad de la economía en forma de inflación y altos índices de desempleo llevan costos económicos y sociales. Los costos económicos pueden ser medidos con el **índice de miseria** o la desigualdad de GDP.
- Los costos sociales incluyen el desempleo, recursos perdidos, posible inestabilidad política, incremento del crimen, y el daño a los valores familiares.
- El fuerte crecimiento económico es más que un ideal económico. Es uno de los fundamentos de una sociedad saludable.

Sección 2
Equilibrio macroeconómico (páginas 442–445)
- El equilibrio macroeconómico es similar al equilibrio en los mercados individuales. Puede ser analizado con **curvas agregadas de oferta** y **curvas agregadas de demanda**.
- Muchos de los factores que influyen en las curvas individuales de oferta y demanda también afectan a las curvas agregadas. Éstas se mueven hacia la derecha para representar un incremento y hacia la izquierda para representar un decremento.
- La intersección de la oferta agregada y la demanda agregada determina el equilibrio macroeconómico. Este equilibrio está definido en términos de una cierta cantidad de GDP real producida en un nivel de precios específico.

Sección 3
Pólizas de estabilización (páginas 447–454)
- La póliza de demanda, o póliza fiscal, es una política diseñada para afectar la curva agregada de demanda a través de decisiones de gastos e impuestos federales. La póliza fiscal es derivada de la **economía de Keynes**. Esta política asigna al gobierno un papel clave en el manejo del gasto fluctuante del sector comercial.
- Los **estabilizadores automáticos** son una parte importante de la economía de demanda, especialmente por el período de tiempo que se requiere para identificar y ejecutar los programas discrecionales.

- La economía de oferta recomienda políticas diseñadas para mover la curva agregada de oferta hacia la derecha. Estas políticas incluyen un papel menor de parte del gobierno, una estructura más baja de impuestos federales, y otras medidas para reducir el papeleo y la reglamentación en el sector empresarial.
- El resultado de la póliza monetaria es el cambio del tamaño del abasto monetario que luego afecta al costo y disponibilidad del crédito. El impacto a corto plazo de la póliza monetaria es sobre las tasas de interés. El impacto a largo plazo es sobre la tasa de la inflación.

Sección 4
Economía y política (páginas 456–460)
- La póliza discrecional se hace cada vez más difícil para ejecutar debido a retrasos de reconocimiento, retrasos de ejecución, embotellamiento en el Congreso, la brevedad de las recesiones, y límites conservativos al presupuesto.
- La póliza fiscal pasiva en forma de los estabilizadores automáticos todavía provee mucha estabilidad, pero la póliza monetaria ha llenado el vacío y ha llegado a ser dominante.
- Los economistas vienen de una variedad de antecedentes, pero están más de acuerdo en asuntos clave de lo que piensa la mayoría de la gente. La economía y la política están entrelazadas muy de cerca. El presidente tiene un **Consejo de Consultores Economistas** pero por razones políticas él no siempre puede seguir sus sugerencias.
- A pesar de su poca acción política de vez en cuando, los economistas han hecho considerable progreso para elevar el entendimiento general de cómo opera la economía.

Comercio internacional

Sección 1

Ventajas absolutas y comparativas (páginas 467–470)

- Estados Unidos está muy involucrado en el comercio internacional. El americano promedio gasta más de $4,200 por año para **importaciones** en forma de productos y servicios.
- El intercambio comercial es necesario porque muchos materiales solamente pueden ser obtenidos en extranjero.
- La **ventaja absoluta** significa que un país puede producir más de un producto que otro país. Pero esto no explica por qué un país con una producción grande puede intercambiar con un país con una producción más pequeña, dando como resultado beneficio de intercambio en ambos países.
- La base del intercambio comercial hoy en día es la **ventaja comparativa**. Si la gente y los países se especializan en las cosas que producen más eficientemente, y si intercambian para obtener las cosas que no producen, el total de la producción mundial incrementará.

Sección 2

Barreras para el comercio internacional (páginas 472–479)

- Las barreras para el intercambio comercial incluyen **tarifas, cuotas,** permisos, certificados de salud, y cuotas voluntarias, todos los cuales han sido usados para restringir el libre flujo de productos.
- Los **proteccionistas** apoyan las barreras para el intercambio comercial por razones de la defensa nacional, industrias infantiles, protección de trabajos domésticos, guardar el dinero en casa, y ayudar el balance de pagos.
- Los **comerciantes libres** creen que todos estos argumentos están defectuosos, con la posible excepción del argumento a favor de las industrias infantiles. Para que el argumento a favor de las industrias infantiles sea válido, la protección debe ser eventualmente removida de manera que la industria pueda competir por si misma.
- Esta es una decisión políticamente difícil. Las altas tarifas fueron una de las causas de la Gran Depresión. El mundo se ha movido hacia el intercambio más libre desde entonces. La **cláusula de nación más favorecida** es importante para muchos países porque les da las mismas reducciones de tarifas que Estados Unidos negocia con otras naciones comerciales.
- GATT fue establecido en 1947 y ha evolucionado en la Organización Mundial del Comercio (WTO, siglas en inglés) la cual administra los acuerdos de GATT, promueve el comercio más libre, y ayuda a arreglar disputas entre gobiernos.
- El **Acuerdo de Libre Comercio de Norte América** (NAFTA, siglas en inglés) eventualmente removerá todas las barreras entre Canadá, México, y Estados Unidos.

Sección 3

Financiamiento y déficits comerciales (páginas 481–485)

- El intercambio extranjero es la sangre de vida del comercio internacional. Su valor está determinado en los mercados de intercambio extranjero donde las divisas son compradas y vendidas.
- Muchos países utilizan un sistema de tipo de cambio flexible, es decir, la oferta y la demanda determinan el valor de las divisas. Algunos países más pequeños también utilizan un sistema de tipo de cambio fijo el cual ata el valor de su moneda con una divisa mayor como el dólar estadounidense.
- Los grandes déficits comerciales en Estados Unidos a mediados de los años 1980 fueron causados parcialmente por un dólar fuerte. Resultó el desempleo en las industrias de exportaciones. El país hubiera tenido un superávit comercial si el valor de sus exportaciones hubiera excedido el valor de sus importaciones.
- Cuando declina el valor del dólar de acuerdo al comercio, el balance de pagos mejora y el desempleo sube en las industrias de importaciones. Cuando se fortalece el valor del dólar, el balance de pagos empeora y el desempleo sube en las industrias de exportaciones.
- Porque los déficits tienden a corregirse por sí mismo, muchas naciones ya no diseñan la póliza económica sólo para mejorar el balance de pagos.

Sistemas económicos comparativos

Sección 1

El espectro de los sistemas económicos
(páginas 491–494)

- Los tres principales tipos de sistemas económicos mundiales son el **comunismo**, **socialismo**, y **capitalismo**.
- Bajo el capitalismo, los recursos productivos son de propiedad y operación privada. El capital es obtenido a través de ganancias en el mercado. La oferta y la demanda determinan los precios. El papel del gobierno es limitado para promover la competencia y proveer los bienes públicos. Bajo el socialismo, muchos de los recursos básicos son de propiedad y operación gubernamental. Los precios toman el papel principal en el reparto de recursos. Muchas sociedades socialistas son democracias en las cuales los oficiales elegidos dirigen el reparto de los recursos en las industrias clave.
- Bajo el comunismo, todos los recursos productivos son de propiedad y operación gubernamental. La planeación central dirige todos los recursos y la mano de obra es organizada para la ventaja común de la comunidad.

Sección 2

El auge y la caída del comunismo (páginas 496–499)

- En 1917 una revolución derrocó el gobierno de Rusia e instituyó un sistema comunista. Para 1927 el país estaba bajo el control del partido comunista y había cambiado su nombre al de Unión Soviética. Bajo una serie de planes de cinco años, Stalín quería realizar una rápida industrialización. Los planes incluyeron la colectivización de la agricultura y la transformación de la industria.
- Cuando el brutal régimen de Stalín terminó en 1953, la Unión Soviética había completado su exitosa transición en una gran potencia industrial. Gosplan, la autoridad de planeación central, determinó cada aspecto de la producción industrial y agrícola, aunque las complejidades de la planeación central se estaban haciendo más difíciles de manejar.
- Al final la economía por mandato fue un fracaso miserable. La baja productividad y falta de incentivos animaron a Mijail Gorbachov a intentar la perestroika, en cambio fundamental de la estructura de la economía y el gobierno. Pero el cambio nunca fue completado y a principios de los años 1990, el sistema económico soviético se colapsó.

Sección 3

La transición al capitalismo (páginas 501–507)

- Los sistemas anteriormente comunistas encaran varios retos al tratar de cambiarse al capitalismo incluso la **privatización** de los recursos de capital, el cambio del poder político de los comunistas a los oficiales electos, y la disciplina y los incentivos de una economía capitalista. Rusia y Europa oriental han tenido varios éxitos en esta transición hacia el capitalismo. Muchas industrias han sido privatizadas usando sistemas de vale y así dando auge al capitalismo en áreas anteriormente dominadas por el comunismo.
- Muchos países en Latinoamérica y hasta China también están cambiándose hacia una economía capitalista. Como resultado, las bolsas han aparecido por todo el mundo, dando la oportunidad de experimentar el capitalismo a millones de accionistas en compañías nuevamente privatizadas.

Sección 4

Las diferentes caras del capitalismo (páginas 509–514)

- Japón alcanzó un crecimiento económico fenomenal con la combinación de lealtad trabajadora y corporativa, tecnología, y bajos impuestos hasta la crisis asiática de 1997.
- Las economías de los "Tigres Asiáticos" (Singapur, Taiwan, Corea del Sur, y Hong Kong antes de su reunificación con China) también deben mucho de su notable éxito al capitalismo aunque son muy diferentes uno del otro en otros aspectos.
- Suecia, antes reconocida como el "estado socialista exitoso," ha cambiado su estructura en el intento de quitarse del socialismo y bajar las tarifas de impuestos sobre corporaciones e individuos.

Países en desarrollo

Sección 1

Desarrollo económico (páginas 521–526)

- Los **países en desarrollo** tienen los mismos problemas que los países industrializados, pero sus problemas son mucho más grandes. Con más de 1.2 mil millones de personas en el mundo que viven con un ingreso de menos de $1 diario, la preocupación por los países en desarrollo es tanto humanitaria como política.
- Los países en desarrollo encaran numerosos obstáculos, incluso las presiones de población por altos índices brutos de natalidad y el incremento de las expectativas de vida.
- La escasez de recursos naturales, limitada educación y tecnología, religión, una gran deuda externa, la fuga del capital, la corrupción, y los resultados de guerra se agregan a los problemas de los países en desarrollo. IMF y el Banco Mundial son dos agencias internacionales que ayudan con el desarrollo.

Sección 2

Un marco para el desarrollo (páginas 528–531)

- Ayuda entender el desarrollo económico como en etapas secuenciales, aunque si esto no siempre describe el patrón experimentado por cada nación. Las etapas incluyen el **equilibrio primitivo**, el rompimiento con el equilibrio primitivo, el despegue, el desarrollo parcial, y el alto desarrollo.
- El Banco Mundial recomienda que las naciones desarrolladas reduzcan las barreras comerciales, reformen la póliza macroeconómica, incrementen el apoyo financiero, y apoyen las reformas de póliza de países en desarrollo. El Banco Mundial también recomienda que los países desarrollados inviertan en su gente, mejoren el clima empresarial, abran sus economías al comercio internacional y revisen su póliza macroeconómica.

Sección 3

Financiamiento del desarrollo económico (páginas 533–537)

- Los países en desarrollo necesitan fomentar el ahorro para asegurar un recurso doméstico de fondos para la inversión. Las economías por mandato a menudo tratan de forzar el ahorro movilizando los recursos de una manera que restringe las libertades individuales.

- Intentos de asegurar el capital a través de la expropiación a menudo se fracasan porque los inversionistas extranjeros llegan a temer la inversión. Algunas veces los fondos externos están disponibles de gobiernos y bancos extranjeros. El Banco Mundial e IMF también proporcionan considerable asistencia.
- Algunos países han podido ayudarse a través de cooperación regional en forma de un área de libre comercio, o una asociación de aduanas tal como la Unión Europea.
- Los diez países ASEAN están trabajando para desarrollar una zona de libre comercio para el año 2008.
- Los países productores de petróleo también organizaron un cártel llamado OPEC (siglas en inglés) para incrementar el precio del petróleo. Corea del Sur es un ejemplo impresionante de una nación en desarrollo que ha realizado el éxito. Se ha desarrollado desde una economía destruida por guerra hasta la economía número 11 en tamaño del mundo.

Retos económicos globales

Sección 1
La demanda global de recursos (páginas 545–550)

• Hace más de 200 años, Thomas Malthus predijo muchos de los problemas de población que algunos países en desarrollo encaran hoy en día tales como altos índices de natalidad, el hambre, y la amenaza de una norma de vida de **subsistencia**.

• Malthus no vislumbró adelantos tecnológicos ni que algunos índices de natalidad bajarían y que algunas poblaciones cesarían de crecer. Muchos **recursos no renovables** como petróleo, gas natural, y carbón son amenazados hoy.

• El **embargo** petrolero a principios de los años 1970 elevó los precios del petróleo y animaron a los americanos a buscar fuentes de energía alternativas y renovables.

• Algunos recursos renovables de energía como la energía hidroeléctrica, biomasa, energía solar, y poder de viento han sido desarrollados inclusive el gasohol, una combinación de gasolina sin plomo y alcohol de grano. Otros recursos como agua y tierra también están bajo presión por el crecimiento de la población.

Sección 2
Incentivos y recursos económicos (páginas 552–556)

• Durante el embargo petrolero de los años 1970, altos precios de gasolina proporcionaron un incentivo para preservar los recursos. Cuando los precios volvieron a bajar, los esfuerzos de conservación declinaron.

• En tanto la población ha crecido y utilizado más recursos energéticos, la gente ha llegado a preocuparse por la contaminación. La respuesta tradicional a la contaminación es que el gobierno apruebe estándares legislados para prohibirla.

• Los economistas argumentan que la contaminación no puede ser controlada hasta que los incentivos económicos para contaminar sean removidos.

• Programas como impuestos sobre la contaminación y permisos para contaminar son diseñados para dar a las compañías el incentivo para no contaminar.

• Los mercados tienen la flexibilidad de ajustarse al cambio, un ajuste que afecta los precios y el reparto de recursos.

Sección 3
Aplicación de la economía en la forma de pensar (páginas 558–561)

• La economía ha llegado a ser una teoría generalizada de alternativas y un marco para la toma de decisión.

• El Consejo Nacional sobre la Educación Económica ha recomendado cinco puntos al respecto de la toma de decisiones. El paso final involucra un análisis de costo y beneficio que compara el costo de una decisión con los beneficios obtenidos.

• Un conocimiento fundamental de la economía ayuda a la gente a enfrentar al futuro, especialmente ahora cuando el capitalismo ha emergido como el tipo dominante de organización económica en el mundo de hoy. El capitalismo moderno no es la versión de eficiencia cruel de los años 1930. El capitalismo moderno ha sido modificado para cumplir con las metas económicas de la gente.

• En los mercados del mundo de hoy, la oferta y la demanda establecen los precios y los precios sirven como señales para los productores y los consumidores.

• Esta flexibilidad permite que la **economía empresarial privada modificada** responda a los eventos del futuro que no se ven hoy.

The following abbreviations are used in the index: *crt* = cartoon; *fig* = figure, chart, graph; *m* = map; *p* = photograph; *q* = quote

A

F

Index

structural unemployment

United Mine Workers of America

structural unemployment, 385–86
study and writing skills: library resources, 230; note taking, 80; outlining, 132; writing process, 441
subsidies, 117, 257
subsistence, 546
substitution effect, 96, 98; and demand, 107
Supplemental Security Income (SSI), 397
supply, 113–20; changes in, 146–47, *fig147;* defined, 113; elasticity of, 118–20; law of, 113
supply curve: individual, 114, *fig114;* market, 114, *fig114*
supply elasticity, 118–20, *fig119;* determinants of, 119–20
supply schedule, 114
supply-side policies, 451–53, 459, *fig450, fig451;* and aggregate supply, 453, *fig452;* limitations of, 453
surcharge, 245
surplus, 143–44, *fig145*
Sweden: capitalism in, 513–14, *p513;* taxes in, 491; welfare state in, 514

T-account, 416
Taft-Hartley Act (1947), 197, 201
Taiwan, capitalism in, 513
takeoff, 529
target prices, 153
tariffs, 472–73; protective, 472–73; revenue, 473
taxable income, 226
tax assessor, 241
tax base, 366
tax credits, 398; investment, 245
taxes: alternative minimum, 245; in controlling pollution, 554–55; corporate, 235; costs of, 231; criteria for effective, 226–27; death, 246; double, 65; economic impact of, 223–26; effect of, on behavior, 224–25; estate, 235; excise, 235, *p235;* FICA, 233–34; flat, 249–50; gift, 235; incidence of, 225–26, *fig225;* individual, 231–33, 240, *fig233, fig234;* individual income, 226; loopholes in, 226, 249; luxury, 224; negative, 400; payroll, 233; pollution, *p181;*

principles of, 227–29; progressive, 229, 450; property, 241–42; proportional, 229; regressive, 229; sales, 226; sin, 224–25; Social Security, 233; state sales, *m240;* and supply curve, 117; and supply-side policies, 452; in Sweden, 491; types of, 229; value-added, 247–49, *fig248*
tax-exempt, 323
Tax Freedom Day, 223, 246
tax reform: inevitability of future, 250; in 1981; 244–45 in 1986, 245–46; in 1993, 246; in 1997, 246, *crt245;* in 2001, 247; *crt246*
tax return, 232; e-filing of, 236
technological monopoly, 170
technological unemployment, 386, *crt386*
technology: as obstacle to economic development, 524; and supply curve, 117
technology skills: database, 495, *p495;* e-mail, 258; Internet, 393, *p393;* multimedia presentations, 299; spreadsheet, 349
telecommunications, 84
Temporary Aid to Needy Families (TANF), 397, 458
Tennessee, as right-to-work law state, *m201;* per capita personal income, *fig399;* growth of real per capita personal income, *fig399*
Tennessee Valley Authority (TVA), 78, 256, 548
terrorism, impact of, 250, 328, 375, 415, 456
Texas, as right-to-work law state, *m201;* per capita personal income, *fig399;* growth of real per capita personal income, *fig399*
Three Mile Island, 548
thrift industry, reforming, 304–5
thrift institutions, 303
Thrift Institutions Advisory Council, 410
tight money policy, 419
time deposits, 417
Tocqueville, Alexis de, 11
total cost, 128
total expenditures: determining, 103–4; test for, 103–5, *fig103*
total product, 123–24, *fig124*
total revenue, 130
trade associations, 78, *p79*

trade deficit: defined, 484; effect of, 484–85
Trade Expansion Act (1962), 478
trade-offs, 19–20, *crt21, fig20*
trade surplus, 484
trade union, 195
trade unions, *fig197*
trade-weighted value of dollar, 484
traditional economies, 33–37, *p34;* advantages, 34; disadvantages, 34–35; examples, 34; simulating trade in, 519
training manual, developing, 160–61
transfer payments, 257
transfer velocity, 287
transparency, 512
Treasury bills, 324
Treasury bonds, 324, 325
Treasury coin notes, 296
Treasury notes, 324
trend line, 376
triangular trade, 289
trough, 376
trust funds, 275
truth in advertising, 182, *crt182*
Truth in Lending Act, 413
two-tier wage system, 211, 212–13

Ukraine, 548
Ulyanov, Vladimir Ilyich, 496–97
underground economy, 343, *crt343*
unemployment, 382; cyclical, 386; frictional, 384–85; during Great Depression, 196; and impact of layoffs, 388, *p388;* kinds of, 384–87; measuring, 382–84, *fig383;* and monetary policies, 454; seasonal, 386; structural, 385–86; technological, 386, *crt386*
unemployment insurance, 449
unemployment rate, 382–83; defined, 383; drop in, 382; limitations of, 383–84
Uniform Resource Locator (URL), 393
unions; See **labor unions**
union shops, 201
United Airlines, 163
United Hatters Union, 196
United Mine Workers of America, 198

Acknowledgments

Cover i Aaron Haupt; **iv** Mark Segal/Stone; **vi** Pat O'Hara/Stone; **vii** (l)Jose Palaez/CORBIS Stock Market, (r)Michael Paras/International Stock; **viii** (tl)courtesy Hard Candy, (bl) Mark Burnett, (r)Steffen Casteel/Getty Images; **ix** (t)Wesley Boxce/Photo Researchers, (b)Orde Eliason/Link Picture Library; **x** (l)Terry Vine/Getty Images, (tr) Tim Flach/Getty Images, (br) Aaron Haupt; **xi** (l)Jim Craigmyle/Masterfile, (c)Joseph Pobereskin/Getty Images, (br)Mark Burnett; **xvi–xxv** Illustration by Guy Crittendon; **xxvi** StudiOhio; **2** SuperStock; **4** Bruce Forster/Stone; **5** Jose Pelaez/The Stock Market; **7** Tom & Dee Ann McCarthy/The Stock Market; **8** (cl)Lester Lefkowitz/The Stock Market, (l)Kirk Anderson/International Stock, (cr)Charlie Westerman/International Stock, (r)George Ancona/International Stock; **11** (t)Alexis Duclos/Liaison Agency, (b)Steven Peters/Stone; **12** Scottish National Portrait Gallery, Edinburgh, Scotland/Bridgeman Art Library, New York/London; **14** Gerald French/FPG; **18** (l)Art Resource, NY, (tr)North Wind Picture Archive, (br)North Wind Picture Archive; **19** Jaques Chenet/Woodfin Camp & Associates; **21** By permission of Johnny Hart and Creators Syndicate, Inc.; **22** Ross Harrison Koty/Stone; **24** Jose Pelaez/The Stock Market; **26** Phil Degginger/Stone; **27** (l)Kirk Anderson/International Stock, (r)Charlie Westerman/International Stock; **30** Mark Burnett; **31** Aaron Haupt; **32** Joseph Nettis/Stone; **33** Milind Ketkar/Dinodia Picture Agency; **34** Margaret Gowan/Stone; **37** Robert S. Semeniuk/The Stock Market; **40** John Lamb/Stone; **41** David Young-Wolff/Stone; **42** Steven Peters/Stone; **43** Tom Uhlman/Liaison Agency; **45** Michael Paras/International Stock; **46** Underwood & Underwood/CORBIS; **48** Chuck Savage/The Stock Market; **49** (l)Cynthia Johnson/Liaison Agency, (r)Bob Daemmrich/Stone; **50** Alan Levenson/Stone; **52** (castle)Dallas & John Heaton/Stock Boston, (Disney)Y. Karsh/Woodfin Camp & Associates, (Lucas)James Wilson/Woodfin Camp & Associates, (Qui-Gon Jinn & Darth Maul)Evan Agostini/Liaison Agency, (Snow White & Dopey)Bill Bachmann/PhotoEdit, (stars bkgd)Kim Westerskov/Stone, (Star Wars logo)Liaison Agency, (Stormtroopers & Boba Fett)Michael Newman/PhotoEdit; **53** (t)Michael Paras/International Stock, (b)Steven Peters/Stone; **56** Andy Sacks/Stone; **57** Michael Nelson/FPG; **59 60** Bob Daemmrich/Stock Boston; **61** Geoff Butler; **62** Dick Luria/FPG; **63** file photo; **65** Peter Langone/International Stock; **67** (bkgd)Mark Burnett, (l)Amilcar/Liaison Agency, (c)Phil Schermeister/Stone, (tr)David Young-Wolff/PhotoEdit; **68** Zigy Kaluzny/Stone; **72** Aaron Haupt; **73** C.R. Rathe/FPG; **74** Bojan Brecelj/CORBIS; **75** George Ancona/International Stock; **77** David Young-Wolff/PhotoEdit; **79** Bob Daemmrich/Stone; **80** Rob Lewine/The Stock Market; **81** (l)Michael Nelson/FPG, (r)Zigy Kaluzny/Stone; **85** VCG/FPG; **86** Mark Segal/Stone; **88** Mark Richards/PhotoEdit; **89** Mark Burnett; **91** Powerstock/Zefa/Index Stock; **94** (bkgd)John Riley/Stone, (Winfrey—bl)Mitchell Gerber/CORBIS; **95** Matt Meadows; **97** Joseph Pobereskin/Stone; **100** (t)David Wade/FPG, (b)David Travers/The Stock Market; **101** Mark Burnett; **104** Karen Moskowitz/Corbis Outline; **108** Mark Ferri/The Stock Market; **109** Mark Burnett; **112** Bohdan Hrynewych/Stock Boston; **113** Geoff Butler; **116** Michael Busselle/Stone; **118** Jeff Isaac Greenberg/Photo Researchers; **120** Courtesy Sidney Harris; **121** (candy) Steven Needham/Envision, (catalog)Bettmann/CORBIS, (Hershey)Bettmann/CORBIS, (Johnson)Johnathan Kirn/Liaison Agency, (magazine)Cynthia Johnson/Liaison Agency, (watch)Mark Harwood/Stone; **122** Phil Hunt/Masterfile; **123** Ulrike Welsch/PhotoEdit; **126** (l)Jose Pelaez/The Stock Market, (r)Mark Burnett; **127** Robert W. Slack/International Stock; **132** Donald C. Johnson/The Stock Market; **133** Ulrike Welsch/PhotoEdit; **136** Geoff Butler; **137** Doug Pensinger/Allsport; **139** Ford Motor Co./FPG; **141** (Becker)Springer-Liaison/Liaison Agency, (bills-tl)Larry Gilpin/Stone, (bills-br) Uli Degwert/International Stock, (coins-bkgd)Matthew Borkoski/Stock Boston, (coins-tr) Walter Schmid/Stone, (Friedman)Chuck Nacke/Woodfin Camp & Associates; **142** J. Bourg/Liaison Agency; **144** David Young-Wolff/PhotoEdit; **149** Bob Daemmrich/Stock Boston; **150** Chad Slattery/Stone; **152** Chuck Savage/The Stock Market; **153** Jeff Greenberg/PhotoEdit; **156** Charles Gupton/Stone; **157** Bob Daemmrich/Stock Boston; **161** Aaron Haupt; **162** Berenholz/The Stock Market; **163** Museun of Flight/CORBIS; **164** Paul Chesley/Stone; **166** Bob Daemmrich/Stone; **168** Courtesy Bozell Worldwide; **170** CALVIN AND HOBBES ©1992 Watterson. Reprinted with permisson of UNIVERSAL PRESS SYNDICATE. All rights reserved.; **171** Barbara Leslie/FPG; **172** (t)Yann Layma/Stone, (l)Claudio Edinger/Liaison Agency, (br)Milind Ketkar/Dinodia Picture Agency; **173** Larry Williams/Masterfile; **175** Etienne de Malglaive/Liaison Agency; **177** (t)Hiroyuki Matsumoto/Stone, (b)Berenholtz/The Stock Market; **178** R.W. Jones/CORBIS; **182** King Features Syndicate. All rights reserved; **184** Phil Schofield/Stone; **185** (l)Paul Chesley/Stone, (r)Etienne de Malglaive/Liaison Agency; **188** Don Smetzer/Stone; **189** David Young-Wolff/Stone; **190** Ralph Mercer/Stone; **192** Bryan F. Peterson/The Stock Market; **193** Kevin Rivolli/AP/World Wide Photos; **196** CORBIS; **198** FPG; **199** Hazel Hankin/Stock Boston; **200** L.M. Otero/AP/World Wide Photos; **202** John Feingersh/The Stock Market; **203** Rob Crandall/Stock Boston; **204** (Chavez)Tim Kelly/Black Star, (coal)Larry Mayer/Liaison Agency, (farm worker)Mark Richards/PhotoEdit, (grapes-t)Eric Sander/Liaison Agency, (grapes-br)Andrew Klapatiuk/Liaison Agency, (Lewis)FPG, (miner)Hulton Getty/Stone, (tools)William Whitehurst/The Stock Market; **205** Ron Chapple/FPG; **210** (t)Pat O'Hara/Stone, (b)Michael Newman/PhotoEdit; **211** Sam Sargent/Liaison Agency; **219** Ron Chapple/FPG; **221** Reprinted by permission–Atlantic Feature Syndicate; **222** Elizabeth Simpson/FPG; **223** PhotoDisc; **227** (l)Roy Morsch/The Stock Market, (r)Richard Hutchings/PhotoEdit; **230** Terry Vine/Stone; **231** Christie's Images; **235** Bob Daemmrich/Stone; **237** (bkgd)Brian Allen/The Stock Market, (Federal Reserve)John Neubauer/PhotoEdit, (Rivlin)Terry Ashe/Liaison Agency, (Yellen notes)Amanita Pictures, (Yellen)Diana Walker/Liaision Agency; **238** Mark Wilson/Liaison; **243** (t)John Mellott/Uniphoto Pictor, (b)Arthur Holeman/International Stock; **244** Bob Daemmrich/Stone; **245** THE BORN LOSER reprinted by permission of Newspaper Enterprise Association, Inc.; **246** TOLES ©2001 The Buffalo News. Reprinted with permission of UNIVERSAL PRESS **249** Jim Craigmyle/Masterfile; **251** Richard Hutchings/PhotoEdit; **254** Chad Ehlers/Stone; **255** Alex Wong/Newsmakers; **259** David Young-Wolff/Stone; **260** Kenneth Lambert/AP/Wide World Photos; **265** Keith Wood/Stone; **266** (tl)Randy Masser/International Stock, (tr)Hulton-Getty/Stone, (bl)Hulton-Getty/Stone, (br)New York Times Co./Archive Photos; **267** Denis Poroy/AP/Wide World Photos; **268** Robert Frerck/Woodfin Camp & Associates; **270** Bill Tucker/International Stock; **271** (t)Stephen Simpson/FPG, (b)Richard Laird/FPG; **272** Mark Wilson/AP/Wide World Photos; **276** Tribune Media Services, Inc. All Rights Reserved. Reprinted with permission; **279** (l)David Young-Wolff/Stone, (r)Richard Hutchings/Photo Researchers; **283** (t)Robert Shafer/Stone, (b)Telegraph Colour Library/FPG; **284** International Stock; **285** Hulton Getty/Stone; **286** Chuck O'Rear/Woodfin Camp & Associates; **287** Michael Newman/PhotoEdit; **288** Reprinted by permission News America Syndicate; **289** Michael J. Howell/International Stock, (br)file photo; **291** Mark Burnett, (Mohajer)courtesy Hard Candy; **292** William Whitehurst/The Stock Market; **293** Amanita Pictures; **294** Geoff Butler; **299** Aaron Haupt; **300** Georgina Bowater/The Stock Market; **301** (l)John Elk III/Stock Boston, (r)Doug Armand/Stone; **304** David Young-Wolff/PhotoEdit; **306** (t)Rob Crandall/The Image Works, (b)Tony Freeman/PhotoEdit; **307** Doug Armand/Stone; **311** Aaron Haupt; **312** Nadia MacKenzie/Stone; **313** SuperStock; **317** (bkgd–Hayes)Alan Schein/The Stock Market, (bkgd–Lewis)Robert Brenner/PhotoEdit, (dress)A. Benainous/Liaison Agency, (Hayes)Larry Lazlo, courtesy Janus, (Lewis)Liaison Agency, (stock-Hayes bkgd)file photo, (stock-tl)Cobalt Productions; **318** David Young-Wolff/Stone; **324** William Taufic/The Stock Market; **326** Courtesy Harley L. Schwadron; **327** Richard Drew/AP/Wide World Photos; **328** Richard Drew/AP/Wide World Photos; **332** From *The Wall Street Journal*–Permission, Cartoon Features Syndicate; **334** Tim Flach/Stone; **335** (l)David Young-Wolff/Stone, (r)William Taufic/The Stock Market; **338** Chad Ehlers/International Stock; **340** John Madere/The Stock Market; **341** Freida Leinward/Woodfin Camp & Associates; **343** Tribune Media Services, Inc. All Rights Reserved. Reprinted with permission; **350** Ed Bock/The Stock Market; **354** From *The Wall Street Journal*–Permission, Cartoon Features Syndicate; **355** (Alvarado)courtesy Alvarado Construction, (bkgd)William R. Sallaz/Duomo, (tools)Don Mason/The Stock Market; **356** Ben Simmons/The Stock Market; **358** Michelle Bridwell/PhotoEdit; **362** (t)Elliot Varner Smith/International Stock, (b)Stan-Pak/International Stock; **363** Bruce Rogovin/Stone; **369** Michelle Bridwell/PhotoEdit; **372** Mark Segal/Stone; **373** Aaron Haupt; **374** Terry Qing/FPG; **375** Sandra Baker/Stone; **381** (Lewis)courtesy George Mason University, (students–bkgd)Beatriz Schiller/International Stock, (students–tr)Ulrike Welsch/PhotoEdit, (bills)Doug Martin; **382** Gabe Palmer/The Stock Market; **384** Michael Keller/The Stock Market; **386** From *The Wall Street Journal*–Permission, Cartoon Features Syndicate; **388** (t)Mitch Kezar/Stone, (b)William Taufic/The Stock Market **389** Don Smetzer/Stone; **393** Geoff Butler; **394** Laima Druskis/Stock Boston; **398** Paul Barton/The Stock Market; **401** Sandra Baker/Stone; **404** John Henley/The Stock Market; **406** P. Aventurier/Liaison Agency; **407** Liaison Agency; **409** Terry Ashe/Liaison Agency, (br)Louis Psihoyos/Matrix; **410** By permission of Johnny Hart and Creators Syndicate, Inc.; **411** From *The Wall Street Journal*–Permission, Cartoon Features Syndicate; **414** (tr)Jeffery Titcomb/Liaison Agency, (bl)Christoph Wilhelm/FPG, (Greenspan)Steffen Casteel/FPG; **415** Tony Freeman/PhotoEdit; **418** Jon Feingersh/The Stock Market; **422** ©1999 Bill Ammend. Distributed by Universal Press Syndicate; **424** Topham/The Image Works; **425** (t)Chuck Savage/The Stock Market, (b)David Young-Wolff/PhotoEdit **426** Carlos Spaventa/FPG; **429** Greg Pease/Stone; **431** Mike Thompson, *The State Journal Register*, Copley News Service; **432** Bruce Ayres/Stone; **433** (l)Liaison Agency, (r)Chuck Savage/The Stock Market; **436** International Stock; **437** Richard Laird/FPG; **440** Jon Riley/Stone; **441** Victor Ramos/International Stock; **442** Bruce Forster/Stone; **446** (tl)Lester Lefkowitz/The Stock Market, (tr)Aaron Haupt, (bills–bkgd)Larry Gilpin/Stone, (Du Pont)Bettmann/CORBIS, (Heinz)Bettmann/CORBIS; **447** Mark Reinstein/FPG; **448** Bob Daemmrich/Uniphoto Pictor; **455** (l)Brian Bhar/AllSport, (r)Jonathan Daniel/AllSport; **456** PhotoDisc; **457** Jiang Jin/SuperStock; **459** Tribune Media Services, Inc. All Rights Reserved. Reprinted with permission; **461** (l)Richard Laird/FPG, (r)Mark Reinstein/FPG; **464** John Zoiner/International Stock; **466** Peter Christopher/Masterfile; **467** Roger M. Smith/International Stock; **471** (br)Michael Grecco/Stock Boston, (Microsoft campus aerial)Brunner Burke/Stone, (Gates)Mark Richards/PhotoEdit, (mouse)Jim Cummins/FPG, (Public Market &

Sapce Needle)Ron Chapple/FPG, (Windows logo)R. Ramirez/PhotoEdit; **472** Steven Needham/Envision; **473** James Wilson/Woodfin Camp & Associates; **475** Gary Payne/Liaison Agency; **477** Joseph Nettis/Stock Boston; **480** Mark Segal/Stone; **481** George Hunter/Stone; **484** Michael Newman/PhotoEdit; **485** Andy Hernandez/Liaison Agency; **486** Robert Brenner/PhotoEdit; **487** (l)James Wilson/Woodfin Camp & Associates, (r)Michael Newman/PhotoEdit; **490** Domenico Ruzza/Envision; **492** Courtesy Electrolux IT Solutions AB; **495** David Young-Wolff/PhotoEdit; **496** Liaison Agency; **498** Bob Daemmrich/Stone; **500** (t)Stone, (br)Stone, (Manifesto)Mark Burnett, (Marx)AKG London; **501** Chuck Nacke/Woodfin Camp & Associates; **504** Robert Frerck/Woodfin Camp & Associates; **505** Jose Pelaez/The Stock Market; **506** (t)Paul S. Howell/Liaison Agency, (b)Jason P. Howe/ South American Pictures; **507** D.E. Cox/Stone; **508** (t)Andrew Holbrooke/The Stock Market, (b)David Ball/The Stock Market; **509** Susana Gonzalez/Getty Images; **510** Fujifotos/ The Image Works; **513** Chad Ehlers/Stone; **515** David Ball/The Stock Market; **519** Aaron Haupt; **520** Keren Su/Stone; **521** Sean Sprague/Stock Boston; **525** Bernard Pierr Wolff/Photo Researchers; **527** (Lewis)courtesy Princeton University, (market)Bruno De Hogues/Stone, (school)Thomas W. Friedmann/Photo Researchers; **528** Bruno De Hogues/Stone; **529** John Olson/The Stock Market; **531** John Moss/Photo Researchers; **532** Stone; **533** John V. Cotter/D. Donne Bryant Stock Photo; **535** Simon Jauncy/Stone; **537** Mark Segal/Stone; **538** Alan Oddie/PhotoEdit; **539** (l) Bernard Pierre Wolff/ Photo Researchers, (r)Mark Segal/Stone; **542** Orde Eliason/Link Picture Library; **543** Wesley Bocxe/Photo Researchers; **544** John Mead/Science Photo Library/Photo Researchers; **545** Wesley Boxce/Photo Researchers; **548** Hans Peter Merten/Stone; **551** (crops)Gregg Mancuso/Stock Boston, (crowd)VCG/FPG, (Malthus)Hulton Getty/Stone; **552** Ruth Dixon/Stock Boston; **553** Simon Fraser/Science Photo Library/ Photo Researchers; **554** Ryan Williams/International Stock; **555** Phil Borden/PhotoEdit; **557** (l)James N. Westwater, (r)Paul Souders/The Image Bank; **559** Glen Allison/Stone; **561** Roberto Arakaki/ International Stock; **562** Michael Scott/Stone; **563** (l)Ryan Williams/International Stock, (r)Paul Souders/The Image Bank; **A34** Uli Degwert/ International Stock.